W9-AQS-589

Webster's
New World Dictionary
of Quotable Definitions
Second Edition

Edited by

Eugene E. Brussell

PRENTICE HALL
Englewood Cliffs, New Jersey 07632

Library of Congress Cataloging-in-Publication Data

Webster's new world dictionary of quotable definitions / edited by
   Eugene E. Brussell.—2nd ed.
      p.   cm.
   Rev. ed. of: Dictionary of quotable definitions. 1970.
   Includes index.
   ISBN 0-13-619057-X—ISBN 0-13-949272-0
    1. Quotations, English.   I. Brussell, Eugene E.   II. Dictionary
of quotable definitions.
PN6081.B77   1988   88-15087
082—dc19   CIP

© 1988, 1970 by Prentice-Hall, Inc.

All rights reserved. No part of this book may be reproduced in any form or by any means, without permission in writing from the publisher.

Printed in the United States of America

10 9 8 7 6 5 4 3 2 1

ISBN 0-13-619057-0

Originally published as ISBN 0-13-949272-0
This edition printed exclusively for Borders Press

PRENTICE HALL
Career & Personal Development
Englewood Cliffs, NJ 07632
A Simon & Schuster Company

Prentice-Hall International (UK) Limited, *London*
Prentice-Hall of Australia Pty. Limited, *Sydney*
Prentice-Hall Canada Inc., *Toronto*
Prentice-Hall Hispanoamericana, S.A., *Mexico*
Prentice-Hall of India Private Limited, *New Delhi*
Prentice-Hall of Japan, Inc., *Tokyo*
Simon & Schuster Asia Pte. Ltd., *Singapore*
Editora Prentice-Hall do Brasil, Ltda., *Rio de Janeiro*

Introduction to This New Edition

When the *Dictionary* first emerged in 1970, I was convinced then that it was a unique work of descriptive definitions in that aphorisms and metaphors replaced straight dictionary meanings. Time has not erased this belief. It was then and remains now in this completely revised and updated edition neither a conventional dictionary nor a mere book of quotations.

This new edition, like the previous one, is primarily for the speaker, writer, businessperson, clergyman, author, lecturer, teacher, student. In short, it is a work suited for anyone attempting to address others effectively, imaginatively but without flat verbiage. I have added, however, almost five thousand new entries as well as many new subject areas.

Many of the definitions will not be located in standard books of quotations. A large number of entries are of a humorous nature. This coincides with the goal of resurrecting whenever possible the pungent line at the expense of the dull or obvious. The selection of each entry was carefully weighed in regard to the practical aspects of communication as well as to the witty or even outrageous connotation.

The *Webster's New World Dictionary of Quotable Definitions* is very easy to use. It is framed in a true dictionary form but also employs two systems of cross-referencing to aid the reader—topically within the subject entry and in an authors' index. Subjects are arranged alphabetically and within each subject entry alphabetically by the author's last name. Anonymous entries are placed under the last known author entry. Translations are tailored for modern usage.

The *Dictionary* will help you in the search for the right comment. You will also enjoy browsing through it in your leisure and professional moments for wisdom and entertainment. That has always been the goal in what has turned out to be a true labor of love.

Eugene E. Brussell

To David, my father loyal

A

ABILITY

(Consists) mainly in a high degree of solemnity.
Ambrose Bierce

(That which distinguishes) able men from dead
ones. *Ambrose Bierce*

The heart to conceive, the understanding to direct,
or the hand to execute. *Junius*

Trying all things; achieving what you can.
Adapted from Herman Melville

The art of getting credit for all the home runs that
somebody else hits. *Casey Stengel*

The explanation of your success.
Harry Thompson

SEE ALSO GENIUS, INSTINCT, SKILL, TAL-
ENT, WORK.

ABNORMAL

Not conforming to standard. In matters of thought
and conduct, to be independent is to be abnormal.
Ambrose Bierce

To have intelligence, character or genius; to be
less stupid than one's neighbor; to be better than
the worst; to be one's self. *Elbert Hubbard*

SEE ALSO ECCENTRICITY, GENIUS, MAD-
NESS.

ABOMINATION

A proud look, a lying tongue, and hands that shed
innocent blood. A heart that devises wicked
imaginations, feet that are swift in running to
mischief, a false witness that speaks lies, and he
that sows discord among brethren.
Bible: Proverbs, VI, 16-19.

ABORTION

Nothing but murder. *Dietrich Bonhoeffer*

Any operation which directly destroys either the
unborn child or the mother.
*Decree of the Tribunal of the
Holy Office, May 28, 1884*

A smutty thing under any circumstances, legal or
illegal. *Rustan Feroze*

Infanticide. *Flavius Josephus*

The direct murder of the innocent.
Pope Pius XI

A capital crime. *Talmud: Sanhedrin, 57b,c.*

A precipitation of murder. He also is a man who is
about to be one. *Tertullian*

SEE ALSO BIRTH CONTROL, POPULATION EX-
PLOSION.

1

ABSENCE

A woman's great strength.   *Emile C. Alain*

(To be) superseded in the consideration and affection of another.   *Ambrose Bierce*

Absence is to love what wind is to fire; it extinguishes the small, it enkindles the great.
        Comte de Bussy-Rabutin

The pain without the peace of death.
        Thomas Campbell

The common cure of love.
        Miguel de Cervantes

(That which) sharpens love.   *Thomas Fuller*

The enemy of love.   *Italian Proverb*

Absence and death are the same—only that in death there is no suffering.
        Walter Savage Landor

The invisible and incorporeal mother of ideal beauty.   *Walter Savage Landor*

That which extinguishes small passions and increases great ones.   *La Rochefoucauld*

Death . . . to them that love.   *Philip Sidney*

The cure for love.   *Spanish Proverb*

That which makes the heart grow fonder—of somebody else.   *Anon.*

ABSOLUTE

The most fatal illusion . . . life is growth and motion.   *Brooks Atkinson*

Nothing more than the deceased spirit of theology and thus a belief in pure phantoms.
        Ludwig A. Feuerbach

The absolute is what it is, regardless of anything else.   *Charles Hartshorne*

Independent or neutral to relational alternatives.
        Charles Hartshorne

The finalities of the earlier ages.
        A. Eustace Haydon

God . . . all else is relative.   *Will Herberg*

Everything absolute belongs to pathology.
        Friedrich W. Nietzsche

Something all-inclusive, and not dependent upon anything outside itself.   *Anon.*

SEE ALSO FANATICISM, IDEALS, TRUTH.

ABSTAINER

A weak person who yields to the temptation of denying himself a pleasure.   *Ambrose Bierce*

Whereby a man refraineth from anything which he may lawfully take.   *Thomas Elyot*

ABSTINENCE

A peculiarly fitting and appropriate method of self-denial and self-discipline.   *John C. Ford*

The best safeguard of morals and health.
        Robert E. Lee

The beginning of saintliness.   *Moses Luzzato*

The surety of temperance.   *Plato*

Something good in its place . . . if forbidden food, forbidden sexual indulgence, forbidden money present themselves.   *Joseph Saiida*

Something that is beneficial as long as it does not harm anybody.   *Adapted from Mark Twain*

The virtue of those too ill or too old to enjoy life.
        Anon.

SEE ALSO ABSTAINER, CONTINENCE, MODERATION, SELF-DENIAL, TEMPERANCE.

ABSTRACTION

The concreteness of Idealists.
        Eugene E. Brussell

What the eye sees before habit sets up its categories.   *John Ciardi*

The intellectual's favorite pastime.
        Aldous Huxley

SEE ALSO IDEALS, PHILOSOPHER, SCIENCE.

ABSURDITY

SEE FOOLISHNESS, RIDICULOUSNESS.

ABYSS

The measureless gulf between literature and the American magazine.   *Elbert Hubbard*

The distance between a thinker and an editorial writer.   *Elbert Hubbard*

ACADEMIC FREEDOM

Simply a way of saying that we get the best results in education and research if we leave their management to people who know something about them.   *Robert M. Hutchins*

Read this to mean imposing by violence anti-academic conditions on our schools and universities. Dissenters are shouted down, not allowed to speak, or the microphone is wrestled from them. Discussion exists only among those who agree. They demand that others follow democratic rules that they themselves defy.   *Henry J. Taylor*

The right...to study, discuss, and write about facts and ideas without restrictions, other than those imposed by conscience and morality.

Yale University, Report
Advisory Committee, 1952.

ACADEMY

A modern school where football is taught.
Ambrose Bierce

An ancient school where morality and philosophy were taught.   *Ambrose Bierce*

A society promoting the love of the static, immobile.   *Adapted from Elbert Hubbard*

Pertaining to fossils; vegetative; parasitic—the opposite of change.   *Elbert Hubbard*

They commit their pupils to the theatre of the world, with just taste enough of learning to be alienated from industrious pursuits, and not enough to do service in the ranks of science.

Thomas Jefferson

SEE ALSO COLLEGE, SCHOOL, UNIVERSITY.

ACCENT

A kind of chanting; all men have accent of their own,—though they only notice that of others.
Thomas Carlyle

The soul of talk; it gives it feeling and verity.
Jean-Jacques Rousseau

SEE ALSO ELOQUENCE, LANGUAGE, SPEECH.

ACCEPTANCE

The truest kinship with humanity.
Gilbert Keith Chesterton

To go with the drift of things,
    To yield with a grace to reason,
And bow and accept the end
    Of a love or a season?   *Robert Frost*

What makes any event put on a new face.
Adapted from Henry S. Haskins

The art of making someone who has just done you a small favor wish that he might have done you a greater one.   *Russell Lynes*

ACCIDENT

An inevitable occurrence due to the action of immutable natural laws.   *Ambrose Bierce*

An event happening unexpectedly and without fault; if there is any fault, there is liability.
Thomas M. Cooley

A condition in which presence of mind is good, but absence of body better.   *Foolish Dictionary*

Accidents exist only in our heads, in our limited perceptions. They are the reflections of the limit of our knowledge.   *Franz Kafka*

Accidents are accidents only to ignorance.
George Santayana

There is no such thing...What we call by that name is the effect of some cause which we do not see.   *Voltaire*

A surprise arranged by nature.   *Anon.*

SEE ALSO CHANCE, FORTUNE, LIFE, LUCK.

ACCOMPLICE

One associated with another in crime, having guilty knowledge and complicity, as an attorney who defends a criminal, knowing him guilty.
Ambrose Bierce

ACHIEVEMENT

That which is socially useful.
Adapted from Alfred Adler

The death of endeavor and the birth of disgust.
Ambrose Bierce

A bondage. It drives us to a higher achievement.
Albert Camus

Finding out what you would be; then doing what you have to do.   *Adapted from Epictetus*

Taking risks and making efforts.   *Karen Horney*

To send a son to Harvard.   *Edgar W. Howe*

Building a house, begetting a son, or writing a book.   *Italian Proverb*

To attempt the impossible.   *Anon.*

SEE ALSO ACTION, DEEDS, SUCCESS.

ACQUAINTANCE

A degree of friendship called slight when its object is poor or obscure, and intimate when he is rich or famous.   *Ambrose Bierce*

A person whom we know well enough to borrow from, but not well enough to lend to.
Ambrose Bierce

Anyone who has refused us a loan.
Elbert Hubbard

A friend who has borrowed money from you.
Anon.

ACTING

Consists of the ability to keep an audience from coughing.   *Jean-Louis Barrault*

Acting is honesty. If you can fake that, you've got it made.   *George Burns*

A poor traditionary fame.   *William Combe*

A voluntary dream.   *William Hazlitt*

The art of speaking in a loud clear voice and the avoidance of bumping into furniture.
Adapted from Alfred Lunt

To seem natural rather than to be natural.
Alan A. Milne

The lowest of art; if it is an art at all.
George Moore

Acting isn't really a creative profession. It's an interpretative one.   *Paul Newman*

Just one version of the unreal after another.
Jack Nicholson

The art of persuasion. The actor persuades himself, first, and through himself, the audience.
Laurence Olivier

Just one big bag of tricks.   *Laurence Olivier*

A masochistic form of exhibitionism. It is not quite the occupation of an adult.
Laurence Olivier

An art which consists of keeping the audience from coughing.   *Ralph Richardson*

The ability to dream on cue. *Ralph Richardson*

Acting is characterization, the process of two entities merging—the actor and the role.
George C. Scott

That attempt to find universality, reality and truth in a world of pretending.   *George C. Scott*

To hold as 'twere, the mirror up to nature.
William Shakespeare

One of the imitative arts.   *William Shenstone*

A sad business where you crawl from hope to hope.   *Walter Slezak*

The moving picture of nature.   *William Winter*

SEE ALSO ACTOR, HOLLYWOOD, MOVIE, THEATER.

ACTION

Coarsened thought—thought become concrete, obscure, and unconscious.   *Henry F. Amiel*

That which gives meaning to the world.
Adapted from Leon Baeck

What matters . . . We are present where we act.
Henri Bergson

Your business.   *Bhagavad-Gita*

A readiness for responsibility.
Dietrich Bonhoeffer

Our epochs.   *Lord Byron*

The proof, the criterion, of the Holy Spirit.
Hermann Cohen

The only things in life in which we can be said to have any property.   *Charles Caleb Colton*

A man's action is only a picture book of his creed.
Ralph Waldo Emerson

Words are also actions, and actions are a kind of words. *Ralph Waldo Emerson*

To think. *Ralph Waldo Emerson*

Our acts our angels are, or good or ill,
Our fatal shadows that walk by us still.
John Fletcher

The soul of all action is blindness. He who knows, cannot act any longer. Knowing means foregoing action. *Egon Friedell*

The proper Fruit of Knowledge. *Thomas Fuller*

That which justifies itself only through morality.
Warren Goldberg

The great end of life. *Thomas Henry Huxley*

The normal completion of the act of will which begins as prayer. That action is not always external, but it is always some kind of effective energy.
William R. Inge

The best interpreters of . . . thoughts.
John Locke

Man's destiny and duty in this life.
Dean Mansel

To befriend any one on God's account, and to be at enmity with whosoever is the enemy of God.
Mohammed

Desire and force . . . desire causes our voluntary acts, force our involuntary. *Blaise Pascal*

(That which) must be shown, by each of us in his appointed place, not merely in the patience, but in the activity of our hope . . . our labor.
John Ruskin

The only road to knowledge.
George Bernard Shaw

The first task of life. *William G. Sumner*

Simply the refuge of people who have nothing whatever to do. *Oscar Wilde*

The basis of action is lack of imagination. It is the last resource of those who know not how to dream. *Oscar Wilde*

A blind thing dependent on external influences, and moved by an impulse of whose nature it is unconscious. *Oscar Wilde*

Action is transitory, a step, a blow,
The motion of a muscle—this way or that.
William Wordsworth

SEE ALSO ACHIEVEMENT, DEEDS, GREAT-NESS, HERO, LIVING, MORALITY, RELIGION, WORK.

ACTOR

Rogues, vagabonds and sturdy beggars.
Act of Parliament, 1597.

A professional (one) is a man who can do his job when he doesn't feel like it. An amateur is (one) . . . who can't do his job when he does feel like it. *James Agate*

A sculptor who carves in snow.
Lawrence Barrett

Casual laborers. *Lillian Braithwaite*

An actor is a guy who, if you ain't talking about him, he ain't listening. *Marlon Brando*

A favored class—as they are merry folk who give pleasure, everyone favors and protects them.
Miguel de Cervantes

The strolling tribe; a despicable race.
Charles Churchill

A wandering, careless, wretched, merry race.
George Crabbe

A nuisance in the earth, the very offal of society.
Timothy Dwight

A musician who plays on a home-made instrument—himself. *Helen Hayes*

The only honest hypocrite. *William Hazlitt*

A paradox who plays when he works and works when he plays. *Lewis C. Henry*

The best . . . is that man who can do nothing extremely well. *Alfred Hitchcock*

No better than creatures set upon tables . . . to make faces and produce laughter, like dancing dogs. *Samuel Johnson*

Compulsive quoters of people who originated the ideas which they have finally come to believe are entirely their own. *Alexander King*

Men who sleep till noon, and spend the afternoon calling on women. *George Jean Nathan*

A man with an infinite capacity for taking praise.
Michael Redgrave

They are the abstract and brief chronicles of the time.   *William Shakespeare*

Actors are like politicians, and politicians are like actors. They both spend time each day contemplating their image. They both have a desire to be loved.   *Gore Vidal*

A child's prerogative. Children are born to act. Usually, people grow out of it. Actors always seem to be people who never did quite grow out of it.   *Joanne Woodward*

One who is no better than the director.   *Anon.*

A man who can walk to the side of a stage, peer into the wings filled with dust...and say "What a lovely view there is from this window."   *Anon.*

A puppet under its own power.   *Anon.*

A person who makes faces for a living.   *Anon.*

One who gets a glazed look in his eye when the conversation drifts away from himself.   *Anon.*

One who creates illusion in order to reveal reality.
Anon.

SEE ALSO ACTING, HOLLYWOOD, MOVIE, STARLET.

ADAM

The luckiest man—he had no mother-in-law.
Sholom Aleichem

A man without a navel.   *Thomas Browne*

God created Adam out of dust and then made Eve to dampen him down.   *Leonard L. Levinson*

(One who) sinned when he fell from Contemplation. Since then, there has been division in man.   *Jacques Maritain*

The goodliest man of men.   *John Milton*

Adam was created single to teach us that to destroy one person is to destroy a whole world, and to preserve one person is to preserve a whole world.   *Mishna*

Originally one, he has fallen, and, breaking up...he has filled the whole earth with the pieces.   *Saint Augustine*

(A man who) when he said a good thing...knew nobody had said it before.   *Mark Twain*

The first great benefactor of our race. He brought death into the world.   *Mark Twain*

The first man to tell anybody about his operation.
Anon.

The only human to escape teething pains.   *Anon.*

The only one who could not say, "Haven't we met before?"   *Anon.*

SEE ALSO CREATION (WORLD), MAN.

ADMIRAL

That part of a war-ship which does the talking while the figure-head does the thinking.
Ambrose Bierce

Admirals extoll'd for standing still
Or doing nothing with a deal of skill.
William Cowper

SEE ALSO GENERAL, MILITARISM, WAR.

ADMIRATION

A very short-lived passion, that immediately decays upon growing familiar with its object.
Joseph Addison

Our polite recognition of another's resemblance to ourselves.   *Ambrose Bierce*

A youthful fancy which scarcely ever survives to mature years.   *Josh Billings*

Ignorance.   *Thomas Fuller*

Things not understood.   *Thomas Fuller*

A form of shamefaced flattery.   *Elbert Hubbard*

Approbation, heightened by wonder and surprise, constitutes the sentiment.   *Adam Smith*

One of the most bewitching, enthusiastic passions of the mind...it arises from novelty and surprise, the inseparable attendants of imposture.
William Warburton

SEE ALSO FAME, REVERENCE.

ADOLESCENCE

A phase of transition from childhood to manhood, a phase of uprootedness and drastic change.
Eric Hoffer

A kind of emotional seasickness. Both are funny, but only in retrospect.   *Arthur Koestler*

Just at the age 'twixt boy and youth. When thought is speech, and speech is truth.
William Shakespeare

Not yet old enough for a man, nor young enough for a boy.   *William Shakespeare*

A house on moving day—a temporary mess.
Julius E. Warren

In America, a period of time spent as if it were the last fling at life, rather than a preparation for it.
Anon.

That period in life in which the young feel a great urge to answer the telephone.   *Anon.*

That period in life when one's parents become more difficult.   *Anon.*

That period in life when a boy refuses to believe that someday he'll be as stupid as his parents.
Anon.

That period when the young feel their parents should be told the facts of life.   *Anon.*

A stage between infancy and adultery.   *Anon.*

SEE ALSO CHILDREN, JUVENILE DELIN-QUENCY, YOUTH.

ADOLESCENT

One who goes from humpty-dumpty to hanky-panky.   *Hyman Maxwell Berston*

Those who are quickest to discern hypocrisy.
Eugene E. Brussell

One who is well informed about anything he doesn't have to study.   *Marcelene Cox*

(One who) looks inward; the adult can look outward.   *Pamela Frankau*

One who has reached the age of dissent.
Harold Leslie

The awkward age when a child is too old to say something cute and too young to say something sensible.   *Anon.*

ADULT

A child blown up by age.   *Simone de Beauvoir*

When childhood dies, its corpses are called adults and they enter society.   *Brian Aldiss*

An obsolete child.   *Theodore Geisel*

(Those who) have forgotten what it is to be a child.   *Randall Jarrell*

To be alone.   *Jean Rostand*

A kernal of instinct surrounded by a vast husk of education.   *Bertrand A. Russell*

A word used to lure children to movies.
Sidney Skolsky

(When) a child . . . realizes he has a right not only to be right but also to be wrong.   *Thomas Szasz*

One who has ceased to grow vertically but not horizontally.   *Anon.*

SEE ALSO AGE, MAN, MATURITY, MIDDLE-AGE, WOMAN.

ADULTERY

Whosoever looks on a woman to lust after her hath committed adultery with her already in his heart.   *Bible: Matthew, V, 28.*

Whosoever shall put away his wife, except it be for fornication, and shall marry another, commits adultery.   *Bible: Matthew, XIX, 9.*

Usually an act done under cover of darkness and secrecy, and in which the parties are seldom surprised.   *Decision of the Maryland Court of Appeals, 1931.*

To set your neighbor's bed a-shaking . . . an ancient and long-established custom.   *Juvenal*

A man is guilty of adultery if he marries a divorced woman; and so is he who divorces his wife, save on the ground of misconduct, to marry again.   *Firmianus Lactantius*

The application of democracy to love.

Henry Louis Mencken

Not only when you look with...desire at a woman who is not your wife, but also if you look in the same manner at your wife.

Pope John Paul 2

If a man leaves his wife and she marries another, she commits adultery. *Saint Augustine*

To leave a wife who is sterile in order to take another by whom children may be had. Anyone doing this is guilty of adultery. *Saint Augustine*

(The) great democratic vice.

George Bernard Shaw

SEE ALSO CUCKOLD, LOVERS, MISTRESS, SEX (LOVE), SIN.

ADVANTAGE

To seize an opportunity...to know when to forego an advantage. *Benjamin Disraeli*

Recognition of opportunity. *Max Gralnick*

To enjoy no advantage at all.

Henry David Thoreau

SEE ALSO ANCESTRY, WEALTH.

ADVENTURE

Rightly considered, only an inconvenience.

Gilbert Keith Chesterton

Something you seek for pleasure, or even for profit, like a gold rush or invading a country...the thing you *will* to occur.

Katherine Ann Porter

ADVENTURER

An outlaw...Adventure must start with running away from home. *William Bolitho*

The tremendous outsider. *William Bolitho*

With the woman-adventurer all is love or hate. Her adventure is man; her type is not the prospector, but the courtesan. That is, her adventure is an escape, developing inevitably into a running fight with the institution of marriage.

William Bolitho

One who has a passion to realize the impossible.

Adapted from Isaac M. Wise

ADVERTISEMENTS

The principal reason why the businessman has come to inherit the earth. *James R. Adams*

The mouthpiece of business. *James R. Adams*

Eighty-five per cent confusion and fifteen per cent commission. *Fred Allen*

The ideals of a nation. *Norman Douglas*

One of the most interesting and difficult of modern literary forms. *Aldous Huxley*

The only truths to be relied on in a newspaper.

Thomas Jefferson

Legalized lying. *Herbert G. Wells*

A creator of false hunger. *Anon.*

SEE ALSO ADVERTISING, NEWSPAPERS, PUBLIC RELATIONS, TELEVISION COMMERCIAL.

ADVERTISING

A sort of tumor, that ends by killing the victim's sympathies. *Henry B. Adams*

The great art in...finding out a proper method to catch the reader's eye. *Joseph Addison*

Instruments of ambition. *Joseph Addison*

Advertising isn't a science. It's persuasion...an art. *William Bernbach*

What you do when you can't go see somebody.

Fairfax Cone

To avoid the concrete promise...and cultivate the delightfully vague. *John Crosby*

The education of the public as to who you are, where you are, and what you have to offer in way of skill, talent, commodity. *Elbert Hubbard*

An organized effort to extend and intensify craving. *Aldous Huxley*

Promise—large promise—is the soul of advertising. *Samuel Johnson*

The science of arresting the human intelligence long enough to get money from it.

Stephen B. Leacock

The cheapest way of selling goods, particularly if the goods are worthless.   *Sinclair Lewis*

The place where the selfish interests of the manufacturer coincide with the interests of society.
David Ogilvy

That essential American strategy.
Richard H. Rovere

The modern substitute for argument; its function is to make the worse appear better.
George Santayana

The art of making whole lies out of half truths.
Edgar A. Shoaff

Millions of dollars . . . spent annually to entice people to dedicate themselves to the "cult of things," nice things which are phony, valueless, glamorous, sinful.   *Rolan Simonitsch*

A campaign of subversion against intellectual honesty and moral integrity.   *Arnold Toynbee*

A technique which makes you believe you've longed all your life for something you've never heard of before.   *Anon.*

The vision which reproaches man for the paucity of his desires.   *Anon.*

The whip which hustles humanity up the road to the Better Mousetrap.   *Anon.*

A paying thought.   *Anon.*

Bragging for profit.   *Anon.*

SEE ALSO ADVERTISEMENTS, NEWSPAPERS, PROPAGANDA, PUBLIC RELATIONS, TELEVISION, TELEVISION COMMERCIAL.

ADVICE

The suggestions you give someone else which you hope will work for your benefit.
Ambrose Bierce

To seek another's approval of a course already decided upon.   *Ambrose Bierce*

A drug on the market; the supply always exceeds the demand.   *Josh Billings*

What is best to yourself given by yourself.
Adapted from Cicero

Like snow; the softer it falls, the longer it dwells upon, and the deeper it sinks into, the mind.
Samuel Taylor Coleridge

Always a confession.   *Emile Herzog*

(Something) offensive, because it shows us that we are known to others, as well as to ourselves.
Samuel Johnson

What we ask for when we already know the answer but wish we didn't.   *Erica Jong*

What a man gives when he gets too old to set a bad example.   *La Rochefoucauld*

A sacred thing.   *Plato*

A thing sought by all, but taken by none, including the one who gives it.   *Harry Ruby*

One of those injuries which a good man ought, if possible, to forgive.   *Horace Smith*

A commodity more blessed to give than receive.
Anon.

Something that costs you nothing unless you act upon it.   *Anon.*

AFFECTATION

A fault.   *Miguel de Cervantes*

It is a form of affectation to emphasize the fact that you do not indulge in it.   *La Rochefoucauld*

An awkward and forced imitation of what should be genuine and easy, wanting the beauty that accompanies what is natural.   *John Locke*

The whole aim of affectation is to cheat you.
Adapted from G. H. Powell

What spoils fine faces.   *Anon.*

SEE ALSO HYPROCRISY.

AFFECTION

A body of enigmas, mysteries, riddles wherein two so become one that they both become two.
Adapted from Thomas Browne

The purest affection the heart can hold is the honest love of a nine-year old.   *Holman Day*

These jets . . . which make a young world for me.
Ralph Waldo Emerson

A bad adviser.   *German Proverb*

A woman's whole life.   *Washington Irving*

SEE ALSO FEELING, HAPPINESS, LOVE.

AFTER-THOUGHT

A tardy sense of prudence that prompts one to try to shut his mouth about the time he has put his foot in it.   *Gideon Wurdz*

SEE ALSO REPARTEE.

AGE

Always 15 years older than I am.

Bernard Baruch

Only a number, a cipher for the records. A man can't retire his experience.   *Bernard Baruch*

(Something that) doesn't matter unless you're a cheese.   *Billie Burke*

Succeeding stages.   *Thomas Campbell*

A matter of feeling, not of years.

George W. Curtis

Youth is a blunder; manhood is a struggle; old age a regret.   *Benjamin Disraeli*

The essence of age is intellect.

Ralph Waldo Emerson

Childhood is ignorant, boyhood is lighthearted, youth is rash, and old age is ill-humored.

Luis de Granada

When a man is young he writes songs; grown up, he speaks in proverbs; in old age he preaches pessimism.   *Hebrew Proverb*

A bad habit which a busy man has no time to form.   *Emile Herzog*

A person's age is not dependent upon the number of years that have passed over his head, but upon the number of colds that have passed through it.

Woods Hutchinson

At eighteen, one adores at once; at twenty, one loves; at thirty, one desires; at forty, one reflects.

Paul de Kock

Age is not all decay; it is the ripening, the swelling, of the fresh life within, that withers and bursts the husks.   *George Macdonald*

Youth is fair, a graceful stag,
Leaping, playing in a park
Age is gray, a toothless hag,
Stumbling in the dark.   *Isaac Peretz*

The first forty years of life give us the text; the next thirty supply the commentary on it.

Arthur Schopenhauer

A matter of arteries.

Adapted from Thomas Sydenham

Youth is a garland of roses; old age a crown of willows.   *Talmud: Sabbath, 152a.*

A man is still young as long as women can make him happy or unhappy. He reaches middle age when they can no longer make him unhappy. He is old when they cease to make him either happy or unhappy.   *Anon.*

At ten, a child; at twenty, wild;
    At thirty, tame if ever;
At forty, wise; at fifty, rich;
    At sixty, good, or never.   *Anon.*

The only thing that comes to us without effort.

Anon.

Your length in years.   *Anon.*

When one begins to exchange emotions for symptoms.   *Anon.*

SEE ALSO MATURITY, MIDDLE AGE, OLD AGE, YOUTH.

AGGRESSION

An innate, independent, instinctual disposition in man...it constitutes the most powerful obstacle to culture.   *Sigmund Freud*

The evil projected by the aggressor into the souls of those he aims to destroy or oppress.

Gustave Thibon

AGNOSTIC

One who doesn't know whether God exists, but is afraid to say so loudly in case God might hear him.   *Eugene E. Brussell*

A man who doesn't know whether there is A God or not, doesn't know whether he has a soul or not, doesn't know whether there is a future life or not, doesn't believe that anyone else knows any more about these matters than he does, and thinks it a waste of time to try to find out.

Richard Henry Dana

A confession of ignorance where honest inquiry might easily find the truth. "Agnostic" is but Greek for "ignoramus."   *Tyron Edwards*

I took thought, and invented what I conceived to be the appropriate title of "agnostic." It came into my head as suggestively antithetic to the "Gnostic" of Church history.

Thomas Henry Huxley

The person who admits that he does not know, and is consequently open to learning.

David E. Trueblood

SEE ALSO AGNOSTICISM, ATHEIST, FREE THINKERS, SKEPTIC.

AGNOSTICISM

The philosophical, ethical, and religious dry rot of the modern world.   *F. E. Abbot*

I do not pretend to know where many ignorant men are sure—that is all that agnosticism means.

Clarence S. Darrow

A shadow cast by the eclipse of the supernatural...Its meaning departs when the intellectual outlook is directed wholly to the natural world.   *John Dewey*

A theory about knowledge and not about religion.

Richard Downey

Not open-mindedness; it is culpable inaction.

Nels F. Ferré

It is wrong for a man to say that he is certain of the objective truth of any proposition unless he can produce evidence which logically justifies that certainty. This is what agnosticism assets.

Thomas Henry Huxley

Not a creed, but a method, the essence of which lies in the rigorous application of a single principle...that every man should be able to give a reason for the faith that is in him.

Thomas Henry Huxley

Simply means that a man shall not say he knows or believes that for which he has no grounds for professing to believe.   *Thomas Henry Huxley*

Help for the living, hope for the dead.

Robert G. Ingersoll

The everlasting perhaps.   *Francis Thompson*

SEE ALSO AGNOSTIC, ATHEISM, SKEPTICISM.

AGREEABLE

A person who agrees with me.

Benjamin Disraeli

He who is endowed with the natural bent to do acceptable things, from a delight he takes in them merely as such.   *Richard Steele*

AGRICULTURE

SEE FARM, FARMING.

ALCOHOL

SEE DRINKING, WINE.

ALCOHOLIC

SEE DRUNKENNESS.

ALIMONY

Buying oats for a dead horse.   *Arthur Baer*

Billing minus cooing.   *Mary Dorsey*

A system which results when two people make a mistake and one of them continues to pay for it.

Jimmy Lyons

Disinterest, compounded annually.

Walter McDonald

The ransom that the happy pay to the devil.

Henry Louis Mencken

The wages of sin is alimony.   *Carolyn Wells*

Matrimonial insurance for women paid by men for having poor judgment.   *Anon.*

The cash surrender value of the American male.

Anon.

The act of giving comfort to the enemy.   *Anon.*

The high cost of leaving.   *Anon.*

The male's best proof that you have to pay for your mistakes.   *Anon.*

The result of marrying in haste and repenting insolvent.   *Anon.*

ALLEGORY

Time balm.   *Anon.*

A form of guaranteed income.   *Anon.*

What a woman who loved a man for all he is worth gets.   *Anon.*

SEE ALSO DIVORCE, MARRIAGE, WIFE.

ALLEGORY

Like so many tracts of light in a discourse, that make everything about them clear and beautiful.
Joseph Addison

A man's life.   *John Keats*

ALLIANCE

SEE TREATY.

ALMS

SEE CHARITY, PHILANTHROPY.

ALONE

SEE LONELINESS, SOLITUDE.

ALTRUISM

Disregarding one's own cause.
Eugene E. Brussell

Inverted egotism.   *Jacob Cohen*

The art of using others with the air of loving them.
Rene Dubreuil

Living largely for the good and happiness of others.   *Adapted from Judah Moscato*

Mowing your neighbor's lawn.
Harry Thompson

Making the common good the mark of one's aim.
Adapted from John Wise

Slavery.   *Anon.*

Desiring nothing for others that you do not desire for yourself.   *Anon.*

The art of doing unselfish things for selfish reasons.   *Anon.*

SEE ALSO CHARITY, IDEALIST, PHI-LANTHROPY, REFORM.

AMATEUR

A public nuisance who confounds his ambition with his ability.   *Ambrose Bierce*

One who practices something without hope of fame and money or of even doing it well.
Adapted from Gilbert Keith Chesterton

SEE ALSO DILETTANTE.

AMBASSADOR

In American politics, a person who having failed to secure an office from the people is given one by the Administration on condition that he leave the country.   *Ambrose Bierce*

(One who) should be versed in all the sciences; he should understand hints, gestures and expressions of the face; he should be honest, skillful and of good family.   *Code of Manu, VII*

A man whose vocabulary becomes three times as extensive and twice as indistinct as any one elses.
Adapted from John Kenneth Galbraith

The eyes and ears of states.
Francesco Guicciardini

A man who had the most money and the fewest votes.   *John D. Lodge*

Ambassadors are, in the full meaning of the term, titled spies.   *Napoleon I*

An honest man, sent abroad to lie for the commonwealth.   *Henry Wotton*

One who makes the world safe for hypocrisy.
Anon.

A paid political tourist.   *Anon.*

A politician who is given a job abroad in order to get him out of the country.   *Anon.*

SEE ALSO DIPLOMAT.

AMBIDEXTROUS

Able to pick with equal skill a right-hand pocket or a left.   *Ambrose Bierce*

AMBITION

The desire of rising.   *Thomas Adams*

(That which) raises a secret tumult in the soul; it inflames the mind, and puts it into a violent hurry of thought. *Joseph Addison*

The excrement of glory. *Pietro Aretino*

(That which) destroys its possessor.
Babylonian Talmud: Yoma, 86a.

Like choler, which is a humor that makes man active, earnest, full of alacrity and stirring, if it be not stopped. But if it be stopped, and cannot have its way, it becomes a dust, and thereby malign and venomous. *Francis Bacon*

An overmastering desire to be vilified by enemies while living and made ridiculous by friends when dead. *Ambrose Bierce*

Not what man does...but what man would do.
Robert Browning

A proud covetousness, or a dry thirst of honor, a great torture of the mind, composed of envy, pride...a gallant madness, one defines it a pleasant poison. *Robert Burton*

The only power that combats love.
Colley Cibber

An insatiable desire for honor, command, power, and glory. *Cicero*

The mind's immodesty. *William D'Avenant*

That worst of deities...queen of wrong.
Euripides

The wings of great actions. *Johann W. Goethe*

A condition inspired by the wish to be first.
Max Gralnick

The desire to excel. *Max Gralnick*

Bondage. *Ibn Gabirol*

To be unhappy at home is the ultimate result of all ambition. *Samuel Johnson*

The last affection a high mind can put off.
Ben Jonson

Avarice on stilts and masked.
Walter Savage Landor

This senseless chasing of rainbows.
Frederick Loewe

In a private man a vice...in a prince...virtue.
Philip Massinger

A secret poison. *Saint Bernard*

The shadow of a dream. *William Shakespeare*

Goaled rush. *Ellis Stewart*

(A vice which) often puts men upon doing the meanest offices; so climbing is performed in the same posture with creeping. *Jonathan Swift*

That which brings the mind into full activity.
Henry J. Taylor

Nets to catch the wind. *John Webster*

The last refuge of the failure. *Oscar Wilde*

Ambition has but one reward for all:
A little power, a little transient fame,
A grave to rest in, and a fading name!
William Winter

Bubbles on the rapid stream of time.
Edward Young

Achievement. *Israel Zangwill*

Aggravated itching of the palm. *Anon.*

A mental condition which compels one to work one's self to death in order to live. *Anon.*

SEE ALSO FAME, SUCCESS.

AMBULANCE

A crash and carry car. *Anon.*

The shuttle between a speeding car and a wheelchair. *Anon.*

AMERICA

An asylum on earth for civil and religious liberty.
Samuel Adams

Half-brother of the world! With something good and bad of every land. *Philip J. Bailey*

A European outpost culturally and spiritually. The whole doctrine of white supremacy comes from Europe. *James Baldwin*

The country where you buy a lifetime supply of aspirin for one dollar, and use it up in two weeks.
John Barrymore

Where humanity, for the first time in modern history, was let loose. *Hans Bendix*

A place where Jewish merchants sell Zen love beads to agnostics for Christmas.

John B. Brimer

We are not a Nation, but a Union, a confederacy of equal and sovereign States. *John C. Calhoun*

A dirty chimney on fire. *Thomas Carlyle*

A commonwealth in which common men and women should count for more than elsewhere.

Lord Charnwood

A huge rescue squad on a twenty-four hour call to any spot on the globe where dispute . . . may erupt.

Eldridge Cleaver

The only nation in history which . . . has gone directly from barbarism to degeneration without the usual interval of civilization.

Georges Clemenceau

The greatest potential force, material, moral, and spiritual, in the world. *G. Lowes Dickinson*

A country of young men.

Ralph Waldo Emerson

America means opportunity, freedom, power.

Ralph Waldo Emerson

(A place where) the geography is sublime, but the men are not: the inventions are excellent, but the inventors one is sometimes ashamed of.

Ralph Waldo Emerson

A wild democracy, the riot of mediocrities . . . Our few fine persons are apt to die.

Ralph Waldo Emerson

A sanctuary on the earth for individual man.

William Faulkner

An anti-paradise, but it has so much room and so many possibilities, and in the end one does come to belong to it. *Sigmund Freud*

A mistake, a magnificent mistake, but a mistake nonetheless. *Sigmund Freud*

A place where an hour is forty minutes.

German Proverb

(A country which) has liberty without license and authority without despotism. *James C. Gibbons*

The land of unlimited opportunities.

Ludwig Goldberger

The only country deliberately founded on a good idea. *John Gunther*

A place where the people have the right to complain about the lack of freedom.

Louis Hirsch

A civilization that operates its economy and government, and satisfies most of its cultural needs without the aid of the typical intellectual.

Eric Hoffer

(A) country (which) gives a man elbow room to do what is nearest to his heart. *Eric Hoffer*

The only place where man is full-grown.

Oliver Wendell Holmes 1

The greatest law factory the world has ever known. *Charles Evans Hughes*

America . . . may be described as a land where the Common Man is perpetually bidding his fellow to go to hell, and at the same time doing his best to get him into heaven. *Lawrence P. Jacks*

Equal and exact justice to all men.

Thomas Jefferson

The general store for the world . . . Most of all, merchants for a better way of life.

Lady Bird Johnson

Not merely a nation, but a nation of nations.

Lyndon Baines Johnson

An economic system prouder of the distribution of its products than of the products themselves.

Murray Kempton

A nation of immigrants.

John Fitzgerald Kennedy

Mother of exiles. *Emma Lazarus*

America is a tune. It must be sung together.

Gerald S. Lee

The last abode of romance and other medieval phenomena. *Eric Linklater*

She of the open soul and open door.

James Russell Lowell

A map of endlessness, of opening out, of forever and ever. *Archibald MacLeish*

A land of boys who refuse to grow up.

Salvador de Madariaga

A great death continent populated only with machines and walking corpses.

Jacques Maritain

A cocktail culture whose unlovely symbol is the ring on the best mahogany.   *Elsa Maxwell*

A nation of twenty-million bathrooms with a humanist in every tub.   *Mary McCarthy*

Not a nation so much as a world.

Herman Melville

(A) conservtive country without any conservative ideology.   *C. Wright Mills*

A dream in the constant process of realization, a vision constantly being fulfilled.   *Judah Nadich*

The largest shopping center in the world.

Richard Milhous Nixon

A country that has leapt from barbarism to decadence without touching civilization.

John O'Hara

Almost a continent and hardly yet a nation.

Ezra Pound

This synagogue is our temple, this city our Jerusalem, this happy land our Palestine.

Gustav Poznanaski

An overdeveloped urban nation with an under-developed system for dealing with its city problems.   *James Reston*

A nation that conceives many odd inventions for getting somewhere but can think of nothing to do when it gets there.   *Will Rogers*

(A land) where law and custom alike are based upon the dreams of spinsters.

Bertrand A. Russell

A young country with an old mentality.

George Santayana

A powerful solvent. It seems to neutralise every intellectual element, however tough and alien it may be, and to fuse it in the native goodwill, complacency, thoughtlessness, and optimism.

George Santayana

A "happy-ending" nation.   *Dore Schary*

The child society *par excellence* . . . the society of all rights and no obligations.   *Karl Shapiro*

This great spectacle of human happiness.

Sydney Smith

In the United States there is more space where nobody is than where anybody is. That is what makes America what it is.   *Gertrude Stein*

The sovereign power of the people, exercised through their representatives in Congress, with the concurrence of the executive.

Thaddeus Stevens

A large, friendly dog in a very small room. Every time it wags its tail, it knocks over a chair.

Arnold J. Toynbee

The finest society on a grand scale that the world has thus far produced.   *Alfred North Whitehead*

The greatest poem.   *Walt Whitman*

If she stands for one thing more than another, it is for the sovereignty of self-governing people.

Woodrow Wilson

The only idealistic nation in the world.

Woodrow Wilson

The place where you cannot kill your government by killing the men who conduct it.

Woodrow Wilson

Not a mere body of traders; it is a body of free men. Our greatest is built upon our freedom . . . moral, not material.   *Woodrow Wilson*

The only fabulous country; it is the only place where miracles not only happen, but where they happen all the time.   *Thomas Wolfe*

God's crucible, the great melting-pot.

Israel Zangwill

A country where all the people are created equal and are free to become otherwise.   *Anon.*

This face of many faces.   *Anon.*

A country where they lock up juries and let defendants out.   *Anon.*

SEE ALSO AMERICANISM, AMERICANS, YANKEE.

AMERICAN CONSTITUTION

Essentially an economic document based upon the concept that the fundamental rights of private property are anterior to government and morally beyond the reach of popular majorities.

Charles A. Beard

Laws of heavenly origin. It was not borrowed from Greece or Rome, but from the Bible.

Lyman Beecher

A way of ordering society, adequate for imaginative statesmanship.   *Felix Frankfurter*

A charter emanating directly from the people.

Arthur Goldberg

The Constitution is what the judges say it is.

Charles Evans Hughes

Our basic law...is distinctive among the basic law of all nations, even the free nations of the West, in that it prescribes no national dogma: economic, social, or religious.

Lyndon Baines Johnson

The Constitution was designed to remedy existing injustices perpetrated by the superior force of an interested and overbearing majority.

James Madison

A superior, paramount law, unchangeable by ordinary means.   *John Marshall*

The charter of all that is distinctively American in our national spirit.   *Edward Mooney*

The most marvelously elastic compilation of rules of government ever written.

Franklin Delano Roosevelt

A Charter of Anarchism. It was not an instrument of government: it was a guarantee to the whole American nation that it never should be governed at all. And that is exactly what the Americans wanted.   *George Bernard Shaw*

Not a mere lawyer's document; it is a vehicle of life, and its spirit is always the spirit of the age.

Woodrow Wilson

SEE ALSO AMERICA, AMERICANS.

AMERICANISM

To respect the rights of others.

William Jennings Bryan

Carry the American flag, and keep step to the music of the Union.   *Rufus Choate*

A mode of living in which we find the joy of life and the joy of work harmoniously combined.

Albert Einstein

Deep involvement in the destiny of men everywhere.   *Dwight David Eisenhower*

A heritage of tolerance, moderation, and individual liberty that was implanted from the very beginnings of European settlement in the New World. America has quite rightly been called a nation that was "born free."

James W. Fulbright

Liberty without license and authority without despotism.   *James Gibbons*

To embody human liberty in workable government.   *Herbert Hoover*

The uncrossed desert and the unclimbed ridge. It is the star that is not reached and the harvest that's sleeping in the unplowed ground.

Lyndon Baines Johnson

We aspire to nothing that belongs to others. We seek no dominion over our fellow man, but man's dominion over tyranny and misery.

Lyndon Baines Johnson

The American system of private enterprise and economic democracy.

Franklin Delano Roosevelt

Those who are Americans and nothing else.

Theodore Roosevelt

A question of principle, or purpose, of Idealism, of Character; it is not a matter of birthplace or creed or line of descent.   *Theodore Roosevelt*

Equalitarianism, love of freedom, and bounding energy.   *Stephen J. Taylor*

'Tis our true policy to steer clear of permanent alliances, with any portion of the foreign world.

George Washington

Consists in utterly believing in the principles of America.   *Woodrow Wilson*

SEE ALSO AMERICA, YANKEE.

AMERICANS

Hardness and materialism, exaggeration and boastfulness...false smartness, a false audacity, a want of soul and delicacy.   *Matthew Arnold*

The American mind...is not formed by books, but...by newspapers and the Bible.

Van Wyck Brooks

A people who are still...but in the gristle, and not yet hardened into the love of manhood.

Edmund Burke

Most Americans are born drunk...They have a sort of permanent intoxication from within, a sort of invisible champagne...Americans do not need to drink to inspire them to do anything.

Gilbert Keith Chesterton

A sort of queer Englishman.   *Agatha Christie*

Fixers rather than preventers.   *James Doolittle*

A puny and fickle folk. Avarice, hesitation, following are our diseases.   *Ralph Waldo Emerson*

Only the continuation of the English genius into new conditions, more or less propitious.
                        Ralph Waldo Emerson

A fortunate people but a very commonsensical people, with vision high but their feet on the earth, with belief in themselves and faith in God.
                        Warren G. Harding

One step forward,—and in that advancing figure you have the American.   *Thomas W. Higginson*

The Romans of the modern world—the great assimilating people.   *Oliver Wendell Holmes 1*

One who will sacrifice property, ease, and security in order that he and his children may retain the rights of free men.   *Harold Ickes*

Not a thoughtful people; they are too busy to stop and question their values.   *William R. Inge*

They are a race of convicts, and ought to be thankful for anything we allow them short of hanging.   *Samuel Johnson*

Enslaved, illogical, elate,
    He greets the embarrassed Gods, nor fears
To shake the iron hand of fate
    Or match with destiny for beers.
                        Rudyard Kipling

The desire for riches is their ruling passion.
                        La Rochefoucauld

(One who is) nomadic in religion, in ideas, in morals.   *James Russell Lowell*

People who prefer the Continent to their own country, but (who) refuse to learn its languages.
                        Edward Lucas

The peculiar, chosen people—the Israel of our time—we bear the ark of liberties of the world.
                        Herman Melville

Simply one who has put out of his mind all doubts and questionings, and who accepts . . . the whole body of official doctrine of his day.
                        Henry Louis Mencken

That singular people who know a little, and but a little, of everything.   *John Neal*

A primitive people camouflaged behind the latest inventions.   *José Ortega y Gasset*

(Those who) make money their pursuit.
                        Richard Parkinson

Cut an American into a hundred pieces and boil him down, you will find him all Fourth of July.
                        Wendell Phillips

The first requisite of a good citizen in this republic of ours is that he shall be able and willing to pull his weight.   *Theodore Roosevelt*

A sane and healthy man, who believes in decency and has a wholesome mind.
                        Theodore Roosevelt

Children of the crucible.   *Theodore Roosevelt*

The great idealist among mankind.
                        Leon Samson

The perfect conformist.   *André Siegfried*

The most materialistic people in the world.
                        George W. Steevens

An Anglo-Saxon relapsed into semibarbarism.
                        Bayard Taylor

(An Englishman is) a person who does things because they have been done before. (An American is) a person who does things because they haven't been done before.   *Mark Twain*

One who gets mad when an alien cusses the institutions he cusses.   *Anon.*

Similar participants in a uniform way of life.
                        Anon.

SEE ALSO AMERICA, AMERICANISM, YANKEE.

AMNESTY

A noble world. What it stands for is the true dictate of wisdom.   *Aeschines*

The state's magnanimity to those offenders whom it would be too expensive to punish.
                        Ambrose Bierce

The most beautiful word in all human speech.
                        Victor Hugo

AMUSEMENT

A metaphysical trick to deceive our anguish.
                        Jean C. De Menasce

Its main purpose is to keep people from vice.

Adapted from Samuel Johnson

Taking your fun where you find it.

Adapted from Rudyard Kipling

The happiness of those who cannot think.

Alexander Pope

When men are rightly occupied . . . their work.

John Ruskin

SEE ALSO ENTERTAINER, SPORTS.

ANALOGY

The least misleading thing we have.

Samuel Butler 2

All perception of truth is the perception of analogy; we reason from our hands to our head.

Henry David Thoreau

ANARCHIST

One who believes people should go about doing just as they please—short of altering any of the things to which he has grown accustomed.

Adapted from Max Beerbohm

One who disaffiliates himself from the machinations of society and government in order to fulfill his personal quest.   *Eugene E. Brussell*

A person more interested in his own fate than in who gets elected to Congress.

Warren Goldberg

One who maps and surveys the air and constructs dainty Utopias with the building-blocks quarried from his . . . credulity.   *Elbert Hubbard*

A militant bourgeois who has deserted both Rome and Reason because he cannot stand the competition.   *Elbert Hubbard*

A bourgeois turned inside out.   *Nikolai Lenin*

The ordinary man . . . wants to do as he likes. He may want his neighbor to be governed, but he himself doesn't want to be governed. He is mortally afraid of government officials and policemen.   *George Bernard Shaw*

One who wants to be left alone.   *Anon.*

ANARCHY

The liberation of the human mind from the dominion of religion; the liberation of the human body from the dominion of property; liberation from the shackles and restraints of government.

Johann W. Goethe

The possibility of organization without discipline, fear or punishment, and without the pressure of property.   *Johann W. Goethe*

An adroit mixture of customs that are beneficial to society, and could be followed even if no law existed.   *Peter A. Kropotkin*

A name given to a . . . theory of life and conduct under which society is conceived without government.   *Pëtr A. Kropotkin*

The doctrine that all the affairs of men should be managed by individuals or voluntary associations, and that the State should be abolished.

Benjamin R. Tucker

ANATOMY

Anatomy is to physiology as geography to history; it describes the theater of events.

Jean F. Fernel

Something everyone has but it looks better on a girl.   *Bruce Raeburn*

SEE ALSO BODY.

ANCESTRY

An account of one's descent from an ancestor who did not particularly care to trace his own.

Ambrose Bierce

The known part of the route from an arboreal ancestor with a swim bladder to an urban descendant with a cigarette.   *Ambrose Bierce*

(Something that) increases in the ratio of distance.

George W. Curtis

Man is descended from a hairy-tailed quadruped, probably arboreal in its habits.

Charles Darwin

The blending of all emotions. How . . . superior to the herd is the man whose father only is famous! Imagine then the feelings of one who can trace his line through a thousand years of heroes and of princes.   *Benjamin Disraeli*

I am my own ancestor.   *Andoche Junot*

The man who has not anything to boast of but his illustrious ancestors is like a potato—the only good belonging to him is underground.
Thomas Overbury

A desirable thing to have, but the glory belongs to our ancestors.   *Adapted from Plutarch*

A lamp to posterity.   *Sallust*

The last people I should choose to have a visiting acquaintance with.   *Richard Brinsley Sheridan*

Those transparent swindles.   *Mark Twain*

If famous, something we all take credit for as if we had something to do with it.   *Anon.*

The bark of a family tree.   *Anon.*

SEE ALSO ARISTOCRACY, BREEDING, GENTLEMAN, HEREDITY, RANK.

ANCIENTS

The wisdom of the cradle.   *Thomas Browne*

People who were really new in everything.
Blaise Pascal

SEE ALSO CLASSICS, HISTORY.

ANGEL

He shall give his angels charge over thee, to keep thee in all thy ways.   *Bible: Psalms, XCI, 2.*

The dispensers and administrators of the Divine beneficence toward us; they regard our safety...and exercise a constant solicitude that no evil befall us.   *John Calvin*

A spiritual creature created by God without a body, for the service of Christendom and of the Church.   *Martin Luther*

Everyone entrusted with a mission is an angel...All forces that reside in the body are angels.   *Moses Maimonides*

Angels may become men or demons, and again from the latter they may rise to be men or angels.
Origen

Guardians.   *Saint Ambrose*

In heaven...nobody in particular.
George Bernard Shaw

Angels are human forms, or men, for I have conversed with them as man to man.
Emanuel Swedenborg

ANGER

A mental imbecility.   *Hosea Ballou*

(A state that) begins with folly, and ends with repentance.   *Henry G. Bohn*

It is the man.   *Cabanis*

An expensive luxury in which only men of a certain income can indulge.   *George W. Curtis*

(Something that) boils at different degrees.
Ralph Waldo Emerson

A vulgar passion directed to vulgar ends, and it always sinks to the level of its object.
Ernest Feuchtersleben

One of the sinews of the soul; he that wants it hath a maimed mind.   *Thomas Fuller*

Overheating the oven.   *Warren Goldberg*

(A state that) starts with madness, and ends with regret.   *Abraham Hasdai*

Momentary insanity.   *Horace*

Before election, the righteous wrath of a candidate in the presence of evils that he has invented; after election day, his wail in the presence of the grave he did not dig.   *Elbert Hubbard*

(Sometimes) a violent blushing and scampering up and down of the blood upon hearing the truth about ourselves.   *Elbert Hubbard*

A wind which blows out the lamp of the mind.
Robert G. Ingersoll

An essential part of the outfit of every honest man.   *James Russell Lowell*

The seducer of thought. No man can think clearly when his fists are clenched.
George Jean Nathan

Brief madness, and, unchecked, becomes protracted madness, bringing shame and even death.
Petrarch

Valour's whetstone.   *Thomas Randolph*

Like those ruins which smash themselves on what they fall.   *Seneca*

Supping upon one's self.   *Anon.*

Something you never get rid of by losing.   *Anon.*

SEE ALSO HATRED.

ANGLO-SAXON

(One who) carries self-government and self-development with him wherever he goes.

Henry Ward Beecher

People who do not know how to enjoy themselves.

Adapted from Henry George

It is the outstanding mark of the Anglo-Saxon's philosophical provincialism that he places sex on the farcial index expurgatories along with his God, his wife, his dog.   *George Jean Nathan*

The qualities of the...race are industry, intelligence, and self-confidence.   *Anthony Trollope*

SEE ALSO AMERICA, CHURCH OF ENGLAND, ENGLAND, ENGLISH LANGUAGE, ENGLISHMEN.

ANIMALS

Agreeable friends—they ask no questions, they pass no criticisms.   *George Eliot*

Every man.   *Frederick the Great*

Nothing but the forms of our virtues and vices, wandering before our eyes, the visible phantoms of our souls.   *Victor Hugo*

Man in a stage of arrested development.

Christian Morgenstern

(Those who) hear about death for the first time when they die.   *Arthur Schopenhauer*

(Those who) never hear the clock strike...die without any idea of death...have no theologians to instruct them, their last moments are not disturbed by unwelcome and unpleasant ceremonies, their funerals cost them nothing, and no one starts lawsuits over their wills.   *Voltaire*

SEE ALSO CAT, DOG.

ANTHOLOGIST

A person who uses scissors and taste.

Philip Van Doren Stern

Praise the wise anthologist,
Who culls the best that's on the shelf.
None of us worthies shall be missed
Including his son, his wife and himself.   *Anon.*

ANTHOLOGY

A complete dispensary of medicine for the more common mental disorders, and may be used as much for prevention as cure.   *Robert Graves*

ANTIQUES

Remnants of history which have casually escaped the shipwrecks of time.   *Francis Bacon*

Glorified scrap.   *Max Gralnick*

Anything that has outlived its usefulness.

Oliver Herford

Beings that had lived for centuries, or else come back from the dead, without suffering any impairment of their integrity.   *Ernest Jones*

An object that has made a round trip to the attic.

Anon.

An object that fetches fancy prices for what grandmother threw out.   *Anon.*

Junk that had a second chance and took advantage of it.   *Anon.*

ANTI-SEMITISM

(A disease that) will die only with the last Jew.

Victor Adler

The socialism of fools.   *August Bebel*

A useful revolutionary expedient.   *Adolf Hitler*

A form of Christian hypocrisy. The Christian whitewashes himself by attributing his views to the Jew.   *Bernard Lazare*

(A belief which) diverts men from the real tasks confronting them...diverts them from the true causes of their woes.   *Jacques Maritain*

The final consequence of Judaism.

Friedrich W. Nietzsche

The most dangerous survival of cannibalism.

Joseph Stalin

A noxious weed.   *William Howard Taft*

A pathological condition, a peculiar form of sexual perversion.   *Leon Tolstoy*

The swollen envy of pigmy minds—meanness, injustice.   *Mark Twain*

One of its fundamental causes is that Jews exist . . . We carry the germs of Anti-Semitism in our knapsack on our backs.   *Chaim Weizmann*

SEE ALSO JEWS, JUDAISM, ZIONISM.

ANXIETY

The essence of conscience.   *Sigmund Freud*

In psychoanalysis . . . it comprehends many forms and degrees of fear, apprehensiveness, dread or even panic.   *Ernest Jones*

The excitement, the *élan vital* which we carry with us, and which becomes stagnated if we are unsure about the role we have to play.

Frederick S. Perls

Fear of one's self.   *Wilhelm Stekel*

Frustrated coitus.   *Anon.*

SEE ALSO WORRY.

APATHY

SEE INDIFFERENCE.

APE

Man is God's ape, and an ape is zany to a man, doing over those tricks (especially if they be knavish) which he sees done before him.

Thomas Dekker

What is the ape to man? A laughingstock, a thing of shame.   *Friedrich W. Nietzsche*

Of beasts, it is confess'd, the ape
Comes nearest us in human shape;
Like man he imitates each fashion,
And malice is his ruling passion.

Jonathan Swift

An animal with the effrontery to resemble man.
Anon.

SEE ALSO EVOLUTION, MAN.

APHORISM

Portable wisdom.   *William R. Alger*

Predigested wisdom.   *Ambrose Bierce*

Boned wisdom for weak teeth.   *Ambrose Bierce*

The largest and worthiest portion of our knowledge . . . and the greatest and best of men is but an aphorism.   *Samuel Taylor Coleridge*

Thoughts one might have . . . expressed . . . by someone recognizedly wiser than oneself.

Marlene Dietrich

The excellence of aphorisms consists . . . in the comprehension of some obvious and useful truth in a few words.   *Samuel Johnson*

A personal observation inflated into a universal truth, a private posing as a general.

Stefan Kanfer

An aphorism is never exactly true; it is either a half-truth or one-and-a-half truths.   *Karl Kraus*

To say in ten sentences what other men say in whole books.   *Friedrich W. Nietzsche*

Aphorisms are salted not sugared almonds at Reason's feast.   *Logan P. Smith*

(That which) drags from obscurity a recognizable intuition by clothing it in words.

Adapted from Logan P. Smith

A proverb with long whiskers.   *Anon.*

APOLLO SPACE PROGRAM

A symbol of the insatiable curiosity of all mankind to explore the unknown.   *Edwin Aldrin*

A majestic milestone of man's quest for the stars, and it is a dramatic reminder of how far we have yet to go in the heavens as well as here on earth.
Joseph Alioto

One small step for man, one giant leap for mankind.   *Neil Armstrong*

The finest tribute to the most dynamic people in the world and their system.   *Vinod K. Bansal*

A circus to distract people's minds from the real problems which are here on the ground.

Eldridge Cleaver

A triumph of the squares.   *Eric Hoffer*

An American triumph.   *Patricia Lepis*

An event apart from the main flow of history.
James MacGregor

An accomplishment of middle America.   *Anon.*

SEE ALSO ASTRONAUTS, SPACE PROGRAM.

APOLOGY

To lay the foundation for a future offense.

Ambrose Bierce

A very desperate habit—one that is rarely cured . . . only egotism wrong side out. Nine times out of ten, the first thing a man's companion knows of his shortcomings is from his apology.

Oliver Wendall Holmes 1

An expression bestowed on a man if you are wrong, on a woman if you are right.   *Anon.*

To repeat an insult with variations.   *Anon.*

APOSTATE

SEE HERETIC.

APOSTLE

Fools for Christ's sake.

Bible: Corinthians, IV, 10.

A person who has grown round-shouldered from following the spoor of another.   *Elbert Hubbard*

Them that the Lord gave the keys of the Kingdom of Heaven.   *Pope Innocent 3*

The Apostles for our sake received the gospel from the Lord Jesus Christ; Jesus Christ was sent from God. Christ then is from God, and the Apostles from Christ. Both therefore came in due order from the will of God.   *Saint Clement*

These whom Christ had set up as masters, Who were His companions, His disciples, His intimates.   *Tertullian*

APPARITION

SEE GHOST.

APPETITE

The most violent appetites in all creatures are lust and hunger; the first is a perpetual call upon them to propagate their kind, the latter to preserve themselves.   *Joseph Addison*

An instinct thoughtfully implanted by Providence as a solution to the labor question.

Ambrose Bierce

A most direct line to the grave for the poor and rich alike.   *Eugene E. Brussell*

The best sauce.   *French Proverb*

Something you always bring to another's table.

Jewish Proverb

SEE ALSO ABSTINENCE, EATING, HUNGER, STOMACH.

APPLAUSE

The echo of a platitude.   *Ambrose Bierce*

The spur of noble minds, the end and aim of weak ones.   *Charles Caleb Colton*

Sweet, seducing charms.   *William Cowper*

The silence that accepts merit as the most natural thing in the world is the highest applause.

Ralph Waldo Emerson

The beginning of abuse.   *Japanese Proverb*

At the start of a lecture, it is a manifestation of faith. If it comes in the middle, a sign of hope. At the end, it is always charity.

Adapted from Fulton J. Sheen

Often less a blessing than a snare.

Edward Young

SEE ALSO FAME, POPULARITY.

APRIL

April is the cruelest month, breeding
Lilacs out of the dead land, mixing
Memory and desire, stirring
Dull roots with spring rain.

Thomas Stearns Eliot

Lovely fickleness.   *William H. Gibson*

A spirit of youth in everything.

William Shakespeare

Love's spring.   *William Shakespeare*

The uncertain weather month.   *Anon.*

The world growing green.   *Anon.*

The month when the green returns to the lawn, the lilac and the IRS.   *Anon.*

SEE ALSO SPRING.

APRIL FOOL

The March fool with another month added to his folly.   *Ambrose Bierce*

The day upon which we are reminded of what we are on the other 364.   *Mark Twain*

ARABS

A man who will pull down a whole temple to have a stone to sit on.   *Arabian Proverb*

Oriental Italians. A gifted, noble people; a people of wild, strong feelings, and of iron restraint over these; the characteristic of noblemindedness, of genius.   *Thomas Carlyle*

Arabs are not heathens. Idolatry was eliminated from their speech and hearts long ago, and they affirm properly the unity of God...Those who worship in mosques today have their hearts directed only toward heaven.   *Moses Maimonides*

SEE ALSO MOHAMMED, MOHAMMEDANISM.

ARCHAEOLOGIST

The best husband any woman can have: the older she gets, the more interested he is in her.

Agatha Christie

One whose career lies in ruins.   *Anon.*

ARCHAEOLOGY

The science of digging a hole and spinning a yarn about it.   *Ralph Alexander*

The Peeping Tom of the sciences...the sand-box of men who care not where they are going; they merely want to know where everybody else has been.   *James Bishop*

Frozen history.   *Gregory Mason*

Digging up the past.   *Leonard Wooley*

ARCHITECT

One who drafts a plan of your house, and plans a draft of your money.   *Ambrose Bierce*

A man who could build a church...by squinting at a sheet of paper.   *Charles Dickens*

The servant of society, of the style and the mores...of the customs of the demands of the time in which he works.   *Philip Johnson*

A fellow who talks you into debt three or four thousand dollars more.   *Abraham Martin*

ARCHITECTURE

The art of creating a space.

Yoshinobu Ashihara

The art of significant forms in space—that is, forms significant of their functions.

Claude Bragdon

The inner-relation and interaction of mass, space, place, and line.   *Craig Ellwood*

The flowering of geometry.

Ralph Waldo Emerson

Frozen music.   *Johann W. Goethe*

A particle is snatched from space, rhythmically modulated by membranes dividing it from surrounding chaos: that is Architecture.

Erno Goldfinger

The art of how to waste space.   *Philip Johnson*

A cultural instrument.   *Louis I. Kuhn*

The printing press of all ages.

La Rochefoucauld

A social art and only makes sense as the promoter and extender of human relations.

Denys Lasdum

The handwriting of man.   *Bernard Maybeck*

The thoughtful housing of the human spirit in the physical world.   *William O. Meyer*

The will of an epoch translated into space.

Ludwig Mies van der Rohe

A sort of oratory of power.

Friedrich W. Nietzsche

The pride of man, his triumph over gravitation, his will to power.   *Friedrich W. Nietzsche*

The art of resolving our needs for physical shelter harmoniously with the environment.

Gustavo de Roza

The manly language of a people inspired by resolute and common purpose.   *John Ruskin*

The frame of human existence...the only record you can read now of those civilizations which have passed into the distance.   *Frank Lloyd Wright*

ARGUMENTS

The longest distance between two points of view.
Daniel Bennett

The hereditary misfortune of thought.
Elias Canetti

The tree of knowledge blasted by dispute.
John Denham

Something you can easily win—with yourself.
Adapted from William Feather

A discussion which has two sides and no end.
Leonard Neubauer

The worst sort of conversation.   *Jonathan Swift*

(Something) vulgar, and often convincing.
Oscar Wilde

SEE ALSO CONTROVERSY, DEBATE, LAW- YERS.

ARISTOCRACY

The rich, the beautiful and well born.
John Quincy Adams

That form of government in which education and discipline are qualifications for suffrage or office- holding.   *Aristotle*

Rectitude, platitude, high-hatitude.
Margot Asquith

A corporation of the best, of the bravest.
Thomas Carlyle

Title...fortune...position.   *Thomas Carlyle*

It is well said, "Land is the right basis of an aristocracy"; whoever possesses the land, he, more...than any other, is the governor, vice-king of the poeple of the land.   *Thomas Carlyle*

What is left over from rich ancestors after the money is gone.   *John Ciardi*

A combination of many powerful men, for the purpose of maintaining and advancing their own particular interests. It is consequently a con- centration of all the most effective parts of a community for a given end; hence its energy, efficiency and success.

James Fenimore Cooper

The immediate power between tyranny and de- mocracy. It saves the people from violating the law, and the king from oppressing the people.

Benjamin R. Haydon

Nothing but ancient riches.   *George Herbert*

Virtue and talents.   *Thomas Jefferson*

A clean tradition, culture, public spirit, honesty, honor, courage—above all, courage.

Henry Louis Mencken

A deeply worldly quality, a profound sophistica- tion, an informed cynicism.   *William S. White*

An almost disdainful private detachment, a long...ancestral memory that rejects both too much love and too much hate; a willingness to die quietly...but never to be caught out in a senti- mentalism or a cliché of thought.

William S. White

SEE ALSO ANCESTRY, BREEDING, HERED- ITY, KING, NOBILITY.

ARISTOCRAT

Fellows that wear downy hats and clean shirts— guilty of education and suspected of bank ac- counts.   *Ambrose Bierce*

Pre-eminence of high descent.   *Robert Blair*

The democrat ripe and gone to seed.

Ralph Waldo Emerson

To be of such character that people do not care to know whether you are or are not.

Jean de La Bruyère

When he fights he fights in the manner of a gentleman fighting a duel, not in that of a long- shoreman cleaning out a waterfront saloon...he carefully guards his *amour propre* by assuming that his opponent is as decent a man as he is, and just as honest.   *Henry Louis Mencken*

Mere accident, and not a virtue.

Pietro Metastasio

One who speaks freely from what is dictated by a clear conscience.   *Adapted from Philo*

I am an aristocrat. I love liberty; I hate equality.

John Randolph

He who is by nature well fitted for virtue.

Seneca

A pedigree reaching as far back as the Deluge.

William Makepeace Thackeray

Anyone conducting himself with dignity and truthfulness.   *Anon.*

SEE ALSO ANCESTRY, ARISTOCRACY, GENTLEMAN, GREAT MAN, NOBILITY, RANK, SUPERIOR MAN.

ARISTOTLE (384-322 B.C.)

A schoolboy who knows the answer to a sum, but cannot get the figures to come to it.

Walter Bagehot

The master of them that know.   *Dante*

This accursed, proud, knavish heathen...God sent him as a plague for our sins.

Martin Luther

(He) who has an oar in every water and meddles with all things.   *Michel de Montaigne*

A man of excellent genius, though inferior in eloquence to Plato.   *Saint Augustine*

A fore-runner of Christian truth.   *Phillip Schaff*

Indistinctness of ideas, confusion of mind, and a confident use of language which led to the delusive notion that he had really mastered his subject...He put words in the place of things, subject in the place of object.   *John Tyndall*

(He) invented science, but destroyed philosophy.

Alfred North Whitehead

(He) discovered all the half-truths which were necessary to the creation of science.

Alfred North Whitehead

ARITHMETIC

SEE MATHEMATICS.

ARMS

Adult toys.   *Jean Follain*

(That which) makes men equal; a citizen's musket fires as well as a nobleman's.   *Heinrich Heine*

(That which) does more for peace than a thousand mild apostles.   *Theodor Herzl*

The props of peace.   *Latin Proverb*

The principal foundations of all states.

Niccolo Machiavelli

SEE ALSO WAR.

ARMY

A body of men assembled to rectify the mistakes of the diplomats.   *Josephus Daniels*

An instrument for bolstering, protecting and expanding the present.   *Eric Hoffer*

A body of humanitarians that seeks to impress on another body of men the beauty of non-resistance—by exterminating them.   *Elbert Hubbard*

Two armies are two bodies which meet and try to frighten each other.   *Napoleon I*

The basis of power, and...power is always in the hands of those who command the army.

Adapted from Leon Tolstoy

SEE ALSO GENERAL, MILITIA, SOLDIER, WAR.

ART

Every art is social...the result of a relation between the artist and his time.

James Truslow Adams

Chance and observation, nursed by use and experience...improved and perfected by reason and study.   *Leon Alberti*

In part, art completes what nature cannot elaborate; and in part, it imitates nature.   *Aristotle*

Consists in bringing something into existence.

Aristotle

Man added to nature.   *Francis Bacon*

Man's nature; nature is God's art.

Philip J. Bailey

Nature concentrated.   *Honoré de Balzac*

Art distills sensation and embodies it with enhanced meaning in memorable form.

Jacques Barzun

The achievement of stillness in the midst of chaos.

Saul Bellow

Art strives for form, and hopes for beauty.
George Bellows

Charm and lightness of form. *Julien Benda*

Not based on actuality; but on the wishes, dreams and aspirations of a people. *Bernard Berenson*

Art is I; science is we. *Claude Bernard*

This word has no definition. *Ambrose Bierce*

Art is made to disturb. Science reassures. There is only one valuable thing in art: the thing you cannot explain. *Georges Braque*

Life upon the larger scale.
Elizabeth Barrett Browning

The one way possible of speaking truth.
Robert Browning

The history of revivals. *Samuel Butler 2*

To create, and in creating live a being more intense, that we endow with form our fancy, gaining as we give the life we image.
Adapted from Lord Byron

Abstract art? A product of the untalented, sold by the unprincipled to the utterly bewildered.
Al Capp

A self-respecting search for the unknown.
Eugenio Carmi

A mould in which to imprison for a moment the shining, elusive element which is life itself—life hurrying past us and running away, too strong to stop, too sweet to lose. *Willa Cather*

The triumph over chaos. *John Cheever*

Consists of limitation. The most beautiful part of every picture is the frame.
Gilbert Keith Chesterton

Like morality, consists in drawing the line somewhere. *Gilbert Keith Chesterton*

The conversation that best listens to itself listening. *John Ciardi*

To draw from the accumulated wisdom of tradition a reasoned and independent sentiment of my own individuality. *Gustave Courbet*

An absolute mistress...she requires the most entire self-devotion, and she repays with grand triumphs. *Charlotte Cushman*

Art imitates nature as well as it can, as a pupil follows his master; thus it is a sort of grandchild of God. *Dante*

Art is vice. One does not wed it, one rapes it.
Edgar Degas

Not what you see but what you must make others see. *Edgar Degas*

The terms of an armistice signed with fate.
Bernard De Voto

The stored honey of the human soul, gathered on wings of misery and travail. *Theodore Dreiser*

International possessions, for the joy and service of the whole world. The nations hold them in trust for humanity. *Havelock Ellis*

A jealous mistress, and if a man have a genius for it, he makes a bad husband and an ill provider.
Ralph Waldo Emerson

The path of the creator to his work.
Ralph Waldo Emerson

By means of appearances, to produce the illusion of a loftier reality. *Ralph Waldo Emerson*

The conscious utterance of thought, by speech or action, to any end. *Ralph Waldo Emerson*

Nature is everything man is born to, and art is the difference he makes in it. *John Erskine*

The increment of the power of the hand.
John Fiske

A side of phantasy-life. *Sigmund Freud*

Certain significant and orderly relations of form.
Roger Fry

Preoccupation with inevitable sequences of cause and effect. *Roger Fry*

Either a plagiarist or a revolutionist.
Paul Gauguin

The handmaids of religion. *James C. Gibbons*

A collaboration between God and the artist, and the less the artist does the better. *André Gide*

Consists in the employment of a...system of laws, commensurate to every purpose within its scope, but concealed from the eye of the spectator.
John Mason Good

That which gives a pure emotion...which invites to neither virtue nor patriotism...nor anything but art itself.   *Remy de Gourmont*

The expression of an emotional experience in some medium—stone, bronze, paint, words, or musical tone—in such a way that it may be transferred to other people.   *F. E. Halliday*

That through which form becomes style.
                                      Emile Herzog

A revolt against man's fate.   *Emile Herzog*

The most exact transcription possible of my most intimate impression of nature.   *Edward Hopper*

Anything done by a man or woman on paper, canvas, marble or a musical keyboard that people pretend to understand, and sometimes buy.
                                      Elbert Hubbard

The antithesis of whatever becomes popular in the cultured world.   *Elbert Hubbard*

Love's by-product.   *Elbert Hubbard*

The expression of man's joy in his work.
                                      Elbert Hubbard

Not a thing: it is a way.   *Elbert Hubbard*

An instant arrested in eternity.
                                      James G. Huneker

(That which makes) it possible for us to know, if only imperfectly and for a little while, what it actually feels like to think subtly and feel nobly.
                                      Aldous Huxley

One of the means whereby man seeks to redeem a life which is experienced as chaotic, senseless, and largely evil.   *Aldous Huxley*

Nothing more than the shadow of humanity.
                                      Henry James

Anything that makes for proportion and perspective, that contributes to a view of all the dimensions.   *Henry James*

(That which) registers the deformities which have not yet penetrated our consciousness.
                                      Franz Kafka

The truest League of Nations, speaking a language and preaching a message understood by all peoples.   *Otto H. Kahn*

The expression of something one has seen which is bigger than oneself.   *Oliver La Farge*

The business of art is to reveal the relation between man and his universe, at the living moment.   *D. H. Lawrence*

(That which happens) wherever deep experience attains intense expression.   *Ludwig Lewisohn*

If it sells, it's art.   *Franklin Lloyd*

The desire of man to express himself, to record the reactions of his personality to the world he lives in.   *Amy Lowell*

The conveyance of spirit by means of matter.
                                      Salvador de Madariaga

Not a caricature of creation, it continues creation.
                                      Jacques Maritain

Always and everywhere the secret confession, and at the same time, the immortal movement.
                                      Karl Marx

The true function of art is to criticise, embellish and edit nature—particularly to edit it, and so make it coherent and lovely.
                                      Henry Louis Mencken

A shadow of the divine perfection.
                                      Michelangelo

The employment of the powers of nature for an end.   *John Stuart Mill*

Sacrifice and self-control.   *Alice D. Miller*

The treating of the commonplace with the feeling of the sublime.   *Jean F. Miller*

Art is not nature. Art is nature digested. Art is a sublime excrement.   *George Moore*

To complete the design of the gods.
                                      George Moore

Man's expression of his joy in labor.
                                      William Morris

To express through the body the mystery of the soul. Through the body—that is to say by way of all the signs—visual, audible, mobile.
                                      Jean Mouroux

A means of addressing humanity.
                                      Modest P. Moussorgsky

The only permanent and immortal religion.

George Jean Nathan

What we know in terms of what we hope.

George Jean Nathan

A kind of subconscious madness expressed in terms of sanity. *George Jean Nathan*

A reaching out into the ugliness of the world for vagrant beauty and the imprisoning of it in a tangible dream. *George Jean Nathan*

The gross exaggeration of natural beauty.

George Jean Nathan

A form of catharsis. *Dorothy Parker*

All art does but consist in the removal of surplusage. *Walter Pater*

Nothing but the highest quality to your moments as they pass. *Walter Pater*

A lie that makes us realize the truth.

Pablo Picasso

There are three arts which are concerned with all things: one which uses, another which makes, and a third which imitates them. *Plato*

The reproduction of what the senses perceive in nature through the veil of the soul.

Edgar Allan Poe

A kind of illness. *Giacomo Puccini*

The economy of feeling; it is emotion cultivating good form. *Herbert Read*

An expansion of monkey imitativeness.

W. Winwood Reade

(Something that) lies hid and works its effect, itself unseen. *Joshua Reynolds*

That in which the hand, the head and heart go together. *John Ruskin*

Sensations of peculiar minds, sensations occurring to them only at particular times, and to a plurality of mankind perhaps never.

John Ruskin

Experience of thoughts which could only rise out of a mass of the most extended knowledge, and of dispositions modified in a thousand ways by peculiarity of intellect. *John Ruskin*

Simply a right method of doing things. The test of the artist does not lie in the will with which he

goes to work, but in the excellence of the work he produces. *Saint Thomas Aquinas*

A delayed echo. *George Santayana*

An enjoyment which requires no appreciable effort, which costs no sacrifice, and which we need not repay with repentance.

Johann C. Schiller

All great art...is propaganda.

George Bernard Shaw

A vice, a pastime which differs from some of the most pleasant vices and pastimes by consolidating and intensifying the organs which it exercises.

Walter Sickert

One long roll of revelation...revealed only to those whose minds are...vacant...not for those whose minds are muddied with the dirt of politics, or heated with the vulgar chatter of society.

Walter Sickert

To let one's self go—that is what art is always aiming at. *Joel E. Spingarn*

Imagination without skill gives us modern art.

Thomas Stoppard

Artlessness. *Henry David Thoreau*

A human activity consisting of this, that one man, usually by means of external signs, hands on to others feelings he has lived through, and that other people are infected by these feelings, and also experience them. *Leon Tolstoy*

The business of art lies just in this—to make that understood and felt which, in the form of an argument, might be incomprehensible and inaccessible. *Leon Tolstoy*

Religion is the everlasting dialogue between humanity and God. Art is its soliloquy.

Franz Werfel

Art has nothing to do with communication between person and person, only with communication between different parts of a person's mind.

Rebecca West

Nothing less than a way of making joys perpetual.

Rebecca West

A goddess of dainty thought—reticent of habit, abjuring all obtrusiveness, purposing in no way to better others. *James McNeill Whistler*

The imposing of a pattern on experience, and our esthetic enjoyment in recognition of the pattern.
Alfred North Whitehead

The perfect use of an imperfect medium.
Oscar Wilde

(Something that) never expresses anything but itself.   *Oscar Wilde*

The most intense mode of individualism that the world has known.   *Oscar Wilde*

Lying, and telling of beautiful untrue things, this is the proper aim of art.   *Oscar Wilde*

To reveal art and conceal the artist is art's aim.
Oscar Wilde

The unique result of a unique temperament. Its beauty comes from the fact that its author is what he is.   *Oscar Wilde*

A corner of creation seen through a temperament.
Emile Zola

A weapon in the class struggle.   *Anon.*

SEE ALSO BEAUTY, CRITICISM, LITER-ATURE, MUSIC, PAINTING, POETRY, WRIT-ING.

ARTISTS

(One whose) work outlives him,—there's his glory.   *Thomas Bailey Aldrich*

The simplifier.   *Henry F. Amiel*

Not a man of action but a maker, a fabricator of objects.   *Wystan H. Auden*

(One who) dips his brush into his own soul, and paints his own nature into his pictures.
Henry Ward Beecher

A man who carries his happiness within him.
Ludwig van Beethoven

His art is a storehouse of values, because he gives body and vitality to what else would remain inert and lifeless.   *Eric Bentley*

The man who never in his mind and thought travelled to heaven, is no artist...Mere enthusi-asm is the all in all...Passion and expression are beauty itself.   *William Blake*

One whose works are expensive posthumously.
Eugene E. Brussell

(He who) must penetrate into the world, feel the fate of human beings, of peoples, with real love. There is no art for art's sake.   *Marc Chagall*

The artist appeals to that part of our being which is not dependent on wisdom; to that in us which is a gift and not an acquisition...He speaks to our capacity for delight, and wonder, to the sense of mystery surrounding our lives; to our sense of pity, and beauty, and pain.   *Joseph Conrad*

He renders clear the sensations that things arouse within us, and which the great run of men, in the presence of nature, only vaguely see and hear.
Eugène Delacroix

(Those who) have a perception not only of the pastness of the past but of its presence.
Thomas Stearns Eliot

The true artist has the planet for his pedestal; the adventurer, after years of strife, has nothing broader than his shoes.   *Ralph Waldo Emerson*

A bad husband, and an ill provider.
Ralph Waldo Emerson

One who is urged on by instinctual needs...He longs to attain to honor, power, riches, fame, and the love of women; but he lacks the means of achieving these gratifications. So, like any other with an unsatisfied longing, he turns away from reality and transfers all his interest...to the creation of his wishes in the life of phantasy.
Sigmund Freud

He possesses the mysterious ability to mould his particular material until it expresses the ideas of his phantasy faithfully.   *Sigmund Freud*

The artist, like the neurotic, has withdrawn from an unsatisfying reality into this world of imagina-tion; but, unlike the neurotic, he knew how to find a way back from it and once more to get a firm foothold in reality. His...works of art were the imaginary gratifications of unconscious wishes.
Sigmund Freud

A man for whom the visible world exists.
Theophile Gautier

An exhibitionist by profession.
Vincent van Gogh

(One who) sees the harmony, the wholeness, the tendencies toward perfection in things every-where.   *Richard H. Guggenheimer*

Fellows with odd haircuts who are partial to floors rather than chairs as sitting places.   *Ben Hecht*

A dissatisfied person.   *Eric Hoffer*

Scratch an artist and you surprise a child.
James G. Huneker

Someone like the God of creation, remaining within or behind or beyond or above his handiwork, invisible, refined out of existence, indifferent, paring his fingernails.
Adapted from James Joyce

A solitary figure . . . In pursuing his perceptions of reality he must often sail against the currents of his time. This is not a popular role.
John Fitzgerald Kennedy

He who draws the things as he sees it for the God of things as they are.   *Rudyard Kipling*

(One who) places more value on the powers which do the forming than on the final forms themselves.   *Paul Klee*

To draw a moral, to preach a doctrine, is like shouting at the north star . . . The great artist sets down his vision of it and is silent.
Ludwig Lewisohn

One to whom all experience is revelation.
Ludwig Lewisohn

A sort of impassioned proof-reader, blue pencilling the bad spelling of God.
Henry Louis Mencken

A man who won't prostitute his art, except for money.   *Henry Meyers*

The unacknowledged legislators of the world.
Jonathan Miller

The artist creates the work of art . . . to free his nervous system from a tension . . . The artist writes, paints, sings or dances the burden of some idea or feeling off his mind.   *Max Nordau*

He . . . who can carry his most shadowy precepts into successful application.   *Edgar Allan Poe*

Almost the only men who do their work with pleasure.   *Auguste R. Rodin*

He . . . who has embodied in the sum of his works, the greatest number of the greatest ideas.
John Ruskin

A dreamer consenting to dream of the actual world.   *George Santayana*

A moralist, though he need not preach.
George Santayana

The only one who has normal vision.
George Bernard Shaw

A regenerative force.   *George Bernard Shaw*

A neurotic who continually cures himself with his art.   *Leon Simonson*

The essence of an artist is that he should be articulate.   *Algernon Charles Swinburne*

Mediocre people who are patient and industrious (enough) to revise their stupidity, to edit themselves into something like intelligence.
Kurt Vonnegut, Jr.

One whose career always begins tomorrow.
James McNeill Whistler

The master of eternity.   *Oscar Wilde*

This is the reason that the artist lives and works and has his being: that from life's clay and his own nature . . . he may distil the beauty of an everlasting form.   *Thomas Wolfe*

(He who makes) comprehensible to mortals the genius of mankind.   *Stefan Zweig*

One who doesn't see things as they are, but as he is.   *Anon.*

SEE ALSO AUTHOR, COMPOSER, CREATIVITY, PAINTER, POET, WRITER.

ASCETICISM

May be a mere expression of organic hardihood, disgusted with too much ease.   *William James*

The vilest blasphemy—blasphemy towards the whole of the human race.   *Richard Jefferies*

The sacrifice of one's personal inclinations . . . the heart of the Christian religion and of all great religions.   *Henry C. Link*

The sacrifice of one part of human nature to another, that it may live more completely in what survives of it.   *Walter Pater*

The sacrifice most acceptable to God . . . complete renunciation of the body . . . the only real piety.
Saint Clement

The denial of the will to live.
Arthur Schopenhauer

A disease.   *Voltaire*

ASPIRATIONS

One long effort to escape from the commonplaces of existence.   *Arthur Conan Doyle*

My only friends.   *Henry Wadsworth Longfellow*

The thing we long for, that we are
For one transcendent moment.
James Russell Lowell

To love the beautiful, to desire the good, to do the
best.   *Moses Mendelssohn*

Aspiration is achievement.   *Israel Zangwill*

Stretching your appetite beyond your natural
sphere.   *Anon.*

SEE ALSO POWER, SUCCESS.

ASSASSIN

Those who have received money to murder.
Antonio Escobar

The extreme form of censorship.
George Bernard Shaw

ASSIMILATION

A makeshift freedom, resulting from a deliberate
loss of memory that never quite lets one forget.
Eugene E. Brussell

An attempt to be on the biggest side.
Eugene E. Brussell

The public admission of a private inferiority.
Eugene E. Brussell

Accepting, either voluntarily or by force, among
the duties of citizenship, an obligation of amnesia,
of becoming oblivious of oneself, of erasing one's
memories, one's past, one's intimate group relationships.   *Adapted from Hayyim Greenberg*

An entrance card into the community.
Heinrich Heine

The only chance of life, liberty, and the pursuit of
happiness to . . . unbeloved stock.
Earnest Hooton

The guise of apes and fools.   *Ludwig Lewisohn*

Any place but home. Any people except one's
own. Any God except the God of one's fathers.
Ludwig Lewisohn

An act of social emancipation.   *Franz Mehring*

Loss of identity.   *Solomon Schechter*

Estrangement from the self.   *Paul Weinberger*

Evaporation . . . dissolution.   *Israel Zangwill*

SEE ALSO CONVERSION.

ASTROLOGY

An adjunct and ally to astronomy.
Johann Kepler

Astrology fosters astronomy. Mankind plays its
way up.   *Georg C. Lichtenberg*

(Something) framed by the Devil to the end that
many people may be scared from entering into the
state of matrimony, and from every divine and
human office and calling.   *Martin Luther*

A disease, not a science . . . it is a tree under the
shadow of which all sorts of superstitions thrive.
Moses Maimonides

The excellent foppery of the world.
William Shakespeare

SEE ALSO STARS.

ASTRONAUTS

Space activists.   *Frank Borman*

(Those who) often seem to be interchangeable
parts of a vast mechanism.
Time Magazine, July 25, 1969.

The first men who went to the airport on a
business trip without their wives pleading, "Take
me along."   *Anon.*

Envoys from mankind.   *Anon.*

The Questers.   *Anon.*

ATHEISM

Atheism must define itself by theism; it is a–theism, that is . . . not theism.

George A. Buttrick

The three great apostles of practical atheism . . . are wealth, health and power.

Charles Caleb Colton

A religion in effect in fair weather.

English Proverb

Philosophically, it is religious, for it makes a huge religious ceremony of denying God.

Charles W. Ferguson

An inhuman, bloody ferocious system, equally hostile to every useful restraint and to every virtuous action . . . Its first object is to dethrone God. *Robert Hall*

Atheism of the heart consists in the living rejection of what we have here found to be God's command and promise to man. *John Hutchison*

To dispute what God can do. *James 1 of England*

That individualism which makes a man feel alone and isolated in a world against which he must defend himself. *John Macmurray*

By positive atheism I mean an active struggle against everything that reminds us of God—that is . . . anti-theism rather than atheism.

Jacques Maritain

Starts in an act of faith in reverse gear and is a full-blown religious commitment . . . it proclaims that all religion must . . . vanish away, and it is itself a religious phenomenon.

Jacques Maritain

The equal toleration of all religions . . . is the same thing as atheism. *Pope Leo XIII*

My atheism . . . is true piety towards the universe and denies only gods fashioned by men in their own image, to be servants of their human interests. *George Santayana*

(Something) that endeavors itself to play the god, and decide what will be good for mankind and what bad. *Herbert Spencer*

Usually a screen for repressed religion.

Wilhelm Stekel

The attempt to remove any ultimate concern—to remain unconcerned about the meaning of one's existence. *Paul Tillich*

All things must speak of God, refer to God, or they are atheistic. *Henry P. Van Dusen*

The vice of a few intelligent people. *Voltaire*

Selfishness is the only real atheism.

Israel Zangwill

SEE ALSO AGNOSTIC, AGNOSTICISM, SKEPTICISM.

ATHEIST

All that impugn a received religion or superstition are . . . branded with the name of atheists.

Francis Bacon

The fool hath said in his heart, There is no God.

Bible: Psalms, XIV, I

The atheist does not say, "There is no God," but he says, "I know not what you mean by God;" the word God is to me a sound conveying no clear or distinct affirmation. *Charles Bradlaugh*

A man who has no invisible means of support.

John Buchan

A guy who watches a Notre Dame—SMU football game and doesn't care who wins.

Dwight David Eisenhower

He only is a true atheist to whom the predicates of the Divine Being—for example, love, wisdom and justice—are nothing. *Ludwig A. Feuerbach*

One point beyond the Devil. *Thomas Fuller*

A religious person. He believes in atheism as though it were a new religion. *Eric Hoffer*

A man who destroys the chimeras which afflict the human race, and so leads men back to nature, to experience and to reason. *Paul H. d' Holbach*

One who sees no reason for believing in the existence of any supernatural Being and who feels no emotional need for such a belief.

Adapted from Ernest Jones

There are only practical atheists. Their atheism consists, not in the denying the truth of God's existence, but in failing to realize God in their actions. *Jules Lagneau*

(Those who) have chosen to stake their lives against divine Transcendence and any vestige of Transcendence whatsoever. *Jacques Maritain*

An orphaned heart, which has lost the greatest of fathers. *Jean Paul Richter*

(One who) is always alone.   *Ignazio Silone*

All atheists are rascals, and all rascals are atheists.   *August Strindberg*

A man who believes himself an accident.

Francis Thompson

Impudent and misguided scholars who reason badly, and who, not being able to understand the Creation, the origin of evil . . . have recourse to the hypothesis of the eternity of things and of inevitability.   *Voltaire*

Frequently . . . a philosophical optimist. Having given up all hope in the very existence of a human soul, he pretends to a glowing faith in man's innate goodness.   *Franz E. Winkler*

One who can be a moral human being by choosing to live on earth rather than in the air.   *Anon.*

A believer in man as the highest being.   *Anon.*

A man related to God without being conscious of the relation.   *Anon.*

SEE ALSO AGNOSTIC, FREE THINKERS, SKEPTIC.

ATHLETE

Th' athletic fool, to whom what Heaven denied of soul, is well compensated in limbs.

Adapted from John Armstrong

A dignified bunch of muscles unable to split wood or sift the ashes.   *Anon.*

One who basks in glory for the moment.   *Anon.*

SEE ALSO SPORTS.

ATOM

A specter threatening us with annihilation.

Max Born

Atomic energy bears that same duality . . . expressed in the Book of Books thousands of years ago: "See, I have set before thee this day life and good, and death and evil . . . therefore choose life."   *David E. Lilienthal*

The conception of the atom stems from the concepts of subject and substance: there has to be "something" to account for any action. The atom is the last descendant of the concept of the soul.

Friedrich W. Nietzsche

ATONEMENT

The blood of Jesus Christ His Son cleanseth us from all sin.   *Bible: John 1, 7.*

To be at one with God, to sink self into the not-self, to achieve a mystic unity with the source of being, wiping out all error and finding peace in self-submergence.   *Issac Goldberg*

An immunity both in preparation for transgressions to come.   *Elbert Hubbard*

To raise a sin from a vice to a virtue.

Elbert Hubbard

On the day of Atonement the pious Jew becomes forgetful of the flesh and its wants and, banishing hatred, ill-feeling and all ignoble thoughts, seeks to be occupied exclusively with things spiritual.

The Jewish Encyclopedia, 11, 1909.

The process of recovering the sinful personality into a life with God, and of neutralizing the moral wrong done by man to man, through the power of self-sacrificing love.   *Eugene W. Lyman*

Atones for sins against God, not for sins against man, unless the injured man has been appeased.

Mishna: Yoma, VIII, 9.

SEE ALSO CHRIST, CROSS, FORGIVENESS, SIN.

ATTORNEY

SEE LAWYERS.

AUCTIONEER

The man who proclaims with a hammer that he has picked a pocket with this tongue.

Ambrose Bierce

One who appreciates the full cost of junk.

Eugene E. Brussell

One who sees esthetics in attic furniture.

Eugene E. Brussell

One who admires all schools of art.

Adapted from Oscar Wilde

A man who incites a mob for profit.   *Anon.*

SEE ALSO ANTIQUES.

AUTHOR

A man with an advantage over all the masters

because he can multiply his originals . . . can make copies of his works . . . which shall be as valuable as the originals themselves.

Adapted from Joseph Addison

He, with his copy-rights and copy-wrongs, in his squalid garret, in his rusty coat; ruling from his grave . . . whole nations and generations who would, or would not, give him bread while living,—is a rather curious spectacle.

Thomas Carlyle

The light of the world; the world's Priest; guiding it, like a sacred pillar of fire, in its dark pilgrimage through the waste of time.

Thomas Carlyle

A person who has a good memory and hopes . . . other people haven't. *Irvin S. Cobb*

The author is of peculiar organization. He is a being born with a predisposition which with him is irresistible, the bent of which he cannot in any way avoid. *Benjamin Disraeli*

A little like the old court jester. He's supposed to speak his vicious paradoxes with some sense in them, but he isn't part of whatever the fabric is that makes a nation. *William Faulkner*

Not those who advance what is new, but those who know how to put what they have to say as if it had never been said before. *Johann W. Goethe*

A person who you can silence by shutting his book. *Max Gralnick*

He who tells us what he heard and saw with veracity. *Thomas Gray*

We male authors write for or against something, for or against an idea, for or against a party; but women always write for or against one particular man, or . . . on account of one particular man.

Heinrich Heine

Something of a black sheep, like a village fiddler. Occasionally a fiddler becomes a violinist, and he is a credit to his family; but as a rule he would have done better had his tendency been toward industry and saving. *Edgar W. Howe*

A baker; it is for him to make the sweets, and others to buy and enjoy them. *Leigh Hunt*

(One whose power) we estimate . . . by his worst performance; and when he is dead, we rate them by his best. *Samuel Johnson*

The chief glory of every people.

Samuel Johnson

(One) skilled equally with voice or pen to stir the hearts or mould the minds of men.

James Russell Lowell

A fool who, not content with having bored those who have lived with him, insists on boring future generations. *Charles de Montesquieu*

A person who departs; he does not die.

Dinah M. Mulock

(One who) possesses not only his own intellect, but also that of his friends.

Friedrich W. Nietzsche

An ordinary guy who happens to write well.

John O'Hara

The Faust of modern society, the sole surviving individualist in a mass age. *Boris Pasternak*

Ninety-nine times out of a hundred, persons of mere address, perseverance, effrontery—in a word, busy-bodies, toadies, quacks.

Edgar Allan Poe

Three classes—shooting stars, planets, and fixed stars. *Arthur Schopenhauer*

The engineer of the human soul. *Joseph Stalin*

A venerable name; How few deserve it, and what numbers claim! *Edward Young*

One who has his head in the clouds and his feet behind the sales-counter. *Anon.*

SEE ALSO BOOK, CLASSICS, FICTION, LITERATURE, NOVEL, PEN, POET, WRITERS.

AUTHORITY

A halter. *Adelard of Bath*

What is founded on tradition or prophetic inspiration. *Solomon Adret*

The negation of liberty. *Mikhail A. Bakunin*

The living Christ speaking through the Holy Spirit. *H. H. Farmer*

The longing for the father that lives in each of us from his childhood days. *Sigmund Freud*

The collective general sense of the wisest men living in the department to which they belong.

James A. Froude

The people. *Thomas Jefferson*

The exercise of power toward some morally affirmed end and in such a reasonable way as to secure popular acceptance and sanction.

Irving Kristol

The only general persuasive in matters of conduct...a judgment which we feel to be superior to our own. *John Henry Newman*

Big Brother. *George Orwell*

It is reason. *James B. Pratt*

The Government. *John Ruskin*

Tyranny unless tempered by freedom.

Stefan Zweig

SEE ALSO CLASSES, DEMOCRACY, GOVERNMENT, LAW, MASSES, PEOPLE.

AUTOBIOGRAPHY

The most respectable form of lying.

Humphrey Carpenter

Recollections of gentlemen who tell us what they please, and amuse us, in their old age, with the follies of their youth. *George Crabbe*

An obituary in serial form with the last installment missing. *Quentin Crisp*

The next thing like living one's life over again.

Benjamin Franklin

An unrivaled vehicle for telling the truth about other people. *Phillip Guedalla*

(A book about) things which no one else will say about you, and which therefore you have to say about yourself. *Elbert Hubbard*

Books which I give away. *Charles Lamb*

Its title should be simple—a few plain words— "My Heart Laid Bare." But—this little book must be true to its title. *Edgar Allan Poe*

An I-witness account. *Anon.*

Plausible fiction. *Anon.*

SEE ALSO BIOGRAPHY.

AUTOMATION

A phenomenon which causes long lines to form at unemployment offices, the unions to rant, pink slips to rain—all for the good of the country.

Anon.

A modern day phenomenon that replaces everyone but the boss's son. *Anon.*

Something that breathes instant firing. *Anon.*

AUTOMOBILE

A walking-stick; and one of the finest things in life is going on a journey with it.

Robert Holliday

An invention which makes people go fast and money faster.

Jimmy Lyons

A secular sanctuary for the individual, his shrine to the self, his mobile Walden Pond.

Edward McDonagh

Man's greatest invention—until he got into the driver's seat.

Anon.

Man's most successful effort to produce the mule.

Anon.

The first sight that strikes you in any large American city. *Anon.*

AUTUMN

The melancholy days are come, the
  saddest of the year,
Of wailing winds, and naked woods,
  and meadows brown and sear.

William Cullen Bryant

A second spring when every leaf's a flower.

Albert Camus

Harvest season of the Goddess of Death.

Horace

The beautiful and death-struck year.

Alfred Edward Housman

(A season which) repays the earth the leaves which summer lent it. *Georg C. Lichtenberg*

Trees leaves dropping on their neighbors.

O. W. Piette

When the frost is on the punkin and the fodder's in the shock. *James Whitcomb Riley*

Leave-taking...the swallows are chattering of destination and departure. *Mary Webb*

AVARICE

(A state) which dissipates energy in war and trade. *Brooks Adams*

A mere madness, to live like a wretch, and die rich. *Robert Burton*

Mother of crimes, greedy for more the more she possesses, every searching open-mouthed for gold. *Claudian*

A universal passion, which operates at all times, at all places, and upon all persons.
David Hume

The spur of industry. *David Hume*

The last passion of those lives of which the first part has been squandered in pleasure, and the second devoted to ambition. *Samuel Johnson*

The last corruption of degenerate man.
Samuel Johnson

The besetting vice of a propertied society.
Max Radin

An itching palm. *William Shakespeare*

Species of madness. *Baruch Spinoza*

SEE ALSO COVETOUSNESS, MISERLINESS.

AXIOM

SEE BELIEF.

B

BABY

An alimentary canal with a loud voice at one end and no responsibility at the other.
Elizabeth I. Adamson

Bits of star-dust blow from the hand of God. Lucky the woman who knows the pangs of birth for she has held a star. *Lawrence Barretto*

A mother's anchor. She cannot swing far from her moorings. *Henry Ward Beecher*

A misshapen creature of no particular age, sex, or condition, chiefly remarkable for the violence of the sympathies and antipathies it excites in others, itself without sentiment or emotion.
Ambrose Bierce

It is all gut and squall. *Charles Brown*

A bald head and a pair of lungs. *Eugene Field*

An angel whose wings decrease as his legs increase. *French Proverb*

A little rivet in the bonds of matrimony.
Arthur Gordon

Frequently can be classified as home accidents.
Max Gralnick

Unwritten history!
Unfathomed mystery! *Josiah G. Holland*

A thing on mother's milk and kisses fed.
Homer

Lumps of flesh. *Samuel Johnson*

A tight little bundle of wailing and flannel.
Frederick Locker-Lampson

Something that gets you down in the daytime and up at night. *Kate M. Owney*

Coiled within the dark womb he sits, the image of an ape; a caricature and a prophecy of the man that is to be. *W. Winwood Reade*

God's opinion that the world should go on.
Carl Sandburg

A well-spring of pleasure. *Martin F. Tupper*

An inestimable blessing and bother.
Mark Twain

Mom and Pop art. *Patricia J. Warner*

Today a premature baby is one that's born before its parents are married. *Earl Wilson*

Someone just the size of a hug. *Anon.*

A perfect example of minority rule. *Anon.*

A disturber of the peace. *Anon.*

SEE ALSO BIRTH, CHILD, CHILDREN.

BACHELOR

A man whom women are still sampling.
Ambrose Bierce

A coward. *Eugene E. Brussell*

A sly old fish, too cunning for the hook.
George Crabbe

The only good husbands...they're too considerate to get married.   *Finley Peter Dunne*

God created them for the consolation of widows and the hope of maids.   *J. De Finod*

An incompleted animal. He resembles the odd half of a pair of scissors.   *Benjamin Franklin*

One who flees unpleasantness wherever it is found.   *Warren Goldberg*

The unsettled, thoughtless condition.
    Samuel Johnson

A man who is foot-loose and fiancé free.
    F. G. Kernan

A man who has never weakened during a weekend.   *G. L. Knapp*

A man who thinks a weekend is something you rest up in.   *Kenneth Kraft*

An average male over twenty-one whom no average female ever has made a serious attempt to marry.   *Henry Louis Mencken*

One who thinks that the only thoroughly justified marriage was the one that produced him.
    Harlan Miller

All reformers.   *George M. Moore*

One who thinks one can live as cheaply as two.
    Eleanor Ridley

(One who) gets tangled up with a lot of women in order to avoid getting tied up to one.
    Helen Rowland

(One) who thinks he is a thing of beauty and a boy forever.   *Helen Rowland*

A man in winter without a fur cap.
    Russian Proverb

Half a man.   *Sanskrit Proverb*

A man who shirks responsibilities and duties.
    George Bernard Shaw

A man who hopes all his courting plans go through without a hitch.   *Albert Spong*

Who travels alone, without lover or friend,
But hurries from nothing, to nought at the end.
    Ella W. Wilcox

A permanent public temptation.   *Oscar Wilde*

A man who never makes the same mistake once.
    Ed Wynn

A man who never Mrs. anybody.   *Anon.*

One who knows the precise psychological moment when to nod his head—no.   *Anon.*

One who is foot-loose and fiancée free.   *Anon.*

One who has never told his wife a lie.   *Anon.*

One who savours the chase but does not eat the game.   *Anon.*

A man who has died before his education began.
    Anon.

One who is nice to women all his life.   *Anon.*

A man with no ties except those that need pressing.   *Anon.*

A souvenir of some woman who found a better one at the last moment.   *Anon.*

A man who lives at his ease.   *Anon.*

A man who tries to avoid the major issue.
    Anon.

One who can have a girl on his knees without having her on his hands.   *Anon.*

A man who would not take yes for an answer.
    Anon.

One who lives in a laundromat, eats in restaurants and wears socks with holes.   *Anon.*

SEE ALSO CELIBACY, HUSBAND, MARRIAGE.

BACH, JOHANN SEBASTIAN (1685-1750)

I have always kept one end in view, namely...to conduct a well-regulated church music to the honour of God.   *Johann Sebastian Bach*

I was obliged to be industrious. Whoever is equally industrious will succeed...equally well.
    Johann Sebastian Bach

Too much counterpoint—and what is worse, Protestant counterpoint.   *Thomas Beecham*

The immortal god of harmony.
    Ludwig van Beethoven

There is always something left to discover in him.
    Pablo Casals

A sublime sewing-machine.   *Colette*

Bach almost persuades me to be a Christian.
                                              Roger Fry

It is as though eternal harmony were conversing with itself...in God's bosom shortly before He created the world.
                               Johann Wolfgang von Goethe

He has said all there is to say.   *Charles Gounod*

He wrote music that has a positive D-Major feeling about life.   *Adapted from Elmer Iseler*

He is characteristic of our era in that his music is equally balanced between mathematics and emotion...technical precision and deep feeling.
                                          Yehudi Menuhin

He taught how to find originality within an established discipline; actually—how to live.
                                         Jean-Paul Sartre

The underlying personality of the man is known only in the most shadowy way.
                                  Time Magazine, Dec., 1968.

He considered himself not an artist, but an artisan, no more elevated in stature than a cabinet-maker with his tools and wood.
                                  Time Magazine, Dec., 1968.

He is a phenomenon of *our* time.   *Rosalyn Turek*

Bach opens a vista to the universe. After experiencing him, people feel there is meaning to life after all.   *Helmut Walcha*

The greatest of preachers.   *Charles M. Widor*

BACON, FRANCIS (1561-1626)

He had the sound, distinct, comprehensive knowledge of Aristotle, with all the beautiful lights, graces and embellishments of Cicero.
                                         Joseph Addison

In Bacon see the culminating prime
Of British intellect and British crime.
                                         Ambrose Bierce

His hearers could not cough or look aside from him without loss...The fear of every man that heard him was lest he should make an end.
                                            Ben Jonson

He seemed to me ever, by his work, one of the greatest men, and most worthy of admiration.
                                            Ben Jonson

The art which Bacon taught was the art of inventing arts. The knowledge in which Bacon excelled all men was a knowledge of the mutual relations of all departments of knowledge.
                                       Thomas B. Macaulay

The wisest, brightest, meanest of mankind.
                                        Alexander Pope

Bacon always seems to write with his ermine on.
                                       Alexander Smith

That great secretary of Nature.   *Izaak Walton*

BAD

The result of speaking and acting without foreseeing the results of words and deeds.   *Franz Kafka*

A bad man is the sort who weeps every time he speaks of a good woman.
                                   Henry Louis Mencken

All that proceeds from weakness.
                                  Friedrich W. Nietzsche

A bad man is the sort of man who admires innocence, and a bad woman is the sort of woman a man never gets tired of.   *Oscar Wilde*

SEE ALSO EVIL, HELL, IMMORALITY, WICKEDNESS.

BALLAD

The gypsy-children of song, born under green hedgerows in the leafy lanes and bypaths of literature,—in the...summertime.
                               Henry Wadsworth Longfellow

(They) show the complexion of the time.
                                           John Selden

SEE ALSO POETRY, SONG.

BALLOT

The rightful and peaceful successors of bullets.
                                         Abraham Lincoln

A paper representative of the bayonet, the billy, and the bullet...a laborsaving device for ascertaining on which side force lies and bowing to the inevitable. *Benjamin R. Tucker*

It is no less the arbitrament of force than is the decree of the most absolute of despots backed by the most powerful of armies.

Benjamin R. Tucker

SEE ALSO DEMOCRACY, MAJORITY, VOTING.

BANDIT

SEE CRIMINAL.

BANK

A power...greater than the people themselves, consisting of many and various and powerful interests combined in one mass, held together by the cohesive power of the vast mass.

John C. Calhoun

A place where they lend you an umbrella in fair weather and ask for it back when it begins to rain.

Robert Frost

Bread box. *Franklin Tyger*

SEE ALSO FINANCE, PARENTS.

BANKER

Bankers Are Just Like Anybody Else, Except Richer. *Ogden Nash*

A fellow who hands you his umbrella when the sun is shining and wants it back the minute it begins to rain. *Mark Twain*

One who lends money to the already affluent.

Anon.

A man who believes in interest, not principles.

Anon.

A pawnbroker nicely dressed. *Anon.*

BAPTISM

Being by nature born in sin, and the children of wrath, we are hereby made the children of grace.

Book of Common Prayer.

A sign of initiation, by which we are admitted into the society of the Church, in order that, being incorporated into Christ, we may be numbered among the children of God. *John Calvin*

God's Wardrobe; in Baptism we put on Christ; there we are invested, appareled in Christ.

John Donne

The strength of baptism, that's within;
It saves the soul by drowning sin.

Robert Herrick

A living, saving water on account of the Word of God which is in it. *Martin Luther*

The vehicle to heaven, the public agent of the Kingdom, the gift of adoption. *Saint Basil*

It is ransom to captives and remission of sins...the death of sin and the soul's regeneration...a garment of light and a holy seal that can never be dissolved. *Saint Cyril*

In Baptism the Holy Spirit, which in the beginning of creation "moved upon the face of the waters," renews its hidden action on water as a primordial and representative element of the material world. *Vladimir Soloviev*

The virtue of cleansing an infant of an enormous sin expiated by the Son of God, and committed thousands of years before the parents of the child dreamed of making him. *Voltaire*

BARBARISM

Not taking others into account...the tendency to disassociation. *Warren Goldberg*

The absence of standards to which appeal can be made...the annulment of all norms.

José Ortega y Gasset

SEE ALSO CIVILIZATION, MASSES, SAVAGE.

BARD

SEE POET.

BARGAIN

Anything a customer thinks a store is losing money on. *Kin Hubbard*

Something you have to find use for, once you've bought it. *Franklin P. Jones*

Something you can't use at a price you can't resist. *Franklin P. Jones*

A transaction in which each participant thinks he has cheated the other. *Anon.*

Something that still costs money. *Anon.*

BASEBALL

Almost the only place in life where a sacrifice is really appreciated.   *Mark Beltaire*

The greatest conversation piece ever invented in America.   *Bruce Catton*

A game which consists of tapping a ball with a piece of wood, then running like a lunatic.
                                            H. J. Dutiel

An island of surety in a changing world.
                                            William Veek

BASHFULNESS

An ornament to youth, but a reproach to old age.
                                            Aristotle

A tough husk in which a delicate organization is protected from premature ripening.
                                            Ralph Waldo Emerson

Oftener the effect of pride than of modesty.
                                            Lord Halifax

Frequently a result of having too high an opinion of our own importance.
                                            Adapted from Samuel Johnson

The protective fluid within which our personalities are able to develop into natural shapes.
                                            Harold Nicolson

A maid's best dress.   *Welsh Proverb*

SEE ALSO MODESTY.

BASTARD

One who inherits his mother's name.
                                            Max Gralnick

The son of no one, or rather the son of all.
                                            Legal Maxim

Those born of sinful intercourse and not counted as legal children.   *Legal Maxim*

The end product of unplanned parenthood.
                                            Caskie Stennett

There are no illegitimate children—only illegitimate parents.   *Leon R. Yankwich*

BATTLE

A method of untying with the teeth a political knot that would not yield to the tongue.
                                            Ambrose Bierce

Iron and blood.   *Otto von Bismarck*

Misunderstanding.   *Thomas Carlyle*

Mechanism; men now even die, and kill one another, in an artificial manner.
                                            Thomas Carlyle

Six or seven thousand of the human species less than there were a month ago, and seems to me to be all.   *Lord Chesterfield*

(Something) insupportably tedious and revolting.
                                            Ralph Waldo Emerson

The caprice of chance.   *William Godwin*

The result of a moment, of a thought; the hostile forces advance with various combinations, they attack each other and fight for a certain time, the critical moment arrives, a mental flash decides, and the least reserve accomplishes the object.
                                            Napoleon I

SEE ALSO ARMY, WAR.

BATTLEFIELD

(Activity that) doesn't determine what is right. Only who is left.   *Peter Bowman*

On fame's eternal camping-ground
    Their silent tents are spread,
And glory guards with solemn round
    The bivouac of the dead.   *Theodore O'Hara*

At once the playroom of all the gods and the dancehall of all the furies.   *Jean Paul Richter*

They there may dig each other's graves,
And call the sad work glory.
                                            Percy Bysshe Shelley

A place of settlement of disputes...gradually yielding to arbitral courts of justice.
                                            William Howard Taft

SEE ALSO ARMY, GENERAL, SOLDIER, WAR.

BEARD

The hair that is commonly cut off by those who justly execrate the absurd Chinese custom of shaving the head.   *Ambrose Bierce*

That ornamental excrement which groweth beneath the chin. *Thomas Fuller*

The glory of a face. *Talmud: Sabbath, 52a.*

A thing worn with gift ties. *Anon.*

To confront in defiance. *Anon.*

Man's ability to overcome social obstacles.

Anon.

SEE ALSO HAIR.

BEAUTY

A gift of God. *Aristotle*

Size as well as symmetry. *Aristotle*

Whatever is in any way beautiful has its source of beauty in itself, and is complete in itself; praise forms no part of it. *Marcus Aurelius*

The divine force which permeates the world.

Israel Baal Shem Tob

Summer fruits which are easy to corrupt and cannot last. *Francis Bacon*

God's trademark in creation.

Henry Ward Beecher

A fading flower. *Bible: Isaiah, XXVIII, 1.*

Vanity. *Bible: Proverbs, XXXI, 30.*

The power by which a woman charms a lover and terrifies a husband. *Ambrose Bierce*

A rainbow—full of promise but shortlived.

Josh Billings

The distilled essence of love—love which suffers and aspires. *John E. Boodin*

The best of all we know. *Robert Bridges*

When purely physical, the sole characteristic of a person that belongs to time.

Eugene E. Brussell

That which remains lovely in vulgar surroundings. *Eugene E. Brussell*

An air of robustness and strength is . . . prejudicial to beauty. An appearance of delicacy, and even of fragility, is almost essential to it.

Edmund Burke

Two kinds of beauty—loveliness and dignity . . . regard loveliness as the quality of woman, dignity that of man. *Cicero*

Beauty is not caused. It is. *Emily Dickinson*

Zest is the secret of all beauty. *Christian Dior*

All heiresses. *John Dryden*

That which is simple; which has no superfluous parts; which exactly answers its end; which stands related to all things; which is the mean of many extremes. *Ralph Waldo Emerson*

The virtue of the body. *Ralph Waldo Emerson*

What is all beauty but the trace
Of my heart shining in my face? *Edmond Fleg*

The most beautiful subjects? The simplest and the least clad. *Anatole France*

Silent eloquence. *French Proverb*

A good letter of introduction. *German Proverb*

Eternity gazing at itself in a mirror.

Kahlil Gibran

Holiness visible, holiness seen, heard, touched, holiness tasted. *Eric Gill*

A manifestation of secret natural laws, which otherwise would have been hidden from us forever. *Johann W. Goethe*

Merely the spiritual making itself known sensuously. *Georg W. Hegel*

The index of a larger fact than wisdom.

Oliver Wendell Holmes 1

Beauty is in the eye of the beholder.

Margaret W. Hungerford

That which apart from concepts is represented as the object of a universal satisfaction . . . the symbol of the morally Good. *Immanuel Kant*

Beauty is truth, truth beauty. *John Keats*

God's handwriting. *Charles Kingsley*

An immense predilection, a perfect conviction of the desirability of a certain thing.

Wyndham Lewis

That . . . which is worthy. *Isaac Linetzki*

Something wonderful and strange that the artist fashions out of the chaos of the world in the torment of his soul.

William Somerset Maugham

The first present Nature gives to women, and the first it takes away. *George Mere*

Beauty is but a flower
Which wrinkles will devour.   *Thomas Nashe*

She is a visitor who leaves behind
The gift of grief, the souvenir of pain.
                                      Robert Nathan

Simply a word; it is not even a concept. In his view of the beautiful, man postulates himself as the standard of perfection. A species has no alternative to saying yea to itself in this way.
                                Friedrich W. Nietzsche

The joy of the eternal youthfulness of the creative mind...it is the sharing of the gladness of the creative discovery of a reawakened life in the universe that constitutes the love of art to us.
                                  Kakuzo Okakura

A harmonious relation between something in our nature and the quality of the object which delights us.   *Blaise Pascal*

Sheer delightful waste to be enjoyed in its own high right.   *Donald C. Peattie*

An ephemoral thing, wasting away almost before it comes to its prime.   *Philo*

'Tis not a lip, or eye, we beauty call,
But the joint force and full result of all.
                                  Alexander Pope

A point of arrival.   *Auguste R. Rodin*

Continual possession of God.   *Saint Gregory*

A pledge of the possible conformity between the soul and nature, and consequently a ground of faith in the supremacy of the good.
                                George Santayana

What is beautiful is good, and who is good will soon be beautiful.   *Sappho*

Beauty is a vain doubtful good;
A shining glass that fadeth suddenly;
A flower that dies when first it 'gins to bud;
A brittle glass that's broken presently.
                              William Shakespeare

If the motion which objects we see communicate to our nerves be conducive to health, the objects causing it are styled beautiful; if a contrary motion be excited, they are styled ugly.
                                  Baruch Spinoza

A finer utility whose end we do not see.
                              Henry David Thoreau

Being...divested of every ornament which was not fitted to endure.   *Henry David Thoreau*

(Something) altogether in the eye of the beholder.
                                    Lew Wallace

Real beauty ends where an intellectual expression begins.   *Oscar Wilde*

A form of genius—is higher than genius, as it needs no explanation.   *Oscar Wilde*

The only thing time cannot harm...What is beautiful is a joy for all seasons and a possession for all eternity.   *Oscar Wilde*

The only beautiful things are the things that do not concern us.   *Oscar Wilde*

The beauty of the world has two edges, one of laughter, one of anguish, cutting the heart asunder.   *Virginia Woolf*

The outward form that dies on earth.   *Anon.*

SEE ALSO ART, COSMETICS, FACE, HEALTH, NATURE, PAINTING, POETRY, TRUTH, WOMAN.

BED

Where we laugh, cry, are born in, and die.
                        Adapted from Isaac de Benserade

A great luxury, disposing to an universal relaxation, and inducing beyond anything else that species called sleep.   *Edmund Burke*

That heaven upon earth to the weary head.
                                    Thomas Hood

The best medicine.   *Italian Proverb*

The happiest part of a man's life.
                                  Samuel Johnson

The bed encompasses our whole life, for we were born in it, we live in it, and we shall die in it.
                                Guy de Maupassant

A place of luxury to me. I would not exchange it for all the thrones in the world.   *Napoleon I*

A chamber deaf to noise, and blind to light.
                                  Philip Sidney

The place where marriages are decided.   *Anon.*

For lovers, a place for bringing together or drifting apart.   *Anon.*

For lovers, a bridge toward something better.

Anon.

The grave of lost illusions.   *Anon.*

SEE ALSO DREAM, DREAMER, SNORING.

BEE

Small among flying things, but her fruit has the chiefest sweetness.

Apocrypha: Ecclesiastes, XI, 3.

Nature's confectioner.   *John Cleveland*

The debouchee of dews!   *Emily Dickinson*

Creatures that by a rule in nature teach
The act of order to a peopled kingdom.

William Shakespeare

The bee...does the whole business of life at once, and at the same time feeds, and works, and diverts itself.   *Jonathan Swift*

A sweet thing that stings.   *Anon.*

BEER

That which drowns all care.   *Robert Herrick*

Life itself.   *Oxfordshire Proverb*

A drink...for all constitutions, but especially for the cholerick and melancholick most wholesome.

Tobias Venner

SEE ALSO DRINKING.

BEETHOVEN, LUDWIG VAN (1770-1827)

I shall hear in heaven.   *Ludwig van Beethoven*

I have not a single friend, I must live alone. But well I know that God is nearer to me than to other artists; I associate with Him without fear; I have always recognized and understood Him and have no fear for my music—it can meet no evil fate.

Ludwig van Beethoven

I have avoided almost all social gatherings because it is impossible for me to say to people: "I am deaf."   *Ludwig van Beethoven*

I know that I am an artist.

Ludwig van Beethoven

I don't want to know anything about...(the) system of ethics. *Power* is the morality of men who stand out from the rest, and it is also mine.

Ludwig van Beethoven

Never show to men the contempt they deserve, one never knows to what use one may want to put them.   *Ludwig van Beethoven*

Tell me nothing of rest. I know of none but sleep, and woe is me that I must give up more time to it than usual.   *Ludwig van Beethoven*

I will take Fate by the throat; it shall not wholly overcome me.   *Ludwig van Beethoven*

Beethoven can write music, thank God—but he can do nothing else on earth.

Ludwig van Beethoven

I feel as if I had written scarcely a few notes.

Ludwig van Beethoven

A more self-contained, energetic, sincere artist I never saw. I can understand right well how singular must be his attitude towards the world.

Johann W. Goethe

An utterly untamed personality, not altogether in the wrong in holding the world...detestable, but who does not make it any the more enjoyable either for himself or for others by his attitude.

Johann W. Goethe

Beethoven is not beautiful. He is dramatic, powerful, a maker of storms...but his speech is the speech of a self-centered egotist.

James G. Huneker

The father of all the modern melomaniacs, who, looking into their own souls, write what they see therein—misery, corruption, slighting, selfishness, and ugliness.   *James G. Huneker*

Again and again he lifts us to a height from which we revaluate not only all music but all life, all emotion, and all thought.   *Ernest Newman*

Beethoven's music is music about music.

Friedrich W. Nietzsche

Beethoven's attitude towards life...(is) to be found in his realization of the heroism of achievement...to realize suffering as one of the great structural lines of human life.   *John W. Sullivan*

He was impervious to criticism; his manners were atrocious; he ignored conventions; he was permanently subject to no social passions, not even sexual love.   *John W. Sullivan*

(He was) primarily concerned to express his personal vision of life...Beethoven the man and Beethoven the composer are not two unconnected entities.   *John W. Sullivan*

We know, from...his music, that Beethoven was a man who experienced all that we can experience, who suffered all that we can suffer. If, in the end, he seems to reach a state "above the battle" we also know no man ever knew more bitterly what the battle is.   *John W. Sullivan*

This small...pock-marked, unkempt German provincial.   *Anon.*

BEGGAR

The happy folk.   *Pierre J. Beranger*

One who has relied on the assistance of his friends.   *Ambrose Bierce*

Vermin that infest the rich.   *French Proverb*

A robber who has lost his nerve—a bandit with a streak of yellow in his ego.   *Elbert Hubbard*

The only free man in the universe.
                                       Charles Lamb

The true king.   *Gotthold E. Lessing*

Someone who breeds while rich men feed.
                                  Adapted from John Ray

SEE ALSO POOR, POVERTY.

BEGINNING

Half the whole.   *Aristotle*

(Something that) bears witness to the end, and the end will at long last bear witness to the beginning.   *Leon Baeck*

A quarter of the journey.   *Henry G Bohn*

Something that is always difficult.
                                  German Proverb

Half way to winning.   *Heinrich Heine*

The hardest step.   *James Howell*

The most important part of the work.   *Plato*

When things are always at their best.   *Anon.*

BEHAVIOR

The sum of behavior is to retain a man's own dignity, without intruding upon the liberty of others.   *Francis Bacon*

A man's ethical behavior should be based effectually on sympathy, education and social ties and needs; no religion basis is necessary.
                                  Albert Einstein

The finest of the fine arts.
                             Ralph Waldo Emerson

Be civil to all; sociable to many; familiar to few; Friend to One; enemy to none.
                                Benjamin Franklin

A mirror, in which everyone shows his image.
                                 Johann W. Goethe

No truer index to intelligence.   *Ibn Gabirol*

What a man does, not what he feels, thinks, or believes.   *Benjamin C. Leeming*

The theory of manners practically applied.
                                  Madame Necker

Live your life, do your work, then take your hat.
                              Henry David Thoreau

SEE ALSO CONDUCT, DEEDS, MANNERS.

BEING

A torrent, in and out of which all bodies pass, coalescing and cooperating with the whole, as the various parts in us do with one another.
                                 Marcus Aurelius

For in Him we live, and move, and have our being.   *Bible: Acts, XVII, 28.*

The nature of things in themselves. A thing "is" whatever it gives us least trouble to think it is. There is no other "is" than this.
                                 Samuel Butler 2

Perfection of power to be.   *John Dewey*

All things come from being, and being comes from non-being.   *Lao-tzu*

SEE ALSO EXISTENCE, LIFE, LIVING, MAN, REALITY.

BELIEF

What a man had rather were true.

Francis Bacon

Mere self-defense to hold that behind...non-rational forces, and above them, guiding them by slow degrees...stands that supreme Reason.

Arthur James Balfour

Life itself. *Thomas Carlyle*

Childish foolishness. *Morris R. Cohen*

The natural possession of beings possessing minds. *Martin D'Arcy*

The most complete of all distinctions between man and the lower animals. *Charles Darwin*

What makes men stronger. *Jerry Dashkin*

Consists in accepting the affirmations of the soul; unbelief, in denying them.

Ralph Waldo Emerson

True belief transcends itself; it is belief in something—in a truth which is not determined by faith, but which...determines faith.

Erich Frank

Truths being in and out of favour. *Robert Frost*

A matter of living what you know to be correct.

Max Gralnick

Consists not in the nature and order of our ideas, but in the manner of their conception, and in their feeling to the mind...something *felt* by the mind, which distinguishes the ideas of the judgment from the fictions of the imagination.

David Hume

Often extremely irrational attempts to justify our instincts. *Thomas Henry Huxley*

Security and guidance. *Koran*

Your own assent to yourself, and the constant voice of your own reason. *Blaise Pascal*

Thought at rest. *Charles S. Peirce*

The demi-cadence which closes a musical phrase in the symphony of our intellectual life.

Charles S. Peirce

A calm and satisfactory state which we do not wish to avoid. *Charles S. Peirce*

The essence...is the establishment of a habit.

Charles S. Peirce

Faith is belief, and belief has...an aspect of firmness, persistence, and subjective certainty.

Ralph Barton Perry

A matter of taste. *George Bernard Shaw*

A passion, or an involuntary operation of the mind, and like other passions, its intensity is precisely proportioned to the degrees of excitement. *Percy Bysshe Shelley*

Religious belief is a total assertion which has for its subject the whole world order. *J. L. Stocks*

Whatever thoughts any human soul is seeking to live by. *William Temple*

SEE ALSO CERTAINTY, CONVICTION, DOGMA, FAITH, RELIGION, TRUTH.

BELIEVER

A songless bird in a cage. *Robert G. Ingersoll*

One in whom persuasion and belief
Had ripened into faith, and faith become
A passionate intuition. *William Wordsworth*

BELIEVING

Not...what a man is made to believe but...what he must believe. *Gilbert Keith Chesterton*

Whatever one likes to see one likes to believe.

German Proverb

What takes place in us when we believe is a phenomenon of intimate and superhuman light.

Jean B. Lacordaire

Not a matter of creed. What a man believes may be ascertained, not from his creed, but from the assumption on which he habitually acts.

George Bernard Shaw

SEE ALSO BELIEF, CREED, FAITH, TRUTH.

BELLS

The publicity of God. In France people say, "God is advertising Himself." *R. L. Bruckberger*

Music's laughter. *Thomas Hood*

The music bordering nearest heaven.

Charles Lamb

The best of preachers.

Henry Wadsworth Longfellow

The voice of the church.

Henry Wadsworth Longfellow

I call the living. I mourn the dead; I break the lightning.   *Johann C. Schiller*

I mourn death, I disperse the lightning, I announce the Sabbath, I rouse the lazy, I scatter the winds, I appease the blood-thirsty.   *Anon.*

BENEVOLENCE

To love all men.   *Confucius*

To act from pure benevolence is not possible for finite beings. Human benevolence is mingled with vanity, interest, or some other motive.

Samuel Johnson

One of the distinguishing characteristics of man. It is the path of duty.   *Mencius*

A natural instinct of human mind; when A sees B in distress, his conscience always urges him to entreat C to help him.   *Sydney Smith*

SEE ALSO CHARITY, GENEROSITY, GIVING, PHILANTHROPY.

BEST-SELLER

The affinity between the mediocrity of the author's ideas and those of the public.

Nicolas Chamfort

All these long-gone-with-the-winded novels.

David McCord

The gilded tomb of a mediocre talent.

Logan P. Smith

A book of momentary interest.   *Anon.*

Usually lots of reading but not much writing.

Anon.

SEE ALSO BOOK, FICTION.

BIBLE

The classical book of the noble ethical sentiment.

Felix Adler

It furnished good Christians an armor for their warfare, a guide for their conduct, a solace in their sorrows, food for their souls.

Gaius G. Atkins

Prosperity is the blessing of the Old Testament, adversity is the blessing of the New.

Francis Bacon

One wisdom which is perfect.   *Roger Bacon*

Not man's word about God, but God's word about man.   *Karl Barth*

Thy word is a lamp unto my feet, and a light unto my path.   *Bible: Psalms, CXIX, 105.*

A respectable book, but I should hardly call it one whose philosophy is of the soundest. All truth, especially historic truth, requires cool...investigation, for which the Jews do not appear to have ever been famous.   *George Borrow*

God's book because it is in a unique and universal sense Man's book. It is the record of and the vehicle for transmitting a great human experience, an experience of God, of human need, and of God's response to that need.   *Richard Brook*

The immortal epic of a people's confused, faltering, but indomitable struggle after a nobler life in a happier world.   *Lewis Browne*

A work too hard for the teeth of time, and cannot perish but in the general flames, when all things shall confess their ashes.   *Thomas Browne*

The school of the Holy Spirit.   *John Calvin*

That divine Hebrew Book,—the word partly of the man Moses, an outlaw tending his...herds, four thousand years ago, in the wilderness of Sinai.   *Thomas Carlyle*

God's wisdom.   *William Ellery Channing*

The religion of Protestants.

William Chillingworth

The unchangeable word of God to which man must bend himself, and not something which he can bend to his own personal ideas.

Jean Danielou

The ascent towards discovery.

Henry Daniel-Rops

A collection of different legends, mutually contradictory and written at different times and full of historical errors, issued by churches as a "holy" book.   *Dictionary of Foreign Words, Soviet Government, 1951.*

A window in this prison-world, through which we may look into eternity.   *Timothy Dwight*

(A book that has) implanted itself in the table-talk and household life of every man and woman in the European and American nations.

Ralph Waldo Emerson

An old Cremona; it has been played upon by the devotion of thousands of years until every word and particle is public and tunable.

Ralph Waldo Emerson

A history of the growth of the idea of God.

St. John Ervine

A book that sweats people into unity.

Adapted from Leon Feuchtwanger

The epic of the world . . . all life's fever is there, its hopes and joys, its suffering and sin and sorrow.

James Frazer

The two-edged sword of God's word.

Thomas Fuller

That great medicine chest of humanity.

Heinrich Heine

The portable fatherland. *Heinrich Heine*

A plain old book, modest as nature itself . . . a book of an unpretending work-day appearance, like the sun that warms or the bread that nourishes us. *Heinrich Heine*

(A book of) shallows where a lamb could wade and depths where an elephant would drown.

Matthew Henry

The book of books, the storehouse and magazine of life and comfort. *George Herbert*

The Magna Charta of the poor and the oppressed.

Thomas Henry Huxley

(The instigator) of revolt against the worst forms of clerical and political despotism.

Thomas Henry Huxley

The Iliad of religion. *Joseph Joubert*

God's Word in that it is a memory of a past revelation of God and an expectation of future revelation. *Adolph Keller*

One mighty representative of the whole spiritual life of humanity. *Helen Keller*

The best gift God has given to man . . . But for it we could not know right from wrong.

Abraham Lincoln

Christ is the master; the Scriptures are only the servant. *Martin Luther*

A book which, if everything else in our language should perish, would alone suffice to show the whole extent of its beauty and power.

Thomas B. Macaulay

The Bible leads us to Jesus, the inexhaustible, the every unfolding Revelation of God.

George Macdonald

The Old Testament is tribal in its provinciality; its god is a local god, and its village police and sanitary regulations are erected into eternal laws.

John Macy

A chronicle of crises in the life of men and nations. *Judah Magnes*

The history of a deliverer; of God proclaiming himself as man's deliverer from the state into which he is ever ready to sink.

Frederick D. Maurice

What Dryden said about Chaucer applies to infinitely greater degree to the Bible: "Here is God's plenty." *Robert J. McCracken*

The revelation of God . . . the supreme revelation of man. *William Lyon Phelps*

Bread that comes down from heaven.

Pope Benedict XV

A hymn to Justice. *Pierre J. Proudhon*

The great book of consolation for humanity.

Ernest Renan

The bone and sinew of nations with the will to live. *Romain Rolland*

A parable of man's advance to the family, to the tribe, to a nation with a national ideal, to a nation with a universal ideal. *Franz Rosenzweig*

A most perfect rule for human life.

Saint Benedict

Literature, not dogma. *George Santayana*

Our patent of nobility. *Solomon Schechter*

The mystery of mysteries! *Walter Scott*

An open town in time of war, which serves indifferently the occasions of both parties.

Jonathan Swift

God experienced in all the length and breadth and height and depth of His revelation and communication to man.   *E. I. Watkin*

(A book which) teaches man his own individual responsibility . . . dignity, and . . . equality with his fellow-man.   *Daniel Webster*

A book of faith, and a book of doctrine, and a book of morals, and a book of religion, of special revelation from God.   *Daniel Webster*

Fear is the denomination of the Old Testament; belief is the denomination of the New.
          Benjamin Whichcote

The people's book of revelation, revelation of themselves not alone, but revelation of life and of peace.   *Woodrow Wilson*

The highest ethical note ever yet sounded . . . by man.   *Israel Zangwill*

SEE ALSO CHRISTIANS, CHRISTIANITY, CHURCHES, COMMANDMENTS, DEISM, GOD, HOLINESS, JEWS, JUDAISM, RELIGION, TEN COMMANDMENTS, THEIST.

BIBLIOMANIA

Collecting an enormous heap of books without intelligent curiosity.   *Isaac D'Israeli*

Desire to have many books, and never use them.
          Henry Peacham

SEE ALSO BOOK, LIBRARY, READING.

BIGAMIST

A man who marries a beautiful girl and a good cook.   *Chicago Herald-American*

Someone who makes the same mistake twice.
          Jimmy Lyons

A lion-tamer working in two cages simultaneously.   *Anon.*

BIGAMY

A mistake in taste.   *Ambrose Bierce*

Respectability carried to criminal lengths.
          Constantine Fitz-Gibbon

Having one wife too many. Monogamy is the same.   *Oscar Wilde*

When two rites make a wrong.   *Anon.*

Taking one two many.   *Anon.*

BIGOT

One . . . obstinately and zealously attached to an opinion that you do not entertain.
          Ambrose Bierce

One who is frequently wrong, but with confidence.   *Eugene E. Brussell*

People who have no convictions at all.
          Gilbert Keith Chesterton

He who will not reason.   *William Drummond*

A person who slams his mind in your face.
          Paul H. Gilbert

A blind man with sight.   *Max Gralnick*

Anyone attached to an opinion you do not entertain.   *Edward Higgins*

A person who, under an atheist king, would be an atheist.   *Jean de La Bruyère*

A man who converts the main issue in piety into a side issue, and a side issue into the main issue.
          Mendel of Kotzk

SEE ALSO ANTI-SEMITISM, PREJUDICE.

BIGOTRY

To take up half on trust, and half to try.
          John Dryden

(When) objects fall into categories . . . and wear little sure channels in the brain.   *David Grayson*

Chronic dogmatism.   *Horace Greeley*

The disease of ignorance, of morbid minds.
          Thomas Jefferson

A form of egoism, and to condemn egosim intolerantly is to share it.   *George Santayana*

Dark convictions.   *Logan P. Smith*

A darkness in the understanding.
          John Woolman

BIOGRAPHY

Dramatic constructions.   *Katherine Anthony*

One of the new terrors.   *John Arbuthnot*

(Something that) should be written by an acute enemy.   *Arthur J. Balfour*

The literary tribute that a little man pays to a big one.   *Ambrose Bierce*

The only true history.   *Thomas Carlyle*

A heroic poem.   *Thomas Carlyle*

The Art of Biography
Is different from Geography.
Geography is about maps,
But Biography is about chaps.
          Gilbert Keith Chesterton

The confession of the man himself to somebody.
          Ralph Waldo Emerson

Material (that) is not to be had and if it were it could not be used.   *Sigmund Freud*

An interpretive, selective, and analytic, not a creative art.   *Claude M. Fuess*

Like big game hunting... one of the recognized forms of sport, and it is as unfair as only sport can be.   *Philip Guedalla*

A region bounded on the north by history, on the south by fiction, on the east by obituary, and on the west by tedium.   *Philip Guedalla*

Nobody can write the life of a man, but those who have eat and drunk and lived in social intercourse with him.   *Samuel Johnson*

Biography is, of the various kinds of narrative writing, that which is most eagerly read and most easily applied to the purpose of life.
          Samuel Johnson

Should be a man's conversation, not his deeds.
          George M. Moore

The history of the lives of individual men as a branch of literature.
          Oxford English Dictionary.

A living voice.   *Samuel Smiles*

SEE ALSO AUTOBIOGRAPHY, HISTORIAN.

BIRDS

Dame nature's minstrels.   *Gavin Douglas*

Only a song machine.   *George Macdonald*

The merry minstrels of the morn.
          James Thomson

A voice, a mystery.   *William Wordsworth*

BIRTH

I was shapen in iniquity; and in sin did my mother conceive me.   *Bible: Psalms, L, 5.*

The first and direct of all disasters.
          Ambrose Bierce

The sudden opening of a window through which you look out upon a stupendous prospect. For what has happened? A miracle. You have exchanged nothing for the possibility of everything.
          William M. Dixon

Wherever a child is born...there the angel's choir chant anew the sweet tidings of glory and peace and good will.   *Hyman Enelow*

The first of all dangers to life, as well as the prototype of all the later ones we fear; and this experience has left its mark behind it on that expression of emotion which we call anxiety.
          Sigmund Freud

The first experience of anxiety.   *Sigmund Freud*

The beginning of death.   *Thomas Fuller*

The coffin is the cradle's brother.
          German Proverb

The glory of God.   *Jewish Proverb*

We begin to die at birth; the end flows from the beginning.   *Marcus Manilius*

A sleep and a forgetting.   *William Wordsworth*

SEE ALSO BABY.

BIRTH CONTROL

A mine disaster...think of all the people lost inside you.   *Richard Brautigan*

The idea that people should be in one respect completely and utterly uncontrolled, so long as they evade everything in that function that is positive and creative.   *Gilbert Keith Chesterton*

The avoidance of pregnancy...within the bounds of reason and morality.   *John A. Goodwine*

Turning marital relations into a form of annual inventory.   *Sydney J. Harris*

The use of unnatural means for the avoidance of conception.   *Lambeth Conference of Anglican Bishops, 1920.*

Complete abstinence from intercourse.   *Lambeth Conference of Anglican Bishops, 1930.*

It means attacking the primary purpose of the marriage act in the very manner of performing it.   *Donald F. Miller*

An act of will whose purpose is to prevent fertilization.   *Otto A. Piper*

Sin against nature...a deed which is shameful and intrinsically vicious...an offense against the law of God and nature.   *Pope Pius XI*

A grave sin.   *Pope Pius XII*

The one sin for which the penalty is national death, race death; a sin for which there is no atonement.   *Theodore Roosevelt*

The most revolutionary invention of the nineteenth century.   *George Bernard Shaw*

Premature murder.   *Tertullian*

Copulation without population.   *Anon.*

The formula by which one plus one equals zero.   *Anon.*

Anti-littering.   *Anon.*

SEE ALSO ABORTION.

BIRTHDAY

A big event in everybody's life. It should be a holiday—with pay.   *Michael Darling*

The funeral of the former year.   *Alexander Pope*

Feathers in the broad wing of time.
          Jean Paul Richter

BISHOP

The power and authority of a bishop ... consist ... in inspecting the manners of the people and clergy, and punishing them in order to reformation, by ecclesiastical censures.
          William Blackstone

Bishops by divine institution have succeeded to the place of the Apostles, as shepherds of the Church, and he who hears them, hears Christ.
          Constitution of the Church, Second Vatican Council, 1964.

The individual Bishops...exercise their pastoral government over the portion of the People of God committed to their care, and not over the churches nor over the universal Church.
          Constitution of the Church, Second Vatican Council, 1964.

Only a surpliced merchant. Through his lawn I can see the bright buttons of the shopman's coat.
          Ralph Waldo Emerson

In their corporate capacity the bishops...have the right to articles of faith. But individually, their sole duty is to dispense with the observation of those articles.   *Charles de Montesquieu*

An ecclesiastical sheriff.   *Chief Justice North*

The politician of churches.   *Maxwell Pont*

Every steward sent by the master to govern his house...wherefore the bishop should be regarded as the Lord Himself.   *Saint Ignatius*

All are successors of the Apostles.
          Saint Jerome

The most solemn and terrible duty of a bishop is the entertainment of the clergy.   *Sydney Smith*

The steward of God.   *Anon.*

The president of a firm dealing in spiritual life, whose days are spent auditing books and hiring and firing the personnel.   *Anon.*

SEE ALSO CATHOLICISM, PRIESTS.

BLACK

SEE NEGRO, SLAVE, SLAVERY.

BLASPHEMY

Thou shalt not take the name of the Lord thy God in vain.   *Bible: Exodus, XX, 7.*

Denying the being or providence of God, contumelious reproaches of our Saviour Christ, profane scoffing at the Holy Scripture, or exposing it to contempt or ridicule.   *William Blackstone*

Injustice.   *Robert G. Ingersoll*

All great truths begin as blasphemies.

George Bernard Shaw

BLESSING

Blessed is the man that walketh not in the counsel of the ungodly, nor standeth in the way of sinners, nor sitteth in the seat of the scournful.

Bible: Psalms, I, 1.

The dead which die in the Lord.

Bible: Revelation, XIV, 13.

Blessed is he who has found his work; let him ask no other blessedness.   *Thomas Carlyle*

God Himself.   *Meister Eckhart*

Long life, riches, serenity, the love of virtue, and the attainment of ambition.   *The Hung-Fan*

The fruits of labor, toil, self-denial, and study.

William G. Sumner

Every misery I miss.   *Izaak Walton*

Good when He gives, nor less when He denies, mere blessings in disguise.   *Anon.*

SEE ALSO SALVATION.

BLONDE

A brunette with a top secret.   *Daniel Bennett*

An abbreviation of "peroxide of hydrogen."

Jimmy Lyons

The cross between a brunette and a drugstore.

Anon.

BLOOD

The blood is the life.

Bible: Deuteronomy, XII, 23.

An inheritance.   *Miguel de Cervantes*

A very special kind of sap.   *Johann W. Goethe*

That fragile scarlet tree we carry within us.

Osbert Sitwell

BLUE

Trueness.   *Ben Jonson*

Blue! Gentle cousin of the forest-green,
    Married to green.   *John Keats*

Not merely a color; it is a mystery.

Israll B. Najara

True love.   *Scottish Proverb*

BLUESTOCKING

A misfortune to a woman.   *Mary W. Montagu*

When we think...ill of a woman, and wish to blacken her character, we merely call her a blue-stocking.   *Edgar Allan Poe*

A scourge to her husband, her children, her friends, her servants, and the whole world.

Jean-Jacques Rousseau

BLUSHING

A sign of guilt or ill-breeding.

William Congreve

Only a dubious flag-signal which may mean either of two contradictories.   *George Eliot*

Virtue's color.   *English Proverb*

Notice to be careful.   *Edgar W. Howe*

(Means) already guilty; true innocence is ashamed of nothing.   *Jean-Jacques Rousseau*

Badges of imperfection. Saints have no shame.

William Wycherley

SEE ALSO BASHFULNESS.

BOASTER

A boaster and a liar are first cousins.

German Proverb

An ass.   *William Shakespeare*

A person with whom it is no sooner done than said.   *Anon.*

Someone invited for dinner who proves that the night has a thousand I's.   *Anon.*

SEE ALSO EGOTIST.

BOASTING

SEE EXAGGERATION, LYING.

BODY

A system of tubes and glands . . . a bundle of pipes and strainers, fitted to one another after so wonderful a manner as to make a proper engine for the soul to work with.   *Joseph Addison*

A bar of soap. It gradually wears down from repeated use.   *Ritchie Allen*

Am I what I seem, more flesh and blood,
A branching channel, with a mazy flood . . .
I call it mine, not me.   *John Arbuthnot*

A healthy body is a guest-chamber for the soul; a sick body is a prison.   *Francis Bacon*

The temple of the Holy Ghost.
          Bible: Corinthians, VI, 19.

A portion of soul discern'd by the five senses, the chief inlets of soul in this age.   *William Blake*

The workhouse of the soul.   *Henry G. Bohn*

A pair of pincers set over a bellows and a stewpan, the whole fixed upon stilts.   *Samuel Butler 1*

A hodge-podge of sagging livers, sinking gall bladders, drooping stomachs, compressed intestines, and squashed pelvic organs.
          John Button 2

An envelope.   *Alexis Carrel*

The . . . form entrusted to you by Heaven and Earth . . . a blended harmony.   *Chuang-tzu*

This house of clay not built with hands.
          Samuel Taylor Coleridge

The tenement of clay.   *John Dryden*

A community made up of its innumerable cells or inhabitants.   *Thomas Alva Edison*

The magazine of inventions, the patent office, where are the models from which every hint is taken. All the tools and engines on earth are only extensions of its limbs and senses.
          Ralph Waldo Emerson

A thing of shreds and patches, borrowed unequally from good and bad ancestors and a misfit from the start.   *Ralph Waldo Emerson*

A pipe through which we tap all the succors and virtues of the material world.
          Ralph Waldo Emerson

Only a prison.   *Mohandas K. Gandhi*

The harp of your soul.   *Kahlil Gibran*

A marvelous machine . . . a chemical laboratory, a power-house. Every movement, voluntary or involuntary, full of secrets and marvels!
          Theodor Herzl

The instrument of the spirit.   *Samson R. Hirsch*

Nothing by objectified will.   *Thomas Landry*

A worthy dwelling for the soul, God's portion from on high.   *Israel S. Lipkin*

The urn of the soul.   *Lucretius*

A machine which winds its own springs.
          Julien O. Mettrie

A bundle of aches, Longing for rest.
          Edna S. Millay

An internal world.   *Jonathan Miller*

A fetid drop.   *Mishna: Abot, III, 1.*

The body is made for the soul to express it.
          Jean Mouroux

A morsel for death.   *Guru Nanak*

A vessel which He wrought, and into which He infused His workmanship and skill.
          Guru Nanak

An affliction of the soul . . . a burden, a necessity, a strong chain, and a tormenting punishment.
          Palladas

The tomb of the soul.   *Plato*

The temple of the Holy Spirit, and is the means whereby alone the soul can establish relations with the universe.   *Harry Roberts*

A tabernacle in which the transmissible human spirit is carried for a while, a shell for the immortal seed that dwells in it and has created it.
          George Santayana

Not a home but an inn—and that only briefly.
          Seneca

The unwilling sport of circumstance and passion.
          Adapted from Percy Bysshe Shelley

A human body is composed of a large number of different entities, and each of them is itself a composite.   *Baruch Spinoza*

A cell state in which every cell is a citizen.
                                          Rudolf Virchow

The best picture of the human soul.
                                       Ludwig Wittgenstein

This heaven-labour'd form, erect, divine.
                                          Edward Young

A little city.   *Anon.*

SEE ALSO CORPSE, FLESH.

BOHEMIA

A bunch of amateurs teaching amateurs to be amateurs.   *Charles Coburn*

A good place in which to camp, but a very poor place in which to settle down.   *Elbert Hubbard*

(A place) not on the map because it is not a money-order office.   *Elbert Hubbard*

People who sit on the floor and drink black coffee when all the time there are chairs and cream in the room.   *Beatrice Lillie*

A place of artistic-minded pretenders.   *Anon.*

BOHEMIAN

A person open to the suspicion of irregular and immoral living.   *Ralph Waldo Emerson*

A person conventionally unconventional.
                                     George Bernard Shaw

An educated hoss-thief.   *Artemus Ward*

A person who works to live but does not live to work.   *Heathcote Williams*

BONAPARTE, NAPOLEON

SEE NAPOLEON 1.

BOOK

The legacies that...genius leaves to mankind, to be delivered down from generation to generation, as presents to those that are yet unborn.
                                        Joseph Addison

That is a good book which is opened with expectation and closed with profit.
                                    Amos Bronson Alcott

A blast from the lungs made visible to the eyes.
                                          Hervey Allen

Most books, indeed, are records less
Of fulness than of emptiness.
                                      William Allingham

A garden carried in the pocket.
                                       Arabian Proverb

Ships which pass through the vast sea of time.
                                          Francis Bacon

A garden, an orchard, a storehouse, a party, a company by the way, a counsellor, a multitude of counsellors.   *Henry Ward Beecher*

The windows through which the soul looks out.
                                     Henry Ward Beecher

The compasses and telescopes and sextants and charts which other men have prepared to help us navigate the dangerous seas of human life.
                                        Jesse L. Bennett

A malevolent literary device for cramping the growth of a language and making it hard and inelastic.   *Ambrose Bierce*

Something to be read, not kept under glass or in a safe.   *John Mason Brown*

Masters who instruct us without rods...without hard words and anger...they conceal nothing.
                                      Richard de Bury

The true university.   *Thomas Carlyle*

All that mankind has done, thought, gained or been...they are the chosen possession of men.
                                       Thomas Carlyle

Friends that never fail me.   *Thomas Carlyle*

The blessed chloroform of the mind.
                                       Robert Chambers

The voices of the distant and the dead, and make us heirs of the spiritual life of past ages.
                                  William Ellery Channing

Leisure for me; they are never engaged.   *Cicero*

A guide in youth and an entertainment for age.
                                        Jeremy Collier

Feeders for brothels.   *Anthony Comstock*

They give new views to life, and teach us how to
live.   *Adapted from George Crabbe*

Accumulated wisdom.   *George W. Curtis*

The most remarkable creation of man; nothing
else that he builds ever lasts...Monuments
fall...civilizations grow old and die out...but in
the world of books are volumes that live on, still
as young and fresh as the day they were written—
still telling men's hearts of the hearts of men
centuries dead.   *Clarence Day*

The curse of the human race. Nine-tenths...are
nonsense, and the clever books are the refutation
of that nonsense.   *Benjamin Disraeli*

The quietest and most constant of friends; they are
the most accessible and wisest of counsellors, and
the most patient of teachers.   *Charles W. Eliot*

The best thing, well used; abused, among the
worst.   *Ralph Waldo Emerson*

The scholar's idle times. When he can read God
directly, the hour is too precious to be wasted in
other men's transcripts of their reading.
          Ralph Waldo Emerson

A work of magic whence escape all the images to
trouble the souls and anger the hearts of men.
          Anatole France

Sweet unreproaching companions to the miserable.   *Oliver Goldsmith*

The most complicated and mightiest of all the
miracles created by man on his path to the
happiness and power of the future.
          Maxim Gorky

My masters and companions.   *Joseph Hall*

A screen to keep us from a knowledge of things.
          William Hazlitt

An inanimate thing, yet it talks...
It gives, and does not take.   *Moses Ibn Ezra*

Books constitute capital. A...book lasts as long
as a house...It is not, then, an article of mere
consumption but...of capital, and often in the
case of professional men, setting out in life, it is
their only capital.   *Thomas Jefferson*

The most effective weapon against intolerance
and ignorance.   *Lyndon Baines Johnson*

A way to lose yourself in other men's minds.
Books think for you.
          Adapted from Charles Lamb

What they make a movie out of for television.
          Leonard L. Levinson

A mirror: if an ass peers into it, you can't expect
an apostle to look out.   *Georg C. Lichtenberg*

Sepulchers of thought.
          Henry Wadsworth Longfellow

The very heart and core of ages past.
          Amy Lowell

All books are either dreams or swords,
You can cut, or you can drug, with words.
          Amy Lowell

Two sorts of books: those that no one reads and
those that no one ought to read.
          Henry Louis Mencken

The precious life-blood of a master spirit, im-
balmed and treasured up on purpose to a life
beyond life.   *John Milton*

A book ought to be like a man or a woman, with
some individual character in it, though eccentric,
yet its own; with some blood in its veins and
speculation in its eyes and a way and will of its
own.   *John Mitchel*

Style and structure are the essence...great ideas
are hogwash.   *Vladimir Nabokov*

They only teach us to talk about things we know
nothing about.   *Jean-Jacques Rousseau*

Windows that frame the wide and luminous view.
          Adapted from Frances C. Sayers

A finer world within the world.
          Alexander Smith

Books extend our narrow present back into a
limitless past. They show us the mistakes of the
men before us and share with us recipes for
human success.   *T. V. Smith*

Funny little portable pieces of thought.
          Susan Sontag

A mighty bloodless substitute for life.
          Robert Louis Stevenson

The treasured wealth of the world, the fit inheritance of generations and nations.
          Henry David Thoreau

The good book is always a book of travel; it is about a life's journey.   *Henry M. Tomlinson*

Life's best business: vocation to these has more emolument coming in than all the other busy terms of life.   *Richard Whitlock*

For company the best friends, in doubts counsellors...time's perspective...the busy man's best recreation, the opiate of idle weariness...the seedplot of immortality.   *Richard Whitlock*

The Meccas of the mind.

George E. Woodberry

The world carried in the hand.   *Anon.*

SEE ALSO AUTHOR, BIBLIOMANIA, FICTION, LITERATURE, NOVEL, PRINTING, READER, STYLE, WRITING.

BORE

A person who talks when you wish him to listen.

Ambrose Bierce

A Bromide.   *Gelett Burgess*

A harmless creature, or of that class of irrational bipeds who hurt only themselves.

Maria Edgeworth

A fellow who opens his mouth and puts his feats in it.   *Henry Ford*

A man who deprives you of solitude without providing you with company.   *Gian Gravina*

A person who has flat feats.   *Joseph Harrington*

The last one to find himself out.

Oliver Wendell Holmes 1

All men...except when we want them.

Oliver Wendell Holmes 1

A man like a spider, spinning conversation incessantly out of his bowels.

Adapted from Samuel Johnson

A person not only dull, but the cause of dullness in others.   *Adapted from Samuel Johnson*

A man who spends so much time talking about himself that you can't talk about yourself.

Melville Landon

(One) who has a fixed idea to impart, and the fixed ideas of the few are the boredom of the many.   *Edward V. Lucas*

Everyone...to someone.   *Llewellyn Miller*

A fellow talking who can change the subject back to his topic...faster than you can change it back to yours.   *Laurence J. Peter*

The kind of man who, when you ask him how he is, tells you.   *Channing Pollock*

A man in love with another woman.

Mary P. Poole

A man who, when you ask him how he is, tells you.   *Bertram L. Taylor*

To tell everything.   *Voltaire*

The coming of age of seriousness.   *Oscar Wilde*

A man who is never unintentionally rude.

Oscar Wilde

A guy who wraps up a two-minute idea in a two-hour vocabulary.   *Walter Winchell*

A person one cannot endure indefinitely.   *Anon.*

One who lights up a room when he leaves.

Anon.

One who thinks he is always at his best.   *Anon.*

One whom even the grave yawns for.   *Anon.*

One who keeps his conversation hohumming.

Anon.

One whose shortcoming is long a-staying.

Anon.

SEE ALSO PHILISTINE.

BOREDOM

The desire of activity without the fit means of gratifying the desire.   *George Bancroft*

The world's second worst crime...the first is being a bore.   *Cecil Beaton*

What happens when we lose contact with the universe.   *John Ciardi*

A feeling of isolation, of alienation from corporate society.   *Jerry Dashkin*

The tedium of life.   *Aurus Gellius*

The curse of those who achieve security.

Max Gralnick

The consciousness of a barren, meaningless existence.   *Eric Hoffer*

The essential nature of monogamy.

Elbert Hubbard

Uniformity of manners and thoughts.

Joseph Jacobs

Time, with all its celerity, moves slowly to him whose whole employment is to watch its flight.

Samuel Johnson

Uniformity. *Lamotte-Houdar*

Something that exists only among those who attach importance to the mind.

Giacomo Leopardi

The fixed ideas of the few. *Edward V. Lucas*

Rent for living in this world. *William Manville*

The yawn of a new day. *Harold Murray*

Complete repose, without passion, occupation, amusement, care. *Blaise Pascal*

A vital problem for the moralist, since at least half the sins of mankind are caused by fear of it.

Bertrand A. Russell

An emptiness filled with insistence. *Leon Stein*

Sentenced to solitary confinement inside our own skins, for life. *Tennessee Williams*

SEE ALSO MONOTONY.

BOSS

The question "Who ought to be boss?" is like asking "Who ought to be the tenor in the quartet?" Obviously, the man who can sing tenor.

Henry Ford

(One who) exists to make sensible exceptions to general rules. *Elting E. Morison*

The one who watches the clock during the coffee break. *Hupp Trevis*

One who does not care for "yes" men. He also appreciates men who can say "no" when he does.

Anon.

A man who can look at both sides: his side and the wrong side. *Anon.*

The man at the office who is early when you are late and late when you are early. *Anon.*

SEE ALSO EXECUTIVE, LEADER.

BOSTON

The town of the cries and the groans, where the Cabots can't see the Kabotschniks and the Lowells won't speak to the Cohns.

Adapted from Franklin P. Adams

The home of the bean and the cod, where the Lowells talk to the Cabots, and the Cabots talk only to God. *Adapted from John C. Bossidy*

A hole. *Robert Browning*

The heart of the world.

Oliver Wendell Holmes 1

The thinking center of the continent, and therefore of the planet. *Oliver Wendell Holmes 1*

A moral and intellectual nursery always busy applying first principles and trifles.

George Santayana

A state of mind. *Mark Twain*

A museum piece. *Frank Lloyd Wright*

The wheel within Massachusetts. Boston therefore is often called the "hub of the world," since it has been the source and fountain of the ideas that have reared and made America. *F. B. Zinckle*

BOSTONIAN

The East wind made flesh.

Thomas G. Appleton

A comfortable man with dividends.

Henry Wadsworth Longfellow

As a race, far inferior in point of anything beyond mere talent to any other set upon the continent of North America. They are decidedly the most servile imitators of the English it is possible to conceive. *Edgar Allan Poe*

If you hear an owl hoot: "To whom" instead of "To who" you can make up your mind he was born and educated in Boston. *Anon.*

Your grave Bostonian, stately of pace, with second-hand English writ in his face. *Anon.*

BOTANY

The art of insulting flowers in Greek and Latin.

Alphonse Karr

BOURGEOISIE

SEE MIDDLE CLASS, PHILISTINE.

BOY

A magical creature—you can lock him out of your workshop, but you can't lock him out of your heart. *Allan Beck*

The appetite of a horse, the digestion of a sword swallower...the curiosity of a cat, the lungs of a dictator...the shyness of a violet, the audacity of a steel trap, the enthusiasm of a firecracker, and when he makes something he has five thumbs on each hand. *Allan Beck*

Someone who wants to grow up fast and be a fireman and eat candy for a living.
Eugene E. Brussell

Hurry on its way to doing nothing. *John Ciardi*

At best, but pretty buds unblown, whose scent and hues are rather guessed at than known.
Adapted from William Cowper

Someone more troublesome than a dozen girls.
English Proverb

One who has a wolf in his stomach.
German Proverb

A young boy is a theory; an old man is a fact.
Edward Howe

Capital fellows in their own way, among their mates; but they are unwholesome companions for grown people. *Charles Lamb*

Nature's raw material. *Hector H. Munro*

Of all the wild beasts, the most difficult to manage. *Plato*

A noise with dirt on it. *Anon.*

A cross between a god and a goat. *Anon.*

An appetite with a skin pulled over it. *Anon.*

SEE ALSO CHILD, YOUTH.

BOYHOOD

A summer sun. *Edgar Allan Poe*

Health that mocks the doctor's rules,
Knowledge never learned in schools.
John Greenleaf Whittier

The time when we crowd years in one brief moon.
Adapted from John Greenleaf Whittier

The sweetest roamer. *George E. Woodberry*

SEE ALSO CHILDHOOD, YOUTH.

BRAHMS, JOHANNES (1833-1897)

When I feel the urge to compose, I begin by appealing directly to my Maker.
Johannes Brahms

I once told Wagner himself that I was the best Wagnerian of our time. *Johannes Brahms*

A landscape torn by mists and clouds, in which I can see ruins of old churches, as well as of Greek temples—that is Brahms. *Evard Grieg*

For the drawing room he is not graceful enough, for the concert hall not fiery enough, for the city not cultured enough. *Anton Rubinstein*

I believe Johannes to be the true Apostle, who will also write Revelations. *Robert Schumann*

(His music) is a verbosity which outfaces its commonplaceness by dint of sheer magnitude.
George Bernard Shaw

I have played over the music of that scoundrel Brahms. What a giftless bastard!
Peter Illyich Tchaikovsky

He seemed to lack liveliness, so that in our meetings he was often scarcely noticed.
Richard Wagner

He can't exult! *Hugo Wolf*

BRAIN

An apparatus with which we think that we think.
Ambrose Bierce

The greatest natural resource. *Karl Brandt*

(Something that) starts working the moment you get up in the morning, and does not stop until you get into the office. *Robert Frost*

Our brains are seventy-year clocks. The angel of life winds them up once for all, then closes the case, and gives the key into the hands of the angel of the resurrection. *Oliver Wendell Holmes 1*

The knapsack of intelligence. *Elbert Hubbard*

A commodity...used to fertilize ideas.

Elbert Hubbard

Only one condition out of many on which intellectual manifestations depend.

Thomas Henry Huxley

An appendage of the genital glands. *Carl G. Jung*

Three kinds of brains: one understands of itself, another can be taught to understand, and the third can neither understand of itself or be taught to understand.   *Niccolo Machiavelli*

The citadel of the senses.   *Pliny 1*

A most unusual instrument of elegant and as yet unknown capacity.   *Stuart L. Seaton*

A part of the body that begins to operate at birth but stops when its owner gets up to make a speech.   *Anon.*

The greatest underdeveloped territory.   *Anon.*

A part of the human mechanism that starts to function at birth and stops when its owner gets up to make an impromptu speech.   *Anon.*

What people are forced to use who don't have college degrees.   *Anon.*

Nature's way of keeping house.   *Anon.*

SEE ALSO HEAD, INTELLIGENCE, MIND, THINKING, UNDERSTANDING.

BRAVERY

Fear sneering at itself.   *Maxwell Bodenheim*

A cheap and vulgar quality, of which the brightest instances are frequently found in the lowest savages.   *Paul Chatfield*

An accident of circumstances.   *Michael Dee*

Falling but not yielding.   *Latin Proverb*

(Physical bravery is) an animal instinct; moral bravery is a much higher and truer courage.

Wendell Phillips

To look into the mirror of your own soul to see written there the disfigurements caused by your own misbehavior.   *Fulton J. Sheen*

The condition you find yourself in after a few drinks.   *Anon.*

SEE ALSO COURAGE, GALLANTRY, HEROISM.

BREAD

The staff of life.   *English Saying*

What the rich occasionally give to the poor as a substitute for cake.

Adapted from Elbert Hubbard

Bread for myself is a material question; bread for my neighbor is a spiritual question.

Jacques Maritain

SEE ALSO FOOD, STOMACH.

BREEDING (MANNERS)

The best security against other people's ill manners.   *Lord Chesterfield*

Surface Christianity.   *Oliver Wendell Holmes 2*

The test of a man or woman's breeding is how they behave in a quarrel.   *George Bernard Shaw*

An expedient to make fools and wise men equals.

Richard Steele

Concealing how much we think of ourselves and how little we think of the other person.

Mark Twain

SEE ALSO GENTLEMAN, MANNERS, WELL-BRED.

BREVITY

Not only the soul of wit, but the soul of making oneself agreeable, and of getting on with people, and...of everything that makes life worth having.

Samuel Butler 1

The soul of drinking, as of wit.   *Charles Lamb*

To say at once whatever is to be said.

Georg C. Lichtenberg

The soul of lingerie.   *Dorothy Parker*

Almost a condition of being inspired.

George Santayana

The soul of wit.   *William Shakespeare*

The next best thing to silence.   *Anon.*

Words that cover more ground than they occupy.

Anon.

SEE ALSO EPIGRAM, TALK.

BRIDE

A woman with a fine prospect of happiness behind her.   *Ambrose Bierce*

A goddess who descends into commonality.
Anon.

SEE ALSO HONEYMOON, NIAGARA FALLS, WEDDING.

BRIDGE (CARDS)

Being miserable together.   *Don Herold*

An unfriendly game of cards.   *Anon.*

The triumph of mind over chatter.   *Anon.*

The most shin-bruising game in America.
Anon.

A war surrounded by politicians.   *Anon.*

BRITAIN

SEE ENGLAND.

BRITISH EMPIRE

Our policy now can only be to sustain the fragments of what was once a glorious empire on which the sun used never to set and on which now it seldom rises.   *Lord Beaverbrook*

A domain created in a moment of world absent-mindedness.   *Eamon de Valera*

SEE ALSO ENGLAND, ENGLISHMEN.

BRITON

SEE ENGLISHMEN.

BROADMINDEDNESS

The result of flattening high-mindedness out.
George Saintsbury

High-mindedness flattened out by experience.
Anon.

BROADWAY

The longest street with the shortest memory.
Maurice Barrymore

A street of ham and aches.   *Hyman Gardner*

America's hardened artery.   *Mark Kelly*

A place where people spend money they haven't earned to buy things they don't need to impress people they don't like.   *Walter Winchell*

SEE ALSO THEATER.

BROTHERHOOD

An injustice righted here, an opportunity extended there.   *Kingsley Amis*

The right hands of fellowship.
Bible: Galantians, II, 9.

Finally, be ye all of one mind.
Bible: Peter, III, 8.

Brotherhood is religion!   *William Blake*

Not an ideal, but a divine reality . . . a spiritual and not a psychic reality.   *Dietrich Bonhoeffer*

When two say to one another with all that they are, "It is Thou."   *Martin Buber*

Owing to your brethren all that it is in your power to give.   *Adapted from John Calvin*

While there is a lower class I am it. While there is a criminal class I am of it. While there is a soul in prison I am not free.   *Eugene V. Debs*

All for one and one for all.   *Alexandre Dumas*

To live vividly together.   *Max Eastman*

Helping yourself by helping others.
Adapted from Elbert Hubbard

(To) live, think, and suffer with the men of your time, as one of them.   *Henry de Lubac*

The crest and crowning of all good.
Edwin Markham

A destiny which makes us brothers.
Edwin Markham

When man to man shall be a friend and brother.
Adapted from Gerald Massey

Mutually mindful of each other, of one heart and one mind.   *Saint Cyprian*

To love God by loving man.
Adapted from Saint Francis de Sales

A feeling of fellowship that should be, but isn't.
Anon.

SEE ALSO BIBLE, CHRIST, CHRISTIANITY, CHRISTIANS, FELLOWSHIP, FRIENDSHIP, GOD, RELIGION.

BRUTALITY

SEE CRUELTY.

BRYAN, WILLIAM JENNINGS
(1860-1925)

The boy orator of the Platte.   *W. J. Connell*

The Platte—six inches deep and six miles wide at the mouth.   *Joseph B. Foraker*

A somewhat greasy bald-headed man with his mouth open.   *Henry Louis Mencken*

A personally honest and . . . attractive man, a real orator and a born demagogue, who has every crank, fool, and putative criminal in the country behind him.   *Theodore Roosevelt*

He was in himself the average man . . . he did not merely resemble that average man, he was that average man.   *Charles W. Thompson*

A progressive who never progressed—mentally.
Charles W. Thompson

BUDDHISM

Their belief . . . that Providence sends down always an Incarnation of Himself into every generation. At bottom some belief in a kind of pope! . . . that there is a Greatest Man; that he is discoverable . . . that we ought to treat him with an obedience which knows no bounds.
Thomas Carlyle

The word used for religion in Buddhism is *brahma-cariya* which may be translated as "the ideal life"—any way of life which anyone may consider to be the ideal as a consequence of his holding a certain set of beliefs about the nature and destiny of man in the universe.
G. P. Malalasekera and K. N. Jayatilleke

The . . . doctrine that real riches consists not in the abundance of goods but in the paucity of wants.
Alfred Marshall

Buddhism . . . may be accepted as a preface to the Gospel . . . and as the most convincing argument withal that truth to be clearly known waits upon Revelation.   *Paul E. Moore*

The product of long centuries of philosophical speculation . . . The things necessary . . . are a very mild climate, customs of great gentleness and liberality, and no militarism.
Friedrich W. Nietzsche

An emphasis on personality which finds its climax in Christianity.   *David E. Trueblood*

BUDGETING

A system of additions and subtractions more honored in breach than in observance.
Eugene E. Brussell

Telling your money where to go instead of wondering where it went.   *C. E. Hoover*

A mathematical confirmation of your suspicions.
A. A. Latimer

A reflection of values in the language of dollars and sense.   *Samuel S. Markowitz*

The art of doing that well with one dollar which any bungler can do with two after a fashion.
Arthur Wellington

A method of worrying before you spend instead of afterwards.   *Anon.*

A system of going into debt systematically.
Anon.

An in-debt activity.   *Anon.*

SEE ALSO ECONOMY.

BUREAUCRACY

A giant mechanism operated by pygmies.
Honoré de Balzac

A continuing congregation of people who must act more or less as one.   *John Kenneth Galbraith*

The antithesis of democracy.   *Jo Grimond*

The cancer-cell of the nation.   *E. S. Haynes*

The anonymous "they," the enigmatic "they" who are in charge. Who is "they"? I don't know. Nobody knows. Not even "they" know.
Joseph Heller

Parasites living on the labor of the industrious.

Thomas Jefferson

More machinery of government than is necessary.

Thomas Jefferson

The nearest thing to immortality in this world.

Hugh S. Johnson

The biggest eater and the biggest loafer that ever oppressed the sons of man.   *David Lubin*

The rule of no one...the modern form of despotism.   *Mary McCarthy*

The work of government has been in the hands of governors by profession; which is the essence and meaning of bureaucracy.   *John Stuart Mill*

SEE ALSO GOVERNMENT, WASHINGTON, D.C.

BURKE, EDMUND (1729-1797)

He was a scientific statesman; and therefore a seer.   *Samuel Taylor Coleridge*

He'd talk to you in such a manner, that, when you parted, you would say, this is an extraordinary man.   *Samuel Johnson*

An out-and-out vulgar bourgeois.   *Karl Marx*

He rose like a rocket, he fell like a stick.

Thomas Paine

BUSINESS

Profit.   *Charles F. Abbott*

The art of extracting money from another man's pocket without resorting to violence.

Max Amsterdam

The place set apart where men may deceive each other.   *Anacharsis*

(Something) more agreeable than pleasure; it interests the whole mind, the aggregate nature of man more continuously, and more deeply.

Walter Bagehot

Swindling.   *August Bebel*

Gambling.   *Ambrose Bierce*

Boldness...is the first, second, and third thing.

Henry G. Bohn

A battle where everything goes, where the only gospel is "get ahead," and never spare friends or foes.   *Adapted from Berton Braley*

(An activity) which should know neither love nor hate.   *Samuel Butler 2*

The business of America is business.

Calvin Coolidge

To make money in an honorable manner.

Peter Cooper

Marketing and innovation.   *Peter Drucker*

Business? That's very simple—it's other people's money.   *Alexandre Dumas*

All business proceeds on beliefs, or judgments of probabilities, and not on certainties.

Charles W. Eliot

A great art involving the selling of wind.

Baltasar Gracian

Punctuality is the soul of business.

Thomas C. Haliburton

The pursuit of gain...in which men can serve the needs of others whom they do not know.

F. A. Hayek

A combination of war and sport.   *Emile Herzog*

Business is war.   *Japanese Saying*

Consists in persuading crowds.   *Gerald S. Lee*

The aim...is service, for profit, at a risk.

Benjamin C. Leeming

A superior economic tool by which to provide those things that constitute the physical basis of living.   *David E. Lilienthal*

The material foundation of a society which can further the highest values known to men.

David E. Lilienthal

A continual dealing with the future...a continual calculation, an instinctive exercise in foresight.

Henry R. Luce

The playthings of our elders.   *Saint Augustine*

The Jungle.   *Upton Sinclair*

The judicious use of sabotage.   *Thorstein Veblen*

(That which) underlies everything in our national life, including our spiritual life. Witness...that in the Lord's Prayer, the first petition is for daily bread. No one can worship God or love his neighbor on an empty stomach.

Woodrow Wilson

Riding a bicycle. Either you keep moving or you fall down.   *John D. Wright*

SEE ALSO CAPITALISM, COMMERCE, CORPORATION, ECONOMICS, ECONOMY, MARKETPLACE.

BUSINESSMAN

(One who) has all the air, the distraction and restlessness and hurry of...a criminal.

William Hazlitt

The most sensible people to be met with in society...who argue from what they see and know.   *William Hazlitt*

One who gets the business and completes the transaction—all the rest are clerks and laborers.

Elbert Hubbard

One who should keep moving about so people will think he is doing big things.   *Jewish Saying*

He who attempts to get people to believe he has something they want.

Adapted from Gerald S. Lee

The only man above the hangman and the scavenger who is forever apologizing for his occupation. He is the only one who always seeks to make it appear, when he attains the object of his labors, i.e., the making of a great deal of money, that it was not the object of his labors.

Henry Louis Mencken

The visionless demigod of our new materialistic myth.   *Eugene O'Neill*

Someone who has read only newspapers since leaving school.

Adapted from George Bernard Shaw

(Those so engaged) because the soul abhors a vacuum and they have not discovered any continuous employment for man's nobler faculties.

Henry David Thoreau

They are not units but fractions.

Woodrow Wilson

SEE ALSO CAPITALIST, MERCHANT, SALESMAN.

BUTLER

SEE SERVANT.

BUTTER

Gold in the morning, silver at noon, lead at night.

English Proverb

Butter is life.   *Sanskrit Proverb*

BUTTERFLY

At best,
He's but a caterpillar, drest   *John Gay*

The butterfly, an idle thing, nor honey makes, nor yet can sting.   *Adapted from Adelaide O'Keefe*

Exquisite child of the air.   *Alice F. Palmer*

First grubs obscene, then wriggling worms, then painted butterflies.

Adapted from Alexander Pope

BYRON, LORD (1788-1824)

I really am the meekest and mildest of men since Moses.   *Lord Byron*

The grand Napoleon of the realms of rhyme.

Lord Byron

A coxcomb who would have gone into hysterics if a tailor had laughed at him.   *Ebenezer Elliott*

Great only as a poet; as soon as he reflects, he is a child.   *Johann W. Goethe*

He is great in so little a way.   *Charles Lamb*

He had a head which statuaries loved to copy, and a foot the deformity of which the beggars in the street mimicked.   *Thomas B. Macaulay*

A star that shot through the firmament.

Samuel Rogers

An exceedingly interesting person...a slave to the vilest and most vulgar prejudices.

Percy Bysshe Shelley

A denaturalized being who, having exhausted every species of sensual gratification, and drained the cup of sin.   *John Styles*

The power of Byron's personality lies in the splendid and imperishable excellence which covers all his offences and outweighs all his defects: the excellence of sincerity and strength.

Charles Algernon Swinburne

C

CAIN

The inventor of murder, the father of art...a man of first-rate genius. *Thomas De Quincey*

CALAMITY

I am poured out like water, and my bones are out of joint: my heart is like wax; it is melted in the midst of my bowels. *Bible: Psalms, XXII, 14.*

Two kinds: misfortune to ourselves, and good fortune to others. *Ambrose Bierce*

A mighty leveller. *Edmund Burke*

The perfect glass wherein we truly see and know ourselves. *William D'Avenant*

The test of integrity. *Samuel Richardson*

Virtue's opportunity. *Seneca*

SEE ALSO MISFORTUNE.

CALENDAR

Events are...the best calendar.
Benjamin Disraeli

Modern calendars mar the sweet simplicity of our lives by reminding us that each day that passes is the anniversary of some perfectly uninteresting event. *Oscar Wilde*

SEE ALSO TIME.

CALIFORNIA

A fine place to live in—if you happen to be an orange. *Fred Allen*

The end of the rainbow. *American Proverb*

A state that's washed by the Pacific on one side and cleaned by Las Vegas on the other.
Albert Cooper

A state so blessed in climate no one ever dies there from a natural death.
Adapted from Robert Frost

The land of perpetual pubescence, where cultural lag is mistaken for renaissance.
Ashley Montagu

God's great exaggerated land. *Anon.*

The congested land of high taxes and good weather. *Anon.*

SEE ALSO HOLLYWOOD, LOS ANGELES.

CALUMNY

Mere dirt—throw a great deal, and some of it will stick. *George Coleman*

Only the noise of madmen. *Diogenes*

To spread suspicion...to propagate scandal...To create an unfavorable impression, it is not necessary that certain things should be true, but that they have been said. *William Hazlitt*

CALVINISM

Diseases of others that break out in your body.
Friedrich W. Nietzsche

A vice of curious constitutions; trying to kill it keeps it alive; leave it to itself and it will die a natural death. *Thomas Paine*

SEE ALSO GOSSIP, SCANDAL.

CALVINISM

A religion without a prelate, a government without a king. *George Bancroft*

Calvinism, or the belief in election, is not simply blasphemy, but the superfetation of blasphemy.
Samuel Taylor Coleridge

You will and you won't—you'll be damned if you do—and you'll be damned if you don't.
Adapted from Lorenzo Dow

The doctrine that an infinite God made millions of people, knowing that they would be damned.
Robert G. Ingersoll

Absurdities. *Thomas Jefferson*

CANDY

A universal food; it speaks all languages; it dries the tears in the eyes of little children . . . it is the advance agent of happiness in every clime.
National Confectioners Association

CANNIBAL

A gastronome of the old school who preserves the simple tastes and adheres to the natural diet of the pre-pork period. *Ambrose Bierce*

Anyone who takes his fellow-being at his physical valuation. *Elbert Hubbard*

One who appreciates his fellow-being at his true worth. *Elbert Hubbard*

A man who loves his neighbor with sauce.
Jean Riguax

An assassin who has an excuse.
Pierre Valdagne

One who goes into a cafe and orders the waiter.
Anon.

CANNON

Cruel and damnable machines . . . the direct suggestion of the Devil. If Adam had seen in a vision the horrible instruments his children were to invent, he would have died of grief.
Martin Luther

The last argument of governments. *Anon.*

SEE ALSO ARMS, WAR.

CANT

Cant means untruthfulness, but joined to the feeling that one is truthful or telling the truth; the deceiving of others which is at the same time a self-deception. *Moritz Busch*

The *grand primum* mobile of England.
Lord Byron

A double-distilled lie, the *material prima* of the devil, from which all falsehoods . . . and abominations body themselves. *Thomas Carlyle*

CAPITAL

Abstinence from enjoyment is the only source of capital. *Thomas Brassey*

A result of labor, and is used by labor to assist it in further production. Labor is the active and initial force, and labor is therefore the employer of capital. *Henry George*

What is left over when the primary needs of a society have been satisfied. *Aldous Huxley*

Only the fruit of labor, and could never have existed if labor had not first existed.
Abraham Lincoln

That part of wealth which is devoted to obtaining further wealth. *Alfred Marshall*

Dead labor that, vampire-like, lives only by sucking living labor, and lives the more, the more labor it sucks. *Karl Marx*

A social power. *Karl Marx*

That part of the wealth of a country which is employed in production, and consists of food, clothing, tools, raw materials, machinery, etc., necessary to give effect to labor.
David Ricardo

CAPITALISM

The result of the secularization of economic life, and by the hierarchical subordination of the material to the spiritual.   *Nicholas Berdyaev*

The power of anonymity over human life.

Nicholad Berdyaev

Production for a market by enterprising individuals or combines with the purpose of making a profit.   *Peter Berger*

Means investment, and investment means the direction of labor toward the production of the greatest returns—returns that so far as they are great show by that very fact that they are consumed by the many, not alone by the few.

Oliver Wendell Holmes 2

Based on private property, where normal economic activity consists of commercial transactions between consulting adults.   *Irving Kristol*

Uneven economic and political development.

Nikolai Lenin

The basic law of capitalism is you or I, not both you and I.   *Karl Liebknecht*

(When) civilization is the monopoly of a privileged minority.   *William Liebknecht*

A spirit of exaltation of active and inventive power, of the dynamic energies of man and of individual enterprise.   *Jacques Maritain*

A system of plunder.   *Karl Marx*

Not merely the production of commodities; it is essentially the production of surplus value.

Karl Marx

A system under which the means of production—industrial plant and tools, raw materials and partly finished products of all kinds in process of manufacture—are owned by private persons.

John Nef

That system which is devoted to securing wealth for its citizens.   *Abraham Rosenblum*

An economic system, resting on the organization of legally free wage-earners, for the purpose of pecuniary profit, by the owners of capital or his agents, and setting its stamp on every aspect of society.   *Richard H. Tawney*

The social counterpart of Calvinism. The central idea is expressed in the ... phrase "a calling." To the Calvinist, the calling is ... a strenuous and exacting enterprise to be chosen by himself, and to be pursued with a sense of religious responsibility.   *Richard H. Tawney*

SEE ALSO AMERICA, BUSINESS, MONEY, RICHES, WEALTH.

CAPITALIST

A man who owns all of the rainbows.

American Saying

The robber barons.   *Matthew Josephson*

What every American hopes to be before he dies.

Adapted from Henry Louis Mencken

One who will do anything for the poor except get off his back.   *Leon Tolstoy*

A man who works not for a living but to stay alive.

Anon.

Every American who works for a living.   *Anon.*

CAPITAL PUNISHMENT

Life shall go for life, eye for eye, tooth for tooth, hand for hand, foot for foot.

Bible: Deuteronomy, XIX, 21.

The infliction of public vengeance.

John Calvin

Only an administrative murder.   *Albert Camus*

An anachronism too discordant to be suffered, mocking with grim reproach all our clamorous professions of the sanctity of life.

Benjamin N. Cardozo

A warning.   *J. Edgar Hoover*

Simply doubles the number of murders.

David Schwartz

The worst form of assassination, because ... it is invested with the approval of society.

George Bernard Shaw

Not ... murder. Murder is an offensive act. The term cannot be applied legitimately to any defensive act.   *Benjamin R. Tucker*

The thirst for vengeance satisfied.   *Anon.*

Legalized murder.   *Anon.*

CAPRICE

The manner in which society rids itself of cancer cells. *Anon.*

SEE ALSO EXECUTION, PUNISHMENT.

CAPRICE

The only difference between a caprice and a lifelong passion is that the caprice lasts a little longer. *Oscar Wilde*

A fancy fancy. *Anon.*

CARDS

A world of pure power politics where rewards and punishments were meted out immediately. A deck of cards was built like the purest of hierarchies, with every card a master to those below it, a lackey to those above it. *Ely Culbertson*

The Devil's books. *English Proverb*

Cards were at first for benefits designed, sent to amuse, not enslave the mind.

Adapted from David Garrick

(An amusement which) generates kindness and consolidates society. *Samuel Johnson*

The safest insurance against the tedium of old age. *William Somerset Maugham*

SEE ALSO GAMBLING.

CAREER

SEE LABOR, VOCATION, WORK.

CARELESSNESS

To have an eye on Eternity, wherein nothing matters. *Elbert Hubbard*

To perform an act wisely, but not too well.

Elbert Hubbard

CARICATURE

The most penetrating of criticisms.

Aldous Huxley

Rough truth. *George Meredith*

The tribute that mediocrity pays to genius.

Oscar Wilde

Exaggeration of a fact. *Robert Zwickey*

CARLYLE, THOMAS (1795-1881)

Carlyle's eye was a terrible organ: he saw everything. *Augustine Birrell*

I lead a most dyspeptic, solitary, self-shrouded life; consuming, if possible in silence, my considerable daily allotment of pain; glad when any strength is left in me for working, which is the only use I can see in myself. *Thomas Carlyle*

A spectre moving in a world of spectres.

Thomas Carlyle

He is like a lover or an outlaw who wraps up his message in a serenade, which is nonsense to the sentinel, but salvation to the ear for which it is meant. *Ralph Waldo Emerson*

The indubitable champion of England.

Ralph Waldo Emerson

At bottom...simply an English atheist who makes it a point of honor not to be one.

Friedrich W. Nietzsche

A poet to whom nature has denied the faculty of verse. *Alfred Lord Tennyson*

Rugged, mountainous, volcanic, he was himself a French Revolution than any of his volumes.

Walt Whitman

CARNALITY

Enmity against God. *Bible: Romans, VIII, 6.*

Death. *Bible: Romans, VIII, 6.*

Treating people as objects to gratify personal needs. *Martin Buber*

The desire for flesh beyond all moral considerations. *Max Gralnick*

SEE ALSO LUST, SEX (LOVE).

CASH

SEE CAPITAL, MONEY, WEALTH.

CAT

A soft, indestructible automaton provided by nature to be kicked when things go wrong in the domestic circle. *Ambrose Bierce*

The only non-gregarious domestic animal. It is retained by its extra-ordinary adhesion to the comforts of the house in which it is reared.

Francis Galton

A pygmy lion who loves mice, hates dogs, and patronizes human beings.   *Oliver Herford*

An example of sophistication minus civilization.

Anon.

SEE ALSO KITTEN.

CATHEDRAL

SEE CHURCHES.

CATHOLICISM

The Church, the Body of Christ, the Kingdom of God.   *Karl Adam*

By far the most elegant worship...with incense, pictures, statues, altars, shrines, relics, and the real presence, confession, absolution,—there is something sensible to grasp at...it leaves no possibility of doubt.   *Lord Byron*

A superstructure within which you can work, like the sonnet.   *Jean Kerr*

The Catholic religion...never wholly lost the spirit of the Great Teacher whose precepts form the noblest code...It is of religions the most poetical.   *Thomas B. Macaulay*

Acceptance of a Supernatural Order, here and now, at every point and turn of daily life, impinging...on all we do, breaking through, always at hand, always real.   *Rosalind Murray*

A vast assemblage of human beings with wilful intellects and wild passion, brought together into one of the beauty and majesty of Superhuman Power.   *John Henry Newman*

Nothing else but simply the legitimate growth and complement, that is, the natural and necessary development of the doctrine of the early Church.

John Henry Newman

A continuous picture of Authority and Private Judgment alternately advancing and retreating in the ebb and flow of the tide.

John Henry Newman

The Catholic religion is the only one that is true.

Pope Leo XIII

It...is called Catholic because it extends over all the world...and because it teaches universally and completely all the doctrines which ought to come to men's knowledge, concerning things both visible and invisible.   *Saint Cyril*

Paganism spiritualised.   *George Santayana*

SEE ALSO CHRISTIANITY, CHURCHES (ROMAN CATHOLIC).

CAUSE

That which follows ever conforms to that which went before.   *Marcus Aurelius*

It's like champagne or high shoes, and one must be prepared to suffer for it.   *Arnold Bennett*

Simply everything which the effect would not result, and with which it must result.

Charles Bradlaugh

Everything is the cause of itself.

Ralph Waldo Emerson

No one effect is ever the effect of a single cause, but only of a combination of causes, and the essence of causation is in the combination.

Herbert L. Samuel

Everything in nature is a cause from which there flows some effect.   *Baruch Spinoza*

God is the free cause of all things.

Baruch Spinoza

SEE ALSO FATE, PREDESTINATION.

CAUTION

Thinking today and speaking tomorrow.

Adapted from Henry G. Bohn

The word of cowardice.   *John Brown*

The prominent feature of weakness of character.

Elbert Hubbard

The eldest child of wisdom.   *Victor Hugo*

(The) feature of genius. Alternately inspired and depressed, its inequalities of mood are stamped upon its labors.   *Edgar Allan Poe*

What we call cowardice in others.   *Oscar Wilde*

The confidential agent of selfishness.

Woodrow Wilson

SEE ALSO COWARDICE, PRUDENCE.

CELEBRITY

A person who works hard all his life to become well known, then wears dark glasses to avoid being recognized. *Fred Allen*

One who is known to many persons he is glad he doesn't know. *Henry Louis Mencken*

Someone who is known for being known.

Studs Terkel

A person thousands of flash bulbs give their lives for. *Anon.*

CELIBACY

The result of a long spiritual maturation in the Church, meditating on the celibate witness of Christ's own priesthood.

America, Editorial, March, 1964.

The worst form of self-abuse. *Peter De Vries*

The ideal state, first because the time is short and detachment from the things of this age is required, and secondly because marriage diverts man and woman alike from the service of God.

C. H. Dodd

The celibate's life taken on for God is an enacted prophecy, shouting to the world that the world is passing away. *Francis J. Filas*

To live without feeling or exciting sympathy, to be fortunate without adding to the felicity of others, or afflicted without tasting the balm of pity.

Samuel Johnson

A state more gloomy than solitude: it is not retreat, but exclusion from mankind.

Samuel Johnson

The man who never in his life has washed the dishes with his wife or polished up the silver plate—he still is largely celibate.

Christopher Morley

Single blessedness. *William Shakespeare*

A celibate, like the fly in the heart of an apple, dwells in a perpetual sweetness, but sits alone, and is confined and dies in singularity.

Jeremy Taylor

To divest yourself of the body. *Anon.*

SEE ALSO ABSTINENCE, CHASTITY.

CEMETERY

An isolated suburban spot where mourners match lies, poets write at a target and stonecutters spell for a wager. *Ambrose Bierce*

Man's final comment on earth.

Eugene E. Brussell

The place which receives all without asking questions. *English Proverb*

The cast-off clothes of God.

Christian Morgenstern

The country home I need. *Mark Twain*

The last resort. *Anon.*

The surest cure for conceit. All get equal billing there. *Anon.*

SEE ALSO COFFIN, FUNERAL, GRAVE.

CENSOR

(One who) believes he can hold back the mighty traffic of life with a tin whistle and a raised right hand. For after all, it is life with which he quarrels. *Heywood Broun*

A person who did not like the movie and burned the book. *Jerry Dashkin*

People with secret attractions to various temptations...they are defending themselves under the pretext of defending others, because at heart they fear their own weaknesses. *Ernest Jones*

The artist and censor differ in this wise: that the first is a decent mind in an indecent body and that the second is an indecent mind in a decent body.

George Jean Nathan

A man who knows more than he thinks you ought to. *Laurence J. Peter*

The guardian of orthodoxy. *Anon.*

CENSORSHIP

Sooner or later a weapon directed against freedom of thought. *Poul Borchsenius*

The courts...duty of protecting the weaker members of society from corrupt, depraving, and lecherous influences...exerted through the guise and medium of literature, drama or art...judged by the mores of the day. *Hyman Bushel*

(To stop) people reading or seeing what we do not want to read or see ourselves. *Lord Diplock*

A caste system of romance, but always with a joinder of antisex and propriety.

Morris Ernst and Alan Schwartz

To prohibit the propagation of opinions which have a dangerous tendency...No member of a society has a right to teach any doctrine contrary to what the society holds to be true.

Samuel Johnson

The tribute that an ignorant age pays to the genius of its time. *Joseph Lewis*

(A) righteous form of sin-hunting.

Thomas Merton

Nothing more than a legal corollary of public modesty. *Jonathan Miller*

Art made tongue-tied by authority.

William Shakespeare

When nobody is allowed to read any books except the books nobody can read.

George Bernard Shaw

SEE ALSO OBSCENITY.

CEREMONY

The superstition of good-breeding, as well as of religion; but yet, being an outwork to both, should not be absolutely demolished.

Lord Chesterfield

The wine of human experience.

Morris R. Cohen

A means for strengthening...religio-ethical sentiments...When ceremonies no longer...fulfill this purpose...they become entirely worthless...and the reign of superstition has been inaugurated. *Abraham Geiger*

Vehicles to spiritual heights. *Judah Halevi*

Ignorance. *Samuel Johnson*

An invention to take off the uneasy feeling which we derive from knowing ourselves to be less the object of love and esteem with a fellow-creature than some other person is. *Samuel Johnson*

It endeavors to make up, by superior attentions in little points, for that invidious preference which it is forced to deny in the greater. *Charles Lamb*

The invention of wise men to keep fools at a distance. *Richard Steele*

A training in self-conquest, while it links the generations...and unifies our atoms dispersed to the four corners of the earth as nothing else could.

Israel Zangwill

CERTAINTY

Mistaken at the top of one's voice.

Ambrose Bierce

Absolute uncertainty. We can no more have this than we can have absolute certainty.

Samuel Butler 2

Certainty generally is illusion, and repose is not the destiny of man. *Oliver Wendell Holmes 2*

I am certain of nothing but the holiness of the heart's affections and the truth of imagination.

John Keats

A dusty answer. *George Meredith*

We can say nothing with certainty about anything, because the picture presented to us is not constant.

Philo

The only certainty is that nothing is certain.

Pliny 1

(One) of the greatest evils that man has inflicted upon man. *Bertrand A. Russell*

SEE ALSO ABSOLUTE, BELIEF, CONVICTION, DOGMA, FAITH, RELIGION.

CERVANTES, MIGUEL DE (1547-1616)

Cervantes smiled Spain's chivalry away; a single laugh demolished the right arm of his own country. *Adapted from Lord Byron*

The man who set the sword back in its sheath.

Gilbert Keith Chesterton

CHAIR

The reward of the aged. *Anon.*

The headquarters for the hindquarters. *Anon.*

CHAMPAGNE

Those bottled windy drinks that laugh in a man's face and then cut his throat. *Thomas Adams*

The drink of least resistance. *Anon.*

Here's to champagne, the drink divine
That makes us forget our troubles;
It's made of a dollar's worth of wine
And three dollar's worth of bubbles. *Anon.*

SEE ALSO DRINKING.

CHANCE

Serves ... as rationalization for every people that is not master of its own destiny. *Hanah Arendt*

A nickname for Providence. *Nicolas Chamfort*

Implies an absolute absence of any principle.
Chuang-tzu

What a capricious man believes in.
Adapted from Benjamin Disraeli

(That which) makes us known to others and to ourselves. *La Rochefoucauld*

(That which) favors the mind that is prepared.
Louis Pasteur

Another master. *Pliny 1*

All chance, direction which thou canst not see.
Alexander Pope

Chance is blind and the sole author of creation.
Joseph X. Saintine

The rude stone which receives its life from the sculptor's hand? Providence gives us chance—and man must mold it to his own designs.
Johann C. Schiller

There is no such thing. *Johann C. Schiller*

A name for our ignorance. *Leslie Stephen*

A word devoid of sense; nothing can exist without a cause. *Voltaire*

The instrument of Providence and the secret agent that counteracts what men call wisdom, and preserves order and regularity, and continuation in the whole. *Horace Walpole*

SEE ALSO ACCIDENT, LUCK.

CHANGE

What is behind the desire of every revolution.
Eugene E. Brussell

What people fear most. *Fëdor M. Dostoievski*

Truths being in and out of favor. *Robert Frost*

The succession of becomings, each of which embodies, objectifies, its predecessors.
Charles Hartshorne

To shift one's position and be bruised in a new place. *Washington Irving*

The only thing that has brought progress.
Charles F. Kettering

To live is to change, and to be perfect is to have changed often. *John Henry Newman*

The seen is the changing, the unseen is the unchanging. *Plato*

Means the unknown. *Eleanor Roosevelt*

This sad vicissitude of things. *Laurence Sterne*

A political catchword for Communist propaganda. *Andries Teurnicht*

SEE ALSO EVOLUTION.

CHARACTER

That which reveals moral purpose, exposing the class of things a man chooses or avoids.
Aristotle

The result of our conduct. *Aristotle*

The highest power of causing a thing to be believed. *Aristotle*

A kingdom established within yourself.
Adapted from Henry Ward Beecher

Character is money; and according as the man earns or spends the money, money in turn becomes character. *Edward Bulwer-Lytton*

Our description of ourselves as we want others to see us. *John Ciardi*

Raising your soul so high that offence cannot reach it. *Adapted from René Descartes*

Not only what one does and says, but what one fails to do and say.
Adapted from Norman Douglas

A development which is higher than intellect.
Norman Elright

That which can do without success.
Ralph Waldo Emerson

Do what you know and perception is converted into character.　　　　*Ralph Waldo Emerson*

Moral order seen through the medium of an individual nature.　　　　*Ralph Waldo Emerson*

A reserved force which acts directly and without means.　　　　*Ralph Waldo Emerson*

Character is centrality, the impossibility of being displaced or overset.　　*Ralph Waldo Emerson*

(A quality) built on the debris of our despair.

Ralph Waldo Emerson

A certain undemonstrable force... genius, by whose impulses the man is guided, but whose counsels he cannot impart.

Ralph Waldo Emerson

A dispensation of Providence, designed to have not merely an immediate, but a continuous, progressive, and never-ending agency.

Edward Everett

Mastery over your thoughts and actions.

Mohandas Gandhi

The stamp on our souls of the free choices of good and evil we have made through life.

John C. Geikie

Means carrying through what you feel able to do.

Johann W. Goethe

Man's... fate.　　　　　　　*Heraclitus*

(That which) must stand behind and back up everything—the sermon, the poem, the picture, the play. None of them is worth a straw without it.

Josiah G. Holland

Not so much where we are, but in what direction we are moving.　　*Oliver Wendell Holmes 1*

The result of two things—mental attitude and the way we spend our time.　　*Elbert Hubbard*

The sum of tendencies to act in a certain way.

Thomas Henry Huxley

What is character but the determination of incident? What is incident but the illustration of character?　　　　*Henry James*

Every man has three characters: that which he exhibits, that which he has, and that which he thinks he has.　　　　*Alphonse Karr*

The decision to take responsibility for being yourself, to make up your mind you're going to

succeed in this life because there's no stopping you.　　　　*Peter Koestenbaum*

Character is built out of circumstances. From exactly the same materials one man builds palaces, while another builds hovels.

George H. Lewes

Character is like a tree and reputation like its shadow. The shadow is what we think of it; the tree is the real thing.　　*Abraham Lincoln*

The measure of a man's real character is what he would do if he knew he would never be found out.

Thomas B. Macaulay

What God and the angels know of us.

Horace Mann

Committing the Golden Rule to memory and to life.　　　*Adapted from Edwin Markham*

(That which is) shaped by deeds, and... partly habit.　　　　*Claude Montefiore*

What you are in the dark.　　*Dwight Moody*

A perfectly educated will.　　　　*Novalis*

What God and the angels know of us.

Thomas Paine

The grand aim of man's creation... and... by its very nature, the product of probationary discipline.　　　　*Austin Phelps*

(Something) made by what you stand for; reputation by what you fall for.　　*Robert Quillen*

The sum of those qualities which make a man a good man and a woman a good woman.

Theodore Roosevelt

The governing element of life, and is above genius.　　　　*Frederick Saunders*

Property.　　　　　　　*Samuel Smiles*

Moral order embodied in the individual.

Samuel Smiles

Not what you are thought to be, but are.

Publilius Syrus

The arbiter of a man's fortune.　*Publilius Syrus*

Portion... potion, and passion.

Talmud: Erubin, 65b.

Fame is what you have taken,
　　Character's what you give.　　*Bayard Taylor*

The power...in...industry, application, and perseverence under the promptings of a brave, determined spirit.   *Mark Twain*

The total of thousands of small daily strivings to live up to the best that is in us...the final decision to reject whatever is demeaning to oneself or to others and with confidence and honesty to choose the right.   *Arthur G. Trudeau*

The sum total of all our capacities and gifts.
        Rahel L. Varnhagen

The spiritual body of the person.
        Edwin P. Whipple

A by-product...produced in the great manufacture of daily duty.   *Woodrow Wilson*

Character is made by what you stand for; reputation by what you fall for.   *Alexander Woollcott*

Intellect associated with moral excellence.
        Theodore D. Woolsey

The stamp on our souls of the free choices of good and evil we have made through life.   *Anon.*

What the public doesn't know about you.
        Anon.

Something tested through business, wine, and conversation.   *Anon.*

A conquest, not a bequest.   *Anon.*

SEE ALSO BREEDING (MANNERS), GENTLEMAN, SUPERIOR MAN.

CHARITY

The perfection and ornament of religion.
        Joseph Addison

The bond of perfectness.
        Bible: Colossians, III, 14.

Charity suffereth long and is kind; charity envieth not; charity vaunteth not itself, is not puffed up.
        Bible: Corinthians, XIII, 4.

Atonement for sin.   *Bible: Ecclesiastes, III, 33.*

A helping hand stretched out to save men from the inferno of their present life.   *William Booth*

The love of God for himself, and our neighbor for God.   *Thomas Browne*

Organized charity is doing good for good-for-nothing people.   *Elizabeth Barrett Browning*

A disciple having asked for a definition of charity, the Master said: Love One Another.   *Confucius*

This only is charity, to do all, all that we can.
        John Donne

To squander...superfluous wealth on those to whom it is sure of doing the least possible good.
        William Hazlitt

The spice of riches.   *Hebrew Proverb*

No man giveth, but with intention of good to himself; because gift is voluntary, and of all voluntary acts the object is to every man his own good.   *Thomas Hobbes*

On a large scale...the worst abuse of private ownership—from the economic point of view.
        Oliver Wendell Holmes 2

A thing that begins at home, and usually stays there.   *Elbert Hubbard*

A debt of honor.   *Immanuel Kant*

Universal benevolence whose fulfillment the wise carry out conformably to the dictates of reason so as to obtain the greatest good.
        Gottfried W. Leibnitz

The bone shared with the dog when you are just as hungry as the dog.   *Jack London*

Helping a man to help himself.
        Moses Maimonides

Charity...is kind, it is not easily provok'd, it thinks no evil, it believes all things, hopes all things.   *Cotton Mather*

A matter on which the immediate effect on the persons directly concerned, and the ultimate consequence to the general good, are apt to be at complete war with one another.
        John Stuart Mill

The perfection of the Christian life...which in some sort unites or joins man to his God.
        Pope John XXIII

(That which) opens in each heart a little Heaven.
        Matthew Prior

A gift of God, and when it is rightly ordered, likens us to God himself, as far as that is possible; for it is charity which makes the man.
        Saint John Chrysostom

(That which) deals with symptoms instead of causes.   *Herbert L. Samuel*

To help the feeble up and support him after.
Adapted from William Shakespeare

Money put to interest in the other world.
Robert Southey

Feeling for others—in your pocket.
Adapted from Charles H. Spurgeon

Whatever capital you divert to the support of a shiftless and good-for-nothing person.
William G. Sumner

The desire to be useful to others without thought of recompense.   *Emanuel Swedenborg*

To will and do what is just and right in every transaction.   *Emanuel Swedenborg*

(That which) equals all the other commandments.
Talmud: Baba Bathra, 9a.

Friendship to all the world . . . friendship expanded like the face of the sun when it mounts above the eastern hills.   *Jeremy Taylor*

Essentially it is a mere act of justice.
William Temple

With one hand I take thousands of dollars from the poor, and with the other I hand back a few dimes.
Leon Tolstoy

Christian charity is the supernatural virtue of the love for God insofar as it extends from God to our fellow men.   *Eberhard Welby*

A religious duty.   *Louis Wirth*

A disguise for the injustice that we mete out to our fellow men.   *Ida A. Wylie*

Good will is the best charity.   *Yiddish Proverb*

A magnet with more power to attract the divine influence than any other precept.
Shneor Zalman

SEE ALSO BENEVOLENCE, GENEROSITY, GIFT, GIVING, PHILANTHROPY.

CHARM

A sort of a bloom on women. If you have it, you don't need to have anything else; if you don't have it, it doesn't much matter what else you have.
James M. Barrie

A glow within a woman that casts a most becoming light on others.   *John Mason Brown*

Lots of soap and water, decent clothes, and a little learning.   *Eugene E. Brussell*

A way of getting the answer yes without having asked any clear question.   *Albert Camus*

Smiles and soap.   *Lewis Carroll*

A sex attribute which has become a habit.
Elbert Hubbard

That extra quality that defies description.
Alfred Lunt

Character exercising its influence.
Edgar Magnin

SEE ALSO BREEDING (MANNERS), MANNERS.

CHASTITY

A virtue . . . and a virtue of high deserving . . . Not because it diminishes, but because it heightens enjoyment.   *Jeremy Bentham*

A supreme form of unselfishness.
John M. Cooper

The cement of civilization and progress.
Mary Baker Eddy

Perhaps the most peculiar of all sexual aberrations.   *Remy de Gourmont*

A woman's chastity consists, like an onion, in a series of coats.   *Nathaniel Hawthorne*

The most unnatural of the sexual perversions.
Aldous Huxley

God's rarest blessing.   *George Meredith*

A virtue in some, but in many almost a vice. These, it is true, are abstinent; but from all that they do the bitch of sensuality looks out with envious eyes.   *Friedrich W. Nietzsche*

She whom no one has asked.   *Ovid*

Chastity, the lily of virtues, makes men almost equal to angels. Nothing is beautiful but what is pure, and the purity of men is chastity.
Saint Francis de Sales

The first degree of chastity is pure virginity; the second is faithful marriage.
Saint John Chrysostom

A monkish and evangelical superstition, a greater foe to natural temperance even than unintellectual sensuality; it strikes at the root of all domestic happiness, and consigns more than half of the human race to misery. *Percy Bysshe Shelley*

A wealth that comes from an abundance of love.
Rabindranath Tagore

Chastity is either abstinence or continence. Abstinence is that of virgins or widows; continence, of married persons. *Jeremy Taylor*

Salvation. *Tertullian*

The spirit of poverty applied to our emotional life—all the clutch and feverishness of desire, the "I want" and "I must have" taken away and replaced by absolute single-mindedness, purity of heart. *Evelyn Underhill*

A woman's lack of temptation and a man's lack of opportunity. *Anon.*

A state peculiar to women—where there are no men. *Anon.*

SEE ALSO ABSTINENCE, CELIBACY, SELF-DENIAL, VIRGINITY.

CHAUCER, GEOFFREY (1340-1400)

And Chaucer, with his infantive
Familiar clasp of things divine.
Elizabeth Barrett Browning

A rough diamond; and must first be polished e'er he shines. *John Dryden*

(A man) glad and erect. *Ralph Waldo Emerson*

The poet of the dawn.
Henry Wadsworth Longfellow

That broad famous English poet.
Thomas Middleton

He is ever master of himself and of his subject. The light upon his page is the light of common day. *Alexander Smith*

The first warbler. *Alfred Lord Tennyson*

CHEERFULNESS

A kind of daylight in the mind, and fills it with a steady and perpetual serenity. *Joseph Addison*

A Habit of the Mind . . . fixed and permanent.
Joseph Addison

A merry heart maketh a cheerful countenance.
Bible: Proverbs, XV, 13.

Health is the condition of wisdom, and the sign of cheerfulness. *Ralph Waldo Emerson*

That modest, hopeful, and peaceful joy which springs from charity and is protected by patience.
F. X. Lasance

The most certain sign of wisdom.
Michel de Montaigne

The principal ingredient in the composition of health. *Arthur Murphy*

One of the very but articles of dress one can wear in society. *William Makepeace Thackeray*

The habit of looking at the good side of things.
W. B. Ullanthorne

The rich and satisfying result of strenuous discipline. *Edwin P. Whipple*

SEE ALSO HAPPINESS, LAUGHTER.

CHEESE

Milk's leap toward immortality.
Clifton Fadiman

Cheese it is a peevish elf,
It digests all things but itself. *John Ray*

CHESS

The movement of pieces eating one another.
Marcel Duchamp

A total kind of warfare. *Robert Fischer*

The touchstone of the intellect.
Johann Wolfgang von Goethe

The art of human reason. *Gustavus Selenus*

A foolish expedient for making idle people believe they are doing something very clever, when they are only wasting their time.
George Bernard Shaw

A game of war in which no element is left to chance. *Anon.*

CHESTERFIELD, EARL OF (1694-1773)

This man I thought had been a lord among wits, but I find he is only a wit among lords.
Samuel Johnson

Lord Chesterfield stands much lower in the estimation of posterity than he would have done if his letters had never been published.

Thomas B. Macaulay

The only Englishman who ever argued for the art of pleasing as the first duty of life. *Voltaire*

A man of much wit, middling sense, and some learning; but as absolutely void of virtue as any Jew, Turk, or heathen that ever lived.

John Wesley

CHEWING GUM

A dentiferous treadmill. *Thomas Alva Edison*

A confection that gratifies the palate and cheats the stomach. *Anon.*

The national anthem without words. *Anon.*

CHICAGO

Where the bulls and the foxes live well and the lambs wind up head-down from the hook.

Nelson Algren

City on the make. *Nelson Algren*

A double Newark. *Heywood Broun*

Queen of the West! *Bret Harte*

The Second City. *A. J. Liebling*

Where the used-car lots succeed one another like a string of past lives. *Sean O'Faolain*

Beautiful, strong and alert, a goddess in purpose and mien. *Wallace Rice*

A Walt Whitman storehouse of democracy come alive, a Sears catalogue of people and occupations endlessly varied in repetitive similarities.

Isaac Rosenfeld

City of big shoulders. *Carl Sandburg*

The Winded City. *William G. Shepherd*

CHICKEN

SEE EGG, HEN.

CHILD

A beam of sunlight from the Infinite and Eternal, with possibilities of virtue and vice—but as yet unstained. *Lyman Abbott*

The best security for old age. *Sholom Asch*

Not to know what happened before one was born is always to be a child. *Cicero*

A man is a small letter, yet the best copy of Adam before he tasted of Eve or the apple. *John Earle*

Nature's fresh picture newly drawn in oil, which time and much handling dims and defaces. His soul is yet a white paper unscribbled with observations of the world, wherewith at length it becomes a blurred notebook. *John Earle*

A curly, dimpled lunatic.

Ralph Waldo Emerson

The beginning of a revolution...But you must have the believing and prophetic eye.

Ralph Waldo Emerson

(One who) thinks twenty shillings and twenty years can scarce ever be spent.

Benjamin Franklin

An ever-bubbling fountain in the world of humanity. *Friedrich Froebel*

Love's by-product. *Warren Goldberg*

The most desirable pest. *Max Gralnick*

A lower animal in the form of a man.

Luis de Granada

The greatest poem ever known.

Christopher Morley

Behold the child, by nature's kindly law, pleased with a rattle, tickled with a straw.

Adapted from Alexander Pope

The creatures of example—whatever surrounding adults do, they will do. *Josiah Warren*

The child is father of the man.

William Wordsworth

One who stands halfway between an adult and a t.v. set. *Anon.*

That which tells in the street what its parents say at home. *Anon.*

Something you can account for before it's born, but once it's here—good Lord! *Anon.*

An island of curiosity surrounded by a sea of question marks. *Anon.*

SEE ALSO BOY, BOYHOOD, GIRLS, YOUTH.

CHILDHOOD

A forward, upward movement.

Simone de Beauvoir

Vanity.   *Bible: Ecclesiastes, XI, 10.*

The period of human life intermediate between the idiocy of infancy and the folly of youth—two removes from the sin of manhood and three from the remorse of age.   *Ambrose Bierce*

Childhood is the country that produces the most nostalgic, contentious and opinionated exiles.

Richard Eder

Health.   *George Herbert*

All mirth.   *John Keble*

The age without pity.   *Jean de La Fontaine*

A forgotten journey.   *Jean de La Varrenne*

A garden of god is our childhood, each day
A festival radiant with laughter and play.

Micah J. Lebensohn

The ability to forget a sorrow.   *Phyllis McGinley*

The sleep of reason.   *Jean-Jacques Rousseau*

A stage in the process of that continual remanufac-ture of the Life Stuff by which the human race is perpetuated.   *George Bernard Shaw*

Days of woe.   *Robert Southey*

To believe in love, to believe in loveliness, to believe in belief...To know not yet that you are under sentence of life, nor petition that it be commuted to death.   *Francis Thompson*

That wonderful time when all you need to lose weight is to bathe.   *Anon.*

SEE ALSO BOYHOOD, GIRLS, YOUTH.

CHILDREN

(They that) increase the cares of life, but...miti-gate the remembrance of death.   *Francis Bacon*

Impediments to great enterprises.

Francis Bacon

A heritage of the Lord: and the fruit of the womb is his reward.   *Bible: Psalms, CXXVII, 3–5.*

My jewels.   *Robert Burton*

Those who always smell of bread and butter.

Lord Byron

Children in a family are like flowers in a bouquet: there's always one determined to face in an opposite direction from the way the arranger desires.   *Marcelene Cox*

All children are by nature children of wrath, and are in danger of eternal damnation in Hell.

Jonathan Edwards

The symbol of the eternal marriage between love and duty.   *George Eliot*

Children are all foreigners. We treat them as such.

Ralph Waldo Emerson

Certain cares and uncertain comforts.

English Proverb

The husband's dangerous rivals.

Sigmund Freud

Poor men's riches.   *Thomas Fuller*

Children we think of affectionately as divided pieces of our own bodies.   *Joseph Hall*

Our most valuable natural resource.

Herbert C. Hoover

Exquisite receptacles of flesh that hold the scrolls of our deeds.   *Adapted from Elbert Hubbard*

Little children, headache; big children, heartache.

Italian Proverb

A great comfort in your old age—and they help you to reach it faster, too.   *Lionel Kaufman*

(Those who) think not of what is past, nor what is to come, but enjoy the present time, which few of us do.   *Jean de La Bruyère*

Not things to be molded, but...people to be unfolded.   *Jess Lair*

God's apostles, day by day sent forth to preach of love and hope and peace.   *James Russell Lowell*

Of all people...the most imaginative. They aban-don themselves without reserve to every illusion.

Thomas B. Macaulay

Those who do not prattle of yesterday. Their interests are all of today.

Adapted from Richard Mansfield

(They) constitute man's eternity.   *Isaac Peretz*

Anchors that hold a mother to life.   *Sophocles*

All children...are God's little enemies at heart.

Samuel Spring

The keys of paradise.   *Richard H. Stoddard*

A torment, and nothing else.   *Leon Tolstoy*

Defective adults.   *Evelyn Waugh*

Children are our immortality—in them we see the story of our life re-written in a fairer hand.
Alfred North Whitehead

God's small interpreters.
John Greenleaf Whittier

A staff for the hand and a hoe for the grave.
Talmud: Yebamot, 65b.

Natural mimics—they act like their parents in spite of every attempt to teach them good manners.   *Anon.*

People which can be raised graciously—if you don't have any.   *Anon.*

SEE ALSO BABY, BOY, GIRLS, YOUTH.

CHINESE

Cunning and ingenious; and have a great talent at bowing out ambassadors who come to visit them.
Leigh Hunt

All Chinese are Confucianists when successful, and Taoists when...failures. The Confucianist in us builds and strives, while the Taoist in us watches and smiles.   *Lin Yutang*

In the United States, everybody's favorite minority.   *Paul Weinberger*

A race whose families are the pivot of their civilization.   *Anon.*

A people who think all caucasions look alike.
Anon.

CHIVALRY

A thing which must be courteously and generously conceded, and must never be pettishly claimed.   *A. C. Benson*

The unbought grace of life, the cheap defence of nations, the nurse of manly sentiment and heroic enterprise.   *Edmund Burke*

The whole of...chivalry is in courtesy.
Ralph Waldo Emerson

The border-land of all romance; where glitter hauberk, helm, and lance, and banner waves, and trumpets sound. Ladies ride with hawk on wrist,

and warriors sweep along magnified by mist. The dusk of centuries and of song.
Adapted from Henry Wadsworth Longfellow

Going about releasing beautiful ladies from other men's castles, and taking them to your own castle.
Henry W. Nevinson

I shall maintain and defend the honest adoes and quarrels of all ladies of honor, widows, orphans and maids of good fame.   *Oath of a Knight*

When every morning brought a noble chance, and every chance brought out a noble knight.
Adapted from Alfred Lord Tennyson

The deportment of a man toward any woman not his wife.   *Anon.*

CHOICE

Life's business.   *Robert Browning*

Trouble.   *Dutch Proverb*

The strongest principle of growth.   *George Eliot*

No choice is also a choice.   *Jewish Proverb*

The difficulty in life.   *George M. Moore*

The power of choice must involve the possibility of error—that is the essence of choosing.
Herbert L. Samuel

CHRIST

The one great word—well worth all languages in earth or heaven.   *Philip J. Bailey*

Christ is all, and in all.
Bible: Colossians, III, 11.

A virgin shall conceive and bear a son, and shall call his name Immanuel.
Bible: Isaiah, VII, 14.

A man of sorrows, and acquainted with grief.
Bible: Isaiah, LIII, 3.

I am the light of the world; he that follow me shall not walk in darkness, but shall have the light of life.   *Bible: John, VII, 12.*

I am the resurrection of the life.
Bible: John, XI, 25.

The incarnation of the genius of Judaism.
Kurt Breysig

The condescension of divinity, and the exaltation of humanity. *Phillips Brooks*

The King of Kings. *Gerald Bullett*

The immeasurably great Unconscious. *Thomas Carlyle*

The best of men...a sufferer, a soft, meek, patient, humble tranquil spirit. The first true gentleman that ever breathed. *Adapted from Thomas Dekker*

The most scientific man that ever trod the globe. He plunged beneath the material surface of things, and found the spiritual cause. *Mary Baker Eddy*

The record of a pure and holy soul, humble, absolutely disinterested, a truthspeaker, and bent on serving, teaching and uplifting men. *Ralph Waldo Emerson*

An era in human history...and its immense influence for good leaves all the perversion and superstition that has accrued almost harmless. *Ralph Waldo Emerson*

The most fascinating figure in history. In him is combined what is best and most mysterious and most enchanting in Israel—the eternal people whose child he was. *Hyman G. Enelow*

A path. *Giles Fletcher*

The one completely harmonious man, unfolding all which was in humanity. *Alice French*

The only one in whom the real and ideal met and were absolutely one. *Alice French*

It is light that enables us to see the differences between things; and it is Christ that gives us light. *Julius and Augustus Hare*

A modest God of the People, a citizen God. *Heinrich Heine*

Shepherd of mortals. *Daniel Henderson*

The world's here, the desire of nations. But besides he is the hero of single souls. *Gerard M. Hopkins*

His parentage was obscure; His condition poor; His education null; His natural endowments great; His life correct and innocent; He was meek, benevolent, patient, firm, disinterested, and of the sublimest eloquence. *Thomas Jefferson*

An abyss filled with light. One must close one's eyes if one is not to fall into it. *Franz Kafka*

A great teacher of morality and an artist in parable. *Joseph Klausner*

The foremost of those who have made humanity divine. *Joseph Krauskopf*

My hope. *Latin Phrase*

The Saviour of men. *Latin Phrase*

A priest and king, though He was never consecrated by any papist bishop or greased by any of those shavelings; but He was ordained and consecrated by God Himself, and by Him anointed. *Martin Luther*

Christ is an example, showing us how to live. *Martin Luther*

The personal embodiment of truths which are permanently central for the spiritual life of mankind. *Eugene W. Lyman*

The immanent Spiritual Life of God focalized in a human personality. *Shailer Mathews*

Expresses both the infinite possibilities of love in human life and the infinite possibilities beyond human life...a true revelation of the total situation in which human life stands. *Reinhold Niebuhr*

A God to whom we can approach without pride, and before whom we may abase ourselves without despair. *Blaise Pascal*

In Politics He was a leveller or communist; in morals He was a monk; He believed that only the poor and despised would inherit the kingdom of God. *W. Winwood Reade*

An inexhaustible principle of moral regeneration. *Ernest Renan*

The best husband. *Saint Augustine*

Know that Our Lord is called in Scripture the Prince of Peace, and hence, wherever He is absolute Master, He preserves peace. *Saint Francis de Sales*

The prototype of a humanity that is yet to be; not the great exception but the great example. *George Seaver*

He is what we should call an artist and a Bohemian in His manner of life. *George Bernard Shaw*

A parish demagogue. *Percy Bysshe Shelley*

He went about to cure poor people who were blind, and many who were sick and lame.
Adapted from Ann and Jane Taylor

The spirit of Compassionate Goodness at the heart of reality. *Harold B. Walker*

God clothed with human nature.
Benjamin Whichcote

SEE ALSO BIBLE, CATHOLICISM, CHRISTIANITY, CHRISTIANS, CHRISTMAS, CROSS, PAPACY, RELIGION, SALVATION.

CHRISTIANITY

God seeking after men. *Thomas Arnold*

The complete negation of common sense and sound reason. *Mikhail A. Bakunin*

An uneasy, a tragic, an impossible faith, in high tension between the real and the ideal, the "is" and the "ought"—that is one of the sources of its strength. *Crane Brinton*

To let Christ lead us to our Father.
Phillips Brooks

The expression of an effort to build up and organize temporal life in accordance with the principles of the Gospel. *R. L. Bruckberger*

An instrument of warfare against vice.
Samuel Butler 1

The bastard progeny of Judaism. It is the basest of all national religions. *Celsus*

Prophetic Judaism. *Hermann Cohen*

Not a theory, or a speculation; but a life;—not a philosophy of life, but a life and a living process.
Samuel Taylor Coleridge

Chistianity is within a man, even as he is a being gifted with reason; it is associated with your mother's chair, and with the first-remembered-tones of her...voice.
Samuel Taylor Coleridge

The religion of loving, speaking, and doing, as well as believing. *John Cumming*

Consists in the reconciliation of the human will with the Divine—the control of the human will as it expresses itself in action.
William Cunningham

Completed Judaism. *Benjamin Disraeli*

Judaism for the multitude. *Benjamin Disraeli*

Undying hope both for this world and the next.
Jonathan Edwards

The triumph of Judaism...to Israel fell the singular privilege of giving a god to the world.
Anatole France

A philosophy which intends to be a rational interpretation of data, but considers as the essential element of these data the religious Faith, the object of which is defined by the Christian revelation. *Etienne Gilson*

Not the religion of Jesus; it is that of the followers of Jesus. *Maurice Goguel*

A system of radical optimism. *William R. Inge*

The highest perfection of humanity.
Samuel Johnson

What was invented two thousand years ago was the spirit of Christianity. *Gerald S. Lee*

The real...Christianity is to be found in its benevolent morality...in the consolation which it bears to the house of mourning, in the light with which it brightens the great mystery of the grave.
Thomas B. Macaulay

Primarily the conversion of all the ancient moral and mystic efforts of humanity into a higher religion, which in fulfilling their aspirations, transcends them. *Eugene Masure*

In great part merely a protest against paganism; its ideal is negative rather than active.
John Stuart Mill

A missionary religion, converting, advancing, aggressive, encompassing the world.
Friedrich M. Müller

At once a philosophy, a political power, and a religious rite: as a religion, it is Holy; as a philosophy, it is Apostolic; as a political power, it is imperial, that is, One and Catholic.
John Henry Newman

The element and principle of all education.
John Henry Newman

Christianity aims at mastering the beasts of prey; its *modus operandi* is to make them ill—to make feeble is the Christian recipe for taming, for "civilizing." *Friedrich W. Nietzsche*

Not so much the pursuit of an ideal as an Ideal that pursues humanity, stooping down in an Incarnation to take up dwelling in the hearts of man.

James E. O'Mahony

The enemy of human love.   *Ouida*

That sweet music which kept in order the rulers of the people.   *Theodore Parker*

A denial of this world...a means of redemption from, not for, life.   *Isaac Peretz*

A battle, not a dream.   *Wendell Phillips*

More than history. It is also a system of truths. Every event which its history records, either is a truth, or...expresses a truth, which man needs to...put into practice.   *Noah Porter*

Simply a "petrifaction" of an alien state of consciousness, projecting into the present from vanished ages.   *Herman Rauschning*

The masterpiece of Judaism, its glory and the fullness of its evolution.   *Ernest Renan*

The relation of the soul to God...not the relation of man to his fellow man.   *Bertrand A. Russell*

The true aim is the acquisition of the Holy Spirit of God.   *Saint Seraphim*

The paganization of monotheism.

George Santayana

The only organization truly potent for the perfection of Society.   *Julius H. Seelye*

Does not remove you from the world and its problems; it makes you fit to live in it, triumphantly and usefully.   *Charles Templeton*

The companion of liberty in all its conflicts, the cradle of its infancy, and the divine source of its claims.   *Alexis de Tocqueville*

Humility, penitence, submissiveness, progress, life.   *Leon Tolstoy*

Requires two things from every man who believes in it; first, to acquire property by just and righteous means, and second, to look not only on his own things, but also on the things of others.

Henry Van Dyke

A too ardent monotheism.   *Edward B. White*

The religion of everyman, the religion for every man, the religion of all conditions.

Maurice Zundel

The name of a number of different religions.

Anon.

SEE ALSO BAPTISM, BIBLE, CATHOLICISM, CHARITY, CHURCHES, COMMANDMENTS, CONVERSION, CROSS, LUTHER, PIETY, PRAYER, PROTESTANTISM, RELIGION, SALVATION, SIN.

CHRISTIANS

A sinful man who has put himself to school to Christ for the honest purpose of becoming better.

Henry Ward Beecher

Every one whose life and disposition are Christ-like, no matter how heretical the denomination may be to which he belongs.

Henry Ward Beecher

The disciples were called Christians first in Antioch.   *Bible: Acts XI, 26.*

One who believes that the New Testament is a divinely inspired book admirably suited to the spiritual needs of his neighbor.   *Ambrose Bierce*

It is not some religious act that makes a Christian what he is, but participation in the suffering of God in the light of the world.

Dietrich Bonhoeffer

One who rejoices in the superiority of a rival.

Edwin Booth

Those Christians best deserve the name who studiously make peace their aim.

Adapted from William Cowper

To be a Christian is not purely to serve God...it is also an ethic, a service to mankind...not merely a theology but also an anthropology.

Albert Dondeyne

A worldly-minded people going to church for recreation and in conformity to custom.

Mohandas K. Gandhi

Like ripening corn; the riper he grows the more lowly he bends his head.   *Thomas Guthrie*

God Almighty's gentleman.

Julius and Augustus Hare

One of several Jewish heresies.   *Eric Hoffer*

To make one a complete Christian he must have the works of a papist, the words of a Puritan, and the faith of a Protestant.   *James Howell*

A man who keeps one day in the week holy and raises hell with folks and fauna the other six.
Elbert Hubbard

Whoever would be a Christian must be a nonconformist. *Martin Luther King 2*

They are infidels who say, Verily God is Christ the son of Mary. *Koran 5.*

A wise man will always be a Christian, because the perfection of wisdom is to know where lies tranquility of mind, and how to attain it, which Christianity teaches. *Walter Savage Landor*

Unhappy men who are persuaded that they will survive death and live forever...they despise death and are willing to sacrifice their lives to their faith. *Lucian*

Not he that has no sin, but he to whom God imputes not his sin because of his faith in Christ.
Martin Luther

A maid, after she had been confirmed, was asked how she knew she was a Christian. "Because," she replied, "now I do not sweep the dirt under the rugs." *John H. Miller*

He that can apprehend and consider vice with all her baits and seeming pleasures, and yet abstain, and yet distinguish and prefer that which is truly better, he is the true warfaring Christian.
John Milton

We are Christians by the same token we are Frenchmen or Germans. *Michel de Montaigne*

The domestic animal, the herd animal.
Friedrich W. Nietzsche

In truth, there was only one Christian, and he died on the cross. *Friedrich W. Nietzsche*

The Jew all over again—he is threefold the Jew.
Friedrich W. Nietzsche

To be like Christ is to be a Christian.
William Penn

The supernatural man who thinks, judges, and acts consistently in accordance with right reason illumined by the supernatural light of the example and teaching of Christ. *Pope Pius XI*

The true citizen, lofty of purpose, resolute in endeavor, ready for a hero's deeds, but never looking down on his task because it is cast in the day of small things. *Theodore Roosevelt*

The heathens, too, believe that Christ died; the belief, the faith in His resurrection makes the Christian Christian...It is faith in this resurrection that justifies us. *Saint Augustine*

A good Christian would rather be robbed than rob others—rather be murdered than murder—martyred than tyrant. *Saint Francis de Sales*

A man who leads on others with him. He must run towards Christ. *Roger Schutz*

A part of a whole, a citizen of the Kingdom of God, a child in the family of the Trinity, a cell in the organism of the Whole Christ and a member of the Mystical Body. *Fulton J. Sheen*

Give, give, give...the best definition of the Christian life I have yet heard. *W. F. Stride*

A man becomes a Christian; he is not born one.
Tertullian

One who so believes in Christ, as that sin hath no more domination over him. *John Wesley*

No man...who does not think constantly of how he can lift his brother, how he can assist his friend, how he can enlighten mankind, how he can make virtue the rule of conduct in the circle in which he lives. *Woodrow Wilson*

The highest style of man. *Edward Young*

Scratch the Christian and you find the pagan—spoiled. *Israel Zangwill*

SEE ALSO BAPTISM, CHARITY, CHURCHES, LUTHER, RELIGION, SAINT, SALVATION, SIN.

CHRISTMAS

Unto you is born this day in the city of David a Saviour, which is Christ the Lord.
Bible: Luke, II, 2.

The hour in which the Prince of Peace was born.
William Cullen Bryant

A lesson of humanity...in every house the Christ is born. *Adapted from Richard W. Gilder*

Glorious time of great Too-Much. *Leigh Hunt*

When children gather round their tree.
Tudor Jenks

This is the happy morn, wherein the Son of Heaven's eternal King, of wedded maid and virgin mother our great redemption from above did bring. *Adapted from John Milton*

If it means anything (it) means the exaltation and glorification of the spirit of the child, which is just another word for humility. *Fulton J. Sheen*

The glory of God and of good-will to man!
John Greenleaf Whittier

Dashing through the dough. *Ralph M. Wyser*

The time when the year comes to a head. *Anon.*

CHURCHES

The actual inner unity of redeemed humanity united with Christ. *Karl Adam*

It is the law of human nature that the Church should wish to do everything and be everything.
Charles Baudelaire

The inner company of those who, under the leadership of Christ, and empowered by Him, insist on living, and if necessary dying, rather than surrender to the selfish, hateful folly of a perishing race of men. *B. I. Bell*

Nothing less than the cosmos Christianized.
Nicholas Berdyaev

And I say also unto thee, That thou art Peter, and upon this rock I will build my church; and the gates of hell shall not prevail against it.
Bible: Matthew, XVI, 18.

Where two or three are gathered together in my name, there am I in the midst of them.
Bible: Matthew, XVIII, 20.

Nothing but a section of humanity in which Christ has really taken form. The Church is the man in Christ, incarnate, sentenced and awakened to new life. *Dietrich Bonhoeffer*

An organization which should fight not for itself but for the salvation of the world.
Adapted from Dietrich Bonhoeffer

A place where one day's truce ought to be allowed to the dissensions and animosities of mankind.
Edmund Burke

Wherever we see the Word of God purely preached and heard, and the sacraments administered according to Christ's institution, there . . . a church of God exists. *John Calvin*

A worshipping, witnessing, confessing community of forgiven sinners who rejoice in the grace that has been given them and who proclaim the word of judgment and redemption to those who have not acknowledged the sovereignty of God over their lives. *Kenneth Cauthen*

A sacred corporation for the promulgation and maintenance in Europe of certain Asian principles which, although local in their birth, are of divine origin and eternal application.
Benjamin Disraeli

Beliefs and practices which unite into one single moral community . . . all those who adhere to them. *Emile Durkheim*

Part of the sky. *Ralph Waldo Emerson*

An anvil that has worn out many hammers.
English Proverb

The only place where someone speaks to me . . . and I do not have to answer back.
Charles de Gaulle

A temple built to God. *George Herbert*

A congregation of baptized believers, associated by a convenant in faith and fellowship of the Gospel; observing the ordinances of Christ; governed by His laws. *E. T. Hiscox*

A community of solitude before God.
Richard Hocking

A church is God between four walls.
Victor Hugo

The community in which men share the process of total evaluation of every aspect of life, arrive at what they conceive to be spiritual judgments on their own lives in the light of an absolute imperative. *Ernest Johnson*

A center of light and leading, of inspiration and guidance, for its specific community.
Rufus M. Jones

The Body of Christian believers and transmitters of Christ's mind and spirit through the centuries.
Rufus M. Jones

The community of destiny operating under a divine mandate. *Edward J. Jurji*

The mansion-house of the Omnipotent God.
Legal Maxim

A voluntary society of men, joining themselves together of their own accord, in order to the public worshipping of God, in such a manner as they judge acceptable to him, and effectual to the salvation of their souls. *John Locke*

It takes *men*, not a creed, to make a church.
Cleland B. McAfee

A totality of segregated and independent units, unknown both to themselves and to others.
A. C. McGiffert

A place in which gentlemen who have never been to heaven brag about it to persons who will never get there. *Henry Louis Mencken*

A hospital for sinners, not a museum for saints.
L. L. Nash

A collection of souls, brought together in one by God's secret grace, though that grace comes to them through visible instruments, and unites them to a visible hierarchy.
John Henry Newman

A people on the move. *John O'Conner*

Wherever one hand meets another helpfully.
John Ruskin

Means convocation, or assembly...because all are called to be members of it. *Saint Isidore*

A Christian church is a body or collection of persons, voluntarily associated together, professing to believe that Christ teaches, to do what Christ enjoins, to imitate his example, cherish his spirit, and make known his gospel to others.
R. F. Sample

The Church should have a tapering spire,
To point to realms where sin's forgiven,
And lead men's thoughts from earth to heaven.
John E. Woodrow

Soul agents for nations. *Anon.*

SEE ALSO BIBLE, CHRISTIANITY, CHURCH (ROMAN CATHOLIC), CROSS, GOD, LUTHER, PRAYER, PREACHING, RELIGION, SALVATION, SYNAGOGUE, WORSHIP.

CHURCH OF ENGLAND

It's pure in doctrine, correct in deeds,
has nought redundant, and nothing needs.
Adapted from George Crabbe

Charity and love is the known doctrine of the Church of England. *Daniel Defoe*

CHURCH (ROMAN CATHOLIC)

Not a mere depository of doctrine. The Church of England is a part of England...part of our strength and...liberties, a part of our national character. *Benjamin Disraeli*

The doctrine of the Old Testament.
Ralph Waldo Emerson

A decorous simplicity. *Justice Lushington*

A popish liturgy, a Calvinistic creed, and an Aminian clergy. *William Pitt*

Ours is the only church where the skeptic stands at the altar, and where St. Thomas is regarded as the ideal apostle. *Oscar Wilde*

CHURCH (ROMAN CATHOLIC)

A sword, the hilt of which is at Rome, and the point everywhere. *André M. Dupin*

The mother and mistress of all the faithful.
Fourth Council of Lateran, 1215.

The work of an Incarnate God. Like all God's works, it is perfect. *James C. Gibbons*

No other than the ghost of the deceased Roman Empire, sitting crowned upon the grave thereof.
Thomas Hobbes

The one great spiritual organization which is able to resist, and must, as a matter of life and death, the progress of science and modern civilization.
Thomas Henry Huxley

A church where there are so many helps to get to Heaven. *Samuel Johnson*

The great fact which dominates the history of modern civilization. *Homer Lea*

Less a religion than a priestly tyranny armed with the spoils of civil power which, on pretext of religion, it hath seized against the command of Christ himself. *John Milton*

Salvation. *Saint Augustine*

The Holy Church, the One Church, the True Church...which fights against all errors.
Saint Augustine

The society of the faithful collected into one and the same body, governed by its legitimate pastors, of whom Jesus Christ is the invisible head—the pope, the successors of St. Peter, being His representative on earth. *Saint John the Baptist*

A faithful and ever watchful guardian of the dogmas which have been committed to her charge. In this sacred deposit she changes nothing, she takes nothing from it, she adds nothing to it.   *Saint Vincent*

SEE ALSO CATHOLICISM, PAPACY, PRIESTS.

CHURCHYARD

SEE CEMETERY, DEATH, GRAVE.

CICERO (106-43 B.C.)

An exalted patriot.   *Thomas Jefferson*

A journalist in the worst sense of the word.
                    Theodor Mommsen

CIGARETTE

Cigarette-smoking is like drinking beer out of a thimble.   *Elizabeth A. Dillwyn*

Killers that travel in packs.   *Mary S. Ott*

The perfect type of a perfect pleasure. It is exquisite, and it leaves one unsatisfied.
                    Oscar Wilde

A neurotic habit that double-times you to the grave.   *Robert Zwickey*

A fire at one end, a fool at the other, and a bit of tobacco in between.   *Anon.*

SEE ALSO TOBACCO.

CIRCUMCISION

Ye shall circumcise the flesh of your foreskin; and it shall be a token of the covenant betwixt me and you.   *Bible: Genesis, XVII, 11.*

An example of the power of poetry to raise the low and offensive.   *Ralph Waldo Emerson*

A sign of the covenant between man and his Creator, not to pollute himself with unchastity.
                    Abraham Ibn Ezra

An institution, not a mere ceremony.
                    Zohar, Genesis, 197a.

SEE ALSO COVENANT.

CIRCUMSTANCE

That unspiritual god and miscreator that makes and helps along our coming evils.
                    Adapted from Lord Byron

Something beyond the control of man.
                    Adapted from Benjamin Disraeli

The creatures of men.   *Benjamin Disraeli*

The fresh banana-peel just around the corner.
                    Elbert Hubbard

Things round about; we are in them, not under them.   *Walter Savage Landor*

The rulers of the weak; they are but the instruments of the wise.   *Samuel Lover*

What determines all our thoughts and acts.
                    Anon.

CIRCUS

A place where horses, ponies and elephants are permitted to see men, women and children acting the fool.   *Ambrose Bierce*

A show as entertaining as the human race.
                    Eugene E. Brussell

An oasis of Hellenism in a world that reads too much to be wise, and thinks too much to be beautiful.   *Oscar Wilde*

Animals acting like the human race, and the human race acting like animals.   *Anon.*

A show that smells.   *Anon.*

An amusement competing for laughs with humanity.   *Anon.*

SEE ALSO CLOWN.

CITIZEN

The most important office.   *Louis D. Brandeis*

It is the function of the citizen to keep the government from falling into error.
                    Robert H. Jackson

The first requisite...is that he shall be able and willing to pull his weight.   *Theodore Roosevelt*

Civis, the most honorable name among the Romans; a citizen, a word of contempt among us.
                    Jonathan Swift

One who accepts his responsibilities in raising his children well, paying taxes, and obeying the law.
Anon.

SEE ALSO PATRIOT.

CITY

The chaos of eternal smoke.   *John Armstrong*

A great mess composed of a multitude of primitive forms of consciousness who are naturally attracted to gore, egoistic grandeur and gross excitement.   *Charles Bolte*

A world of men for me.   *Robert Browning*

Struggling tides of life that seem in wayward, aimless course to tend.
Adapted from William Cullen Bryant

Torture.   *Lord Byron*

Nowadays...the only desert within our means.
Albert Camus

The abiding place of wealth and luxury.
Grover Cleveland

Where works of man are clustered close around, and works of God are hardly to be found.
Adapted from William Cowper

The centre of a thousand trades.
William Cowper

(A place which will) force growth and make men talkative and entertaining, but...artificial.
Ralph Waldo Emerson

The first requisite to happiness.   *Euripides*

Not that which shows the palace of government as the origin and climax of every radiating avenue; the true city is that of a burgher people, governing themselves from their own town hall and yet expressing also the spiritual ideal which governs them.   *Patrick Geddes*

Any place where men have built a jail, a bagnio, a gallows, a morgue, a church, a hospital, a saloon, and laid out a cemetery—hence a center of life.
Elbert Hubbard

Any part of the earth where ignorance and stupidity integrate, agglomerate and breed.
Elbert Hubbard

A herding region.   *Elbert Hubbard*

A settlement that consistently generates its economic growth from its own local economy.
Jane Jacobs

America's glory and sometimes America's shame.   *John Fitzgerald Kennedy*

A great solitude.   *Latin Proverb*

A river leading nowhere.   *Amy Lowell*

A prison for speculative minds.   *Franz Mehring*

Where homes thick and sewers annoy the air.
Adapted from John Milton

A busy hum of men.   *John Milton*

(A phenomenon) growing so fast its arteries are showing through its outskirts.   *Clyde Moore*

A human zoo.   *Desmond Morris*

Has always been the fireplace of civilization, whence light and heat radiated out into the dark.
Theodore Parker

Any city...is...divided into two, one the city of the poor, the other of the rich; these are at war with one another.   *Plato*

A stone forest.   *John B. Priestly*

A natural territory for the psychopath with histrionic gifts.   *Jonathan Raban*

(A place where) there is no room to die.
Felix Riesenberg

The sink of the human race.
Jean-Jacques Rousseau

The people are the city.   *William Shakespeare*

The greatest diversion from external circumstances.   *Sydney Smith*

A magnet—the bigger it is, the greater the drawing power.   *Samuel Tenenbaum*

Millions of people being lonesome together.
Henry David Thoreau

It is men who make a city, not walls or ships.
Thucydides

(A place) of conventions and artificialities ... where the friends of today will fall upon one another tomorrow.   *Joseph Trumpeldor*

The place where men are constantly seeking to find their door and where they are doomed to wandering forever.   *Thomas Wolfe*

A place so big that no one counts.   *Anon.*

SEE ALSO LONDON, LOS ANGELES, NEW YORK CITY, PARIS.

CIVILIZATION

A method of living, an attitude of equal respect for all men. *Jane Addams*

The lamb's skin in which barbarism masquerades. *Thomas Bailey Aldrich*

A constant quest for nonviolent means of solving conflicts. *Max Ascoli*

The beginning is marked by an intense legality; that legality is the very condition of its existence, the bond which ties it together. *Walter Bagehot*

Mankind's struggle upwards, in which millions are trampled to death, that thousands may mount their bodies. *Clara Balfour*

Trade and law. *Jacques Barzun*

Civilization does not lie in a greater or lesser degree of refinement, but in an awareness shared by a whole people. *Albert Camus*

Gunpowder, printing and the Protestant religion. *Thomas Carlyle*

A society based on the opinion of civilians. *Winston S. Churchill*

Civilization and profits go hand in hand. *Calvin Coolidge*

A strange heterogeneous assemblage of vices and virtues, and of a variety of other principles, for ever at war, for ever jarring, for ever producing some dangerous, some distressing extreme. *Saint John de Crèvecoeur*

The cooperation of regional societies under a common spiritual influence. *Christopher Dawson*

Increased means and leisure are the two civilizers of man. *Benjamin Disraeli*

Order and freedom promoting cultural activity. *Will Durant*

(That which) exists by geological consent, subject to change without notice. *Will Durant*

A stream with banks. The stream is sometimes filled with blood from people killing, stealing, shouting and doing the things historians usually record, while on the banks, unnoticed, people build homes, make love, raise children, sing songs, write poetry and even whittle statues. The story of civilization is what happened on the banks. *Will Durant*

Civilization is carried on by superior men, and not by people in the mass; if nature sends no such men, civilization declines. *Victor Duruy*

Quality...not...speed. *Irwin Edman*

A decent provision for the poor is the true test. *Ralph Waldo Emerson*

The test...is the power of drawing the most benefit out of the cities. *Ralph Waldo Emerson*

Consists in progressive renunciation. *Sigmund Freud*

Consists in an ever increasing subjection of our instincts to repression. *Sigmund Freud*

Consists not in the multiplication, but in the deliberate and voluntary reduction of wants. *Mohandas K. Gandhi*

Paralysis. *Paul Gauguin*

Simply a series of victories over nature. *William Harvey*

The process of reducing the infinite to the finite. *Oliver Wendell Holmes 2*

Nothing more than politeness, industry and fairness. *Edgar W. Howe*

A device for increasing human ills. *Elbert Hubbard*

Jesus wept; Voltaire smiled. Of that divine tear and of that human smile is composed the sweetness of the present civilization. *Victor Hugo*

An arrangement for domesticating the passions and setting them to do useful work. *Aldous Huxley*

Details the steps by which men have succeeded in building up an artificial world within the cosmos. *Thomas Henry Huxley*

A condition of mankind which neither embodies any worthy ideal nor even possesses the merit of stability. *Thomas Henry Huxley*

True civilization is where every man gives to every other every right that he claims for himself. *Robert G. Ingersoll*

The history of the slow and painful enfranchisement of the human race. *Robert G. Ingersoll*

The organization of all those faculties that resist the mere excitement of sport. *William James*

All the civilization we know has been created and directed by small intellectual aristocracies, never by people in the mass. The power of crowds is only to destroy. *Gustave Lebon*

Teaching men to govern themselves by letting them do it. *Abraham Lincoln*

(Securing) the largest possible measure of individual liberty consistent with the welfare of society. *Meyer London*

A slow process of learning to be kind. *Charles Lucas*

Our common heritage. *Mike Mansfield*

The degree of a nation's disregard for the necessities of existence. *William Somerset Maugham*

A concerted effort to remedy the blunders and check the practical joking of God. *Henry Louis Mencken*

Consists in the multiplication and refinement of human wants. *Robert A. Millikan*

Found in the softening of manners, in growing urbanity, in politer relations and in the spreading of knowledge in such ways that decency and seemliness are practiced until they transcend specific and detailed laws. *Comte de Mirabeau*

The outcome of a spiritual work...born of man's need to fulfill himself by bringing the universe to fulfillment. *Jean Mouroux*

The development of art out of nature, and of self-government out of passion, and of certainty out of opinion, and of faith out of reason. *John Henry Newman*

To convert man, a beast of prey, into a tame and civilized animal, a domestic animal. *Friedrich W. Nietzsche*

Respect for human life, the punishment of crimes against property and persons, the equality of all good citizens before the law—or, in a word, justice. *Max Nordau*

Nothing else but the attempt to reduce force to being the last resort. *José Ortega y Gasset*

Restrictions, standards, courtesy, indirect methods, justice, reason. *José Ortega y Gasset*

A coat of paint that washes away when the rain falls. *Auguste Rodin*

The making of civil persons. *John Ruskin*

A heritage of beliefs, customs, and knowledge slowly accumulated in the course of centuries. *Antoine de Saint-Exupéry*

The aim of civilization is to make politics superfluous and science and art indispensable. *Arthur Schnitzler*

Man is at bottom a wild, terrific animal. We know him only in connection with taming and training, which is called civilization. *Arthur Schopenhauer*

Heaps of agonizing human maggots, struggling with one another for scraps of food. *George Bernard Shaw*

The sum total of man's material acquisitions. *C. Bezalel Sherman*

A progress from an indefinite, incoherent homogeneity toward a definite, coherent heterogeneity. *Herbert Spencer*

A movement and not a condition. *Arnold J. Toynbee*

A limitless multiplication of unnecessary necessaries. *Mark Twain*

Rich, luxuriant, varied personalism. *Walt Whitman*

The art and practice of living equally in the community. *Thornton Wilder*

A long hard fight to maintain and advance. *Thornton Wilder*

A primary basis of any kind of civilization is destruction of the absurd belief that in government and the ordering of human society the end justifies the means. *Leonard Woolf*

The semblance of peace by manifold illusion. *William Butler Yeats*

One aim—to liberate man from all that is mystic ...and to cultivate the purely rational side of his being. *Ignaz Zollschan*

A slow process of getting rid of our prejudices. *Anon.*

The time when men learn to live off one another instead of off the land.   *Anon.*

A slow process of adopting the ideas of the minority.   *Anon.*

SEE ALSO CULTURE, EDUCATION, GREAT MEN, GREATNESS, HERITAGE, MINORITY, THINKING, THOUGHT.

CIVILIZED

When you take a bath. When you don't take a bath, you are cultured.   *Lin Yutang*

A certain list of things about which we permit a man to have an opinion different from ours. Usually they are things which we have ceased to care about: for instance, the worship of God.

Aubrey Menen

The radical progressive desire on the part of each individual to take others into consideration.

José Ortega y Gasset

To be incapable of giving unnecessary offense, to have some quality of consideration for all who cross our path.   *Agnes Repplier*

A man's ability to remain in one place and linger in his own company.   *Seneca*

Preferring the best not only to the worst but to the second best.   *Anon.*

SEE ALSO GENTLEMAN, MANNERS.

CLARITY

The supreme politeness of him who wields a pen.
Jean Henri Fabré

The greatest of legislative and judicial virtues, like the sunshine, revealing and curative.

Charles Evans Hughes

So clearly one of the attributes of truth that very often it passes for truth.   *Joseph Joubert*

Care should be taken, not that the reader may understand, but that he must understand.

Quintilian

The good faith of philosophers.

Luc de Vauvenargues

To speak without erring, and to be brief without repeating.   *Joseph Zabara*

SEE ALSO ART, LANGUAGE, STYLE, WRITING.

CLASSES

One soweth, and another reapeth.

Bible: John, IV, 37.

He that has, to him shall be given; and he that has not, from him shall be taken even that which he has.   *Bible: Mark, IV, 25.*

Men of low degree are vanity, and men of high degree are a lie.   *Bible: Psalms, LXII, 9.*

The rich and the poor—the have-nots and the haves.   *Edward G. Bulwer-Lytton*

The Washed and the Unwashed.

Thomas Carlyle

Those who consume more than they create, and those who create more than they consume.

Adapted from Edward Carpenter

There are but two families in the world—Have-much and Have-little.   *Miguel de Cervantes*

Three classes of citizens. The first are the rich, who are indolent and yet always crave more. The second are the poor, who have nothing, are full of envy, hate the rich, and are easily led by demagogues. Between the two extremes lie those who make the state secure and uphold the laws.

Euripides

All communities divide themselves into the few and the many. The first are the rich and well-born, the other the mass of people.

Alexander Hamilton

There must be a class to do the menial duties, to perform the drudgery of life. Its requisites are vigor, docility, fidelity. Such a class you must have, or you would not have that other class which leads progress, civilization and refinement.

James H. Hammond

We are, by our occupations, education and habits of life, divided...into different species, which regard one another...with scorn and malignity.

Samuel Johnson

Jupiter placed two tables in the world. The cunning, the vigilant and the strong eat at the first: the inferior have the leavings at the second.

Jean de La Fontaine

Some men labor with their minds and some with their muscles. Those who labor with their minds govern those who labor with their muscles.

Mencius

Merely the ratification of an order of nature, of a natural law of the first rank, over which no arbitrary flat, no "modern idea" can exert any influence. *Friedrich W. Nietzsche*

To the church there are only two kinds of men—those who follow Christ and those who do not.
Franklin M. North

Two or more orders of people who are believed to be, and are accordingly ranked by the members of the community, in socially superior and inferior positions. *W. Lloyd Warner*

Two classes, those who believe the incredible, and those who do the improbable. *Oscar Wilde*

The working class and the employing class.
Anon.

SEE ALSO ARISTOCRAT, MIDDLE CLASS, MULTITUDE, WEALTH, WORKERS.

CLASSICS

Examples of *how* to think, not of *what* to think.
Jacques Barzun

A work which gives pleasure to the minority which is intensely and permanently interested...It lives on because the minority...is eternally curious and is therefore engaged in an eternal process of rediscovery. *Arnold Bennet*

In science, read by preference the newest works; in literature, the oldest. The classics are always modern. *Edward G. Bulwer-Lytton*

The literature of which we do not expect anything new. *Karel Čapek*

Primitive literature. *Stephen B. Leacock*

A true classic is an author who has enriched the human mind, augmented its treasure, and made it advance a step. *Charles A. Sainte-Beuve*

(That which teaches one to) love the instrument better than the end...not what may be read in Greek, but Greek itself. *Sydney Smith*

The noblest recorded thoughts of man...the only oracles which are not decayed.
Henry David Thoreau

Something that everybody wants to have read and nobody wants to read. *Mark Twain*

A book which people praise and don't read.
Mark Twain

Truth and clarity, logically arranged, is classic style in all languages. *Isaac M. Wise*

Something people know by name but never read.
Anon.

A good art work neglected by too much appreciation. *Anon.*

SEE ALSO BOOK, LITERATURE, WRITING.

CLASSIFICATION

A repertory of weapons for attack upon the future and the unknown. *John Dewey*

A bore, both to the describer and the describee.
Benjamin Disraeli

CLASS, MIDDLE

SEE MIDDLE CLASS, PHILISTINE.

CLEANLINESS

Cleanness of body was ever deemed to proceed from a due reverence to God, to society, and to ourselves. *Francis Bacon*

(An act which) leads to the sanctification of the soul. *Moses Maimonides*

Respect for God. *Talmud: Sabbath, 50b.*

Next to godliness. *John Wesley*

A fine life-preserver. *Anon.*

CLEMENS, SAMUEL

SEE TWAIN, MARK.

CLERGYMEN

Not so much what a man says in the pulpit, but what he does out of the pulpit, gives power to his ministry. *Henry Berkowitz*

We are ambassadors for Christ, as though God did beseech you by us. *Bible: Corinthians, V, 20.*

A man who undertakes the management of our spiritual affairs as a method of bettering his temporal ones. *Ambrose Bierce*

It is his profession to support one side.
Samuel Butler 2

The clergyman is expected to be a kind of human Sunday. *Samuel Butler 2*

He that negotiates between God and man, as God's ambassador, the grand concerns of judgment and mercy.

Adapted from William Cowper

Three classes of clergy: Nimrods, ramrods and fishing-rods. *English Proverb*

(Those) who are set apart to the care of sacred matters, and the conducting (of) our public devotions with greater decency and order.

David Hume

An immense body who are ignorant and speak out; a small proportion who know and are silent; and a minute minority who know and speak according to their knowledge.

Thomas Henry Huxley

A man who is good enough to go to heaven.

Samuel Johnson

They think nobly of the Universe, and believe in Souls and Eternal Happiness. *Logan P. Smith*

A landscape painter of Christianity.

Oliver H. Smith

A man...thrown into life with his hands tied, and bid to swim; he does well if he keeps his hands above water. *Sydney Smith*

SEE ALSO BISHOP, CLERICALISM, PREACHERS, PREACHING, PRIESTS, RABBI

CLERICALISM

The utilization of a church, a faith, and the discipline of the faithful for political ends.

R. L. Bruckberger

The pursuit of power, especially political power, by a religious hierarchy, carried on by secular methods and for purposes of social domination.

John Mackay

One of the chief hindrances to social progress.

Herbert L. Samuel

CLEVERNESS

(That which is) serviceable for everything, sufficient for nothing. *Henry F. Amiel*

Often annoying, like a lamp in a bedroom.

Ludwig Boerne

A tool used to fetch foolish admirers.

Jewish Proverb

Consists in knowing perfectly the price of things.

La Rochefoucauld

A quality you distrust when it becomes self-conscious. *Anon.*

A quality which is entertaining but is never confused with trust or wisdom. *Anon.*

Thinking of a bright remark in time to say it. The other consists in not saying it. *Anon.*

The tool with which bad men work. *Anon.*

SEE ALSO CUNNING, WIT.

CLICHÉ

Hush little bright line
Don't you cry...
You'll be a cliché
Bye and bye. *Fred Allen*

To make a cliché is to make a classic.

James Borne

An expression of the lowest common denominator which fits you for the company of the lowest common denominator. *Eugene E. Brussell*

Only something well said in the first place.

William Granger

SEE ALSO PLATITUDE.

CLIMATE

A theory. Weather is a condition.

Oliver Herford

What lasts all the time; weather only lasts a few days. *Anon.*

SEE ALSO WEATHER.

CLOCK

A machine of great moral value to man, allaying his concern for the future by reminding him what a lot of time remains to him. *Ambrose Bierce*

A heart. Its ticks indicate the passing of time—only the clock is apt to keep ticking longer.

Jerry Dashkin

A device which owns no more than sixty minutes an hour. *Samuel Liptzin*

The symbol of man. His heart, too, beats incessantly ... and his moods, swinging between hope and despair, may be brought to a sudden halt by the least jar.   *Eliakim Zunser*

A device which measures out our life.   *Anon.*

SEE ALSO CALENDAR, DAY, LIFE, TIME.

CLOTHES

The woman shalt not wear that which pertaineth unto a man, neither shalt a man put on a woman's garment.   *Bible: Deuteronomy, XXII, 5.*

The intellect of the dandy.   *Josh Billings*

The greatest provocations of lust.
                                        Robert Burton

Clothes gave us individuality, distinctions, social polity; clothes have made men of us.
                                        Thomas Carlyle

Ought to be ... remembrances of our lost innocency.   *Thomas Fuller*

An expression of the social life of the time.
                                        Elizabeth Hawes

(Items) good only as they supply the want of other means of procuring respect.   *Samuel Johnson*

The imprint of sin; we ought therefore to ... cover with decency in accordance with the law of God.
                                        Saint John the Baptist

Clothes keep my various selves buttoned up together, and enable all these otherwise irreconcilable aggregates of psychological phenomena to pass themselves off as one person.
                                        Logan P. Smith

Two-thirds of beauty.   *Welsh Proverb*

Wrappings worn by men for warmth, women for spite, and children because they have to.   *Anon.*

Always the reflection of one's self-respect.
                                        Anon.

SEE ALSO DRESS, FASHION.

CLOUDS

The only birds that never sleep.   *Victor Hugo*

A roof beautifully painted but unable to satisfy the mind.   *Charles Lamb*

Clouds are like Holy Writ, in which theologians cause the faithful or the crazy to see anything they please.   *Voltaire*

CLOWN

It is meat and drink to me.
                                        William Shakespeare

A man who acts too natural.   *Anon.*

A person with a sixth sense who fortunately for mankind doesn't have the other five.   *Anon.*

SEE ALSO COMEDIAN.

CLUB

The scene of savage joys, the school of coarse good-fellowship and noise.
                                        Adapted from William Cowper

An assembly of good fellows, meeting under certain conditions.   *Samuel Johnson*

Mausoleums of inactive masculinity ... places for men who prefer armchairs to women.
                                        Victor S. Pritchett

The feeble coxcombry.   *John Ruskin*

A place where we sleep.   *Anon.*

A wealthy man's saloon.   *Anon.*

COCKTAIL

A pleasant drink. It's mild and harmless—I don't think. When you've had one, call for two, and then you don't care what you do.
                                        Adapted from George Ade

A cocktail is to a glass of wine as rape is to love.
                                        Paul Claudel

All the disagreeability, without the utility, of a disinfectant.   *Shane Leslie*

Drinks that passion the night.   *Anon.*

A little whiskey to make it strong,
A little water to make it weak,
A little lemon to make it sour,
A little sugar to make it sweet.   *Anon.*

SEE ALSO DRINKING.

COCKTAIL PARTY

A gathering held to enable forty people to talk about themselves at the same time. The man who remains after the liquor is gone is the host.

Fred Allen

The form of friendship without the warmth.

Brooks Atkinson

A device...for making overtures towards more serious social relationships, as in the etiquette of whoring. *Brooks Atkinson*

An affair where you meet old friends you never saw before. *Fulton Bryan*

Midst meatless platters of little treats, the pitiless patter of little feats. *Fanklin Malone*

A device for paying off obligations to people you don't want to invite to dinner.

Charles M. Smith

A gathering at which drinks mix people. *Anon.*

An excuse to drink for those who don't need excuses. *Anon.*

A gathering where sandwiches and friends are cut into small pieces. *Anon.*

Drinks supporting bores. *Anon.*

COED

A girl sent to college to find a husband. *Anon.*

A girl who didn't get her man in high school.

Anon.

COFFEE

Break fluid. *R. R. Anderson*

Coffee in England is just toasted milk.

Christopher Fry

(A drink which) should be black as Hell, strong as death, and sweet as love. *Turkish Proverb*

COFFIN

The end of the legend. *Elbert Hubbard*

An ornamental...box which no one cares to open. *Elbert Hubbard*

A room without a door or a skylight.

Elbert Hubbard

A costly container for which even the poor gladly pay. *Anon.*

A container small enough for bums, large enough for presidents. *Anon.*

SEE ALSO DEATH, GRAVE.

COIN

SEE DOLLAR, MONEY.

COLD (ILLNESS)

An ailment cured in two weeks with a doctor's care, and in fourteen days without it.

C. C. Furnas

Both positive and negative. Sometimes the eyes have it and sometimes the nose.

William Lyon Phelps

COLD (TEMPERATURE)

The source of more suffering to all animal nature than hunger, thirst, sickness, and all the other pains of life and of death itself put together.

Thomas Jefferson

SEE ALSO WINTER.

COLERIDGE, SAMUEL TAYLOR (1772-1834)

How great a possibility; how small a realized result! *Thomas Carlyle*

My instincts are so far dog-like that I love being superior to myself better than my equals.

Samuel Taylor Coleridge

He talked on for ever; and you wished him to talk on for ever. *William Hazlitt*

A subtle-souled psychologist. *Charles Lamb*

To tell the story of Coleridge without the opium is to tell the story of Hamlet without...the ghost.

Leslie Stephen

His general appearance would have led me to suppose him a dissenting minister. *J. C. Young*

COLLEGE

A place where learned professors conduct research and talk mainly to themselves.

Eugene E. Brussell

Not an education, but the means of education.

Ralph Waldo Emerson

(A place where one) may learn the 'principles' of salesmanship from a Ph.D. who has never sold anything, or the 'principles' of marketing from a Ph.D. who has never marketed anything.

Abraham Flexner

A refuge from hasty judgment.   *Robert Frost*

A student on one end of a log and Mark Hopkins on the other.   *James A. Garfield*

A place to keep warm between high school and an early marriage.   *George Gobel*

A place where you have to go in order to find out that there is nothing in it.   *Elbert Hubbard*

A place where pebbles are polished and diamonds are dimmed.   *Robert G. Ingersoll*

An experience which seldom hurts a fellow if he is willing to learn a little something after he graduates.   *Anon.*

An institution which holds your children until they decide what they want to do in life.   *Anon.*

A place to pursue knowledge under a handicap.

Anon.

A place where a pigskin is as valuable as a sheepskin.   *Anon.*

A four year plan for confusing the mind methodically.   *Anon.*

A social advantage, as compared with proof of excellence.   *Anon.*

SEE ALSO ACADEMY, PROFESSOR, UNIVERSITY.

COLUMBUS, CHRISTOPHER (1451-1506)

If Columbus had not sailed westward with the obstinacy of a maniac, he would not have encountered some pieces of wood, worked by the hand of man...and he would have had to swallow his shame, return to Europe, and count himself lucky to get there.   *Hector Berlioz*

A patient master, for whom the far is near.

Adapted from Louis J. Block

Columbus discovered no isle or key so lonely as himself.   *Ralph Waldo Emerson*

Every ship that comes to America got its chart from Columbus.   *Ralph Waldo Emerson*

Columbus found a world, and had no chart, save one that faith deciphered in the skies. To trust the soul's invincible surmise was all his science and his only art.   *Adapted from George Santayana*

He gave the world another world.

George Santayana

World-finder.   *Lydia H. Sigourney*

When he started out he didn't know where he was going; when he got there he didn't know where he was; and when he got back he didn't know where he had been.   *Anon.*

SEE ALSO AMERICA.

COMEDIAN

A fellow who finds other comedians too humorous to mention.   *Jack Herbert*

Man...happy under any fate, and he says funny things at funerals, and when the bailiffs are in the house, or the hero is waiting to be hanged.

Jerome K. Jerome

The test of a real comedian is whether you laugh at him before he opens his mouth.

George Jean Nathan

One who is no better than his script.   *Louis Reid*

(One who) can only last till he either takes himself seriously or his audience takes him serious.

Will Rogers

A man on the slow slide to oblivion.   *Anon.*

A hilarity of one.   *Anon.*

COMEDY

(That which) ridicules persons by drawing them in their proper characters.   *Joseph Addison*

Comedy aims at representing men as worse, and tragedy as better, than in real life.   *Aristotle*

Comedy is tragedy interrupted.

Alan Ayckbourn

A sad business.   *Charles Chaplin*

The essence...seems to be an honest...halfness; a nonperformance of what is pretended to be performed, at the same time that one is giving loud pledges of performance. The balking of the intellect, the frustrated expectation, the break of continuity in the intellect, is comedy and it announces itself in the pleasant spasms we call laughter. *Ralph Waldo Emerson*

Comedy like sodomy is an unnatural act.
Martin Feldman

An escape, not from truth but from despair; a narrow escape into faith. *Christopher Fry*

Tragedy viewed from the wings.
Elbert Hubbard

Comedy is criticism. *Louis Kronenberger*

Comedy takes place in a world where the mind is always superior to the emotions.
Joseph Wood Krutch

The debauching of virgins and the amours of strumpets are the subject of comedy.
Firmianus Lactantius

A man in trouble. *Jerry Lewis*

The very last alternative to despair.
Franklin Marcus

The fountain of sound sense. *George Meredith*

Society protecting itself—with a smile.
John B. Priestly

(When) life is caught in the act.
George Santayana

The last refuge of the non-conformist mind.
Gilbert Seldes

The chastening of morals with ridicule.
Adapted from George Bernard Shaw

Simply a funny way of being serious.
Peter Ustinov

Comedy is a clash of character. Eliminate character from comedy and you get farce.
William Butler Yeats

SEE ALSO HUMOR, LAUGHTER, WIT.

COMFORT

A state of mind produced by contemplation of a neighbor's uneasiness. *Ambrose Bierce*

That stealthy thing that enters the house as a guest, and then becomes a host, and then a master.
Kahlil Gibran

To be beyond all bounds of shame.
Philip Sydney

Positive hindrances to the elevation of mankind.
Henry David Thoreau

SEE ALSO CONTENTMENT.

COMMANDMENTS

Precepts...given expressly to purify mankind.
Abba Arika

Not in heaven...nor beyond the sea...But the word is very nigh to you, in your mouth and heart, that you may do it.
Bible: Deuteronomy, XXX, 11.

(They) are divided first into those which effect the welfare of the body and those which effect the welfare of the soul, and secondly into the practical and the speculative. *Joseph Caspi*

The essence...is to make the heart upright.
Abraham Ibn Ezra

All the commandments follow three ways: faith, word, and deed...the essence of every commandment...is faith of heart.
Abraham Ibn Ezra

The pillars of the service of God.
Joseph Ibn Pakuda

The mighty stream of spirituality. *Moses Jung*

The canals through which flow constantly the Torah's abundant faith and love. *Abraham Kook*

The purpose...is...to promote compassion, loving-kindness and peace in the world.
Moses Maimonides

That which obliges us to live after a certain fashion. *José Ortega y Gasset*

Their purpose is to unify the nation and refine man's nature. *Jehiel Pines*

The Eleventh Commandment: Thou shalt not be found out. *George Whyte-Melville*

SEE ALSO CHRISTIANITY, GOD, JUDAISM, RELIGION, TEN COMMANDMENTS.

COMMERCE

A kind of transaction in which A plunders from B the goods of C, and for compensation B picks the pocket of D of money belonging to E.

Ambrose Bierce

A transaction which is good for both parties.

Louis D. Brandeis

The willingness to accept one another's mistakes at a discount. *John Ciardi*

The greatest meliorator of the world.

Ralph Waldo Emerson

That pride and darling of our ocean, that educator of nations, that benefactor in spite of itself.

Ralph Waldo Emerson

The principle of liberty . . . it settled America, and destroyed feudalism, and made peace and keeps peace. *Ralph Waldo Emerson*

A plant which grows wherever there is peace, as soon as there is peace, and as long as there is peace. *Ralph Waldo Emerson*

The equalizer of the wealth of nations.

William Gladstone

The great civilizer. We exchange ideas when we exchange fabrics. *Robert G. Ingersoll*

That spirit which knows no countries, feels no passion or principle but that of gain.

Adapted from Thomas Jefferson

A social act. *John Stuart Mill*

Really nothing but a refinement of piratical morality. *Friedrich W. Nietzsche*

The propensity to truck, barter, and exchange.

Adam Smith

The school of cheating. *Luc de Vauvenargues*

SEE ALSO BUSINESS, MERCHANT.

COMMITTEE

A mutual protection society formed to guarantee that no one person can be held to blame for a botched . . . job that one man could have performed satisfactorily. *Russell Baker*

A group of the unfit, appointed by the unwilling, to do the unnecessary. *Henry Cooke*

A thing which takes a week to do what one good man can do in an hour. *Elbert Hubbard*

An arrangement enabling one to share the blame with others. *Franklin P. Jones*

A cul-de-sac to which ideas are lured and then quietly strangled. *John A. Lincoln*

A simple cure for insomnia. *Red O'Donnell*

A group which succeeds in getting something done only when it consists of three members, one of whom happens to be sick and another absent.

Hendrick W. Van Loon

A body of people formed to delay progress.

Anon.

A group of people who talk for hours to produce a result called minutes. *Anon.*

A group that keeps minutes and wastes hours.

Anon.

SEE ALSO GROUP.

COMMON MAN

SEE MASSES, PEOPLE (THE)

COMMON SENSE

A kind of ultimate validation after science has completed its work. *Russell L. Ackoff*

The measure of the possible. *Henry F. Amiel*

Common sense is instinct, and enough of it is genius. *Josh Billings*

The voice of the Lord is the voice of common sense, which is shared by all that is.

Samuel Butler 1

The best sense I know of. *Lord Chesterfield*

What the world calls wisdom.

Samuel Taylor Coleridge

The most widely shared commodity in the world, for every man is convinced that he is well supplied with it. *René Descartes*

The deposit of prejudice laid down in the mind before the age of 18. *Albert Einstein*

The shortest line between two points.

Ralph Waldo Emerson

Genius dressed in its working clothes.

Ralph Waldo Emerson

The ability to detect values—to know a big thing from a little one. *Elbert Hubbard*

Our secret gift. *George Meredith*

What makes men; the rest is all rubbish.

Petronius

The knack of seeing things as they are, and doing things as they ought to be done.   *C. E. Stowe*

The rare quality to detect what is right.

Joan Tepperman

Genius is homespun.   *Alfred North Whitehead*

The one unteachable gift in life.   *Anon.*

SEE ALSO EXPERIENCE, JUDGMENT.

COMMUNISM

Nobody's got nothing, but everybody's working.

Fred Allen

A depository of granite solidity under a guardianship that resolves all ethical and moral problems.   *Marquis W. Childs and Douglass Cater*

A disease of the heart.   *Chinese Saying*

A quasi-religion... It competes with any and all other ultimate loyalties, or religions for men's very souls.   *Merrimon Cunningham*

The real "opium of the people," distracting men's minds from their essential task...the...myth of an earthly paradise.   *Jean Danielou*

The full-blown fruit of secularism.

Lester De Koster

A necessity of sacrificing the ideal of what is excellent for the individual to the ideal of what is excellent for the whole.   *Thomas De Quincey*

That type of totalitarianism which consists of three basic factors for controlling the people...power...ownership...ideology.

Milovan Djilas

A means of integration to men whose souls and social structures are obviously disintegrating, who have lost their absolutes and hence are lonely and afraid.   *W. R. Forrester*

An untenable illusion.   *Sigmund Freud*

(In Russia) autocracy turned upside down.

Alexander Herzen

A monolithic company—the Communist party takes possession of a whole country...The aim of this super-Capitalistic company is to turn the captive population into skilled mechanics and so shape their souls that they would toil from sunup to sunset.   *Eric Hoffer*

A capitalist heresy.   *Eric Hoffer*

A race in which all competitors come in first with no prizes.   *Lord Inchcape*

A combination of two things which Europeans have kept for some centuries in different compartments of the soul—religion and business.

John Maynard Keynes

A mighty, unifying thunderstorm, marking the springtime of mankind.   *Nikita Khrushchev*

Hatred is the basis of Communism. Children must be taught to hate their parents if they are not Communists.   *Nikolai Lenin*

The opiate of the intellectuals.   *Clare B. Luce*

A hammer which we use to crush the enemy.

Mao Tse-tung

A Christian heresy—the ultimate and altogether radical Christian heresy...Collective revolution renewing history and society only for the life here below.   *Jacques Maritain*

May be summed up in one sentence: Abolish all private property.

Karl Marx and Friedrich Engels

A fanatical foe who has become the high priest of a new religion.   *Laurence J. McGinely*

Whenever it ceases to be true that mankind...prefer themselves to others, and those nearest to them to those more remote, from that moment Communism is not only practicable, but the only defensible form of society.

John Stuart Mill

An apostasy from civilization.   *John C. Murray*

Treason...not against governments but against humanity.   *Richard Milhous Nixon*

A monotonous repetition of the eternal revolution...the perfect common-place of revolutions.

José Ortega y Gasset

The theory which teaches that the labor and the income of society should be distributed equally among all its members by some constitutional authority.   *Robert Palgrave*

What is thine is mine, and all of mine is thine.

Plautus

The fatal plague which insinuates itself into the very marrow of human society only to bring about its ruin.   *Pope Leo XIII*

The exploitation of the strong by the weak . . . inequality springs from placing mediocrity on a level with excellence.   *Pierre J. Proudhon*

Communism to me is one-third practice and two-thirds explanation.   *Will Rogers*

What's your is mine, what's mine's my own.
                    Scottish Saying

Left-wing fascism.   *Susan Sontag*

The dictatorship of the proletariat is the rule—unrestricted by law and based on force.
                    Joseph Stalin

The organization of total conformity—in short, of tyranny—and it is committed to making tyranny universal.   *Adlai Ewing Stevenson*

An ideal that can be achieved only when people cease to be selfish and greedy and when everyone receives according to his needs from communal production.   *Josef B. Tito*

The worship of collective human power.
                    Arnold J. Toynbee

The devil's imitation of Christianity.
                    A. W. Tozer

A system that is based on the belief that man is so weak and inadequate that he is unable to govern himself, and therefore requires the rule of strong masters.   *Harry S. Truman*

Absence of freedom and an endless vista of free false teeth with nothing to bite on.   *Anon.*

SEE ALSO SOCIALISM.

COMMUNISTS

A socialist without a sense of humor.
                    George Cutton

One who has yearnings for equal division of unequal earnings. Idler or bungler, or both, he is willing to fork out his copper and pocket your shilling.   *Adapted from Ebenezer Elliot*

A socialist in a violent hurry.   *G. W. Gough*

Frustrated capitalists.   *Eric Hoffer*

A surgeon who takes a sharp knife and operates on a man's body to cut out malignant growths and thus makes possible the further development and strengthening of the organisms.
                    Nikita Khrushchev

The theory of the communists may be summed up in one sentence: Abolition of private property.
                    Karl Marx

An intensely proud person who proposes to enrich the common fund instead of to sponge from it.
                    George Bernard Shaw

One who has given up hope of becoming a capitalist.   *Anon.*

One who has nothing and is eager to share it with the world.   *Anon.*

SEE ALSO COMMUNISM, SOCIALISTS.

COMMUNITY

A fictitious body, composed of the individual persons who are considered as constituting . . . its members.   *Jeremy Bentham*

Tiny fountain-heads of democracy, rising among the rocks, sometimes lost altogether in their course, sometimes running underground to reappear at last in fuller volume.   *Lord Bryce*

The being no longer side by side, but with one another.   *Martin Buber*

The real . . . community is when its members have a common relation to the center overriding all other relations.   *Martin Buber*

The first link in the series by which we proceed towards a love for our country and mankind.
                    Edmund Burke

(That) by which alone your work can be made universal and eternal in its results.
                    Samson R. Hirsch

A kind of group association in which, through being ourselves, we may get to something greater than ourselves.   *Milton J. Rosenberg*

We who are united in heart and soul.   *Tertullian*

Something that man seeks to form by virtue of his nature.   *Adapted from Edward B. White*

The Church alone; not in the helplessness of spiritual isolation but in the strength of his communion with his brothers and with his Savior.
                    Alexander Yelchaninov

A social unit which binds together the collective experience of its individual members.   *Anon.*

A place where people plan and work together, bound by a cohesive past and future.   *Anon.*

SEE ALSO BROTHERHOOD, CHRISTIANITY, CITY, NATION, STATE, WORLD.

COMMUTER

One who spends his life in riding to and from his wife; a man who shaves and takes a train and then rides back to shave again.

Adapted from Edward B. White

A traveling man who pays short visits to his home and office. *Anon.*

One who never knows how a show comes out because he has to leave early to catch a train to get him back to the country in time to catch a train to bring him back to the city. *Anon.*

One who rides himself to an early grave in order that the wife and children may thrive. *Anon.*

SEE ALSO SUBURBIA.

COMPANION

SEE COMPANY, FRIEND.

COMPANY

An extreme provocative to fancy; and like a hot bed in gardening, is apt to make our imagination sprout too fast. *Anthony A. Cooper*

The mind is depraved by the company of the low; it rises to equality with equals; and to distinction with the distinguished. *The Hitopadesa*

The best is always with men more excellent than myself. *Adapted from Charles Lamb*

Hearts that are delicate and kind and tongues that are neither. *Logan P. Smith*

Good discourse. *Isaac Walton*

SEE ALSO CITY, CROWD, GUEST, SOCIETY.

COMPASSION

SEE MERCY, PITY, SYMPATHY.

COMPENSATION

Every sweet has its sour, every evil its good.

Ralph Waldo Emerson

The whole of what we know is a system of compensations. Every suffering is rewarded; every sacrifice is made up; every debt is paid.

Ralph Waldo Emerson

This marvellous balance of beauty and disgust, magnificence and rats. *Ralph Waldo Emerson*

All our works. *Robert Herrick*

COMPETITION

The total amount of the supply is increased, and by increase of the supply a competition in the sale ensues, and this enables the consumer to buy at lower rates. Of all human powers operating on the affairs of mankind, none is greater. *Henry Clay*

The most extreme expression of that war of all against all which dominates modern middle-class society. *Friedrich Engels*

Nothing more than a partially conventionalized embodiment of primeval selfishness...the supremacy of the motive of self-interest.

Federal Council of Churches of Christ in America, Social Creed, 1932

The keen cutting edge of business, always shaving away at costs. *Henry Ford 2*

A fine, wholesome direction of energy.

Nathan Holman

The life of trade, and the death of the trader.

Elbert Hubbard

The very life of science. *Horace M. Kallen*

The lifeblood of democracy. *Anon.*

An economic struggle for survival among businessmen in which the consumer benefits the most. *Anon.*

The way in which the general welfare of all can be obtained. *Anon.*

SEE ALSO AMERICANISM, BUSINESS, COMMERCE, NATURAL SELECTION.

COMPLACENCY

SEE SELF-SATISFACTION.

COMPLAINT

(An utterance that) is wearisome alike to the wretched and the happy. *Samuel Johnson*

The largest tribute heaven receives and the sincerest part of our devotion.   *Jonathan Swift*

A grief résumé.   *Anon.*

COMPLIMENTS

(Something) taken literally only by the savage. The accuracy of compliment is not that of algebra.
                                        William C. Brownell

A sarcastic remark with a flavor of truth.
                                            Elbert Hubbard

A kiss through a veil. Pleasure sets her soft seal there, even while hiding herself.   *Victor Hugo*

Things you say to people when you don't know what else to say.   *Constance Jones*

A thing often paid by people who pay nothing else.   *Horatio Smith*

I have heard say that complimenting is lying.
                                            Jonathan Swift

This barren verbiage.   *Alfred Lord Tennyson*

All of us are so hard up, that the only pleasant things to pay are compliments. They're the only things we can pay.   *Oscar Wilde*

Lies in court clothes.   *Anon.*

The applause that refreshes.   *Anon.*

SEE ALSO EULOGY, FLATTERY, PRAISE.

COMPOSER

Almost the only creative artist who must depend upon a horde of intermediate agents to present his work...all capable, from first to last, of either augmenting the brilliance of his work, or of disfiguring it, misrepresenting it, even destroying it altogether.   *Hector Berlioz*

A builder and maker of houses not made with hands.   *Adapted from Robert Browning*

SEE ALSO MUSIC.

COMPOSITION

SEE ESSAY, WRITING.

COMPROMISE

An adjustment of conflicting interests as gives each adversary the satisfaction of thinking he has got what he ought not to have.   *Ambrose Bierce*

The sacrifice of one right or good in the hope of retaining another, too often ending in the loss of both.   *Tyron Edwards*

All of the usable surface. The extremes, right or left, are in the gutters.
                                Dwight David Eisenhower

Surrender.   *Ralph Waldo Emerson*

Reciprocal concessions.   *Samuel Johnson*

Never anything but an ignoble truce between the duty of a man and the terror of a coward.
                                        Reginald W. Kauffman

A temporary expedient, often wise in party politics, almost sure to be unwise in statesmanship.
                                        James Russell Lowell

A good umbrella but a poor roof.
                                        James Russell Lowell

Simply changing the question to fit the answer.
                                            Merrit Malloy

The art of slicing a piece of cake in such a way that everyone believes he received the biggest piece.   *Jan Peerce*

(That which) tempts us to believe that injustice, when it is halved, becomes justice.
                                        Herbert L. Samuel

To passionate natures...a surrender...to intellectual natures...a confusion.
                                        George Santayana

A temporary compromise is a diplomatic act, but a permanent compromise is the abandonment of a goal.   *Leon Stein*

Any decision by two or more persons.   *Anon.*

A deal in which two people get what neither of them wanted.   *Anon.*

Things half done.   *Anon.*

SEE ALSO DIPLOMACY.

CONCEIT

God's gift to little men.   *Bruce Barton*

The most incurable disease that is known to the human soul.   *Henry Ward Beecher*

A conceited man is (one who is) satisfied with the effect he produces on himself.   *Max Beerbohm*

The greatest liars.   *Michael Drayton*

Conceit lies in thinking you lack nothing.

Epictetus

(That which) forms the greatest menace to our spiritual integrity.   *Jonathan Eybeshitz*

The quicksand of success.   *Arnold H. Glasow*

The finest armor a man can wear.

Jerome K. Jerome

Conceit...is rebellion to God.

Moses Maimonides

When someone attributes to himself a perfection which is not found in him.   *Baruch Spinoza*

Equivalent to all other sins.

Talmud: Sukka, 29b.

Being enclosed entirely by yourself.   *Anon.*

A swelling head and a shrinking brain.   *Anon.*

SEE ALSO EGOISM, SELF-LOVE, SELF-SATIS-FACTION, VANITY.

CONCENTRATION

The secret of strength in politics, in war, in trade, in short in all management of human affairs.

Ralph Waldo Emerson

The Eternal secret...of every mortal achievement.   *Stefan Zweig*

SEE ALSO STUDY, THOUGHT.

CONDITIONS

When we describe our sensations of another's sorrows.   *Samuel Johnson*

Something no one is content with.   *Anon.*

Something that is never just right.   *Anon.*

The now that prevails.   *Anon.*

CONDUCT

Conduct is three-fourths of our life and its largest concern.   *Matthew Arnold*

(That which) lies in masterful administration of the unforeseen.   *Robert Bridges*

The force that rules the world...whether it be moral or immoral.   *Nicholas Murray Butler*

Suiting our behavior to the occasion.

Miguel de Cervantes

The voice of God, who comes down to dwell in our souls, who knows all our thoughts.

John E. Dalberg-Acton

(Something based on) imitating those we cannot resemble.   *Adapted from Samuel Johnson*

How we behave when no one is watching.

Anon.

How we behave when others are watching.

Anon.

When practiced, the only effective sermon.

Anon.

SEE ALSO BEHAVIOR, DEEDS, RELIGION.

CONFERENCE

A gathering of important people who singly can do nothing, but together can decide that nothing can be done.   *Fred Allen*

A meeting to decide when the next meeting will be held.   *Henry Ginsberg*

A coffee break with real napkins.   *Anon.*

The confusion of the loudest talking character multiplied by the number present.   *Anon.*

CONFESSION

The Scripture moveth us, in sundry places to acknowledge and confess our manifold sins and wickedness.   *Book of Common Prayer.*

A medicine to the erring.   *Cicero*

A palliative rather than a remedy.

Peter De Vries

The first step to repentance.   *Edmund Gayton*

The purpose of sacramental Confession is atonement—at-onement with God.

Caryll Houselander

The Catholic practice...is...little more than a systematic method of keeping healthy-minded-ness on top.   *William James*

To bring to light the unknown, the unconscious darkness, and the underdeveloped creativity of our deeper layers.   *Fritz Kunkel*

Consists of two parts: first, to confess our sins, and secondly, to receive the absolution or forgiveness by the confessor, as from God Himself.
Martin Luther

When we are on our knees, speaking to Him about ourselves. *Vincent McNabb*

To confess a folly freely is the next thing to being innocent of it. *Publilius Syrus*

A Hospital of Souls, where the Good Samaritan, through the instrumentality of the priest, goes about binding up wounds and pouring in oil and wine; a hospital where the Divine Physician displays His healing art. *Alfred Wilson*

A fault more than half mended. *Anon.*

SEE ALSO ATONEMENT, PRIESTS, REPENTANCE.

CONFIDENCE

That feeling by which the mind embarks in great and honorable courses with a sure hope and trust in itself. *Cicero*

That which underlies the whole scheme of civilization. *Adapted from W. Bourke Cockran*

An unconquered army. *George Herbert*

The one big lesson the world needs most to learn.
Elbert Hubbard

The feeling that makes one believe a man, even when one knows that one would lie in his place.
Henry Louis Mencken

A plant of slow growth in an aged bosom.
William Pitt

What every great pioneering people have.
Benjamin Yehuda

The feeling you have before you know better.
Anon.

That which compels you to do the thing you think you cannot do. *Anon.*

SEE ALSO SECURITY, SELF-CONFIDENCE.

CONFLICT

The adventurer is within us, and he contests for our favour with the social man we are obliged to be. These two sorts of life are incompatible; one we hanker after, the other we are obliged to.
William Bolitho

The gadfly of thought . . . a *sine qua non* of reflection and ingenuity. *John Dewey*

CONFORMITY

(The result of) happy men whose natures sort with their vocation. *Francis Bacon*

The herd-fear. *E. Stanley Jones*

The jailer of freedom and the enemy of growth.
John Fitzgerald Kennedy

The chief danger of the time. *John Stuart Mill*

No . . . other faculty than the apelike one of imitations. *John Stuart Mill*

To think and do as your neighbors do. *Anon.*

SEE ALSO FASHION.

CONFUSION

A work where nothing is just or fit—one glaring chaos. *Adapted from Alexander Pope*

Primarily the anxiety of a people who no longer know what the bounds are, who can no longer distinguish truth from falsehood.

William Strickland

The devil is the author of confusion.

Jonathan Swift

CONGRESS

The great commanding theatre of this nation, and the threshold to whatever department of office a man is qualified to enter. *Thomas Jefferson*

The very purpose . . . is to arrive at national decisions by bringing together some . . . individuals, representing . . . individuals, to achieve consent on the way the nation should go.

Lyndon Baines Johnson

One-third, more or less, scoundrels; two-thirds, more or less, idiots; and three-thirds, more or less, poltroons. *Henry Louis Mencken*

A body of men who meet.

*New York Times Editorial,
Jan. 1, 1964.*

Bingo with billions. *Red Skelton*

This is not a government of kings and satraps, but a government of the people, and...Congress is the people. *Thaddeus Stevens*

(A) native American criminal class.

Mark Twain

The stronghold of provincialism. *Anon.*

A body of men who meet to vote on unpopular laws. *Anon.*

A body of men brought together to slow down the government. *Anon.*

SEE ALSO PUBLIC OFFICE.

CONGRESSMAN

A hog. You must take a stick and hit him on the snout. *Henry B. Adams*

A man who votes for all appropriations and against all taxes. *Henry Ashurst*

Reader, suppose you were an idiot. And suppose you were a member of Congress. But I repeat myself. *Mark Twain*

A body of gentlemen charged with high duties and misdemeanors. *Anon.*

SEE ALSO POLITICS.

CONQUER

We wholly conquer only what we assimilate.

André Gide

(That which) is rated by the difficulty.

Michel de Montaigne

Yield if you are opposed; by yielding you conquer. *Ovid*

SEE ALSO VICTORY.

CONQUERORS

A cruel fame, that arises from the destruction of the human species. *Lord Chesterfield*

The greatest...is he who overcomes the enemy without a blow. *Chinese Proverb*

A conqueror is always a lover of peace. He would like to make his entry into our state unopposed.

Karl von Clausewitz

The powerful mixers of cultures and races, they loosen the bonds binding the spirit of the supernatural, and prepare the way for liberty and individuality. *Friedrich Hertz*

The acquiring of the right of sovereignty by victory. *Thomas Hobbes*

The conqueror would rather burst a city gate than find it open to admit him; he would rather ravage the land with fire and sword than overrun it without protest...He scorns to advance by an unguarded road or to act like a peaceful citizen.

Lucan

The Chief who in triumph advances.

Walter Scott

The conquered in the hereafter. *Sefer Hasidim.*

SEE ALSO VICTORY, WAR.

CONQUEST

SEE VICTORY.

CONSCIENCE

A man's judgment of himself according to the judgment of God of him. *William Ames*

An imitation within ourselves of the government without us. *Alexander Bain*

The perfect interpreter of life. *Karl Barth*

A thing of fictitious existence, supposed to occupy a seat in the mind. *Jeremy Bentham*

That inner tribunal. *Anton T. Boisen*

One's soul companion. *Evelyn Brenzel*

Another man within me. *Thomas Browne*

The great beacon light God sets in all.

Robert Browning

(Something that) is thoroughly well-bred, and soon leaves off talking to those who do not wish to hear it. *Samuel Butler 2*

An inward witness and monitor, reminding us of what we owe to God, pointing out the distinction of good and evil. *Adapted from John Calvin*

An actuated or reflex knowledge of a superior power and an equitable law; a law impressed, and a power above impressing it.

Stephen Charnock

What your mother told you before you were six years old. *Brock Chisholm*

The pulse of reason. *Samuel Taylor Coleridge*

All that a man can betray. *Joseph Conrad*

Conscience emphasizes the word ought.
Joseph Cook

The unknown is an ocean. What is conscience? The compass of the unknown. *Joseph Cook*

The still small voice. *William Cowper*

Your own judgment of the right and wrong of our actions. *Tyron Edwards*

What real human progress depends on.
Albert Einstein

A coward, and those faults it has not strength to prevent it seldom has justice enough to accuse.
Oliver Goldsmith

The *advocatus Dei* in our soul.
Dietrich von Hildebrand

The dirty and degrading chimaera.
Adolf Hitler

A man's conscience and his judgment is the same thing. *Thomas Hobbes*

The muzzle of the will. *Elbert Hubbard*

The furnace of dreams, the lurking-place of ideas we are ashamed of . . . the battlefield of the passions. *Victor Hugo*

Simply my whole nature articulate . . . the voice, changing and never stationary, that results from my faith, my actual way of living. *Bede Jarrett*

The moral sense. *Thomas Jefferson*

That small inner voice that gives you the odds.
Franklin P. Jones

The voice of our ideal self, our complete self, our real self, laying its call upon the will.
Rufus M. Jones

An instinct to judge ourselves in the light of moral laws. *Immanuel Kant*

The glory of a good man. *Thomas à. Kempis*

A sacred sanctuary where God alone may enter as judge. *Felicite R. Lamennais*

The most painful wound in the world.
John Large

The guardian in the individual of the rules which the community has evolved for its own preservation. *William Somerset Maugham*

The inner voice that warns us that someone may be looking. *Henry Louis Mencken*

A mother-in-law whose visit never ends.
Henry Louis Mencken

The accumulated sediment of ancestral faintheartedness. *Henry Louis Mencken*

Custom. *Michel de Montaigne*

The voice of your neighbor.
Adapted from Friedrich W. Nietzsche

The belief in authority is the source of conscience; which is . . . not the voice of God in the heart of man, but the voice of some men in man.
Friedrich W. Nietzsche

Nothing but other people inside you.
Luigi Pirandello

My heart. Whatever I feel to be good is good. Whatever I feel to be evil is evil. Conscience is the best of casuists. *Jean-Jacques Rousseau*

The voice of the soul. *Jean-Jacques Rousseau*

A mental possession of ours which enables us to pass some sort of judgment, correct or mistaken, upon moral questions as they arise.
Josiah Royce

The still small voice that makes you feel still smaller. *James A. Sanaker*

The fantastic thing which serves to make men cowards. *Adapted from Thomas Shadwell*

A blushing, shamefaced spirit that mutinies in a man's bosom. *William Shakespeare*

That undying serpent. *Percy Bysshe Shelley*

All inhibitions of a religion and ethical character.
Wilhelm Stekel

God's presence in man. *Emanuel Swedenborg*

A thousand witnesses. *Richard Taverner*

In most men, an anticipation of the opinion of others. *Henry J. Taylor*

Instinct bred in the house.
Henry David Thoreau

That little spark of celestial fire.
George Washington

Conscience and cowardice are really the same thing. *Oscar Wilde*

The soft whispers of the God in man.
Edward Young

Love is the source and substance . . . If it were not for our . . . need to love and to be loved there would be no conscience; there would remain only animal fear and animal aggression. *Gregory Zilboorg*

A voice doing its duty. *Anon.*

A thinking man's filter. *Anon.*

A cur that will let you get past it but that you cannot keep from barking. *Anon.*

Your moral personality. *Anon.*

Something that does not keep you from doing things, but from enjoying them. *Anon.*

That small inner voice that tells you that the tax collector might check your return. *Anon.*

That small inner voice that does not speak your language. *Anon.*

SEE ALSO BIBLE, BRAIN, CONFESSION, GUILT, MORALITY, REPENTANCE.

CONSCIOUSNESS

Evolution looking at itself and reflecting.
Pierre T. de Chardin

An illness—a real thorough-going illness.
Fedor M. Dostoievski

The name of a nonentity, and has no right to a place among first principles. *William James*

The inner light kindled in the soul . . . a music, strident or sweet, made by the friction of existence. *George Santayana*

CONSERVATION

The wise use of the earth and its resources for the lasting good of men. *Gifford Pinchot*

CONSERVATISM

A bag with a hole in it. *Josh Billings*

The politics of reality. *William F. Buckley 2*

Old ways . . . the safest and surest ways.
Edward Coke

An organized hypocrisy. *Benjamin Disraeli*

(That which) stands on man's confessed limitations . . . (It) has no inventions; it is all memory . . . believes in negative fate.
Ralph Waldo Emerson

To keep what progressiveness has accomplished.
R. H. Fulton

The search for a superior moral justification for selfishness. *John Kenneth Galbraith*

Distrust of the poeple tempered by fear.
William Gladstone

A philosophy that takes into account the essential differences between men, and, accordingly, makes provision for developing the different potentialities of each man. *Barry M. Goldwater*

Something that starts with the purchasing of a home and the birth of a child. *Max Gralnick*

On the whole, their policy meant that people had to fill up fewer forms than under the policies of other parties. *Alan P. Herbert*

Sometimes a symptom of sterility. Those who have nothing in them that can grow and develop must cling to what they have in beliefs, ideas and possessions. The sterile radical, too, is basically conservative. He is afraid to let go the ideals and beliefs he picked up in his youth lest his life be seen as empty and wasted. *Eric Hoffer*

Adherence to the old and tried, against the new and untried. *Abraham Lincoln*

Traditionalism become self-conscious and forensic. *C. Wright Mills*

To believe in thinking as you were brought up to think. *Charles S. Peirce*

Not the first by whom the new are tried, nor yet the last to lay the old aside.
Adapted from Alexander Pope

The worship of dead revolutions.
Clinton Rossiter

Those coercive arrangements which a still-lingering savageness makes requisite.
Herbert Spencer

An instinctive revulsion at any departure from the accepted way of doing and of looking at things.

Thorstein Veblen

The maintenance of conventions already in force.

Thorstein Veblen

SEE ALSO REPUBLICAN PARTY.

CONSERVATIVE

(A) quiet, equable, deadly holderon.

Stephen Vincent Benet

A statesman who is enamored of existing evils, as distinguished from the liberal, who wishes to replace them with others.   *Ambrose Bierce*

Victorians, Tudorians, ghosts surviving from the Middle Ages, and multitudes whose minds properly belong to palaeolithic times.

Robert Briffault

All great peoples ... slow to believe in novelties; patient of much error in actualities; deeply and forever certain of the greatness that is in law, in custom once solemnly established, and now recognized as just and final.   *Thomas Carlyle*

All conservatives are such from personal defects. They have been effeminated by position or nature, born halt and blind, through luxury of their parents, and can only, like invalids, act on the defensive.   *Ralph Waldo Emerson*

A conservative ... has a philosophy based upon proven values of the past. When we seek answers for the problems of today we look to the past to see if those problems existed. Generally, they have. So we ask: What was the answer? Did it work? If it did, let us try again.

Barry M. Goldwater

One who desires to retain the wisdom and the experience of the past and who is prepared to apply the best of that wisdom and experience to meet the changes which are inevitable in every new generation.   *Barry M. Goldwater*

The conservative doubts that the present can be bettered, and he tries to shape the future in the image of the present. He goes to the past for reassurance about the present.   *Eric Hoffer*

One who will not look at the new moon, out of respect for that ancient institution, the old one.

Douglas Jerrold

A man becomes a conservative at that moment in his life when he suddenly realises he has something to conserve.   *Eric Julber*

The "religious man" ... for he appeals to an authority beyond the vanity of Demos or Expediency and he trusts in the wisdom of our ancestors and in enduring values.   *Russell Kirk*

Very largely ... fear (of the future), with Anti-Communism replacing belief in freedom as a national cause and a whole list of hatreds and rejections and denials as ultimate objectives.

Archibald MacLeish

A man who wants the rules enforced so no one can make a pile the way he did.   *Gregory Nunn*

He learns how stocks will fall or rise, holds poverty the greatest vice. He thinks wit the bane of conversation, and says that learning spoils a nation.   *Adapted from Matthew Prior*

A man with two perfectly good legs who has never learned to walk.

Franklin Delano Roosevelt

One who admires radicals a century after they're dead.   *Leo C. Rosten*

A man who believes in reform, but not now.

Mort Sahl

The stalwart defender of things as they are.

Arthur M. Schlesinger 1

A man who thinks things ought to progress, but would rather they remained as they are.

James F. Stephen

The man for whom the law exists—the man of forms ... a tame man.   *Henry David Thoreau*

No man can be a conservative unless he has something to lose.   *James Warburg*

That staid come-over-with-the-conqueror type of mind.   *Adapted from William Watson*

(One) warmly, and unalterably, compassionate to the individual; his essential respect goes not so much to mankind as to Man.   *William S. White*

A man who believes nothing should be done for the first time.   *Alfred E. Wiggam*

A man who just sits and thinks, mostly sits.

Woodrow Wilson

One who is against the Democrats for what they are, and against the Republicans for what they are not.   *Anon.*

One who wears both belt and suspenders.

Anon.

One who can't see the difference between radicalism and an idea.   *Anon.*

SEE ALSO REPUBLICAN PARTY.

CONSISTENCY

To be as ignorant today as you were a year ago.

Bernard Berenson

To act in conformity with circumstances, and not to act always the same way under a change of circumstances.   *John C. Calhoun*

The hobgoblin of little minds, adored by little statesmen and philosophers and divines. With consistency a great soul has simply nothing to do.

Ralph Waldo Emerson

The quality of a stagnant mind.   *John Sloan*

A paste jewel that only cheap men cherish.

William Allen White

The last refuge of the unimaginative.

Oscar Wilde

The foundation of great statesmen.   *Anon.*

One who wears both belt and suspenders.

Anon.

CONSTANCY

A virtue particular to those who are about to be betrayed.   *Ambrose Bierce*

A dull sleepy quality at best.   *George Farquhar*

Merely an invention of self-love to win confidence; a method to place us above others and to render us depositories of the most important matters.   *La Rochefoucauld*

Two kinds...in love: one arises from continually discovering in the loved person new subjects for love, the other arises from our making a merit of being constant.   *La Rochefoucauld*

The besetting sin of the human race...the cause of most wars and practically all persecutions.

Freya Stark

That which is practiced best by the old and indifferent.   *Anon.*

CONSTITUTION

A vestment which accommodates itself to the body.   *Edmund Burke*

A law for rulers and people, equally in war and in peace, and covers with the shield of its protection all classes of men, at all times and under all circumstances.   *David Davis*

Should consist only of general provisions; the reason is...they must necessarily be permanent, and that they cannot calculate for the possible change of things.   *Alexander Hamilton*

The...constitution of a society is at once the expression and the consecration of its economic constitution.   *Pëtr A. Kropotkin*

A means of assuring that depositories of power cannot misemploy it.   *John Stuart Mill*

The work of time; one cannot provide in it too broad a power of amendment.   *Napoleon I*

A thing antecedent to a government, and a government is only the creature of a constitution. The constitution is not the act of its government, but of the people constituting a government.

Thomas Paine

Scraps of paper.   *Wilhelm I*

SEE ALSO AMERICAN CONSTITUTION, DEMOCRACY, GOVERNMENT, LAW, LIBERTY, SUPREME COURT.

CONSTITUTION, UNITED STATES

SEE AMERICAN CONSTITUTION.

CONTEMPLATION

SEE REFLECTION, SILENCE, STUDY, THOUGHT.

CONTEMPT

SEE LAUGHTER, RIDICULE, SATIRE.

CONTENTMENT

The utmost we can hope for in this world.

Joseph Addison

Enjoying one's labor.   *Jehiel Anav*

A kind of moral laziness. *Josh Billings*

The very epitome of depravity. *Max Brod*

The mind satisfied. *Eugene E. Brussell*

The all-in-all of life. *Thomas Campbell*

The power of getting out of any situation all that there is in it. *Gilbert Keith Chesterton*

The best powder for women's faces.
Dutch Proverb

More than kingdom. *English Proverb*

An impregnable fortress. *Epictetus*

The Philosopher's Stone, that turns all it touches into gold. *Benjamin Franklin*

Does not consist in heaping up more fuel, but in taking away some fire. *Thomas Fuller*

Simply refined indolence. *Richard Haliburton*

(The) feeling you are bearing with heroic resignation the irritating folly of others.
Jerome K. Jerome

The smother of invention. *Ethel W. Mumford*

A warm sty for eaters and sleepers.
Eugene O'Neill

Not what we have, but what we enjoy.
J. Petit-Senn

The only riches, the only quietness, the only happiness. *George Pettie*

Natural wealth. *Plato*

My crown. *William Shakespeare*

Our best having. *William Shakespeare*

To accept change gracefully. *James Stewart*

The conventional trinity of wine, woman and song. *Rexford G. Tugwell*

Being satisfied with what you haven't got.
Anon.

SEE ALSO FAITH, HAPPINESS.

CONTRACEPTION

SEE BIRTH CONTROL.

CONTRAST

This marvelous balance of beauty and disgust, magnificence and rats. *Ralph Waldo Emerson*

(That which) increases the splendor of beauty, but it disturbs its influence; it adds to its attractiveness, but diminishes its power. *John Ruskin*

CONTROVERSY

A battle in which spittle or ink replace the ... cannon ball. *Ambrose Bierce*

What is it but the falsehood flying off from all manner of conflicting true forces, and making such a loud dust-whirlwind,—that so the truths alone may remain, and embrace brother-like in some true resulting force? *Thomas Carlyle*

That which makes a subject interesting. *Anon.*

SEE ALSO ARGUMENTS, QUARRELING.

CONVALESCENCE

That part of the illness in which the patient is still alive. *Adapted from Leo Michel*

The part that makes the illness worth while.
George Bernard Shaw

CONVENT

Supreme egotism resulting in supreme self-denial. *Victor Hugo*

(A place which exists) not for the love of virtue, but the fear of vice. *Samuel Johnson*

They should only be retreats for persons unable to serve the public, or who have served it.
Samuel Johnson

CONVERSATION

Debate is masculine; conversation is feminine.
Amos Bronson Alcott

The feminine of silence. *Roland Alix*

A fair for the display of the minor mental commodities. *Ambrose Bierce*

Something that disappears into the television set.
Eugene E. Brussell

Consists in building on another man's observation, not overturning it.
Edward G. Bulwer-Lytton

To be prompt without being stubborn, to refute without argument, and to clothe great matters in motley garb. *Benjamin Disraeli*

An art in which a man has all mankind for his competitors. *Ralph Waldo Emerson*

A game of circles. *Ralph Waldo Emerson*

The last flower of civilization...our account of ourselves. *Ralph Waldo Emerson*

Where only such things are spoken and heard as we can reflect upon afterward with satisfaction; and without any mixture either of shame or repentance. *Desiderius Erasmus*

The soul of conversation is sympathy. *William Hazlitt*

Silence is the one great art of conversation. *William Hazlitt*

The best kind...is that which may be called thinking aloud. *William Hazlitt*

A few raisins...into the tasteless dough of existence. *O. Henry*

The slowest form of human communication. *Don Herold*

(Something that) could be enormously improved by the constant use of four simple words: "I do not know." *Emile Herzog*

Building a house, room by room, while we take visitors through it. *Emile Herzog*

The enemy of good wine and food. *Alfred Hitchcock*

Like playing on the harp; there is as much in laying the hands on the strings to stop their vibration as in twanging them to bring out the music. *Oliver Wendell Holmes 1*

The happiest...is that of which nothing is distinctly remembered, but a general effect of pleasing impression. *Samuel Johnson*

No competition, no vanity, but a calm quiet interchange of sentiments. *Samuel Johnson*

Telling people a little less than they want to know. *Franklin P. Jones*

Consists much less in showing a great deal of it than in bringing it out in others. *Jean de La Bruyère*

Anecdote, tempered by interruption. *Raymond Mortimer*

A game played with pruning shears in which each player cuts off his neighbor's voice as soon as it sprouts. *Jules Renard*

Like a salad, should have various ingredients and should be well stirred with salt, oil and vinegar. *Joaquin Setanti*

A phonograph with half-a-dozen records. You soon get tired of them all. *George Bernard Shaw*

The image of the mind. As the man is, so is his talk. *Publilius Syrus*

The secret...is never to open your mouth unless you have nothing to say. *Adapted from Oscar Wilde*

The profession of the mentally unemployed. *Oscar Wilde*

(An art which) should touch everything but concentrate on nothing. *Oscar Wilde*

The only proper intoxication. *Oscar Wilde*

Consists as much in listening as in talking agreeably. *Anon.*

Something that starts the moment you put your foot through the television set. *Anon.*

SEE ALSO ELOQUENCE, LANGUAGE, ORATOR, SPEECH, TALK, TONGUE, WORDS.

CONVERSION

(Not) repairing of the old building; but it takes all down and erects a new structure. *Joseph Alleine*

For all that psychology has to say, conversion might be what the convert thinks it is—the soul's discovery of God...To say that "the subconscious did it" does not prevent one from saying "God did it." *Charles A. Bennett*

A method of confirming others in their errors. *Ambrose Bierce*

(When) a man is wholly given unto God, body, soul, and spirit. *Robert Bolton*

"Regeneration," literally "to be reborn." *John S. Bonnell*

In the exchange of religions, the result of fear or opportunism. *Eugene E. Brussell*

May be estimated a gift. *William Cowper*

Self-purification, self-realization...a revolution in one's life. *Mohandas K. Gandhi*

Consists basically in the inculcation and fixation of proclivities and responses indigenous to the frustrated mind.   *Eric Hoffer*

To execute a mental and moral pirouette from one absurdity to a worse one.   *Elbert Hubbard*

A backslider from your own ideas to those of an inferior.   *Elbert Hubbard*

For one man conversion means the slaying of the beast within him; in another it brings the calm of conviction to an unquiet mind; for a third it is the entrance into a larger liberty and a more abundant life; and yet again it is the gathering into one of the forces of a soul at war with itself.

George Jackson

Conversion simply means turning around.

Vincent McNabb

Conversion is not implanting eyes, for they already exist; but giving them a right direction.

Plato

The process by which a man is received into the presence of God.   *Erik Routley*

Where a profound change in philosophy, ideology, or ethics occurs.   *Leon Salzman*

Primarily an unselfing.   *Edwin T. Starbuck*

SEE ALSO ASSIMILATION, MISSIONARY.

CONVICTION

What the boss thinks.   *Michael Farring*

At eighteen our convictions are hills from which we look; at forty-five they are caves in which we hide.   *F. Scott Fitzgerald*

Opinions which circumstances have temporarily backed.   *Henry S. Haskins*

The mainsprings of action, the driving powers of life. What a man lives are his convictions.

Francis C. Kelley

(The) dangerous enemies of truth.

Friedrich W. Nietzsche

Every conviction has it history, its primitive forms, its stage of tentativeness and error: it becomes a conviction only after having been, for a long time, not one, and then, for an even longer time, hardly one.   *Friedrich W. Nietzsche*

The conscience of the mind.

Mrs. Humphrey Ward

A belief which can be explained without getting angry. The opposite is prejudice.   *Anon.*

SEE ALSO BELIEF, CREED, DOCTRINE, DOGMA, FAITH.

COOKING

A way of giving and of making yourself desirable.

Michel Bourdin

An art, a noble science: cooks are gentlemen.

Robert Burton

An act of love.   *Alain Chapel*

A process of preparing food which would be speeded up fifty years by the use of zippers on canned goods.   *Russel Crouse*

The art of poisoning mankind by rendering the appetite still importunate, when the wants of nature are supplied.   *François de Fénelon*

One of those arts which most require to be done by persons of a religious nature.

Alfred North Whitehead

A scheme of shortening human life through overeating.   *Anon.*

With women a weapon to catch men by the stomach and watch it grow with the years.

Anon.

SEE ALSO FOOD, HUNGER, STOMACH, WIFE.

COOPERATION

A principle of specialization requiring man to work as one in common purpose with others in order to accomplish more.   *Eugene E. Brussell*

Cooperation, and not competition, is the life of trade.   *William Fitch*

Not a sentiment—it is an economic necessity.

Charles Steinmetz

COQUETRY

A circulating library in which we seldom ask twice for the same volume.   *Christian N. Bovee*

Waving fans, coy glances, cringes, and all such simpering humors.   *Ben Jonson*

The glances of a sinful eye, wavings of fans, treading of toes, biting the lip, the wanton gait.

Adapted from Thomas Middleton

A political institution; its purpose is the creation of legitimate power in the industrial sphere.

Peter Drucker

The thorn that guards the rose—easily trimmed off when once plucked.   *Donald G. Mitchell*

(A quality) of advantage only to the beautiful.

Propertius

The gentle art of making a man feel pleased with himself.   *Helen Rowland*

Mostly innocent cruelty.   *Anon.*

The art of gaining attention without intention.

Anon.

COQUETTE

A vain, foolish . . . girl who after a pretty thorough sampling of oneself prefers another.

Ambrose Bierce

Her pleasure is in lovers coy; when hers, she gives them not a thought; but, like the angler, takes more joy in fishing than in fishes caught.

Adapted from George Birdseye

A woman without any heart, who makes a fool of a man that hasn't got any head.

Madame Deluzy

A young lady of more beauty than sense, more accomplishments than learning, more charms of person than graces of the mind, more admirers than friends, more fools than wise men for attendants.   *Henry Wadsworth Longfellow*

(One) fair to no purpose, artful to no end.

Alexander Pope

Young without lovers, old without a friend; a fop their passion, but their prize a sot.

Adapted from Alexander Pope

A wishful winker.   *Anon.*

A woman to turn the head of a dolt.   *Anon.*

A female who believes that it is every man for herself.   *Anon.*

Self-lovers, and this lifelong passion is something no one can dislodge.   *Anon.*

CORPORATION

An ingenious device for obtaining individual profit without individual responsibility.

Ambrose Bierce

Corporations cannot commit treason, nor be outlawed, nor excommunicated, for they have no souls.   *Edward Coke*

Many lesser commonwealths in the bowels of a greater, like worms in the entrails of a natural man.   *Thomas Hobbes*

Corporations are invisible, immortal, and have no soul.   *Roger Manwood*

An artificial being, invisible, intangible, and existing only in the contemplation of the law . . . the mere creature of the law.

John Marshall

It is a body . . . has certainly a head—a new one every year; arms it has and very long ones, for it can reach anything . . . a throat to swallow the rights of the community, and a stomach to digest them . . . but who ever yet discovered . . . either bowels or a heart?   *Howel Walsh*

Like any natural person, except that it has no pants to kick or soul to damn, and, by God, it ought to have both.   *Anon.*

An artificial entity that can do everything but make love.   *Anon.*

SEE ALSO BUSINESS, CAPITALISM, COMMERCE.

CORPSE

(Something) like the cover of an old book, its contents torn out, and stript of its lettering and gilding . . . yet the work itself shall not be lost, for it will appear once more in a new and more beautiful edition.   *Benjamin Franklin*

A human been.   *Kay Goodman*

A human with no problems.   *Anon.*

A forgivable person.   *Anon.*

SEE ALSO DEATH, GRAVE.

CORRESPONDENCE

SEE LETTERS.

CORRUPTION

Everything we see before us today.   *Karl Barth*

God looked upon the earth, and, behold, it was corrupt; for all flesh had corrupted his way upon the earth.   *Bible: Genesis, VI, 12.*

The most infallible symptom of constitutional liberty. *Edward Gibbon*

An evil that grows respectable with age.

Voltaire

A tree whose branches are of an unmeasurable length. *Anon.*

COSMETICS

(That which) makes most women appear not as young as they are painted.

Adapted from Max Beerbohm

Crease paint. *Raymond J. Cvikota*

Cold water, morning and evening, is the best of all cosmetics. *Hebrew Proverb*

The act of tormenting skin with potions, staining cheeks with rouge, extending the line of the eyes with black coloring because of a dissatisfaction with God's plastic skill.

Adapted from Tertullian

The Devil's looking-glass. *Anon.*

Putting on another face on top of the one God has given you. *Anon.*

COSMOPOLITANISM

A citizen of the world. *Francis Bacon*

If a man be gracious and courteous to strangers.

Francis Bacon

Our country is the world—our countrymen are all mankind. *William L. Garrison*

To be really cosmopolitan a man must be at home even in his own country. *Thomas W. Higginson*

Signifies being polite to every country except your own. *Thomas Hood*

(An attitude) likely to be an alibi for not doing one's duty to one's own people.

Mordecai M. Kaplan

Only a parliament of nations, with law and power...that...will bring on earth the rule which is in heaven, the rule of Equity.

David Lubin

A luxury which only the upper classes can afford; the common people are hopelessly bound to their native shores. *Benito Mussolini*

My country is the world, and my religion is to do good. *Thomas Paine*

International integration of an individual's mind.

Anon.

Living within a plurality of loyalties. *Anon.*

COSMOS

SEE UNIVERSE.

COUGH

A convulsion of the lungs, vellicated by some sharp serosity. *Samuel Johnson*

A dry cough is the trumpeter of death.

John Ray

COUNSEL

SEE ADVICE.

COUNTERFEITER

SEE PLAGIARIST.

COUNTRY

The country of every man is that one where he lives best. *Aristophanes*

That which is created with one's own toil and sweat. *David Ben-Gurion*

A land flowing with milk and honey.

Bible: Exodus, III, 8.

The common parent of all. *Cicero*

I...do not call the sod, under my feet my country. But language, religion, laws, government, blood—identity of these makes men of one country. *Samuel Taylor Coleridge*

A return to self, to one's own roots, to growth.

Franz Kafka

The token of the mission which God has given you to fulfill in humanity. *Giuseppe Mazzini*

A fellowship of free and equal men bound together in a brotherly concord of labor towards a single end. *Giuseppe Mazzini*

Our country is wherever we are well off.

John Milton

The world. *Thomas Paine*

That spot to which our heart is bound. *Voltaire*

That which focuses a people. *Israel Zangwill*

SEE ALSO NATION, STATE.

COUNTRYSIDE

The country, as distinguished from the woods, is of man's creation. The savage has no country.
Amos Bronson Alcott

A place no wise man will choose to live in, unless he has something to do which can be better done there. *Samuel Johnson*

The country is lyric,—the town dramatic.
Henry Wadsworth Longfellow

A series of lonely walks and sitting around.
George Bernard Shaw

A kind of healthy grave. *Sydney Smith*

A damp sort of place where all sorts of birds fly about uncooked. *Anon.*

SEE ALSO FARM, NATURE.

COURAGE

I think the Romans call it Stoicism.
Joseph Addison

Not to die but to live. *Vittorio Alfieri*

The lovely virtue—the rib of Himself that God sent down to His children. *James M. Barrie*

The integrating strength that causes one to overcome tragedy. *Eugene E. Brussell*

(That which) lies half-way between rashness and cowardice. *Miguel de Cervantes*

A contradiction in terms. It means a strong desire to live taking the form of readiness to die.
Gilbert Keith Chesterton

The quality which guarantees all others.
Winston S. Churchill

That virtue which champions the cause of right.
Cicero

Generosity of the highest order, for the brave are prodigal of the most precious things
Charles Caleb Colton

Courage is clearly a readiness to risk self-humiliation. *Nigel Dennis*

Courage is fire, and bullying is smoke.
Benjamin Disraeli

Consists in equality to the problems before us.
Ralph Waldo Emerson

Consists in the power of self-recovery.
Ralph Waldo Emerson

Inventions, inspirations, flashes of genius.
Ralph Waldo Emerson

A virtue only so far as it is directed by prudence. *François de Fénelon*

Grace under pressure. *Ernest Hemingway*

A matter of red corpuscles. *Elbert Hubbard*

A quality so necessary for maintaining virtue, that it is always respected, even when it is associated with vice. *Samuel Johnson*

A peculiar kind of fear. *Charles Kennedy*

Never to let your actions be influenced by your fears. *Arthur Koestler*

Doing unwitnessed what one would be capable of doing before the whole world.
La Rochefoucauld

The power to let go of the familiar.
Raymond Lindquist

The ladder on which all the other virtues mount. *Clare Boothe Luce*

The most common and vulgar of the virtues.
Herman Melville

To live dangerously. *Benito Mussolini*

Knowing what not to fear. *Plato*

What preserves our liberty, safety, life, and our homes and parents, our country and children. Courage comprises all things. *Plautus*

To take hard knocks like a man when occasion calls. *Plautus*

Doing what you are afraid to do. There can be no courage unless you're afraid.
Edward V. Rickenbacker

Indifference to personal misfortunes.
Bertrand A. Russell

Personal courage is really a very subordinate virtue—merely the distinguishing mark of a subaltern—a virtue...in which we are surpassed by the lower animals. *Arthur Schopenhauer*

A scorner of things which inspire fear. *Seneca*

A perfect sensibility of the measure of danger, and a mental willingness to endure it. *William T. Sherman*

The footstool of the Virtues, upon which they stand. *Robert Louis Stevenson*

Resistance to fear, mastery of fear—not absence of fear. *Mark Twain*

Being scared to death—and saddling up anyway. *John Wayne*

Fear that has said its prayers. *Anon.*

Being afraid yet pushing on. *Anon.*

Merely the animal instinct to survive. *Anon.*

SEE ALSO BRAVERY, GALLANTRY, HEROISM.

COURT

SEE JUSTICE, JURY, LAW, LAWYERS.

COURTESAN

In all ages a popular woman with men, hence, a woman who never dies. *Albert Benson*

Women with maids who wear kimonos all day and read French novels. *Anon.*

The aristocracy of whoredom. *Anon.*

A woman whom a fortune makes. *Anon.*

A fund loving girl. *Anon*

SEE ALSO MISTRESS, PROSTITUTE.

COURTESY

Subduing our inner state while presenting to the world an agreeable creature. *Eugene E. Brussell*

The courtly manners of any two-legged predatory animal. *Adapted from Elbert Hubbard*

Fictitious benevolence. *Samuel Johnson*

Benevolence in trifles. *William Pitt*

The art of choosing among one's real thoughts. *Abel Stevens*

The art of concealing natural impulses. *Anon.*

A gift notable in well-bred people and courtesans. *Anon.*

SEE ALSO BREEDING, MANNERS, POLITENESS.

COURTSHIP

Courtship to marriage is but as the music in the playhouse till the curtain's drawn. *William Congreve*

Courtship (is) to marriage, as a very witty prologue to a very dull play. *William Congreve*

On the higher physical level...serves the extremely important function of deepening the channels of higher psychical and spiritual love. *John M. Cooper*

To take aim kneeling. *Douglas Jerrold*

The art of the girl not showing her hand till you ask for it. *Franklin P. Jones*

Sweet reluctant amorous delay. *John Milton*

A snappy introduction to a tedious book. *Wilson Mizner*

A number of quiet attentions, not so pointed as to alarm, nor so vague as not to be understood. *Lawrence Sterne*

It is natural for a man to woo a woman, not for a woman to woo a man: the loser seeks what he has lost (the rib). *Talmud: Nidda, 31b.*

That period during which the female decides whether or not she can do any better. *Anon.*

That part of a woman's life that comes between the lipstick and the broomstick. *Anon.*

A lively period before a sentence. *Anon.*

A man pursuing a woman until she catches him. *Anon.*

SEE ALSO HONEYMOON, MARRIAGE.

COVENANT

That day the Lord made a covenant with Abraham, saying: "Unto thy seed have I given this land." *Bible: Genesis, IX, 15.*

I will establish my covenant between me and thee, and thy seed after thee, in their generations, for an everlasting covenant, to be a God unto thee, and to thy seed after thee.

Bible: Genesis, XVII, 7.

A symbolic act of the highest pregnancy, revived three thousand years later as the root of modern nationalism and democracy. For the Covenant was concluded . . . between God and the whole people, every member in complete equality.   *Hans Kohn*

The Magna Charta of Judaism.

George M. Moore

Torah, God, and circumcision are all called Covenant. All three are inseparably linked together.

Zohar: Leviticus, 73b.

SEE ALSO CIRCUMCISION, JEWS, JUDAISM.

COVETOUSNESS

Covetousness has for its mother unlawful desire, for its daughter injustice, and for its friend violence.   *Arabian Proverb*

The moving spirit of civilization from its first dawn to the present day; wealth, and again wealth . . . wealth, not of society, but of the puny individual, was its only and final aim.

Friedrich Engels

The greatest of all monsters, as well as the root of all evil.   *William Penn*

If you have a longing desire to possess the goods which you have not, though you may say you would not possess them unjustly, you are . . . covetous.   *Saint Francis de Sales*

SEE ALSO AVARICE, ENVY.

COWARD

One who in a perilous emergency thinks with his legs.   *Ambrose Bierce*

No . . . man is born a coward . . . Truth makes a man of courage, and guilt makes that man of courage a coward.   *Daniel Defoe*

(One who) only threatens when he is safe.

Johann W. Goethe

Sinners.   *John G. Neihardt*

The summer soldier and the sunshine patriot.

Thomas Paine

One who is always in danger.

Portuguese Proverb

You are the hare of whom the proverb goes, whose valor plucks dead lions by the beard.

Adapted from William Shakespeare

The coward calls himself cautious.

Publilius Syrus

A man in whom the instinct of self-preservation acts normally.   *Sultana Zoraya*

One who is brave only when he is safe.   *Anon.*

Caution is ourselves, despicableness in others.

Anon.

Those who fear death the most.   *Anon.*

SEE ALSO BRAVERY, FEAR, PACIFIST.

COWARDICE

To know what is right and not do it.   *Confucius*

Almost always simply a lack of ability to suspend the functioning of the imagination.

Ernest Hemingway

One too weak to face the world and too weak to leave it.   *Adapted from Charles Kingsley*

To sin by silence.   *Abraham Lincoln*

Defined on the basis of acts performed.

Jean-Paul Sartre

The surest protection against temptation.

Mark Twain

CRAZY

SEE INSANITY, MADNESS.

CREATION (WORLD)

It is not difficult for one seal to make many impressions exactly alike, but to vary shapes almost infinitely, which is what God has done in creation.   *Robert Bellarmine*

Creation took place in eternity as an interior act of the divine mystery of life. The biblical conception of creation is only the reflection of this interior act in the consciousness of primitive man.

Nicholas Berdyaev

In the beginning God created the Heaven and the earth. And the earth was without form, and void; and darkness was upon the face of the deep. And the Spirit of God moved upon the face of the waters. And God said, Let there be light; and there was light.   *Bible: Genesis, I, 1.*

In the beginning was the Word, and the Word was with God, and the Word was God.
                                                    Bible: John I, 1.

The transformation of an otherwise chaotic world into a thing of order and beauty . . . the shaping of an indifferent matter into a world of value.
                                                    John E. Boodin

A mystery.   *Thomas Browne*

The intention of God that all created things should represent the likeness of God, so far as their proper nature will admit.   *Dante*

Means . . . that He has infused His own being into another thing which thereby has taken an independent existence of its own.   *Erich Frank*

Simply an overwhelming outpouring, the overflow of infinite goodness.   *Thomas J. Higgins*

Allah created men of congealed blood.
                                                    Koran, XCVI.

Heaven and earth, center and circumference were made in the same instant of time . . . and man was created by the Trinity on the 26th of October, 4004 B.C. at 9 o'clock in the morning.
                                                    John Lightfoot

The will of God.   *Moses Maimonides*

The only admissable moral theory of Creation is that the Principle of Good cannot at once and altogether subdue the powers of evil, either physical or moral.   *John Stuart Mill*

With ten utterances was the world created.
                                                    Mishna: Abot, V, 1.

The bible of the Deist. He there reads in the handwriting of the Creator himself, the certainty of his existence, and the immutability of his power.
                                                    Thomas Paine

He but spoke the word, and by that intelligible and eternal one . . . were all things created.
                                                    Saint Augustine

Love which works good to all things pre-existing overflowingly in the Good . . . moved itself to creation.   *Saint Augustine*

God has made all things out of nothing: because . . . even although the world has been made of some material, that very same material has been made out of nothing.   *Saint Augustine*

God created heaven and earth only . . . that men should fear.   *Talmud: Sabbath, 31b.*

SEE ALSO ADAM, EVOLUTION, UNIVERSE, WORLD.

CREATIVITY

To strive consciously for an object and to engage in engineering—that is, incessantly and eternally to make new roads, wherever they may lead.
                                                    Fëdor M. Dostoievski

In the creative state a man is taken out of himself. He lets down . . . a bucket into his subconscious, and draws up something which is normally beyond his reach. He mixes this thing with his normal experiences, and out of the mixture he makes a work of art.   *Edward M. Forster*

Discontent translated into art.   *Eric Hoffer*

The ability to "introduce order into the randomness of nature."   *Eric Hoffer*

Psychologically it appears to be closely associated with the sense of security and the desire for perfection.   *Ernest Jones*

A type of learning process where the teacher and pupil are located in the same individual.
                                                    Arthur Koestler

The defeat of habit by originality.   *George Lois*

It is not the finding of a thing, but the making something out of it after it is found.
                                                    James Russell Lowell

A thing of degree, not of kind . . . all persons possess it to a greater or less degree in each of the many areas of human expression.
                                                    F. G. Macomber

(When) the individual has made something new to himself that is satisfying and . . . useful to him, if he has related things that were previously unrelated in his experience, and if the product is 'surprising' (that is, new) to him.   *Alice Miel*

The power to connect the seemingly unconnected.
                                                    William Plomer

To think more efficiently.   *Pierre Reverdy*

The movement of the internal towards the external and not a movement of the external on the surface.
Pierre Reverdy

To live means to create. *Milton Steinberg*

Merely a plus name for regular activity... any activity becomes creative when the doer cares about doing it right, or better. *John Updike*

A method of progress. Conformity... maintains the *status quo*. *Kimball Wiles*

The impulse to find some possibilities of rest in the bewildering phantasmagoria of the outer world. *W. R. Worringer*

SEE ALSO ART, ARTISTS, COMPOSER, INVENTION, MUSIC, PAINTING, SCULPTURE, WRITING.

CREDIT

The only enduring testimonial to man's confidence in man. *James Blish*

A promise to pay. *Ralph Waldo Emerson*

The lifeblood of commerce. *Elbert Hubbard*

(Something) proportioned to the cash which a man has in his chest. *Adapted from Juvenal*

The economic judgment on the morality of a man.
Karl Marx

That canker at the heart of national prosperity, the imaginary riches of paper credit.
Thomas Love Peacock

A condition of human relationships. It binds the future to the present by the confidence we have in the integrity of those with whom we deal.
James T. Shotwell

The life blood of industry, and the control of credit is the control of all society.
Upton Sinclair

A socially irresponsible act to induce people to get deeper into debt. *Anon.*

A device that gets better the less it is used.
Anon.

CREDITOR

Creditors are a superstitious sect, great observers of set days and times. *Benjamin Franklin*

A creditor is worse than a master; for a master owns only your person, a creditor owns your dignity, and can belabor that. *Victor Hugo*

A body without a soul. *Anon.*

The people who come because the customers didn't. *Anon.*

CREDULITY

The characteristic of the present age.
Benjamin Disraeli

To swallow and follow. *Charlotte P. Gilman*

Man's weakness, but the child's strength.
Charles Lamb

The most costly of all follies... It is the chief occupation of mankind. *Henry Louis Mencken*

The only disadvantage of honest hearts.
Philip Sidney

CREED

Man's creed is that he believes in God, and therefore in mankind, but not that he believes in a creed. *Leon Baeck*

The best... is charity toward the creeds of others.
John Billings

My creed is: he is safe that does his best, and death's a doom sufficient for the rest.
William Cowper

A disease of the intellect.
Ralph Waldo Emerson

The grammar of religion. *Henry Fielding*

A sacred total to which nothing may be added, and from which nothing may be taken away.
James A. Froude

To hate man and worship God seems to be the sum of all creeds. *Robert G. Ingersoll*

Nothing but the mere result of chance and temperament. *Joseph H. Shorthouse*

I use the creeds to express, to conserve, and to deepen my belief in God. *William Temple*

Creeds are but branches of a tree.
Ella W. Wilcox

SEE ALSO BELIEF, DOCTRINE, DOGMA.

CRIME

The greatest . . . are caused by surfeit, not by want. Men do not become tyrants in order that they may not suffer cold.   *Aristotle*

An act committed or omitted in violation of a public law either forbidding or commanding it.
                              William Blackstone

The culmination of a complex series of inevitable forces at work in the physical and social environment of the individual.   *Abraham A. Brill*

A line you adopt to make money you don't deserve.   *John Coates*

A breach of faith with the community of mankind.   *Joseph Conrad*

A name for the most obvious, extreme, and directly dangerous forms of . . . departure from the norm in manners and customs.   *Havelock Ellis*

Whoever profits by crime is guilty of it.
                                  French Proverb

The . . . source of crime consists in . . . one man's possessing in abundance that of which another man is destitute.   *William Godwin*

The source of every crime is some defect of the understanding, or some error in reasoning, or some sudden force of the passions.
                                  Thomas Hobbes

A product of social excess.   *Nikolai Lenin*

An overhead you have to pay if you want to live in the city.   *George Moscone*

A logical extension of the sort of behavior that is often considered perfectly respectable in legitimate business.   *Robert Rice*

Only the retail department of what, in wholesale, we call penal law.   *George Bernard Shaw*

The only big business to escape government meddling.   *Anon.*

SEE ALSO JUDGE, JUSTICE, LAW, LAWYERS, MURDER, PRISON, PUNISHMENT.

CRIMINAL

An atheist, though he doesn't always know it.
                              Honoré de Balzac

To the liberal, a victim of society. To the conservative, a person of weak character.
                              Eugene E. Brussell

One who does by illegal means what all the rest of us do legally.   *Elbert Hubbard*

Those who turn preachers under the gallows.
                                  Italian Proverb

An enemy of the human race.   *Latin Proverb*

The type of the strong man in unfavorable surroundings, the strong man made sick.
                              Friedrich W. Nietzsche

Creatures who write crooked lines in the book of their lives.   *Adapted from Karl Rahner*

A person with predatory instincts who has not sufficient capital to form a corporation.
                                  Howard Scott

It could probably be shown by facts and figures that there is no distinctly native American criminal class except Congress.   *Mark Twain*

Those who, along with some judges, take the law into their own hands.   *Anon.*

In the USA, he who knows his rights rather than his wrongs.   *Anon.*

Someone who gets caught.   *Anon.*

SEE ALSO MURDERER, PRISON.

CRISIS

Crises refine life. In them you discover what you are.   *Allan Chalmers*

May be nothing less than God's call to us to reach a new level of humanity.   *Samuel H. Miller*

Times that try men's souls.   *Thomas Paine*

The crisis of yesterday is the joke of tomorrow.
                              Herbert G. Wells

The peacetime relationship between two nations.
                                      Anon.

SEE ALSO TROUBLE.

CRITICISM

The avocation of assessing the failures of better men.   *Nelson Algren*

A gift, an intuition, a matter of tact and flair; it cannot be taught or demonstrated,—it is an art.
Henry F. Amiel

A disinterested endeavor to learn and propagate the best that is known and thought in the world.
Matthew Arnold

The test of a democracy. *David Ben-Gurion*

(Something that) does not depend upon a superior principle in men, but upon superior knowledge.
Edmund Burke

That in which the critic is not the antagonist so much as the rival of the author. *Isaac D'Israeli*

An instinctive activity of the civilized mind.
Thomas Stearns Eliot

Literary criticism is an art, like the writing of tragedies or the making of love, and, similarly, does not pay. *Clifton Fadiman*

The adventure of the soul among masterpieces.
Anatole France

To appreciate, to appropriate, to take intellectual possession, to establish in fine a relation with the criticised thing and make it one's own.
Henry James

Growing important and formidable at very small expense. *Samuel Johnson*

Distorting the general scope and purpose of an author to one's own particular and private spleen.
Adapted from Ben Jonson

The most agreeable of all amusements.
Henry H. Kames

(That which) takes from us that of being deeply moved by very beautiful things.
Jean de La Bruyère

A wise scepticism. *James Russell Lowell*

The art of appraising others at one's own value.
George Jean Nathan

The art wherewith a critic tries to guess himself into a share of the artist's fame.
George Jean Nathan

To distinguish, to analyze, and separate from its adjuncts, the virtue by which a picture, a landscape, a fair personality in life or in a book, produces this special impression of beauty or pleasure, to indicate what the source of that impression is, and under what conditions it is experienced. *Walter Pater*

Regarding the author's end, since none can encompass more than they intend.
Adapted from Alexander Pope

A practice which strips the tree of both caterpillars and blossoms.
Adapted from Jean Paul Richter

A sort of indirect self-exhibition.
Paul Rosenfeld

A serious and public function; it shows the race assimilating the individual, dividing the immortal from the mortal part of a soul.
George Santayana

An attempt to express what the artist tried to express. *Adapted from Joel E. Spingarn*

(That which) recognizes in every work of art an organism governed by its own law.
Joel E. Spingarn

The aim . . . is to distinguish what is essential.
Arthur Symons

You do not get a man's most effective criticism until you provoke him. Severe truth is expressed with some bitterness. *Henry David Thoreau*

Records the adventures of one's soul among masterpieces. *John Wain*

A majestic office, perhaps an art, perhaps even a church. *Walt Whitman*

Three questions are essential . . . What is the author's object? How far has he accomplished it? How far is that object worthy of approbation?
Nathaniel P. Willis

Something you can avoid by saying nothing, doing nothing and being nothing. *Anon.*

Impolite writing in the presence of humbug.
Anon.

SEE ALSO REVIEWERS.

CRITICS

A bundle of biases held loosely together by a sense of taste. *Whitney Balliett*

Eunuchs in harem: they know how its done, they've seen it done every day, but they're unable to do it themselves. *Brendan Behan*

A person who boasts himself hard to please because nobody tries to please him.

Ambrose Bierce

Those cut-throat bandits in the paths of fame.

Robert Burns

A servile race, who in mere want of fault all merit place; who blind obedience pay to ancient schools, bigots to Greece, and slaves to musty rules. *Adapted from Charles Churchill*

Usually people who would have been poets, historians, biographers, if they could; they have tried their talents at one or the other, and have failed; therefore they turn critics.

Samuel Taylor Coleridge

Disinterested thieves of our good name; cool, sober murderers of their neighbor's fame.

Adapted from Samuel Taylor Coleridge

Fools...I write at them, not to them.

William Congreve

He (who) is forced to be literate about the illiterate, witty about the witless and coherent about the incoherent. *John Crosby*

Venomous serpents that delight in hissing.

W. B. Daniel

Men who have failed in literature and art.

Benjamin Disraeli

They who write ill, and they who never dared to write. *Adapted from John Dryden*

The clerk. *Henry Fielding*

He who relates the adventures of his soul among masterpieces. *Anatole France*

Brushers of noblemen's clothes.

George Herbert

The critic takes a book in one hand, and uses the other to paint himself with. When his work is done, we may fail to find the book in it, but we are sure to find him. *Josiah G. Holland*

Nature, when she...manufactured and patented her authors, contrived to make critics out of the chips that were left. *Oliver Wendell Holmes 1*

Men who quarrel over the motive of a book that never had any. *Elbert Hubbard*

A man who expects miracles.

James G. Huneker

A torch-bearing outrider, the interpreter par excellence. *Henry James*

An insect. *Samuel Johnson*

A certain race of men that either imagine it their duty, or make it their amusement, to hinder the reception of every work of learning or genius.

Samuel Johnson

The only independent source of information. The rest is advertising. *Pauline Kael*

Sentinels in the grand army of letters, stationed at the corners of newspapers and reviews to challenge every new author.

Henry Wadsworth Longfellow

A reading-machine, always wound up and going.

James Russell Lowell

He who would write and can't write.

James Russell Lowell

The sorcerer who makes some hidden spring gush forth unexpectedly under our feet.

François Mauriac

The lot of critics is to be remembered by what they failed to understand. *George M. Moore*

(Something) no chronically happy man is.

George Jean Nathan

A man of such infinite wisdom and flawless taste that any opinion he may utter is to be accepted immediately and without question—unless you happen to disagree with him.

George Oppenheimer

A legless man who teaches running.

Channing Pollock

The men with muck-rake. *Theodore Roosevelt*

The secretary of the public...who does not wait to take dictation...who divines, who decides, who expresses every morning what everybody is thinking. *Charles A. Sainte-Beuve*

A man whose watch is five minutes ahead of other people's watches. *Charles A. Sainte-Beuve*

A man who leaves no turn unstoned.

George Bernard Shaw

A most stupid and malignant race...an unsuccessful author turned critic.

Percy Bysshe Shelley

(One who) gives directions to the town to cry it up or run it down.   *Jonathan Swift*

What we ask of him is that he should find out for us more than we can find out for ourselves.

Arthur Symons

The public is the only critic whose opinion is worth anything at all.   *Mark Twain*

A necessary evil, and criticism is an evil necessity.   *Carolyn Wells*

One who tells the artist what he really meant.

Robert Zwickey

Detractors of their betters.   *Anon.*

Someone you read to discover whether you liked it or not.   *Anon.*

A eunuch—he knows what to do but can't do it.

Anon.

The stupid who discuss the wise.   *Anon.*

CROMWELL, OLIVER (1599-1658)

A perfect master of all the arts of simulation and of dissimulation.   *George Bate*

A man in whom ambition had not wholly suppressed, but only suspended, the sentiments of religion.   *Edmund Burke*

He stood bare, not cased in...coat-of-mail: he grappled like a giant, face to face, heart to heart, with the naked truth of things. I plead guilty to valuing such a man beyond all other sorts of men.

Thomas Carlyle

A strong-minded, rough-built Englishman, with a character thoroughly English, and exceedingly good-natured.   *Thomas De Quincey*

He works, plots, fights, in rude affairs, with squires, lords, kings, his craft compares.

Adapted from Ralph Waldo Emerson

A brave bad man.   *Edward Hyde*

He nothing common did, or mean,
Upon that memorable scene,

But with his keener eye
The axe's edge did try.   *Andrew Marvell*

A practical mystic, the most formidable and terrible of all combinations. A man who combines inspiration...derived...from close communion with the supernatural and the celestial, a man who has that inspiration and adds to it the energy of a mighty man of action.

Lord Rosebery

In appearance extremely religious, he preaches eloquently to the soldiers, persuading them to live according to God's laws; and to render his persuasions more efficacious he avails himself of tears.

Giovanni Sagredo

The most terrible of all charlatans.   *Voltaire*

CROSS

The death of death, and the defeat of sin, the beautification of martyrdom, the raising to the skies of voluntary sacrifice, the defiance of pain.

Henry F. Amiel

The symbol of an Elder Brother who went into the far country to manifest the Father's forgiving love.

Henry S. Coffin

There and there only is the power to save.

William Cowper

We do not attach any intrinsic virtue to the Cross; this would be sinful and idolatrous. Our veneration is referred to Him who died upon it.

James C. Gibbons

God's way of uniting suffering with love.

Georgia Harkness

A throne of God's revelation.

Cleland B. McAfee

The way of light.   *Medieval Latin Proverb*

The inversion of all human values. The human is put to death; and out of death comes life.

John C. Murray

The way to bliss.   *Francis Quarles*

By the wood of the Cross the work of the Word of God was made manifest to all.   *Saint Irenaeus*

The only valid symbol for the life of good men.

J. C. Schroeder

A union of the perfect justice and love in response to the sacrifice demanded by the Father.

Sister Mary Immaculate Creek

The symbol and the reality of the immense labor of the centuries which has little by little raised up the created spirit and brought it back to the depths of the divine context.

Sister Mary Immaculate Creek

Ladders that lead to Heaven.   *Samuel Smiles*

Either the darkest spot of all in the mystery of existence, or a searchlight by the aid of which we may penetrate the surrounding gloom.

B. H. Streeter

The fitting close of a life of rejection, scorn, and defeat.   *James Thomson*

The Jacob's ladder by which we ascend into the highest heaven.   *Thomas Traherne*

The victorious struggle of Life over and through death.   *E. I. Watkin*

SEE ALSO CHRIST, CHRISTIANITY, HOLINESS, RELIGION, SALVATION.

CROWD

A crowd is not company, and faces are but a gallery of pictures, and talk but a tinkling cymbol, where there is no love.   *Francis Bacon*

The collective wisdom of individual ignorance.

Thomas Carlyle

Accumulated cruelty.   *Lord Halifax*

The worst of tyrants.   *Homer*

Wherever there is...untruth.

Sören Kierkegaard

A mind without subtlety, a mind without compassion, a mind, finally, uncivilized.

Robert Lindner

(A body that) is always caught by appearance and the crowd is all there is in the world.

Niccolo Machiavelli

A quick way of loosing one's identity.   *Anon.*

A body of people who are more likely to err than individuals.   *Anon.*

A fatal condition to thought.   *Anon.*

SEE ALSO MASSES, MOB, MULTITUDE, PEOPLE (THE), POPULACE.

CRUELTY

The first attribute of the Devil.   *Henry G. Bohn*

To beat a cripple with his own crutches.

Thomas Fuller

A tyrant that's always attended with fear.

Thomas Fuller

(That which) proceeds from a vile mind, and often from a cowardly heart.   *John Harington*

Pleasure in forcing one's will upon other people.

Bertrand A. Russell

SEE ALSO MOB, SAVAGE, TYRANNY.

CRYING

SEE TEARS.

CUCKHOLD

Company makes cuckolds.   *John Clarke*

Cuckolds are Christians the world over.

Thomas Fuller

To wear a horn and not know it.   *John Lyly*

The one who is the last to know about it.   *Anon.*

SEE ALSO ADULTERY.

CULTURE

The best that has been said and thought in the world.   *Matthew Arnold*

Culture is...properly described not as having its origin in curiosity, but as having its origin in the love of perfection: it is a study of perfection.

Matthew Arnold

The passion for sweetness and light...the passion for making them prevail.   *Matthew Arnold*

There is no better motto which it can have than these words of Bishop Wilson, "To make reason and the will of God prevail."   *Matthew Arnold*

The acquiring of culture is the developing of an avid hunger for knowledge and beauty.

Jesse L. Bennett

A way of coping with the world by defining it in detail.   *Malcolm Bradbury*

The great law of culture is: Let each become all that he was created capable of being...casting off all...noxious adhesions, and show himself at length in his own shape and stature, be these what they may. *Thomas Carlyle*

Keeping up six conversations when there are twelve in the room. *Ernest Dimnet*

To overpower nationality.

Ralph Waldo Emerson

All that which gives the mind possession of its own powers. *Ralph Waldo Emerson*

A product of sublimation. *Sigmund Freud*

To...do with our own hands all the necessary labor, from the highest and most complicated...to the coarsest and hardest and meanest.

Aaron D. Gordon

Always a product of mixing. *Friedrich Hertz*

The sum of all the forms of art, of love and of thought, which, in the course of centuries, have enabled man to be less enslaved. *Emile Herzog*

The sum of special knowledge that accumulates in any large united family and is the common property of all its members. *Aldous Huxley*

(That which) is commissioned to convert, as far as lies within its power, pain into enjoyment, necessity into freedom. *Jacob Klatzkin*

To have known the best, and to have known it for the best. *John W. Mackail*

An order of sensory preferences.

Marshall McLuhan

The essence of a self-reliant and autonomous culture is an unshakable egoism.

Henry Louis Mencken

Man's adaptive dimension. *Ashley Montagu*

Man's achievement...exists within the world of grace—God's Kingdom. *Helmut R. Niebuhr*

It is what, seven centuries from now, writers of dreadful texts will instruct college freshmen what we meant, even if now we don't know what we mean. *Michael Novak*

The concrete expression of values too pervasive to be expressed only in words, except centuries later in academic circles. *Michael Novak*

What the rich and the new-rich try to fill their lives with when sexuality falls short.

Michael Novak

Religion externalized...and bears the imprints of its molding by Christianity. *Edmund A. Opitz*

The harmonious development of all the powers and capacities of man. *Felix Perles*

(That which) imparts both light and sweetness to the soul which has the eyes to see. *Philo*

What your butcher would have if he were a surgeon. *Mary P. Poole*

To enhance and intensify one's vision of that synthesis of truth and beauty which is the highest and deepest reality. *John C. Powys*

An acquired taste. *John C. Powys*

The final wall, against which one leans one's back in a god-forsaken chaos. *John C. Powys*

To prevent the expression of everything: that is the...function of culture. *Philip Rieff*

The sum total of man's spiritual values.

C. Bezalel Sherman

The substance...is religion and the form of religion is culture. *Paul Tillich*

An instrument wielded by professors to manufacture professors, who when their turn comes, will manufacture professors. *Simone Weil*

Anything that people do and monkeys don't.

Anon.

The product of versatility and leisure, aided and abetted by some cash. *Anon.*

SEE ALSO CIVILIZATION, CLASSICS, LITERATURE, RELIGION.

CUNNING

The dwarf of wisdom. *William R. Alger*

A sinister or crooked wisdom. *Francis Bacon*

The faculty that distinguishes a weak animal or person from a strong one. *Ambrose Bierce*

Refined policy. *Edmund Burke*

The dark sanctuary of incapacity.

Lord Chesterfield

Knowledge that is divorced from justice. *Cicero*

Strength withheld. *Ralph Waldo Emerson*

A characteristic of animals which is called discretion in men.   *Jean de La Fontaine*

What you are when you rush to get ahead and are not wise.   *Anon.*

SEE ALSO CLEVERNESS.

CUPID

A blind gunner.   *George Farquhar*

The greatest little enemy.
                                        Oliver Wendell Holmes 1

A murderous boy.   *Meleager*

A fiery archer making pain his joy.   *Meleager*

Love's heralds.   *William Shakespeare*

Regent of love.   *William Shakespeare*

A knavish lad.   *William Shakespeare*

The greatest little god.   *Robert Southey*

SEE ALSO LOVE, LOVERS.

CURIOSITY

The first and simplest emotion which we discover in the human mind.   *Edmund Burke*

An itching humor or a kind of longing to see that which is not to be seen, to do that which ought not to be done, to know that secret which should not be known, to eat of the forbidden fruit.
                                            Robert Burton

That low vice.   *Lord Byron*

Delight.   *Walter Charleton*

Free-wheeling intelligence.   *Alistair Cooke*

The secret of happiness.   *Norman Douglas*

Ill manners in another's house.   *Thomas Fuller*

Envy and idleness married together.
                                            Thomas Fuller

Little more than another name for hope.
                                    Julius and Augustus Hare

The lust of the mind.   *Thomas Hobbes*

At its lowest, the instinct that boosts us up to peep over our neighbor's transom.   *Elbert Hubbard*

A monstrous antenna that feels its way through matter and mind, and founders in the infinite.
                                            Elbert Hubbard

A peep-hole in the brain.   *Elbert Hubbard*

In great and generous minds, the first passion and the last.   *Samuel Johnson*

One of the permanent and certain characteristics of a vigorous intellect.   *Samuel Johnson*

Two sorts . . . one is from interest, which makes us desire to know what may be useful to us; another is from pride, and arises from a desire of knowing what others are ignorant of.   *La Rochefoucauld*

Only vanity.   *Blaise Pascal*

This disease.   *Saint Augustine*

The mother of science.   *Charles Singer*

Disinterested intellectual curiosity is the life blood of real civilization.   *George M. Trevelyan*

The foundation of science and progress.   *Anon.*

SEE ALSO EDUCATION, KNOWLEDGE, PHILOSOPHY, SCIENCE, WONDER.

CURRENCY

SEE DOLLAR, MONEY.

CURSE

SEE PROFANITY.

CUSTOM

The coward's plea.   *Charles Churchill*

The best master.   *Cicero*

A sort of second nature.   *Cicero*

The best interpreter of the law.
                                    The Code of Cannon Law, 2

That unwritten law, by which the people keep even kings in awe.   *Adapted from William D'Avenant*

Customs constitute moral standards.
                                            John Dewey

The plague of wise men and the idol of fools.
                                            Thomas Fuller

The ancient roots which control the law.

Max Gralnick

Something that serves to contract our ideas, like our movements, within the circle it has traced for us; it governs us by the terror it inspires for any new and untried condition.   *François Guizot*

The great guide to human life.   *David Hume*

(It) has furnished the only basis which ethics have ever had.   *Joseph Wood Krutch*

Great things astonish us, and small dishearten us. Custom makes both familiar.

Jean de La Bruyère

The tyrant.   *Latin Proverb*

The standing hindrance to human advancement.

John Stuart Mill

Long suffering begets custom...(It is) consent and imitation.   *Michel de Montaigne*

A violent and deceiving schoolmistress.

Michel de Montaigne

The original content of duty.   *Friedrich Paulsen*

Unwritten laws...impressed on the souls of those living under the same constitution.   *Philo*

The world's great idol.   *John Pomfret*

The worst disease to which religion is liable, and the most difficult to cure.   *Solomon Schechter*

Being used to a thing.

Richard Brinsley Sheridan

All that lies buried under fifty years.

John Greenleaf Whittier

Custom is another law.   *Anon.*

SEE ALSO CONFORMITY, HABIT, LAW, TRADITION.

CYNIC

One who never sees a good quality in a man, and never fails to see a bad one. He is the human owl, vigilant in darkness, and blind to light, mousing for vermin, and never seeing noble game.

Henry Ward Beecher

A blackguard whose faulty vision sees things as they are, and not as they ought to be.

Ambrose Bierce

Just a man who found out when he was about ten that there wasn't any Santa Claus, and he's still upset.   *James Gould Cozzens*

A man who tells you the truth about your own motives.   *Russell Green*

One who reads bitter lessons from the past...One who is prematurely disappointed in the future.

Sydney J. Harris

(One who) is only seeking to escape his own inadequacies.   *Edgar F. Magnin*

If to look truth in the face and not resent it when it's unpalatable, and take human nature as you find it...is to be cynical, then I suppose I'm a cynic.   *William Somerset Maugham*

A man who, when he smells flowers, looks around for a coffin.   *Henry Louis Mencken*

(Those who) are only happy in making the world as barren for others as they have made it for themselves.   *George Meredith*

Those canine philosophers.   *Saint Augustine*

A man who looks at the world with a monocle in his mind's eye.   *Carolyn Wells*

A man who knows the price of everything, and the value of nothing.   *Oscar Wilde*

One who detaches himself from the broad stream of humanity and feels superior about it.   *Anon.*

One who looks down on his equals and superiors.

Anon.

A child who goes through life sneering at Santa Claus.   *Anon.*

An organized sarcasm.   *Anon.*

One who is married to his first love—himself.

Anon.

SEE ALSO MISANTHROPE, PESSIMIST.

CYNICISM

A small brass fieldpiece that eventually breaks and kills the cannoneer.   *Henry Aldrich*

The temptation shared by all forms of intelligence.   *Albert Camus*

The anticipation of the historical perspective.

Russell Green

Idealism gone sour.   *Will Herberg*

The intellectual cripple's substitute for intelligence...the dishonest businessman's substitute for conscience...the communicator's substitute...for self-respect.   *Russell Lynes*

Intellectual dandyism.   *George Meredith*

The form in which base souls approach what they call honesty.   *Friedrich W. Nietzsche*

A euphemism for realism. Seeing things as they really are, instead of the way we'd like them to be.
Harry Ruby

Cynicism such as one finds...frequently among the most highly educated young men and women of the West results from the combination of comfort with powerlessness.

Bertrand A. Russell

The only deadly sin I know.   *Henry L. Stimson*

D

DAMNATION

The region of the vile. *Bhagavad-Gita*

Everlasting fire. *Bible: Matthew, XV, 41.*

Continual dying. *John Donne*

The damned come into fatal collision with God, the infinite Good, in whom their beatitude was to be found: that is the pain of damnation.

Charles Journet

The damned are in the abyss of Hell, as within a woeful city, where they suffer unspeakable torments in all their senses and members, because as they have employed all their senses and their members in sinning, so shall they suffer in each of them the punishment due to sin.

Saint Francis de Sales

Everlasting torments. *John Sergieff*

Were's not for gold and women, there would be no damnation. *Cyril Tourneur*

SEE ALSO HELL, PREDESTINATION, SIN.

DAMSEL

A young person of unfair sex addicted to clewless conduct and views that madden to crime.

Ambrose Bierce

(Those who) want nothing but husbands, and when they have them, they want everything.

William Shakespeare

A genius in the daytime and a beauty at night.

Oscar Wilde

One who exists for two major blisses: being missed and being Mrs. *Anon.*

A female who has devised more defensive plays than football coaches. *Anon.*

A female who prepares a man for marriage.

Anon.

A female who brightens a man's life by sitting in the dark with him. *Anon.*

SEE ALSO COQUETTE, LOVERS, SEXES (MEN AND WOMEN), WOMEN.

DANCE

A dance is a measured pace, as a verse is a measured speech. *Francis Bacon*

To leap about to the sound of . . . music, preferably with arms about your neighbor's wife or daughter.

Ambrose Bierce

The child of Music and of Love. *John Davies*

The one physical performance for women that frees them from either moral responsibility or physical hazard. *Agnes De Mille*

The last word in life . . . in dancing one draws nearer to oneself. *Jean Dubuffet*

A pious act of faith. *Heinrich Heine*

The only art of which we ourselves are the stuff of which it is made. *Theodore Shawn*

DANCING

A public revelation of the secrets of the sub-conscious mind and its revelations are often disastrous. *Gelett Burgess*

Certainly a Barbarian exercise, and of savage origin. *Fanny Burney*

The poetry of the foot. *John Dryden*

A necessary accomplishment, although of short use. *Thomas Jefferson*

A touchstone that true beauty tries.

Soame Jenyns

Wonderful training for girls. It's the first way you learn to guess what a man is going to do before he does it. *Christopher Morley*

Through dancing many maidens have been un-maidened, whereby I may say it is the storehouse and nursery of bastardy. *John Northbrooke*

(When the) play of limbs succeeds the play of wit.

Horace and James Smith

That act which tells you about a country. *Anon.*

DANGER

The only one is in taking too many precautions.

Adapted from Alfred Adler

The anger of a great man...the tumult of a mob...a widow that has been thrice married...a wind that comes in at a hole...a reconciled enemy. *Henry G. Bohn*

The spur of all great minds. *George Chapman*

Man himself. *Carl Jung*

In worst extremes. *John Milton*

A mule's hind foot, a dog's tooth, and a woman's tongue. *Charles H. Spurgeon*

When we learn all that a man may be. *Anon.*

DANTE ALIGHIERI (1265-1321)

Not...a large catholic mind; rather...a narrow, even sectarian mind. *Thomas Carlyle*

His greatness has...concentrated itself into fiery emphasis and depth. He is world-great not because he is world-wide, but because he is world-deep. *Thomas Carlyle*

Dante dared to write his autobiography in colossal cipher, or into universality.

Ralph Waldo Emerson

Dante's imagination is the nearest to hands and feet that we have seen. He clasps the thought as if it were a tree or a stone, and describes as mathematically. *Ralph Waldo Emerson*

This man descended to the doomed and the dead for our instruction; then to God ascended.

Adapted from Henry Wadsworth Longfellow

A superior poet to Milton...he runs neck and neck with Homer...none but Shakespeare has gone decidedly beyond him.

Thomas B. Macaulay

The hyena poetizing in tombs.

Friedrich W. Nietzsche

No dream his life was—but a fight!

Thomas W. Parsons

He used Rome's harlot for his mirth; plucked hypocrisy and crime bare—but valiant souls transmitted to the rolls of Time.

Adapted from Thomas W. Parsons

DARWINISM

SEE EVOLUTION, NATURAL SELECTION.

DAUGHTER

A daughter is to her father a treasure of sleep-lessness. *Apocrypha: Ben Sira, VII, 24.*

An embarrassing and ticklish possession.

Menander

The plague of your life.

Richard Brinsley Sheridan

The companion, the friend, and confidant of her mother, and the object of a pleasure something like the love between the angels to her father.

Richard Steele

A headache till they get married—if they get married. *Preston Sturges*

SEE ALSO DAMSEL, GIRLS, WOMAN.

DAWN

The time when men of reason go to bed.

Ambrose Bierce

That single hour of the twenty-four, when crime ceases, debauchery is exhausted, and even desolation finds a shelter. *Banjamin Disraeli*

The time when artists decide to call it a day.

Max Gralnick

The beginning of a daily installment in a serial story that will never end.   *Elbert Hubbard*

The friend of the muses.   *Latin Proverb*

A kind of backward sunset.   *George T. Strong*

DAY

A period of twenty-four hours, mostly misspent.

Ambrose Bierce

What runs through a person like water through a sieve.   *Adapted from Samuel Butler 2*

Is not every meanest day the confluence of two eternities?   *Thomas Carlyle*

A day's endless when you're young, whereas when you grow old it's very soon over.

Louis-Ferdinand Céline

A miniature Eternity.   *Ralph Waldo Emerson*

The days are made on a loom whereof the warp and woof are past and the future time.

Ralph Waldo Emerson

Scrolls: write on them what you want to be remembered for.   *Joseph Ibn Pakuda*

Out of the shadows of night.
The world rolls into light.

Henry Wadsworth Longfellow

If you have lived one day you have seen everything; one day is the same as all others.

Michel de Montaigne

Every day is a messenger of God.

Russian Proverb

Each day is a little life.   *Arthur Schopenhauer*

A little space of time before time expires; a little way of breath.

Adapted from Algernon Swinburne

A span of time no one is wealthy enough to waste.

Anon.

SEE ALSO LIFE, TIME.

DEAD

The dead know not anything, neither have they any more reward; for the memory of them is forgotten.   *Bible: Ecclesiastes, IX, 5.*

Man lieth down, and riseth not; till the heavens be no more, they shall not awake, nor be raised out of their sleep.   *Bible: Job, XIV, 12.*

Done with the work of breathing; the mad race run through to the end; the golden goal attained and found to be a hole.

Adapted from Ambrose Bierce

To be unable to understand that one is alive.

Samuel Butler 2

The life of the dead consists in being present in the minds of the living.   *Cicero*

The end of commentary.   *Jerry Dashkin*

Those who have neither relatives nor friends.

French Proverb

The wind blows out, the bubble dies; the Spring entombed in Autumn lies. The dew dries up, the star is shot, the flight is past—and man forgot.

Adapted from Henry King

The majority.   *Latin Proverb*

The dead don't die. They look on and help.

D. H. Lawrence

Horror.   *Edgar Allan Poe*

In England...names in school-books.

John Ruskin

SEE ALSO DYING, EPITAPH, ETERNAL RECURRENCE, GRAVE, HEAVEN, HELL.

DEATH

A black camel, which kneels at the gates of all.

Abd-El-Kader

The port where all may refuge find.

William Alexander

The end of labour, entry into rest.

William Alexander

A little heap of dust.   *Anacreon*

A release from the impressions of the senses, and from desires that make us their puppets, and from the vagaries of the mind, and from the hard service of the flesh.   *Marcus Aurelius*

When the soul shall emerge from its sheath.

Marcus Aurelius

A friend of ours; and he that is not ready to entertain him is not at home.   *Francis Bacon*

When a human being sees nothing but the past and the present moment. *Leon Baeck*

The sole equality on earth. *Philip J. Bailey*

The universal salt of states. *Philip J. Bailey*

The mystery. *Henry Ward Beecher*

Man goeth to his long home, and the mourners go about the streets. *Bible: Ecclesiastes, XII 5.*

Then shalt dust return to the earth as it was: and the spirit shalt return unto God who gave it.
Bible: Ecclesiastes, XII, 1-7.

He shall return no more to his house, neither shall his place know him any more.
Bible: Job, VII, 10.

The king of terrors. *Bible: Job, XVII, 14.*

All flesh shall perish together, and man shall turn again into dust. *Bible: Job, XXXIV, 15.*

A little sleep, a little slumber, a little folding of the hands to sleep. *Bible: Proverbs, VI, 10.*

His breath goeth forth, he returneth to his earth; in that very day his thoughts perish.
Bible: Psalms, CXLVI, 4.

A pale horse. *Bible: Revelations, VI, 8.*

That blessing which men fly from.
George Henry Boker

Earth to earth, ashes to ashes, dust to dust, in sure and certain hope of the Resurrection.
Book of Common Prayer.

A leap in the dark. *William Brodie*

The cure for all diseases. *Thomas Browne*

The grand perhaps. *Robert Browning*

Only a larger kind of going abroad.
Samuel Butler 1

The way of all flesh. *Samuel Butler 2*

For the unhappy... the commutation of a sentence of life imprisonment. *Alexander Chase*

Rest from labor and misery. *Cicero*

The absence of life... there is no evil in it.
Morris R. Cohen

The liberator of him whom freedom cannot release, the physician of him whom medicine cannot cure, and the comforter of him whom time cannot console. *Charles Caleb Colton*

A law, not a punishment. *Jean-Baptiste Dubos*

The repose of sleep. *Yair Eleazar*

The great reconciler. *George Eliot*

Really nothing, for so long as we are, death has not come, and when it has come we are not.
Epicurus

The debt of nature. *Robert Fabyan*

The certain end of all pain, and of all capacity to suffer pain. Of all the things that man thinks of as evils, this is the least. *Johann G. Fichte*

A friend and comforter to man.
Karl E. Franzos

The goal of all life. *Sigmund Freud*

The most beautiful adventure in life.
Charles Frohman

A low chemical trick played on everybody except sequoia trees. *J. J. Furnas*

The poor man's doctor. *German Proverb*

The inevitable hour. *Thomas Gray*

A delightful hiding-place for weary men.
Herodotus

The Destroyer. *Joseph Hiyya*

The last limit of all things. *Horace*

A readjustment to life's forces. *Elbert Hubbard*

Our redeemer. *Solomon Ibn Gabirol*

The irreversible cessation of total brain function according to the usual and customary standards of medicine. *Illinois State Law.*

One brief sigh. *Italian Proverb*

Emigrated to another star! *Helen H. Jackson*

(When) existence goes out in a lonely spasm of helpless agony. *William James*

We are but tenants, and... shortly the great Landlord will give us notice that our lease has expired.
Joseph Jefferson

The great silence. *Jewish Saying*

That which defies the doctor. *Jewish Saying*

Kind Nature's signal of retreat.

Samuel Johnson

Not the cessation of life, but an incident in it...the "narrows,"...through which the soul passes on its fateful voyage.   *Morris Joseph*

Unwilling sleep.   *John Keats*

A terrible permanence.   *Aline Kilmer*

An illusion...What people call death is the intensification and reinvigoration of life.

Abraham Kook

There is no death. What seems so is transition. This life of mortal breath is but a suburb of the life elysian, whose portal we call death.

Adapted from Henry Wadsworth Longfellow

A tavern on our pilgrimage.   *John Masefield*

The tender clasp of God that loves.

Vincent McNabb

A matter of going from one room to another, ultimately to the most beautiful room.

Mendel of Kotzk

To us here...the most terrible word we know. But when we have tasted its reality, it will mean to us birth, deliverance, a new creation of ourselves.

George S. Merriam

But a name, a date, a milestone by the stormy road, where you may lay aside your load, and bow your face and rest and wait, defying fear and fate.

Adapted from Joaquin Miller

Death is a lengthened prayer, a longer night, a larger end.   *Adapted from Joaquin Miller*

Life's last practical joke.   *Stuart Palmer*

The scion of the house of hope.   *Dorothy Parker*

A path that must be trod, if man would ever pass to God.   *Adapted from Thomas Parnell*

Death is but crossing the world, as friends do the seas; they live in one another still.

William Penn

When you get sick one day and you don't get well again.   *John Phillips*

When nature reclaims its own.   *Philo*

To repay a debt or deposit.   *Philo*

(That which) restores man to the state he was in before he was born; neither soul nor body has any feeling more.   *Pliny 1*

What we call death is merely the bursting of a cell.   *W. Winwood Reade*

The means of transition to future life...the ultimate goal of mortal existence.   *Joseph Saiida*

The gate of life.   *Saint Bernard*

Forgetfulness and silence.   *Saint Gregory*

A journey for a season; a sleep longer than usual.

Saint John Chrysostom

The final awakening.   *Walter Scott*

The dawn of ampler life.   *Owne Seaman*

A punishment to some, to some a gift, and to many a favor.   *Seneca*

Nothingness.   *Seneca*

Dust.   *William Shakespeare*

The undiscovered country, from whose bourne no traveler returns.

Adapted from William Shakespeare

A mockery.   *Percy Bysshe Shelley*

The Messiah.   *Isaac B. Singer*

The ugly fact which nature has to hide, and she hides it well.   *Alexander Smith*

The sleeping partner of life.   *Horace Smith*

The longest sleep.   *Thomas Southerne*

A single death is a tragedy, a million deaths is a statistic.   *Joseph Stalin*

God made death so we'd know when to stop.

Steven Stiles

An eternal night.   *Algernon Charles Swinburne*

When two worlds meet with a kiss: this world going out, the future world coming in.

Talmud: YeBamot, 15.2.

A quiet hour.   *Alfred Lord Tennyson*

We fall asleep and never wake again.

James Thomson

The only immortal who treats us all alike, whose pity and whose peace and whose refuge are for all.   *Mark Twain*

A great leap in the dark.   *John Vanbrugh*

An arrest of life, from which no revival, of any length, whether of the whole or of any part, can take place.   *August Weismann*

Death is frozen time. Time is molten death.
          Franz Werfel

The consciousness of a common inheritance of frailty and weakness.   *John Greenleaf Whittier*

The Dark Cavalier...the Last Lover.
          Margaret Widdemer

Some delightful journey that I shall take when all my tasks are done.
          Adapted from Ella W. Wilcox

The terror of the rich, the desire of the poor.
          Joseph Zabara

When man is put to bed with a shovel.   *Anon.*

The great equalizer of mankind.   *Anon.*

SEE ALSO COFFIN, GRAVE, HEAVEN, HELL, IMMORTALITY, MONUMENT.

DEBATE

Debate is masculine; conversation is feminine.
          Amos Bronson Alcott

The shortest cut between two minds.
          Kahlil Gibran

The death of conversation.   *Emil Ludwig*

Feud for thought.   *Cynthia Scott*

SEE ALSO CONVERSATION.

DEBT

A trap which a man sets and baits himself, and then deliberately gets into.   *Josh Billings*

An evil conscience.   *Henry G. Bohn*

That climax of all human ills.   *Lord Byron*

A bottomless sea.   *Thomas Carlyle*

The end of freedom.   *Michael Cohen*

A prolific mother of folly and of crime.
          Benjamin Disraeli

A preceptor whose lessons are needed most by those who suffer from it most.
          Ralph Waldo Emerson

The way to pay double.   *Thomas Fuller*

The devil in disguise.   *Elbert Hubbard*

Small debts are like small shot; they are rattling on every side, and can scarcely be escaped without a wound; great debts are like cannon; of loud noise but little danger.   *Samuel Johnson*

The first and mightiest force to undermine governments and corrupt the people.
          Adapted from Wendell Phillips

The slavery of the free.   *Publilius Syrus*

Something that shortens hope and life.   *Anon.*

The certain outcome of an uncertain income.
          Anon.

SEE ALSO CREDIT.

DEBT (PUBLIC)

The contracting of debts which a nation never can pay.   *William Cobbett*

If...not excessive...a national blessing.
          Alexander Hamilton

A national curse.   *Andrew Jackson*

The greatest of the dangers to be feared.
          Thomas Jefferson

The principle of spending money to be paid by posterity...swindling futurity on a large scale.
          Thomas Jefferson

DECEIT

To throw dust into other people's eyes.
          Richard Bagot

Comprehends a lie; but a deceit is more than a lie, on account of the view with which it is practiced, its being coupled with some dealing, and the injury which it is calculated to occasion, and does occasion, to another person.   *Justice Butler*

The smiler with the knife under the cloak.
          Geoffrey Chaucer

The game of small minds, and is thus the proper pursuit of women.   *Pierre Corneille*

Water in one hand, fire in the other.
          Gabriel Harvey

The silence of a friend.   *William Hazlitt*

Double-minded, kind in words, but a foe in...conduct.   *Palladas*

That glib and oily art,
To speak and purpose not.
William Shakespeare

Quicksand.   *William Shakespeare*

A taught trick to gain credit with the world for more sense and knowledge than a man is worth.
Laurence Sterne

The deliberate creation of a false impression.
Anon.

SEE ALSO FRAUD, HYPOCRISY, LIE.

DECEMBER

When employees everywhere are working their fingers to the bonus.   *Paul Steiner*

The time when Christmas comes but once a year—to stay a month or so.   *Anon.*

The month of snow and ice and mirth.   *Anon.*

SEE ALSO CHRISTMAS, WINTER.

DECISION

The fine art of executive decision consists in not deciding questions that are not now pertinent, in not deciding prematurely, in not making decisions that cannot be made effective, and in not making decisions that others should make.
Chester I. Barnard

What a man makes when he can't find anybody to serve on a committee.   *Fletcher Knebel*

The action an executive must take when he has information so incomplete that the answer does not suggest itself.   *Arthur W. Radford*

The point...to be decided.
Robert Louis Stevenson

Action based largely on not what to do.   *Anon.*

SEE ALSO ACTION, COMMITTEE, EXECUTIVE, FREE WILL.

DEEDS

(How) God reveals Himself in life.   *Leon Baeck*

An infinite conjugation of the verb to do.
Thomas Carlyle

Deeds are males, words females are.
John Davies

A step toward God.   *Josiah G. Holland*

The normal completion of the act of will which begins as prayer.   *William R. Inge*

Always some kind of effective energy.
William R. Inge

The production of the goods to be delivered.
L. P. Jacks

Something attempted, something done.
Henry Wadsworth Longfellow

Man's destiny and duty in this life.
Dean Mansel

Deeds are facts, and are forever and ever.
Thomas B. Reed

A life spent worthily.
Richard Brinsley Sheridan

A freeway to self-esteem and worth.   *Anon.*

The action part of theory.   *Anon.*

Actions that stand in relation to the faith professed.   *Anon.*

SEE ALSO ACTION, ETHICS, MORALITY.

DEFEAT

SEE FAILURE.

DEFINITION

A definition is the enclosing a wilderness of idea within a wall of words.   *Samuel Butler 1*

A kind of scratching, and generally leave a sore place more sore than it was before.
Samuel Butler 1

Every definition is dangerous.   *Erasmus*

To define is to exclude and negate.
José Ortega y Gasset

That which so describes its object as to distinguish it from all others; it is no definition of any one thing if its terms are applicable to any one other.   *Edgar Allan Poe*

A statement intended to put a word in its place.

Anon.

SEE ALSO DICTIONARY.

DEISM

The enemies of Christianity...the Worship of the God of this world by means of...Natural Religion and Natural Philosophy, and of Natural Morality or Self-Righteousness, the Selfish Virtues of the Natural Heart.   *William Blake*

Nothing but a ghost of religion which haunts the grave of dead faith and lost hope.

Christopher Dawson

Deism, from the Latin word Deus, God, is the belief of a God, and this belief is the first article of every man's creed.   *Thomas Paine*

Consists in contemplating the power, wisdom, and benignity of the Deity in his works, and in endeavoring to imitate him in everything moral, scientifical, and mechanical.   *Thomas Paine*

Slave to no sect, who takes no private road, but looks through nature up to nature's God.

Adapted from Alexander Pope

The only religion that ought to be professed...the religion of worshipping God and being a good man.   *Voltaire*

DEITY

SEE GOD.

DELIGHT

SEE PLEASURE.

DEMAGOGUE

The qualities...are these: to be foulmouthed, base-born, a low, mean fellow.   *Aristophanes*

Mountebanks for the politic body; men that have undertaken great cures, and...have been lucky in two or three experiments, but want the grounds of science, and therefore cannot hold out.

Francis Bacon

One who maximizes his appeal to the frustrated, to the dispossessed of the earth. He offers vivid and dramatic, simplistic solutions to all of life's problems.   *Eugene E. Brussell*

(One who) appeals to passions and prejudices rather than to reason...(He) is in all respects a man of intrigue and deception, of sly cunning and management.   *James Fenimore Cooper*

One who advances his own interests by affecting a deep devotion to the interests of the people.

James Fenimore Cooper

A detractor of others, a professor of humility and disinterestedness, a great stickler for equality as respects all above him, a man who acts in corners, and avoids open and manly expositions of his course, calls blackguards gentlemen, and gentlemen folks.   *James Fenimore Cooper*

Incidents to a free and constitutional country, and you must put up with these inconveniences or do without many important advantages.

Benjamin Disraeli

(One) intemperate, trusting to tumult, leading the populace to mischief with empty words.

Euripides

An undetected liar.   *Walter Lippmann*

The vilest specimens of human nature.

Thomas B. Macaulay

A person with whom we disagree as to which gang should mismanage the country.

Don Marquis

One who preaches doctrines he knows to be untrue to men he knows to be idiots.

Henry Louis Mencken

One who tells you what you want to hear. A statesman tells you what you need to hear.

Max Rafferty

Men who have flattered the people.

William Shakespeare

A speaker who seeks to make capital of social discontent to gain political influence.

Philip F. Stevenson

A new race of men is springing up to govern the nation; they are the hunters after popularity, men ambitious, not of the honor so much as the profits of office...whose principles hang laxly upon them, and who follow not so much what is right as what leads to a temporary vulgar applause.

Joseph Story

He who writes, or speaks, or signs...as those thousands would have him.   *Anthony Trollope*

A member of the rabble in good standing.

Anon.

One who reassures the mass of men that they are better than anyone else. *Anon.*

SEE ALSO DESPOT, DICTATORS, TYRANTS.

DEMOCRACY

An infinite mass of conflicting minds and...interests...which loses in collective intellectual energy in proportion to the perfection of its expansion. *Brooks Adams*

Democracy is Lovelace and the people is Clarissa.

John Quincy Adams

Government by amateurs. *Maxwell Anderson*

Where the poor rule. *Aristotle*

(A system which) arose from men's thinking that if they are equal in any respect, they are equal absolutely. *Aristotle*

Government in the hands of men of low birth, no property, and vulgar employments. *Aristotle*

Means government by discussion but it is only effective if you can stop people talking.

Clement Attlee

The best liberty for all to aspire to the best that is in him, or that ever has been. *James Baldwin*

Practical Christianity. *George Bancroft*

Democracy is evangelical in essence and its motive power is love. *Henri Bergson*

An aristocracy of blackguards. *Lord Byron*

Means despair of finding any heroes to govern you, and contented putting up with the want of them. *Thomas Carlyle*

By the nature of it, a self-cancelling business: it gives in the long run a net result of zero.

Thomas Carlyle

The attainment of a truer and truer Aristocracy or Government of the Best. *Thomas Carlyle*

The art of saying "nice doggie" until you can find a rock. *Wynn Catlin*

A condition where people believe that other people are as good as they are. *Stuart Chase*

Means government by the uneducated, while aristocracy means government by the badly educated. *Gilbert Keith Chesterton*

The...faith is this: that the most...important things must be left to ordinary men themselves— the mating of the sexes, the rearing of the young, the laws of the state. *Gilbert Keith Chesterton*

An attempt (like that of a jolly hostess) to bring the shy people out. *Gilbert Keith Chesterton*

(The belief) that all men are interesting.

Gilbert Keith Chesterton

The will of the governed after it has been subjected to federal probate. *John Ciardi*

The worst form of government, except for all those other forms that have been tried from time to time. *Winston S. Churchill*

The healthful life-blood which circulates through the veins and arteries, which supports the system.

Samuel Taylor Coleridge

A device for maintaining in perpetuity the rights of the people, with the ultimate extinction of all privileged classes. *Calvin Coolidge*

Equal participation in rights as is practicable.

James Fenimore Cooper

To substitute public opinion for law. This is the usual form in which masses of men exhibit their tyranny. *James Fenimore Cooper*

Consists of choosing your dictators after they've told you what you think it is you want to hear.

Alan Coren

That form of government where everybody gets what the majority deserves.

James D. Davidson

A moral and religious creed.

Christopher Dawson

Primarily a mode of associated living, of conjoint communicated experience. *John Dewey*

The fatal drollery. *Benjamin Disraeli*

The premise that the mass of democratic citizens will make right decisions most of the time in response to critical issues.

Milton S. Eisenhower

(That system which) tends to equalize the responsibility, to atomize it into responsibility of the whole population—and therefore everyone becomes equally irresponsible.

Thomas Stearns Eliot

A raft, which would never sink, but then your feet are always in the water. *Ralph Waldo Emerson*

A government of bullies tempered by editors.

Ralph Waldo Emerson

Democracy is essentially anti-authoritarian—that is, it not only demands the right but imposes the responsibility of thinking for ourselves.

Bergen Evans

When the multitude have government.

Abraham Fleming

A system of government that admits variety and permits criticism.

Adapted from Edward M. Forster

The conviction that there are extraordinary possibilities in ordinary people.

Harry Emerson Fosdick

Always a beckoning goal, not a safe harbor.

Felix Frankfurter

A system that creates the . . . conditions for the full development of the individual. *Erich Fromm*

A true democracy rests on the differences between its citizens, as individuals or as groups.

Hayyim Greenberg

A process, not a static condition. It is becoming, rather than being. It can easily be lost; but never is fully won. Its essence is eternal struggle.

William H. Hastie

The conviction . . . that no man is good enough or wise enough to be entrusted with irresponsible power over his fellow-men. *Will Herberg*

No more than an aristocracy of orators.

Thomas Hobbes

A form of government by popular ignorance.

Elbert Hubbard

(A political system where) votes are substitutes for brains. *Elbert Hubbard*

The climate of civilization. *Victor Hugo*

On board a ship in which the voices of the cook and the loblolly boys counted for as much as those of the officers. *Thomas Henry Huxley*

The ballot box. *William R. Inge*

The forged compromise of the majority with the minority. *Daniel K. Inouye*

(That system which) encourages the nimble charlatan at the expense of the thinker, and prefers the plausible wizard . . . to the true statesman.

James Jeans

The only form of government which is not externally at open or secret war with the rights of mankind. *Thomas Jefferson*

Secularism is Democracy and Democracy is Secularism, both as a way of life and as a form of government. *Horace M. Kallen*

Despotism, as it establishes an executive power contrary to the general will. *Immanuel Kant*

A state which recognizes the subjection of the minority to the majority, that is, an organization for the systematic use of violence by one class against the other, by one part of the population against another. *Nikolai Lenin*

Citizen participation. *David E. Lilienthal*

A . . . society . . . in which the majority is always prepared to put down a revoluntionary minority.

Walter Lippmann

A chance to fight for improvement.

Meyer London

Gives every man the right to be his own oppressor.

James Russell Lowell

This faith . . . that . . . does not depend on power, but on the consensus that leaves other faiths free and still provides a ground on which the diversities of faith can stand. *R. M. MacIver*

That state in which the greatest number of men feel an interest in expressing opinion upon political questions, and in which the greatest number of judgments and wills concur in influencing public measures. *James Mackintosh*

The very child of Jesus' teachings of the infinite worth of every personality.

Francis J. McConnell

Liberty plus groceries. *Maury Maverick*

The theory that the common people know what they want, and deserve to get it good and hard.

Henry Louis Mencken

The argument that it is a crime for any man to hold himself out as better than other men, and, above all, a most heinous offense for him to prove it.   *Henry Louis Mencken*

To make kings and queens out of a hundred people.   *F. C. Morehouse.*

Means government of the mentally unfit by the mentally mediocre tempered by the saving grace of snobbery.   *Hector H. Munro*

The essential doctrine...is that each man, as a free human soul, lives of his free will in the service of the whole people.   *Gilbert Murray*

Direct, self-government, over all the people, for all the people, by all the people.
                          Theodore Parker

Means not "I am as good as you are," but "You are as good as I am."   *Theodore Parker*

A system of self-determination...the right to make the wrong choice.   *John Patrick*

A process by which the people are free to choose the man who will get the blame.
                          Laurence J. Peter

A state in which the poor, gaining the upper hand, kill some and banish others, and then divide the offices among the remaining citizens equally, usually by lot.   *Plato*

A charming form of government, full of variety and disorder, and dispensing a kind of equality to equals and unequals alike.   *Plato*

(A system which) agrees better with mere talent than with genius.   *Edgar Allan Poe*

The fairest of names, but the worst of realities— mob rule.   *Polybius*

An institution in which the whole is equal to the scum of all the parts.   *Keith Preston*

Nothing but a constitutional arbitrary power that has succeeded another constitutional arbitrary power.   *Pierre J. Proudhon*

The triumph of bad quality. *Guido de Ruggiero*

(The system which) substitutes election by the incompetent many for appointment by the corrupt few.   *George Bernard Shaw*

It has come to mean whatever anyone wants it to mean.   *Bernard Smith*

A method of getting ahead without leaving any of us behind.   *T. V. Smith*

An attempt to apply the principles of the Bible to a human society.   *Wallace Speers*

The highest form of government: but because of this it requires the highest type of human nature— a type nowhere at present existing.
                          Herbert Spencer

A society which wields all its power as a whole.
                          Baruch Spinoza

A society where it is safe to be unpopular.
                          Adlai Ewing Stevenson

Where everyone is master and tyrannizes over the others.   *Adapted from Max Stirner*

It's not the voting that's democracy, it's the counting.   *Thomas Stoppard*

(The system) founded by the people, managed by the people.   *Joseph Story*

The sense of spiritual independence which nerves the individual to stand alone against the powers of the world.   *Richard H. Tawney*

The people's government made for the people...by the people, and answerable to the people.   *Daniel Webster*

The recurrent suspicion that more than half of the people are right more than half of the time.
                          Edward B. White

A religious faith. For some it comes close to being the only formal religion they have.
                          Edward B. White

A society in which the unbeliever feels undisturbed and at home.   *Edward B. White*

The bludgeoning of the people, by the people, for the people.   *Oscar Wilde*

Letting the mob in to vote.   *Anon.*

That form of society, no matter what its political classification, in which every man has a chance and knows he has it.   *Anon.*

A state of mind in which every man is as good as every other man, provided he really is.   *Anon.*

Careers open to talent.   *Anon.*

A small firm core of common agreement surrounded by a rich diversity of individual differences.   *Anon.*

A political system which can face the truth about itself and yet survive.   *Anon.*

SEE ALSO AMERICA, AMERICAN CONSTITU-
TION, AMERICANISM, AMERICANS, ENG-
LAND, EQUALITY, FREE PRESS, GOVERN-
MENT, LAW, LIBERTY, MAJORITY, PEOPLE
(THE), VOTING.

DEMOCRAT

The proper antipode of a gentleman is to be sought
for among the Anglo-American democrats.

Samuel Taylor Coleridge

He always attacks his opponents, not only with all
arms, but also with snorts and objurations . . . he is
always filled with moral indignation . . . he is incapable of imagining honor in an antagonist, and
hence is incapable of honor.

Henry Louis Mencken

One who believes in the patriotism and energy
and initiative of the average man.   *Anon.*

SEE ALSO POLITICIAN, POLITICS.

DEMOCRATIC PARTY

Like a man riding backward in a carriage. It never
sees a thing until it has gone by.

Benjamin F. Butler

Like a mule. It has neither pride of ancestry nor
hope of posterity.   *Ignatius Donnelly*

I never said all Democrats were saloon-keepers.
What I said was that all saloon-keepers were
Democrats.   *Horace Greeley*

That party never had but two objects—grand and
petit larceny.   *Robert G. Ingersoll*

Troubadours of trouble and crooners of catastrophe.   *Clare Boothe Luce*

A hopeless assortment of discordant differences,
as incapable of positive action as it is capable of
infinite clamor.   *Thomas B. Reed*

I am not a member of any organized political
party. I am a Democrat.   *Will Rogers*

The taxing party.   *Anon.*

DEMONS

The creatures of God.   *Celsus*

Demonology is the shadow of theology.

Ralph Waldo Emerson

The products of the psychic activity of man.

Sigmund Freud

The belief in a demonic world is inculcated
throughout the Gospels and the rest of the books
of the New Testament; it pervades the whole
patristic literature; it colors the theory and practice of every Christian church down to modern
times.   *Thomas Henry Huxley*

Purely spiritual beings, fallen angels, at work
upon human history.   *Josef Pieper*

Their great business is the ruin of mankind . . .
Invisible and intangible . . . demons breathe into
the soul, and rouse up its corruptions with furious
passions and vile excesses.   *Tertullian*

SEE ALSO DEVIL, HELL, WITCH.

DENTIST

A man who, putting metal in your mouth, pulls
coins out of your pocket.

Adapted from Ambrose Bierce

A man who puts tools in your mouth and stale
jokes in your ear.   *Anon.*

Those who are always ready for the old grind.

Anon.

Those who are often driven to extraction.

Anon.

A collector of old National Geographic Maga-
zines.   *Anon.*

Drilling, filling, billing.   *Anon.*

DEPRAVITY

SEE SIN, WICKEDNESS.

DESERT

These drear wastes of sea-born land.

Richard Burton

Something of the eternal mystery of the universe;
burning sun, lambent air, and glowing sand, sand,
sand.   *Marcus Ehrenpreis*

The sea-like, pathless, limitless waste.

Henry Wadsworth Longfellow

DESIRE

Like columns of sunshine radiating through a musty window, nothing tangible, nothing there.
Nahman Bratzlav

A perpetual rack. *Robert Burton*

The warm beast...that lies curled up in our loins and stretches itself with a fierce gentleness.
Albert Camus

Desire and love are the same thing; save that by desire we always signify the absence of the object; by love, most commonly the presence of the same. *Thomas Hobbes*

A viper in the bosom, who, while he was chill, was harmless; but when warmth gave him strength, exerted it in poison. *Samuel Johnson*

The uneasiness a man finds in himself upon the absence of anything whose present enjoyment carries the idea of delight with it. *John Locke*

The greatest feature which distinguishes man from animals. *William Osler*

A forest fire...consuming and destroying everything. *Philo*

The inward sign of a physical proclivity to act.
George Santayana

The desire of love, Joy;
The desire of life, Peace;
The desire of the soul, Heaven. *William Sharp*

The essence of a man. *Baruch Spinoza*

The hankering after pleasure, or existence, or success...the germ from which springs all human misery. *Mahavagga Vinaya*

SEE ALSO LOVE, PASSION.

DESPAIR

The corpse-like bride. *Robert Browning*

An epitome of hell, an extract, a quintessence, a compound, a mixture of all feral maladies ... perplexities. *Robert Burton*

A form of laziness. *Peter Gay*

One of Hell's catchpolls. *Thomas Dekker*

The conclusion of fools. *Benjamin Disraeli*

The end of visioning. *Thomas Hardy*

Bleak encounter with silence and futility and nonbeing. *Julian N. Hartt*

The worst poison. *Heinrich Heine*

The thought of the unattainableness of any good.
John Locke

A wilful business, common to corrupt blood, and to weak woeful minds. *George Meredith*

The rejection of God within oneself.
Antoine de Saint-Exupéry

No change, no pause, no hope!
Percy Bysshe Shelley

An ultimate or "boundary-line" situation. One cannot go beyond it...No way out into the future appears. Non-being is felt absolutely victorious.
Paul Tillich

The pain...that "being" is aware of itself as unable to affirm itself because of the power of non-being. *Paul Tillich*

(A mental state which) exaggerates not only our misery but also our weakness.
Luc de Vauvenargues

A frightful queerness...that there is no way out, or around, or through the impasse. It is the end.
Herbert G. Wells

The sin which cannot find—because it will not look for it—forgiveness. *Hubert van Zeller*

SEE ALSO MISERY, SORROW.

DESPOT

Three kinds...the despot who tyrannizes over the body...the despot who tyrannizes over the soul...the despot who tyrannizes over the soul and body alike. The first is called the prince. The second is called the pope. The third is called the people. *Oscar Wilde*

A harangatanger. *Anon.*

SEE ALSO DEMAGOGUE, DICTATORS, TYRANTS.

DESPOTISM

Efforts to freeze history, to stop change, to solidify the human spirit. *Charles A. Beard*

DESTINY

A late development and very often...the end of societies that have been highly democratic. A despotism may almost be defined as a tired democracy. *Gilbert Keith Chesterton*

To live by one man's will. *Richard Hooker*

Whatever crushes individuality.

John Stuart Mill

When the savages of Louisiana want to gather fruit, they chop down the tree. This is precisely the course of a despotic government.

Charles de Montesquieu

SEE ALSO DICTATORSHIP, TOTALI-TARIANISM, TYRANNY.

DESTINY

Whatever befalls you was preordained for you from eternity. *Marcus Aurelius*

A tyrant's authority for crime and a fool's excuse for failure. *Ambrose Bierce*

Something we create. *Eugene E. Brussell*

A matter of choice; it is not a thing to be waited for, it is a thing to be achieved.

William Jennings Bryan

To leave the known for the unknown.

Christopher Dawson

God. *Thomas Stearns Eliot*

The one inexorable thing! *Louise I. Guiney*

Man's feet are his destiny: they lead him to where he is wanted. *Hama*

That shall be, shall be. *John Heywood*

Men heap together the mistakes of their lives, and create a monster which they call Destiny.

John O. Hobbes

Providence is in God, and attributed to Him alone: Destiny is in the things, and to them ascribed. *Justus Lipsius*

A divinity that shapes our ends.

William Shakespeare

An invention of the cowardly and the resigned.

Ignazio Silone

SEE ALSO DETERMINISM, FATALISM, PRE-DESTINATION.

DESTRUCTION

A creative passion. *Mikhail A. Bakunin*

Still the strongest instinct of our nature.

Max Beerbohm

The outcome of unlived lives. *Erich Fromm*

A primitive instinct which occasionally comes out despite our veneer of civilization. *Anon.*

SEE ALSO CRITICISM, WAR.

DETERMINATION

SEE FORTITUDE.

DETERMINISM

The whole is in each and every part, and welds it with the rest into an absolute unity, an iron block, in which there can be no equivocation or shadow of turning. *William James*

Nothing happens without a cause. Everything has a cause and is necessary. *Leucippes*

To learn to understand the causes of evil, so that we may induce the causes of reform...to antici-pate and plan like a worker and collaborater of God. *Thomas G. Masaryk*

Your sitting-place written by God. *Mohammed*

When the cards are dealt and you pick up your hand, that is determinism; there's nothing you can do except to play it out for whatever it may be worth. And the way you play your hand is free will. *Jawaharlal Nehru*

Propaganda of a souless stupidity...representing man as a dead object driven hither and thither by his environment, antecedents, circumstances.

George Bernard Shaw

There is no free will in the human mind: it is moved to this or that volition by some cause, and that cause has been determined by some other cause, and so on infinitely. *Baruch Spinoza*

SEE ALSO CALVINISM, EVOLUTION, FATE, FATALISM, PREDESTINATION, PROVIDENCE.

DEVIL

A liar, and the father of it.

Bible: John, VIII, 44.

Your adversary.   *Bible: Peter, V, 8.*

The Devil as a roaring lion, walketh about, seeking whom he may devour.
Bible: Peter, V, 8.

The father of lies, but he neglected to patent the idea, and the business now suffers from competition.   *Josh Billings*

The heart of man is the place the Devil's in: I feel sometimes a Hell within myself.
Thomas Browne

The author of confusion and lies.
Robert Burton

The accomplice if not the direct inspirer of all human crimes, from that of Cain down to those of our own time, and the instigator...of all that is evil and, as we say so glibly, "infernal in our civilizations!"   *Nicholas Corte*

I think the devil doesn't exist, but man has created him, he has created him in his own image and likeness.   *Fëdor M. Dostoievski*

God's ape.   *English Proverb*

In heaven he scorns to serve, so now in hell he reigns.   *Adapted from John Fletcher*

The devil is an egotist.   *Johann W. Goethe*

Anything that dehumanizes.   *Eric Hoffer*

One of the principal objects of American reverence.   *Josiah G. Holland*

A god who has been bounced for conduct unbecoming a gentlemen.   *Elbert Hubbard*

Compromise.   *Henrik Ibsen*

The most diligent preacher of all others; he is never out of his diocese.   *Hugh Latimer*

The horrible co-existence of a subtle and incessant intellectual activity with an incapacity to understand anything.   *Clive S. Lewis*

A gentlemen who never goes where he is not welcome.   *John Lincoln*

The Arch-Enemy.   *John Milton*

It was he whose guile, stirred up with envy and revenge, deceived the mother of mankind.
Adapted from John Milton

The strongest and fiercest Spirit that fought in Heaven, now fiercer by despair.
Adapted from John Milton

The patron saint of mere negativistic revolt.
José Ortega y Gasset

A myth, hence he exists and continues to be active. A myth is a story which describes and illustrates in dramatic form certain deep structures of reality.   *Denis de Rougemont*

The devil has power to suggest evil, but he was not given the power to compel you against your will.   *Saint Cyril*

The Devil enters into me through impure, evil, blasphemous thoughts, through doubt, fear, pride, irritability, malice, avarice, envy; therefore his power over me entirely depends upon myself.
John Sergieff

The prince of darkness is a gentleman.
William Shakespeare

He is described as an angel fallen from heaven, and as "the Prince of this world," whose business is to tell us that there is no other world.
Fulton J. Sheen

SEE ALSO CHRISTIANITY, DAMNATION, DEMONS, HELL, TEMPTATION.

DEVOTION

SEE LOVE, PRAYER, WORSHIP.

DIAGNOSIS

A physician's forecast of disease by the patient's pulse and purse.   *Ambrose Bierce*

One of the commonest diseases.   *Karl Kraus*

The first stages of an autopsy.   *Anon.*

An art involving guesswork.   *Anon.*

SEE ALSO DISEASE, DOCTORS.

DIAPER

The eternal triangle.   *J. W. White*

The most functional garment in family life.
Anon.

Trousers worn during the age of indiscretion.
Anon.

DIARY

A daily record of that part of one's life which he can relate to himself without blushing.

Ambrose Bierce

The lavatory of literature.   *Elbert Hubbard*

To see one's self as no one else cares to see us.

Elbert Hubbard

A secret book about pimples, dirt between the toes, and belly-button lint.   *Anon.*

Penned-up emotions.   *Anon.*

SEE ALSO AUTOBIOGRAPHY.

DICKENS, CHARLES (1812-70)

The good, the gentle, high-gifted, ever-friendly, noble Dickens—every inch of him an honest man.

Thomas Carlyle

Dickens, with preternatural apprehension of the language of manners, and the varieties of street life, with pathos and laughter...writes tracts. He is a painter of English details, like Hogarth; local and temporary in his tints and style, and local in his aims.   *Ralph Waldo Emerson*

He has risen like a rocket and he will come down like a stick.   *John G. Lockhart*

He violated every rule of art except the feeling mind and the thinking heart.

Adapted from John Macy

The incarnation of cockneydom, a caricaturist who aped the moralist.   *George Meredith*

Dickens writes too often and too fast...If he persists much longer in this course, it requires no gift of prophecy to foretell his fate.

Quarterly Magazine, 1838.

If Columbus found a new world, Dickens created one—and peopled it with men and women.

Arthur Quiller-Couch

DICTATORS

(Those who) ride to and fro upon tigers which they dare not dismount. And the tigers are getting hungry.   *Gilbert Keith Chesterton*

Men, acting like gods...appointed to establish heaven on earth...To fulfill their mission they must assume a godlike omnipotence. They must be jealous gods, monopolizing power, destroying all rivals, compelling exclusive loyalty.

Walter Lippmann

Rulers who always look good until the last ten minutes.   *Jan Masaryk*

A milder preliminary form of the State of Anti-God as embodied in an individual.

Robert Zwickey

A man with generals in good standing.   *Anon.*

SEE ALSO DESPOT, TOTALITARIANISM.

DICTATORSHIP

A government under which everything which is not prohibited is compulsory.   *Sergei Arutunoff*

A great beech tree, nice to look at, but nothing grows under it.   *Stanley Baldwin*

This unnatural power.   *Edmund Burke*

A great adventure...which crumbles in misery and blood.   *Charles de Gaulle*

Power based directly upon force, and unrestricted by any laws.   *Nikolai Lenin*

An aria, never an opera.   *Emil Ludwig*

Nothing more or less than power which directly rests on violence, which is not limited by any laws or restricted by any absolute rules.

Joseph Stalin

Unlimited power, resting on violence and not on law.   *Joseph Stalin*

Whenever you have an efficient government.

Harry S. Truman

A place where public opinion can't even be expressed privately.   *Walter Winchell*

A system of government where everything that is not forbidden is obligatory.   *Anon.*

A system of government where the politics has been removed from politics.   *Anon.*

General poverty relieved by enthusiasm and maintained by terror.   *Anon.*

SEE ALSO DESPOTISM, RABBLE, TYRANNY.

DICTIONARY

A malevolent literary device for cramping the growth of a language and making it hard and inelastic.   *Ambrose Bierce*

It is full of suggestion,—the raw material of possible poems and histories. Nothing is wanting but a little shuffling, sorting, ligature, and cartilage.   *Ralph Waldo Emerson*

The responsibility of a dictionary is to record the language, not set its style.   *Philip Gove*

(A device that) permits us to hide from ourselves and others the extent of our ignorance.
                                            H. H. Hulse

Like watches; the worst is better than none, and the best cannot be expected to be quite true.
                                            Samuel Johnson

An index to the literature of a given speech . . . it bears to language the relation which a digest bears to a series of legal reports.   *George P. Marsh*

The most interesting book in our language.
                                            Albert Nock

A guide to the spelling of words, provided you know how to spell them.   *Anon.*

SEE ALSO LEXICOGRAPHER.

DIE

SEE DEATH, DYING.

DIETING

(An activity which) shows what bad losers we all are.   *Michael Cohen*

Feeding by measure.   *John Heywood*

A change that not even a healthy man can suffer.
                                            Michel de Montaigne

A system of starving yourself to death so you can live a little longer.   *Jan Murray*

Consists in placing both hands against the table edge and pushing back.   *Robert Quillen*

(A time when) the days seem longer and the meals shorter.   *Earl Wilson*

A serious game wherein you are the umpire.
                                            Anon.

Merely a matter of keeping your mouth shut at the correct time: breakfast, lunch and dinner.
                                            Anon.

The time when the days seem longer and the meals shorter.   *Anon.*

Something you went off yesterday—or expect to start tomorrow.   *Anon.*

The only discipline that shows a gain by showing a loss.   *Anon.*

DIFFICULTY

God's errands and trainers, and only through them can one come to the fullness of manhood.
                                            Henry Ward Beecher

The nurse of greatness—a harsh nurse, who roughly rocks her foster-children into strength and athletic proportion.   *William Jennings Bryan*

A severe instructor.   *Edmund Burke*

Educators.   *Ralph Waldo Emerson*

Obstacles that show what men are.   *Epictetus*

The excuse that history never accepts.
                                            Samuel Grafton

A politician trying to save both sides of his face at once.   *John Lincoln*

That which can be done immediately; the impossible, that which takes a little longer.
                                            George Santayana

SEE ALSO PROBLEM.

DIGESTION

The conversion of victuals into virtues.
                                            Ambrose Bierce

Happiness.   *Lin Yutang*

The great secret of life.   *Sydney Smith*

SEE ALSO COOKING, EATING, HUNGER.

DIGNITY

Consists not in possessing honors, but in the consciousness that we deserve them.   *Aristotle*

The absence of ludicrous and debasing associations.   *Samuel Taylor Coleridge*

Ability to face reality in all its meaninglessness.
Martin Esslin

There is only one terminal dignity—love.
Helen Hayes

A state of . . . emotional starchiness that precedes a bluff. *Elbert Hubbard*

The bodily attitude of a speaker or preacher in the presence of people whose duty it is to believe he is not lying to them. *Elbert Hubbard*

A mask we wear to hide our ignorance.
Elbert Hubbard

Consists in thought. *Blaise Pascal*

The quality that enables a man who says nothing, does nothing and knows nothing to command . . . respect. *John W. Raper*

Our dignity is not in what we do, but what we understand. *George Santayana*

A veil between us and the real truth.
Edwin P. Whipple

True dignity abides with him alone who, in the silent hour of the inward thought can still suspect, and still revere himself, in lowliness of heart.
Adapted from William Wordsworth

Window dressing for a vacant store. *Anon.*

DILEMMA

SEE DIFFICULTY, PROBLEM.

DILETTANTE

A product of where wealth and literature meet.
Douglas Dunn

A philanderer who seduces the several arts and deserts each in turn for another. *Oliver Herford*

An idler who kills time by study.
George Bernard Shaw

One who never finishes anything. *Anon.*

DILIGENCE

SEE PERSEVERANCE.

DIPLOMACY

The atmosphere of accredited mendacity.
Lord Acton

The patriotic art of lying for one's country.
Ambrose Bierce

To speak French, to speak nothing, and to speak falsehood. *Ludwig Boerne*

A disguised war. *Randolph Bourne*

The art of keeping cool.
William Jennings Bryan

The art of saying "Nice doggie" till you can find a rock. *Wynn Catlin*

A continuation of war by other means.
Chou En-lai

Activity that isn't too hard on the brain, but hell on the feet. *Charles G. Dawes*

To do and say the nastiest thing in the nicest way.
Adapted from Isaac Goldberg

Lying in state. *Oliver Herford*

The art of fishing tranquilly in troubled waters.
J. Christopher Herold

(Something that) sees to it that a nation does not perish heroically but maintains itself in a practical way. *Adolf Hitler*

The art of restraining power. *Henry Kissinger*

A game in which the nations are checkmated.
Karl Kraus

Spheres of action. *George Leveson-Gower*

Forever poised between a cliché and an indiscretion. *Harold Macmillan*

The art of jumping into trouble without treading on anyone's toes. *Patricia Stone*

The art of letting someone have your way.
Daniele Vare

A complicated endeavor to sidestep an issue.
Anon.

The art of jumping into trouble without making a splash. *Anon.*

The art of saying things in such a way that nobody knows exactly what you mean. *Anon.*

Saying nothing nicely. *Anon.*

The art of taking while making the other party believe you are giving. *Anon.*

The art of taking sides without anyone knowing it. *Anon.*

The art of making others believe that you believe what you don't believe. *Anon.*

SEE ALSO AMBASSADOR, STATESMANSHIP, TACT.

DIPLOMAT

Lie and deny. *Jacques Baeyens*

Emptiness and quackery. *Otto von Bismarck*

A ward politician with a frock coat.
Smedley D. Butler

Divided into three classes: (1) ambassadors, legates or nuncios; (2) envoys, ministers or other persons accredited to sovereigns; (3) chargés d'affaires accredited to ministers for foreign affairs.
Congress of Vienna

One who lessens tension and promotes understanding. *Anthony Eden*

(Those who) approach every problem with an open mouth. *Arthur Goldberg*

A person who knows the answers, but gives such as he chooses. *Max Gralnick*

The eye and ear of states.
Francesco Guicciardini

Creatures, who when they seem to be coming are going, and when they seem to be going are coming. *Adapted from John Hay*

A man who says "perhaps" when he means no.
Elbert Hubbard

One who can cut his neighbor's throat without having his neighbor notice it. *Trygve Lie*

One whose qualifications consists of keeping a good table and seeing to the ladies. *Napoleon I*

A sort of unconnected atom, continually repelling and repelled. *Thomas Paine*

Protocol, alcohol, and Geritol.
Adlai Ewing Stevenson

A person who can tell you to go to hell in such a way that you actually look forward to the trip.
Caskie Stinnett

Nothing but a headwaiter who's allowed to sit down occasionally. *Peter Ustinov*

Babies in silk hats playing with dynamite.
Alexander Woollcott

An honest man sent abroad to lie for his country.
Henry Wooton

A man who knows when to laugh or cry in company. *Anon.*

One who is held upright by pressure from every side. *Anon.*

One who can put in his oar without rocking the boat. *Anon.*

One who says what will please, not what he knows and feels. *Anon.*

One who knows what it isn't safe to laugh at.
Anon.

One who can keep his shirt on while getting something off his chest. *Anon.*

One who remembers a lady's birthday but forgets her age. *Anon.*

A person who is appointed to avert situations that would never occur if there were no diplomats.
Anon.

One who can yawn with his mouth closed.
Anon.

Usually a wealthy person assigned to meddle in other people's business. *Anon.*

One who says, "I will take the matter under advisement," instead of saying no. *Anon.*

SEE ALSO AMBASSADOR, POLITICIAN.

DIRT

The by-product of a systematic ordering and classification of matter. *Mary Douglas*

Matter in the wrong place. *Lord Palmerston*

DISAPPOINTMENT

A sort of bankruptcy—the bankruptcy of a soul that expends too much in hope and expectation.
Eric Hoffer

The final issue of any act begun yesterday, today or tomorrow. *Elbert Hubbard*

The little "daily dyings" which cloud over the sunshine of life. *John Lubbock*

The nurse of wisdom. *Boyle Roche*

SEE ALSO FAILURE.

DISARMAMENT

Argument between nations to scuttle all weapons that are obsolete. *Leonard L. Levinson*

DISASTER

SEE CALAMITY, TRAGEDY.

DISCIPLE

If any man come to me, and hate not his father, and mother, and wife, and children, and brethren, and sisters, yea, and his own life also, he cannot be my disciple. *Bible: Luke, XIV, 26.*

Keeping to the narrow road true to the jingling of the leader's bells.
Adapted from William Cowper

Ciphers. *Friedrich W. Nietzsche*

One who is always behind. *Anon.*

To be thrown out of one's own orbit and be made a satellite. *Anon.*

DISCIPLINE

SEE AUTHORITY, SELF-CONTROL.

DISCONTENT

The source of trouble, but also of progress.
Berthold Auerbach

A perverse and fretful disposition. *Cicero*

The first step of progress. Show me a thoroughly satisfied man—and I will show you a failure.
Thomas Alva Edison

The want of self-reliance: it is infirmity of will.
Ralph Waldo Emerson

Two kinds...the discontent that works, and the discontent that wrings its hands. The first gets what it wants, and the second loses what it had.

There is no cure for the first but success, and there is no cure at all for the second.
Gordon Graham

The starting-point in every man's career.
Elbert Hubbard

The mainspring in progress. *Elbert Hubbard*

The first step in the progress of a man or a nation.
Oscar Wilde

The road to discovery. *Anon.*

Wanting what others have; hating what we have.
Anon.

Comparison. *Anon.*

DISCORD

Political rivals shaking hands after an election.
Eugene E. Brussell

Harmony not understood. *Alexander Pope*

Firing at each other. *Theodore Roosevelt*

To empty the vials of bitterness into hearts, stirring up one against the other.
Fulton J. Sheen

A sleepless hag who never dies. *John Wolcot*

Noise out of place. *Anon.*

SEE ALSO ARGUMENTS, CONFLICT, WAR.

DISCOURAGEMENT

Nothing resembles pride so much.
Henry F. Amiel

Simply the despair of wounded self-love.
François de Fénelon

Often the last key in the bunch that opens the lock. *Anon.*

SEE ALSO FAILURE.

DISCOVERY

SEE GENIUS, HERO, INVENTION.

DISCRETION

The saying that "There he goes" rather than "Here he lies" sums up the meaning.
American Saying

Be civil to all; sociable to many; familiar with few; friend to one; enemy to none.

Benjamin Franklin

Leaving a few things unsaid.   *Elbert Hubbard*

What is called discretion in men is called cunning in animals.   *Jean de La Fontaine*

Seeing as much as you ought, not as much as you can.   *Adapted from Michel de Montaigne*

Not a matter of rhetoric but of right and wise conduct.   *Dean Rusk*

That honorable stop.   *William Shakespeare*

The art of closing your eyes to a situation before someone closes them for you.   *Earl Wilson*

When you are sure you are right but still check with your spouse.   *Anon.*

Putting two and two together and keeping your mouth shut.   *Anon.*

To be indiscreet discreetly.   *Anon.*

SEE ALSO CAUTION, DIPLOMACY.

DISCRIMINATION

SEE ANTI-SEMITISM, BIGOTRY, NEGRO, PREJUDICE.

DISCUSSION

SEE CONVERSATION, SPEECH, TALK, WORDS.

DISEASE

Not species, such as dogs and cats, but abnormal, though not altogether irregular, behavior of animals and plants.   *Thomas C. Allbutt*

One foot in the grave.   *Beaumont and Fletcher*

The whipping post and branding iron of luxury.

Josh Billings

Self-contemplation is infallibly the symptom of disease.   *Thomas Carlyle*

The taxes laid upon this wretched life; some are taxed higher, and some lower, but all pay something.   *Lord Chesterfield*

An image of thought externalized... We classify disease as error, which nothing but Truth or Mind can heal.   *Mary Baker Eddy*

An experience of...mortal mind. It is fear made manifest on the body.   *Mary Baker Eddy*

The price of ill pleasures.   *Thomas Fuller*

May, after all, be but a symptom of some ailment in the spiritual part.   *Nathaniel Hawthorne*

(That which) begins that equality which death completes.   *Samuel Johnson*

Devil's spells.   *Martin Luther*

The tax on pleasures.   *John Ray*

Death's servant.   *Francis Rous*

Purpose, and the purpose is beneficent. The processes of disease aim not at the destruction of life, but at the savings of it.   *Frederick Treves*

A conflict of citizens in a cell state, brought about by external forces.   *Rudolf Virchow*

SEE ALSO DOCTORS, HEALTH, ILLNESS, MEDICINE.

DISGRACE

Does not consist in the punishment, but in the crime.   *Vittorio Alfieri*

The mark of a base man, and belongs to a character capable of disgraceful acts.   *Aristotle*

To stumble twice against the same stone.

Cicero

That and that alone is a disgrace to a man, which he has deserved to suffer.   *Phaedrus*

(Something) immortal, and lives long after one thinks it is dead.   *Plautus*

To die and not be missed.   *Anon.*

DISINHERIT

The prankish action of the ghosts in cutting the pockets out of trousers.   *Elbert Hubbard*

To leave great sums of money to lawyers.

Elbert Hubbard

A method of insuring post mortem notoriety.

Elbert Hubbard

SEE ALSO HEIR.

DISOBEDIENCE

The rarest and the most courageous of the virtues, is seldom distinguished from neglect, the laziest and most common of the vices.

George Bernard Shaw

Man's original virtue. It is through disobedience that progress has been made.   *Oscar Wilde*

SEE ALSO REBELLION.

DISPOSSESSED

Those who demand a place in the sun, or in more vulgar language, a share in the loot.

Aldous Huxley

DISTANCE

The only thing the rich are willing for the poor to call theirs, and keep.   *Ambrose Bierce*

The thing that lends a warm nostalgia to one's relatives and ex-lovers.   *Eugene E. Brussell*

The great promoter of admiration.

Denis Diderot

SEE ALSO NOSTALGIA.

DISTINCTION

The consequences, never the object, of a great mind.   *Washington Allston*

A desire...which inclines every man first to hope, and then to believe, that Nature has given him something peculiar to himself.

Samuel Johnson

SEE ALSO INDIVIDUALITY.

DIVINITY

SEE GOD, HOLINESS.

DIVORCE

If she go not as you would have her, cut her off from your flesh, and give her a bill of divorce, and let her go.   *Bible: Ecclesiastes, XXV, 26.*

The function of the state.

Doctrines and Discipline of the Methodist Episcopal Church, 11, 1932.

The sacrament of adultery.   *French Proverb*

Holy deadlock.   *A. P. Herbert*

A legal separation of two persons of the opposite sex who desire to respect and honor each other.

Elbert Hubbard

From board and bed.   *Legal Phrase*

There are two causes...first adultery...The second cause is much like: when one runs away from the other, and after returning runs away again.

Martin Luther

Divorce is born of perverted morals, and leads, as experience shows, to vicious habits in public and private life.   *Pope Leo XIII*

The union of man and wife is from God, so divorce is from the devil.   *Saint Augustine*

Divorces are made in heaven.   *Oscar Wilde*

A hash made of domestic scraps.   *Ed Wynn*

An act of disengagement for trivial reasons because the couple was married for trivial reasons.

Anon.

The result of much "I do" about nothing.

Anon.

A check on the population explosion.   *Anon.*

The past tense of marriage.   *Anon.*

A resumption of diplomatic relations and rectification of boundaries.   *Anon.*

What happens when the marriage you thought was a merger turns out to be a conglomerate.   *Anon.*

A severance caused by matrimony and followed by alimony.   *Anon.*

SEE ALSO ALIMONY.

DOCTORS

(One who) is constantly striving for a balance between personal, human values (and) scientific realities and the inevitabilities of God's will.

David Allman

Someone who may be called off the golf course at a moment's notice.   *American Saying*

One upon whom we set our hopes when ill and our dogs when well.   *Ambrose Bierce*

Nature, time, and patience.   *Henry G. Bohn*

God's agents of healing, whether or not they acknowledge this fact.   *John S. Bonnell*

A falcon's eye, a girl's hand, a lion's heart.
      Dutch Proverb

An angel when he comes to cure, a devil when he asks for pay.   *English Proverb*

The cobblers ... of men's bodies; as the one patches our tattered clothes, so the other solders our diseased flesh.   *John Ford*

The first part of the cure.   *French Proverb*

Oxydable products, and the schools must keep furnishing new ones as the old ones turn into oxyds; some of first-rate quality that burn with a great light; some of a lower grade of brilliancy; some honestly ... by the grace of God, of moderate gifts, or in simple phrase, dull.
      Oliver Wendell Holmes 1

The first step toward a cure.   *Latin Proverb*

One of the few who have a mission. To cure incurable diseases.
      Henry Wadsworth Longfellow

A man who gets no pleasure out of the health of his friends.   *Michel de Montaigne*

Those who practice with their brains, and those who practice with their tongues.   *William Osler*

The servant of nature.   *Paracelsus*

Only a consoler of the mind.   *Petronius*

Not infrequently death's pilot-fish.
      G. D. Prentice

The middleman between the bird with the big bill and the guy with the big sickle.   *Donald Quinn*

A traffic cop to direct ailing people.
      Will Rogers

A conspiracy, not a profession ... Every doctor will allow a colleague to decimate a whole countryside sooner than violate the bond of professional etiquette by giving him away.
      George Bernard Shaw

He who calls when God has cured.
      Spanish Proverb

He is the flower (such as it is) of our civilization.
      Robert Louis Stevenson

One who grants the husband's prayers, or gives relief to long-expecting heirs.
      Adapted from Jonathan Swift

Men who prescribe medicines of which they know little, to cure diseases of which they know less, in human beings of whom they know nothing.
      Voltaire

The mark of a true doctor is usually illegible.
      Anon.

The only man who hasn't a guaranteed cure for a cold.   *Anon.*

SEE ALSO DISEASE, HEALTH, ILLNESS, MEDICINE, SURGEON.

DOCTRINE

There is no revealed doctrine proclaimed by the Church which is not contained in its exact substance in the sources of revelation, that is, in Scriptures and Tradition.   *Karl Adam*

The skin of truth set up and stuffed.
      Henry Ward Beecher

There is no Doctrine of Faith, but it perfectly accords with the Principles of True Reason.
      Charles Chauncy

The true doctrine is a master key to all the world's problems. With it the world can be taken apart and put together.   *Eric Hoffer*

(That which) insulates the devout not only against the realities around them but also against their own selves.   *Eric Hoffer*

A guidepost for weaklings.   *James Jacobson*

No doctrine is defined until it is violated.
      John Henry Newman

Religious doctrine is scientific poetry.   *Novalis*

Something that is explained by one's life.
      Matthew Prior

The most fearful tyrants to which men ever are subject, because doctrines get inside a man's own reason and betray him against himself. Civilized men have done their fiercest fighting for doctrines.   *William G. Sumner*

Something that won't make you happy unless it is translated into life.   *Henry Van Dyke*

Something that nails your faith. *Anon.*

SEE ALSO COMMUNISM, DOGMA, RELIGION, THEOLOGY.

DOG

The god of frolic. *Henry Ward Beecher*

(It) teaches a boy fidelity, perseverance, and to turn around three times before sitting down.

Robert Benchley

A . . . deity designed to catch the overflow and surplus of the world's worship. *Ambrose Bierce*

The only thing on this earth that loves you more than he loves himself. *Josh Billings*

In life the firmest friend, the first to welcome, foremost to defend. *Adapted from Lord Byron*

The dog alone, of all brute animals, has an affection upwards to man.

Samuel Taylor Coleridge

He has affection and character, he can enjoy equally the field and the fireside . . . a good fellow.

Leigh Hunt

Every man is Napoleon to him, hence the dog's constant popularity. *Aldous Huxley*

A liberal. He wants to please everybody.

William Kunstler

(That which is) fierce in the woods, gentle in the house. *Martial*

The dog is man's best friend,
He has a tail on one end.
Up in front he has teeth.
And four legs underneath. *Ogden Nash*

To be a high-mannered and high-minded gentleman, careless, affable, and gay, is the inborn pretension of the dog. *Robert Louis Stevenson*

If you pick up a starving dog and make him prosperous, he will not bite you. This is the principal difference between a man and his dog.

Mark Twain

The filthiest of the domestic animals. For this he makes up in a servile, fawning attitude towards his master. *Thorstein Veblen*

The one absolutely unselfish friend that man can have in this selfish world, the one that never deserts him, the one that never proves ungrateful or treacherous . . . When all other friends desert, he remains. *George G. Vest*

A heart-beat At my feet. *Edith Wharton*

A friend. *Xenophanes*

The only animal who has seen his god. *Anon.*

SEE ALSO ANIMALS, ETC.

DOGMA

Individual conviction. *Felix Adler*

The convictions of one man imposed authoritatively upon others. *Felix Adler*

Dogmatic theology is an attempt at both literary and scientific criticism of the highest order; and the age which developed dogma had neither the resources nor the faculty for such a criticism.

Matthew Arnold

The end of thought. *Gilbert Keith Chesterton*

It is only truth. *Romano Guardini*

The view that truth consists in a proposition which is a fixed and final result, or again which is directly known. *Georg W. Hegel*

A hard substance which forms in a soft brain.

Elbert Hubbard

A lie reiterated and authoritatively injected into the mind of one or more persons who believe that they believe what someone else believes.

Elbert Hubbard

Puppism come to its full growth.

Douglas Jerrold

Nothing more or less than emergency measures to which the Church is driven by heresies.

Hans Küng

Gross ignorance. *Jean de La Bruyère*

Catholic dogma is merely the witness, under special symbolism, of the enduring facts of human nature and the universe. *Arthur Machen*

The divine deposit of revelation.

Jacques Maritain

The belief of the Church as she herself has defined it . . . only the Church herself can do this.

John L. McKenzie

Theological dogmas are propositions expressive of the judgments which the mind forms, or the impressions which it receives, of revealed truth.

John Henry Newman

The fundamental principle of my religion.

John Henry Newman

What is dogma to the ordinary man is experience to the pure in heart.   *S. Radhakrishnan*

Authority . . . as the source of opinion.

Bertrand A. Russell

Today there is but one religious dogma in debate: What do you mean by "God"? . . . This is the fundamental religious dogma, and all the other dogmas are subsidiary to it.

Alfred North Whitehead

The ark within which the Church floats safely down the flood-tide of history.

Alfred North Whitehead

SEE ALSO BELIEF, CHURCH (ROMAN CATHOLIC), FAITH, ORTHODOXY, RELIGION.

DOLLAR

A soldier that does your bidding.   *Vincent Astor*

A piece of green paper having healing properties.

Jerry Dashkin

A sacred . . . object, contact with which is looked upon a curative and prophylactic.

Elbert Hubbard

That great object of universal devotion throughout our land.   *Washington Irving*

A friend that opens doors.   *Anon.*

The only object of worship.   *Anon.*

SEE ALSO GOLD, MONEY, RICHES, WEALTH.

DOUBT

The accomplice of tyranny.   *Henry F. Amiel*

Where doubt, there truth is—'tis her shadow.

Philip J. Bailey

An incentive to truth.   *Hosea Ballou*

A greater mischief than despair.   *John Denham*

Seeking to know is only too often learning to doubt.   *Antoinette Deshoulières*

The first step towards philosophy.

Denis Diderot

The trouble of a soul left to itself, which wants to see what God hides from it, and out of self-love.

François de Fénelon

The beginning, not the end of wisdom.

George Iles

What we see first when we look into a region hitherto unknown, unexplored, unannexed.

George Macdonald

Nothing but a trivial agitation on the surface of the soul.   *François Mauriac*

What gets you an education.   *Wilson Mizner*

The key to knowledge.   *Persian Proverb*

To suspend judgment.   *Philo*

(A) dissatisfied state from which we struggle to free ourselves and pass into the state of belief.

Charles S. Peirce

The beacon of the wise.   *William Shakespeare*

Confirmation of faith. It indicates the seriousness of the concern, its unconditional character.

Paul Tillich

(That which) makes men wise.   *Samuel Uceda*

Doubt is certainly not a pleasant condition, but certainly is an absurd one.   *Voltaire*

SEE ALSO AGNOSTICISM, ATHEISM, SKEPTICISM.

DRAMA

The absorption of the ideas by the characters, the dramatic or comic force which the characters give to the ideas.   *Henry Becque*

You crowd a mass of people together, not as you would crowd them in the streets, but as you would crowd them in a prison, in such a manner that it is humiliating for anybody present to make any protest.   *Gilbert Keith Chesterton*

The business . . . is to recommend virtue, and discountenance vice.   *Jeremy Collier*

A just and lively image of human nature, representing its passions and humors, and the changes of fortune to which it is subject, for the delight and instruction of mankind.   *John Dryden*

A slice of life artistically put on the boards.

Jean Jullien

In all ages the drama...through its portrayal of the acting and suffering spirit of man, has been more closely allied than any other art to his deeper thoughts concerning his nature and destiny.   *Ludwig Lewisohn*

What literature does at night.

George Jean Nathan

All really great drama is a form of scandal.

George Jean Nathan

The reflection of a great doubt in the heart and mind of a great, sad, gay man.

George Jean Nathan

Thoughtful rest.   *John Ruskin*

Rhetoric, irony, argument, paradox, epigram, parable, the rearrangement of haphazard facts into orderly and intelligent situations.

George Bernard Shaw

Seeking out the points where great battles take place.   *August Strindberg*

(Something) like the symphony...(It) does not teach or prove anything.   *John M. Synge*

SEE ALSO ACTING.

DRAMATIST

He is usually thought of as a slightly benighted child of nature who somehow or other did it all on a ouija board.   *Maxwell Anderson*

Either a rebel and an artist or a yes man and a hack.   *Eric Bentley*

Like any other writer, he must be somebody—in order to write the somebody he is—and in order to write the world in which he is.   *Eric Bentley*

The business of the dramatist is to keep out of sight, and to let nothing appear but his characters. As soon as he attracts notice to his personal feelings, the illusion is broken.

Thomas B. Macaulay

Of all the imitators, the dramatists are the most perverse, the most unconscionable, of the most unconscious, and have been so time out of mind.

Edgar Allan Poe

(Those who) express their times and guide the public through the complexities of these times.

Robert Sherwood

A congenital eavesdropper with the instincts of a Peeping Tom.   *Kenneth Tynan*

One who believes that the pure event, as an action involving human beings, is more arresting than any comment that can be made upon it.

Thornton Wilder

SEE ALSO THEATER.

DREAM

Excursions to the limbo of things, a semi-deliverance from the human prison.   *Henry F. Amiel*

A vision of the night.   *Bible: Job, XXXIII, 15.*

Children of night, of indigestion bred.

Charles Churchill

(That which) permits each and every one of us to be quietly and safely insane every night of our lives.   *William Dement*

The ghost of a shadow.   *Joseph Devlin*

All dreams are from repletion and complexion bred, from rising fumes of undigested food.

Adapted from John Dryden

A dream only reflects the dreamer's thoughts.

Jonathan Eleazar

Dreams retain the infirmities of our character. The good genius may be there or not; our evil genius is sure to stay.   *Ralph Waldo Emerson*

What makes existence tolerable.

Anatole France

Fiction that helps to sleep.   *Sigmund Freud*

The imaginary gratification of unconscious wishes.   *Sigmund Freud*

A microscope through which we look at the hidden occurrences in our soul.   *Erich Fromm*

What one covets awake.   *German Proverb*

The incomplete form of prophecy.

Isaac Hanina

Daydreams are the gaseous decomposition of true purpose.   *Henry S. Haskins*

A sixtieth part of prophecy.   *Hebrew Proverb*

Dreams are made up mainly of matters that have been in the dreamer's thoughts during the day.

Herodotus

Part of an eternal life.   *Henry Holt*

A private theater where indigestion is the prompter.   *Elbert Hubbard*

A translation of waking life.   *René Magritte*

For what one has dwelt on by day, these things are seen in visions of the night.   *Menander*

The true interpreters of our inclinations, but ... art is required to sort and understand them.
Michel de Montaigne

Each age.   *Arthur O'Shaughnessy*

What we wish for waking.   *George Pettie*

All that we see or seem
Is but a dream within a dream.
Edgar Allan Poe

You eat, in dreams, the custard of the day.
Alexander Pope

To think by moonlight by the light of an inner moon.   *Jules Renard*

Children of an idle brain.   *William Shakespeare*

Nothing but vain fantasy, which is as thin of substance as the air and more inconstant than the wind.   *Adapted from William Shakespeare*

A secretion of our thoughts, and through them our thought is purified.   *Pinhas Shapiro*

Mere productions of the brain, and fools consult interpreters in vain.   *Jonathan Swift*

Where thought in fancy's maze runs mad.
Adapted from Edward Young

Disguised conflict within the individual.   *Anon.*

A secret code, different for each person, which we learn to decipher.   *Anon.*

SEE ALSO ILLUSION, SLEEP.

DREAMER

All men of action.   *James G. Huneker*

One who can only find his way by moonlight, and his punishment is that he sees the dawn before the rest of the world.   *Oscar Wilde*

DRESS

Mirrors a nation's pain and sorrow, its pleasures and joys.   *Adolf Brüll*

(What) the tailor shapes.   *John Bulwer*

The fashion of the country wherein one lives.
Saint John the Bapist

The soul of a man.   *William Shakespeare*

The desire to please by outward charms.
Tertullian

Woman's first duty in life ... what the second duty is no one has yet discovered.   *Oscar Wilde*

Woman's never-ending endeavor to improve on her skin.   *Anon.*

SEE ALSO CLOTHES, FASHION.

DRINKING

Drinking is bad taste but tastes good.
Franklin P. Adams

(An activity which) washes off the daub and discovers the man.   *Henry G. Bohn*

Something to do while getting drunk.
Peggy Bracken

A mere pause from thinking!   *Lord Byron*

Drink drives out the man and brings out the beast.
Albert Camus

The soldier's pleasure.   *John Dryden*

(That which) does not drown care, but waters it, and makes it grow faster.   *Benjamin Franklin*

Medicine to the sorrowful.   *Max Gralnick*

Makes one noisy and absurd. It makes men speak the truth, but that is of little value unless the person is a liar when he's sober.
Adapted from Samuel Johnson

Wild anarchy.   *Ben Jonson*

One of the worst evils in our sensate culture.
Albion R. King

There are two reasons for drinking ... when you are thirsty, to cure it; the other, when you are not thirsty, to prevent it.   *Thomas L. Peacock*

The happiness that it brings is merely negative, a momentary cessation of unhappiness.
Bertrand A. Russell

The social lubricant.   *Edward Strecker*

The occupational disease of the reporter.
Stanley Walker

A way to make other people interesting.   *Anon.*

Something that makes one lose inhibitions and render exhibitions.   *Anon.*

Putting an enemy in your stomach to steal away your brains.   *Anon.*

SEE ALSO WHISKEY, WINE.

DRUNKARD

A person who tries to pull himself out of trouble with a corkscrew.   *Edward Baldwin*

Fools...beasts...devils.   *Henry G. Bohn*

(One who can) always beer up under misfortune.   *Marcelene Cox*

The Devil's swill-tub walking upright.   *Lorenzo Dow*

He is a drunkard who takes more than three glasses, though he be not drunk.   *Epictetus*

A fool's tongue and a knave's heart.   *Thomas Fuller*

Like a whiskey bottle, all neck and belly and no head.   *Austin O'Malley*

A living corpse.   *Saint John Chrysostom*

One who can live neither with alcohol nor without it.   *Anon.*

A red nose, white liver, a blue outlook.   *Anon.*

One who beats everyone to the punch.   *Anon.*

DRUNKENNESS

Shame lost and shame found.   *Josh Billings*

A joy reserved for the gods: so men do partake of it impiously, and so they are very properly punished for their audacity.   *James Branch Cabell*

A foul record.   *Geoffrey Chaucer*

Sepulchre of a man's wit and his discretion.   *Geoffrey Chaucer*

(A vice which) spoils health, dismounts the mind, and unmans men. It reveals secrets, is quarrelsome, lascivious, impudent, dangerous and mad.   *Lord Chesterfield*

(A condition which) insulates us in thought, whilst it unites us in feeling.   *Ralph Waldo Emerson*

The failure of a man to control his thoughts.   *David Grayson*

The variety of behavior...is the same with that of madmen: some of them being raging, others loving, others laughing, all extravagantly, but according to their several domineering passions.   *Thomas Hobbes*

An expression identical with ruin.   *Pythagoras*

Temporary suicide.   *Bertrand A. Russell*

The ruin of reason. It is premature old age ... temporary death.   *Saint Basil*

Simply voluntary insanity.   *Seneca*

The result of an inability to accommodate oneself ... to reality.   *John W. Sullivan*

A vice which is painful and sickly in the very acting of it.   *Jeremy Taylor*

The wrath of grapes.   *Anon.*

Suicide on the installment plan.   *Anon.*

DULLARD

The secret of their power is their insensibility to blows; tickle them with a bludgeon and they laugh with a platitude.   *Ambrose Bierce*

(One whom) nature delights in punishing.   *Ralph Waldo Emerson*

The dull man who is always sure, and the sure man who is always dull.   *Henry Louis Mencken*

One who likes to think with other people's heads.   *Anon.*

One who is less than meets the eye.   *Anon.*

SEE ALSO BORE.

DUTY

Never to tire, never to grow cold; to be patient, sympathetic, tender; to look for the budding flower and the opening heart; to hope always; like God, to love always—this is duty.   *Henry F. Amiel*

Fear God, and keep his commandments: for this is the whole duty of man.
Bible: Ecclesiastes, XII, 13.

That which...impels us in the direction of profit, along the line of desire.   *Ambrose Bierce*

The dominant conception of life.
Louis D. Brandeis

I recognize only one...and that is to love.
Albert Camus

To do what lies clearly at hand.
Thomas Carlyle

What you should do.   *Claudian*

What I must do...not what the people think.
Ralph Waldo Emerson

To represent in my own person, in so far as I am able, the most complete and perfect humanity.
Johann G. Fichte

Consists of pretending that the trivial is critical.
John Fowles

The true source of rights.   *Mohandas K. Gandhi*

That mode of action on the part of the individual which constitutes the best possible application of his capacity to the general benefit.
William Godwin

Whatever the day calls for.   *Johann W. Goethe*

The great highway men call "I ought."
Adapted from Ellen S. Hooper

A pleasure which we try to make ourselves believe is a hardship.   *Elbert Hubbard*

"Learn what is true in order to do what is right," is the summary.   *Thomas Henry Huxley*

To serve society; and, after we have done that, we may attend wholly to the salvation of our own souls.   *Samuel Johnson*

The obligation to act in reverence for law.
Immanuel Kant

A road to bring us, daily, nearer to God.
John Keble

A divine law.   *Douglas C. Macintosh*

A cold and cheerless business, but it does give one a queer sort of satisfaction.
Adapted from William Somerset Maugham

The sole standard of life.   *Giuseppe Mazzini*

The common collective faith.
Giuseppe Mazzini

Every mission.   *Giuseppe Mazzini*

Seeking only to do...work in life honestly and well.   *George S. Merriam*

That action which will cause more good to exist in the universe than any possible alternative.
George M. Moore

A path which all men may tread.
William Morris

(Something that) is useful in work, but offensive in personal relations.   *Bertrand A. Russell*

Doing what we ought.   *Saint Augustine*

To submit ourselves with all humility to the established limits of our intelligence; and not perversely to rebel against them.
Herbert Spencer

The way to glory.   *Alfred Lord Tennyson*

A man performs but one duty—the duty of continuing his spirit, the duty of making himself agreeable to himself.   *Mark Twain*

To be unattached and to work as free beings, to give up all work unto God.   *Vivekananda*

Law in practice.   *Benjamin Whichcote*

Duty is what one expects from others—it is not what one does oneself.   *Oscar Wilde*

Obligations with a dash of resentment.   *Anon.*

SEE ALSO RESPONSIBILITY.

DYING

That dreadful season.   *Joseph Addison*

A momentary pang.   *John André*

One of the things that nature wills.
Marcus Aurelius

The act of dying is also one of the acts of life.
Marcus Aurelius

An awfully big adventure.   *James M. Barrie*

He gathered up his feet into the bed, and yielded up the ghost, and was gathered unto his people.
Bible: Genesis, XLIX, 33.

The last gasp.   *Bible: Maccabees, II, 32.*

Just one more step down the road of life.

Jesse Bishop

Going the way of all flesh.

Thomas Dekker and John Webster

That breakdown in an organism which throws it out of correspondence with some necessary part of the environment.   *Henry Drummond*

We do not die wholly at our deaths: we have mouldered away gradually long before. Death only consigns the last fragment of what we were to the grave.   *William Hazlitt*

A great leap in the dark.   *Thomas Hobbes*

A natural appointment from which there is no hope of escape.   *Jonathan Miller*

What nature teaches you in proper time.

Michel de Montaigne

I have careful records of about 500 deathbeds, studied particularly with reference to the modes of death and the sensations of the dying ... The great majority gave no sign one way or the other; like birth, their death was a sleep and a forgetting.

William Osler

To put off a garment. For the body is about the soul as a garment; and after laying this aside for a short time by means of death, we shall resume it again with the more splendor.

Saint John Chrysostom

Something ghastly, as being born is something ridiculous.   *George Santayana*

Ceasing to be afraid.   *William Wycherley*

On the way to a great perhaps.   *Anon.*

SEE ALSO DEATH, GRAVE, MONUMENT.

E

EAR

Something we can not close at will, and we are the poorer for it.   *Emile Brian*

A bony labyrinthean cave.   *Abraham Coles*

Two music-rooms.   *Thomas Dekker*

The only true writer and the only true reader.
Robert Frost

The gates to the mind.   *Moses Ibn Ezra*

The road to the heart.   *Voltaire*

EARTH

That point equally near to heaven and to the infinite.   *Henry F. Amiel*

Something that you are on today, but it is on you tomorrow.   *Adapted from Isaac Benjacob*

A lump of clay surrounded by water.
Bhartrihari: The Vairagya Sataka.

The heaven is my throne, and the earth is my footstool.   *Bible: Isaiah, LXVI, 1.*

The earth is the Lord's, and the fullness thereof.
Bible: Psalms, XXIV, 1.

The heavens are the heavens of the Lord; but the earth has He given to the children of men.
Bible: Psalms, CXV, 6.

The great tomb of man.   *William Cullen Bryant*

The lunatic asylum of the solar system.
Samuel P. Cadman

A globe carelessly hurled into the Universe to annoy the Heavens.   *Elias Canetti*

Mother of numberless children.
Samuel Taylor Coleridge

The best investment on earth.   *Louis Glickman*

The frozen echo of the silent voice of God.
S. M. Hageman

A stage which God and nature do with actors fill.
Thomas Heywood

A small...planet, full of noise, nonsense ... created in order to swell the pockets of politicians.
Elbert Hubbard

The heritage of the strong...the future belongs to the victorious people who have a right to life.
Ahmad Hussein

The earth is given as a common stock for man to labor and live on.   *Thomas Jefferson*

The only heaven.   *Arthur Keith*

The earth is round, and is inhabited on all sides...is insignificantly small, and is borne through the stars.   *Johann Kepler*

The grave ... wherein all things that live must rot.
John Marston

The draught wherein the heavenly bodies discharge their corruption; the very muckhill on which the sublunary orbs cast their excrements.   *John Marston*

Just a dusty road.   *John Masefield*

A spot, a grain, an atom.   *John Milton*

Only a ball-bearing in the hub of the universe.   *Christopher Morley*

A round body in the center of the heavens.   *Plato*

This congregated ball.   *Alexander Pope*

A bawdy planet.   *William Shakespeare*

A water-covered sphere, crusted here and there with continents upon which there is the fragile green hue of life.   *Walter Sullivan*

A dying cinder.   *Alpheus H. Verrill*

Footstool of our God...our house, our parent, and our nurse.   *Isaac Watts*

The dream of God.   *John H. Wheelock*

The final tomb of all that is good, bad, and indifferent.   *Anon.*

SEE ALSO UNIVERSE, WORLD.

EATING AND DRINKING

The gift of God.   *Bible: Ecclesiastes, III, 13.*

What you are.   *Antheime Brillat-Savarin*

There is no heaven but this.   *Arthur H. Clough*

My recreation.   *Chauncey Depew*

The way to a man's heart.   *Fanny Fern*

The demagogic demands of the belly.   *Elbert Hubbard*

A sacred rite among the rich.   *Elbert Hubbard*

An artificial aid to conversation and the repetition of threadbare stories.   *Elbert Hubbard*

A universal law...most persistent and inexorable.   *Mendel of Kotz*

The function that kills more people than wars.   *Anon.*

SEE ALSO APPETITE, COOKING, DIET, FOOD, GOURMAND, GOURMET, STOMACH.

ECCENTRICITY

A method of distinction so cheap that fools employ it to accentuate their incapacity.   *Ambrose Bierce*

Eccentricity is originality without sense.   *John S. Blackie*

(That which) has always abounded when and where strength of character has abounded; and the amount of eccentricity in a society has been proportional to the amount of genius, mental vigor, and moral courage it contained.   *John Stuart Mill*

All strangeness and self-particularity in our manners and condition.   *Michel de Montaigne*

An enemy to society and civil conversation.   *Michel de Montaigne*

An outlaw.   *Alexander Smith*

Oddities and singularities of behavior.   *William Temple*

ECCLESIASTES

Modern...skeptical...blasé...so fashionably free from enthusiasm, from all fervor or deep conviction.   *Leon Harrison*

Nowhere else can we see so plainly the singularity, the variety, the unexpectedness of Jewish genius.   *Ernest Renan*

Nothing grander...in its impassioned survey of mortal pain and pleasure, its estimate of failure and success...no poem working more indomitably for spiritual illumination.   *Edmund C. Steadman*

ECHO

The pleasure of hearing yourself talk.   *William Congreve*

The voice divine of human loyalty.   *George Eliot*

Something that always has the last word.   *German Proverb*

The voice of a reflection in the mirror.   *Nathaniel Hawthorne*

The shadow of a sound—a voice without a mouth, and words without a tongue.   *Horace Smith*

ECONOMICS

The savage struggle for a crumb that has converted mankind into wolves and sheep.

Alexander Berkman

The savage struggle for a crumb that has converted mankind into wolves and sheep.

Alexander Berkman

The ever recurring decisive forces, the chief points in the process of history.

Eduard Bernstein

The dismal science. *Thomas Carlyle*

The very foundation of social and moral well-being. *Felix Frankfurter*

Like theology...economics deal with matters which men consider very close to their lives.

John Kenneth Galbraith

The science of the production, distribution and use of wealth, best understood by college professors on halfrations. *Elbert Hubbard*

The science of managing one's household.

Seneca

SEE ALSO BUDGETING, CREDIT, MONEY.

ECONOMIST

A guy with a Phi Beta Kappa key on one end of his watch chain and no watch on the other end.

Alben W. Barkley

A man who states the obvious in terms of the incomprehensible. *Alfred A. Knopf*

The economist must concern himself with the ultimate aims of man. *Alfred Marshall*

Theologians. *Karl Marx*

A person who knows all about money but has none. *J. Marvin Peterson*

One who guesses wrong with confidence.

Anon.

ECONOMY

Mere parsimony is not economy...Expense, and great expense, may be an essential part of true economy. *Edmund Burke*

One of the highest essentials of a free government...always a guarantee of peace.

Calvin Coolidge

The wealth of the poor, and the wisdom of the rich. *Alexandre Dumas*

To spend less than you get. *Benjamin Franklin*

Going without something you do want, in case you should someday want something which you probably won't like. *Anthony Hope*

The doctrine of proportion reduced to practice...foreseeing contingencies and providing against them...expecting contingencies and being prepared for them. *Hannah More*

Cutting down other people's wages.

John B. Morton

The carefulness and detail of thrift.

Theodore T. Munger

A great revenue. *John Ray*

The art of making the most of life.

George Bernard Shaw

To pitch your scale of living one degree below your means. *Henry J. Taylor*

The poor man's mint. *Martin F. Tupper*

Denying yourself a necessity today that you may buy a luxury tomorrow. *Anon.*

The art of spending money without getting any fun out of it. *Anon.*

EDINBURGH

That most picturesque (at a distance) and nastiest (when near) of all capital cities. *Thomas Gray*

A modern Athens—fit for modern Greeks.

James Hannay

SEE ALSO SCOTLAND.

EDISON, THOMAS ALVA (1847-1931)

My father thought I was stupid, and I almost decided I must be a dunce.

Thomas Alva Edison

I used never to be able to get along at school. I was always at the foot of the class. I used to feel that the teachers did not sympathize with me.

Thomas Alva Edison

Deafness probably drove me to reading.

Thomas Alva Edison

My refuge was the Detroit Public Library. I read the library. *Thomas Alva Edison*

I don't care so much about making my fortune as I do for getting ahead of the other fellows.

Thomas Alva Edison

It has been just so in all my inventions. The first step is an intuition—and comes with a burst, then difficulties arise...I have the right principle...time, hard work and some good luck are necessary. *Thomas Alva Edison*

I would construct a theory and work on its lines until I found it untenable, then it would be discarded and another theory evolved.

Thomas Alva Edison

Edison's first thought, in approaching a problem...was to evaluate the matter in terms of helpfulness to others. *Harvey S. Firestone 2*

His inventions created millions of new jobs ... Edison has done more toward abolishing poverty than all the reformers and statesmen.

Henry Ford

A mere mechanic. *Cardinal Gibbons*

A central figure of this age of applied science.

The Independent, May 1, 1913.

He ate at his desk and slept in a chair. In six weeks he had gone through the books, written a volume of abstracts, and made two thousand experiments...and produced a solution.

Edward H. Johnson

A rough-hewn, old-fashioned American individualist...one of the most prolific inventors known to history. *Matthew Josephson*

He was indeed hard to teach. Whatever he learned in his own way...though his mother inspired him, no one ever *taught* him anything; he taught himself. *Matthew Josephson*

To my mind, Edison's greatest "invention" was organized research. *Charles F. Kettering*

Edison (is) famous for such inventions as the cylinder phonograph, the carbon microphone, multiplex telegraphy, the motion picture camera...and, greatest of all, the development of a complete system for the generation, distribution and utilization of electric power.

Sherman R. Knapp

The indispensable man of the two centuries which his life spanned. *Thomas W. Martin*

The great research-minded genius who gave the first practical start to the electric industry.

Thomas W. Martin

A discoverer. *Nature, Mar. 20, 1879.*

He wields a power and magnitude of which no warrior ever dreamed. This democratic, kindly, modest man...is humanity's friend.

Arthur J. Palmer

The great intuitive and practical inventor.

David Sarnoff

The poet of technology, seeking out hidden rhythms in nature, combining them in symphonies of invention. *David Sarnoff*

One of the wonders of the world...He produces accomplished facts.

Scientific American, Dec., 1878.

A practical scientist. *Anon.*

The inventor who willed himself into being different. *Anon.*

The peaceful revolutionary. *Anon.*

EDITOR

One whose editorials are forgotten by the time circumstances prove him wrong. *Jerry Dashkin*

A man who knows what he wants, but doesn't know what it is. *Walter Davenport*

A person employed on a newspaper, whose business it is to separate the wheat from the chaff, and to see that the chaff is printed. *Elbert Hubbard*

A bit of sandpaper applied to all forms of originality. *Elbert Hubbard*

A delicate instrument for observing the development and flowering of the...mediocre and encouraging its growth. *Elbert Hubbard*

Who would not be an editor? To write the magic *we* of such enormous might; to be so great beyond the common span that it takes the plural to express the man. *Adapted from J. G. Saxe*

One whose profession is arguing with writers.

Anon.

A reporter whose legs have gone back on him.

Anon.

He who makes a long story short. *Anon.*

SEE ALSO NEWS, PRESS (THE).

EDUCATION

There are...two educations. One should teach us how to make a living and the other how to live.

James Truslow Adams

A companion which no misfortune can depress, no crime can destroy, no enemy can alienate, no despotism can enslave...Without it, what is man? A splendid slave, a reasoning savage.

Joseph Addison

Observation more than books, experience rather than persons. *Amos Bronson Alcott*

The whole object of education is...to develop the mind. The mind should be a thing that works.

Sherwood Anderson

First, religious and moral principles; secondly, gentlemanly conduct; thirdly, intellectual ability.

Thomas Arnold

Training for duty. *Berthold Auerbach*

The aim...should be to teach us rather how to think, than what to think. *James Beattie*

To make a tool of every faculty—how to open it, how to keep it sharp, and how to apply it to all practical purposes. *Henry Ward Beecher*

Our sixth sense. *Clive Bell*

Self-education. *Jessie L. Bennett*

That which discloses to the wise and disguises from the foolish their lack of understanding.

Ambrose Bierce

Learning what you didn't know you didn't know.

Daniel J. Boorstin

Work 'em hard, play 'em hard, feed 'em up to the nines, and send 'em to bed so tired that they are asleep before their heads are on the pillow.

Franklin Boyden

(Something which) makes a people easy to lead, but difficult to drive; easy to govern, but impossible to enslave. *Lord Brougham*

Not to be frightened by the best but to treat it as part of daily life. *John Mason Brown*

One of the few things a person is willing to pay for and not get. *William L. Bryan*

The cheap defense of nations. *Edmund Burke*

Reeling and writhing and different branches of arithmetic—ambition, distraction, uglification, and derision. *Lewis Carroll*

The task...is to bring the young and the great together. *John Jay Chapman*

Not an object, but a method.

Gilbert Keith Chesterton

The development of desirable traits and characteristics. *Franklin Cody*

An ornament to the fortunate, a haven of refuge to the unfortunate. *Democritus*

Capacity for further education. *John Dewey*

The true center of correlation on the school subject is...the child's own social activities.

John Dewey

The acquisition of those habits that effect an adjustment of an individual and his environment.

John Dewey

The stimulation of the child's powers by the demands of the social situations in which he finds himself. *John Dewey*

The methodical creation of the habit of thinking.

Ernest Dimnet

A progressive discovery of our own ignorance.

Will Durant

The seeing of things in the making.

Thomas Alva Edison

To discipline rather than to furnish the mind; to train it to the use of its own powers, rather than fill it with the accumulation of others.

Tyron Edwards

In a Christian society education must be religious...in the sense that its aims will be directed by a Christian philosophy of life.

Thomas Stearns Eliot

A better safeguard of liberty than a standing army.

Edward Everett

Being able to differentiate between what you do know and what you don't. It's knowing where to go to find out what you need to know; and it's knowing how to use the information once you get it. *William Feather*

Driving a set of prejudices down your throat.

Martin Fisher

Without ideals, without effort, without scholarship, without philosophical continuity, there is no such thing as education. *Abraham Flexner*

The liberation, organization, and direction of power and intelligence, with the development of taste, with culture. *Abraham Flexner*

All the minds of past ages.

Bernard de Fontenelle

Helping the child realize his potentialities.

Erich Fromm

The root of the word education is *e-ducere*, literally, to lead forth, or to bring out something which is potentially present. *Erich Fromm*

Hanging around until you've caught on.

Robert Frost

The ability to listen to almost anything without losing your temper or your self-confidence.

Robert Frost

A decent home...honest virtuous parents.

Mohandas K. Gandhi

Every man who rises above the common level has received two educations: the first from his teachers; the second, more personal and important, from himself. *Edward Gibbon*

The only real education comes from what goes counter to you. *André Gide*

To stimulate the child's impulses and call forth the best and noblest tendencies. *Emma Goldman*

Education is Making Men. *Arthur Guiterman*

(That which) shows a man how little other people know. *Thomas C. Haliburton*

What remains when we have forgotten all that we have been taught. *Lord Halifax*

To be able to be caught up into the world of thought. *Edith Hamilton*

(The purpose of a liberal one) is to make one's mind a pleasant place to spend one's leisure.

Sydney Harris

Burning into the heart and brain of youth...an instinctive and comprehended sense of race.

Adolf Hilter

A form of self-delusion. *Elbert Hubbard*

The instruction of the intellect in the laws of Nature, under which name I include not merely things and their forces, but men and their ways; and the fashioning of the affections and of the will into an earnest and loving desire to move in harmony with those laws.

Thomas Henry Huxley

The development of the memory at the expense of the imagination. *Owen Johnson*

The first resort as well as the last, for a world-wide solution of the problem of freedom.

Horace M. Kallen

The aim (of Jewish education) is to develop a sincere faith in the holiness of life and a sense of responsibility for enabling the Jewish people to make its contribution to the achievement of the good life. *Mordecai M. Kaplan*

A chest of tools. *Herbert Kaufman*

A kind of state-supported baby-sitting service.

Gerald Kennedy

To develop the personality of the individual and the significance of his life to himself and to others. *Grayson Kirk*

A kind of begetting. *Georg C. Lichtenberg*

(That which leads) one to the right loves and hatreds. *Lin Yutang*

(It conducts) us to that enjoyment which is...the best in quality and infinite in quantity.

Horace Mann

To convert the mind into a living fountain, and not a reservoir. *John M. Mason*

That which fits a man to perform justly, skilfully, and magnanimously all the offices, both private and public, of peace and war. *John Milton*

The contact of ideas with events.

Felix M. Morley

(That which) gives a man a clear, conscious view of his own opinions and judgments, a truth in developing them, an eloquence in expressing them, and a force in urging them.

John Henry Newman

A conscious, methodical application of the best means in the wisdom of the ages to the end that youth may know how to live completely.

Austin O'Malley

Character development.   *William J. O'Shea*

Being afraid at the right time.   *Angelo Patri*

A debt due from present to future generations.

George Peabody

Nothing more than the polishing of each single link in the great chain that binds humanity together and gives it unity.   *Johann H. Pestalozzi*

A method whereby one acquires a higher grade of prejudices.   *Laurence J. Peter*

The only interest worthy of the deep, controlling anxiety of the thoughtful man.   *Wendell Phillips*

The noisy jargon of the schools.   *John Pomfret*

The role and object . . . is the formation of a new human being, reborn in baptism, into a perfect Christian.   *Pope Pius XII*

Real education must ultimately be limited to men who insist on knowing—the rest is mere sheepherding.   *Ezra Pound*

The acquiring of a life style.   *Kenneth Rexroth*

Ephemeral knowledge and tenacious dislike.

Jean Rostand

Leading human souls to what is best, and making what is best out of them.   *John Ruskin*

To help the child in its own battle, to strengthen it and equip it, not for some outside end proposed by the state, or by any other impersonal authority, but to the ends which the child's own spirit is obscurely seeking.   *Bertrand A. Russell*

A change effected in the organism to satisfy the desires of the operator.   *Bertrand A. Russell*

One of the chief obstacles to intelligence and freedom of thought.   *Bertrand A. Russell*

The established church of the United States.

Michael E. Sadler

To get experience out of ideas.

George Santayana

Education is what you read in fine print; experience is what you get when you don't.

Peter Seeger

That which gives a man his liberty.   *Seneca*

What we call education and culture is for the most part nothing but the substitution of reading for experience . . . obsolete fictions for contemporary experience.   *George Bernard Shaw*

To direct vanity to proper objects.   *Adam Smith*

To give children resources that will endure as long as life endures.   *Sidney Smith*

To live under the dominion of one's own reason.

Baruch Spinoza

A weapon, whose effect depends on who holds it in his hands and at whom it is aimed.

Joseph Stalin

The inculcation of the incomprehensible into the ignorant by the incompetent.   *Josiah Stamp*

The great end . . . to raise ourselves above the vulgar.   *Richard Steele*

Training through love.   *Wilhelm Stekel*

The raising of character by the broadening of vision and the deepening of feeling.

Mayer Sulzberger

Its purpose is . . . the discipline of the mind for its own sake.   *Allen Tate*

Something said in private conversation one day in the street, a remark by a teacher in the middle of a discussion, a book picked up in someone's room.

Harold Taylor

To give us confidence, and to make us think ourselves on a level with other men.

J. Horne Took

(That which) has produced a vast population able to read but unable to distinguish what is worth reading.   *George M. Trevelyan*

Consists mainly in what we have unlearned.

Mark Twain

The thing (when formal) that enables a man to get along without the use of his intelligence.

Alfred Wiggam

(A process) which makes one rogue cleverer than another.   *Oscar Wilde*

An educated man is one who can entertain a new idea, entertain another person and entertain himself.   *Sydney Wood*

Teaching people to behave as they prefer not to behave.   *Anon.*

A continuing dialogue assuming different points of view.   *Anon.*

Job training.   *Anon.*

Teaching a child how to talk—and then how to keep quiet.   *Anon.*

What's left over after you've forgotten the facts.
Anon.

To reverence superiority and accept a fact though it slay him is the final test of an educated man.
Anon.

SEE ALSO COLLEGE, EXPERIENCE, GENTLEMAN, KNOWLEDGE, LEARNING, MOTHER, NATURE, PEDANT, PEDANTRY, PROFESSOR, SCHOOL, TEACHER, UNIVERSITY.

EGG

The egg is smooth and very pale;
It has no nose, it has no tail;
It has no ears that one can see;
It has no wit, no repartee.   *Roy Bishop*

A hen is only an egg's way of making another egg.
Samuel Butler 2

Every living thing comes from an egg.
William Harvey

A chicken *in potentia*.   *Ben Jonson*

Always an adventure: it may be different.
Oscar Wilde

A potential omelette.   *Anon.*

SEE ALSO HEN.

EGO

The only trip. You are who you are because of your ego.   *John Cassavetes*

The immediate dictate of human consciousness.
Max Planck

The monstrous appetite of the self, requiring no nourishment to grow.   *Anon.*

That which makes you judge yourself and turn in a favorable verdict.   *Anon.*

The personality as the center of the universe.
Anon.

Some spark within us which leads us to believe that we are better than we are, and which is often instrumental in proving it.   *Anon.*

SEE ALSO CONCEIT, SELF-ESTEEM, SELF-LOVE, VANITY.

EGOISM

Frozen compassion.   *Ludwig Boerne*

The anesthetic given by a kindly nature to relieve the pain of being a damned fool.
Bellamy Brooks

The tongue of vanity.   *Nicolas Chamfort*

An amiable illusion, which the shape of our planet prompts, that every man is at the top of the world.   *Ralph Waldo Emerson*

(A quality which) centers and concentrates man upon himself, but at the same time...limits his theoretical outlook because he is indifferent to everything which is not directly related to his own welfare.   *Ludwig A. Feuerbach*

The characteristic of self-taught men.
William Hazlitt

A mind that is full, and full of itself.
Joseph Joubert

The anesthetic that dulls the pain of stupidity.
Franklin Leahy

(A) kind of religion in which the more devoted a man is, the fewer proselytes he makes, the worship of himself.   *George Macdonald*

The essence of a self-reliant and autonomous culture.   *Henry Louis Mencken*

The very essence of a noble soul.
Friedrich W. Nietzsche

To identify consciousness with that which merely reflects consciousness.   *Patanjali*

To curry favor with myself.   *Phaedrus*

When a man is wrapped up in himself.
John Ruskin

A case of mistaken nonentity.
Barbara Stanwyck

An alphabet of one letter.   *Anon.*

Believing that you are always the center of observation.   *Anon.*

When nothing is more to yourself than yourself.
Anon.

A great love affair involving one actor—unassisted.
Anon.

Self-confidence looking for trouble.   *Anon.*

The anesthesia that keeps people on living terms with themselves.
Anon.

SEE ALSO SELF-ESTEEM, SELF-LOVE, VANITY.

EGOTIST

One who's always me-deep in conversation.
William Bertolotti

A person of low taste, more interested in himself than in me.
Ambrose Bierce

A person who thinks he knows as much as you do.
Ambrose Bierce

A self-made man who worships his creator.
John Bright

(One who) worships his creator.
William Cowper

A cock who thinks the sun has risen to hear him crow.
Adapted from George Eliot

The pest of society.   *Ralph Waldo Emerson*

One who is always letting off esteem.
Paul Gilbert

(One who) does not tolerate egoism.
Joseph Roux

The man whose eye is ever on himself.
Adapted from William Wordsworth

One who talks about himself so much that he gives you no time to talk about yourself.   *Anon.*

One whose only good feature is that he seldom gossips about other people.   *Anon.*

One who is law unto himself.   *Anon.*

EINSTEIN, ALBERT (1879-1955)

I remind myself that my inner and outer life depend on the labor of other men, living and dead, and that I must exert myself in order to give the same measure as I have received.
Albert Einstein

I am strongly drawn to the simple life.
Albert Einstein

I have never looked upon ease and happiness as ends in themselves...The ordinary objects of human endeavor—property, outward success, luxury—have always seemed to me contemptible.
Albert Einstein

I gang my own gait and have never belonged to my country, my home, my friends, or even my immediate family.   *Albert Einstein*

It is necessary for the success of any complex undertaking that one man should do the thinking and directing and in general bear the responsibility.   *Albert Einstein*

The really valuable thing in...life (is) the creative, sentient, individual, the personality; it alone creates the noble and sublime, while the herd remains dull in thought and dull in feeling.
Albert Einstein

He is cheerful, sure of himself and agreeable. He understands as much about psychology as I do about physics, so we had a very pleasant talk.
Sigmund Freud

A man...whose achievements can be measured only by the few who are able to follow his reasoning and challenge his conclusions.
Alan Harris

From the point of view of his teachers he was an unsatisfactory pupil, apparently incapable of progress in languages, history, geography, and other primary subjects.   *Alan Harris*

A man who does not go to the barber, who does not wear a tie or socks, whose eyes seem to be directed away from the little things of our world. He does not toil for personal comfort.
Leopold Infeld

He gazed at the stars, yet he also tried to look at his fellow men with kindness and compassion.
Leopold Infeld

The aloof conscience of the world.
Leopold Infeld

EISENHOWER, DWIGHT DAVID (1890-1969)

In the first year of the war we had a desperate need for a hero...Eisenhower was chosen to be that hero.   *Marquis W. Childs*

The symbol of a warmhearted, friendly, simple America. *Marquis W. Childs*

Our hostage against ill fortune, our warranty that all would be well. *Marquis W. Childs*

Represented strength, triumph, unswerving confidence. Millions were happy to take him on faith. *Marquis W. Childs*

He was more like a big industrial executive who, on the day the plant is breaking production records, will show visitors around the mill as if he had nothing else to do. *Raymond Clapper*

I don't believe a man should try to pass his historical peak. I think I pretty well hit my peak in history when I accepted the German surrender in 1945. *Dwight David Eisenhower*

In spite of the difficulties we have, I ask you this one question: If each of us in his own mind would dwell more upon those simple virtues—integrity, self-confidence, an unshakeable belief in his Bible—would not some of these problems tend to simplify themselves? *Dwight David Eisenhower*

A good man of decent sensibilities, rather dull, living the manifestation of the American dream. *Warren Goldberg*

The apotheosis of mediocrity. *Douglas MacArthur*

The greatest leader of the atomic age. *Richard Milhous Nixon*

A man who ranks among the greatest legendary heroes of this nation. *Richard Milhous Nixon*

(A) fancy khaki-colored package being sold by the political hucksters. *Adlai Ewing Stevenson*

A glamorous military hero, glorified by the press. *Harry S. Truman*

The Great Golfer. *Gore Vidal*

A man above politics. *Anon.*

EJACULATION

Short prayers darted up to God on emergent occasions. *Thomas Fuller*

ELECTIONEERING

A realm, peopled only by villains or heroes, in which everything is black and white.
John Mason Brown

The only time one is likely to see his congressman in the flesh. *Eugene E. Brussell*

A refresher course in kissing babies and other parts. *Max Gralnick*

The very essence of the constitution. *Junius*

A war in which everybody shoots from the lip.
Raymond Moley

Emotional orgies which endeavor to distract attention from the real issues involved.
James H. Robinson

(The process of) giving a public figure a character which, in fact, he doesn't have. *Mort Sahl*

Saluting rows of old women, drinking with clowns, and being upon a level with the lowest part of mankind. *Richard Steele*

Democracy's ceremonial, its feast, its great function. *Herbert G. Wells*

A time when the streets are infested with politicians selling their wares. *Anon.*

When the air is filled with speech and vice-versa.
Anon.

SEE ALSO BALLOT, POLITICIAN, POLITICS, VOTING

ELECTRICITY

The power that causes all natural phenomena not known to be caused by something else.
Ambrose Bierce

We call that fire of the black thundercloud electricity, and lecture learnedly about it, and grind the like of it out of the glass and silk: but *what* is it? What made it? Whence comes it? Whither goes it? *Thomas Carlyle*

Carrier of light and power, devourer of time and space, bearer of human speech over land and sea, greatest servant of man, itself unknown.
Charles W. Eliot

SEE ALSO RADIO, TELEPHONE, TELEVISION.

ELEPHANT

The animal with no natural enemies except man . . . truly, the king of beasts. *Jerry Dashkin*

A mouse built to government specifications.
Robert Heinlein

Although a gross beast, is yet the most decent and most sensible of any upon the earth.

Saint Francis de Sales

ELOPEMENT

To elope is cowardly; it is running away from danger; and danger has become so rare in modern life.   *Oscar Wilde*

An act which bears no presents.   *Anon.*

Getting married without a shower or parental consent.   *Anon.*

ELOQUENCE

The gift of making any color appear white.

Ambrose Bierce

Thought warmed over by acting talent.

Eugene E. Brussell

Vehement simplicity.   *Richard Cecil*

He is an eloquent man who can treat subjects of an humble nature with delicacy, lofty things impressively, and moderate things temperately.

Cicero

Power to translate a truth into language perfectly intelligible to the person to whom you speak.

Ralph Waldo Emerson

Not what the speaker says but who he is.

Euripides

The finest...is that which gets things done; the worst is that which delays them.

David L. George

What one thinks he has after a cocktail.

Warren Goldberg

The transference of thought and emotion from one heart to another, no matter how it is done.

John B. Gough

A powerful instrument.   *Thomas Jefferson*

Talking and eloquence are not the same: to speak, and to speak well are two things. A fool may talk, but a wise man speaks.   *Ben Jonson*

A gift of the mind, which makes us master of the heart and spirit of others.   *Jean de La Bruyère*

Consists of saying all that is necessary, and nothing but what is necessary.

La Rochefoucauld

Saying the proper thing and stopping.

Stanley Link

Often...a silent look.   *Ovid*

The art of saying things in such a way that those to whom we speak may listen to them with pleasure.

Blaise Pascal

The painting of thought.   *Blaise Pascal*

More thought in less words.   *David Schwartz*

Speech is the body; thought, the soul, and suitable action the life of eloquence.   *Charles Simmons*

Does not consist in speech. Words and phrases may be marshalled in every way, but they cannot compass it. It must consist in the man, in the subject, and in the occasion.   *Daniel Webster*

It comes...like the outbreaking of a fountain from the earth, or the bursting forth of volcanic fires, with spontaneous, original, native force.

Daniel Webster

Something an orator waves with.   *Anon.*

Logic on fire.   *Anon.*

The art of orally persuading the multitude that one and one equals three.   *Anon.*

SEE ALSO CONVERSATION, LANGUAGE, ORATORY, SPEECH.

EMANCIPATION

When the mind is permitted to form, to express, and to employ its own convictions of truth on all subjects, as it chooses.   *Henry Ward Beecher*

All persons held as slaves within said designated states and parts of states are henceforward shall be free.   *Abraham Lincoln*

EMERSON, RALPH WALDO (1803-1882)

A young man...after failing in the everyday avocation of a Unitarian preacher and schoolmaster, starts a new doctrine of Transcendentalism, declares all the old revelations superannuated and worn out, and announces the approach of new revelations and prophecies.

John Quincy Adams

A voice oracular.   *Matthew Arnold*

His thought rounded the spheres, his dreams topped the Cosmos. He walks in ether and is part of the barred and crimson sunset.

Benjamin de Casseres

For though he builds glorious temples, it is odd he leaves never a doorway to get in a god.
Adapted from James Russell Lowell

A primitive pagan in whose mind all creation is duly respected as parts of himself.
Adapted from James Russell Lowell

He is willing to worship the stars and the sun—a convert to nothing but Emerson.
Adapted from James Russell Lowell

The Codfish Moses. *Henry Louis Mencken*

One who lives instinctively on ambrosia—and leaves everything indigestible on his plate.
Friedrich W. Nietzsche

A gap-toothed and hoary-headed ape, carried at first into notice on the shoulders of Carlyle, and who now in his dotage spits and chatters from a dirtier perch of his own finding and fouling.
Algernon Charles Swinburne

A just man, poised on himself, all-loving, all-inclosing, and sane and clear as the sun.
Walt Whitman

EMINENCE

He who surpasses or subdues mankind.
Lord Byron

Nearest to the gallows. *Chinese Proverb*

That which shortens life. *Hebrew Proverb*

They that stand high. *William Shakespeare*

SEE ALSO DISTINCTION, GREATNESS.

EMOTION

SEE FEELING.

EMPLOYMENT

SEE LABOR, WORK.

END

Death. *Anuzita*

The great and chief end of men... is the preservation of their property. *John Locke*

Great is the art of beginning, but greater is the art of ending. *Henry Wadsworth Longfellow*

(That which) directs and sanctifies the means.
Justice Wilmot

Something that proves everything. *Anon.*

SEE ALSO DESTINY, FATE.

ENEMY

Every man is his own chief enemy. *Anacharsis*

He that is not with me is against me.
Bible: Luke, XI, 23.

A man's enemies are the men of his own house.
Bible: Micah, VII, 6.

Lack of friends, and empty purse.
Nicholas Breton

Yet is every man his greatest enemy, and...his own executioner. *Thomas Browne*

(One who) strengthens our nerves and sharpens our skill...our helper. *Edmund Burke*

The greatest enemy to man is man.
Robert Burton

Anger watching the opportunity for revenge.
Cicero

Everyone needs a warm personal enemy...to keep him free of rust in the movable parts of his mind. *Gene Fowler*

Those who have more accurate insights about you than you do yourself. *Max Gralnick*

Our own hands. *Joseph Hall*

Those who rob us of our good opinion of ourselves. *William Hazlitt*

A father who contracts debts is an enemy, and a mother false to her bed; a beautiful wife is an enemy; an ignorant son. *The Hitopadesa*

If any two men desire the same thing, which ... they cannot both enjoy, they become enemies.
Thomas Hobbes

The friend who stings you into action.
Elbert Hubbard

Any one who tells you the truth about you.
Elbert Hubbard

An injured friend. *Thomas Jefferson*

Man's chief enemy is his own unruly nature and the dark forces pent up within him.
Ernest Jones

None but yourself.
Henry Wadsworth Longfellow

Who are your bitterest enemies? The unknown who suspect how much you would despise them if you knew them.   *Arthur Schnitzler*

My best friend...the man who keeps me up to the mark.   *George Bernard Shaw*

To be an enemy is a sin; to have one is a temptation.   *Benjamin Whichcote*

SEE ALSO DANGER, HATRED, WAR.

ENGAGEMENT

In love, a period of occupation without possession.   *Leonard L. Levinson*

In war, a battle. In love, the salubrious calm that precedes the hostilities.   *Gideon Wurdz*

A snappy introduction to a tedious book.   *Anon.*

SEE ALSO COURTSHIP.

ENGLAND

A nation of shopkeepers.   *Samuel Adams*

(A nation) divided from all the world...united in itself.   *Francis Bacon*

The mother of parliaments.   *John Bright*

An artificial country: take away her commerce, and what has she?   *Edmund Burke*

A low, newspaper, humdrum country.
Lord Byron

Sixty different religions and only one gravy, melted butter.   *Francesco Caraccioli*

The world's busybody.   *Thomas Carlyle*

Divided into three classes: Knaves, Fools, and Revolutionists.   *Gilbert Keith Chesterton*

The head of modern civilization.
James Fenimore Cooper

A domestic country: there the home is revered, the hearth sacred.   *Benjamin Disraeli*

(A country) unrivaled for two things—sporting and politics.   *Benjamin Disraeli*

The paradise of women, the purgatory of men, and the hell of horses.   *John Florio*

The great Mother Empire...splendidly isolated in Europe.   *George Foster*

A good land with bad people.   *French Proverb*

A prison for men, a paradise for women, a purgatory for servants, a hell for horses.
Thomas Fuller

A cemetery with ornamental tombstones.
Asher Ginzberg

A land of scholars.   *Oliver Goldsmith*

A foul-mouthed nation.   *William Hazlitt*

A nation which nothing but views of interest can govern.   *Thomas Jefferson*

A pirate spreading misery and ruin over the face of the ocean.   *Thomas Jefferson*

A pleasant place for them that's rich and high...a cruel place for such folks as I.
Adapted from Charles Kingsley

(An) accursed bucket-shop of a refrigerator.
Rudyard Kipling

A little garden full of sour weeds.   *Louis XIV*

Preëminently the country of pauperism.
Karl Marx

(A land of) men with thoughts above their station.
John Masefield

A Conservative country that votes Labour from time to time.   *Reginald Maudling*

The country in which social discipline has most succeeded, not so much in conquering, as in supressing whatever is most liable to conflict with it. The English, more than any other people, not only act but feel according to rule.
John Stuart Mill

The champion of justice and right.
Lord Palmerston

A land severed from the world by nature's wise indulgence.   *Adapted from John Phillips*

A nation of amateurs.   *Lord Rosebery*

A world by itself.   *William Shakespeare*

(A nation in which) there are only two classes in good society: the equestrian classes and the neurotic classes.   *George Bernard Shaw*

The one voice in Europe.   *Alfred Lord Tennyson*

A power which had dotted over the surface of the whole globe with her possessions and military posts.   *Daniel Webster*

A museum of style.   *Tom Wolfe*

Oh, it's a snug little island!
A right little, tight little island.

William Wordsworth

SEE ALSO PARLIAMENT

ENGLISH LANGUAGE

The language with which we are swaddled and rocked asleep.   *John Eachard*

The sea which receives tributaries from every region under heaven.   *Ralph Waldo Emerson*

Most English words are of one syllable, so that the more monosyllables you use, the truer Englishman you shall seem.   *George Gascoigne*

A useful instrument for a country setting out to learn the habits of democracy. It is most convenient for the politician to be able to employ a language with only one word (instead of three or even four) for *you.*   *R. C. Goffin*

Expressly masculine...the langauge of a grown-up man and has very little childish or feminine about it.   *Otto Jespersen*

Good English is plain, easy and smooth in the mouth of an unaffected English gentleman.

Samuel Johnson

The most difficult, arbitrary and careful of all languages.   *Matthew F. Maury*

The language of men ever famous and foremost in the achievements of liberty.   *John Milton*

Our language hath no law but use.

Joshua Sylvester

The accretion and growth of every dialect, race and range of time, and is both free and compacted composition of all.   *Walt Whitman*

The king's English.   *Thomas Wilson*

ENGLISHMEN

(They) instinctively admire any man who has no talent and is modest about it.   *James Agate*

A man who had never been able to tell a lie about others and who is never willing to face the truth about himself.   *Michael Arlen*

A race that binds its body in chains and calls it liberty.   *Adapted from Robert Buchanan*

(People that have) sixty different religions, and only one sauce.   *Francesco Caraccioli*

The stupidest in speech, the wisest in action.

Thomas Carlyle

A dumb people.   *Thomas Carlyle*

One who dines by himself in a room filled with other hermits.   *James Fenimore Cooper*

Germans pretending to be French.

Max Eastman

Not an inventive people; they don't eat enough pie.   *Thomas Alva Edison*

I find the Englishman to be him of all men who stands firmest in his shoes.

Ralph Waldo Emerson

There is in his manners a suspicion of insolence...his belief...that he shall not find his superiors elsewhere.   *Ralph Waldo Emerson*

A solid people, wearing good hats and shoes, and owners of land whose title-deeds are properly recorded.   *Ralph Waldo Emerson*

This selfish race aim to extend their empire over the ball; subject, destroy, absorb and conquer all.

Adapted from Philip Freneau

(Those who) travel about all the time, looking at battlefields, waterfalls, ruined masonry, and dull classical relics.   *Johann W. Goethe*

A man who lives on an island in the North Sea governed by Scotsmen.   *Phillip Guedalla*

The real English resemble Romans. They do not want London to be...famous for her lectures...halls of science...or her national galleries. These things we prefer bad. We pride ourselves on our train service, our shops, our policemen, our Rugby football matches and our race meetings.   *Viscount Harberton*

The only people to whom the term blackguard is peculiarly applicable—by which I understand a reference of everything to violence, and a contempt for the feelings and opinions of others.

William Hazlitt

Ill manners make the Englishman.

William Hazlitt

The best at weeping and the worst at laughing.

Thomas Hearne

The Englishman's strong point is a vigorous insularity which he carries with him, portable and sometimes insupportable.

Thomas W. Higginson

Our natural enemies...the only nation on earth who wish us ill from the bottom of their souls.

Thomas Jefferson

(People who) sniff for doctrine everywhere.

Henry Arthur Jones

The maddest of all mankind.   *Rudyard Kipling*

Nearly all people in England are of the superior sort, superiority being an English ailment.

D. H. Lawrence

Three qualities: he can suffer no partner in his love, no stranger to be his equal, nor to be dared by any.   *John Lyly*

A quick, ingenious, and piercing spirit; acute to invent, subtile and sinewy to discourse, not beneath the reach of any point the highest that human capacity can soar to.   *John Milton*

A busy people. They haven't the time to become polished.   *Charles de Montesquieu*

Not only England, but every Englishman is an island.   *Novalis*

(One who) has all the qualities of poker except its occasional warmth.   *Daniel O'Connell*

The only letter which Englishmen write is capital I. This...is the most pointed comment on their national character.   *Anton Rubinstein*

He does everything on principle. He fights you on patriotic principles; he robs you on business principles; he enslaves you on imperial principles.

George Bernard Shaw

(Those who) do not know what to think until they are coached, laboriously and insistently for years, in the proper and becoming opinion.

George Bernard Shaw

(One who) thinks he is moral when he is only uncomfortable.   *George Bernard Shaw*

(One who) imagines God is an Englishman.

George Bernard Shaw

(Those who) will never be slaves; they are free to do whatever the government and public opinion allow them to do.   *George Bernard Shaw*

The English are eminently a nation of vagabonds. The sun paints English faces with all the colors of his climes. The Englishman is ubiquitous.

Alexander Smith

The most disagreeable of all the nations of Europe—more surly and morose, with less disposition to please, to exert themselves for the good of society, to make small sacrifices, and to put themselves out of their way.   *Sydney Smith*

The English are mentioned in the Bible: Blessed are the meek, for they shall inherit the earth.

Mark Twain

A person who does things because they have been done before.   *Mark Twain*

They are like their own beer: froth on top, dregs on the bottom, the middle excellent.   *Voltaire*

People who say what they think.   *Voltaire*

Generally the most extraordinary persons that we meet with, even out of England.

Horace Walpole

(Those who) have everything in common with the Americans...except language.   *Oscar Wilde*

A strong being who takes a cold bath in the morning and talks about it for the rest of the day.

Ellen Wilkinson

SEE ALSO ANGLO-SAXON, SCOTLAND.

ENOUGH

You never know what is enough unless you know what is more than enough.   *William Blake*

Something as good as a feast.   *English Proverb*

Abundance to the wise.   *Euripides*

Enough is enough.   *John Heywood*

Whatever suffices.   *Latin Proverb*

ENTHUSIASM

A distemper of youth, curable by small doses of repentance in connection with outward applications of experience.   *Ambrose Bierce*

The genius of sincerity, and truth accomplishes no victories without it.   *Edward G. Bulwer-Lytton*

Nothing but a moral inebriety.   *Lord Byron*

That secret and harmonious spirit which hovers over the production of genius.   *Isaac D'Israeli*

Every great and commanding moment in the annals of the world is the triumph of some enthusiasm.   *Ralph Waldo Emerson*

Energy that boils over and runs down the side of the pot.   *Arnold H. Glasow*

The great hill-climber.   *Elbert Hubbard*

The most beautiful word on earth.
          Christian Morgenstern

A force no less destructive and incalculable than logic; for, like wine, it puts the judgment in a heat.   *F. S. Oliver*

Fire under control.   *Norman Vincent Peale*

The best protection in any situation.
          David Seabury

The sense of this word among the Greeks affords the noblest definition of it: enthusiasm signifies God in us.   *Anna Louise de Staël*

(That which) exaggerates the importance of important things and overlooks their deficiencies.
          Hugh Tigner

That temper of the mind in which the imagination has got the better of the judgment.
          William Warburton

That kindling spark which marks the difference between the leaders in every activity and the laggards who put in just enough to get by.
          Anon.

Seeing only the down payment.   *Anon.*

SEE ALSO FANATICISM, PASSION, SUCCESS, ZEAL.

ENVIRONMENT

SEE LIFE, NATURE, SOCIETY, WORLD.

ENVY

Deformed persons and eunuchs, and old men and bastards, are envious, for he that cannot possibly mend his own case, will do what he can to impair another's.   *Francis Bacon*

A coal come hissing hot from hell.
          Philip J. Bailey

The most corroding of the vices, and also the greatest power in any land.   *James M. Barrie*

The rottenness of the bones.
          Bible: Proverbs, XXVII,4.

The beginning of hell in this life, and a passion not to be excused.   *Robert Burton*

A fly that passes all a body's sounder parts, and dwells upon the sores.   *George Chapman*

The sincerest form of flattery.   *John C. Collins*

Ignorance.   *Ralph Waldo Emerson*

The adversary of the fortunate.   *Epictetus*

Nothing but a row of hooks to hang up grudges on.   *John Foster*

A kind of praise.   *John Gay*

The sorrow of fools.   *German Proverb*

Envy is but the smoke of low estate, ascending still against the fortunate.
          Adapted from Fulke Greville

A torment.   *Horace*

A thousand eyes, but none with correct vision.
          Isacher Hurwitz

Almost the only vice which is practicable at all times, and in every place; the only passion which can never lie quiet from want of irritation.
          Samuel Johnson

Poisoning the banquet one cannot taste; blasting the harvest one has no right to reap.
          Adapted from Samuel Johnson

Envy and hatred are always united. They gather strength from each other by being engaged upon the same object.   *Jean de La Bruyère*

A timid and shameful passion which we never dare avow.   *La Rochefoucauld*

The enemy of honor.   *Latin Proverb*

The natural, necessary and unavoidable effect of emulation, or a desire of glory.   *William Law*

Uneasiness of the mind, caused by the consideration of a good we desire, obtained by one we think should not have it before us.   *John Locke*

That most odious and anti-social of all the passions.   *John Stuart Mill*

A pain of mind that successful men cause their neighbors.   *Onasander*

The vulture who explores our inmost liver, and drags out our heart and nerves.   *Petronius*

Envy always implies conscious inferiority wherever it resides.   *Pliny 1*

Self-made hurts.   *Shaikh Saadi*

To bark at eminent men, as little dogs do at strangers.   *Seneca*

The green sickness.   *William Shakespeare*

Hatred without a cure.   *Anon.*

A negative mental condition of being lean from seeing others eat.   *Anon.*

SEE ALSO COVETOUSNESS, JEALOUSY.

EPICUREAN

An opponent of Epicurus, an abstemious philosopher who, holding that pleasure should be the chief aim of man, wasted no time in gratification of the senses.   *Ambrose Bierce*

Everything rational in moral philosophy which Greece and Rome left us.   *Thomas Jefferson*

EPIGRAM

A short, sharp saying in prose or verse, frequently characterized by acidity or acerbity and sometimes by wisdom.   *Ambrose Bierce*

A dwarfish whole, its body brevity, and wit its soul.   *Adapted from Samuel Taylor Coleridge*

A catered to platitude.   *Eugene E. Brussell*

(Something) useful to attract attention to ideas.   *Mandell Creighton*

Three things must epigrams, like bees, have ... a sting, and honey, and a body small.   *Latin Distich*

Weapons ... carried ... into literature.   *H. P. Dodd*

Short, it is easily retained in the memory; pithy, it contains in the compass of a few lines the sum of an argument; and the result of experience it often expresses the wisdom of ages.   *H. P. Dodd*

The epigram has been compared to a scorpion, because as the sting of the scorpion lies in the tail, the force of the epigram is in the conclusion.   *Lilius Gyraldus*

A dash of wit and a jigger of wisdom, flavored with surprise.   *Elbert Hubbard*

A vividly expressed truth that is so, or not, as the case may be.   *Elbert Hubbard*

A beautiful meaning in few and clear words ... It slings at the mark without delay.   *Moses Ibn Ezra*

A light vessel holding a heavy load.   *Jacob Klatzkin*

A gag that's played Carnegie Hall.   *Oscar Levant*

Striking a verbal match on the seat of your intellectual pants.   *John A. Lincoln*

Half truth so stated as to irritate the person who believes the other half.   *Shailer Mathews*

A platitude with vine-leaves in its hair.   *Henry Louis Mencken*

(Requires) wit, occasion, and good luck.   *Christopher Morley*

A solemn platitude gone to a masquerade ball.   *Lionel Strachey*

EPITAPH

An inscription showing that virtues acquired by death have a retroactive effect.   *Ambrose Bierce*

My name alone.   *Lord Byron*

A belated advertisement for a line of goods that has been permanently discontinued.   *Irvin S. Cobb*

The last word.   *Homer Croy*

A sumptuous pyramid of golden verse
Over the ruins of an ignoble hearse.   *John Day*

A statement that usually lies above about the one who lies beneath.   *Foolish Dictionary*

Praise too late.   *Max Gralnick*

Postponed compliments.   *Elbert Hubbard*

A tongueless mouth.   *William Shakespeare*

EQUALITY

Men of culture are the true apostles of equality.   *Matthew Arnold*

The absolutely necessary condition of freedom.

Mikhail A. Bakunin

No last nor first. *Robert Browning*

All men are created equal; but that does not mean that all men are or can be equal in possessions, in ability, or in merit; it simply means that all shall stand equal before the law.

William Jennings Bryan

Equality reposes on this: that there is no man really clever who has not found that he is stupid.

Gilbert Keith Chesterton

May be divided into that of condition and rights. Equality of condition is incompatible with civilization, and is found only to exist in those communities that are but slightly removed from the savage state. In practice, it can only mean a common misery. *James Fenimore Cooper*

The portion of everyone at their advent upon the earth; and equality is also theirs when put beneath it. *Enclos*

Today it means "sameness," rather than "oneness." *Erich Fromm*

(A) classless society. *Mohandas K. Gandhi*

The graveyard. *German Proverb*

Merely idealizing envy.

Oliver Wendell Holmes 1

A proposition to which, at ordinary times, no sane person has ever given his assent.

Aldous Huxley

An utterly baseless fiction.

Thomas Henry Huxley

The foundation on which all (our constitutions) are built. *Thomas Jefferson*

The denial of every preëminence but that annexed to legal office, and particularly the denial of preëminence by birth. *Thomas Jefferson*

Better that some should be unhappy than that none should be happy, which would be the case in a general state of equality. *Samuel Johnson*

Equality is the share of everyone at their advent upon earth; and equality is also theirs when placed beneath it. *Anne Lenclos*

The centre and circumference of all democracy.

Herman Melville

The chief groundwork of equity.

Michel de Montaigne

Consists only in this: that all men have their origin in God the Creator, have been redeemed by Jesus Christ, and are to be judged and rewarded or punished by God exactly according to their merits or demerits. *Pope Pius X*

The right, granted by the Constitution, of rich and poor, black and white, to bathe in champagne and winter on the Riviera. *Leo C. Rosten*

The contemplation of God...for it was in God that men were equal...as the manifestation of God, men were equal in rights. As the servants of God, they were also equal in their duties.

Adapted from Antoine de Saint-Exupéry

(A condition) essential to good breeding.

George Bernard Shaw

The offspring of envy and covetousness.

William G. Sumner

Death. *Publilius Syrus*

(Means) equal opportunities for becoming unequal. *Richard H. Tawney*

The greatest of all doctrines and the most difficult to understand. *Mark Van Doren*

A pleasant dream: the law cannot equalize men in spite of nature. *Luc de Vauvenargues*

Giving others the same chances and rights as myself. *Walt Whitman*

A chance to be more or less equal than others.

Anon.

A condition we desire only with our superiors.

Anon.

SEE ALSO BROTHERHOOD, CLASSES, DEMOCRACY, LIBERTY.

EQUITY

Not legal justice, but a rectification of legal justice. *Aristotle*

That exact rule of righteousness or justice which is to be observed between man and man.

Charles Buck

Simply a matter of the length of the judge's ears.

Elbert Hubbard

Equity considers that to have been done which ought to have been done. *Legal Maxim*

A roguish thing; for law we have a measure. Equity is according to the conscience of him that is chancellor; and as that is larger or narrower, so is equity. *John Selden*

What every one pleases to make it. *John Selden*

Abatement of legal right upon reasonable considerations. *Benjamin Whichcote*

ERASMUS, DESIDERIUS (1466-1536)

The enemy to true religion, the open adversary of Christ, the complete and faithful picture and image of Epicurus and Lucian. *Martin Luther*

That great injured name—the glory of the priesthood and the shame. *Alexander Pope*

Erasmus laid the egg of the Reformation and Luther hatched it. *R. C. Trench*

ERROR

A false notion involving a principle of faith.
Judah Abravanel

Cosmic powers, but relative in their nature, not absolute, since they depend for existence upon the perversion or contradiction of their opposites, and are not like truth and good, self-existing absolutes, inherent aspects of the supreme Self-Existent. *Sri Aurobindo*

Evidence that something has tried to accomplish something. *John E. Babcock*

The pursuit of absolute truth. *Samuel Butler 2*

Simply a failure to adjust immediately from a preconception to an actuality. *John Cage*

The discipline through which we advance.
William Ellery Channing

Feeling where we ought to think, and thinking where we ought to feel. *Churton Collins*

Ignorance is a blank sheet on which we may write; but error is a scribbled one from which we must first erase. *Charles Caleb Colton*

The prejudices picked up in childhood.
René Descartes

The best teachers. *James A. Froude*

The errors of sages are regarded as willful sins; the sins of the ignorant are accounted as unwitting errors. *Judah Ilai*

To follow something which does not lead to that at which we wish to arrive. *Saint Augustine*

The things that are not. *William Shakespeare*

The force that welds men together. *Leon Tolstoy*

A hardy plant; it flourishes in every soil.
Martin F. Tupper

The only things one never regrets. *Oscar Wilde*

The world's first product. *Anon.*

SEE ALSO FAULT, RIGHT AND WRONG.

ESSAY

Like organizing a meal. The various dishes must be so arranged as to rouse the appetite and renew the pleasure with each course. *Moses Ibn Ezra*

The little which holds much, that instructs and does not weary. *Moses Ibn Ezra*

A meditative journey in quest of self.
Donald Frame

A loose sally of the mind; an irregular undigested piece. *Samuel Johnson*

Primarily a personal, subjective, individual form of prose expression—a reflection of the author . . . sometimes expressed formally, sometimes informally. *Russell Nye*

(A literary form where) there is no room for the impurities of literature. *Virginia Woolf*

A piece of writing principally for reflection and the recharging of the brain. *Anon.*

SEE ALSO WRITING.

ESSAYIST

A tatler, spectator, rambler, lounger.
Charles Copeland

Some turn over all books, and they are equally searching in all papers; they write out of what they presently find or meet, without choice.
Ben Jonson

A lucky person who has found a way to discourse without being interrupted. *Charles Poore*

ETERNAL RECURRENCE

The thing that has been, it is that which shall be; and that which is done is that which shall be done: and there is no new thing under the sun.

Bible: Ecclesiastes, I, 9.

While the earth remains, seed-time and harvest, and cold and heat, and summer and winter, and day and night shall not cease.

Bible: Genesis, VIII, 22.

All things return eternally, and ourselves with them: We have already existed times without number, and all things with us.

Friedrich W. Nietzsche

Round and round we go, all of us, and ever come back thither.   *Walt Whitman*

SEE ALSO DEATH, PREDESTINATION.

ETERNITY

For ever and ever.   *Bible: Galatians, I, 5.*

Yesterday, and today, and forever.

Bible: Hebrews, XIII, 8.

The simultaneous and complete possession of infinite life.   *Boethius*

Not an unending continuance of this life—that would perhaps be Hell—but...a quite different life, divine not mundane, perfect not earthly, true life not corrupt half-life.   *Emil Brunner*

It is timeless, present with and in all times.

Samuel Taylor Coleridge

Not something that begins after you are dead; it is going on all the time.   *Charlotte P. Gilman*

Another word for change.   *Gerald Gould*

Implies unborn as well as undying, or without beginning or ending in time.

Charles Hartshorne

Every instant.   *Heinrich Heine*

Now is eternity; now is the immortal life.

Richard Jefferies

The sum of all sums.   *Lucretius*

I am the things that are, and those that are to be, and those that have been.   *Proclus*

Nothing passeth but the whole is present, whereas no time is all at once present.   *Saint Augustine*

Where there is no where and no when.

Arthur Schopenhauer

Eternity consists of opposites.   *Seneca*

If the human mind, by any future improvement of its sensibility, should become conscious of an infinite number of ideas in a minute, that minute would be eternity.   *Percy Bysshe Shelley*

Our destination.   *Alfred E. Taylor*

The life beyond the world...the inspiration of the life that is now.   *E. Troeltsch*

Eternity is a thrust upon
A bit of earth, a senseless stone.
A grain of dust, a casual clod
Receives the greatest gift of God.

Louis Untermeyer

Beyond the stars.   *Henry K. White*

A succession of todays.   *Israel Zangwill*

Death only.   *Anon.*

The lifetime of the Almighty.   *Anon.*

SEE ALSO DEATH, HEAVEN, HELL, IMMORTALITY, INFINITY, LIFE, PREDESTINATION, PROVIDENCE, SALVATION, SOUL.

ETHICS

The distinctive element in Christian ethics is the primacy of love, the self-giving love that is known fully to Christian faith in the cross of Christ.

John Bennett

The attempt to think through the implications of Christian faith for the moral life.   *John Bennett*

The ethical attitude...taken over from the formerly dominant religion, and then justified by a philosophical construction.

Christopher Dawson

Christian ethics is not a scheme of codified conduct. It is a purposive effort to relate love to a world of relativities through a casuistry obedient to love.   *Joseph Fletcher*

A therapeutic effort which deals predominantly with the point which is easily seen to be the sorest in any scheme of civilization.   *Sigmund Freud*

Jewish ethics is rooted in the doctrine of human responsibility, that is, freedom of the will.

Joseph H. Hertz

A body of imperfect social generalizations expressed in terms of emotions.

Oliver Wendell Holmes 2

I have but one system of ethics for men and for nations—to be grateful, to be faithful to all engagements and under all circumstances, to be open and generous, promoting in the long run even the interests of both.   *Thomas Jefferson*

The obligations of morality.   *Lajos Kossuth*

The doctrine of manners...which teaches men their duty.   *Maunder*

The art of living well and happily.   *Henry Moore*

To think well.   *Blaise Pascal*

The science which investigates the general principles for determining the true worth of the ultimate ends of human conduct.   *Reginald A. Rogers*

Obeying the compulsion to help all life which one is able, while shrinking from injuring anything that lives.   *Albert Schweitzer*

To render scientific...and...systematic—the apparent cognitions that most men have of the rightness or reasonableness of conduct.

Henry Sidgwick

Their cardinal ideas: (1) the character of the agent; (2) the nature of the motive; (3) the quality of his deeds: (4) the results.   *Herbert Spencer*

The science of human duty.   *David Swing*

The Ten Commandments and the Sermon on the Mount are all the ethical code anybody needs.

Harry S. Truman

The ethic of Jesus seeks human development directly through the limitation of self-interest by mutual adjustment and mutual aid.

Harry F. Ward

The Word of God as contained in the writings of the Old and New Testaments and the traditions of the Church.   *Eberhard Welby*

Ethics and aesthetics are one and the same.

Ludwig Wittgenstein

SEE ALSO BEHAVIOR, CONDUCT, DEEDS, DUTY, MORALITY, PHILOSOPHY, RELIGION, RIGHT AND WRONG.

ETIQUETTE

Getting sleepy in company and not showing it.

Eugene E. Brussell

Behaving yourself a little better than is absolutely essential.   *William Cuppy*

In the human world etiquette is known both before and after eating, and, in a certain restricted circle, during eating.   *Jerry Dashkin*

The conventionalities of society...the ripened results of a varied and long experience.

Archibald A. Hodge

The noise you don't make while eating soup.

Leonard L. Levinson

(That which) requires us to admire the human race.   *Mark Twain*

SEE ALSO MANNERS.

EUGENICS

The systematic breeding of the best minds and bodies.   *Eugene E. Brussell*

Scientific breeding for a superior product, which in turn will produce a better world.

Max Gralnick

The best of either sex should be united with the best as often, and the inferior with the inferior as seldom as possible.   *Plato*

To replace the reckless or haphazard direction of human evolution with intelligent and carefully planned guidance.   *Amram Scheinfeld*

The selective breeding of Man.

George Bernard Shaw

EULOGY

Praise of a person, who has either the advantage of wealth and power, or the consideration to be dead.

Ambrose Bierce

The tribute that we pay to achievements that resemble, but do not equal, our own.

Ambrose Bierce

Praise attained by merit or by wealth.

Samuel Johnson

Praise that is too much and too late.   *Anon.*

EUNUCH

He that is wounded in the stones, or has his privy member cut off.   *Bible: Deuteronomy, XXIII, 1.*

There are some eunuchs, which were so born from their mother's womb: and there are some ... which were made eunuchs of men: and there be eunuchs, which have made themselves eunuchs for the kingdom of heaven's sake.

Bible: Matthew, XIX, 12.

Those who make themselves sexless for the kingdom of heaven's sake. *Anon.*

EUROPE

A continent which does not feel free until it succeeds in enslaving and oppressing others.

Adapted from Bernard Berenson

(Where) all educated Americans, first or last, go.

Ralph Waldo Emerson

A continent of energetic mongrels.

Herbert Fisher

The great American sedative. *Henry James*

A great mad house. *Thomas Jefferson*

A peninsula occupying the northwestern portion of Asia. *Raymond Mortimer*

The state system of Europe is a system akin to the system of cages in an improverished provincial zoo. *Leon Trotsky*

A rag-yard of old bones. *Anon.*

A place we go to be Americanized. *Anon.*

EVE

SEE ADAM.

EVERYBODY

The square root of zero. *Elbert Hubbard*

Nobody in toto. *Elbert Hubbard*

Normally the complex unit of the mass and the divergent, specialized minorities. Nowadays, "everybody" is the mass alone.

José Ortega y Gasset

He that is everybody and nobody. *Anon.*

SEE ALSO MASSES, PEOPLE (THE).

EVIDENCE

SEE FACT, SCIENCE.

EVIL

Misplaced good. *Samuel Alexander*

The footstool of good. *Israel Baal-Shem Tob*

A form of good, of which the results are not immediately manifest. *Honoré de Balzac*

A proof of God's existence, a challenge to turn towards that in which love triumphs over hatred, union over division, and eternal life over death.

Nicholas Berdyaev

The bond of iniquity. *Bible: Acts, VIII, 23.*

I make peace, and create evil. I the Lord do all these things. *Bible: Isaiah, XIV, 7.*

The active springing from energy.

William Blake

That which God does not will. *Emil Brunner*

To do nothing. *Edmund Burke*

A moral evil is an evil that has its origin in the will. *Samuel Taylor Coleridge*

Evil is not being; it is a hole in being, a lack. That is why there can be no absolute evil: evil can exist only in what is itself good. *Yves M. Congar*

It means subtraction, deprivation, failure.

Martin C. D'Arcy

There are three all-powerful evils: lust, anger and greed. *Tulsi Das*

Neither person, place, nor being, but simply a belief, an illusion of material sense.

Mary Baker Eddy

Good tortured by its own hunger and thirst.

Kahlil Gibran

Either sin or the consequence of sin.

Etienne Gilson

The three evils are the sea, fire, and woman.

Greek Proverb

A wrong function ... the use of a good impulse at the wrong time, in the wrong place, towards a wrong end. *J. A. Hadfield*

The loss of good. *Robert Herrick*

A fact not to be explained away, but to be accepted; and accepted not to be endured, but to be conquered. It is a challenge...to our courage.

John H. Holmes

That which makes for separateness.

Aldous Huxley

Only good perverted.

Henry Wadsworth Longfellow

Negations.   *Moses Maimonides*

Evil as such is the only thing. I am able to do without God, by withdrawing myself...as if by an initiative emanating from my nothingness, from the current of Divine causality.

Jacques Maritain

That which one believes of others. It is a sin to believe evil of others, but it is seldom a mistake.

Henry Louis Mencken

Evil has no substance of its own, but is only the defect, excess, perversion, or corruption of that which has substance.   *John Henry Newman*

Whatever springs from weakness.

Friedrich W. Nietzsche

That which perverts the mind and shackles the conscience.   *Saint Ambrose*

The privation of a particular good, inherent in a particular good.   *Saint Thomas Aquinas*

A disposition of the soul which is contrary to virtue and comes from a heedless desertion of good.   *Saint Basil*

Destroying life, doing it injury, hindering its development.   *Albert Schweitzer*

That which we certainly know hinders us from possessing anything that is good.

Baruch Spinoza

Whatever hinders man's perfecting his reason and capability to enjoy the rational life.

Baruch Spinoza

Ignorance, hatred and prejudice.

Charles W. Steckel

Lack of money is the root of all evil.

Mark Twain

The brute motive force of fragmentary purpose, disregarding the eternal vision...overruling, retarding, hurting.   *Alfred North Whitehead*

SEE ALSO BAD, DEVIL, GOOD AND BAD, HELL, SIN, WAR, WICKEDNESS.

EVOLUTION

The notion of a gradual rise in Beings from the meanest to the most High...a vain imagination.

Joseph Addison

Men first appeared as fishes. When they were able to help themselves they took to the land.

Anaximander

A disreputable episode on one of the minor planets.   *Lord Balfour*

The religion of the irreligious.

William Baumgartner

Simply means continuous growth; a tree growing from a seedling is an example of evolution.

Hilaire Belloc

Dissociation and division.   *Henri Bergson*

The theory that puts men with an immortal soul in the same circle with the wolf, the hyena, and the skunk.

Adapted from William Jennings Bryan

Gorilla damnifications of humanity.

Thomas Carlyle

A face turned from the clod—
Some call it Evolution,
    And others call it God.   *W. H. Carruth*

A process of self-realizing a moral purpose; the correlation of mind and brain is just the phenomenal aspect of the real correlation of our mind with the divine power.   *George A. Coe*

The story of man, traced for us by the scientist, is seen as the travail of God's energy, creating man in His own image.   *C. A. Coulson*

Natural selection.   *Charles Darwin*

Man is descended from a hairy, tailed quadruped, probably arboreal in its habits. *Charles Darwin*

These new-fangled theories.   *Benjamin Disraeli*

Interpretation which would make a text of Holy Writ a Divine instruction upon a subject belonging to the physical or natural sciences.

Henry Dordolot

Striving to be a man, the worm mounts through all the spires of form.   *Ralph Waldo Emerson*

The hypothesis that any subhuman animal organism gradually took on a human type of mind.

Ulrich A. Hauber

Staggering from one error to the other.

Henrik Ibsen

A brutal philosophy—to wit, there is no God, and the ape is our Adam. *Henry E. Manning*

Men risen out of the mire. *Don Marquis*

Nevertheless, it is even harder for the ape to believe that he has descended from man.

Henry Louis Mencken

Not a force but a process; not a cause but a law.

John Morley

A shabby-genteel sentiment...which makes men prefer to believe that they are degenerated angels rather than elevated apes. *W. Winwood Reade*

The preservation of favored races in the struggle for life. *Herbert Spencer*

Survival of the fittest, which I have here sought to express in mechanical terms is that which Mr. Darwin has called "natural selection."

Herbert Spencer

A change from an incoherent homogeneity to a coherent heterogeneity, accompanying the dissipation of motion and integration of matter.

Herbert Spencer

The ages that have gone into the making of a man.

Alfred Lord Tennyson

Far more a philosophical concept than a scientific one. *David E. Trueblood*

Every individual...the highest as well as the lowest, is derived in an unbroken line from the first and lowest forms. *August Weismann*

One of the many theories...of profoundest value...yet leaving the divine secrets just an inexplicable and unreachable as before—maybe more so. *Walt Whitman*

Man was produced by successive and spontaneous transformations of less perfect forms into more perfect forms. This is the essence of evolution.

Anon.

The descent of man from monkey, which some people forgot to make. *Anon.*

A jungle of fanciful assumption. *Anon.*

SEE ALSO CREATION (WORLD), NATURAL SELECTION.

EXAGGERATION

The peculiar property of young men; they betray a vehement nature. *Aristotle*

A blood relation of falsehood and nearly as blamable. *Hosea Ballou*

The definition of art. *Gilbert Keith Chesterton*

Truth that has lost its temper. *Kahlil Gibran*

A branch of lying. *Baltasar Gracian*

EXAMINATIONS

(That which is) formidable even to the best prepared, for the greatest fool may ask more than the wisest man can answer.

Charles Caleb Colton

When the foolish ask questions that the wise cannot answer. *Oscar Wilde*

EXAMPLE

Every life. *Henry F. Amiel*

The school of mankind. *Edmund Burke*

Not only the best way of propagating an opinion, but...the only way worth taking into account.

Samuel Butler 2

An eloquent orator. *Czech Proverb*

The greatest of all seducers.

Collin D'Harleville

The only way of educating. *Albert Einstein*

The best sermon. *Benjamin Franklin*

Footprints on the sands of time.

Henry Wadsworth Longfellow

The only bible which millions of people read today. *James E. Murray*

Example is not the main thing in life—it is the only thing. *Albert Schweitzer*

A lesson that all men can read. *Gilbert West*

SEE ALSO ACTION, DEEDS.

EXCLUSIVENESS

SEE ARISTOCRACY, SNOBBERY, WEALTH.

EXCOMMUNICATION

The chief weapon of ecclesiastical discipline, and very useful for keeping the people to their duties.
Decrees of the Council of Trent, Dec. 4, 1563.

Merely external punishment.   *Martin Luther*

EXECUTION

Executions are intended to draw spectators. If they do not draw spectators they don't answer their purpose.   *Samuel Johnson*

Sheer horror to all concerned...but out of all this, and towering behind the vulgar and hideous accessories of the scaffold, gleams the majesty of the law.   *Alexander Smith*

SEE ALSO CAPITAL PUNISHMENT, HANGING.

EXECUTIVE

If a man has an office with a desk on which there is a buzzer, and if he can press that buzzer and have somebody come dashing in response—then he's an executive.   *Elmer Adams*

A true executive is one who regards attractive stenographers as stenographers.
Eugene E. Brussell

A man who isn't worried about his own career but rather the careers of those who work for him.
Henry S. Burns

A "born executive" is someone whose father owns the business.   *Shannon Carse*

A man who can make quick decisions and is sometimes right.   *Elbert Hubbard*

Men of measured merriment...with careful smiles...that run the shops.   *Sinclair Lewis*

(One who is) by profession a decision maker. Uncertainty is his opponent. Overcoming it is his mission.   *John McDonald*

The world-builder.   *Plato*

The best executive is the one who has some sense enough to pick men to do what he wants done, and self-restraint enough to keep from meddling with them while they do it.   *Theodore Roosevelt*

A good executive believes in sharing credit with the one who did the work.   *William Rotsler*

One who can delegate all the responsibility, shift all the blame, and appropriate all the credit.
Bobby Vinton

The ability to get the credit for the work others do.
Anon.

An artist delegating duties.   *Anon.*

One who knows how to delegate duties, reserving the grand decision for himself.   *Anon.*

One who doesn't have to share the credit with the one who does the work.   *Anon.*

Someone with an office between two expediters.
Anon.

SEE ALSO BOSS, LEADER.

EXERCISE

A poor substitute for diet.   *Blake Clark*

A modern superstition, invented by people who ate too much, and had nothing to think about.
George Santayana

Health.   *James Thomson*

To talk, not to walk.   *Oscar Wilde*

EXILE

The three great causes of exile: lack of courage, of honor, and of government.   *Isaac Abravanel*

The deep, unutterable woe.   *William E. Aytoun*

He shall return no more to his house, neither shall his place know him any more.
Bible: Job, VII, 10.

One who serves his country by residing abroad, yet is not an ambassador.   *Ambrose Bierce*

A form of punishment, giving rise to peculiar and primitive forms of social behavior.
Eugene E. Brussell

A wanderer who begs his daily bread.   *Diogenes*

Life.   *Victor Hugo*

A form of imprisonment.   *Moses Ibn Ezra*

Death.   *Ovid*

He suffers exile who denies himself to his country.   *Publilius Syrus*

EXISTENCE

A succession of Paradises successively denied.
                                        Samuel Beckett

A few years of youth and grace and then you fall flat on your face.   *Wolf Biermann*

A practical joke.   *Paul Bocuse*

A temporal series of events of facts...a form of the appearance of the Real.   *Francis H. Bradley*

A bad serial by which we let ourselves be bewitched.   *Michel Butor*

A funny thing that happened to me on the way to the grave.   *Quentin Crisp*

A dull routine   *Arthur Conan Doyle*

All existence is co-existence.
                                    Martin Heidegger

A party. You join after its started and you leave before its finished.   *Elsa Maxwell*

Mystery: the narrow region of our experience is a small island in the midst of a boundless sea.
                                    John Stuart Mill

A series of footnotes to a vast, obscure, unfinished masterpiece.   *Vladimir Nabokov*

A mystery wilder than the dreams of Devil or God.   *Llewelyn Powys*

The entire sum of existence is the magic of being needed by just one person.   *Vii Putnam*

An inconclusive experiment.   *Kenneth Rexroth*

To act.   *Jean-Jacques Rousseau*

A man is involved in life, leaves his impress on it, and outside of that there is nothing.
                                    Jean-Paul Sartre

Something which has its roots far down below in the dark, and its branches stretching out into the immensity above.   *Oliver Schreiner*

A flash of occasional enjoyments lighting up a mass of pain and misery.
                                Alfred North Whitehead

We come. We go. And in between we try to understand.   *Rod Steiger*

A pilgrimage toward a better world.
                                    Arthur J. Zuckerman

SEE ALSO LIFE, LIVING, NATURAL SELEC-
TION, REALITY.

EXISTENTIALISM

A vision of a man as a stranger in the universe—a stranger to himself and to others.
                                        John L. Brown

The Sartre brand...is an atheist who sees man as helpless, flung without knowing why or how into a world he cannot understand, endowed with liberty...which he may betray but which he cannot deny, to make his way as best he can in fear and trembling, in uncertainty and anguish.
                                        John L. Brown

The substitute for religion of men who are lonelier and more isolated than human individuals have ever been before, "without hope and without God in this world."   *Aelred Graham*

Atheistic existentialism...reflects and declares the longing of man for nothingness.
                                    Jacques Maritain

The endeavour to understand man by cutting below the cleavage between subject and object.
                                        Rollo May

Its method...is to leave the unchanging essence of things out of sight, and concentrates all its attention on particular existence.   *Pope Pius XII*

An attempt to draw all consequences from a consistent atheistic position.   *Jean-Paul Sartre*

Man exists, turns up, appears on the scene, and, only afterwards, defines himself.
                                    Jean-Paul Sartre

To make every man aware of what he is and to make the full responsibility of his existence rest on him.   *Jean-Paul Sartre*

An ethics of action and involvement.
                                    Jean-Paul Sartre

A doctrine which makes human life possible and...declares that every truth and every action implies a human setting and a human subjectivity.
                                    Jean-Paul Sartre

The central preoccupation of existentialism can be defined in one phrase: the stature of man. Is he a god or a worm?   *Colin Wilson*

EXODUS

The defiant proclamation of the rights of man.
                                        Moses George

The center of Jewish history and thought.

Eric Gutkind

The exodus of the Hebrews from Egypt was a slave revolt, a religious movement and a nationalistic movement.   *Eric Hoffer*

Forever the springtime of the entire world.

Abraham I. Kook

SEE ALSO JEWS, MOSES.

EXPERIENCE

What you've got when you're too old to get a job.

Leon Abramson

An arch to build upon.   *Henry B. Adams*

The reward of suffering.   *Aeschylus*

The best proof.   *Francis Bacon*

The comb nature gives us when we are bald.

Belgian Proverb

The wisdom that enables us to recognize as an undesirable old acquaintance the folly that we have already embraced.   *Ambrose Bierce*

A school where men learn what a big fool he has been.   *Josh Billings*

Like a pitiless beauty. Years pass before you win her, and by the time she finally surrenders, you have both grown old and no longer need one another.   *Ludwig Boerne*

A dim lamp, which only lights the one who bears it.   *Louis-Ferdinand Céliné*

To most men, experience is . . . the stern lights of a ship, which illumine only the track it has passed.

Samuel Taylor Coleridge

Our guide.   *Henry Steele Commager*

That precarious gait.   *Emily Dickinson*

The child of thought, and thought is the child of action. We cannot learn men from books.

Benjamin Disraeli

A jewel that I have purchased at an infinite rate.

Thomas Ford

A good school, but the fees are high.

Heinrich Heine

The extract of suffering.   *Arthur Helps*

(Something that) teaches us that experience teaches us nothing.   *Emile Herzog*

Nothing but memory.   *Thomas Hobbes*

A divine summons, exalting passion.

William E. Hocking

Awareness of the encompassing totality of things.

Sidney Hook

Stinging and getting stung.   *Elbert Hubbard*

Not what happens to a man. It is what a man does with what happens to him.   *Aldous Huxley*

A comb given to a man when he is bald.

Irish Proverb

A . . . thing that enables you to recognize a mistake whenever you make it again.

Franklin P. Jones

Our only teacher, both in war and peace.

Walter Savage Landor

(That which) makes a person better or bitter.

Samuel Levenson

Experience: in all that our knowledge is founded; and from that it ultimately derives itself.

John Locke

What really happens to you in the long run; the truth that finally overtakes you.

Katherine Ann Porter

The fruit of the tree of errors.

Portuguese Proverb

A poor hut constructed from the ruins of the palace of gold and marble called our illusions.

Joseph Roux

Composed rather of illusions lost than of wisdom acquired.   *Joseph Roux*

One thing you can't get for nothing.

Oscar Wilde

(That which) demonstrates that the future will be the same as the past.   *Oscar Wilde*

The name everyone gives to their mistakes.

Oscar Wilde

The knowledge that enables you to recognize a mistake when you make it again.   *Anon.*

The yeast of success.   *Anon.*

A practical school where man graduates hard-boiled.   *Anon.*

What you have left over after everything else is gone.   *Anon.*

A hard teacher, and there are no graduates, degrees, or survivors. *Anon.*

SEE ALSO EDUCATION, KNOWLEDGE, LEARNING, THOUGHT.

EXPERIMENT

Pursuing not only what you seek but also what you do not seek. *Adapted from Claude Bernard*

The observer listens to nature; the experimenter questions and forces her to reveal herself.
George L. Cuvier

No facts are to me sacred; none are profane. I . . . an endless seeker, with no past at my back.
Ralph Waldo Emerson

A hard teacher because she gives the test first, the lesson afterwards. *Vernon Law*

SEE ALSO INVENTION, RESEARCH, SCIENCE.

EXPERT

One who knows more and more about less and less. *Ambrose Bierce*

The one who predicts the job will take the longest and cost the most. *Arthur Bloch*

A man who has made all the mistakes which can be made in a very narrow field. *Niels Bohr*

The function . . . is not to be more right than other people, but to be wrong for more sophisticated reasons. *David Butler*

One who knows too much about one subject.
Leonard L. Levinson

A damned fool a long way from home.
Carl Sandburg

A person who avoids small errors as he sweeps on to the grand fallacy. *Benjamin Stolberg*

An ordinary man away from home giving advice.
Oscar Wilde

A mechanic away from home.
Charles E. Wilson

A man who has stopped thinking.
Frank Lloyd Wright

One who can take something you already know and make it sound confusing. *Anon.*

SEE ALSO SPECIALIST.

EXTRAVAGANCE

The passion of acquiring riches in order to support a vain expense. *François de Fénelon*

Anything you buy that is of no earthly use to your wife. *Franklin P. Jones*

The way the other fellow spends his money.
Harry Thompson

The luxury of the poor. *Oscar Wilde*

SEE ALSO LUXURY.

EYE

The pulse of the soul; as physicians judge the heart by the pulse, so we by the eye.
Thomas Adams

Man was created with two eyes, so that with one he may see God's greatness, and with the other his own lowliness. *Samuel Y. Agnon*

The light of the body. *Bible: Matthew, VI, 22.*

Sentinels. *Cicero*

(The) windows of the soul.
Guillaume Du Bartas

Love's tongue. *Phineas Fletcher*

The heart's letter. *George Herbert*

The spectacles of the brain; the peephole of the consciousness. *Elbert Hubbard*

The balls of sight are so formed, that one man's eyes are spectacles to another, to read his heart with. *Samuel Johnson*

That which tells what the heart means.
Judah L. Lazerov

The windows of our souls, by which . . . all dishonest concupiscence gets into our hearts.
Salvianus

The traitor of the heart. *Thomas Wyatt*

SEE ALSO SIGHT.

F

FABLE

The first pieces of wit that made their appearance in the world.   *Joseph Addison*

A bridge which leads to truth.   *Arabian Proverb*

The most effective means of presenting and impressing both truth and duty.   *Tyron Edwards*

A lie that has attained the dignity of age.
                                                        Warren Robertson

A horror story to prepare children for the daily newspaper.   *Anon.*

SEE ALSO MYTHOLOGY.

FACE

The tablet of unutterable thoughts.   *Lord Byron*

The portrait of the mind.   *Cicero*

A history.   *Samuel Taylor Coleridge*

The shorthand of the mind, and crowds a great deal in a little room.   *Jeremy Collier*

Often only a smooth imposter.
                                                        Pierre Corneille

The index of a feeling mind.   *George Crabbe*

The best criterion of value.   *William Hazlitt*

A convenience rather than an ornament.
                                            Oliver Wendell Holmes 1

Oftentimes a true index of the heart.
                                                        James Howell

The masterpiece of God. The eyes reveal the soul, the mouth the flesh. The chin stands for purpose, the nose means will; but over and behind all is that fleeting something we call "expression."
                                                        Elbert Hubbard

Outward show.   *Juvenal*

Some tell a story, some speak not. They are books in which not a line is written, save perhaps a date.
                        Henry Wadsworth Longfellow

The title-page which heralds the contents of the human volume.   *William Matthews*

The index to joy and mirth, to severity and sadness.   *Pliny 1*

My landscape.   *Joshua Reynolds*

Books, with this in their favor, that they may be perused in much less time, and are less liable to be misunderstood.   *Frederick Saunders*

A book where men may read strange matters.
                                                William Shakespeare

A pleasant face is a silent recommendation.
                                                        Publilius Syrus

They trace the operations of the mind with the iron pen of fate, and tell us not only what powers are within, but how they have been employed.
                                                Mary Wollstonecraft

A mystery.   *William Wordsworth*

The mould of the heart.   *Zohar: Genesis, 96b.*

Something that can be lifted, but falls when you get the bill.   *Anon.*

FACT

Facts, when combined with ideas, constitute the greatest force in the world.   *Carl W. Ackerman*

Nothing. It is valuable only for the idea attached to it, or for the proof which it furnishes.

Claude Bernard

A great thing—a sentence printed, if not by God, then at least by the Devil.   *Thomas Carlyle*

The theories we believe we call facts and the facts we disbelieve we call theories.   *Felix Cohen*

Not truths...not conclusions...not even premisses, but in the nature and parts of premisses. The truth depends on, and is arrived at, by a legitimate deduction from all facts which are truly material.   *Samuel Taylor Coleridge*

God's arguments; we should be careful never to misunderstand or pervert them.   *Tyron Edwards*

(Something) established by two or three good testimonies.   *Nathaniel Emmons*

All solid facts were originally mist.

Henry S. Haskins

The toys of men who live and die at leisure. They who are engrossed in the rapid realization of an extravagant hope tend to view facts as something base and unclean. Facts are counterrevolutionary.

Eric Hoffer

Ventriloquist's dummies. Sitting on a wise man's knee they may be made to utter words of wisdom; elsewhere, they say nothing, or talk nonsense, or indulge in sheer diabolism.   *Aldous Huxley*

Working tools only.   *Clarence B. Randall*

A fact, in science, is not a mere fact, but an instance.   *Bertrand A. Russell*

Nothing is so fallacious as facts, except figures.

Adapted from Sydney Smith

Stubborn things.   *Tobias Smollett*

The refuge of those who have no imagination.

Luc de Vauvenargues

Every fact is what it is, a fact of pleasure, of joy, of pain, or of suffering. In its union with God that fact is not a total loss, but on its finer side is an element to be woven immortally into the rhythm of mortal things.   *Alfred North Whitehead*

The hardest thing in this world to get.

Walter Yost

A datum of experience as distinct from conclusions.   *Anon.*

SEE ALSO RESEARCH, SCIENCE, TRUTH.

FAILURE

All failures...are failures because they are lacking in social interest.   *Alfred Adler*

They fail, and they alone, who have not striven.

Thomas Bailey Aldrich

An inability to stay quiet, an irritable desire to act directly.   *Adapted from Walter Bagehot*

A school in which the truth always grows strong.

Henry Ward Beecher

Man's historical experience...and there are no grounds for supposing it will ever be anything else.   *Nicholas Berdyaev*

(Something) made only by those who fail to dare, not by those who dare to fail.   *Louis Binstock*

Failure is an event, never a person.

William D. Brown

A sign that man has tried to surpass himself.

Adapted from Georges Clemenceau

Not to be true to the best one knows.

Frederic W. Farrar

Any man who has $10,000 left when he dies.

Errol Flynn

The opportunity to begin again, more intelligently.   *Henry Ford*

An excuse for idling.   *Max Gralnick*

The fear of failure.   *Max Gralnick*

Pulling in one's horse as he is leaping.

Julius and Augustus Hare

The greedy search for money or success...Why? Because that kind of life makes them depend upon things outside themselves.   *Emile Herzog*

Often that early morning hour of darkness which precedes the dawning of the day of success.
Leigh M. Hodges

God's own tool for carving some of the finest outlines in the character of his children.
Thomas Hodgkin

The man who can tell others what to do and how to do it, but never does it himself.
Elbert Hubbard

A man who has blundered but is not able to cash in the experience.   *Elbert Hubbard*

The highway to success, inasmuch as every discovery of what is false leads us to seek...after what is true.   *John Keats*

Lack of application.   *La Rochefoucauld*

It is always too late, or too little, or both.
David Lloyd George

Failure comes only when we forget our ideals and objectives and principles.   *Jawaharlal Nehru*

Nothing but education, nothing but the first step to something better.   *Wendell Phillips*

Not the falling down, but the staying down.
Mary Pickford

Never anything but an invitation to have recourse to God.   *Antonin Sertillanges*

I can give you the formula for failure—which is: Try to please everybody.   *Herbert B. Swope*

The path of least persistence.   *Anon.*

Anyone seen on a bus after the age of thirty.
Anon.

To die and not be missed.   *Anon.*

SEE ALSO ERROR, FAULT, SUCCESS.

FAIR PLAY

Hearing what both sides have to say.
Adapted from Aristophanes

Turn about is fair play.   *English Proverb*

Hear the other side.   *Saint Augustine*

FAIRY-TALE

SEE FABLE, FOLKLORE, MYTHOLOGY.

FAITH

A certitude without proofs...a sentiment, for it is a hope; it is an instinct, for it precedes all outward instruction.   *Henry F. Amiel*

The capacity of the soul to perceive the abiding...in the transitory, the invisible in the visible.
Leon Baeck

The proper name of religious experience.
John Baillie

Nothing but spiritualized imagination.
Henry Ward Beecher

The substance of things hoped for, the evidence of things not seen.   *Bible: Hebrews, XI, 1.*

Faith without works is dead.
Bible: James, II, 26.

I know that my redeemer liveth.
Bible: Job, XIX, 25.

The soul riding at anchor.   *Josh Billings*

An outward and visible sign of an inward and spiritual grace.   *Book of Common Prayer*

Where reason ends.   *Nahman Bratzlav*

The soul's adventure.   *William Bridges*

Faith is obedience, nothing else.   *Emil Brunner*

A kind of betting or speculation.
Samuel Butler 2

The response of our spirits to beckonings of the eternal.   *George A. Buttrick*

A knowledge of the benevolence of God toward us, and a certain persuasion of His veracity.
John Calvin

Consists, not in ignorance, but in knowledge, and that, not only of God, but also of the divine will.
John Calvin

Loyalty to some inspired teacher, some spiritual hero.   *Thomas Carlyle*

Love taking the form of aspiration.
William Ellery Channing

Believing things when common sense tells you not to.   *Valentine Davis*

The matrix of formulated creeds and the inspiration of endeavor.   *John Dewey*

To me faith means not worrying.   *John Dewey*

Reason grown courageous.   *Sherwood Eddy*

A certain beginning by which knowledge of the Creator begins to be produced in the rational nature.   *John S. Erigena*

The function of the heart.
Mohandas K. Gandhi

Building on what you know is here, so you can reach what you know is there.
Cullen Hightower

An assent of the mind and a consent of the heart, consisting mainly of belief and trust.
E. T. Hiscox

A gift of God which man can neither give nor take away by promise of rewards or menaces of torture.
Thomas Hobbes

Primarily a process of identification; the process by which the individual ceases to be himself and becomes part of something eternal.
Eric Hoffer

Faith in a holy cause is to a considerable extent a substitute for the lost faith in ourselves.
Eric Hoffer

Faith, as an intellectual state, is self-reliance.
Oliver Wendell Holmes 1

Implies the disbelief of a lesser fact in favor of a greater.   *Oliver Wendell Holmes 1*

The great act of faith is when a man decides that he is not God.   *Oliver Wendell Holmes 2*

The effort to believe what your common sense tells you is not true.   *Elbert Hubbard*

The little night-light that burns in a sick-room; as long as it is there, the obscurity is not complete, we turn towards it and await the daylight.
Abbé Huvelin

The summit of the Torah.   *Solomon Ibn Gabirol*

An act of self-consecration, in which the will, the intellect, and the affections all have their place.
William R. Inge

A man's religious faith...means for me essentially his faith in the existence of an unseen order of some kind in which the riddles of the natural order may be found explained.   *William James*

Faith is not faith without believing.
Thomas Jefferson

An encounter in which God takes and keeps the initiative.   *Eugene Joly*

Often the boast of a man who is too lazy to investigate.   *F. M. Knowles*

The assent to any proposition not...made out by the deductions of reason; but upon the credit of the proposer, as coming from God, in some extraordinary way of communication.   *John Locke*

That which is woven of conviction and set with the sharp mordant of experience.
James Russell Lowell

A practical attitude of the will.
John MacMurray

A total attitude of the self.   *John Macquarrie*

Nothing else than trust in the divine mercy promised in Christ.   *Philip Melanchthon*

The most...ecstatic faith is almost agnostic. It trusts absolutely nothing without professing to know it all.   *Henry Louis Mencken*

An illogical belief in the occurrence of the impossible.   *Henry Louis Mencken*

Every man's true faith is the one he finds customary wherever he happens to be.
Michel de Montaigne

Faith is courage; it is creative while despair is always destructive.   *David S. Muzzey*

The result of the act of the will, following upon a conviction that to believe is a duty.
John Henry Newman

The final triumph over incongruity, the final assertion of the meaningfulness of existence.
Reinhold Niebuhr

Not wanting to know what is true.
Friedrich W. Nietzsche

Whoever has theological blood in his veins is shifty and dishonorable in all things. The pathetic thing that grows out of this condition is called faith.   *Friedrich W. Nietzsche*

Intellect on the wing.   *Charles Parkhurst*

God felt by the heart, not by reason.
Blaise Pascal

An attitude of the person. It means you are prepared to stake yourself on something being so.
Arthur M. Ramsey

The only known cure for fear.   *Lena K. Sadler*

God's work within us.   *Saint Thomas Aquinas*

Faith has to do with things that are not seen, and hope with things that are not in hand.

Saint Thomas Aquinas

The foretaste of that knowledge which hereafter will make us happy.   *Saint Thomas Aquinas*

To believe that which you do not yet see; and the reward of faith is to see that which you believe.

Saint Augustine

The subtle chain which binds us to the infinite.

Adapted from Elizabeth O. Smith

Nothing but obedience and piety.

Baruch Spinoza

A theological virtue that inclines the mind, under the influence of the will and grace, to yield firm assent to revealed truths, because of the authority of God.   *Adolphe Tanqueray*

Believing where we cannot prove.

Alfred Lord Tennyson

What's up is faith, what's down is heresy.

Alfred Lord Tennyson

A rock with roots.   *Puzant K. Thomajan*

An act of a finite being who is grasped by and turned to the infinite.   *Paul Tillich*

Believing what you know ain't so.   *Mark Twain*

Consists of believing things because they are impossible.   *Voltaire*

As faith is the evidence of things not seen, so things that are seen are the perfection of faith.

Arthur Warwick

The divine evidence whereby the spiritual man discerneth God and the things of God.

John Wesley

A passionate intuition.   *William Wordsworth*

A bridge across the gulf of death.

Edward Young

Verification by the heart; confession by the tongue; action by the limbs.   *Anon.*

SEE ALSO BELIEF, CERTAINTY, CHRISTIANITY, PIETY, RELIGION, SALVATION.

FALSEHOOD

SEE CALUMNY, LIE, LYING.

FAME

A parasite of pride, ever scornful to meekness, and ever obsequious to insolent power.

John Quincy Adams

Vanity.   *Marcus Aurelius*

A river, that beareth up things light and swoln, and drowns things weighty and solid.

Francis Bacon

An ego-building but back-breaking state of being which—rather like love—is most comfortable in private, and most frightening when its loss is contemplated.   *Phyllis Battelle*

Loneliness.   *Vicki Baum*

A bubble that often comes from blowing your own horn.   *Bishop Berry*

(To be) conspicuously miserable.

Ambrose Bierce

Climbing a greasy pole for $10 and ruining trousers worth $15.   *Josh Billings*

A few words upon a tombstone, and the truth of those not to be depended on.

Christian N. Bovee

The thirst of youth.   *Lord Byron*

It is no sure test of merit, but only a probability of such: it is an accident, not a property of man.

Thomas Carlyle

Fame isn't a thing. It's a feeling. Like what you get after a pill.   *Joyce Cary*

The advantage of being known to those who do not know us.   *Nicolas Chamfort*

Something that comes legitimately after death. So I'm not in any hurry for it.   *Gower Champion*

Solitude.   *Coco Chanel*

When you have done your best with what you know how to do best—and people everywhere look at you with a friendly smile.

Maurice Chevalier

Nothing but an empty name.   *Charles Churchill*

Wind.   *Thomas Coryate*

A host of expendable sycophants, a lack of privacy and the alienation of old friends.

Morton Da Costa

A breath of wind that blows now this way, now that, and changes name as it changes sides.

Dante

Fame is a fickle flood
Upon a shifting plate.   *Emily Dickinson*

Food that dead men eat.   *Austin Dobson*

What someone writes on your tombstone.

Finley Peter Dunne

As a projection of one's ego...mere vanity. True fame is not the projection of one's self but the selfless service of humanity.   *James A. Farley*

The deep current of man's progress on this earth.

James A. Farley

The breath of the people, and that often unwholesome.   *Thomas Fuller*

A magnifying glass.   *Thomas Fuller*

The echo of actions, resounding them to the world, save that the echo repeats only the last part, but fame relates all, and often more than all.

Thomas Fuller

An empty bubble.   *James Grainger*

That which compels us to live not as we want, but as our fans want.   *Max Gralnick*

The inheritance not of the dead, but of the living. It is we who look back with lofty pride to the great names of antiquity.   *William Hazlitt*

Not popularity...It is the spirit of a man surviving himself in the minds and thoughts of other men.   *William Hazlitt*

(When) you are known by people you don't know.

Eric Hoffer

A giddy whirlwind's fickle gust.

Oliver Wendell Holmes 1

Fame...though in itself one of the most dangerous things to man, is nevertheless the true and appointed air, element, and setting of genius and its works.   *Gerard Manley Hopkins*

To have your name paged in a fashionable hotel.

Adapted from Elbert Hubbard

A recognition of excellence which must be felt but need not be spoken.   *Anna Jameson*

(That which is) known to exist by the echo of its footsteps through congenial minds.

Anna Jameson

To get a name.   *Samuel Johnson*

Footprints on the sands of time.

Henry Wadsworth Longfellow

A revenue payable only to our ghosts.

George Mackenzie

Being known by more people than you know.

Jonathan Miller

When the phone rings in your flat and you're told "Sir, you have a transatlantic call", and without even thinking, you say, "And who is it calling?"

Laurence Olivier

To be pointed at with the finger and to have it said, "There goes the man."   *Persius*

The perfume of heroic deeds.   *Plato*

The achievements of the mind.   *Propertius*

A goddess capricious.   *Douglas Reed*

Fame is a bugle call
Blown past a crumbling wall.   *Lizette W. Reese*

The aggregate of all the misunderstandings that collect around a new name.   *Ranier M. Rilke*

The beginning of the fall of greatness.

Vasily V. Rozanov

A foolish image by which worth is reckoned.

George Santayana

The outward sign of recognition of an inward representative authority residing in genius or good fortune.   *George Santayana*

Consists in the immortality of a man's work, his spirit, his efficacy, in the perpetual rejuvenation of his soul in the world.   *George Santayana*

Something which must be won.

Arthur Schopenhauer

Nothing but what a man is in comparison with others...it vanishes the moment other people become what the famous man is.

Arthur Schopenhauer

An inscription on a grave.   *Alexander Smith*

The advantage of being known by people of whom you yourself know nothing, and for whom you care as little.   *Stanislaus*

Fame and rest are utter opposites.

Richard Steele

An echo, a shade, a dream, a flower that is blasted with every wind and spoiled with every shower.   *Torquato Tasso*

A heavy burden.   *Voltaire*

Chiefly a matter of dying at the right time.
                                          Bud Walters

The shade of immortality.   *Edward Young*

Something which comes to those who are thinking about something else.   *Anon.*

To live in poverty and end up as a statue.   *Anon.*

SEE ALSO ARTISTS, DEEDS, EMINENCE, GLORY, HONOR.

FAMILIARITY

The first step toward parenthood.
                              Hyman Maxwell Berston

A relation into which fools are providentially drawn for their mutual destruction.
                                      Ambrose Bierce

(A condition which) either offends your superiors, or else dubs you their dependent...It gives your inferiors just, but troublesome and improper claims of equality.   *Lord Chesterfield*

The deadly effect of enabling one to predict the other person's responses; and when that happens, the stimulating quality and creative tension of a relationship are finished.   *Arthur Koestler*

The aphides that...suck out the juices intended for the germ of love.   *Walter Savage Landor*

A magician that is cruel to beauty, but kind to ugliness.   *Ouida*

The opiate of the imagination.   *Arnold Toynbee*

FAMILY

The school of duties...founded on love.
                                          Felix Adler

The miniature commonwealth upon whose integrity the safety of the larger commonwealth depends.   *Felix Adler*

The only preserving and healing power counteracting any historical, intellectual or spiritual crisis no matter of what depth.   *Ruth N. Anshen*

A kind of discipline of humanity.
                                      Francis Bacon

An earlier heaven.   *John Bowring*

A court of justice which never shuts down for night or day.   *Malcolm de Chazal*

A good institution because it is uncongenial.
                              Gilbert Keith Chesterton

It starts with a young man falling in love with a girl—no superior alternative has yet been found.
                                  Winston S. Churchill

The prime objects of civilization, and the ultimate ends of all industry.   *Charles W. Eliot*

A manufacture very little above the building of a house of cards. Time and accidents are sure to furnish a blast to blow them down.
                                        Lord Halifax

The native soil on which performance of moral duty is made easy through natural affection...and then is widened to include human relationships in general.   *I Ching*

Consists of those who live under the same roof with the paterfamilias; those who form...his fireside.   *Lord Kenyon*

The we of me.   *Carson McCullers*

A unit composed not only of children, but of men, women, an occasional animal, and the common cold.   *Ogden Nash*

The first and essential cell of human society.
                                      Pope John XXIII

A society limited in numbers, but nevertheless a true society, anterior to every state or nation, with rights and duties of its own, wholly independent of the commonwealth.   *Pope Leo XIII*

The family is...begotten...for Heaven and eternity.   *Pope Pius XI*

One of nature's masterpieces.
                                  George Santayana

If well ordered...they are the springs from which go forth the streams of national greatness and prosperity—of civil order and public happiness.
                                      William Thayer

SEE ALSO CHILD, DAUGHTER, FATHER, HOME, MARRIAGE, MOTHER, PARENTS, SON, WIFE.

FAMINE

SEE HUNGER, STOMACH.

FANATIC

The Devil's plaything.   *Armenian Proverb*

One compelled to action by the need to find a strong meaning in life. The fanatic determines for himself what role he is to play in life, and his intense devotion to a cause is the means.

Eugene E. Brussell

(One who) is nearer to the heart of things than the cool and slippery disputant.   *Edwin H. Chapin*

One who can't change his mind and won't change the subject.   *Winston S. Churchill*

One who does what he thinks the Lord would do if only He knew the facts of the case.

Adapted from Finley Peter Dunn

The gadflies that keep society from being too complacent.   *Abraham Flexner*

(One who) is perpetually incomplete and insecure. He cannot generate self-assurance out of his individual resources—out of his rejected self—but finds it only by clinging passionately to whatever support he happens to embrace.

Eric Hoffer

Whence come the fanatics? Mostly from the ranks of the noncreative man of words...the eternal misfits and the...contemners of the present.

Eric Hoffer

Often selfish people who were forced, by innate shortcomings or external circumstances, to lose faith in their own selves.   *Eric Hoffer*

A man who consciously over-compensates a secret doubt.   *Aldous Huxley*

Scratch a fanatic and you will find a wound that never healed.   *William N. Jayme*

A lunatic with a hobby.   *Leonard L. Levinson*

The outgrowth of yesterday's false preachments.

Carl E. Sanders

The subject of strong delusions.

Richard Whately

The insecure person anywhere, at any time, who gives himself without reservation to any movement that promises him meaning through action.

Robert Zwickey

One who is highly enthusiastic about something in which you are not even remotely interested.

Anon.

One with an all-devouring interest.   *Anon.*

SEE ALSO BIGOT.

FANATICISM

That which is founded on pride and which glories in persecution.   *Marchese di Beccaria*

That temperament which can only repose in fixed sanctities.   *Hilaire Belloc*

Zeal run wild.   *Eugene E. Brussell*

False fire of an overheated mind.

William Cowper

There is only one step from fanaticism to barbarism.   *Denis Diderot*

The essence of faith...the faith that works miracles.   *Gustave Flaubert*

Not a characteristic of mature societies but of unstable and politically primitive societies.

James W. Fulbright

A flight from the self.   *Eric Hoffer*

Fanaticism (when not a mere expression of ecclesiastical ambition) is only loyalty carried to convulsive extreme.   *William James*

The more ardent zeal of others.

Henry Wadsworth Longfellow

The child of persecution.   *Napoleon 1*

What is fanaticism today is the fashionable creed tomorrow, and trite is the multiplication table a week later.   *Wendell Phillips*

Redoubling your effort when you have forgotten your aim.   *George Santayana*

The effect of a false conscience, which makes religion subservient to the caprices of the imagination, and the excesses of the passions.

Voltaire

Religion caricatured.   *Edwin P. Whipple*

A fire which heats the mind...but heats without purifying. It stimulates and foments all the passions, but it rectifies none.   *Anon.*

SEE ALSO BIGOTRY, ZEAL.

FANTASY

What reality becomes when we ask enough questions of it.   *John Ciardi*

Weak, serious drama filtered through a poetic imagination into beauty.   *George Jean Nathan*

FAREWELL

A sound which makes us linger.   *Lord Byron*

Death seems in the word—farewell.
Thomas Campbell

Wasted sadness. One should leave quietly.
Adapted from Jerome K. Jerome

That bitter word, which closed all earthly friendships, and finished every feast of love.
Robert Pollock

FARM

A parcel of land ripe for subdivision.
Edward Bellis

Today a manufacturing center wherein the utilization of mechanical devices is the highest good.
Eugene E. Brussell

An irregular patch of nettles bounded by short term notes, containing a fool and his wife who didn't know enough to stay in the city.
Sidney J. Perelman

What a city man dreams of at 5 p.m., never at 5 a.m.   *Anon.*

A hunk of land on which...you'll make a fortune—if you strike oil on it.   *Anon.*

FARMER

The best citizens, the staunchest soldiers. Farmers are, of all men, the least given to vice.   *Cato*

It is his part to create. All trade rests at last on his primitive activity.   *Ralph Waldo Emerson*

(One who) is covetous of his dollars, and with reason...He knows how many strokes of labor it represents. His bones ache with the day's work that earned it.   *Ralph Waldo Emerson*

A man who makes his money in the country and blows it when he comes to town.
Elbert Hubbard

The chosen people of God.   *Thomas Jefferson*

The best fertilizer for a piece of land.
Lyndon Baines Johnson

Often worthless fellows. They have all the sensual vices of the nobility, with cheating into the bargain.   *Samuel Johnson*

Slave of the wheel of labor.   *Edwin Markham*

A sullen prayer, like the soil he tills.
Joseph Roux

When tillage begins, other arts follow. The farmers, therefore, are the founders of civilization.
Daniel Webster

A handy man with a sense of humus.
Edward B. White

A man whose sons and daughters move to the city.
Anon.

A man who wakes up surrounded by work.
Anon.

A man who believes in the eight-hour day: eight hours in the forenoon and eight hours in the afternoon.   *Anon.*

FARMING

A school of patience: you can't hurry the crops or make an ox in two days.   *Emile C. Alain*

A kind of continual miracle wrought by the hand of God.   *Benjamin Franklin*

(Something that) looks nice—from a car window.
Kin Hubbard

To plow is to pray—to plant is to prophesy.
Robert G. Ingersoll

The first and most precious of all the arts.
Thomas Jefferson

Redemption.   *Mendel of Kotz*

The first and most respectable of all the arts.
Jean-Jacques Rousseau

A senseless pursiut, a mere laboring in a circle. You sow that you may reap, and then you reap that you may sow. Nothing ever comes out of it.
Joannes Stobaeus

The most important labor of man.
Daniel Webster

The best business a man can do.   *Noah Webster*

Some people tell us there ain't no Hell, but they never farmed, so how can they tell?   *Anon.*

To plow and to sow, and to reap and to mow.

Anon.

FASCISM

A dictatorship...possessing irresponsible power ...an effort to freeze the economic crisis arising from the application of great technology—to freeze it by the pressure of military forces sustained openly or tacitly by the middle classes.

Charles A. Beard

Dictatorship from the extreme right...a government which is run by a small group of large industrialists and financial lords.

Heywood Broun

A lie told by bullies.   *Ernest Hemingway*

Capitalism in decay.   *Nikolai Lenin*

A religious conception in which man is seen in his immanent relationship with a superior law and with an objective will that transcends the particular individual and raises him to conscious membership of a spiritual society.

Benito Mussolini

An army on the march.   *Benito Mussolini*

Action and sentiment...the unconscious re-awakening of our profound racial instinct.

Alfredo Rocco

Ownership of government by an individual, by a group, or by any other controlling private power.

Franklin Delano Roosevelt

Capitalism plus murder.   *Upton Sinclair*

Nothing but capitalist reaction; from the point of view of the proletariat the differences between types of reaction are meaningless.   *Leon Trotsky*

SEE ALSO DICTATORSHIP, TOTALITAR-
IANISM.

FASHION

A despot whom the wise ridicule and obey.

Ambrose Bierce

Something that goes out of style as soon as most people have one.   *Sylvia S. Bremer*

An idiot painter that seems industrious to place staring fools and unprincipled knaves in the foreground of its picture, while men of sense and honesty are too often thrown in the dimmest shades.   *Robert Burns*

The tax which the industry of the poor levies on the vanity of the rich.   *Nicolas Chamfort*

Fashion is an architecture—it is a matter of proportions.   *Coco Chanel*

The science of appearances, and it inspires one with the desire to seem rather than to be.

Edwin H. Chapin

Beautiful things which always become ugly in time.   *Jean Cocteau*

A kind of elevated vulgarity.   *George Darley*

The love of change for its own sake, the desire for something new.   *Thomas Stearns Eliot*

All that fashion demands is composure and self-content.   *Ralph Waldo Emerson*

Something that goes in one year and out the other.

Thomas Graham

Gentility running away from vulgarity, and afraid of being overtaken.   *William Hazlitt*

The abortive issue of vain ostentation and exclusive egotism.   *William Hazlitt*

(That which) constantly begins and ends in the two things it abhors most—singularity and vulgarity.   *William Hazlitt*

The attempt to realize art in living forms and social intercourse.   *Oliver Wendell Holmes 1*

A barricade behind which men hide their nothingness.   *Elbert Hubbard*

A woman's compromise between the admitted desire to dress and the unadmitted desire to undress.   *Lin Yutang*

For the most part, nothing but the ostentation of riches.   *John Locke*

Something barbarous, for it produces innovation without reason and imitation without benefit.

George Santayana

(Something that) wears out more apparel than the man.   *William Shakespeare*

Nothing but an induced epidemic.

George Bernard Shaw

(That by which) the fantastic becomes for a moment the universal.   *Oscar Wilde*

A form of ugliness so intolerable that we have to alter it every six months.   *Oscar Wilde*

What one wears oneself; what is unfashionable is what other people wear.   *Oscar Wilde*

SEE ALSO CLOTHES, DRESS.

FASTING

The general bequest of the East to religion—an aspect of the general ascetic discipline of sense life.   *Gaius G. Atkins*

He fasts enough who eats with reason.
Archibald J. Cronin

When the table is covered with fish.
Danish Proverb

A medicine.   *Saint John Chrysostom*

A sort of self-punishment, usually for religious reasons.   *Robert Zwickey*

SEE ALSO ABSTINENCE, SELF-DENIAL.

FAT

SEE OBESITY.

FATALISM

The refuge of a conscience-stricken mind, maddened at the sight of evils which it has brought upon itself, and cannot remove.
John Henry Newman

An excuse for practical inaction or mental indolence.   *Ralph Barton Perry*

(A belief in) a rigid chain of infinitely predestined causes.   *Lytton Strachey*

Always apt to be a double-edged philosophy; for while ... it reveals the minutest occurrences as the immutable result of a rigid chain of infinitely predestined causes ... it invests the wild incoherencies of conduct or of circumstance with the sanctity of eternal law.   *Lytton Strachey*

The wine-soaked premise of the earth-trapped mortal ... the device of a lazy and evasive thinker who denies the existence of a free will.
Alan M. Sullivan

Futility in trust and the compensation for defeat.
Alan M. Sullivan

The doctrine that action is futile.   *Anon.*

What shall be, shall be.   *Anon.*

SEE ALSO CALVINISM, PREDESTINATION.

FATE

The Karma, good or bad, acquired by an embodied being in the past life.   *Atmanushasana*

Whatever the universal nature assigns to any man at any time.   *Marcus Aurelius*

The heart is its own fate.   *Philip J. Bailey*

A disposition inherent in changeable things, by which Providence connects all things in their due order.   *Boethius*

Fate is not the ruler, but the servant of Providence.
Edward G. Bulwer-Lytton

Whatever limits us.   *Ralph Waldo Emerson*

Nothing but the deeds committed in a prior state of existence.   *Ralph Waldo Emerson*

Events not in our power.
Adapted from Robert Herrick

(That which) turns out the doom of high and low; her capacious urn is constantly shaking out the names of all mankind.   *Horace*

The gunman that all gunmen dread.
Don Marquis

What I will.   *John Milton*

If by fate anyone means the will or power of God, let him keep his meaning but mend his language: for fate commonly means a necessary process which will have its way apart from the will of God and men.   *Saint Augustine*

What must be shall be.   *Seneca*

What is decreed must be.   *William Shakespeare*

A personified idea of those characteristics of life that call out the heroic in man. *John W. Sullivan*

The outward wayward life we see, the hidden springs we may not know.

Adapted from John Greenleaf Whittier

The endless chain of causation, whereby things are; the reason or formula by which the world goes on.   *Zeno*

A name for facts not yet passed through the processes of thought.   *Anon.*

SEE ALSO CALVINISM, DESTINY, PRE-DESTINATION, WILL.

FATHER

He who brings up, not he who begets, is the father.
Bible: Exodus, XXXIV, 3.

Call no man your father upon the earth: for one is your Father, which is in heaven.
Bible: Matthew, XXIII, 9.

A man who expects his son to be as good a man as he meant to be.   *Franklin A. Clark*

A banker provided by nature.   *French Proverb*

One . . . is more than a hundred school-masters.
George Herbert

He is the father whom the marriage points to.
Legal Maxim

He who raises the child is called the father, not the one who had begotten the child.
Midrash Rabbah

The quietest member of the family unit.   *Anon.*

A man who can't get on the phone, into the bathroom, or out of the house.   *Anon.*

One whose love should be for his children; the children's love is for their children.   *Anon.*

One whose daughter marries a man vastly her inferior mentally, but then gives birth to unbelievably brilliant granchildren.   *Anon.*

The kin you love to touch.   *Anon.*

SEE ALSO DAUGHTER, PARENTS.

FAULT

One of my offenses, as distinguished from one of yours, the latter being crimes.   *Ambrose Bierce*

The greatest of faults is to be conscious of none.
Thomas Carlyle

Your failings.   *Confucius*

Errors in the brain.   *William Cowper*

The grumbling business.   *Robert West*

SEE ALSO ERROR, FAILURE.

FEAR

Pain arising from the anticipation of evil.
Aristotle

The soul's signal for rallying.
Henry Ward Beecher

Safety.   *Edmund Burke*

An instructor of great sagacity, and the herald of all revolutions . . . there is rottenness where he appears.   *Ralph Waldo Emerson*

Good sense.   *Dorothy Fosdick*

That which gives intelligence even to fools.
French Proverb

The greatest of all inventors.   *French Proverb*

The lengthened shadow of ignorance.
Arnold H. Glasow

The needle that pierces us that it may carry a thread to bind us to heaven.   *James Hastings*

The beadle of the law.   *George Herbert*

Uncertainty.   *Eric Hoffer*

The thought of admitted inferiority.
Elbert Hubbard

Nature's warning signal to get busy.   *Henry Link*

An uneasiness of the mind, upon the thought of future evil likely to befall us.   *John Locke*

The first thing on earth to make gods.
Lucretius

The one permanent emotion of the inferior man.
Henry Louis Mencken

The highest fence.   *Dudley Nichols*

Worry is a form of fear, and all forms of fear produce fatigue.   *Bertrand A. Russell*

The main source of superstition, and one of the main sources of cruelty.   *Bertrand A. Russell*

A slinking cat I find beneath the lilacs of my mind.   *Sophie Tunnell*

The start of wisdom.   *Miguel de Unamuno*

Fear follows crime and is its punishment.
Voltaire

A cloak which old men huddle about their love, as if to keep it warm.
Adapted from William Wordsworth

The darkness where negatives are developed.
Anon.

Expectation of evil.   *Anon.*

The tax that conscience pays to guilt.   *Anon.*

SEE ALSO CAUTION, GOD, SAFETY, WORRY.

FEBRUARY

February brings the rain,
Thaws the frozen lake again.   *Sara Coleridge*

The shortest month in the year...also the worst.
Italian Proverb

The most serious charge which can be brought against New England is not Puritanism but February.   *Joseph Wood Krutch*

When winter's back has been broken—after everybody else's.   *William Vaughan*

SEE ALSO WINTER.

FEELING

The emotion which drives the intelligence forward in spite of obstacles.   *Henri Bergson*

A prostrating disease caused by a determination of the heart to the head.   *Ambrose Bierce*

The *unconscious* conversion of instinctual impulses.   *Carl Jung*

A supremely valid phase of humanity at its noblest and most mature.   *Joshua L. Liebman*

Hidden impulses.   *Joshua L. Liebman*

The hardest thing in the world to put...into words.   *Jack London*

Not the Cinderella of our inner life, to be kept in her place among the cinders in the kitchen. Our emotional life is *us* in a way our intellectual life cannot be.   *John MacMurray*

The naked truth.   *John Ray*

The ennobling difference between one man and another...is precisely in this, that one feels more than another.   *John Ruskin*

Any portion of consciousness which occupies a place sufficiently large to give it a perceivable individuality.   *Herbert Spencer*

SEE ALSO HEART, LOVE, PASSION.

FELLOWSHIP

Charity.   *James C. Gibbons*

There are three kinds...some are like food, indispensable; some are like medicine, good sometimes; and some are like poison, unnecessary at any time.   *Samuel HaNagid*

A make-believe compact for purposes of piffle.
Elbert Hubbard

The ability to unite.   *Berl Katznelson*

The final grounds of holy fellowship are in God. Persons in the Fellowship are related to one another through Him...They get at one another through Him.   *Thomas R. Kelly*

Fellowship is Heaven, and lack of fellowship is Hell; fellowship is life, and lack of fellowship is death.   *William Morris*

The virtue of pigs in a litter which lie close together to keep each other warm.
Henry David Thoreau

A snobbish agreement whereby the right people are certain to meet other right people.   *Anon.*

The means whereby the Christian Church interprets human nature.   *Anon.*

God's gift of personal survival.   *Anon.*

SEE ALSO BROTHERHOOD.

FEMALE

SEE LADY, MOTHER, WOMAN, WOMEN.

FEMINIST

One who believes in the liberation of that which has been suppressed as female in a man.
Betty Friedan

A woman who assumes self-dependence as a basic condition of her life.   *Erica Jong*

A man or woman who already knows for a fact that men and women are equal and wants society to wake up to that fact, so the world can stop operating at half-strength. *Marlo Thomas*

FESTIVAL

SEE HOLIDAY.

FEUDALISM

A religious horror of letters and knowledge...human nature chained fast for ages in a cruel, shameful, and deplorable servitude.
John Quincy Adams

(A time when) only the convent and the castle appear to be alive...The convent prays and the castle sings; the cottage hungers and groans and dies. *W. Winwood Reade*

Nothing but a brief eclipse of the sun.
Jean Paul Richter

SEE ALSO CHIVALRY.

FEVER

Errors of various types. The quickened pulse, coated tongue, febrile heat, dry skin, pain in the head and limbs, are pictures drawn on the body by a mortal mind. *Mary Baker Eddy*

A superabundance of bile.
Saint John Chrysostom

FICTION

Fact distorted into truth. *Edward Albee*

The phantasmagorical world. *Matthew Arnold*

Imagining based on facts, and the facts must be accurate or the work of imagining will not stand up. *Margaret C. Banning*

Fiction...partakes more than we suspect, of the nature of lying. *Thomas Carlyle*

Transcendent genius accommodating itself to the character of the age. *William Ellery Channing*

The world of our dreams come true.
Courtney Riley Cooper

Writing in effect for the stage. *Charles Dickens*

The fanciful and dramatic grouping of real traits around imaginary scenes or characters.
Tyron Edwards

A writer is congenitally unable to tell the truth and that is why we call what he writes fiction.
William Faulkner

Fiction...has the softenings of fancy and sentiment; and we read on in the hope of something like poetical justice to be done at last, which is more than we can reckon upon in reality.
William Hazlitt

Always the particular situation between individuals, never the silent wish to illustrate a general truth. *William Somerset Maugham*

Character in decay is the theme of the great bulk of superior fiction. *Henry Louis Mencken*

Writing about the human heart.
James A. Michener

The most influential books, and the truest in their influence. *Robert Louis Stevenson*

They show us the web of experience, but with a singular change—that monstrous, consuming ego of ours being...struck out.
Robert Louis Stevenson

They repeat, they re-arrange, they clarify the lessons of life; they disengage us from ourselves, they constrain us to the acquaintance of others.
Robert Louis Stevenson

(A form which) reveals truths that reality obscures. *Jessamyn West*

The good end happily, the bad unhappily—that is what fiction means. *Oscar Wilde*

A kind of magic trickery...trying to make people believe something is true that isn't.
Angus Wilson

What happens when truth changes hands a few times. *Anon.*

SEE ALSO LITERATURE, NOVEL.

FIFTY

SEE MIDDLE AGE.

FIGHTING

When a man fights it means that a fool has lost his argument. *Chinese Proverb*

It is the ignorant and childish part of mankind that is the fighting part. Idle and vacant minds want excitement, as...boys kill cats.

Ralph Waldo Emerson

A radical instinct; if men have nothing else to fight over they will fight over words, fancies, or women, or they will fight because they dislike each other's looks, or because they have met walking in opposite directions.

George Santayana

The joy of life. *Norman Thomas*

SEE ALSO AGGRESSION, ARGUMENTS, BATTLE, QUARRELING, WAR.

FINANCE

The art or science of managing revenues and resources for the best advantage of the manager.

Ambrose Bierce

The cohesive power of the vast surplus in the banks. *John C. Calhoun*

Cohesive power of public plunder.

Grover Cleveland

The art of passing money from one hand to another until it finally disappears.

Leonard L. Levinson

The octopus. *Frank Norris*

The system. *Lincoln Steffens*

SEE ALSO BANK, BUSINESS, MONEY, WEALTH.

FIRE

The symbol of civilization. *Joseph H. Hertz*

The most tangible of all visible mysteries.

Leigh Hunt

God's unfailing charity. *John Oxenham*

A live thing in a dead room. *Sydney Smith*

The most tolerable third party.

Henry David Thoreau

FISHERMAN

Meek, quiet-spirited men...free from those high, those restless thoughts which corrode the sweets of life. *Izaak Walton*

A brother of the angle. *Izaak Walton*

A man who spends rainy days sitting around on the muddy banks of rivers doing nothing because his wife won't let him do it at home. *Anon.*

A man who baits and sees. *Anon.*

FISHING

That solitary vice. *Lord Byron*

An excuse to drink in the daytime.

James Cannon

The art of taking more fish out of a stream than were ever in it. *Oliver Herford*

The great occasion when we may return to the fine simplicity of our forefathers.

Herbert C. Hoover

The chance to wash one's soul with pure air.

Herbert C. Hoover

A delusion entirely surrounded by liars in old clothes. *Don Marquis*

An affair of luck. *Henry Van Dyke*

An art worthy the knowledge and patience of a wise man. *Izaak Walton*

Content and pleasure. *Izaak Walton*

May be said to be so like the mathematics that it can never be fully learnt. *Izaak Walton*

Somewhat like poetry—men are to be born so.

Izaak Walton

An employment for my idle time, which is then not idly spent. *Henry Wotton*

A rest to my mind, a cheerer of my spirits, a diverter of sadness, a calmer of unquiet thoughts, a moderator of passions, a procurer of contentedness. *Henry Wotton*

Incessant expectation, and perpetual disappointment. *Arthur Young*

A stick and a string with a fly on one end and a fool at the other. *Anon.*

An idle sport that makes men and truth strangers.

Anon.

The art of doing almost nothing. *Anon.*

The art of the wrist with a twist. *Anon.*

FLAG

A kind of idolatry which it would be 'a sin to destroy. For a flag represents an ideal.
Mohandas K. Gandhi

That which leads a people. *Theodor Herzl*

A deathless creed. *Julia Ward Howe*

The trademark of a nation.
Leonard L. Levinson

The embodiment of our ideals and (it) teaches us not only how to live but how to die.
Douglas MacArthur

The embodiment...of history. It represents the experiences made by men and women, the experiences of those who do and live under that flag.
Woodrow Wilson

The emblem of our unity, our power, our thought and purpose as a nation. *Woodrow Wilson*

The power of nations. *Anon.*

SEE ALSO NATIONALISM, PATRIOTISM.

FLATTERER

A friend who is your inferior, or pretends to be so.
Aristotle

All...are mercenary, and all low-minded men are flatterers. *Aristotle*

Their throat is an open coffin; they flatter with their tongues. *Bible: Psalms, V, 9.*

Flatterers look like friends, as wolves like dogs.
George Chapman

That agreeable animal which you meet every day in civilized society. *Benjamin Disraeli*

Those who destroy the souls of the living by blinding their eyes. *Epictetus*

Flatterers, like cats, lick and then scratch.
German Proverb

The flatterer is blear-eyed to ill; and cannot see vices, and his tongue walks ever in one track of unjust praises, and can no more tell how to discommend than to speak true. *Joseph Hall*

(One who) lives at the expense of the person who listens to him. *Jean de La Fontaine*

One who says things to your face that he would not say behind your back. *G. Millington*

Those worst of enemies. *Tacitus*

An esteem-fitter. *P. K. Thomajan*

One who extremely exaggerates in his opinion of your qualities so that it may come nearer to your opinion of them. *Oscar Wilde*

SEE ALSO EULOGY, PRAISE.

FLATTERY

Like cologne water, to be smelt of, not swallowed.
Adapted from Josh Billings

(That which) corrupts both the receiver and the giver. *Edmund Burke*

No more than what raises in a man's mind an idea of a preference which he has not.
Edmund Burke

To lay on with a trowel. *William Congreve*

The destruction of all good fellowship: it is like a qualmish liqueur in the midst of a bottle of wine.
Benjamin Disraeli

Implicit assent. *William Hazlitt*

Something nice someone tells you about yourself that you wish were true. *Frank Malester*

Witchcraft...if artfully performed.
Bernard de Mandeville

(Something) that exhausts you in your effort to believe it. *Wilson Mizner*

To take advantage of the foibles of the great, to foster their errors, and never to give advice which may annoy. *Jean Baptiste Molière*

Baloney is the unvarnished lie laid on so thick you hate it. Blarney is flattery laid on so thin you love it. *Fulton J. Sheen*

An instance of ill-manners. *Jonathan Swift*

The worst poison of true feeling. *Tacitus*

One who extremely exaggerates in his opinion of your qualities so that it may come nearer to your opinion of them. *Oscar Wilde*

Telling the other guy what he already thinks of himself. *Hal Wilshire*

The turnpike road of Fortune's door.
John Wolcot

The art of patting a person on the back in order to turn his head. *Anon.*

A commodity that makes everyone sick except those that swallow it. *Anon.*

Hearing from others what you have always thought about yourself. *Anon.*

SEE ALSO COMPLIMENTS, EULOGY, PRAISE.

FLEAS

Fleas are, like the remainder of the universe, a divine mystery. *Anatole France*

The bravest of all the creatures of God, if ignorance of fear were courage. *Mark Twain*

FLESH

All flesh is not the same flesh: but there is one kind of flesh of men, another flesh of beasts, another of fishes, and another of birds.
Bible: Corinthians, XV, 39.

The works of the flesh are manifest, which are these, Adultery, fornication ... hatred ... murders, drunkenness, revellings, and such like.
Bible: Galatians, V, 19-21.

All flesh is grass, and all the goodliness thereof is as the flower of the field. *Bible: Isaiah, XL, 6.*

Dust that measures all our time.
Adapted from George Herbert

SEE ALSO BODY, CORPSE.

FLIRT

SEE COQUETTE, WOMAN.

FLOWERS

The sweetest thing God ever made, and forgot to put a soul into. *Henry Ward Beecher*

Words which even a baby may understand.
Adapted from Arthur C. Coxe

The Amen! of Nature.
Oliver Wendell Holmes 1

An exquisite invention. *Leigh Hunt*

Heaven's masterpiece. *Dorothy Parker*

The Infinite has written its name on the heavens in shining stars, and on the earth in tender flowers. *Jean Paul Richter*

The reproductive organs of the plants they grow on. *Logan P. Smith*

Love's truest language. *Anon.*

FLY

A ... stylist who puts a period after each utterance. *Elbert Hubbard*

The reincarnation of our own dirt and carelessness. *Woods Hutchinson*

A lunch-counter irritant. *Leonard L. Levinson*

The Lord in His wisdom made the fly
And then forgot to tell us why. *Ogden Nash*

FOLKLORE

It reveals their (the people's) characteristic efforts to explain and deal with the strange phenomena of nature; to understand and interpret the ways of human beings with each other; and to give expression to deep, universal emotions.

Mary Hill Arbuthnot

An educational "must" for adults, married or single, for the reader who has once come to know and love these tales will never be able again to endure the insipid rubbish of contemporary entertainment. *Wystan H. Auden*

Stories that never run out of editions. *Anon.*

The cement of society. *Anon.*

The mirror of a people. *Anon.*

SEE ALSO FABLE, MYTHOLOGY.

FOLK SINGER

Someone who sings through his nose by ear.
Anon.

Singers who keep alive ethnic music by directing them at college educated intellectuals. *Anon.*

An intellectual who sings songs that nobody ever wrote. *Anon.*

A middle class person who warbles about the working classes and poverty. *Anon.*

FOLLY

The foolishness of fools.
Bible: Proverbs, XIV, 24.

That gift...whose creative and controlling energy inspires man's mind, guides his actions and adorns his life. *Ambrose Bierce*

Folly in youth is sin, in age 'tis madness.
Samuel Daniel

A vigorous plant, which sheds abundant seed.
Isaac D'Israeli

Wisdom spun too fine. *Benjamin Franklin*

The first degree of folly is to conceit one's self wise; the second to profess it; the third to despise counsel. *Benjamin Franklin*

(Something that) grows without watering.
George Herbert

The chief characteristic...is that it mistakes itself for wisdom. *Fray de Leon*

An accelerated velocity downwards.
Shemarya Levin

A self-chosen misfortune. *Menander*

The common curse of mankind.
William Shakespeare

The direct pursuit of Happiness and Beauty.
George Bernard Shaw

The prettiest word in the language.
William Shenstone

Every man's follies are the caricature resemblances of his wisdom. *John Sterling*

SEE ALSO FOOLISHNESS.

FOOD

Edibles that will give you heartburn immediately, instead of at three o'clock in the morning.
John Barrymore

Part of the spiritual expression of the French, and I do not believe that they have ever heard of calories. *Beverley Baxter*

God—to a man with an empty stomach.
Mohandas K. Gandhi

The first enjoyment of life. *Lin Yutang*

A weapon. *Maxim Litvinov*

What is food to one man is bitter poison to others.
Lucretius

(That which explains) half the emotions of life.
Sydney Smith

The commonest cause of domestic strife. *Anon.*

SEE ALSO DIET, EATING, HUNGER.

FOOL

You can tell when a fool speaks: he grinds much and produces little. *Sholom Aleichem*

(One who) contributes nothing worth hearing and takes offense at everything. *Aristotle*

The fool hath said in his heart, There is no God.
Bible: Psalms, XIV, 1.

A person who pervades the domain of intellectual speculation and diffuses himself through the channels of moral activity. *Ambrose Bierce*

A learned fool is one who has read everything and simply remembered it. *Josh Billings*

Every man a little beyond himself.
Henry G. Bohn

(One who) always finds one still more foolish to admire him. *Nicolas Boileau*

All men...and in spite of all their pains.
Nicolas Boileau

(Something hard to describe) without much patient self-inspection. *Frank M. Colby*

The majority. *Casmir Delavigne*

(One who) could never hold his peace; for too much talking is ever the indice of a fool.
Demacatus

One who expects things to happen that never can happen. *George Eliot*

You are not a fool just because you have done something foolish—only if the folly of it escapes you. *James Fibig*

One who is without anxiety. *Johann W. Goethe*

A fool hath no dialogue within himself; the first thought carrieth him without the reply of a second. *Lord Halifax*

He...that thinks not that another thinks.
George Herbert

Every man is a damn fool for at least five minutes every day; wisdom consists in not exceeding the limit. *Elbert Hubbard*

Anybody who feels at ease in the world today.

Robert Maynard Hutchins

There are two kinds: One says, "This is old, therefore it is good"; the other says, "This is new, therefore it is better." *William R. Inge*

Someone who is clever—to himself.

Jewish Proverb

A person who grows without the help of rain.

Jewish Saying

A disease incurable. *Ben Jonson*

A fool does not enter a room, nor leave it, nor sit down, nor rise up, nor is he silent, nor does he stand on his legs, like a man of sense.

Jean de La Bruyère

An automaton...a machine worked by a spring...natural forces make him move and turn, always at the same pace and never stopping. He is never inconsistent with himself ...He is fixed and immovable by nature. *Jean de La Bruyère*

Ladies' playfellows. *Brian Melbancke*

A...man that hears all he hears.

Austin O'Malley

One who does not suspect himself.

José Ortega y Gasset

He thinks himself the most prudent of men, hence the enviable tranquility with which the fool settles down, thereby installing himself in his own folly.

José Ortega y Gasset

(Whoever) writes his name upon a wall.

John Ray

Those who want to kill space and time.

Adapted from John Ruskin

The whetstone of the wits.

William Shakespeare

(One whose) intellect is improperly exposed.

Sydney Smith

Every man in some man's opinion.

Spanish Proverb

A big enough majority in any town.

Mark Twain

People who think themselves rich with little.

Luc de Vauvenargues

A man may know a fool by his much chattering.

Richard Wydeville

A misfortune. *Yiddish Proverb*

One who always laughs.

Zabara: Sefer Shaashuim, 13c, Ch.9.

One whom no advice will help. *Anon.*

SEE ALSO MORON.

FOOLISHNESS

The wish to be wiser than everybody else is the biggest foolishness. *Sholom Aleichem*

God hath chosen the foolish things of the world to confound the wise. *Bible: Corinthians, I, 27.*

A statement or belief manifestly inconsistent with one's own opinion. *Ambrose Bierce*

(A condition which) arises from the imitation of those whom we cannot resemble.

Samuel Johnson

To excommunicate the world.

George Santayana

When the body or tongue outraces the brain.

Anon.

A combination of laziness and a dislike for enforced knowledge. *Anon.*

SEE ALSO IGNORANCE.

FOOTBALL

A beastly game played by beasts. *Henry Blaha*

A game to keep coal miners off the streets.

James Breslin

A function of a quasi-religious nature performed by a few experts but followed in spirit by the whole university world.

Charles Horton Cooley

(Serves) as a symbol to arouse in the students and in the alumni certain congregate and hieratic emotions. *Charles Horton Cooley*

Nothing but beastly fury and extreme violence.

Thomas Elyot

One of the last great strongholds of genuine, old-fashioned American hypocrisy. *Paul Gallico*

FOOTNOTE

A game where one watches the figures on sweaters instead of in them.   *Arnold Glasow*

A sport that bears the same relation to education that bullfighting does to agriculture.

Elbert Hubbard

A friendly kind of fight.   *Philip Stubbes*

FOOTNOTE

Like running downstairs to answer the doorbell during the first night of marriage.

John Barrymore

Tedious information set aside where it can be easily skipped.   *Leonard L. Levinson*

Scholarly barbed wire.   *Edmund Wilson*

FOREBEARANCE

A part of justice.   *Marcus Aurelius*

To forgive an enemy who has been shorn of power.   *Elbert Hubbard*

To buy golden opinions of one's self.

Elbert Hubbard

Knowing when to forego an advantage.   *Anon.*

SEE ALSO FORGIVENESS, MERCY, TOLERANCE.

FORCE

Force and right are the governors of this world; force till right is ready.   *Matthew Arnold*

The vital principle . . . of despotism.

Thomas Jefferson

The midwife of every old society which is pregnant with the new.   *Karl Marx*

An economic power.   *Franz Mehring*

Force rules the world, and not opinion; but opinion is that which makes use of force.

Blaise Pascal

The enemy of civilization.   *T. V. Smith*

The blind wild-beast.   *Alfred Lord Tennyson*

A disclosure of the failure of civilization, either in the general society or in a remnant of individuals.

Alfred North Whitehead

SEE ALSO FIGHTING, MILITARISM.

FORD, HENRY (1863-1947)

He could get anything out of the men becasue he just talked and would tell them stories. He'd never say, "I want this done!" He'd say, "I wonder if we can do it."   *George Brown*

He's a thinking, sensible person—serious-minded. He's worked out something different.

Clara J. Bryant

We often wondered when Henry Ford slept because he was putting in long hours working and when he went home at night he was always experimenting or reading.   *Charles T. Bush*

Once in awhile you might get the echo of what someone else had just said to him, but most of what came up was his own. He was a thinker; he wasn't a repeater.   *W. J. Cameron*

I always said he had a twenty-five track mind. He had a few gadgets in his mind that the rest of us didn't have. He'd see further and see it faster.

W. J. Cameron

(I am) afraid of him, for I find him most right where I thought him most wrong.

Thomas Alva Edison

Even when I was very young I suspected that much might be done in a better way. That is what took me to mechanics . . . I had a kind of workshop with odds and ends of metal for tools before I had anything else . . . My toys were all tools—they still are!   *Henry Ford*

It is not possible to learn from books how everything is made—and a real mechanic ought to know how nearly everything is made.

Henry Ford

I was never tired. I was always enjoying what I was doing, and always had plenty of energy for it.

Henry Ford

The Lord is working and will clear the land of those who do not go ahead.   *Henry Ford*

I have never know what to do with money after my expenses were paid. I can't squander it on myself without hurting myself, and nobody wants to do that.   *Henry Ford*

We'll build this as well as we know how, and if we don't use it, somebody will use it. Anything that is good enough will be used.   *Henry Ford*

A man can never leave his business. He ought to think of it by day and dream of it by night.

Henry Ford

He didn't do much. He only told them what to do, and they very willingly did it.   *Margaret Ford*

He was always tinkering.   *William Ford*

His was a sensitive heart and . . . an understanding mind . . . He had sympathy and pity for the woes of others.   *Edgar A. Guest*

He was endowed with a fine engineering talent . . . a fierce will to power; nevertheless he was an exceedingly simple being at bottom.

Matthew Josephson

Ford was extremely sentimental; he kept the most trivial memorabilia of his boyhood days, loved rustic dances, old tunes and country folkways.

Matthew Josephson

A thinker of an original kind.

Samuel S. Marquis

A man of highly original mind and personality, quite different from anybody else, and that he was a very complicated man, every intimate agreed.

Allan Nevins

He read little . . . was not a good conversationalist, and, feeling a certain uneasiness . . . in the presence of highly literate men, he got little out of talk with others. But he was that rare person, a man who took time to think.   *Allan Nevins*

The apostle of rural virtues and the prophet of mass production; the isolationist and the internationalist; the plodder and the seer.   *Allan Nevins*

A first class mechanical engineer.

James Scholes

FOREIGN RELATIONS
(UNITED STATES)

Peace, commerce and honest friendship with all nations—entangling alliances with none.

Thomas Jefferson

I have ever deemed it fundamental . . . never to take active part in the quarrels of Europe.

Thomas Jefferson

An open book—generally a checkbook.

Will Rogers

To have nothing to do with the political intrigues, or the squabbles of European nations.

George Washington

To keep the United States free from political connections with every other country, to see them independent of all and under the influence of none.   *George Washington*

It is our true policy to steer clear of permanent alliance with any portion of the foreign world.

George Washington

FORGIVENESS

Ought to be like a cancelled note, torn in two and burned up, so that it can never be shown against the man.   *Henry Ward Beecher*

Man's deepest need and highest achievement.

Horace Bushnell

The sweetest revenge.   *Isaac Friedmann*

God's business.   *Heinrich Heine*

The highest and most difficult of all moral lessons.   *Joseph Jacobs*

God's command.   *Martin Luther*

The giving, and so the receiving of life.

George Macdonald

Forgiving love is a possibility only for those who know they are not good, who feel themselves in need of divine mercy.   *Reinhold Niebuhr*

The remission of sins. For it is by this that what has been lost, and was found, is saved from being lost again.   *Saint Augustine*

Not the enthusiasm of Humanity alone, nor the great sentences of the Sermon on the Mount alone, but both together, the creative meeting of the Spirit and the Word.   *John R. Seeley*

The most tender part of love.   *John Sheffield*

The fragrance the violet sheds on the heel that has crushed it.   *Mark Twain*

FORGOTTEN

I am forgotten as a dead man out of mind: I am like a broken vessel.   *Bible: Psalms, XXXI, 12.*

Unminded, unmoaned.   *John Heywood*

Who is the Forgotten Man? He is the clean, quiet, virtuous, domestic citizen, who pays his debts and his taxes and is never heard of out of his little circle.   *William G. Sumner*

FORM

(That which) has value only in what it suggests.
Felix Adler

Social experience solidified.   *Ernst Fischer*

Those simple outward laws which have been sanctioned by the experience of mankind.
James A. Froude

The unity of geometrical balance and of successive relations.   *Roger Fry*

Vehicles and expressions of the spirit, as well as a means of fortifying it.   *Abraham Geiger*

That which lends expression to every sentiment and thought.   *Adapted from Max Nordau*

The balance between tension and relaxation.
Ernest Toch

The regular order of law and the inevitability of necessity.   *W. R. Worringer*

SEE ALSO ART, MUSIC, STYLE.

FORNICATION

SEE ADULTERY, SEX (LOVE).

FORTITUDE

To bear all inward and outward sufferings in silence, complaining only to God.
E. L. Gruber

That quality of mind which does not care what happens so long as it does not happen to us.
Elbert Hubbard

Something best shown when others are put to the test.   *Anon.*

SEE ALSO COURAGE, HEROISM.

FORTUNE

Sovereign of all the gods . . . and these other names are given her in vain; for she alone disposes all things as she will.   *Aeschylus*

A deep nick in time's restless wheel for each man's good.   *Adapted from George Chapman*

A shadow upon a wall.   *Geoffrey Chaucer*

Not exceptions, but fruits.
Ralph Waldo Emerson

An evil chain to the body, and vice to the soul.
Epictetus

Little advantages that occur every day.
Benjamin Franklin

A harvest day. We must be busy when the corn is ripe.   *Adapted from Johann W. Goethe*

(Something) never permanently . . . adverse or favorable; one sees her veering from one mood to the other.   *Herod, King of Judea*

Fortune is a woman, and therefore friendly to the young, who with audacity command her.
Niccolo Machiavelli

Arbiter of half our actions, but she still leaves the control of the other half to us.
Niccolo Machiavelli

A tide in the affairs of men.
William Shakespeare

That arrant whore.   *William Shakespeare*

An aim in life.   *Robert Louis Stevenson*

Like glass, the brighter the glitter, the more easily broken.   *Publilius Syrus*

A man's own character.   *Publilius Syrus*

A bitch!   *John Vanbrugh*

A right whore: if she gives at all she deals in small parcels, that she may take away all at one swoop.
John Webster

SEE ALSO ACCIDENT, CHANCE, DESTINY, FATE.

FORTY

Any man of forty who is endowed with moderate intelligence has seen . . . the entire past and future.
Marcus Aurelius

The dangerous age.   *Karin Michaelis*

Every man at forty is a fool or physician.
John Ray

Every man over forty is a scoundrel.

George Bernard Shaw

Then you know a boy is an ass,
Then you know the worth of a lass.

William Makepeace Thackeray

At thirty man suspects himself a fool—knows it at forty, and reforms his plan.

Adapted from Edward Young

SEE ALSO MIDDLE AGE.

FOX-HUNTER

(Those) who have all day long tried in vain to break their necks join at night in a second attempt on their lives by drinking.

Bernard de Mandeville

(Those who pursue) with earnestness and hazard something not worth catching.   *Alexander Pope*

The world may be divided into people that read, people that write, people that think, and fox-hunters.   *William Shenstone*

The English country gentleman galloping after a fox—the unspeakable in full pursuit of the uneatable.   *Oscar Wilde*

SEE ALSO HUNTING.

FRANCE

The most frivolous and fickle of civilized nations—they pass from the game of war to the game of peace, from the game of science to the game of art, from the game of liberty to the game of slavery, from the game of slavery to the game of licence.   *Walter Bagehot*

The dial of Europe.   *Ludwig Boerne*

A relatively small and eternally quarrelsome country in Western Europe.   *William Buckley 2*

A despotism tempered by epigrams.

Thomas Carlyle

A country where it is often useful to exhibit one's vices, and invariably dangerous to exhibit one's virtues.   *Nicolas Chamfort*

Where mankind lives in haste, and thrives by chance.   *Daniel Defoe*

A dancing nation, fickle and untrue.

Daniel Defoe

A slight unseason'd country.   *John Fletcher*

Land of mirth and social ease.

Oliver Goldsmith

France is sacred territory,
Blessed fatherland of freedom.   *Heinrich Heine*

The only country in the world where the rich are sometimes brilliant.   *Lillian Hellman*

A country where the practice of governing too much has taken root and done much mischief.

Adapted from Thomas Jefferson

Worse than Scotland in everything but climate.

Samuel Johnson

A conservative nation which likes even its disorders to have a cachet of organized continuity.

Arthur Koestler

Half artist and half anchorite,
Part siren and part Socrates.   *Percy Mackaye*

The land that has taught us six-hundred-and-eighty-five ways to dress eggs.

Adapted from Thomas Moore

A fickle nation.   *Napoleon 1*

A nation of monkeys with the throat of parrots.

Joseph Sieyes

The faithless vain disturber of mankind.

Edward Thomson

France has neither winter nor summer nor morals—apart from these drawbacks it is a fine country.   *Mark Twain*

(A country where) every bourgeois wants to be an artist.   *Oscar Wilde*

The only country where the money falls apart and you can't tear the toilet paper.   *William Wilder*

A country where the impossible always happens and the inevitable never does.   *Anon.*

SEE ALSO FRENCH LANGUAGE, FRENCHMAN, PARIS.

FRANKLIN, BENJAMIN (1706-1790)

Incarnation of the peddling, tuppenny Yankee.

Davis Jefferson

The greatest man and ornament of the age and country in which he lived.   *Thomas Jefferson*

A philosophical Quaker full of mean and thrifty maxims. *John Keats*

The mighty genius, who, to the advantage of mankind, compassing in his mind the heavens and earth, was able to restrain alike thunderbolts and tyrants. *Conte de Mirabeau*

He snatched the thunderbolt from heaven, then the sceptre from tyrants. *A. R. Turgot*

FRATERNITY

SEE ALSO BROTHERHOOD, FELLOWSHIP.

FRAUD

The homage that force pays to reason.

Charles P. Curtis

No court has ever attempted to define fraud.

Nathaniel Lindley

Fraud is infinite in variety; sometimes it is audacious and unblushing; sometimes it pays a sort of homage to virtue, and then it is modest and retiring; it would be honesty itself if it could only afford it. *Lord MacNaughten*

SEE ALSO DECEIT, LYING.

FREEDOM

Emancipation from the arbitrary rule of other men. *Mortimer J. Adler*

Obedience to the law. *American Army Motto*

Entire independence of all authority, prescription and routine—fullest room to expand as it will.

Matthew Arnold

Only he is free who cultivates his own thoughts ... and strives without fear of man to do justice to them. *Berthold Auerbach*

Room to enlarge. *C. A. Bartol*

Man's freedom is his inner worth.

Michael Beer

When we unbind ourselves from slavery within.

Nicholas Berdyaev

Exemption from the stress of authority.

Ambrose Bierce

A political condition that every nation supposes itself to enjoy in virtual monopoly.

Ambrose Bierce

The cause of God. *William L. Bowles*

To be free from everything is to be—nothing. Only nothing is quite free, and freedom is abstract nothingness. *F. H. Bradely*

Nothing else but a chance to be better.

Albert Camus

The one purport, wisely aimed at, or unwisely, of all man's struggles, toilings and sufferings, on this earth. *Thomas Carlyle*

Perfect freedom is reserved for the man who lives by his own work and in that work does what he wants to do. *R. G. Collingwood*

The amount of security enjoyed by minorities.

John E. Dalberg

The greatest gift conferred by God on human nature; for through it we have our felicity here as men, through it we have our felicity elsewhere as deities. *Dante*

Means the power to carry out your own emotions.

Clarence Darrow

Keeping open the channels of revelation, preserving the Word of Truth and communicating the Spirit of Life. *Christopher Dawson*

Diversity of opinion is the essence of freedom.

Joseph Devlin

The right to hold, maintain and transport slaves.

Jonah Enright

The discipline that is identical with trained power...Genuine freedom...is intellectual; it rests in the trained power of thought.

John Dewey

The right to be wrong, not the right to do wrong.

John Diefenbaker

The right to live as we wish. *Epictetus*

Not emancipation but isolation and exposure, destruction of community patterns.

Michael Fisher

Consists in the spontaneous activity of the total, integrated personality. *Erich Fromm*

When you're easy in your harness.

Robert Frost

If society fits you comfortably enough.

Robert Frost

The royal kinship of all men in God.

Robert I. Gannon

The principles of the Bible are the groundwork of human freedom. *Horace Greeley*

God's service spells freedom. *Judah Halevi*

Nothing but the recognition and adoption of such universal and substantial objects as Right and Law, and the production of a reality that is accordant with them—the State.

Georg W. Hegel

Freedom presupposes order, and order presupposes rules and the ability to enforce them.

Roger W. Heyns

Political power divided into small fragments.

Thomas Hobbes

To some, freedom means the opportunity to do what they want to do. To most it means not to do what they do not want to do. *Eric Hoffer*

The open window through which pours the sunlight of the human spirit and of human dignity.

Herbert C. Hoover

Man's self-transcendence, the capacity of the human mind to stand clear of itself...to determine his action and to manipulate objects as he wills. *John Hutchison*

Only necessity understood, and bondage to the highest is identical with true freedom.

William James

A man is free in proportion to his virtues, and the extent to which he is free determines what his virtues can accomplish. *John of Salisbury*

To be free is to be bound—bound in the fetters of obligation...To live in a free country...and be...the plaything of vicious desires, is to be a slave. *Morris Joseph*

That faculty which enlarges the usefulness of all other faculties. *Immanuel Kant*

There are two freedoms, the false where one is free to do what he likes, and the true where he is free to do what he ought. *Charles Kingsley*

A way of life which requires authority, discipline, and government of its own kind.

Walter Lippmann

A liberty to follow my own will in all things, when the rule prescribes not, and not to be subject to the inconstant, uncertain unknown, arbitrary will of another man. *John Locke*

Freedom is re-created year by year in hearts wide open on the Godward side.

Adapted from James Russell Lowell

True freedom is to share all the chains our brothers wear.

Adapted from James Russell Lowell

Mastery, through knowledge, of historic conditions and race character. *Hamilton W. Mabie*

The right to choose: the right to create for oneself the alternatives of choice. *Archibald MacLeish*

The right to one's dignity as a man.

Archibald MacLeish

Pursuing our own good in our own way, so long as we do not attempt to deprive others of theirs, or impede their efforts to obtain it.

John Stuart Mill

Where justice reigns, 'tis freedom to obey.

James Montgomery

Freedom from interruption may be counted by artists as not the least of the five freedoms.

Charles Morgan

Good wages, short hours, security in employment, good homes, opportunity for leisure and recreation with family and friends.

Oswald Mosely

To live under a government by law.

William Murray

Freedom is the freedom to say that two plus two makes four. If that is granted, all else follows.

George Orwell

The greatest of all blessings. *Philo*

Let me live my own, and die so too.

Alexander Pope

See what friends, and read what books I please.

Alexander Pope

The fountainhead and origin of many evils.

Pope Leo XIII

When it is established that man's soul is immortal and endowed with reason and not bound up with things material. *Pope Leo XIII*

Being able to turn down an invitation to dinner without giving an excuse.   *Jules Renard*

The supremacy of human rights everywhere.

Franklin Delano Roosevelt

The absence of obstacles to the realization of desires.   *Bertrand A. Russell*

That we sin not—and that is freedom.

Saint Augustine

(Something which) exits only in the land of dreams.   *Johann C. Schiller*

Not being a slave to any circumstance, to any constraint, to any chance; it means compelling Fortune to enter the lists on equal terms.

Seneca

Christian freedom is neither the lonely rebellion of an atheistic existentialist nor the self-will of the rugged individualist. It is freedom-in-community.

Roger L. Shinn

To move forward towards a worthy objective across a fierce terrain of resistance, to be vital and aglow in the exercise of a great enterprise.

Abba Hillel Silver

A man is free only when he has an errand on earth.   *Abba Hillel Silver*

To do what (one) will, provided he infringes not upon the equal freedom of any other man.

Herbert Spencer

Only that thing is free which exists by the necessities of its own nature, and is determined in its actions by itself alone.   *Baruch Spinoza*

He alone is free who lives with free consent under the entire guidance of freedom.

Baruch Spinoza

True freedom consists with the observance of law.

Bonnell Thornton

Being able to determine your being through history.   *Paul Tillich*

A curse inasmuch as it is the source of spiritual evil in Man, but at the same time...an inestimable treasure inasmuch as it is also the source, the only source, in Man, of spiritual good.

Arnold J. Toynbee

The possibility of change.   *Johanan Twerski*

The power of doing what we will.   *Voltaire*

Plenty to eat, and time and ability to read and think and talk things over.   *Henry A. Wallace*

We are only so free that others may be free as well as we.   *Benjamin Whichcote*

To walk free and own no superior.

Walt Whitman

To have achieved your life.   *Tennessee Williams*

The history of limitation of governmental power and not its increase.   *Woodrow Wilson*

(That which) exists only where the people take care of the government.   *Woodrow Wilson*

The right of a man to think and feel honestly.

Richard Wright

SEE ALSO AMERICA, AMERICAN CONSTITUTION, AMERICANISM, EMANCIPATION, FREE MAN, FREE PRESS, FREE SPEECH, FREE WILL, GOVERNMENT, INDEPENDENCE, INDIVIDUALISM, LIBERTY.

FREE GOVERNMENT

Consists in an effectual control of rivalries.

John Quincy Adams

If any ask me what a free government is, I answer that...it is what the people think so.

Edmund Burke

(When) the people is the true legislator.

Edmund Burke

The combined wisdom and folly of the people.

James A. Garfield

Freedom of religon, freedom of press, and freedom of person under the protection of the habeas corpus.   *Thomas Jefferson*

To have a standing rule to live by, common to every one of that society, and made by the legislative power vested in it.   *John Locke*

Government over all, by all, and for the sake of all.   *Theodore Parker*

The creature of volition.   *A. H. Stephens*

The right of the people to make and to alter their constitutions.   *George Washington*

SEE ALSO AMERICA, AMERICAN CONSTITUTION, DEMOCRACY, LIBERTY.

FREE MAN

He is the freeman whom the truth makes free, and all are slaves beside. *William Cowper*

Those who live under a government so constitutionally checked and controlled that proper provision is made against its being otherwise exercised. *John Dickinson*

So far as a man thinks, he is free. *Ralph Waldo Emerson*

One who realizes his ambition. *Joseph Emery*

He is free who lives as he chooses. *Epictetus*

No man...He is a slave to wealth, or to fortune, to the laws, or the people restrain him from acting according to his will alone. *Euripides*

He that in those things which by his strength and wit he is able to do, is not hindered to do what he has a will to. *Thomas Hobbes*

(He who) relies wholly on himself, whose angular points of character have all been rounded off and polished. *Horace*

The wise who can command his passions, who fears not want, nor death, nor chains, firmly resisting his appetites and despising the honors of the world. *Horace*

He...who knows how to keep in his own hands the power to decide, at each step, the course of his life. *Salvador de Madariaga*

He...who wishes only for that which he is able to accomplish, and does whatever pleases him. *Jean-Jacques Rousseau*

That man is free who is protected from injury. *Daniel Webster*

A man working for himself, with choice of time, and place, and object. *Adapted from William Wordsworth*

FREE PRESS

The palladium of all the civil, political, and religious rights of an Englishman. *William Blackstone*

Merely the liberty of discussing the propriety of public measures and political opinions. *Benjamin Franklin*

Who can give it any definition which does not leave the utmost latitude for evasion? I hold it to be impracticable, and from this I infer that its security...must altogether depend on public opinion...on the general spirit of the people and of the government. *Alexander Hamilton*

Publishing the truth, from good motives and for justifiable ends, though it reflect on the government, on magistrates, or individuals. *Alexander Hamilton*

Freedom from any deleterious influence, whether imposed by interests too strong for the publisher to resist, or self-imposed for benefits received or hoped for. *Harold L. Ickes*

The palladium of all the civil, political, and religious rights. *Junius*

Not a privilege but an organic necessity in a great society. *Walter Lippmann*

A man must print what he pleases without license. *Lord Mansfield*

One of the great bulwarks of liberty and can never be restrained but by desperate governments. *George Mason*

The liberty of thinking and of publishing whatever one likes...the fountainhead of many evils. *Pope Leo XIII*

The staff of life for any vital democracy. *Wendell L. Willkie*

SEE ALSO NEWSPAPERS, PRESS (THE).

FREE SPEECH

No such thing ever existed. No such thing now exists. *John Quincy Adams*

Means that you shall not do something to people either for the views they have, or to the views they express, or the words they speak or write! *Hugo Black*

In England little else than the right to...say anything which a jury consisting of twelve shopkeepers think it expedient should be said or written. *Albert V. Dicey*

The reasonable expression of one's opinions, including constructive criticism of the policy followed by public officials. *Francis J. McConnell*

To know, to utter, and argue freely according to conscience.   *John Milton*

(When) men can speak in whatever way given them to utter what their hearts hold—by voice, by posted card, by letter or by press.

William A. White

SEE ALSO FREEDOM, FREE PRESS, LIBERTY, SPEECH.

FREE THINKERS

He who does not fear to go to the end of his thought.   *Leon Blum*

Generally those who never think at all.

Laurence Sterne

FREE THINKING

The use of the understanding in endeavoring to find out the meaning of any proposition whatsoever, in considering the nature of the evidence for or against, and in judging of it according to the seeming force or weakness of the evidence.

Anthony Collins

In itself a good; but it gives an opening to false liberty.   *John Henry Newman*

FREE TRADE

Not a principle; it is an expedient.

Benjamin Disraeli

Free commerce with all nations.

Thomas Jefferson

To throw open the doors of commerce, and to knock off all its shackles, giving perfect freedom to all persons for the vent of whatever they may choose to bring into our ports, and asking the same in theirs.   *Thomas Jefferson*

FREEWAY

Something that is not free when one considers the emotional toll.   *Anon.*

A system that hurls cars off at improper exits.

Anon.

A stretch of concrete that permits you to go anywhere and see nothing.   *Anon.*

A delightful place to drive—if you like speed and don't want to stop.   *Anon.*

SEE ALSO COMMUTER, SUBURBIA.

FREE WILL

God . . . created man; He also created the circumstances under which he lives and acts; but still he has endowed man with discretion to choose how to act.   *Muhammad Ali*

A kind of *coup d'état* which our mind foresees and which it tries to legitimate beforehand by a formal deliberation.   *Henri Bergson*

(God) produces not only our choice, but also the very freedom that is our choice.

Jacques Bossuet

God . . . wills us to be free . . . He wills not only that we should be free in power, but that we should be free in its exercise.   *Jacques Bossuet*

A man can be said to exercise free will in a morally significant sense only so far as his chosen act is one in which he is the sole cause or author, and only if . . . he "could have chosen otherwise."

Charles A. Campbell

I am a free agent, inasmuch as . . . I have a will, which renders me justly responsible for my actions, omissive as well as commissive.

Samuel Taylor Coleridge

That by which my mind chooses anything.

Jonathan Edwards

God's gift of a do-it-yourself kit.

Lawrence Eisenberg

The principle of this our life.   *Johann G. Fichte*

(Something) determined by the organization of the brain; and that in turn acquires its individual character by the laws of heredity and the influence of environment.   *Ernst Haeckel*

The will is motivated; but since there is a conflict of motives, the choice is free . . . Free will involves a genuine indeterminacy, but it is plainly distinct from chance or caprice.   *D. J. Hawkins*

Freedom is a fundamental character of the will . . . That which is free is the will. Will without freedom is an empty word.   *Georg W. Hegel*

It merely says that of alternatives that really *tempt* our will more than one is really possible.

William James

Autonomy, that is, the property of the will to be a law unto itself.   *Immanuel Kant*

The will of a rational being can be his own only if he acts on the idea that it is free, and therefore this idea must, as a practical matter, be ascribed to all rational beings.   *Immanual Kant*

Humanism believes . . . that human beings possess true freedom of creative action and are within reasonable limits, the masters of their own destiny.   *Corliss Lamont*

The only thing that makes possible any love of goodness or joy worth having.   *Clive S. Lewis*

The power which makes humans fit subjects to be caught up by the Spirit and touched by God's grace, as creatures made for eternal life or eternal death.   *Martin Luther*

I confess that mankind has a free will, but it is to milk kine, to build houses, etc., and no further.
                                          Martin Luther

Not the liberty to do whatever one likes, but the power of doing whatever one sees ought to be done.   *George Macdonald*

To be able to determine the indeterminate; that is the, the future—this is implied in the very conception of action. The Agent is the determiner.
                                      John Macmurray

That which tends to whatever side a man wishes.
                                  Moses Maimonides

Evolution knows nothing of free will, all our actions are the necessary outcome of chemical processes.   *Ilya I. Metchnikoff*

An egregious theological trick for making mankind "responsible" in the theological sense— which is to say, responsible to theologians.
                                Friedrich W. Nietzsche

The power of choosing good and evil.   *Origen*

One of the principal organs of belief, not that it forms belief, but because things are true or false according to the side on which we look at them.
                                      Blaise Pascal

The freedom of the ego here and now, and its independence of the casual chain.   *Max Planck*

A truth that comes from the immediate dictate of the human consciousness.   *Max Planck*

There is no such thing . . . The mind is induced to wish this or that by some other cause, and that cause is determined by another cause, and so on back to infinity.   *Baruch Spinoza*

Not a faculty which can be called free. "Free-will" is a word . . . devoid of sense, and that which scholars have called "indifference."   *Voltaire*

FRENCH

Irreconcilable, savage foes . . . if you strip them of the cook, the tailor, and the hairdresser, you will find nothing left in them but copper-skinned Indians.   *Otto von Bismarck*

Like gunpowder, each by itself smutty and contemptible; but mass them together, they are terrible indeed.   *Samuel Taylor Coleridge*

Easy, debonair, and brisk, give him his lass, his fiddle, and his frisk. He's always happy, reign whoever may, and he laughs the sense of misery away.   *Adapted from William Cowper*

A dancing nation, fickle and untrue.
                                        Daniel Defoe

They are all slaves and wear wooden shoes.
                                      Oliver Goldsmith

Honor the French! They have taken good care of the two greatest human needs—good eating and civic equality.   *Heinrich Heine*

The only people . . . who have been at once philosophers, poets, orators, historians, painters, architects, sculptors, and musicians.
                                          David Hume

An amiable and intelligent people . . . not an imaginative one. The greatest height they go is in a balloon.   *Leigh Hunt*

A nation of right merry fellows, possessing the true secret of being happy, which is nothing more than thinking of nothing, talking about anything, and laughing at everything.   *Washington Irving*

They do everything; they know nothing.
                                      Italian Proverb

Italians with bad tempers.   *Dennis McEvoy*

These fashion-mongers.   *William Shakespeare*

Two species: the one of idle monkeys who mock at everything; and the other of tigers who tear.
                                          Voltaire

A people on the down grade.
                                  William 2 of Germany

A pleasure-loving people, fond of dancing and light wines.   *Anon.*

SEE ALSO FRANCE, PARIS.

FRENCH LANGUAGE

The most perspicuous and pointed language in the world.   *Samuel Taylor Coleridge*

The speech of the clear, the cheerful, or the august among men.   *John Morley*

(A language) badly fitted for music.

Wolgang Amadeus Mozart

The true and native language of insincerity.

Alfred Sutro

The most meagre and inharmonious of all languages.   *Horace Walpole*

FRENCHMAN

A Frenchman who...has the manners and good breeding of his country is the perfection of human nature.   *Lord Chesterfield*

A peculiar race.   *Anon.*

FREUD, SIGMUND (1856-1939)

The childhood fantasies...of Freud...do not foretell the future originator of psychoanalysis. They fit a general, a reformer, or a business executive rather than the patient, full-time listener to petty complaints.   *Sigfried Bernfeld*

An artist rather than a scientist.   *Havelock Ellis*

That boy will never amount to anything.

Jacob Freud

I have never done anything mean or malicious and cannot trace any temptation to do so.

Sigmund Freud

When I ask myself why I (act) honorably...I have no answer...why I—and...my six children—have to be thoroughly decent human beings is a mystery to me.   *Sigmund Freud*

A have always been dissatisfied with my gifts.

Sigmund Freud

I am not really a man of science...I am by temperament...a conquistador.

Sigmund Freud

A not very agreeable man.   *Sigmund Freud*

I have not really been ambitious. I sought in science the satisfactions offered during research and at the moment of discovery.   *Sigmund Freud*

I am no genius...not even very talented; my whole capacity for work...lies in my character attributes and in the lack of any marked intellectual deficiency.   *Sigmund Freud*

I regard myself as one of the most dangerous enemies of religion.   *Sigmund Freud*

The Jews are treating me like a national hero, although my service to the Jewish cause is confined to the single point that I have never disowned my Jewishness.   *Sigmund Freud*

Freud hardly ever indulged in controversy...he responded to criticism...by continuing his researches and producing more and more evidence.

Ernest Jones

His greatest strength...was the quite extraordinary respect he had for the singular fact.

Ernest Jones

There are few psychologists of any school who do not admit their debt to him.   *The Lancet*

The pathfinder toward a humanism of the future.

Thomas Mann

The first irreligious moralist in history.

Philip Rieff

The most incorruptible *savant* in a time of corruption.   *Gilbert Robin*

A most moral—even prudish—bourgeois, an exemplary father and husband who loved to walk in the mountains...collect modest antiquities...He disliked small talk, hated quarrels, disapproved of even mildy off-color jokes.   *Leo C. Rosten*

This man totally transformed psychology. He gave sociology the long-missing bridge between individual and group behavior, and anthropology a process by which child rearing projects itself into culture patterns.   *Leo C. Rosten*

A mystic-philosopher who spun fantasies about human nature based upon his own assumptions.

Anon.

FREUDIANISM

A magnificent castle in the air.   *Sals W. Baron*

He showed...the enormous importance of man's unconscious in his everyday activities of thought and action. Carried to its extreme conclusion,

Freud and his followers have seen in this discovery the end of free will.   *J. Dominian*

Freud's discarding of moral values has contributed toward making the analyst just as blind as the patient.   *Karen Horney*

Anti-Christian...In setting up the infantile appetites as the basis of all life of the soul and the spirit it ranges virtue...under sin, it places the ultimate origins of the recognition of the highest values in the flesh.   *John Huizinga*

A reactionary idealistic trend widespread in bourgeois psychological science...now in the service of imperialism.

Short Philosophic Communist Dictionary

Freud's selection of religious data is almost as unfair as could be arranged. All of his major illustrations are of three related kinds, the pathological, the primitive and infantile.

David E. Trueblood

The fleshy science.   *Anon.*

FRIEND

The medicine of life.
Apochrypha: Ecclesiastes, VI, 16.

A single soul dwelling in two bodies.   *Aristotle*

A strong defense: and he that hath found such an one hath found a treasure.
Bible: Ecclesiastes, VI, 14.

The thermometers by which we may judge the temperature of our fortune.
Countess of Blessington

One who is willing to endorse your banknote. Laying down one's life is nothing in comparison.
Adapted from Gamaliel Bradford

One who forgives you when you have overtaken him professionally and financially.
Eugene E. Brussell

Someone to laugh with me, someone to be grave with me, someone to please me and help my discrimination with his...own remark, and at times, no doubt, to admire my acuteness and penetration.   *Robert Burns*

A second self.   *Cicero*

A man's...ten fingers.   *Robert Collyer*

A person with whom you dare to be yourself.
Franklin Crane

My well-spring in the wilderness.   *George Eliot*

We walk alone in the world. Friends, such as we desire, are dreams and fables.
Ralph Waldo Emerson

Do with your friends as you would do with your books. Have them where you can find them, but seldom use them.   *Ralph Waldo Emerson*

A person with whom I may be sincere. Before him I may think aloud.   *Ralph Waldo Emerson*

Fictions founded on some single momentary experience.   *Ralph Waldo Emerson*

A man's friends are his magnetisms.
Ralph Waldo Emerson

Our greatest joy and our greatest sorrow.
Francois de Fénelon

An old wife, an old dog, and ready money.
Benjamin Franklin

They only are true friends who think as one.
French Proverb

The enemy of my enemy.   *French Proverb*

The best mirror.   *George Herbert*

(Those who) love not mine, but me.
Robert Herrick

Two bodies with one soul inspired.   *Homer*

One who knows all about you and loves you just the same.   *Elbert Hubbard*

Thieves of time.   *Latin Proverb*

One who has the same enemies you have.
Abraham Lincoln

(One who) is long a-getting, and soon lost.
John Lyly

In prosperity a pleasure, a solace in adversity, in grief a comfort, in joy a merry companion, at all times an other I.   *Adapted from John Lyly*

Fellowship in joy, not sympathy in sorrow, is what makes friends.   *Friedrich W. Nietzsche*

A true friend unbosoms freely, advises justly, assists readily, adventures boldly, takes all patiently, defends courageously, and continues a friend unchangeably.   *William Penn*

People who borrow my books and set wet glasses on them.   *Edwin Arlington Robinson*

That part of the human race with which one can be human.   *George Santayana*

A present you give yourself.
                                                    Robert Louis Stevenson

One who walks in when the rest of the world walks out.   *Walter Winchell*

A name for more constant acquaintance.
                                                    Horace Walpole

Another I.   *Zeno*

One who excuses you when you have made a fool of yourself.   *Anon.*

One who doesn't buy your child a drum or horn for his birthday.   *Anon.*

One who is here today and here tomorrow.
                                                    Anon.

A foul-weather person.   *Anon.*

One who forgives you your defects, and if he really likes you, he fails to see any.   *Anon.*

Someone you can be silent with.   *Anon.*

Trouble is a big sieve through which we sift our acquaintances; those who are too big to pass through are friends.   *Anon.*

One who wants to be with us, even as we want to be with him.   *Anon.*

SEE ALSO LOVERS, WIFE.

FRIENDSHIP

A certain parallelism of life, a community of thought.   *Henry B. Adams*

Confederacies of vice, or leagues of pleasure.
                                                    Joseph Addison

A very taxing and arduous form of leisure activity.
                                                    Mortimer Adler

(Something) not known in prosperity.
                                          Apocrypha: Ben Sira, XII, 8.

To love a man that you cannot bear to see a stain upon him . . . to speak painful truth through loving words.   *Henry Ward Beecher*

A ship big enough to carry two in fair weather, but only one in foul.   *Ambrose Bierce*

A word the very sight of which in print makes the heart warm.   *Augustine Birrell*

Cement of the soul.   *Robert Blair*

Simply one who proves himself in time of need.
                                                    Eugene E. Brussell

A strong and habitual inclination in two persons to promote the good and happiness of one another.
                                                    Eustace Budgell

Sharing the prejudice of experience.
                                                    Charles Bukowski

Like money, easier made than kept.
                                                    Samuel Butler 2

Love refined.   *Susannah Centlivre*

That rectitude which will shrink from no truth.
                                                    William Ellery Channing

A slow grower, and never thrives unless ingrafted upon a stock of known and reciprocal merit.
                                                    Lord Chesterfield

Can only exist where men harmonize in their views of things human and divine.   *Cicero*

Nothing else than an accord in all things, human and divine, conjoined with mutual good-will and affection.   *Cicero*

Complete unity of aim.   *Cicero*

A holy tie.   *John Dryden*

Forgetting what one gives, and remembering what one receives.   *Alexander Dumas*

Good understanding.   *Ralph Waldo Emerson*

Without confidence there is no friendship.
                                                    Epicurus

A name, a charm that lulls to sleep; a shade that follows wealth or fame, and leaves a wretch to weep.   *Adapted from Oliver Goldsmith*

A disinterested commerce between equals.
                                                    Oliver Goldsmith

(Something that) cannot live with ceremony, nor without civility.   *Lord Halifax*

A loneliness relieved of the anguish of loneliness.
                                                    Dag Hammarskjöld

Like wine, raw when new, ripened with age, the true old man's milk and restorative cordial.
                                                    Thomas Jefferson

A state that must be kept in constant repair.
Adapted from Samuel Johnson

The feeling of friendship is like that of being comfortably filled with roast beef; love, like being enlivened with champagne.
Samuel Johnson

The hobby-horse of all the moral rhethoricians; it is nectar and ambrosia to them.
Immanual Kant

An alliance, a reciprocal accommodation of interests, an exchange of good offices.
La Rochefoucauld

Nothing but a system of traffic, in which self-love always proposes to itself some advantage.
La Rochefoucauld

A treasury: you cannot take from it more than you put into it.
Max Mandelstamm

Friendship is but a word.
Philip Massinger

The highest degree of perfection in society.
Michel de Montaigne

A union of spirits, a marriage of hearts, and the bond thereof of virtue.
William Penn

Among women only a suspension of hostilities.
Comte de Rivarol

The vital air of friendship is composed of confidence. Friendship perished in proportion as this air diminishes.
Joseph Roux

To desire the same things and to reject the same things.
Sallust

Almost always the union of a part of one mind with the part of another; people are friends in spots.
George Santayana

To feel as one while remaining two.
Anne S. Swetchine

The ally of our sorrows, the ease of our passions, the counsellor of our doubts, the clarity of our minds, the emission of our thoughts, the exercise and improvement of what we meditate.
Jeremy Taylor

Only a little more honor among rogues.
Henry David Thoreau

A holy passion, so sweet and steady and loyal and enduring in its nature that it will last through a whole lifetime, if not asked to lend money.
Mark Twain

The marriage of the soul...subject to divorce.
Voltaire

A plant of slow growth, and must undergo and withstand the shocks of adversity before it is entitled to the appelation.
George Washington

The wine of life.
Edward Young

One heart in two bodies.
Joseph Zabara

The voluntary discipline of ignoring faults in one another.
Anon.

Consists in the number of things friends need no longer mention.
Anon.

The relationship some women accept from men when they would rather knot.
Anon.

Expecting a great deal from one another but never asking for it.
Anon.

Two clocks keeping time.
Anon.

FROG

The frog by nature is both damp and cold. Her mouth is large, her belly much will hold.
Adapted from John Bunyan

The nicest little rabbity things you ever tasted.
Charles Lamb

FUNERAL

In the city a funeral is just an interruption of traffic. In the country it is a form of popular entertainment.
George Ade

Man goeth to his long home, and the mourners go about the streets.
Bible: Ecclesiastes, XII, 5.

A pageant whereby we attest our respect for the dead by enriching the undertaker.
Ambrose Bierce

Solemn mockery.
William H. Ireland

The last bedtime story.
Leonard L. Levinson

To stop smoking, drinking, overeating and chasing women all at the same time.
Adapted from Robert Orben

A consolation to the living than of any service to the dead.
Saint Augustine

(An occasion when) we are apt to comfort ourselves with the happy difference that is betwixt us and our dead friend.   *Thomas Wilson*

SEE ALSO DEATH, GRAVE.

FUTILITY

Most men eddy about
Here and there—eat and drink,
Chatter and love and hate,
Gather and squander, are raised
Aloft, are hurl'd in the dust,
Striving blindly, achieving
Nothing; and then they die.   *Matthew Arnold*

All is vanity and vexation of the spirit.
                          Bible: Ecclesiastes, 1, 14.

All human effort.   *Robert Browning*

The effort it took to put this book together.
                               Eugene E. Brussell

To attack windmills.   *Miguel de Cervantes*

To go into the water and grasp the foam.
                                  Chinese Proverb

Our greatest sorrow—but also our greatest consolation.   *Jacob Klatzkin*

Two baldheaded men fighting over a comb.
                                  Russian Proverb

To waste your labor.   *Terence*

To complain to a stepmother.   *Anon.*

FUTURE

That period of time in which our affairs prosper, our friends are true and our happiness is assured.
                                  Ambrose Bierce

An opaque mirror. Anyone who tries to look into it sees nothing but the dim outlines of an old worried face.   *James Bishop*

A place where the radical spends most of his time.
                               Eugene E. Brussell

The past in preparation.   *Pierre Dac*

To the being of fully alive, the future is not ominous but a promise; it surrounds the present like a halo.   *John Dewey*

Hope!   *John Fiske*

(A time that) is hidden even from those who make it.   *Anatole France*

The past returning through another gate.
                                Arnold H. Glasow

An unwelcomed guest.   *Edmund W. Gosse*

Something which everyone reaches at the rate of sixty minutes an hour, whatever he does, whoever he is.   *Clive S. Lewis*

A world limited by ourselves; in it we discover only what concerns us and, sometimes, by chance, what interests those whom we love the most.   *Maurice Maeterlinck*

A great land; a man cannot go around it in a day; he cannot measure it with a bound; he cannot bind its harvests into a single sheaf. It is wider than the vision, and has no end.   *Donald G. Mitchell*

The past and present are only our means; the future is always our end. Thus we never really live, but only hope to live.   *Blaise Pascal*

Only the past again, entered through another gate.
                               Arthur Wing Pinero

States unborn and accents yet unknown.
                              William Shakespeare

The shape of things to come.   *Herbert G. Wells*

Something that comes one day at a time.   *Anon.*

SEE ALSO TOMORROW.

G

GADGETS

Objects which now cost more to maintain than their inital cost. *Hyman Maxwell Berston*

The modern inconveniences. *Mark Twain*

GAIETY

Often the reckless ripple over depths of despair. *Edwin H. Chapin*

(The state) of a poor person on learning of the death of a rich relative. *Elbert Hubbard*

The hard cash of happiness; everything else is just a promissory note. *Arthur Schopenhauer*

SEE ALSO CHEERFULNESS, HAPPINESS.

GALLANTRY

To do a perfectly unselfish act from selfish motives. *Elbert Hubbard*

To remember one is a gentleman in spite of one's birth and training. *Elbert Hubbard*

Saying empty things in an agreeable manner. *La Rochefoucauld*

SEE ALSO CHIVALRY, HEROISM.

GALLOWS

SEE HANGING.

GAMBLER

One begins by being a dupe and ends by being a rascal. *Edward E. Descamps*

(One who) transgresses all the Ten Commandments. *Leon of Modena*

(One who) always loses. He loses money, dignity, and time. And if he wins, he weaves a spider's web round himself. *Moses Maimonides*

The better the gambler the worse the man. *Publilius Syrus*

One who plays the fool. *Anon.*

GAMBLING

Life's one real charm. *Adapted from Charles Baudelaire*

A principle inherent in human nature. It belongs to us all. *Edmund Burke*

A revolt against boredom. *Stuart Chase*

A disgrace. *Lord Chesterfield*

This tyrant vice. *David Garrick*

The strength of Monaco...the weakness of the world. *Herbert A. Gibbons*

A compulsive weakness. *Max Gralnick*

A disease of barbarians superficially civilized. *William R. Inge*

GARBAGE

A form of robbery. *Moses Maimonides*

The sure way of getting nothing for something.
Wilson Mizner

A door and window into all theft, murder, whoredom, swearing...deceit.
John Northbrooke

(That which) promises the poor what property preforms for the rich—something for nothing.
George Bernard Shaw

An activity you recall when and where but not why. *Anon.*

SEE ALSO BRIDGE (CARDS), CARDS.

GARBAGE

A fact of life which must be carried out once a day by the husband. *Anon.*

The verbal kind is found in daily newspapers.
Anon.

GARDEN

God almighty first planted a garden. And, indeed, it is the purest of human pleasures.
Francis Bacon

The richer realm. *Alice Brown*

A garden is like those pernicious machineries which catch a man's coat...or his hand, and draw in his arm, his leg, and his whole body to irresistible destruction. *Ralph Waldo Emerson*

What makes a garden
And why do gardens grow?
Love lives in gardens—
God and lovers know! *Carolyn Giltinan*

The one spot on earth where history does not assert itself. *Edmund Gosse*

The market is the best garden. *George Herbert*

The best place to seek God...You can dig for Him there. *George Bernard Shaw*

A more lasting pleasure than building.
William Shenstone

(Early ones) are planted on the pray-as-you sow plan. *Edythe Soper*

A thing of beauty and a job forever. *Anon.*

Something that is healthy exercize if one can straighten up afterwards. *Anon.*

A place where the mind goes to seed. *Anon.*

Soil sport. *Anon.*

Man's effort to improve his lot. *Anon.*

A thing that dies if you water it and rots if you don't. *Anon.*

GENEALOGY

An account of one's descent from an ancestor who did not...care to trace his own.
Ambrose Bierce

A perverse preoccupation of those who seek to demonstrate that their forebears were better people than they are. *Sydney J. Harris*

Tracing back your family as far as the money will go. *Anon.*

SEE ALSO ANCESTRY, HEREDITY.

GENERAL (MILITARY)

They always remind me of parakeets, for mammals don't usually dress in such colors.
Sigmund Freud

The best...are those who have served in the artillery. *Napoleon I*

I made all my generals out of mud. *Napoleon I*

Those who make war without leaving anything to hazard. *Adapted from Maurice de Saxe*

A man whose single reputation is made out of ten thousand corpses. *Sung Ts'ao*

The proper arts of a general are judgment and prudence. *Tacitus*

(One who) must be skillfull in preparing the materials of war and in supplying his soldiers; he must be a man of mechanical ingenuity...kind and yet severe, open yet crafty, careful of his own but ready to steal from others, profuse yet rapacious, cautious yet enterprising.
Xenophon

The man you have to stick close to if you don't want to get hurt. *Anon.*

One who doesn't have to fight for his medals.
Anon.

Someone who always dies in bed.   *Anon.*

One who stands at the head of his troops, drawn salary in hand.   *Anon.*

SEE ALSO ARMY, BATTLE, MILITARISM, WAR.

GENERALIZATION

A life-saver.   *George Ade*

Something vital for daily discourse.
        Jerry Dashkin

The passionate faith of the common man.
        Robert Lynd

(That which) is necessary to the advancement of knowledge; but particularly is indispensable to the creations of the imagination.
        Thomas B. Macaulay

A plateau where a tired mind rests.
        Witt H. Pearson

Only what is in the particular is in the general.
        Talmud: Sota, 46b.

GENERATION

The period between the time a town tears down a historic landmark and the time it has a fund-raising drive to build an authentic reproduction of it.   *William Vaughan*

GENEROSITY

Giving handsomely where it is proper to give at all.   *Lord Chesterfield*

Giving more than you can.   *Kahlil Gibran*

Consists less in giving much than in giving at the right moment.   *Jean de La Bruyère*

Most often only the vanity of giving, which we like better than the thing we give.
        La Rochefoucauld

The giving away of other men's goods.
        John Northbrooke

Giving help rather than advice.
        Luc de Vauvenargues

GENIUS

To do what is impossible for talent is the mark of genius.   *Henry F. Amiel*

Mainly an affair of energy.   *Matthew Arnold*

Perseverance in disguise.   *Henry Austin*

The power to be a boy again at will.
        James M. Barrie

The capacity for productive reaction against one's training.   *Bernard Berenson*

The recapturing of childhood.
        Charles Baudelaire

That which forces the inertia of humanity to learn.   *Henry Bergson*

To know without having learned; to draw just conclusions from unknown premises; to discern the soul of things.   *Ambrose Bierce*

Elegant common sense.   *Josh Billings*

A dependent quality. It cannot put forth its whole powers nor claim all honors without aid from the talents and labors of others.
        William Cullen Bryant

Patience.   *George de Buffon*

Ever a secret to itself.   *Thomas Carlyle*

The most precious gift that Heaven can give to the earth...the soul of man actually sent down from the skies with a God's-message to us.
        Thomas Carlyle

The clearer presence of God Most High in a man. Dim, potential in all men; in this man it has become clear, actual.   *Thomas Carlyle*

The transcendent capacity of taking trouble.
        Thomas Carlyle

Reason made sublime.   *Joseph de Chénier*

Carrying the feelings of childhood into the powers of manhood.   *Samuel Taylor Coleridge*

Unconscious activity.   *Samuel Taylor Coleridge*

You will find this a good...criterion of genius— whether it progresses and evolves, or only spins upon itself.   *Samuel Taylor Coleridge*

To Christ, genius was simply an instrument for service, to be displayed only so far as it might be useful.   *William H. Crawshaw*

When human power becomes so great and original that we can account for it only as a kind of divine inspiration. *William H. Crawshaw*

Someone who can accept society without denying himself. *Richard Crutchfield*

(Something that) must be born, and never can be taught. *John Dryden*

(One who) sees the world at a different angle from his fellows, and there is his tragedy.
Havelock Ellis

(Genius rests) on profound convictions, which refuse to be analyzed. *Ralph Waldo Emerson*

Genius is religious. It is a larger imbibing of the common heart. *Ralph Waldo Emerson*

To believe your own thought, to believe that what is true for you in your private heart is true for all men. *Ralph Waldo Emerson*

That superior alchemy that alters the vices of nature into the elements of destiny.
Pierre Emmanuel

Mediocrities sweat blood to produce rubbish. Geniuses create wonder without effort.
Anatole France

God's work in great minds to pull the people up.
Johann W. Goethe

The talent of a man who is dead.
Edmond de Goncourt

Genius...diagnoses the situation...supplies the answer. *Robert Graves*

Genius...excels his fellow in nothing save the knack of expression; he throws out...a lucky hint at truths of which every human soul is profoundly though unutterably conscious.
Nathaniel Hawthorne

Genius melts many ages into one, and thus effects something permanent...A work of genius is but the newspaper of a century, or perchance of a hundred centuries. *Nathaniel Hawthorne*

Nothing more than our common faculties refined to a greater intensity. *Benjamin R. Haydon*

(It) forms itself on another...less by assimilation than by friction. One diamond polishes another.
Heinrich Heine

Nothing but labor and diligence.
William Hogarth

An infinite capacity for taking pains.
Jane Hopkins

One who stands at both ends of a perspective.
Elbert Hubbard

The ability to act wisely without precedent—the power to do the right thing for the first time.
Elbert Hubbard

One who offends his time, his country, his relatives. *Elbert Hubbard*

A promontory jutting out into the future.
Victor Hugo

A child up to the age of ten. *Aldous Huxley*

To be able to see and feel what will come to pass ten years hence. *Vladimir Jabotinsky*

The capacity for seeing relationships where lesser men see none. *William James*

Little more than the faculty of perceiving in an unhabitual way. *William James*

A mind of large general powers, accidentally determined to some particular direction.
Samuel Johnson

That energy which collects, combines, amplifies, and animates. *Samuel Johnson*

A man of genius makes no mistakes. His errors are volitional and are the portals of discovery.
James Joyce

Ethereal chemicals operating on the mass of neutral intellect. *John Keats*

Originality, the opening of new frontiers.
Arthur Koestler

What everybody is at least once a year.
Adapted from Georg C. Lichtenberg

One who shoots at something no one else can see, and hits it. *Lutheran Digest*

As a rule, a response to apparently hostile limitations. *Robert Lynd*

Geniuses reach their goal with one step, whereas common minds must be led to it through a long row of objectives. *Moses Mendelssohn*

Energy and activity. *Donald G. Mitchell*

Genius, cried the commuter,
As he ran for the 8:13,
Consists of an infinite capacity
For catching trains. *Christopher Morley*

(Something) not seen with the eyes, but with the mind. *Blaise Pascal*

To...achieve complete possession of one's own experience, body, rhythm, and memories.
Cesare Pavese

The state of mental disease arising from the undue predominance of some one of the faculties.
Edgar Allan Poe

An infinite capacity for taking life by the scruff of the neck. *Christopher Quill*

A power which no precepts can teach, and which no industry can acquire. *Joshua Reynolds*

Nothing but a sublime storm. *George Sand*

Geniuses must be...fed and raised on the shoulders of some old tradition. *George Santayana*

Genius learn only from itself; talent chiefly from others. Genius learns from nature, from its own nature; talent learns from art.
Arnold Schoenberg

(One who possesses) not only greater depths, but...more levels of existence than the ordinary man. *John W. Sullivan*

A man who is exceptionally rich in recoverable contexts. *John W. Sullivan*

Abundance of life or health.
Henry David Thoreau

To pose new questions which time and mediocrity can resolve. *H. R. Trevor-Roper*

There is a certain characteristic common to all ...Each of them has a consciousness of being a man apart. *Miguel de Unamuno*

The faculty of acquiring poverty.
Edwin P. Whipple

Of these three requisites of genius, the first is soul, and the second, soul, and the third, soul.
Edwin P. Whipple

Talent repeats, genius creates. Talent is a cistern; genius a fountain. *Edwin P. Whipple*

A combination of great powers.
Edwin P. Whipple

(A condition which) is inconsiderate, self-relying, and...without any intention to please.
Isaac M. Wise

The introduction of a new element into the universe. *William Wordsworth*

That which generates heat and progress. *Anon.*

A fugitive from the law of averages. *Anon.*

A quality which arises out of the disproportionate power and size of the total faculties. *Anon.*

Anyone who has a Jewish grandmother. *Anon.*

Something you can't be by trying. *Anon.*

SEE ALSO ARTISTS, BOOK, GREAT MEN, GREATNESS, HERO, INTELLIGENCE, INVENTOR, MIND, ORIGINALITY, TALENT.

GENOCIDE

A denial of the right of existence of human groups...contrary to moral law.
United Nations Assembly Resolution 96, Dec. 11, 1946.

GENTLEMAN

Any man who wouldn't hit a woman with his hat on. *Fred Allen*

(Merely) elegant living. *James Allen*

To speak as the common people do, to think as wise men do. *Roger Ascham*

(One who leaves) the world untainted with falsehood, or dissimulation, or wantonness, or conceit. *Marcus Aurelius*

He is a gentleman who is kind and affable to every creature. *Adapted from Richard Barnfield*

Gentleness, absence of browbeating or overbearing manners, absence of fuss, and...consideration for other people. *Samuel Butler 2*

Genteel in personage,
Conduct, and equipage;
Noble by heritage,
Generous and free. *Henry Carey*

He...that doth gentle deeds. *Geoffrey Chaucer*

A man who hasn't made love to his wife in five years, and is prepared to shoot any other man who tries. *Frank M. Colby*

He who can live unknown and not fret.
Confucius

Liberal in his attainments, opinions, practices and concessions. He asks for himself no more than he is willing to concede to others.

James Fenimore Cooper

Repose and cheerfulness are the badges of the gentleman—repose in energy.

Ralph Waldo Emerson

A gentleman must be incapable of a lie.

Ralph Waldo Emerson

Manners and money. *Thomas Fuller*

Education begins a gentleman; conversation completes him. *Thomas Fuller*

To make a gentleman, several trades are required, but chiefly a barber. *Oliver Goldsmith*

What's a gentleman but his pleasure?

Gabriel Harvey

One who understands and shows every mark of deference to the claims of self-love in others, and exacts it in return from them. *William Hazlitt*

A little God over against the Cosmos.

Oliver Wendell Holmes 2

One who is gentle toward the friendless.

Elbert Hubbard

To ignore, to disdain to consider, to overlook, are the essence of the gentleman. *William James*

A man who helps a woman across the street even if she does need help. *Franklin P. Jones*

One who may love like a lunatic, but not like a beast. *Adapted from La Rochefoucauld*

(One who) is mindful no less of the freedom of others than of his own dignity. *Livy*

When an Englishman is totally incapable of doing any work whatsoever, he describes himself in the income-tax form as a "gentleman."

Robert Lynd

One who listens with interest to things he knows all about, when they are told to him by a person who knows nothing about them.

Philippe de Moray

One who never inflicts pain.

John Henry Newman

A gentleman is one who never heard the story before. *Adapted from Austin O'Malley*

(He who has) respect for those who can be of no possible service to him. *William Lyon Phelps*

A sort of modest, inoffensive people, who neither have sense nor pretend to any, but enjoy a jovial sort of dullness. *Alexander Pope*

Stand the gaff, play fair, and be a good man to camp out with. *Theodore Roosevelt*

A...first characteristic is that fineness of structure in the body which renders it capable of the most delicate sensation; and of structure in the mind which renders it capable of the most delicate sympathies. *John Ruskin*

Fineness of nature. *John Ruskin*

Another word for intense humanity.

John Ruskin

The qualifications are to eat *á la mode*, drink champagne, dance jigs, and play at tennis.

Thomas Shadwell

We are gentlemen that neither in our hearts nor outward eyes envy the great, nor do the low despise. *Adapted from William Shakespeare*

Blood and breeding. *William Shakespeare*

A man, more often a woman, who owes nothing and leaves the world in debt to him.

George Bernard Shaw

One who has money enough to do what every fool would do if he could afford it: that is, consume without producing. *George Bernard Shaw*

Make money; and the whole nation will conspire to call you a gentleman. *George Bernard Shaw*

A gentleman ain't a man—leastways not a common man—the common man bein' but the slave wot feeds and clothes the gentleman beyond the common. *George Bernard Shaw*

(Those) who can live idly and without manual labor, and will bear the port, charge and countenance of a gentleman, he alone should be called master and be taken for a gentleman.

Thomas Smith

Well born, well dressed, and moderately learned.

Statue of All Souls College, Oxford

The only infallible rule we know is, that the man who is always talking about being a gentleman never is one. *R. S. Surtees*

A patient wolf.   *Henrietta Tiarks*

One who does not tell the naked truth in the presence of ladies.   *Adapted from Mark Twain*

If a man is a gentleman, he knows quite enough, and if he is not a gentleman, whatever he knows is bad for him.   *Oscar Wilde*

One who never hurts anyone's feelings unintentionally.   *Oscar Wilde*

One who remembers a woman's birthday but forgets her age.   *Anon.*

One who never strikes a woman without provocation.   *Anon.*

One who can like and respect those who can be of no possible service to him.   *Anon.*

One who makes it a cinch for a woman to remain a lady.   *Anon.*

Platitudes plus manners.   *Anon.*

A man who can disagree without being disagreeable.   *Anon.*

One who can tell you all about his problems but does not.   *Anon.*

God's servant, the world's master, and his own man.   *Anon.*

A man who doesn't pretend to be anything he isn't.   *Anon.*

One who holds the door open while his wife carries in the groceries.   *Anon.*

SEE ALSO ARISTOCRAT, CLASSES, MANNERS.

GEOMETRY

Geometry existed before the Creation, is coeternal with the mind of God, is God himself.
Johannes Kepler

The purest realization of human reason; but Euclid's axioms cannot be proven. He who does not believe in them sees the whole building crash.
Arthur Koestler

That part of universal mechanics which accurately proposes and demonstrates the art of measuring.   *Issac Newton*

SEE ALSO MATHEMATICS.

GERMAN

A mind that has a talent for making no mistakes but the very greatest.
Adapted from Clifton Fadiman

A slave who obeys the mere nod or word of his master and needs neither whips nor chains. Servility is inherent in him—it is in his soul.
Heinrich Heine

Everything that is ponderous, vicious and pompously clumsy.   *Friedrich W. Nietzsche*

A hero born, and believes that he can hack and hew his way through life.
Heinrich von Treitschke

One who loves fighting for its own sake.
Adapted from Horace Walpole

The chosen of God.   *William 2 of Germany*

All wisdom derives from the German, and he himself remains a fool.   *Yiddish Proverb*

SEE ALSO NIETZSCHE, WAGNER.

GERMANY

The source of all European revolutions, the mother of those discoveries which transformed the shape of the world. Gunpowder, printing, religious reform came out of its womb.
Ludwig Boerne

Europe's ghetto.   *Ludwig Boerne*

The First Nation of the Universe.
Thomas Carlyle

The only country I have visited where the hands of the men are better cared for than the hands of the women.   *Price Collier*

Germany is Hamlet.   *Ferdinand Freiligrath*

(A country which needs) neither freedom nor equality. They are a speculative race...dreamers who live only in the past and future, and have no present.   *Heinrich Heine*

The paramount workshop of modern anti-Semitism.   *Vladimir Jabotinsky*

The spiritual battlefield of European antagonisms.   *Thomas Mann*

This natural foe to liberty.   *Woodrow Wilson*

GHETTO

That which divides the universe into two: this world for the gentiles—the hereafter for the Jews.
David Ben-Gurion

Only a negative way of saying community.
Eugene E. Brussell

A place of poverty, dirt, ignorance and immorality—the seat of the sweatshop, the tenement house...where the people are queer and repulsive.
Hutchins Hapgood

The ghetto...was for the Jew...not a prison, but a refuge.
Max Nordau

The first spot on the pogrom.
Anon.

The politician's paradise.
Anon.

A concrete reservation.
Anon.

SEE ALSO ANTI-SEMITISM, JEWS, JUDAISM.

GHOST

The outward and visible sign of an inward fear.
Ambrose Bierce

Are we not Spirits, that are shaped into a body, into an Appearance...we not only carry a future Ghost within us; but are, in very deed, Ghosts!
Thomas Carlyle

The disembodied.
William Motherwell

The sheeted dead.
William Shakespeare

Thy bones are marrowless, thy blood is cold; thou hast no speculation in those eyes which thou dost glare with.
Adapted from William Shakespeare

A dancing shape, an image gay, to haunt, to startle, and way-lay.
Adapted from William Wordsworth

A shadow of its former self.
Anon.

GIFT

Every good gift and every perfect gift is from above, and cometh down from the Father of lights.
Bible: James, I, 17.

A precious stone in the eyes of him that hath it.
Bible: Proverbs, XVII, 8.

The only gift is a portion of thyself...the poet brings his poem; the shepherd his lamb...the girl, a hankerchief of her own sewing.
Ralph Waldo Emerson

The only gift is a portion of yourself. The gift without the giver is bare.   *James Russell Lowell*

The merest trifle set apart from honest gains, and sanctified by faith.   *Mahabharata*

Gifts are like fish-hooks.   *Martial*

A synonym of trade.   *Austin O'Malley*

Consists not in what is done or given, but in the intention of the giver or doer.   *Seneca*

A bribe with bells.   *John Steinbeck*

Whatever man has.   *Christoph M. Wieland*

SEE ALSO GIVING, PHILANTHROPY.

GIRLS

Innocence playing in the mud, beauty standing on its head, and motherhood dragging a doll by the foot.   *Allan Beck*

Certainly the best idea that any boy has had to date.   *John Ciardi*

Something old men love for what they are, and young men for what they promise to be.
Adapted from Johann W. Goethe

A vision in the evening and a sight in the morning.   *Anon.*

Those who will scream at a mouse and smile at a wolf.   *Anon.*

A very common species. But when we find the "right" one she never reminds us of the others.
Anon.

SEE ALSO DAUGHTER.

GIVING

He that hath pity upon the poor lendeth unto the Lord.   *Bible: Proverbs, XIX, 17.*

Social action.   *WIlliam Bolitho*

The only thing we ever have.   *Louis Ginsberg*

The busines of the rich.   *Johann W. Goethe*

One glorious chain of love.   *Samson R. Hirsch*

When I give I give myself.   *Walt Whitman*

Not giving beyond the possibility of return.

Anon.

SEE ALSO CHARITY, GENEROSITY, PHILANTHROPY.

GLORY

To honor God.   *Apocrypha: Aristeas, 234.*

Goads and spurs to virtue.   *Francis Bacon*

(That which) lies in noble deeds, and in the recognition alike by leading men and by the nation at large of valuable services rendered to the State.

Cicero

Consists not in never failing, but in rising every time we fall.   *Ralph Waldo Emerson*

Where great men rise.   *William D. Foulke*

Largely a theatrical concept. There is no striving for glory without a vivid awareness of an audience—the knowledge that our mighty deeds will come to the ears of our contemporaries or "of those who are to be."   *Eric Hoffer*

A torch to kindle the noble mind.

Silius Italicus

God created three glories: Childhood, Youth, and Woman.   *Vladimir Jabotinsky*

The glory of good men is in their conscience and not in the mouths of men.   *Thomas á Kempis*

The deeds of our saints and sages.

Jacob Klatzkin

The glory of great men should always be measured by the means which they have used to acquire it.   *La Rochefoucauld*

The true and honorable recompense of gallant actions.   *Alain R. Lesage*

Military glory—the attractive rainbow that rises in showers of blood.   *Abraham Lincoln*

Anything that God has made.

George Macdonald

To leave our names afterwards.

Philip Massinger

A circle in the water which never ceases to enlarge itself until, by broad spreading, it disperses to nought.   *Adapted from William Shakespeare*

To become a literary theme, or a common noun, or an epithet.   *Paul Valéry*

The estimation of lookers-on.   *Anon.*

SEE ALSO CELEBRITY, FAME, VICTORY.

GLUTTON

A poor man who eats too much, as contradistinguished from a gourmand, who is a rich man who "lives well."   *Ambrose Bierce*

He needs no more than birds and beasts to think; all his occasions are to eat and drink.

Adapted from John Dryden

One who digs his grave with his teeth.

French Proverb

The first in banquets, but the last in fight.

Homer

One who takes the piece of pastry you wanted.

Anon.

SEE ALSO EATING, GOURMAND, OBESITY.

GOD

That which has no definition.   *Joseph Albo*

The voice which says, "It's not good enough"— that's what God is.   *William Alfred*

An infantile fantasy, which was necessary when men did not understand what lightening was.

Edward Anhalt

For science, God is simply the stream of tendency by which all things seek to fulfill the law of their being.   *Matthew Arnold*

A term of poetry and eloquence...a literary term...and mankind mean different things by it as their consciousness differs.   *Matthew Arnold*

A convenient way of expressing our wonder in the vast splendor of the universe, and our humility over the modesty of man's achievements.

Brooks Atkinson

A never sleeping eye that reads the heart, and registers our thoughts.   *Francis Bacon*

The foundation and guarantee of morality.

Leon Baeck

The eternal Father.   *Karl Barth*

A reality of spirit...God cannot...be conceived as an object, not even as the very highest object. God is not to be found in the world of objects.

Nicholas Berdyaev

A spirit who is intimately present to our minds, producing in them all that variety of ideas or sensations which continually affect us.

George Berkeley

I am that I am. *Bible: Exodus, III, 14.*

A consuming fire. *Bible: Hebrews, XII, 29.*

God is love; and he that dwelleth in love dwelleth in God, and God in him.

Bible: John, IV, 16.

I am Alpha and Omega, the beginning and the end, the first and the last.

Bible: Revelation, XXII, 13.

He is...called God, because He alone is the Good, the Heart, or (that which) is best.

Jacob Boehme

A substance, but it is a substance that is super-substantial. *Boethius*

God is not one thing because He is, and another thing because He is just; with Him to be just and to be God are one and the same. *Boethius.*

Not an absolute but a limited monarch, limited by the rule which infinite wisdom prescribes to infinite power. *Henry Bolingbroke*

The perfect poet, who in His person acts His own creations. *Adapted from Robert Browning*

The necessary and total solution of the problem posed by a universally absurd world.

R. L. Bruckberger

The universal substance in existing things. He comprises all things. He is the fountain of all being. In Him exists everything that is.

Giordano Bruno

Our expression for all forces and powers which we do not understand, or with which we are unfamiliar. *Samuel Butler 2*

God cannot be conceived without His eternity, power, wisdom, goodness, truth, right and mercy.

John Calvin

Another name for human intelligence raised above all error and imperfection, and extended to all possible truth. *William Ellery Channing*

The creative Force, behind and in the universe, who manifests Himself as energy, as life, as order, as beauty, as thought, as conscience, as love. *Henry S. Coffin*

An independent, unique, infinite, eternal, omnipotent, immutable, intelligent, and free First Cause, whose power extends over all things.

Etienne B. Condillac

That inner presence which makes us admire the beautiful, which rejoices us when we have done right. *Eugene Delacroix*

God implies necessary and eternal existence.

René Descartes

It denotes the unity of all ideal ends arousing us to desire and actions. *John Dewey*

Power with intelligence. *Benjamin Disraeli*

The life, mind, order, and law of the world.

Will Durant

God is Mind, and God is infinite; hence all is Mind. *Mary Baker Eddy*

A superior reasoning power...revealed in the incomprehensible universe. *Albert Einstein*

A knowledge of the existence of something we cannot penetrate...it is this knowledge and this emotion that constitute the truly religious attitude.

Albert Einstein

A superior mind that reveals itself in the world of experience. *Albert Einstein*

An unutterable sign in the human heart.

Havelock Ellis

He is beyond our ken—infinite, immense, and His real greatness is known to Himself alone. Our mind is too limited to understand Him.

Marcus M. Felix

I learned from a hillbilly revivalist that God is the *croupier*, and never loses. *Martin H. Fischer*

An idealized superman. *Sigmund Freud*

The personalized God is psychologically nothing other than a magnified father. *Sigmund Freud*

One of the many different poetic expressions of the highest value in humanism, not a reality in itself. *Erich Fromm*

God is a verb,
Not a noun. *Richard Fuller*

The highest, remotest, most infinite, and final ... emotional speculation of which man is capable.   *John Galsworthy*

God is conscience. He is even the atheism of the atheist.   *Mohandas K. Gandhi*

God and happiness are one.   *André Gide*

The order in which life takes on meaning.
                                    Langdon Gilkey

The hero of a book called the Bible.
                                     Nelson Glueck

Existence is God!   *Johann W. Goethe*

The uncreated creator of everything.
                                   Simon Gruenberg

A Leveler, who renders equal small and great.
                                  Johanan HaCohen

A gaseous vertebrate.   *Ernst Haeckel*

The Creator.   *Eliezer Halevi*

God is by definition worshipful, and this means exalted beyond all possible rival or superior.
                                Charles Hartshorne

The object of worship in the high religions.
                                Charles Hartshorne

The beginning and end of all things.
                                    Heinrich Heine

The God of the Hebraic religion is either a living, active, "feeling" God or He is nothing.
                                      Will Herberg

What God is we cannot show.   *Robert Herrick*

The sculptor who chisels on the rough block of stone the general outline of what the finished pieces will be.   *Thomas J. Higgins*

The Other Mind which in creating Nature is also creating me.   *William E. Hocking*

That which makes man human.   *Eric Hoffer*

Anything that humanizes.   *Eric Hoffer*

The great soul that sits on the throne of the universe.   *Josiah G. Holland*

A pure Spirit, distinct from the creature He has called into existence.   *Joseph Huby*

The perfect fulfillment of all our capacities and powers.   *Jay W. Hudson*

The Perfect Person of our ideal ... He ever exists on earth in the degree that life unfolds towards His perfection.   *Jay W. Hudson*

The latent EGO of the visible Infinite ... the invisible made evident. The world concentrated is God.   *Victor Hugo*

An ever-present spirit guiding all that happens to a wise and holy end.   *David Hume*

A product of the human mind. As an independent or unitary being active in the affairs of the universe, he does not exist.   *Julian Huxley*

A spectator, benevolent perhaps but ineffective, of the workings of the cosmic machine ... his sole occupation throughout eternity is to enjoy the verification of his predictions ... Instead of ruling a kingdom he merely holds a watching brief.
                                     Julian Huxley

The sum of the forces acting in the cosmos as perceived and grasped by the human mind.
                                     Julian Huxley

Is is essential that God be conceived as the deepest power in the universe; and second, he must be conceived under the form of a mental personality.
                                    William James

Something lying outside of my own and other than me, and whose existence I simply come upon and find.   *William James*

The normal object of the mind's belief. Whether over and above this he be really the living truth is another question.   *William James*

The God of many men is little more than their court of appeal against the damnatory judgment passed on their failures by the opinion of the world.   *William James*

A superintending power to maintain the Universe in its course and order.   *Thomas Jefferson*

God, to be God, must transcend what is. He must be the maker of what ought to be.
                                    Rufus M. Jones

We know God easily, if we do not constrain ourselves to define him.   *Joseph Joubert*

The sum of the animating, organizing forces and relationships which are forever making a cosmos out of chaos.   *Mordecai M. Kaplan*

The sum total of all the forces in the universe that work for man's salvation.   *Mordecai M. Kaplan*

The whole solace and comfort of the soul.

Thomas á Kempis

The reconciliation of the many in the One.

Hans Kohn

Personified incomprehensibility.

Georg C. Lichtenberg

A single and complete essence, which consists of no diversity of parts or of accidents.

Peter Lombard

A mighty fortress is our God,
    A bulwark never failing.   *Martin Luther*

A voice in the wind I do not know; a meaning on the face of the high hills whose utterance I cannot comprehend.

Adapted from George Macdonald

The conception of a personal ground of all that we experience.   *John Macmurray*

The object of all our desires, the end of all our actions . . . and the governing power of our whole souls.   *Jean B. Massillon*

The Person who, as over against our own personalities, expresses Himself in the Whole.

Sheiler Mathews

God is not in a book . . . he *is* . . . he must reveal himself to us.   *Frederick D. Maurice*

The word God is a theology in itself, indivisibly one . . . from the vastness and simplicity of its meaning. Admit a God, and you introduce among the subjects of your knowledge a fact encompassing, closing in upon, absorbing, every other fact conceivable.   *John Henry Newman*

A Being endowed with intelligence and wisdom.

Isaac Newton

The eminently relative One, whose openness to change contingently on the actions of others is literally boundless.   *Schubert Ogden*

He is pure mind. He moves and acts without needing any corporeal space, or size, or form, or color, or any other property of matter.   *Origen*

A first cause, and the cause of all things.

Thomas Paine

The eternal Being.   *Blaise Pascal*

Ultimate reality.   *Philo*

The Reality undergoing and penetrating through the whole derived creation.   *Norman Pittenger*

Not the author of all things, but of a few things only, and not of most things that occur to man.

Plato

Truth itself.   *Pope Leo XIII*

The unshaken foundation of all social order and of all responsible action on earth.   *Pope Pius XI*

God is not the name of God, but an opinion about Him.   *Pope Sixtus*

A radical being of all goodness.

Francis Quarles

A light that is never darkened.   *Francis Quarles*

The anonymous presence.   *Karl Rahner*

An unutterable sigh, planted in the depths of the soul.   *Jean Paul Richter*

I don't say what God is, but it's a name that somehow answers us when we are driven.

Edwin Arlington Robinson

That thing than which nothing greater can exist.

Saint Thomas Aquinas

We can know what God is not, but we cannot know what He is.   *Saint Augustine*

He alone is God who can never be sought in vain.

Saint Bernard

God does not exist . . . We are precisely on a plane where nothing exists but men.   *Jean-Paul Sartre*

Call it nature, fate, fortune: all are but names for the one and same God.   *Seneca*

A divinity that shapes our ends.

William Shakespeare

A vengeful, pitiless, and almighty fiend.

Percy Bysshe Sheeley

A veil woven by philosophical conceit, to hide the ignorance of philosophers.

Percy Bysshe Shelley

The process which created and sustains me.

Upton Sinclair

A power, operating at the center of the universe, which creates, maintains, and comprehends my personality and all other personalities.

Upton Sinclair

An infinite and Eternal energy.

Herbert Spencer

Moses conceived the Deity as a Being who has always existed, does exist, and always will exist, and he therefore called Him Jehovah, which in Hebrew signifies these three phases.

Baruch Spinoza

A being absolutely infinite; a substance consisting of infinite attributes, each of which expresses His Eternal and infinite essence.

Baruch Spinoza

Man is an organ of life, and God alone is life.

Emanuel Swedenborg

The ruler of all.   *Tacitus*

A social God, a concentrated projection of all the qualities useful to the herd in a supreme supernatural personality—the supreme herd leader of humanity.   *A. G. Tansley*

The name of this infinite and inexhaustible depth and ground of all being...That depth is what the word God means...It...speaks of the depths of your life, of the source of your being.

Paul Tillich

He is being—itself beyond essence and existence.

Paul Tillich

A circle everywhere and circumference nowhere.

Timaeus

Every man recognizes within himself a free and rational spirit, independent of his body. This spirit is what we call God.   *Leon Tolstoy*

The living God is within you...The only God to worship is the soul in the human body.

Swami Vivekananda

The eternal subject of everything.

Swami Vivekananda

I can never know what he is.   *Voltaire*

A force representing a sort of distillation of the best instincts of men, which inspires them and somehow triumphs in human events in the end.

Herbert G. Wells

(That which) is in the world, or nowhere, creating continually in us and around us.

Alfred North Whitehead

The binding element in the world.

Alfred North Whitehead

The poet of the world, with tender patience leading it by his vision of truth, beauty, and goodness.   *Alfred North Whitehead*

That character of events to which man must adjust himself in order to attain the greatest goods and avoid the greatest evils.   *Henry N. Wieman*

The identifying mark of God is organic unity, found functioning preeminently in Jesus, which operates in the world to make us brothers; that is, functional members of one another.

Henry N. Wieman

That interaction between individual groups and ages which generates and promotes the greatest possible mutuality of good.   *Henry N. Wieman*

The idea of an unsurpassable maximum.   *Anon.*

SEE ALSO AGNOSTICISM, ATHEISM, BIBLE, CHRISTIANITY, CHURCHES, CHURCH OF ENGLAND, CHURCH (ROMAN CATHOLIC), COMMANDMENTS, DEATH, DEVIL, ETERNAL RECURRENCE, FAITH, HEAVEN, HELL, IMMORTALITY, JUDAISM, MOHAMMEDANISM, MONOTHEISM, MOSES, THEOCRACY, THEOLOGY, SYNAGOGUE.

GOLD

A wonderful clearer of the understanding; it dissipates every doubt and scruple in an instant, accomodates itself to the meanest capacities...and brings over the most obstinate and inflexible.   *Joseph Addison*

A deep-persuading orator.   *Richard Barnfield*

The touchstone whereby to try men.

Thomas Fuller

A transient, shining trouble.   *James Grainger*

Price of many a crime untold.   *Thomas Hood*

The money of monarchs.   *John J. Ingalls*

A living god.   *Percy Bysshe Shelley*

A metal men dig out of holes for dentists and governments to put back in.   *Anon.*

SEE ALSO MONEY, WEALTH.

GOLDEN AGE

Never the present age.   *Thomas Fuller*

From the days of the first grandfather, everybody has remembered a golden age behind him.

James Russell Lowell

Unadorned fiction.   *Anon.*

Nostalgia embroidered. *Anon.*

SEE ALSO NOSTALGIA.

GOLDEN RULE

Love thy neighbor. *Akiba*

Do others or they will do you.
American Proverb

Be considerate of your companion as of yourself.
Apocrypha: Ben Sira, XXXI, 15.

What you yourself hate, do to no man.
Apocrypha: Tobit, IV, 14.

As you would that men should do to you, do you also to them likewise. *Bible: Luke, VI, 31.*

Seek for your neighbor what you would seek for yourself. *Abraham Hasdai*

What you're unwilling to receive, be sure you never do. *The New England Primer*

The rule of proportion. *Robert Recorde*

Treat your inferiors as you would be treated by your betters. *Seneca*

The golden rule is that there are no golden rules.
George Bernard Shaw

If it be a duty to respect other men's claims, so also is it a duty to maintain our own.
Herbert Spencer

Desire nothing for yourself which you do not desire for others. *Baruch Spinoza*

Moderation in all things. *Terence*

Hurt not others with that which pains yourself.
Udanavarga

Do unto the other feller the way he'd like to do unto you, an' do it fust. *E. N. Westcott*

Do unto others as they would do unto you if they had the chance. *Anon.*

GOLF

The most...perfect expression of national stupidity. *Max Beerbohm*

If you watch a game, it's fun. If you play it, it's a recreation. If you work at it, it's golf. *Bob Hope*

The playthings of childhood. *Samuel Johnson*

A form of moral effort. *Stephen B. Leacock*

Essentially an exercize in masochism conducted out of doors. *Paul O'Neil*

The most useless outdoor game ever devised to waste the time and try the spirit of man.
Westbrook Pegler

A plague invented by the Calvinistic Scots as a punishment for man's sins. *James Reston*

The only game which has a moral purpose and is definitely tinged with a touch of the spiritual.
Henry H. Shires

A good walk spoiled. *Mark Twain*

A lot of walking, broken by disappointments and bad arithmetic. *Earl Wilson*

A game in which one endeavors to control a ball with implements ill adapted for the purpose.
Woodrow Wilson

A game that begins with a golfball and ends with a highball. *Anon.*

Cussing and cheating mostly. *Anon.*

The game that turned the cows out of the pasture and let the bull in. *Anon.*

A game where the ball lies poorly and the player well. *Anon.*

A sport in which many impressive scores are attained by a lead pencil. *Anon.*

The most popular method of beating around the bush. *Anon.*

GOOD

Has two meanings: it means both that which is good absolutely and that which is good for somebody. *Aristotle*

One of mankind's most inexplicable perversions.
Ingmar Bergman

Full of the Holy Ghost and of faith.
Bible: Acts, II, 24.

To be zealously affected always in a good thing.
Bible: Galatians, IV, 18.

Whatsoever every man chiefly loves above all other things, that, he persuades himself is best for him. *Boethius*

Many meanings. For examples, if a man were to shoot his grandmother at a range of five hundred yards, I should call him a good shot, but not necessarily a good man.

Gilbert Keith Chesterton

That is good which commands me to my country, my climate, my means and materials, my associates. *Ralph Waldo Emerson*

There are three sorts of good: the profitable, the pleasurable, and the virtuous. *Leon Hebraeus*

Whatsoever is the object of any man's appetite or desire, that it is which he...calleth good.

Thomas Hobbes

Good is when I steal other people's wives and cattle; bad is when they steal mine.

Hottentot Proverb

That which makes for unity. *Aldous Huxley*

The ethical and spiritual artistry of individuals; it cannot be mass-produced. *Aldous Huxley*

To be true to the best. *Morris Joseph*

That which is pleasant, agreeable and well-suited to any perceptive life or grade of such life, and which involves the preservation of the recipient.

Henry Moore

All that elevates the feeling of power, the will to power, the power itself in man.

Friedrich W. Nietzsche

That which contributes to the course of ascending evolution and leads us away from the animal toward freedom. *Lecomte de Noüy*

A special kind of truth and beauty...truth and beauty in human behavior. *Harry A. Overstreet*

Thinking right, and meaning well.

Alexander Pope

That is good which does me good. *John Ray*

Action, and action prescribed. *Leon Roth*

Happiness for each man after his own heart, and for each hour according to its inspiration.

George Santayana

The greatest...is the knowledge of the union which the mind has with the whole of Nature.

Baruch Spinoza

That which...is useful to us. *Baruch Spinoza*

Everything which we are certain is a means by which we may approach nearer and nearer to the model of human nature we set before us.

Baruch Spinoza

It merely requires a certain amount of sordid terror, a certain lack of imaginative thought, and a certain low passion for middle-class respectability. *Oscar Wilde*

SEE ALSO BEAUTY, RIGHT, VIRTUE

GOOD AND BAD

The good is that which is closer to God and the bad that which is farther from Him. Bad is therefore a lower degree of good.

Israel Baal Shem Tob

Evil and good are God's right hand and left.

Philip J. Bailey

Pleasure...the only good, Pain...the only evil.

Jeremy Bentham

Nothing but by comparison. *Henry G. Bohn*

What can perpetuate itself is good and what is evil destroys itself. *Lyman Bryson*

The essence of good and evil is a certain kind of moral purpose. *Epictetus*

When good befalls a man he calls it Providence, when evil fate. *Knut Hamsun*

We are all ready to be savage in some cause. The difference between a good man and a bad one is the choice of the cause. *William James*

Evil is only good perverted.

Henry Wadsworth Longfellow

Efficiency and inefficiency.

George Bernard Shaw

Nothing out of its place is good and nothing in its place is bad. *Walt Whitman*

SEE ALSO EVIL, RIGHT AND WRONG

GOODBYE

SEE FAREWELL.

GOSSIP

Murder by language. *Roland Barthes*

What no one claims to like but what everybody enjoys. *Joseph Conrad*

A sort of smoke that comes from the dirty tobacco-pipes of those who diffuse it; it proves nothing but the bad taste of the smoker.

George Eliot

A personal confession either of malice or imbecility. *Josiah G. Holland*

What people say behind your back . . . your standing in the community. *Edgar W. Howe*

Vice enjoyed vicariously. *Elbert Hubbard*

The opiate of the oppressed. *Erica Jong*

The world's cheapest form of compensation.

Stefan Kanfer

The mixture of detraction and prophecy.

Henry E. Manning

Social sewage. *George Meredith*

Cutting honest throats by whispers.

Walter Scott

Foul whisperings. *William Shakespeare*

(Talk which) turns an earful into a mouthful.

George Bernard Shaw

The henchman of rumor and scandal.

Richard Brinsley Sheridan

Idle talk about other persons not present.

Patricia Spacks

What some invent and the rest enlarge.

Jonathan Swift

The art of saying nothing in a way that leaves practically nothing unsaid. *Walter Winchell*

The lengthening of the tongue to hammerlike proportions. *Anon.*

Anything that goes in one ear and out over the back fence. *Anon.*

Ear pollution. *Anon.*

The joy of recall and rearrangement. *Anon.*

Conversation is when three people are talking. Gossip is when one of them leaves. *Anon.*

Nothing more than mouth-to-mouth recitation.

Anon.

Winding your tongue up and letting go. *Anon.*

SEE ALSO SCANDAL, TONGUE.

GOSSIPERS

Those who depend on the characters and lives of their neighbors for all their amusement.

George Bancroft

Little people who like to about what the great are doing. *German Proverb*

Gossips are frogs—they drink and talk.

George Herbert

A professional athlete—of the tongue.

Aldous Huxley

A cannibal. *Moses Ibn Ezra*

A person who puts two and two together— whether they are or not. *Mary McCoy*

(Those) who murder characters to kill time.

Richard Brinsley Sheridan

Sociologists on a mean and petty scale.

Woodrow Wilson

A newscaster without a sponsor. *Anon.*

The spies of life. *Anon.*

Those who reinforce what you already suspected.

Anon.

Those who have a sense of rumor. *Anon.*

Negatives that develop and then enlarge. *Anon.*

GOURMAND

An adult who can eat almost as much as a small child. *Cynic's Cyclopaedia*

A rich man who eats well, as distinguished from a poor man who eats too much.

Adapted from Elbert Hubbard

One who weeps because he cannot eat when asleep. *Anon.*

SEE ALSO EATING, GLUTTON, STOMACH.

GOURMET

A glutton in a dress suit. *Shannon Carse*

Just a glutton with brains. *Philip W. Haberman*

Usually little more that a glutton festooned with charge cards. *Sydney J. Harris*

One who eats himself into the grave.

Twentieth Century Proverb

A man invited for an evening of wine, women and song—and asks what kind of wine.   *Anon.*

GOUT

The distemper of a gentleman.
                                    Lord Chesterfield

Pangs arthritic that infest the toe Of libertine excess.   *William Cowper*

The only enemy that I do not wish to have at my feet.   *Sydney Smith*

A very singular disease...It seems as if the stomach fell down into the feet.   *Sydney Smith*

GOVERNMENT

The people. From this element spring all governments.   *John Quincy Adams*

The essence of a free government consists in effectual control of rivalries.
                                 John Quincy Adams

A group of men organized to sell protection to the inhabitants of a limited area at monopolistic prices.   *Maxwell Anderson*

The art of the momentarily feasible, of...the least bad attainable.   *Bernard Berenson*

Security to possessors, facility to acquirers, and liberty and hope to the people.
                                    William Blackstone

Accountancy.   *Louis D. Brandeis*

A contrivance of human wisdom to provide for human wants.   *Edmund Burke*

Compromise and barter.   *Edmund Burke*

A machine: to the discontented a "taxing machine," to the contented a "machine for securing property."   *Thomas Carlyle*

The most conspicuous object in society...called upon to give signal of what shall be done; and...to preside over...and command the doing of it.   *Thomas Carlyle*

The exact symbol of its people, with their wisdom and unwisdom.   *Thomas Carlyle*

(Something which gives) men the opportunity to work out happiness for themselves.
                                William Ellery Channing

To create restraint but to do good.
                                    Rufus Choate

A trust, and the offices of the government are trustees; and both the trust and trustees are created for the benefit of the people.
                                    Henry Clay

An instrumentality by which the people's affairs should be conducted upon business principles, regulated by the public needs.
                                    Grover Cleveland

A device for maintaining in perpetuity the rights of the people, with the ultimate extinction of all privileged classes.   *Calvin Coolidge*

To further and promote human strivings.
                                    Wilbur L. Cross

The expression of what cultivation exists in the population which permits it. The law is only a memorandum.   *Ralph Waldo Emerson*

The principal obstruction and nuisance with which we have to contend.
                                Ralph Waldo Emerson

Making men live together in peace and with reasonable happiness.   *Felix Frankfurter*

The biggest organized social effort for dealing with social problems.   *Felix Frankfurther*

An evil...we should have as little of it as the general peace of human society will permit.
                                    William Godwin

Two legitimate purposes—the suppression of injustice against individuals within the community, and the common defense against external invasion.   *William Godwin*

That which teaches us to govern ourselves.
                                    Johann W. Goethe

The Santa Claus of something-for-nothing and something-for-everyone.   *Barry M. Goldwater*

(Something that) enforces and defends all of man's natural rights and protects him against wrongs of his fellow men.   *Galusha A. Grow*

A grant of power from the governed.
                                    William Harrison

An evil, but of the two forms of that evil, democracy or monarchy, the sounder is monarchy; the more able to do its will, democracy.
                                    Benjamin R. Haydon

The very basis of representative government is a two-party system. It is one of the essential checks and balances against inefficiency, dishonesty, and tyranny.   *Herbert Hoover*

Mainly an expensive organization to regulate evildoers, and tax those that behave: government does little for fairly respectable people except annoy them.   *Edgar W. Howe*

Legalized pillage.   *Elbert Hubbard*

The agency charged with responsibility for the common good.   *Robert Maynard Hutchins*

Freedom of religion...press...person under the protection of *habeas corpus.*   *Thomas Jefferson*

The only orthodox object...is to secure the greatest degree of happiness possible to the general mass of those associated under it.

Thomas Jefferson

Just a device to protect man so that he may earn his bread in the sweat of his labor.

Hugh S. Johnson

Exists to protect freedom and enlarge the opportunities of every citizen.

Lyndon Baines Johnson

Government is a rancher from Montana, a banker from New York, an automobile maker from Detroit; government is the son of a tenant farmer from Texas who is speaking to you tonight.

Lyndon Baines Johnson

Exists for the purpose of keeping peace ... compelling us to settle our disputes by arbitration instead of...blows.   *Thomas B. Macaulay*

That is the best government which desires to make the people happy, and knows how to make them happy.   *Thomas B. Macaulay*

The whole duty...is to prevent crime and to preserve contracts.   *Lord Melbourne*

The common enemy of all decent citizens.

Henry Louis Mencken

A conspiracy against the superior man.

Henry Louis Mencken

Exists to protect the rights of minorities. The loved and the rich need no protection.

Wendell Phillips

The greatest happiness of the whole, and not that of any one class.   *Plato*

Inspected, spied on, directed, legislated at...assessed...censored...hoaxed, robbed...bullied, beaten...insulted, dishonored. That's government.   *Pierre J. Proudhon*

A baby. An alimentary canal with a big appetite at one end and no sense of responsibility at the other.

Ronald Reagan

Government is a referee, and it shouldn't try to be a player in the game.   *Ronald Reagan*

To have one party govern and the other party watch.   *Thomas Reed*

Us; we are the government, you and I.

Theodore Roosevelt

A form of association that defends and protects the person and property of each with the common force of all.   *Jean-Jacques Rousseau*

The art of government is the organization of idolatry.   *George Bernard Shaw*

Wisdom and virtue...all government is but an imperfect remedy for the deficiency of these.

Adam Smith

When the people obey the judge, and the judges obey the law.   *Solon*

An association of men who do violence to the rest of us.   *Leon Tolstoy*

The assumption of authority over a given area and all within it, exercised generally for the double purpose of more complete oppression of its subjects and extension of its boundaries.

Benjamin R. Tucker

Consists in taking as much money as possible from one party of citizens to give to the other.

Voltaire

The right of the people to make and to alter their constitutions of government.

George Washington

Government...is force.   *George Washington*

Laws.   *Daniel Webster*

An attempt to express the conscience of everybody...in the rules that everybody is commanded to obey.   *Woodrow Wilson*

A kind of gangsterism.   *Frank Lloyd Wright*

Apathy at the circumference and apoplexy at the center.   *Anon.*

SEE ALSO AMERICA, AMERICAN CONSTITUTION, ANARCHY, CONSERVATISM, CONSTITUTION, DEMOCRACY, DEPOTISM, FREEDOM, LIBERALISM, LIBERTY, MONARCHY, PUBLIC OPINION, TOTALITARIANISM.

GRACE

The gift of God.   *Bible: Ephesians, II 8.*

Fitting into what one is doing.   *Marcia Cavell*

Grace is but glory begun, and glory is but grace perfected.   *Jonathan Edwards*

The seed of the life of heaven.

Reginald Garrigou-Lagrange

The outward expression of the inward harmony of the soul.   *William Hazlitt*

The love that gives, that loves the unlovely and the unlovable.   *Oswald C. Hoffmann*

The inspiration from on high...the spirit of the law.   *Victor Hugo*

It is the gift of God which is only given to us to draw us on to God Himself.   *Bede Jarrett*

The divine transformation of the soul, the action of God upon the soul.   *Jacques Leclercq*

Nothing else than the forgiveness or remission of sins.   *Philip Melanchthon*

In every gesture dignity and love.   *John Milton*

Nothing but the heavenly light, which from the depths of the Divinity diffuses itself over the rational creatures.   *Mathias J. Scheeben*

The good which God puts into each concrete situation over and above all that man can do or plan or even imagine.   *Henry N. Wieman*

"What is grace?" was asked of an old colored man... "Grace," he replied, "is what I should call giving something for nothing."   *Anon.*

GRAMMAR

A science or nothing. It has the outward forms of a science and its difficulties spring out of its scientific character.   *Alexander Bain*

It is not the business of grammar...to give law to the fashions which regulate our speech. On the contrary, from its conformity to these, and from that alone, it derives all its authority and value.

George Campbell

My grammar, 'tis of thee,
Sweet incongruity,
Of thee I sing.
I love each mood and tense,
Each freak of accidence,

Protect me from common sense,
Grammar, my king!   *Isaac Goldberg*

The grave of letters.   *Elbert Hubbard*

Common speech formulated.

William Somerset Maugham

The art of speaking and writing correctly.

Medieval Definition

The means by which the forms of language are made to correspond with the universal forms of thought.   *John Stuart Mill*

The analysis of language.   *Edgar Allan Poe*

Like other sciences, (it) deals only with what can be brought under general laws and stated in the form of general rules.   *Henry Sweet*

The science of putting language in its place.

Anon.

SEE ALSO LANGUAGE, RHETORIC, SPEECH.

GRASS

The hair of the earth.   *Thomas Dekker*

The beautiful uncut hair of graves.

Walt Whitman

The green stuff that wilts on the lawn and thrives in the garden.   *Anon.*

GRATITUDE

A sentiment lying midway between a benefit received and a benefit expected.

Ambrose Bierce

A burden upon our imperfect nature.

Lord Chesterfield

One of the least articulate of the emotions, especially when it is deep.   *Felix Frankfurter*

A lively sense of anticipation concerning favors about to be received.   *Elbert Hubbard*

The fruit of great cultivation; you do not find it among gross people.   *Samuel Johnson*

Only a secret wish to get greater benefits.

La Rochefoucauld

To thank God for all His infinite goodness with all our heart.   *Ottokar Prohaszka*

A blessing we give to one another.

Robert Raynolds

A duty which ought to be paid, but which none have a right to expect.   *Jean-Jacques Rousseau*

To practice thanksgiving.   *Sad Dar*

The exchequer of the poor.

William Shakespeare

A lively sense of future favors.   *Robert Walpole*

The memory of the heart.   *Anon.*

GRAVE

(A place of) oblivion, dust and an endless darkness.   *Beaumont and Fletcher*

The grave is mine house; I have made my bed in the darkness.   *Bible: Job, XVII, 13.*

A place in which the dead are laid to await the coming of the medical student.   *Ambrose Bierce*

Heaven's golden gate.   *William Blake*

The last inn of all travelers, where we shall meet worms instead of fleas.   *William D'avenant*

Where human folly sleeps.   *John Dyer*

A rut with ends.   *Daniel Easton*

Those hillocks of mortality, where proud man is only found by a small swelling in the ground.

Adapted from Thomas Flatman

The general meeting place.   *Thomas Fuller*

A grave is but a plain suit, and a rich monument is one embroidered.   *Thomas Fuller*

That shabby corner of God's allotment where He lets the nettles grow, and where all unbaptized infants, notorious drunkards, suicides, and others of the conjecturally damned are laid.

Thomas Hardy

A piece of churchyard fitting everybody.

Adapted from George Herbert

(A place that) buries every error—covers every defect—extinguishes every resentment!

Washington Irving

A covered bridge leading from light to light through a brief darkness.

Adapted from Henry Wadsworth Longfellow

The footprints of angels.

Henry Wadsworth Longfellow

The field and Acre of our God, the place where human harvests grow.

Adapted from Henry Wadsworth Longfellow

Nature's busy old democracy.

William Vaughn Moody

Little houses in a row,
Down a quiet lane;
Neither doors nor windows know,
Peace and darkness reign.
Though you cannot pay the rent,
You will dwell there with the best.
Where the weary, broken, spent,
Find eternal rest!   *Isaac Peretz*

Every land is a grave for famous men...graven not so much on stone as in the hearts of men.

Pericles

The best shelter.   *John Ray*

That small model of the barren earth which serves as paste to cover our bones.

Adapted from William Shakespeare

My peace.   *William Shakespeare*

All roads end at the grave, which is the gate of nothingness.   *George Bernard Shaw*

The threshold of eternity.   *Robert Southey*

(That which) levels all distinctions and makes the whole world kin.

Union Prayer Book, 1922, 11:325.

The low green tent
Whose curtain never outward swings.

John Greenleaf Whittier

Your own quiet room when the journey's done.

Adapted from Humbert Wolfe

What each passing day brings you closer to.

Yiddish Proverb

The last resort.   *Anon.*

What everyone ends up owning.   *Anon.*

The abode appointed for all the living.   *Anon.*

What awaits us at the end of the march.   *Anon.*

The place where beauty fades.   *Anon.*

SEE ALSO CEMETERY, COFFIN, DEATH, FU-
NERAL, MONUMENT.

GRAVITY

The very essence of imposture.
Anthony A. Cooper

The ballast of the soul, which keeps the mind steady. *Thomas Fuller*

A trick of the body invented to conceal the lack of mind. *La Rochefoucauld*

A taught trick to gain credit of the world for more sense and knowledge than a man was worth.
Laurence Sterne

SEE ALSO SERIOUSNESS.

GREAT MEN

Something you don't have to be big to become.
Sholom Aleichem

The true men, the men in whom nature has succeeded. They are not extraordinary—they are in the true order. It is the other species of men who are not what they ought to be. *Henry F. Amiel*

Thrice servants: servants of the . . . state, servants of fame, and servants of business; so they have no freedom, neither in their persons, nor in their actions, nor in their times. *Francis Bacon*

The fellow that does his job every day. The mother who has children and gets up and gets the breakfast and keeps them clean and sends them off to school. The fellow who keeps the streets clean . . . The Unknown Soldier. Millions.
Bernard M. Baruch

Three signs—generosity in the design, humanity in the execution, moderation in success.
Otto von Bismarck

One who is in advance of his age.
Adapted from Henry P. Brougham

The commissioned guides of mankind, who rule their fellows. *Thomas Carlyle*

The real great man is the man who makes every man feel great. *Gilbert Keith Chesterton*

He . . . who rises to a high position by his own merit, and not one who climbs up by the injury and disaster of another. *Cicero*

The man who does his work, any work, conscientiously, must always be in one sense a great man. *Dinah M. Craik*

He . . . who never reminds us of others.
Ralph Waldo Emerson

They who see that spiritual is stronger than material force, that thoughts rub the world.
Ralph Waldo Emerson

He who in the midst of the crowd keeps with perfect sweetness the independence of solitude.
Ralph Waldo Emerson

He who can alter my state of mind.
Ralph Waldo Emerson

I count him a great man who inhabits a higher sphere of thought, into which other men rise with labor and difficulty. *Ralph Waldo Emerson*

Instruments by which the Highest One works out his designs; light-radiators to give guidance and blessing to the travelers of time. *Moses Harvey*

(He who) is endowed with a higher degree of sensitiveness, so that seeing a little sooner and farther than his fellows the coming situations, he can size them up in advance. *Lewis B. Hershey*

One who perceives the unseen, and knows the obvious. *Elbert Hubbard*

A man who lives a long way off.
Elbert Hubbard

He . . . that is little in himself, and that makes no account of any height of honors.
Thomas á Kempis

Not those who have fewer passions and greater virtue than ordinary men, but those who have the greater aims. *La Rochefoucauld*

The man who can get himself made and who will get himself made out of anything he finds at hand.
Gerald S. Lee

Solitary towers in the city of God.
Henry Wadsworth Longfellow

A great man is made up of qualities that meet or make great occasions. *James Russell Lowell*

He who has not lost the heart of a child.
Mencius

That man is great, and he alone, who serves a greatness not for his own, for neither praise nor pelf: content to know and be unknown: whole in himself. *Adapted from Owen Meredith*

He alone...who either does great things, or teaches how they may be done, or describes them with a suitable majesty when they have been done.

John Milton

Meteors designed to burn so that the earth may be lighted.   *Napoleon I*

Only an actor playing out his own ideal.

Friedrich W. Nietzsche

The select men...the only ones who are active and not merely reactive, for whom life is a perpetual striving, an incessant course of training.   *José Ortega y Gasset*

The "well known," that is, known by everyone...he who has made himself known by excelling the anonymous mass. It implies an unusual effort as the course of his fame.

José Ortega y Gasset

That man...who can use the brains of others to carry on his work.   *Donn Piatt*

He who forms the taste of a nation; the next greatest is he who corrupts it.   *Joshua Reynolds*

That man...who has never grieved in evil days and never bewailed his destiny.   *Seneca*

There is no such thing...People believe in them, just as they used to believe in unicorns and dragons. The greatest man or woman is 99 per cent just like yourself.   *George Bernard Shaw*

The man who does a thing for the first time.

Al Smith

Those who wear at their hearts the fire's center.

Stephen Spender

Born of the sun, they traveled a short while towards the sun, and left the vivid air signed with their honor.   *Adapted from Stephen Spender*

He only...who can neglect the applause of the multitude, and enjoy himself independent of its favour.   *Richard Steele*

He who cares not to be great, but as he saves or serves the state.

Adapted from Alfred Lord Tennyson

Instructive and attractive text-books, whose paragraphs are deeds.   *Isaac M. Wise*

SEE ALSO ARISTOCRACY, GENIUS, HERO, HEROISM, MINORITY, NOBILITY, SUPERIOR MAN.

GREATNESS

A generous concern for the good of mankind, and the exercise of humility.   *Joseph Addison*

A spiritual condition worthy to excite love, interest, and admiration; and the outward proof of possessing greatness is that we excite love, interest, and admiration.   *Matthew Arnold*

The right using of strength.

Henry Ward Beecher

Not so much a certain size as a certain quality in human lives. It may be present in lives whose range is very small.   *Phillips Brooks*

The freemasonry of the enlightened, whatever their condition may be or wherever they live.

Van Wyck Brooks

That pompous misery.   *William Broome*

The outer material result, the practical realization and embodiment of Thoughts that dwell in the Great Men sent into the world.   *Thomas Carlyle*

True greatness...is filled with awe and reverence in the face of dark and mysterious fate, it is mindful of the ever-rolling wheel of destiny, and never allows itself to be counted great or happy before its end.   *Johann G. Fichte*

To forgive no enemy; but to be cautious and often dilatory in revenge.   *Henry Fielding*

To maintain a constant gravity in...countenance and behavior, and to effect wisdom on all occasions.   *Henry Fielding*

Consists in power, pride, insolence, and doing mischief to mankind...A great man and a great rogue are synonymous.   *Henry Fielding*

A strong will and a good heart.

Karl E. Franzos

The capacity, not necessity, to forgive in heart, mind and soul.   *Warren Goldberg*

So often a courteous synonym for great success.

Philip Guedalla

Saying what is true.   *Heraclitus*

To think greatly and to nobly dare.

Adapted from Homer

A retentive memory is a good thing, but the ability to forget is the true token of greatness.

Elbert Hubbard

The hour (and) the man.   *William James*

Too huge for mortal tongue, or pen of scribe.
                                John Keats

Dignity without pride was formerly the characteristic of greatness; the revolution in morals is completed, and it is now pride without dignity.
                    Walter Savage Landor

Honorable conduct and noble disposition.   *Ovid*

To get good out of all things and all persons.
                                John Ruskin

To have the fraility of a man with the security of a god.   *Seneca*

A function of circumstances.
                        Ralph de Toledano

The dream of youth realized in old age.
                        Alfred de Vigny

SEE ALSO ARISTOCRACY, GENIUS, HEROISM, MINORITY, NOBILITY, SUPERIOR MAN.

GREECE

The Holy Land.   *Georg Brandes*

Sad relic of departed worth!   *Lord Byron*

Immortal, though no more: though fallen, great!
                                Lord Byron

'Tis haunted, holy ground.   *Lord Byron*

Freedom's home or Glory's grave!   *Lord Byron*

The first garden of Liberty's tree.
                            Thomas Campbell

From heroes to shopkeepers—that has been sad Greece's history.   *Max Gralnick*

The fountain of knowledge.   *Samuel Johnson*

GREED

SEE ALSO AVARICE, COVETOUSNESS, MISERLINESS.

GREEKS

Plausible rascals—with all the Turkish vices, without their courage.   *Lord Byron*

Of all the peoples, the Greeks have best dreamed the dream of life.   *Johann W. Goethe*

An actor.   *Juvenal*

One of the most excitable of the races of mankind.
                            John Stuart Mill

Little more than splendid savages.
                            Charles Sumner

GRIEF

An iron chain.   *Stephen Vincent Benét*

The instructor of the wise.   *Lord Byron*

Grief is itself a medicine.   *William Cowper*

The pleasure that lasts the longest.
                            Elbert Hubbard

The vice of weakness and the virtue of strength.
                            Elbert Hubbard

A divine and terrible radiance which transfigures the wretched.   *Victor Hugo*

A species of idleness.   *Samuel Johnson*

Nothing becomes offensive so quickly as grief. When fresh, it finds someone to console it, but when it becomes chronic, it is ridiculed, and rightly.   *Seneca*

Beauty's canker.   *William Shakespeare*

SEE ALSO SORROW, TEARS.

GROUCH

(One who) escapes so many little annoyances that it almost pays to be one.   *Kin Hubbard*

GROUP

An extension...of the original family situation.
                            Sigmund Freud

A group is best defined as a dynamic whole based on inter-dependence rather than on similarity.
                                Kurt Lewin

The group to which an individual belongs is the (psychological) ground on which he stands, which gives or denies him status...security and help.
                                Kurt Lewin

SEE ALSO COMMITTEE, SOCIETY.

GROWTH

A man's growth is seen in the successive choirs of his friends.   *Ralph Waldo Emerson*

Coherence capable of moving itself.   *Philo*

SEE ALSO MATURITY.

GUEST

One who hates the other guests, and the host hates them all.   *Albanian Proverb*

The first day a man is a guest, the second a burden, the third a pest.
                                Edward R. Laboulaye

A nuisance after three days in a friend's house.
                                                Plautus

(Those who) are often welcomest when they are gone.   *William Shakespeare*

Someone who begins to smell like a dead herring after three days.   *Adapted from Mark Twain*

A wise one is someone who arrives late but makes up for it by leaving early.   *Anon.*

GUILT

The guilty is he who merely meditates a crime.
                                        Vittorio Alfieri

Never a rational thing; it distorts all the faculties of the human mind, it perverts them, it leaves a man no longer in the free use of his reason, it puts him into confusion.   *Edmund Burke*

The natural reaction from behavior which contravenes the sense of right and wrong.
                                        J. Dominian

Specifically the response to repressed aggressiveness.   *Ernest Jones*

In law a man is guilty when he violates the rights of another. In ethics he is guilty if he only thinks of doing so.   *Immanuel Kant*

The source of sorrow, the avenging fiend that follows us behind with whips and stings.
                            Adapted from Nicholas Rowe

Guilt proceeds from the free will of the person who is reprobated and deserted by grace.
                                Saint Thomas Aquinas

The unfortunate circumstance that hangs people.
                                Robert Louis Stevenson

Guilty is what the man says when your luck runs out.   *Joseph Wambaugh*

Men's minds.   *Anon.*

SEE ALSO CONFESSION, CONSCIENCE, ORIGINAL SIN, SIN.

GUN

SEE ARMS, WAR.

H

HABEAS CORPUS

A writ by which a man may be taken out of jail when confined for the wrong crime.

Ambrose Bierce

The most stringent curb that ever legislation imposed on tyranny.   *Thomas B. Macaulay*

HABIT

(Acquiring) a particular quality by constantly acting in a particular way.   *Aristotle*

The source of all working ... apprenticeship ... practice ... learning in the world.

Thomas Carlyle

Something you can do without thinking—which is why most of us have so many of them.

Franklin Clark

The test of truth: It must be right, I've done it from my youth.   *Adapted from George Crabbe*

That beneficent harness of routine, which enables silly men to live respectable and happy men to live calmly.   *George Eliot*

(A chain that) coils itself around the heart like a serpent, to know and stifle it.   *William Hazlitt*

The approximation of the animal system to the organic. It is a confession of failure in the highest function of being, which involves a perpetual self-determination, in full view of all existing circumstances.   *Oliver Wendell Holmes 1*

The great economizer of energy.

Elbert Hubbard

Servants that regulate your sleep, your work and your thought.   *Elbert Hubbard*

(That which) converts luxurious enjoyments into dull and daily necessities.   *Aldous Huxley*

The enormous fly-wheel of society, its most precious conservative agent.   *Henry James*

What keeps us all within the bounds of ordinance.

William James

(Chains that are) too small to be felt till they are too strong to be broken.   *Samuel Johnson*

A cable. We weave a thread of it every day, and at last we cannot break it.   *Horace Mann*

First cobwebs, then chains.   *Spanish Proverb*

A thought—good or evil—an act, in time a habit—so runs life's law.   *Ralph W. Trine*

(Something which) makes everything, even love.

Luc de Vauvenargues

(That which) rules the unreflecting herd.

William Wordsworth

Armor that protects our nerve-force.   *Anon.*

SEE ALSO CUSTOM, TRADITION.

HAIR

The only thing that will really prevent baldness.

Drew Berkowitz

The most delicate and lasting of our materials.

Leigh Hunt

The beauty of women.   *Italian Proverb*

The finest ornament women can have.

Martin Luther

HAM (ACTOR)

Any actor who has not been successful in repressing his natural instincts.   *George Jean Nathan*

An actor who makes a fat line seem greasy.

Anon.

SEE ALSO ACTING, ACTOR.

HANDEL, GEORGE FREDERIC
(1685-1759)

Handel, to him I bow the knee.

Ludwig van Beethoven

Handel is so great and so simple that no one but a professional musician is unable to understand him.   *Samuel Butler*

(On composing The Messiah) I did think I did see all Heaven before me and the great God Himself.

George Frederic Handel

(On composing the Hallelujah Chorus) Whether I was in my body or out of my body as I wrote it I know not. God knows.

George Frederic Handel

He is the master of us all.   *Joseph Haydn*

HANGING

A necktie party.   *American Saying*

To kick the wind.   *John Florio*

To choke a poor scamp for the glory of God.

James Russell Lowell

The worst use a man can be put to.

Henry Wotton

SEE ALSO CAPITAL PUNISHMENT, EXECUTION.

HANGOVER

A dark brown taste, a burning thirst, a head that's ready to split and burst...not time for mirth, no time for laughter—the cold gray dawn of the morning after.   *Adapted from George Ade*

Something to occupy a head that wasn't used the night before.   *Howard W. Newton*

When the brew of the night meets the cold of the day.   *Anon.*

HAPPINESS

The quality of your thoughts.   *Marcus Aurelius*

Very little is needed...it is all within yourself, in your way of thinking.   *Marcus Aurelius*

Courage and work...energy, and above all...illusions.   *Honoré de Balzac*

This is the greatest happiness a man can feel—that he could be a partner with the Lord in creation...creative life, conquest of nature, and a great purpose.   *David Ben-Gurion*

To live with a purpose greater than yourself, and to see it slowly fulfilled with the passing years.

David Ben-Gurion

The end of human action.   *Jeremy Bentham*

He that keepeth the law, happy is he.

Bible: Proverbs, XXIX, 18.

Possessing what others can't get.   *Josh Billings*

(When one) is in red-hot pursuit of a dollar with a reasonable prospect of overtaking it.

Josh Billings

The greatest cosmetic for beauty.

Countess of Blessington

To admire without desiring.

Francis M. Bradley

Travel into a very far country, and even out of ourselves.   *Thomas Browne*

Enjoying the realities as well as the frivolities of life.   *Edward G. Bulwer-Lytton*

When a man can put on his shoes and go to work.

John Burnes

Happiness is but a name.   *Robert Burns*

To see that heaven lies about us here in this world.

John Burroughs

The absence of pain.   *Chinese Proverb*

The absence of the striving for happiness.

Chuang-Tse

Tranquility of mind.   *Cicero*

Made up of minute fractions...countless infinitesimals of pleasurable and genial feeling.

Samuel Taylor Coleridge

To find out what one is fitted to do and to secure an opportunity to do it.   *John Dewey*

Happiness is really found in giving and in serving others.   *Henry Drummond*

Consists largely in not wanting something that is out of your reach.   *Robert C. Edwards*

To fill the hour, and leave no crevice for a repentance or an approval.

Ralph Waldo Emerson

It is the chief point of happiness that a man is willing to be what he is.   *Erasmus*

To shut yourself up in art, and count everything else as nothing.   *Gustave Flaubert*

A good stomach and an evil heart.

Bernard de Fontenelle

What a man was born for.   *Jacob Frank*

Little advantages that occur every day.

Benjamin Franklin

(Something that) makes up in height for what it lacks in length.   *Robert Frost*

He is happy that knoweth not himself to be otherwise.   *Thomas Fuller*

A...life spent in learning, earning and yearning.

Lillian Gish

Consists in activity; such is the constitution of our nature: it is a running stream, and not a stagnant pool   *John M. Good*

A direction and not a place.   *Sydney J. Harris*

It is a method of life.   *Burton Hillis*

Forgetting self in usual effort.   *Elbert Hubbard*

It's pretty hard to tell what does bring happiness; poverty and wealth have both failed.

Kin Hubbard

The conviction that we are loved...in spite of ourselves.   *Victor Hugo*

Happiness is like coke—something you get as a by-product in the process of making something else.   *Aldous Huxley*

The sense of having worked according to one's capacity and light to make things clear and get rid of cant and shams.   *Thomas Henry Huxley*

The calm, glad certainty of innocence.

Henrik Ibsen

Happiness is not a reward—it is a consequence.

Robert G. Ingersoll

For most men at all times the secret motive of all they do, and of all they are willing to endure.

William James

To be not pained in body, nor troubled in mind.

Thomas Jefferson

Tranquility and occupation.   *Thomas Jefferson*

Consists in the multiplicity of agreeable consciousness. A peasant has not the capacity for having equal happiness with a philosopher.

Samuel Johnson

Consists not in having temporal things in abundance, but a moderate competency.

Thomas á Kempis

The full use of your powers along lines of excellence in a life affording scope.

John Fitzgerald Kennedy

Thinking of the welfare of others first, and not taking one's self too seriously.   *J. Kindleberger*

Happiness is in the taste, and not in the things themselves.   *La Rochefoucauld*

To know nothing.   *Latin Proverb*

Ease from pain.   *John Locke*

Happiness, to some elation;
Is to others, mere stagnation.   *Amy Lowell*

We must not look outside for happiness, but in ourselves, in our own minds. "The kingdom of God is within you."   *John Lubbock*

The art of relaxation.   *Maxwell Maltz*

A perfume which you cannot pour on others without getting a few drops on yourself.

Louis L. Mann

To struggle.   *Karl Marx*

The first requisite for the happiness of the people is the abolition of religion. *Karl Marx*

Friends, books, a cheerful heart, and a conscience clear. *William Mather*

Days...rigorously planned, nights left open to chance. *Mignon McLaughlin*

To be happy one must be (a) well fed, unhounded by sordid cares, at ease in Zion, (b) full of a comfortable feeling of superiority to the masses of one's fellow men, and (c) delicately and unceasingly amused according to one's taste.
Henry Louis Mencken

That pleasure that flows from the sense of virtue and from the consciousness of right deeds.
Henry Moore

To be very busy with the unimportant.
A. Edward Newton

The feeling that power increases—the resistance is being overcome. *Friedrich W. Nietzsche*

Happiness is a woman. *Friedrich W. Nietzsche*

No one is happy unless he is reasonably well satisfied with himself, so that the quest for tranquillity must of necessity begin with self-examination. *William S. Ogdon*

Absorption in some vocation which satisfies the soul. *William Osler*

The putting of one's self outside one's self into another self or personality.
Harry A. Overstreet

A by-product of an effort to make some one else happy. *Gretta Palmer*

Liking what we have to do. *Wilfred Peterson*

He truly possesses it who lives in the anticipation of honest fame, and the glorious figure he shall make in the eyes of posterity. *Pliny 2*

A way-station between two little and too much.
Channing Pollock

Health, peace, and competence.
Alexander Pope

A good bank account, a good cook, and a good digestion. *Jean-Jacques Rousseau*

A quiet life, for it is only in an atmosphere of quiet that true joy can live. *Bertrand A. Russell*

When we have peace, such little peace as can be had in a good life. *Saint Augustine*

Happiness lies in the consciousness we have of it, and by no means in the way the future keeps its promises. *George Sand*

To be out of jail. To eat and sleep regular. To get what I write printed in a free country for free people. To have a little love in the home and esteem outside the home. *Carl Sandburg*

The only sanction of life; where happiness fails, existence remains a mad and lamentable experience. *George Santayana*

Knowing that you do not need happiness.
William Saroyan

Not having what you want, but wanting what you have. *Hyman J. Schachtel*

Nothing more than freedom from suffering.
Arthur Schopenhauer

The only ones among you who will be really happy are those who will have sought and found how to serve. *Albert Schweitzer*

Not to have enough leisure to wonder whether you are happy or not. *George Bernard Shaw*

Being used for a purpose recognized by yourself as a mighty one. *George Bernard Shaw*

Essentially a state of going somewhere, wholeheartedly, one-directionally, without regret or reservation. *William H. Sheldon*

The ability to overlook. *Roy L. Smith*

The most powerful of tonics. *Herbert Spencer*

Happiness is added Life, and the giver of Life
Herbert Spencer

Little health,
Much wealth,
And a life by stealth. *Jonathan Swift*

The mastery of passions. *Alfred Lord Tennyson*

Consists in life, and life is in labor.
Leon Tolstoy

A Swedish sunset—it is there for all, but most of us look the other way and lose it. *Mark Twain*

Good friends, good books and a sleepy conscience. *Mark Twain*

Good habits, amiability, and forbearance.
Welsh Proverb

The grace of being permitted to unfold...all the spiritual powers planted within us.
Franz Werfel

A mental state aided by wine, women and tobacco.   *Anon.*

Enjoying doing and enjoying what is done.
                                              Anon.

Not what we have, but what we enjoy.   *Anon.*

Something to do, something to love, something to hope for.   *Anon.*

Success is getting what you want; happiness is wanting what you get.   *Anon.*

Getting what you want—not what you want others to think you want.   *Anon.*

Happiness is not created by what happens to us but by our attitude toward each happening.
                                              Anon.

A balance between what one is and what one has.
                                              Anon.

An outlook created by problem-solving.   *Anon.*

SEE ALSO FRIEND, FRIENDSHIP, HOPE, LAUGHTER, LOVE, MARRIAGE, PLEASURE, WISDOM.

HAT

A creation that will never go out of style; it will just look ridiculous year after year.   *Fred Allen*

The *ultimatum moriens* of respectability.
                                Oliver Wendell Holmes 1

HATRED

(A state that makes you) irritable, gloomy, and prematurely old.   *Berthold Auerbach*

Self-punishment.   *Hosea Ballou*

Darkness.   *Bible: John II, 11.*

An eternity withdrawn from love.
                                Ludwig Boerne

Medicine for the frustrated.
                                Eugene E. Brussell

The great cohesive among the frustrated.
                                Eugene E. Brussell

Madness of the heart.   *Lord Byron*

Inveterate anger.   *Cicero*

Burning down your own house to get rid of a rat.
                            Harry Emerson Fosdick

The greatest unilateral passion. It comes from you alone.   *Warren Goldberg*

The most accessible and comprehensive of all unifying agents.   *Eric Hoffer*

A habit.   *Elbert Hubbard*

A dark happiness.   *Victor Hugo*

The piquant sauce which accelerates both the swallowing and the digestion of ideas and policies.   *Vladimir Jabotinsky*

We must hate because hatred is Communism. Children must be taught to hate their parents if they are not Communists.   *Nikolai Lenin*

Always a clash between our spirit and someone else's body.   *Cesare Pavesé*

The cinders of affection.   *Walter Raleigh*

Our spiritual defeat and our likeness to what we hate.   *George W. Russell*

The coward's revenge for being intimidated.
                            George Bernard Shaw

Pain accompanied by the idea of an external cause.   *Baruch Spinoza*

A prolonged form of suicide.   *Douglas V. Steere*

Just a standing reproach to the hatred person, and owes all its meaning to a demand for love.
                                Ian Suttie

Life's fitful fever.   *Anon.*

The most sublime force in life. To love is to surrender; to hate is to carry on.   *Anon.*

SEE ALSO BIGOTRY, REVENGE.

HEAD

The dome of thought, the palace of the soul.
                            Adapted from Lord Byron

The dupe of the heart.   *La Rochefoucauld*

Majestic box! O wondrous can, from labels free!
                                Walter Mason

SEE ALSO BRAIN, MIND.

HEALTH

The thing that makes you feel that now is the best time of the year.   *Franklin P. Adams*

A man's own observation (of) what he finds good and what he finds hurt of.   *Francis Bacon*

The absence of disease, and...of all those kinds of pain which are among the symptoms of disease.   *Jeremy Bentham*

The beginning of health is to know the disease.
Miguel de Cervantes

Diet.   *A. B. Cheales*

Not a condition of matter, but of Mind.
Mary Baker Eddy

A sound mind in a manly body.   *Homer*

The blessings of the rich! The riches of the poor!
Ben Jonson

Simply a state in which the individual happens transiently to be perfectly adapted to his environment. Obviously such states cannot be common, for the environment is in constant flux.
Henry Louis Mencken

Objection, evasion, distrust and irony are signs of health.   *Friedrich W. Nietzsche*

An appropriate balance of the coordination of all of what we are.   *Frederick S. Perls*

To wish to be healthy is a part of being healthy.
Seneca

The sound body is a product of the sound mind.
George Bernard Shaw

Beauty, and the most perfect health is the most perfect beauty.   *William Shenstone*

The soul that animates all the enjoyments of life, which fade and are tasteless without it.
William Temple

To eat what you don't want, drink what you don't like and do what you'd rather not.   *Mark Twain*

A blessing that money cannot buy.   *Izaak Walton*

The one condition taken for granted by those who have it.   *Anon.*

SEE ALSO BODY, DIET, EXERCISE, MENTAL HEALTH.

HEARING

SEE EAR.

HEART

Where your treasure is, there will your heart be also.   *Bible: Matthew, VI, 21.*

An organ that grows hard quicker in riches than an egg boiling in water.   *Ludwig Boerne*

The place the Devil dwells in.   *Thomas Browne*

A brittle thing, and one false vow can break it.
Edward G. Bulwer-Lytton

The mirror of the things that are near and far.
Adapted from Alice Cary

It is the whole of women, who are guided by nothing else: and it has so much to say, even with men...that it triumphs in every struggle with the understanding.   *Lord Chesterfield*

The heart asks pleasure first,
And then, excuse from pain;
And then, those little anodynes
That deaden suffering.
And then, to go to sleep;
And then, if it should be
The will of its Inquisitor,
The liberty to die.   *Emily Dickinson*

A viper, hissing, and spitting poison at God.
Jonathan Edwards

The alarm watch, your pulse.   *Matthew Green*

The beginning of life...the household divinity which...nourishes, cherishes, quickens the whole body, and is indeed the foundation of life, the source of all action.   *William Harvey*

The great conservative.   *Nathaniel Hawthorne*

The heart of man is made to reconcile contradictions.   *David Hume*

May be compared to a wurst: no one can tell exactly what's inside.   *Jewish Saying*

A free and fetterless thing—a wave of the ocean, a bird on the wing.   *Henry Wadsworth Longfellow*

A millstone in a mill: when you put wheat under it, it turns and grinds and bruises the wheat to flour; if you put no wheat, it still grinds on, but then it is itself it grinds and wears away.
Martin Luther

The tabernacle of the human intellect.
Moses Maimonides

That abyss.   *Saint Augustine*

The most noble member of our body.
Saint John Chrysostom

A lonely hunter that hunts on a lonely hill.
William Sharp

The hearts of holy men are temples in the truth of things, and, in type and shadow, they are heaven itself.   *Jeremy Taylor*

The organ that sees better than the eye.
                                          Yiddish Proverb

A pump.   .   *Anon.*

HEATHEN

SEE PAGAN.

HEAVEN

The Holy of Holies, the dwelling of the Lord.
                          Apocrypha: Jubilees, VIII, 19.

The common conception . . . is that of . . . a kind of middle-class home, with goodness all around, the lost ones restored, hymnody incessant.
                                          Matthew Arnold

Where imperfection ceaseth, heaven begins.
                                          Philip J. Bailey

The glory of God.   *Bible: Psalms, XIX, 2.*

To be one with God.   *Confucius*

Who has not found the heaven below
   Will fail of it above.
God's residence is next to mine,
   His furniture is love.   *Emily Dickinson*

The happy land where they that love are blest.
                          Adapted from Frederick W. Faber

Fulfilled desire.   *Edward Fitzgerald*

The place where the donkey finally catches up with his carrot: hell is the eternity while he waits for it.   *Russell Green*

The better land.   *Felicia D. Hemans*

A quire of blest Souls circling in the Father.
                                          Robert Herrick

That glorious land above the sky.   *Joe Hill*

Largely a matter of digestion.   *Elbert Hubbard*

A penitential colony where the virtuous and the good are condemned to eternal fellowship for their stupidities uttered on earth.
                                          Elbert Hubbard

A place where one is permitted to continue one's . . . inanities for an eternity.
                                          Elbert Hubbard

To rest in God eternally . . . Indeed, Heaven has no meaning but that.   *Bede Jarrett*

A consciousness of the favor of God . . . the contemplation of truth . . . the possession of felicitating ideas.   *Samuel Johnson*

There is no place of toil, no burning heat, no piercing cold, nor any briars there . . . this place we call the Bosom of Abraham.
                                          Flavius Josephus

In the heaven-world there is no fear; thou art not there, O Death, and no one is afraid on account of old age. Leaving behind both hunger and thirst, and out of the reach of sorrow, all rejoice in the world of heaven.   *Katha Upanishad*

The vision of fulfilled desire.   *Omar Khayyám*

Only metaphors for the agony of sin and the happiness of virtue.   *Kaufman Kohler*

Gardens and vineyards
Damsels with swelling breasts . . .
And a brimming cup.   *Mahomet, Sara, 78*

A fair blue stretch of sky.   *John Masefield*

Heaven is to believe in it.   *Catulle Mendés*

There is a world above
   Where parting is unknown;
A whole eternity of love,
   Form'd for the good alone.

                                          James Montgomery

It will fit in any space you give to it . . . So broad— it takes in all things true; so narrow—it can hold but you.   *Adapted from John R. Moreland*

Heaven is our heritage
Earth but a player's stage.   *Thomas Nashe*

(What) every beloved object is the center of.
                                          Novalis

The next world.   *Plautus*

Nothing else than the well-ordered society of those who enjoy the vision of God.
                                          Saint Thomas Aquinas

The perfectly ordered and harmonious enjoyment of God, and of one another in God.
                                          Saint Augustine

Eating *foie gras* to the sound of trumpets.
                                          Sydney Smith

The land that ends our dark uncertain travel.
                                          Edmund C. Stedman

Heaven is such that all who have lived well, of whatever religion, have a place there.

Emanuel Swedenborg

Heaven is doing good from good-will; hell is doing evil from ill-will.   *Emanuel Swedenborg*

In heaven there is no eating, drinking, propagation, business, jealousy, hatred or competition, but the righteous sit, with their crowns on their heads, enjoying the brilliance of the Divine Presence.   *Talmud: Berakot, 17a.*

Might be defined as the place which men avoid.

Henry David Thoreau

There is a land of pure delight,
  Where saints immortal reign;
Infinite day excludes the night,
  And pleasures banish pain.   *Isaac Watts*

'Tis like a little heaven below.   *Isaac Watts*

A small American community composed of white Anglo-Saxon Protestants.   *Anon.*

SEE ALSO DEATH, JUDGMENT DAY, RESURRECTION, SOUL.

HEBREWS

SEE JEWS.

HEBREW LANGUAGE

(A language which) has about thirty words to express justice and humanity, but not a single one for slave.   *Joseph S. Bloch*

The tongue of God, the tongue of angels, the tongue of the prophets.   *Johann Buxtorf*

A shield against assimilation in all its forms.

Isaac H. Herzog

The original tongue of mankind.

Dunash Ibn Tamin

The beginning of all human speech.

Father Jerome

"The middle bar" which embraces all the scattered children of Israel.   *Moses Luzzatto*

The golden hinge upon which our national and religious existence turns.   *Sabato Morais*

The Hebrew language has been set apart by God as the receptacle of truths destined to sway mankind and humanize the world.   *Sabato Morais*

The language in whiich God, angels and men spoke together . . . as friends talk face to face.

Johannes Reuchlin

Primarily a language of the senses . . . There is a prevalence . . . of the harder, heavier consonants.

George A. Smith

SEE ALSO JEWS, JUDAISM.

HEIR

He who gets what's left.   *Leonard L. Levinson*

One whose tears are masked laughter.

Publilius Syrus

One who is always suspected and disliked.

Anon.

HELL

A place where there are no fans.

Arabian Proverb

The home of incurables.   *J. P. Arendzen*

A mass-production factory.   *Wystan H. Auden*

Hell is the wrath of God—His hate of sin.

Philip J. Bailey

Where their worm dies not, and the fire is not quenched.   *Bible: Mark, IX, 44.*

Present pain of mind, spiritual torment which neither sleep nor time nor any distraction can alleviate.   *R. V. Bodley*

A lake of fire and brimstone whose flame are unquenchable, and whose smoke ascendeth up forever and ever.   *Book of Mormon, 1830.*

A vast, unbottom'd, boundless pit.

Robert Burns

The religion of Hell is patriotism, and the government is an enlightened democracy.

James Branch Cabell

The suffering of being unable to love.

Fëdor M. Dostoievski

Hell is truth seen too late—duty neglected in its season.   *Tryon Edwards*

Hell is oneself. Hell is alone, and the other figures in it merely projections. There is nothing to escape from and nothing to escape to. One is always alone.   *Thomas Stearns Eliot*

The final desolation of solitude in the phantasmal world of imagination, shuffling memories, and desires. *Thomas Stearns Eliot*

A half-filled auditorium *Robert Frost*

To begin over and over again the tasks left unfinished in your lifetime. *André Gide*

A place paved with women's tongues.

Abbé Guyon

No other but a soundless pit, where no one beam of comfort peeps in.

Adapted from Robert Herrick

The place where whipping-cheer abounds, but no jailer there to wash the wounds.

Adapted from Robert Herrick

An ancient conflagration that was checked when Voltaire invented the asbestos intellect.

Elbert Hubbard

Fashioning our characters in the wrong way.

William James

God's penitentiary. *Charles Jaynes*

Failure in a great object. *John Keats*

The Shadow from a Soul on fire.

Omar Khayyam

A fire that flames! None shall broil there, but the most wretched, who says it a lie and turns his back. But the pious shall be kept away from it.

Koran.

A circle about the unbelieving. *Koran.*

Profound abyss of utter misery—into the depths of which bad men shall fall headlong and mourn their doom for countless years. *Mahabharata*

Hell is when you're dumb. Hell is when you're a slave. Hell is when you don't have freedom and when you don't have justice. And when you don't have equality, that's hell. *Malcolm X*

All places shall be hell that are not heaven.

Christopher Marlowe

Every man is his own hell.

Henry Louis Mencken

Hell begins on the day when God grants us a clear vision of all that we might have achieved, of all the gifts which we have wasted, of all that we might have done which we did not do. For me, the conception of hell lies in two words: "too late."

Gian-Carlo Menotti

A dungeon horrible on all sides round.

John Milton

Torture without end. *John Milton*

Myself am Hell. *John Milton*

The place where the satisfied compare disappointments. *Philip Moeller*

The idea of eternal punishment. *John Morley*

A brimstone sea of boiling fire.

Francis Quarles

The infliction of cruelty with a good conscience is a delight to moralists. That is why they invented Hell. *Bertrand A. Russell*

A city involved in darkness, burning with brimstone and stinking pitch, and full of inhabitants who cannot make their escape.

Saint Francis de Sales

Hell is other people. *Jean-Paul Sartre*

A place where you have nothing to do but amuse yourself . . . the paradise of the worthless.

George Bernard Shaw

The ego, sated with its own satisfied wishes, having to consume itself forever with no hope of release. *Fulton J. Sheen*

Hell is a city much like London.

Percy Bysshe Shelley

Self-love and the love of the world.

Emanuel Swedenborg

The despair of accursed souls. *Jeremy Taylor*

Nothing but self-will, and if there were no self-will there would be no Devil and no hell.

Theologica Germanica.

Where sinners must with devils dwell in darkness, fire, and chains.

Adapted from Isaac Watts

Lack of something to feel important about.

Anon.

SEE ALSO DAMNATION, DEMONS, DEVIL, JUDGMENT DAY, SIN.

HEN

A foul way of laying around and making money.

Paulette Brussell

An egg's way of making another egg.

Samuel Butler 2

SEE ALSO EGG.

HEREDITY

Nothing but stored environment.

Luther Burbank

The thing a child gets from the other side of the family.   *Marceline Cox*

Congenital predisposition.   *Sigmund Freud*

Acquired qualities . . . transmitted to descendants.
Sigmund Freud

Our reanimated ancestors.   *Joseph Glanvill*

A legacy of traits.   *Warren Goldberg*

The road travelled by genes.   *Warren Goldberg*

An omnibus in which all our ancestors ride, and every now and then one of them puts his head out and embarrasses us.   *Oliver Wendell Holmes 1*

Not only what we have inherited from our fathers that exists in us again, but all sorts of old dead ideas and . . . old dead beliefs.   *Henrik Ibsen*

The tenth transmitter of a foolish face.

Richard Savage

Something everyone believes in until his children start acting like fools.   *Anon.*

Something you believe in when you child's grades are good.   *Anon.*

SEE ALSO ANCESTRY.

HERESY

The great hearesy in the world of religion is a cold heart, not a luminous head.

Henry Ward Beecher

The dislocation of some complete and self-supporting scheme by the introduction of a novel denial of some essential part therein.

Hilaire Belloc

Strange doctrines.   *Bible: Hebrews, XIII, 9.*

Whosoever transgresseth, and abideth not in the doctrine of Christ.   *Bible: John, 1, 9.*

The over-confident . dogmatic assumption that men, themselves . . . are in a position to know all about God.   *J. V. Casserley*

That the office sanctifies the holder of it.

John E. Dalberg

The law knows no heresy.

*Decision of the Supreme Court,
Watson vs. Jones, Dec., 1871.*

To believe that we have reached finality and can settle down with a completed system.

Harry Emerson Fosdick

Only another word for freedom of thought.

Graham Greene

A refutation of that which is.   *Warren Goldberg*

A form of spiritual treason.   *Warren Goldberg*

An act of the will, not of reason, and is indeed a lie, not a mistake.   *John Hales*

The school of pride.   *George Herbert*

No more than private opinion.   *Thomas Hobbes*

What the minority believe; it is the name given by the powerful to the doctrines of the weak.

Robert G. Ingersoll

Consists not in teaching actual error, but in the failure to teach all the truth that there is to be known.   *Franklin J. Sheed*

What's up is faith, what's down is heresy.

Alfred Lord Tennyson

An attack on the divinity of the divine. It gives to something finite infinite validity.   *Paul Tillich*

Experiments in man's unsatisfied search for truth.
Herbert G. Wells

An unconventional by-product of exuberance.

Anon.

SEE ALSO AGNOSTICISM, ATHEISM, FREE THINKERS, PAGAN.

HERETIC

Those who speak of worldly and religious matters as though they were distinct.

Israel Baal Shem Tob

A peculiar and highly pronounced representative of ecclesiasticism, who is possessed by a desire to cut an exclusive ecclesiastical figure and to be alone in the right with regard to the religious truth he professes.   *Nicholas Berdyaev*

A Christian in Constantinople.   *Ambrose Bierce*

A fellow who disagrees with you regarding something neither of you knows anything about.
William C. Brann

The less numerous party.   *Edward Gibbon*

The only real . . . heretics are the purely selfish.
Wilfred T. Grenfell

An impugner of fundamentals.
Thomas Jefferson

A man who wishes to see with his own eyes. The only question is whether he has good eyes.
Georg E. Lessing

Every human being at those moments of his life when he resigns momentarily from the herd and thinks for himself.   *Archibald MacLeish*

Too often . . . a tender-hearted advocate of spiritual first aid.   *Vincent McNabb*

A man may be a heretic in the truth; and if he believes things only because his pastor says so . . . without knowing other reason, though his belief be true, yet the very truth he holds becomes his heresy.   *John Milton*

(Those who) do away with the true doctrine of the Lord, not interpreting and transmitting the Scriptures agreeably to the dignity of God.
Saint Clement

Mad dogs, biting secretly.   *Saint Ignatius*

A viperous worm.   *William Shakespeare*

Among theologians . . . those who are not backed with a sufficient array of battalions to render them orthodox.   *Voltaire*

SEE ALSO ATHEIST, PAGAN.

HERITAGE

Scriptures . . . which have become absorbed into our blood.   *Sholom Asch*

(Something) we receive with our life the mind of centuries.   *Berthold Auerbach*

The sanctuaries of God.   *Judah Halevi*

All of the positive past values that hold a civilization together.   *Robert Zwickey*

SEE ALSO CIVILIZATION, CULTURE, TRADITION.

HERMIT

A person whose vices and follies are not sociable.
Abrose Bierce

Anyone without an automobile.   *Anon.*

HERO

Men . . . who take hold of . . . circumstances, force them upon their own actions and personalities, and transforms them along the lines of their own dreams.   *Tawfig Al-Hakim*

(Those) who give us a far view into the realm of the spirit.   *Berthold Auerbach*

The world-man in whose heart one passion stands for all.   *Adapted from Philip J. Bailey*

The hero . . . is "sincere" and does his "duty", i.e., he acts intuitively, without interference of mechanical philosophies or restrictive codes.
Eric Bentley

The man who conquers his senses.
Bhartrihari: the Niti Sataka.

Mighty men of valour.   *Bible: Joshua, VI, 2.*

Essential men.   *Elizabeth Barrett Browning*

Essentially a dissatisfied person thirsting for glory. The contented do not voluntarily seek adventurous tasks.   *Eugene E. Brussell*

The great thinker . . . the original man, the seer; whose shaped spoken thought awakes the slumbering capability of all into thought.
Thomas Carlyle

He who lives in the inward sphere of things, in the True, Divine and Eternal, which exists always, unseen to most, under the Temporary, Trivial: his being is in that.   *Thomas Carlyle*

A God-created soul which will be true to its origin.   *Thomas Carlyle*

The Hero can be a Poet, Prophet, King, Priest or what you will, according to the kind of world he finds himself born into.   *Thomas Carlyle*

I am convinced that a light supper, a good night's sleep, and a fine morning, have sometimes made a hero of the same man, who, by an indigestion, a restless night, and rainy morning, would have proved a coward.   *Lord Chesterfield*

To believe in the heroic makes heroes.
Benjamin Disraeli

The memory of a great name, and the inheritance of a great example.   *Benjamin Disraeli*

(Those who) exterminate each other for the benefit of people who are not heroes.   *Havelock Ellis*

A hero is no braver than an ordinary man, but he is brave five minutes longer.

Ralph Waldo Emerson

The hero is not fed on sweets,
Daily his own heart he eats.

Ralph Waldo Emerson

One who is afraid to run away.   *English Proverb*

Some are even three men—the actual man, the image, and the debunked remains.

Esther Forbes

Not men of battle, but men of faith.

Moses Gaster

Clear-sighted ones; their deeds, their words are the best of the period. Heroes have formed purposes to satisfy themselves, not others.

Georg W. Hegel

He who despises this world, and a weakling is he who honors it.   *Moses Ibn Ezra*

(Those) created by popular demand, sometimes out of the scantiest materials.

Gerald White Johnson

A man who has fought impressively for a cause of which we approve.   *Dumas Malone*

The man who really stands up and is counted, ethically, morally and humanly, and so becomes larger than himself.   *Marya Mannes*

The ordinary man is involved in action. The hero acts. An immense difference.   *Henry Miller*

Who is a hero? He who conquers his will.

Mishna: Abot, IV, 1.

One who believes that all women are ladies, whereas a villain believes that all ladies are women.   *Adapted from George Jean Nathan*

A being of angry greatness, with the bravest eye and the keenest will.   *Friedrich W. Nietzche*

The man who establishes values and controls the wills of epochs.   *Friedrich W. Nietzsche*

The man of action who strips from himself and from others habits which have lasted thousands of years and sets a better example for posterity to follow.   *Friedrich W. Nietzsche*

One who knows how to hang on one minute longer.   *Norwegian Proverb*

The shortest lived profession on earth.

Will Rogers

One who thinks slower than a coward.

William Rotsler

The person who has the courage to make a good thing of his whole life.   *Georges Simenon*

Who'er excels in what we prize.   *Jonathan Swift*

Those who do not feel the impotence of man.

Paul Valéry

One who enters a battle feat first.   *Anon.*

SEE ALSO BRAVERY, GREAT MEN, HEROISM, SUPERIOR MAN.

HEROISM

Unbounded courage and compassion joined.

Joseph Addison

The compliance of history, the coming together of special events and situations with unusual men.

Tawfig Al-Hakim

The brillian triumph of the soul over the flesh ... over fear: fear of poverty, of suffering, of calumny, of sickness, of isolation, and of death.

Henry F. Amiel

The dazzling and glorious concentration of courage.   *Henry F. Amiel*

An urge which seems to compel.

George Bernanos

To stand held only by the invisible chains of higher duty, and, so standing, to let the fire creep up to the heart.   *Phillips Brooks*

The experience of despair transformed into victory by a conscious effort of the will.

Eugene E. Brussell

The divine relation which ... unites a great man to other men.   *Thomas Carlyle*

To arrive at a point in history when the only gift you have to offer has suddenly become relevant.

Quentin Crisp

A heroic act measured by its contempt for some external good.   *Ralph Waldo Emerson*

Self-trust is the essence.   *Ralph Waldo Emerson*

The charateristic of...heroism is its persistency...The heroic cannot be the common, nor the common heroic.   *Ralph Waldo Emerson*

Active genius...the self-devotion of genius manifesting itself in action.
                              Julius and Augustus Hare

To resist the doubt, and the...wisdom to know when it ought to be resisted, and when obeyed.
                              Nathaniel Hawthorne

It is always either doing or dying.
                              Roswell D. Hitchcock

(Proving) to ourselves and others that we are not what we and they thought we were.   *Eric Hoffer*

When honor scorns to compromise with death.
                              Robert G. Ingersoll

To make heroic decisions and to be prevented by "circumstances beyond your control" from even trying to execute them.   *William James*

Endurance for one moment more.
                              George Kennan

Consists in being superior to the ills of life in whatever shape they may challenge you to combat.
                              Napoleon 1

(Deeds) which are performed within four walls and in domestic privacy.   *Jean Paul Richter*

Ambition and vanity.   *Seneca*

Not giving a damn before witnesses.   *Anon.*

SEE ALSO BRAVERY, COURAGE, GREAT MEN, GREATNESS, HERO, NOBILITY, SUPERIOR MAN.

HERO-WORSHIP

Transcendent admiration of a great man.
                              Thomas Carlyle

(That which) gives the masses models of mankind that tend to lift humanity above the commonplace manners of ordinary life.   *Donn Piatt*

HIGHBROW

A seeker and sustainer of all that is excellent in the world.   *Myron Byrne*

The kind of a person who looks at a sausage and thinks of Picasso.   *Alan P. Herbert*

A person who has grown so wise that the obvious escapes him.   *Elbert Hubbard*

One who reveres knowledge with superstitious awe.   *Elbert Hubbard*

A person who...often believes that a good book is bad.   *Robert Lynd*

A person educated beyond his intelligence.
                              Brander Matthews

A man who has found something more interesting than women.   *Edgar Wallace*

SEE ALSO INTELLECTUAL, PEDANT.

HISTORIAN

Historians undertake to arrange sequences,—called stories, or histories—assuming in silence a relation of cause and effect.   *Henry B. Adams*

The true office...to represent the events themselves...and to leave the observations and conclusions thereupon to the liberty and faculty of every man's judgment.   *Francis Bacon*

A broad-gauge gossip.   *Ambrose Bierce*

(One who) must be precise, faithful...unprejudiced; and neither interest nor fear, hatred nor affection, should make him swerve from the way of truth.   *Miguel de Cervantes*

(One who) must have some conception of how men who are not historians behave.
                              Edward M. Forster

Historians relate, not so much what is done, as what they would have believed.
                              Benjamin Franklin

The first quality...is to be true and impartial; the next to be interesting.   *David Hume*

Every great writer.   *Walter Savage Landor*

(He who) can see the nobler meaning of events that are near him.   *James Russell Lowell*

A man of independence, loving frankness and truth.   *Lucian*

An impartial judge, giving each side all it deserves but no more. He should know in his writings no country and no city; he should bow to no authority and acknowledge no king.   *Lucian*

An unsuccessful novelist.
                              Henry Louis Mencken

The historian's first duties are sacrilege and the mocking of false gods. They are his indispensable instruments for establishing the truth.

Jules Michelet

One who looks backward and in the end believes backward. *Friedrich W. Nietzsche*

A noble employment to rescue from oblivion those who deserve to be remembered, and by extending the reputation of others, to advance at the same time our own. *Pliny 2*

A prophet in retrospect. *August W. von Schlegel*

The historian reports to us, not events themselves, but the impressions they have made on him.

Heinrich von Sybel

An editor of yesterday's news. *Anon.*

A sort of talking ghost from out of the past.

Anon.

HISTORY

To get behind men and grasp ideas. *Lord Acton*

A sort of mask, richly colored.

John Quincy Adams

The sum total of things that could have been avoided. *Konrad Adenauer*

That which is written by the victor.

Adapted from Maxwell Anderson

That huge Mississippi of falsehood.

Matthew Arnold

Petrified imagination. *Arthur Baer*

The mere scum of events. *Walter Bagehot*

A record of the gradual negation of man's original bestiality by the evolution of his humanity.

Mikhail A. Bakunin

A series of accepted judgments.

Geoffrey Barraclough

Not that which men do worthily, but that which they do successfully. *Henry Ward Beecher*

Economic facts are...the chief points in the process of history. *Edward Bernstein*

An account mostly false...which is brought about by rulers mostly knaves, and soldiers mostly fools. *Ambrose Bierce*

The great dust heap. *Augustine Birrell*

A piece of paper covered with print; the main thing is still to make history, not to write it.

Otto von Bismarck

The record of the periodical crusades for or against some bogey which believing men have evolved out of their credulity or fear.

Ernest Boyd

The result of exceptional men willing themselves in desired directions. *Eugene E. Brussell*

The record of that which one age finds worthy of note in another. *Jacob Burckhardt*

Dialogue between God and man-in-pilgrimage in the language of Event; and Christ is...the key to the translation. *George A. Buttrick*

The sum total of...successive rebellions.

Albert Camus

A mighty drama, enacted upon the theatre of time, with suns for lamps and eternity for a background. *Thomas Carlyle*

The essence of innumerable biographies.

Thomas Carlyle

A distillation of rumor. *Thomas Carlyle*

Distilled newspapers. *Thomas Carlyle*

The only real poetry...could we tell it right.

Thomas Carlyle

The first distinct product of man's spiritual nature; his earliest expression of what can be called Thought. *Thomas Carlyle*

A confused heap of facts. *Lord Chesterfield*

History is a sacred kind of writing, because truth is essential to it, and where truth is, there God himself is. *Miguel de Cervantes*

The witness of the times...the messenger of antiquity. *Cicero*

Little more than a graveyard in which one reads the epitaphs of buried states. *Edgar Cowan*

The record of an encounter between character and circumstance. *Donald Creighton*

Philosophy teaching by examples. *Dionysius*

An endless repetition of the wrong way of living.

Lawrence Durrell

A pattern of timeless moments.
Thomas Stearns Eliot

A record of the power of minorities, and of minorities of one. *Ralph Waldo Emerson*

All history resolves itself very easily into the biography of a few stout and earnest persons.
Ralph Waldo Emerson

Class struggles, of struggles between dominated and dominating classes at various stages of social development. *Friedrich Engels*

History deals with the irregular effects of the passions and caprices of men.
Bernard de Fontenelle

Bunk. *Henry Ford*

Essentially a series of race murders.
Sigmund Freud

A voice forever sounding across the centuries the laws of right and wrong. *James A. Froude*

The unrolled scroll of prophecy.
James A. Garfield

A relay race in which each of us, before dropping in his tracks, must carry one stage further the challenge of being a man. *Romain Gary*

The history of the world is only the opinion of the world. *German Proverb*

An argument without end. *Pieter Geyl*

Little more than the register of crimes, follies, and misfortunes of mankind. *Edward Gibbon*

An absurd happening into which more or less gifted people attempt to introduce some perspective. *Günter Grass*

The study of other people's mistakes.
Philip Guedalla

The progress of the consciousness of freedom.
Georg W. Hegel

God governs the world; the actual working of His government—the carrying out of His plan—is the History of the World. *Georg W. Hegel*

History is all improvisation, all will, all extempore—there are no frontiers. *Alexander Herzen*

Made by men who have the restlessness, impressionability, credulity, capacity for make-believe, ruthlessness, and self-righteousness of children.
Eric Hoffer

(Something) usually played by the best and the worst over the heads of the majority in the middle.
Eric Hoffer

One long record of giving revolution another trial, and limping back at last to sanity, safety, and work. *Edgar W. Howe*

Gossip well told. *Elbert Hubbard*

A collection of epitaphs. *Elbert Hubbard*

A branch of speculation, connected (often rather arbitrarily and uneasily) with certain facts about the past. *Aldous Huxley*

Events which do not matter and events which probably never occurred. *William R. Inge*

A register of the crimes and miseries that man has inflicted on his fellow man. *Washington Irving*

Ideas are...forces. Infinite, too, is the power of personality. A union of the two always makes history. *Henry James*

History...only informs us what bad government is. *Thomas Jefferson*

The knowledge which gives dimension to the present, direction to the future, and humility to the leaders of men. *Lyndon Baines Johnson*

A narrative of misery. *Samuel Johnson*

The making of man. *Mordecai M. Kaplan*

The works of man. *John Keats*

Determined not by what happens in the skies, but by what takes place in the hearts of men.
Arthur Keith

A logical whole which unfolds step by step under the guidance of inexorable laws.
Ferdinand Lassalle

The visible effects of invisible changes in human thought. *Gustave Lebon*

The record of a man in quest of his daily bread and butter. *Henrik van Loon*

Clarified experience. *James Russell Lowell*

The story of the magnificent rearguard action fought during several thousand years by dogma against curiosity. *Robert Lynd*

A compound of poetry and philosophy.
Thomas B. Macaulay

Not what happened but what people thought or said about it. *Frederic W. Maitland*

The histories of mankind...are histories only of the higher classes.   *Thomas R. Malthus*

Class struggles.   *Karl Marx*

Nothing but the activity of man in pursuit of his ends.   *Karl Marx*

That excited and deceitful old woman!

Guy de Maupassant

The course of life is like the sea; men come and go; tides rise and fall; and that is all of history.

Adapted from Joaquin Miller

Invention.   *Catherine Morland*

A fraud agreed upon.   *Napoleon 1*

Centuries of systematic exploration of the riddle of death, with a view of overcoming death.

Boris Pasternak

A people's memory.   *Isaac Peretz*

The crystallization of popular beliefs.

Donn Piatt

The record of the follies of the majority.

Lindsay Rogers

The category of human phenomena which tends to catastrophe.   *Jules Romains*

An attempt to seize occurrences in their pattern.

Leon Roth

To see...a moral purpose and a task for a people on earth.   *Jacob Singer*

That terrible mill in which sawdust rejoins sawdust.   *Edith Sitwell*

The incessant conflict between liberty and authority.   *Charles T. Spradling*

To prevent virtuous actions from being forgotten, and that evil words and deeds should fear an infamous reputation with posterity.   *Tacitus*

A view of events as they really happened, and as they are very likely...to repeat themselves at some future time—if not exactly the same, yet very similar.   *Thucydides*

A collection of fables and useless trifles.

Leon Tolstoy

Consists of a series of encounters between individual human beings and God in which each man or woman or child...is challenged by God to make his free choice between doing God's will and refusing to do it.   *Arnold J. Toynbee*

A vision of the whole universe on the move in the four-dimensional framework of space-time

Arnold J. Toynbee

The science of what never happens twice.

Paul Valéry

Only a picture of human crimes and misfortunes.

Voltaire

A list of those who have accommodated themselves with the property of others.   *Voltaire*

A recital of mistakes.   *Voltaire*

In essence...ideas.

Herbert G. Wells

A race between education and catastrophe.

Herbert G. Wells

Human history is similar to the heroic tales pigs relate of swine.   *Welsh Proverb*

The progress of thought.

Alfred North Whitehead

Merely gossip.   *Oscar Wilde*

Those old credulities.   *William Wordsworth*

Legend and romance.   *Thomas Wright*

History is what the historian thinks the past was.

Robert Zwickey

The propaganda of the victorious.   *Anon.*

What enables each nation to use the other fellow's past record as an alibi.   *Anon.*

A hard core of interpretation surrounded by a pulp of disputable facts.   *Anon.*

Facts that never happened, written by ghosts.

Anon.

HISTORY WRITING

The science of human degradation.

Henry B. Adams

Living half in a cemetery.   *Aristide Briand*

A way of getting rid of the past.

Johann W. Goethe

Sin writes histories, goodness is silent.

Johann W. Goethe

At present a disease of the self-appointed elite of the educated.   *Eric Hoffer*

The old man's business of looking back and casting up his accounts, of seeking consolation in the memories of the past.

Friedrich W. Nietzsche

(Something that) always needs to be rewritten.

George Santayana

History is past politics and politics present history.

John Seeley

Opinions rather than actual events.

Baruch Spinoza

Merely fluid prejudice.

Mark Twain

A most unprofitable trade.

John Wolcot

HOBBY

(That which) puts to work those unused talents which might otherwise become restless, and it provides us with a form of activity in which there is no need whatever to strive for success.

Hal Falvey

Hard work one wouldn't do for a living. *Anon.*

HOLE

Nothing at all, but you can break your leg in it.

Austin O'Malley

HOLIDAY

Overrated disturbances of routine, costly and uncomfortable, and...in need of another holiday to correct the ravages. *Edward Lucas*

(A time which) promotes the good feeling that men should have toward each other in their social and political relations. *Moses Maimonides*

Occasions for social intercourse. *Joseph Saadia*

A good working definition of hell.

George Bernard Shaw

A day when father works twice as hard as he does at the office. *Anon.*

HOLINESS

Everything created by God.

Israel Baal Shem Tob

Everything that lives. *William Blake*

A sweet, pleasant, charming, serene, calm nature.

Jonathan Edwards

To have friends whose lives we can elevate or depress by our influences.

Harry Emerson Fosdick

Religious principle put into action. It is faith gone to work. It is love coined into conduct.

Frederick D. Huntington

A primal reality as the individual feels impelled to respond to solemnly and gravely, and neither by a curse nor a jest. *William James*

The merest gesture...if it is filled with faith.

Franz Kafka

The perfect accordance of the will to the moral law...a perfection of which no rational being ... is capable of at any moment of his existence.

Immanuel Kant

The essence of all moral perfection.

Kaufmann Kohler

Consists in use and practice.

Martin Luther

The "wholly other" transcending all worldly values. *I. Maybaum*

A holy person is one who is sanctified by the presence and action of God within him.

Thomas Merton

A fire whose outgoing warmth pervades the Universe. *Plotinus*

Holiness comes by holy deeds, not by starving flesh of daily needs. *Shaikh Saadi*

The architectural plan upon which God buildeth up His living temple. *Charles H. Spurgeon*

"Holy" has the same root as "wholly"; it means complete. A man is not complete in spiritual stature if all his mind, heart, soul, strength are not given to God. *R. J. Stewart*

SEE ALSO CHRIST, DEEDS, PIETY, SABBATH, SAINT.

HOLLAND

A country that draws fifty foot of water, in which men live as in the hold of nature.

Samuel Butler 1

A land that rides at anchor, and is moor'd.

Samuel Butler 1

The water-land of Dutchman and of ditches.

Lord Byron

God made the ocean, but the Dutch made Holland.   *Dutch Proverb*

Where the broad ocean leans against the land.

Oliver Goldsmith

Proof of what man can create on the most thankless soil.   *Theodor Herzl*

The very cockpit of Christendom.

James Howell

A country naturally cold, moist, and unpleasant.

William Petty

HOLLYWOOD

A place where people from Iowa mistake each other for movie stars.   *Fred Allen*

Being nowhere and talking to nobody about it.

Michelangelo Antonioni

Where great-grandmothers dread to grow old.

Phyllis Battelle

A place where you can get along by knowing two words—swell and lousy.   *Vicki Baum*

A place where your best friend will plunge a knife in your back and then call the police to tell them that you are carrying a concealed weapon.

George Frazier

The only place...where you can go to a formal dinner dressed for a picnic and feel thoroughly at ease.   *William Gargan*

An emotional Detroit.   *Lillian Gish*

The Holy Grail of the nineteen-thirties and forties.   *Warren Goldberg*

A place which builds beautiful cans without sardines.   *Max Gralnick*

A place where the stars employ doubles to do all their dangerous jobs for them, excepting marriage.   *Thomas Jenk*

A place where everyone is a genius until he loses his job.   *Erskine Johnson*

Strip away the phony tinsel (and) you can find the real tinsel underneath.   *Oscar Levant*

A place where the inmates are in charge of the asylum.   *Edward MacNamara*

The town where inferior people have a way of making superior people feel inferior.

Dudley F. Malone

A gold rush in dinner jackets.   *Boris Morros*

A place where you spend more than you make, on things you don't need, to impress people you don't like.   *Kenneth Murray*

Ten million dollars worth of intricate and high ingenious machinery functioning elaborately to put skin on baloney.   *George Jean Nathan*

The place bad guys go when they die.

George Jean Nathan

A dreary industrial town controlled by hoodlums of enormous wealth, the ethical sense of a pack of jackels, and taste so degraded that it befouled everything it touched.   *Sidney J. Perelman*

(A place) full of people that learned to write but evidently can't read.   *Will Rogers*

An extraordinary kind of temporary place.

John Schlesinger

There are two Hollywoods: the Hollywood where people live and work, and the Hollywood which lives in the mind of the public like a fabulous legend.   *Leo C. Rosten*

A state of mind surrounded by Los Angeles.

Morton Thompson

A town where they place you under contract instead of observation.   *Walter Winchell*

A place where they shoot too many pictures and not enough actors.   *Walter Winchell*

The place where blood is thicker than talent.

Anon.

A place where a grand opening can be anything from a new movie to a new grave.   *Anon.*

A warm Siberia.   *Anon.*

SEE ALSO MOVIE, MOVIE-FAN.

HOLLYWOOD PRODUCER

An ulcer with authority.   *Fred Allen*

A person who gets too much credit if a show is good and too much blame if it's bad.   *Fred Coe*

An executive who wears a worried look on his assistant's face.   *Leonard L. Levinson*

A fellow who found it more profitable to sell ham on film than ham on rye. *Bert Lytell*

HOLY

SEE HOLINESS.

HOME

A place where you can scratch any place you itch. *Henry Ainsley*

An instrument for measuring the degree of civilization a people has attained. *Moritz Alsberg*

Any old place I hang my hat. *American Saying*

The place of last resort, open all night. *Ambrose Bierce*

The one wild place in the world of rules and set tasks. *Gilbert Keith Chesterton*

A school of power. *Ralph Waldo Emerson*

The place where, when you go there, they have to take you in. *Robert Frost*

Something you somehow haven't to deserve. *Robert Frost*

Where we love is home. *Oliver Wendell Holmes 1*

A place we go to change our clothes so as to go somewhere else. *Elbert Hubbard*

The abode of the heart. *Elbert Hubbard*

The first boon of Heaven; and it is well it is so, since it is that which is the lot of the mass of mankind. *Thomas Jefferson*

The ultimate result of all ambition, the end to which every enterprise and labor tends, and of which every desire prompts to prosecution. *Samuel Johnson*

That's the part of the world where people know when you're sick, miss you when you die, and love you while you live. *Samuel Johnson*

(A place where) hearts are of each other sure. *John Keble*

Books and a garden of flowers. *Andrew Lang*

Home is where you go when other places close. *Joseph Laurie*

Home means wife. *Mishna: Yoma, I, 1.*

Not where you live but where they understand you. *Christian Morgenstern*

The girl's prison and the woman's workhouse. *George Bernard Shaw*

The strength of a nation. *Lydia H. Sigourney*

A great source of happiness. It ranks immediately after health and a good conscience. *Sydney Smith*

The modern idea of home has been well expressed as the place one goes from the garage. *George Wickersham*

Where the mortgage is. *Anon.*

A restaurant which never closes. *Anon.*

Where you live with your loved ones. *Anon.*

A place where the great are small, and the small are great. *Anon.*

No place is home until two people have latchkeys. *Anon.*

A shelter from all terror, doubt, division. *Anon.*

SEE ALSO FAMILY, HUSBAND, MOTHER, WIFE.

HOMELAND

SEE NATION, PATRIOTISM.

HONESTY

The precondition for genuine scientific and scholarly work. *Leon Baeck*

The rarest wealth anyone can possess, and yet all the honesty in the world ain't lawful tender for a loaf of bread. *Josh Billings*

Not discovered. *Susanna Centlivre*

The ability to resist small temptations. *John Ciardi*

To remain faithful to the truth, to be continually unfaithful to all the successive, indefatigable renascent errors. *Adapted from Charles Péguy*

To subdue one's party spirit, one's vanity, one's prepossessions, ideals—stating things fairly, not humoring your argument—doing justice to your enemies...refusing unmerited praise. *Aubrey de Vere*

Looking painful truths in the face. *Aubrey de Vere*

Showing your breast to the world.   *Anon.*

SEE ALSO SINCERITY, TRUTH.

HONEYMOON

Applied to those married persons that love well at first, and decline in affection afterward; it is honey now, but it will change as the moon.

Thomas Blount

A good deal like a man laying off to take an expensive vacation, and coming back to a different job.   *Edgar W. Howe*

A happiness not quite worn out.

Elbert Hubbard

A postlude to a wedding march and a prelude to a funeral ditty.   *Elbert Hubbard*

The first month after marriage, when there is nothing but tenderness and pleasure.

Samuel Johnson

The time during which the bride believes the bridegroom's word of honor.

Henry Louis Mencken

Short periods of adjustment; marriages are long ones.   *Richard Sullivan*

A period of time which makes one weak.   *Anon.*

The morning after the knot before.   *Anon.*

SEE ALSO NIAGARA FALLS.

HONOR

In men...courage, in women chastity.

Joseph Addison

The kind of thing that comes to you when you've outlived your critics.   *Thomas H. Benton*

Afflicted with an impediment in one's reach.

Ambrose Bierce

A rocky island without a landing-place; once we leave it we can't get back.   *Nicolas Boileau*

Honour is like a widow, won
With brisk attempt and putting on.

Samuel Butler 1

What is fitting is honorable, and what is honorable is fitting.   *Cicero*

Our own heart, and not other men's opinions forms...true honor.

Samuel Taylor Coleridge

A very fine medieval inheritance, which women never get hold of.   *Joseph Conrad*

The moral conscience of the great.

William D'Avenant

Purity is the feminine, truth is the masculine of honor.   *Julius and Augustus Hare*

Posts of danger and of care.   *Josiah G. Holland*

An itch in youthful blood of doing acts extravagantly good.   *Samuel Howard*

Honour is purchased by the deeds we do.

Christopher Marlowe

Simply the morality of superior men.

Henry Louis Mencken

The difference between a moral man and a man of honor is that the latter regrets a discreditable act, even when it has worked and he has not been caught.   *Henry Louis Mencken*

Act well your part: there all the honour lies.

Alexander Pope

Without money...nothing but a malady.

Jean Racine

The honors of this world, what are they but puff, and emptiness, and peril of falling?

Saint Augustine

On its objective side, other people's opinion of what we are worth; on its subjective side, it is the respect we pay to this opinion.

Arthur Schopenhauer

A mistress all mankind pursue.   *Paul Whitehead*

SEE ALSO HONESTY, TRUTH, VIRTUE.

HOPE

The Promised Land...the land where one is not.

Henry F. Amiel

Desire and expectation rolled into one.

Ambrose Bierce

Grief's best music.   *Henry G. Bohn*

One of the ways in which what is merely future and potential is made vividly present and actual to us.   *Emil Brunner*

The positive mode of awaiting the future.
Emil Brunner

The gay, skylarking pajamas we wear over yesterday's bruises.   *Benjamin de Casseres*

Of all ills that men endure, the only cheap and universal cure.   *Abraham Cowley*

To hope is to enjoy.   *Jacques Delille*

That very popular trust in flat things coming round!   *Charles Dickens*

Hope is the thing with feathers
That perches in the soul.   *Emily Dickinson*

The soul of the unhappy.   *Johann W. Goethe*

A kind of cheat: in the minute of our disappointment we are angry; but upon the whole matter there is no pleasure without it.   *Lord Halifax*

The poor man's bread.   *George Herbert*

Appetite, with an opinion of attaining, is called hope; the same, without such opinion, despair.
Thomas Hobbes

A substitute for yesterday.   *Elbert Hubbard*

A mask the dying person wears.
Elbert Hubbard

The word which God has written on the brow of every man.   *Victor Hugo*

Faith holding out its hands in the dark.
George Iles

The last thing ever lost.   *Italian Proverb*

That star of life's tremulous ocean.
Paul M. James

A species of happiness, and perhaps, the chief happiness which this world affords.
Samuel Johnson

As it was preached by the first apostles, it meant nothing more or less than a confidence on the part of the Christian that he or she would attain happiness in a future life.   *Ronald A. Knox*

A more gentle name for fear.   *Letitia E. Landon*

Some extraordinary spiritual grace that God gives us to control our fears, not to oust them.
Vincent McNabb

A pathological belief in the occurrence of the impossible.   *Henry Louis Mencken*

The major weapon against the suicide impulse.
Karl Menninger

An adventure, a going forward—a confident search for a rewarding life.   *Karl Menninger*

The worst of evils, for it prolongs the torment of man.   *Friedrich W. Nietzsche*

An instinct which we cannot repress, and which lifts us up.   *Blaise Pascal*

The patent medicine
For disease, disaster, sin.   *Wallace Rice*

Eating the air on promise of supply.
William Shakespeare

A flatterer: but the most upright of all parasites; for she frequents the poor man's hut as well as the palace of his superior.   *William Shenstone*

The fawning traitor of the mind, while, under colour of friendship, it robs it of its chief force of resolution.   *Philip Sidney*

The belief, more or less strong, that joy will come; desire is the wish it may come.
Sydney Smith

Hope tell a flattering tale,
Delusive, vain and hollow.   *Mary Wrother*

SEE ALSO BELIEF, CERTAINTY, FAITH, OPTIMISM, SUCCESS.

HOSPITAL

The only place where people aren't plotting to get something from you. The only place where man sympathizes with his fellow man.

Adapted from Louis-Ferdinand Celine

The only place you can get into without having baggage.   *Will Rogers*

That blend of penitentiary and third-class hotel.
Henry E. Sigerist

A place where friends of the patient go to talk to other friends of the patient.   *Francis O. Walsh*

A place where you go to be born.   *Anon.*

A large building full of patients discussing their operations.   *Anon.*

SEE ALSO DOCTORS, ILLNESS.

HOSPITALITY

Sweet courtesy has done its most
if you have made each guest forget
That he himself is not the host.

Thomas Bailey Aldrich

The virtue which induces us to feed and lodge
certain persons who are not in need of food and
lodging.   *Ambrose Bierce*

A little fire, a little food, and an immense quiet.

Ralph Waldo Emerson

Welcome in your eye, your hand, your tongue.

Adapted from William Shakespeare

The most charming torture we have devised.

John Steinbeck

A genial hearth, a hospitable board,
And a refined rusticity.   *William Wordsworth*

HOST

A host is like a general: it takes a mishap to reveal
his genius.   *Horace*

The master of the feast. The man who sits in the
lowest place, and who is always industrious in
helping everyone.   *David Hume*

HOTEL

A house kept for those who are not housekeepers.

Paul Chatfield

An establishment where a guest often gives up
good dollars for poor quarters.

Foolish Dictionary

A refuge from home life.   *George Bernard Shaw*

HOUSE

My castle... I have my own four walls.

Thomas Carlyle

The house of everyone is to him as his castles and
fortress, as well as for his defence against injury
and violence as for his repose.   *Edward Coke*

A master, and a task for life: he is to furnish,
watch, show it, and keep it in repair, the rest of his
days.   *Ralph Waldo Emerson*

A castle which the King cannot enter.

Ralph Waldo Emerson

The difference between a house and a home is
this: a house may fall down, but a home is broken
up.   *Elbert Hubbard*

A rendezvous for burglars.   *Elbert Hubbard*

Man's best refuge.   *Legal Maxim*

A great source of happiness. It ranks immediately
after health and good conscience.

Sydney Smith

My castle, from which the law does not compel
me to flee.   *William Staunford*

A noble consort to man and the trees. The house
should have repose and such texture as will quiet
the whole and make it graciously one with external nature.   *Frank Lloyd Wright*

The thing that keeps a man running to the
hardware store.   *Robert Zwickey*

SEE ALSO FAMILY, HOME.

HUG

A roundabout way of expressing emotion.

Gideon Wurdz

Energy gone to waist.   *Anon.*

HUMAN BEINGS

Three classes: those who are billed to death, those
who are worried to death and those who are bored
to death.   *Winston S. Churchill*

(That which) makes us human is the power to
work with symbolic images: the gift of imagination.   *Jacob Bronowski*

I may define man as a male human being and a
woman as a female human being. What the early
Christians did was to strike the "male" out of the
definition of man, and "human being" out of the
definition of woman.   *James Donaldson*

The greatest of the earth's parasites.

Martin H. Fischer

Animated matter than thinks.

Adapted from Frederick the Great

The only animal that can be bored.

Erich Fromm

A miserable little pile of secrets.   *Emile Herzog*

The playwrights and stage managers of our lives: they cast us in a role and we play it whether we will or no.   *Eric Hoffer*

Two distinct races: the men who borrow, and the men who lend.   *Charles Lamb*

A thinking intelligent being, that has reason and reflection, and can consider itself as itself.
John Locke

A little cave-dwelling virus mutated.
John D. MacDonald

An ingenious assembly of portable plumbing.
Christopher Morley

Nothing else than a series of undertakings...the sum, the organization, the ensemble of the relationships which make up these undertakings.
Jean-Paul Sartre

Anxiety ridden animals.   *Iris Murdoch*

The only animals of which I am thoroughly and cravenly afraid.   *George Bernard Shaw*

A very complicated physical mechanism and nothing more.   *J. C. Smart*

Frankenstein's monster who periodically gets out of control.   *Patrick White*

A more complex structure than any social system to which he belongs.   *Alfred North Whitehead*

More or less random collections of borrowed emotions and borrowed ideas.   *Robert Zwickey*

SEE ALSO HUMANITY, MAN, MANKIND.

HUMANISM

Faith in the dignity of the human soul.
Jacob Agus

An act of will, which has a way of proving itself through the kind of deeds and policies that it inspires.   *Jacob Agus*

Puritanism with a sense of humor.
J. Auer and Julian Hartt

That spiritual heresy...by which man came to see himself as a whole, instead of as a spiritual-social-biological organism in living relation to the real world of spirit.   *V. A. Demant*

It rejects supernaturalism and moral absolutism, and argues that the best possibililities of human beings can be achieved only by a combination of informed intelligence and the candid recognition that man must bear the responsibility for whatever standards he adopts.   *Charles Frankel*

A popular, bland, respectable faith...the orthodoxy of the nonbeliever, but it is a ready refuge for the half-believer too...It simply says: "Take up your credit card and follow me."
Paul J. Hallinan

Man is the cornerstone.   *Emil G. Hirsh*

It dwells on no new facts. It is rather a slow shifting in the philosophic perspective, making things appear as from a new centre of interest or point of sight.   *William James*

Meant originally...concerned with worldly rather than with divine things, or more narrowly still, with the literature of Greece and Rome which ... was naturally irrelevant to religion.
Joseph Wood Krutch

Duty to Man has replaced Duty to God. It is the central point of Humanism.   *Rosalind Murray*

To liberate and help emancipate mankind, with the result that man becomes an absolute for man.
Jean-Paul Sartre

The religion of one who says yea to life here and now.   *R. W. Sellars*

SEE ALSO EXISTENTIALISM.

HUMANITY

Something more than a mere species—it is a historical development.   *Simone de Beauvoir*

God's outer church. Its needs and urgencies are priests and pastors.   *Henry Ward Beecher*

A body of organisms that preys on itself.
Jerry Dashkin

People packed in an automobile which is traveling down hill without lights on a dark night at terrific speed and driven by a four-year-old child. The signposts along the way are all marked "Progress."   *Lord Dunsany*

Man is the will, and woman the sentiment.
Ralph Waldo Emerson

One undivided and indivisible family.
Mohandas K. Gandhi

A living organism, of which races and peoples are the members.   *Moses Hess*

The only religion. *Robert G. Ingersoll*

The mould to break away from.

Robinson Jeffers

A pigsty where liars, hypocrites and the obscene in spirit congregate. *George M. Moore*

Only cave men who have lost their cave.

Christopher Morley

Two classes...Those who make great demands on themselves, piling up difficulties and duties; and those who demand nothing special of themselves, but for whom to live is to be every moment what they already are, without imposing on themselves any effort towards perfection.

José Ortega y Gasset

Condemned clay. *Saint Augustine*

Composed of two categories, the invalids and the nurses. *Walter Sickert*

Woman, above all other educators, educates humanly. Man is the brain, but woman is the heart of humanity. *Samuel Smiles*

The products of editing, rather than authorship.

George Wald

A mere local incident in an endless and aimless series of cosmical changes. *Robert Zwickey*

SEE ALSO MAN, MANKIND, MASSES, WOMAN.

HUMILITY

True humility is contentment. *Henry F. Amiel*

Whosoever shall smite thee on thy right cheek, turn to him the other also.

Bible: Matthew, V, 39.

(That which) cannot be degraded by humiliation.

Edmund Burke

The realization of our awful nearness to a claim earned in the blood of his followers and the sacrifice of his friends.

Dwight David Eisenhower

The most essential point in lowliness.

François de Fénelon

Knowing God. *John Flavel*

To superiors...duty, to equals courtesy, to inferiors nobleness. *Benjamin Franklin*

The substitution of one pride for another.

Eric Hoffer

The first of virtues—for other people.

Oliver Wendell Holmes 1

Grogginess of the Ego. *Elbert Hubbard*

To recede to...littleness. *Elbert Hubbard*

The odor of sanctity. *Elbert Hubbard*

Censure of a man's self. *Samuel Johnson*

Man making himself a worm.

Adapted from Immanuel Kant

A state of mind appropriate to the truth of things. A soul that has not attained humility is not prepared to grasp the truth of the world in its fullness. *Jacob Klatzkin*

Often only a pretended submission, an artifice of pride, which abases itself in order to exalt itself.

La Rochefoucauld

The altar upon which God wishes us to offer him sacrifices. *La Rochefoucauld*

Nothing else but a right judgment of ourselves.

William Law

A kind of moral jiu-jitsu. *Gerald S. Lee*

(An) old monk who, asked to define humility, replied: "If you forgive a brother who has wronged you before he is penitent towards you."

Geddes MacGregor

The realization of our awful nearness to a magnificence of which we are unworthy.

Alistair MacLean

To walk humbly with God, never doubting, whatever befall, that His will is good, and His law is right. *Paul Elmer More*

An actual participation or assumption of the condition of those to whom we stoop...to feel and behave as if we were low.

John Henry Newman

The trodden worm curls up. Thus it reduces its chances of being stepped on again. In the language of morality—humility.

Friedrich W. Nietzsche

(A state which is) highest when it stoops.

Channing Pollock

A noble mind in a low estate. *Jane Porter*

(Something that is) preached by the clergy, but practiced only by the lower classes.

Bertrand A. Russell

A Divine veil which covers our good deeds, and hides them from our eyes.   *Saint John Climacus*

Keeping your eyes off other people's faults, and fixing them on your own.

Saint Alphonse Rodriguez

Being able to laugh at our own foibles.

Fulton J. Sheen

To make a right estimate of one's self.

Charles H. Spurgeon

The modesty of the soul...the antidote to pride.

Voltaire

The grace that makes every grace amiable.

Anon.

The pride of the humble.   *Anon.*

To be low in one's esteem.   *Anon.*

SEE ALSO MODESTY, PRIDE.

HUMOR

Falling downstairs if you do it while in the act of warning your wife not to.   *Kenneth Bird*

Not a gift of the mind, but of the heart.

Ludwig Boerne

(A) warm tender fellow-feeling with all forms of existence.   *Thomas Carlyle*

Its essence is love; it issues not in laughter, but in still smiles, which lie far deeper.

Thomas Carlyle

The finest perfection of poetic genius.

Thomas Carlyle

Playful aggression.   *Emil Draitser*

Grown-up play.   *Max Eastman*

An affirmation...of man's superiority to all that befalls him.   *Romain Gary*

The faculty which corrects exaggerations and extravagance.   *John R. Green*

The exploitation of disproportion.

Russell Green

The oil and wine of merry meeting.

Washington Irving

A type of stimulation which tends to elicit the laughter reflex.   *Arthur Koestler*

Humour is really laughing off a hurt.

William Mauldin

The contemplation of the finite from the point of view of the infinite.   *Christian Morgenstern*

Truth in an intoxicated condition.

George Jean Nathan

The ability to see three sides of one coin.

Ned Rorem

The red thread in the gray linen.

Jonah Rosenfeld

Pleasantry in pain.   *Moritz Saphir*

An ornament and safeguard...It is a genius itself, and so defends from the insanities.

Walter Scott

Closely related to faith; it bids us not to take anything too seriously.   *Fulton J. Sheen*

A peerless weapon of the British when dealing with foreign countries.   *Walter Starkie*

Humor is odd, grotesque, and wild,
Only by affectation spoiled;
'Tis never by invention got;
Men have it when they know it not.

Jonathan Swift

The very best articles of dress worn in society.

William Makepeace Thackeray

The other side of tragedy...one of our greatest and earliest national resources which must be preserved at all costs.   *James Thurber*

A kind of emotional chaos told calmly and quietly in retrospect.   *James Thurber*

Emotional chaos remembered in tranquility.

James Thurber

The secret source of Humor itself is not joy but sorrow. There is no humor in heaven.

Mark Twain

Gravity concealed behind the jest.   *John Weiss*

The irregular, the incongruous and the bizarre in human nature and human behavior treated in a kindly manner.   *Robert Zwickey*

What makes you laugh at something which would make you mad if it happened to you.   *Anon.*

SEE ALSO LAUGHTER, SATIRE, WIT.

HUMORIST

I think funny.   *Abe Burrows*

The man who sees the inconsistency in things.
    Gilbert Keith Chesterton

A comedian who doesn't tell dirty stories.
    Gordon Currie

One who threatens one's values yet evokes laughter in the process.   *Anon.*

SEE ALSO COMEDIAN, SATIRIST, WITS.

HUNGER

Not only the best cook, but the best physician.
    Peter Altenberg

(A state) sharper than the sword.
    Beaumont and Fletcher

A peculiar disease afflicting all classes of mankind and commonly treated by dieting.
    Ambrose Bierce

The best sauce in the world.
    Miguel de Cervantes

The worst political advisor.   *Albert Einstein*

The best cook.   *Seligman Ginzberger*

The mother of fascism.   *Joseph F. Gould*

The best cook.   *Latin Proverb*

A kind of suffering like burning slowly and incessantly on a still fire.   *Mendel of Kotz*

The teacher of the arts and the inspirer of invention.   *Persius*

One of the few cravings that cannot be appeased with another solution.   *Anon.*

SEE ALSO DIET, POVERTY, STOMACH.

HUNTING

The slaughter of animals made ferocious by the presence of man.   *James Cannon*

(A sport which) owes its pleasures to another's pain.   *William Cowper*

Fire your little gun.
Bang! Now the animal
    Is dead and dumb and done.
    Walter De La Mare

A passion...deeply implanted in the human breast.   *Charles Dickens*

The most important business in the life of a gentleman.   *John Dryden*

Wild animals never kill for sport. Man is the only one to whom the torture and death of his fellow creatures is amusing in itself.   *James A. Froude*

It is very strange, and very melancholy, that the paucity of human pleasures should persuade us ever to call hunting one of them.
    Samuel Johnson

Cruelty.   *Ezekiel Landau*

The least honorable form of war on the weak.
    Paul Richard

When a man wants to murder a tiger he calls it sport: when the tiger wants to murder him he calls it ferocity.   *George Bernard Shaw*

(The) image of war without its guilt.
    William Somerville

The way of sinners.   *Talmud: Aboda Zara, 18b.*

The labor of savages, the amusement of gentlemen.   *Anon.*

SEE ALSO FOX-HUNTER.

HURRY

The dispatch of bunglers.   *Ambrose Bierce*

The weakness of fools.   *Baltasar Gracian*

HUSBAND

Something no respectable family should be without.   *Fred Allen*

An orangoutang trying to play the violin.
    Honoré de Balzac

A whole-time job. That is why so many husbands fail. They cannot give their entire attention to it.
    Arnold Bennett

For the husband is the head of the wife, even as Christ is the head of the church.

Bible: Ephesians, V, 23.

And thy desire shall be to thy husband, and he shall rule over thee.   *Bible: Genesis, III, 16.*

One who, having dined, is charged with the care of the plate.   *Ambrose Bierce*

Optimists. They go through life believing that somehow, somewhere, they will eventually arrive someplace on time—with their wife. It never happens.   *Hal Boyle*

A mute testament to woman's innate superiority.

Eugene E. Brussell

A hero in his own home until the company leaves.

Warren Goldberg

The first man up, and the last in bed.

Robert Herrick

A booby prize in life's lottery.   *Elbert Hubbard*

(A) man of placid and conforming mind.

Henry Louis Mencken

A plaster which cures all girl's complaints.

Moliere

One who has several small mouths to feed and one big one to listen to.   *Vincent Montemora*

The chief of the family and the head of the wife.

Pope Leo XIII

What is left of the lover after the nerve has been extracted.   *Helen Rowland*

A male with an inferiority complex.

Paul Weinberger

A sort of promissory note—a woman is tired of meeting him.   *Oscar Wilde*

A man who feels disloyal when he thinks on his own.   *Anon.*

A man who has chased a woman until she has caught him.   *Anon.*

A lover with a two-day's growth of beard, his collar off, and a bad cold in the head.   *Anon.*

One who lays down the law to his wife, and then accepts all her amendments.   *Anon.*

The last to know the dishonor of his house.

Anon.

SEE ALSO ALIMONY, BACHELOR, DIVORCE, FATHER, MARRIAGE, WIFE.

HYGIENE

SEE CLEANLINESS.

HYPOCHONDRIA

Sham pain.   *Howard Elliott*

A knack for extracting, for personal application, the greatest amount of venom from any and every incident of life, no matter what it may be.

Georg C. Lichtenberg

Groundless anxiety on the score of future misfortunes entirely of our own manufacture.

Arthur Schopenhauer

A species of torment which not only makes us unreasonably cross with the things of the present... but also leads to unmerited self-reproach for what we have done in the past.

Arthur Schopenhauer

HYPOCRISY AND HYPOCRITE

A mouth that prays, a hand that kills.

Arabian Proverb

There is no sincerity in their mouth; their inward part is a yawning gulf, their throat is an open sepulchre; they make smooth their tongue.

Bible: Isaiah, XXIX, 13.

One who, professing virtues that he does not respect, secures the advantage of seeming to be what he despises.   *Ambrose Bierce*

A source of pain, and the happy time of life starts as soon as we give them up.   *Nicolas Chamfort*

A hypocrite is in himself both the archer and the mark, in all actions shooting at his own praise or profit.   *Thomas Fuller*

A hypocrite despises those whom he deceives, but he has no respect for himself. He would make a dupe of himself, too, if he could.

William Hazlitt

The only vice that cannot be forgiven... The repentance of a hypocrite is itself hypocrisy.

William Hazlitt

He that hides one thing in his heart and utters another.   *Homer*

The most exhausting thing in life.

Ann Morrow Lindbergh

An awkward and forced imitation of what should be genuine and easy, wanting the beauty that accompanies what is natural.   *John Locke*

Hypocrisy, the only evil that walks invisible, except to God alone.   *Adapted from John Milton*

Those who daub both sides of a wall.   *Petronius*

Merely a method by which we can multiply our personalities.   *Oscar Wilde*

Pretending to be wicked, and being really good all the time.   *Oscar Wilde*

SEE ALSO AFFECTATION, CANT, LIAR.

HYPOTHESIS

SEE THEORY.

I

IDEALIST

(Those who) give the distant view.

Cannon Barnett

One who is seldom forced to confront practical problems head-on. *Eugene E. Brussell*

A person who helps other people to be prosperous. *Henry Ford*

A sleepwalker who insists on stepping out of a solid window into the air.

Adapted from Elbert Hubbard

One who, on noticing that a rose smells better than a cabbage, concludes that it will also make a better soup. *Henry Louis Mencken*

(One who) pursues what his heart says is right in a way that his head says will work.

Richard Milhous Nixon

That implies you are not going to achieve something. *Arthur Scargill*

When they come downstairs from their Ivory Towers, Idealists are apt to walk straight into the gutter. *Logan P. Smith*

The court jesters of Providence, who even pay for their own fool's caps. *Isaac M. Wise*

Those who gaze at the moon and fall in the gutter.

Anon.

One who is for anything so long as it does not hurt business—his business. *Anon.*

One who demands that you live up to his ideals.

Anon.

SEE ALSO REFORMERS, UTOPIA.

IDEALS

Our better selves. *Amos Bronson Alcott*

A flaming vision of reality. *Joseph Conrad*

Beautiful pictures on the walls of our souls, mental images that establish us in the habitual companionship of the highest that we know.

Harry Emerson Fosdick

The world's masters. *Josiah G. Holland*

An excuse for murder, tyranny or self-aggrandizement. *Elbert Hubbard*

Any theory that justifies our secret itch.

Elbert Hubbard

The noble toga that political gentlemen drape over their will to power. *Aldous Huxley*

Ideas or beliefs when these are objects not only of contemplation or affirmation but also of hope, desire, endeavor, admiration, and resolve.

Ralph Barton Perry

Like stars; you will not succeed in touching them with your hands. But like the seafaring man on the desert waters, you choose them as your guides, and following them you will reach your destiny.

Carl Schurtz

Ideals are thoughts. So long as they exist merely as thoughts, the power in them remains ineffective.   *Albert Schweitzer*

The projection before us of what is behind impelling us, of what is above guiding us, of what is within creating us.   *Antonin Sertillanges*

SEE ALSO PERFECTION, REFORMERS, UTOPIA.

IDEAS

Set hands about their several tasks.
Amos Bronson Alcott

The ancients left them for us and we are building the homes for them.   *Amos Bronson Alcott*

One of the greatest pains to human nature.
Walter Bagehot

The thing that gives people courage.
Georges Clemenceau

Tramps...knocking at the back-door of your mind, each taking a little of your substance, each carrying away some crumb of that belief in a few simple notions you must cling to if you want to live decently.   *Joseph Conrad*

(Something a) man is always ready to die for...provided that idea is not quite clear to him.
Paul Eldridge

(Something that) must work through the brains and arms of good and brave men, or they are no better than dreams.   *Ralph Waldo Emerson*

A feast of association, and the height of it is a good metaphor.   *Robert Frost*

The great warriors of the world.
James A. Garfield

An incitement.   *Oliver Wendell Holmes 2*

Madness or heroism.   *Victor Hugo*

Something that usually comes like firemen—too late.   *Jewish Saying*

Direct emanations of the material state.
Adapted from Karl Marx

Intelligence plus experience.   *Felix M. Morley*

(Something) we build up on the sunken piers of obsolete wisdom.   *Donald C. Peattie*

Only an imperfect induction from fact.
Ezra Pound

The very coinage of your brain.
William Shakespeare

Beards—men do not have them until they grow up.   *Voltaire*

(Thoughts that) won't keep. Something must be done about them.   *Alfred North Whitehead*

Salvation by imagination.   *Frank Lloyd Wright*

An idea that is not dangerous is unworthy of being called an idea at all.   *Oscar Wilde*

SEE ALSO BRAIN, MIND, THEORY.

IDEOLOGY

SEE CREED, DOCTRINE, THEORY.

IDIOT

SEE FOOL, MORON.

IDLENESS

A kind of monster in the creation. All nature is busy about him; every animal he sees reproaches him.   *Joseph Addison*

The tempter that beguiles and expels from paradise.   *Amos Bronson Alcott*

Emptiness.   *Hosea Ballou*

The well-spring and root of all vice.
Thomas Becon

The canker of the mind.   *John Bodenham*

Doing ill.   *Henry G. Bohn*

(Inactivity which) fills up a man's time much more completely, and leaves him less his own master, than any sort of employment whatever.
Edmund Burke

The badge of gentry.   *Robert Burton*

Perpetual despair.   *Thomas Carlyle*

A sort of suicide.   *Lord Chesterfield*

The refuge of weak minds, and the holiday of fools.   *Lord Chesterfield*

Doing nothing.   *Ella Colum*

Doing nothing with a deal of skill.
William Cowper

Being free to do anything. *Floyd Dell*

That man is idle who can do something better.
Ralph Waldo Emerson

He is idle that might be better employed.
Thomas Fuller

The occupation most becoming to a civilized man. *Theophile Gautier*

A . . . genius for doing nothing, and doing it assiduously. *Thomas C. Haliburton*

The ruin of most men. *George Hillard*

The sepulchre of a living man.
Josiah G. Holland

Masterly inactivity. *Horace*

The way to be nothing. *Nathaniel Howe*

The ultimate purpose of the busy.
Samuel Johnson

An infirmity of the mind. *La Rochefoucauld*

A chance of future misfortune. *Napoleon 1*

The mistress of wanton appetites, and fortress of lust's gate. *John Northbrooke*

To fritter away the whole day inconsequently and incoherently, and to follow nothing but the whim of the moment. *Jean-Jacques Rousseau*

The stupidity of the body, and stupidity is the idleness of the mind. *Johann G. Seume*

Stagnant satisfaction. *Samuel Smiles*

The insupportable labor of doing nothing.
Richard Steele

Does not consist in doing nothing, but in doing a great deal not recognized in the dogmatic formularies of the ruling class.
Robert Louis Stevenson

To kill the time. *James Thomson*

Rust that attaches itself to the most brilliant metals. *Voltaire*

The most difficult thing in the world, the most difficult and the most intellectual. *Oscar Wilde*

Disciplined inaction. *Anon.*

The art of being a vegetable. *Anon.*

SEE ALSO LAZINESS, LEISURE, LOAFER.

IDOLATRY

Thou shalt not make unto thee any graven image, or any likeness of anything that is in heaven above, or that is in the water under the earth.
Bible: Exodus, XX, 4.

Gods of silver or of gold ye shalt not make unto you. *Bible: Exodus, XX, 20.*

Words can become idols, and machines ... Science and the opinions of one's neighbors can become idols, and God has become an idol for many. *Erich Fromm*

To worship the State or the man is idolatry.
James M. Gillis

Worship of the self projected and objectified: all idolization is self-idolization. *Will Herberg*

Not only the adoration of images . . . but also trust in one's own righteousness, works and merits, and putting confidence in riches and power.
Martin Luther

The position of identifying God with our own particular system and beliefs.
Albert T. Mollegen

To make gods by the dozen.
Michel de Montaigne

Idolatry is in a man's own thought, not in the opinion of another. *John Selden*

He who slays a king and he who dies for him.
George Bernard Shaw

The modern idol maker goes not to the forest but to the laboratory, and there, with the help of scientific concepts moulds the kind of God he will adore. *Fulton J. Sheen*

SEE ALSO PAGAN.

IF

One of the shortest and most important words in the English language. *Gertrude Holtz*

A tightrope that stretches from but to but.
Elbert Hubbard

A fatality endowed with free will.
Elbert Hubbard

IGNORAMUS

A person unacquainted with certain kinds of knowledge familiar to yourself, and having certain other kinds that you know nothing about.

Ambrose Bierce

Any man who flatters himself that he is educated.

Elbert Hubbard

Those who despise education.   *Anon.*

Someone who can't explain what he doesn't like.

Anon.

Someone who doesn't know about what you learned yesterday.   *Anon.*

SEE ALSO FOOL, IGNORANCE, MORON, STUPIDITY.

IGNORANCE

Not innocence, but sin.   *Robert Browning*

Innocence and certitude compounded.

Eugene E. Brussell

Vanity, and pride, and arrogance.

Samuel Butler 2

Ignorance lies at the bottom of all human knowledge, and the deeper we penetrate the nearer we arrive unto it.   *Charles Caleb Colton*

Ignorance and superstition ever bear a close, and even a mathematical relation to each other.

James Fenimore Cooper

The condition necessary . . . for existence itself. If we knew all, we could not endure life for an hour.

Anatole France

The dominion of absurdity.   *James A. Froude*

A body without knowledge.   *Hebrew Proverb*

The recipe . . . is: be satisfied with your opinions and content with your knowledge.

Elbert Hubbard

Most ignorance is vincible ignorance. We don't know because we don't want to know.

Aldous Huxley

The only slavery.   *Ralph G. Ingersoll*

Mere privation by which nothing can be produced.   *Samuel Johnson*

A vacuity in which the soul sits motionless and torpid for want of attraction.   *Samuel Johnson*

I know of no disease of the soul but ignorance . . . a pernicious evil, the darkener of man's life, the disturber of his reason, and the common confounder of truth.   *Ben Jonson*

A soft . . . easy . . . pillow.   *Michel de Montaigne*

It is not . . . a thing of itself, but . . . only the absence of knowledge.   *Thomas Paine*

The beginning of knowledge; knowledge is the beginning of wisdom; wisdom is the awareness of ignorance.   *William Rotsler*

Condemnation before investigation.

Herbert Spencer

The solidified wisdom of the ages.

John Steinbeck

The first requisite of the historian—ignorance which simplifies and clarifies, which selects and omits, with a placid perfection unattainable by the highest art.   *Lytton Strachey*

Something that gains strength and certainty as it goes along.   *Anon.*

The only thing more costly than an education.

Anon.

SEE ALSO FOOLISHNESS, STUPIDITY.

IGNORANT

The finest and most useful of the arts but one that is rarely and poorly practiced.   *Ludwig Boerne*

What everybody is, only on different subjects.

Will Rogers

Confident in everything.   *Charles H. Spurgeon*

To walk in the night.   *Anon.*

Answering all questions put to you.   *Anon.*

SEE ALSO FOOL, ILLITERACY.

ILLEGITIMATE

SEE BASTARD.

ILLITERATE

One who goes down to posterity talking and writing bad grammar.

Adapted from Benjamin Disraeli

Unseeing, unthinking—an animal, an excretion.
Anon.

The condition of relying on experts.   *Anon.*

ILLNESS

A second chance, not only at health but at life itself!   *Louis E. Bisch*

One of the great pleasures of life, provided one is not too ill and is not obliged to work till one is better.   *Samuel Butler 2*

The taxes laid upon this wretched life; some are taxed higher, and some lower, but all pay something.   *Lord Chesterfield*

A belief which must be annihilated by the divine mind.   *Mary Baker Eddy*

That which tells us what we are.   *Italian Proverb*

To enjoy monarchal prerogatives.
Charles Lamb

A state of languor and an image of death.
Francois Rabelais

Often a blessing. By ravaging the body it frees the soul and purifies it.   *Romain Rolland*

A great leveler. At its touch, the artificial distinctions of society vanish away.   *Max Thorek*

SEE ALSO DISEASE, DOCTORS, HEALTH, INSANITY, MEDICINE.

ILLUSION

The most dangerous of our calculations.
Georges Bernanos

They save us pain and allow us to enjoy pleasure instead. We must...accept it without complaint when they sometimes collide with...reality against which they are dashed to pieces.
Sigmund Freud

An illusion is not the same as an error...We call a belief an illusion when wish-fulfillment is a prominent factor in its motivation.
Sigmund Freud

Nothing can justly be called an illusion which is a permanent and universal human experience.
John C. Powys

The first of all pleasures.   *Voltaire*

SEE ALSO DREAM, FANTASY.

IMAGINATION

A sort of faint perception.   *Aristotle*

The air of mind.   *Philip J. Bailey*

A warehouse of facts, with poet and liar in joint ownership.   *Ambrose Bierce*

The real and eternal world of which this vegetable universe is but a faint shadow.   *Willilam Blake*

Means to make images and to move them about inside one's head in new arrangements.
Jacob Bronowski

A specifically human gift...the characteristic act...of the mind of man.   *Jacob Bronowski*

The living Power and prime agent of all human Perception.   *Samuel Taylor Coleridge*

A good horse to carry you over the ground—not a flying carpet to set you free from probability.
Robertson Davies

The act of taking up residence in someone else's point of view.   *Adapted from John Erskine*

The wide-open eye which leads us always to see truth more vividly.   *Christopher Fry*

The one weapon in the war against reality.
Jules de Gaultier

One of the truest conditions of communion with heaven.   *Nathaniel Hawthorne*

Imagination and memory are but one thing, which for divers considerations hath divers names.
Thomas Hobbes

A ladder to the fourth dimension.
Elbert Hubbard

The giant enemy of reality.   *Elbert Hubbard*

Sympathy illumined by brains.
Elbert Hubbard

The thing which prevents us from being as happy in the arms of a chambermaid as in the arms of a duchess.   *Samuel Johnson*

The eye of the soul.   *Joseph Joubert*

What the imagination seizes...must be truth—whether it existed before or not.   *John Keats*

Not only the creative source of artistic production, but also the root of religious experience.
Richard Kroner

The true magic carpet.   *Norman Vincent Peale*

To form competent, adequate images of reality, most especially human reality. Fantasy does the very opposite. *William Lynch*

Reaching, by intuition and intensity of gaze... a more essential truth than is seen at the surface of things. *John Ruskin*

My mind's eye. *William Shakespeare*

The beginning of creation. You imagine what you desire; you will what you imagine; and at last you create what you will. *George Bernard Shaw*

The great instrument of moral good.
Percy Bysshe Shelley

What makes some politicians think they are statesmen. *Roberta Tennes*

The result of heredity. It is simply concentrated race-experience. *Oscar Wilde*

The mightiest lever
Known to the moral world.
William Wordsworth

What makes a cartoonist think he is an artist.
Anon.

Unspoiled instinct. *Anon.*

SEE ALSO FANTASY, POETRY, VISION.

IMITATION

Go, and do thou likewise. *Bible: Luke, X, 37.*

Criticism. *William Blake*

To admire on principle is the only way to imitate without loss of originality.
Samuel Taylor Coleridge

The sincerest form of flattery.
Charles Caleb Colton

"Adapted" from other men's lore.
Austin Dobson

Echoes, repeating involuntarily the virtues, the defects, the movements, and the characters of those among whom we live. *Joseph Joubert*

To do exactly the opposite is also a form of imitation. *Georg C. Lichtenberg*

(When good) the most perfect originality.
Voltaire

The sincerest form of plagiarism. *Anon.*

SEE ALSO PLAGIARISM.

IMMIGRANT

SEE PIONEER

IMMORTALITY

Not only the doing of certain things, but the deception of self in refusing to see what should and should not be done. *Eric Bentley*

Inexpedient. Whatever... men find to be generally inexpedient comes to be considered ... immoral. *Ambrose Bierce*

To show things really as they are. *Lord Byron*

The morality of those who are having a better time. *Henry Louis Mencken*

To accept the fashion of the day no matter what it be. *Anon.*

SEE ALSO EVIL, SIN, VICE.

IMMORALITY

Not the future life; it is life in harmony with the true order of things—life in God. *Henry F. Amiel*

God created man to be immortal, and made him to be an image of his own eternity.
Apocrypha: Wisdom of Solomon, II, 23.

The bravest gesture of our humanity toward the unknown. It is always a faith, never a demonstration. *Gaius G. Atkins*

Then shalt the dust return to the earth as it was: and the spirit shalt return unto God who gave it.
Bible: Ecclesiastes, XII, 12.

And though after my skin worms destroy this body, yet in my flesh shalt I see God.
Bible: Job, XIX, 26.

This is the promise that He hath promised us, even eternal life. *Bible: John, II, 25.*

A toy which people cry for,
And on their knees apply for,
Dispute, contend and lie for,
    And if allowed
    Would be right proud
Eternally to die for. *Ambrose Bierce*

A great affirmation of the soul of man.
Hugh Black

The resurrection. *Book of Common Prayer*

That which is the foundation of all our hopes and all our fears...which are of any consideration: I mean a Future Life.   *Joseph Butler*

When a man dies but his words live.   *Carl Crow*

The power to live.   *Fëdor M. Dostoievski*

Belief in the worthlessness and nothingness of this life.   *Ludwig A. Feuerbach*

Salvation for the righteous.   *Louis Finkelstein*

A supreme act of faith in the reasonableness of God's work.   *John Fisk*

A condition sought by political officeholders where the incumbent never...dies or resigns.
Elbert Hubbard

Divine compensation for the starving.
Elbert Hubbard

A superfluous addition to life; to go on living after one desires and hopes to remain dead.
Elbert Hubbard

It is the rainbow—Hope, shining upon the tears of grief.   *Robert G. Ingersoll*

To ascend in essence to an ecstatic meeting with the friends we have loved and lost, and whom we shall still love and never lose again.
Thomas Jefferson

A government bureau.   *Hugh S. Johnson*

The postulate of immortality...must lead to the supposition of the existence of a cause adequate to this effect; in short, it must postulate the existence of a God.   *Immanuel Kant*

A hope beyond the shadow of a dream.
John Keats

A better world.   *August von Kotzebue*

The great world of light that lies behind all human destinies.
Adapted from Henry Wadsworth Longfellow

The thought of life that ne'er shall cease.
Henry Wadsworth Longfellow

To rise upon some fairer shore.   *J. L. McCreery*

A framework within which earthly ways of life are judged and changed, lived and abandoned.
Margaret Mead

The condition of a dead man who doesn't believe that he is dead.   *Henry Louis Mencken*

The survival of personality.   *Max Nordau*

The genius to move others long after you yourself have stopped moving.   *Franklin Rooney*

Sleep that no pain shall wake,
Night that no morn shall break.
Christina Rossetti

After the royal throne comes death; after the dunghill comes the Kingdom of Heaven.
Saint John Chrysostom

The natural continuation of life *per se*.
Harry B. Scholefield

To desire the perpetuation of a great mistake.
Arthur Schopenhauer

When Judaism speaks of immortality...its primary meaning is that man contains something independent of the flesh and surviving it; his consciousness and moral capacity, his essential personality; a soul.   *Milton Steinberg*

When I can read my title clear
To mansions in the skies.   *Isaac Watts*

The good hereafter.   *John Greenleaf Whittier*

When someone dies but his creations live.
Anon.

Life after death in a better world where friends and dear ones shall meet again.   *Anon.*

The idea of the survival of the spirit after death in some form, whether clear or vague.   *Anon.*

SEE ALSO DEATH, ETERNITY, HEAVEN, RESURRECTION, SALVATION, SOUL.

IMPERIALISM

A policy of acquisition of new and distant territory or the incorporation of remote interests with our own.   *Grover Cleveland*

The conquest of the earth...taking it away from those who have a different complexion or slightly flatter noses than ourselves.   *Joseph Conrad*

The fashion of shooting everybody who doesn't speak English.   *Richard Croker*

International kleptomania.
Cynic's Cyclopaedia

The desire to gain a more extensive territory, to conquer or to hold in awe our neighboring states, to surpass them in arts or arms...A desire founded on prejudice and error.
William Godwin

The endeavor of the great controllers of industry to broaden the channel for the flow of their surplus wealth by seeking foreign markets and foreign investments to take off the goods and capital they cannot use at home.   *John A. Hobson*

Tyranny, hiding behind the...name of humanity.
Elbert Hubbard

Take up the white man's burden—
   Send forth the best ye breed—
Go bind your sons to exile
   To serve your captive's need.
Rudyard Kipling

The transition stage from capitalism to socialism...It is capitalism dying, not dead.
Nikolai Lenin

Benevolent assimilation.   *Willliam McKinley*

Spiritual as well as economic expansion.
Benito Mussolini

National egotism, where love of one's own nation leads to the suppression of other nationalities.
Report of the Oxford Conference, 1938.

The white's land. The cannon! One must submit to baptism, clothes, work.   *Arthur Rimbaud*

The rich man gains a market; the poor man loses a leg.   *Russian Proverb*

To found a great empire for the sole purpose of raising up a people of customers.   *Adam Smith*

The highest phase of capitalist development.
Joseph Stalin

The possession of such lands as are void of Christian inhabitants, for Christ's sake.
William Strachey

With a hero at head, and a nation
Well gagged and well drilled and well
   cowed,
And a gospel of war and damnation.
Algernon Charles Swinburne

IMPOSSIBILITY

Most of the things worth doing.
Louis D. Brandeis

Not a lucky word...no good comes of those that have it often in their mouths.   *Thomas Carlyle*

And what's impossible, can't be,
And never, never comes to pass
George Coleman 2

The lowest percentage of the word attempt.
Jerry Dashkin

A word that I never utter.   *Colin D'Harleville*

Nothing...to a willing heart.   *John Heywood*

A word only to be found in the dictionary of fools.
Napoleon 1

That which takes a little longer.
George Santayana

The word for weakling.   *Anon.*

INCOME

Something that you can't live without or within.
Harry B. Behrmann

The natural and rational gauge...of respectability.   *Ambrose Bierce*

Not to be eager to buy.   *Cicero*

Something to live beyond.   *Anon.*

SEE ALSO MONEY, RICHES, WEALTH.

INCREDIBLE

SEE FANTASY.

INDEPENDENCE

The truly independent person—in whom creative thinking is at its best—is someone who can accept society without denying himself.
Richard Crutchfield

To be let alone.   *Jefferson Davis*

Accountable to none.   *Benjamin Franklin*

The course I mark out for myself, guided by such knowledge as I can obtain.
Robert M. La Follette

(Following) your own path, no matter what people say.   *Karl Marx*

Resistance to the herd spirit.   *Daniel Mason*

A rocky island without a beach.   *Napoleon 1*

The privilege of the strong.
Friedrich W. Nietzsche

Middle class blasphemy. We are all dependent on one another. *George Bernard Shaw*

To know what you prefer, instead of humbly saying Amen to what the world tells you you ought to prefer. *Robert Louis Stevenson*

To breathe after your own fashion, to live after your own nature. *Henry David Thoreau*

Living in a manner that you can look any man in the eye and tell him to go to hell. *Anon.*

SEE ALSO AMERICANS, FREEDOM, INDIVID-UALISM, LIBERTY.

INDEX

A necessary implement...Without this, a large author is but a labyrinth, without a clue to direct the reader therein. *Thomas Fuller*

A pitiful piece of knowledge. *Joseph Glanville*

(Something that) tells us the contents of stories and directs us to the particular chapters.
Philip Massinger

The index, by which the whole book is governed and turned, like fishes by the tail.
Jonathan Swift

Consulting indexes...is to read books Hebraically, and begin where others usually end. *Jonathan Swift*

INDIAN (AMERICA)

A race in the process of growth, with probably a higher spiritual endowment and potential than any other primitive people. *J. Donald Adams*

Impassive—fearing but the name of fear—a stoic in the woods—a man without a tear.
Thomas Campbell

Master of all sorts of woodcraft, he seemed a part of the forest and lake, and the secret of his amazing skill seemed to be that he partook of the nature and fierce instincts of the beasts he slew.
Ralph Waldo Emerson

Savages we call them, because their manners differ from ours. *Benjamin Franklin*

The ruins of mankind. *Thomas Hooker*

The only ones to be conquered by the United States and not come out ahead. *Harry Olive*

An untutored mind who sees God in the clouds, or hears Him in the winds.
Adapted from Alexander Pope

The silent, exploited race. *Anon.*

Those who approach like foxes, fight like lions, and fly away like birds. *Anon.*

INDIANA

The Hoosier State. *John W. Davis*

Blest Indiana! in whose soil
Men seek the sure rewards of toil,
And honest poverty and worth
Find here the best retreat on earth. *John Finley*

The home of more first-rate second-class men than any State in the Union.
Thomas R. Marshall

INDIFFERENCE

The malady of the cultivated classes.
Henry F. Amiel

Neither cold nor hot. *Bible: Revelation, III, 5.*

Guilt by omission. *Arthur Koestler*

Political repletion. *Nikolai Lenin*

The tragedy of love.
William Somerset Maugham

'Tis lack of kindly warmth.
William Shakespeare

The worst sin towards our fellow creatures.
George Bernard Shaw

The only infidelity. *Israel Zangwill*

Vigor mortis. *Anon.*

INDIGESTION

An excellent commonplace for two people that never met before. *William Hazlitt*

Indigestion is charged by God with enforcing morality on the stomach. *Victor Hugo*

A falling out between the head and the stomach.
Anon.

INDISCRETION

The guilt of woman.   *Ambrose Bierce*

Nothing looks so like innocence as an indiscretion.   *Oscar Wilde*

To speak and act the truth.   *Anon.*

INDIVIDUAL

Humanity is alone real; the individual is an abstraction.   *Auguste Comte*

All that is valuable in human society.
                                    Albert Einstein

It is only to the individual that a soul is given. And the high destiny of the individual is to serve rather than to rule.   *Albert Einstein*

A bundle of possiblities and he is worth what life may get out of him before he is through.
                    Ralph Waldo Emerson

The cornerstone of our culture and our civilization.   *Joseph Proskauer*

The Creator made all men different in features, intelligence and voice, in order to promote honesty and chastity.   *Tosefta: Sanhedrin, VIII, 6.*

SEE ALSO GREAT MEN, HERO, MINORITY.

INDIVIDUALISM

The death of individuality . . . if only because it is an "ism."   *Gilbert Keith Chesterton*

The system in which human stupidity can do the least harm.   *John B. Clark*

The sin of political liberty.
                    James Fenimore Cooper

Leaving to the citizen as much freedom of action and of being as comports with order and the rights of others.   *James Fenimore Cooper*

To clap copyright on the world.
                    Ralph Waldo Emerson

The axiom that the individual was capable of realizing his own spiritual salvation . . . the individual was equally competent to attain his own economic salvation.   *John E. Hughes*

The special way a man responds to an elemental and recurrent cycle of experiences.
                    Robert C. Wood

SEE ALSO PERSONALITY.

INDIVIDUALITY

Acquiring a particular quality by acting in a particular way.   *Aristotle*

The image you get when you remember a single personality from all the rest after one meeting—that personality can lay claim to individuality.
                    Eugene E. Brussell

(Something) founded in feeling.   *William James*

The salt of common life. You may have to live in a crowd, but you do not have to live like it, not subsist on its food. You may have your own orchard. You may drink at a hidden spring.
                    Henry Van Dyke

SEE ALSO DISTINCTION, PERSONALITY.

INDUSTRY

SEE AMERICA, BUSINESS, CAPITALISM, WORK.

INEQUALITY

Mind. It is not income levels but differences in mental equipment that keep people apart, breed feelings of inferiority.   *Jacquetta Hawks*

The nature of things.   *Mencius*

What you relish best in others.   *Anon.*

INFANT

SEE BABY.

INFERIORITY

Exaggerated sensitiveness.   *Alfred Adler*

(That which) rules the mental life and can be clearly recognized as the sense of incompleteness and unfulfillment.   *Alfred Adler*

(A state owned by) one who knows nothing that is not known to every adult, who can do nothing that could not be learned by anyone in a few weeks, and who meanly admires mean things.
                    Henry Louis Mencken

What people make you feel—with your consent.
                    Adapted from Eleanor Roosevelt

To be weighed in the balance and to be found wanting.   *Anon.*

A quality relished mostly in competitors.

Anon.

SEE ALSO CLASSSES, MASSES, MOB.

INFIDEL

SEE PAGAN.

INFIDELITY

SEE ADULTERY, CUCKOLD.

INFINITY

A fathomless gullf, into which all things vanish.

Marcus Aurelius

If the doors of perception were cleansed, everything would appear to man as it is, infinite.

William Blake

Man always sees the infinite shadowed forth in something finite. *Thomas Carlyle*

The source of joy. There is no joy in the finite. Infinite is immortal. *Chandogya Upanishad.*

Whatever we imagine. *Thomas Hobbes*

When we say anything is infinite, we signify only that we are not able to conceive the ends and bounds of the thing named. *Thomas Hobbes*

A dark illimitable ocean, without bound.

John Milton

A floorless room without walls or ceiling.

Anon.

That dimension without end which the human mind cannot grasp. *Anon.*

SEE ALSO EINSTEIN, ETERNITY, TIME.

INFLATION

The most important economic act of our time— the single greatest peril to our economic health.

Bernard M. Baruch

Being broke with a lot of money in your pocket.

Paulette Brussell

Inflation is repudiation. *Calvin Coolidge*

Prosperity with high blood pressure.

Arnold H. Glasow

The first panacea for a mismanaged nation is inflation of the currency; the second is war. Both bring a temporary prosperity; both bring a permanent ruin. *Ernest Hemingway*

(Something) like a . . . pregnancy—it keeps growing. *Leon Henderson*

When you never had it so good or parted with it so fast. *Max Hess*

The world's most successful thief.

Carl E. Person

(When) we do more for the dollar than it does for us. *Robert Quillen*

(The cause): too much money going to somebody else. *William Vaughan*

Seeing a youngster get his first job at a salary you dreamed of as the culmination of your career.

William Vaughan

When one can live cheaper than two. *Anon.*

When the buck does not stop anywhere. *Anon.*

That which makes it possible for people from all walks of life to live in more expensive neighborhoods without even moving. *Anon.*

A fate worse than debt. *Anon.*

SEE ALSO BUDGET, TAXES.

INFORMATION

SEE FACT, KNOWLEDGE, SCIENCE.

INGRATE

One who receives a benefit from another, or is otherwise an object of charity. *Ambrose Bierce*

Any person who has got something for nothing, and wants more on the same terms.

Elbert Hubbard

He . . . who denies that he has received a kindness; he . . . who conceals it; he . . . who makes no return for it; he . . . who forgets it. *Seneca*

INGRATITUDE

To bite the hand that feeds us. *Edmund Burke*

A weed of every climate. *Samuel Garth*

Too great haste in repaying an obligation is a species of ingratitude. *La Rochefoucauld*

Treason to mankind.   *James Thomson*

SEE ALSO INGRATE.

INHERITANCE

SEE HEIR.

INITIATIVE

Doing the right thing without being told.
                                  Elbert Hubbard

INJUSTICE

Impiety.   *Marcus Aurelius*

The definition of injustice is no other than the not
performance of covenant.   *Thomas Hobbes*

Blasphemy.   *Robert G. Ingersoll*

Delay in justice.   *Walter Savage Landor*

(That which is) relatively easy to bear; what stings
is justice.   *Henry Louis Mencken*

SEE ALSO JUSTICE, LAW.

INNOCENCE

The truly innocent are those who not only are
guiltless themselves but who think others are.
                                  Josh Billings

The unbounded hope, the heavenly ignorance.
                                  Lord Byron

Folly and innocence are so alike, the difference,
though essential, fails to strike.
                        Adapted from William Cowper

A new-laid egg.   *Wiiliam S. Gilbert*

To have no guilt at heart, no wrong-doing to turn
us pale.   *Horace*

Innocence is an armed heel
To trample accusation.   *Percy Bysshe Shelley*

The child unborn.   *Anon.*

The age when a man thinks of all the wicked
things he is going to do.   *Anon.*

SEE ALSO BABY, VIRGINITY.

INSANITY

The man who cannot believe his senses, and the
man who cannot believe anything else are both
insane.   *Lord Chesterfield*

Power of fancy over reason.   *Samuel Johnson*

Insanity is what a majority of people say is
insanity.   *R. D. Laing*

A perfectly rational adjustment to the insane
world.   *R. D. Laing*

Consists of building major structures upon foundations which do not exist.   *Norman Mailer*

No free will.   *Legal Maxim*

To art what garlic is to salad.
                        Augustus Saint-Gaudens

SEE ALSO MADNESS.

INSINCERITY

SEE HYPOCRISY AND HYPOCRITE.

INSPIRATION

A force that poets have invented to give themselves importance.   *Jean Anouilh*

To see a world in a grain of sand, and heaven in a
wild flower; hold infinity in the palm of your hand
and eternity in an hour.
                        Adapted from William Blake

A spark o' nature's fire.   *Robert Burns*

I become a transparent eyeball; I am nothing; I see
all . . . I am part or particule of God.
                        Ralph Waldo Emerson

Inspiration presupposes revelation . . . may be
called the guardian of revelation.
                        Vincent McNabb

A subjective light.   *Vincent McNabb*

Holy rapture . . . from the seeds of the divine mind
sown in man.   *Ovid*

All the affection, attraction, inward reproaches
and regrets, perceptions and illuminations with
which God moves, working in our hearts through
His fatherly love and care, in order to awaken, to
kindle, lead and draw us to heavenly love and holy
desires.   *Saint Francis de Sales*

**SEE ALSO IDEAS, IMAGINATION, REVELA-
TION, VISION.**

INSTINCT

The not ourselves, which is in us and all around us...The enduring power, not ourselves, which makes for righteousness.   *Matthew Arnold*

Untaught ability.   *Alexander Bain*

The unfathomable Somewhat, which is Not we.
Thomas Carlyle

The psychical representative of an endosomatic, continuously flowing, source of stimulation.
Sigmund Freud

The source of an instinct is a process of excitation occurring in an organ, and the immediate aim of the instinct lies in the removal of this organic stimulus.   *Sigmund Freud*

The nose of the mind.   *Emile de Girardin*

Action taken in pursuance of a purpose, but without conscious perception of what the purpose is.   *Karl R. von Hartmann*

Intelligence, incapable of self-consciousness.
John Sterling

INSTITUTION

It is institutions alone that can create a nation.
Benjamin Disraeli

The lengthened shadow of one man.
Ralph Waldo Emerson

A vast mass of routine, petty malice, self-interest, carelessness.   *George Santayana*

Where there is a lull of truth an institution springs up.   *Henry David Thoreau*

INSULT

When a blockhead's remark points the dart.
Adapted from Samuel Johnson

Bad coins: we cannot help their being offered to us, but we need not take them.
Charles H. Spurgeon

(An act which) stigmatizes others with one's own blemishes.   *Talmud: Kiddushim, 70b.*

SEE ALSO RIDICULE, SATIRE.

INSURANCE

A guarantee that, no matter how many necessities a person had to forgo all through life, death was something to which he could look forward.

Fred Allen

An ingenious modern game of chance in which the player is permitted to enjoy the comfortable conviction that he is beating the man who keeps the table.   *Ambrose Bierce*

Paying for catastrophe on the installment plan.
Anon.

INTEGRATION

That period in a neighborhood's life when the first Negro family moves in and the last white family moves out.   *Adapted from Saul Alinsky*

Complete acceptance of the fact that *in order to have* a decent house or education, blacks must move into a white neighborhood or send their children to a white school. This reinforces...the idea that "white" is automatically better and "black" is by definition inferior.
Stokely Carmichael

Integration today means the man who "makes it," leaving his black brothers behind in the ghetto as fast as his new sportscar will take him.
Stokely Carmichael

A subterfuge for the maintenance of white supremacy.   *Stokely Carmichael*

A subterfuge only for those blacks who still suffer from a sense of inferiority.   *Robert Gordis*

SEE ALSO NEGRO.

INTELLECTUAL

A man who carries a briefcase.   *Jacques Barzun*

Someone whose mind watches itself.
Albert Camus

Someone who can listen to the "William Tell Overture" without thinking of the Lone Ranger.
John Chesson

Our most anxious social class is that known by courtesy as the intellectuals.   *Frank M. Colby*

One who has microscopes before his eyes.
Adapted from Albert Einstein

A man who takes more words than necessary to tell us more than he knows.

Dwight David Eisenhower

One who stands firmly on both feet in mid-air on both sides of an issue. *Henri Ferguson*

Man's attempt to be as absolute as God is, to know absolutely and to refuse the creaturehood of partial knowledge and of veiled choices.

Nels F. Ferré

People for whom ideas, concepts, literature, music, painting, the dance have intrinsic meaning.

Milton M. Gordon

A poor relation...(who) has to pick up the crumbs. He usually ekes out a living by teaching, journalism, or some white-collar job.

Eric Hoffer

A would-be aristocrat who loathes the sight, the sound and smell of common folk. *Eric Hoffer*

A literate person who feels himself a member of the educated minority. *Eric Hoffer*

Someone who forms his judgment on the basis of second-hand experience and who deals with ideas more than actions and things. *Herman Kahn*

(Those who) get their ideas and concepts second-hand from instruction and information systems rather than experience. *Herman Kahn*

(One) constantly betrayed by his own vanity. Godlike, he blandly assumes he can express everything in words. *Ann Morrow Lindbergh*

Swollen in head, weak in legs, sharp in tongue.

Mao Tse-tung

(Those who) have lost the sense of human weakness. *Francois Mauriac*

A person educated beyond his intellect.

Horace Porter

(They who) preserve a cool and unbiased judgment in the face of all solicitations to passion.

Bertrand A. Russell

Those who are all head but can't sew on a button.

Anon.

One who racks his brains as to whether a flea has a bellybutton. *Anon.*

A seeker of complexities. *Anon.*

One who produces endless quandaries for himself and others by sleight of brain. *Anon.*

A class more highly estimated by itself than by anyone else. *Anon.*

One who reads another's works—a non-creative man. *Anon.*

Powerless men of words. *Anon.*

SEE ALSO HIGHBROW, PROFESSOR.

INTELLIGENCE

Making the noblest and best in our curious heritage prevail. *Charles A. Beard*

The faculty of manufacturing artificial objects, especially tools to make tools. *Henry Bergson*

The faculty of making and using unorganized instruments. *Henry Bergson*

'Tis good-will makes intelligence.

Ralph Waldo Emerson

The test...is the ability to hold two opposed ideas in the mind at the same time, and still retain the ability to function. *F. Scott Fitzgerald*

(There are) two forms of intelligence, that of the brain and that of the heart. *George Gissing*

Discrimination between the probable and improbable, and acceptance of the inevitable.

Solomon Ibn Gabirol

To perceive things in the germ. *Lao-tse*

Honest, unaffected distrust of the powers of man is the surest sign. *Georg C. Lichtenberg*

The link that joins us to God.

Moses Maimonides

A function of integration within a single brain.

Charlton Ogburn

To be able to discern that what is true is true, and that what is false is false. *Emanuel Swedenborg*

All men see the same objects, but do not equally understand them. Intelligence is the tongue that discerns and tastes them. *Thomas Traherne*

The thing that enables a man to get along without an education. *Albert Wiggam*

The test of what we do with our leisure time.

Anon.

SEE ALSO MAN, MIND, THOUGHT.

INTELLIGENT PERSON

A man who enters with ease and completeness into the spirit of things and the intention of persons, and who arrives at an end by the shortest route.   *Henry F. Amiel*

The best encyclopedia.   *Johann W. Goethe*

(Those who) are always on the unpopular side of anything.   *Kin Hubbard*

Simply a question of organic chemistry, nothing more. One is no more responsible for being intelligent as for being stupid.   *Paul Leautaud*

To be open-minded, active-memoried, and persistently experimental.   *Leon Stein*

(One who) never snubs anybody.

Luc de Vauvenargues

An intelligent person will seek knowledge in details before venturing to discourse on great subjects.   *Leopold Zunz*

SEE ALSO BRAIN, SUPERIOR MAN.

INTEREST

Interest speaks all sorts of tongues, plays all sorts of parts, even that of disinterestedness.

La Rochefoucauld

A man's interest consists of whatever he takes interest in. He is a good man or a bad, according as he prefers one class of his interests to another.

John Stuart Mill

INTOLERANCE

SEE BIGOTRY, PREJUDICE.

INTUITION

The supra-logic that cuts out all routine processes of thought and leaps straight from problem to answer.   *Robert Graves*

The power of direct spiritual insight into the reason of things.   *J. Gurnhill*

Women's intuition is the result of millions of years of not thinking.   *Rupert Hughes*

Reason in a hurry.   *Holbrook Jackson*

Insight information.   *Alyce Misner*

What passes for woman's intuition is often nothing more than man's transparency.

George Jean Nathan

The strange instinct that tells a woman she is right, whether she is or not.   *Oscar Wilde*

The gift which enables a woman to arrive . . . at an infallible and irrevocable decision without the aid of reason, judgment, or discussion.   *Anon.*

SEE ALSO INSTINCT, MIND, REASON, UNDERSTANDING.

INVENTION

Bringing out the secrets of nature and applying them for the happiness of man.

Thomas Alva Edison

What does invention do but place the blocks of a child's game to make it whole.

Adapted from Robert U. Johnson

Consists in avoiding the constructing of useless combinations and in constructing the useful combinations which are in infinite minority. To invent is to discern, to choose.   *Henri Poincaré*

The basis . . . is science.

Alfred North Whitehead

The greatest invention of the nineteenth century was the invention of the method of invention.

Alfred North Whitehead

Trial and error.   *Anon.*

SEE ALSO EDISON, THOMAS ALVA, PROGRESS, SCIENCE.

INVENTOR

He that . . . augments the power of a man and the well-being of mankind.   *Henry Ward Beecher*

(One who) knows the world, half-enthusiast, half-rouge.   *Jeremy Bentham*

A person who makes an ingenious arrangement of wheels, levers and springs, and believes it civilization.   *Ambrose Bierce*

(One who) thinks only of what is in his own mind and not of the calculations and anxieties of his prospective patrons.   *Matthew Josephson*

A man with wheels in his head.   *Anon.*

A man who knows how to borrow from his experiences.   *Anon.*

A whirlwind of activity.   *Anon.*

SEE ALSO EDISON, THOMAS ALVA, FORD, HENRY, SCIENCE.

IRELAND

A little bit of heaven.   *J. Keirn Brennan*

That domestic Irish giant, named of Despair.
                                        Thomas Carlyle

A country in which the political conflicts are at least genuine...They are about patriotism, about religion, or about money: the three great realities.
                                Gilbert Keith Chesterton

A state of social decomposition.
                                    Benjamin Disraeli

The bane of England, and the opprobrium of Europe.   *Benjamin Disraeli*

A country in which the probable never happens and the impossible always does.
                                        John P. Mahaffy

A fatal disease—fatal to Englishmen and doubly fatal to Irishmen.   *George Moore*

A little Russia in which the longest way round is the shortest way home, and the means more important than the end.   *George Moore*

The Land of Youth.   *George W. Russell*

IRISHMEN

The cry-babies of the western world. Even the mildest quip will set them off into resolutions and protest.   *Heywood Broun*

An imaginative race, and it is said that imagination is too often accompanied by somewhat irregular logic.   *Benjamin Disraeli*

A fair people, they never speak well of one another.   *Samuel Johnson*

(One who) can be worried by the consciousness that there is nothing to worry about.
                                        Austin O'Malley

An Irishmen's heart is nothing but his imagination.   *George Bernard Shaw*

Irascible, prone to debt, and to fight, and very impatient of the restraints of law.   *Sydney Smith*

A servile race in folly nursed,
Who truckle most when treated worst.
                                        Jonathan Swift

The best hearts.   *Horace Walpole*

The Texans of Europe.   *Anon.*

IRONY

The gaiety of reflection and the joy of wisdom.
                                        Anatole France

The last phase of disillusion.   *Anatole France*

The cactus-plant that sprouts over the tomb of our dead illusions.   *Elbert Hubbard*

The weapons of the weak when persecuted or degraded.   *Anatole Leroy-Beaulieu*

Jesting hidden behind gravity.   *John Weiss*

To appreciate the joke which is on oneself.
                                        Jessamyn West

Insult conveyed in the form of a compliment.
                                        Edwin P. Whipple

Giving father a billfold for his birthday.   *Anon.*

SEE ALSO SATIRE.

ISLAM

SEE KORAN, MOHAMMED.

ISOLATION

SEE SOLITUDE.

ISRAEL

The core of the human race and the rest of humanity is like the peeling.   *Isaac Abravanel*

The Holy Land, where land is made holy and holiness made land. It is the homeland of holiness.   *Meir Ben-Horin*

A land flowing with milk and honey
                                    Bible: Exodus, III, 8.

I will give unto you and your seed after you, the land wherein your are a stranger, all the land of Canaan, for an everlasting possession.
                                    Bible: Genesis, XVII, 8.

A proverb and a by-word among all peoples.
                                    Bible Kings, IX, 7.

A people that shall dwell alone, and shall not be reckoned among the nations.
                                    Bible: Numbers, XXIII, 9.

The embodiment of the re-awakening corporate spirit of the whole Jewish nation.

Albert Einstein

He who says Israel says civilization.

Paul Eldridge

The people of Revelation...It must have had a native endowment that it could produce...such heroes of the spirit.   *Abraham Geiger*

Not merely an ethnic group, a racial entity, or some historically conditioned society, but...indeed a servant of God.   *Simon Greenberg*

Israel was made to be a "holy people." This is the essence of its dignity and the essence of its merit.

Abraham J. Heschel

A rare refuge; it is home and family, synagogue and congregation, nation, and revolutionary party all in one.   *Eric Hoffer*

Land of the muses, perfection of beauty, wherein every stone is a book, every rock a graven tablet.

Micah J. Lebensohn

An activating ferment injected into the mass, it gives the world no peace, it bars slumber, it teaches the world to be discontented and restless as long as the world has not God.

Jacques Maritain

A school of the knowledge of God to all nations.

Clement C. Webb

SEE ALSO JEWS, JUDAISM, ZIONISM.

ITALY

Classic ground.   *Joseph Addison*

A great prison where children are taught to adore their chains and to pity those who are free.

Lauro de Bosis

A paradise for horses, a hell for women.

Robert Burton

Inn of grief, ship without pilot in a mighty storm, no longer queen of provinces, but a brothel.

Dante

The country where opera and organ-grinders originated.   *Max Gralnick*

Home of the arts!   *Felicia D. Hermans*

A man who has not been in Italy, is always conscious of an inferiority, from his not have seen what it is expected a man should see.

Samuel Johnson

Only a geographical expression.

Clemens von Metternich

This world of beauty, color, and perfume, hoary with age, yet of unchanging bloom.

Adapted from Ada F. Murray

The Creator made Italy from designs by Michelangelo.   *Mark Twain*

Great mother of earth's fruits, great mother of men!   *Vergil*

A paradise inhabited with Devils.

Henry Wotton

SEE ALSO PAPACY, ROME.

J

JACKSON, ANDREW (1767-1845)

One of our tribe of great men who turn disease to commodity . . . he craves the sympathy for sickness as a portion of his glory.

John Quincy Adams

A chief magistrate of whom so much evil has been predicted, and from whom so much good has come. *Thomas H. Benton*

A great general, an incorruptible judge, and a capable president. *William G. Brownlow*

I feel much alarmed at the prospect of seeing General Jackson President. He is one of the most unfit men I know of for such a place.

Thomas Jefferson

The most American of Americans—an embodied Declaration of Independence—the Fourth of July incarnate. *James Parton*

JAIL

SEE PRISON.

JAMES, HENRY (1843-1916)

He has created a genre of his own. He has the distinction that makes the scientist a savant; he has contributed something to the common stock.

W. C. Brownell

He writes like an old woman. *William Faulkner*

Poor Henry . . . spending eternity wandering round and round a stately park and the fence is just too high for him to peep over and they're having tea just too far for him to hear what the countess is saying.

William Somerset Maugham

(One who) writes fiction as if it were a painful duty. *Oscar Wilde*

JANUARY

SEE WINTER.

JAZZ

When you got to ask what it is, you'll never get to know. *Louis Armstrong*

The primrose path to Hell! *Francis Beckman*

It's like an act of murder; you play with intent to commit something. *Duke Ellington*

American folk music. *George Gershwin*

The result of energy stored up in America.

George Gershwin

Your own experience, your thoughts, your wisdom. *Charles Parker*

A man telling the truth about himself.

Quincy Jones

A current that bubbled forth from a spring in the slums of New Orleans to become the mainstream of the twentieth century. *Henry Pleasants*

(Either) a thrilling communion with the primitive soul, or an ear-splitting bore. *Winthrop Sargent*

What they call jazz is just the music of people's emotions. *William Smith*

Music that will endure as long as people hear it through their feet instead of their brains.
John P. Sousa

Music invented by demons for the torture of imbeciles. *Henry Van Dyke*

The opposite of square. *Anon.*

An appeal to the emotions by an attack on the nerves. *Anon.*

SEE ALSO MUSIC.

JEALOUSY

Concerned about the preservation of that which can be lost only if not worth keeping.
Ambrose Bierce

(A state that) makes a man silly...and a woman more subtle. *Ludwig Boerne*

Jealousy is all the fun you think they had.
Erica Jong

Jealousy is fed by doubt, and becomes madness or ends when it passes from doubt to certainty.
La Rochefoucauld

More self-love than love. *La Rochefoucauld*

Wedlock's yellow sickness. *Thomas Middleton*

The injured lover's hell. *John Milton*

A kind of civil war in the soul. *William Penn*

The great exaggerator. *Johann C. Schiller*

The green-eyed monster. *William Shakespeare*

The fear or apprehension of superiority.
William Shenstone

Moral indignation is jealousy with a halo.
Herbert G. Wells

It is the hydra of calamities,
The sevenfold death. *Edward Young*

The friendship one woman has for another.
Anon.

A way to get rid of everything you are afraid of losing. *Anon.*

SEE ALSO ENVY.

JEFFERSON, THOMAS (1743-1826)

If not an absolute atheist, he had no belief in a future existence. All his ideas of obligation were bounded by the present life.
John Quincy Adams

His duties to his neighbor were under no stronger guarantee than the laws of the land and the opinions of the world. The tendency of this condition upon a mind of great compass...is to produce insincerity and duplicity, which were his besetting sins through life.
John Quincy Adams

Jefferson's mind was...flexible and open. It is in this sense that he was a great liberal ...His end was always the life, the liberty, and the happiness of individual human beings. *Stuart G. Brown*

A thoughtfully active man, as close as we are likely to come to Emerson's American Scholar.
Stuart G. Brown

His mind was restless and curious, active rather than reflective, given to the search for practical applications rather than to grand speculations.
Stuart G. Brown

The second founder of the liberties of the people.
Henry Clay

A man of profound ambition and violent passions.
Alexander Hamilton

He had a steadfast and abiding faith in justice, righteousness and liberty as the prevailing ... forces in the conduct of States, and that justice and righteousness were sure to prevail where any people bear rule in perfect liberty.
George F. Hoar

Author of the Declaration of American Independence, of the statute of Virginia for religious freedom, and father of the University of Virginia.
Thomas Jefferson

I have the consolation to reflect that during the period of my administration not a drop of the blood of a single fellow citizen was shed by the sword of war or of the law. *Thomas Jefferson*

I have such reliance on the good sense of the body of the people...that I am not afraid of their letting things go wrong to any length in any cause.
Thomas Jefferson

The most extraordinary collection of talent, of human knowledge, that has ever been gathered

together at the White House—with the possible exception of when Thomas Jefferson dined alone.
John Fitzgerald Kennedy

The principles of Jefferson are the definitions and axioms of a free society.   *Abraham Lincoln*

A speculative theorist.   *John Marshall*

An idealist with sense.   *Richard Milhous Nixon*

A gentleman...who could calculate an eclipse, survey an estate, tie an artery, plan an edifice, try a cause, break a horse, dance a minuet, and play the violin.   *James Parton*

JERUSALEM

The capital of the Jewish people.
David Ben-Gurion

City of truth.   *Bible: Zechariah, VIII, 3.*

The city of God, mystics, and religions.
Eugene E. Brussell

God's renewed embrace with a people with whom He was once intimately acquainted.
Harry Halperin

Jerusalem the golden,
With milk and honey blest,
Beneath thy contemplation
Sink heart and voice oppressed.   *Saint Bernard*

Jerusalem, like Heaven, is more a state of mind than a place.   *Israel Zangwill*

JESTER

SEE CLOWN, COMEDIAN.

JESUS

SEE CHRIST, CROSS.

JEWELRY

Something people use in order to appear better than other people.   *Hugh R. Cullen*

Orators of love.   *Samuel Daniel*

A woman's best friend.   *Edna Ferber*

Infinite riches in a little room.
Christopher Marlowe

JEWS

A people that adopts an unsocial way of life, refuses to sit at table with others, or to take part in the common prayers and offerings.
Apollonius

To be a Jew is a destiny.   *Vicki Baum*

A people of saviors, anointed for thorns and chosen for pain.   *Richard Beer-Hofmann*

A peoplehood.   *David Ben-Gurion*

The unrestrainable escapees from all the world's Egypts...the trembling, fearing, and daring visionaries at the foot of Mount Sinai these three thousand years; and the dreaming, praying, fighting, working, and singing builders of Zion.
Meir Ben-Horin

Those who see whatever is visible by the light of nature and culture, like all other men and women, and, like no other men.   *Meir Ben-Horin*

Ye shall be a peculiar treasure unto me above all people.   *Bible: Exodus, XIX, 5.*

A stiff-necked people.
Bible: Exodus, XXXII, 9.

I will make of thee a great nation, and I will bless thee, and make thy name great.
Bible: Genesis, XII, 2.

A race by religion, not a race by blood.
Hayyim Block

The great despoiled ones of history.   *Leon Blum*

A distinct nationality of which every Jew, whatever his country, his station or his shade of belief, is necessarily a member.   *Louis D. Brandeis*

A people of glaring faults and shining virtues.
Max Brod

(A people) held together by common remembering.   *Martin Buber*

A creative strain.   *Pearl Buck*

A weather-beaten, wasp-like fellow, sometimes a frenetic and lunatic person, sometimes one discontented.   *Thomas Coryat*

A people still, whose common ties are gone;
Who, mixed with every race, are lost in none.
George Crabbe

A people of artists, of intrinsic dreamers...that is why they have survived.   *Gabriele D'Annunzio*

An ancient people, a famous people, an enduring people, and a people who in the end have generally attained their objects.   *Benjamin Disraeli*

A race which can do anything but fail.

Benjamin Disraeli

Those enemies of the human race. Haughty and at the same time base, combining an invincible obstinacy with a spirit despicably mean, they weary alike your love and your hatred.

Anatole France

It is not birth that makes the Jew, but conviction, the profession of faith.   *Abraham Geiger*

A phenomenon the like of which has never been seen: a peasantry not given to drink...laborers not given to brawls.   *Judah L. Gordon*

Three are the marks of a Jew—a tender heart, self-respect, and charity.   *Hebrew Proverb*

When people talk about a wealthy man of my creed, they call him an Israelite; but if he is poor they call him a Jew.   *Heinrich Heine*

(One who) is obligated by his birth; Judaism is inalienable.   *Samuel Holdheim*

One cannot be a Jew without actively belonging to the Jewish people, even as one cannot be a soldier without belonging to an army.

Mordecai M. Kaplan

A piece of stubborn antiquity.   *Charles Lamb*

His cup is gall, his meat is tears,
His passion lasts a thousand years.

Emma Lazarus

A group whose fate has a positive meaning.

Kurt Lewin

A distinct people even though they abandon their own vernacular.   *Thomas G. Masaryk*

The only people in their world who conceived the idea of a universal religion, and labored to realize it by a propaganda often more zealous than discreet.   *George Moore*

The chosen people of the world's hatred.

Leon Pinsker

The Jews, like Cain, are doomed to wander the earth as fugitives and vagabonds, and their faces are covered with shame.   *Pope Innocent III*

Leaven in the progress of every country.

Ernest Renan

A people who can't sleep themselves and let nobody else sleep.   *Isaac B. Singer*

A people of the spirit, whose Torah was...a land, government and laws.   *Peretz Smolenskin*

(Those who have) firm faith in the living God, an intense feeling of their human and national personality, and an irresistible striving to realize and materialize their faith and feeling.

Vladimir Solovyov

Someone who weeps when the shofar sounds before the Temple Wall.   *Shmuel Stehman*

The Jews are a fact...and they need no definition.   *Mayer Sulzberger*

A people given to superstition and opposed to religion.   *Tacitus*

Scapegoats of revolution.   *Judd Teller*

He who has never been persecuted is not a Jew.

Talmud: Haggadah, 5a.

The emblem of eternity.   *Leon Tolstoy*

A creative minority.   *Arnold J. Toynbee*

Manifestly fossils of the Syriac Society.

Arnold J. Toynbee

The Jews of what their history has made them.

Louis Wirth

The eldest-born of time, touching the creation and reaching forward into the future, the true blasé of the universe.   *Israel Zangwill*

The great misunderstood of history.

Israel Zangwill

The work of eighteen hundred years of idiotic persecution.   *Emile Zola*

SEE ALSO HEBREW LANGUAGE, ISRAEL, JUDAISM, RABBI, SYNAGOGUE, TEN COMMANDMENTS, TORAH, ZIONISM.

JOHNSON, LYNDON BAINES (1908-1973)

A hard-working politician, noted for his expertise in the cloakrooms of the senate, who found the Presidency too big a game to handle. In the end he pleased neither the middle-classes nor the lower classes.   *Jerry Dashkin*

A genius in the art of legislative process.

Hubert H. Humphrey

My own philosophy...I believe every American has something to say and...a right to an audience...I believe there is always a national answer to each national problem.

Lyndon Baines Johnson

By personal choice, I am a Democrat, for I can in that party best apply and express my beliefs. As for being anything else, the definitions of what I am will have to be applied by others.

Lyndon Baines Johnson

I am...a liberal, a conservative, a Texan, a taxpayer, a rancher, a businessman, a consumer, a parent, a voter, and not as young as I used to be—and I am all these things in no fixed order.

Lyndon Baines Johnson

I am reminded always in my work at Washington of my own origins. I was born in the hill country of Texas, a remote region then, still remote today...My neighbors, friends, relatives there live independent, self-contained lives.

Lyndon Baines Johnson

I am a yes man for anything that will aid in the defense of this Republic.

Lyndon Baines Johnson

Mr. Johnson's Presidency was the first ever to carry on simultaneously a major war and the establishment of a major domestic program of social reform.   *Louis W. Koenig*

An incredibly potent mixture of persuasion, badgering, flattery, threats, reminders of past favors and future advantages.   *Mary McGrory*

A man who liked people for themselves...but who also was consciously on the lookout for the political main chance.   *Booth Mooney*

A good man to help out with naval matters.

Franklin Delano Roosevelt

He doesn't have the best mind on the Democratic side...he isn't the best orator; he isn't the best parliamentarian. But he's the best combination of all these qualities.   *Richard Russell*

A Senator's Senator.   *Theodore C. Sorensen*

He meant to put young men to work...to restore their morale.   *William S. White*

Physically and geographically, he is a southerner. In emotion, in basic point of view, in personal background he is the westerner.

William S. White

A man of no particular depth. When faced with a problem, he consulted with those he believed experts on the subject. He then acted on the view he thought the brightest. He never evolved a philosophy which could serve as a yardstick.

Robert Zwickey

JOHNSON, SAMUEL (1709-1784)

One of the great heroes of England. He bore poverty, the critics, ingratitude, personal loss stoically. He should be studied as a model of what the self-educated man can become in spite of fate.

Eugene E. Brussell

One of our great English souls. A strong and noble man; so much left undeveloped in him to the last: in a kindlier element what might he not have been.   *Thomas Carlyle*

A sage, by all allow'd.   *William Cowper*

All other wits are nothing compared with him...Johnson gives you a forcible hug, and shakes laughter out of you, whether you will or no.   *David Garrick*

Envy...was the bosom serpent of this literary despot.   *William Hayley*

A scholar and a Christian, yet a brute.

Soame Jenyns

I can now look back...in which little has been done, and little...enjoyed; a life diversified by misery, spent part in the sluggishness of penury, and part under the violence of pain, in gloomy discontent or...distress.   *Samuel Johnson*

The union of great powers with low prejudices.

Thomas B. Macaulay

One of those who left a personal seduction behind him in the world and retains, after death, the art of making friends.

Adapted from Robert Louis Stevenson

His style is a mixture of Latin and English; an intolerable composition of Latinity, affected smoothness, scholastic accuracy, and roundness of periods.   *Noah Webster*

JOKE

Jokes that give no pain are jokes.

Miguel de Cervantes

The cayenne of conversation, and the salt of life.
Paul Chatfield

The essence...seems to be an honest or well-intended halfness; a non-performance of what is pretended to be performed, at the same time that one is giving loud pledges of performance.
Ralph Waldo Emerson

Sport to one...death to another.
William Hazlitt

A kind of *coitus interruptus* between reason and emotion.   *Arthur Koestler*

Often only indulgence of intellect.
Jean de La Bruyère

Verbal mementoes of the communal experience.
Jonathan Miller

The radioactive tracers in human history. By their light, we can make out cardinal moments in the pulse and growth of feeling.   *George Steiner*

Something you must share with someone else.
Anon.

SEE ALSO COMEDY, HUMOR, LAUGHTER, SATIRE, WIT.

JOURNALISM

Literature in a hurry.   *Matthew Arnold*

The first power in the land.   *Samuel Bowles*

The business of presenting the news of the day to the mass man.   *Eugene E. Brussell*

Consists largely in saying "Lord Jones Dead" to people who never knew that Lord Jones was alive.
Gilbert Keith Chesterton

Buying white paper at 2¢ a pound and selling it at 10¢ a pound.   *Charles A. Dana*

Organized gossip.   *Edward Eggleston*

The science of beating the sense out of words.
Henry James

Our...impossible task of providing every week a first rough draft of a history that will never be completed about a world we can never understand.   *Philip Graham*

The sole aim...should be service.
Mohandas K. Gandhi

A profession whose business it is to explain to others what it personally does not understand.
Lord Northcliffe

(That which) forces us to take an interest in some fresh triviality or other every day.
Marcel Proust

A news sense is really a sense of what is important, what is vital, what has color and life—what people are interested in. That's journalism.
Burton Roscoe

In America, journalism is apt to be regarded as an extension of history; in Britain, as an extension of conversation.   *Anthony Sampson*

Exaggeration...for the object of journalism is to make events go as far as possible.
Arthur Schopenhauer

An ability to meet the challenge of filling the space.   *Rebecca West*

The survival of the vulgarest.   *Oscar Wilde*

Instant garbage.   *Robert Zwickey*

A trade, not a profession.   *Anon.*

SEE ALSO NEWS, PRESS (THE).

JOURNALIST

Assassins who sit with loaded blunder-busses at the corner of streets and fire them off for hire or for sport at any passenger they select.
John Quincy Adams

An effete corps of impudent snobs who characterize themselves as intellectuals.   *Spiro Agnew*

A writer who guesses his way to the truth and dispels it with a tempest of words.
Ambrose Bierce

A man who has missed his calling.
Otto von Bismarck

A hired buffoon, a daily scribbler of some low lampoon condemned to drudge.
Adapted from Lord Byron

To serve thy generation, this thy fate.
Mary Clemmer

(One who) is partly in the entertainment business and partly in the advertising business—advertising either goods, or a cause, or a government. He just has to make up his mind whom he wants to entertain, and what he wants to advertise.

Claud Cockburn

(One who is) too busy with the news of the day to lay aside the mental habits of fifty years before.

Frank M. Colby

Puppets. They simply respond to the pull of the most powerful strings.　*Lyndon Baines Johnson*

A man without virtue, who writes lies at home for his own profit. To these compositions is required neither genius nor knowledge...but contempt of shame and indifference to truth are absolutely necessary.　*Samuel Johnson*

The highest reach of a journalist is an empty reasoning on policy, and vain conjectures on the public management.　*Jean de La Bruyère*

A man who writes a piece of news which corrupts before morning, and which he is obliged to throw away as soon as he awakes.

Adapted from Jean de La Bruyère

(One who) is called upon to deliver his judgment point-blank and at the word of command on every conceivable subject of human thought.

James Russell Lowell

A grumbler, a censurer, a giver of advice...a tutor of nations.　*Napoleon 1*

All journalists are...alarmists; this is their way of making themselves interesting.

George A. Riddell

(People who) cover you, yet you are never covered.　*Felix Riesenberg*

Nameless men and women whose scandously low payment is a guarantee of their ignorance and their servility to the financial department.

George Bernard Shaw

The thorn in the cushion of the editorial chair.

William Makepeace Thackeray

An ambassador is a man of virtue sent to lie abroad for his country; a news-writer is a man without virtue who lies at home for himself.

Henry Wotton

Bad manners make a journalist.　*Oscar Wilde*

SEE ALSO NEWSPAPERS, PRESS (THE).

JOY

The true joy of man is in doing that which is most proper to his nature.　*Marcus Aurelius*

Every joy is gain
And gain is gain, however small.

Robert Browning

Perfectly to will what God wills, to want what He wants.　*Meister Eckhart*

To put one's power in some natural and useful or harmless way...and the real misery is not to do this.　*Oliver Wendell Holmes 2*

The function of creating and acting and changing, living intensely through each day.

Charles E. Jeanneret

To begin.　*Cesare Pavese*

An elation of spirit—of a spirit which trusts in the goodness and truth of its own possessions.

Seneca

The realization of the truth of oneness, the oneness of our soul with the world and of the world.　*Rabindranath Tagore*

The life of a man's life.　*Benjamin Whichcote*

A fruit that Americans eat green.

Amando Zegri

SEE ALSO HAPPINESS, PLEASURE.

JUDAISM

The principle of Divine Unity, which signifies the unity and equality of all men.

Elie-Aristide Astruc

A total approach to one's family, the world and one's self, to the values one holds and the aspirations one cherishes. These are dramatized through the regular discipline of worship, ritual and ceremony and the recognition that the blessings of life come from God.　*Sidney H. Brooks*

Judaism is a religion of ideals, Christianity, of an ideal person.　*Francis C. Burkitt*

Not a creed; the Jewish God is simply a negation of superstition, an imaginary result of its elimination.　*Albert Einstein*

A way of life which endeavors to transform virutally every human action into a means of communication with God. *Louis Finkelstein*

Utilitarianism...It asserts...a God who...is here and now; a God of the living as well as of the dead; a God of the market place as well as of the temple. *Henry George*

The national creative power, which expresses itself primarily in a religious culture. *Ahad HaAm*

The religion of the Bible...the classical paradigm of a God-made religion. *Arthur Hertzberg*

A religion of time aiming at the sanctification of time...The Sabbaths are our great cathedrals. *Abraham J. Heschel*

The track of God in the wilderness of oblivion. *Abraham J. Heschel*

The funded cultural activity which the Jewish people has transmitted from generation to generation. *Mordecai M. Kaplan*

An evolving religious civilization. *Mordecai M. Kaplan*

Belief in the divine origin of the Torah and the acceptance of the yoke of the commandments. *Samuel D. Luzzatto*

(A religion which) looks upon all human beings as children of one Father; thinks of them all created in the image of God, and insists a man be judged not by his religion, but by his action. *Samuel D. Luzzatto*

(A religion which) has no symbolical books, no articles of faith...and, according to the spirit of true Judaism, must hold them inadmissible. *Moses Mendelssohn*

A tendency rather than a doctrine...the attitude of...viewing life and death, man and the world, from the point of view of eternity. *Adolph S. Oko*

A divine religion, not a mere complex of racial peculiarities and tribal customs. *Solomon Schechter*

SEE ALSO COVENANT, JEWS, MOSES, RABBI, SYNAGOGUE, TEN COMMANDMENTS.

JUDGE

The function of the judge is to restore equality. *Aristotle*

Their office is...to interpret law, and not to make law, or give law. *Francis Bacon*

(One) more learned than witty, more reverend than plausible, and more advised than confident. Above all things, integrity is their portion and proper virtue. *Francis Bacon*

To compress, to shape, to label the erratic sequences of life is the perennial function of the judges. *Sybille Bedford*

A member of the bar who once knew a governor. *Curtis Bok*

A man of cold neutrality. *Adapted from Edmund Burke*

A speaking law. *Cicero*

It is the province of the judge to expound the law only—the written from the statute, the unwritten or common law from the decisions of our predecessors and of our existing courts...Not to speculate upon what is best, in his opinion, for the advantage of the community. *Samuel Taylor Coleridge*

(One who) weighs the arguments, and puts a brave face on the matter, and since there must be a decision, decides as he can, and hopes he has done justice. *Ralph Waldo Emerson*

One who learns law from lawyers. *Elbert Hubbard*

The duty of a judge is to administer justice, but his practice is to delay it. *Jean de La Bruyère*

It is for a judge to declare, not to make the law. *Legal Maxim*

A law student who marks his own papers. *Henry Louis Mencken*

God's minister, and a father of the country, appointed of God to punish offenders. *John Northbrooke*

It is a judge's duty to investigate both the circumstances and time of an act. *Ovid.*

Men who...should be free from hatred and friendship, anger and pity. *Sallust*

He who decides a case. *Seneca*

(One) dressed in a little brief authority...most ignorant of what he's most assured. *William Shakespeare*

Nothing but the ego speaking. *Michele Simpson*

Judges... are picked out from the most dextrous lawyers, who are grown old or lazy.

Jonathan Swift

Nothing but the law speaking.

Benjamin Whichcote

One who populates the city jails by grave decisions—head or tails.   *Anon.*

A referee between two lawyers.   *Anon.*

SEE ALSO JURY, JUSTICE, LAW, LAW (COMMON), LAW (NATURAL), LAWSUIT, SUPREME COURT, TRIAL.

JUDGMENT

We judge others according to results; how else?—not knowing the process by which results are arrived at.   *George Eliot*

Not conclusions of reasoning, but immediate sensations like those of seeing and hearing.

James A Froude

The dark line in the face of God.   *Billy Graham*

Consists not in seeing through deceptions and evil intentions but in being able to waken the decency dormant in every person.   *Eric Hoffer*

Knowledge is the treasure, but judgment the treasurer of a wise man. He that has more knowledge than judgment is made for another man's use more than his own.   *William Penn*

To pronounce the verdict in regard to a person, to anticipate... the punishment that the sinner deserves from God.   *John Ruskin*

JUDGMENT DAY

The wrath to come.   *Bible: Matthew, III, 7.*

Day of wrath, that day of burning

Tommaso di Celano

The last loud trumpet's wondrous sound shall through the tombs resound, and wake the nations under ground.   *Adapted from Wentworth Dillon*

When rattling bones together fly
From the four corners of the sky.   *John Dryden*

(When God scans you) not for medals, degrees, and diplomas, but for scars.   *Elbert Hubbard*

(When) God will not ask to what sect you belonged, but what manner of life you led.

Israel Kagan

The day when we shall not be asked what we have read, but what we have done.

Adapted from Thomas á Kempis

The world's last session.   *John Milton*

We have reached a point in history where the unchecked pursuit of truth, without regard to its social consequences, will bring to a swift end the pursuit of truth... by wiping out the very civilization that has favored it. That would indeed be the judgment of God.   *Lewis Mumford*

That dreadful day when heaven and earth shall pass away.   *Adapted from Walter Scott*

When all this old world and its generations shall be consumed in one fire.   *Tertullian*

When the silence of death will descend upon our planet.   *E. I. Watkin*

When the saints and sinners
Shall be parted right and left.   *Anon.*

SEE ALSO DEATH, SIN, SINNER.

JUDICIARY

SEE JUDGE, JURY, LAWYERS, SUPREME COURT, TRIAL.

JUNE

The leafy month.   *Samuel Taylor Coleridge*

The month of leaves and roses, when pleasant sights salute the eyes and pleasant scents the noses.   *Adapted from Nathaniel P. Willis*

The rebirth of the earth.   *Anon.*

For many couples, the end to a marry chase.

Anon.

JUNK

SEE ANTIQUES.

JURY

Twelve persons chosen to decide who has the better lawyer.   *Robert Frost*

The stupidity of one brain multiplied by twelve.

Elbert Hubbard

A collection of sedentary owls.   *Elbert Hubbard*

The judges of fact.   *Legal Maxim*

A group of twelve people of average ignorance.

Herbert Spencer

A group which must be touched before it can be reached.   *Anon.*

JUSTICE

The only true principle for mankind.

Henry F. Amiel

A faculty that may be developed. This development is what constitutes the education of the human race.   *Henry F. Amiel*

Eye for eye, tooth for tooth, hand for hand, foot for foot.   *Bible: Exodus, XXI, 24.*

A commodity which in a more or less adulterated condition the State sells to the citizen as a reward for his allegiance, taxes and personal service.

Ambrose Bierce

The great standing policy of civil society.

Edmund Burke

Consists in the compliance with custom in all matters of difference between men.

James C. Carter

That no one shall suffer wrong, and that the public good is served.   *Cicero*

To give everyone his due.   *Cicero*

It is the function of justice not to wrong one's fellow men.   *Cicero*

Compliance with the written laws.   *Cicero*

There is no such thing as justice—in or out of court.   *Clarence Darrow*

The end of government.   *Daniel Defoe*

(Something) always violent to the party offending, for every man is innocent in his own eyes.

Daniel Defoe

Truth in action.   *Benjamin Disraeli*

Never anything in itself, but in the dealings of men with one another in any place whatever and at any time . . . a kind of compact not to harm or be harmed.   *Epicurus*

When you are awarded the verdict.

Max Gralnick

The end of government . . . the end of civil society.

Alexander Hamilton

Whereas in Greek the idea of justice was akin to harmony, in Hebrew it is akin to holiness.

Joseph H. Hertz

Taking from no man what is his.

Thomas Hobbes

A system of revenge wherein the State imitates the criminal.   *Elbert Hubbard*

To fulfill the fair expectations of man.

Lyndon Baines Johnson

The earnest and constant will to render to every man his due. The precepts of the law are these: to live honorably, to injure no other man, to render to every man his due.   *Justinian 1*

A virtue of the soul distributing that which each person deserves.   *Diogenes Laertius*

A name for certain classes of mortal rules, which concern the essentials of human well-being.

John Stuart Mill

All strength and activity . . . to use against all violence and oppression on the earth.

John Milton

What is established.   *Blaise Pascal*

The insurance which we have on our lives and property. Obedience is the premium which we pay for it.   *William Penn*

A certain rectitude of mind whereby a man does what he ought to do in the circumstances confronting him.   *Saint Thomas Aquinas*

Fairness is what justice really is.   *Potter Stewart*

Every virtue is included in the idea of justice.

Theognis

That side of love which affirms the independent right of persons within the love relation.

Paul Tillich

The hope of all who suffer.
The dread of all who wrong.

John Greenleaf Whittier

The only thing that allowed the human race to stop living as animals and to start living as human beings.   *Frank W. Wilson*

The heart and spirit of men who resist power.

Woodrow Wilson

SEE ALSO EQUALITY, JUDGE, JUDGMENT, JURY, LAW, LAW (COMMON), LAW (NATURAL), LAWYERS.

JUVENILE DELINQUENCY

A product of the lack of worthy goals to offer our young. Lack of worthiness—the source of our major problem with the anti-social youngster.

Jerry Dashkin

A product of sickness in our society. It is largely an urban phenomenon and its most fertile breeding place in the slums of the great cities.

Life Magazine

(Something which) starts in the high chair and ends in the death chair.   *James D. Murray*

JUVENILE DELINQUENT

Other people's children in trouble.

Jerry Dashkin

A child who starts acting like his parents.   *Anon.*

A person with primitive social behavior.   *Anon.*

K

KANGAROO

An animal that carries its brood in a snood.

Harry McNaughton

A pogo stick with a pouch. *Anon.*

KENNEDY, JOHN FITZGERALD
(1917-1963)

The television personality...a boy Democrat whose only assets are juvenile charm and $300 million. *Lucius Beebe*

An engaging personality primarily, whose popularity rested on good looks and a pleasing style rather than on specific programs.

Eugene E. Brussell

The bright charm is only skin deep; underneath there is a core of steel—metallic, sometimes cold, sometimes unbending, usually durable.

James M. Burns

A serious, driven man—about as casual as a cash register. *James M. Burns*

Egotism and a fierce will to succeed are his ruling characteristics. In the service of his ambition, he is wily and coldly calculating, but not hypocritical. Candor is probably his most engaging personal trait. *Economist*

A rationalist, a man who deals in reality rather than rhetoric. He's not what you would call an all-outer. He's not an all-outer on anything.

Fortune Magazine, Oct., 1960.

I got Jack into politics...I told him Joe was dead and therefore it was his responsibility to run for Congress. He didn't want to. He felt he didn't have the ability and he still feels that way.

Joseph P. Kennedy

People just seem to like Jack. He'll put on a pair of old dungarees and go out and talk to the gardener or anybody...He looks just like some hayseed from Kansas. *Joseph P. Kennedy*

I don't have an organized philosophy of life. I just have my family and my work. I subscribe to the Greek idea of "full use of your powers along the ideas of excellence," and I love politics.

John Fitzgerald Kennedy

I grew up in a very strict house where there were no free riders. *John Fitzgerald Kennedy*

Whatever one's religion in his private life may be, for the office-holder nothing takes precedence over his oath to uphold the Constitution and all its parts. *John Fitzgerald Kennedy*

Two personalities. One is the sandy-haired, boyish politician with the blue eyes and the easy informality with all comers. The other is the politician who stands aside, studies the politician and tries to decide what makes him tick. He is, in fact, a kind of junior edition of Adlai Stevenson.

Fletcher Knebel

The "matinee idol" of the United States Senate. He has few political rivals in the good-looks department. Six feet tall, tanned and handsome, he has an engaging smile and a shock of unruly brown hair that has become his trade-mark.

Victor Lasky

The product of an age in which men felt they could achieve special distinction by the techniques of superpress-agentry rather than by the espousal of serious ideas. *Victor Lasky*

Kennedy has a dozen faces...Kennedy's most characteristic quality is the remote and private air of a man who has traversed some lonely terrain of experience, of loss and gain, of nearness to death, which leaves him isolated from the mass of others. *Norman Mailer*

Something in his appearance suggests to the suggestible that he is lost...a prince in exile...or a very wealthy orphan. *Mary McGory*

One whom many conservatives will believe to be conservative, but whom 'liberals' will know to be otherwise. *Raymond Moley*

A Democrat and a liberal without any touches of Marxism...His voting record might qualify him as an independent...He is one of the few...who isn't angry at anyone. *W. E. Mullins*

Kennedy, in the supercilious arrogance which Harvard inculcates in lace-curtain Irish, doggedly mispronounced ordinary words...This was the Rooseveltian contempt for the common man. He seems afraid to be taken as a valid American.

Westbrook Pegler

Kennedy grimly believes in the right to dissent. In fact, he will tell you what you can dissent about.

Robert G. Spivack

Here is Everywoman's son, and perhaps her lover...His boyishness invites protection and solicitude. *James Wechsler*

A curious blend of Boston conservatism and New Deal liberalism. *Anon.*

A remarkable quality of shy, sense-making sincerity. *Anon.*

A curious reversal of the law of the log cabin.

Anon.

KILL

SEE MURDER.

KINDNESS

Gladdening the hearts of those who are travelling the dark journey with us. *Henry F. Amiel*

Kindness is wisdom. There is none in life but needs it and may learn. *Philip J. Bailey*

A brief preface to ten volumes of exaction.

Ambrose Bierce

A language which the dumb can speak, the deaf can understand. *Christian N. Bovee*

Good will. *Charles F. Dole*

The golden chain by which society is bound together. *Johann W. Goethe*

Charity minus money. *Max Gralnick*

Loving people more than they deserve.

Joseph Joubert

SEE ALSO ALTRUISM, FOREBEARANCE, MERCY.

KING

What is the essence of kingship? To rule oneself well, and not to be led astray by wealth or fame.

Apocrypha: Aristeas, 178.

To do well and be ill spoken of.

Marcus Aurelius

A human being who has few things to desire and many things to fear.

Adapted from Francis Bacon

The representatives of divine majesty, deputed by Providence to execute its designs.

Jacques Bossuet

The animal known as king is by nature carnivorous. *Marcus Cato*

Nothing resembles a man more than a king.

Charles XII of Sweden

A feather in a man's cap: let children enjoy their rattle. *Oliver Cromwell*

Grasshoppers; they are nothing, and less than nothing: both their love and their hatred is to be despised. *Jonathan Edwards*

A king is appointed to protect his subjects in their lives, properties and laws. For this purpose he has a delegation of power from the people, and he has no just claim to any other power.

John Fortesque

A very ordinary kind of man who has to live in a very extraordinary kind of way that sometimes seems to have little sense to it. *King George V*

The least independent man in his dominions.
Julius and Augustus Hare

Divine Right tempered by bombs.
Elbert Hubbard

A public servant.   *Ben Jonson*

A royalist by trade.   *Joseph 2 of Austria*

One who never dies.   *Legal Maxim*

Good kings are slaves and their subjects are free.
Marie of France

A name of dignity and office, not of person.
John Milton

An official who today has become a vermiform
appendix: useless when quiet; when obtrusive, in
danger of removal.   *Austin O'Malley*

Scratch a king and find a fool.   *Dorothy Parker*

A man condemned to bear the public burden of a
nation's care.   *Adapted from Matthew Prior*

The king is not the nation's representative, but its
clerk.   *Maximilien F. Robespierre*

He is one whom all good men can praise without
compunction not only during his life, but even
afterwards.   *Saint John Chrysostom*

A thing men have made for their own sakes, for
quietness' sake.   *John Selden*

Kings are not born: they are made by universal
hallucination.   *George Bernard Shaw*

Like stars—they rise and set, have the worship of
the world, but no repose.
Adapted from Percy Bysshe Shelley

Kings is mostly rapscallions.   *Mark Twain*

Everyone is born a king, and most people die in
exile, like most kings.   *Oscar Wilde*

A highly paid model for postage stamps.   *Anon.*

SEE ALSO LEADER, MONARCHY, QUEEN.

KISS

A lovely trick designed by nature to stop speech
when words become superfluous.
Ingrid Bergman

A word invented by the poets as a rhyme for
"bliss."   *Ambrose Bierce*

Traditional Hollywood style greeting for friend
and foe alike.   *Eugene E. Brussell*

Something made of nothing, tasting very sweet; a
most delicious compound, with ingredients complete.   *Adapted from Mary E. Buell*

"Kiss" rhymes to "bliss" in fact as well as verse.
Lord Byron

Kisses are keys; wanton kisses are keys of sin.
John Clarke

Something that often leads to marriage because it
leaves something to be desired.
Adapted from Robert Fontaine

The anatomical juxtaposition of two orbicularis
oris muscles in a state of contraction.
Henry Gibbons

Lip service to love.   *Warren Goldberg*

A course of procedure, cunningly devised for the
mutual stoppage of speech at a moment when
words are superfluous.   *Oliver Herford*

The sure, sweet cement, glue, and lime of love.
Robert Herrick

When women kiss it always reminds one of
prizefighters shaking hands.
Henry Louis Mencken

A kiss can be a comma, a question mark or an
exclamation point. That's basic spelling that every
woman ought to know.   *Mistinguette*

Unspoken promise of a soul's allegiance.
Marion Phelps

A pleasant reminder that two heads are better than
one.   *Rex Prouty*

(When) soul meets soul on lover's lips.
Percy Bysshe Shelley

To a young girl, faith; to a married woman, hope;
and to an old maid, charity.   *V. P. Skipper*

A thing of use to no one, but prized by two.
Robert Zwickey

A contraction of the mouth due to an enlargement
of the heart.   *Anon.*

A vigorous exchange of saliva.   *Anon.*

Something which you cannot give without taking,
and cannot take without giving.   *Anon.*

SEE ALSO LOVE, LOVERS.

KITCHEN

SEE COOKING.

KITTEN

The trouble with a kitten is
THAT
Eventually it becomes a
CAT.   *Ogden Nash*

A kitten is so flexible that she is almost double;
the hind parts are equivalent to another kitten with
which the forepart plays. She does not discover
that her tail belongs to her until you tread upon it.
                              Henry David Thoreau

SEE ALSO CAT.

KNOWLEDGE

Emancipation from error.   *Henry F. Amiel*

A rich storehouse for the glory of the Creator, and
the relief of man's estate.   *Francis Bacon*

Knowledge and human power are synonymous.
                                       Francis Bacon

Reasoning and Experience.   *Roger Bacon*

The fear of the Lord is the beginning of knowledge.   *Bible: Proverbs, I, 7.*

The small part of ignorance that we arrange and
classify.   *Ambrose Bierce*

An unending adventure at the edge of uncertainty.
                                   Jacob Bronowski

There is knowledge and knowledge: knowledge
that resteth in the bare speculation of things, and
knowledge that is accompanied with the grace of
faith and love, which puts a man upon doing even
the will of God from the heart.   *John Bunyan*

Recorded Experience, and a product of History;
of which...Reasoning and Belief, no less than
Action and Passion, are essential materials.
                                   Thomas Carlyle

The first step...is to know that we are ignorant.
                                       David Cecil

A comfortable and necessary retreat and shelter
for us in advanced age; and if we do not plant it

while young it will give us no shade when we
grow old.   *Lord Chesterfield*

The only instrument of production that is not
subject to diminishing returns.   *J. M. Clark*

When you know a thing, to hold that you know it,
and when you do not know it, to admit that you do
not—this is true knowledge.   *Confucius*

Learning well retained.   *Dante*

The key that first opens the hard heart, enlarges
the affections, and opens the way for men into the
kingdom of heaven.   *Jonathan Edwards*

Knowing that we cannot know.
                              Ralph Waldo Emerson

The amassed thought and experience of innumerable minds.   *Ralph Waldo Emerson*

A process of piling up facts; wisdom lies in their
simplification.   *Martin H. Fischer*

The intellectual manipulation of carefully verified
observations.   *Sigmund Freud*

Not to know more than all men, but to know more
at each moment than any particular man.
                                   Johann W. Goethe

Remembrance.   *Thomas Hobbes*

All knowledge resolves itself into probability.
                                       David Hume

Two kinds; we know a subject ourselves, or we
know where we can find information upon it.
                                   Samuel Johnson

(Something) needful to thinking people—it takes
away the heat and fever; and helps, by widening
speculation, to ease the burden of the mystery.
                                       John Keats

History tells us what man has done; art, what man
has made; literature, what man has felt; religion,
what man has believed; philosophy, what man has
thought.   *Benjamin C. Lemming*

Experience.   *John Locke*

Nothing but the perception of the connection and
agreement or disagreement and repugnancy, of
any of our ideas.   *John Locke*

Our senses.   *Lucretius*

A living contact with truth, a transformation in
love. An encounter with God.   *Peter Minard*

Her business is not to find a man's eyes, but to guide, govern, and direct his steps, provided he has found feet and straight legs to go upon.

Michel de Montaigne

Power, if you know it about the right person.

Ethel Mumford

Recognition of something absent.

George Santayana

The wing wherewith we fly to heaven.

William Shakespeare

Understanding the evidence that establishes a fact, not in the belief that it is a fact.

Charles T. Sprading

Nothing but the continually burning up of error to set free the light of truth.   *Rabindranath Tagore*

To know that we know what we know, and that we do not know what we do not know, that is true knowledge.   *Henry David Thoreau*

A conceit that we know something which robs us of the advantage of our actual ignorance.

Henry David Thoreau

The great sun of the firmament. Life and power are scattered with all its beams.   *Daniel Webster*

The toupee which covers our baldness.   *Anon.*

SEE ALSO EDUCATION, EXPERIENCE, FAIL-URE, LEARNING, SCIENCE, SELF-KNOWL-EDGE, TRUTH.

KORAN

It (the Koran) was not the Prophet who spoke under the influence of the Holy Spirit; it was a Divine Message brought by the Holy Spirit; it was a Divine Message brought by the Holy Spirit or Gabriel, and delivered in words to the Holy Prophet, who delivered it to Mankind.

Muhamed Ali

The Koran preaches the oneness of God and emphasizes divine mercy and forgiveness.

N. J. Dawood

The Revelation (sending down) of this Book is from the Mighty, the Wise.   *Koran*

SEE ALSO MOHAMMED, MOHAMMEDANISM.

L

LABOR

A high human function . . . the basis of human life, the most dignified thing in the life of man.

David Ben-Gurion

In the sweat of thy face shalt thou eat bread, till thou return unto the ground; for out of it wast thou taken. *Bible: Genesis III, 19.*

Profit. *Bible: Proverbs, XIV, 23.*

One of the processes by which A acquires the property of B. *Ambrose Bierce*

A surmounting of difficulties, an exertion of the contracting power of the muscles; and as such resembles pain, which consists in tension . . . in everything but degree. *Edmund Burke*

(When) the whole soul of a man is composed into a kind of real harmony the instant he sets himself to work. *Thomas Carlyle*

The grand conqueror, enriching and building up nations more surely than the proudest battles.

William Ellery Channing

The capital of our workingmen.

Grover Cleveland

The duty of all citizens of the republic.

Constitution of the U.S.S.R., 1924.

Every man's . . . life-preserver.

George B. Emerson

Nature's physician. *Galen*

The curse of the world, and nobody can meddle with it without becoming proportionately brutified. *Nathaniel Hawthorne*

To walk in the golden track that leads to God.

Josiah G. Holland

Everything in the world is purchased by labor, and our passions are the only causes of labor.

David Hume

To labor is to pray. *Motto of the Benedictines*

Rest from the sorrows that greet us; rest from petty vexations that meet us; rest from sin-promptings that ever entreat us.

Adapted from Frances S. Osgood

Our portion lest we should make this world our rest and not hope for the hereafter.

Saint John Chrysostom

(Activity which) serves to mortify and subdue the flesh. *Saint Francis de Sales*

The real measure of the exchangeable value of all commodities. *Adam Smith*

The happiness of men consists in life. And life is in labor. *Leon Tolstoy*

Nature is inexhaustible and untiring labor is a god which rejuvenates her. *Voltaire*

The best form of prayer. *Israel Zangwill*

An activity by which money is pumped from one pocket into another. *Anon.*

LABORER

SEE WORKERS.

LABOR UNIONS

The worst thing that ever struck the earth because they take away a man's independence.

Henry Ford

Trade unions are islands of anarchy in a sea of chaos.　　*Aneurin Bevin*

An elemental response to the human instinct for group action in dealing with group problems.

William Green

A formula for national misery.　　*Paul Johnson*

(They) are about individuals and the right to answer back to the boss.　　*Leonard Murray*

The best and most suitable means for attaining what is aimed at, that is...for helping each individual member to better his condition to the utmost in body, mind and property.

Pope Leo XIII

LADY

No lady is ever a gentleman.

James Branch Cabell

One who never shows her underwear unintentionally.　　*Lilian Day*

A woman who always remembers others, and never forgets herself.　　*Charles D. Gibson*

The result of that perfect education in taste and manner, down to every gesture.

Charles Kingsley

One man's lady is another man's woman; sometimes, one man's lady is another man's wife.

Russell Lynes

One who makes a man behave like a gentleman.

Russell Lynes

A gentleman's woman.　　*Jimmy Lyons*

That monster of European civilization and Teutonic-Christian stupidity.　*Arthur Schopenhauer*

To have nothing to do, but listlessly to go they scarcely care where, for they cannot tell what.

Mary Wollstonecraft

SEE ALSO MISTRESS, WIFE, WOMAN.

LAKE

The landscape's most beautiful and expressive feature. It is the earth's eye; looking into which the beholder measures the depth of his own nature.　　*Henry David Thoreau*

LAND

SEE COUNTRY, FARMING, PROPERTY.

LANGUAGE

Spirit crystallized and substantiated.

Hayyim N. Bialik

A man's language is an unerring index of his nature.　　*Laurence Binyon*

Established custom...is the standard to which we must at last resort for determining every controverted point in language.　　*Hugh Blair*

A species of fashion, in which by the general, but tacit, consent of the people of a particular state or country, certain sounds come to be appropriate to certain things as their signs.　*George Campbell*

Language is called the Garment of Thought: however, it should rather be, Language is the Flesh-Garment, the Body, of Thought.

Thomas Carlyle

What is it all but metaphors.　　*Thomas Carlyle*

(That which is) established by the usage of people of fashion.　　*Lord Chesterfield*

The armory of the human mind; and at once contains the trophies of its past, and the weapons of its future conquests.

Samuel Taylor Coleridge

The apparel in which your thoughts parade before the public.　　*George W. Crane*

The half-art, half-instinct.　　*Charles Darwin*

A city to the building of which every human being brought a stone.　　*Ralph Waldo Emerson*

Little better than the croak and cackle of fowls, and other utterances of brute nature—sometimes not so adequate.　　*Nathaniel Hawthorne*

The blood of the soul...into which our thoughts run, and out of which they grow.

Oliver Wendell Holmes 1

The picture and counterpart of thought.

Mark Hopkins

The tool of the mind. *Elbert Hubbard*

The only instrument of science, and words are but the signs of ideas. *Samuel Johnson*

The pedigrees of nations. *Samuel Johnson*

Mankind's worst obstacle. *Fletcher Knebel*

Man's deadliest weapon. *Arthur Koestler*

An organism. To digest it one must be, paradoxically, swallowed up by it. *Shemarya Levin*

A form of organized stutter.

Marshall McLuhan

After a speech is fully fashioned to the common understanding, and accepted by consent of a whole country and nation, it is called a language.

George Puttenham

(Something that) should be employed as the means, not as the end; language is the instrument, conviction is the work. *Joshua Reynolds*

A purely human and non-instinctive method of communicating ideas, emotions and desires by means of a system of voluntarily produced symbols. *Edward Sapir*

A sacred trust and a most important privilege of the higher orders of society.

Friedrich von Schlegel

The memory of the human race. *William Smith*

A thread or nerve of life running through all the ages, connecting them into one common, prolonged and advancing existence. *William Smith*

Magic forces of nature and of blood . . . a heritage of emotions, habits of thought, traditions of taste, inheritances of will—the imperative of the past.

Shalom Spiegel

The main instrument of man's refusal to accept the world as it is. *George Steiner*

A poor bull's-eye lantern wherewith to show off the vast cathedral of the world.

Robert Louis Stevenson

The expression of ideas by means of speech-sounds combined into words. *Henry Sweet*

The amber in which a thousand precious and subtle thoughts have been safely imbedded and preserved. *Richard C. Trench*

Custom. *Isaac Watts*

The expression of ideas, and if the people of one country cannot preserve an identity of ideas they cannot retain an identity of language.

Noah Webster

A series of squeaks. *Alfred North Whitehead*

Certain instrumentalities whereby men consciously and with intention represent their thought to the end, chiefly, of making it known to other men. *William D. Whitney*

The bloodline that transmits our culture from one generation to the next. *Guy Wright*

The refined use of the tongue for the expression of opinion. *Anon.*

SEE ALSO CONVERSATION, ORATORY, RHETORIC, SPEECH, STYLE, WRITING.

LAUGHTER

A universal bond that draws all men closer.

Nathan Ausubel

Laughter is satanic, and, therefore, profoundly human. It is born of Man's conception of his own superiority. *Charles Baudelaire*

The spectacle of a human being being responding mechanically to an unexpected situation.

Henri Bergson

The corrective force which prevents us from becoming cranks. *Henri Bergson*

An interior convulsion, producing a distortion of the features and accompanied by inarticulate noises. *Ambrose Bierce*

(Something) that rushes out of a man's soul like the breaking up of a Sunday School.

Josh Billings

The sensation of feeling good all over and showing it principally in one spot.

Adapted from Josh Billings

(When tolerant) the cruelest form of contempt.

Pearl Buck

The cipher-key wherewith we decipher the whole man. *Thomas Carlyle*

Frequent and loud laughter is the characteristic of folly and ill manners: it is the manner in which the mob expresses their silly joy at silly things.

Lord Chesterfield

Has its source in some kind of meanness or deformity. *Cicero*

A convulsion of the nerves.

Samuel Taylor Coleridge

A vulgar expression of the passion.

William Congreve

An instrument of happiness. *John Dryden*

A noisy smile. *Steven Goldberg*

We only laugh at those instances of moral absurdity to which we are conscious we ourselves are not liable. *Oliver Goldsmith*

The mind's intonation. There are ways of laughing which have the sound of counterfeit coins.

Edmond de Goncourt

Convulsive and involuntary movement, occasioned by mere surprise or contrast...before it has time to reconcile its belief to contradictory appearances. *William Hazlitt*

Little more than an expression of self-satisfied shrewdness. *Georg W. Hegel*

Nothing else but sudden glory arising from some sudden conception of some eminency in ourselves, by comparison with the infirmity of others, or with our own formerly. *Thomas Hobbes*

The bark of delight of a gregarious animal at the proximity of his kind. *Wyndham Lewis*

A confession of the sins and silliness of the world, but is also a kind of genial acquiescence in these sins and silliness. *Robert Lynd*

The first thing that ages on a woman.

Adapted from George Jean Nathan

A smile that burst. *Patricia Nelson*

The innocent, youthful side of repentance, of disillusion, of understanding.

George Santanyana

The sudden perception of the incongruity between a concept and the real cbject.

Arthur Schopenhauer

The older and greater church to which I belong: the church where the oftener you laugh the better, because by laughter only can you destroy evil without malice, and affirm good fellowship without mawkishness. *George Bernard Shaw*

Sunshine in a house. *William Makepeace Thackeray*

A kind of joyousness that is incompatible with contempt or indignation. *Voltaire*

Instant vacation. *Robert Zwickey*

A convulsion arising from the sudden transformation of a strained expectation into nothing.

Anon.

An orgasm triggered by the intercourse of reason and unreason. *Anon.*

SEE ALSO COMEDY, HUMOR, JOKE, SATIRE, WIT.

LAW

The expression of the will of the strongest for the time being, and therefore laws have no fixity, but shift from generation to generation.

Brooks Adams

The sober second thought of the people.

Fisher Ames

Spider's webs; they hold the weak and delicate who are caught in their meshes, but are torn in pieces by the rich and powerful. *Anacharsis*

A form of order, and good law must necessarily mean good order. *Aristotle*

A pledge that the citizens of a state will do justice to one another. *Aristotle*

Reason free from from passion. *Aristotle*

The beginning of the law is benevolence, and with benevolence it ends.

Babylonian Talmud: Sotah.

Things captious, and oracles not well inspired.

Francis Bacon

Certain in meaning, just in precept, convenient in execution, agreeable to the form of government, and productive of virtue in those that live under it.

Francis Bacon

That tendency to impose a settled customary yoke upon all men and all actions. *Walter Bagehot*

A mouse-trap: easy to enter but not easy to get out of. *Arthur J. Balfour*

The effort of men to organize society.

Henry Ward Beecher

Every law is an infraction of liberty.

Jeremy Bentham

Not made for a righteous man, but for the lawless and disobedient, for the ungodly and for sinners.

Bible: Timothy, 1, 9.

Medicines: they usually cure the disease only by setting up another that is lesser or more transient.

Otto von Bismarck

A rule of civil conduct, prescribed by the supreme power in a state, commanding what is right and prohibiting what is wrong.   *William Blackstone*

The embodiment of the moral sentiments of the people.   *William Blackstone*

Law is not justice, but the sacrifice of singular virtues to the dull world's ease of mind.

Adapted from Gordon Bottomley

A means to serve what we think is right.

William J. Brennan 2

Equity and utility.   *Edmund Burke*

There is but one law for all, namely, that law which governs all law, the law of our Creator, the law of humanity, justice, equity,—the law of nature and of nations.   *Edmund Burke*

Whatever is boldly asserted and plausibly maintained.   *Aaron Burr*

The law of God, which we call the moral law, must alone be the scope, and rule, and end of all laws.   *John Calvin*

The expression and the perfection of common sense.   *Joseph H. Choate*

The absolute justice of the State, enlightened by the perfect reason of the State.   *Rufus Choate*

The welfare of the people is the chief law.

Cicero

Nothing but a correct principle drawn from the inspiration of the gods, commanding what is honest, and forbidding the contrary.   *Cicero*

Right reason calling up imperiously to our duty, and prohibiting every violation of it.   *Cicero*

Supernatural entities which do not have a verifiable existence except to the eyes of faith.

Felix S. Cohen

A formless mass of isolated decisions.

Morris Cohen

The common good of all is the supreme law.

Richard Cumberland

A bum profession. It is utterly devoid of idealism and almost poverty stricken as to any real ideas.

Clarence Darrow

Like clothes. They should be made to fit the people they are meant to serve.

Clarence Darrow

The law is for the protection of the weak more than the strong.   *William Erle*

Nothing else but the will of him that hath the power of the supreme father.   *Robert Filmer*

A system in which the state must establish guilt by evidence independently and freely secured.

Felix Frankfurter

All we have standing between us and the tyranny of mere will.   *Felix Frankfurter*

The might of the community. Yet, it, too, is nothing else than violence . . . it is the communal, not individual, violence that has its way.

Sigmund Freud

Our human laws are but the copies, more or less imperfect, of the eternal laws, so far as we can read them.   *James A. Froude*

Possession is nine points of the law.

Thomas Fuller

A majestic edifice, sheltering all of us, each stone of which rests on another.   *John Galsworthy*

An institution of the most pernicious tendency . . . Law was made that a plain man might know what he had to expect, and yet the most skillful practitioners differ.   *William Godwin*

To govern all alike—those opposed as well as those who favour them.   *Ulysses S. Grant*

Obliges us to do what is proper, not simply what is just.   *Hugo Grotius*

The maximum gratification of the nervous system of man.   *Learned Hand*

Words and paper without the hands of swords of men.   *James Harrington*

Common power.   *Thomas Hobbes*

That which is needful for the good of the people.

Thomas Hobbes

The very bulwarks of liberty; they define every man's rights, and defend the individual liberties of all men.   *Josiah G. Holland*

A statement of the circumstances in which the public force will be brought to bear upon men through the courts.   *Oliver Wendell Holmes 2*

What a judge dispenses.   *Gerhart Husserl*

The standard and guardian of our liberty; it circumscribes and defends it.   *Edward Hyde*

The precepts...are these: to live honorably, to injure no other man, to render to every man his due.   *Institutes of Justinian*

An alliance of those who have farsight and insight against the shortsighted.   *Rudolf von Jhering*

The last result of human wisdom acting upon human experience for the benefit of the public.

Samuel Johnson

One precedent creates another. They soon accumulate and become law.   *Junius*

An adroit mixture of customs that are beneficial to society, and would be followed even if no law existed.   *Pëtr A. Kropotkin*

Simulation of reality.   *John C. Lilly*

The multitude of little decisions made daily by millions of men.   *Walter Lippmann*

Laws are the sovereigns of sovereigns.

Louis XIV

Expressions of the opinion of some class which has power over the rest.   *Thomas B. Macaulay*

The glorious uncertainty.   *Charles Macklin*

Merely the expression of the will of the strongest for the time being, and therefore laws have no fixity, but shift from generation to generation.

Charles A. Madison

Consists of principles which govern specific and individual cases as they happen to arise.

Lord Mansfield

Nothing but the recognition of economic conditions.   *Adapted from Karl Marx*

Laws undertake to punish only overt acts.

Charles de Montesquieu

A business whose outlook is shared by its major clients.   *Laura Nader*

(Law is) grounded on the thesis: God gave it, and the fathers lived it.   *Friedrich W. Nietzche*

The purpose...is to prevent the strong always having their way.   *Ovid*

The despot of mankind, often compels us to do many things which are against nature.   *Plato*

There is a written and unwritten law. Written law is that under which we live in different cities, but that which has arisen from custom is called unwritten law.   *Plato*

Force first made conquest, and that conquest was then made into law.

Adapted from Alexander Pope

Laws only bind when they are in accordance with right reason, and hence with the eternal law of God.   *Pope Leo XIII*

Experience developed by reason and applied continually to further experience.   *Roscoe Pound*

Nothing but a declaration and application of what is already just.   *Pierre J. Proudhon*

Rules imposed on man by constituted authority.

Adapted from Emery Reves

To a noble nation, not chains, but chain mail—strength and defence, though something also of an encumbrance.   *John Ruskin*

An ordinance of reason for the common good, made by him who has care of the community.

Saint Thomas Aquinas

Precisely what I am in my barnyard, a bridle and check to prevent the strong and greedy from oppressing the timid and weak.

Saint John de Crèvecoeur

A voice...sent down from heaven; it should command, not discuss.   *Seneca*

Nets of such a texture as the little creep through, the great break through, and the middle-sized alone are entangled in.   *William Shenstone*

The wisdom of our ancestors.   *Sydney Smith*

The determination of the majority of those who have property in land.   *Jonathan Swift*

That codeless myriad of precedent,
That wilderness of single instances.

Alfred Lord Tennyson

The products of selfishness, deception and party prejudice.   *Leon Tolstoy*

Something which must have a moral basis, so that there is an inner compelling force for every citizen to obey.   *Chaim Weizmann*

The crystallization of the habit and thought of society.   *Woodrow Wilson*

Merely the summing up in legislative form of the moral judgment that the community has already reached.   *Woodrow Wilson*

The backbone which keeps man erect.
                                      S. C. Yuter

That which protects everybody who can afford a good lawyer.   *Anon.*

The second oldest profession.   *Anon.*

SEE ALSO CRIME, CRIMINAL, JUDGE, JURY, JUSTICE, LAWYERS, LITIGATION, PROSECUTOR, SUPREME COURT.

LAW (COMMON)

Nothing but reasons.   *Edward Coke*

The articulate voice of some sovereign or quasi-sovereign that can be identified.
                         Oliver Wendell Holmes 2

The custom of the kingdom.   *Justice North*

A bullet which is instantaneously and charmingly effective.   *Anon.*

LAW (NATURAL)

A force working in history which tends to keep human beings human.   *J. V. Casserley*

That which God at the time of creation of the nature of man infused into his heart, for his preservation and direction ... the moral law.
                                    Edward Coke

Those rights to which every man is entitled equally.   *Patrick Colquhoun*

(That which) is merely responsible for uniformity in sustaining what has been originated and what is being sustained.   *Henry Drummond*

They are great lines running ... through the world ... reducing it like parallels of latitude to intelligent order.   *Henry Drummond*

The law of sympathy, of fellowship, of mutual help and service.   *Washington Gladden*

That naive state of mind that accepts what has been familiar.   *Oliver Wendell Holmes 2*

The general and perpetual voice of men ... a sentence of God himself.   *Richard Hooker*

The ensemble of things to do and not to do.
                                  Jacques Maritain

Moral law.   *Jacques Maritain*

The laws of God.   *George Mason*

The only law of laws truly and properly to all mankind fundamental; the beginning and the end of all government.   *John Milton*

The forces with which God has endowed His creatures, and by reason of which they must, when left to themselves, always act the same way if placed under the same circumstances.
                                  Bernard J. Otten

The law of nature is the same thing as the eternal law, implanted in rational creatures, and inclining them to their right action and end; and can be nothing else but the eternal reason of God.
                                   Pope Leo XIII

The moral law of God made clear to us through the judgments of human reason and the dictates of conscience.
                  Roman Catholic Bishops of the U.S., Nov., 1948.

Natural reasoning, keeping control over sense appetite and eliminating that irrational behavior which is the disruption of what is naturally coherent.   *Saint Maximus*

The unwritten and undying laws of the Gods.
                                      Sophocles

The instinct by which we feel justice.   *Voltaire*

Temporary habits of nature.
                         Alfred North Whitehead

SEE ALSO JUSTICE, LAW.

LAWSUIT

A machine which you go into as a pig and come out as a sausage.   *Ambrose Bierce*

To set an attorney to work to worry and torment another. man.   *William Cobbett*

To go to law is for two persons to kindle a fire, at their own cost, to warm others and singe themselves to cinders.   *Owen Felltham*

To gain a case by parting with your money.
Max Gralnick

That which consumers time and money and rest and friends.   *Adapted from George Herbert*

A fruit-tree planted in a lawyer's garden.
Italian Proverb

A method of collecting half the debt by compelling twice the payment.   *Anon.*

SEE ALSO JUDGE, JURY, JUSTICE, LAW, LAWYERS, LITIGATION, TRIAL.

LAWYERS

Lawyers are just like physicians: what one says, the other contradicts.   *Sholom Aleichem*

The only persons in whom ignorance of the law is not punished.   *Jeremy Bentham*

One skilled in the circumvention of the law.
Ambrose Bierce

A learned gentleman who rescues your estate from your enemies and keeps it himself.
Henry Brougham

One who defends you at the risk of your pocket-book, reputation and life.   *Eugene E. Brussell*

A chimney-sweeper who has no objection to dirty work, because it is his trade.
Charles Caleb Colton

The only civil delinquents whose judges must of necessity be chosen from (amongst) themselves.
Charles Caleb Colton

By law's dark by-ways he has stored his mind with wicked knowledge on how to cheat mankind.
Adapted from George Crabbe

These are the mountebanks of state
The mastiffs of a government,
To worry and run down the innocent.
Daniel Defoe

Not the man who has an eye to every side and angle of contingency...but who throws himself on your part so heartily that he can get you out of a scrape.   *Ralph Waldo Emerson*

One whose opinion is worth nothing unless paid for.   *English Proverb*

(Those who) lie, conceal and distort everything and slander everybody.   *Jean Giraudoux*

Where there is a rift in the lute, the business of the lawyer is to widen the rift and gather the loot.
Arthur G. Hays

Those who earn a living by the sweat of their browbeating.   *James G. Huneker*

It is the trade of lawyers to question everything, yield nothing, and to talk by the hour.
Thomas Jefferson

I think we may class the lawyer in the natural history of monsters.   *John Keats*

He is no lawyer who cannot take two sides.
Charles Lamb

Those who use the law as shoemakers use leather; rubbing it, pressing it, and stretching it with their teeth, all to the end of making it fit their purposes.   *Louis XII*

Men who hire out their words and anger.
Martial

One who protects us against robbery by taking away the temptation.   *Henry Louis Mencken*

People whose profession it is to disguise matters.
Thomas More

A lawyer without history or literature is a mechanic, a mere working mason; if he possesses some knowledge of these, he may venture to call himself an architect.   *Walter Scott*

Perilous mouths.   *William Shakespeare*

Those whose interests and abilities lie in perverting, confounding and eluding the law.
Adapted from Jonathan Swift.

A college trained person appointed by the court or client to take what's left.   *Anon.*

One who helps you get what's coming to him.
Anon.

SEE ALSO CRIME, CRIMINAL, JUDGE, JURY, JUSTICE, LAW, LITIGATION.

LAZINESS

Unwarranted repose of manner in a person of low degree.   *Ambrose Bierce*

A bodily affliction which mostly the young indulge in, and only the old can afford.

Cynic's Cyclopaedia

The greater part of human misery.

Georg C. Lichtenberg

The habit of resting before fatigue sets in.

Jules Renard

A premature death.   *Stanislaus*

The sleep of the mind.   *Luc de Vauvenargues*

The mental alertness to avoid hard work.   *Anon.*

SEE ALSO IDLENESS, LEISURE.

LEADER

Men before God and gods before men.

Nathaniel Ames

(One who is) best when people barely know he exists.   *Witter Bynner*

Lights of the world and stars of the human race.

William Cowper

Lord of human kind.   *John Dryden*

He gets men to go along with him because they want to do it for him and they believe in him.

Dwight David Eisenhower

To be a leader of men one must turn one's back on men.   *Havelock Ellis*

A man who has tastes like mine, but in greater power.   *Ralph Waldo Emerson*

The foremost horse in the team.   *John Fletcher*

To put up with...distortions and to stick to one's guns come what may—this is the...gift of leadership.   *Mohandas K. Gandhi*

The ability to recognize a problem before it becomes an emergency.   *Arnold H. Glasow*

One who strives to turn his followers into children.   *Eric Hoffer*

The leader has to be practical and a realist, yet must talk the language of the visionary and the idealist.   *Eric Hoffer*

The leader personifies the certitude of the creed and the defiance and grandeur of power. He articulates and justifies the resentment damned up in the souls of the frustrated. He kindles the vision of a breath-taking future so as to justify the sacrifice of a transitory present. He stages a world of make-believe so indispensable for the realization of self-sacrifice and united action.

Eric Hoffer

One who breaks new paths into unfamiliar territory.   *Gerald White Johnson*

The final test of a leader is that he leaves behind him in other men the conviction and the will to carry on.   *Walter Lippmann*

The other side of the coin of loneliness, and he who is a leader must always act alone. And acting alone, accept everything alone.

Ferdinand E. Marcos

Great leaders have something in them which inspires a whole people and makes them do great deeds.   *Jawaharlal Nehru*

(His) character and qualifications...are refelcted in the men he selects, develops and gathers around him.   *Arthur Newcomb*

One who implements noble ideals and principles with practical accomplishments.

Richard Milhous Nixon

(One who) must always conserve his resources for the battles that count. He must look at the major objectives of his administration...and must never become involved in a fight on a minor issue which might prejudice his chance to win on a major issue.   *Richard Milhous Nixon*

(He who) must know, must know that he knows, and must be able to make it abundantly clear to those about him that he knows.

Clarence B. Randall

Whoever is foremost.   *Johann C. Schiller*

Reason and calm judgment, the qualities specially belonging to a leader.   *Tacitus*

The wave pushed ahead by the ship.

Leon Tolstoy

A man who has the ability to get other people to do what they don't want to do and like it.

Harry S. Truman

One who, out of madness or goodness, volunteers to take upon himself the woe of a people.

John Updike

SEE ALSO AUTHORITY, BOSS, DICTATORS, EXECUTIVE, GENIUS, GREAT MEN, GREATNESS, HERO, KING, MASTER, PRESIDENT.

LEARNED

The wisdom of a learned man cometh by opportunity of leisure; and he that hath little business shalt become wise.

Apocrypha: Ecclesiastes, XXXVIII, 24.

He...who knows the most of what is farthest removed from the common life and actual observation, that is of the least practical utility, and least liable to be brought to the test of experience.

William Hazlitt

What people become from reading five hours a day. *Samuel Johnson*

One who voluntarily does more thinking than is necessary for his own survival.

Mildred McAffee

One who is never bored.

Adapted from Jean Paul Richter

An idler who kills time by study. Beware of his false knowledge: it is more dangerous than ignorance. *George Bernard Shaw*

Some...have only one book in them; others, a library. *Sydney Smith*

The learned tradition is not concerned with truth, but with the learned adjustment of learned statements of antecedent people.

Alfred North Whitehead

SEE ALSO BOOK, INTELLECTUAL, KNOWLEDGE, LEARNING, SCHOLAR.

LEARNING

To unlearn what is nought. *Antisthenes*

What we have to learn to do, we learn by doing.

Aristotle

Learning hath its infancy, when it is but beginning and almost childish; then his youth, when it is luxuriant and juvenile; then his strength of years, when it is solid and reduced; and lastly his old age, when it waxeth dry and exhaust.

Francis Bacon

Dust shaken out of a book and into an empty skull. *Ambrose Bierce*

The kind of ignorance distinguishing the studious.

Ambrose Bierce

The art of knowing how to use common sense to advantage. *Josh Billings*

Learning, the knowledge of the world, is only to be acquired by reading men, and studying all the various editions of them. *Lord Chesterfield*

The knowledge of that which none but the learned know. *William Hazlitt*

In doing we learn. *George Herbert*

A companion on a journey to a strange country ...a strength inexhaustible. *Hitopadesa*

The end...is to repair the ruins of our first parents by regaining to know God aright.

John Milton

Learning is by nature curiosity...prying into everything, reluctant to leave anything, material or immaterial unexplained. *Philo*

Serves to confirm what we believe on the authority of God. *Pope Leo XIII*

To know how to navigate in a forest of facts, ideas, and theories. *Raymond Queneau*

History taken up. *John Selden*

Words are but wind; and learning is nothing but words; ergo, learning is nothing but wind.

Jonathan Swift

Consists in preserving man's clear character, in giving new life to the people, and in dwelling in perfection, or the ultimate good. *Ta Hsüeh*

Direct intercourse and sympathy.

Henry David Thoreau

(Something that) preserves the errors of the past as well as its wisdom. *Alfred North Whitehead*

A matter of reading books no one ever heard of.

Anon.

LECTURER

One with his hand in your pocket, his tongue in your ear, and his faith in your patience.

Ambrose Bierce

Traveling men who express themselves and collect. *Shannon Fife*

One who makes talk money. *Anon.*

LEGEND

SEE FABLE, MYTHOLOGY.

LEGISLATURE

SEE CONGRESS, PARLIAMENT.

LEISURE

The goal . . . of business.   *Aristotle*

The time you don't get paid for and enjoy spending.   *Hyman Maxwell Berston*

Man's one opportunity to satisfy whatever appetites he happens to have.   *George Boas*

Ease . . . with dignity.   *Cicero*

An empty cup. It all depends what we put into it.   *Raphael Demos*

Is not true leisure one with true toil?   *John S. Dwight*

The best test of the quality of a civilization . . . the criterion of a people's life.   *Irwin Edman*

Those periods when daydreaming is legitimatized.   *Warren Goldberg*

The rest period between the rounds of life.   *Warren Goldberg*

The time for doing something useful.   *Nathaniel Howe*

More time to waste.   *Robert Maynard Hutchins*

The opiate of the masses.   *Malcolm Muggeridge*

The reward of labour.   *John Ray*

The last product of civilization.   *Bertrand A. Russell*

Without study . . . a tomb for the living man.   *Seneca*

Doing nothing.   *Gertrude Stein*

Rejoicing in the pursuits of an inglorious ease.   *Vergil*

SEE ALSO IDLENESS, VACATION.

LETTERS

The heart's warm dictates to the distant friend.   *George Crabbe*

Letters mingle souls, thus absent friends speak.   *Adapated from John Donne*

Messenger of sympathy and love,
Servant of parted friends,
Consoler of the lonely,

Bond of the scattered family,
Enlarger of the common life.   *Charles W. Eliot*

Carrier of news and knowledge.   *Charles W. Eliot*

A deliberate and written conversation.   *Baltasar Gracian*

Love is the marrow of friendship, and letters are the elixir of love.   *James Howell*

Friendship is the great chain of human society, and intercourse of letters is one of the chiefest links in that chain.   *James Howell*

A conversation between the absent and the present.   *Wilhelm von Humboldt*

Letters are like bodies, and their meanings like souls.   *Abraham Ibn Ezra*

Kind messages that pass from land to land that betray the heart's deep history.
Adapted from Henry Wadsworth Longfellow

That most delightful way of wasting time.   *John Morley*

An unannounced visit.   *Friedrich W. Nietzsche*

Soft interpreters of love.   *Matthew Prior*

Like smallclothes before the invention of suspenders; it is impossible to keep them up.   *Sydney Smith*

SEE ALSO PEN.

LEXICOGRAPHER

The navvy of scholarship, carrying his head backward and forward from one learned library to another.   *Osbert Burdett*

A writer of dictionaries, a harmless drudge.   *Samuel Johnson*

SEE ALSO DICTIONARY.

LIAR

A thief.   *Thomas Adams*

He that denies that Jesus is the Christ.
Bible: John, II, 22.

A lawyer with a roving commission.   *Ambrose Bierce*

The greatest fools.   *Lord Chesterfield*

(He who) is not believed even when he tells the truth.   *Cicero*

Show me a liar, and I will show you a thief.
George Herbert

One who tells an unpleasant truth.
Oliver Herford

One who tells the truth about something that never happened; hence a poet, a preacher, or a politician.   *Elbert Hubbard*

One who fools himself most of all when he imagines people believe him.   *Jewish Saying*

(One who) should have a good memory.
Quintilian

If you want to be thought a liar, always tell the truth.   *Logan P. Smith*

A liar is a man who does not know how to deceive.   *Luc de Vauvenargues*

The aim of the liar is simply to charm, to delight, to give pleasure. He is the very basis of civilized society.   *Oscar Wilde*

SEE ALSO LIE, LYING, SLANDER, SOPHISTRY.

LIBEL

It is not the truth or falsehood that makes a libel, but the temper with which it is published.
Justice Best

I despair of any definition of libel which shall exclude no publications which ought to be suppressed, and include none which ought to be omitted.   *John Campbell*

Everything printed or written which reflects on the character of another, and is published without lawful justification or excuse...whatever the intention may have been.   *Justice Parke*

SEE ALSO CALUMNY, LYING, SLANDER.

LIBERAL

A man who cultivates the skills that make freedom operational. He is always a man on special assignment.   *Max Ascoli*

Anyone whose ideas coincide with yours.
Russell Baker

A man who leaves a room when the fight begins.
Heywood Broun

(Those who) can understand everything but people who don't understand them.   *Leonard Bruce*

The true liberal is liberal in human relations and conservative in his economics. He seeks to conserve a capitalistic system characterized by free enterprise and the profit motive because it is essential to liberty.   *Harry J. Carman*

A mind that is able to imagine itself believing anything.   *Max Eastman*

A man too broadminded to take his own side in a quarrel.   *Robert Frost*

A man who is willing to spend somebody else's money.   *Carter Glass*

A man who tells other people what to do with their money.   *Le Roi Jones*

A man who wants to be accepted as a black but not mistaken for one.   *John Killens*

A man who defends the rights of conservatives.
Arnold Lunn

They believe in each and every quack who sets up his booth on the fair-grounds, including the Communists. The Communists have some talents, too, but they always fall short of believing in the liberals.   *Henry Louis Mencken*

A man who is right most of the time, but he's right too soon.   *Gregory Nunn*

A power worshipper without power.
George Orwell

A person whose interests aren't at stake at the moment.   *Willis Parker*

(A person) hotly compassionate toward people in the abstract and in the mass.   *William S. White*

A radical with family and children.   *Anon.*

A man with his mind open at both ends.   *Anon.*

One who believes in more laws and more jobholders, therefore in higher taxes and less liberty.   *Anon.*

SEE ALSO REFORMERS.

LIBERALISM

An attitude...human sympathy, a receptivity to change...a scientific willingness to follow reason rather than faith or any fixed ideas.
Chester Bowles

Complete and courageous devotion to the freedom of inquiry.   *John Dewey*

The tone and tendency ... is to attack the institutions of the country under the name of reform and to make war on the manners and customs of the people under the pretext of progress.

Benjamin Disraeli

The conviction that nothing fundamentally matters in religion except those things which create private and public goodness.

Harry Emerson Fosdick

Trust in the people qualified by prudence.

William E. Gladstone

Moral extortion ... touch a person's guilt and you open him up to a cause.   *Warren Goldberg*

The wrong prognosis for a correct diagnosis.

Warren Goldberg

That which tries to make what is minority, foremost.   *Warren Goldberg*

A mode of expression for comfortably situated citizens who wish to appear progressive in outlook without having to pay too high a price for their principles.   *Andrew Hacker*

A force truly of the spirit proceeding from the deep realization that economic freedom cannot be sacrificed if political freedom is to be preserved.

Herbert C. Hoover

An autonomous, self-sustaining conception of man's relationship of God, his universe, his society. In this sense is Liberalism a faith, and by virtue of this fact it has been forced to fight other faiths.   *John E. Hughes*

Too often merely a way of speaking.

Oscar Janowsky

An uncompromising devotion to the idea of equal liberty as both the means and the end of life.

Henry M. Kallen

Genius ... making change serve the eternal unchanging values we cherish. *David E. Lilienthal*

An aristocratic notion founded upon the historic laws of chivalry and *noblesse oblige*.

John Morse

Denying the State in the interests of the particular individual.   *Benito Mussolini*

False liberty of thought ... the exercise of thought upon matters, in which ... thought cannot be brought to any successful issue ... Among such matters are first principles of any kind.

John Henry Newman

The mistake of subjecting to human judgment those revealed doctrines which are in their nature beyond and independent of it.

John Henry Newman

In religion ... the doctrine that there is no positive truth in religion but that one creed is as good as another.   *John Henry Newman*

A religious optimism which is true to the facts of neither the world of nature nor the world of history.   *Reinhold Niebuhr*

The supreme form of generosity ... the right which the majority concedes to minorities.

José Ortega y Gasset

That principle of political rights, according to which the public authority, in spite of being all-powerful, limits itself and attempts, even at its own expense, to leave room in the State ... for those to live who neither think nor feel as it does, that is to say as do the stronger, the majority.

José Ortega y Gasset

The first refuge of political indifference and the last refuge of Leftists.   *Harry Roskolenko*

Socialism—in the generic sense.

Joseph Sobran

The function of liberalism in the past was that of putting a limit to the powers of kings. The function ... in the future will be that of putting a limit to the powers of Parliament.

Herbert Spencer

SEE ALSO DEMOCRAT, REFORMERS.

LIBERALITY

SEE CHARITY, GENEROSITY, PHILAN-THROPY.

LIBERTY

A power to do as we would be done by.

John Adams

A self-determining power in an intellectual agent. It implies thought and choice and power.

John Adams

Means that a man is recognized as free and treated as free by those who surround him.

Mikhail A. Bakunin

Where the Spirit of the Lord is, there is liberty.

Bible: Corinthians, III, 17.

One of Imagination's most precious possessions.
Ambrose Bierce

The great half truth.   *William Blake*

To do everything that is right, and...being restrained from doing anything that is wrong.
Jonathan Boucher

The only liberty I mean, is a liberty connected with order; that not only exists along with order and virtue, but which cannot exist at all without them.   *Edmund Burke*

In the most liberal sense it is the negation of law, for law is restraint, and the absence of restraint is anarchy.   *Benjamin N. Cardozo*

The penalty of sins that are past, the pledge of inestimable benefits that are coming.
Thomas Carlyle

A state of the social compact as permits the members of the community to lay no more restraints on themselves, than are required by their real necessities, and obvious interests.
James Fenimore Cooper

The assurance that every man shall be protected in doing what he believes his duty against the influence of authority and majorities, custom and opinion.   *John E. Dalberg*

The unhampered translation of will into act.
Dante

Effective power to do specific things.
John Dewey

The right to elect people to make restrictions for you.   *Dublin Opinion*

To do each as he pleases; to care for nothing and nobody, and cheat everybody.   *William Faux*

The power of doing whatever does not injure another.   *French National Assembly, 1789.*

There is no generalized idea of liberty...since the liberty of a particular man is exercised only at the expense of other people's.
Remy de Gourmont

The power that we have over ourselves.
Hugo Grotius

A gift of the beneficent Creator to the whole human race.   *Alexander Hamilton*

The absence of external impediments.
Thomas Hobbes

The breath of progress.   *Robert G. Ingersoll*

By physical liberty I mean the right to do anything which does not interfere with the happiness of another. By intellectual liberty I mean the right to think and the right to think wrong.
Robert G. Ingersoll

Unobstructed action according to our will within the limits drawn around us by the equal rights of others.   *Thomas Jefferson*

Liberty in the lowest rank of every nation is little more than the choice of working or starving.
Samuel Johnson

A bourgeois dream.   *Nikolai Lenin*

A combination of principles and laws which acknowledge, protect, and favor the dignity of man.   *Francis Lieber*

The world has never had a good definition of the word liberty.   *Abraham Lincoln*

To be under no other legislative power but that established by consent in the commonwealth.
John Locke

When complaints are freely heard, deeply considered, and speedily reformed, then is the utmost bound of civil liberty attained that wise men look for.   *John Milton*

Consists in every man's being allowed to speak his thoughts, and lay open his sentiments.
Charles de Montesquieu

The right to do what the laws allow.
Charles de Montesquieu

A compensation for the heaviness of taxation. In despotic states the equivalent for liberty is the lightness of taxation.   *Charles de Montesquieu*

The right to tell people what they do not want to hear.   *George Orwell*

The fountain-head of many evils.   *Pope Leo XIII*

Obedience to the law which one has laid down for oneself.   *Jean-Jacques Rousseau*

That treacherous phantom.   *John Ruskin*

To be unable to sin.   *Saint Augustine*

Liberty is conforming to the majority.
Hugh Scanlon

To be slave to nothing, to no necessity, to no accident.   *Seneca*

Liberty means responsibility. That is why most men dread it.   *George Bernard Shaw*

The possibility of doubting...of making a mistake...of searching and experimenting...of saying "No" to any authority. *Ignazio Silone*

The right of any person to stand up anywhere and say anything whatsoever that everybody thinks. *Lincoln Steffens*

The status of the man who is guaranteed by law and civil institutions the exclusive employment of all his own powers for his own welfare. *William G. Sumner*

Believing what men please...also of endeavoring to propagate that belief as much as they can. *Jonathan Swift*

Independence, maintained by force. *Voltaire*

The sovereignty of the individual. *Josiah Warren*

Exists in proportion to wholesome restraint; the more restraint on others to keep off from us, the more liberty we have. *Daniel Webster*

The only thing you cannot have unless you are willing to give it to others. *William Allen White*

When you define liberty you limit it, and when you limit it you destroy it. *Brand Whitlock*

Does not consist in mere declarations of the rights of man. It consists in the translation of those declarations into definite actions. *Woodrow Wilson*

A free field and no favor. *Woodrow Wilson*

The proper end and object of authority. *John Winthrop*

Something that everybody believes in as long as its application does not bother anybody. *Anon.*

A state of being free from the things we don't like in order to be slaves to the things we do like. *Anon.*

SEE ALSO AMERICA, AMERICAN CONSTITUTION, AMERICANISM, DEMOCRACY, EQUALITY, EQUITY, FREEDOM, FREE MAN, FREE PRESS.

LIBRARIAN

A factor and trader for helps to learning. *John Dury*

Unlearned men of books assume the care, as eunuchs are the guardians of the fair *Adapted from Edward Young*

A keeper of the books. *Anon.*

LIBRARY

A room frought with books and people. *Fred Allen*

The soul's burial-ground. *Henry Ward Beecher*

The true university. *Thomas Carlyle*

The delivery room for the birth of ideas—a place where history comes to life. *Norman Cousins*

The tombs of such as cannot die. *George Crabbe*

The diary of the human race. *George Dawson*

A company of the wisest and wittiest men that could be picked out of all civil countries...set in best order. *Ralph Waldo Emerson*

A well-chosen library has innumerable dishes, and all of admirable flavor. *William Godwin*

A place where the dead lie. *Elbert Hubbard*

No place affords a more striking conviction of the vanity of human hopes. *Samuel Johnson*

A hospital for the mind. *Library at Alexandria*

The ruins of an antique world and the glories of a modern one. *Henry Wadsworth Longfellow*

A palace where the lofty spirits of all nations and generations meet. *Samuel Niger*

The enormous institution itself serving as instructor. *Philip Roth*

An evergreen tree of diabolical knowledge. *Richard Brinsley Sheridan*

A theatre—the stage is time, the play is the play of the world. *Alexander Smith*

Mummied authors. *Bayard Taylor*

A rest-home for the mind. *Anon.*

A collection of 15,000 mystery novels and 35 other books. *Anon.*

SEE ALSO BOOK, EDUCATION, READING.

LIE

Truth in masquerade. *Lord Byron*

The refuse of fools and cowards.

Lord Chesterfield

Terminological inexactitude.

Winston S. Churchill

The most terrible of lies is not that which is uttered but that which is lived. *W. G. Clarke*

Fire in the stubble—it turns all the light stuff around into its own substance for a moment...and then dies; and all its converts are scattered in the wind, without place or evidence of their existence. *Samuel Taylor Coleridge*

Not only a sort of suicide in the liar, but...a stab at the health of human society.

Ralph Waldo Emerson

A...poor substitute for the truth but the only one discovered up to date. *Foolish Dictionary*

Half the truth is often a great lie.

Benjamin Franklin

Merely corroborative detail, intended to give artistic verisimilitude to a bold and unconvincing narrative. *William S. Gilbert*

Sin has many tools, but a lie is the handle which fits them all. *Oliver Wendell Holmes 1*

That which you do not believe.

Holbrook Jackson

The whole way to hell. *William Penn*

A fault in a boy, an art in a lover, an accomplishment in a bachelor, and second nature in a married woman. *Helen Rowland*

The essence...is in deception, not in words; a lie may be told by silence, by equivocation, by the accent on a syllable...and all these kinds of lies are worse and baser...than a lie plainly worded.

John Ruskin

Something that handles the present, but has no future. *Anon.*

A weapon of the ego and of defense. *Anon.*

SEE ALSO DECEIT, DIPLOMACY, FLATTERY, LIAR, LYING.

LIFE

A series of relapses and recoveries. *George Ade*

My college. May I graduate well, and earn some honors! *Louisa May Alcott*

A blister on top of a tumor, and a boil on top of that. *Sholom Aleichem*

A document to be interpreted. *Henry F. Amiel*

A fair-tale written by God's fingers.

Hans Christian Anderson

Preoccupation and anxiety...Nothing but anger and jealousy, strife and contention.

Apocrypha: Ben Sira, XL, 1-3.

Short to the fortunate, long to the unfortunate.

Apollonius

A theater in which the worst people often have the best seats. *Aristonymus*

This strange disease...with its sick hurry, its divided aims. *Matthew Arnold*

A battle, sojourning in a strange land; and the fame that comes after is oblivion.

Marcus Aurelius

A tragedy at last, because it ends with death.

Alfred Austin

A school of probability. *Walter Bagehot*

A means unto an end—that end...God.

Philip J. Bailey

A bridge of groans across a stream of tears.

Philip J. Bailey

A cup of tea; the more heartily we drink the sooner we reach the dregs. *James M. Barrie*

A long lesson in humility. *James M. Barrie*

The life of every man is a diary in which he means to write one story, and writes another, and his humblest hour is when he compares the volume as it is with what he vowed to make it.

James M. Barrie

A hospital in which every patient is possessed by the desire to change his bed.

Charles Baudelaire

Dissimulation, equivocation and mental reservation. *Aphra Behn*

A one-way street. *Bernard Berenson*

Tendency, and the essence of tendency is to develop in the form of a sheaf, creating, by its very growth, divergent directions among which its impetus is divided. *Henri Bergson*

Half of it is spent in night, and of the rest half is lost by childhood and old age. Work, grief, longing an illness make up what remains.
Bhartrihari

To love the Lord...that is your life and length of days.   *Bible: Deuteronomy, XXX, 20.*

A vapor, that appeareth for a little time, and then vanisheth away.   *Bible: James, IV, 14.*

A warfare.   *Bible: Job, VII, I.*

We are but of yesterday, and know nothing, because our days upon earth are a shadow.
Bible: Job, VIII, 9.

A spiritual pickle preserving the body from decay.
Ambrose Bierce

Life consists not in holding good cards but in playing those you do hold well.   *Josh Billings*

The two-fold internal movement of composition and decomposition, at once general and continuous.   *Henry M. Blainville*

A temporary ill, to be soon cured by that dear old doctor, Death.   *Edwin Booth*

Any life...is made up of a *single moment*—the moment in which a man finds out...who he is.   *Jorge L. Borges*

Now that I've come
　To this place—alone
Life is a spent dream
　And a gray stone.   *Verne Bright*

Life is a copycat and can be bullied into following the master artist who bids it come to heel.
Heywood Broun

I count life just a stuff
To try the soul's strength on.   *Robert Browning*

All real life is meeting.   *Martin Buber*

A day at most.   *Robert Burns*

The art of drawing sufficient conclusions from insufficient premises.   *Samuel Butler 2*

One long process of getting tired.
Samuel Butler 2

Playing a violin solo in public and learning the instrument as one goes on.   *Samuel Butler 2*

Life is not 99% chance. It is 100% chance.
Adapated from Samuel Butler 2

A matter about which we are lost if we reason either too much or too little.   *Samuel Butler 2*

A kind of partial death—a long, lingering death-bed...of stagnation and nonentity on which death is but the seal.   *Samuel Butler 2*

A sentence man has to serve for being born.
Pedro Calderon

A dusty corridor...shut at both ends.
Roy Campbell

A little gleam of time between two eternities.
Thomas Carlyle

We emerge from the Inane; haste stormfully across the astonished Earth; then plunge again into the Inane.   *Thomas Carlyle*

A fragment, a moment between two eternities, influenced by all that has preceded, and to influence all that follows. The only way to illumine it is by extent of view.   *William Ellery Channing*

The art of drawing without an eraser.
John Christian

Hurried and worried until we are buried—there's no curtain call—life's a very funny proposition after all.   *Adapted from George M. Cohan*

Thought.   *Samuel Taylor Coleride*

A maze in which we take the wrong turning before we have learned to walk.   *Cyril Connolly*

A garish, unrestful hotel.   *Joseph Conrad*

An endless race against death.
Jacques-Yves Cousteau

A sense of fancied bliss and heartfelt care, closing at last in darkness and despair.
Adapted from William Cowper

A simple loan.   *Eugue Delacroix*

That long and cruel malady.   *Emile Deschamps*

A tumble-about thing of ups and downs.
Benjamin Disraeli

A mystery as deep as ever death can be.
Mary M. Dodge

Like eating artichokes—you've got to go through so much to get so little.   *T. A. Dorgan*

A B-picture script.   *Kirk Douglas*

A very grim and dangerous contest, relieved . . . by an illusion of pleasure, which is the bait, and the lure for all in this internecine contest.

Theodore Dreiser

Life seems to be divided into two periods: in the first we indulge, in the second we preach.

Will Durant

A little rule, a little sway,
A sunbeam in a winter's day,
Is all the proud and mighty have
Between the cradle and the grave.   *John Dyer*

A fatal adventure. It can have only one end. So why not make it as far ranging and free as possible?   *Alexander Eliot*

A series of surprises, and would not be worth taking or keeping if it were not.

Ralph Waldo Emerson

An experiment. The more experiments you make the better.   *Ralph Waldo Emerson*

March weather, savage and serene in one hour.

Ralph Waldo Emerson

A longish doze, interrupted by fits and starts of bewildered semi-alertness.   *Clifton Fadiman*

For most men . . . a search for the proper manila envelope in which to get themselves filed.

Clifton Fadiman

A series of little deaths, out of which life always returns.   *Charles Feidelson 2*

That power in the individual which can force external forces to obey an internal law.

Ernst von Feuchtersleben

An art as any other, and the great incidents in it are no more to be considered as mere accidents than the severest members of a fine statue or a noble poem.   *Henry Fielding*

Life is work, and everything you do is so much more experience.   *Henry Ford*

Consists not simply in what heredity and environment do to us but in what we make out of what they do to us.   *Harry Emerson Fosdick*

A library owned by an author. In it are a few books which he wrote himself, but most of them were written for him.   *Harry Emerson Fosdick*

An onion, and one peels it crying.

French Proverb

A republic where the individuals are for the most part unconscious that while they are working for themselves they are also working for the public good.   *Francis Galton*

An endless series of experiments.

Mohandas K. Gandi

A drink of salt water, which seems to quench, but actually inflames.   *Elijah Gaon*

A series of vexations and pains, and sleepless nights are the common lot.   *Elijah Gaon*

A terrible disease cured only by death.

Hai Gaon

Life is a jest, and all things show it; I thought so once and now I know it.

Adapted from John Gay

The only riddle that we shrink from giving up.

William S. Gilbert

A quarry, out of which we are to mold and chisel and complete a character.   *Johann W. Goethe*

Life at the greatest and best is but a forward child, that must be humored and coaxed a little till it falls asleep, and then all the care is over.

Oliver Goldsmith

An experiment in the art of living, but you die before you see the result.   *Russell Green*

Life is something like this trumpet. If you don't put anything it it, you don't get anything out.

W. C. Handy

Life is a game of whist. From unseen sources the cards are shuffled, and the hands are dealt.

Eugene Hare

A succession of frontispieces. The way to be satisfied is never to look back.   *William Hazlitt*

Sobs, sniffles, and smiles, with sniffles predominating.   *O. Henry*

(Something) half spent before we know what it is.

George Herbert

From diapers to dignity to decomposition.

Don Herold

A great bundle of little things.

Oliver Wendell Holmes 1

An end in itself, and the only question as to whether it is worth living is whether you have had enough of it.   *Oliver Wendell Holmes 1*

A fatal complaint, and an eminently contagious one.   *Oliver Wendell Holmes 1*

Action and passion.   *Oliver Wendell Holmes 2*

The interval between the time your teeth are almost through and you are almost through with your teeth.   *Elbert Hubbard*

An onion: you peel off layer after layer and then you find there is nothing in it.

James G. Huneker

An art; and, to practice it well, men need not only acquired skill, but also a native tact and taste.

Aldous Huxley

At any given moment life is completely senseless. But viewed over a long period, it seems to reveal itself as an organism existing in time, having a purpose, tending in a certain direction.

Aldous Huxley

Routine punctuated by orgies.   *Aldous Huxley*

A shadowy, strange, and winding road.

Robert G. Ingersoll

A predicament which precedes death.

Henry James

The great use of life is to spend it for something that outlasts it.   *William James*

A real fight.   *William James*

The art of avoiding pain.   *Thomas Jefferson*

Nothing but a dream, but few want to wake up.

Jewish Proverb

The cheapest bargain. You get it for nothing.

Jewish Proverb

A progress from want to want.   *Samuel Johnson*

A state in which much is to be endured and little to be enjoyed.   *Samuel Johnson*

A pill which none of us can bear to swallow without gilding.   *Samuel Johnson*

The main of life is composed of small incidents and petty occurrences.   *Samuel Johnson*

The faculty of spontaneous activity, the awareness that we have powers.   *Immanuel Kant*

A man's life of any worth is a continual allegory, and very few eyes can see the mystery of his life.

John Keats

Either a daring adventure, or nothing.

Helen Keller

An exciting business and most exciting when it is lived for others.   *Helen Keller*

Only play, and idle talk, and pageantry, and boasting among you, and rivalry in respect of wealth and children.   *Koran*

A tragedy for those who feel, a comedy for those who think.   *Jean de La Bruyère*

One line in a deathless poem.

Joshua L. Liebman

A loom, weaving illusion.   *Vachel Lindsay*

A leaf of paper white whereon each one of us may write his word or two, and then comes night.

Adapted from James Russell Lowell

Our sad condition, our only consolation is the expectation of another life. Here below all is incomprehensible.   *Martin Luther*

A tragedy full of joy.   *Bernard Malamud*

A long headache in a noisy street.

John Masefield

A scrambled egg.   *Don Marquis*

A few brief, flying years.   *Walt Mason*

Like one of those modern kindergartens in which children are left to their own devices and work only at the subjects that arouse their interest.

William Somerset Maugham

A mission...an aim.   *Giuseppe Mazzini*

A voyage that's homeward bound.

Herman Melville

Not a tragedy, but...a bore.

Henry Louis Mencken

(Not) one damn thing after another—it's one damn thing over and over.

Edna St. Vincent Millay

That bad bargain.   *Michel de Montaigne*

Partly folly, partly wisdom.

Michel de Montaigne

Life is but play;
A throb, a tear:
A sob, a sneer;
And then—good day.   *Leon de Montenaeken*

Pleasures and woe.   *Thomas Moore*

A foreign language: all men mispronounce it.

Christopher Morley

✓ To be, to do, to do without, and to depart.

John Morley

A party: one arrives long after it's started, and one's going to leave long before it's over.

Robert Morley

A single letter in the alphabet. It can be meaningless. Or it can be part of a great meaning.

*National Planning Committee, Jewish
Theological Seminary of America*

An instinct of growth, for survival, for the accumulation of forces, for power.

Friedrich W. Nietzsche

Essentially appropriation, injury, conquest of the strange and weak, suppression, severity, obtrusion of peculiar forms, incorporation, and . . . exploitation.   *Friedrich W. Nietzsche*

To accept the impossible, do without the indispensable, and bear the intolerable.

Kathleen Norris

Strange interlude!   *Eugene O'Neill*

A petty thing unless it is moved by the indomitable urge to extend its boundaries.

José Ortega y Gasset

A campaign, not a battle, and has its defeats as well as its victories.   *Donald Piatt*

A mighty maze, but not without a plan.

Alexander Pope

A rivulet, constantly passing away, and yet constantly coming on.   *Alexander Pope*

To look about us and to die.   *Alexander Pope*

The life of man is a winter's day, and a winter's way.   *John Ray*

To procure life, to obtain a mate, and to rear offspring: such is the real business of life.

W. Winwood Reade

Love, work and knowledge.   *Wilhelm Reich*

Life is what our character wants it to be.

Jules Renard

A surgeon: It wounds, and administers no anesthetic. It cuts out . . . the heart of us sometimes.

Winifred Rhoades

A little work, a little sleep, a little love and it is all over.   *Mary Roberts Rinehart*

A game that must be played.

Edwin Arlington Robinson

A combat without grandeur, without happiness, fought in solitude and silence.   *Romain Rolland*

A long second best, a perpetual compromise between the ideal and the possible.

Bertrand A. Russell

Mere accident, and of the worst kind: we are born to be victims of diseases and passions, of mischances and death.   *Saint John de Crèvecoeur*

An onion; you peel it off one layer at a time, and sometimes you weep.   *Carl Sandburg*

Not a spectacle or a feast; it is a predicament.

George Santayana

That incurable disease from which all have thus far died, and only those survive who are never born.   *Moritz Saphir*

Only a constant struggle for mere existence, with the certainty of losing it at last.

Arthur Schopenhauer

An unprofitable disturbance in the calm of nonexistence.   *Arthur Schopenhauer*

A play! It's not its length, but its performance that counts.   *Seneca*

And so, from hour to hour, we ripe and ripe, and then, from hour to hour, we rot and rot.

Adapted from William Shakespeare

✓ This great stage of fools. *William Shakespeare*

A disease; and the only difference between one man and another is the stage of the disease at which he lives.   *George Bernard Shaw*

A flame that is always burning itself out, but it catches fire again every time a child is born.

George Bernard Shaw

No brief candle to me. It is a sort of splendid torch that I have got hold of for the moment.

George Bernard Shaw

A series of inspired follies. The difficulty is to find them to do. Never lose a chance: it doesn't come every day.   *George Bernard Shaw*

To get what you want; and, after that, to enjoy it.
                                                      Logan P. Smith

✓ One long dirty trick.   *Thorne Smith*

Desire of flesh and incurable loneliness of the soul.   *Hjalmar Söderberg*

A precious, impermanent gift.
                                                Theodore C. Sorensen

The coordination of actions.   *Herbert Spencer*

The continuous adjustment of internal relations to external relations.   *Herbert Spencer*

Is it not to shift from side to side—from sorrow to sorrow?—to button up one cause of vexation, and unbutton another?   *Laurence Sterne*

Our last cruise.   *Robert Louis Stevenson*

A battle in which we fall from the wounds we receive in running away.   *William L. Sullivan*

A ridiculous tragedy...the worst kind of composition.   *Jonathan Swift*

A tragedy wherein we sit as spectators for a while and then act our part in it.   *Jonathan Swift*

A dark night and an ill guide, a boisterous sea and a broken cable, a hard rock and a rough wind.
                                                      Jeremy Taylor

A jest, a dream, a shadow, bubble, air, a vapor at the best.   *Adapted from George W. Thornbury*

A tale told in an idiom, full of unsoundness and fury, signifying nonism.   *James Thurber*

Consists in penetrating the unknown, and fashioning our actions in accord with the new knowledge thus acquired.   *Leon Tolstoy*

Creation and cremation.
                                          Herbert Beerbohm Tree

To keep breathing.   *Sophie Tucker*

A wave which in no two consecutive moments of its existence is composed of the same particles.
                                                      John Tyndall

An arrow—therefore you must know what mark to aim at, how to use the bow—then draw it to the head, and let go.
                                          Adapted from Henry Van Dyke

Our own work. It is a thing of beauty, or a thing of shame, as we ourselves make it.   *Henry Ware*

Next to death, the saddest thing.
                                                      Edith Wharton

An offensive, directed against the repetitious mechanism of the universe.
                                            Alfred North Whitehead

A suck and a sell.   *Walt Whitman*

Our lives are songs: God writes the words and we set them to music at pleasure; and the song grows glad, or sweet or sad as we choose to fashion the measure.   *Adapted from Ella Wheeler Wilcox*

Far too important a thing ever to talk seriously about.   *Oscar Wilde*

To most of us the real life is the life we do not lead.   *Oscar Wilde*

Simply an accumulation of all the forces that resist death.   *Heathcote Williams*

An unanswered question, but let's still believe in the dignity and importance of the question.
                                                  Tennessee Williams

A process of burning oneself out and time is the fire that burns you.   *Tennessee Williams*

Not a matter of extent but of content.
                                                    Stephen S. Wise

The one supreme thing that interests us all, because we all have to live it.   *Ida A. Wylie*

Dust, which frugal nature lends man for an hour.
                                          Adapted from Edward Young

Bubbles on the rapid stream of time.   ✓
                                                      Edward Young

Man's life's a vapor,
And full of woes;
He cuts a caper,
And down he goes.   *Anon.*

A span of time in which the first half is ruined by our parents and the second half by our children.
                                                              Anon.

Consists in wanting something. When a man is satisfied he is as good as dead.   *Anon.*

A jig-saw puzzle with most of the pieces missing.
                                                              Anon.

A one way street.   *Anon.*

Spending most of your day doing what you do not want to do in order to earn the right, at brief moments, to do what you desire.   *Anon.*

School tablet, aspirin tablet, stone tablet.   *Anon.*

SEE ALSO BODY, EXISTENCE, GOD, HUMAN BEINGS, HUMANITY, IMMORTALITY, LIVE, LIVING, MAN, TIME.

LIFE INSURANCE

Providing for the widows and orphans—of the officers and directors.   *Harry Thompson*

An investment in disaster.   *Anon.*

LIGHT

The first creature of God, in the works of the days, was the light of the sense: the last was the light of reason: and his sabbath work ever since is the illumination of his Spirit.   *Francis Bacon*

And God said, Let there be light: and there was light.   *Bible: Genesis, I, 3.*

Light is sown for the righteous.
Bible: Psalms, XCVII, 11.

The first of painters. There is no object so foul that intense light will not make beautiful.
Ralph Waldo Emerson

The prime work of God.   *John Milton*

The symbol of the divine.
Union Prayer Book, 1940.

SEE ALSO ELECTRICITY.

LIMERICK

The limerick is furtive and mean;
You must keep her in close quarantine,
   Or she sneaks to the slums
   And promptly becomes
Disorderly, drunk, and obscene.   *Morris Bishop*

No matter how grouchy you're feeling,
You'll find that a limerick is healing.
   It grows in a wreath
   All around the front teeth,
Thus preserving the face from congealing.
Anon.

The limerick packs laughs anatomical
Into space that is quite economical.

But the good ones I've seen
So seldom are clean,
And the clean ones so seldom are comical!
Anon.

LINCOLN, ABRAHAM (1809-1865)

A nature, modeled on a higher plan.
George H. Boker

Uncommon commoner... unschooled scholar.
Edmund V. Cooke

One of those peculiar men who perform with admirable skill everything which they undertake.
Stephen A. Douglas

A martyr to the cause of man.
Charles G. Halpin

Not a type. He stands alone—no ancestors, no followers, no successors.   *Robert G. Ingersoll*

Strange mingling of mirth and tears, of the tragic and grotesque, of cap and crown...Lincoln, the gentlest memory of the world.
Robert G. Ingersoll

That mystic mingling of star and clod.
Frederick Landis

The first American.   *James Russell Lowell*

A man to match the mountains and the sea.
Edwin Markham

Cinderella in prairie boots.
Henry Louis Mencken

Lincoln had a very deep feeling for people, but...he could be tough in a crisis. No one pushed him around. He was a very skillful political operator.   *Richard Milhous Nixon*

Steel and velvet...hard as rock and soft as drifting fog, who holds in his heart and mind the paradox of terrible storm and peace.
Carl Sandburg

One of the people! born to be
Their curious epitome;
To share yet rise above
Their shifting hate and love.
Richard H. Stoddard

An enemy of the human race, and deserves the execration of all mankind.   *Robert Toombs*

I never see the man without feeling that he is one to become personally attach'd to, for his combination of purest, heartiest tenderness, and native western form of manliness.   *Walt Whitman*

A very normal man with very normal gifts, but all upon a great scale, all knit together in loose and natural form, like the great frame in which he moved and dwelt.   *Woodrow Wilson*

Fox Populi.   *Anon.*

Blackguard and buffoon as he is, he has pursued his end with an energy as untiring as an Indian, and a singleness of purpose that might almost be called patriotic.   *Anon.*

LION

(The) predator-in-chief.   *Michael Bailey*

Strongest among beasts, and turns not away for any.   *Bible: Proverbs, XXX, 30.*

Lions are king of beasts, yet their power is not to rule and govern but to devour.

Adapted from Samuel Butler 1

The lion is (beyond dispute)
Allow'd the most majestic brute;
His valor and his gen'rous mind
Prove him superior of his kind.   *John Gay*

LIQUOR

SEE COCKTAIL PARTY, DRINKING, DRUNK-ARD, WINE.

LISTENING

The only way to entertain some folks.
Kin Hubbard

To persuade others . . . with your ears.
Dean Rusk

To listen well is a second inheritance.
Publilius Syrus

A very dangerous thing. If one listens one may be convinced.   *Oscar Wilde*

Growing in stature through the ears.   *Anon.*

A declining art.   *Anon.*

LITERATURE

A challenge to despair.   *Eric Bentley*

Exists to please—to lighten the burden of men's lives; to make them for a short while forget their sorrows and their sins . . . their disappointed hopes, their grim futures—and those men of letters are the best loved who have best performed literature's truest office.   *Augustine Birrell*

A pleasure which arises not only from the things said, but from the way in which they are said; and that pleasure is only given when the words are carefully or beautifully put together into sentences.   *Stopford Brooke*

An investment of genius which pays dividends to all subsequent times.   *John Burroughs*

The thought of thinking Souls.   *Thomas Carlyle*

To reveal tongues with the fingers, silently to give salvation to men, to fight with pen and ink against the attacks of the devil.   *Cassiodorus*

When a book . . . reaches a certain intensity of artistic performance . . . That intensity may be a matter of style, situation, character, emotional tone, or idea.   *Raymond Chandler*

The expression of a nation's mind in writing.
William Ellery Channing

Literature and fiction are two entirely different things. Literature is a luxury; fiction is a necessity.   *Gilbert Keith Chesterton*

Literature is but language.
Gilbert Keith Chesterton

Has always been allegorical.
Gilbert Keith Chesterton

The art of writing something that will be read twice.   *Cyril Connolly*

A transmission of power. Textbooks, and treatises, dictionaries and encyclopedias, manuals and books of instruction—they are communications; but literature is a power line, and the motor . . . is the reader.
Charles P. Curtis

A generation and an incarnation, an earthly likeness of the eternal utterance and its manifestation in time.   *Peter J. Dempsey*

There is first the literature of *knowledge,* and . . . the literature of *power.* The function of the first is to *teach*; the function of the second is to *move*...The first speaks to the mere discursive understanding; the second speaks ultimately...to the higher understanding of reason.

Thomas De Quincey

Literature should stand by itself, of itself, and for itself.
Charles Dickens

The mystery of the human heart and its passage through time.
Hugh Dinwiddy

An avenue of glory ever open to those ingenious men who are deprived of honors or of wealth.

Isaac D'Israeli

Literature, has been, and probably always will be judged by moral standards.

Thomas Stearns Eliot

When a writer arranges the circumstances of experience to figure forth large themes...leaping the barriers of custom and language...to be heard by men of many countries and many ages.

George P. Elliot

The effort of man to indemnify himself for the wrongs of his condition. *Ralph Waldo Emerson*

An idea with a glow. *Oscar Firkins*

The only occupation in which wages are not given in proportion to the goodness of the work done.

James A. Froude

It is life that shakes and rocks us; it is literature which stabilizes and confirms.

Heathcote W. Garrold

The grand line of demarcation between the human and the animal kingdoms. *William Godwin*

A noble calling, but only when the call obeyed by the aspirant issues from a world to be enlightened and blessed. *Horace Greeley*

(Writing that has the) ability to survive the stupidity of the people who teach it and the indifference of the pupils who study it. *Sydney J. Harris*

A kind of intellectual light which, like the light of the sun, may sometimes enable us to see what we do not like. *Samuel Johnson*

A legitimate function...escape from the provincial into the universal, from the here to the there, from today to yesterday. *Halford Luccock*

An idealization of quarrels. Cut quarrels out of literature, and you will have very little history or drama or fiction or epic poetry left.

Robert Lynd

The expression, through the aesthetic medium of words, of the dogmas of the Catholic Church, and that which is in any way out of harmony with these dogmas is not literature. *Arthur Machen*

Language put to its best purpose, used at its utmost power...and recorded that it may not pass away. *John W. MacKail*

An art, a science, a profession, a trade, and an accident. The literature that is of lasting value is an accident. It is something that happens.

S. McCrothers

The product of inquiring minds in revolt against the immovable certainties of the nation.

Henry Louis Mencken

The sudden expression of the fierce, hilarious lives of human beings. *Christopher Morley*

Only what people would say to each other if they had the chance. *Christopher Morley*

The most seductive, the most deceiving, the most dangerous of professions. *John Morley*

All that enhances, by means of the word, both your knowledge and your ability to employ that knowledge. *Samuel Niger*

News that stays news. *Ezra Pound*

Language charged with meaning to the utmost possible degree. *Ezra Pound*

An occupation in which you have to keep proving your talent to people who have none.

Jules Renard

Literature was formerly an art and finance a trade: today it is the reverse. *Joseph Roux*

The immortality of speech.

August W. von Schlegel

Literature in many of its branches is no other than the shadow of good talk.

Robert Louis Stevenson

Simply the appropriate use of language.

Evelyn Waugh

An analysis of experience and a synthesis of the findings into a unity. *Rebecca West*

Literature always anticipates life. It does not copy it, but moulds it to its purpose. *Oscar Wilde*

The notation of the heart. *Thornton Wilder*

The orchestration of platitudes.

Thornton Wilder

A monumental proof enough against death.

Anon.

SEE ALSO BOOK, CLASSICS, FICTION, NOVEL, READING, STYLE, WRITERS, WRITING.

LITIGATION

A machine which you go into as a pig and come out of as a sausage.   *Ambrose Bierce*

A form of hell whereby money is transferred from the pockets of the proletariat to that of lawyers.

Elbert Hubbard

SEE ALSO LAWSUIT, LAWYERS, TRIAL.

LIVE

To live is like to love—all reason is against it, and all healthy instinct for it.   *Samuel Butler 2*

To live is to function. That is all there is in living.

Oliver Wendell Holmes 2

To feel ourselves fatally obliged to exercise our liberty, to decide what we are going to be in this world.   *José Ortega y Gasset*

To have something definite to do—a mission to fulfill.   *José Ortega y Gasset*

SEE ALSO EXISTENCE, LIFE.

LIVING

Activity.   *James Truslow Adams*

To stand firm and be ready for an unforeseen attack.   *Marcus Aurelius*

(Identifying) ourselves with the struggles and problems, individual and social, as well as with the hopes and ideals of the age in which we live.

Anita Block

We live in deeds, not years; in thoughts, not breaths, in feelings, not figures on the dial.

Gamaliel Bailey

Living is throwing theory into the fire.

Adapted from Mikhail A. Bakunin

To take things as they be.   *John K. Bangs*

The state which makes one unwilling to exchange what one has, no matter how grim, for the uncertainties of death, no matter how attractive.

Eugene E. Brussell

To make the most of life, and to make the best of it.   *Edwin H. Chapin*

A form of not being sure, not knowing what next or how.   *Agnes De Mille*

Communion with God, or . . . doing good.

John Donne

Struggle for worthy causes.

Dwight David Eisenhower

A never-ending conflict between the impulse to find freshly available forms of gratification of the primary instincts and the constant tendency to revert to older forms even when these had proven less successful.   *Sigmund Freud*

Consists of mutual service.

Charlotte P. Gilman

What you get is a living—what you give is a life.

Lillian Gish

To put out one's power in some natural and useful or harmless way.   *Oliver Wendell Holmes 2*

Action and passion; therefore, it is required of a man that he should share the passion and action of his time at peril of being judged not to have lived.

Oliver Wendell Holmes 2

Love, laughter and work.   *Elbert Hubbard*

A constant readjustment to our surroundings.

Okakura Kakuzo

To live in an English country home, engage a Chinese cook, marry a Japanese wife, and take a French mistress.   *Lin Yutang*

The finest art, and the most difficult to learn.

John Macy

Working.   *Karl Marx*

Allowing happiness to change its form without being disappointed by the change.

Charles Morgan

Three kinds . . . one is occupied in action and doing; the second in knowledge and study; the third in . . . fruition of pleasures and wanton pastimes.   *John Northbrooke*

Any exquisite passion.   *Walter Pater*

The art of knowing how to believe lies.

Cesare Pavese

Internal dramas, instantaneous and sensational, played to an audience of one.   *Anthony Powell*

Reasoning on the past, complaining of the present, and trembling for the future.

Antoine Rivarol

To succeed in giving life some weight without making it too heavy.   *Jean Rostand*

To act...to make use of our organs, senses, faculties, of all those parts of ourselves which give us the feeling of existence.

Jean Jacques Rousseau

Transcribed patterns of milieu.

Dagobert Runes

The process of reacting to stress.

Stanley J. Sarnoff

Struggle and take risks.   *Ignazio Silone*

First...get what you want; and, after that...enjoy it.   *Logan P. Smith*

A living thing is distinguished from a dead thing by the multiplicity of the changes at any moment taking place in it.   *Herbert Spencer*

Tearing up one rough draft after another.

John J. Sullivan

To go alone, and not to require a constant supervision.   *Henry David Thoreau*

To be able to create one's own terms for what one does.   *Kenneth Tynan*

To move about in a cloud of ignorance.

Thornton Wilder

A serious attempt to make something of oneself and one's surroundings.   *Angus Wilson*

Surrendering your ego to the service of your fellow men.   *Walter B. Wolfe*

SEE ALSO ETHICS, EXISTENCE, LIFE, LONGEVITY, THOUGHT, WORK.

LOAFER

The man who is usually busy keeping some one else from working.   *Elbert Hubbard*

(One who) always has the correct time.

Kin Hubbard

A person who is trying to make weekends meet.

Anon.

SEE ALSO IDLENESS.

LOGIC

A large drawer, containing some useful instruments, and many more that are superfluous.

Charles Caleb Colton

The armory of reason, furnished with all offensive and defensive weapons.   *Thomas Fuller*

An instrument used for bolstering a prejudice.

Elbert Hubbard

Neither a science nor an art, but a dodge.

Benjamin Jowett

The art of going wrong with confidence.

Joseph Wood Krutch

The art of convincing us of some truth.

Jean de La Bruyère

Nothing more than a knowledge of words.

Charles Lamb

The anatomy of thought.   *John Locke*

A gamble, at terrible odds—if it was a bet you wouldn't take it.   *Thomas Stoppard*

Simply the architecture of human reason.

Evelyn Waugh

LOGICIAN

The rapt saint.   *Ralph Waldo Emerson*

He deposits on a sheet of paper a certain assemblage of syllables, and fancies that their meaning is riveted by the act of deposition.

Edgar Allan Poe

LONDON

A place to plunder!   *Gebhard L. Blücher*

That pleasant place, where every kind of mischief's brewing.   *Adapted from Lord Byron*

A mighty mass of brick, and smoke, and shipping, dirty and dusty but as wide as the eye can see.   *Adapted from Lord Byron*

That monstrous tuberosity of civilized life.

Thomas Carlyle

A huge immeasurable spirit of a thought, embodied in brick, in iron, smoke, dust, palaces, parliaments...Not a brick was made but some man had to think of the making of that brick.

Thomas Carlyle

The clearing-house of the world.

Joseph Chamberlain

The centre of a thousand trades.

William Cowper

Resort and mart of all the world.

William Cowper

A stony-hearted step-mother.

Thomas De Quincey

A roost for every bird.   *Benjamin Disraeli*

A nation, not a city.   *Benjamin Disraeli*

A city of cities, an aggregate of humanity.

Benjamin Disraeli

The epitome of our times, and the Rome of today.

Ralph Waldo Emerson

Crowds without company, and dissipation without pleasure.   *Edward Gibbon*

The only place in which the child grows completely up into the man.   *William Hazlitt*

The needy villian's gen'ral home.

Samuel Johnson

A city whose day begins when day is done.

Adapted from Richard Le Gallienne

The dining-room of Christendom.

Thomas Middleton

Dear, damn'd, distracting town.

Alexander Pope

That great sea.   *Percy Bysshe Shelley*

The worst place in the world for a good woman to grow better in.   *John Vanbrugh*

The city San Francisco thinks it is.   *Anon.*

SEE ALSO CITY.

LONELINESS

The surest sign of age.   *Amos Bronson Alcott*

Man's real condition.   *Wystan H. Auden*

A game of pretense; for the essential lonliness is an escape from an inescapable God.

Walter Farrell

The peculiar feeling caused by the presence of one or more bores.   *Elbert Hubbard*

Being broke and among relatives.

Adapted from Frank M. Hubbard

The first thing which God's eye nam'd not good.

John Milton

The stuff of hell.   *Gerald Vann*

The central and inevitable experience of every man.   *Thomas Wolfe*

Really a homesickness for God.

Hubert van Zeller

SEE ALSO SOLITUDE.

LONGEVITY

Uncommon extension of the fear of death.

Ambrose Bierce

Barring hanging and accidents, is largely a matter of heredity.   *Howard Haggard*

Protracted woe.   *Samuel Johnson*

The result of freedom from grief and worry.

Moses Maimonides

One of the more dubious rewards of virtue.

Ngaio Marsh

To live twice.   *Martial*

The longer one lives, the less importance one attaches to things, and also the less importance to importance.   *Jean Rostand*

SEE ALSO OLD AGE.

LOS ANGELES

A place where the only cultural advantage is that you can turn right on a red light.   *Woody Allen*

A parking lot for used cities.   *Wilson Mizner*

Too many freeways, too much sun, too much abnormality taken normally, too many pink stucco houses and pink stucco consciences.

Clancy Sigal

Detroit with grapefruits.   *Anon.*

A sunny Des Moines.   *Anon.*

Many suburbs in search of a city.   *Anon.*

Where neon goes to die.   *Anon.*

A place where they arrest you for doing 80 miles per hour on the freeway for holding up traffic.

    Anon.

SEE ALSO CALIFORNIA, HOLLYWOOD.

LOVE

A perpetual hyperbole.   *Francis Bacon*

When a couple of young people strongly devoted to each other commence to eat onions.

    James M. Bailey

The union of a want and a sentiment.

    Honoré de Balzac

A kind of vaccination which saves a man from catching the complaint a second time.

    Honoré de Balzac

A find, a fire, a heaven, a hell, where pleasure, pain, and sad repentance dwell.

    Richard Barnfield

Two minds without a single thought.

    Philip Barry

The delightful interval between meeting a beautiful girl and discovering that she looks like a haddock.   *John Barrymore*

The need to escape from oneself.

    Charles Baudelaire

To endure for others.   *Henry Ward Beecher*

A load: blessed is he who bears heavy ones.

    Richard Beer-Hofmann

God is love.   *Bible: John, IV, 8.*

The fulfilling of the law.

    Bible: Romans, XIII, 10.

A temporary insanity curable by marriage or by removal of the patient from the influences under which he incurred the disorder.   *Ambrose Bierce*

(A) disease...prevalent only among civilized races living under artificial conditions.

    Ambrose Bierce

To live is to love.   *Ludwig Boerne*

A form of flattery which pleases all.

    Ludwig Boerne

Truth made vulnerable to logic and sense.

    Eugene E. Brussell

When a liberal wants to marry a conservative or visa-versa.   *Eugene E. Brussell*

A beautiful dream with glandular activity.

    Eugene E. Brussell

The business of the idle, but the idleness of the busy.   *Edward G. Bulwer-Lytton*

When another person's needs are as important as your own.   *Abe Burrows*

A sort of hostile transaction, very necessary to keep the world going, but by no means a sinecure to the parties concerned.   *Lord Byron*

Man's love is of man's life a part; it is woman's whole existence.   *Lord Byron*

Not altogether a delirium, yet it has many points in common.   *Thomas Carlyle*

The beginning of knowledge.   *Thomas Carlyle*

Something you have to make...It's all work, work.   *Joyce Cary*

The blinding revelation that some other being can be more important to the lover than he is to himself.   *J. V. Casserley*

Love and war are the same thing, and stratagems and policy are as allowable in the one as in the other.   *Miguel de Cervantes*

In young men...simply sexual desire and its accomplishment is its end.

    Miguel de Cervantes

The exchange of two momentary desires and the contact of two skins.   *Nicolas Chamfort*

Either the shrinking remnant of something which was once enormous; or...part of something which will grow in the future into something enormous.   *Anton Chekhov*

The word used to label the sexual excitement of the young, the habituation of the middle-aged, and the mutual dependence of the old.   *John Ciardi*

Love is always the first time again. Whatever comes after that is only habituation.

    John Ciardi

An alliance of friendship and animalism.
Charles Caleb Colton

A sickness full of woes, all remedies refusing.
Samuel Daniel

A hell!   *Thomas Dekker*

An ocean of emotions, entirely surrounded by expenses.   *Thomas R. Dewar*

A season pass on the shuttle between heaven and hell.   *Donald Dickerman*

The principle of existence and its only end.
Benjamin Disraeli

(Something that) comes unseen; we only see it go.
Austin Dobson

Suffering divinized.   *James W. Douglass*

Love is not...a noun. It is a verb.
Hugh Downs

Sex to the last.   *John Dryden*

A gracious and beautiful erotic art.
Havelock Ellis

Only the reflection of a man's own worthiness from other men.   *Ralph Waldo Emerson*

The affirmative of affirmatives.
Ralph Waldo Emerson

Our highest word, and the synonym of God.
Ralph Waldo Emerson

(That which) teaches letters to a man unlearned.
Euripides

To be always doing things for God, and not to mind because they are such little ones.
Frederick W. Faber

A word properly applied to our delight in particular kinds of food; sometimes metaphorically spoken of the favorite objects of all our appetites.
Henry Fielding

Desperate madness.   *John Ford*

Union under the condition of preserving one's integrity.   *Erich Fromm*

An act of faith, and whoever is of little faith is also of little love.   *Erich Fromm*

To love means to commit oneself without guarantee, to give oneself completely in the hope that our love will produce love in the loved person.
Erich Fromm

(A state which) has to be blinding to make things right.   *Robert Frost*

The effort a man makes to be satisfied with only one woman.   *Paul Geraldy*

It is the special quality of love not to be able to remain stationary, to be obliged to increase under pain of diminishing.   *André Gide*

A platform upon which all ranks meet.
William S. Gilbert

Yesterday's illusion, today's allusion, and tomorrow's delusion.   *Warren Goldberg*

A non-possessive empathy and respect for the feelings of the loved one.   *Max Gralnick*

To stop comparing.   *Bernard Grasset*

The drug which makes sexuality palatable in popular mythology.   *Germaine Greer*

A freely given emotion...that is made stronger by its being returned.   *Roger Grimsby*

Loving in the other sex what you lack in yourself.
Adapted from G. Stanley Hall

Love in your heart wasn't put there to stay. Love isn't love till you give it away.
Oscar Hammerstein 2

Love at first sight is only realizing an imagination that has always haunted us.   *William Hazlitt*

Three kinds of love: of pleasures, of profit, and of virtue.   *Leon Hebraeus*

A hole in the heart.   *Ben Hecht*

A fan club with only two fans.   *Adrian Henri*

A combination of sex and sentiment.
Emile Herzog

A conflict between reflexes and reflections.
Magnus Hirschfeld

A game in which both players always cheat.
Edgar W. Howe

A portion of the soul itself, and it is of the same nature as...the celestial breathing of the atmosphere of paradise.   *Victor Hugo*

The reduction of the universe to a single being, the expansion of a single being. *Victor Hugo*

The more subtle form of self-interest. *Holbrook Jackson*

Like the measles—all the worse when it comes late in life. *Douglas Jerrold*

Only one of the many passions...and has no great influence on the sum of life. *Samuel Johnson*

The wisdom of the fool and the folly of the wise. *Samuel Johnson*

Love means that the attributes of the lover are changed into those of the Beloved. *Junayd of Bagdad*

The most terrible, and also the most generous of all the passions; it is the only one which includes in its dreams the happiness of someone else. *Alphonse Karr*

A sport in which the hunter must contrive to have the quarry in pursuit. *Alphonse Karr*

The form of selection most conducive to the ennoblement of the species. *Ellen Key*

Sentimental measles. *Charles Kingsley*

The beginning, the middle, and the end of everything. *Jean B. Lacordaire*

True love is like ghosts, which everybody talks about and few have seen. *La Rochefoucauld*

The cure of coquetry. *La Rochefoucauld*

Love is getting home after a day's work and not needing a martini to unwind. *Julius La Rosa*

A thing to be *learned*. It is a difficult, complex maintenance of individual integrity throughout the incalculable process of inter-human polarity. *D.H. Lawrence*

The great asker. *D. H. Lawrence*

 To place our happiness in the happiness of another. *Gottfried von Leibnitz*

Habit causes love. *Lucretius*

An image of God...the living essence of the divine nature which beams full of all goodness. *Martin Luther*

A feeling that has the power of making you believe what you would normally treat with the deepest suspicion. *Pierre Marivaux*

The conjunction of the mind, and opposition of the stars. *Andrew Marvell*

A mutual admiration society consisting but of two members...the one whose love is less intense will become president. *Joseph Mayer*

Like war: easy to begin but very hard to stop. *Henry Louis Mencken*

The delusion that one woman differs from another. *Henry Louis Mencken*

The triumph of imagination over intelligence. *Henry Louis Mencken*

An expression of the communion between persons. *Thomas Merton*

The pill that leaves the heart sick and overturns the will. *Adapted from Thomas Middleton*

To communicate to the other that you are all for him, that you will never fail him or let him down when he needs you, but that you will always be standing by with all the necessary encouragements. *Ashley Montague*

Nothing else but an insatiate thirst of enjoying a greedily desired object. *Michel de Montaigne*

Immortality struggling within a mortal frame. *A. Victor Murray*

The association of two beings for the benefit of one. *Countess Nathalie*

The privilege of emperors, kings, soldiers and artists; it is the butt of democrats, traveling salesmen, magazine poets and the writers of American novels. *George Jean Nathan*

A barbarity, for it is exercised at the expense of all others. *Friedrich W. Nietzsche*

The state in which a man sees things most decidedly as they are not. *Friedrich W. Nietzsche*

A kind of warfare. *Ovid*

Quicksilver in the hand. Leave the fingers open and it stays in the palm; clutch it and it darts away. *Dorothy Parker*

When a person's...own boundary expands to include the you, or the other, that was previously outside himself. *Frederick S. Perls*

A grave mental disease. *Plato*

An appetite of generation by the mediation of beauty. *Plato*

The mood of believing in miracles.

John C. Powys

Space and time measured by the heart.

Marcel Proust

An attempt to change a piece of a dream-world into reality. *Theodore Reik*

Consists in this: that two solitudes protect and touch and greet each other. *Rainer M. Rilke*

A ghastly wine freshening and fortifying the minds of its chosen, and raising them beyond thought or care of worldly allurements.

Richard Rolle

The fairest and most profitable guest a reasonable creature can entertain. *Richard Rolle*

To love is to choose. *Joseph Roux*

Woman's eternal spring and man's eternal fall.

Helen Rowland

A little haven of refuge from the world.

Bertrand A. Russell

Looking outward together in the same direction.

Antoine de Saint-Exupéry

An egotism of two. *Antoine de Salle*

A most important function in propagation of the human species and is all the more interesting because it is involuntary and shows a readiness to be courted. *Joseph Sandler*

Only half an illusion; the lover, but not his love, is deceived. *George Santayana*

A spirit all compact of fire.

William Shakespeare

A little foolishness and a lot of curiosity.

George Bernard Shaw

A gross exaggeration of the difference between one person and everybody else.

George Bernard Shaw

A mutual self-giving which ends in self-recovery.

Fulton J. Sheen

Its very essence is liberty: it is compatible neither with obedience, jealousy, nor fear: it is...most pure, perfect, and unlimited where its votaries live in confidence, equality, and unreserve.

Percy Bysshe Shelley

That...sentiment...the universal thirst for a communion not merely of the senses, but of our whole nature. *Percy Bysshe Shelley*

The supreme value around which all moral values can be integrated into one ethical system valid for the whole of humanity. *Pitirim Sorokin*

Like war: you begin when you like and leave off when you can. *Spanish Proverb*

A symbol of eternity. It wipes out all sense of time, destroying all memory of a beginning and all fear of an end. *Anna Louise de Staël*

The whole history of a woman's life; it is only an episode in man's. *Anna Louise de Staël*

Spiritual fire. *Emanuel Swedenborg*

Consists in desiring to give what is our own to another and feeling his delight as our own.

Emanuel Swedenborg

A reality in the domain of the imagination.

Charles de Talleyrand

Friendship set on fire. *Jeremy Taylor*

The strange bewilderment which overtakes one person on account of another person.

James Thurber and Edward B. White

What you've been through with somebody.

James Thurber

Renunciation of one's personal comfort.

Leon Tolstoy

The true means by which the world is enjoyed.

Thomas Traherne

The child of illusion and the parent of disillusion...the sole medicine against death, for it is death's brother. *Miguel Unamuno*

An act of endless forgiveness, a tender look which becomes a habit. *Peter Ustinov*

The heart's immortal thirst to be completely known and all forgiven. *Henry Van Dyke*

Not getting, but giving. *Henry Van Dyke*

The fire. *Vergil*

To believe, to hope, to know—a taste of heaven below. *Adapted from Edmund Waller*

Belief in the existence of other human beings as such. *Simone Weil*

A mutual misunderstanding. *Oscar Wilde*

An energy which exists of itself. It is its own value.   *Thornton Wilder*

Love...remains among the sharpest expressions of self-interest. Not until it has passed through long servitude...through great doubts, can it take its place among the loyalties.   *Thornton Wilder*

There is a land of the living and a land of dead and the bridge is love, the only survival, the only meaning.   *Thorton Wilder*

Just another four-letter word.
   Tennessee Williams

A talkative passion.   *Thomas Wilson*

The ultimate expression of the will to live.
   Thomas Wolfe

A man's insane desire to become a woman's meal ticket.   *Gideon Wurdz*

The dawn of marriage, and marriage is the sunset of love.   *Anon.*

The star men look up to as they walk along. (Marriage is the coal-hole they fall into.)   *Anon.*

To some people, only the last word in a telegram.
   Anon.

Love is such a funny thing;
   It's very like a lizard;
It twines itself round the heart
   And penetrates your gizzard.   *Anon.*

SEE ALSO ALIMONY, COURTSHIP, CUPID, MARRIAGE, MOTHER, PASSION, PLATONIC LOVE, SEX (LOVE), SEXES (MEN AND WOMEN).

LOVERS

A lover teaches a wife all her husband kept hidden from her.   *Honoré de Balzac*

A man who tries to be more amiable than it is possible for him to be.   *Nicolas Chamfort*

Sick people.   *Jeremy Collier*

Unconscious comedians.   *Elbert Hubbard*

Madmen.   *Latin Proverb*

A kind of soldier.   *Ovid*

Scratch a lover, and fine a foe.   *Dorothy Parker*

All lovers swear more performance than they are able, yet reserve an ability that they never per-

form; vowing more than the perfection of ten, discharging less than the tenth part of one.

   William Shakespeare

When two people are under the influence of the most violent, most insane, most delusive, and most transient of passions, they are required to swear that they will remain in that excited, abnormal, and exhausting condition continuously until death do them part.   *George Bernard Shaw*

SEE ALSO COURTSHIP, HUSBAND, MARRIAGE, ROMANCE, SEX (LOVE), SEXES (MEN AND WOMEN), WIFE, WOMAN.

LOYALTY

SEE FRIENDSHIP, PATRIOTISM.

LUCK

The success of people you don't like.
   Hyman, Maxwell, Berston

What you have left over after you give 100%.
   Langston Coleman

When the bread falls on the floor with the buttered side up.   *Max Gralnick*

Tenacity of purpose.   *Elbert Hubbard*

The hardships and privations which you have not hestitated to endure.   *Max O'Rell*

An explanation of the other fellow's success.
   Harry Thompson

Money in the bank.   *Walter Winchell*

Good and bad luck is but a synonym, in the great majority of instances, for good and bad judgment.
   Anon.

Hard work and a stubborn conviction that you deserve to succeed.   *Anon.*

A lazy man's estimate of a worker's success.
   Anon.

SEE ALSO CHANCE, SUCCESS.

LUDICROUS

SEE RIDICULOUSNESS.

LUNATIC

SEE MADMAN.

LUST

War against the soul.   *Bible: Peter, II, 11.*

The brutish passion.   *Robert Burton*

A means for the satisfaction of animal needs.
                             Mohandas K. Gandhi

Only a careless distribution of superfluous time.
                                Samuel Johnson

Lewd and lavish arts of sin.   *John Milton*

The act...gross and brief, and brings loathing
after it.   *Petronius*

A corrosive to conscience...a mortal bane to all
the body.   *Pliny 1*

An appetite of the mind by which temporal goods
are preferred to eternal goods.   *Saint Augustine*

A disease of nature.   *Saint Augustine*

The expense of spirit in a waste of shame.
                             William Shakespeare

The sages figured lust in the form of a satyr; of
shape, part human, part bestial; to signify that the
followers of it prostitute the reason of a man to
pursue the appetites of a beast.   *Richard Steele*

Snares and poison.   *Jonathan Swift*

A short pleasure, bought with long pain, a hon-
eyed poison, a gulf of shame.   *John Taylor*

A breeder of diseases, a gall to the conscience, a
corrosive to the heart.   *John Taylor*

The body's bane, and the soul's perdition.
                                     John Taylor

A game never postponed by darkness.   *Anon.*

When the body is used carnally in a carnal
situation.   *Anon.*

SEE ALSO CARNALITY, LOVE, SEXES (LOVE).

LUTHER, MARTIN (1483-1546)

His words are half battles.   *Thomas Carlyle*

The only fit commentator on Paul...not by any
means such a gentleman as the Apostle, but
almost as great a genius.
                           Samuel Taylor Coleridge

Luther, taking into account nothing but his own
violent and personal experience, projected into an
abstract and universal theological doctrine.
                                    Yves Congar

Luther was guilty of two great crimes—he struck
the Pope in his crown, and the monks in their
belly.   *Desiderius Erasmus*

The solitary monk who shook the world from
pagan slumber.
              Adapted from Robert Montgomery

SEE ALSO PROTESTANTISM, REFORMATION.

LUXURY

A rich man's superfluities.   *George Coleman 2*

Superfluities.   *John Gay*

A mark of pride and a cause of envy.
                                    Enoch Hanok

(Something which) makes a man so soft, that it is
hard to please him, and easy to trouble him; so
that his pleasures at last become his burden.
Luxury is a nice master, hard to be pleased.
                                 Henry Mackenzie

A wild beast, first made fiercer with tying and
then let loose.   *Michel de Montaigne*

An enticing pleasure, a bastard mirth, which hath
honey in her mouth, gall in her heart, and a string
in her tail.   *Francis Quarles*

A criminal affection for pleasures opposed to
Christian chastity.   *Saint John the Baptist*

Superfluous things.   *Seneca*

Positive hindrances to the elevation of mankind.
                             Henry David Thoreau

LYING

Abomination to the Lord.
                          Bible: Proverbs, XII, 22.

A kind of self-denying.   *Samuel Butler 1*

The art of survival.   *Benjamin de Casseres*

A very monster.   *Thomas Dekker*

Not only a sort of suicide in the liar...a stab at
the health of human society.
                           Ralph Waldo Emerson

Violation of truth. *Ralph Waldo Emerson*

An indispensable part of making life tolerable.

Bergen Evans

The strongest acknowledgement of the force of truth. *William Hazlitt*

A form of creativitity; talking the truth is being only a reporter. *Eric Hoffer*

A medicine to men. *Plato*

Essential to humanity. They are...as important as the pursuit of pleasure and moreover are necessary to that pursuit. *Marcel Proust*

Who speaks not truly, lies.

William Shakespeare

A moral category...a pillar of the state.

Alexander Solzhenitsyn

Lying and boasting are the same.

Welsh Proverb

An abomination unto the Lord, but a very present help in time of trouble. *Anon.*

SEE ALSO DECEIT, EXAGGERATION, FLAT-TERY, LIAR, LIE, SLANDER, SOPHISTRY.

M

MACAULAY, THOMAS BABINGTON (1800-1859)

I settled that he was some obscure man of letters or of medicine...and here I had been sitting next to him, hearing him talk, and setting him down for a dull fellow. *Charles C. Greville*

It is impossible to mention any book in any language with which he is not familiar; or to touch upon any subject...on which he does not know everything that is to be known.
Charles C. Greville

His history is partial, his criticism superficial, his style fantastic. *Walter Savage Landor*

A Scottish sycophant and a fine talker.
Karl Marx

A sentence of Macaulay's may have no more sense in it than a blot pinched between doubled paper.
John Ruskin

A book in breeches. He has occasional flashes of silence that make his conversation perfectly delightful. *Sydney Smith*

I wish I was as sure of everything as Macaulay is of everything. *William Windham*

An ugly, cross-made, splay-footed, shapeless little dumpling of a fellow, with featureless face.
Anon.

MADMAN

The man who has lost everything except his reason. *Gilbert Keith Chesterton*

People who never grow gray. *German Proverb*

A crippled mind which says that we are the ones who limp. *Max Gralnick*

(One who) thinks all other men are crazy.
Publilius Syrus

SEE ALSO INSANITY.

MADNESS

Lucid intervals and happy pauses.
Francis Bacon

Affected with...intellectual independence; not conforming to standards of thought, speech and action derived by the conformants...at odds with the majority; in short, unusual. *Ambrose Bierce*

The refusal to develop, to adjust, to dilute one's true self in the sordid mush of the world.
Gerald Brennan

The brain...destroy'd by thought.
Charles Churchill

A mental stain. *Cicero*

The extreme limits of wisdom. *Jean Cocteau*

The human mind in ruins. *S. B. Davies*

Much madness is divinest sense
  To a discerning eye;
Much sense the starkest madness.
Emily Dickinson

That reckless fire. *Edmund W. Gosse*

The final outcome of all that is wrong with a culture.   *Jules Henry*

Often the logic of an accurate mind overtaxed.

Oliver Wendell Holmes 1

What everyone is, more or less, on one point.

Adapted from Rudyard Kipling

Liberation and renewal as well as enslavement and existential death.   *R. D. Laing*

A common calamity; we are all mad at some time or other.   *Johannes B. Mantuanus*

Man's state implies a necessary curse: when not himself, he's mad; when most himself, he's worse.

Adapted from Francis Quarles

To think of too many things in succession too fast, or of one thing exclusively.   *Voltaire*

SEE ALSO INSANITY, MENTAL HEALTH.

MAJORITY

He who has the truth, even though he be one.

Arabian Proverb

A force which is invariably on the wrong side.

Jasper Bergstrum

Ninety and nine.   *Bible: Matthew, XVIII, 13.*

The dead.   *Samuel Butler 2*

The will of a rabble.   *John C. Calhoun*

To be in the weakest camp.

Gilbert Keith Chesterton

One with the law is a majority.   *Calvin Coolidge*

The best repartee.   *Benjamin Disraeli*

(That which) is lazy-minded, incurious, absorbed in vanities, and tepid in emotion, and is therefore incapable of either much doubt or much faith.

Thomas Stearns Eliot

A few powerful leaders, a certain number of accommodating scoundrels and subservient weaklings, and a mass of men who trudge after them without in the least knowing their own minds.

Johann W. Goethe

The forgotten American, the man who pays his taxes, prays, behaves himself, stays out of trouble and works for his government.

Barry Goldwater

A herd, and not a nice one.   *William Hazlitt*

The most dangerous foe to truth and freedom in our midst.   *Henrik Ibsen*

(A factor which) never has truth on its side.

Henrik Ibsen

One man with courage makes a majority.

Andrew Jackson

One of God's side is a majority.

Wendell Phillips

One, with God, is always a majority, but many a martyr has been burned at the stake while the votes were being counted.   *Thomas B. Reed*

(Those who) are negligent and supine.

Jonathan Swift

Any man more right than his neighbor.

Henry David Thoreau

All the fools in town.   *Mark Twain*

SEE ALSO CROWD, MASSES, MOB, MULTITUDE, PEOPLE (THE), PUBLIC OPINION, RABBLE.

MALE

SEE BACHELOR, HUSBAND, MAN.

MALICE

SEE EVIL, HATRED, REVENGE.

MAN

Partly the animal from which he has come...partly the God who is coming to him.

Lyman Abbott

The merriest species of the creation; all above or below him are serious.   *Joseph Addison*

An ape with possibilities.   *Roy C. Andrews*

Mere veins and flesh wedded to bones.

Apocrypha: Sibl, Frag. 1.

The only animal who injures his mate.

Lodovico Ariosto

At his best...the noblest of all animals; separated from law and justice, he is the worst.   *Aristotle*

An animal until his immediate material and economic needs are satisfied, he cannot develop further.   *Wystan H. Auden*

A little flesh, a little breath, and the part which governs.   *Marcus Aurelius*

(One whose) life is dyed to his imagination.

Marcus Aurelius

As the image of God he belongs to that other, the higher life; he is "a child of the world to come."

Leon Baeck

An act of God.   *Philip J. Bailey*

A military animal.   *Philip J. Bailey*

Man is wholly the product of the environment that nourishes and raises him—an inevitable, involuntary and consequently irresponsible product.

Mikhail A. Bakunin

A brief and transitory episode in the life of one of the meanest of the planets.   *Arthur J. Balfour*

The religious animal.   *William C. Barrett*

The second strongest sex in the world.

Philip Barry

The creature on the boundary between heaven and earth.   *Karl Barth*

The cruellest foe.   *Richard Baxter*

A foundling in the cosmos, abandoned by the forces that created him.   *Carl L. Becker*

A chance deposit on the surface of the world, carelessly thrown up between two ice ages by the same forces that rust iron and ripen corn.

Carl L. Becker

The only creature endowed with reason...also the only creature to pin its existence on things unreasonable.   *Henri Bergson*

The Lord God formed man of the dust of the ground, and breathed into his nostrils the breath of life; and man became a living soul.

Bible: Genesis, II, 7.

They that dwell in the house of clay.

Bible: Job, IX, 17.

A worm.   *Bible: Job, XXV, 6.*

A member of the unconsidered, or negligible sex...The genus has two varieties: good providers and bad providers.   *Ambrose Bierce*

Live dirt.   *Josh Billings*

An intellect served by organs.

Louis G. de Bonald

A cooking animal. The beasts have memory, judgment, and all the faculties and passions of our mind in a certain degree; but no beast is a cook.

James Boswell

Ever a contingent being in search of necessity.

George Brantl

The sum of all the social conditions of all times.

Bertolt Brecht

A puny, slow, awkward, unarmed animal.

Jacob Bronowski

That amphibious piece between a corporeal and spiritual Essence, the middle form that links those two together.   *Thomas Browne*

A composition of man and beast.

Thomas Browne

A noble animal, splendid in ashes, and pompous in the grave.   *Thomas Browne*

The only creature that knows he will die, besides the elephant.   *Eugene E. Brussell*

Uniqueness is the essential property of man, and it is given to him in order that he may unfold it.

Martin Buber

A religious animal.   *Edmund Burke*

An inferior part of the creation of God.

Joseph Butler

God's highest present development. He is the latest thing in God.   *Samuel Butler 2*

The only animal that can remain on friendly terms with the victims he intends to eat until he eats them.   *Samuel Butler 2*

(A) pendulum between a smile and a tear.

Lord Byron

That heritage of woe.   *Lord Byron*

Half dust, half deity.   *Lord Byron*

A digestive tube.   *Pierre Cabanis*

Animals used by words.   *James Branch Cabell*

Something that feels happy, plays the piano, likes going for a walk and, in fact, wants to do a whole lot of things that are really unnecessary.

Karel Capek

The miracle of miracles, the great inscrutable mystery of God.   *Thomas Carlyle*

What is man? A foolish baby,
Daily strives, and fights, and frets;
Demanding all, deserving nothing;
One small grave is what he gets.

Thomas Carlyle

A feeble unit in the middle of a threatening infinitude.   *Thomas Carlyle*

A tool-using animal.   *Thomas Carlyle*

The most...plastic of creatures.

Thomas Carlyle

An omniverous biped that wears breeches.

Thomas Carlyle

A mouse...running in and out of every hole in the cosmos hunting for the Absolute Cheese.

Benjamin de Casseres

A volume, if you know how to read him.

William Ellery Channing

Something that feels happy, plays the piano, likes going for a walk, and, in fact, wants to do a whole lot of things that are really unnecessary.

Karel Chapek

Man is Creation's masterpiece. Who says so?— Man!   *Adapted from Sulpice G. Chevalier*

An embodied paradox, a bundle of contradictions.   *Charles Caleb Colton*

A self-compulsive bundle of 126 instincts.

William T. Costello

A genuine offspring of revolt.   *William Cowper*

The only animal that eats when he is not hungry.

Jerry Dashkin

A proud, and yet a wretched thing.   *John Davies*

The point at which the world of spirit touches the world of sense, and it is through him and in him that the material creation attains to intelligibility and becomes enlightened and spiritualized.

Christopher Dawson

A passive instrument in the hands of necessity.

Paul H. D'Holbach

A creature constituted to be a profound secret and mystery to every other.

Adapted from Charles Dickens

The most intelligent of the animals—and the most silly.   *Diogenes*

A pliable animal, a being who gets accustomed to everything.   *Fëdor M. Dostoievski*

The ungrateful biped.   *Fëdor M. Dostoievski*

If you can remove the word "human"...you can view him...as no more than an extremely clever, adaptable and mischievous little animal.

Thomas Stearns Eliot

Lenses through which we read our own minds.

Ralph Waldo Emerson

A bundle of relations, a knot of roots, whose flower and fruitage is the world.

Ralph Waldo Emerson

An intelligence served by organs.

Ralph Waldo Emerson

Inventors sailing forth on voyages of discovery.

Ralph Waldo Emerson

A bundle of ancestors.   *Ralph Waldo Emerson*

Foolish children, who...see everything in the most absurd manner, and are the victims at all times of the nearest object.

Ralph Waldo Emerson

A little soul carrying around a corpse.

Epictetus

A certain intellectual idea formed eternally in the divine Mind.   *John Scotus Erigena*

Man is not a being different from the animals, nor superior to them.   *Sigmund Freud*

The worst animal.   *Thomas Fuller*

The descendant of every king and every slave that ever lived.   *Kahlil Gibran*

Nature's sole mistake.   *William S. Gilbert*

The purpose of creation.   *Goan of Saadin*

A recording animal.   *Robert Gourlay*

The inventor of stupidity.   *Remy de Gourmont*

Man is sin.   *Robert Greene*

A tiny grain of protoplasm in the perishable framework of organic nature.   *Ernest Haeckel*

A reasoning rather than a reasonable animal.

Robert B. Hamilton

Two distinct orders of men—the lovers of freedom and the devoted advocates of power.

Robert Y. Hayne

The only animal that laughs and weeps; for he is the only animal that is struck with the difference between what things are, and what they ought to be.   *William Hazlitt*

Creatures of imagination, passion, and self-will, more than of reason or even self-interest.

William Hazlitt

An intellectual animal, and therefore an everlasting contradiction to himself.   *William Hazlitt*

The aristocrat among the animals.

Heinrich Heine

All men are either Jews or Greeks: either they are driven by ascetic, image-hating, spiritualizing impulses, or they are cheerful, taking pride in self-government.   *Heinrich Heine*

A world which is born and which dies . . . beneath every gravestone lies a world's history.

Heinrich Heine

Sleep and dust.   *George Herbert*

The only animal that plays poker.   *Don Herold*

The only animal that contemplates death, and the only animal that shows any sign of doubt of its finality.   *William E. Hocking*

Eminently a storyteller. His search for a purpose, a cause, an ideal, a mission and the like is largely a search for a plot and a pattern in the development of his life story—a story that is basically without meaning or pattern.   *Eric Hoffer*

Nature's only unfinished animal.   *Eric Hoffer*

An omnibus in which his ancestors ride.

Oliver Wendell Holmes 1

A super-age savage, predatory, acquisitive, primarily interested in himself.

Earnest A. Hooton

Dust and shadow.   *Horace*

A super-simian.   *Elbert Hubbard*

Anything allowed to stand at a public bar.

Elbert Hubbard

A being said to be the highest work of God and who admits it.   *Elbert Hubbard*

An intelligence in servitude to his organs.

Aldous Huxley

The great Alps and Andes of the living world.

Thomas Henry Huxley

Very queer animals—a mixture of horse-nervousness, ass-stubbornness and camel-malice.

Thomas Henry Huxley

A machine into which we put what we call food and produce.   *Robert G. Ingersoll*

Man passes away; his name perishes from record and recollection; his history is as a tale that is told, and his very monument becomes a ruin.

Washington Irving

The only animal that can be a fool.

Holbrook Jackson

A dog's ideal of what God should be.

Holbrook Jackson

Man, biologically considered . . . is the most formidable of all the beasts of prey, and, indeed, the only one that preys systematically on its own species.   *William James*

An imitative animal.   *Thomas Jefferson*

(One who) is under absolute mandate to express divinity in his own life and his whole nature.

F. Ernest Johnson

The only being that can properly be called idle.

Samuel Johnson

An inquiring animal.   *Arthur Keith*

The most extraordinary computer of all.

John Fitzgerald Kennedy

The being that is aware of the world as a whole. Man is therefore a metaphysical or a religious being. He is religious not accidentally but essentially.   *Richard Kroner*

A character in a comedy.   *Jean de La Bruyère*

The cause for women's dislike for one another.

Jean de La Bruyère

A fallen god who remembers the heavens.

Alphonse M. de Lamartine

A pugnacious animal.   *Harold J. Laski*

A confounded, corrupt, and poisoned nature, both in body and soul. *Martin Luther*

The hearts of men are their books; events are their tutors; great actions are their eloquence.

Thomas B. Macaulay

Man is not the creature of a drawing room or the Stock Exchange, but a lonely soul confronted by the Source of all souls. *Arthur Machen*

A being out of joint and wounded—wounded by the devil with the wound of concupiscence and by God's wound of love. *Jacques Maritain*

The slime of this dung-pit. *John Marston*

Some are good, some are middling, the most are bad. *Martial*

Body, mind, and imagination. His body is faulty, his mind untrustworthy, but his imagination has made him remarkable...has made life on this planet an intense practice of all the lovelier energies. *John Masefield*

A wolf—a wolf with his own refinement who often enjoys befouling those whom he tortures.

Francois Mauriac

We are rational creatures; our virtue and perfection is to love reason...to love order.

Nicolas Melebranche

Some are fine fellows, some right scurvy; most, a dash between the two. *George Meredith*

A kind of miscarriage of the ape.

Ilya I. Metchnikoff

A little world, in which we may discern a body mingled of earthly elements, and a heavenly spirit and the vegetable soul of plants...the senses of the lower animals, and reason...and the likeness of God. *Pico Mirandola*

A crawling, and ever-moving ant.

Adapted from Michele de Montaigne

An ingenious assembly of portable plumbing.

Christopher Morley

To say that man is made up of certain chemical elements is a satisfactory description only for those who intend to use him as a fertilizer.

Herbert J. Muller

A distracted atom in a growing chaos made poor by his wealth, made empty by his fullness, reduced to monotony by his very opportunities for variety. *Lewis Mumford*

A mosaic of characteristics and qualities that only rarely achieve an internal and intrinsic harmony.

Abraham Myerson

A meteor designed to burn so that the earth may be lighted. *Napoleon 1*

Merely a more perfect animal than the rest. He reasons better. *Napoleon 1*

Our days begin with trouble here,
  Our life is but a span,
And...death is always near,
  So frail a thing is man.

New England Primer.

A rope connecting animal and superman.

Friedrich W. Nietzsche

The earth has a skin and that skin has diseases; one of its diseases is called man.

Friedrich W. Nietzsche

A walking argument of God's existence, a moving advertisement of God's power, an articulate herald of God's intelligence. *John A. O'Brien*

The bad child of the universe.

James Oppenheim

Basically there are two kinds of men—the quick and the wed. *Robert Orben*

One who goes out of this world as he came in—on milk. *William Osler*

False, dissembling, subtle, cruel, and inconstant.

Thomas Otway

The creature of circumstances. *Robert Owen*

A reed, the weakest thing in nature, but he is a thinking reed. *Blaise Pascal*

Depository of truth, a sink of uncertainty and error, the glory and the shame of the universe.

Blaise Pascal

Bladders of wind. *Petronius*

A wild beast who walks upright. *Philemon*

One who will give a woman anything except his seat on the streetcar.

Adapted from Horace Porter

The measure of all things. *Protagoras*

God's last, best and so far as we know, final expression of himself. *William S. Rainford*

The aspirations of creators and the propensities of quadrupeds. *W. Winwood Reade*

The medium between spirit and matter ... between the visible and the invisible world. He sums them up in his person, as in a universal center.
Adrien-Emanuel Roquette

There are only two kinds of men—the dead and the deadly. *Helen Rowland*

One who loses his illusions first, his teeth second, and his follies last. *Helen Rowland*

A rational soul using a mortal and earthly body.
Saint Augustine

An earthly animal, but worthy of Heaven.
Saint Augustine

A sack of dung, the food of worms.
Saint Bernard

The keystone in the arch of the community.
Antoine de Saint-Exupéry

Man is described by science not as being "a little lower than the angels" but rather as being a bit higher than the apes. *Paul E. Sabine*

The greatest miracle and the greatest problem on this earth. *David Sarnoff*

Man is nothing else but what he makes of himself.
Jean-Paul Sartre

The being who hurls himself toward a future and who is conscious of imagining himself as being in the future. *Jean-Paul Sartre*

A precious stone: cut and polished by morals, adorned by wisdom. *Isaac F. Satanov*

An imitative creature, and whosoever is foremost leads the herd. *Johann C. Schiller*

A ball tossed betwixt the wind and the billows.
Johann C. Schiller

A burlesque of what he should be.
Arthur Schopenhauer

At bottom a wild and terrible animal.
Arthur Schopenhauer

Children of a larger size. *Seneca*

A social animal. *Seneca*

A reasoning animal. *Seneca*

Weak, watery being, standing in the midst of unrealities. *Seneca*

The paragon of animals. *William Shakespeare*

The only joker in the deck of nature.
Fulton J. Sheen

An animal that makes bargains; no other animal does this—no dog exchanges bones with another.
Adam Smith

A creature who lives not upon bread alone, but principally by catchwords.
Robert Louis Stevenson

A somewhat altered fish, a slightly remodeled ape. *George R. Stewart*

Every man is a history of the world for himself.
Max Stirner

Science gives us the low view of man—man as matter, man as animal, at best, man as one of the mass. *F. Sherwood Taylor*

A map of misery. *John Taylor*

The artificer of his own happiness.
Henry David Thoreau

A human being—that is enough for me; he can't be any worse. *Mark Twain*

The only animal that blushes—or needs to.
Mark Twain

A hard, laborious species. *Vergil*

Poor silly animals. *Horace Walpole*

The only animal which even attempts to have anything to do with his half-grown young.
George R. Wells

A constant puzzle. *Walt Whitman*

A rational animal who always loses his temper when he is called upon to act in accordance with the dictates of reason. *Oscar Wilde*

The favorite animal on earth. *John Wise*

A creature squalid, vengeful, and impure.
William Wordsworth

The organ of the accumulated smut and sneakery of 10,000 generations of weaseling souls.
Philip Wylie

The smallest part of nothing. *Edward Young*

A composite of the heavenly and earthly.
Zohar: Genesis, 20b.

The only animal that eats when he is not hungry, drinks when he is not thirsty, and makes love at all seasons. *Anon.*

The only animal that can be skinned more than once. *Anon.*

The only animal that goes to sleep when it is not sleepy and gets up when it is. *Anon.*

That foolish animal that tries to get even with its enemies—and ahead of its friends. *Anon.*

SEE ALSO DEATH, EVOLUTION, FATE, HUMAN BEINGS, HUMANITY, LIFE, PEOPLE (THE), SOCIETY, WOMAN.

MANKIND

Divided into three classes: those that are immovable, those that are movable, and those that move.
Arabian Proverb

A dog's mistake in theology. *John Ciardi*

A series of conspiracies to win from nature some advantage without paying for it.
Ralph Waldo Emerson

An incorrigible race. Give them but bugbears and ideals—it is all they ask. *William Hazlitt*

It has left many traces of its life—barrooms, brothels, jails, churches, gallows, best sellers.
Elbert Hubbard

Mankind has honored its destroyers and persecuted its benefactors, building palaces for living brigands, and tombs for long dead prophets.
William R. Inge

The history of mankind is little else than a narrative of designs which have failed, and hopes that have been disappointed. *Samuel Johnson*

Parts of a developing whole, all enfolded in an embracing and interpenetrating love.
Oliver Lodge

A devourer one of another. *John Northbrooke*

A tribe of animals, living by habits and thinking in symbols; and it can never be anything else.
George Santayana

A child with a stolen dynamite cap.
John Steinbeck

The most pernicious race of little odious vermin that nature ever suffered to crowd upon the surface of the earth. *Jonathan Swift*

A farce. *Mark Twain*

That factor in nature which exhibits in its most intense form the plasticity of nature.
Alfred North Whitehead

An irrational collection of animals. *Anon.*

SEE ALSO HUMANITY, MAN.

MANNERS

A hardened form of morality.
Berthold Auerbach

Your station in life. *Eugene E. Brussell*

What vex or soothe, corrupt or purify, exalt or debase, barbarize or refine us, by a constant, steady . . . operation. *Edmund Burke*

Good manners are made up of petty sacrifices.
Ralph Waldo Emerson

A contrivance of wise men to keep fools at a distance. *Ralph Waldo Emerson*

An impassible wall of defence.
Ralph Waldo Emerson

The society of women is the foundation of good manners. *Johann W. Goethe*

The art of wearing appropriate masks.
Max Gralnick

. . . manners may in Seven
  Words be found:
Forget Yourself and think of
  Those Around. *Arthur Guiterman*

Oil that lubricates social contacts.
Leon Harrison

The test is being able to bear patiently with bad ones. *Solomon Ibn Gabirol*

Self-respect is at the bottom of all good manners. They are the expression of discipline, of goodwill, of respect for other people's rights and comforts and feelings. *Edward S. Martin*

The technic of expressing consideration for the feelings of others. *Alice D. Miller*

Consists of not shaking hands too eagerly.
Adapted from Pythagoras

The great secret is not having bad manners or good manners or any other particular sort of manners, but having the same manners for all human souls. *George Bernard Shaw*

Behaving as if you were in Heaven, where there are no third-class carriages, and one soul is as good as another.   *George Bernard Shaw*

The art of making those people easy with whom we converse.   *Jonathan Swift*

Training in everything. The peach was once a bitter almond; cauliflower is nothing but cabbage with a college education.   *Mark Twain*

An expression of the relation of status—symbolic pantomime of mastery on the one hand and of subserviance on the other.   *Thorstein Veblen*

The final and perfect flower of noble character.
          William Winter

Simply to cherish such an habitual respect for mankind as may prevent us from disgusting a fellow-creature for the sake of a present indulgence.   *Mary Wollstonecraft*

The combination of the mind of a gentleman with the emotions of a bum.   *Anon.*

The noise not made while eating soup.   *Anon.*

SEE ALSO BREEDING (MANNERS), ETIQUETTE, GENTLEMAN, LADY, POISE, POLITENESS, TACT.

MARCH

A month that comes in like a lion and goes out like a lamb.   *English Proverb*

Blossom on the plum,
  Wild wind and merry;
  Leaves upon the cherry,
And one swallow come.   *Nora Hopper*

Slayer of the winter.   *William Morris*

A kind of interregnum, winter's sovereignty relaxing, spring not yet in control.
          New York Times Editorial, Mar. 1, 1964.

Like an army defeated
The snow hath retreated,...
The Ploughboy is whopping...
There's joy in the mountains:
There's life in the fountains...
The rain is over and gone.   *William Wordsworth*

A warm breath blown through icy fingers.
          Anon.

SEE ALSO SPRING.

MARKETPLACE

The place set apart where men may deceive each other.   *Anacharsis*

The best garden.   *George Herbert*

Three women and a goose make a marketplace.
          Italian Proverb

Two women make a market; three make a fair.
          Ukrainian Proverb

The women's courthouse.   *West Indian Proverb*

MARRIAGE

(An arrangement which) enlarges the scene of our happiness and miseries.   *Joseph Addison*

An act of purification...the foundation of all morality.   *Felix Adler*

A taste of paradise.   *Sholom Aleichem*

That relation between man and woman in which the independence is equal, the dependence mutual, and the obligation reciprocal.
          Louis K. Anspacher

A sad barnyard when the hen crows lounder than the cock.   *G. L. Apperson*

An exclusive relation of one or more men to one or more women, based on custom, recognized and supported by public opinion, and where law exists, by law.   *Lord Avebury*

The end of man.   *Honoré de Balzac*

Our last, best chance to grow up.
          Joseph Barth

And they too shall be one flesh.
          Bible: Ephesians, V, 31.

Bone of my bones, and flesh of my flesh.
          Bible: Genesis, II, 23.

The state or condition of a community consisting of a master, a mistress and two slaves, making in all, two.   *Ambrose Bierce*

Earning a living...sleeping, shaving, eating, walking the dog and obeying...children.
          Hal Boyle

The making of a home, the rearing of children—the working together for economic security.
          Barnett R. Brickner

The best method for getting acquainted.

Heywood Broun

The commercial prostitution of love...the last outcome of our whole social system, and its most clear condemnation.   *Edward Carpenter*

The Christian ideal of marriage is that of indissoluble unity.   *Sydney Cave*

An armed alliance against the outside world.

Gilbert Keith Chesterton

Man and woman coupled together for the sake of strife.   *Adapted from Charles Churchill*

Marriage belongs to society; it is a social contract.

Samuel Taylor Coleridge

A feast where the grace is sometimes better than the dinner.   *Charles Caleb Colton*

To share the bitter-sweet of life.   *George Crabbe*

A lane where there is no turning.

Dinah M. Craik

The destiny offered to women by society.

Simone de Beauvoir

Going through so much to learn so little.

Charles Dickens

To think together.   *Robert C. Dodds*

An absurdity imposed by society.

Armantine Dudevant

A relation either of sympathy or of conquest.

George Eliot

The most natural state of man, and...the state in which you will find solid happiness.

Benjamin Franklin

The means to eat, drink and sleep together.

French Proverb

A school in which the student learns too late.

German Proverb

Fever in reverse: it starts with heat and ends with cold.   *German Proverb*

The most inviolable and irrevocable of all contracts that were ever formed. Every human compact may be...dissolved but this.

James C. Gibbons

Being united in one life.   *Henry Gilbert*

An experiment frequently tried.

William S. Gilbert

To publicly announce you are going to bed together.   *Warren Goldberg*

To make love without tryst.   *Warren Goldberg*

Flagellation with care.   *Warren Goldberg*

The only evil men pay for.   *Greek Proverb*

A deal in which a man gives away half his groceries in order to get the other half cooked.

John Gwynne

The high sea for which no compass has yet been invented.   *Heinrich Heine*

A mistake of youth—which we should all make.

Don Herold

An honorable agreement among men as to their conduct toward women, and it was devised by women.   *Don Herold*

A woman's hair net tangled in a man's spectacles on top of the bedroom dresser.   *Don Herold*

An edifice that must be rebuilt every day.

Emile Herzog

A legal or religious ceremony by which two persons of the opposite sex solemnly agree to harass and spy on each other...until death do them join.   *Elbert Hubbard*

Love's demitasse.   *Elbert Hubbard*

A very sea of calls and claims, which have but little to do with love.   *Henrik Ibsen*

Something you have to give your whole mind to.

Henrik Ibsen

The torment of one, the felicity of two, the strife and enmity of three.   *Washington Irving*

To propagate understanding.   *Samuel Johnson*

The best state for man in general; and every man is a worse man, in proportion as he is unfit for the married state.   *Samuel Johnson*

The most expensive way to get your laundry done.

Charles Jones

A lottery.   *Ben Jonson*

Like buying something you've been admiring for a long time in a shop window. You may love it when you get it home, but it doesn't always go with everything else in the house.   *Jean Kerr*

The self-begetting wonder.   *Charles Kingsley*

A lottery, but you can't tear up your ticket if you lose.   *Farquhar M. Knowles*

Something that the bachelor misses and the widower escapes.   *Farquhar M. Knowles*

To decide independently to live with an equal partner, and to subordinate oneself to the formation of a new subject, a "we."   *Fritz Kunkel*

A monopoly, and not of the least invidious sort.   *Charles Lamb*

A dull meal, with the dessert at the beginning.   *Pierre La Mure*

The great puzzle of our day . . . Solve it, or be torn to bits, is the decree.   *D. H. Lawrence*

Consent, not cohabitation, constitutes marriage.   *Legal Maxim*

A triumph of habit over hate.   *Oscar Levant*

Neither Heaven nor Hell. It is simply Purgatory.   *Abraham Lincoln*

Physic against incontinence.   *Martin Luther*

A perfect moment frozen for a dull eternity.   *William Manville*

To transmute romantic love . . . into real and indestructible human love.   *Jacques Maritain*

The fusion of two hearts—the union of two lives—the coming together of two tributaries.   *Peter Marshall*

A process that makes for strange bedfellows.   *Groucho Marx*

An evil, but . . . a necessary evil.   *Menander*

Quiet slavery.   *Henry Louis Mencken*

An economic matter . . . it also concerns . . . the husband's cigars.   *Henry Louis Mencken*

Slavery, and man is the slave.   *Adapted from Henry Louis Mencken*

Unashamed mornings.   *Thomas Middleton*

One flesh.   *John Milton*

Friendship.   *Michel de Montaigne*

May be compared to a cage: the birds without despair to get in, and those within despair to get out.   *Michel de Montaigne*

A covenant which has nothing free but the entrance.   *Michel de Montaigne*

The only known example of the happy meeting of the immovable object and the irresistible force.   *Ogden Nash*

A book of which the first chapter is written in poetry and the remaining chapters in prose.   *Beverley Nichols*

An end of many short follies—being one long stupidity.   *Friedrich W. Nietzsche*

A job. Happiness or unhappiness has nothing to do with it.   *Kathleen Norris*

A kind of cosmic, bored familiarity in which everyone watches television, and lives and lets live.   *Michael Novak*

The butt of many jokes, an irrepressible font of complaints, a fecund source of ribaldry and delight, and an agony of too much beauty and comfort, too much anger and despair.   *Michael Novak*

The condition of life between man and woman most adequately symbolized by the act of sexual intercourse.   *Michael Novak*

Two kinds . . . where the husband quotes the wife, or where the wife quotes the husband.   *Clifford Odets*

A meal where the soup is better than the dessert.   *Austin O'Malley*

A sublimation of physical passion, in which the intensity and warmth of natural appetite is retained on the higher level of domestic life, and there enriched with the values of parentage, companionship, and fidelity.   *Ralph Barton Perry*

The greatest educational institution on earth.   *Channing Pollock*

Its chief . . . purpose . . . is to increase and multiply.   *Pope Leo XIII*

A deliberate act of will, and from this union of souls by God's decree a sacred and inviolable bond arises.   *Pope Pius XI*

Paying an endless visit in your worst clothes.   *John B. Priestly*

The only state left in which practically everything is legal.   *Nancy Randolph*

The first month is honeymoon or smick smack; the second is hither and thither; the third is thwick thwock; the fourth, the Devil take them that brought thee and I together.   *John Ray*

Wedlock is padlock.   *John Ray*

A lottery in which men stake their liberty, and women their happiness.   *Madame de Rieux*

A scheme for looting the male.   *Lord Riley*

Not a union merely between two creatures—it is a union between two spirits.
      Frederick W. Robertson

The first union to defy management.
      Will Rogers

A process by which the grocer gets an account the haberdasher once had.
      Franklin Delano Roosevelt

An institution that simplifies life and complicates living.   *Jean Rostand*

A souvenir of love.   *Helen Rowland*

The miracle that transforms a kiss from pleasure into a duty, and a life of luxury into a necessity.
      Helen Rowland

A bargain, and somebody has to get the worst of it.   *Helen Rowland*

Often . . . hardly differs from prostitution, except being harder to escape from.
      Bertrand A. Russell

The tomb of love.   *Russian Proverb*

A vice; all that can be done is to excuse and sanctify it; therefore it was made a religious sacrament.   *Saint Jerome*

The nursery of Christianity, which supplied the earth with faithful souls, to complete the number of the elect in heaven.   *Saint Francis de Sales*

Sexual companionship and an equality in duty and labor.   *Olive Schreiner*

An institution which is popular because it combines the maximum of temptation with the maximum of opportunity.   *George Bernard Shaw*

A system . . . hostile to human happiness.
      Percy Bysshe Shelley

An institution that turns a night owl into a homing pigeon.   *Glenn Shelton*

The thing that makes loving legal.
      Simone Signoret

A lottery.   *Samuel Smiles*

A pair of shears, so joined that they cannot be separated, often moving in opposite directions, yet always punishing anyone who comes between them.   *Sydney Smith*

A ceremony in which rings are put on the finger of the lady and through the nose of the gentleman.
      Herbert Spencer

A rain of rice along the hall—Tears on my cheeks—and that is all.   *Ann Spicer*

A vow to please one another.   *Stanislaus*

The completest image of Heaven and Hell we are capable of receiving in this life.   *Richard Steele*

One long conversation, chequered by disputes.
      Robert Louis Stevenson

A friendship recognized by the police.
      Robert Louis Stevenson

A step so grave and decisive that it attracts light-headed variable men by its very awfulness.
      Robert Louis Stevenson

A field of battle, not a bed of roses.
      Robert Louis Stevenson

Two lives bound fast in one.
      Alfred Lord Tennyson

A poor sordid slavery.   *John Vanbrugh*

The only adventure open to the cowardly.
      Voltaire

(An arrangement) instituted by God himself for the purpose of preventing promiscuous intercourse of the sexes, for promoting domestic felicity, and for securing the maintenance and security of children.   *Noah Webster*

A more or less durable connection between male and female lasting beyond the mere act of propagation till after the birth of the offspring.
      Edward Westermarck

The consequence of a misunderstanding between yourself and another person.
      Adapted from Oscar Wilde

The one subject on which all women agree and all men disagree.   *Oscar Wilde*

A status of antagonistic coöperation.
      John M. Woolsey

Entering (into life) through the personality of another.   *Alexander Yelchaninov*

A romantic novel in which the hero dies in the preface.   *Anon.*

The only business arrangement whereby one partner continues to receive increment after the partnership has been dissolved.   *Anon.*

Like a prizefight. The preliminaries are better than the main event.   *Anon.*

A chain, golden or otherwise, which bind a man and woman together.   *Anon.*

The process by which love blossoms into vengeance.   *Anon.*

A dinner—the appetite is always keener at the start.   *Anon.*

Like taking a bath—not so hot once you get accustomed to it.   *Anon.*

Too often much "I do" about nothing.   *Anon.*

The banalization of love.   *Anon.*

The only life sentence that is suspended by bad behavior.   *Anon.*

A two-handed game of solitaire.   *Anon.*

By day an endless noise; by night the echo of forgotten joys.   *Anon.*

Something that makes two one—but which one?
                                                  Anon.

It begins with a prince kissing an angel. It ends with a baldheaded man looking across the table at a fat woman.   *Anon.*

A tourniquet: it stops your circulation.   *Anon.*

Something made in heaven, but lived on the ground.   *Anon.*

SEE ALSO ALIMONY, BACHELOR, BRIDE, DIVORCE, FATHER, HOME, HONEYMOON, HUSBAND, MOTHER, MOTHERHOOD, WEDDING, WIDOW, WIFE, WOMAN.

MARTYR

(Those who) look down on people who aren't.
                                            Samuel N. Behrman

One who moves along the line of least reluctance to a desired death.   *Ambrose Bierce*

To dare to say what others only dare to think makes men martyrs or reformers—or both.
                                          Elizabeth R. Charles

He who has become the instrument of God, who has lost his will in the will of God...has found freedom in submission to God.
                                        Thomas Stearns Eliot

Any man who is willing to sacrifice others for his cause.   *Elbert Hubbard*

(He) who falls for the love of God.   *Ben Jonson*

I look on martyrs as mistakes, yet they still burned for it at stakes.
                                  Adapted from John Masefield

The cause, not the death, make martyrs.
                                             Napoleon I

It is martyrs who create faith rather than faith that creates martyrs.   *Miguel de Unamuno*

These Christs that die upon the barricades.
                                            Oscar Wilde

A self-made hero.   *Anon.*

MARTYRDOM

The archetypal form of conflict with evil, the summit of Christian sanctity through conformation to Christ, and...the official proclamation of the Gospel to the accredited representatives of the earthly city.   *Jean Danielou*

To die for an idea is to place a pretty high price on conjectures.   *Anatole France*

The only method by which religous truth can be established.   *Samuel Johnson*

Blood as verification to the truth.
                                        Friedrich W. Nietzsche

The perfection and crown of Christian sanctity and Christian life.   *Saint Jean Eudes*

Proof of the intensity, never of the correctness of a belief.   *Arthur Schnitzler*

The only way in which a man can become famous without ability.   *George Bernard Shaw*

The blood of martyrs is the seed of the Church.
                                      Adapted from Tertullian

Three kinds...the first both in will and deed, which is the highest; the second in will but not in deed; the third in deed but not in will.

Charles Wheatly

MARX, KARL (1818-1883)

The leader of the people's movement...behind his moderation and reserve one could detect the passionate fire of a daring spirit.

Albert Brisbane

A romantic realist, a man of many faces.

John W. Burrow

The best-hated and most-slandered man of his age...although he had many opponents he had hardly a personal enemy. *Friedrich Engels*

The greatest head of our times.

Friedrich Engels

A man who examined everything to discover its historical origin and the conditions of its development. *Friedrich Engels*

A revolutionary, and his great aim in life was to cooperate in this or that fashion in the overthrow of capitalist society and the State institutions which it has created. *Friedrich Engels*

My affairs have now reached the...point at which I can no longer leave the house because my clothes are in pawn and I can no longer eat meat because my credit is exhausted. *Karl Marx*

I must follow my goal through thick and thin, and I shall not permit bourgeois society to turn me into a money-making machine. *Karl Marx*

Half a century on my back and still a pauper!

Karl Marx

Marx throughout his life...as far as accounts were concerned...could never quite balance his budget. *Franz Mehring*

His tremendous industry matched his...powers, and it was not long before his overworked days and nights began to undermine a constitution originally of iron. *Franz Mehring*

He declared that incapacity to work was a death sentence on any human being not really an animal. *Franz Mehring*

Never in my life have I met a man whose attitude was so hurtfully and intolerably arrogant.

Karl Schurz

He is the first and only one amongst us to whom I would ascribe the quality of leadership, the capacity to master a big situation without losing himself in...details. *Adolph T. Techov*

The man who studied the proletariat assiduously without earning a living as one—or being one.

Robert Zwickey

MASSES

Characterless reflections of the environment.

Eugene E. Brussell

The mass are animal...and near chimpanzee. But the units, whereof the mass is composed, are neuters, every one of which may be grown to a queen bee. *Ralph Waldo Emerson*

Rude, lame, unmade, pernicious in their demands and influence, and need not be flattered but schooled. *Ralph Waldo Emerson*

(Those who will) never come of age, and will always be at the bottom of the social scale.

Gustave Flaubert

That which gives vent to its impulses.

Adapted from Sigmund Freud

Mute, inglorious men and women who made no nuisance of themselves in the world.

Philip Howard

The raw material from which a people is formed.

Henrik Ibsen

(They who exert) an immense gravitational pull which seems...to paralyze every upward step... with their attributes of mediocrity.

Karl Jaspers

(Those) not only moderate in intellect, but also moderate in inclinations. *John Stuart Mill*

They have no tastes or wishes strong enough to incline them to do anything unusual, and they consequently do not understand those who have.

John Stuart Mill

Individuals minus quality.

José Ortega y Gasset

The pseudo-intellectual, unqualified, unqualifiable, and, by his very mental texture, disqualified.

José Ortega y Gasset

A type of man who is not interested in the principles of civilization. Not of this or that civilization but...of any civilization.

José Ortega y Gasset

The spoiled child...the primitive in revolt...the barbarian. *José Ortega y Gasset*

(That which) crushes beneath it everything that is different...excellent, individual, qualified and select. Anybody who is not like everybody, who does not think like everybody, runs the risk of being eliminated. *José Ortega y Gasset*

The psychological state of feeling lord and master of oneself and equal to anybody else.

José Ortega y Gasset

He whose life lacks any purpose, and simply goes drifting along...though his possibilities and powers be enormous, he constructs nothing.

José Ortega y Gasset

Those who are only concerned with their own well-being, and at the same time they remain alien to the cause of that well-being.

José Ortega y Gasset

The unqualified individual...the human being as such, generically. *José Ortega y Gasset*

(Those who) neither should nor can direct their own personal existence, and still less rule society in general. *José Ortega y Gasset*

The common social quality, man as undifferentiated from other men, but as repeating in himself a generic type. *José Ortega y Gasset*

All that sets no value on itself—good or ill—based on specific grounds, but which feels itself "just like everybody," and nevertheless is not concerned about it. *José Ortega y Gasset*

(That which) never comes up to the standard of its best member, but on the contrary degrades itself to a level with the lowest.

Henry David Thoreau

The nondistinctive bulk of human kind—the average man. *Robert Zwickey*

The peoples of perpetual dawn. *Anon.*

SEE ALSO CROWD, MAJORITY, MAN, MULTITUDE, PEOPLE (THE), RABBLE.

MASTER

The measure of a master is his success in bringing all men round to his opinion twenty years later.

Ralph Waldo Emerson

The man who gives me employment, which I must have or suffer, that man is my master, let me call him what I will. *Henry George*

He is master of his brothers who is worthier and wiser than they.

Adapted from Algernon Charles Swinburne

One who accepts responsibility and serves well.

Robert Zwickey

SEE ALSO EXECUTIVE, LEADER, SUPERIOR MAN.

MATERIALISM

Calvinism without God. *Edward Bernstein*

The quest for things as things that promises satisfaction but in the end leaves you unsatisfied.

Eugene E. Brussell

There is nothing in the universe but matter and force; and...all the phenomena of nature are explicable by deduction from the properties assignable to these two primitive factors.

Thomas Henry Huxley

The denial that there is a higher and lower in existence and that the higher is completely independent of the lower and can never be reduced to it...When the whole—any whole—is looked upon as only the sum total of its parts—that is materialism. *Charles Malik*

The doctrine that nothing exists except matter and its movements and modifications: also that the phenomena of consciousness and will are wholly due to the operation of material agencies.

Oxford Dictionary, 1951.

An implication that there is nothing else in existence except the material universe which we know so well. *John C. Powys*

Organized emptiness of the spirit. *Franz Werfel*

SEE ALSO COMMUNISM, MATTER, SCIENCE.

MATHEMATICIAN

(One who) proceeds upon propositions which he has once demonstrated, and though the demonstration may have slipped out of his memory he builds upon the truth, because he knows it was demonstrated.   *Joseph Addison*

Often only blockheads.   *Georg C. Lichtenberg*

MATHEMATICS

Ways for the imagination to travel and the wings...or vehicles to take you where you want to go.   *Scott M. Buchanan*

Like the Nile, begins in minuteness, but ends in magnificence.   *Charles Caleb Colton*

The multiplied necessity...the supreme arbiter. From its decisions there is no appeal.
Tobias Dantzig

The tool specially suited for dealing with abstract concepts of any kind and there is no limit to its power in this field.   *Paul A. Dirac*

Mathematics deals exclusively with the relations of concepts to each other without consideration of their relation to experience.   *Albert Einstein*

A tentative agreement that two and two make four.
Elbert Hubbard

A study independent of the actual world.
Adapted from Cassius J. Keyser

Contains much that will neither hurt one if one does not know it nor help one if one does not know it.   *Johann B. Mencken*

The only science where one never knows what one is talking about nor whether what is said is true.
Bertrand A. Russell

The region of absolute necessity, to which not only the actual world, but every possible world must conform.   *Bertrand A. Russell*

A stern perfection such as only the greatest art can show.   *Bertrand A. Russell*

The music of reason.   *James J. Sylvester*

In its modern developments, may claim to be the most original creation of the human spirit.
Alfred North Whitehead

MATRIMONY

SEE MARRIAGE, WEDDING.

MATTER

Unthinking, unperceiving, inactive substance.
George Berkeley

Matter is not just the weight that drags us down...It is simply the slope on which we can go up as well as go down, the medium that can uphold just as well as give way.
Pierre T. de Chardin

The immediate unity of existence with itself.
Georg W. Hegel

Bodies which are not myself: there are other existences...I call them matter. Where there is an absence of matter, I call it void.
Thomas Jefferson

Every portion of matter may be looked upon as a garden full of plants, and a pond full of fishes.
Gottfried W. von Leibnitz

A kind of non-being, a mere potency or ability to receive forms and undergo substantial mutations; in short, an avidity for being.   *Jacques Maritain*

Everything is more or less organized matter.
Napoleon 1

Exists only as attraction and repulsion—attraction and repulsion are matter.   *Edgar Allan Poe*

SEE ALSO MATERIALISM, SCIENCE.

MATURITY

The ability to live in someone else's world.
Oren Arnold

The day you have your first real laugh at yourself.
Ethel Barrymore

To mature is to go on creating oneself endlessly.
Henri Bergson

Riper years.   *Book of Common Prayer*

When you start to check on your illusions.
Eugene E. Brussell

A frank acceptance of barren realities.
Eugene E. Brussell

The ability to postpone gratification.
Sigmund Freud

Means neither "too soon" nor "too late."
Aulus Gellius

Implies otherness...the art of living with.
Julius Gordon

The slowness in which a man believes.
Baltasar Gracian

When keeping a secret gives you more satisfaction than passing it along.   *John Henry*

To face, and not evade, every fresh crisis that comes.   *Fritz Künkel*

When something means more to you than satisfying your own personal desires.
Hugh Missildine

A person is mature when he is free to love and be loved.   *Hugh Missildine*

When we can treat ourselves in our own way rather than within the automatic ways of our parents in childhood.   *Hugh Missildine*

To have reacquired the seriousness that one had as a child at play.   *Friedrich W. Nietzsche*

The characteristic of the mature person is that he affirms life.   *Harry Emerson Overstreet*

Having the ability to escape categorization.
Kenneth Rexroth

Not being taken in by oneself.
Katjetan von Schlaggenberg

Awareness of the ambiguity of one's highest achievements, as well as one's deepest failures.
Paul Tillich

To live with fear and not be afraid is the final test.
Edward Weeks

The day we don't need to be lied to about anything.   *Franklin Yerby*

When you can sense your concern for others outweighing your concern for yourself.   *Anon.*

Not the absence of conflict, but knowing how to cope with it.   *Anon.*

Crying alone.   *Anon.*

SEE ALSO ADULT, RESPONSIBILITY.

MAXIM

Little sermons.   *Gelett Burgess*

The clue in the labyrinth, or the compass in the night.   *Joseph Joubert*

Maxims are to intellect what laws are to actions; they do not enlighten, but they guide and direct, and, although themselves blind, are protective.
Joseph Joubert

The condensed good sense of nations.
James Mackintosh

MAY

Follows April and redeems many promises that April has forfeited.
Adapted from Brooks Atkinson

The voice of one who goes before, to make the paths of June more beautiful.
Adapted from Helen Hunt Jackson

A perfumed word...an illuminated initial. It means youth, love, song, and all that is beautiful in life.   *Henry Wadsworth Longfellow*

A pious fraud of the almanac.
James Russell Lowell

The month of gladness.   *John Lydgate*

Spring's sweet month.   *Anon.*

SEE ALSO SPRING.

MAYOR

It's a mad life...a stirring life, a fine life, a velvet life, a careful life.   *Thomas Dekker*

A chaste...person whose private life is made inviolable by the libel laws.   *Elbert Hubbard*

The culmination...of self-sufficient mediocrity.
Elbert Hubbard

A crow's nest from which one may see the perpetually receding horizons of the Governorship and the Presidency.   *Elbert Hubbard*

A chef of morality.   *Elbert Hubbard*

A nebulous cluster of thought...resolved into a gaseous state.   *Elbert Hubbard*

The alter ego of organized cant.
Elbert Hubbard

MEDICINE

Nothing else but the substitute of exercise or temperance.   *Joseph Addison*

The Lord hath created medicines out of the earth; and he that is wise will not abhor them.

Apocrypha: Ecclesiastes, XXXVIII, 4.

The only profession that labors to destroy the reason for its own existence.   *James Bryce*

A conjectural art. It has almost no rules.   *Celsus*

They do not heal, but only relieve suffering temporarily, exchanging one disease for another.

Mary Baker Eddy

Patience is the best medicine.   *John Florio*

Not only a science; it is also an art . . . it deals with the very process of life, which must be understood before it may be guided.

Theophrastus B. Hohenheim

A good laugh and a long sleep.   *Irish Proverb*

There is no medicine; there are only medicine men.   *Salvador de Madariaga*

A healing art.   *Walter Martin*

One of the chief objects of medicine is to save us from the natural consequences of our vices and follies.   *Henry Louis Mencken*

The arts that promise to keep our body and mind in good health.   *Michel de Montaigne*

A collection of uncertain prescriptions, the results of which, taken collectively, are more fatal than useful to mankind.   *Napoleon 1*

Time is the best medicine.   *Ovid*

The knowledge of the loves and desires of the body, and how to satisfy them.   *Plato*

The department of witchcraft.

George Bernard Shaw

Consists of amusing the patient while nature cures the disease.   *Voltaire*

SEE ALSO DISEASE, DOCTORS, SURGEON.

MEDIOCRITY

A colorless and odorless gas; allow it to accumulate undisturbed, and suddenly it explodes with a force beyond all belief.   *George Bernanos*

Having lived without praise or blame.   *Dante*

The universal subjugator.   *Johann W. Goethe*

(One who) adds two and two, and gets only four.

Henry S. Haskins

Excellence to the mediocre.   *Joseph Joubert*

Minds (which) generally condemn everything which passes their understanding.

La Rochefoucauld

To the mediocre mediocrity is a form of happiness; they have a natural instinct for mastering one thing, for specialization.

Friedrich W. Nietzsche

Innate hermetism of the soul. Refusal to compare oneself with others, to get out of oneself for a moment and transfer to a neighbor's level.

José Ortega y Gasset

SEE ALSO MASSES, MOB.

MEDITATION

SEE PRAYER, RELIGION, SILENCE, THOUGHT, WORSHIP.

MEEKNESS

Not a contemplative virtue, it is maintaining peace and patience in the midst of pelting provocation.   *Henry Ward Beecher*

Taking injuries like pills, not chewing, but swallowing them down.   *Thomas Browne*

Nought else but a true knowing and feeling of man's self as he is.

Cloud of the Unknowing, 14 century.

(Those who have it in them to) inherit the earth. They won't have the nerve to refuse.

John Henry

Inheriting the earth—six or more feet of it.

Adapted from Abraham Myerson

Those who are never at all angry, for such are insensible . . . Meekness excludes revenge.

Theophylact

(Those who will) inherit the earth—they have it coming to them.   *James Thurber*

SEE ALSO HUMILITY.

MELANCHOLY

To be sad.   *Robert Burns*

A hell upon earth.   *Robert Burton*

There is no greater cause...than idleness; no better cure than business. *Robert Burton*

The mind's disease. *John Ford*

The pleasure of being sad. *Victor Hugo*

A kind of happiness to know just how unhappy we are. *La Rochefoucauld*

A feeling of sadness and longing that is not akin to pain, and resembles sorrow only as the mist resembles rain.
Adapted from Henry Wadsworth Longfellow

The nurse of frenzy. *William Shakespeare*

Dejection. *William Wordsworth*

SEE ALSO SORROW.

MELODRAMA

The blood of the stage. *George Jean Nathan*

Drama aged in wood. *Anon.*

MELODY

SEE MUSIC, SONG.

MEMOIRS

Published memories indicate the end of a man's activity, and that he acknowledges the end.
George Meredith

To speak ill of everybody except oneself.
Marechal Petain

When you put down the good things you ought to have done, and leave out the bad ones you did do—that's memoirs. *Will Rogers*

They are generally written by people who have either entirely lost their memories, or have never done anything worth remembering.
Oscar Wilde

What a person suffered that the world should know about. *Anon.*

SEE ALSO AUTOBIOGRAPHY, DIARY.

MEMORY

What God gave us so that we might have roses in December. *James M. Barrie*

The editor of one's sense of life.
Elizabeth Bowen

The receptacle and sheath of all knowledge.
Cicero

Card indexes consulted, and then put back in disorder by authorities whom we do not control.
Cyril Connolly

A hidden cord that is touched when we listen to our friend's original stories.
Cynic's Cyclopaedia

The secret of a good memory is attention, and attention to a subject depends upon our interest in it. *Tyron Edwards*

Some call her memory and some call her tradition. *Adapted from George Eliot*

The library of the mind.
Francis Fauvel-Gourand

What it takes to understand.
Edward M. Forster

A form of meeting. *Kahlil Gibran*

A sepulchre furnished with a load of broken and discarnate bones. *Joseph Glanvill*

A child walking along a seashore. You never can tell what small pebble it will pick up and store away among its treasured things. *Pierce Harris*

Imagination and memory are but one thing, which for divers considerations have divers names. *Thomas Hobbes*

Each man's memory is his private literature.
Aldous Huxley

The one who thinks over his experiences most, and weaves them into systematic relations with each other will be at one with the best memory.
William James

The art of attention. *Samuel Johnson*

The substance of personal identity.
Horace Kallen

(That which) tempers prosperity, lessens adversity, controls youth, and delights old age.
Firmianus Lactantius

All we really own. *Elias Lieberman*

It performs in preserving and storing up things gone by. *Plutarch*

The art of understanding. *Roscoe Pound*

The tombs of our buried hopes.
Marguerite Power

A kind of pharmacy or chemical laboratory in which chance guides our hand now to a calming drug and now to a dangerous poison.

Marcel Proust

A treasurer to whom we must give funds, if we would draw the assistance we need.

Nicholas Rowe

A man's memory may almost become the art of continually varying and misrepresenting his past, according to his interest in the present.

George Santayana

Soul of joy and pain.   *Richard Savage*

The warder of the brain.   *William Shakespeare*

A man's real possession...In nothing else is he rich, in nothing else is he poor.

Alexander Smith

Storehouse of the mind, garner of facts and fancies.   *Martin F. Tupper*

Holds together past and present, gives continuity and dignity to human life...the companion ... the tutor, the poet, the library, with which you travel.   *Mark Van Doren*

The diary we all carry about with us.

Mary H. Waldrip

The diary that chronicles things that never have happened and couldn't possibly have happened.

Oscar Wilde

The treasure of the mind.   *Thomas Wilson*

Something you forget details with.   *Anon.*

A beaten path in the brain.   *Anon.*

SEE ALSO AUTOBIOGRAPHY, BIOGRAPHY, HISTORY, KNOWLEDGE, PAST.

MENTAL HEALTH

The moment of unconscious creative synthesis, when, without thinking about it at all, we know that we make sense to ourselves and to others.

Franklin Barron

The feeling that one is free and that life and its outcome are in one's own hands. *Franklin Barron*

A deeper sense of relaxed participation in the present moment...Life ceases to be a course between birth and death, and becomes instead a fully realized experience of change.

Franklin Barron

Facing what we fear.

Adapted from Max Lerner

Feeling comfortable.   *Darold Treffert*

SEE ALSO NEUROSIS, NEUROTIC, PSYCHI-ATRIST.

MERCHANT

One engaged in a commercial pursuit. A commercial pursuit is one in which the thing pursued is the dollar.   *Ambrose Bierce*

The least virtuous citizens and possess the least *amor patriae.*   *Thomas Jefferson*

One who likes nobody.   *Anon.*

MERCY

An attribute beloved of detected offenders.

Ambrose Bierce

In war a universal mode of subjugating people.

Elbert Hubbard

Mercy is not...pronouncing judgment on another man's deserts, but in relieving his necessities; in giving aid to the poor, not in inquiring how good they are.   *Saint Ambrose*

Nobility's true badge.   *William Shakespeare*

An attribute to God himself.

Willliam Shakespeare

A virtue of the weak.   *Anon.*

The charity of those who can afford it.   *Anon.*

SEE ALSO CHRISTIANITY, FOREBEARANCE.

MERIT

Purity of life and heart.   *Horace*

Man's chief merit consists in resisting the impulses of his nature.   *Samuel Johnson*

What you do.   *Saint Thomas Aquinas*

In the use, not in the possession, lies the merit.

Adapted from Gilbert West

METAPHOR

When it is placed to an advantage, casts a kind of glory round it, and darkens a lustre through a whole sentence.   *Joseph Addison*

The highest value in both prose and poetry.

Aristotle

The greatest thing in style...a mark of genius, for to make good metaphors implies an eye for resemblances. *Aristotle*

The language of poetry. *Raphael Kraus*

SEE ALSO POETRY.

METAPHYSICIAN

A man who goes into a dark cellar at midnight without a light looking for a black cat that is not there. *Bowen of Colwood*

Men with no taste for exact facts, but only a desire to transcend and forget them as quickly as possible. *Henry Louis Mencken*

A man who excels in writing with black ink on a black ground. *Charles de Talleyrand*

METAPHYSICS

Valid knowledge of both sensible and suprasensible being. *Mortimer Adler*

An elaborate, diabolical invention for mystifying what was clear, and confounding what was intelligible. *William E. Aytoun*

The science of any half-lie.

Mikhail A. Bakunin

The science of proving what we don't understand.

Josh Billings

Merely our human attempt to decipher the meaning of things. *John E. Boodin*

The anatomy of the soul.

Catherine S. de Boufflers

The finding of bad reasons for what we believe upon instinct; but to find these reasons is no less an instinct. *Francis H. Bradley*

An attempt to define what is truly and completely real. *Edgar S. Brightman*

The attempt of the mind to rise above the mind.

Thomas Carlyle

A science which treats of...forms abstracted from matter; of immaterial things, as God, angels, etc. *Zachary Grey*

An attempt to define a thing and by so doing escape the bother of understanding.

Elbert Hubbard

Nothing but an inventory of all our possessions acquired through Pure Reason, systematically arranged. *Immanuel Kant*

The art of being sure of something that is not so.

Joseph Wood Krutch

An immensity of nonsense.

Henry Louis Mencken

An attempt to prove the incredible by an appeal to the unintelligible. *Johann B. Mencken*

The art of bewildering oneself methodically.

Jules Michelet

Consists of two parts, first, that which all men of sense already know, and second, that which they can never know. *Voltaire*

When the man speaking and the man spoken to do not understand each other, that is metaphysics.

Voltaire

An attempt to define the indefinable. *Anon.*

Much wrangling in things needless to be known.

Anon.

MIDDLE AGE

When you are too young to take up golf and too old to rush up to the net. *Franklin P. Adams*

Middle age is a time of life that a man first notices in his wife. *Richard Armour*

Having a choice of two temptations and choosing the one that will get you home earlier.

Daniel Bennett

You know you are there when your gray hair isn't premature. *Eugene E. Brussell*

My days are in the yellow leaf;
  The flowers and fruits of love are gone;
The worm, the canker and the grief
  Are mine alone. *Lord Byron*

That age which hovers between the fool and sage.

Adapted from Lord Byron

When you begin to exchange your emotions for symptoms. *Irvin S. Cobb*

In the middle of the journey of your life. *Dante*

Youth without its levity and age without decay.

Daniel Defoe

When a narrow waist and a broad mind begin to change places.   *Glenn Dorenbush*

When your age starts to show around your middle.   *Bob Hope*

The old age of youth and youth of old age.

Nunally Johnson

When you don't have to have fun to enjoy yourself.   *Franklin P. Jones*

When you are sitting home on Saturday night and the telephone rings and you hope it isn't for you.

Ring Lardner

When our judgment ripens and our imagination decays.   *Thomas B. Macaulay*

The time when a man is always thinking that in a week or two he will feel as good as ever.

Don Marquis

That time of life when a person has learned how to have a little fun in spite of his troubles.

Adapted from Don Marquis

When work is no longer play and play is getting to be work.   *Arthur Moger*

When you are not inclined to exercise anything but caution.   *Arthur Murray*

When you have met so many people that every new person you meet reminds you of someone else and usually is.   *Ogden Nash*

When anything new you feel is . . . likely to be a symptom.   *Laurence J. Peter*

The time when you'll do anything to feel better, except give up what's hurting you.

Robert Quillen

(A time when) you discover you keep on growing older, even after you are old enough.

Donald Raddle

That period in a man's life when he'd rather not have a good time than have to get over it.

Oscar Wilde

Later than you think and sooner than you expect.

Earl Wilson

When a man stops dodging temptation and temptation starts dodging him.   *Anon.*

A time when you can call a man clever but not handsome.   *Anon.*

When you start eating what is good for you instead of what you like.   *Anon.*

A period of life when a man begins to feel friendly toward insurance agents.   *Anon.*

The five B's of middle age: baldness, bridgework, bifocals, bay windows and bunions.   *Anon.*

A period of life when one can do as much as ever but would rather not.   *Anon.*

When your money is shorter, experience longer, stamina lower, and forehead higher.   *Anon.*

When everything starts to wear out, fall out or spread out.   *Anon.*

When your body goes to waist.   *Anon.*

MIDDLE CLASS

Those who make the state secure and uphold the laws.   *Euripides*

An epithet which the riff-raff apply to what is respectable, and the aristocracy to what is decent.

Anthony Hope

That prisoner of the barbarian 20th century.

Sinclair Lewis

Living for others and not yourself—that's middle class morality.

Adapted from George Bernard Shaw

A moderately honest man with a moderately faithful wife, moderate drinkers both, in a moderately healthy house: that is the true middle class unit.   *George Bernard Shaw*

Those who make up the backbone of a country. Any country lacking a middle class is a poor country and in trouble.   *Robert Zwickey*

SEE ALSO SUBURBIA.

MIDNIGHT

The noon of thought.   *Anna L. Barbauld*

The noon of night.   *Dante*

The witching hour of night.   *John Keats*

The outpost of advancing day, the frontier town and citadel of night.

Adapted from Henry Wadsworth Longfellow

This is the dumb and dreary hour, when injured ghosts complain; when graves give up their dead to haunt the faithless swain.

Adapted from David Mallet

The dead vast and middle of the night.

William Shakespeare

Fairy time. *William Shakespeare*

SEE ALSO WITCH.

MILITARISM

It means conquest abroad and intimidation and oppression at home. It means the strong arm which has ever been fatal to free institutions. It is what millions of our citizens have fled from in Europe. *Democratic National Platform, 1900.*

A fever for conquest, with peace for a shield, using music and brass buttons to dazzle and divert the populace. *Elbert Hubbard*

A fixed, fighting mental attitude that will never know when the war is over. *Elbert Hubbard*

The great preserver of our ideals of hardihood.

William James

Defeatism in the moral sphere.

Herbert L. Samuel

The Gospel of Force. *Fulton J. Sheen*

That which is not civil. *Charles de Talleyrand*

Does not consist in the existence of any army ... Militarism is a spirit...a point of view ... a purpose. The purpose ... is to use armies for aggression. *Woodrow Wilson*

SEE ALSO ARMY, GENERAL, SOLDIER, WAR.

MILITIA

The security of a free state.

Constitution of the United States, Amendment 2.

Mouths without hands maintained at vast expense; in peace a charge, in war a weak defense.

Adapted from John Dryden

For a people who are free...their best security.

Thomas Jefferson

MILTON, JOHN (1608-1674)

He was a true poet, and of the Devil's party without knowing it. *William Blake*

On his anointed eyes, God set his seal and gave him blindness and inward light that he might see as never man saw.

Adapted from Richard R. Bowker

The words of Milton are true in all things, and were never truer than in this: "He who would write heroic poems must make his whole life a heroic poem." *Thomas Carlyle*

The stair...to let down the English genius from the summits of Shakespeare.

Ralph Waldo Emerson

He saw; but blasted with excess of light, closed his eyes in endless night.

Adapted from Thomas Gray

A genius that could cut a colossus from rock, but could not carve heads upon cherry-stones.

Samuel Johnson

An acrimonious and surly republican.

Samuel Johnson

Of all the poets who have introduced into their works the agency of supernatural beings, Milton has succeeded the best. *Thomas B. Macaulay*

The character of Milton was peculiarly distinguished by loftiness of spirit.

Thomas B. Macaulay

God-gifted organ-voice of England.

Alfred Lord Tennyson

Mighty-mouth'd inventor of harmonies.

Alfred Lord Tennyson

Exquisite Puritan, grave Cavalier!

Henry Van Dyke

Lover of liberty at heart. *Henry Van Dyke*

A great poet, but a bad divine, and a miserable politician. *John Wilson*

A notorious traitor. *William Winstanley*

MIND

The unit and measure of things visible and invisible. *Amos Bronson Alcott*

Man's sacred guide in all things.

Apocrypha: Maccabees, II, 23.

Mind seems to be an independent substance implanted within the soul and to be incapable of being destroyed. *Aristotle*

A very citadel, for a man has no fortress more impregnable wherein to find refuge and be untaken forever. *Marcus Aurelius*

There is one radical distinction between different minds...that some minds are stronger and apter to mark the differences of things, others to mark their resemblances. *Francis Bacon*

The mind is the man. *Francis Bacon*

The mind of man is far from a clear and equal glass...it is rather like an enchanted glass, full of superstition and imposture. *Francis Bacon*

A mysterious form of matter secreted by the brain. *Ambrose Bierce*

A kingdom. *Edward Dyer*

God is Mind, and God is infinite; hence all is Mind. *Mary Baker Eddy*

Living ray of intellectual fire. *William Falconer*

A fountain playing in the sun and falling back into the great subterranean pool of the subconscious from which it rises. *Sigmund Freud*

An iceberg—it floats with only one-seventh of its bulk above water. *Sigmund Freud*

A sheet of white paper in this, that the impressions it receives the oftenest, and retains the longest, are black ones.

Julius and Augustus Hare

A clock that is always running down, and requires to be as constantly wound up. *William Hazlitt*

Seventy-year clocks. The Angel of life winds them up once for all, then closes the case, and gives the key into the hand of the Angel of the Resurrection. *Oliver Wendell Holmes 1*

Nothing but a heap or collection of different perceptions, united together by certain relations, and supposed, though falsely, to be endowed with a perfect simplicity and identity. *David Hume*

The creator and governor of the realm of matter—not ... our individual minds, but the mind in which the atoms out of which our individual minds have grown exist as thought.

James Jeans

The atmosphere of the soul. *Joseph Joubert*

What is mind? No matter. What is matter? Never mind. *T. H. Key*

Our mind is God. *Menander*

The apex in the pyramid of values to be found in the universe. It is this which constitutes the dignity of man as a moral personality, and makes him a being of surpassing worth.

John A. O'Brien

Our mind holds the same position in the world of thought as our body occupies in the expanse of nature. *Blaise Pascal*

My mind's my kingdom. *Francis Quarles*

A barren soil—a soil which is soon exhausted, and will produce no crop...unless it be continually fertilized and enriched with foreign matter. *Joshua Reynolds*

That little world. *Samuel Rogers*

An empire. *Robert Southwell*

A mirror...of heavenly sights.

Robert Southwell

A musical instrument with a certain range of tones, beyond which in both directions we have an infinite silence. *John Tyndall*

The mind's the standard of the man.

Isaac Watts

My own church. *Anon.*

SEE ALSO BRAIN, INTELLIGENCE, THINKING, THOUGHT.

MINORITY

Every new opinion, at its starting, is precisely in a minority of one. *Thomas Carlyle*

Those by which we judge a country.

Ralph Waldo Emerson

Minorities are the stars of the firmament; majorities, the darkness in which they float.

Martin Fischer

(They) that have...achieved all that is noble in the history of the world. *J. B. Gough*

That which is always in the right. *Henrik Ibsen*

Individuals or groups of individuals which are specially qualified. *José Ortega y Gasset*

(What forms when) each member separates himself from the multitude for special, relatively personal, reasons . . . an attitude of singularity.

José Ortega y Gasset

Not the petulant person who thinks himself superior to the rest, but the man who demands more of himself than the rest, even though he may not fulfil in his person those higher exigencies.

José Ortega y Gasset

Every man who adopts a serious attitude before his own existence and makes himself fully responsible for it.   *José Ortega y Gasset*

The chosen heroes of the world.   *Anon.*

SEE ALSO ARISTOCRACY, GREAT MEN, HERO, SUPERIOR MAN.

MIRACLE

The true miracles are those of man.

Emile C. Alain

Every believer is God's miracle.

Philip J. Bailey

Miracles are to those who believe in them.

William G. Benham

Prayer and pains, through faith in Christ Jesus.

John Eliot

Ancient history merely; they are not in the belief, nor in the aspiration of society.

Ralph Waldo Emerson

Life itself.   *Christopher Fry*

The swaddling-clothes of infant churches.

Thomas Fuller

The dearest child of faith.   *Johann W. Goethe*

A happening seen by four men at once, but by no one man in particular—hence, a collective, but otherwise untrue fact.   *Elbert Hubbard*

A physical event described by men who did not see it.   *Elbert Hubbard*

A transgression of a law of nature by a particular volition of the Divinity, or by the interposition of some invisible agent.   *David Hume*

The bastard child of faith and reason, which neither parent can afford to own.

William R. Inge

The children of mendacity.   *Robert G. Ingersoll*

A particular case of the immanence of the divine in matter.   *C. E. M. Joad*

God's signature, appended to His masterpiece of creation; not because they ought to be needed, but because they are needed.   *Ronald A. Knox*

A sensible operation, which being above the comprehension of the spectator, and in his opinion contrary to the established course of nature, is taken by him to be divine.   *John Locke*

The simplest features of the world about us.

Carl W. Miller

Miracles appear to be so, according to our ignorance of nature, and not according to the essence of nature.   *Michel de Montaigne*

The miraculous displays of God's power.

Andrews Norton

An effect which exceeds the natural force of the means employed for it.   *Blaise Pascal*

(Something which) happens only in times and in countries in which miracles are believed in, and in the presence of persons who are disposed to believe them.   *Ernest Renan*

Propitious accidents, the natural causes of which are too complicated to be readily understood.

George Santayana

An event which creates faith; that is the purpose and nature of miracles.   *George Bernard Shaw*

A work exceeding the power of any created agent, consequently being an effect of the divine omnipotence.   *Robert South*

Signifies nothing more than an event . . . the cause of which cannot be explained by another familiar instance, or . . . which the narrator is unable to explain.   *Baruch Spinoza*

Signs pointing to the presence of a divine power in nature and history.   *Paul Tillich*

The principal external proof and confirmation of the divinity of a doctrine.   *John Tillotson*

All is miracle. The . . . order of nature, the revolution of a hundred millions of worlds around a million of suns, the activity of light, the life of animals, all are grand and perpetual miracles.

Voltaire

A law-abiding event by which God accomplishes His redemptive purposes through the release of

energies which belong to a plane of being higher than any with which we are normally familiar.
Leslie D. Weatherhead

Something one has to work hard for.
Adapted from Chaim Weizmann

Every cubic inch of space.   *Walt Whitman*

A woman who won't talk.   *Gideon Wurdz*

SEE ALSO BABY, LIFE.

MIRROR

Largely the cause of love at first sight.
George Linn

A device which tells us the truth is a terrible thing.   *Abraham Pollock*

The conscience of women. They never do a thing without first consulting it.   *Moritz Saphir*

Thy glass will show thee how thy beauties wear.
William Shakespeare

All mirrors are magical...never can we see our faces in them.   *Logan P. Smith*

I change, and so do women too; but I reflect, which women never do.   *Anon.*

A device which makes you appear always imperfect.   *Anon.*

A device which shows everyone his best friend.
Anon.

MISANTHROPE

Lean, hungry, savage anti-everything.
Oliver Wendell Holmes 1

I consider him an unhappy man whom no one pleases.   *Martial*

One who loves nothing.   *Plautus*

MISER

An imposter who cannot bear to deal through his own tariff wall.   *John Ciardi*

One who is miserable.   *Tyron Edwards*

One who is always poor.   *French Proverb*

Misers are neither relations, nor friends, nor citizens, nor Christians, nor perhaps even human beings.   *Jean de La Bruyère*

A guy with unready cash.   *Stanley Levinson*

Misers are very good people; they amass wealth for those who wish their death.   *Stanislaus*

MISERLINESS

A handsome income.   *Desiderius Erasmus*

A disease in which a dollar obstructs the vision to the exclusion of a higher denomination.
Elbert Hubbard

Misery in disguise.   *Publilius Syrus*

Being mean to yourself and others.   *Anon.*

SEE ALSO AVARICE.

MISERY

To have few things to desire, and many things to fear.   *Francis Bacon*

To have a stomach and lack meat, to have meat and lack a stomach, to lie in bed and cannot rest.
William Camden

To have once been happy.   *John Clark*

A communicable disease.   *Martha Graham*

Not knowing what we want and killing ourselves to get it.   *Don Herold*

To be afflicted with habitual indecision.
Adapted from William James

Almost always the result of thinking.
Joseph Joubert

Myself my sepulchre, a moving grave.
John Milton

The chief cause of our misery is less the violence of our passions than the feebleness of our virtues.
Joseph Roux

The secret...is to have leisure to bother about whether you are happy or not. The cure for it is occupation.   *George Bernard Shaw*

To be hated, and to know that we deserve to be hated.   *Adam Smith*

MISFORTUNE

The kind of fortune that never misses.
Ambrose Bierce

The ballast which maintains our equilibrium on the sea of life, when we no longer have fortunes to carry.   *Ludwid Boerne*

The most direct way of getting to know yourself and your friends.   *Max Gralnick*

Something we should treasure; they constitute our bank of fortitude.   *Eric Hoffer*

(Something which evokes) talents which in prosperous circumstances would have lain dormant.
                    Horace

The state in which a man most easily becomes acquainted with himself, being especially free from admirers then.   *Samuel Johnson*

Interest and vanity are the usual sources.
                    La Rochefoucauld

When theory outstrips performance.
                    Leonardo da Vinci

Knives, that either serve us or cut us, as we grasp them by the blade or the handle.
                    Herman Melville

That which makes one man superior to another.
                    Philemon

With man, most of his misfortunes are occasioned by man.   *Pliny 1*

A tonic and bracer.   *Walter Scott*

(They) occur only when a man is false to his genius...They spring from seeds which we have sown.   *Henry David Thoreau*

(Something) we can easily learn to endure ... another man's, I mean.   *Mark Twain*

A state which introduces a man to himself.
                    Anon.

Man's true touchstone.   *Anon.*

A time when you decide upon religion or suicide.
                    Anon.

The great educator.   *Anon.*

SEE ALSO CALAMITY, SUFFERING.

MISSIONARY

The messengers of the churches, and the glory of Christ.   *Bible: Corinthians, VIII, 23.*

A machine for converting the heathen.
                    Thomas Carlyle

Our noble society for providing the infant Negroes in the West Indies with flannel waistcoats and moral pocket handkerchiefs.   *Charles Dickens*

Things are scattered with moral law...Every cause in Nature is nothing but a disguised missionary.   *Ralph Waldo Emerson*

Sincere...persons suffering from the meddler's itch.   *Elbert Hubbard*

A person sent by the ruling church...for religious propaganda among backward peoples (for example, in colonial or semi-colonial countries); he is usually an advance espionage agent of the imperialist usurpers.   *Slovar I. Slov*

The divinely provided food for destitute and underfed cannibals.   *Oscar Wilde*

MISTAKE

SEE ERROR, FAILURE.

MISTRESS

Mutability.   *Lord Byron*

Hath she thin hair, hath she none, she's to me a paragon.   *Robert Herrick*

A female who has rights, as distinguished from a married woman, who has duties.
                    Elbert Hubbard

A little country retreat near the town—not to dwell in constantly, but only for a night and away.
                    William Wycherley

MOB

Every numerous assembly is mob, let the individuals who compose it be what they will.
                    Lord Chesterfield

A society of bodies voluntarily bereaving themselves of reason...man voluntarily descending to the nature of the beast.   *Ralph Waldo Emerson*

A Monster; Heads enough, but no Brains.
                    Benjamin Franklin

Many heads, but no brains.   *Thomas Fuller*

One of the bloodiest noises in the world.
                    Lord Halifax

A many-headed beast.   *Horace*

Fickle citizens.   *Horace*

Only the voice of madness and not the voice of the people.   *Robert Kennedy*

A few men may make a mob as well as many.
    Wendell Phillips

All ... are different from the men themselves. Neither intelligence nor culture can prevent a mob from acting as a mob. The wise man and the knave lose their identity and merge themselves into a new being.   *Thomas B. Reed*

A vulgar and anonymous tyranny ... Such a headless people has the mind of a worm and the claws of a dragon.   *George Santayana*

Our supreme governors.   *Horace Walpole*

Humanity going the wrong way.
    Frank Lloyd Wright

The scum that rises when the water boils.
    Anon.

SEE ALSO CROWD, MASSES, MULTITUDE, PEOPLE (THE), POPULACE, RABBLE.

MODERATION

Nothing to excess.   *Anacharsis*

The inseparable companion to wisdom.
    Charles Caleb Colton

The noblest gift of Heaven.   *Euripides*

The silken string running through the pearl—chain of all virtues.   *Thomas Fuller*

A little with quiet.   *George Herbert*

To live on little.   *Horace*

The belief that you will be a better man tomorrow than you were yesterday.   *Murray Kempton*

A virtue wherewith to curb the ambition of the great, and to console men of moderate means for their small fortunes and insignificant merits.
    La Rochefoucauld

The languor and sloth of the soul; ambition is its activity and heat.   *La Rochefoucauld*

The rule of the *Not too Much.*   *John Milton*

The middle road.   *Ovid*

Life's middle state.   *Alexander Pope*

A fatal thing; nothing succeeds like excess.
    Oscar Wilde

SEE ALSO TEMPERANCE.

MODESTY

A feeling rather than a disposition. It is a kind of fear of falling into disrepute.   *Aristotle*

An invention by which pleasure is augmented. Modesty dictates concealment; concealment stimulates curiosity; curiosity augments desire, and with previous desire subsequent gratification increases.   *Jeremy Bentham*

The only sure bait when you angle for praise.
    Lord Chesterfield

That feeling by which honorable shame acquires a valuable and lasting authority.   *Cicero*

An ornament, but you go further without it.
    German Proverb

The lowliest of the virtues, and is a confession of the deficiency it indicates.   *William Hazlitt*

The natural butt of impertinence.
    William Hazlitt

Enhancing your charm by pretending not to be aware of it.   *Oliver Herford*

A beau-catcher that young ladies wear and women affect.   *Elbert Hubbard*

Among men ... the will-to-wait and seize.
    Elbert Hubbard

The attitude of mind that precedes the pounce.
    Elbert Hubbard

Egotism turned wrong side out.
    Elbert Hubbard

Meekness and wisdom combined.
    Solomon Ibn Gabirol

An index to nobility.   *Solomon Ibn Gabirol*

Once a wise man was asked, What is intelligence? He answered, modesty. Then he was asked, What is modesty? And he answered, intelligence.
    Solomon Ibn Gabirol

Modesty is to merit what shadows are to a painting; it gives it force and relief.
    Jean de La Bruyère

The respectful unobtrusiveness of one whose mission in life is to be ignored.

Hector H. Munro

With people of only moderate ability modesty is mere honesty; but with those who possess great talent it is hypocrisy.   *Arthur Schopenhauer*

The virtue of those who are deficient in other virtues.   *Stanislaus*

The highest instance of a noble mind.

Richard Steele

One of the seven deadly virtues.   *Alfred Sutro*

The beauty of women.   *Anon.*

The art of drawing attention to whatever it is you are being humble about.   *Anon.*

Placing a higher private estimate on your achievements than you are willing to show in public.

Anon.

The polite concession worth makes to inferiority.

Anon.

SEE ALSO HUMILITY, MEEKNESS.

MOHAMMED (570-632)

A rough self-helping son of the wilderness; does not pretend to be what he is not. There is no ostentatious pride in him; but neither does he go much upon humility: he is there as he can be, in cloak and shoes of his own clouting.

Thomas Carlyle

Mohammed starts out as a man of words, develops into an implacable fanatic and finally reveals a superb practical sense.   *Eric Hoffer*

The kingdom of Mohammed is a kingdom of revenge, of wrath, and desolation.

Martin Luther

I am only the Lord's servant; then call me the servant of God, and his messenger.   *Mohammed*

Mohammed gave his Arabs the best religion he could, as well as the best laws.   *George Sale*

SEE ALSO KORAN.

MOHAMMEDANISM

A bastard kind of Christianity, but a living kind; with a heart-life in it; not dead, chopping barren logic merely.   *Thomas Carlyle*

Faith in Allah and His apostle, prayers, almsgiving, fasting, and pilgrimage to the Sacred House at Mecca, built by Abraham for the worship of the One God.   *N. J. Dawood*

The kingdom of Mohammed is a kingdom of revenge, of wrath, and desolation.

Martin Luther

MOMENTS

An edifice which the Omnipotent cannot rebuild.

Ralph Waldo Emerson

The crutch on which the hour leans as it limps into eternity.   *Elbert Hubbard*

A space of time in which we dream of something that will never come true, or form a resolution that another minute effaces.   *Elbert Hubbard*

SEE ALSO DAY, TIME.

MONARCH

SEE KING.

MONARCHY

An absolute monarchy is one in which the monarch does as he pleases so long as he pleases the assassins.   *Ambrose Bierce*

The most expensive of all forms of government, the regal state requiring a costly parade, and he who depends on his own power to rule must strengthen that power by bribing the active and enterprising whom he cannot intimidate.

James Fenimore Cooper

(Something) natural to man, because it is an instinct to nature: the very bees have it.

Leigh Hunt

The true pattern of Divinity. *James 1 of England*

A piece of wood covered with velvet.

Napoleon 1

The master fraud, which shelters all others.

Thomas Paine

All the monarchical governments are military. War is their trade; plunder and revenue their objects.   *Thomas Paine*

Wisely limited...the surest safeguard of the rights and liberties of a great nation.

Thomas Paine

(Something) natural to men, as it is to bees, ants, migratory birds, wandering elephants, wolves on the prowl, and other animals, all of which appoint one to lead their undertakings.

Arthur Schopenhauer

In monarchies things go by whimsy.

John Vanbrugh

SEE ALSO KING.

MONASTICISM

A brothel rather than a sanctuary of chastity.

John Calvin

Not godliness, but a kind of life, either useful or useless to anyone, depending on one's habit of body and temperament. *Desiderius Erasmus*

(Represents) something more positive than a protest against the world. We believe it to have been the realization of the infinite loveliness and beauty of personal purity. *James A. Froude*

Castration. *Victor Hugo*

A life of luxury that even a king would envy.

John Huss

MONEY

Sweet balm. *Arabian Proverb*

A guarantee that we may have what we want in the future. Though we need nothing at the moment, it insures the possibility of satisfying a necessary desire when it arises. *Aristotle*

The sovereign queen of all delights—for her the lawyer pleads, the soldier fights.

Adapted from Richard Barnfield

A dream...a piece of paper on which is imprinted in invisible ink the dream of all the things it will buy, all the trinkets and all the power over others. *David T. Bazelon*

A kind of institutionalized dream which... constitutes the main fantasy on which our way of life has been built. *David T. Bazelon*

The symbol of everything that is necessary for man's well-being and happiness...Money means freedom, independence, liberty.

Edward E. Beals

(That which) speaks sense in a language all nations understand. *Alfred Behan*

What things run into and people run out of.

Mark Beltaire

A defense. *Bible Ecclesiastes, VII, 12.*

A good servant but a bad master.

Henry G. Bohn

The sinews of art and literature.

Samuel Butler 2

The last enemy that shall never be subdued. While there is flesh is money—or the want of money, but money is always on the brain so long as there is a brain in reasonable order. *Samuel Butler 2*

Aladdin's lamp. *Lord Byron*

The best foundation in the world.

Miguel de Cervantes

That which gives a man thirty years more of dignity. *Chinese Proverb*

The sinews of war. *Cicero*

A circulating medium. *W. Bourke Cockran*

Enables a man to get along without an education, and education enables him to get along without money. *Marcelene Cox*

Something which is never out of season.

Adapted from Thomas Draxe

The representative of a certain quantity of corn or other commodity. Its value is in the necessities of the animal man. It is so much warmth, so much bread. *Ralph Waldo Emerson*

The price of life. *Ralph Waldo Emerson*

The greatest temptation. *Jonathan Eybeshitz*

The fruit of evil as often as the root of it.

Henry Fielding

Like an arm or a leg—use it or lose it.

Henry Ford

Money is just what we use to keep tally.

Henry Ford

The sinew of love as well as of war.

Thomas Fuller

What you'd get on beautifully without if only other people weren't so crazy about it.

Margaret Harriman

The god of our time. *Heinrich Heine*

Money is life to us wretched mortals. *Hesiod*

Slave or master. *Horace*

The principle of commercial nations.

Thomas Jefferson

Health, and liberty, and strength.

Charles Lamb

Ready medicine. *Latin Proverb*

Another kind of blood. *Latin Proverb*

Something that talks. Most of us can't keep it long enough to hear what it says. *Jimmy Lyons*

A kind of disease which those who have it don't like to spread. *Mendel Maranz*

Man's work and being, alienated from himself, and this alien being rules him, and he prays to it.

Karl Marx

The sixth sense which enables you to enjoy the other five. *William Somerset Maugham*

The chief value of money lies in the fact that one lives in a world in which it is overestimated.

Henry Louis Mencken

The best advocate. *Mendele*

(That which) brings honor, friends, conquest, and realms. *John Milton*

The only substance which can keep a cold world from nicknaming a citizen "Hey, you!"

Wilson Mizner

Something that is more troublesome to watch than forget. *Adapted from Michel de Montaigne*

The cause of good things to a good man, of evil things to a bad man. *Philo*

A metal shoe elevator for small people to make them look as tall as others. *Moritz Saphir*

Human happiness in the abstract.

Arthur Schopenhauer

A good soldier. *William Shakespeare*

The most important thing in the world.

George Bernard Shaw

The stuff with which one purchases time.

Thomas Stoppard

The best broker. *Talmud: Baba Metzia, 63b.*

A new form of slavery. *Leon Tolstoy*

An article which may be used as a universal passport to everywhere except heaven, and as a universal provider of everything except happiness.

Wall Street Journal

The root of all good. *Rudolf Wanderone*

A deception and a disappointment.

Herbert G. Wells

An eel in the hand. *Welsh Proverb*

The monomania of the century. *Isaac M. Wise*

The best messenger. *Yiddish Proverb*

A device which permits people to get into debt a little further. *Anon.*

What gives value to it is work exchanged.

Anon.

An evidence of culture and a passbook into polite society. *Anon.*

The only true aristocracy. *Anon.*

The fringe benefit of a job you like. *Anon.*

SEE ALSO CAPITALISM, DOLLAR, ECONOMICS, GOLD, INFLATION, PROPERTY, RICHES, WEALTH.

MONKEY

An organized sarcasm upon the human race.

Henry Ward Beecher

An arboreal animal which makes itself at home in genealogical trees. *Ambrose Bierce*

Comedians. *Heinrich Heine*

They always remind me of poor relations.

Henry Luttrell

A malicious mirror. *Anon.*

MONOLOGUE

The egotist's version of a scintillating conversation. *Anon.*

When one woman is talking. When two are talking it's a catalog. *Anon.*

A conversation between two people, such as, a husband and wife. *Anon.*

MONOPOLY

A power...greater than the people themselves, consisting of many and various and powerful interests...held together by the cohesive power of the vast surplus in the banks. *John C. Calhoun*

The organization of industrial consolidations.
Adapted from Charles R. Flint

Combinations of capital. *Benjamin Harrison*

Special privilege. *Robert M. La Follette*

Undigested securities. *John P. Morgan*

The octopus. *Frank Norris*

The system. *Lincoln Steffens*

SEE ALSO CORPORATION.

MONOTHEISM

One Lord, one faith, one baptism, one God and Father of all, who is above all, and through all, and in you all. *Bible: Ephesians, IV, 5.*

The immovable bulwark of moral culture for all future ages. *Hermann Cohen*

It...revealed the father nucleus which had always lain hidden behind every divine figure.
Sigmund Freud

A return to the historical roots of the idea of God...the intimacy and intensity of the child's relation to the father. *Sigmund Freud*

Rationalism; it is the negation of all the absurdities by which the religious views...of the ancient nations were dominated. *Heinrich Graetz*

The adherence to a one and only God, truth, cause, leader, nation...usually the end result of a search for pride. *Eric Hoffer*

Not only the positive search for unity but also, negatively, the refusal to set man in the throne of God. *Leon Roth*

One God, to whom the name of God alone belongs, from which all things come, and who is Lord of the whole universe. *Tertullian*

SEE ALSO CHRISTIANITY, GOD, JUDAISM.

MONOTONY

The awful reward of the careful.
A. G. Buckham

The law of nature...The monotony of necessary occupations is exhilarating and life-giving.
Mohandas K. Gandhi

One wife at a time. *Anon.*

MONUMENT

The final and funniest folly of the rich.
Ambrose Bierce

Monuments are made for victories over strangers.
Julius Caesar

The monuments of noble men are their virtues.
Euripides

Poor remembrances. *John Florio*

The clothes of the dead; a grave is but a plain suit; a rich monument is an embroidered one.
Thomas Fuller

Merely a cold and sad memory of a man who would else be forgotton. No man who needs a monument ever ought to have one.
Nathaniel Hawthorne

A remembrance for those who do not need one.
Adapted from William Hazlitt

Towers of silence. *Robert X. Murphy*

A forted residence 'gainst the tooth of time.
William Shakespeare

The only thing that can stand upright and lie on its face at the same time. *Anon.*

A boast in stone. *Anon.*

A remembrance for those who do not need one.
Adapted from William Hazlitt

SEE ALSO COFFIN, DEATH, EPITAPH, GRAVE.

MOON

A collection of just about every variety of shapes. Angularities, granularities, every variety of rock you could find. *Edwin Aldrin*

A very natural and very pleasant environment in which to work.   *Edwin Aldrin*

Magnificent desolation.   *Edwin Aldrin*

It has a stark beauty all its own. It's like much of the high desert of the United States. It's different, but it's very pretty out here.   *Neil Armstrong*

There's nothing there.   *Frederick Bissell*

The lesser light, the lover's lamp, a ruined world, a globe burned out, a corpse upon the road of night.   *Adapted from Richard Burton*

The moon certainly isn't pretty. It was exotic and it was different and it was challenging...I don't think it's forbidding.   *Eugene Cernan*

The first milestone on the road to the stars.
                    Arthur C. Clarke

The passionless bright face.   *Dinah M. Craik*

Fair regent of the night.   *Erasmus Darwin*

A little physical evidence of eternity.
                    Jerry Dashkin

A golden sickle reaping darkness down.
                    James B. Hope

A Rosetta Stone of the planets.   *Robert Jastrow*

The newest frontier.   *Selwyn O. Juter*

Maker of sweet poets.   *John Keats*

Silver evasion.   *Archibald MacLeish*

Nothing but a ball of rocks and dirt.
                    Paul O'Neil

The remains of a huge, seething dust cloud whose center had already condensed to form the earth.
                    Science News, August 16, 1969

Sovereign mistress of true melancholy.
                    William Shakespeare

Everyone is a moon, and has a dark side which he never shows to anybody.   *Mark Twain*

A sphere of dust rolling in outer space.   *Anon.*

MORALITY

A private and costly luxury.   *Henry B. Adams*

The greatest part of morality is of a fixed eternal nature, and will endure when faith shall fail.
                    Joseph Addison

The idea of human conduct regulated in a human manner.   *Matthew Arnold*

A terribly thin covering of ice over a sea of primitive barbarity.   *Karl Barth*

Character and conduct such as is required by the circle or community in which man's life happens to be placed.   *Henry Ward Beecher*

Not only to do right but to discover what *is* right.
                    Eric Bentley

Conforming to a local and mutable standard of right.   *Ambrose Bierce*

Morality may consist solely in the courage of making a choice.   *Leo Blum*

The grammar of religion.   *Ludwig Boerne*

A complicated gesture learnt from books.
                    Robert Bolt

The custom of one's country and the current feeling of one's peers.   *Samuel Butler 2*

All systems of morality are based on the idea that an action has consequences that legitimize or cancel it.   *Albert Camus*

Not only the way in which we behave towards our neighbors, but also the way in which we cling to the integrity of our own thinking.
                    J. V. Casserley

To enjoy and give enjoyment, without injury to yourself or others.   *Nicolas Chamfort*

The taste for what is pure and (for) what defies the era.   *Jacques Chardonne*

Drawing the line somewhere.
                    Gilbert Keith Chesterton

Two principles...that self-interest is the mainspring of all our actions...that utility is the test of their value.   *Charles Caleb Colton*

I ought, or I ought not, constitute the whole of morality.   *Charles Darwin*

The social feelings which are instinctive or innate in the lower animals.   *Charles Darwin*

A moral being is one who is capable of reflecting on his past actions and their motives—of approving of some and disapproving of others.
                    Charles Darwin

An endeavor to find for the manifestation of impulse in special situations an office of refreshment and renewal.   *John Dewey*

Morality, said Jesus, is kindness to the weak; morality, said Nietzsche, is bravery of the strong; morality, said Plato, is the effective harmony of the whole. *Will Durant*

Blind obedience to words of command.
Havelock Ellis

The direction of the will on universal ends.
Ralph Waldo Emerson

Feeling temptation but resisting it.
Sigmund Freud

A document written in alternative ciphers, which change from line to line. *James A. Froude*

The outward and visible form of the inner essence of the State. *Georg W. Hegel*

What is moral is what you feel good after and what is immoral is what you feel bad after.
Ernest Hemingway

The love of God, through Christ, with Christ, and in Christ. *Dietrich von Hildebrand*

Doing the kind, generous, splendid thing.
Oliver Wendell Holmes 2

Simply another means of living, but the saints make it an end in itself.
Oliver Wendell Holmes 2

The line of conduct that pays. *Elbert Hubbard*

The formaldehyde of theology. *Elbert Hubbard*

Implies some sentiment common to all mankind, which recommends the same object to general approbation, and makes every man...agree in the same opinion...concerning it.
David Hume

To have done, once and for all, with lying.
Thomas Henry Huxley

To...give up pretending to believe that for which there is no evidence, and repeating unintelligible propositions about things beyond the possibilities of knowledge. *Thomas Henry Huxley*

Not properly the doctrine of how we may make ourselves happy, but how we may make ourselves worthy of happiness. *Immanuel Kant*

In every case I must so act that I can at the same time will that the maxim behind my act should become a universal law. *Immanuel Kant*

Man's most fundamental myth.
Joseph Wood Krutch

Morality, if it is not fixed by custom and authority, becomes a mere matter of taste determined by the idiosyncrasies of the moralist.
Walter Lippmann

A compendium of the minimum of sacrifices necessary for man to live in company with other men, without suffering too much or causing others to suffer. *Gina Lombroso*

Without religion (it) is only a kind of dead reckoning—an endeavor to find our place on a cloudy sea. *Henry Wadsworth Longfellow*

A hollow tooth which must be propped with gold.
Edgar Lee Masters

The theory that every human act must be either right or wrong, and that ninety-nine per cent of them are wrong. *Henry Louis Mencken*

Acquired feelings. *John Stuart Mill*

To do as one would be done by, and to love one's neighbor as one's self. *John Stuart Mill*

Merely statements that certain kinds of actions will have good effects. *George F. Moore*

The best of all devices for leading mankind by the nose. *Friedrich W. Nietzsche*

A means of preserving the community and saving it from destruction. Next it is a means of maintaining the community on a certain plane and in a certain degree of benevolence.
Friedrich W. Nietzsche

A means for the satisfaction of human wants. In other words, morality must justify itself at the bar of life, not life at the bar of morality.
Max C. Otto

Behaving as you were brought up to behave.
Charles S. Peirce

To obey the traditional maxims of your community without hesitation or discussion.
Charles S. Peirce

Has to do with the definition of right *conduct,* and this not simply by way of the ends of action. *How* we do *what* we do is as important as our goals.
Paul Ramsey

Morality involves the correct and careful regulation of three relationships: man to God, man to himself, and man to his fellow men.

> *Roman Catholic Bishops of the*
> *United States, Nov., 1951.*

The meeting-place between the human and divine.   *Leon Roth*

Reverence for life.   *Albert Schweitzer*

What is morality? Gentility.

> *George Bernard Shaw*

You can draw a line and make other chaps toe it. That's what I call morality.

> *George Bernard Shaw*

Only social habits and circumstantial necessities.

> *George Bernard Shaw*

Keeping up appearances in this world, or becoming suddenly devout when we imagine that we may be shortly summoned to appear in the next.

> *Horace Smith*

The regulation of conduct in such a way that pain shall not be inflicted.   *Herbert Spencer*

Morality is moral only when it is voluntary.

> *Lincoln Steffens*

A personal affair; in the war of righteousness every man fights for his own hand.

> *Robert Louis Stevenson*

For those who adopt a scientific view... present expediency.   *F. Sherwood Taylor*

The act of defining your principles to oppose your practices.   *Francis Thompson*

What the majority then and there happen to like and immorality is what they dislike.

> *Alfred North Whitehead*

Simply the attitude we adopt towards people whom we personally dislike.   *Oscar Wilde*

Consists in accepting the standard of one's age.

> *Oscar Wilde*

Conduct which is not dependent upon the whims of the politicians, the majority.   *Anon.*

SEE ALSO BIBLE, CHRISTIANITY, CONDUCT, ETHICS, GOLDEN RULE, GOOD AND BAD, JUSTICE, RELIGION, TEN COMMANDMENTS.

MORON

Those whose mental development is above that of an imbecile (7 years) but does not exceed that of a normal child of twelve years.

> *American Association for the Study*
> *of the Feeble-Minded*

A thing that grieves not and that never hopes; stolid and stunned, a brother of the ox.

> *Adapted from Edwin Markham*

One who is content with a serene state.   *Anon.*

SEE ALSO FOOL.

MOSES

The father of civil liberty for all humanity.

> *Lyman Abbott*

This was the truest worrier
  That ever buckled sword;
This the most gifted poet
  That ever breathed a word.

> *Cecil F. Alexander*

Now the man Moses was very meek, above all the men which were upon the face of the earth.

> *Bible: Numbers, XII, 3.*

A merciful, meek man, and yet with what fury did he run through the camp, and cut throats of three-and-thirty thousand of his dear Israelites that were fallen into idolatry.   *Daniel Defoe*

The man... who created the Jews.

> *Sigmund Freud*

A pillar of light on the threshold of history.

> *Asher Ginzberg*

The founder of his nation and the creator of its religion.   *Ernest Jones*

Moses with his law is most terrible; there never was any equal to him in perplexing, affrighting, tyrannizing, threatening, preaching, and thundering.   *Martin Luther*

A colossus among the great mythical figures of humanity.   *Ernest Renan*

An Egyptian priest... who possessed a portion of Lower Egypt, being dissatisfied with the established institutions there, left it and came to Judea with a large body of people who worshipped the Most High.   *Strabo*

The author of the great principle that the governments and religions of nations must be built upon the same basis of truth as is individual character.

Isaac M. Wise

SEE ALSO TEN COMMANDMENTS.

MOSLEMS

SEE MOHAMMEDANISM.

MOTHER

The child's schoolroom.   *Henry Ward Beecher*

The holiest thing alive.

Samuel Taylor Coleridge

The child's supreme parent.   *Havelock Ellis*

Not a person to lean on but a person to make leaning unnecessary.   *Dorothy C. Fisher*

God could not be everywhere so he therefore made mothers.   *Jewish Proverb*

A woman who doesn't mind her son becoming a boxer as long as he becomes a doctor or lawyer first.   *Jewish Saying*

The best academy.   *James Russell Lowell*

The obese multipara in her greasy kimono.

Henry Louis Mencken

She who can take the place of all others, but whose place no one else can take.

Gaspard Mermillod

One moment makes a father, but a mother is made by endless moments, load on load.

John C. Neihardt

The name for God in the lips and hearts of little children.   *William Makepeace Thackeray*

God's deputy on earth.   *Rahel L. Varnhagen*

The hand that rocks the cradle
Is the hand that rules the world.

William Wallace

The woman who decorates her life with babies.

Anon.

SEE ALSO BABY, FATHER, WOMAN.

MOTHERHOOD

Womanliness means only motherhood;
All love begins and ends there.

Robert Browning

The greatest privilege of life.   *May R. Coker*

The headliner in God's great vaudeville.

Elbert Hubbard

The keystone of the arch of matrimonial happiness.   *Thomas Jefferson*

The pleasing punishment that women bear.

William Shakespeare

Woman's wisdom.   *Alfred Lord Tennyson*

The way that humanity can satisfy its desire for physical immortality and triumph over its fear of death.   *Rebecca West*

An incident, an occupation, a career according to the mettle of the woman.   *Anon.*

MOUNTAIN

The palaces of nature.   *Lord Byron*

Good neighbours.   *George Herbert*

A holy altar; an organ breathes in every grove.

Thomas Hood

The beginning and end of all natural scenery.

John Ruskin

An affront to man's conquest of nature.

Edward Whymper

MOURNING

SEE GRIEF.

MOUTH

In man, the gateway to the soul; in woman, the outlet of the heart.   *Ambrose Bierce*

A hole under a drunkard's nose that all his money runs into.   *English Proverb*

A snare of death.   *Anon.*

Something that is shallowest where it babbles.

Anon.

MOVIE

An extension of gossip and daydream.

Eric Bentley

A petrified fountain of thought.   *Jean Cocteau*

The only art which cannot, or will not, use intelligence.   *Franklin Craven*

A collaborative art.   *Kirk Douglas*

(Something) written by the half-educated for the half-witted.   *Saint John Ervine*

A battleground...love, hate, violence, action, death—in a word, emotion.   *Samuel Fuller*

A term used by one who enjoys rather than "appreciates" motion-pictures.

Warren Goldberg

In picture-making the writer is the most important clog in the wheel.   *Samuel Goldwyn*

Life with the dull parts cut out.

Alfred Hitchcock

A business of making mud pies and playing Indian.   *Grover Jones*

A dog: the head is commerce, the tail is art. And only rarely does the tail wag the dog.

Joseph Losey

(Hollywood movies) were the American dream ... a Dream in terms of material satisfactions and sensual love, whose requisite happy ending was always a long drawn-out embrace.

Malcolm Muggeridge

Art simplified, purified, and hogtied.

Anon.

SEE ALSO HOLLYWOOD, STARLET.

MOVIE-FAN

One who sees the movie first, then reads the book.   *Warren Goldberg*

One who prefers seeing the movie to reading the book.   *Warren Goldberg*

One who enjoys the pop-corn as much as the movie.   *Anon.*

MOZART, WOLFGANG AMADEUS (1756-1791)

He emancipated music from the bonds of a formal age, while remaining the true voice of the eighteenth century.   *Thomas Beecham*

Raphael is the same man as Mozart.

Georges Bizet

Mozart is sunshine.   *Antonin Dvorak*

This boy will cause us all to be forgotten.

Johann Hasse

The greatest composer I know, either personally or by repute.   *Joseph Haydn*

I pay no attention whatever to anybody's praise or blame...I simply follow my own feelings.

Wolfgang Amadeus Mozart

I like an aria to fit a singer as perfectly as a well-tailored suit of clothes.

Wolfgang Amadeus Mozart

Beethoven is the greatest composer—but Mozart is the only one.   *Gioacchino Rossini*

MUCKRAKER

One who sits on the fence and defames American enterprise as it marches by.   *Elbert Hubbard*

MULTITUDE

That great enemy of reason, virtue, and religion.

Thomas Browne

That numerous piece of monstrosity, which, taken asunder, seem men, and the reasonable creatures of God, but, confused together, make but one great beast.   *Thomas Browne*

A net result of zero.   *Thomas Carlyle*

This many-headed monster.   *Samuel Daniel*

(A body which) is always in the wrong.

Wentworth Dillon

A beast of many heads.   *Desiderius Erasmus*

(That which) grows neither old nor wise; it always remains in its infancy.   *Johann W. Goethe*

SEE ALSO CROWD, MAJORITY, MASSES, MOB.

MURDER

To create a vacancy without nominating a successor. *Ambrose Bierce*

(An act) committed by men who, as they shaved in the morning, had no idea they would kill before the day was out. *Albert Camus*

When a person of sound memory and discretion unlawfully killeth any reasonable creature in being, and under the king's peace, with malice aforethought, either express or implied.
Edward Coke

Simply to kill a man is not murder.
Thomas De Quincey

A break in the monotony of things.
Adapted from Robert Lynd

Murder, gentlemen, is when a man is murderously killed. *Liam Mathews*

(Acts that) long survive their commission, and, like the ghosts of the murdered, forever haunt the steps of the malefactor. *Walter Scott*

Glorified assault. *Arthur Train*

To destroy. *Edward Young*

Retroactive birth control. *Anon.*

SEE ALSO ASSASSIN, CAIN, EXECUTION.

MURDERER

Whosoever hates his brother is a murderer.
Bible: John III, 15.

A man of violent passions, bloodshot eyes, and swollen veins that alone can grasp the knife of murder. *Percy Bysshe Shelley*

One who is presumed to be innocent until he is proven insane. *Anon.*

MUSEUM

Cemeteries of the arts. *Alphonse M. de Lamartine*

Seldom a cheerful place—oftenest induces a feeling that nothing could ever have been young.
Walter Pater

The home of a pedant. *Anon.*

MUSIC

There's only two ways to sum up music: either it's good or it's bad. If it's good you don't mess about it; you just enjoy it. *Louis Armstrong*

A universal language, and need not be translated.
Berthold Auerbach

That which penetrates the ear with facility and quits the memory with difficulty.
Thomas Beecham

Music *per se* means nothing; it is sheer sound.
Thomas Beecham

Tones that sound, and roar and storm about me until I have set them down in notes.
Ludwig van Beethoven

The one incorporeal entrance into the higher world of knowledge which comprehends mankind but which mankind cannot comprehend.
Ludwig van Beethoven

The beating of the pulse, the rhythm of the blood that accompanies a given order of ideas.
Henry Brailsford

God is its author, and not man; he laid the keynote of all harmonies...and he made us so that we could hear and understand.
John G. Brainard

There is music wherever there is harmony, order, or proportion. *Thomas Browne*

There is something in it of divinity more than the ear discovers. *Thomas Browne*

Noise with a beat. *Eugene E. Brussell*

Melody, time, consonance, dissonance.
Charles Burney

Organisation of sound. *John Cage*

A kind of inarticulate unfathomable speech which leads us to the edge of the Infinite and lets us for moments gaze into that. *Thomas Carlyle*

The speech of angels. *Thomas Carlyle*

See deep enough, and you see musically; the heart of nature being everywhere music.
Thomas Carlyle

Noble sounds that never lie, brag, flatter or malign.
Adapted from Gilbert Keith Chesterton

The soul of geometry.   *Paul Claudel*

Cocktail music...(is) audible wallpaper.
Alistair Cooke

A system of proportions in the service of a spiritual impulse.   *George Crumb*

Another planet.   *Alphonse Daudet*

The arithmetic of sounds as optics is the geometry of light.   *Claude Debussy*

An outburst of the soul.   *Frederick Delius*

The best, most beautiful, and most perfect way that we have of expressing a sweet concord of mind to each other.   *Jonathan Edwards*

The only language in which you cannot say a mean or sarcastic thing.   *John Erskine*

Various synchronized sounds into time and tune.
Max Gralnick

Fused emotions.   *Edmund Gurney*

Music is non-illustrative...a form of Ideal Motion...it is apprehended by a special and isolated Musical Faculty.   *Edmund Gurney*

Music means itself.   *Edward Hanslick*

A fluid architecture of sound.   *Roy Harris*

Emotion, not thought, is the sphere of music.
Hugh R. Haweis

It is spirit, yet in need of time, rhythm; it is matter, yet independent of space.
Heinrich Hein

Geometry in time.   *Arthur Honeggar*

A safe kind of high.   *Jimi Hendrix*

An attempt to express emotions that are beyond speech.   *Elbert Hubbard*

Classic music is the kind that we keep thinking will turn into a tune.   *Kin Hubbard*

The only art...wherein originality may reveal itself in the face of fools and not pierce their mental opacity.   *James G. Huneker*

After silence that which comes nearest to expressing the inexpressible.   *Aldous Huxley*

One of the ways God has of beating in on man.
Charles Ives

The human treatment of sounds.
Jean-Michel Jarré

The only sensual pleasure without vice.
Samuel Johnson

Love in search of a word.   *Sidney Lanier*

A kind of counting performed by the mind without knowing that it is counting.
Gottfried W. von Leibnitz

There are three worlds of music—the composer's, the performer's, and the critic's.
Erich Leinsdorf

The universal language of mankind.
Henry Wadsworth Longfellow

The art of the prophets, the only art that can calm the agitations of the soul; it is one of the most magnificent and delightful presents God has given us.   *Martin Luther*

A magic marriage between theology and the so diverting mathematics.   *Thomas Mann*

The half-articulate art, the dubious, the irresponsible, the insensible.   *Thomas Mann*

There are only two kinds of music; German music and bad music.   *Henry Louis Mencken*

(A balance) between mathematics and emotion...technical precision and deep feeling.
Yehudi Menuhin

A beautiful opiate, if you don't take it too seriously.   *Henry Miller*

Should never be painful to the ear but should flatter and charm it, and thereby always remain music.   *Wolfgang Amadeus Mozart*

The ideal of all art...whatever, because...it is impossible to distinguish the form from the substance...the subject from the expression.
Walter Pater

A principal means of glorifying our merciful Creator.   *Henry Peacham*

An example of order, or a less muddied congeries and proportion than we have yet about us in daily life.   *Ezra Pound*

Moonlight in the gloomy night of life.
Jean Paul Richter

Music is essentially useless, as life is.
George Santayana

A sort of dream architecture which passes in filmy clouds and disappears into nothingness.

Percy Scholes

A living application of mathematics.

Gino Severini

The brandy of the damned.

George Bernard Shaw

The only cheap and unpunished rapture upon earth.   *Sydney Smith*

The organization of a certain finite number of variables.   *Stephen Sondheim*

An elaboration of emotional speech.

Herbert Spencer

Music alone can be purely religious.

Anne Louise de Staël

Feeling . . . not sound.   *Wallace Stevens*

Nothing more than a succession of impulses that converge towards a definite point of repose.

Igor Stravinsky

(The communication of) valuable spiritual states which testify to the depth of the artist's nature and to the quality of his experience of life.

John W. Sullivan

The sound of universal laws promulgated.

Henry David Thoreau

The crystallisation of sound.

Henry David Thoreau

The noblest among the mathematical arts.

Johannes Tinctoris

Music is made up of a large number of individual sounds, and is either a single melody or a partsong.   *Johannes Tinctoris*

The shorthand of emotion.   *Leon Tolstoy*

Natural law as related to the sense of hearing.

Anton von Webern

All music is what awakes from you when you are reminded by the instruments.   *Walt Whitman*

The art which is most nigh to tears and memory.

Oscar Wilde

What Beethoven heard clearest when deaf.

Anon.

The shaped sounds between silences.   *Anon.*

The planned sound evironment.   *Anon.*

Music is what feelings sound like.   *Anon.*

Mathematics for the soul.   *Anon.*

SEE ALSO JAZZ, OPERA, SONG.

MYSTERY

Things which are strange and unknown.

Julius Caesar

Another name for our ignorance.

Tyron Edwards

The fundamental emotion which stands out at the cradle of true art and true science.

Albert Einstein

Life.   *Albert Einstein*

The unknown . . . powers which transcend the ken of the understanding.   *Ralph Waldo Emerson*

Not the prison of the mind of man, it is his home.

Adapted from Walter Farrell

How God rules the universe.

Moses Maimonides

If you go directly at the heart of a mystery, it ceases to be a mystery, and becomes only a question of drainage.   *Christopher Morley*

The standard device for getting around a logical contradiction by elevating it to the status of a truth beyond logic.   *Max C. Otto*

The antagonist of truth . . . a fog of human invention that obscures truth, and represents it in distortion.   *Thomas Paine*

Only a theological term for religious allegory . . . a dogma which is plainly absurd, but which, nevertheless conceals in itself a lofty truth.

Arthur Schopenhauer

The wisdom of blockheads.   *Horace Walpole*

MYSTIC

A person who is puzzled before the obvious, but who understands the non-existent.

Elbert Hubbard

A gymnast who turns flip-flops between the here and not-here.   *Elbert Hubbard*

Not one who sees God in nature, but one for whom God and nature fit into one plane.
Bede Jarrett

One of the marks of the true mystic is the tenacious and heroic energy with which he pursues a definite moral idea.   *James A. Leuba*

The mystic sees the ineffable, and the psychopathologist the unspeakable.
William Somerset Maugham

They...desire to know, only that they may love; and their desire for union with the principle of things in God...is founded on a feeling which is neither curiosity nor self-interest.   *E. Recejac*

His spirit is...sunk and lost in the Abyss of Deity, and loses the consciousness of all creature-distinctions.   *John Tauler*

To be a mystic is simply to participate here and now in that real and eternal life.
Evelyn Underhill

The visionary...when his vision mediates to him an actuality beyond the reach of the senses.
Evelyn Underhill

One too full of God to speak intelligibly to the world.   *Anon.*

SEE ALSO VISION.

MYSTICISM

Nothing but an overwhelming concentration of religious experience.   *Jacob B. Agus*

The hyphen between paganism and Christianity.
Charles Baudelaire

Gossip grown old.   *Richard P. Blackmur*

Myths are public dreams, dreams are private myths.   *Joseph Campbell*

That which is somehow interesting, though somewhat incomprehensible.   *Warren Goldberg*

From mystics proceed religious revelations; from mystics, philosophy; mysticism is the common source of both.   *Karl R. von Hartmann*

Mysticism is essentially...leading to immediate contact with God.   *Thomas Hughes*

A consciousness of the beyond.
William R. Inge

Communion with God.   *William R. Inge*

The concentration of reason in feeling, the enthusiastic love of the good, the true, the one.
Benjamin Jowett

The sense of the infinity of knowledge and of the marvel of the human faculties.   *Benjamin Jowett*

The union of scepticism and yearning.
Friedrich W. Nietzsche

The science of ultimates...the science of self-evident Reality.   *Coventry Patmore*

Not a religion but a religious disease.
George Santayana

Any profound view of the world.
Albert Schweitzer

The very pinnacle of individualism.
Bernard Smith

Sentimentality taken seriously.   *Leon Stein*

The expression of the innate tendency of the human spirit towards complete harmony with the transcendental order.   *Evelyn Underhill*

The pursuit of private heavens.   *Anon.*

SEE ALSO RELIGION, SUPERSTITION.

MYTHOLOGY

A myth contains the story that is preserved in popular memory and that helps bring to life some deep stratum buried in the depths of the human spirit.   *Nicholas Berdyaev*

The body of a primitive people's beliefs concerning its origin, early history, heroes, deities...as distinguished from the true accounts which it invents later.   *Ambrose Bierce*

To express man's understanding of himself in the world in which he lives.   *Rudolf Bultmann*

The use of imagery to express the other-worldly in terms of this world, and the divine in terms of human life, the other side in terms of this side.
Rudolf Bultmann

Dream stories that reveal to us the inner meanings of life.   *Jerry Dashkin*

Nothing other than psychological processes projected into the outer world.   *Sigmund Freud*

The permanent and universal aspirations of men, such as the dream of a future human fraternity.

William E. Hocking

The value-impregnated beliefs and notions that men hold, that they live by or live for.

R. M. MacIver

A description of a pattern of life, arising out of the unconscious, that carries the values for a society and gives a person the ability to handle anxiety, to face death, to deal with guilt.   *Rollo May*

A story which describes and illustrates in dramatic form certain deep structures of reality.

Denis de Rougemont

Nothing more than ancient gossip.   *Stanislaw*

Stories that everyone accepts but on one believes.

Anon.

N

NAME

Every man has three names: one his father and mother gave him, one others call him, and one he acquires himself.   *Bible: Ecclesiastes, VII, 13.*

As his name is, so is he.

Bible: Samuel XXV, 25.

Glory and . . . nothing.   *Lord Byron*

The invisible thing called a Good Name is made up of the breath of numbers that speak well of you.

Lord Halifax

The marks of things.   *Legal Maxim*

I have said everything when I have named the man.   *Pliny 2*

Nothing.   *Edgar Allan Poe*

God created things by naming them; the artist recreates them by taking their name off or giving them a new one.   *Marcel Proust*

Labels, plainly printed on the bottled essence of our past behavior.   *Logan P. Smith*

One's life.   *Talmud: Berakot, VII, 7b.*

SEE ALSO FAME, NICKNAME, REPUTATION.

NAPOLEON 1 (1769-1821)

There never was a human being who united against himself such a mass of execration and abhorrence . . . There is indeed . . . an admiration of him equally enthusiastic . . . but I have never yet seen the person by whom he was regarded with affection.   *John Quincy Adams*

His game was empires, his stakes were thrones, his dice were human bones.

Adapted from Lord Byron

The instinct of active, brave, able men, throughout the middle class everywhere, has pointed out Napoleon as the incarnate Democrat.   *Ralph Waldo Emerson*

An imposter and a rogue.

Ralph Waldo Emerson

Napoleon had himself the illusions which he gave to the people. This was his strength and his weakness, this was his beauty.   *Anatole France*

He wore everyone out. He was not a man, but a machine.   *Anatole France*

A genius to whom every trace of nobility was so alien . . . a classical anti-gentleman. But he was built on a grandiose scale.   *Sigmund Freud*

Always enlightened, always clear and decided, he was endowed at every hour with enough energy to carry into effect whatever he considered . . . necessary.   *Johann W. Goethe*

His life was the stride of a demigod, from battle to battle, and from victory to victory.

Johann W. Goethe

Napoleon healed through sword and fire the sick nation.   *Heinrich Heine*

A lion in the field only. In civil life, a cold-blooded, calculating . . . usurper, without a virtue

...supplying ignorance by bold presumption.
Thomas Jefferson

Bonaparte's wisdom was in his thoughts, and his madness in his passions.   *Joseph Joubert*

A miraculous child.   *Thomas B. Macaulay*

A mediocre and grotesque individual who played at the role of hero.   *Karl Marx*

I shall be considered as an extraordinary man. I have fought fifty pitched battles, almost all of which I have gained. I have framed and carried into effect a code of laws that will bear my name to the most distant posterity.   *Napoleon 1*

I rose from being a private person to the astonishing height of power I possessed without having committed a single crime to obtain it.
Napoleon 1

The synthesis of brute and superman.
Friedrich W. Nietzsche

Grand, gloomy, and peculiar, he sat upon the throne a sceptred hermit, wrapped in the solitude of his own originality.   *Charles Phillips*

Although too much of a soldier among sovereigns, no one could claim with better right to be a sovereign among soldiers.   *Walter Scott*

This young man does everything, can do every thing, and will do everything.
Emmanuel J. Sieyes

No law but his own headstrong will he knew.
Robert Southey

This dark little archaic personage, hard, compact, capable, unscrupulous, imitative, and neatly vulgar.   *Herbert G. Wells*

NATION

Men and women.   *Richard Aldington*

A totality of men united through community of fate into a community of character.   *Otto Bauer*

And hath made of one blood all nations.
Bible: Acts, XVII, 26.

The nations are as a drop of a bucket, and are counted as the small dust of the balance.
Bible: Isaiah, XL, 15.

The unity of a people. King and parliament are the unity made visible.
Samuel Taylor Coleridge

A work of art and a work of time.
Benjamin Disraeli

Institutions alone...create nations.
Benjamin Disraeli

A body of people who feel they are a nation.
Rupert Emerson

The sense of common identity, the sense of a singularly important national 'we' which is distinguished from all others who make up an alien 'they.'   *Rupert Emerson*

Nations are what their deeds are.
Georg W. Hegel

A people possessing a developed national consciousness.   *Friedrich Hertz*

A historical group of men of recognizable cohesion, held together by a common enemy.
Theodor Herzl

A thing that lives and acts like a man, and men are the particles of which it is composed.
Josiah G. Holland

May be said to consist of its territory, its people and its laws. The territory is the only part which is of certain durability.   *Abraham Lincoln*

Nations are the citizens of humanity, as individuals are the citizens of the nation.
Giuseppe Mazzini

The offspring of a common birth, a clan...It enables men to relate their lives to the lives of others.   *John Nef*

A self-defined human community.   *John Nef*

A detour of nature to arrive at six or seven great men—and then get around them.
Friedrich W. Nietzsche

A group of men who speak one language and read the same newspapers.   *Friedrich W. Nietzsche*

Two classes—the nations in which the government fears the people, and the nations in which the people fear the government.   *Amos R. Pinchot*

A geographical problem divided from the others by nationalism.   *Irwin W. Smith*

A licensed predatory concern...not bound by the decencies of that code of laws and morals that governs private conduct. *Thorstein Veblen*

SEE ALSO COUNTRY, PATRIOTISM, STATE.

NATIONALISM

A silly cock crowing on its own dunghill.
Richard Aldington

A mighty affirmation of life, and with it a sense of unshakable rootedness. *Kurt Blumenfeld*

That ridiculous and hurtful vanity, by which the people of each country are apt to prefer themselves to those of every other. *Henry Bolingbroke*

An infantile disease. It is the measles of mankind.
Albert Einstein

A defensive movement against the crude encroachments of civilization. *Franz Kafka*

The essense of a people's spirituality.
Nahman Krochmal

A religion and a theory of state-absolutism.
Edwin Lewis

The complete subjugation of the individual to the group and the predominance of the interest of the group over the claims of humanity.
Israel I. Mattuck

One of the effective ways in which the modern man escapes life's ethical problems.
Reinhold Niebuhr

The juvenile delinquency of the contemporary world. *Laurens Van der Post*

National egotism. *Anon.*

SEE ALSO COUNTRY, PATRIOTISM.

NATIONALITY

Likeness between members is the essence of nationality. *Louis D. Brandeis*

Nationality is the miracle of independence. Race is the principle of physical analogy.
Benjamin Disraeli

A portion of mankind...united among themselves by common sympathies which do not exist between them and any others—which makes them coöperate with each other more willingly than with other people. *John Stuart Mill*

Desire to be under the same government, and desire that it should be government by themselves or a portion of themselves exclusively.
John Stuart Mill

NATURAL

Healthiness in every speech and action...free from all doubt and vexation, all thought of ways and means and all pretense. *Marcus Aurelius*

Simply a pose. *Oscar Wilde*

A very difficult pose to maintain. *Oscar Wilde*

NATURAL SELECTION

From the war of nature, from famine and death, the most exaulted object which we are capable of conceiving, namely, the production of the higher animals, directly follows. *Charles Darwin*

Implies that the individuals which are best fitted for the complex and changing conditions to which, in the course of ages, they are exposed, generally survive and procreate their kind.
Charles Darwin

I have called this principle, by which each slight variation, if useful, is preserved, by the term Natural Selection. *Charles Darwin*

Nature has made up her mind that what cannot defend itself shall not be defended.
Ralph Waldo Emerson

The means whereby evolution has been brought about. *Ernest Jones*

Of all the animals that are born a few only can survive; and it is owing to this law that development takes place. The law of murder is the law of growth. *W. Winwood Reade*

The survival of the fittest. *Herbert Spencer*

A dishonoring view of nature.
Samuel Wilberforce

SEE ALSO EVOLUTION, SURVIVAL.

NATURE

The never idle workshop.   *Matthew Arnold*

Nature is the nature of all things that are; things that are have a union with all things from the beginning.   *Marcus Aurelius*

The only love that does not deceive human hopes.
        Honoré de Balzac

A step-mother.   *Guillaume du Bartas*

The visible series of effects or sensations imprinted on our minds according to certain fixed and general laws.   *George Berkeley*

What I call God.   *Robert Browning*

The system of law established by the Creator for the existence of things and the succession of beings.   *George L. Buffon*

The big fish eat the little fish, the little fish eat the water insects, and the water insects eat the weeds and the mud.   *Chinese Proverb*

The term in which we comprehend all things that are representable in the form of time and space, and subjected to the relations of cause and effect.
        Samuel Taylor Coleridge

A name for an effect, whose cause is God.
        William Cowper

The art of God eternal.   *Dante*

An endless combination and repetition of a very few laws.   *Ralph Waldo Emerson*

A mutable cloud which is always and never the same.   *Ralph Waldo Emerson*

A rag-merchant, who works up every shred and ort and end into new creations.
        Ralph Waldo Emerson

Everything that man is born to.   *John Erskine*

One connected whole. At any given moment every part must be precisely what it is, because all other parts are what they are.   *Johann G. Fichte*

A great spectacle, somewhat resembling the opera.   *Bernard de Fontenelle*

The universal language. *Chistopher W. von Gluck*

The living, visible garment of God.
        Johann W. Goethe

A volume of which God is the author.
        Moses Harvey

Seen from within, nature is a war of living powers of will.   *Karl Heim*

Visible thought.   *Heinrich Heine*

The unseen intelligence which loved us into being, and is disposing of us by the same token.
        Elbert Hubbard

That...which no one can define.
        Elbert Hubbard

An infinite pleasure-ground, where all may graze, and where the more bite, the longer the grass grows, the sweeter is its flavor, and the more it nourishes.   *Thomas Henry Huxley*

A conjunction of the verb to eat, in the active and passive.   *William R. Inge*

Nothing but the exercise of the divine omnipotence.   *Immanuel Kant*

A house to dwell in.   *Charles Lamb*

(Something that) resolves everything into its component elements, but annihilates nothing.
        Lucretius

The sum of all phenomena, together with the causes which produce them; including not only all that happens, but all that is capable of happening.
        John Stuart Mill

A hymn of praise to God.   *Maria Mitchell*

The background and theatre of the tragedy of man.   *John Morley*

One grand cosmic book describing the power and majesty of God.   *John A. O'Brien*

The image of God.   *Blaise Pascal*

God under a disguise.   *A. E. Taylor*

A structure of evolving processes. The reality is in the process.   *Alfred North Whitehead*

A hanging judge.   *Anon.*

SEE ALSO BEAUTY, EVOLUTION, GOD, NATURAL SELECTION.

NAZISM

Big business gone hydrophobia.
        Oscar Ameringer

An idolatry.   *Karl Barth*

Pathology in politics.   *Walter Bartz*

A community bound by blood ties.

Brockhaus Encyclopedia

The foremost principle...is the leader principle. This means victory over the parliamentary system and over majority rule in all spheres of life and consolidation of all politically and productively superior forces of the nation.

Brockhaus Encyclopedia

Revolutionary ideals...purely medieval and reactionary. *Sigmund Freud*

The St. Vitus dance of the Twentieth Century.

Hermann Rauschning

SEE ALSO FASCISM, TOTALITARIANISM.

NECESSITY

The art of rushing to the defense of the winning side. *Henry F. Amiel*

The spur of genius. *Honoré de Balzac*

God, the World and Love. *Richard Garnett*

The last and strongest weapon. *Livy*

The mother of an empty stomach. *Jimmy Lyons*

The tyrant's plea. *John Milton*

A violent school-mistress.

Michel de Montaigne

The plea for every infringement of human freedom. It is the argument of tyrants; it is the creed of slaves. *William Pitt*

The constant scourge of the lower orders.

Arthur Schopenhauer

The mother of "taking chances." *Mark Twain*

Today's three basic necessities—food, clothing and a tax shelter. *William Vaughan*

A better pain-killer than anything.

Luc de Vauvenargues

(That which) frees us from the embarrassment of choice. *Luc de Vauvenargues*

Not only the tyrant's plea, but the patriot's defense, and the safety of the state. *James Wilson*

The mother of tension. *Anon.*

NECK

A tower of ivory.

Bible: Solomon's Song, VII, 4.

A place to get it in; or what you usually get at a chicken dinner when your mother-in-law is serving. *Jimmy Lyons*

Something that looks like a pickled peach with age. *Anon.*

NEGLIGENCE

SEE CARELESSNESS.

NEGRO

Any person who has in his or her veins any Negro blood whatever.

Arkansas State Constitution, Acts, 1911.

(Those who) are taught really to despise themselves from the moment their eyes open on the world. *James Baldwin*

(One) superior to the white race.

Henry Ward Beecher

A caricature of the white man.

Otto von Bismarck

A merry-hearted, grinning, dancing, singing, affectionate kind of creature, with a great deal of melody and amenability in his composition.

Thomas Carlyle

They're human beings, just like anybody else.

Kenneth Cass

Someone who lives in dread of being pushed into a bottomless pit where he ceases to matter.

Price Cobbs

A life of tragedy, of injustice, of oppression. The law has made him equal, but man has not.

Clarence S. Darrow

The Problem of the twentieth century.

W. E. B. Du Bois

The greatest amount of happiness out of the smallest capital. *Ralph Waldo Emerson*

Every person having one-eighth or more of African or Negro blood.

Florida State Constitution, 1927.

The sons of Africa. *Benjamin Franklin*

Meaning black—hard, strong, fierce Black—in other tongues; meaning only the property, the slaves, the wards, the clowns in this sad, twisted, frightened tongue. *Vincent Harding*

The fact of namelessness. *Vincent Harding*

A man whom God made and loves.

Kyle Haselden

An exile in his own land.

Martin Luther King 2

All persons with any appreciable mixture of Negro blood.

Lee vs. New Orleans Great Northern R. Co.

(One who) is compelled to loiter around the edges of industry. *Kelley Miller*

A social and conventional, not a biological concept. *Gunnar Myrdal*

The "Negro race" is defined in America by the white people... in terms of parentage. Everybody having a *known* trace of Negro blood in his veins... is classified as a Negro.

Gunnar Myrdal

He is of all races the most gentle and kind. The man, the most submissive; the woman, the most affectionate. *Arthur R. Ropes*

Their mental processes are different.

John C. Stennis

Black is not needing a psychiatrist to tell you what is wrong. *Anon.*

A man who has lost his identity. *Anon.*

SEE ALSO EMANCIPATION, EQUALITY, SLAVERY.

NEIGHBOR

Every neighbor is a teacher. *Arabian Proverb*

A good neighbor is a fellow who smiles at you over the back fense but doesn't climb over it.

Arthur Baer

A person who can get to your house in less than one minute and take two hours to go back home.

O. A. Battista

One whom we are commanded to love as ourselves, and who does all he knows to make us disobedient. *Ambrose Bierce*

(He is) not a man; he is an environment... the barking of a dog... the noise of a pianola... a dispute about a party wall.

Gilbert Keith Chesterton

Every man's neighbor is his looking-glass.

English Proverb

The man who knows more about you than you know about yourself. *Elbert Hubbard*

Just the man who is next to you at the moment, the man with whom any business has brought you into contact. *George Macdonald*

Someone who cuts your mornings into mincemeat for the smallest talk. *Anon.*

NEIGHBORHOOD

A residential area that is changing for the worse.

John Ciardi

Not a geographic term. It is a moral concept. It means our collective responsibility for the preservation of man's dignity and integrity.

Joachim Prinz

NEPOTISM

Appointing your grandmother to office for the good of the party. *Ambrose Bierce*

A $10 word meaning to stow your relatives in a soft berth. *Ilka Chase*

Perverting public office into family property.

Adapted from Thomas Jefferson

When your opponent puts a relative on the payroll.

Samuel Stewart

Putting on heirs. *Anon.*

NETHERLANDS

SEE HOLLAND.

NEUROSIS

A metaphysical problem. *Rudolf Allers*

A human privilege. *Sigmund Freud*

Without exception disturbances of the sexual function. *Sigmund Freud*

The result of a conflict between the ego and the id; the person is at war with himself.

Sigmund Freud

An inner cleavage—the state of being at war with oneself.   *Carl G. Jung*

Work and love . . . Without them there is neurosis.

Theodore Reik

SEE ALSO PSYCHIATRIST.

NEUROTIC

A man who has been forced to adjust to the way we all live. A psychotic is a man who has failed to adjust to the way a psychiatrist lives. A psychiatrist is a man who has been forced to adjust to his own adjustment.   *John Ciardi*

To be always unhappy, engrossed with oneself, ungrateful and malignant, and never quite in touch with reality.   *Cyril Connolly*

The true believer.   *Sigmund Freud*

A self-taut person.   *Shelby Friedman*

Simply persons whose attempted solutions of their difficulties takes a clinical form resulting in what are called symptoms.   *Ernest Jones*

One who doesn't know what he wants and won't be satisfied until he gets it.   *Leon Mortimer*

Everything great in the world comes from neurotics. They alone have founded our religions and composed our masterpieces.   *Marcel Proust*

A saint minus his saintliness.

Alexander Yelchaninov

A person who, when you ask him how he is, tells you.   *Anon.*

One who knows he is upset, but it makes him nervous.   *Anon.*

A person of the world; the trouble is in discovering which world.   *Anon.*

One who usually prefers a psychiatrist's couch to a double bed.   *Anon.*

A person in a clash by himself.   *Anon.*

SEE ALSO PSYCHIATRIST, PSYCHIATRY, PSYCHOANALYSIS.

NEUTRALITY

Without engaging . . . assent to one side or the other.   *Joseph Addison*

An evidence of weakness.   *Louis Kossuth*

Impartial in thought as well as action.

Woodrow Wilson

Not indifference . . . not self-interest. The basis . . . is sympathy for mankind. It is fairness, it is good will . . . it is impartiality of spirit and of judgment.   *Woodrow Wilson*

Not taking sides in public.   *Anon.*

NEW ENGLAND

A place of as serious piety as any I can hear of under Heaven.   *Richard Baxter*

Any well-established village in New England . . . could afford a town drunkard, a town atheist, and a few democrats.

Denis Brogan

A finished place . . . the first permanent civilization in America.   *Bernard De Voto*

Originally a plantation of religion, not a plantation of trade.   *John Higginson*

A people of God, settled in those areas which were once the Devil's territories.

Cotton Mather

NEWS

If a man bites a dog, that is news.   *John Bogart*

An emergency.   *Turner Catledge*

News is almost by definition bad news.

Marquis W. Childs

When a dog bites a man that is not news, but when a man bites a dog that is news.

Charles A. Dana

That which comes from the North, East, West and South, and if it comes from only one point of the compass, then it is a class publication and not news.   *Benjamin Disraeli*

History shot on the wing. The huntsmen from the Fourth Estate seek to bag only the peacock or the eagle of the swifting day.   *Gene Fowler*

The first rough draft of history. *Philip Graham*

The manna of a day. *Matthew Green*

Anything that makes a woman say: "For heaven's sake!" *Edward Howe*

The cultivation of disquietude for disquietude's sake. *Aldous Huxley*

Whatever a good editor chooses to print.

Arthur McEwen

If it's far away, it's news, but if it's close to home, it's sociology. *James Reston*

When shallow noodles publish shallow views.

John G. Saxe

The hodge-podge of a day. *Bonnell Thornton*

Women, wampum and wrongdoing.

Stanley Walker

Anything that concerns people, and interests them. *George Washburn*

The atmosphere of events. *Woodrow Wilson*

The disasters of the day. *Anon.*

The same thing happening every day to different people. *Anon.*

Nobody's business in print. *Anon.*

SEE ALSO FREE PRESS, JOURNALISM, PRESS (THE).

NEWSPAPERS

A circulating library with high blood pressure.

Arthur Baer

The schoolmasters of the common people.

Henry Ward Beecher

One form of continuous fiction. *Aneurin Bevan*

A medium that presents facts, not ideas; events, not the happenings which led to the events.

Eugene E. Brussell

Satan's Invisible World Displayed.

Thomas Carlyle

A weapon in somebody's hands.

Claud Cockburn

(An) ever bubbling spring of endless lies.

William Cowper

Vehicles of much amusement: but this does not outweigh the evil they do to society.

George Crabbe

The world's mirrors. *James Ellis*

Does its best to make every square acre of land and sea give an account of itself at your breakfast table. *Ralph Waldo Emerson*

A sponge or invention for oblivion.

Ralph Waldo Emerson

Consists of just the same number of words, whether there be any news in it or not.

Henry Fielding

A permanent crime wave. *Max Gralnick*

A figment factory. *Elbert Hubbard*

The best instrument for enlightening the mind of man, and improving him as a rational, moral and social being. *Thomas Jefferson*

(They) always excite curiosity. No one ever lays one down without a feeling of disappointment.

Charles Lamb

A servile instrument of wealthy men

Harold J. Laski

A daily spiritual death. *Ferdinand Lassalle*

A device for amusing one half of the world with the other half's troubles. *Leonard L. Levinson*

A device for making the ignorant more ignorant and the crazy crazier. *Henry Louis Mencken*

A good newspaper . . . is a nation talking to itself.

Arthur Miller

(A device) more to be feared than a thousand bayonets. *Napoleon I*

One of the chief enemies of the Kingdom of God.

*Northwest Conference of the
Methodist Episcopal Church, 1933.*

A forum for the consideration of all public questions of public importance, and, to that end, to invite intelligent discussion from all shades of opinion. *Adolph S. Ochs*

We live under a government of men and morning newspapers. *Wendell Phillips*

A chartered libertine. *William Pitt*

The cemeteries of ideas. *Pierre J. Proudhon*

The second hand in the clock of history . . . it is not only made of baser metal than those which point to the minute and the hour, but it seldom goes right.   *Arthur Schopenhauer*

Something of a monopoly, and its first duty is to shun the temptations of monopoly.
                                                Charles P. Scott

(A device) unable . . . to discriminate between a bicycle accident and the collapse of civilization.
                                            George Bernard Shaw

(A vehicle) to print the news, and raise hell.
                                                Wilbur F. Storey

I have been reading the morning paper. I do it every morning—well knowing that I shall find in it the usual depravations and basenesses . . . that make up civilization, and cause me to put in the rest of the day pleading for the damnation of the human race.   *Mark Twain*

Ought to be the register of the times, and faithful recorder of every species of intelligence . . . like a well-covered table, it should contain something suited to every palate.   *John Walker*

A private enterprise, owing nothing to the public, which grants it no franchise. It is therefore affected with no public interest. It is emphatically the property of its owner, who is selling a manufactured product at his own risk.
                                    Wall Street Journal, Jan. 20, 1925.

It is always the unreadable that occurs.
                                                    Oscar Wilde

In the old days men had the rack. Now they have the press.   *Oscar Wilde*

(Something to) comfort the afflicted, and afflict the comfortable.   *John Winkler*

To diffuse among people correct information on all interesting subjects, to inculcate just principles in religion, morals and politics, and to cultivate a taste for sound literature.   *Anon.*

Half ads and the other half lies between the ads.
                                                        Anon.

A medium excellent in the knowledge of life's meanest things.   *Anon.*

Where immorality runs into many editions.
                                                        Anon.

Where the mass of men get their opinions and polysyllables.   *Anon.*

SEE ALSO FREE PRESS, JOURNALISM, JOURNALIST, PRESS (THE).

NEWTON, ISAAC (1642-1727)

Newton dived into nature's hidden springs and laid bare the principles of things and gave us worlds unknown before.
                                    Adapted from Charles Churchill

Patient of contradiction as a child,
Affable, human, diffident, and mild,
Such was Sir Isaac.   *William Cowper*

I seem to have been only like a boy playing on the seashore, and diverting myself in now and then finding a smoother pebble or a prettier shell than ordinary, whilst the great ocean of truth lay all undiscovered before me.   *Isaac Newton*

A mind forever voyaging through strange seas of thought alone.
                                    Adapted from William Wordsworth

NEW YORK CITY

This giant asparagus bed of alabaster and rose and green skyscrapers.   *Cecil Beaton*

The Jerusalem of journalism.   *Jim Bishop*

A detective story.   *Agatha Christie*

The shrine to which the lords of capitalism commute in cattle cars.   *John Ciardi*

A city without baths or plumbing, lighted by gas and scavenged by pigs.   *Charles Dickens*

A sucked orange.   *Ralph Waldo Emerson*

An island in the Atlantic.
                                                    Waldo Frank

Stream of the living world.   *Richard W. Gilder*

A town that's shut off from the world by the ocean on one side and New Jersey on the other.
                                                        O. Henry

Little old Noisyville-on-the-Subway.
                                                        O. Henry

A city where everyone mutinies but no one deserts.   *Harry Hershfield*

A beautiful catastrophe.   *Charles E. Jeanneret*

A cloacina of all the depravities of human nature.
                                                Thomas Jefferson

This capital city of high-tension activity.

Stanley Levey

Truly the City of Man. It is humanity in microcosm, reflecting the infinite variety as well as the infinite capacity for good or evil of the human race.   *Diosdado Macapagal*

The nation's thyroid gland.   *Christopher Morley*

Delirium.   *Byron R. Newton*

A place where everyone will stop watching a championship fight to look at an usher giving a drunk the bum's rush.   *Damon Runyon*

A nightmare in stone.   *Edgar Saltus*

A separate nation in spirit.   *Eric Sevareid*

(A city composed of) people who get acquainted with their neighbors by meeting them in Miami.

Marjorie Steele

A city of 7,000,000 so decadent that when I leave it I never dare look back lest I turn into salt and the conductor throw me over his left shoulder for good luck.   *Franklin Sullivan*

The fullest expression of our modern age.

Leon Trotsky

A Technicolor bazaar.   *Kenneth Tynan*

A little strip of an island with a row of well-fed folks up and down the middle, and a lot of hungry folks on each side.   *Harry L. Wilson*

Prison towers and modern posters for soap and whiskey.   *Frank Lloyd Wright*

The great stone desert.   *Israel Zangwill*

A place where people never have a moment to themselves.   *Anon.*

A place where the inhabitants consider anyone outside of the city mere hicks.   *Anon.*

The city of Brotherly Shove.   *Anon.*

SEE ALSO CITY.

NIAGARA FALLS

The miracle that sense appalls.   *Morris Bishop*

The start of a tedious soap-opera.   *Irwin Smith*

Every American bride is taken there, and the sight of the stupendous waterfall must be one of the earliest if not the keenest disappointments in American married life.   *Oscar Wilde*

Simply a vast unnecessary amount of water going the wrong way and then falling over unnecessary rocks.   *Oscar Wilde*

SEE ALSO BRIDE, HONEYMOON.

NICKNAME

The heaviest stone that the Devil can throw at a man.   *William Hazlitt*

Of all eloquence a nickname is the most concise; of all arguments is the most unanswerable.

William Hazlitt

A terse, pointed, shorthand mode of reasoning, condensing a volume of meaning into an epithet.

William Mathews

The propensity to approach a meaning not directly and squarely, but by circuitous styles of expression.   *Walt Whitman*

SEE ALSO NAME.

NIETZSCHE, FRIEDRICH W. (1844-1900)

Here is this one great man that Germany has, and nobody values him in Germany, hardly anybody knows him.   *Georg Brandes*

I am the Anti-Donkey *par excellence,* a monster in the history of the world. I am... the Antichrist.

Friedrich W. Nietzsche

The greatest European event since Goethe.

A. R. Orage

An agile but unintelligent and abnormal German, possessed of mania of grandeur.   *Leo Tolstoy*

NIGHT

A stealthy evil raven.   *Thomas Bailey Aldrich*

Night, when deep sleep falleth on men.

Bible: Job, IV, 13.

When no man can work.   *Bible: John, IX, 4.*

Night is the sabbath of mankind,
To rest the body and the mind.   *Samuel Butler 1*

When the shadow of death is darkest, when despondency is strongest, and when hope is weakest.   *Charles Dickens*

The mother of thoughts.   *John Florio*

The half of life, and the better half.

Johann W. Goethe

Love's mart of kisses.   *Marlowe and Chapman*

The time for rest.   *James Montgomery*

Vast sin-concealing chaos.

William Shakespeare

Black stage for tragedies and murders.

William Shakespeare

Millions of suns, and sleep and restoring
darkness.   *Walt Whitman*

NIGHT CLUB

A place where the tables are reserved and the
guests aren't.   *Frederick Casper*

A place where people with nothing to remember
go to forget.   *Grove Patterson*

A saloon with an orchestra.

Matthew Weinstock

An ash tray with music.   *Anon.*

An unrestaurant.   *Anon.*

NIHILISM

The annihilation of everything as it now exists.

Mikhail A. Bakunin

When you have freed your mind from the fear of
God, and that childish respect for the fiction of
right.   *Mikhail A. Bakunin*

A cult which denies the fundamental discrimination between good and bad, between higher and
lower...the debasement of justice and the disregard of law.   *Lewis Mumford*

SEE ALSO ANARCHY.

NIHILIST

A man who does not bow down before any
authority; who does not take any principle on
faith, whatever reverence that principle may be
enshrined in.   *Ivan S. Turgenev*

That strange martyr who has no faith, who goes to
the stake without any enthusiasm, and dies for
what he does not believe in, is a purely literary
product. He was invented by Turgenev, and completed by Dostoyevsky.   *Oscar Wilde*

NIXON, RICHARD MILHOUS (1913-)

He was a leader in scholastic and student activities—a self-starter—very popular. I think of
Dick as a "fighting Quaker."   *O. C. Albertson*

A very high type of American who would make a
good, positive President.   *James Berryman*

A master at politics whose skill encompasses a
knowledge of how the system works, an appreciation of the importance of personal contacts, an
ability to keep factions together, and the capacity
to win nominations and exert leadership.

Herbert Brownell 2

A naive, inept, maladjusted Throttlebottom.

Emanuel Celler

My children have caught him lovingly in a nickname...To them, he is always "Nixie," the kind
and the good...His somewhat martial Quakerism
sometimes amused and always heartened me.

Whittaker Chambers

Unquestionably...the leader of the conservative
forces.   *Lucius D. Clay*

The embodiment of dedicated tenacity. His voice
was low and vibrant except when he laced into the
opposition...He never smoked, ate sparingly...and seldom drank coffee or liquor.

William T. Costello

As a salesman with a high coefficient of bellig-
erency, he has been a man of many issues...His
sole purpose and preoccupation has been politics...he has made himself a worldwide symbol
of conflict.   *William T. Costello*

To some he is a hatchet man pure and simple...to
others, a "cardboard man," often with two sides
but without depth as a person.

William T. Costello

His inner self remains an enigma.

William T. Costello

A good soldier.

Dwight David Eisenhower

There is no man in the history of America who
has had such careful preparation as has...Nixon
for carrying out the duties of the Presidency.

Dwight David Eisenhower

He knows when to keep quiet...When he did
speak, he spoke on things he knew about...he
grew in status in the eyes of all the administration.
And his judgment became more and more respected.   *James Hagerty*

The conviction of Alger Hiss was due to your patience and persistence alone.

J. Edgar Hoover

A man in his own right. No father, mother, brother or sister finances his campaigns or runs around the country for him; no million-dollar trust fund is ready for him if he gets licked.

Konrad Kellen

He's a conservative... and if he became President, we could expect Republican policy would switch to the right.   *John Fitzgerald Kennedy*

A Pepsodent smile, a ready quip... an actor's perfection with lines.   *William F. Knowland*

He belongs to no party cliques, and his voting record defies classification.   *Victor Lasky*

A ruthless partisan.   *Walter Lippmann*

A fatalist, to the point of believing that whether he becomes president will depend more on "circumstances" than on anything he, his friends or his opponents (do).   *Earl Mazo*

A practical individual, careful to master details and alternatives... he is at his best in a crisis.

Earl Mazo

Basically he is shy and taciturn. He broods and abhors back-slapping and gives the appearance of being a friendless "loner."   *Earl Mazo*

None of us had too much time to play. Dick has had a lot to make him serious.   *Donald Nixon*

I knew he would be successful in whatever he undertook.   *Patricia R. Nixon*

We came from typical everyday American families that have had to work for what they got out of life but always knew there was unlimited opportunity.   *Patricia R. Nixon*

A simple soldier in the Republican ranks.

Richard Milhous Nixon

I never in my life wanted to be left behind.

Richard Milhous Nixon

I will be an old-fashioned kind of lawyer, a lawyer who can't be bought.   *Richard Milhous Nixon*

My grandmother set the standards for the whole family. Honesty, hard work, do your best at all times—humanitarian ideals.

Richard Milhous Nixon

I am for a government living within its means— the so-called balanced budget.

Richard Milhous Nixon

I know what it is to be poor.

Richard Milhous Nixon

I'm a pessimist, but if I figure I've got a chance, I'll fight for it.   *Richard Milhous Nixon*

A liberal in foreign policy and a conservative in domestic policy.   *Richard Milhous Nixon*

You don't win campaigns with a diet of dishwater and milktoast.   *Richard Milhous Nixon*

I'm not necessarily a respecter of the status quo in foreign affairs. I am a chance taker... I would take chances for peace—the Quakers have a passion for peace.   *Richard Milhous Nixon*

There is a certain naiveté about him that is as misleading as it is charming... Cynics who make light (of his true personality) must reckon with the fact that it is an enormously attractive personality to millions of the uncynical.   *Cabell Phillips*

He has a fantastic capacity to communicate with people eye to eye, shoulder to shoulder.

Paul S. Smith

A little man in a big hurry.

Robert A. Taft

He is a man of exceptional abilities and solid virtues, but somehow his many parts have always added up to less than a convincing whole.

Time Magazine, Aug. 16, 1968.

An unusual phenomenon in American politics— not because of his amazing rise to pre-eminence, but because in that rise he was always his own man.   *Ralph de Toledano*

A political figure who has consistently neutralized efforts of friend and foe to mold him to a form alien to his own nature.

Ralph de Toledano

The easiest man to beat.

Harry S. Truman

(A) "loser" who came back.

U.S. News and World Report, Nov. 18, 1968.

Since high school Nixon has had an uncommon ability to take advantage of a situation before and after it develops... His success is due to knowing what to do and when to do it, perfect timing in everything.   *Merton G. Wray*

He was one guy who knew where he was going...Dick's plans were concise, concrete and specific. *Lester Wroble*

The All-American Boy Demagogue.

Anon. Democrat

One thing about Mr. Nixon—as far as his temper is concerned—he has a rather short fuse. This may cause him trouble as President. *Anon.*

The jugular orator. *Anon.*

A haze of impressions left by political speeches and fostered by political opponents. *Anon.*

The most conspicuous opponent of communism in Congress. *Anon.*

The village boy who came such a long way in so short a time. *Anon.*

NOBILITY

The true standard of quality...seated in the mind; those who think nobly are noble.

Isaac Bickerstaffe

He is noble who has a priority among free-men, not he who has a sort of wild liberty among slaves. *Edmund Burke*

Real nobility is based on scorn, courage, and profound indifference. *Albert Camus*

Inner superiority to world fortune.

Morris R. Cohen

All nobility in its beginnings was somebody's natural superiority. *Ralph Waldo Emerson*

The possession of land. *Henry George*

An accident of fortune; noble actions are the chief mark. *Carlo Goldoni*

A dignity based on the presumption that we shall do well because our fathers did well.

Joseph Joubert

To be regarded a blameless person, stalwart for the right in word and in deed. *Juvenal*

The noble soul has reverence for itself.

Friedrich W. Nietzsche

Nobility is defined by the demands it makes on us—by obligations, not by rights.

José Ortega y Gasset

A generous mind. *Plato*

Nothing but ancient riches. *John Ray*

True nobility is exempt from fear.

William Shakespeare

SEE ALSO ARISTOCRACY, GREAT MEN, GREATNESS, HERO, MINORITY, SUPERIOR MAN.

NOISE

A stench in the ear. Undomesticated music. The chief product and authenticating sign of civilization. *Ambrose Bierce*

Any undesired sound...sound at the wrong time and the wrong place. *N. W. McLachlan*

The most impertinent of all forms of interruption.

Arthur Schopenhauer

Audible grime.

Anon.

NOMINATE

To designate for the heaviest political assessment.

Ambrose Bierce

The call of the vile. *Elbert Hubbard*

The art of molding figures in plaster.

Elbert Hubbard

NON-CONFORMIST

To be indecent. *American Saying*

Whoso would be a man must be a non-conformist. *Ralph Waldo Emerson*

He who refuses to be satisfied to go along with the continuance of things as they are, and insists upon attempting to find new ways of bettering things.

Josiah W. Gitt

The grouping together of those who agree only in their disagreement in regard to the limitless multitude. *José Ortega y Gasset*

One whom the world hates.

Saint Jerome

Merely a person of conformity in reverse.

Anon.

SEE ALSO ECCENTRICITY, GENIUS.

NONSENSE

Good nonsense is good sense in disguise.

Josh Billings

A kind of exuberant capering round a discovered truth. *Gilbert Keith Chesterton*

The ropy drivel of rheumatic brains.

William Gifford

An assertion of man's spiritual freedom in spite of all the oppression of circumstance.

Aldous Huxley

Often the wisest form of allegory.

Joseph Leftwich

NORTH CAROLINA

A strip of land lying between two states. *Anon.*

A valley of humiliation lying between two mountains of conceit. *Anon.*

NOSE

The extreme outpost of the face.

Ambrose Bierce

The bone and gristle penthouse.

Stewart Robertson

Thou canst tell why one's nose stands i' the middle of one's face?...Why, to keep one's eyes on either side. *William Shakespeare*

NOSTALGIA

A seductive liar. *George W. Ball*

Yesterdaze. *Leonard Bossard*

A love for one's former self. *Jerry Dashkin*

Only a longing for your lost childhood.

Jerry Dashkin

An atavistic longing for a simpler condition, for a childhood of innocence...remembered in all its crystalline purity precisely because it never existed. *Peter Gay*

Something pleasant we feel for places we were uncomfortable in at an earlier age.

Adapted from William Rotsler

That which makes things seem a hundred times more wonderful now than they did when they were taking place. *Walter Slezak*

Old, unhappy, far-off things.

William Wordsworth

The longing to go back to the good old days when you were neither good nor old. *Anon.*

Dreaming of a place you grew up in that you wouldn't live in as an adult. *Anon.*

The realization that things were not as unbearable as they seemed at the time. *Anon.*

SEE ALSO GOLDEN AGE, PAST.

NOTHING

A good thing to say, and always a clever thing to say. *Will Durant*

Imposssible. The mind, let it stretch its conceptions ever so far, can never so much as bring itself to conceive of a state of perfect nothing.

Jonathan Edwards

Something that has density without weight, like a barber's breath. *Elbert Hubbard*

Man's noblest works. *Thomas Moore*

Out of nothing nothing can come, and nothing can become nothing. *Persius*

Nothing is but what is not.

William Shakespeare

The cause of most worries. *Anon.*

A bunghole without a barrel around it. *Anon.*

SEE ALSO HOLE.

NOVEL

The phantasmagorical world. *Matthew Arnold*

A work in which the greatest powers of the mind are displayed, in which the most thorough knowledge of human nature, the happiest delineation of its varieties, the liveliest effusions of wit and humor are conveyed to the world in the best chosen language. *Jane Austen*

A detector of mined experience.

John F. Bardin

False notions of life. *James Beattie*

A species of composition bearing the same relation to literature that the panorama bears to art.

Ambrose Bierce

A short story padded.   *Ambrose Bierce*

Exaggerated pictures, impossible ideals, and specimens of depravity.   *Mary Baker Eddy*

All novels are about certain minorities: the individual is a minority.   *Ralph Ellison*

Every novel is a debtor to Homer.

Ralph Waldo Emerson

The object...is to enlarge experience, not to convey facts.   *David Garnett*

Receipts to make a whore.   *Matthew Green*

The highest example of subtle interrelatedness that man has discovered.   *D. H. Lawrence*

The representation of human beings at their follies and villainies.   *Henry Louis Mencken*

A mirror carried along a main road.   *Stendhal*

Novels are sweets. All people with healthy literary appetites love them.

William Makepeace Thackeray

American dry goods.   *Oscar Wilde*

The only relaxation of the intellectually unemployed.   *Oscar Wilde*

SEE ALSO FICTION, LITERATURE.

NOVELISTS

The novelist is concerned with types and with the eminent case among the types, and the great man is...only the most eminent case of the average type, and is...the type that the novelist can do the most with.   *Richard P. Blackmur*

Children talking to children—in the dark.

Bernard De Voto

The historian of the present. The historian is the novelist of the past.   *Georges Duhamel*

The object of the novelist is to keep the reader entirely oblivious of the fact that the author exists—even of the fact that he is reading a book.

Ford Maddox Ford

The only writer who can make a name without a style.   *Robert Frost*

In the old days, a spare-time genius. Nowadays, a man who can write 2,000 words a day on the same subject.   *Leonard L. Levinson*

The cardinal rule is to treat one's characters as if they were chessmen, and not try to win the game by altering the rules—for example, by moving the knight as if he were a pawn.

Georg C. Lichtenberg

A sort of itinerant glazier, transporting a mirror along the highway of the world to reflect impartially its sunsets and mud puddles.

Donald Malcolm

The function of the novelist...is to comment upon life as he sees it.   *Frank Norris*

The historian of conscience.   *Frederic Raphael*

Generally great liars.   *Saint John the Baptist*

The business of the novelist is not to relate great events, but to make small ones interesting.

Arthur Schopenhauer

SEE ALSO FICTION, LITERATURE, WRITERS.

NOVELTY

Nothing...except what has been forgotten.

Mademoiselle Bertini

The thing that hath been, it is that which shall be, and that which is done is that which shall be done: and there is no new thing under the sun.

Bible: Ecclesiastes, I, 9.

An essential attribute of the beautiful.

Benjamin Disraeli

Things that are curious and unfamiliar.

Adapted from Robert Herrick

The one thing that the public dislike.

Oscar Wilde

The one thing that human nature craves.   *Anon.*

SEE ALSO CUSTOM, FASHION.

NOVEMBER

The gloomy month...when the people of England hang and drown themselves.   *Joseph Addison*

The eleventh twelfth of a weariness.

Ambrose Bierce

NUDIST COLONY

A place where no one can say they hope to see more of you. *James Ball*

A place for the woman who has everything.
James Ball

A place where people can be themselves—in the altogether. *Eugene E. Brussell*

A place which makes a religion of the body.
Jerry Dashkin

A group of sunbathers who, in their search for a perfect tan, are determined to leave no stern untoned. *Charles Dwelley*

A place where costumes are forbidden—even on Halloween. *Anon.*

NUDITY

A state in which a bit of the mystery goes.
James Ball

The work of God. *William Blake*

When beauty is clothed best. *Phineas Fletcher*

The chaste state. *Max Gralnick*

In a state of nature. *Latin Proverb*

Innocence. *Emanuel Swedenborg*

NUMBER

The obvious distinction between the beast and man. Thanks to number, the cry becomes song, noise acquires rhythm, spring is changed to dance, force becomes dynamic, and outlines figures. *Joseph de Maistre*

O

OATH

In law, a solemn appeal to the deity, made binding upon the conscience by a penalty for perjury.

Ambrose Bierce

Words, and words but wind.   *Samuel Butler 1*

Playthings or convenient tools.

William Cowper

Crutches, upon which lies go.

Adapted from Thomas Dekker

The fossils of piety.   *George Santayana*

SEE ALSO TREATY.

OBEDIENCE

The sensible alternative for those who cannot lead.   *Eugene E. Brussell*

Not only the first law of God, but also the first tenet of a revolutionary party and of fervent nationalism.   *Eric Hoffer*

The key to every door.   *George Macdonald*

Not servitude of man to man, but submission to the will of God, who governs through the medium of men.   *Pope Leo XIII*

Makes slaves of men, and of the human frame a mechanized automation.

Adapted from Percy Bysshe Shelley

The primary and irremissible motive and the foundation of all morality.   *Friedrich J. Stahl*

The courtesy due to kings.

Alfred Lord Tennyson

SEE ALSO AUTHORITY.

OBESITY

The weight that eventually compells you to bow to time.   *James Ball*

A disease brought on by boredom and disappointment.   *Cyril Connolly*

A lot of fat that does not fit.   *Herbert G. Wells*

A tale of horror told by the bathroom scale.

Anon.

The great equalizer. The more bodily weight carried around the shorter the time left to carry it.

Anon.

The condition of not only keeping your figure, but doubling it.   *Anon.*

SEE ALSO EATING, GOURMET.

OBITUARY

SEE DEATH.

OBLIGATION

SEE DUTY.

OBLIVION

Our name shall be forgotten in time, and no man shall have our works in remembrance, and our life shall pass away as the trace of a cloud, and shall be dispersed as a mist.

Apocrypha: Wisdom of Solomon, II, 4.

Fame's eternal dumping ground. Cold storage for high hopes. *Ambrose Bierce*

The dark page whereon memory writes her light-beam characters; were it all light, nothing could be read there, any more than if it were all darkness. *Thomas Carlyle*

The only certainty. *Horace Greeley*

A place where the human race and politicians are as one. *Elbert Hubbard*

The hell of a good idea. *Leonard L. Levinson*

Cancell'd from Heav'n and sacred memory.

John Milton

The world forgetting, by the world forgot.

Alexander Pope

The flower that grows best on graves.

George Sand

The swallowing gulf. *William Shakespeare*

Out of the world's way, out of the light, out of the ages of worldly weather, forgotten by all men altogether.

Adapted from Algernon Charles Swinburne

The skull of Pharaoh staring at the sky. *Anon.*

SEE ALSO DEATH, GRAVE.

OBSCENITY

Violence concerned with sex. *John D. Black*

I can't define it, but I know it when I see it.
William J. Brennan 2

Material which deals with sex in a manner appealing to prurient interest. *William J. Brennan 2*

Pornography is virulent propaganda against women. *Susan Brownmiller*

A category of offenses . . . of a polluting character.
John Campbell

Material that seeks to excite the libido without attempting to reach the higher centers of the mind. *Jon Carroll*

A book . . . when it is offensive to decency or chastity, which is immodest, which is indelicate, impure, causing lewd thoughts of an immoral tendency. *Justice Clark*

The test . . . is . . . whether the tendency of the matter . . . is to deprave and corrupt those whose minds are open to such immoral influences, and into whose hands a publication of this sort may fall. *Alexander J. Cockburn*

(Catering) to the lowest and most sensual part of human nature. *Judge Crane*

Porn is men's control of women.

Andrea Dworkin

It smacks . . . of fantasy and unreality, of sexual perversion and sickness and represents, according to one thoughtful scholar, "a debauchery of the sexual faculty." *Stanley Field*

Depicting dirt for dirt's sake . . . the vile rather than the coarse, the blow to sense. *Stanley Ford*

It must . . . be such as actually to arouse or calculated to arouse in the viewer or reader . . . venereal pleasure. *Harold C. Gardiner*

The present critical point in the compromise between candor and shame at which the community may have arrived here and now.

Learned Hand

Not . . . words, or matters . . . but . . . base minds, filthy conceits, or lewd intents.

John Harington

Immodest; not agreeable to chastity of the mind; causing lewd ideas. *Samuel Johnson*

Pornography . . . a predominantly male fantasy involving the sadistic humiliation of women.

Irving Kristol

(Recognizable) by the insult it offers to sex and the human spirit. *D. H. Lawrence*

Dirt for dirt's sake. *Matthew Levy*

(Something) unfit for general circulation.

Morgan J. O'Brien

Material which deals with sex in a manner appealing to prurient interest. *Edmund L. Palmieri*

Whatever happens to shock some elderly and ignorant magistrate. *Bertrand A. Russell*

Not a quality inherent in a book or picture, but solely and exclusively a contribution of the reading mind, and hence cannot be defined in terms of the qualities of a book or picture.

Theodore Schroeder

The shame-psychology of the accusing persons.

Theodore Schroeder

That form of immorality which has relation to sexual impurity. *George Shiras*

Offensive to chastity, delicacy, or decency ... offensive to morals.

U.S. Congressional Act, 1873.

Tending to stir the sex impulses or to lead to sexually impure and lustful thoughts.

John M. Woolsey

That which tends to corrupt or debase. *Anon.*

The judgment of material according to the average person's application of contemporary community standards. *Anon.*

Poison of the mind made public. *Anon.*

Actions against public decency tending to corrupt the public morals. *Anon.*

SEE ALSO VULGARITY.

OBSCURITY (LACK OF CLARITY)

The principal ingredient of the sublime.

Benjamin Disraeli

The realm of error. *Luc de Vauvenargues*

OBSCURITY (UNKNOWN)

To be found in the register of God, not in the record of man. *Thomas Browne*

The greatest praise. *Charles Churchill*

The pleasantest condition of life.

Abraham Cowley

A secluded journey along the pathway of a life unnoticed. *Horace*

The life that is best worth living. *Mark Twain*

OBSOLESCENCE

A factor which says that the new thing I bring you is worth more than the unused value of the old thing. *Charles F. Kettering*

OBSTINACY

Idolatry. *Bible: Samuel, XV, 23.*

Stiff in opinions. *John Dryden*

To stick to your favorite lie or truth.

Elbert Hubbard

Error in armor. *Leonard L. Levinson*

The surest trial of folly and self-conceit.

Michael de Montaigne

The result of the will forcing itself into the place of the intellect. *Arthur Schopenhauer*

The name of perseverance in a good cause, and of obstinacy in a bad one. *Laurence Sterne*

OBVIOUS

That which is never seen until someone expresses it. *Kahlil Gibran*

The course of every intellectual...ends in the obvious, from which the non-intellectuals have never stirred. *Aldous Huxley*

Usually what is most thoroughly forgotten and most rarely done. *Christian Morgenstern*

The most difficult question to answer. *Anon.*

OCEAN

SEE SEA.

OLD AGE

One of the most difficult chapters in the great art of living. *Henry F. Amiel*

The pegs fall out, the tone is gone, and the harmony becomes dissonance. *Aristophanes*

The time to make pronouncements.

James T. Baker

Life's parody. *Simone de Beauvoir*

When all girls look alike to you. *Mac Benoff*

Wisdom; and in the length of days understanding.

Bible: Job, XII, 12.

That period...in which we compound for the vices that we still cherish by reviling those that we have no longer the enterprise to commit.

Ambrose Bierce

A glorious thing when one has not unlearned what it means to begin.   *Martin Buber*

Good thoughts his only friends,
   His wealth a well-spent age,
The earth his sober inn
   And quiet pilgrimage.   *Thomas Campion*

To be left alone at a banquet—the lights dead and the flowers faded.
                Adapted from Gilbert Keith Chesterton

A second child by nature.   *Charles Churchill*

Twice a child.   *Cratinus*

Old men are only walking hospitals.
                                    Wentworth Dillon

To take in sail.   *Ralph Waldo Emerson*

A good advertisement.   *Ralph Waldo Emerson*

To be out of war, out of debt, out of the drouth . . . out of the dentist's hands.
                            Ralph Waldo Emerson

Voice and shadow.   *Euripides*

An emotion which comes over us at almost any age.   *Edward M. Forster*

When a man outlives his body.   *Sigmund Freud*

The happiest time in a man's life. The worst of it is, there's so little of it.   *William S. Gilbert*

Aches.   *John Harington*

In the prime of senility.   *Joel Chandler Harris*

A good and pleasant time. It is true you are shouldered off the stage, but then you are given such a comfortable front stall as spectator, and, if you have really played your part, you are more content to sit down and watch.
                                    Jane E. Harrison

No more than a bad habit which a busy man has no time to form.   *Emile Herzog*

The time to hear the kind voice of friends and to say to one's self: "The work is done."
                            Oliver Wendell Holmes 2

A bloodless race that sends a feeble voice.
                                        Homer

To steal yourself from life by slow decays.
                                        Homer

A natural disease.   *Immanuel of Rome*

Whenever a man's friends begin to compliment him about looking young.   *Washington Irving*

Beyond all grace of youth.   *Robinson Jeffers*

To wait and remember.   *Robinson Jeffers*

A mere monument of the times which are past.
                                    Thomas Jefferson

Body decay.   *Thomas Jefferson*

Protracted woe.   *Samuel Johnson*

(When) shame and grief are of short duration.
                                    Samuel Johnson

(When) the possibilities of life get smaller and smaller.   *Franz Kafka*

(A time of) inveterate dislike of interruption.
                                    Charles Lamb

A tyrant who forbids, upon pain of death, all the pleasures of youth.   *La Rochefoucauld*

When our vices quit us.   *La Rochefoucauld*

Near the end.   *James Russell Lowell*

A man is old when he can pass an apple orchard and not remember the stomach-ache.
                            James Russell Lowell

The time when a man is always thinking that in a week or two he will feel as good as ever.
                                    Don Marquis

It liberates you from envy, hatred, and malice.
                        William Somerset Maugham

An infectious chronic disease, characterized by the degeneration or enfeebling of the noble elements and by the excessive activity of the phagocytes.   *Elié Metchnikoff*

Senescence begins
And middle age ends
The day your descendants
Outnumber your friends.   *Ogden Nash*

A dreary solitude.   *Plato*

A great sense of calm and freedom. When the passions have relaxed their hold you have escaped, not from one master, but from many.   *Plato*

A bed full of bones.   *John Ray*

The end of hope.   *Jean Paul Richter*

When it's not so hard to avoid temptation as it is to find it.   *Cosmo Sardo*

Like the end of the mask-ball, when the masks are dropped.   *Arthur Schopenhauer*

The downward slope.   *Seneca*

An incurable disease.   *Seneca*

Sans teeth, sans eyes, sans taste, sans everything.
                                        William Shakespeare

(When) it is not the intelligence that deteriorates but the character.   *C. P. Snow*

The most unexpected of all things that happen to a man.   *Leon Tolstoy*

Nobody grows old by merely living a number of years. People grow old by deserting their ideals.
                                            Samuel Ullman

The road's last turn.   *Henry Van Dyke*

Nearing our journey's end, where time and eternity meet and blend.   *Rollin J. Wells*

The estuary that enlarges and spreads itself grandly as it pours in the Great Sea.
                                            Walt Whitman

That period in a man's life when he'd rather not have a good time than have to get over it.
                                            Oscar Wilde

A bad sickness.   *Joseph Zarfati*

You have reached old age when you no longer care where your wife goes, providing you don't have to go along.   *Anon.*

The time when men pay more attention to their food than to waitresses.   *Anon.*

When your dreams about sex are reruns.   *Anon.*

When you feel like the morning after the night before—and you haven't even been anywhere.
                                                Anon.

When one begins to exchange emotions for symptoms.   *Anon.*

SEE ALSO AGE, LONGEVITY, OLD-TIMER, RETIREMENT, SIXTY.

OLD MAID

A woman who has been engaged once too seldom.
                                        Cynic's Cyclopaedia

A lady of uncertain age and uneasy virtue.
                                            Elbert Hubbard

An unposted letter.   *Hungarian Proverb*

A woman who knows all the answers but has never been asked the question.   *Earlene White*

Between the age of consent and collapse.   *Anon.*

A bachelor's wife.   *Anon.*

A debutante who overdid it.   *Anon.*

Slipping beauty.   *Anon.*

OLD-TIMER

One who can remember when a juvenile delinquent was a child who owed eight cents on an overdue library book.   *Leonard L. Levinson*

One who can recall when a bureau was a piece of furniture.   *Carey MacWilliams*

A fellow who remembers when, if a woman had to be carried out of a place, she had either fainted or died.   *Abraham Martin*

One who can recall when a man was not labeled a reactionary when he had a good word for free enterprise.   *Anon.*

One who remembers when the most shocking novels contained asterisks.   *Anon.*

SEE ALSO OLD AGE, SIXTY.

OMEN

A sign that something will happen if nothing happens.   *Ambrose Bierce*

Prophesying with accents terrible.
                                        William Shakespeare

Invisible handwriting on the wall.   *Anon.*

OPERA

Its only design is to gratify the senses, and keep up an indolent attention in the audience.
                                            Joseph Addison

Like a husband with a foreign title: expensive to support, hard to understand, and therefore a supreme social challenge.   *Cleveland Amory*

A play representing life in another world whose inhabitants have no speech but song, no motions but gestures, and no postures but attitudes.
                                            Ambrose Bierce

A magic scene contrived to please the eyes and the ears at the expense of the understanding.

Lord Chesterfield

A concert in fancy dress. *Paul Claudel*

A form of entertainment where there is always too much singing. *Claude Debussy*

When a guy gets stabbed in the back and instead of bleeding, he sings. *Edward Gardner*

One of the most magnificent and expenseful diversions the wit of man can invent.

John Evelyn

Theatrical music. *Christoph W. von Gluck*

(Something) noble and elevated, neither mingling, torturing nor destroying the life and sense of the words, but rather enforcing their energy and spirit. *Angelo Grillo*

A rendezvous for the bored. *Elbert Hubbard*

A melodic curve which will...reveal immediately a human being in one definite phase of his existence. *Leos Janacek*

An exotic and irrational entertainment.

Samuel Johnson

Distracting torment. *Charles Lamb*

A disease which breaks out in society every winter and can be cured only by the inner satisfaction of a seat in a box and the outer application of diamonds on the chest. *Jimmy Lyons*

The opera...is to music what a bawdy house is to a cathedral. *Henry Louis Mencken*

A fatuity laden with music, with dances, with machinery and scenery...but fatuous nontheless.

Sieur de Saint-Evremond

A bizarre mixture of poetry and music.

Sieur de Saint-Evremond

A musical scenery, a musical atmosphere in which the characters move and talk. *Erik Satie*

The not-true. *Peter I. Tschaikovsky*

Nothing but a public gathering place where we assemble on certain days without precisely knowing why. *Voltaire*

Music set to melodrama. *Anon.*

SEE ALSO MUSIC, WAGNER.

OPINION

The mistress of fools. *William G. Benham*

Circumstances are the creators of most opinions.

Albert V. Dicey

That which affects the whole character and fortune of the individual.

Adapted from Ralph Waldo Emerson

The foundation of all temporal happiness.

Owen Falltham

Flexible prejudices. *Gerald Horton*

That great lady which rules the world.

James Howell

(That which) gives the mind a great deal of flexibility, and strengthens it in its preferences.

Joseph Joubert

Sounding the words of another's talk.

Adapted from David Lloyd

The world's master always. *Gervase Markham*

In good men...knowledge in the making.

John Milton

Truth filtered through the moods, the blood, the disposition of the spectator. *Wendell Phillips*

Between knowledge of what really exists and ignorance of what does not exist lies the domain of opinion. It is more obscure than knowledge, but clearer than ignorance. *Plato*

Something wherein I go about to give reasons why all the world should think as I think.

John Selden

Nothing but the result of chance and temperament. *Joseph H. Shorthouse*

Opinion is ultimately determined by the feelings, and not by the intellect. *Herbert Spencer*

That vagrant leader of the mind.

Jonathan Swift

The thought of the day. *Anon.*

SEE ALSO BELIEF, LAW, PUBLIC OPINION, SENTIMENT.

OPPORTUNIST

One who goes ahead and does what you always intended to do. *K. L. Krichbaum*

One who sees what is coming and avoids it by taking all sides.   *Joan Tepperman*

(One) who is always able to land on somebody else's feet.   *Earl Wilson*

One who counts his fingers after shaking hands with another opportunist.   *Anon.*

One frequently skilled in making his greed sound like altruism.   *Anon.*

One who remains neutral until he discovers who is holding the gun.   *Anon.*

OPPORTUNITY

A favorable occasion for grasping a disappointment.   *Ambrose Bierce*

The start of great enterprises.   *Demosthenes*

What is opportunity to the man who can't use it? An unfecundated egg, which the waves of time wash away into nonentity.   *George Eliot*

Health and a job.   *Elbert Hubbard*

(To) catch a good that is within our reach.
                                      Samuel Johnson

The tools to him that can handle them.
                                    John G. Lockhart

A tide in the affairs of men, which, taken at the flood, leads on to fortune.
                                 William Shakespeare

The best captain of all endeavor.
                                        Sophocles

The right moment.   *Spanish Proverb*

It depends . . . upon talent and energy, it depends still more upon birth, social position, access to education and inherited wealth; in a word, upon property.   *Richard H. Tawney*

The only weapon of advantage.   *John Udall*

A combination of the right psychological moment and some capital.   *Robert Zwickey*

An hour in most men's lives appointed to make their happiness.   *Anon.*

Making the most from one's resources.   *Anon.*

A knock on the door.   *Anon.*

A knock that usually comes when we are out.
                                            Anon.

SEE ALSO ADVANTAGE, SUCCESS.

OPPRESSION

SEE DICTATORSHIP, IGNORANCE, POVERTY, TOTALITARIANISM, TYRANNY.

OPTIMISM

Believing that what will come, and must come, shall come well.   *Adapted from Edwin Arnold*

Whatever happens at all, happens as it should.
                                      Marcus Aurelius

Nine times out of ten, optimism is a sly form of selfishness, a method of isolating oneself from the unhappiness of others.   *Georges Bernanos*

We know that all things work together for good to them that love God.   *Bible: Romans, VIII, 28.*

The doctrine or belief that everything is beautiful, including what is ugly.   *Ambrose Bierce*

God's in his Heaven—
All's right with the world!   *Robert Browning*

The noble temptation to see too much in everything.   *Gilbert Keith Chesterton*

Whatever is right.   *Democritus*

Full of faith that something will turn up.
                            Adapted from Benjamin Disraeli

Whatever is, is in its causes just.   *John Dryden*

The content of small men in high places.
                                   F. Scott Fitzgerald

To look up and not down
To look forward and not back,
To look out and not in,—
    and
To lend a hand.   *Edward E. Hale*

Everything that is, is reasonable.
                                     Georg W. Hegel

A kind of heart stimulant.   *Elbert Hubbard*

Fatty degeneration of intelligence.
                                     Elbert Hubbard

The instinct to lie.   *Elbert Hubbard*

(The belief) in the capacity for the procreation and development of ideals.   *William James*

A sunny mood.   *James Russell Lowell*

(The belief) that somehow good shall be the final goal of ill.   *Alfred Lord Tennyson*

A mania of maintaining that everything is right when it is wrong. *Voltaire*

What will be will be well, for what is well.

Walt Whitman

The state of mind which believes matrimony will be less expensive than the engagement. *Anon.*

Making the most of all that comes and the least of all that goes. *Anon.*

To believe that disasters celebrate and enhance the glory of God. *Anon.*

The belief that even when worst comes to worst, it won't be so bad. *Anon.*

SEE ALSO CHEERFULNESS, CONFIDENCE, HOPE, SELF-CONFIDENCE, SUCCESS.

OPTIMIST

The Pollyanna pest who says that all is for the best. *Adapted from Franklin P. Adams*

One who can always see the bright side of other people's troubles. *Mac Benoff*

A proponent of the doctrine that black is white.

Ambrose Bierce

The human personification of spring.

Susan Bissonette

One who doesn't care what happens, as long as it doesn't happen to him. *Curt Bois*

A believer in the best. *Phillips Brooks*

One who believes a change in political regime will lower taxes. *Max Gralnick*

A neurotic person . . . trying hard to be brave.

Elbert Hubbard

A fellow who believes what's going to happen will be postponed. *Kin Hubbard*

One who thinks he knows what the world would be like if it went the way he wants. A pessimist knows what it will be like if it stays the way it is.

John A. Lincoln

A guy that has never had much experience.

Don Marquis

The sort of man who marries his sister's best friend. *Henry Louis Mencken*

Someone who tells you to cheer up when things are going his way. *Edward R. Murrow*

A fellow who believes a housefly is looking for a way out. *George Jean Nathan*

Anybody who expects change. *John J. Plomp*

A great renovator and disinfectant in the world.

George Santayana

The fellow who talks about what a fool he used to be. *Buddy Satz*

A man who sees a green light everywhere.

Albert Schweitzer

One who knows exactly how bad a place the world can be; a pessimist is one who finds out anew every morning. *Peter Ustinov*

A man who hasn't gotten around to reading the morning papers.

Earl Wilson

'Twixt optimist and pessimist
   The difference is droll;
The optimist sees the doughnut,
   The pessimist, the hole.

McLandburgh Wilson

A man who gets treed by a lion but enjoys the scenery. *Walter Winchell*

One who sees an opportunity in every calamity; a pessimist sees a calamity in every opportunity.

Anon.

A man who says the bottle is half full when it's half empty. *Anon.*

A bridegroom who thinks he has no bad habits.

Anon.

A man not to borrow money from. He always expects to get it back. *Anon.*

One who takes a frying-pan on a fishing trip.

Anon.

A man who sees the brighter side of your misfortune. *Anon.*

One who makes the best of it when you get the worst of it. *Anon.*

SEE ALSO CHEERFULNESS, SUCCESS.

ORATOR

One who can make men see with their ears.

Arabian Proverb

ORATORY

One who convinces you to lay down your life for his cause. *Eugene E. Brussell*

A man who says what he thinks and feels what he says. *William Jennings Bryan*

Glitterings and sounding generalities. *Rufus Choate*

A person who doesn't let mere facts stand in the way of producing a pleasant sound. *Franklin Clark*

There is no true orator who is not a hero. *Ralph Waldo Emerson*

He who has no hands
Perforce must use his tongue;
Foxes are so cunning
Because they are not strong. *Ralph Waldo Emerson*

(A person) with a flood of words and a drop of reason. *Benjamin Franklin*

(One) waving in the wind of his own eloquence. *Bertram Herridge*

(One who) must make use of violent affirmations, stated in abusive terms. His methods are to exaggerate, to repeat, to avoid any attempt to produce reasonable proof. *Gustave Lebon*

A two-legged gab-machine. *Adapted from James Russell Lowell*

One with judgment and the wit to express it. *Adapted from William Penn*

He possesses the utmost facility and copiousness of expression, and though always extempore, his discourses have all the propriety and elegance of the most studied and elaborate compositions. *Pliny 2*

A man skilled in moving to tears. *Pliny 2*

Fire in each eye, and papers in each hand, they rave, recite, and madden round the land. *Adapted from Alexander Pope*

The mouth of a nation. *Joseph Roux*

A man...that hath a mint of phrases in his brain. *William Shakespeare*

One who knows that the brain can absorb only what the seat can endure. *Anon.*

SEE ALSO RHETORIC, SPEECH, TONGUE.

A conspiracy between speech and action to cheat the understanding. A tyranny tempered by stenography. *Ambrose Bierce*

The power to talk people out of their sober and natural opinions. *Paul Chatfield*

The management with grace, of voice, countenance, and gesture. *Cicero*

The huffing and blustering spoiled child of a semi-barbarous age. *Charles Caleb Colton*

Condensing some daily experience into a glowing symbol. *Ralph Waldo Emerson*

The lullaby of the intellect. *Elbert Hubbard*

The power of beating down your adversary's arguments, and putting better in their place. *Samuel Johnson*

Forceful speech. *John Keble*

Begin low, speak low;
Take fire, rise higher;
When most impressed
Be self-possessed;
At the end wax warm,
And sit down in a storm. *John Leifchild*

Not truth, but persuasion. *Thomas B. Macaulay*

Oratory is just like prostitution; you must have little tricks. *Vittorio E. Orlando*

The art of making deep noises from the chest sound like important messages from the brain. *H. I. Phillips*

The art of making pleasant sounds, which cause the hearers to say "Yes, Yes" in sympathy with the performer, without inquiring too closely exactly what he means. *Samuel Tucker*

Platitudes plus personality. *Anon.*

A solitary vice performed in public. *Anon.*

An art in which nothing you say reveals the fact that you are saying nothing. *Anon.*

To cover indefinite facts with infinite words. *Anon.*

The sole career that gives a man a woman's privileges. *Anon.*

SEE ALSO ELOQUENCE, RHETORIC, SPEECH.

ORDERLINESS

The dream of man.   *Henry Adams*

Light and peace, inward liberty and free command over oneself; order is power...man's greatest need, and his true well-being.
      Henry F. Amiel

A place for everything and...everything in its place.   *Henry G. Bohn*

The foundation of all good things.
      Edmund Burke

Ligaments by which the members of the body are joined together and kept each in its proper place.
      John Calvin

The eternal fitness of things.   *Samuel Clarke*

Power at command; mastery of the resources available for carrying through the actions undertaken.   *John Dewey*

To know what one is to do and to move to do it promptly and by the use of the requisite means.
      John Dewey

In its narrowest conception, order means obedience.   *John Stuart Mill*

Heaven's first law.   *Alexander Pope*

A tyrant in the hands of bad men.   *Anon.*

The basis for conservatism.   *Anon.*

SEE ALSO AUTHORITY, CONSERVATISM.

ORIENT

The cradle of all infamies and all wisdom.
      Elbert Hubbard

A place where God and the home have an esoteric meaning.   *Elbert Hubbard*

SEE ALSO CHINESE.

ORIGINALITY

Sincerity.   *Thomas Carlyle*

Merely the step beyond.   *Louis Danz*

The originality of a subject is in its treatment.
      Benjamin Disraeli

Being one's self, and reporting accurately what we see and are.   *Ralph Waldo Emerson*

Simply a pair of fresh eyes.
      Thomas W. Higginson

What we do with what we did not originate.
      Eric Hoffer

Undetected plagiarism.   *William R. Inge*

The art of concealing your source.
      Franklin P. Jones

The one thing which unoriginal minds cannot feel the use of.   *John Stuart Mill*

The fine art of remembering what you hear but forgetting where you heard it.   *Laurence J. Peter*

Consists not only in doing things differently, but also in doing things better.
      Adapted from Edmund C. Steadman

Does not consist in saying what no one has ever said before, but in saying exactly what you think yourself.   *James Stephen*

Nothing but judicious imitation. The most original writers borrowed one from the other.
      Voltaire

Not taking things at second hand; not looking through the eyes of the dead; not feeding on experience alone through books.   *Anon.*

SEE ALSO CREATIVITY, GREATNESS, INVENTORS.

ORIGINAL SIN

A hereditary depravity and corruption of our nature, diffused into all parts of the soul, which first makes us liable to God's wrath.
      John Calvin

The malice that is ever flickering within us.
      Eric Hoffer

Original Sin...is no positive taint or corruption inherent in our nature, but a negative fact, the deprivation of an unowned super-human gift intended by God for us—namely, *Ultimate Redemption.*   *C. C. Martindale*

A term denoting Adam's sin as transferred to us or the state to which Adam reduced his children.
      John Henry Newman

An inevitable fact of human existence, the inevitability of which is given by the nature of man's spirituality.   *Reinhold Niebuhr*

The really massive and primordial fact of all human history. *Marc Oraison*

The effect of Adam's sin.

Arthur Schopenhauer

The term...should be replaced by existential description of the universal and tragic character of man's estrangement. *Paul Tillich*

SEE ALSO ADAM, SALVATION, SIN.

ORPHANS

Prisoners of charity. *Joseph Harrington*

Those who enjoy peace and freedom—without love. *Anon.*

ORTHODOXY

The anchor which holds the world in its place.

Benjamin Blazer

Characterized by a spirit, and a very proper one, of reverent agnosticism towards the central mysteries of the faith. *J. V. Casserley*

If you go to church and like the singing better than the preaching, that's not orthodox.

Edward Howe

The state of mind which congratulates itself on being absolutely right...that all who think otherwise are wholly wrong. *Elbert Hubbard*

A worship of the static. *Elbert Hubbard*

A corpse that does not know it is dead.

Elbert Hubbard

Where the patient can neither eliminate an old idea or absorb a new one. *Elbert Hubbard*

The Bourbon of the world of thought. It learns not, neither can it forget.

Thomas Henry Huxley

Means not thinking—not needing to think.

George Orwell

Unconsciousness. *George Orwell*

The grave of intelligence. *Bertrand A. Russell*

A refuge of consistency in a world of nonsense and chaos. *Robert Zwickey*

SEE ALSO CUSTOM, RELIGION.

OSTEOPATH

One who argues that all human ills are caused by the pressure of hard bone upon soft tissue. The proof of this theory is to be found in the heads of those who believe it. *Henry Louis Mencken*

OWNERSHIP

SEE CAPITALISM, PROPERTY, WEALTH.

OXFORD UNIVERSITY

Home of lost causes, and forsaken beliefs, and unpopular names, and impossible loyalties.

Matthew Arnold

Half way to Rome.

William Black

A sanctuary in which exploded systems and obsolete prejudices find shelter and protection after they have been hunted out of every corner of the world. *Adam Smith*

I wonder anyone does anything here but dream and remember; the place is so beautiful one expects the people to sing instead of speaking.

William Butler Yeats

OYSTER

Amatory food. *Lord Byron*

A cruel meat because we eat them alive; then they are an uncharitable meat, for we leave nothing to the poor. *Jonathan Swift*

A fish built like a nut which may frequently be a he or a she. *Anon.*

P

PACIFIST

He giveth his cheek to him that smiteth him.
Bible: Lamentations, III, 30.

Resist not evil; but whosoever shall smite thee on thy right cheek, turn to him the other also.
Bible: Matthew, V, 39

A dead Quaker. *Ambrose Bierce*

A canting impotence. *Ralph Waldo Emerson*

Undisguised cowardice. *Adolf Hitler*

There are pacifists in pleasure as well as pacifists in war. The latter are called cowards. The former are called leading moral citizens.
George Jean Nathan

The peace-at-any-price, non-resistance, universal arbitration people. *Theodore Roosevelt*

The unlovely, senile side of civilization.
Theodore Roosevelt

A traitor to his country and humanity.
Theodore Roosevelt

"Resist not evil" means "Do not resist the evil man," which means "Do no violence to another," which means "Commit no act that is contrary to love." *Leon Tolstoy*

A peace coward. *Anon.*

A deceased pacifist. *Anon.*

One who fights with everybody but the enemy.
Anon.

One who does not strike anything but an attitude.
Anon.

PAGAN

The heathen spirit is wingless. It cannot lift itself to heights from which the totality of being is visible, and it therefore loses itself in details. It lacks fantasy for that which it cannot apprehend with the senses; it must hold the thing in its hand.
Sholem Asch

(Means) free to imagine divinities.
Gilbert Keith Chesterton

(To be) suckled in a creed outworn.
William Wordsworth

PAIN

A new idea. *Walter Bagehot*

The only evil. *Jeremy Bentham*

The birth of personality, its fight for its own nature. *Nicholas Berdyaev*

Pain has an element of blank;
It cannot recollect
When it began, or if there were
A day when it was not.
It has no future but itself,
Its infinite realms contain
Its past, enlightened to perceive
New periods of pain. *Emily Dickinson*

The wages of ill pleasures. *Thomas Fuller*

The deepest thing we have in nature, and union through pain and suffering has always seemed more real and holy than any other.

Henry Hallam

The price that God putteth upon all things.

James Howell

A form of salvation.   *Elbert Hubbard*

Life—the sharper, the more evidence of life.

Charles Lamb

Perfect misery.   *John Milton*

The means of redemption and sanctification for every man who does not deny God.

Pope Pius XII

The greatest evil.   *Saint Augustine*

The scourge of life, and death's extreme disgrace.

Adapted from Philip Sidney

The correlative of some species of wrong—some kind of divergence from that course of action which perfectly fills our requirements.

Herbert Spencer

A natural heritage.   *Anon.*

The breaking of the crust that encloses all understanding.   *Anon.*

SEE ALSO SUFFERING.

PAINTER

The painter thinks in form and colors...to constitute a pictorial fact.   *Georges Braque*

The most lively observers of what passes in the world about them, and the closest observers of what passes in their own heads. *William Hazlitt*

A king in his realm.   *Georges Rouault*

One who can paint a great picture on a small canvas.   *Adapted from Charles D. Warner*

One who doodles for a living.   *Anon.*

SEE ALSO ARTISTS.

PAINTING

Painting is color acting.   *Josef Albers*

A fight with yourself and the material.

Karel Appel

A strategem by which we conquer life's disorder.

Alfred Barr

Every artist dips his brush in his own soul, and paints his own nature into his pictures.

Henry Ward Beecher

To give body to our desires.   *John Berger*

The art of protecting flat surfaces from the weather and exposing them to the critic.

Ambrose Bierce

Dead speakers.   *Nicholas Breton*

Abstract art? A product of the untalented, sold by the unprincipled to the utterly bewildered.

Al Capp

The intermediate somewhat between a thought and a thing.   *Samuel Taylor Coleridge*

A poem without words.   *Confucius*

A science, and should be pursued as an inquiry into the laws of nature.   *John Constable*

A flat surface covered with colors arranged in a certain order.   *Maurice Denis*

A picture of paint.   *William Gold*

(Landscape) The obvious resource of
misanthropy.   *William Hazlitt*

A continual creation out of nothing.

William Hazlitt

A record of emotion.   *Edward Hopper*

A poem without words.   *Horace*

An exploration of the self which becomes translated into an exploration of the world.

Peter Hutchinson

(Fit) only for the eyes, and does not correspond to reality.   *Moses Ibn Ezra*

A thundering collision of different worlds, intended to create a new world in, and from, the struggle with one another. *Wassily Kandinsky*

A sum of destructions.   *Pablo Picasso*

Another way of keeping a diary. *Pablo Picasso*

A way to forget life...a cry in the night...a strangled laugh.   *Georges Rouault*

Nothing but a noble and expressive language, invaluable as the vehicle of thought, but by itself nothing.   *John Ruskin*

Silent poetry.   *Simonedes of Amorgos*

My ideal . . . is that every part of it should oblige the looker-on who has any real sense for a whole to see it.   *Leon Stein*

Not wrought by hands alone, but also by thought.
          Adapted from W. W. Story

Like good cooking—it can be tasted, but not explained.   *Maurice de Vlaminck*

A beautifully colored surface, nothing more.
          Oscar Wilde

A picture wrought by thought.   *Anon.*

SEE ALSO ART.

PANIC

SEE TERROR.

PANTHEISM

There is the fact of the nearness of God, what the books call his *immanence*. Push it too far and you have *pantheism*—a God lost in the world to which he is near.   *Cleland B. McAfee*

The religion of beauty, imagination, and philosophy, without constraint moral or intellectual, a religion speculative and self-indulgent . . . the great deceit which awaits the Age to come.
          John Henry Newman

(Religions) which tend to sanctify the real rather than to inspire the ideal.   *Reinhold Niebuhr*

An impiety monstrous to confound God and nature.   *Walter Raleigh*

It says nothing. To call the world God is not to explain it; it is only to enrich our language with a superfluous synonym for the word world.
          Arthur Schopenhauer

PAPACY

No other than the ghost of the deceased Roman Empire, sitting crowned upon the grave thereof.
          Thomas Hobbes

The hope of Italy and of the whole world.
          Pope Leo XIII

That sacred repository of all truths.
          Pope Pius XI

The primacy is given to Peter that it may be shown that the Church is one and the See of Christ is one.
          Saint Cyprian

SEE ALSO CATHOLICISM, CHURCH (ROMAN CATHOLIC).

PAPIST

SEE CATHOLICISM.

PARADISE

SEE HEAVEN.

PARADOX

A cheat: it gains attention at first by its novelty, but later it is discredited, when its emptiness becomes apparent.   *Baltasar Gracian*

The source of the thinker's passion, and the thinker without a paradox is like a lover without feeling: a paltry mediocrity.   *Sören Kierkegaard*

When premature insight clashes with prevailing nonsense.   *Karl Kraus*

The truest sayings.   *Lao-tse*

PARASITE

We humans are the greatest of the earth's parasites.   *Martin H. Fischer*

One who goes through a revolving door on another's push.   *Anon.*

Creatures who live off the earned increment of others.   *Anon.*

SEE ALSO MAN.

PARENTS

What children never think of when falling in love.
          Eugene E. Brussell

People who use the rhythm system of birth control.   *Mary Flink*

Children aren't happy with nothing to ignore, and that's what parents were created for.
          Adapted from Ogden Nash

The bones on which children cut their teeth.
          Peter Ustinov

Those who think they are old enough to know better. *Anon.*

The hardships of a child's life. *Anon.*

The definition of this word is always a matter of opinion. *Anon.*

Those who spend half their time wondering how their children will turn out, and half the time wondering when they will turn in. *Anon.*

Something to grow out of. *Anon.*

Those who learn from their parents. *Anon.*

SEE ALSO CHILD, FAMILY, FATHER, MOTHER.

PARIS

A veritable ocean. Take as many soundings in it as you will, you will never know its depth.
Honoré de Balzac

A city where great ideas perish, done to death by a witticism. *Honoré de Balzac*

A city of gaieties and pleasures where four-fifths of the inhabitants die of grief.
Nicolas Chamfort

(A city) terribly derisive of all absurd pretensions but its own. *Ralph Waldo Emerson*

The cafe of Europe. *Abbé Galiani*

Here nobody sleeps; it is not the way.
Thomas Gray

France is a man, Paris is the heart. *Henry IV*

An immense hospitality. *Victor Hugo*

A sinister Chicago. *Joris K. Huysmans*

Old, crumbling walls and the pleasant sound of water running in the urinals. *Henry Miller*

A circus, a fair. *Joaquin Miller*

The middle-aged woman's paradise.
Arthur Wing Pinero

Where the only good talkers are found.
Francois Villon

The French disease. *Horace Walpole*

The city and the people are uncanny. They seem to be of another species from us. *Anon.*

SEE ALSO FRENCH, FRENCHMAN.

PARLIAMENT

Nothing less than a big meeting of more or less idle people. *Walter Bagehot*

Mostly fools. *Thomas Carlyle*

A mock...compos'd of a people that are only suffer'd to sit there because they are known to have no virtue. *Edward Soxby*

What are they but pimps of tyranny, who are only employed to draw in the people to prostitute their liberty. *Edward Soxby*

The House of Lords in the British Outer Mongolia for retired politicians. *Lord Stansgate*

Only a means to an end, and when it fails to achieve that end other means must be employed.
Carl Stürgkh

SEE ALSO CONGRESS.

PARODY

SEE CARICATURE.

PARTY

SEE COCKTAIL PARTY, POLITICAL PARTY.

PASSION

That state which shows people at their sincerest. It is the antonym of fake. *Eugene E. Brussell*

A lover's glory. *Lord Byron*

They incite and persuade the mind to will the events for which they prepare the body.
René Descartes

The winds necessary to put everything in motion, though they often cause storms.
Bernard de Fontenelle

Nothing more than human activity resulting from private interests—special...self-seeking designs.
Georg W. Hegel

Passions unguided are for the most part mere madness. *Thomas Hobbes*

The passionate attitude is less a response to stimuli from without than an emanation of an inner dissatisfaction. *Eric Hoffer*

Passions are spiritual Rebels, and raise sedition against the understanding.   *Ben Jonson*

A burning forehead and a parching tongue.
John Keats

The only advocates which always persuade.
La Rochefoucauld

Lasting passion is the dream of the harlot and from it we wake in despair.   *Clive S. Lewis*

The experience of being carried along by a power greater than controlled conscious willing.
Rollo May

To be totally caught up in love.   *Rollo May*

Power.   *William Vaughan Moody*

A sort of fever in the mind, which leaves us weaker than it found us.   *William Penn*

It may...be termed the mob of the man, that commits a riot upon reason.   *William Penn*

The elements of life.   *Alexander Pope*

Wild Nature's vigour working at the root.
Alexander Pope

Passions are like floods and streams. The shallow murmur, the deep are dumb.
Adapted from Walter Raleigh

(That which) makes the best observations and draws the most wretched conclusions.
Jean Paul Richter

An unnatural movement of the soul that is the result of a love without reason, or of an irrational aversion for some concrete object.
Saint Maximus

The quintessence of every passion is selfishness.
Moritz Saphir

The Master Passion, the hunger for self-approval.
Mark Twain

Riding a horse that runs away with you.   *Anon.*

SEE ALSO LOVE, ZEAL.

PAST

A work of art, free of irrelevancies and loose ends.   *Max Beerbohm*

Our very being.   *David Ben-Gurion*

That part of Eternity with some small fraction of which we have a slight and regrettable acquaintance.   *Ambrose Bierce*

The pearl-gift thrown to hogs.
Robert Browning

The best prophet of the future.   *Lord Byron*

The "good old times"—all times, when old, are good.   *Lord Byron*

The misty black and bottomless pit of time.
Thomas Duffett

Time that always looks better than it was. It is only pleasant because it isn't now.
Adapted from Finley Peter Dunn

That which we possess fully and in whole.
Isidor Eliashev

A funeral gone by.   *Edmund W. Gosse*

The best way to suppose what may come.
Lord Halifax

That is the land of lost content,
I see it shining plain,
The happy highways where I went
And cannot come again. *Alfred Edward Housman*

What men believed happened.
Gerald White Johnson

That which will not tell us what we ought to do, but...what we ought to avoid.
José Ortega y Gasset

Whatever the records and the memories agree upon.   *George Orwell*

A bucket of ashes.   *Carl Sandburg*

The...abysm of time.   *William Shakespeare*

What's past is prologue.   *William Shakespeare*

One's past is what one is. It is the only thing by which people should be judged.   *Oscar Wilde*

Old, unhappy, far-off things,
And battles long ago.   *William Wordsworth*

Our cradle, not our prison, and there is danger as well as appeal in its glamor. The past is for inspiration, not imitation, for continuation, not repetition.   *Israel Zangwill*

The wreckage of days departed.   *Anon.*

SEE ALSO ANCESTRY, HISTORY, MEMORY, TRADITION, YESTERDAY.

PASTOR

SEE CLERGYMEN.

PATIENCE

Passion tamed.   *Lyman Abbott*

A minor form of despair, disguised as a virtue.
Ambrose Bierce

Faith waiting for a nibble.   *Josh Billings*

A plaster for all sores.   *Miguel de Cervantes*

The virtue of those who lack courage and strength.   *Christina of Sweden*

Sorrow's salve.   *Charles Churchill*

The ability to care slowly.   *John Ciardi*

A poor man's remedy.   *John Clarke*

Patience is the virtue of an ass,
That trots...his burden, and is quiet.
George Granville

Pride walling itself up.   *Elbert Hubbard*

To go to sleep in the lap of the inevitable.
Elbert Hubbard

The strongest of strong drinks, for it kills the giant Despair.   *Douglas Jerrold*

The art of concealing your impatience.
Franklin P. Jones

The life-long martyrdom.
Henry Wadsworth Longfellow

The principal part of faith.   *George Macdonald*

The quality that is needed most just as it is exhausted.   *Cary MacWilliams*

The beggar's virtue.   *Philip Massinger*

A gift that God gives only to those He loves.
Moroccan Proverb

The best remedy for every trouble.   *Plautus*

Means waiting without anxiety.
Saint Francis de Sales

Confirmed desperation.   *Henry David Thoreau*

The key to Paradise.   *Turkish Proverb*

The art of hoping.   *Luc de Vauvenargues*

Remaining forever in the rear.   *Anon.*

SEE ALSO PERSEVERANCE, SUCCESS.

PATIENT

SEE DISEASE, DOCTORS, HOSPITAL, ILLNESS.

PATRIOT

One to whom the interests of a part seem superior to those of the whole.   *Ambrose Bierce*

The dupe of statesmen and the tool of conquerors.
Ambrose Bierce

The best preventive of crime.   *George Borrow*

He who is proud of his country.   *George Borrow*

The seed of Freedom's tree.   *Thomas Campbell*

The unknown, steadfast citizen who year after year quietly and unselfishly benefits his nation.
Albert Carr

Noble stubbornness resisting might.
John Dryden

Those that (are) intelligent, courageous, decisive and tireless in their support of high principle.
Dwight David Eisenhower

His first, best country ever is at home.
Oliver Goldsmith

A fool in every age.   *Alexander Pope*

Those who go willingly when their country calls.
Anon.

SEE ALSO AMERICANISM, FLAG, PATRIOTISM.

PATRIOTISM

A lively sense of collective responsibility.
Richard Aldington

The first resort of a scoundrel.   *Ambrose Bierce*

Bearing ourselves humbly before God, but conscious that we serve an unfolding purpose.
Winston S. Churchill

Looking out for yourself by looking out for your country.   *Calvin Coolidge*

The love and respect I owe to my country.

Francois A. de Thou

Patriotism means equipped forces and a prepared citizenry.   Dwight David Eisenhower

Patriotism has its roots deep in the instincts and the affections. Love of country is the expansion of filial love.   David D. Field

The love of humanity.   Mohandas K. Gandhi

To love one's country in spite of its climate.

Warren Goldberg

Patriotism varies, from a noble devotion to a moral lunacy.   William R. Inge

The last refuge of a scoundrel.   Samuel Johnson

To most men, a moral necessity. It meets and satisfies that desire for a strong, disinterested enthusiasm in life which is deeply implanted in our nature.   William E. Lecky

Love of the good things we ate in our childhood.

Lin Yutang

Hope is the mainspring of patriotism.

David Lloyd George

That pernicious sentiment, "Our country right or wrong."   James Russell Lowell

The egg from which all wars are hatched.

Guy de Maupassant

Patriotism is classified under the virtue of piety. Filial piety makes us respect and love our parents; patriotic piety makes us true, loyal citizens, loving our country as our parent.

John T. McNicholas

A variety of hallucination.

Henry Louis Mencken

Often an arbitrary veneration of real estate above principles.   George Jean Nathan

The rationalized expression of something which has nonrational but true sources.   William Pfaff

Old men's lies.   Ezra Pound

Public duty parodied.   James E. Rogers

The willingness to be killed for trivial reasons.

Bertrand A. Russell

To serve one's country by deeds, and . . . to serve her by words.   Sallust

A soul controlled by geography.

George Santayana

The passion of fools and the most foolish of passions.   Arthur Schopenhauer

Our country, right or wrong. When right, to be kept right; when wrong, to be put right.

Carl Schurz

Your conviction that this country is superior to all other countries because you were born in it.

George Bernard Shaw

True patriotism is of no party.

Tobias G. Smollett

Nothing more than a feeling of welfare, and the dread of seeing it disturbed.   Stanislaus

(To) love America enough to wish to see her as a model to mankind.   Adlai Ewing Stevenson

Not a short and frenzied outburst of emotion, but the tranquil and steady dedication of a lifetime.

Adlai Ewing Stevenson

Patriotism knows neither latitude nor longitude. It is not climate.   E. A. Storrs

To be patriotic, hate all nations but your own.

Lionel Strachey

A sense of partisan solidarity in respect of prestige.   Thorstein Veblen

Our country, our whole country, and nothing but our country.   Daniel Webster

A mere national self-assertion, a sentimentality of flag-cheering with no constructive duties.

Herbert G. Wells

The virtue of the vicious.   Oscar Wilde

The finest flower of Western Civilization as well as the refuge of the scoundrel.   Leonard Woolf

Geographic loyalty.   Anon.

Self-interest multiplied by population.   Anon.

Unconditional loyalty to one's country.   Anon.

SEE ALSO AMERICANISM.

PATRON

The first resort of a scoundrel.   Ambrose Bierce

The first part of painting.   William Blake

One who looks with unconcern on a man struggling for life in the water, and, when he has reached ground, encumbers him with help.

Samuel Johnson

A wretch who supports with insolence, and is paid with flattery. *Samuel Johnson*

The last resort of a scoundrel. *Samuel Johnson*

My soul's earth's god. *William Shakespeare*

The whole art of life. *George Bernard Shaw*

PAUSE

The most precious things in speech.

Ralph Richardson

That impressive...eloquent...that geometrically progressive silence which often achieves a desired effect where no combination of words howsoever felicitous could accomplish it. *Mark Twain*

SEE ALSO SILENCE.

PAWNBROKER

A man who takes an interest in things.

Fred Allen

One who lives off the flat of the land.

Lionel Shelly

One who asks you to see him at your earliest inconvenience. *Anon.*

PEACE

A decay of spirit and political courage.

Friedrich von Bernhardi

Abandoning all desires, moving about without attachment and longing, without the sense of "I" and "mine." *Bhagavad-Gita*

The work of righteousness.

Bible: Isaiah, XXXII, 17.

A period of cheating between two periods of fighting. *Ambrose Bierce*

That state in which fear of any kind is unknown.

John Buchan

Your own self. *Simha Bunam*

Implies reconciliation. *Edmund Burke*

Liberty in tranquility. *Cicero*

A moribund condition, caused by a surplus of civilians, which war seeks to remedy.

Cyril Connolly

In His will is our peace. *Dante*

The rising flame of man daring to become truly human. *James W. Douglass*

War in Masquerade. *John Dryden*

Poor reading. *Thomas Hardy*

A quiet life. *Thomas Heywood*

The first and fundamental law of nature...to seek peace and follow it. *Thomas Hobbes*

A monotonous interval between fights.

Elbert Hubbard

The *summum bonum* of old age.

Thomas Jefferson

The creation of a world community in which every nation can follow its own course without fear of its neighbors. *Lyndon Baines Johnson*

A process—a way of solving problems.

John Fitzgerald Kennedy

A short pause between wars for enemy identification. *Clemens Kirchner*

The white space between the chapters in the history books. *Leonard L. Levinson*

A state brought about by having no opinions whatever about anything.

Adapted from Georg C. Lichtenberg

The nurse of drones and cowards.

Philip Massinger

'Peace' is when nobody's shooting. A 'just peace' is when our side gets what it wants.

William Maudlin

A dream, and not even a beautiful one.

Helmuth von Moltke

Order based on law. *Emery Reves*

Time out. *Leo C. Rosten*

Ineradicable seeds of future decline.

John Ruskin

Our final good. *Saint Augustine*

Peace is when time doesn't matter as it passes by.
Maria Schell

This weak piping time.   *William Shakespeare*

The essence of all prophecies.
Eleazar Shammua

Not the absence of war; it is a virtue, a state of mind, a disposition of benevolence, confidence, and justice.   *Baruch Spinoza*

An act of reconciliation.   *Luigi Sturzo*

The blessing of the Holy One.
Talmud: Megilla, 18a.

The state of things in which the natural hostility of man toward man is manifested by creation instead of . . . destruction.   *Paul Valéry*

The period of creative competition and the struggle of inventions.   *Paul Valéry*

Self-control at its widest—at the width where the "self" has been lost, and interest has been transferred to coordinations wider than personality.
Alfred North Whitehead

Our gift—to each other.   *Elie Wiesel*

The healing and elevating influence of the world.
Woodrow Wilson

Peace begins just where ambition ends.
Edward Young

God is peace, His name is peace, and all is bound together in peace.   *Zohar: Leviticus, 10b.*

A temporary suspension of hostilities.   *Anon.*

SEE ALSO CHRISTIANITY, PACIFIST, VICTORY.

PEDANT

One whose impudence will overrule his ignorance to talk of learned principles.
Adapted from Thomas Adams

A man who has been brought up among books, and is able to talk of nothing else . . . a very indifferent companion.   *Joseph Addison*

One who has read everything and remembered it.
Josh Billings

A talkative footnote.   *Eugene E. Brussell*

A gatherer and disposer of other men's ideas.
Eugene E. Brussell

(One) with various readings stored (in) his empty skull, learned without sense, and venerably dull.
Charles Churchill

A man who studies a vacuum through instruments that allow him to draw cross-sections of the details.   *John Ciardi*

(One who) can hear nothing but in favor of the conceits he is amorous of, and cannot see but out of the grates of his prison.   *Joseph Glanvill*

A person who knows all the answers but doesn't understand the questions.   *Warren Goldberg*

A person with more education than he can use.
Elbert Hubbard

The unseasonable ostentation of learning.
Samuel Johnson

One educated beyond his intellect.
Milton Keiser

A reading-machine always wound up and going.
James Russell Lowell

(One) deep versed in books and shallow in himself.   *John Milton*

A pedant is always throwing his system in your face, and applies it equally to all things, times, and places, just like the tailor who would make a coat out of his own head, without any regard to the bulk or figure of the person that must wear it.
Mary W. Montagu

(One) with loads of learned lumber in his head.
Alexander Pope

A person suffering from first-degree knowledge.
Anon.

An ignoramus who read a book.   *Anon.*

One who thinks he thinks.   *Anon.*

An expert on the misapprehensions of others.
Anon.

A mockery of the learned gentleman.   *Anon.*

A donkey who always carries books on his shoulders.   *Anon.*

SEE ALSO PROFESSOR.

PEDANTRY

Consists of the use of words unsuitable to the time, place, and company.

Samuel Taylor Coleridge

To be blind with light. *Benjamin Franklin*

Laying so many books on the head that the brains cannot move except along narrow roads.

Max Gralnick

To suppose that there is no knowledge in the world but that of books. *William Hazlitt*

Pretending not to be pedantic. *William Hazlitt*

The dotage of knowledge. *Holbrook Jackson*

Knowledge that puffs up the possessor's mind.

William Mather

A reasoning, self-sufficing thing,
An intellectual All-in-all. *William Wordsworth*

Shiny pants acquired at a seat of learning.

Anon.

PEDESTRIAN

A car owner who has found a parking space.

Hawley R. Everhart

A zombie (who) has no mind of his own and walks around without knowing where he's going or what he's doing. *Bob Hope*

One who always has the right of way—to the hospital. *Warren Goldberg*

A man with a wife and three grown daughters.

Jan Murray

A man who has two cars, a wife, and a son in high school. *Anon.*

A man whose children are home from college.

Anon.

Two classes: the quick and the dead. *Anon.*

SEE ALSO AUTOMOBILE.

PELICAN

A wonderful bird is the pelican.
His mouth can hold more than his belican.
  He can take in his beak
  Enough food for a week
I'm darned if I know how the hellican.

Dixon L. Merritt

PEN

That mighty instrument of little men.

Lord Byron

Slave of my thoughts. *Lord Byron*

The tongue of the mind. *Miguel de Cervantes*

Wit's plough. *John Clarke*

The interpreter of the heart. *Elijah Delmedigo*

A clarion. *Henry Wadsworth Longfellow*

A formidable weapon, but a man can kill himself with it a great deal more easily than he can other people. *George Prentice*

Most dangerous tools. *John Taylor*

SEE ALSO AUTHOR, WRITING.

PENALTY

SEE PRISON, PUNISHMENT.

PENNSYLVANIA

Can be called "the mother of dissension." Rebels are constantly being born in Pennsylvania, although they seldom remain there.

Struthers Burt

(A state that) has produced but two great men: Benjamin Franklin, of Massachusetts; and Albert Gallatin of Switzerland. *John J. Ingalls*

The cradle of tolerance and freedom of religion.

Thomas Jefferson

The keystone of the democratic arch.

Pennsylvania Democratic Committee, 1803.

PENSION

A roll of honor. *Grover Cleveland*

Pay for the work we keep on doing in our dreams after we retire. *Eric Hoffer*

An allowance made to anyone without an equivalent. *Samuel Johnson*

SEE ALSO RETIREMENT.

PEOPLE, THE

Little dogs biting one another. *Marcus Aurelius*

There are two kinds...in one's life—people whom one keeps waiting and the people for whom one waits.   *Samuel N. Behrman*

Two classes of people in the world: those who constantly divide the people of the world into two classes, and those who do not.   *Robert Benchley*

Two classes: the righteous and the unrighteous. The classifying is done by the righteous.
                                    Ambrose Bierce

That numerous piece of monstrosity.
                                    Thomas Browne

The attempt of many to rise to the completer life of one.   *Robert Browning*

The vulgar popular cattle.   *Robert Buchanan*

The great unwashed.   *Edmund Burke*

A beast of muddy brain that knows not its own strength.   *Tommasso Campanella*

An old woman. Let her maunder and mumble.
                                    Thomas Carlyle

The man in the street.   *Ralph Waldo Emerson*

(Those) who have something to say and can't, and the other half who have nothing to say and keep on saying it.   *Robert Frost*

The many. (Hoi polloi).   *Greek Proverb*

A monster full of confusion and mistake.
                                    Francesco Guicciardini

Two classes...those who consider things in the abstract, or with a reference to truth, and those who consider them only with reference to themselves, to the main chance.   *William Hazlitt*

That part of the state which does not know what it wants.   *Georg W. Hegel*

The only righteous source of power.
                                    Heinrich Heine

The only sure reliance for the preservation of our liberty.   *Thomas Jefferson*

The venal herd.   *Juvenal*

A wild beast.   *Niccolo Machiavelli*

The patient thrust of the activities of the human intellect and human labor multiplying in individual lives at the ground level of civilized existence.
                                    Jacques Maritain

A herd confused, a miscellaneous rabble, who extol vulgar things.   *Adapted from John Milton*

The moving force of history.   *I. E. Petrov*

A many-headed beast.   *Alexander Pope*

Honest brothers, but they think like soap-boilers.
                                    Johann C. Schiller

The voice of humbug.   *William T. Sherman*

The rulers and the ruled, the law-givers and the law-abiding, the beginning and the end.
                                    Adlai Ewing Stevenson

A venal pack.   *Suetonius*

Three kinds—commonplace men, remarkable men, and lunatics.   *Mark Twain*

There are only two kinds of people who are really fascinating—people who know absolutely everything and people who know absolutely nothing.
                                    Oscar Wilde

It is absurd to divide people into good or bad. People are either charming or tedious.
                                    Oscar Wilde

Animals plus a wealth of fantasy, psyche, soul.
                                    D. W. Winnicott

The first human subject and original of civil power.   *John Wise*

An assish, mulish, packhorse clan.
                                    John Wolcot

Animals boasting but few members who desire to be different.   *Anon.*

SEE ALSO CROWD, MAN, MASSES, MOB, MULTITUDE, POPULACE, RABBLE.

PERFECTION

An imaginary state...distinguished from the actual by an element known as excellence.
                                    Ambrose Bierce

To do one or two things well.
                                    Eugene E. Brussell

Use.   *William Bullein*

The worst disease that ever afflicted the human mind.   *Louis Fontanes*

Nothing.   *Heinrich Heine*

Does not consist in any singular state or condition of life...but in holy and religious conduct of ourselves in every state of Life.   *William Law*

Man, being incomplete, is not at rest and is therefore always striving for his completion ... And this itself is his perfection. *Judah Löw*

The line of conduct that presents the fewest drawbacks. *Niccolo Machiavelli*

What American women expect to find in their husbands...but English women only hope to find in their butlers. *William Somerset Maugham*

Nothing more than a complete adaptation to the environment; but the environment is constantly changing, so perfection can never be more than transitory. *William Somerset Maugham*

Trifles make perfection, and perfection is no trifle. *Michelangelo*

Consists not in surrendering vice out of slavish fear of punishment...but...in having one fear, the loss of God's friendship. *Saint Gregory*

Being, not doing; it is not to effect an act but to achieve a character. *Fulton J. Sheen*

What alone gives meaning to life.
Logan P. Smith

Only modes of thought...notions which we are in the habit of forming from the comparison with one another of individuals of the same species.
Baruch Spinoza

(That which) just precedes a change, and signifies the approaching end of an epoch.
Alfred North Whitehead

To be like God...in unity of spirit.
William of St. Thierry

Such a nuisance that I often regret having cured myself of using tobacco. *Emile Zola*

SEE ALSO PERSEVERANCE, SUCCESS.

PERFUME

Any smell that is used to drown a worse one.
Elbert Hubbard

To stink. *Michel de Montaigne*

Chemical warfare. *Anon.*

SEE ALSO COSMETICS.

PERSECUTION

A bad and indirect way to plant religion.
Thomas Browne

A history of endeavors to cheat nature, to make water run up hill, to twist a rope of sand.
Ralph Waldo Emerson

The business of fanatics who think they hear the whisperings of God. *Max Gralnick*

To punish a man because we infer from the nature of some doctrine which he holds...that he will commit a crime. *Thomas B. Macaulay*

Always the strongly marked feature of all law-religions, or religions established by law.
Thomas Paine

Punishment inflicted on those who are somehow different. *Joan Teppermann*

SEE ALSO BIGOTRY.

PERSEVERANCE

The greatest of all teachers. *Arabian Proverb*

Never say die. *Richard H. Barham*

A lowly virtue whereby mediocrity achieves an inglorious success. *Ambrose Bierce*

Patience concentrated. *Thomas Carlyle*

The mother of good luck, and God gives all things to industry. *Benjamin Franklin*

A silent power that grows irresistibly greater with time. *Johann W. Goethe*

Victory. *Max Gralnick*

To ascend the ladder step by step.
Adapted from George Herbert

The duration of tastes and opinions which we can neither give nor take away from ourselves.
La Rochefoucauld

The crowning quality...of great hearts.
James Russell Lowell

The first thing a child should learn...It is what he will have most need to know.
Jean-Jacques Rosseau

Neither to change, nor falter, nor repent.
Percy Bysshe Shelley

'Tis known by the name of perseverance in a good cause—and of obstinacy in a bad one.
Laurence Sterne

A mighty good luck piece. *Anon.*

Another name for success. *Anon.*

To finish the job you start. *Anon.*

The eternal try-angle. *Anon.*

To deprive misfortune of its power. *Anon.*

SEE ALSO SUCCESS.

PERSON

SEE HUMAN BEINGS, INDIVIDUAL, MAN.

PERSONALITY

The gland of creativity. *Sholem Asch*

That single spark of divinity that sets you off and makes you different from every other living creature. *Bruce Barton*

The unique person of a man, with his unique destiny. *Nicholas Berdyaev*

The very intention of the evolution of life. *Henri Bergson*

Selfhood, self-consciousness, self-control, and power to know. *Borden P. Browne*

A byway of your own. *Dante*

A *fact* of evolution. *Julian Huxley*

What we are able to realize of the infinite wealth which our divine human nature contains hidden in its depths. *William R. Inge*

A human being in whom all the different aspects of man's nature...are dovetailed into an harmonious whole, with the result that the whole force of the man is behind his every act, thought and wish. *C. E. M. Joad*

The subsistence of the spiritual soul communicated to the human composite. *Jacques Maritain*

A person that is real, a person who takes a stand. *Frederick S. Perls*

The secret of the universe, as by slow degrees it reveals itself to us, turns out to be personality. *John C. Powys*

The aggregate of the spirit's self-consciousness and of the liberty which rests thereon. *M. J. Scheeben*

Personality is to a man what perfume is to a flower. *Charles M. Schwab*

A synthetic, an organic whole...not a mere collection of its constituent elements. *John W. Sullivan*

Man's awareness of being...under obligation to something greater than himself. *Paul Tillich*

A complex balance of many conflicting claims, forces, tensions, compunctions, distractions, which yet manages somehow to.be a functioning entity. *Allen Wheelis*

That alone that endows a man to stand before presidents or generals, or in any distinguished collection, with aplomb. *Walt Whitman*

The name we give to our collection of eccentricities. *Anon.*

The art of making people admire in you those qualities which you do not possess. *Anon.*

What you are when people are around; character is what you are when everybody goes home. *Anon.*

The name we give to our queer habits. *Anon.*

The indefinable something that enables us to get by without ability. *Anon.*

SEE ALSO CHARACTER, GREATNESS, INDIVIDUALISM, INDIVIDUALITY.

PESSIMISM

(The) one ism which kills the soul. *John Buchan*

A thing like opium, that may often be a poison and sometimes a medicine, but never a food for us, who are driven by an inner command not only to think but to live, not only to live but to grow, and not only to grow but to build. *Gilbert Keith Chesterton*

The name that men of weak nerves give to wisdom. *Bernard De Voto*

Essentially a religious disease. *William James*

Every line in my face. *Richard Jefferies*

Not a philosophy, but a temperament. *Max Nordau*

A mental disease...It means illness in the person who voices it, and in the society which produces that person. *Upton Sinclair*

PESSIMIST

Nothing is right and nothing is just; we sow in ashes and reap in dust.

Adapted from Mary M. Singleton

SEE ALSO CYNICISM, OPTIMIST.

PESSIMIST

(One who) burns his bridges before he gets to them. *Sidney Ascher*

(One who) feels that all women are bad; an optimist hopes so. *Shannon Carse*

Miserable fellows...who see a black star always riding through the light and colored clouds in the sky. *Ralph Waldo Emerson*

People who have an appetite for grief.

Ralph Waldo Emerson

One who makes the worst out of the best.

Warren Goldberg

One who has been intimately acquainted with an optimist. *Elbert Hubbard*

A man who looks both ways when...crossing a one-way street. *Laurence J. Peter*

A man who tells the truth prematurely.

Edmond Rostand

A Buddhist who has strayed from the Orient, and who in his exodus has left behind him all his fantastic shackles, and has brought with him, together with ethical laws, only the cardinal tenet, "Life is evil." *Edgar E. Saltus*

A man who thinks everybody as nasty as himself, and hates them for it. *George Bernard Shaw*

A poor sleeper. *Paul Weinberger*

One who builds dungeons in the air.

Walter Winchell

The triumph of worry over matter. *Anon.*

One who, when he has the choice of two evils, chooses both. *Anon.*

One who makes difficulties of his opportunities.

Anon.

One who lives with an optimist. *Anon.*

A gloomy person who spends all his days in expectation of the worst. *Anon.*

One who is never happy unless he is miserable and even then he is not pleased. *Anon.*

One who is tied in nots. *Anon.*

A man to borrow money from. He never expects to get it back. *Anon.*

SEE ALSO CYNIC, OPTIMISM.

PHARISEE

A great attempt to achieve the full domination of religion over life. *Leon Baeck*

A person who pretends to believe that Christianity is an easy thing and asks of the Christian...more than he asks of himself. *Albert Camus*

Prophecy in action. *Louis Finkelstein*

Judaism is the monument of the Pharisees.

George F. Moore

(Those who) permitted no discord between religion and life. *Vladimir Solovyov*

PHARMACIST

The Physician's accomplice. *Ambrose Bierce*

They bear the same relation to physicians that priests do to philosophers; the ignorance of the former makes them positive and dogmatical, and assuming, and enterprising...and consequently much more taking with people. *David Hume*

The man in the white coat who stands behind the counter selling cosmetics and watches. *Anon.*

PHILANTHROPIST

A rich...old gentleman who has trained himself to grin while his conscience is picking his pocket.

Ambrose Bierce

The friend of man, to vice alone a foe.

Robert Burns

Friend to the friendless, to the sick man health.

Samuel Taylor Coleridge

Those who go about doing good.

Mandell Creighton

A man born not for himself, but for the whole world. *Adapted from Lucan*

A bandit who is kind to beggars. *Anon.*

A man who gives away what he should be giving back. *Anon.*

A man whose life is a bowl of charities.   *Anon.*

SEE ALSO BENEVOLENCE, CHARITY.

PHILANTHROPY

This is our special duty, that if anyone specially needs our help, we should give him such help to the utmost of our power.   *Cicero*

An American habit...to make human beings healthier, happier, wiser, more conscious of the rich possibilities of human existence.
Charles Dollard

A certain air of quackery.
Ralph Waldo Emerson

The wish to scatter joy and not pain around us.
Ralph Waldo Emerson

The most acceptable service of God.
Benjamin Franklin

Mere vanity and love of distinction, gilded over to others and to themselves with some show of benevolent sentiment.   *Walter Scott*

Almost the only virtue which is sufficiently appreciated by mankind.
Henry David Thoreau

To befriend the unhappy.   *Vergil*

Philanthropy is the refuge of people who wish to annoy their fellow-creatures.   *Oscar Wilde*

Penance for secret guilt.   *Anon.*

Help to others out of a fellow-feeling.   *Anon.*

SEE ALSO CHARITY.

PHILISTINE

The people who believe most that our greatness and welfare are proved by our being very rich, and who most give their lives and thoughts to becoming rich.   *Matthew Arnold*

Philistine must have originally meant...a strong, dogged, unenlightened opponent of the children of the light.   *Matthew Arnold*

One whose mind is the creature of his environment, following the fashion in thought, feeling and sentiment.   *Ambrose Bierce*

What we call bores, dullards, children of darkness.   *Thomas Carlyle*

A hollow gut
Filled with fear and hope.   *Johann W. Goethe*

A term of reproach used by prigs to designate certain people they do not like.   *Elbert Hubbard*

A term of contempt applied by prigs to the rest of their species.   *Leslie Stephen*

A low practical man who pays his debts.
Artemus Ward

Consumer-oriented people who give little thought to the qualitative and serious side of life.
Paul Weinberger

PHILOSOPHER

Immense masses of absurdities, vices and lies.
John Quincy Adams

(One who) aspires to explain away all mysteries, to dissolve them into light.   *Henry F. Amiel*

(Those who) make imaginary laws for imaginary commonwealths, and their discourses are as the stars, which give little light because they are so high.   *Francis Bacon*

The servants of posterity.   *Francis Bacon*

Adults who persist in asking childish questions.
Isaiah Berlin

He who can analyze his delusions is called a philosopher.   *Ambrose Bierce*

A blind man in a dark room looking for a black cat which isn't there.   *Lord Bowen of Colwood*

One you never go to for advice.
Eugene E. Brussell

(One who) succeeds in raising genuine doubts.
Morris R. Cohen

A fool who torments himself while he is alive, to be talked about after he is dead.
Jean D'Alembert

The cartographer of human life.   *René Daumal*

A person who will not believe what he sees because he is too busy speculating about what he does not see.   *La Bovier de Fontenelle*

An ignorant sot to the simplest Christian.
Joseph Hall

The pioneers of revolution.   *Robert Harper*

(One) who can forget himself.   *William Hazlitt*

He who regards another's wife as his mother, another's goods as clods of earth, and all mankind as himself.   *Hitopadesa, IV.*

Those hired by the comfortable class to prove that everything is all right.

Adapted from Oliver Wendell Holmes 2

One who thinks in order to believe.

Elbert Hubbard

One who formulates his prejudices and systematizes his ignorance.   *Elbert Hubbard*

One who contradicts other philosophers.

William James

(One who) knows the universe but not himself.

Jean de la Fontaine

May be described in four words, much hope, little faith; a disposition to believe that anything, however extraordinary, may be done; an indisposition to believe that anything extraordinary has been done.   *Thomas B. Macaulay*

One who doubts.   *Michel de Montaigne*

To make light of philosophy is to be a true philosopher.   *Blaise Pascal*

One who desires to discern the truth.   *Plato*

Not merely to have subtle thoughts, nor even to found a school, but so to love wisdom as to live according to its dictates, a life of simplicity, independence, magnanimity, and trust.

Henry David Thoreau

A philosopher's duty is not to pity the unhappy—it is to be of use to them.   *Voltaire*

People who talk about something they don't understand, and make you think it's your fault.

Anon.

One who always knows what to do until it happens to him.   *Anon.*

One who can size himself up and forget the result.

Anon.

Anyone who can survive the madness of his times.

Anon.

PHILOSOPHY

Unintelligible answers to insoluble problems.

Franklin P. Adams

The complete liberty of the mind... It loves one thing only—truth.   *Henry F. Amiel*

Means, first doubt; and afterwards the consciousness of what knowledge means, the consciousness of uncertainty and of ignorance... limit, shade, degree, possibility.

Henry F. Amiel

To deliberate well in reference to any question that emerges.   *Apocrypha: Aristeas, 256.*

Never to be carried away by impulses, but to ponder over the injuries that result from the passions, and to act rightly as the circumstances demand, practicing moderation.

Apocrypha: Aristeas, 256.

The science which considers truth.   *Aristotle*

A little philosophy inclines a man's mind to atheism; but depth in philosophy brings men's minds about to religion.   *Francis Bacon*

When superficially studied excites doubt; when thoroughly explored, it dispels it.

Francis Bacon

The common sense of the next century.

Henry Ward Beecher

To assist men to understand themselves and thus operate in the open and not wildly in the dark.

Isaiah Berlin

A route of many roads leading from nowhere to nothing.   *Ambrose Bierce*

Common-sense in a dress suit.

Oliver S. Braston

A system of thought which supplies answers for the past and future, but none for the present.

Eugene E. Brussell

All philosophies, if you ride them home, are nonsense.   *Samuel Butler 2*

Philosophy...is like stirring mud or not letting a sleeping dog lie.   *Samuel Butler 2*

An attempt to deny, circumvent or otherwise escape from the way in which the roots of things interlace with one another.   *Samuel Butler 2*

A continual battle against custom; an ever-renewed effort to transcend the sphere of blind custom, and so become transcendental.

Thomas Carlyle

An antidote to sorrow.   *Cicero*

The cultivation of the mental faculties; it roots out vices and prepares the mind to receive proper seed. *Cicero*

Inner superiority to worldy fortune. *Morris R. Cohen*

The middle state between...knowledge and wisdom. *Samuel Taylor Coleridge*

The science of sciences. *Samuel Taylor Coleridge*

A method, cultivated by philosophers, for dealing with the problems of men. *John Dewey*

The thoughts of men about human thinking, reasoning and imagining, and the real values in human existence. *Charles W. Eliot*

That account which the human mind gives to itself of the constitution of the world. *Ralph Waldo Emerson*

A consciousness of man's own weakness and impotence with reference to the things of real importance in life. *Epictetus*

A recognition of the conflict between the opinions of men. *Epictetus*

Preparation to face the things which may come upon us. *Epictetus*

Good health or bad makes our philosophy. *French Proverb*

Philosophy goes no further than probabilities, and every assertion keeps a doubt in reserve. *James A. Froude*

A modest confession of ignorance. *Roswell D. Hitchcock*

Such knowledge of effects or appearances as we acquire by true ratiocination from the knowledge we have first of their causes or generation. *Thomas Hobbes*

If it isn't common sense, it isn't philosophy. *Edgar W. Howe*

Our highest conception of life, its duties and its destinites. *Elbert Hubbard*

The reflections of common life, methodized and corrected. *David Hume*

Devices for making it possible to do, cooly, continuously, and with good conscience, things which otherwise one could do only in the heat of

passion...and under the threat of subsequent remorse. *Aldous Huxley*

The practical realization of all moral purposes, and this is the essence of religion. *Moses Ibn Daud*

To care and think and deal with death. *Moses Ibn Ezra*

The object of studying philosophy is to know one's own mind, not other people's. *William R. Inge*

To find out what definite difference it will make to you or me, at definite instants of our life, if this world-formula or that world-formula be the true one. *William James*

The term...signifies that which philosophers are doing...The meaning of the term is a function of two variables—time and clime. *Cassius J. Keyser*

The art of lying about the art of living. *D. G. Kin*

Playing a game, with a fixed set of axioms and rules, whether we are aware of them or not. *Arthur Koestler*

What am I? What ought I to do? What may I hope and believe? All philosophy may be reduced to this. *Georg C. Lichtenberg*

Consists largely of one philosopher arguing that all others are jackasses. He usually proves it, and I should also add that he also usually proves that he is one himself. *Henry Louis Mencken*

The algebra of history. *Maurice Merleau-Ponty*

Nothing else but a sophisticated poetry. *Michel de Montaigne*

Philosophy is doubt. *Michel de Montaigne*

Looking at things which one takes for granted and suddenly seeing that they are very odd indeed. *Iris Murdoch*

The confession of its originator, and a species of involuntary and unconscious autobiography. *Friedrich W. Nietzsche*

Philosophy is at bottom homesickness—the longing to be at home everywhere. *Novalis*

Inertia rides and riddles...
That which is called Philosophy. *Dorothy Parker*

Not one that passes final judgments and establishes ultimate truth. It is one that causes uneasiness and starts commotion.

Charles Péguy

An attempt to give a reasonable account of our own personal attitude toward the more serious business of life. *Josiah Royce*

The search for the indefinable.

Dagobert Runes

Should be piecemeal and provisional like science; final truth belongs to heaven, not to this world.

Bertrand A. Russell

Viewed from a sufficient distance, all systems of philosophy are seen to be personal, temperamental, accidental, and premature.

George Santayana

Thinking spirals: we go higher but get no farther.

Arthur Schnitzler

Discretion. *John Selden*

The love of wisdom and the endeavor to attain it.

Seneca

Completely unified knowledge.

Herbert Spencer

Philosophy has no end in view save truth.

Baruch Spinoza

To ascertain those established conjunctions of successive events which constitute the order of the universe. *Dugald Stewart*

To record the phenomena which it exhibits to our observation, and to refer them to their general laws, is the . . . business of philosophy.

Dugald Stewart

A history of falsehood. *August Strindberg*

The outcome of the belief in the supernatural held by man in his more or less primitive state.

Paul Topinard

The discovery of what is true, and the practice of that which is good. *Voltaire*

When he who hears does not know what he who speaks means, and when he who speaks does not know what he himself means. *Voltaire*

Philosophy asks the simple question: What is it all about? *Alfred North Whitehead*

(Teaches) us to bear with equanimity the misfortune of our neighbors. *Oscar Wilde*

Simply puts everything before us and neither explains nor deduces anything.

Ludwig Wittgenstein

Something that enables the rich to say there is no disgrace in being poor. *Gideon Wurdz*

The substance of the world's wisdom.

Robert Zwickey

A filter turned upside down, where what goes in clear comes out cloudy. *Anon.*

Any systematic scheme of thought which allows you to be unhappy intelligently. *Anon.*

Like a pigeon, something to admire as long as it isn't over your head. *Anon.*

A general view of things from the standpoint of reason. *Anon.*

An individual's way of seeing the total thrust and pressure of the universe. *Anon.*

A systematization of all things according to worth. *Anon.*

Passionate vision. *Anon.*

Unified knowledge tying together the tagends of chaotic life. *Anon.*

The quest for God. *Anon.*

The quest for a value for all things in the natural world. *Anon.*

PHOTOGRAPHY

A penetrating statement, which can be described in a very simple term—selectivity.

Berenice Abbott

A true expression of what one feels about life in its entirety. *Ansel Adams*

To see beneath the surfaces and record the qualities of nature and humanity which live or are latent in all things. *Ansel Adams*

Instantaneous art for busy people, simplified art for people without artistic training, mechanical skill and genius for mass production turned to art.

M. F. Agha

To capture a moment that people cannot always see. *Henry Callahan*

A way of drawing...Our unique moment of creation is the one twenty-fifth of a second when we press the button. *Henri Cartier-Bresson*

A...notebook for recording sketches made in time and space. *Henri Cartier-Bresson*

The essence lies not in its fixation of the visible and actual but...in...the external projection ... of an inner vision of the artist. *Helmar Lerski*

The notebook of a trained reporter.
Stefan Lorant

(To) set free the *human contents* of objects ... imparts humanity to the inhuman world.
Clarence J. Loughlin

The most rigorously logical of man's methods of making images. *Henry H. Smith*

Significant details, illuminated in a flash, fixed for ever. *Susan Sontag*

A major force in explaining man to man.
Edward Steichen

A form of voyeurism. *Joseph Strick*

The "art form" of the untalented. *Gore Vidal*

An art form which isolates single moments for all time *Anon.*

PHYSICIAN

SEE DOCTORS, MEDICINE.

PICTURE

SEE PAINTING.

PIETY

One that feared God, and eschewed evil.
Bible: Job, 1, 1.

Reverence for the Supreme Being, based upon His supposed resemblance to man. *Ambrose Bierce*

Something that grows as potency declines.
Max Gralnick

The tinfoil of pretense. *Elbert Hubbard*

(Something that) is determined by one's attitude to money. *Aaron S. Kaidanover*

To look on all things with a master eye and mind at peace. *Lucretius*

Continence is the foundation of genuine piety.
Pope Sixtus 1

Renunciation of the body and its passions. This is the only real piety. *Saint Clement*

Piety to mankind must be three-fourths pity.
George Santayana

The consciousness of being absolutely dependent, or...of being in relation with God.
F. Schliermacher

SEE ALSO HOLINESS, RELIGION, REVERENCE, WORSHIP.

PIG

An animal closely allied to the human race by the splendor and vivacity of its appetite, which...is inferior in scope, for it sticks at pig.
Ambrose Bierce

Pigs is pigs. *Ellis Butler*

The pig, if I am not mistaken,
Supplies us sausage, ham, and bacon.
Let others say his heart is big—
I call it stupid of the pig. *Ogden Nash*

PIONEER

Tramps forced out of corporate societies onto the frontiers of human experience. *James Baker*

Whoever does a thing first. *Greek Proverb*

(One who) has no specialty, no likes and dislikes, no "ego." He is but a nail, driven wherever the country demands. *Vladimir Jabotinsky*

Generally a man who has outlived his credit or fortune in the cultivated parts. *Benjamin Rush*

The difference between a refugee and a pioneer is a difference of prepositions. A pioneer goes *to*, and a refugee comes *from*. *Maurice Samuel*

The (American) pioneer...is...a highly civilized being, who consents, for a time, to inhabit the backwoods, and who penetrates into the wilds of the New World with the Bible, an axe, and a file of newspapers. *Alexis de Tocqueville*

The poorer sort of people that commonly begin to improve remote deserts.   *John Woolman*

One who remembers when he could have bought the town for a thousand dollars.   *Anon.*

SEE ALSO WEST (THE OLD).

PIPE

The pipe draws wisdom from the lips of the philosopher, and shuts up the mouths of the foolish; it generates a style of conversation contemplative, thoughtful, benevolent, and unaffected.   *William Makepeace Thackeray*

A device to make dullards appear more cultured than they are.   *Anon.*

SEE ALSO TOBACCO.

PITY

The deadliest feeling that can be offered to a woman.   *Vicki Baum*

(That which) costs nothing, and it ain't worth nothing.   *Josh Billings*

The very basis of genius.   *Anatole France*

Fiction of future calamity to ourselves, proceeding from the sense of another man's calamity.
                    Thomas Hobbes

The feeling which arrests the mind in the presence of whatsoever is grave and constant in human sufferings and unites it with the human sufferer.
                    James Joyce

A perception of our own troubles through the woes of others.   *La Rochefoucauld*

When you feel pity, you don't ask other people first whether you ought to.
                    Georg C. Lichtenberg

A depressant. A man loses power when he pities.
                    Friedrich W. Nietzsche

When a man suffers himself, it is called misery; when he suffers in the misery of another, it is called pity.   *Saint Augustine*

A mental illness induced by the spectacle of other people's miseries.   *Seneca*

The scavenger of misery.

                    George Bernard Shaw

Remembering yourself.   *Anon.*

SEE ALSO SYMPATHY, TOLERANCE.

PLAGIARISM

To take the thought or style of another writer.
                    Ambrose Bierce

Another man's ideas dressed up.
                    Solomon Bushkin

If we steal thoughts from the moderns, it will be cried down as plagiarism; if from the ancients, it will be cried up as erudition.
                    Charles Caleb Colton

Stealing a ride on someone else's train of thought.
                    Russell E. Curran

Borrowing, if it be not bettered by the borrower.
                    John Milton

Taking something from one man and making it worse.   *George M. Moore*

The only 'ism' Hollywood believes in.
                    Dorothy Parker

An act which aids the novice.   *Anon.*

Something acceptable solely in regard to manners.   *Anon.*

SEE ALSO IMITATION.

PLAGIARIST

A rival aspirant to public honors.
                    Ambrose Bierce

They lard their lean books with the fat of others' works.   *Robert Burton*

Every man...life is theatrical and literature a quotation.   *Ralph Waldo Emerson*

Slavish herd!   *Horace*

A man who succeeds in being an imitation.
                    Elbert Hubbard

All the makers of dictionaries.   *Voltaire*

A stand-in for a stand-out.   *Anon.*

A literary body-snatcher.   *Anon.*

Educated pickpockets.   *Anon.*

SEE ALSO IMITATION.

PLANET

SEE EARTH, WORLD.

PLATITUDE

Simply a truth repeated till people get tired of hearing it. *Stanley Baldwin*

The wisdom of a million fools in the diction of a dullard. *Ambrose Bierce*

All that is mortal of a departed truth.
Ambrose Bierce

The cackle surviving the egg. *Ambrose Bierce*

The concentrated experience of the race.
Norman Douglas

The nearest approach to immortality for any truth. *Paul Eldridge*

An observation that is too true to be good.
Max Gralnick

A truth we are tired of hearing.
Godfrey Nicholson

The moral commonplaces. *Philip Sidney*

In modern life nothing produces such an effect as a good platitude. It makes the whole world kin.
Oscar Wilde

Saying an undisputed thing in a solemn way.
Anon.

A dull old saw that everyone borrows but no one sharpens. *Anon.*

SEE ALSO CLICHÉ.

PLATO (428-347 B.C.)

Plato's works are logical exercises for the mind. Little that is positive is advanced in them.
Samuel Taylor Coleridge

From a wedding-banquet he has passed to that city which he had founded for himself and planted in the sky. *Diogenes*

The sum of Plato's wonderful wisdom is: This is not that, and therefore, that is not this.
Adapted from Robert Dodsley

Out of Plato come all things that are still written and debated among men of thought.
Ralph Waldo Emerson

Plato is philosophy and philosophy is Plato.
Ralph Waldo Emerson

At once the glory and the shame of mankind, since neither Saxon nor Roman have availed to add any idea to his categories.
Ralph Waldo Emerson

Plato has no external biography. If he had lover, wife, or children, we hear nothing of them. He ground them all into paint.
Ralph Waldo Emerson

His foggy mind is forever presenting the semblances of objects which, half seen through a mist, can be defined neither in form nor dimensions. *Thomas Jefferson*

He can put light into our eyes. *Joseph Joubert*

A bore. *Friedrich W. Nietzsche*

PLATONIC LOVE

An impossible state between a man and a woman.
Charles Elson

A purely spiritual eroticism. *Thomas Merton*

Sex above the ears. *Thyra S. Winslow*

A type of love affected by women who feared mustaches were contagious. *Anon.*

The gun you didn't know was loaded. *Anon.*

The name given to the period between the first look and the first kiss. *Anon.*

Being invited down into the cellar for a glass of ginger ale. *Anon.*

Sex minus glands. *Anon.*

Something possible—but only between a husband and wife. *Anon.*

SEE ALSO LOVE, SEX (LOVE).

PLAY

The exultation of the possible. *Martin Buber*

One of the main bases of civilization.
John Huizinga

Joy unrefined. *Anon.*

A carry-over from childhood. *Anon.*

SEE ALSO AMUSEMENT.

PLAYGIRL

A heart stimulant for elderly gentlemen.
Hyman Maxwell Berston

A vision at night and a real sight in the morning.
George Kirby

One who smokes, swears, drinks, and plays around. Antonym: wife.   *Anon.*

She who provides all things to all men except a stable relationship.   *Anon.*

A female who is afflicted with the lamentable problem of saying "no."   *Anon.*

A female who says "perhaps" when she means yes.   *Anon.*

The kind of woman men poke funds at.   *Anon.*

One who provides the sweets which others buy.
Anon.

SEE ALSO MISTRESS, PROSTITUTE.

PLAYWRIGHT

SEE DRAMATIST.

PLEASURE

What people say you cannot do.   *Walter Bagehot*

The only good.   *Jeremy Bentham*

The gift of God.   *Bible: Ecclesiastes, III, 12.*

The least hateful form of dejection.
Ambrose Bierce

Pleasure's a sin, and sometimes sin's a pleasure.
Lord Byron

A siren that lures to flay alive the young beginner.
Adapted from Lord Byron

The rock which most young people split upon.
Lord Chesterfield

Not...the business of a man of sense and character; but it may be, and is, his relief, his reward.   *Lord Chesterfield*

The harmony between the specific excitability of a living creature and the exciting causes correspondent thereto.   *Samuel Taylor Coleridge*

The greatest blessing.   *Epicurus*

The alpha and omega of a blessed life...our first and kindred good.   *Epicurus*

The absence of pain in the body and of trouble in the soul.   *Epicurus*

Marshy lands that we must travel nimbly, hardly daring to put down our feet.
Bernard de Fontenelle

The most real good in this life.
Friedrich the Great

Pain past.   *Thomas Fuller*

Every perfect action.   *André Gide*

There are only three pleasures in life pure and lasting, and all derived from inanimate things— books, pictures, and the face of nature.
William Hazlitt

An intensity exquisite.   *Heinrich Heine*

The greatest...is to do a good action by stealth, and to have it found out by accident.
Charles Lamb

One of the major kinds of profit.
Michel de Montaigne

The bait of sin.   *Plato*

Our greatest evil or our greatest good.
Alexander Pope

Sleep, riches and health.   *Jean Paul Richter*

That which cannot be described.
Jean-Jacques Rousseau

Nothing else but the intermission pain.
John Selden

The true pleasure of life is to live with your inferiors.   *William Makepeace Thackeray*

Simple pleasures are the last refuge of the complex.   *Oscar Wilde*

Nature's test, her sign of approval. When we are happy we are always good, but when we are good we are not always happy.   *Oscar Wilde*

SEE ALSO ART, DEEDS, HAPPINESS, LABOR, LOVE.

PLUMBER

An adventurer who traces leaky pipes to their source.   *Arthur Baer*

One who'll look at Niagara Falls and say, "Give me time and I could fix it."   *Meyer Davis*

A man who gets paid for sleeping under sinks.
                                                   Anon.

A craftsman who forces you to cash in your savings bonds.   *Anon.*

POE, EDGAR ALLAN (1809-1849)

A meteor that has lost its way!
                                        Thomas Bailey Aldrich

Proud, mad, but not defiant,
   He touched at heaven and hell.   *J. H. Boner*

There is no more effective way of realizing Poe's genius than my imagining American literature without him.   *William C. Brownell*

The jingle-man.   *Ralph Waldo Emerson*

He had...that desire to rise which is vulgarly called ambition, but no wish for the esteem of the love of his species.   *Rufus W. Griswold*

There comes Poe, with his raven, like
   Barnaby Rudge,
Three fifths of him genius and two
   fifths sheer fudge.   *James Russell Lowell*

He walked with shadows.   *Clinton Scollard*

Hawthorne with delirium tremens.
                              Adapted from Leslie Stephen

I have a distinct and pleasing remembrance of his looks, voice, manner and matter; very kindly and human, but subdued, perhaps a little jaded.
                                        Walt Whitman

An evanescent mystic whose mysticism breaks down.   *Anon.*

POET

A person...passionately in love with language.
                                        Wystan H. Auden

All who love, who feel great truths, and tell them.
                                        Philip J. Bailey

People who despise money except what they need for today.   *James M. Barrie*

(One who must have) sincerity and depth of vision.   *Thomas Carlyle*

Through him all men see.
                              William Ellery Channing

One who, in the excursions of his fancy between Heaven and earth, lights upon a kind of fairyland, in which he places a creation of his own, where he embodies shapes, and gives action and adventure to his ideal offspring.   *George Crabbe*

The painter of the soul.   *Isaac D'Israeli*

He announces that which no man has foretold.
                                        Ralph Waldo Emerson

The poet's business is not to save the soul of a man but to make it worth saving.
                                        James E. Fletcher

The mere wastepaper of mankind.
                                        Benjamin Franklin

The truest historian.   *James A. Froude*

Buffoons.   *Johann W. Goethe*

To be a poet is a condition rather than a profession.   *Robert Graves*

The first teachers of mankind.   *Horace*

Prophets whose prophesying never comes true.
                                        Edgar W. Howe

A person born with the instinct of poverty.
                                        Elbert Hubbard

A worthless, shiftless chap whose songs adorn the libraries of...shopkeepers...one hundred years after the chap has died of malnutrition.
                                        Elbert Hubbard

A maker, or a fainer; his art, an art of imitation, of faining, expressing the life of man in fit measure, numbers, and harmony.   *Ben Jonson*

The most unpoetical of anything in existence, because he has no identity; he is continually filling some other body.   *John Keats*

(Those) who simply tell the most hearteasing things.   *John Keats*

The dreaming doer.   *John G. Neihardt*

The true poet is all-knowing! He is an actual world in miniature.   *Novalis*

One who should always be hungry or in love.
                                        Donald Peattie

Every man...when he is in love.   *Plato*

(Those who) utter great and wise things which they do not themselves understand. *Plato*

Of all mankind the creatures most absurd.

Alexander Pope

God's most candid critics are those of his children whom he has made poets. *Walter Raleigh*

A person who puts . . . life into action.

John Ruskin

The combined product of such internal powers as modify the nature of others; and of such external influences as excite and sustain these powers; he is not one, but both. *Percy Bysshe Shelley*

A nightingale, who sits in darkness and sings to cheer its own solitude with sweet sounds.

Percy Bysshe Shelley

The priest of the invisible. *Wallace Stevens*

Liars by profession. *Jonathan Swift*

A man who lives . . . by watching his moods.

Henry David Thoreau

(One whose works) have never yet been read by mankind, for only great poets can read them.

Henry David Thoreau

A man is a poet if the difficulties inherent in his art provide him with ideas; he is not a poet if they deprive him of ideas. *Paul Valéry*

The spectator of all time and of all existence. For him no form is obsolete, no subject out of date.

Oscar Wilde

(One who) can survive anything but a misprint.

Oscar Wilde

A man speaking to men, endowed with more lively sensibility, more enthusiasm and tenderness, who has a greater knowledge of human nature, and a more comprehensive soul than are supposed to be common among mankind.

William Wordsworth

A man pleased with his own passions and volitions, and who rejoices more than other men in the spirit of life that is in him.

William Wordsworth

One that would peep and botanize upon his mother's grave. *William Wordsworth*

The eternal bane of landlords. *Anon.*

SEE ALSO ARTISTS, METAPHOR, RHYME.

Imaginative metrical discourse.

Raymond M. Alden

The art of representing human experiences . . . in metrical language, usually with chief reference to the emotions and by means of the imagination.

Raymond M. Alden

The most beautiful, impressive, and widely effective mode of saying things. *Matthew Arnold*

A criticism of life under the conditions fixed for such a criticism by the laws of poetic truth and beauty. *Matthew Arnold*

A form looking for a subject and a subject looking for a form. *Wystan H. Auden*

Seeks to accommodate the show of things to the desires of the mind, and to create an ideal world better than the world of experience.

Francis Bacon

A kind of ingenious nonsense. *Isaac Barrow*

A bygone phase in the history of the human kind.

Clifford Bax

The impish attempt to paint the color of the wind.

Maxwell Bodenheim

The succession of experiences—sounds, images, thoughts, emotion—through which we pass when we are reading. *Andrew Bradley*

Life distilled. *Gwendolyn Brooks*

That art which selects and arranges the symbols of thought in such a manner as to excite the imagination the most powerfully and delightfully.

William Cullen Bryant

The product of the smaller intestines.

Pierre Cabanis

Man's rebellion against being what he is.

James Branch Cabell

All poetry is but a giving of names.

Thomas Carlyle

Poetry is at bottom a biography, the life of a man.

Thomas Carlyle

Musical thought. *Thomas Carlyle*

The expression of the hunger for elsewhere.

Benjamin de Casseres

The utterance of deep and heart-felt truth.

> *Edwin H. Chapin*

The communication of pleasure.

> *Samuel Taylor Coleridge*

The best words in their best order.

> *Samuel Taylor Coleridge*

That to which we return, with the greatest pleasure, possesses the genuine power, and claims the name of essential poetry.

> *Samuel Taylor Coleridge*

The art of producing pleasure by the just expression of imaginative thought and feeling in metrical language. *William J. Courthope*

The language of feeling. *Benedetto Croce*

A literary gift—chiefly because you can't sell it.

> *Cynic's Cyclopaedia*

A latency of meaning beyond the simple statement of facts. *E. Dallas*

If I feel physically as if the top of my head were taken off, I know that is poetry.

> *Emily Dickinson*

Delight is the chief if not the only end...instruction can be admitted but in the second place, for poetry only instructs as it delights.

> *John Dryden*

The intolerable wrestle with words and meanings.

> *Thomas Stearns Eliot*

Not a turning loose of emotion, but an escape from emotion...not the expression of personality, but an escape from personality.

> *Thomas Stearns Eliot*

Only that is poetry which cleanses and mans me.

> *Ralph Waldo Emerson*

The expression of a sound mind speaking after the ideal, not after the apparent.

> *Ralph Waldo Emerson*

The concrete and artistic expression of the human mind in emotional and rhythmical language.

> *Encyclopaedia Britannica*

An ordered voice, one which tries to tell you about a vision in the unvisionary language of farm, city and love. *Paul Engle*

Ordinary language raised to the nth power. Poetry is boned with ideas, nerved and blooded with emotions, and held together by the delicate, tough skin of words. *Paul Engle*

What is poetry? Who knows?
Not the rose, but the scent of the rose.

> *Eleanor Farjeon*

Not myself, but what makes me
See, hear, and feel something that prose
Cannot: and what is, who knows.

> *Eleanor Farjeon*

Imagination. *Owen Felltham*

It begins in delight and ends in wisdom.

> *Robert Frost*

An extravagance you hope to get away with.

> *Robert Frost*

(When) an emotion has found its thought and the thought has found words. *Robert Frost*

Language in which man explores his own amazement. *Christopher Fry*

Plucking at the heartstrings, and making music with them. *Dennis Gabor*

Truth dwelling in beauty. *Robert Gilfillan*

Thoughts that breathe, and words that burn.

> *Thomas Gray*

A wonderful game with words.

> *Irene W. Grisson*

Science sees signs; Poetry the thing signified.

> *Julius and Augustus Hare*

All that is worth remembering of life.

> *William Hazlitt*

To suggest; to imply, to employ words with auras of association, with a reaching out toward a vision, a probing down into an emotion, beyond the compass of explicit definition.

> *Harold Hobson*

The utterance of a passion for truth, beauty, and power, embodying and illustrating its conceptions by imagination and fancy, and modulating its language on the principle of variety in uniformity.

> *Leigh Hunt*

What is poetry? Why, Sir, it is much easier to say what it is not. We all know what light is, but it is not easy to tell what it is. *Samuel Johnson*

Impromptus made at leisure. *Joseph Joubert*

A friend to soothe the cares, and lift the thoughts of men. *Adapted from John Keats*

A drainless shower of light. *John Keats*

Nothing else than each poet's innermost feeling issuing in rhythmic language. *John Kebble*

A powerful piece of imposture. It masters the fancy, and hurries it nobody knows whither. *Firmianus Lactantius*

Concentration is the very essence of poetry. *Amy Lowell*

It is not the finding of a thing, but the making something out of it after it is found that is of consequence. *James Russell Lowell*

Something to make us better and wiser by continually revealing those types of beauty and truth which God has set in all men's souls. *James Russell Lowell*

The truth of madness. The reasonings are just, but the premises are false. *Thomas B. Macaulay*

The art of employing words in such a manner as to produce an illusion of the imagination. *Thomas B. Macaulay*

A poem should not mean but be. *Archibald MacLeish*

The language of a state of crisis. *Stéphane Mallarmé*

That intercommunication between the inner being of things and the inner being of the human Self which is a kind of divination. *Jacques Maritain*

What Milton saw when he went blind. *Don Marquis*

Poetry has done enough when it charms. *Henry Louis Mencken*

A comforting piece of fiction set to more or less lascivious music. *Henry Louis Mencken*

Its purpose is not to establish facts, but to evade and deny them. *Henry Louis Mencken*

Talking on tiptoe. *George Meredith*

A peerless proficiency of the imagination. *Marianne Moore*

An honesty unfeigned,
A heart unchained.
A madness well restrained. *Christopher Morley*

A disease of the spirit. *Christopher Morley*

The mysteries of the irrational perceived through rational words. *Vladimir Nabokov*

All literary production which attains the power of giving pleasure by its form, as distinct from its matter. *Walter Pater*

The rhythmical creation of beauty. *Edgar Allan Poe*

The revelation of a feeling that the poet believes to be interior and personal (but) which the reader recognizes as his own. *Salvatore Quasimodo*

A full sister of religion, of genuine, soulful piety. *Joshua Rapoport*

The cadence of consenting feet. *Herbert Read*

Language that tells us, through a more or less emotional reaction, something that cannot be said. *Edwin Arlington Robinson*

Truth in its Sunday clothes. *Joseph Roux*

The presentment, in musical form, to the imagination, of noble grounds for the noble emotions. *John Ruskin*

Devil's wine. *Saint Augustine*

A spot about half-way between where you listen and where you wonder what it was you heard. *Carl Sandburg*

The journal of a sea animal living on land, wanting to fly in the air. *Carl Sandburg*

A search for syllables to shoot at the barriers of the unknown and unknowable. *Carl Sandburg*

The achievement of the synthesis of hyacinths and biscuits. *Carl Sandburg*

What makes the invisible appear. *Nathalie Sarraute*

A damned weed, and will let nothing good or profitable grow by it. *Thomas Shadwell*

A mimetic art. It creates, but it creates by combination and representation. *Percy Bysshe Shelley*

The record of the best and happiest moments of the best and happiest minds. *Percy Bysshe Shelley*

The most elegant of youthful accomplishments; but it is entirely a youthful one. *William Shenstone*

Vocal painting. *Simonides*

The deification of reality. *Edith Sitwell*

The natural language of all worship.

Anne Louise Staël

Rhythmical, imaginative language expressing the invention, taste, thought, passion, and insight of the human soul. *Edmund C. Stedman*

An art...the easiest to dabble in, the hardest in which to reach true excellence.

Edmund C. Stedman

A vocal picture. *Anthony Stubbing*

Nothing but healthy speech.

Henry David Thoreau

The music of the soul; and, above all, of great and feeling souls. *Voltaire*

Concrete and artistic expression of the human mind in emotional and rhythmical language.

Theodore Watts-Dunton

Wisdom married to immortal verse.

William Wordsworth

The imaginative expression of strong feeling usually rhythmical. *William Wordsworth*

SEE ALSO LITERATURE, METAPHOR, RHYME, WRITING.

POISE

Something attractive only when one is on a tightrope; seated on the ground, and there is nothing wonderful about it. *André Gide*

The art of raising the eyebrows instead of the roof.

Howard W. Newton

The ability to be ill at ease inconspicuously.

Earl Wilson

The ability to face the guillotine without losing your head. *Anon.*

The art of raising your eyebrows instead of your temper. *Anon.*

SEE ALSO BREEDING (MANNERS), MANNERS.

POLAND

Hope of the half-defeated. *Hilaire Belloc*

The symbol of all who have loved the loftiest ideals of humanity and have fought for them.

Georg M. Brandes

POLICEMAN

An armed force for protection and participation.

Ambrose Bierce

Men fully able to meet and compete with criminals. *John F. Hylan*

Policemen are soldiers who act alone; soldiers are policemen who act in unison. *Herbert Spencer*

A...watcher of the public weal.

Alfred Lord Tennyson

The bane of anarchists and criminals. *Anon.*

The thin line that stands between us and the barbarians. *Anon.*

The folk-hero of small town America. *Anon.*

POLITENESS

An easy virtue, and has great purchasing power.

Amos Bronson Alcott

The most acceptable hypocrisy.

Ambrose Bierce

A necessary check on animality.

Eugene E. Brussell

The chief sign of culture. *Baltasar Gracian*

Not speaking evil of people with whom you have just dined until you are...a hundred yards from their house. *Emile Herzog*

The screen of language. *Elbert Hubbard*

A substitute for war. *Elbert Hubbard*

Artificial good humor. *Thomas Jefferson*

Fictitious benevolence. *Samuel Johnson*

One of those advantages which we never estimate rightly but by the inconvenience of its loss.

Samuel Johnson

One half good nature and the other half good lying. *Mary W. Little*

Benevolence in small things.

Thomas B. Macaulay

A desire to so contrive it, by word and manner, that others will be pleased with us and with themselves.   *Charles de Montesquieu*

That roguish and cheerful vice.

Friedrich W. Nietzsche

Consists in being easy about one's self, and in making everyone about one as easy as one can.

Alexander Pope

A liberating constraint. It makes it possible to say everything that rudeness couldn't.

Sigismund von Radecki

A form of behavior often mistaken for good manners.   *Harry Ruby*

A tacit agreement that people's miserable defects...shall on either side be ignored and not be made the subject of reproach.

Arthur Schopenhauer

An air-cushion: there is nothing inside, but it softens the shocks of life.

Arthur Schopenhauer

Pretended liking.   *Logan P. Smith*

Politeness has been defined as artificial good nature; with much greater propriety it may be said that good nature is natural politeness.

Stanislaus

Hope and trust in men.   *Henry David Thoreau*

Organized indifference.   *Paul Valéry*

Sleep not when others speak, sit not when others stand, speak not when you should hold your peace, walk not on when others stop.

George Washington

The art of choosing among your thoughts.

Anon.

To please others and ourselves.   *Anon.*

SEE ALSO BREEDING (MANNERS), CHARACTER, CHARM, COURTESY, DIPLOMACY, ETIQUETTE, GENTLEMEN, LADY, MANNERS.

POLITICAL CAMPAIGN

SEE ELECTIONEERING, POLITICIAN.

POLITICAL CANDIDATE

SEE ELECTIONEERING, PUBLIC OFFICE

POLITICAL PARTY

A dreadful spirit of division as rends a government into two distinct people, and makes them greater strangers and more averse to one another than if they were actually two different nations.

Joseph Addison

Things inseparable from free government.

Edmund Burke

Leads to viscious, corrupt and unprofitable legislation, for the sole purpose of defeating a party.

James Fenimore Cooper

Organized opinion.   *Benjamin Disraeli*

To pair off into insane parties, and learn the amount of truth each knows by the denial of an equal amount of truth.   *Ralph Waldo Emerson*

An elegant incognito devised to save a man from the vexation of thinking.

Ralph Waldo Emerson

A kind of conspiracy against the rest of the nation.

Lord Halifax

The organized power of one class to oppress the other.   *Karl Marx and Friedrich Engels*

The madness of the many, for the gain of a few.

Alexander Pope

All parties without exception, when they seek for power, are varieties of absolutism.

Pierre J. Proudhon

The historical organ by means of which a class becomes class conscious.   *Leon Trotsky*

SEE ALSO ELECTIONEERING.

POLITICIAN

An eel in the fundamental mud upon which the superstructure of organized society is reared.

Ambrose Bierce

A calculating person who never shows feeling— unintentionally.   *Eugene E. Brussell*

One who likes what the majority likes.

Eugene E. Brussell

An honest politician is one who when he's bought stays bought.   *Simon Cameron*

A dealer in promises.   *Gabriel Chevallier*

(One who) thinks of the next election; a statesman, of the next generation.   *James Clarke*

Trustees of the people.   *Grover Cleveland*

Any man with a fine shock of hair, a good set of teeth, and a bewitching smile, can park his brains, if he has any, and run for public office.
Franklin Dane

A man who can be verbose in fewer words than anyone else.   *Peter De Vries*

(One who expresses) a minimum of thought in a maximum amount of words.   *Abba Eban*

A public slave.   *Baltasar Gracian*

One who has the shortcomings of his constituency.   *Max Gralnick*

(One who) will do anything to keep his job—even become a patriot.   *William Randolph Hearst 1*

A man who identifies the sound of his own voice with the infallible voice of the public.
Joseph K. Howard

Men who volunteer the task of governing us for a consideration.   *Elbert Hubbard*

Public property.   *Thomas Jefferson*

This struggle and scramble...for a way to live without work.   *Abraham Lincoln*

A set of men who have interests aside from the interests of the people and who...are, taken as a mass, at least one step removed from honest men.
Abraham Lincoln

Insecure and intimidated men.
Walter Lippmann

A person with whose politics you won't agree; if you agree with him he is a statesman.
David Lloyd George

Somebody that any bloke can come to—no matter what he's done—and get help. Help, you understand, none of your law and justice, but help.
Martin Lomasney

One who talks himself red, white and blue in the face.   *Clare Boothe Luce*

Any citizen with influence enough to get his old mother a job as charwoman in the City Hall.
Henry Louis Mencken

Men who, at some time or other, have compromised with their honor, either by swallowing their convictions or by whooping for what they believe to be untrue.   *Henry Louis Mencken*

(One who) divides mankind into two classes: tools and enemies. That means that he knows only one class: enemies.   *Friedrich W. Nietzsche*

Quicksilver; if you try to put your fingers on him, you will find nothing under it.   *Austin O'Malley*

The semi-failures in business and the professions, men of mediocre mentality, dubious morals, and magnificent commonplaceness.
Walter B. Pitkin

The slave of pomp, a cipher in the state.
Richard Savage

One that would circumvent God.
William Shakespeare

A man who has to shave twice a day.
Adlai E. Stevenson

A man who understands government, and it takes a politician to run a government.
Harry S. Truman

Just men at play, with us as counters to be moved about.   *Gore Vidal*

(One who) toils but for a momentary rattle.
Horace Walpole

Lord of the golden tongue and smiting eyes, whose virtue, genius wrings deadlier ills than ages can undo.   *Adapted from William Watson*

An animal who can sit on a fence and yet keep both ears to the ground.   *Oscar Wilde*

A person who realizes you can't fool all of the people all of the time but is willing to give it a try.
Robert Zwickey

One with the tutored capacity to produce serious pronouncements in a sonorous voice.
Robert Zwickey

One who shrinks from the duties of private life to seek the publicity of public office.   *Anon.*

One who takes a firm stand on matters that he knows the public will endorse.   *Anon.*

One who thinks twice before saying nothing.
Anon.

A man who never met a tax he didn't like or try to hike.   *Anon.*

One who gets money from the rich and votes from the poor to protect them from each other.   *Anon.*

All things to all men and to all men nothing.
Anon.

One who keeps the masses loyal to him by keeping them angry at someone else.   *Anon.*

One who approaches every subject with an open mouth.   *Anon.*

He who belongs to the opposite party.   *Anon.*

One who has a good memory and hopes other people haven't.   *Anon.*

One who is willing to do anything on earth for the common folk except become one.   *Anon.*

Two classes: the appointed and the disappointed.
Anon.

A puppy attempting to follow three children at the same time.   *Anon.*

One who stands for what he thinks others will fall for.   *Anon.*

One who shakes your hand before the election and your acquaintance afterwards.   *Anon.*

SEE ALSO BALLOT, DEMOCRACY, ELEC-TIONEERING, STATESMAN.

POLITICS

The systematic organization of hatreds.
Henry B. Adams

Practical politics consists in ignoring facts.
Henry B. Adams

A struggle not of men but of forces.
Henry B. Adams

The gentle art of getting votes from the poor and campaign funds from the rich, by promising to protect each from the other.   *Oscar Ameringer*

The good of man must be the end of the science of politics.   *Aristotle*

The art of putting people under obligation to you.
Jake Arvey

The art of looking for trouble, finding it everywhere, diagnosing it wrongly, and applying unsuitable remedies.   *Ernest Benn*

A strife of interests masquerading as a contest of principles. The conduct of public affairs for private advantage.   *Ambrose Bierce*

The doctrine of the possible.
Otto von Bismarck

The art of the next best.   *Otto von Bismarck*

A realm, peopled only by villains or heroes, in which everything is black or white and gray is a forbidden color.   *John Mason Brown*

An art where a sense of humor is absolutely forbidden.   *Eugene E. Brussell*

To young men it is the worthiest ambition...the greatest and the most honourable adventure.
John Buchan

Vain hope.   *Thomas Carlyle*

War without violence. War is politics with violence.   *Stokeley Carmichael*

The moral man's compromise, the swindler's method, and the fool's hope.   *John Ciardi*

Turning a complex problem of the head into a simple moral question of the heart.
Frank M. Colby

One of the most corrupting of the influences to which men are exposed.
James Fenimore Cooper

The diplomatic name for the law of the jungle.
Ely Culbertson

This career of plundering and blundering.
Benjamin Disraeli

The possession and distribution of power.
Benjamin Disraeli

A deleterious profession.
Ralph Waldo Emerson

A lot of mirrors and blue smoke.   *Wych Fowler*

A sickbed on which people toss from side to side, thinking they will be more comfortable.
Adapted from Johann W. Goethe

The arena of interests, not morals.
Warren Goldberg

The highly ceramic art of molding scum to your own desires.   *Francis L. Golden*

A cruel trade; good nature is a bunglar in it.
Lord Halifax

Politics—where they pat you on the back so they'll know where to stick the knife.
Harry Hershfield

Persuading the public to vote for this and support that and endure these for the promise of those.

Gilbert Highet

The science of how who gets what, when and why.

Sidney Hillman

The glad hand, and a swift kick in the pants.

Elbert Hubbard

(An art that) makes strange postmasters.

Kin Hubbard

A torment.   *Thomas Jefferson*

Nothing more than the means of rising in the world.   *Samuel Johnson*

Politics is property.   *Murray Kempton*

It beats following the dollar . . . First, there is the great chess game—the battle, the competition. There's the strategy and which piece you move . . . And then in government you can do something about what you think.

John Fitzgerald Kennedy

Economics in action.   *Robert M. La Follette*

A form of astrology—and money is its sign.

John Leonard

Concealment, evasion, factious combinations, the surrender of convictions to party objects, and the systematic pursuit of expediency.   *Robert Lowe*

The hard dealing of hard men over properties; their strength is in dealing and their virility.

Norman Mailer

War without bloodshed.   *Mao Tse-tung*

The whole aim . . . is to keep the populace alarmed (and hence clamorous to be led to safety) by an endless series of hobgoblins.

Henry Louis Mencken

Consists wholly of a succession of unintelligent crazes, many of them so idiotic that they exist only as . . . shibboleths and are not reducible to logical statement at all.   *Henry Louis Mencken*

The first business of men, the school of mediocrity, to the covetously ambitious a sty, to the dullard his amphitheatre . . . Olympus to genius.

George Meredith

An activity in which the choice is constantly between two evils.   *John Morley*

The diversion of trivial men who, when they succeed at it, become important in the eyes of more trivial men.   *George Jean Nathan*

Consists in directing rationally the irrationalities of men.   *Reinhold Niebuhr*

A mass of lies, evasions, folly, hatred, and schizophrenia.   *George Orwell*

The science of exigencies.   *Theodore Parker*

A profession in which you cannot be true to all of your friends all of the time.   *Michael Pazaine*

The common pulse-beat, of which revolution is the fever-spasm.   *Wendell Phillips*

I used to say that politics was the second oldest profession, and I have come to know that it bears a gross similarity to the first.   *Ronald Reagan*

Mostly pill-taking.   *Thomas B. Reed*

A perpetual emergency.   *Ralph Roeder*

All politics is apple sauce.   *Will Rogers*

At its worst . . . a device for keeping people—and peoples—apart. At its best . . . a means of bringing them together.   *César Saerchinger*

The premises of politics lie in the conclusions of ethics.   *Herbert L. Samuel*

Nothing but good manners in public.

Lincoln Steffens

Perhaps the only profession for which no preparation is thought necessary.

Robert Louis Stevenson

Nothing but corruptions.   *Jonathan Swift*

The madness of many for the gain of a few.

Jonathan Swift

The cigar-smoke of a man.

Henry David Thoreau

Reader, suppose you were an idiot. And suppose you were a member of Congress. But I repeat myself.   *Mark Twain*

The art of making possible that which is necessary.   *Paul Valéry*

The first act of the professional politician is to accuse the other side of being professional politicians.   *William Vaughan*

The greatest of all sciences.

Luc de Vauvenargues

A pen in a stockyard.   *Herbert G. Wells*

An art not merely of compromise but of . . . what might be called an impersonal and inherent . . . cruelty.   *William S. White*

A clever game, and sometimes a great nuisance.
Adapted from Oscar Wilde

The science of the ordered progress of society along the lines of greatest usefulness and convenience to itself.   *Woodrow Wilson*

A popularity contest...mass merchandising.
Franklin Zappa

The disease of the ego which causes you to swell without growing.   *Anon.*

The craft of appeasing the voter without giving him what he wants.   *Anon.*

The relentless pursuit of the voter.   *Anon.*

SEE ALSO BALLOT, CONSERVATISM, DEMOCRACY, DEMOCRAT, ELECTIONEERING, LIBERALISM, POLITICAL PARTY, POLITICIAN, PUBLIC OFFICE, RADICALISM, REPUBLICAN PARTY, VOTING.

POLYGAMY

A bore.   *Lord Byron*

An endeavor to get more out of life than there is in it.   *Elbert Hubbard*

Like a man who is attached to more churches than one, whereby his faith is so distracted that it becomes no faith.   *Emanuel Swedenborg*

POOR

God's people.   *Bible: Exodus, XXXI, 5.*

Those who are *excluded* from participating in the economy.   *John Kenneth Galbraith*

Man is God's image; but a poor man is Christ's stamp to boot.   *George Herbert*

The only consistent altruists; they sell all that they have and give to the rich.   *Holbrook Jackson*

Those who have nothing and are always eager to share it with others.   *Jewish Proverb*

Those who have dry throats and wet shoes.
Jewish Proverb

A man who eats chicken when he is sick or when the chicken is.   *Jewish Saying*

He is poor whose expenses exceed his income.
Jean de La Bruyère

He who sees the world in the purse.
Samuel Liptzin

Not the man who has little, but he who desires more.   *Seneca*

A frame of mind.   *Mike Todd*

To always want more than you have.   *Anon.*

Those who expect no change for the worse.
Anon.

The non-possession of much.   *Anon.*

The only class of people who have time to cutivate the intellect.   *Anon.*

A very real, a very active condition.   *Anon.*

A class of people with a permanent crime wave.
Anon.

SEE ALSO CLASSES, MONEY, PHILANTHROPY, POVERTY, RICHES, WEALTHY.

POPE, ALEXANDER (1688-1744)

The splendid high priest of our excellent and indispensable eighteenth-century.
Matthew Arnold

One whom it was easy to hate, but still easier to quote.   *Augustine Birrell*

The moral poet of all civilization.   *Lord Byron*

He had all the genius of one of the first masters. Never...were such talents and such drudgery united.   *William Cowper*

Pope...wrote poetry fit to put round frosted cake.   *Ralph Waldo Emerson*

Ten razor blades in one neat couplet case!
John Macy

A madman or...a very great poet.
Raymond Smith

POPULACE

They are such as are not likely to be remembered a moment after their disappearance: they leave behind them no traces of their existence, but are forgotten as though they had never been.
Joseph Addison

A sickly progeny...too poor to tax, too numerous to feed.   *Colin Ellis*

The small change of glory.   *French Proverb*

The mutable, rank-scented many.

William Shakespeare

Herds and flocks of people that follow anybody that whistles to them, or drives them to pasture.

Jeremy Taylor

SEE ALSO CROWD, MAJORITY, MASSES, MOB, PEOPLE (THE), PUBLIC (THE), RABBLE.

POPULARITY

The people's chosen flower.   *Quintus Ennius*

A crime from the moment it is sought; it is only a virtue where men have it whether they will or no.

Lord Halifax

The triumph of the commonplace.

Elbert Hubbard

Glory's small change.   *Victor Hugo*

The capacity for listening sympathetically when men boast of their wives and women complain of their husbands.   *Henry Louis Mencken*

To mingle with the erring throng.

Robert Nugent

That empty and ugly thing.

Robert Louis Stevenson

Always an exhausting business.   *Anon.*

A pleasant visitor who always leaves in the morning.   *Anon.*

SEE ALSO APPLAUSE, FAME.

POPULATION

About the only thing left that discriminates in favor of the plain people.   *Kin Hubbard*

Humanity considered as statistics.   *Anon.*

POPULATION EXPLOSION

The political problem of problems.

Thomas Henry Huxley

A condition that has led to all the modern evils, from bureaucracy on down.   *Anon.*

The result of overbearing women.   *Anon.*

That phenomenon that will eventually convert beauty spots to amusement parks.   *Anon.*

SEE ALSO BIRTH CONTROL.

PORNOGRAPHY

SEE OBSCENITY.

POSSESSIONS

Nine points of the law.   *English Proverb*

Something that hinders enjoyment and increases annoyance whether you lend or borrow.

Adapted from Baltasar Gracian

Possession means to sit astride of the world, instead of having it astride you.

Adapted from Charles Kingsley

All the possessions of mortals are mortal.

Metrodorous

Moses expressed it by the name of Cain, meaning "possession," a feeling foolish to the core...for instead of regarding all possessions as God's, Cain fancied that they were his own, though he could not possess securely even himself.   *Philo*

To know how to do without.   *Jean F. Regnard*

Outward things.   *Saint Clement*

We only possess what we renounce; what we do not renounce escapes from us.   *Simone Weil*

It...gives one position, and prevents one from keeping it up.   *Oscar Wilde*

Only what you yourself are.   *Anon.*

SEE ALSO PROPERTY, SELF, WEALTH.

POSTERITY

A most limited assembly. Those gentlemen who reach posterity are not much more numerous than the planets.   *Benjamin Disraeli*

The consequence of the necessity of death. If a man were sure of living forever here, he would not care.   *Nathaniel Hawthorne*

The author's favorite.   *Samuel Johnson*

The patriotic name for grandchildren.

Art Linkletter

That high court of appeal which is never tired of eulogising its own justice and discernment.

Thomas B. Macaulay

(That which) gives every man his true value.

Tacitus

Our children's children, and those who shall be descended from them.   *Vergil*

SEE ALSO CHILDREN.

POSTMAN

A civil servant whose legs taste sweet to dogs.

Anon.

A man who delivers the mail and reads other people's post-cards.   *Anon.*

POVERTY

(That which) was created only to provide the well-to-do with an opportunity for charity.

Jehiel Anav

The non-possession of much.   *Antipater*

A curse of the heart.

Apocrypha: Ben Sira, XXXVIII, 19.

The discoverer of all the arts.   *Apollonius*

The parent of revolution and crime.   *Aristotle*

A shirt of fire.   *Armenian Proverb*

A file provided for the teeth of the rats of reform.

Ambrose Bierce

The wicked man's tempter, the good man's perdition, the proud man's curse, the melancholy man's halter.   *Edward G. Bulwer-Lytton*

The reward of honest fools.   *Colley Cibber*

We can call only the want of what is necessary poverty.   *Clement 1*

Not only a great evil, but tends to its own increase by leading to recklessness in marriage.

Charles Darwin

Poverty consists in feeling poor.

Ralph Waldo Emerson

The lack of ability, in any given circumstances, to get whatever is necessary for comfortable living.

Edward H. Faulkner

No vice, but an inconvenience.   *John Florio*

The best thing that can happen to a young man.

James A. Garfield

The open-mouthed, relentless hell which yawns beneath civilized society. And it is hell enough.

Henry George

A state of mind not of income. The key ways of overcoming this state of mind are marriage and work.   *George Gilder*

To be poor, and seem to be poor.

Oliver Goldsmith

The strenuous life—without brass bands, or uniforms, or hysteric popular applause, or lies.

William James

The worst moral disease from which our civilization suffers.   *William James*

People come to poverty in two ways: accumulating debts and paying them off.   *Jewish Saying*

Our failure to give our fellow citizens a fair chance to develop their own capabilities.

Lyndon Baines Johnson

A great enemy to human happiness; it . . . destroys liberty, and it makes some virtues impracticable, and others extremely difficult.   *Samuel Johnson*

Nothing but gloom and melancholy.

Samuel Johnson

Half laziness.   *Yugoslavian Proverb*

A virtue greatly overrated by those who no longer practice it.   *Barnaby C. Keeney*

To have nothing is not poverty.   *Martial*

The hospital of the labor army.   *Karl Marx*

A soft pedal upon all branches of human activity, not excepting the spirit.   *Henry Louis Mencken*

(A condition which) keeps together more homes than it breaks up.   *Hector H. Munro*

The most deadly and prevalent of all diseases.

Eugene O'Neill

A kind of disease which is called lack of money.

Francois Rabelais

A great radiance from within.

Rainer Maria Rilke

The only thing wrong with the poor.

George Bernard Shaw

No disgrace to a man, but it is confoundedly inconvenient.   *Sydney Smith*

Life near the bone, where it is sweetest.
                                    Henry David Thoreau

No disgrace—and that's about all that can be said for it.   *R. M. Tucker*

Nothing but self-denial.   *Oscar Wilde*

What sticks to a man after all of his friends have left him.   *Anon.*

Rude inelegance.   *Anon.*

SEE ALSO POOR.

POWER

Power is poison.   *Henry B. Adams*

When wielded by abnormal energy...the most serious of facts.   *Henry B. Adams*

Power is like a woman you want to stay in bed with forever.   *Patrick Anderson*

The morality of men who stand out from the rest.
                                Ludwig van Beethoven

There is no power but from God.
                                Bible: Romans, XIII, 1

Religion.   *Phillips Brooks*

The right word and the right accent.
                                    Joseph Conrad

The application of intelligence to force.
                                    Arthur F. Corey

The most constant and the most active of all the causes which degrade and demoralize men.
                            Adapted from John E. Dalberg

All power is trust.   *Benjamin Disraeli*

Accomplishment, aided and abetted by money.
                                    Jake W. Ehrlich

The god of the one who accepts only himself.
                                        Waldo Frank

The perception of power *is* power.   *David Garth*

Heavier toil, superior pain.   *Thomas Gray*

To attempt to produce any effect, and to succeed.
                                    William Hazlitt

The power of a man is his present means to obtain some future apparent good.   *Thomas Hobbes*

The measure of manhood.   *Josiah G. Holland*

Patience and gentleness is power.   *Leigh Hunt*

Gradually stealing away from the many to the few, because the few are more vigilant and consistent.
                                    Samuel Johnson

The ultimate aphrodisiac.   *Henry Kissinger*

To be able to do without.   *George Macdonald*

A Dead Sea fruit. When you achieve it, there is nothing there.   *Harold Macmillan*

Political power is...the organized power of one class to oppress another.
                        Karl Marx and Friedrich Engels

Power is not a means, it is an end.
                                    George Orwell

Unbridled ambition for domination.
                                    Pope Pius XI

A drug, the desire for which increases with the habit.   *Bertrand A. Russell*

Self-reverence, self-knowledge, self-control.
                                Alfred Lord Tennyson

SEE ALSO AUTHORITY, FAITH, GREATNESS, LEADER, SOVEREIGNTY, STATE, WEALTH.

PRAISE

A debt we owe unto the virtue of others, and due unto our own from all whom malice hath not made mutes, or envy struck dumb.
                                    Thomas Browne

The shipwreck of historians.   *John E. Dalberg*

Incense to the wisest of us.   *Benjamin Disraeli*

That which makes good men better and bad men worse.   *Thomas Fuller*

When you praise someone you call yourself his equal.   *Johann W. Goethe*

The beginning of blame.   *Japanese Proverb*

A debt, but flattery is present.   *Samuel Johnson*

Blind guide with siren voice.   *John Keble*

Praise to the face
Is open disgrace.   *V. S. Lean*

Our praises are our wages.
                                William Shakespeare

Rebuke to the man whose conscience alloweth it
not.   *Martin F. Tupper*

The art of praising began the art of pleasing.
                                        Voltaire

We are praised only as men in us do recognise
some image of themselves, an abject counterpart
of what they are, or the empty thing that they
would wish to be.

Adapted from William Wordsworth

The sweetest of all sounds.   *Zenophon*

Something a person tells you about yourself that
you suspected all along.   *Anon.*

SEE ALSO APPLAUSE, COMPLIMENTS, EU-
LOGY.

PRAYER

The pillow of religion.   *Arabian Proverb*

An energy of aspiration towards the eternal *not
ourselves* that makes for righteousness, of aspiration towards it, and of cooperation with it.

Matthew Arnold

A window to Heaven.   *Israel Baal Shem Tob*

An act of daring.   *Israel Baal Shem Tob*

The spirit speaking to Truth.   *Philip J. Bailey*

An actuation of an intellective soul towards God,
expressing... an entire dependence on Him as the
author and fountain of all good, a will and
readiness to give Him his due.

Augustine Baker

A direct approach to the throbbing heart of the
universe.   *Israel Bettan*

Asking that the laws of the universe be annulled in
behalf of a single petitioner confessedly unworthy.

Adapted from Ambrose Bierce

Prayer represents commitment. To pray is to say,
"I'm willing to get with it—love, responsibility,
action."   *Malcolm Boyd*

A wish turned God-ward.   *Phillips Brooks*

Not a vain attempt to change God's will; it is a
filial desire to learn God's will and to share it.

George A. Buttrick

Prayer is and remains always a native and deepest
impulse of the soul of man.   *Thomas Carlyle*

A binding necessity in the lives of men and
nations.   *Alexis Carrel*

A mystical elevation, an absorption of consciousness in the contemplation of the principle
both permeating and transcending our world.

Alexis Carrel

The effort of man to reach God to commune with
an invisible being.   *Alexis Carrel*

Identifying oneself with the divine Will by the
studied renunciation of one's own.   *Paul Claudel*

The very highest energy of which the mind is
capable.   *Samuel Taylor Coleridge*

The sign of faith.   *Franklin Conklin*

That incense of the heart whose fragrance smells
to Heaven.   *Adapted from Nathaniel Cotton*

Prayer is the little implement
Through which men reach
Where presence is denied them.

Emily Dickinson

The highest prayer is not one of faith merely; it is
demonstration. Such prayer heals sickness, and
must destroy sin and death.   *Mary Baker Eddy*

The contemplation of the facts of life from the
highest point of view.   *Ralph Waldo Emerson*

The soliloquy of a beholding and jubilant soul.

Ralph Waldo Emerson

A disease of the will.   *Ralph Waldo Emerson*

A cry of hope.   *French Proverb*

The key of the day and the lock of the night.

Thomas Fuller

The very soul and essence of religion and therefore prayer must be the very core of the life of
man, for no man can live without religion.

Mohandas K. Gandhi

The result of a racketeer asking the gods for
special protection.

Adapted from Henry S. Haskins

A technique for contacting and learning to know
Reality... the exploration of Reality by exploring
the Beyond, which is within.   *Gerald Heard*

Prayer is not asking for things—not even for the
best things; it is going where they are.

Gerald Heard

The end of preaching.   *George Herbert*

Reversed thunder.   *George Herbert*

Putting to death of the self that God may reign.
                                     E. Herman

A ladder on which thoughts mount to God.
                                     Abraham J. Heschel

Our humble answer to the inconceivable surprise
of living.   *Abraham J. Heschel*

A sermon to our own selves.   *Emil G. Hirsch*

A rising desire of the heart into God by withdrawing of the heart from all earthly thoughts.
                                     Walter Hylton

Religion in act.   *William James*

The vital act by which the entire mind seeks to
save itself by clinging to the principle from which
it draws its life.   *William James*

The very moment itself of the soul, putting itself
into a personal relation of contact with the mysterious power—of which it fills the presence.
                                     William James

I do not mean a request proffered to a deity; I
mean . . . intense aspiration.   *Richard Jefferies*

Conversation with God.   *Josippon*

A pressing forth of the soul out this earthly
life . . . a stretching with all its desire after the life
of God.   *William Law*

The greatest simplicity, speaking to Him frankly
and plainly, and imploring His assistance in our
affairs, just as they happen.   *Brother Lawrence*

A single grateful thought toward heaven is the
most perfect prayer.   *Georg E. Lessing*

A goodly Christian's weapon.   *Martin Luther*

That passion of the soul which catches the gift it
seeks.   *George Meredith*

The upward glancing of an eye
    When none but God is near.
                                     James Montgomery

Communion with God.   *A. Victor Murray*

The heralds to prepare a better life.
                                     Francis Rous

The drowning and unconsciousness of the soul.
                                     Jala al-Din Rumini

Religion in act.   *Auguste Sabatier*

The unfolding of one's will to God that He may
fulfill it.   *Saint Thomas Aquinas*

Conversation with God.   *Saint Clement*

When the spirit leaves the body and the world,
and, in the act of prayer, loses all matter and all
form.   *Saint Maximus*

A desperate effort to work further and to be
efficient beyond the range of one's powers.
                                     George Santayana

God's own psychotherapy for His sinful children.
                                     Raphael Simon

Refuge from the degradation of self-love.
                                     William L. Sullivan

Truth is what prays in man, and a man is
continually at prayer when he lives according to
the truth.   *Emanuel Swedenborg*

The service of the heart.   *Talmud: Taanit, 2a.*

Releasing the energies of God. For prayer is
asking God to do what we cannot do.
                                     Charles Trumbull

Every prayer reduces itself to this: "Great God,
grant that two be not four."   *Ivan Turgeniev*

Search without vanity.   *Rahel L. Varnhagen*

The deep personal testament that increases faith
and knowledge.   *Paul Weinberger*

The sum total of religion and morals.
                                     Duke of Wellington

An appeal which must never be answered; if it is,
it ceases to be prayer and becomes correspondence.   *Oscar Wilde*

Man's rational prerogative.
                                     William Wordsworth

Communion which shuts out the noise of the
world.   *Anon.*

The words you use to sigh over your own life
directed upward.   *Anon.*

Opening the gate to heaven.   *Anon.*

**SEE ALSO CHURCHES, GOD, PIETY, RELI-
GION, WORSHIP.**

PREACHERS

For we preach not ourselves, but Christ Jesus the
Lord.   *Bible: Corinthians, IV, 5, 7.*

An agent of a higher power with a lower responsibility.   *Ambrose Bierce*

He that negotiates between God and man, as God's ambassador.

Adapted from William Cowper

Like torches, a light to others, waste and destruction to themselves.   *Richard Hooker*

(One who) works orally.   *Elbert Hubbard*

A man who advises others concerning things about which he knows nothing.

Elbert Hubbard

The heart of a lion, the skin of a hippopotamus, the agility of a greyhound, the patience of a donkey, the wisdom of an elephant, the industry of an ant, and as many lives as a cat.

Edgar D. Jones

Both a soldier and a shepherd. He must nourish, defend, and teach; he must have teeth in his mouth, and be able to bite and to fight.

Martin Luther

The first duty of a preacher of the gospel is to declare God's law and describe the nature of sin.

Martin Luther

The test...is that his congregation goes away saying, not what a lovely sermon, but, I will do something!   *Saint Francis de Sales*

He ought to preach to his own flock exclusively, and nowhere else.   *Edwin Sandys*

(Those who) remind mankind of what mankind are constantly forgetting.   *Sydney Smith*

The task...is to lift men above the low view of their times, to give them the elevation and outlook which enables them to distinguish currents from eddies.   *Ralph W. Sockman*

A messenger, not an actor.   *Ralph W. Sockman*

(One who leads) men from what they want to what they need.   *Ralph W. Sockman*

SEE ALSO CLERGYMEN, PRIESTS, RABBI.

PREACHING

The most ephemeral form of literature.

Norman Bentwich

The best...is always the natural overflow of a ripe mind.   *James Black*

Proclaiming the word of God.

Orestes Brownson

A proclamation which claims to be the call of God through the mouth of man.   *Rudolf Bultmann*

An embarrassed stammering...Do not call it difficult...call it impossible.   *A. C. Craig*

A religious pep-talk.   *Frederic S. Fleming*

My preaching at its best has itself been personal counseling on a group scale.

Harry Emerson Fosdick

An art, and in this, as in all the arts, the bad performers far outnumber the good.

Aldous Huxley

Babbling.   *Moses Maimonides*

The great object is to hazard nothing; their characteristic is decent debility.   *Sydney Smith*

The deep soul-moving sense
Of religious eloquence.   *William Wordsworth*

Too often a message of sorrow making its way into otherwise happy homes.   *Anon.*

Having a sermon to preach, not preaching a sermon.   *Anon.*

Soul Food.   *Anon.*

SEE ALSO CLERGYMEN, PREACHERS, PRIESTS.

PREDESTINATION

The eternal decree of God whereby He has determined what He would have to become of every individual of mankind. Eternal life is ordained for some, and eternal damnation for others.

John Calvin

That God has foreordained everything.

René Descartes

The elect are chosen for eternal happiness, the rest are left graceless and damned to everlasting hell.   *Martin Luther*

The recognition of God's absolute sovereignty in the natural and moral worlds, and especially the absolute sovereignty of His free grace as the only ground of human salvation.   *Jan H. Scholten*

PREFACE

A talk with the reader.   *Charles Lamb*

Speeches before the curtain; they make even the most self-forgetful performers self-conscious.

William A. Neilson

PREJUDICE

Weighing the facts with your thumbs on the scales. *Leon Aikman*

A vagrant opinion without visible means of support. *Ambrose Bierce*

Our mistresses; reason is at best our wife, very often needed, but seldom minded.

Lord Chesterfield

A way of thinking that has dogmatized the notion that one ethnic group is condemned by the laws of nature to hereditary inferiority and another group is marked off as hereditarily superior.

Joseph F. Doherty

The props of civilization. *André Gide*

Feeling without reason. *Max Gralnick*

Circles of inclusion and exclusion.

Kyle Haselden

Prejudice, put theologically, is one of man's several neurotic and perverted expressions of his will to be God. *Kyle Haselden*

The child of ignorance. *William Hazlitt*

A raft onto which the shipwrecked mind clambers and paddles to safety. *Ben Hecht*

Our method of transferring our own sickness to others. It is our ruse for disliking others rather than ourselves. *Ben Hecht*

To be weak. *Samuel Johnson*

Likings and dislikings. *Charles Lamb*

Opinions adopted before examination.

Joseph de Maistre

False race pride which commits whole segments of our population to a role of inferiority.

Julian J. Reiss

The very ink with which all history is written.

Mark Twain

The king of the vulgar crowd. *Voltaire*

An opinion without judgment. *Voltaire*

The reasoning of the stupid. *Voltaire*

A disease characterized by hardening of the categories. *William A. Ward*

The dislike for all that is unlike.

Israel Zangwill

An opinion that holds a man. *Anon.*

Being down on something you are not up on.

Anon.

SEE ALSO BIGOTRY, FANATICISM, JEWS, NEGRO, RADICALISM, REACTIONARY.

PRESENT, THE

An isthmus or narrow neck of land that rises in the midst of an ocean, immeasurably diffused on either side of it. *Joseph Addison*

Elastic to embrace infinity. *Louis Anspacher*

Nothing more than the past, and what was found in the effect was already in the cause.

Henri Bergson

The time spent in suffering now for a better future. *Eugene E. Brussell*

The Now, that indivisible point which studs the length of infinite line whose ends are nowhere.

Adapted from Richard Burton

The living sum-total of the whole Past.

Thomas Carlyle

An eternal now. *Abraham Cowley*

All the ready money Fate can give.

Abraham Cowley

An indivisible point which cuts in two the length of an infinite line. *Denis Diderot*

An edifice which God cannot rebuild.

Adapted from Ralph Waldo Emerson

The necessary product of all the past, the necessary cause of all the future. *Robert G. Ingersoll*

Never a happy state to any being.

Samuel Johnson

The present hour. *Samuel Johnson*

The now, the here, through which all future plunges to the past. *James Joyce*

The blocks with which we build.

Henry Wadsworth Longfellow

The symbol and vehicle of the future.

Joseph McSorely

A growth out of the past. *Walt Whitman*

The living now. *William Wordsworth*

Such as is. *Anon.*

All you have for your certain possession. *Anon.*

SEE ALSO PAST, TIME

PRESIDENCY

The U.S. Presidency is a Tudor monarchy plus telephones. *Anthony Burgess*

To eat dust before the real masters who stand erect behind the throne. *Ralph Waldo Emerson*

The symbol of American ideals.

Herbert Hoover

The instrument by which national conscience is livened and it must under the guidance of the Almighty interpret and follow that conscience.

Herbert Hoover

The natural aristocracy. *Sidney Hyman*

A splendid misery. *Thomas Jefferson*

The key office. *John Fitzgerald Kennedy*

What a lousy, fouled-up job this has turned out to be. *John Fitzgerald Kennedy*

You need two things—wide factual knowledge and the ability to make decisions, and to make them stick. *Joseph P. Kennedy*

The worst job in the world. *Joseph P. Kennedy*

A place where priorities are set and goals determined. *Richard Milhous Nixon*

That goldfish bowl. *Harry S. Truman*

The finest jail in the world. *Harry S. Truman*

To be lonely, very lonely at times of great decisions. *Harry S. Truman*

PRESIDENT

President means chief servant.

Mohandas K. Gandhi

The last person in the world to know what the people really want and think.

James A. Garfield

The duty of the President (is) to see that the laws be executed . . . a duty that does not go beyond the laws or require him to achieve more than Congress sees fit to leave within his power.

Oliver Wendell Holmes 2

A link in the long chain of his country's destiny, past and future. *Herbert Hoover*

(He) alone must make the decisions. The President cannot share his power, cannot delegate. He alone is the chief of state.

John Fitzgerald Kennedy

The President's chief function is to lead . . . not to oversee every detail, but to put the right people in charge, to provide them with the basic guidance and direction, and to let them do the job.

Richard Milhous Nixon

A public monument. *Eleanor Roosevelt*

A glorified public relations man who spends his time flattering . . . and kicking people to get them to do what they are supposed to do anyway.

Harry S. Truman

The loneliest man in the world. *Anon.*

A yes-man to the majority. *Anon.*

The postage stamp of tomorrow. *Anon.*

SEE ALSO LEADER.

PRESS, FREE

SEE FREE PRESS

PRESS, THE

The hired agent of a monied system, and set up for no other purpose than to tell lies where the interests are involved. *Henry B. Adams*

A forum for the people, through which the people may know freely what is going on.

Louis D. Brandeis

The servant of human intellect and its ministry is for good or evil, according to the character of those who direct it. *William Cullen Bryant*

A method of educating people to approach printed matter with distrust.

Adapted from Samuel Butler 2

A mirror—albeit a distorting mirror, according to its politics or the smallness of its purpose.

James Cameron

A Fourth Estate.   *Thomas Carlyle*

A sort of wild animal in our midst—restless, gigantic, always seeking new ways to use its strength.   *Zechariah Chaffe 2*

An excellent servant, but a terrible master.
                              James Fenimore Cooper

The instrument of elevating man to the highest point of which his faculties admit, or of depressing him to the lowest.   *James Fenimore Cooper*

The wisdom of the age.   *Stephen Crane*

One of our great out-sentries.   *Thomas Erskine*

That polluted vehicle.   *Thomas Jefferson*

Our chief ideological weapon. Its duty is to strike down the enemies of the working class.
                              Nikita Khrushchev

A collective propagandist and a collective agitator . . . a collective organizer of the masses.
                              Nikolai Lenin

A chartered libertine.   *William Pitt*

The only weapon with whose aid the party every day speaks to the working class in the language of the party.   *Joseph Stalin*

The protagonist and preserver of all rights, the foe and destroyer of all tyrannies.   *Edmunds Travis.*

The mouth-organ of the masses.   *Anon.*

SEE ALSO FREE PRESS, JOURNALISM, NEWS, NEWSPAPERS.

PRIDE

Haughtiness of soul.   *Joseph Addison*

Pampered vanity.   *Joanna Baillie*

A mortal enemy to charity—the first and father sin.   *Thomas Browne*

What we now call the lust for power.
                                   Colin Clark

The first peer and president of hell.
                                   Daniel Defoe

The sworn enemy to content.   *Thomas Fuller*

The truly proud man knows neither superiors nor inferiors. The first he does not admit of: the last

he does not concern himself about.
                                William Hazlitt

A sense of worth derived from something that is not organically part of us.   *Eric Hoffer*

The core of pride is self-rejection.   *Eric Hoffer*

That solemn vice of greatness.   *Ben Jonson*

A sign of self-centered view, of a lack of objectivity.   *Fritz Kunkel*

The spring of malice and desire of revenge, and of rash anger and contention.   *Robert Leighton*

Man's malady.   *A. T. Mollegen*

The never failing vice of fools.   *Alexander Pope*

He that is proud eats himself up; pride is his own mirror, his own trumpet, his own chronicle.
                    Adapted from William Shakespeare

A kind of pleasure produced by a man thinking too well of himself.   *Baruch Spinoza*

To be vain of one's rank or place.   *Stanislaus*

Cap and bells for a fool.   *Alfred Lord Tennyson*

Littleness.   *William Wordsworth*

That impartial passion, reigns through all, attends our glory, fails to desert our fall.
                         Adapted from Edward Young

SEE ALSO EGOISM, VANITY.

PRIESTS

He who speaks what all feel.   *Felix Adler*

The essence . . . is that he should believe himself, however humbly and secretly, to be set in a certain sense between humanity and God.
                              Arthur C. Benson

A sworn officer of the pope.
                              Otto von Bismarck

Vows can't change nature; priests are only men.
                              Robert Browning

My profession is to keep secrets.
                              Miguel de Cervantes

Priests are extremely like other men, and neither the better or worse for wearing a gown or surplice.   *Lord Chesterfield*

The profession of a gentleman.   *Jeremy Collier*

A piece of mere church-furniture at best.

William Cowper

Every one shall be his own priest, his own mediator between himself and God.

Abraham Geiger

Crutches for the crippled life of the soul.

Franz Kafka

Every baptized Christian is a priest already, not by appointment or ordination from the pope or any other man, but because Christ himself has begotten him as a priest and has given birth to him in baptism. *Martin Luther*

Christ's priests...are merely His shadows and organs, they are His outward signs; and what they do, He does. *John Henry Newman*

One of the necessary types of humanity...It is his triumph to achieve as much faith as possible in an age of negation. *Walter Pater*

The minister of Christ, an instrument in the hands of the Divine Redeemer. *Pope Pius XI*

He who is entrusted with the care of men.

Saint John Chrysostom

The minister of disquietude, the dispenser of a new hunger and thirst. *Emmanuel Suhard*

The priest should be a man above human weakness...a stranger to every diversion. *Synesius*

All men...in virtue of their vocation to be "Christ" among their brethren.

Maurice Zundel

The instruments of God. *Anon.*

SEE ALSO CHURCH (ROMAN CATHOLIC), PAPACY, ROME.

PRIMA DONNA

'Tis strange how the newspapers honor a creature that is called prima donna. They say not a thing of how she can sing, but write reams about the clothes she has on her.

Adapted from Eugene Field

Merely tone and technique without intelligence.

Ernest Newman

Temper with a voice. *Anon.*

PRINCE

Princes are like to heavenly bodies, which cause good or evil times, and which have much veneration, but no rest. *Francis Bacon*

(Men) whose breasts are all agleam and aglimmer with the symbols of fifty victories at which they were not present. *Max Beerbohm*

The Prince exists for the sake of the State, not the State for the sake of the Prince.

Desiderius Erasmus

The first servant and the first magistrate of the state. *Frederick the Great*

Those who have long hands and many ears.

German Proverb

Those who forget themselves and serve mankind.

Woodrow Wilson

PRINCIPLE

Every principle contains in itself the germs of a prophecy. *Samuel Taylor Coleridge*

(Those which) become modified in practice by facts. *James Fenimore Cooper*

A passion for truth. *William Hazlitt*

Something that has no real force except when one is well fed. *Anon.*

Prejudices whitewashed and surmounted by a neon halo. *Anon.*

SEE ALSO IDEALS, THEORY.

PRINTING

Either the greatest blessing or the greatest curse of modern times, one forgets which.

James M. Barrie

The universal monarch. *Richard Carlile*

A multiplication of mind. *Richard Carlile*

Ready-writing. *Thomas Carlyle*

Printing broke out in the province of Kansu in 868 A.D. The Early Chinese simply could not let well enough alone. *Will Cuppy*

The greatest misfortune that ever befell man.

Benjamin Disraeli

Things printed can never be stopped; they are like babies baptized, they have a soul from that moment, and go on forever.   *George Meredith*

The art which enables one man to write with many pens.   *Moritz Steinschneider*

The art preservative of all arts.   *Anon.*

The angles and curves used to convey or obscure events.   *Anon.*

SEE ALSO BOOK, FREE PRESS, JOURNALISM, NEWSPAPERS, PRESS (THE).

PRISON

A place of punishment and rewards.

Ambrose Bierce

Stones of law.   *William Blake*

The place where an offender without funds or social prestige is sent.   *Max Gralnick*

The place where a lady may have a baby without fear of social ostracism.   *Elbert Hubbard*

An institution where even crooks go wrong.

Elbert Hubbard

A Socialist's Paradise, where equality prevails, everything is supplied, and competition is eliminated.   *Elbert Hubbard*

A hostelry where the guest is always wrong.

James A. Johnston

Paying with your body when you cannot pay with money.   *Legal Maxim*

One long gob of nothing. Complete monotony ... No hope, reward or advancement.

Nathan Leopold

Double grills with great nails, triple doors, heavy bolts, to wicked souls you represent hell; but to the innocent you are only wood, stones, iron.

Pellisson-Fontanier

(Something) designed to improve ethics by herding together the sinners.   *Dagobert Runes*

Our cage.   *William Shakespeare*

A worse crime than any of those committed by its victims.   *George Bernard Shaw*

PROCRASTINATION

Endless durance.   *Edmund Spenser*

A house of study, and of contemplation: a place of discipline and reformation.   *John Taylor*

A school to which criminals are sent to figure out what went wrong.   *Anon.*

A monument to neglected youth.   *Anon.*

SEE ALSO CRIME, JUSTICE, PUNISHMENT.

PRIVATE ENTERPRISE

An economy open to new ideas, new products, new jobs, new men.   *William Benton*

Consists of harnessing men, money, and ideas, and the genius of inventors and technologists with the savings of the thousands.   *Malcolm Muir*

SEE ALSO AMERICA, CAPITALISM.

PROBLEM

When two and two isn't four.   *Warren Goldberg*

Most ... are test questions.

Henry S. Haskins

An opportunity in work clothes.

Henry J. Kaiser 2

The price of progress.   *Anon.*

SEE ALSO PROGRESS, QUESTION.

PROCESS

The process itself is the actuality.

Alfred North Whitehead

PROCRASTINATION

One of these days is none of these days.

Henry G. Bohn

Struggling with ruin.   *Hesiod*

Procrastination is the art of keeping up with yesterday.   *Don Marquis*

The thief of time. Year after year it steals, till all are fled, and to the mercies of a moment leaves the vast concerns of an eternal scene.

Adapted from Edward Young

Hardening of the oughteries.   *Anon.*

PROCREATION

SEE BIRTH, POPULATION EXPLOSION, SEX (LOVE), SEXES.

PRODIGY

If anything happens which a man has not seen before, he calls it a prodigy.   *Cicero*

A child who plays the piano when he ought to be in bed.   *John B. Morton*

A child who is just as smart at four as he will be at forty.   *Anon.*

PROFANITY

A meaningless use of words which allows the speaker to vocalize and exercise his tone code. Since he has reached the linguistic stage of development he swears. Otherwise he would coo.
Kenneth Bartlett

The bad man's charity.   *Beaumont and Fletcher*

A kind of prayers.   *Samuel Butler 1*

A phase of resurrected adolescence in adulthood.
Robert Zwickey

Explosive expressions that have saved many a man and woman from nervous breakdowns.   *Anon.*

What is said when one doesn't know what to say.
Anon.

SEE ALSO VULGARITY.

PROFESSION

SEE VOCATION.

PROFESSOR

One who talks in someone else's sleep.
Wystan H. Auden

One who helps you discover his own nature, rather than your own.   *Eugene E. Brussell*

A library wired for sound.   *Eugene E. Brussell*

A man who avoids reality by teaching in a college.
Muriel Cohen

In New England (they) guard the glory that was Greece.   *Clarence Day*

Owls are not really wise—they only look that way. The owl is a sort of college professor.
Elbert Hubbard

Learned gentlemen who receive the cash that remains after the coaches are paid off.
James Smith

An overeducated thought-controller.   *Anon.*

An absent-minded fellow who slams his wife and kisses the door.   *Anon.*

A master of whatever is not worth knowing.
Anon.

These are two types: the dead and the buried.
Anon.

SEE ALSO COLLEGE, UNIVERSITY.

PROGRESS

Where the force of legality has gone far enough to bind the nation together, but not far enough to kill out all varieties and destroy nature's perpetual tendency to change.   *Walter Bagehot*

A lazy man's creed . . . It is the individual counting on his neighbors to perform his task for him.
Charles Baudelaire

The Bible shows how the world progresses. It begins with a garden, but ends with a holy city.
Phillips Brooks

The law of life.   *Robert Browning*

All progress is based upon a universal innate desire on the part of every organism to live beyond its income.   *Samuel Butler 2*

The victory of laughter over dogma.
Benjamin de Casseres

Does not consider in looking for a direction in which one can go on indefinitely. True progress consists in looking for a place where we can stop.
Gilbert Keith Chesterton

The encouragement of variety . . . the ferment of ideas, the clash of disagreeing judgments.
Calvin Coolidge

The privilege of the individual to develop his own thoughts and shape his own character.
Calvin Coolidge

An advance into truth, a deeper appreciation and love of what is familiar be it a birthright, or a gift such as Revelation.   *Martin C. D'Arcy*

What we call progress is the exchange of one nuisance for another.   *Havelock Ellis*

Every line of history.   *Ralph Waldo Emerson*

The activity of today and the assurance of tomorrow.   *Ralph Waldo Emerson*

An unfolding, like the vegetable bud. You have first an instinct, then an opinion, then a knowledge.   *Ralph Waldo Emerson*

Learning to travel faster on errands not conspicuously improved over past ones.
          Warren Goldberg

Committing different errors.   *Warren Goldberg*

Man's ability to complicate simplicity.
          Thor Heyerdahl

Cost is the father, and compensation the mother of progress.   *Josiah G. Holland*

What we have mastered of good and gain; the pride deposed and the passion slain.
          Adapted from Josiah G. Holland

Getting free from theology, and substituting psychology instead.   *Elbert Hubbard*

The onward stride of God.   *Victor Hugo*

Call it Tomorrow.   *Victor Hugo*

The consequence of rapidly spending the planet's irreplaceable capital.   *Aldous Huxley*

The hope and faith (in the teeth of all human progress) that one can get something for nothing.
          Aldous Huxley

The history of progress is written in the lives of infidels.   *Robert G. Ingersoll*

Rushing straight ahead and leaving yourself behind.   *Adapted from Karl Kraus*

In antiquity...the appearance of great men; in modern times...the appearance of great inventions.   *William E. Lecky*

To act, that each to-morrow
Find us farther than to-day.
          Henry Wadsworth Longfellow

Morality and knowledge.   *Luigi Luzzatti*

The open or indirect action of Christianity upon the human spirit.   *Jacques Maritain*

The elevation of punishment from the base rank of vengeance to the exalted level of justice.
          R. H. Markham

The time when one pays twice as much in taxes as he formerly got in wages.
          Adapted from Henry Louis Mencken

The idea of progress is the underlying presupposition of what may be broadly defined as "liberal culture."   *Reinhold Niebuhr*

The effect of an even more rigorous subjugation of the beast in man, of an ever tenser self-restraint, an ever keener sense of duty and responsibility.
          Max Nordau

To make conscientious use of the gifts received from God, to avoid all injustice, and to seize every opportunity for doing works of love and kindness.   *Pope Pius XII*

It is based on perfect technology.   *Jean Renoir*

Onward! Full speed ahead! without asking whether directly before you was a bottomless pit.
          George Santayana

All progress is initiated by challenging current conceptions, and executed by supplanting existing institutions.   *George Bernard Shaw*

Not an accident, but a necessity...It is a part of nature.   *Herbert Spencer*

People taking unpopular positions.
          Adlai Ewing Stevenson

What happens when inevitability yields to necessity.   *Adlai Ewing Stevenson*

All the modern inconveniences.   *Mark Twain*

Life means progress, and progress means suffering.   *Hendrik W. Van Loon*

A continuing effort to make the things we eat, drink and wear as good as they used to be.
          William Vaughan

To preserve order amid change, and to preserve change amid order.   *Alfred North Whitehead*

The realization of Utopias.   *Oscar Wilde*

Swapping old troubles for new.   *Anon.*

SEE ALSO CHANGE, EVOLUTION, HERO, INVENTION, RADICAL, REFORM, SCIENCE.

PROGRESSIVE SCHOOL

(Where) none of the teachers ever raised his voice. None of the children ever lowered his, except through hoarseness. *Emily Hahn*

(The) cult of immediacy.

Robert Maynard Hutchins

A place where they teach children the identical things they teach in other schools—only the teacher is pilloried and naked. *Anon.*

Tot rule. *Anon.*

SEE ALSO EDUCATION, SCHOOL.

PROHIBITION

There is a crying for wine in the streets; all joy is darkened, the mirth of the land is gone.

Bible: Isaiah, XXIV, 11.

A great social and economic experiment, noble in motive and far-reaching in purpose.

Herbert C. Hoover

Equivalent to allowing free liquor, plus lawlessness. *Theodore Roosevelt*

(A law which) drives drunkenness behind doors and into dark places, and does not cure it or even diminish it. *Mark Twain*

A species of intemperance itself, for it goes beyond the bounds of reason, in that it attempts to control a man's appetite by legislation, and makes a crime out of things that are not crimes. *Anon.*

PROLETARIAT

SEE COMMUNISM, LABORER.

PROOF

SEE FACT, SCIENCE.

PROPAGANDA

The art of persuading others of what one does not believe oneself. *Abba Eban*

Persuading people to make up their minds while withholding some of the facts from them.

Harold Evans

A seeding of the self in the consciousness of others. *Elizabeth Drew*

To identify one's cause with values which are unquestioned. *Timothy Garton-ash*

(That which) serves more to justify ourselves than to convince others; and the more reason we have to feel guilty, the more fervent our propaganda.

Eric Hoffer

To make one set of people forget that certain other sets of people are human. *Aldous Huxley*

Enables people to do in cold blood things they could otherwise do only in the heat of passion.

Adapted from Aldous Huxley

The diminution of the love of truth by the falsehoods which interest dictates.

Samuel Johnson

Education by means of pre-fabricated ideas.

Mordecai M. Kaplan

Polished lying. *Lin Yutang*

A polite euphemism for deception.

Walter Lippmann

(When the) complex is made into the simple, the hypothetical into the dogmatic, and the relative into an absolute. *Walter Lippmann*

To make lies sound truthful and murder respectable and to give an appearance of solidity to pure wind. *George Orwell*

All propaganda is lies—even when it's telling the truth. *George Orwell*

A lie told to millions. *Anon.*

SEE ALSO DICTATORS, NEWSPAPERS.

PROPAGANDIST

A specialist in selling attitudes and opinions.

Hans Speier

PROPERTY

At once the consequence and the basis of the state.

Mikhail A. Bakunin

That which tends most to the perpetuation of society itself. *Edmund Burke*

The great end for which men entered into society.

William Camden

The art of democracy. It means that every man should have something that he can shape in his own image.   *Gilbert Keith Chesterton*

The agent in all that distinguishes the civilized man from the savage.   *James Fenimore Cooper*

The ground work of moral independence.
                          James Fenimore Cooper

A legal relation by virtue of which someone has, within a certain group of men, the exclusive privilege of ultimately disposing of a thing.
                                Paul Eltzbacher

Man's labor. That is property, and that alone, which labor of man has made such.
                              Galusha A. Grow

What we call real estate—the solid ground to build a house on . . . the broad foundation on which nearly all the guilt of this world rests.
                            Nathaniel Hawthorne

Only a means of doing what is pleasing in the sight of God.   *Samson R. Hirsch*

A form of power.   *Sidney Hook*

That which is necessary in all civil society.
                                  David Hume

The fruit of labor; property is desirable; is a positive good in the world.   *Abraham Lincoln*

The only dependable foundation of personal liberty.   *Walter Lippmann*

The original source of freedom. It still is its main bulwark.   *Walter Lippmann*

The reason why men enter into society.
                                  John Locke

A social right.
                              James Madison

The safeguard of family life, the stimulus and the reward of work.
              Pastoral Letter of the French Roman Catholic Hierarchy, 1919.

An incontrovertible natural right.   *Pope Pius X*

Theft.   *Pierre J. Proudhon*

The right to use and abuse. It is the absolute, irresponsible dominion of man over his person and goods.   *Pierre J. Proudhon*

A sacred trust expressly granted by God, the Bible, and the Recorder's Office. *Leo C. Rosten*

The pivot of civilization.   *Leon Samson*

Exists by the grace of law. It is not a fact, but a legal fiction.   *Max Stirner*

The most fundamental and complex of social facts, and the most important of human interests.
                            William G. Sumner

Faith is in this world the best property for a man.
                                Sutta-Nipata

SEE ALSO POSSESSIONS, RICHES, WEALTH.

PROPHECY

Your old men shall dream dreams, your young men shall see visions.   *Bible: Joel, II, 28.*

The art . . . of selling one's credibility for future delivery.   *Ambrose Bierce*

The passion of prying into futurity . . . a striking part of the history of human nature.
                                Robert Burns

A sacred gift to man.   *William Campbell*

To "discern the signs of the times," to see what God is bringing to pass as the history of peoples and societies unfolds, to point to the judgment he brings upon all institutions.   *John B. Coburn*

To observe that which has passed, and guess it will happen again.   *Elbert Hubbard*

To anticipate the future by guessing at the past.
                                Elbert Hubbard

Consists in the most perfect development of the imaginative faculty . . . an emanation from God.
                              Moses Maimonides

The prophesying business is like writing figures; it is fatal to everyone save the man of absolute genius.   *Henry Louis Mencken*

Dreaming on things to come.
                            William Shakespeare

To deal in lies.   *Welsh Proverb*

SEE ALSO REVELATION, VISION.

PROPHETS

The doctors of the diseases of the soul.
                                  Al-Ghazali

I am the voice of one crying in the wilderness.

Bible: John, 1, 23.

Always a minority and always judged wrong at the time by the majority. *Irving Cohen*

The first to utter this cry of justice and pity, and they did so for all time. *Arsene Darmsteter*

He who anticipates his century is generally persecuted when living, and is always pilfered when dead. *Benjamin Disraeli*

Essentially a man of the future: he did not live in the past, the past lived in him.

Hyman G. Enelow

He who conjectures well. *Euripides*

The best guesser. *Greek Proverb*

One with a good memory.

Adapted from Lord Halifax

He who reads and reveals the present.

Eric Hoffer

The advance couriers of time. *Elbert Hubbard*

(Those) who led the way...to the truly monotheistic conception of one sole God of the whole world...disregarding all barriers of race and space and time. *David Hume*

The man of God *par excellence*. *Edmond Jacob*

The noble characters in each generation.

Hamilton W. Mabie

He who dares oppose his own people on great moral and social and political issues.

Judah L. Magnes

The interpreters of God.

Philo

The beating hearts of the Old Testament.

Walter Rauschenbusch

The oldest advocates of the opposed.

Ernest Renan

Men who were happy, upright, and beloved of God, who spoke by the divine Spirit and gave oracles of the future which are now coming to pass. *Saint Justin Martyr*

If you keep saying things are going to be bad, you have a chance of being a prophet.

Isaac B. Singer

A social worker who is absolutely independent, and neither fears nor submits to anything external. *Vladimir S. Soloviev*

A money-getting tribe. *Sophocles*

One whose forecasts are forgotten by the time events prove him correct. *Anon.*

PROSE

Prose is where all the lines but the last go on to the margin—poetry is where some of them fall short of it. *Jeremy Bentham*

Prose: words in their best order; poetry: the best words in the best order.

Samuel Taylor Coleridge

The last word in literature, since it contains every kind of rhythm to be found in verse, and other rhythms as well. *A. R. Orage*

Order, precision, directness are the radical merits of prose thought. *Walter Pater*

SEE ALSO ESSAY, GRAMMAR, WRITING.

PROSECUTOR

An oratorical censor that precedes the coming of the hangman. *Elbert Hubbard*

A nose that can sniff the gallows long before the wood is cut for it in the forest. *Elbert Hubbard*

The righteous arm of the state. *Anon.*

SEE ALSO LAWYER.

PROSPERITY

A feeble reed. *Daniel d'Ancheres*

The blessing of the Old Testament.

Francis Bacon

Something gauged by a country's treatment of the aged. *Adapted from Nahman Bratzlav*

When the stream of life flows according to our wishes. *Cicero*

An instrument to be used; not a deity to be worshipped. *Calvin Coolidge*

The greatest enemy a man can have.

Samuel David

The severest test that can come to a people.

John Foster Dulles

Means that we are able to appreciate and use God's spiritual ideas of abundance.

Lowell Fillmore

Writing on water.　　　　　　*Hindu Proverb*

That which comes about when men believe in other men.　　　　　　*Elbert Hubbard*

That condition which attracts the lively interest of lawyers, and warrants your being sued for damages or indicted, or both.　*Elbert Hubbard*

The consequence of rapidly spending the planet's irreplaceable capital.　　　　*Aldous Huxley*

The child of peace.　　　　*William Prynne*

If the period of prosperity could be expressed in a single word, that word would be confidence.

Thomas B. Reed

(A period when) never have so many people lived so well so far behind before.　　*A. Sapient*

The surest breeder of insolence.　*Mark Twain*

A fairyland of exorbitance.　　　　*Anon.*

A time when people buy things they can't afford.

Anon.

SEE ALSO HAPPINESS, MONEY, RICHES, SUCCESS, WEALTH.

PROSTITUTE

A furnace of love, burning youth and money.

Bhartrihari: the Sringa Sataka

Arises out of the domination of man in matters of sex.　　　　　　*Edward Carpenter*

Every man's Cleopatra!　　　　*John Dryden*

The naughtipacks or offscourings of men.

Arthur Golding

Wanton look and twinkling,
Laughing and tickling,
Open breast and singing,
These without lying
Are tokens of whoring.　　*William Hazlitt*

He who marries his daughter to an old man makes a prostitute of her.　　　*Hebrew Proverb*

An ancient and more or less honorable profession.

Rudyard Kipling

The pavement to every man that walketh.

William Langland

The eternal priestess of humanity, blasted for the sins of the people.　　　*William E. Lecky*

A necessity. Without them, men would attack responsible women in the streets.　*Napoleon 1*

A young whore, an old saint.　　*John Ray*

A devoted part of the sex—devoted for the salvation of the rest.　　*Mary Wollstonecraft*

A woman footloose and fanny free.　　*Anon.*

A woman engaged in social service work of a sort.

Anon.

Usually a night solicitor.　　　　*Anon.*

A female with a community chest.　　*Anon.*

A woman who has no anxiety about her reputation. The worse it gets the better her income.

Anon.

SEE ALSO COURTESAN, MISTRESS.

PROTESTANT

A person who has examined the evidences of religion for himself, and who accepts them because, after examination, he is satisfied of their genuineness and sufficiency.

Philip G. Hamerton

The religion of the Scotch Protestants is simply pork-eating Judaism.　　*Heinrich Heine*

We seek our pardons from our heavenly hope, and not by works, or favor from the pope; to saints we make no prayer, or intercession, and unto God alone we make confession.

Adapted from John Taylor

PROTESTANTISM

The true force of Protestantism was its signal return to the individual conscience—to the method of Jesus.　　　*Matthew Arnold*

A sort of dissent.　　　　*Edmund Burke*

The belief that God deals directly with man as a person, so that salvation is gained "by faith alone." *J. Leslie Dunstan*

What we call Protestantism was really a free thought movement; a revolt against religion.

Edgar W. Howe

A proposal to change masters. From being the slave of the papacy the intellect was to become the serf of the *Bible.* *Thomas Henry Huxley*

A reaffirmation of the Old Testament and of Judaism. *Thomas G. Masaryk*

The feeling of a direct responsibility of the individual to God. *John Stuart Mill*

A positive affirmation of Christian gospel rather than an anti-Catholic movement.

Helmut Niebuhr

A great congeries of historic movements.

Reinhold Niebuhr

An opposition in the name of individual responsibility before God. *Gerhard Ritter*

A continuous history of the breaking of images.

Paul Tillich

SEE ALSO CHRISTIANITY, CHURCHES, LU-THER.

PROVERBS

Instruction. *Apocrypha: Ecclesiastes, VIII, 8.*

Pointed speeches. *Francis Bacon*

The wisdom of the streets. *William G. Benham*

A short sentence based on long experience.

Miguel de Cervantes

A racial aphorism which has been, or still is, in common use, conveying advice or counsel, invariably camouflaged figuratively, disguised in metaphor or allegory. *S. G. Champion*

The flowers of the rhetoric of a vulgar man.

Lord Chesterfield

Art—cheap art. As a general rule they are not true; unless they happen to be mere platitudes.

Joseph Conrad

The literature of the illiterate.

Frederick S. Cozzens

The steps by which we walk in all our businesses.

Kenelm Digby

The sanctuary of the intuitions.

Ralph Waldo Emerson

Consist usually of a natural fact selected as a picture or parable of a moral truth.

Ralph Waldo Emerson

Much matter decocted into few words.

Thomas Fuller

They are all made by men, for their own advantage. *Thomas Hardy*

Invaluable treasures to dunces with good memories. *John Hay*

To repeat what has been said a thousand times.

William Hazlitt

The proverbs of a nation furnish the index to its spirit, and the results of its civilization.

Josiah G. Holland

The philosophy of the common people.

James Howell

Few words, right sense, fine imagery.

Moses Ibn Ezra

A proverb is no proverb to you till your life has illustrated it. *John Keats*

The ready money of human experience.

James Russell Lowell

One man's wit and all men's wisdom.

John Russell

A little gospel. *Spanish Proverb*

Pocket wisdom...conceived for the use of mediocre people, to discourage them from ambitious attempts. *Robert Louis Stevenson*

SEE ALSO APHORISM, EPIGRAM, MAXIM.

PROVIDENCE

The lost assigned to every man.

Marcus Aurelius

Providence has been called the baptismal name of Chance, but a devout person would say that Chance is a nickname of Providence.

Nicolas Chamfort

Experience joined to common sense
To mortals is a providence.   *Matthew Green*

It means that there is significance to everything
that happens in the world, and a heart, a concern,
and a power stronger than all the powers of the
world which is able to fulfill the purpose of its
care for man.   *Romano Guardini*

When good befalls a man he calls it Providence,
when evil, Fate.   *Knut Hamsun*

This viewless, voiceless Turner of the wheel.
                                   Thomas Hardy

Divine Providence is Wisdom, endowed with an
infinite Power, which realizes its aim, viz., the
absolute rational design of the world.
                                   Georg W. Hegel

The care God takes of all things.
                              Saint John Damascene

The will of God through which all existing things
receive their fitting issue.
                              Saint John Damascene

God's will from which all existing things receive
fitting ends.   *Saint Gregory*

A judgment of God.   *Johann C. Schiller*

A greater power than we can contradict.
                              William Shakespeare

The most popular scapegoat for our sins.
                                   Mark Twain

The mighty power of the gods.   *Vergil*

SEE ALSO CALVINISM, DESTINY, FATE.

PRUDE

A native of Boston.   *Foolish Dictionary*

A virgin hard of feature, old, and void of all good-
nature; lean and fretful and would seem wise, yet
plays the fool before she dies.
                         Adapted from Alexander Pope

The outrageously virtuous.   *Richard Steele*

A virtuous exhibitionist.   *Anon.*

A person who manages to repress one's natural
instincts.   *Anon.*

PRUDENCE

A rich, ugly old maid courted by incapacity.
                                   William Blake

Provident fear.   *Edmund Burke*

Consists in a certain judgment (of) how to choose
God.   *Baldassare Castiglione*

The practical knowledge of things to be sought,
and of things to be avoided.   *Cicero*

To know the useful art of acting dumb.
                                   George Crabbe

The greatest good ... from it spring all the other
virtues.   *Epicurus*

Neither the hope nor the fear of anything from the
uncertain events of the future.   *Anatole France*

Steering by the wind.   *Baltasar Gracian*

Wise venturing.   *Lord Halifax*

A presumption of the future, contracted from the
experience of time past.   *Thomas Hobbes*

(The attitude that) keeps life safe, but does not
often make it happy.   *Samuel Johnson*

Consists in the power to recognize the nature of
disadvantages and to take the less disagreeable as
good.   *Niccolo Machiavelli*

The first thing to desert the wretched.   *Ovid*

SEE ALSO CAUTION, DISCRETION.

PSALMS

The anatomy of the soul.   *John Calvin*

The prayer-book and the hymn-book of the whole
world ... they are religion itself put into speech.
                                   Carl L. Cornill

(Where) men speak to God and to their own
hearts.   *Matthew Henry*

A "little Bible" since it contains, set out in the
briefest and most beautiful form, all that is to be
found in the whole Bible.   *Martin Luther*

Our Bread of Heaven in the wilderness of our
Exodus.   *Thomas Merton*

The whole music of the heart of man, swept by the
hand of his Maker.   *Rowland E. Prothero*

A mirror in which each man sees the motions of his own soul. *Rowland E. Prothero*

The songs of the human soul, timeless and universal. *Theodore H. Robinson*

The confessional of half mankind.

George A. Smith

PSYCHIATRIST

To him it is given to "prepare the ways of the Lord and make straight His paths." *Rudolf Allers*

A doctor with a queasy stomach.

Eugene E. Brussell

A wealthy man retired from the practice of medicine. *Eugene E. Brussell*

A debris digger. *Paulette Brussell*

A man who goes to a burlesque show and watches the musicians. *Robert Fontaine*

Someone who will listen to you as long as you don't make sense. *Maxwell Hyman*

One who has an inner-calm system in his office.

William Kennedy

Physicians of the mind. *Pope Gregory I*

A doctor who tells you what everybody knows in language nobody can understand. *John Proctor*

A priestly man...For with him the relation to the patient and the inner activities of the patient have been lifted out of the realm of the subjectivity of the finite and into the inclusive life of the eternal.

Paul Tillich

A trauma critic. *Anon.*

One who does not have to worry as long as other people do. *Anon.*

An eavesdropper with a college degree. *Anon.*

A person you give your headaches to. *Anon.*

One who analyzes your unhappiness so that you may know why you are unhappy. *Anon.*

One who lets you see why you are unhappy.

Anon.

An ambivalence chaser. *Anon.*

SEE ALSO FREUD, NEUROSIS.

PSYCHIATRY

The troubled science. *R. H. Berg*

The art of teaching people how to stand on their own feet while reclining on couches.

Shannon Fife

A terrible waste of couches. *Rosina Pagan*

The art of making a man take his medicine lying down. *Anon.*

Enables us to correct our faults by confessing our parent's shortcomings. *Laurence J. Peter*

The care of the id by the odd. *Anon.*

PSYCHOANALYSIS

A wonderful discovery...Makes quite simple people feel they're complex.

Samuel N. Behrman

Confession without absolution.

Gilbert Keith Chesterton

An impartial tool both priest and layman can use in the service of the sufferer. *Sigmund Freud*

Consists precisely in having extended research to the region of the mind. *Sigmund Freud*

Neither religious nor the opposite.

Sigmund Freud

The task of making conscious the shadowside and the evil within us. It simply brings into action the civil war that was latent, and lets it go at that.

Carl G. Jung

The disease it purports to cure. *Karl Kraus*

The approach is a technique, not a substitute for a moral code, and to confuse the two is to invite catastrophe. *Louis Linn and Leon Schwartz*

Freud's scientific label permits the nicest girl to discuss intimate sexual details with any man, the two stimulating each other erotically during the talk while wearing poker faces, and at the same time proving themselves learned and liberated.

Emil Ludwig

One of the greatest foundation stones of a structure of the future. *Thomas Mann*

(To) tolerate a stranger at the bedside of my mind.

Vladimir Nabokov

The confessional technique developed by the psychiatrist in the probing of psychic disturbances and in effecting their removal.

John A. O'Brien

Yet another method of learning how to endure the loneliness produced by culture.   *Philip Rieff*

(A method wherein) a neutral figure...neither advises nor consoles nor condemns, to whom the patient "transfers" his deepest affections and hostilities.   *Leo C. Rosten*

A method of treatment.   *Fulton J. Sheen*

An expression of the predicament of modern man.

Paul Tillich

The means for ultimate health.

Gregory Zilboorg

Calvinism in Bermuda shorts.   *Anon.*

SEE ALSO FREUD, FREUDIANISM, MENTAL HEALTH, NEUROSIS, NEUROTIC, PSYCHIATRIST.

PSYCHOLOGY

Psychology must supply us with the facts about the human mind and its experiences.

F. R. Barry

A mass of cant...of superstition worthy of the...medicine man.   *John Dewey*

A form of myth making, whereby men supply the place of knowledge by converting their conjectures into dogma, and then do battle on behalf of the dogmas.   *C. E. M. Joad*

Like all other sciences, it formulates no moral goal; it is not a philosophy of life, nor did its pioneers ever intend it to be. It is a key to the temple, not the temple itself.

Joshua L. Liebman

The business of psychology is to tell us what actually goes on in the mind. It cannot possibly tell us whether the beliefs are true or false.

Hastings Rashdall

A word dragged in when the explaining gets difficult.   *Anon.*

SEE ALSO BRAIN, MIND, PSYCHIATRY.

PUBLIC OFFICE

The end of the private man.   *Eugene E. Brussell*

Public trusts, bestowed for the good of the country, and not for the benefit of an individual or a party.   *John C. Calhoun*

Government is a trust and the officers of the government are trustees...both...are created for the benefit of the people.   *Henry Clay*

A trust.   *Charles J. Fox*

It is but honorable exile from one's family and affairs.   *Thomas Jefferson*

(Not) a reward, but an increased responsibility.

Lyndon Baines Johnson

That in which the interest of the functionary is entirely coincident with his duty.

John Stuart Mill

The last refuge of the incompetent.

Boise Penrose

SEE ALSO DEMOCRACY, GOVERNMENT, POLITICIAN, POLITICS.

PUBLIC OPINION

What people think that other people think.

Alfred Austin

A people's invincible armor.   *Ludwig Boerne*

Something that is gotten by reiteration.

Adapted from Elizabeth Barrett Browning

The greatest lie in the world.   *Thomas Carlyle*

The law of nature.   *Cicero*

What we call public opinion is generally public sentiment.   *Benjamin Disraeli*

That bloated vanity.   *Ralph Waldo Emerson*

Everybody knowing better than anybody.

French Proverb

What the multitude says is so, or soon will be so.

Baltasar Gracian

The judgment of the incapable many opposed to that of the discerning few.   *Elbert Hubbard*

A vulgar, impertinent, anonymous tyrant who deliberately makes life unpleasant for anyone who is not content to be the average man.

William R. Inge

Like the pressure of the atmosphere; you can't see it—but, all the same, it is sixteen pounds to the square inch.   *James Russell Lowell*

The immemorial form of the mob's fears.

Henry Louis Mencken

A compound of folly, weakness, prejudice, wrong feeling, right feeling, obstinacy and newspaper and newspaper paragraphs.   *Robert Peel*

Private gossip which has reached epidemic proportions.   *Anon.*

The people's tyranny.   *Anon.*

Something formulated when judgment is at its weakest and most narrow.   *Anon.*

SEE ALSO DEMOCRACY, MAJORITY, MASSES, MOB, POPULACE, PUBLIC (THE), TYRANNY.

PUBLIC RELATIONS

An engineering of consent.   *Robert Bedingfield*

The attempt, by information, persuasion, and adjustment, to engineer public support for an activity, cause, movement, or institution.

Edward L. Bernays

Hiring someone who knows what he is doing to convince the public that you know what you are doing.   *Hyman Maxwell Berston*

Serving the public well or ill and letting the public know only about the well part.

Warren Goldberg

The craft of arranging the truth so that people will like you.   *Alan Harrington*

Serving the public well and letting the public know about it.   *Herman Kerr*

Press agentry on a yearly basis.

Leonard L. Levinson

Hard work.   *Richard Milhous Nixon*

The management function which evaluates public attitudes, identifies the policies and procedures of an individual or an organization with the public interest, and executes a program of action to earn public understanding and acceptance.

Public Relations News, New York City, 1954.

The art of winning friends and getting people under the influence.   *Jeremy Tunstall*

SEE ALSO ADVERTISEMENTS, ADVERTISING.

PUBLIC SERVANT

One who serves the public for his own good.

Art Linkletter

Persons chosen by the people to distribute the graft.   *Mark Twain*

SEE ALSO PUBLIC OFFICE.

PUBLIC, THE

The wisest critic.   *George Bancroft*

A piano. You just have to know what keys to poke.

Al Capp

An old woman. Let her maunder and mumble.

Thomas Carlyle

A bad guesser.   *Thomas De Quincey*

The monkeys outside the cage.   *Max Gralnick*

One immense ass.   *Horace Greeley*

The greatest of cowards, for it is afraid of itself.

William Hazlitt

A great dunce...it has no opinions but upon suggestion.   *William Hazlitt*

A scurvy master.   *Italian Proverb*

That miscellaneous collection of a few wise and many foolish individuals.   *John Stuart Mill*

A fool.   *Alexander Pope*

A great baby.   *John Ruskin*

The public is merely a multiplied "me."

Mark Twain

A ferocious beast. One must either chain it up or flee from it.   *Voltaire*

SEE ALSO MAJORITY, MASSES, MOB, MULTITUDE, PEOPLE (THE), POPULACE, RABBLE.

PUBLISHER

A bookmaker in search of a longshot.

Harold Coffin

One of a band of panders which sprang into existence soon after the death of Gutenberg and which now overruns the world. *Elbert Hubbard*

The patron saint of the mediocre.

Elbert Hubbard

Publishers are demons. *William James*

A smart merchant who takes a block of spruce, slices it into 500 sheets, sprays ink on it, and sells it at $5.00 a copy. *Leonard L. Levinson*

One who may find a message for the world from time to time. *Anon.*

SEE ALSO PRESS (THE), PRINTING.

PUBLISHING

The most difficult game to master and predict.

Anon.

A guessing game with ulcers. *Anon.*

PULPIT

SEE CLERGYMEN, PREACHERS, PREACHING.

PUN

Among the smaller excellencies of lively conversation. *James Boswell*

A paltry, humbug jest; those who have the least wit make them best.

Adapted from William Combe

(To) torture one poor word ten thousand ways.

John Dryden

Two strings of thought tied with an acoustic knot.

Arthur Koestler

A pistol let off at the ear; not a feather to tickle the intellect. *Charles Lamb*

A noble thing *per se*. It fills the mind, it is as perfect as a sonnet; better. *Charles Lamb*

The lowest form of humor—when you don't think of it first. *Oscar Levant*

A joke based on the infirmities of language.

Leonard L. Levinson

Language on vacation. *Christopher Morley*

The wit of words. They are exactly the same to words which wit is to ideas, and consist in the sudden discovery of relations in language.

Sydney Smith

A talent which no man affects to despise but he that is without it. *Jonathan Swift*

Something every person belittles and everyone attempts. *Louis Untermeyer*

A low species of wit. *Noah Webster*

SEE ALSO HUMOR, WIT.

PUNCTUALITY

The soul of business. *Henry G. Bohn*

The cheapest virtue which can give force to an otherwise utterly insignificant character.

John F. Boyes

The politeness of kings. *Louis XVIII*

A form of self-indulgence. *Robert Lynd*

The virtue of the bored. *Evelyn Waugh*

The thief of time. *Oscar Wilde*

The craft of ascertaining how late the other fellow is going to be. *Anon.*

The practice of making you too early for any appointment. *Anon.*

The art of arriving for an appointment in time to be indignant at the tardiness of the other party.

Anon.

The state of being lonely. *Anon.*

PUNISHMENT

A sort of medicine. *Aristotle*

To make sure that the guilty man does not repeat his crime, and to deter others . . . from committing it. *Cesare Beccaria*

All punishment is mischief. All punishment in itself is evil. *Jeremy Bentham*

An artificial consequence annexed by political authority to an offensive act. *Jeremy Bentham*

An eye for an eye, a tooth for a tooth, a hand for a hand. Burning for burning, wound for wound, and stripe for stripe. *Bible: Exodus, XXI, 24.*

The main strength and force of a law.

William Blackstone

The sword of heaven.   *Dante*

The preventive of crime.   *Tyron Edwards*

The greatest...is to be despised by your neighbors, the world, and members of your family.
Edgar W. Howe

The justice that the guilty deal out to those that are caught.   *Elbert Hubbard*

A perpetual fine, imposed hourly during the lifetime of a human being for his temerity in living.   *Elbert Hubbard*

That one should be turned loose in society and remain absolutely unnoticed by all the members thereof.   *William James*

To silence, not to confute.   *Samuel Johnson*

Preventative pain.   *Leonard L. Levinson*

Prevention from evil.   *Horace Mann*

The healing art of wickedness.   *Plato*

Being abandoned to one's self.
Pasquier Quesnel

Justice for the unjust.   *Saint Augustine*

Sin is a suppurating wound; punishment is the surgeon's knife.   *Saint John Chrysostom*

The notion of a remedy, and has the place of a mean, not of an end.   *Benjamin Whichcote*

The most severe punishment—finding out you are wrong.   *Walter Winchell*

To wear the yoke of our own wrong doing.
Anon.

SEE ALSO CAPITAL PUNISHMENT, HANGING, PRISON.

PUNISHMENT, CAPITAL

SEE CAPITAL PUNISHMENT.

PUPPETS

Puppets are people, and the way they play depends on how they are made and the way their strings are pulled. Through them we see ourselves in miniature.   *Catherine Reighard*

PURITANISM

Puritanism restricted natural pleasures; it substituted the Jeremiad for the Paean.
Samuel Butler 2

A State without kings or nobles...a church without a bishop.   *Rufus Choate*

The whole history of English progress since the Restoration, on its moral and spiritual sides.
John R. Green

The rebirth of the Hebrew spirit in the Christian conscience.   *Reuben Kaufman*

Alienation of the body...the use of the body as a machine.   *Rollo May*

The haunting fear that someone, somewhere, may be happy.   *Henry Louis Mencken*

The impulse to punish the man with a superior capacity for happiness—to bring him down to the miserable level of "good" men, i.e., stupid, cowardly and chronically unhappy men.
Henry Louis Mencken

An American heritage to be grateful for and not to be sneered at because it required everyone to attend divine worship and maintained a strict code of moral ethics.   *Samuel E. Morison*

A passion for righteousness; the desire to know and do God's will.   *Samuel E. Morison*

A Protestant renaissance of the Old Testament and a reversion to the biblical precedents for the regulation of the minutest details of daily life.
Oscar Strauss

A determined and varied effort to erect the holy community.   *A. S. Woodhouse*

SEE ALSO CALVINISM, NEW ENGLAND.

PURITANS

A popular scapegoat...a catch basin for undeserved reproaches.   *Silas Bent*

Those pious pioneers who voluntarily subjugated themselves to a rigid set of duties in order to create an orderly and just society.
Eugene E. Brussell

A sect, whose chief diversion lies
In odd perverse antipathies.   *Samuel Butler 1*

A person who pours righteous indignation into the wrong things.   *Gilbert Keith Chesterton*

A very wonderful people...If they were narrow it was not a...destructive narrowness, but a vital and productive narrowness.   *Calvin Coolidge*

He had stiff knees, the Puritan,
That were not good at bending.
James Russell Lowell

Two different men, the one all selfabasement, penitence, gratitude, passion; the other proud, calm, inflexible, sagacious. He prostrated himself in the dust before his Maker; but he set his foot on the neck of his king.
Thomas B. Macaulay

One who uses the cross as a hammer to knock in the heads of sinners.   *Henry Louis Mencken*

Not one who tries to make us think as he does, but one who tries to make us do as he does.
Henry Louis Mencken

Not a man of speculation. He originated nothing... The distinction between his case and that of others was simply that he practiced what he believed.   *Wendell Phillips*

The Puritan did not stop to think; he recognized God in his soul, and acted.   *Wendell Phillips*

A solemn and unsexual man.
Percy Bysshe Shelley

One, who, all doubts, allayed, is conscious that he is a sealed and chosen vessel. *Richard H. Tawney*

Wild opportunists, swarmed into a remote wilderness to find elbow-room for... fanatic doctrines and practices.   *Nathaniel Ward*

(Those who) are interesting for their costumes and not for their convictions.   *Oscar Wilde*

One who always thinks below the belt and suspects evil.   *Anon.*

PURITY

Using your life in the way God wants, exercising constant restraint.   *Francis Devas*

Consists... in possessing a pure heart but what there is in the heart comes out also and is shown in outward acts and... behavior.
Mohandas K. Gandhi

A rapt... aloofness toward natural processes.
Elbert Hubbard

A condition that causes one to snoop around in garbage-dumps.   *Elbert Hubbard*

Simplicity reaches out after God; purity discovers and enjoys Him.   *Thomas á Kempis*

The sum of all loveliness.   *Francis Thompson*

To be saved, atrophied and pickled.   *Anon.*

The condition for a higher love—for a possession superior to all possessions: that of God.   *Anon.*

SEE ALSO CHASTITY, INNOCENCE.

PURPOSE

SEE END, LIVING, SUCCESS.

Q

QUARRELING

Dog-snap and cat-claw, curse and counterblast.
Robert Browning

The weapon of the weak. *Hebrew Proverb*

Three principal causes... First, competition; second, diffidence; thirdly, glory. The first maketh men invade for gain; the second for safety; and the third for reputation. *Thomas Hobbes*

(They) have something of familiarity, and a community of interest; they imply acquaintance; they are of resentment, which is of the family of dearness. *Charles Lamb*

For souls in growth, great quarrels are great emancipations. *Logan P. Smith*

SEE ALSO ARGUMENTS, WAR.

QUEEN

A woman by whom the realm is ruled when there is a king, and through whom it is ruled when there is not. *Ambrose Bierce*

A widow for life. *Welsh Proverb*

SEE ALSO KING, MONARCHY.

QUEER

SEE ECCENTRICITY.

QUESTION

Something that ignorant men raise which wise men answered a thousand years ago.
Adapted from Johann W. Goethe

The "silly question" is the first intimation of some totally new development.
Alfred North Whitehead

The start of knowledge. *Anon.*

QUESTIONING

Man's finest quality. *Solomon Ibn Gabirol*

Not the mode of conversation among gentlemen.
Samuel Johnson

The beginning of genius without which no progress would flow. *Anon.*

QUIET

Quiet to quick bosoms is a hell. *Lord Byron*

Noise you don't mind. *Leonard L. Levinson*

A happy life... for it is only in an atmosphere of quiet that true joy can live. *Bertrand A. Russell*

That blessed mood. *William Wordsworth*

SEE ALSO SILENCE.

QUOTATIONS

The act of repeating erroneously the words of another. *Ambrose Bierce*

The wisdom of the wise and the experience of ages. *Isaac D'Israeli*

Every book . . . and every house is a quotation out of all forests and mines and stone-quarries, and every man is a quotation from all his ancestors.

Ralph Waldo Emerson

The parole of literary men all over the world.

Samuel Johnson

Something that somebody said that seemed to make sense at the time. *Leonard L. Levinson*

Other people's flowers. *Michel de Montaigne*

A diamond on the finger of a man of wit, and a pebble in the hand of a fool. *Joseph Roux*

Scraps of learning. *Edward Young*

An excellent way to begin or end a speech.

Anon.

Something that exists only to better express yourself. *Anon.*

SEE ALSO PLAGIARISM.

R

RABBI

Men distinguished for superior erudition and the blamelessness of their lives, and these qualities form their only title to distinction.   *Felix Adler*

The legitimate successors and continuators of the prophets.   *Robert T. Herford*

He who joins with the common man in order to lift him to a higher level.

Adapted from Jacob J. Katz

The foundation of the world...No revelation is possible except through him.   *Abraham Malak*

Primarily a teacher.   *David Philipson*

God-fearing men.   *Sefer Hasidim, 13c.*

SEE ALSO JUDAISM, SYNAGOGUE.

RABBLE

In a republic, those who exercise a supreme authority tempered by fraudulent elections.

Ambrose Bierce

The dregs of the people.   *Cicero*

The venal herd.   *Juvenal*

Nothing. It can do nothing on its own.

Napoleon 1

An entity which few care to admit they are a part of.   *Anon.*

The greater part of the masses.   *Anon.*

SEE ALSO CROWD, DEMOCRACY, MASSES, MULTITUDE, PEOPLE (THE), PUBLIC (THE)

RACE

God hath made of one blood all nations of men.
Bible: Acts, XVIII, 26.

The key of history, and why history is so often confused is that it has been written by men who were ignorant of this principle and all the knowledge it involves.   *Benjamin Disraeli*

Two or more persons who see some difference between themselves and other people.

Leonard L. Levinson

There is but one race—humanity.

George Moore

The cheap explanation tyros offer for any collective trait that they are too stupid or too lazy to trace to its origin.   *Edward A. Ross*

SEE ALSO NATIONALITY, NEGRO

RACE CONFLICT

A denial of human dignity and man's essential unity.   *Catholic Bishops of South Africa, July, 1957.*

Pigment of the imagination.   *Sandra Griffiths*

A national issue and a national disgrace.

Paul J. Hallinan

Man's gravest threat to man, the maximum of hatred for a minimum of reason, the maximum of cruelty for a minimum of thinking.

Abraham J. Heschel

This blasphemy attributes to God that which is of the devil. *Martin Luther King 2*

SEE ALSO BIGOTRY, NEGRO, PREJUDICE.

RADICAL

The conservative of tomorrow injected into the affairs of today. *Ambrose Bierce*

What makes a radical radical is not that he discomfits others, but *how* he does it.

Daniel J. Boorstin

The nonconformists of every age.

Commonweal, Editorial, July 1, 1955.

An obstructionist who grows fat on conservatism and conversation. *Elbert Hubbard*

A hungry or unsuccessful person.

Elbert Hubbard

One who wants to tackle all evil at the root.

Dwight MacDonald

An idealist who feels impelled to right existing wrongs. *Charles A. Madison*

A man with both feet planted firmly in the air.

Franklin Delano Roosevelt

The radical of one century is the conservative of the next. The radical invents the views. When he has worn them out the conservative adopts them.

Mark Twain

One who insists on recognizing the facts, adjusting policies to facts and circumstances as they arrive. *Woodrow Wilson*

A man who knows where he is going when he moves. *Woodrow Wilson*

Those who see the total destruction of the present structure of society as an immediate end to a better future. *Robert Zwickey*

A conservative out of a job. *Anon.*

SEE ALSO REFORM, REFORMERS, REVOLUTION.

RADICALISM

Involves a commitment to the interdependence of men, and to the sharing of their concerns.

Daniel J. Boorstin

A passionate faith in the infinite perfecibility of human nature. *Eric Hoffer*

A plan for going forward by backing up to mob rule. *Elbert Hubbard*

(A position which) endeavors to realize a state more in harmony with the character of the ideal man. *Herbert Spencer*

That attitude which looks toward the future for answers and hates the present and the past. The desire for immediate and total change is central.

Robert Zwickey

SEE ALSO REFORM, REVOLUTION.

RADIO

A toy to tickle the ears of fools.

Francis Beeding

The rape of the elements. *James Cannon*

A laughingstock of intelligence...a stench in the nostrils of the gods of the ionosphere.

Lee De Forest

The triumph of illiteracy. *John Dos Passos*

Of unique usefulness for bringing peoples together...the radio shows them as they are, and reveals their most attractive side.

Albert Einstein

Television without eye-strain. *Max Gralnick*

A conduit through which prefabricated din can flow into our homes. *Aldous Huxley*

Death in the afternoon and into the night.

Arthur Miller

A creative theatre of the mind. *Jack Smith*

An instrument perfectly suited to a prison.

Leon Trotsky

SEE ALSO TELEVISION.

RAILROAD

The greatest blessing that the ages have wrought out for us. They give us wings; they annihilate the toil and dust of pilgrimage; they spiritualize travel!   *Nathaniel Hawthorne*

Not...traveling at all; it is merely being sent to a place, and very little different from becoming a parcel.   *John Ruskin*

Only a device for making the world smaller.
John Ruskin

RAINBOW

God's glowing covenant.   *Hosea Ballou*

I do set my bow in the cloud, and it shall be for a token of a covenant between me and the earth.
Bible: Genesis, IX, 13.

A midway station given
For happy spirits to alight
   Betwixt the earth and heaven.
Thomas Campbell

The ribbon nature puts on after washing her hair.
Ramón Gómez de la Serna

Arch of promise.   *Robert Southey*

Heaven's promise in technicolor.   *Anon.*

RANK

Relative elevation in the scale of human worth.
Ambrose Bierce

A great beautifier.   *Edward G. Bulwer-Lytton*

In the main...a consequence of property.
James Fenimore Cooper

Rank is to merit what dress is to a pretty woman.
La Rochefoucauld

SEE ALSO ARISTOCRACY, CLASSES.

RATIONALISM

Devoid of all delusions save those of observation, experience and reflection.   *Ambrose Bierce*

The exercise of reason instead of faith in matters of faith.   *John Henry Newman*

The growth and gradual diffusion...of the supremacy of reason.   *Mark Pattison*

The attempt to establish a system of human rights and a general theory of law in the light of the nature of man as a being standing by himself, with no necessary reference whatever to a superior Being.   *Pope Pius XII*

The mental attitude which unreservedly accepts the supremacy of reason and aims at establishing a system of philosophy and ethics verifiable by experience and independent of all arbitrary assumptions of authority.
Rationalist Press Association

(Rejecting) the claims of "revelation," the idea of a personal God, the belief in personal immortality, and in general the conceptions logically accruing to the practices of prayer and worship.
John M. Robertson

The attempt to live on Christian ethical capital without Christ.   *Ralph Russell*

SEE ALSO REASON, SCIENCE, THOUGHT.

RATIONALIZING

The self-exculpation which occurs when we feel ourselves, or our group, accused of misapprehension or error.   *James Harvey Robinson*

REACTION

The consequence of a nation waking from its illusions.   *Benjamin Disraeli*

A state of moving away from something.   *Anon.*

REACTIONARY

People whose notion of a satisfactory future is, in fact, a return to an idealized past.
Robertson Davies

He sees the future as a glorious restoration rather than an unprecedented innovation.   *Eric Hoffer*

A person who sits in his easy chair on Sunday, never thinking that tomorrow is Monday, but only that yesterday was Saturday.   *Ferdinand Pecora*

A somnambulist walking backward.
Franklin Delano Roosevelt

One who can't see the difference between radicalism and an idea.   *Anon.*

READER

Some read to think, these are rare; some to write, these are common; and some read to talk, and these form the great majority.

Charles Caleb Colton

Two sorts: one who carefully goes through a book, and the other who as carefully lets the book go through him.   *Douglas Jerrold*

A reading-machine, always wound up and going, master of whatever was not worth knowing.

Adapted from James Russell Lowell

One who thinks with someone else's head instead of his own.   *Anon.*

SEE ALSO BOOK, PEDANT.

READING

To weigh and consider.   *Francis Bacon*

Using all one's engine-power. If we are not tired after reading, common-sense is not in us.

Arnold Bennett

(To) mark, learn, and inwardly digest.

Book of Common Prayer.

Seeing an author's object, whatever it may be, as he saw it.   *Thomas Carlyle*

Blood that enters letters.   *Miguel de Cervantes*

That intense excitement and sense of enlargement and liberation which comes from a discovery which is also a discovery of oneself.

Thomas Stearns Eliot

I wish only to read that book it would have been a disaster to omit.   *Ralph Waldo Emerson*

A dynamic act: the creative coming together of minds.   *Waldo Frank*

He that loves reading, has everything within his reach. He has but to desire, and he may possess himself of every species of wisdom to judge and power to perform.   *William Godwin*

To skip judiciously.   *Philip G. Hamerton*

The greatest pleasure in life...while we are young.   *William Hazlitt*

(A) device for avoiding thought.   *Arthur Helps*

An acquirement which means more than the pronunciation of words, more than repetition of sentence. It plays an important part in education itself and leads the way to a broad, deep culture.

Alice Jordan

If you will receive profit, read with humility, simplicity and faith; and seek not at any time the fame of being learned.   *Thomas á Kempis*

Reading means borrowing.

Georg C. Lichtenberg

Reading furnishes our mind only with materials of knowledge; it is thinking makes what we read ours.   *John Locke*

The key which admits us to the whole world of thought and fancy and imagination.

James Russell Lowell

To see with the keenest eyes, hear with the finest ears, and listen to the sweetest voices of all time.

James Russell Lowell

Too much reading makes one deep versed in books and shallow as a person.

Adapted from John Milton

To exchange hours of ennui for hours of delight.

Charles de Montesquieu

An oppression of the mind.   *William Penn*

Thinking with a strange head instead of with one's own.   *Arthur Schopenhauer*

It is quality rather than quantity that matters.

Seneca

This polite and unpunishable vice, this selfish, serene, life-long intoxication.   *Logan P. Smith*

Living with the best company.

Adapted from Sydney Smith

Seeing by proxy.   *Herbert Spencer*

A continuous conversion...The real question is what changes will be made in you as a result of really reading a book.   *Leon Stein*

To take a great and dangerous step.

Robert Louis Stevenson

Coming to know in personal terms what is in the mind of the writer.   *Harold Taylor*

A noble intellectual exercise.

Henry David Thoreau

The only enjoyment in which there is no alloy; it lasts when all other pleasures fade.

Anthony Trollope

The work of the alert mind, is demanding, and under ideal conditions produces finally a sort of ecstasy. This gives the experience of reading a sublimity and power unequaled by any other form of communication.   *Edward B. White*

An exercise, a gymnast's struggle.

Walt Whitman

SEE ALSO EDUCATION, KNOWLEDGE, LEARNING.

REALISM

What men do, and not what they ought to do.

Francis Bacon

The art of depicting nature as it is seen by toads.

Ambrose Bierce

A way of seeing ear-wax, belly-button lint, and dirt between the toes. It is looking at life too close up.   *Eugene E. Brussell*

An attitude of mind on the part of the writer toward his material, a vague indication of the sympathy and candor with which he accepts, rather than chooses, his theme.   *Willa Cather*

A record of life at low pitch and ebb viewed in the sunless light of day.   *Walter De La Mare*

To think that two and two are four
And neither five nor three.   *Alfred E. Housman*

Nothing more and nothing less than the truthful treatment of material.   *William Dean Howells*

To attempt to explain what is mysterious by mental maladies.   *Joris K. Huysmans*

SEE ALSO LIVING.

REALIST

A man who insists on making the same mistakes his grandfather did.   *Benjamin Disraeli*

When a man begins to call himself a "realist," he is preparing to do something he is secretly ashamed of doing.   *Sydney Harris*

The man, who having weighed all the visible factors in a given situation and having found that the odds are against him, decides that fighting is useless.   *Raoul de Sales*

Somebody who thinks the world is simple enough to be understood. It isn't.   *Donald Westlake*

REALITY

What I "come up against," what takes me by surprise, the other-than-myself which pulls me up and obliges me to reckon with it and adjust myself to it because it will not consent simply to adjust itself to me.   *John Baillie*

Religious consciousness.   *Francis H. Bradley*

All existence, and all thought and feeling.

Francis H. Bradley

A narrow little house which becomes a prison to those who can't get out of it.   *Joyce Cary*

All our interior world . . . and that . . . more so than our apparent world.   *Marc Chagall*

Atoms and empty space.   *Democritus*

A sliding door.   *Ralph Waldo Emerson*

(Something that) will always remain unknowable.

Sigmund Freud

God or Spirit.   *Charles E. Garman*

Spirit is the only Reality. It is the inner being of the world, that which essentially is, and is *per se*.

Georg W. Hegel

The things that really are in the world . . . those motions by which these seemings are caused.

Thomas Hobbes

The existentialist responsibility of remaking ourselves every morning.   *Clive James*

The things we cannot possibly not know, sooner or later, in one way or another.   *Henry James*

A feeling of objective presence, a perception of what we may call "something there," more deep and more general than any of the special and particular senses.   *William James*

The pure concept of the understanding, that which corresponds to a sensation in general.

Immanuel Kant

What is felt and believed.   *Felix Mendelssohn*

That unmovable something which lies...behind the changing show of facts on which our minds feed.   *Joseph S. Needham*

What is before your eyes.   *Ovid*

A staircase going neither up nor down. We don't move, today is today.   *Octavio Paz*

That...which abides unchanged.

Saint Augustine

The well-known, often-discussed, but, to my mind, as yet unexplained Universe.

Logan P. Smith

In general what truths have to take account of.

A. E. Taylor

Reality is just itself, and it is nonsense to ask whether it be true or false.

Alfred North Whitehead

Nothing but a collective hunch   *Anon.*

SEE ALSO LIFE, LIVING.

REASON

The only oracle of man.   *Ethan Allen*

A spark kindled by the beating of our heart.

Apocrypha: Wisdom of Solomon, II, 2.

That by which the soul thinks and judges.

Aristotle

To act according to nature and according to reason is the same thing.   *Marcus Aurelius*

(That which) governs the wise man and cudgels the fool.   *Henry G. Bohn*

Every man's reason is every man's oracle.

Henry Bolingbroke

Life's sole arbiter.   *Richard Burton*

The only faculty we have wherewith to judge concerning anything, even revelation itself.

Joseph Butler

Nine times in ten, the fettered and shackled attendant of the triumph of the heart and the passions.   *Lord Chesterfield*

The light and lamp of life.   *Cicero*

Reason always means what someone else has got to say.   *Elizabeth Cleghorn*

The life of law.   *Edward Coke*

The servant of instinct.   *Clarence Day*

Reason is not measured by size or height, but by principle.   *Epictetus*

Reason always means what someone else has got to say.   *Elizabeth C. Gaskell*

Reason exercises merely the function of preserving order, is...the police in the region of art. In life it is mostly a cold arithmetician summing up our follies.   *Heinrich Heine*

Nothing else but to conceive a sum total from addition of parcels, or to conceive a remainder from subtraction of one sum from another.

Adapted from Thomas Hobbes

The arithmetic of the emotions.

Elbert Hubbard

God's emissary.   *Abraham Ibn Ezra*

The only oracle given you by heaven, and you are answerable for, not the rightness, but the uprightness of the decision.   *Thomas Jefferson*

A free activity of the mind, reaching conclusions under no compulsion save that of evidence.

C. E. M. Joad

True religion.   *Morris Josesph*

The constant condition of all free actions by which man takes his place in the phenomenal world.

Immanuel Kant

Natural revelation, whereby the eternal Father of light...communicates to mankind that portion of truth which he has laid within the reach of their natural faculties.   *John Locke*

The discovery of the certainty or probability of such...truths, which the mind arrives at by deduction made from such ideas, which it has got by the use of its natural faculties: viz., by sensation or reflection.   *John Locke*

The greatest enemy that faith has.

Martin Luther

Reason is but choosing.   *John Milton*

What is now reason was formerly impulse.

Ovid

My augury, and my interpretation of the future; by it I have practiced divination, and obtained knowledge.   *Ovid*

That dreary shed, that hutch for grubby schoolboys.   *Theodore Roethke*

The norm of the human will, according to which its goodness is measured, because reason derives from the eternal law which is the divine reason itself.   *Saint Thomas Aquinas*

(The faculty which) establishes lines of moral cleavage everywhere and makes right eternally different from wrong.   *George Santayana*

No fair reproduction of the universe, but the expression of man alone.   *George Santayana*

A harmony among irrational impulses.
                                    George Santayana

The analysis of belief.   *Franz Schubert*

A portion of the divine spirit set in a human body.
                                    Seneca

A promising child—it surprises, may improve or stop short, but it is not come to maturity.
                                    Horace Walpole

Passion and prejudice govern the world; only under the name of reason.   *John Wesley*

An emotion for the sexless.   *Heathcote Williams*

Upright stature in the soul.   *Edward Young*

SEE ALSO JUDGMENT, MIND, RATIONALISM, THINKING, THOUGHT.

REBELLION

A manly and glorious struggle in opposition to the lawless power of rebellious kings and princes.
                                    Samuel Adams

The sin of witchcraft.   *Bible: Samuel, XV, 23.*

(Consists) in the fact that man surrenders his claim to freedom and received his true freedom from dependence upon God.   *Emil Brunner*

Now and then...a good thing, and as necessary in the political world as storms in the physical.
                                    Thomas Jefferson

A medicine necessary for the sound health of government.   *Thomas Jefferson*

The despot's code, and has no terror for others than slavish souls.   *Benjamin Judah*

The very word is a confession; an avowal of tyranny, outrage, and oppression.
                                    Benjamin Judah

An art.   *Karl Marx*

A few determined leaders and a sound cause.
                                    Henry Louis Mencken

Creation—the revolt against nothingness.
                                    José Ortega y Gasset

Rebellion to tyrants is obedience to God.   *Anon.*

SEE ALSO RADICAL, REVOLUTION.

RECOLLECTION

SEE AUTOBIOGRAPHY, BIOGRAPHY, DIARY, HISTORY WRITING, MEMORY, REFLECTION.

RECREATION

SEE AMUSEMENT, SPORTS.

REFLECTION

The state of man being above himself and under his God.
                Cloud of the Unknowing, 14th century.

The path of immortality.   *Dhammapada*

Creating the thing contemplated.
                                    Benjamin Disraeli

Second thoughts.   *Euripides*

The highest form of human life on condition that it is centered upon the object, the knowledge of which is the end of that life.   *Etienne Gilson*

To think again.   *Warren Goldberg*

The return into itself...of the individuality of any state following upon its being proved...by something other than itself which is shown to depend on it or presuppose it.   *Georg W. Hegel*

That conditioning of alert passivity, in which the soul lays itself open to the divine Ground within and without, the immanent and transcendent Godhead.   *Aldous Huxley*

That notice which the mind takes of its own operations, and the manner of them, by reason whereof there come to be ideas of the operations in the understanding.   *John Locke*

Simply the experience of God that is given to a soul purified by humility and faith.

Thomas Merton

Wisdom's ... best nurse.   *John Milton*

Remembrance.   *Alexander Pope*

Joyful song of God's love taken in mind, with sweetness of angel's praise. This is jubilation, this is the end of perfect prayer and high devotion in this life.   *Richard Rolle*

The foundation of any creative work.

Gershon Shofman

Any state in which the mind considers its own content.   *Anon.*

SEE ALSO PHILOSOPHY, THINKING.

REFORM

A trade—with some a swindling trade—with others an honest but yet lucrative trade.

John Quincy Adams

The clearing away of an old rather than ... the making of a new law.   *Henry Thomas Buckle*

A correction of abuses.

Edward G. Bulwer-Lytton

To innovate is not to reform.   *Edmund Burke*

In hope to merit heaven by making earth a hell.

Adapted from Lord Byron

The utopium of the people.   *Arthur Case*

A good replete with paradox; it is a cathartic which our political quacks recommend to others, but will not take themselves; it is admired by all who cannot effect it, and abused by all who can.

Charles Caleb Colton

The dictates of a man's genius and constitution.

Ralph Waldo Emerson

A mask under cover of which a more terrible reform, which dares not yet name itself, advances.   *Ralph Waldo Emerson*

Every reform was once a private opinion.

Ralph Waldo Emerson

A transition from the past into a regenerated future. Such reform does not break with the past but rather preserves carefully the bond which connects the present with the past.

Abraham Geiger

(Something that) must come from within, not from without. You cannot legislate for virtue.

James C. Gibbons

The craving to change ourselves.   *Eric Hoffer*

The pursuit of other people's happiness.

Elbert Hubbard

A concern with the perfectibility of mankind.

Hugh Kingsmill

Always a symptom of thwarted or perverted development.   *Hugh Kingsmill*

Catholic reform is *not revolution* ... Catholic reform is intent on preserving the continuity of historical development, and hence is not innovation but *renewal*.   *Hans Küng*

Like patriotism, a favorite device of persons with something to sell.   *Henry Louis Mencken*

Bending a crooked stick the opposite way.

Michel de Montaigne

An indefinable something to be done, in a way nobody knows how, at a time nobody knows when, that will accomplish nobody knows what.

Thomas B. Reed

That desire for change which arises from below. No man with four aces demands a new deal.

Anon.

Wishing to correct other people's habits.   *Anon.*

SEE ALSO CHANGE, PROGRESS.

REFORMATION, THE

A judgment day for Europe, when all the nations were presented with an open Bible and all the emancipation of the heart and intellect which an open Bible involves.   *Thomas Carlyle*

(That which) destroyed the unity of faith and ecclesiastical organization of the Christian peoples of Europe.

Catholic Encyclopedia, Reformation, 1913.

A liberation of man from the corporate pattern of an all-embracing Church.   *Michael Fisher*

Not...chiefly a religious movement. It involved a break with the historical ecclesiastical institution and the organization of new churches independent of Rome, but the break was as much political as religious.   *A. C. McGiffert*

In essence...not protest but affirmation, not reform but conservation, not reaction, but propulsion. Its best name is "evangelical."
                    A. R. Mentz

The religious phase of the Renaissance.
                    Harry A. Overstreet

A time when prophetic voices spoke out but to reaffirm for their own time those great and original Christian convictions which are the wellspring of our Christian life.   *James A. Pike*

The Reformation in England was a parliamentary transaction.   *Maurice Powicke*

Not only a religious gain but also a religious loss.
                    Paul Tillich

The Reformation meant not the elimination of the church's control over everyday life, but rather the substitution of a new form of control for the previous one.   *Max Weber*

SEE ALSO LUTHER, PROTESTANTISM.

REFORMERS

Earnest believers in the world.   *Walter Bagehot*

A virtuous person with a mean mind.
                    Walter Bagehot

Those who are seeking not so much to "make people good" as to share an enthusiasm.
                    Charles A. Bennett

The loudest complainers for the public.
                    Edmund Burke

A believer in the divine truth of things.
                    Thomas Carlyle

A priest first of all...He appeals to Heaven's invisible justice against earth's visible force.
                    Thomas Carlyle

Socrates drinking the hemlock,
    And Jesus on the road.   *W. H. Carruth*

The canting moralist.   *John Davidson*

Souls that plague the gentle world.
                    John Davidson

A man who thinks men can be turned into angels by an election.   *Finley Peter Dunne*

The Reformer believes that there is no evil coming from Change.   *Ralph Waldo Emerson*

A remaker of what man has made.
                    Ralph Waldo Emerson

One who, when he smells a rat, is eager to let the cat out of the bag.   *Foolish Dictionary*

Those who are fond of setting things to rights.
                    William Hazlitt

The man who does what he can, and thanks heaven that things are not worse.
                    Elbert Hubbard

One who causes the rich to band themselves against the poor.   *Elbert Hubbard*

One who educates the people to appreciate the things they need.   *Elbert Hubbard*

A man with but one idea, and that a wrong one.
                    Adapted from Samuel Johnson

One who is trying to make the world a better place to die in.   *Leonard L. Levinson*

When A annoys or injures B on the pretense of improving B, A is a scoundrel.
                    Henry Louis Mencken

People who think it a shame when anything goes wrong—who rush to the conclusion that the evil could and ought to have been prevented.
                    John Stuart Mill

Those who...do most to make the world better.
                    John Stuart Mill

One who insists on his conscience being your guide.   *Milard Miller*

All reformers are bachelors.   *George Moore*

We must do what we can, improve every opportunity...We must take the present social order and build upon it.   *William Morris*

Merely devils turned inside out.
                    Edgar Allan Poe

A saint run mad.   *Alexander Pope*

Wild enthusiasts, projectors, politicians.
                    Alexander Pope

Men who form the lunatic fringe in all reform movements.   *Theodore Roosevelt*

Moralists on the scent of evil.

George W. Russell

The faithful preachers of Christianity.

Julius H. Seelye

Nine parts of self-interest gilt over with one part philanthropy.   *Herbert Spencer*

A hound-dog to scent out evil.   — *John T. Stone*

People that bear a commission from no one, who, as a rule, are least informed on the principles of government, but who insist on exercising the power of government to make their neighbors live the lives they desire to prescribe for them.

Oscar W. Underwood

A guy who rides through a sewer in a glass bottom boat.   *James J. Walker*

One who demands the most from himself.

Anon.

SEE ALSO LIBERALS, PROGRESS, RADICAL, SOCIALIST.

REFUGEE

SEE PIONEER.

REGRET

The beginning of a new life.   *George Eliot*

These poor Might-Have-Beens.

William E. Henley

The sum of life's bewailing.   *Letitia E. Landon*

An appalling waste of energy; you can't build on it; it's only good for wallowing in.

Katherine Mansfield

A woman's natural food—she thrives on it.

Arthur Wing Pinero

Make the most of your regrets. To regret deeply is to live afresh.   *Henry David Thoreau*

SEE ALSO REMORSE, REPENTANCE.

REINCARNATION

SEE ETERNAL RECURRENCE.

RELATIVES

What everyone has except the poor.

Italian Proverb

A tedious pack of people who haven't got the remotest knowledge of how to live nor the smallest instinct about when to die.   *Oscar Wilde*

Persons who live too near and die too seldom.

Anon.

SEE ALSO FAMILY, PARENTS.

RELATIVITY

When a man sits with a pretty girl for an hour, it seems like a minute. But let him sit on a hot stove for a minute—and it's longer than any hour. That's relativity.   *Albert Einstein*

Nothing more and nothing less than the admission that a complex state of affairs cannot be described in over-simplified language.   *Philip Frank*

RELAXATION

SEE REST, VACATION.

RELIGION

The life of God in the soul of man.

Lyman Abbott

The cultivation of occult forces whether in detail or mass.   *Henry B. Adams*

The ten commandments and the sermon on the mount.   *John Quincy Adams*

Two general heads. The first comprehends what we are to believe, the other what we are to practice.   *Joseph Addison*

The sense of outgoing to the whole universe in its process towards the quality of deity.

Samuel Alexander

The search for a value underlying all things.

Gordon W. Allport

A man's religion is the audacious bid he makes to bind himself to creation and to the Creator.

Gordon W. Allport

An elective in the university of life.

Amercian Saying

The language of the heart, which is the language of friends, lovers, children, and parents.

E. S. Ames

Its value is measured by the sacrifices which it can extract from the individual.

Henry F. Amiel

The unforeseen, the miraculous, the extraordinary.
Henry F. Amiel

Morality touched by emotion. *Matthew Arnold*

The voice of the deepest human experience.

Matthew Arnold

Doing as little harm as possible, in doing good in abundance, in the practice of love, of compassion, of truthfulness and purity, in all walks of life.

Asoka's Edicts

An attempt to express... what is essentially inexpressible. *Leon Baeck*

The divinity within us reaching up to the divinity above. *Bahai Saying*

An adequate definition of religion is unattainable. It remains the supreme symbol of what is perhaps its most fundamental quality, which is mystery.

Herschel Baker

The product of the fancy and credulity of men who have not yet reached the full development and complete personality of their intellectual powers.

Mikhail A. Bakunin

The root, without which morality would die.

C. A. Bartol

Man's search... for strength and courage to be gained from the heart of spiritual matter, greater than an individual man, greater than the more or less human race. *B. I. Bell*

Less a fear than a reaction against fear.

Henri Bergson

To visit the fatherless and widows in their affliction, and to keep himself unspotted from the world. *Bible: James, I, 27.*

Hope and fear, explaining to Ignorance the nature of the unknowable. *Ambrose Bierce*

Devoted and loyal commitment to the best that reason and insight can discover.

Julius S. Bixler

You cannot be a whole unless you join a whole. This... is religion. *Bernard Bosanquet*

A phase of a people's total interaction with the objective world of nature, organized society and the accumulated tradition of an historic past.

William C. Bower

Too often that which is good enough for the children. *Eugene E. Brussell*

The basis of civil society, and the source of all good and of all comfort. *Edmund Burke*

Obedience to the will of the Sovereign of the world, in a confidence in His declarations, and in imitation of His perfections. *Edmund Burke*

A sense of divine Truth, as enters into a Man, and becomes a Spring of a new Nature within him, reforming his Thoughts and Designs, purifying his Heart. *Gilbert Burnet*

The way we set our personalities for the purpose of meeting the whole stream of events.

Herbert Butterfield

The holy service of God. *William Camden*

The submergence of self in the pursuit of an ideal, the readiness to spend oneself without measure, prodigally... for something intuitively apprehended as great and noble.

Benjamin N. Cardozo

The thing that a man does practically believe; the thing a man does practically lay to heart, and know for certain, concerning his vital relations to this mysterious Universe, and his duty and destiny there. *Thomas Carlyle*

A man's religion is the chief fact with regard to him. *Thomas Carlyle*

Religion is knight-errantry.

Miguel de Cervantes

The sense of ultimate reality, of whatever meaning a man finds in his own existence or the existence of anything else. *Gilbert Keith Chesterton*

A matter of loyalty to the accepted ways hallowed by our ancestors. *Morris R. Cohen*

The most gentlemanly thing in the world. It will alone gentilize, if unmixed with cant.

Samuel Taylor Coleridge

The link between soul and body, the point where heaven and earth meet in friendly encounter.

Israel Deutsch

Any activity pursued in behalf of an ideal end against obstacles and in spite of threats of personal loss because of conviction. *John Dewey*

A bridge between the visible and the invisible and should primarily be regarded as the key to a riddle, the explanation of a mystery.
Ernest Dimnet

The rule of life, not a casual incident of it.
Benjamin Disraeli

Not mere conformity to moral law, it is an espousal of moral ideals, a dedication of the heart, a loyal devotion, the perpetual renewal of a right spirit within us. *Durant Drake*

A bandage that man has invented to protect a soul made bloody by circumstance.
Theodore Dreiser

The soul of civilization. *Will and Ariel Durant*

A unified system of beliefs and practices relative to sacred things...things set apart and forbidden.
Emile Durkheim

The consecration of individual life, at first for love and spiritual ends, but finally for humanitarian ends. *Charles A. Ellwood*

Civilizing power. *Ralph Waldo Emerson*

The ethics of one or another holy person.
Ralph Waldo Emerson

Well-doing and daring. *Ralph Waldo Emerson*

The emotion of reverence which the presence of the universal mind ever excites in the individual.
Ralph Waldo Emerson

The ejaculations of a few imaginative men.
Ralph Waldo Emerson

(That which serves) to enngender in us a sense of human worth. *Jonathan Eybeshitz*

The way we react to what we cannot evade.
Nels F. Ferré

The dream of waking consicousness.
Ludwig A. Feuerbach

A...conciliation of powers superior to man which are believed to control the course of nature or of human life. *James G. Frazer*

A universal obsessional neurosis.
Sigmund Freud

A derivative of the more primitive instincts.
Sigmund Freud

A parallel to the neurosis which the civilized person must pass through on his way from childhood to maturity. *Sigmund Freud*

An attempt to get control over the sensory world, in which we are placed, by means of the wish-world which we have developed inside us as a result of biological and psychological necessities.
Sigmund Freud

Any system of thought and action shared by a group which gives the individual a frame of orientation and an object of devotion.
Erich Fromm

The intellectual resolution of the unknown.
Buckminster Fuller

A good life is the only religion. *Thomas Fuller*

What can be followed out in day-to-day practice.
Mohandas K. Gandhi

Attachment to the whole, soaring up to the infinite, despite our finiteness and limitedness.
Abraham Geiger

Consists not in knowing many things but in practicing the few plain things we know.
Joseph Glanvill

The method you choose of getting to heaven.
Max Gralnick

Faith in an ordainer. *Asa Gray*

A sociology conceived as a physical, meta-physical and moral explanation of all things.
Marie J. Guyau

The power to escape from the power and service of the transitory. *Adolf Harnack*

The mother of dreams. Over the gray world, ruined by deluge and death, it has sought ever, and found, the arching rainbow of hope.
A. E. Haydon

Moral life rising to think. *Georg W. Hegel*

A disease, but a noble disease. *Heraclitus*

Not a dogma, nor an emotion, but a service.
Roswell D. Hitchcock

Fear of power invisible, feigned by the mind or imagined from tales publicly allowed (is) religion; not allowed, superstition. *Thomas Hobbes*

The forerunner of international law; because it alone can create the international spirit, the international obligation.　　　*William E. Hocking*

A speculative hypothesis of an extremely low order of probability.　　　*Sidney Hook*

(A) challenge to aspiration and hope in the mind of man.　　　*Ernest M. Hopkins*

Not an intelligence, but a faith.
　　　　　　　　　　Edgar W. Howe

A desperate attempt to find an escape from the truly dreadful situation in which we find ourselves.　　　*Fred Hoyle*

Formal religion was organized for slaves; it offered them consolation which earth did not provide.　　　*Elbert Hubbard*

Philosophy touched with emotion.
　　　　　　　　　　Elbert Hubbard

Consists of those actions, purposes, and experiences which are humanly significant.
　　　　　　　Humanist Manifesto, 1933.

The alcohol of the soul.　　　*Robert Hume*

A consciously accepted system of make-believe.
　　　　　　　　　　Aldous Huxley

Our own religion is what life has taught us.
　　　　　　　　　　William R. Inge

The mind and will of God, existing as God exists, objectively outside of men and of peoples, superior to all men, exacting from man the obedience due by the creature to the Creator.　　*John Ireland*

The feelings, acts, and experiences of individual men in their solitude, so far as they apprehend themselves to stand in relation to whatever they may consider the divine.　　　*William James*

A man's total reaction upon life.　　*William James*

A monumental chapter in the history of human egotism.　　　*William James*

The natural belief in a Power or Powers beyond our control, and upon whom we feel ourselves dependent.　　　*Morris Jastrow*

Personal cooperation with a trusted Creator of Values.　　　*Paul E. Johnson*

Our religion is in a book; we have an order of men whose duty it is to teach it; we have one day in the week set apart for it.　　　*Samuel Johnson*

An experience which no definition exhausts.
　　　　　　　　　　Rufus M. Jones

The only philosophy which the common mind is able to understand and adopt.　　*Joseph Joubert*

A discipline, a law, a yoke, an indissoluble engagement.　　　*Joseph Joubert*

The recognition of our duties as divine commands.　　　*Immanuel Kant*

Morals in reference to God as legislator.
　　　　　　　　　　Immanuel Kant

The organized quest of a people for salvation, for helping those who live by the civilization of that people to achieve their destiny as human beings.
　　　　　　　　　　Mordecai M. Kaplan

There are two branches of religion—high and low, mystical sleep-walkers and practical idealists.
　　　　　　　　　　John M. Keynes

The elder sister of philosophy.
　　　　　　　　　　Walter Savage Landor

A doctrine which resolves the problem of the afterlife and, based on this doctrine, a discipline which establishes relationship between man and the powers which rule over him.
　　　　　　　　　　Jacques Leclercq

A man's religion is the truth he lives habitually, subconsciously and consciously.
　　　　　　　　　　Benjamin C. Leeming

(That which ties) the soul of man up with some permanent reality beyond the show of sense.
　　　　　　　　　　J. A. Leighton

A clumsy sort of spiritual whiskey in which the slaves of capital drown their human being and their revenge for an existence little worthy of man.
　　　　　　　　　　Nikolai I. Lenin

The process whose distinguishing feature is to seek in the deepest part of the soul an increasing participation in the primal energy of things, to ask love to identify us with the supreme generosity of the spirit.　　　*R. L. Le Senne*

That mode of behavior in the struggle for life in which use is made of powers characterized here as psychic, super-human and usually personal.
　　　　　　　　　　James A. Leuba

Life, more life, a larger, richer, more satisfying life is...the end of religion.　　*James A. Leuba*

Only so many religious dialects.

Georg C. Lichtenberg

The accumulated spiritual wisdom and ethical precepts dating from the time of the earliest Prophets and gradually formulated into a body of tested truth for man's moral guidance and spiritual at-homeness in the universe.

Joshua L. Liebman

Conscience in action. Henry D. Lloyd

A sense of something transcending the expected or natural. Robert H. Lowie

An experience of securing spiritual integrity.

Eugene W. Lyman

The opium of the people. Karl Marx

An emotion resting on a conviction of a harmony between ourselves and the universe at large.

John E. McTaggart

Simply a concerted effort to deny the most obvious realities. Henry Louis Mencken

A respectable distraction from the sourness of life. C. Wright Mills

The acceptance of neither a primitive absurdity nor of a sophisticated truism, but of a momentous possibility—the possibility namely that what is highest in spirit is deepest in nature.

W. P. Montague

The friend of him who has no friend.

James Montgomery

A noble attempt to suggest in human terms more-than-human realities. Christopher Morley

Mutual erotic love, erotic adoration, is the most natural religion. Henry A. Murray

A species of mental disease. Benito Mussolini

Instruments of insights into what civilization means. Mohammed Naguib

The vaccine of the imagination; she preserves it from all dangerous and absurd beliefs.

Napoleon 1

The idea of a Moral Governor, and a particular Providence. John Henry Newman

A system; it is a rite, a creed, a philosophy, a rule of duty, all at once. John Henry Newman

The Life of God in the Soul of Man.

Joseph F. Newton

The best armor in the world, but the worst cloak.

Joseph F. Newton

A process of turning your skull into a tabernacle, not of going up to Jerusalem once a year.

Austin O'Malley

(That which) teaches man to be good.

Thomas Paine

To do good. Thomas Paine

Consists in believing that everything that happens is extraordinarily important. It can never disappear from the world, precisely for this reason.

Cesare Pavese

A deep recognition of a something in the circumambient ALL. Charles S. Peirce

Nothing else but love to God and man.

William Penn

Man's sense of the disposition of the universe to himself. Ralph Barton Perry

That realm that is inviolable before the law of causation and therefore closed to science.

Max Planck

(Something which) converts despair, which destroys, into resignation, which submits.

Marguerite Power

Ritual and the truth of dogma. John C. Powys

A sum of scruples which impede the free exercise of our faculties. Solomon Reinach

A direction of the heart. Rainer Maria Rilke

The interpretation both of the eternal and of the spirit of loyalty through emotion, and through fitting activity of the imagination. Josiah Royce

The dedication of them...to Him who will raise them up at the last day. John Ruskin

The sum of ties or relations which bind men to God. John A. Ryan

An intercourse, a conscious and voluntary relation, entered into by a soul in distress with the mysterious power upon which it feels itself to depend, and upon which its fate is contingent.

Auguste Sabatier

Human experience interpreted by human imagination. George Santayana

Consists of conscious ideals, hopes, enthusiasms, and objects of worship; it operates by grace and flourishes by prayer. George Santayana

The metaphysics of the people.

Arthur Schopenhauer

The masterpiece of the art of animal training, for it trains people as to how they shall think.

Arthur Schopenhauer

An array of legendary personages.

George Bernard Shaw

The reaction of mankind to something apprehended but not comprehended.   *J. Shotwell*

Popular religion may be summed up as a respect for ecclesiastics.   *Baruch Spinoza*

The hunger of the soul for the impossible, the unattainable, the inconceivable.   *W. T. Stace*

A *feeling adjustment* to the deeper things of life, and to the larger reality that encompasses the personal life.   *Edwin Starbuck*

The fear of the many and the cleverness of the few.

Stendhal

All religion relates to life, and the life of religion is to do good.   *Emanuel Swedenborg*

(Something) too often talked of, but too little known.   *Jonathan Swift*

A personal relation with God.   *William Temple*

That which is never spoken.

Henry David Thoreau

The substance of culture.   *Paul Tillich*

The establishment by man of such a relation to the Infinite Life around him.   *Leo Tolstoy*

Man's attempt to get in touch with an absolute spiritual Reality behind the phenomena of the Universe, and, having made contact with It, to live in harmony with It.   *Arnold J. Toynbee*

A set of things which the average man thinks he believes and wishes he was certain.

Mark Twain

Worship of God and the practice of justice.

Adapted from Voltaire

The everlasting dialogue between humanity and God.   *Franz Werfel*

Consists in a profound humility, and a universal charity.   *Benjamin Whichcote*

World loyalty.   *Alfred North Whitehead*

What the individual does with his own solitariness.   *Alfred North Whitehead*

The fashionable substitute for belief.

Oscar Wilde

I would rather think of my religion as a gamble than to think of it as an insurance premium.

Stephen S. Wise

A faith which sides with poverty.   *Anon.*

The greatest tonic ever conceived for perplexity.

Anon.

A decoration in prosperity and a refuge in adversity.   *Anon.*

A perception of the divine existence issuing in duty.   *Anon.*

SEE ALSO ATHEISM, BELIEF, BIBLE, CHRIST, CHRISTIANITY, CHRISTIANS, COMMANDMENTS, FAITH, GOD, JEWS, JUDAISM, MOHAMMEDANISM, MORALITY, PIETY, PREACHERS, PREACHING, RABBI, TEN COMMANDMENTS, THEOLOGY, TORAH, WORSHIP.

REMEMBRANCE

SEE MEMORY, REFLECTION, THOUGHT.

REMORSE

The reproaches of your own heart.

Adapted from Joseph Addison

The echo of a lost virtue.

Edward G. Bulwer-Lytton

That inward hell!   *Lord Byron*

The fatal egg by Pleasure laid.   *William Cowper*

Remorse is memory awake.   *Emily Dickinson*

The anticipation of the pain to which our offense has exposed us.   *Helvetius*

A vivid awareness of our weakness and worthlessness.   *Eric Hoffer*

The form that failure takes when it has made a grab and got nothing.   *Elbert Hubbard*

Pride's ersatz for repentance.   *Aldous Huxley*

When the scourge and the torturing hour calls us to penance.   *Adapted from John Milton*

Beholding heaven and feeling hell.

George Moore

The pain of sin.   *Theodore Parker*

The torturer of the brave!   *Walter Scott*

Rats in the belfrey.   *Anon.*

The price of a good time.   *Anon.*

To carry your own accuser within your breast.

Anon.

A poison in your mind that will not let you rest.

Anon.

SEE ALSO CONSCIENCE, MIND, REGRET, RE-
PENTANCE.

REPARTEE

Prudent insult...Practiced by gentlemen with a
constitutional aversion to violence, but a strong
disposition to offend.   *Ambrose Bierce*

The highest order of wit, as it bespeaks the coolest
yet quickest exercise of genius at a moment when
the passions are aroused.

Charles Caleb Colton

A duel fought with the points of jokes.

Max Eastman

What you could have used before it was too late.

Warren Goldberg

Any remark which is so clever that it makes the
listener wish he had said it himself.

Elbert Hubbard

Something we think of twenty-four hours too late.

Mark Twain

A remark that is better never than late.   *Anon.*

SEE ALSO RIDICULE, WIT.

REPENTANCE

Recoil not from the bad act and its painful
consequences, but from the principle underlying
the act.   *Felix Adler*

Contrition felt for the crime.   *Vittorio Alfieri*

The voice of God.   *Israel Baal Shem Tob*

Another name for aspiration.

Henry Ward Beecher

A change of heart produced in a sinner by the
word of the gospel and the Holy Spirit.

Henry Bullinger

When prodigals return.   *A. A. Dowty*

Repentance is but want of power to sin.

John Dryden

The end of passion.   *Owen Felltham*

Acknowledging...former transgressions.

Edward Hyde

To up and act for righteousness, and forget that
you ever had relations with sin.   *William James*

A kind of leavetaking, looking backward indeed,
but yet in such a way as precisely to quicken the
steps toward that which lies before.

Sören Kiekegaard

Repentance was perhaps best defined by a small
girl: "It's to be sorry enough to quit."

C. H. Kilmer

Not so much regret for the ill we have done as fear
of the ill that may happen to us in consequence.

La Rochefoucauld

A truce with sin.   *Leonard L. Levinson*

To do so no more is the truest repentance.

Martin Luther

Means that the sinner forsake his sins, cast them
out of his mind, and resolve in his heart to sin no
more.   *Moses Maimonides*

Two parts: contrition and faith.

Philip Melanchthon

Religious doctrine viewed on its illuminated side.

John Henry Newman

The manifestation of the Invisible Divine Power.

John Henry Newman

The moment in our history through which we
know ourselves to be known from beginning to
end, in which we are apprehended by the knower.

Helmut R. Niebuhr

The most dishonorable belief against the character
of the Divinity.   *Thomas Paine*

The record of God's acts in time, His often violent
intrusions into human history.   *Philip Scharper*

All that man sees.   *Marvin Schrage*

Not self-regarding, but God-regarding. It is not
self-loathing, but God-loving.   *Fulton J. Sheen*

Pain, accompanied by the idea of oneself as
cause.   *Baruch Spinoza*

A determination not to fail the good again.

Douglas V. Steere

Predicting the yet future manifestations of God through His appointed channels.

James E. Talmage

God willed that to the interior help of the Holy Spirit, there should be joined exterior facts, and especially miracles and prophecies.

Vatican Council, Session III, 1870.

SEE ALSO FAITH, MIRACLE, PROPHECY, VISION.

REPETITION

Reality...it is the seriousness of life.

Sören Kiekegaard

A good means of making or keeping impressions vivid, and almost the only means of keeping them unchanged.   *George Santayana*

REPORTER

SEE JOURNALIST.

REPUBLICAN PARTY

The first party that was not founded on some compromise with the Devil. It is the first party of pure, square, honest principles.

Robert G. Ingersoll

The stale, dank atmosphere of "normalcy."

John Fitzgerald Kennedy

We should make no bones at all about our basic belief that private enterprise generally is more efficient and desirable than government enterprise.   *Richard Milhous Nixon*

The Greater Opportunity party.

Richard Milhous Nixon

Anybody can be a Republican when the market is up. But when stocks are selling for no more than they're worth, let me tell you, being a Republican is a sacrifice.   *Will Rogers*

A party with one idea; but that is a noble idea ... the idea of equality—the equality of all men before human tribunals and human laws.

William H. Seward

The party that gets most of its campaign funds from Wall Street and Big Business...the party that gave us the phony Wall Street boom of the nineteen twenties and the Hoover depression that followed.   *Harry S. Truman*

Grand Old Platitudes.   *Harry S. Truman*

The party that doesn't believe anything new should be tried for the first time.   *Anon.*

The Party that endorses the Democratic plank twenty years later.   *Anon.*

The Party that upholds and strengthens the traditional values which made this country great.

Anon.

SEE ALSO CONSERVATISM, POLITICAL PARTY.

REPUTATION

What people gossip behind your back.

Henry Banks

At once the most beautiful and most brittle of all human things.   *Fanny Burney*

A bubble which a man bursts when he tries to blow it for himself.   *Emma Carleton*

A mirror of crystal, shining and bright, but liable to be sullied by every breath that comes near it.

Miguel de Cervantes

What the world thinks of us.   *Cicero*

Something that never corresponds with the amount of your labor.   *Adapted from Horace*

Your standing in the community.

Edgar W. Howe

A synonym of popularity: dependent on suffrage, to be increased or diminshed at the will of the voters.   *Anna Jameson*

Only a...candle, of a wavering and uncertain flame, and easily blown out, but it is the light by which the world looks for and finds merit.

James Russell Lowell

What others are not thinking about you.

Thomas Masson

A great noise: the more there is made, the farther off it is heard.   *Napoleon 1*

What men and women think of us.   *Plato*

RESEARCH

An idle and most false imposition; oft got without merit, and lost without deserving.

William Shakespeare

What you seem to be like. *Anon.*

SEE ALSO FAME, HONOR, NAME.

RESEARCH

The ability to investigate systematically and truly all that comes under your observation in life.

Marcus Aurelius

Scientific activity dedicated to discovering what makes grass green. *Russell Baker*

The process of going up alleys to see if they are blind. *Marston Bates*

When I'm doing what I don't know (what) I'm doing. *Wernher von Braun*

To give each and every element its final value by grouping them in the unity of an organized whole.

Pierre T. de Chardin

A blind date with knowledge. *Will Henry*

An organized method of finding out what you are going to do when you can't keep on doing what you are doing now. *Charles F. Kettering*

An organized method for keeping you reasonably dissatisfied with what you have.

Charles F. Kettering

Something that tells you that a jackass has two ears. *Albert D. Lasker*

The art of the soluble. *Peter Medawar*

If you steal from one another, it's plagiarism; if you steal from many, it's research.

Wilson Mizner

A duty. *Moses Nahawendi*

Not to find truth but to investigate and search after it. *Max Nordau*

The beginning of research is curiosity, its essence is discernment, and its goal truth and justice.

Isaac H. Satanov

Means going out into the unknown with the hope of finding something new to bring home.

Albert Szent-Gyorgyi

The opium of the biographers. *Anon.*

A way of life dedicated to discovery. *Anon.*

RESPECTABILITY

The pretense that no one really knows about us.

John Ciardi

(Something) accorded only to a personality which respects itself, to character...not to a servile creature which surrenders its all and permits the effacement of its own individuality.

Simon M. Dubnow

The dickey on the bosom of civilization.

Elbert Hubbard

Implies a multitude of little observances, from the strict keeping of Sunday down to the careful tying of a cravat. *Victor Hugo*

Respectable means rich, and decent means poor.

Thomas L. Peacock

Public acclaim, the reward of scoundrels.

Bertrand A. Russell

SEE ALSO GENTLEMAN, LADY, WEALTH.

RESPONSIBILITY

A detachable burden easily shifted to the shoulders of God, Fate, Fortune, Luck, or one's neighbor. *Ambrose Bierce*

The great developer. *Louis D. Brandeis*

Work to carry on within, duties to perform abroad, influences to exert which are peculiarly ours, and which no conscience but our own can teach. *Adapted from William Ellery Channing*

The price of greatness. *Winston S. Churchill*

The high price of self-ownership.

Eli J. Schleifer

A way of doing the right thing—and of shortening life. *Anon.*

SEE ALSO GREATNESS, MATURITY, SUPERIOR MAN.

REST

The end and reward of toil. *James Beattie*

Six days may work be done; but in the seventh is the sabbath. *Bible: Exodus, XXXI, 15.*

Come unto me, all ye that labor and are heavy laden, and I will give ye rest.

Bible: Matthew, XI, 28.

Rest is for the dead.   *Thomas Carlyle*

The fitting of self to one's sphere.
                                           John S. Dwight

A pain.   *Homer*

Moonlight of the spirit!   *Jean Paul Richter*

To lie fallow for a while.   *Martin F. Tupper*

SEE ALSO DEATH, IDLENESS, LEISURE, RE-
TIREMENT, SABBATH.

RESTAURANT

A place where the smell is usually better than the
food.   *Eugene E. Brussell*

Where one goes to rest and rant.   *Walter Lee*

An institution for the distribution of indigestion.
                                        Leonard L. Levinson

RESURRECTION

Many of them that sleep in the dust of the earth
shall awake, some to everlasting life, and some to
shame and everlasting contempt.
                                        Bible: Daniel, XII, 2

The hour . . . in which all that are in the grave shall
hear His voice, and shall come forth; they that
have done good, unto the resurrection of life; and
they that have done evil, unto the resurrection of
damnation.   *Bible: John, V, 28–29.*

The sea gave up the dead which were in it; and
death and hell delivered up the dead which were in
them: and they were judged every man according
to his works.   *Bible: Revelation, XX, 13.*

A stable apprehension that our ashes shall enjoy
the fruits of our pious endeavors.
                                        Thomas Browne

A revival of the dead at a time when it shall please
the Creator.   *Moses Maimonides*

The re-establishment of personal life on the farther side of the grave, the conviction that the total
personality, invested by God with a perfect organism, lives on.   *Robert J. McCracken*

We would not call it resurrection unless the soul
returned to the same body, for resurrection means
a second rising.   *Saint Thomas Aquinas*

That the bodies of all men—both those who have
been born and those who shall be born, both those
who have died and those who shall die—shall be
raised again.   *Saint Augustine*

This visible flesh . . . will rise again.
                                        Saint Augustine

The glory of the Holy Spirit *comes out from
within*, decking and covering the bodies of the
saints—the glory which they had before, but
hidden within their souls.   *Saint Macarius*

SEE ALSO CHRIST, CHRISTIANITY, DEATH,
ETERNAL RECURRENCE, JUDGMENT DAY.

RETIREMENT

One sure way of shortening life. *Franklin Conklin*

Friend to life's decline.   *Oliver Goldsmith*

The only true retirement is that of the heart.
                                        William Hazlitt

(When one) shrivels up into a nuisance to all
mankind.   *Herbert C. Hoover*

Statutory senility.   *Emmett O'Donnell*

Since no one has found Utopia, perhaps this is
what it is meant to be.   *Paul Weinberger*

The bane of longevity.   *Anon.*

The reward for a lifetime of labor consisting of the
grandchildren, hobbies and travel.   *Anon.*

SEE ALSO LEISURE, OLD AGE.

REVELATION

Events occurring in the historical experience of
mankind, events which are apprehended by faith
as the "mighty acts" of God.   *John Baillie*

Knowledge of the divine will as cannot be found
through submersion in myself or in the secret of
the world . . . an act of personal self-impartation
from outside our own range, in which God gives
us himself.   *Emil Brunner*

Primarily . . . conduct and supernatural life and
not . . . speculative answers to speculative questions.   *Martin C. D'Arcy*

The Eternal speaking time.   *Martin C. D'Arcy*

Made . . . for the purpose of showing that which
the moral darkness of man will not, without
supernatural light, allow him to perceive.
                                        Thomas De Quincey

True revelation comes through the clear intellect.

Solomon B. Freehof

The record of the immediate experience of those who are pure enough in heart and poor enough in spirit to be able to see God.   *Aldous Huxley*

The silent, imperceptible manifestation of God in history. It is the still, small voice: it is the inevitableness, the regularity of nature.

Herbert M. Loewe

An act whereby God speaks to men through Himself or through his messenger, making a statement the truth of which He guarantees.

William J. McGucken

Something more than mere remorse for sins; it comprehends a change of nature befitting heaven.

Lew Wallace

SEE ALSO CONSCIENCE, GUILT, REGRET, REMORSE.

REVENGE

A kind of wild justice, which the more man's nature runs to, the more ought law to weed it out.

Francis Bacon

Eye for eye, tooth for tooth, hand for hand, foot for foot.   *Bible: Deuteronomy, XIX, 21.*

As you have done, it shall be done to you.

Bible: Obadiah, I, 15.

The noblest . . . is to forgive.   *Henry G. Bohn*

A debt in the paying of which the greatest knave is honest and sincere, and, so far as he is able, punctual.   *Charles Caleb Colton*

That recoil of Nature, not to be guarded against, which ever surprises the most wary transgressor.

Ralph Waldo Emerson

Nothing which we don't invite.

Ralph Waldo Emerson

That thirsty dropsy of our souls.

Fletcher and Massinger

One of the grand principles in the divine administration of human affairs. There is everywhere the working of the everlasting law of requital: man always gets as he gives.   *John Foster*

A luscious fruit which you must leave to ripen.

Emile Gaboriau

The only debt people wish to pay promptly.

Max Gralnick

Living well is the best revenge.   *George Herbert*

A morsel reserved for God.   *Italian Proverb*

The poor delight of little minds.   *Juvenal*

The road I made.   *John Masefield*

Biting a dog because the dog bit you.

Austin O'Malley

Forgiveness and a smile.   *Samuel Palmer*

To forget a wrong.   *John Ray*

To obtain a second life.   *Publilius Syrus*

SEE ALSO PUNISHMENT.

REVERENCE

The spiritual attitude of a man to a god and a dog to man.   *Ambrose Bierce*

A man is ethical only when life . . . is sacred to him, that of plants and animals as that of his fellow man, and when he devotes himself helpfully to all life that is in need of help.

Albert Schweitzer

The most complicated, the most direct, and the most elegant of all compliments.

William Shenstone

A feeling of overpowering awe in regard to the mysteries of the universe.   *Robert Zwickey*

SEE ALSO GOD, PIETY, WORSHIP.

REVIEWERS

Intellectual prostitutes.   *Max Beerbohm*

Usually people who would have been poets, historians, biographers, if they could: they have tried their talents at one or the other, and have failed.   *Samuel Taylor Coleridge*

Men who quarrel over the motive of a book that never had any.   *Elbert Hubbard*

A kind of children's disease which more or less attacks newborn books.   *Georg C. Lichtenberg*

Sentinels in the grand army of letters, stationed at the corners of newspapers . . . to challenge every new author.   *Henry Wadsworth Longfellow*

He who would write and can't write.

James Russell Lowell

A barker before the door of a publisher's circus.

Austin O'Malley

The actual definition of reviewmanship is now...stabilized. In its shortest form it is "How to be up on the author without actually tampering with the text." Stephen Potter

Sextons, who...can tell you to what John Thompson or to what Tom Matthews such a skull or such belonged—but who wishes to know?

Horace Walpole

A necessary evil, and criticism is an evil necessity. Carolyn Wells

One who gives the best jeers of his life to the author. Anon.

A failure at creativity. Anon.

SEE ALSO CRITICS.

REVOLUTION

They arrive through the force of circumstances, and are independent of any deliberate will or conspiracy. They can be foreseen, but their explosion can never be accelerated.

Mikhail A. Bakunin

An abrupt change in the form of misgovernment.

Ambrose Bierce

Legality on vacation. Leon Blum

A transfer of power. Edward G. Bulwer-Lytton

The first step to empire. Edmund Burke

All modern revolutions have ended in a reinforcement of the power of the State. Albert Camus

A phoenix...rising like a flame from the bodies of the wretched. Luis Cernuda

Every revolution is the consequence of one revolution and the beginning of another.

Francois de Chateaubriand

Longing not so much to change things as to overturn them. Cicero

(When) an oppressed people are authorized...to rise and break their fetters. Henry Clay

Power...in the hands of nobodies.

George Danton

(Something which) creates illusions and is conducted in the name of unrealizable ideals.

Milovan Djilas

Creating through the crisis of vision and shared agony the kind of power which rises to meet a torn world anew with the world of love and the act of transformation. James W. Douglass

A thought is one man's mind.

Ralph Waldo Emerson

A natural phenomenon governed by physical laws different from the rules which govern the development of society in normal times.

Friedrich Engels

Revolution is war, a zoological rather than a human method. Hayyim Greenberg

A conspicuous instrument of change.

Eric Hoffer

Would you realize what Revolution is, call it progress. Victor Hugo

The larva of civilization. Victor Hugo

Broadening—for all Americans—the material and spiritual benefits of the democratic heritage.

Lyndon Baines Johnson

(That which) evaporates, leaving behind only the slime of a new bureaucracy.

Adapted from Franz Kafka

The creation of an alternative. Ron Karenga

The language of the unheard.

Martin Luther King 2

A fighting cow, its vital organs constituted of one stomach for the digestion of food, the other for the digestion of revenge. Deirdre Levinson

The change of power from the hands of one class into the hands of the other. Deirdre Levinson

A complete renovation and reopening under new management. Leonard L. Levinson

The common refuge which God hath provided for all men against force and violence. John Locke

Violent and sudden usurpations.

James Madison

The will to act against this world and to seek ways of changing it. René Magritte

Only a false-front for the urge to rule.

Henry Louis Mencken

An activity which begins in the best heads, and runs steadily down to the populace.

Klemens von Metternich

An idea which has found bayonets. *Napoleon 1*

Derives from the agitation of elites.

Edward Norman

The setting up of a new order contradictory to the old one. *José Ortega y Gasset*

To undermine the established customs, by going back to their origin, in order to mark their want of justice. *Blaise Pascal*

Insurrection of thought. *Wendell Phillips*

Painful yet fruitful gestations of a people; they shed blood but create light; they eliminate men, but elaborate ideas. *Manuel Prada*

Revolution is just like one cocktail—it gets you organized for the next. *Will Rogers*

To dare: that is the whole secret of revolutions.

Antoine Saint-Just

A transfer of property from one class to another class. *Leon Samson*

The result of an old society pregnant with a new one. *Schurmann and Schell*

Revolution within the soul is the Christian adventure...The sword it carries is not turned against our neighbor, but against our absurd over-valuation of the self. *Fulton J. Sheen*

Inexorable confrontation in the refusal of the privileged to relinquish their power, and the recognition of the victimized that without power they are lost. *William Strickland*

Repression is the seed of revolution.

Daniel Webster

(An) effort to get rid of a bad government and set up a worse. *Oscar Wilde*

The right to refuse allegiance to, and to resist, the government when its tyranny or its inefficiency are great and unendurable. *Anon.*

A mass movement which travels on an empty stomach. *Anon.*

When wrongs are rioted. *Anon.*

SEE ALSO COMMUNISM, REBELLION.

REVOLUTIONIST

Those who know when power is lying in the street and when they can pick it up. *Hannah Arendt*

A doomed man. He has no personal interests, no affairs, sentiments, attachments, property, not even a name of his own. *Mikhail A. Bakunin*

Everything in him is absorbed by one exclusive interest, one thought, one passion—the revolution...He knows only one science, the science of destruction. *Mikhail A. Bakunin*

Every revolutionist ends up either by becoming an oppressor or a heretic. *Albert Camus*

(One who) must be able to do anything.

Joseph Goebbels

One who adopts certain speculative *a priori* conceptions of political right, with the fanaticism and proselytizing fervor of religious belief.

Adapted from William E. Lecky

Potential Tories, because they imagine that everything can be put right by altering the shape of society; once that change is effected...they see no need for any other. *George Orwell*

Life's champion and avenger. *Boris Pasternak*

A man who dislikes himself and so attaches his passion to the violent overthrow of existing order.

Robert Zwickey

SEE ALSO RADICAL.

RHETORIC

The power of determining in a particular case what are the available means of persuasion.

Aristotle

For all the rhetorician's rules
Teach nothing but to name his tools.

Samuel Butler 1

Rigmarole. *Lord Byron*

That pestilent cosmetic. *Thomas Henry Huxley*

It lays down laws for the writing of sentences and paragraphs about as reasonable and as useful as a set of directions telling how to be a gentleman, or how to have a taste for tomatoes.

Stephen B. Leacock

SEE ALSO ORATORY, WRITING.

RHINE RIVER

A blending of all beauties.   *Lord Byron*

The beautifulest river in the earth...and my first idea of a world-river.   *Thomas Carlyle*

RHYME

Agreeing sounds in the terminals of verse, mostly bad.   *Ambrose Bierce*

The rudder of verses.

Adapted from Samuel Butler 1

The most obvious way of externalizing sound.

Robert Zwickey

SEE ALSO POETRY.

RICHES

A gift from God.   *Jehiel Anav*

The "baggage" of virtue; the Roman word is better, "impediment."   *Francis Bacon*

Larger means to gratify the will.

William Congreve

A mind released from anxious thoughts.

William Cowper

The savings of many in the hands of one.

Eugene Debs

Consists not in industry, much less in saving, but in a better order, a timeliness, being at the right spot.   *Ralph Waldo Emerson*

Not the end, but only a change of worries.

Epicurus

The one word that contradicts everything you can say against a man.

Adapted from Henry Fielding

Who is rich? He that is content. Who is that? Nobody.   *Benjamin Franklin*

Neither to flatter nor to borrow.   *Thomas Fuller*

I am indeed rich, since my income is superior to my expense, and my expense is equal to my wishes.   *Edward Gibbon*

The seat of the human soul.   *Elbert Hubbard*

An illusion.   *Solomon Ibn Gabirol*

The longest road.   *Jewish Proverb*

That which gives us time.

Adapted from Charles Lamb

To live sparingly with an open mind.   *Lucretius*

The most valuable of all human possessions, next to a superior and disdainful air.

Henry Louis Mencken

A contented mind.   *Mohammed*

A sort of duty...that it may be in one's power to do good.   *Mary W. Montagu*

The incentives to evil.   *Ovid*

A gift from Heaven signifying, "This is my beloved son, in whom I am well pleased."

John D. Rockefeller

My brother.   *Russian Proverb*

Not...possession of much, but giving much.

Saint John Chrysostom

A great slavery.   *Seneca*

That man is richest whose pleasures are the cheapest.   *Henry David Thoreau*

A man is rich in proportion to the number of things which he can afford to let alone.

Henry David Thoreau

Lack of needs.   *Franz Werfel*

What lies underneath your hat.   *Anon.*

SEE ALSO ARISTOCRACY, DOLLAR, GOLD, MONEY, POSSESSIONS, PROPERTY, WEALTH.

RIDICULE

The qualification of little ungenerous minds.

Joseph Addison

The sharpest reproof.   *Henry G. Bohn*

The language of the devil.   *Thomas Carlyle*

Egotism in ill humor.   *Samuel Taylor Coleridge*

The test of truth.   *Anthony A. Cooper*

The subtlest form of revenge.   *Baltasar Gracian*

To turn serious matters to sport.   *Horace*

A kind of gangrene, which if it seizes one part of a character corrupts all the rest.

Samuel Johnson

Poverty of wit. *Jean de La Bruyère*

The weapon of those who have no other.

Hubert Pierlot

(Something that) often checks what is absurd, and fully as often smothers that which is noble.

Walter Scott

These paper bullets of the brain.

William Shakespeare

The first and last argument of fools.

C. Simmons

The fume of little hearts. *Alfred Lord Tennyson*

Barbed ire. *Anon.*

SEE ALSO CARICATURE, LAUGHTER, SATIRE, WIT.

RIDICULOUSNESS

Merely a subdivision of the ugly. It consists in some defect which is neither painful nor destructive. *Aristotle*

(Something) produced by any defect that does not involve pain or death. *Aristotle*

One step above the sublime makes the ridiculous, and one step above the ridiculous makes the sublime again. *Thomas Paine*

Extreme wisdom or extreme folly. *Anon.*

SEE ALSO FOOLISHNESS.

RIGHT

The greatest good to the greatest number.

Jeremy Bentham

Something other people grant after you've fought tooth and nail for them. *Brendan Francis*

A moral quality annexed to the person, justly entitling him to possess some particular privilege, or to perform some particular act.

Hugo Grotius

The liberty each man hath to use his own power as he will himself for the preservation of his own nature. *Thomas Hobbes*

Faithful to the light within.

Oliver Wendell Holmes 1

That which tends to the universal good.

Francis Hutcheson

We will consider nothing right unless it advances our revolution. *Nikolai I. Lenin*

The eternal sun; the world cannot delay its coming. *Wendell Phillips*

Whatever is, is right. *Alexander Pope*

If it be right to me, it is right. *Max Stirner*

A delusion created by a ghost. *Max Stirner*

The side Everyman thinks he is on. *Anon.*

To do whatever you least want to do. *Anon.*

SEE ALSO ETHICS, GOOD, MORALITY.

RIGHT AND WRONG

Right is the opposite of wrong; and wrong consists of inflicting injuries on other people.

Robert Briffault

The only right is what is after my constitution, the only wrong what is against it.

Ralph Waldo Emerson

To be engaged in opposing wrongs affords, under the conditions of our mental constitution, but a slender guarantee for being right.

William E. Gladstone

Right and wrong exist in the nature of things. Things are not right because they are commanded, nor wrong because they are prohibited.

Robert G. Ingersoll

Actions are right in proportion as they tend to promote happiness; wrong as they tend to produce the reverse of happiness. *John Stuart Mill*

SEE ALSO ETHICS, GOOD AND BAD, MORALITY.

RIGHTEOUS

A lover of men.

Apocrypha: Wisdom of Solomon, XII, 19.

A form of common sense. Wise expediency.

Elbert Hubbard

Whosoever believes in God. *Koran, II.*

Priests of the Holy One.

Seder Eliyahu Zuta, ch. 20.

Severe judges and impossible mates. *Anon.*

RISK

SEE DANGER.

RITUAL

SEE BELIEF, CHRISTIANITY, CHURCHES, JUDAISM, PRAYERS.

RIVER

The cosiest of friends.   *George W. Curtis*

A wet highway.   *Leonard L. Levinson*

Roads that move and carry us where we wish to go.   *Blaise Pascal*

An aspect of nature which lies behind the cottages and billboards.   *Anon.*

A benefaction to the towns they visit and to the people they recreate.   *Anon.*

ROBBER

SEE THIEF.

ROBESPIERRE, MAXIMILIEN (1758-1794)

A fanatic, a monster, but he was incorruptible, and incapable of robbing, or of causing the deaths of others.   *Napoleon 1*

An enthusiast, but one who really believed that he was acting right, and he died not worth a sou.
Napoleon 1

Robespierre came out of the pages of Rousseau.
Oscar Wilde

ROGUE

A man who gives women a past.   *Henry Best*

Lewd fellows of the baser sort.
Bible: Acts, XVII, 5.

A roundabout fool.   *Samuel Taylor Coleridge*

A man who treats all women as sequels.   *Anon.*

A man who is always ready to give up a passing fancy for something fancier.   *Anon.*

A man with a perfect sense of two-timing.
Anon.

A man with a little black book of cancelled chicks.
Anon.

SEE ALSO SCOUNDREL.

ROMAN CATHOLIC

SEE CATHOLICISM, CHURCH (ROMAN CATHOLIC), PAPACY.

ROMANCE

In love, one first deceives oneself and then others —and that is what is called romance.
John L. Balderston

They that have had it have slipped in and out of heaven.   *James M. Barrie*

This will that stirs in us to have the creatures of earth and the affairs of earth, not as they are, but "as they ought to be," which we call romance.
James Branch Cabell

Romance, like a ghost, eludes touching. It is always where you were, not where you are.
George W. Curtis

The offspring of fiction and love.
Benjamin Disraeli

Every form of human life.
Thomas W. Higginson

Where the hero begins by deceiving himself and ends by deceiving others.   *Elbert Hubbard*

Consists of the things that can reach us only through a beautiful circuit and subterfuge of our thoughts and desires.
Adapted from Henry James

A celestial crown.   *George Meredith*

The essential elements...are curiosity and the love of beauty.   *Walter Pater*

A love affair in other than domestic surroundings.
Walter Raleigh

The spirit of adventure, the code of honour, both masculine and feminine.   *George Santayana*

(Something) always young.
John Greenleaf Whittier

There is no such thing...in our day, women have become too brilliant; nothing spoils a romance so much as a sense of humor in the woman.
Oscar Wilde

A self-induced state of hallucination that leaves one finally unromantic.   *Anon.*

SEE ALSO LOVE, LOVERS, NOVEL.

ROMAN PEOPLE

The Roman nature was fierce, rugged, almost brutal.   *James A. Froude*

A blunt, flat people.   *Walter Savage Landor*

At heart, more of a farmer than a soldier.

John Ruskin

Lords of the world.   *Vergil*

ROME

The queen of nations.   *William Alexander*

First among cities, home of the gods.   *Ausonius*

The vanquished.   *Joachim du Bellay*

The Niobe of nations! There she stands, childless and crownless, an empty urn within her withered hands, whose holy dust was scattered long ago.

Adapted from Lord Byron

Lone mother of dead empires.   *Lord Byron*

A city greater than any upon earth, whose amplitude no eye can measure, whose beauty no imagination can picture.   *Claudian*

Mother of arms and of law, who extends her sway over all the earth and was the earliest cradle of justice.   *Claudian*

The lie of salvation.   *Sigmund Freud*

The city of all time, and of all the world.

Nathaniel Hawthorne

Smoke, wealth, and noise.   *Horace*

Where the Pope is, Rome is.   *Italian Proverb*

A city for sale, and doomed to speedy destruction, if it finds a purchaser.   *Jugurtha*

The wild waste of all-devouring years.

Alexander Pope

The capital of the world.   *Pope Innocent II*

At once the paradise, the grave, the city, and the wilderness.   *Anon.*

Weakness of the great, folly of the wise, her very speech is dead.   *Anon.*

SEE ALSO ITALY, PAPACY, ROMAN PEOPLE.

ROOSEVELT, FRANKLIN (1882-1945)

To him men were so many tools to be used for the accomplishment of what he believed to be a good purpose.   *James F. Byrnes*

A hypocrite who beguiled the masses.

Ben Hecht

He was always like a daddy to me.

Lyndon Baines Johnson

The leader of his people in a great war, he lived to see the assurance of the victory but not to share it.

Archibald MacLeish

All that is within me cries out to go back to my home on the Hudson River to avoid public responsibilites.   *Franklin Delano Roosevelt*

A bridge between the old and the new America.

Franklin Delano Roosevelt

My answer is democracy—and more democracy. And...I am of the firm belief that the nation...supports my opposition to vesting supreme power in the hands of any class.

Franklin Delano Roosevelt

It was not easy for a crippled man to carry on this kind of campaign...The simple job of getting up and sitting down several times was almost as much exercise as the ordinary man takes during an entire day...He always went through this harrowing experience smiling.

Samuel I. Rosenman

The architect of an era.   *Rexford G. Tugwell*

A tremendous leader...one with strange gifts to mobilize opinion *anywhere*.   *William S. White*

The master politician. He left it impossible for any conceivable successor wholly to ignore his incredible technical skill as a politician.

William S. White

The President who helped to defeat fascism, only to encourage communism in a compromised peace settlement.   *Robert Zwickey*

A man who never worked for a living, never had to meet a payroll, yet an unabated spendor of other people's money.   *Robert Zwickey*

The Anglo-Dutch patroon.   *Anon.*

ROOSEVELT, THEODORE (1859-1919)

He entered all the portals of the world, a vibrant, thrilled, exhaustless, restless soul, riding at last to the very stars.   *Adapted from Robert H. Davis*

That damned cowboy.   *Mark Hanna*

He was very likeable, a big figure, a rather ordinary intellect, with extraordinary gifts, a shrewd and I think pretty unscrupulous politician.
Oliver Wendell Holmes 1

(He) seemed to be forcing himself all the time; acting, as it were, and successfully.   *Ike Hoover*

The Constitution rides behind
  And the Big Stick rides before,
Which is the rule of precedent
In the reign of Theodore.   *Wallace Irwin*

His greatest work was inspiring and actually beginning a world movement for staying territorial waste.   *Robert M. La Follette*

A combination of St. Paul and St. Vitus.
John Morley

Roosevelt is not an American...He is America.
John Morley

One of the most illustrious psychological examples of the distortion of conscious mental processes through the force of subconscious wishes.
Morton Prince

He has subjugated Wall Street.   *Joseph Pulitzer*

I'm just an ordinary man.   *Theodore Roosevelt*

And when I make up my mind to do a thing, I act.
Theodore Roosevelt

The greatest teacher of the essentials of popular government the world has ever known.
Elihu Root

A megalomaniac.   *William Howard Taft*

Pilot and Prophet!   *Charles H. Towne*

ROUSSEAU, JEAN-JACQUES (1712-1778)

The self-torturing sophist.   *Lord Byron*

A first-rate writer who espoused a second-rate philosophy. He simply ignored the dark places of the human mind.   *Jerry Dashkin*

His self-portraiture is a lie, admirably executed, but still only a brilliant lie.   *Heinrich Heine*

Surely the blackest and most atrocious villain...that now exists in the world.

David Hume

(He) clothed passion in the garb of philosophy, and preached the sweeping away of injustice by the perpetuation of further injustice.
Thomas Henry Huxley

A very bad man.   *Samuel Johnson*

The grand model for the emotional excesses of romanticism.   *Anon.*

RUDENESS

The worst of all diseases.   *Euripides*

The weak man's imitation of strength.
Eric Hoffer

Rudeness is now serving as a substitute for power, for faith, and for achievement.   *Eric Hoffer*

Right now the paragons of rudeness are found on the campuses and among people who fancy themselves in the vanguard of society.   *Eric Hoffer*

Sovereignty without a crown.
Talmud: Sanhedrin, 105a.

A negation of the social spirit.   *Anon.*

SEE ALSO VULGARITY.

RUINS

Time's slow finger written in the dust.
Anna L. Barbauld

Long decay.   *Earl Richard of Carlisle*

The hope of the ancient yesterday.
Elbert Hubbard

Civilization's fallen arch.   *Leonard L. Levinson*

Our monuments.   *Ludwig Lewisohn*

Worldly immortality.   *Anon.*

RULE

SEE AUTHORITY, GOVERNMENT, KING, MON-ARCHY, STATE.

RULER

SEE DICTATORS, LEADER, MONARCHY.

RUMOR

A great traveller.   *William G. Benham*

A favorite weapon of the assassins of character.
                                          Ambrose Bierce

Half a lie.   *Thomas Fuller*

Mischievous, light, and easily raised, but hard to bear and difficult to escape.   *Hesiod*

A report different in form from the original.
                                              Plautus

A pipe blown by surmises, jealousies, conjectures.   *William Shakespeare*

Something invented and enlarged upon.   *Anon.*

SEE ALSO CALUMNY, GOSSIP.

RUSSIA

A country devoid of a humanistic tradition, which kills its creative minds in one way or another.
                                        Eugene E. Brussell

A riddle wrapped in a mystery inside an enigma.
                                      Winston S. Churchill

An immense prison.   *Oscar I. Grusenberg*

The purest and most colossal example of monopolistic capitalism.   *Eric Hoffer*

A patchwork of bolshevism, czarism, nationalism, pan-Slavism, dictatorship, and borrowings from Hitler, and monopolistic capitalism.
                                            Eric Hoffer

A colossus of brass on a pedestal of clay.
                                      Joseph II of Austria

The land of conscious willful hope.
                                        Lincoln Steffens

Their whole society is based on a succession of lies which nobody really believes.
                                          Auberon Waugh

A fit partner for a League of Honor.
                                        Woodrow Wilson

A place where nobody sits up all night to see how the elections came out.   *Anon.*

The land of possibilities.   *Anon.*

RUSSIAN

A person with a Caucasian body and a Mongolian soul.   *Ambrose Bierce*

Scratch a Russian, and you will wound a Tartar.
                                        Joseph de Maistre

One who is clever, but always too late.
                                        Russian Proverb

S

SABBATH

To give to man peaceful hours, hours completely diverted from everyday life. *Leon Baeck*

A sponge to wipe out all the sins of the week.
Henry Ward Beecher

The great organ of the divine administration—the only means provided by God to give ubiquity and power to his moral government.
Lyman Beecher

God blessed the seventh day, and sanctified it: because that in it he had rested from all his work which God created and made.
Bible: Genesis, II, 3.

The still day devoted to God.
Eugene E. Brussell

The quintessence of the doctrine of ethical monotheism . . . It is the epitome of the love of God.
Hermann Cohen

The Lord's day. *Jonathan Edwards*

The day of peace between man and nature . . . By not working—by not participating in the process of natural and social change—man is free from the chains of nature and from the chains of time.
Erich Fromm

One of the main pillars of Priest-craft and superstition, and the strong-hold of a merely ceremonial Religion. *William L. Garrison*

The hallow'd day. *James Grahame*

An opportunity for fellowship with God, and for glad, not austere, service of Him.
Judah Halevi

The incomplete form of the world to come.
Isaac Hanina

A day of mirth. *George Herbert*

The Sabbaths are our great cathedrals.
Abraham J. Heschel

Signifies an abdication on that day of the right to be master of certain things enjoyed during the six other days . . . an essential affirmation of faith.
Israel Kagan

Day of the Lord, as all our days should be.
Henry Wadsworth Longfellow

The attuning of the heart to the comprehension of God. *Moses Maimonides*

Day of all the week the best, Emblem of eternal rest. *John Newton*

The visible sign of the insufficiency of the material and the need for its re-integration with the spiritual. *Louis Roth*

Once a week to do our small devotion and then to follow any merry notion.
Adapted from Edmund Spenser

The hub of the Jew's universe. *Israel Zangwill*

SEE ALSO CHRISTIANITY, CHURCHES, JUDAISM, SUNDAY.

SACRED

SEE BIBLE, HOLINESS.

SACRIFICE

SEE SELF-SACRIFICE.

SADNESS

SEE GRIEF, MELANCHOLY, SORROW.

SAFETY

Never to feel secure. *Henry G. Bohn*

Never to be secure. *Thomas Fuller*

The trodden path. *Legal Maxim*

Safety lies in the middle course. *Ovid*

The best safety lies in fear.
William Shakespeare

Our own honest hearts and chainless hands.
Thomas N. Talfourd

SEE ALSO CAUTION, FEAR, SECURITY.

SAILOR

They that go down to the sea in ships, that do business in great waters.
Bible: Psalms, CVII, 23–24.

(Those who) are nearest to death and the farthest from God. *Thomas Fuller*

(Those) not fit to live on land. *Samuel Johnson*

(Those who) get money like horses and spend it like asses. *Tobias Smollett*

A wolf in ship's clothing. *Anon.*

The personification of restlessness. *Anon.*

SEE ALSO SEA, SHIP.

SAINT

He who says, what is mine is yours and what is yours is yours.
Babylonian Talmud: Aboth, V, 13.

A dead sinner, revised and edited.
Ambrose Bierce

We can never begin to be saints, until we realize that all sanctity consists in the replacing of ourselves and our lives by Christ and His life.
Eugene Boylan

A saint's of th' heav'nly realm a peer.
Samuel Butler 1

Those sacred on earth become saints above it.
Adapted from Samuel Daniel

Saintliness does not come from occupation; it depends upon what one is. *Meister Eckhart*

A skeptic once in every twenty-four hours.
Ralph Waldo Emerson

The word . . . means a man called out from among sinners, and in this sense all good men are saints.
François de Fénelon

One whose humanistic compassion derives from his previous life as a sinner. *Max Gralnick*

The exclusive possession of those who have either worn out or never had the capacity to sin.
Elbert Hubbard

They are impregnators of the world, vivifiers and animators of potentialities of goodness which but for them would lie forever dormant.
William James

One who succeeds in giving us at least a glimpse of eternity, despite the thick opacity of time.
Henry de Lubac

Each stands alone, letting his life flow forth in a reckless torrent that is apparently controlled only by the uncontrollable passion of love to God and love to man. *B. W. Maturini*

A window through which God's mercy shines on the world. And for this he strives to be holy . . . in order that the goodness of God may never be obscured by any selfish act of his.
Thomas Merton

Mainly . . . insane people. *Benito Mussolini*

A person of heroic virtue whose private judgment is privileged. *George Bernard Shaw*

A golden chain, in which each saint is a separate link, united to the next by faith, works, and love.
Symeon the New Theologian

Neither special creations nor spiritual freaks, but those who have learned St. Augustine's aspiration: "My life shall be a real life, being wholly full of Thee." *Evelyn Underhill*

The great teachers of the loving-kindness and fascination of God.   *Evelyn Underhill*

A man of convictions, who has been dead a hundred years, canonized now, but cannonaded while living.   *H. L. Wayland*

The only difference between the saint and the sinner is that every saint has a past and every sinner has a future.   *Oscar Wilde*

God's showmen.   *Anon.*

A sinner who kept on trying.   *Anon.*

SEE ALSO HERO, HOLINESS, JUDGMENT DAY.

SALAD

Four persons are wanted to make a good salad: a spendthrift for oil, a miser for vinegar, a counselor for salt, and a madman to stir all up.

Abraham Hayward

SALESMAN

A successful sales executive is a man who can keep both feet firmly implanted on the desk—and give the impression they belong there.

Franklin Dane

An optimist who finds the world full of promising potential.   *Jerry Dashkin*

Someone who it is always a pleasure to bid good-bye to.   *Anon.*

The high-priest of profits.   *Anon.*

One who sells goods that won't come back to customers who will.   *Anon.*

The foot-soldier of free enterprise.   *Anon.*

SEE ALSO ADVERTISING, BUSINESS.

SALT

It is a covenant of salt for ever before the Lord unto thee and to thy seed with thee.

Bible: Numbers, XVIII, 19.

The policeman of taste: it keeps the various flavors of a dish in order and restrains the stronger from tyrannizing over the weaker.

Malcolm de Chazal

What makes things taste bad when it isn't in them.   *Anon.*

SALVATION

The Catholic faith.   *Athanasian Creed*

Salvation is not putting a man into Heaven, but putting Heaven into man.   *Maltbie D. Babcock*

Obedience, judgment, witness.   *Stephen Bayne*

The fearless man is his own salvation.

Robert Bridges

Science.   *Luther Burbank*

Salvation and Christian obedience are one and the same.   *William Ellery Channing*

Love of God expressed in action.

Hasdai Crescas

Good faith.   *Archibald J. Cronin*

The knowledge of sin is the start of salvation.

Epicurus

The state of grace.

Formulary of the Presbyterian Church of Scotland, 1643.

Faith in Christ, and obedience to laws.

Thomas Hobbes

Redemption from a belief in miracles.

Elbert Hubbard

The essence of religion.   *Mordecai M. Kaplan*

The cross.   *Thomas á Kempis*

Salvation is an act of forgiveness coming from God alone.   *Latin Saying*

God's will.   *Martin Luther*

The Christian Church.   *Martin Luther*

Salvation...ultimately can be constructed upon knowledge gained by reason.

Moses Mendelssohn

Not an instantaneous deed, but a life-long adventure.   *Max C. Otto*

This is the way Jesus saves us: by revealing the nature of God and by creating within us the desire for fellowship with Him; by exhibiting life as it ought to be and may be and thus inspiring us to nobler conduct.   *Kirby Page*

Outside the Church, no salvation: that is to say...outside the congregation of the just, outside of good faith responding to grace, outside of the quest for truth in a sincere and pure heart.

H. L. Perreyve

SAN FRANCISCO

To be subject to the Roman pontiff.

Pope Boniface VIII

The Church.   *Roman Catholic Maxim*

The Catholic Church.   *Saint Augustine*

Must be effected in a social environment in which love of God and man must be in constant operation.   *Roland Simonitsch*

Salvation is actualized in history whenever a demonic power in social or individual existence is overcome by the divine power which has become visible in Christ.   *Paul Tillich*

A present deliverance from sin, a restoration of the soul to its primitive health, its original purity, a recovery of the divine nature.   *John Wesley*

Being alive to God and to every good which God's world can bring us.   *Anon.*

SEE ALSO ATONEMENT, BAPTISM, CATHOLICISM, CHRIST, CHRISTIANITY, CHURCH (ROMAN CATHOLIC), CONFESSION, CROSS, FAITH, GRACE, RELIGION, WORSHIP.

SAN FRANCISCO

A hilly Detroit.   *Euguene E. Brussell*

A cosmopolitan labyrinth of infinite surprises.

Barnaby Conrad

A city of no seasons but that of wet, wind and cold.   *Jerry Dashkin*

A condition of love with itself.   *Jerry Dashkin*

A large fog gap on the coast of California.

Warren Goldberg

A city with eleven months and several odd days of Indian Summer.   *Charles Groves*

A city of four seasons every day.   *Bob Hope*

The gayest, lightest-hearted, most pleasure-loving city in the Western continent.   *Will Irwin*

A mad city inhabited by perfectly insane people whose women are of a remarkable beauty.

Rudyard Kipling

Nothing but a three-day city—including all the museums.   *Leonard Lyons*

The cool grey city of love.   *George Sterling*

A city of misfits and neurotics.   *Anon.*

SANITY

Not being subdued by your means.

Ralph Waldo Emerson

Who then is sane? He who is not a fool.   *Horace*

The ability to do teamwork.   *Elbert Hubbard*

He who can simulate sanity will be sane.   *Ovid*

Madness put to good uses.   *George Santayana*

SEE ALSO MADNESS, MENTAL HEALTH.

SARCASM

SEE CARICATURE, RIDICULE, WIT.

SARONG

A simple garment carrying the implicit promise that it will not long stay in place.

Edward B. White

SATAN

SEE DEVIL.

SATIRE

Sarcastic levity of tongue.   *Lord Byron*

Not the sneering substance that we know, but satire that includes the satirist.   *Frank M. Colby*

A lonely and introspective occupation, for nobody can describe a fool to the life without much patient self-inspection.   *Frank M. Colby*

When scandal has new minted an old lie, or taxed invention for a fresh supply.

Adapted from William Cowper

Something which must lance wide the wounds of men's corruptions, open the side of vice, and search deep for dead flesh and rank cores.

Adapted from John Day

The boldest way to tell men freely of their foulest faults, and to laugh at their vain deeds and vainer thoughts.   *Adapted from John Dryden*

Creating a logical argument that, followed to its basic end, is absurd.   *Jules Feiffer*

When there's more malice shown than matter.

Benjamin Franklin

Sarcasm...barbed with contempt.

Washington Gladden

(That which) attacks stuffed shirts, hypocrisies, aping merit.　　　*Edgar Johnson*

A play that closes Saturday night.

George S. Kaufman

(That form) in which ridicule is combined with so little malice and so much conviction that it even rouses laughter in those who are hit.

Georg C. Lichtenberg

My little gift of words twisted into a scourge of rough and knotted cords that whistle as they swing to leave on backs their purple sting.

Adapted from James Russell Lowell

A polished razor keen that wounds with a touch that's scarcely felt or seen.

Adapted from Mary W. Montagu

The most aggressive form of flattery. In it imitation is fired by indignation. The satirist elevates the importance of what he is tearing down. He cannot ignore what he sets out to deplore.

Charles Poore

My weapon.　　　　　　　　　　*Alexander Pope*

Moral outrage transformed into comic art.

Philip Roth

A...glass wherein beholders...discover everybody's face but their own.　　*Jonathan Swift*

Lies about literary men while they live, and eulogy lies about them when they die.　*Voltaire*

The last flicker of originality in a passing epoch as it faces the onroad of staleness and boredom. Freshness has gone: bitterness remains.

Alfred North Whitehead

SEE ALSO IRONY, RIDICULE, SATIRIST, WIT.

SATIRIST

A being with an eye in the back of his head who fills up with straw and sawdust all illusions.

Elbert Hubbard

A man who discovers unpleasant things about himself and then says them about other people.

Peter McArthur

(One who) holds a place half-way between the preacher and the wit. He has the purpose of the

first and uses the weapons of the second. He must both hate and love.　　　*Hubert Wolfe*

SATISFACTION

SEE CONTENTMENT, HAPPINESS.

SAVAGE

A man of one story, and that one story a cellar...The civilized man is thirty stories deep.

Henry Ward Beecher

A human organism that has not received enough news from the human race.　　*John Ciardi*

(Those) extemporizing from hand to mouth.

Ralph Waldo Emerson

Animals in human shape.

Bernard de Fontenelle

A person whose manners differ from ours.

Benjamin Franklin

Hapless children of the moment.

Sigmund Freud

Your new-caught, sullen peoples, Half-devil and half-child.　　　　*Rudyard Kipling*

The most conservative of human beings.

A. H. Sayce

People who don't know what is wrong until missionaries show them.　　　　　*Anon*

Those who are content to be what they are.

Anon.

SEE ALSO INDIAN (AMERICAN), MASSES, MOB, RABBLE.

SAVANT

A professor being quoted by the newspaper.

Leonard L. Levinson

A man you come to for advice.　*Robert Zwickey*

A man single-minded and specialized in speculative philosophy.　　　　　　　*Anon.*

One who walks into other people's homes by mistake while engrossed in thought.　*Anon.*

A practical dreamer.　　　　　　　*Anon.*

SEE ALSO PHILOSOPHER, PROFESSOR, SCHOLAR, TEACHER.

SAVIOUR

SEE CHRIST, CROSS.

SCANDAL

That abominable tittle-tattle. *Lord Byron*

The main feature...as the term is used in Catholic theology, is that it furnishes a bad example to someone, furnishing him with an occasion of sin.
Francis Connell

The babbler's trade. *William Cowper*

(Something) caused only by matters that no one can tolerate and everyone is curious about.
Alan Dodd

The gabble of today's opinion.
Ralph Waldo Emerson

Gossip related by a small bore. *Elbert Hubbard*

Vice enjoyed vicariously. *Elbert Hubbard*

Every whisper of infamy is industriously circulated, every hint of suspicion eagerly improved, and every failure of conduct joyfully published by those whose interest it is that the eye and voice of the public should be employed on any rather than on themselves. *Samuel Johnson*

An occasion of spiritual harm to the neighbor.
Gerald Kelley

The mud we throw. *James Russell Lowell*

Merely the compassionate allowance which the gay make to the humdrum. *Hector H. Munro*

Amusing ourselves with the faults, foibles, follies and reputations of our friends. *Royall Tyler*

The basis of every scandal is an immoral certainty. *Oscar Wilde*

Gossip made tedious by morality. *Oscar Wilde*

The sweetener of a female feast. *Oscar Wilde*

Something that has to be bad to be good. *Anon.*

SEE ALSO CALUMNY, GOSSIP, SLANDER.

SCAPEGOAT

Scapegoats for economic sins are called Jews.
Bernard Berenson

Someone who has to be there when things go wrong. *Eugene E. Brussell*

The goat...shall...go for a scapegoat into the wilderness. *Bible: Leviticus, XVI, 9–10.*

A convenient release from inner tension.
Max Gralnick

SEE ALSO BIGOTRY, PREJUDICE.

SCHOLAR

"What does it all mean?" There lies the true responsibility of the scholar—not to a ritual but to the reality of a subject. *Jacques Barzun*

The scholar's mission is to instruct and inspire the race in reference to the general end,—progress,— for which God has made and placed us here.
Orestes Brownson

A poor person; money runs from them headlong to the boor. *Adapted from Robert Burton*

There are only two kinds...those who love ideas and those who hate them. *Emile Chartier*

Those book learned fools who mess the world.
John Drinkwater

They are thin and pale, their feet are cold, their heads are hot, the night is without sleep, the day a fear of interruption,—pallor, squalor, hunger, and egotism. *Ralph Waldo Emerson*

The office of the scholar is to cheer, to raise, and to guide men by showing them facts amidst appearances. *Ralph Waldo Emerson*

The student of the world; and of what worth the world is, and with what emphasis it accosts the soul of man, such is the worth, such the call of the scholar. *Ralph Waldo Emerson*

He must be solitary, laborious, modest, and charitable...He must embrace solitude as a bride...that he may become acquainted with his thoughts. *Ralph Waldo Emerson*

The favorite of Heaven and earth, the excellency of his country, the happiest of men.
Ralph Waldo Emerson

Every man is a scholar potentially, and does not need any one good so much as this of right thought. *Ralph Waldo Emerson*

A man of learning, of habits, of whims and crotchets...the double flowers of college culture, their stamina all turned to petals, their stock in the life of the race all funded in the individual.

Oliver Wendell Holmes 1

A deadly ptomain that infests all forms of dynamic thought.   *Elbert Hubbard*

One who draws his breath and salary.

Elbert Hubbard

Anybody with a bulging brow and no visible means of support.   *Elbert Hubbard*

A medieval owl that roosts in universities, especially those that are endowed.

Elbert Hubbard

A man, long on advice but short on action, who thinks he thinks.   *Elbert Hubbard*

To talk in public, to think in solitude, to read and to hear, to inquire and to answer inquires, is the business of the scholar.   *Samuel Johnson*

The scholar digs his ivory cellar in the ruins of the past and lets the present sicken as it will.

Archibald MacLeish

An unmannered species.   *George Meredith*

One who reads, reflects, and enjoys learning.

David Riesman

Men who write Latin verses.

George Bernard Shaw

One who takes pains and gives them to others.

Anon.

One who demands more of himself than the majority of mankind.   *Anon.*

A person always too busy for his family.   *Anon.*

One who wraps himself in quotations.   *Anon.*

SEE ALSO INTELLECTUAL, STUDY.

SCHOLARSHIP

A record of disagreements.

Charles Evans Hughes

Polite argument.   *Philip Rieff*

SEE ALSO RESEARCH.

SCHOOL

A cap and bell for fools.   *William Cowper*

The dull study of hieroglyphs.

Thomas Alva Edison

A system of despair.   *Ralph Waldo Emerson*

The nurseries of all vice and immortality.

Henry Fielding

The major component of the system of consumer production . . . necessary to produce the habits and expectations of the managed consumer society.

Ivan Illich

Vast factories for the manufacture of robots.

Robert M. Lindner

Dull, unintelligible tasks, new and unpleasant ordinances, brutal violations of common sense and common decency.   *Henry Louis Mencken*

The free school is the promoter of that intelligence which is to preserve us a free nation.

Republican National Platform, 1888.

A prison. But it is in some respects more cruel than a prison. In a prison . . . you are not forced to read books written 'by the warders . . . In prison they may torture your body; but they do not torture your brains.   *George Bernard Shaw*

A place where parents send their very best efforts.

Anon.

SEE ALSO ACADEMY, COLLEGE, EDUCATION, UNIVERSITY.

SCHOPENHAUER, ARTHUR (1788-1860)

Logic and learning and wit, teaching pessimism,—teaching that this is the worst of all possible worlds, and inferring that sleep is better than waking, and death than sleep,—all the talent in the world cannot save him from being odious.

Ralph Waldo Emerson

The last German to be really reckoned with. He is not a mere local or national phenomenon, but a European event.   *Friedrich W. Nietzsche*

SCIENCE

To be acceptable as scientific knowledge a truth must be a deduction from other truths.   *Aristotle*

An experience which contradicts the communal experience.   *Gaston Bachelard*

The labor and handicraft of the mind.

Francis Bacon

The . . . goal of the sciences is the endowment of human life with new inventions and riches.

Francis Bacon

A chief, an invisible Christ.

Mikhail A. Bakunin

A faith to bind men together.   *Louis Berman*

A substitute for the moribund old mythologies which kept them sundered.   *Louis Berman*

That which increases our power in proportion to its lowering of our pride.

Adapted from Claude Bernard

The literature of truth.   *Josh Billings*

The essence of science: ask an important question and you are on the way to a pertinent answer.

Jacob Bronowski

Signifies some faith's about to die.

Robert Browning

An allegory that asserts that the relations between the parts of reality are similar to the relations between terms of discourse.   *Scott Buchanan*

An exchange of ignorance for another kind of ignorance.   *Adapted from Lord Byron*

A flickering light in our darkness.

Morris Cohen

The faith, ideals, and ethics of science constitute a form of natural religion.   *Edwin G. Conklin*

One aspect of God's presence.   *C. A. Coulson*

(That which) equips man, but does not guide him. It illuminates the world for him to the region of the most distant stars, but it leaves night in his heart. It is invincible, but indifferent, neutral, unmoral.   *James Darmsteter*

Practical philosophy.   *René Descartes*

Not a mere record of isolated discoveries; it is a narrative of the conflict of two contending powers, the expansive force of the human intellect on one side, and the compression arising from traditionary faith and human interest on the other.

John W. Draper

A series of judgments, revised without ceasing.

Pierre Duclaux

All science . . . rests on a basis of faith, for it assumes the permanence and uniformity of natural laws—a thing which can never be demonstrated.   *Tyron Edwards*

Science can only ascertain what *is,* but not what *should be,* and outside of its domain value judgments of all kinds remain necessary.

Albert Einstein

The grand aim . . . is to cover the greatest number of empirical facts by logical deduction from the smallest number of hypotheses or axioms.

Albert Einstein

Nothing more than a refinement of everyday thinking.   *Albert Einstein*

Men love to wonder, and that is the seed of our science.   *Ralph Waldo Emerson*

The increment of the power of the eye.

John Fiske

My kingdom is as wide as the world, and my desire has no limit. I go forward always, freeing spirits and weighing worlds, without fear, without compassion, without love, and without God. Men call me science.   *Gustave Flaubert*

Science does not deny God, she goes one better. She makes him unnecessary.

Freethinkers of Liege, 1865.

Any discipline in which the fool of this generation can go beyond the genius of the last generation.

Max Gluckman

Just one of those great flights of altar stairs that lead through darkness up to God.

Edgar J. Goodspeed

A branch of knowledge which gives us truth, not always of the consoling kind.   *Max Gralnick*

Faith in order.   *Asa Gray*

(Something) vastly more stimulating to the imagination than the classics.   *John Haldane*

The desire to know causes.   *William Hazlitt*

Great science labored to increase the people's joys, but every new invention seemed to add another noise.   *Adapted from Alan P. Herbert*

An imaginative adventure of the mind seeking truth in a world of mystery.   *Cyril Hinshelwood*

The skill of proceeding upon general and infallible rules.   *Thomas Hobbes*

The knowledge of consequences, and dependence of one fact upon another.   *Thomas Hobbes*

Knowledge of the truth of propositions, and how things are called.   *Thomas Hobbes*

Science can only deal with what is, and nothing about what ought to be, which is the concern of ethics; science can tell us means to ends, but not about what the ends should be.
Leonard Hodgson

Piecemeal revelation.   *Oliver Wendell Holmes 1*

The topography of ignorance.
Oliver Wendell Holmes 1

A first-rate piece of furniture for a man's upper-chamber, if he has common-sense on the ground floor.   *Oliver Wendell Holmes 1*

Classified superstition.   *Elbert Hubbard*

The knowledge of the common people classified and carried one step further.   *Elbert Hubbard*

Equipped with his five senses, man explores the universe around him and calls the adventure Science.   *Edwin Powell Hubble*

Simply common sense at its best—that is, rigidly accurate in observation, and merciless to fallacy in logic.   *Thomas Henry Huxley*

Trained and organized common sense.
Thomas Henry Huxley

The discovery of identity amidst diversity.
William S. Jevons

A search for the principles of law and order in the universe, and as such an essentially religious endeavor.   *Arthur Koestler*

Science is spectrum analysis. Art is photosynthesis.   *Karl Kraus*

The only acceptable method of dealing with those things which can be investigated experimentally, and . . . measured.   *Joseph Wood Krutch*

The creation of dilemmas by the solution of mysteries.   *Leonard L. Levinson*

The backward undoing of the tapestry web of God's science.   *George Macdonald*

Only an episode of religion—and an unimportant one at that.   *Christian Morgenstern*

To foresee, and not . . . to understand.
Pierre Lecomte de Nouy

The dry husks of facts.   *William Osler*

Every science has for its basis a system of principles as fixed and unalterable as those by which the universe is regulated . . . Man cannot make principles; he can only discover them.
Thomas Paine

A selective system of cognitive orientations to reality.   *Talcott Parsons*

A continual analysis of facts of rough and general observation into groups of facts more precise and minute.   *Walter Pater*

The only faith . . . consonant with reason, with the dignity of man.   *Karl Pearson*

Nothing but perception.   *Plato*

Science confers power, not purpose. It is a blessing, therefore, if the purpose which it serves is good; it is a curse, if the purpose is bad.
William L. Poteat

The total absorption of the individual event in the generalization is the goal.   *Moody E. Prior*

A way of thinking, but it can only advance on a basis of technique.   *Magnus Pyke*

A great game. It is inspiring and refreshing. The playing field is the universe itself.
Isidor I. Rabi

Science is a religion, science alone will henceforth make the creeds . . . alone can solve for men the eternal problems.   *Ernest Renan*

Science is for those who learn; poetry, for those who know.   *Joseph Roux*

To substitute facts for appearances, and demonstrations for impression.   *John Ruskin*

All exact science is dominated by the idea of approximation.   *Bertrand Russell*

The miracles best authenticated by history and by daily life.   *George Santayana*

Nothing but developed perception, interpreted intent, common sense rounded out and minutely articulated.   *George Santayana*

Neither a potential for good or evil. It is a potential to be harnessed by man to do his bidding.   *Glenn T. Seaborg*

Science is always wrong—it never solves a problem without creating ten more.
George Bernard Shaw

A knowledge of matter.   *Fulton J. Sheen*

The great antidote to the poison of enthusiasm and superstition.   *Adam Smith*

Organized knowledge.   *Herbert Spencer*

Scientific truths, of whatever order, are reached by eliminating perturbing or conflicting factors, and recognizing only fundamental factors.

Herbert Spencer

Pearls strung on a cord of faith.

Joshua Steinberg

Consists of a haphazard heap of information, united by nothing, often utterly unnecessary.

Leon Tolstoy

A cemetery of dead ideas.

Miguel de Unamuno

(A system which) robs men of wisdom and usually converts them into phantom beings loaded up with facts.   *Miguel de Unamuno*

A collection of successful recipes.   *Paul Valéry*

The task of science is to stake out the limits of the knowable, and to center consciousness within them.   *Rudolf Virchow*

Almost wholly the outgrowth of pleasurable intellectual curiosity.   *Alfred North Whitehead*

The record of dead religions.   *Oscar Wilde*

That false secondary power by which we multiply distinctions.   *William Wordsworth*

Only the tools in a box.   *Frank Lloyd Wright*

Not belief, but the will to find out.   *Anon.*

That which shows us what is possible, not what is right.   *Anon.*

SEE ALSO FACT, KNOWLEDGE, RESEARCH.

SCIENTIST

A lover of truth for the very love of truth itself, wherever it may lead.   *Luther Burbank*

There are two classes, those who want to know, and do not care whether others think they know or not, and those who do not much care about knowing, but care very greatly about being reputed as knowing.   *Samuel Butler 2*

My mind seems to have become a kind of machine for grinding general laws out of large collections of facts.   *Charles Darwin*

(Those who) find in nature what is there.

Eugene Delacroix

I pull a flower from the woods,—
A monster with a glass
Computes the stamens in a breath,
And has her in a class.   *Emily Dickinson*

A man always studying one subject.

Benjamin Disraeli

The world's greatest army devoted to good works...the scientists attack falseness of every kind, and accept no doctrine until the last doubt has been disposed of.   *Edgar W. Howe*

Peeping toms at the keyhole of eternity.

Arthur Koestler

Not the master magician he thinks he is, but only a sorcerer's apprentice who does not know how to turn off what he has turned on—or even how to avoid blowing himself up.   *Joseph Wood Krutch*

A man who would rather count than guess.

Leonard L. Levinson

Not the *possession* of knowledge, of irrefutable truths, that constitutes the man of science, but the disinterested, incessant *search* for truth.

Karl Popper

Their business is not with the possible, but the actual...with a world that is. They have but one desire—to know the truth. They have but one fear—to believe a lie.   *John Tyndall*

A team...one doesn't need to know their names.

John Wilmot

A fingering slave, one that would peep and botanize upon his mother's grave.

Adapted from William Wordsworth

SCOTLAND

A barren soil where nature's germs confined to stern sterility, can stint the mind.

Adapted from Lord Byron

A land of meanness, sophistry, and mist.

Lord Byron

The birth-place of song.   *Alexander Crawford*

Only...a worse England.   *Samuel Johnson*

A nation just rising from barbarity.

Samuel Johnson

Land of brown heath and shaggy wood,
Land of the mountain and the flood.

Walter Scott

The land of the plaided warriors of the North.
Walter Scott

That knuckle-end of England, that land of Calvin, oatcakes and sulphur.   *Sydney Smith*

A window washer of the mind.   *Anon.*

SEE ALSO EDINBURGH.

SCOTSMAN

A dark, carnal people.   *George Fox*

The noblest prospect which a Scotchman ever sees is the high road that leads him to England.
Samuel Johnson

No McTavish
Was ever lavish.   *Ogden Nash*

SCOUNDREL

He who slanders an absent friend, he who does not defend him when he is attacked, he who seeks eagerly to raise the senseless laugh and acquire the fame of wit, he who cannot keep a friend's secret.
Horace

When A annoys or injures B on the pretense of improving B, A is a scoundrel.
Henry Louis Mencken

Every man over forty.   *George Bernard Shaw*

A man who won't stay bought.
William M. Tweed

SCRIPTURE

SEE BIBLE.

SCULPTURE

Not pure form, but pure plastic rhythm; not the construction of bodies, but the construction of the action of bodies.   *Umberto Boccioni*

Mud pies which endure.   *Cyril Connolly*

To raise the dead to life.
Henry Wadsworth Longfellow

An art that takes away superfluous material.
Michelangelo

Images, lifelike but lifeless, wonderful but dead.
William Morris

Not the mere cutting of the form of anything in stone; it is the cutting of the *effect* of it.
John Ruskin

SEE ALSO ART.

SEA

The great devourer of men.   *Pio Baroja*

A body of water occupying about two-thirds of the world made for man—who has no gills.
Ambrose Bierce

Gray and melancholy waste.
William Cullen Bryant

A fluid world.   *Charles Caleb Colton*

That great fishpond.   *Thomas Dekker*

The nourisher of kings.   *Ralph Waldo Emerson*

The sea drowns out humanity and time; it has no sympathy with either, for it belongs to eternity, and of that it sings its monotonous song for ever and ever.   *Oliver Wendell Holmes 1*

The wavy waste.   *Thomas Hood*

A highway between the doorways of the nations.
Franklin K. Lane

Seas but join the regions they divide.
Alexander Pope

My fellow-creature.   *Francis Quarles*

The sea is the world's great heart,
    Beating eternally,
And bearing on its gloomy tide
    The sky diurnally.   *Julius Rodenberg*

The fishman's farm.   *Russian Proverb*

The herring-pond.   *Walter Scott*

The waste basket of the world.   *Rodger Simons*

A wavy waste of waters!   *Robert Southey*

Dirty, wobbly and wet.   *Wallace Stevens*

The world of waters wild.   *James Thomson*

A secret world of wonders.   *James Thomson*

A continual miracle.   *Walt Whitman*

A huge body of water entirely surrounded by rumors of everlasting peace.   *Anon.*

The parent of all substance, the cradle of all life.
Anon.

SEAMAN

SEE SAILOR.

SEASONS

SEE AUTUMN, SPRING, SUMMER, WINTER.

SECRET

Your slave if you keep it, your master if you lose it.   *Arabian Proverb*

A thing we give to others to keep for us.
Elbert Hubbard

Something known only to a few.
Elbert Hubbard

Your secret is your prisoner; if you let it go you are a prisoner to it.   *John Ray*

The seal of speech.   *Solon*

A weapon and a friend.   *James Stephens*

Something known only to a few at a time.
Anon.

Something a woman tells everybody not to tell anybody.   *Anon.*

Something that is hushed about from place to place.   *Anon.*

Something three people keep if two of them are dead.   *Anon.*

SEE ALSO GOSSIP, MYSTERY.

SECT AND SECTARIANISM

Most sects represent something real—the satisfaction of some fundamental need of the human spirit.   *Charles S. Braden*

The maggots of corrupted texts.
Samuel Butler 1

Stoves, but fire keeps its old properties through them all.   *Ralph Waldo Emerson*

Sectarianism is part of original sin.
Walter Rauschenbusch

Sect and error are synonymous.   *Voltaire*

SEE ALSO CREED, DOCTRINE, THEOLOGY.

SECULARISM

The view of life that limits itself not to the material in exclusion of the spiritual, but to the human here and now in exclusion of man's relation to God and hereafter.
Catholic Bishops of the United States, 1947.

Hell-bent for nowhere.   *William T. Costello*

Neutrality toward God.   *John D. Fee*

The conviction that man has power of control over his world and can exercise it without sin—without corruption, disaster, and despair.
M. Holmes Hartshorne

The form in which the fallen world demonically seeks to replace God, from whom it receives its being in each moment of its existence.
Karl Heim

The divorcement of large areas of life from effective religious and moral sanctions.
F. Ernest Johnson

Man's religious life is conceived as an inner and private affair, having no necessary relevance to his business or political activities and incapable of furnishing him with sanctions to guide his organized social relationships.
F. Ernest Johnson

The product of an abnormal condition, the disruption of the spiritual unity of Christianity.
John La Farge

A final achievement in the evolution of mankind.
Harold J. Laski

Practical atheism . . . Its nature is neither to affirm nor to deny religious faith, but to live indifferently to it.   *Leroy E. Loemker*

The practical atheism that lies in the affirmation that God is not relevant to all the activities of men.
G. Bromley Oxnam

A perspective on life and reality taken on faith which includes men and things, but not God; time and history, but not eternity.   *James A. Pike*

To live without God.   *Paul Scherer*

The stance of mind assumed by those who decide that they can have what they desire without departing from any "sensible" code of morals; that . . . it is possible subtly to revamp standards of conduct without losing the right to a Christian coat of varnish.   *George N. Shuster*

The sawdust of the mills of science.

Alan M. Sullivan

The demoralization of personal and family life.

Hazen G. Werner

The attempt to organize and run society without reference to the divine will.   *Anon.*

The practice of the absence of God.   *Anon.*

SECURITY

Stability within ourselves.   *Bernard M. Baruch*

A feeling that there is a larger and more enduring life surrounding, appreciating, upholding the individual, and guaranteeing that his efforts and sacrifice will not be in vain.

Charles H. Cooley

Friendships.   *David H. Fink*

Emancipation from the security of Paradise.

Erich Fromm

The warm enfoldment of the natural and social environment.   *A. Eustace Haydon*

A superstition. It does not exist in nature, nor do the children of men...experience it.

Helen Keller

Yourself and your own vigor.

Niccolo Machiavelli

An invitation to indolence.   *Rod McKuen*

A glasscase that keeps out all happiness, pain, awareness, change.   *Paul Williams*

When I'm in love with somebody extraordinary who loves me back.   *Shelley Winters*

SELF

The disease we all have and that we have to fight against all our lives.   *Sherwood Anderson*

The arch-flatterer.   *Francis Bacon*

Unborn, eternal, changeless, ancient. It is never destroyed even when the body is destroyed.

Bhagavad-Gita

The Self is not to be described as not this, not *that*. It is incomprehensible, for it cannot be comprehended.   *Brihadaranayaka Upanishad*

The only corner of the universe that one can be certain of improving.   *Aldous Huxley*

It is part of man's very nature to think of his real self as soul, and to think of that soul as imperishable.   *Morris Joseph*

The only prison that can even bind the soul.

Henry Van Dyke

SEE ALSO EGOISM, SOUL.

SELF-COMPLACENCY

The death of the artist.

William Somerset Maugham

Pleasure accompanied by the idea of oneself as a cause.   *Baruch Spinoza*

SEE ALSO SELF-SATISFACTION.

SELF-CONFIDENCE

A dependence upon one's self.   *John Gay*

The first requisite to great undertakings.

Samuel Johnson

A strong feeling of being part and parcel of the group and having a positive attitude toward it.

Kurt Lewin

SEE ALSO CONFIDENCE.

SELF-CONTROL

The highest form of rulership.

Apocrypha: Aristeas, 222.

The hardest victory.   *Aristotle*

Lord of himself—that heritage of woe!

Lord Byron

Self-worth controlling.   *Morris R. Cohen*

Coolness and absence of heat and haste.

Ralph Waldo Emerson

Ability to restrain a laugh at the wrong place.

Elbert Hubbard

To remain always cool and unruffled under all circumstances.   *Thomas Jefferson*

Presence of mind in untried emergencies.

James Russell Lowell

Full power and command of myself.   *Rabelais*

The quality that distinguishes the fittest to survive.   *George Bernard Shaw*

SELF-DEFENSE

To take my own part.   *George Borrow*

The first law of nature.   *Samuel Butler 1*

A virtue and sole bulwark of all right.
Adapted from Lord Byron

The sum of the right of Nature, which is, "by all means...to defend ourselves."
Thomas Hobbes

The clearest of all laws, and for this reason: the lawyers didn't make it.   *Douglas Jerrold*

And one who attacks, you, attack him in like manner.   *Koran, 2.*

The sole end for which mankind are warranted, individually or collectively, in interfering with the liberty of action of any of their number.
John Stuart Mill

SEE ALSO SELF-PRESERVATION, SURVIVAL.

SELF-DENIAL

Indulgence of a propensity to forego an advantage.
Ambrose Bierce

To be forgetful of self.   *Ovid*

Only the effect of prudence on rascality.
George Bernard Shaw

A method by which man arrests his progress.
Oscar Wilde

Feeling your oats without sowing them.   *Anon.*

SEE ALSO ABSTINENCE, CELIBACY.

SELF-DETERMINATION

An imperative principle of action, which statesmen will henceforth ignore at their peril.
Woodrow Wilson

SEE ALSO DEMOCRACY, FREEDOM, LIBERTY.

SELF-ESTEEM

A poor center of a man's actions.
Francis Bacon

The most voluble of the emotions.
Frank M. Colby

Every new adjustment is a crisis in self-esteem.
Eric Hoffer

Derives from the potentialities and achievements of the self.   *Eric Hoffer*

Self-esteem = $\frac{\text{Success}}{\text{Pretensions}}$ *William James*

An erroneous appraisement of the self.   *Anon.*

SEE ALSO CONCEIT, EGOISM.

SELFISHNESS

The survival of the animal in us. Humanity only begins for a man with self-surrender.
Henry F. Amiel

The strongest barrier to faith.   *Joseph L. Baron*

That detestable vice which no one will forgive in others and no one is without in himself.
Henry Ward Beecher

Devoid of consideration for the selfishness of others.   *Ambrose Bierce*

The root and source of all natural and moral evils.
Nathaniel Emmons

Full of self.   *Francois de Fénelon*

The dynamo of our economic system...which may range from mere petty greed to admirable types of self-expression.   *Felix Frankfurter*

The greatest curse of the human race.
William E. Gladstone

A form of infantilism.   *Julius Gordon*

A state of mine.   *Timothy Markus*

The man who lives by himself and for himself.
Charles H. Parkhurst

To seek our own profit.   *Baruch Spinoza*

A force of nature.   *Robert Louis Stevenson*

The enemy of all true affection.   *Tacitus*

When someone places his own comfort before your convenience.   *Joan Tepperman*

Consuming happiness without producing any.
Joan Tepperman

To clutch at things and use them only for my own pleasure or profit.   *Gerald Vann*

A man is called selfish, not for pursuing his own good, but for neglecting his neighbor's.
Richard Whately

Selfishness is not living as one wishes to live. It is asking other people to live as one wishes to live.
Oscar Wilde

The only real atheism.   *Israel Zangwill*

Seeking your own good at the world's cost.
Anon.

Taking care of number one in all situations.
Anon.

Keeping all you have and trying for all you can.
Anon.

Using people as objects.   *Anon.*

SEE ALSO SELF-LOVE, VANITY.

SELF-KNOWLEDGE

What I seem to myself.   *Robert Browning*

The great puzzle.   *Lewis Carroll*

The most difficult lesson in the world.
Miguel de Cervantes

That which grows out of man's self-confrontation with God.   *Dietrich von Hildebrand*

What other people say we are. We know ourselves chiefly by heresay.   *Eric Hoffer*

Only by knowledge of that which is not Thyself, shall thyself be learned.   *Owen Meredith*

To understand oneself . . . th classic form of consolation.   *George Santayana*

To see one's equation written out.
George Santayana

The only thing a man knows . . . The world outside he can know only by heresay.   *Alexander Smith*

Self-inquiries . . . that lead to virtue and to God.
Isaac Watts

To talk with our past hours.   *Edward Young*

Knocking at your own bosom for answers.
Anon.

To be intimate at home.   *Anon.*

SEE ALSO KNOWLEDGE, WISDOM.

SELF-LOVE

Every man for himself, the devil for all.
Robert Burton

A principle of action.   *Isaac D'Israeli*

The state of having no rivals.
Adapted from Benjamin Franklin

A cup without any bottom; you might pour all the great lakes into it, and never fill it up.
Oliver Wendell Holmes 1

A busy prompter.   *Samuel Johnson*

The greatest of all flatterers.   *La Rochefoucauld*

The deceiving mirror.   *Philip Massinger*

Self-love and love of the world constitute hell.
Emanuel Swedenborg

Nothing more than natural self-affirmation.
Paul Weinberger

The instrument of our preservation; it resembles the provision for the perpetuity of mankind.
Voltaire

The beginning of a lifelong romance.
Oscar Wilde

Concentration on self-auto-eroticism.
Alexander Yelchaninov

SEE ALSO CONCEIT, EGOISM, SELF-ESTEEM, SELFISHNESS, VANITY.

SELF-PITY

One of the last things that any woman surrenders.
Irvin S. Cobb

Our worst enemy.   *Helen Keller*

SEE ALSO PITY.

SELF-PRESERVATION

An animal's first impulse.   *Diogenes*

Natural law.   *John Donne*

The first of laws.   *John Dryden*

Prey on others, or become a prey.   *Howard Fish*

The first principle of nature.   *Charles Shadwell*

SEE ALSO NATURAL SELECTION, SURVIVAL.

SELF-RESPECT

The chiefest bridle of all vices.   *Francis Bacon*

That corner-stone of all virtue.   *John Herschell*

The secure feeling that no one, as yet, is suspicious.   *Henry Louis Mencken*

The noblest garment with which a man may clothe himself, the most elevating feeling with which the mind can be inspired.   *Samuel Smiles*

When strong within the individual, a feeling which will admit no acts of a detrimental nature to the self-image. Barbarians lack such a feeling in depth.   *Robert Zwickey*

To be mentally faithful to yourself.   *Anon.*

SEE ALSO PRIDE, SELF-ESTEEM.

SELF-SACRIFICE

The real miracle out of which all the reported miracles grew.   *Ralph Waldo Emerson*

The first element of religion, and resolves itself in theological language into the love of God.
James A. Froude

Positive duty.   *James A. Froude*

The most conspicuous element of a virtuous and religious character.   *William E. Lecky*

An arranged scheme of self-deliverance from evil.
John Oman

Neither amputation nor repentance. It is, in essence, an act...the gift of oneself to the being of which one forms a part.
Antoine de Saint-Exupéry

Only the effect of prudence on rascality.
George Bernard Shaw

(That which) enables us to sacrifice other people without blushing.   *George Bernard Shaw*

SELF-SATISFACTION

The state of mind of those who have the happy conviction that they are not as other men.
Adapted from Margery Allingham

To please myself.   *Gustave Flaubert*

Believing that the ace of trumps is up your sleeve and that God Almighty put it there.
Henry Labouchere

When all one's faults are locked securely in the chest of one's mind.
Adapted from Sara Teasdale

To pardon your misconduct.   *Anon.*

SEE ALSO CONTENTMENT.

SELF-TRUST

The essence of heroism.   *Ralph Waldo Emerson*

The first secret of success.
Ralph Waldo Emerson

SEMANTICS

To know and recognize not merely the direct but the secret power of the word.   *Knut Hamsun*

The art of telling a man you don't know what he's talking about when you know very well what he's talking about but don't like what he's saying.
Charles Poore

SEE ALSO WORDS.

SEMINAR

A place where you can learn in three hours what it takes a professor three months to teach.
Richard Evarts

SENATORS

The citadel of liberty.   *Calvin Coolidge*

One who owes a duty to his state and to the opinions, and even prejudices of its people...But, after all, a senator is, in the end, a senator of the United States—*all* the United States.   *Lyndon Baines Johnson*

Men of individual honor and personal character, and of absolute independence. We know no masters, we acknowledge no dictators.
Daniel Webster

Men who attempt to please everyone all of the time.   *Anon.*

Men who have risen from obscurity to something worse.   *Anon.*

A man who is so busy talking he hasn't the time to think about it.   *Anon.*

SEE ALSO CONGRESS.

SENECA (54 B.C—39 A.D.)

You may get a motto for every sect in religion, or line of thought in morals or philosophy...but nothing is ever thought out by him.

Samuel Taylor Coleridge

The toreador of virtue.   *Friedrich W. Nietzsche*

SENILITY

SEE OLD AGE.

SENTENCE

A word or set of words followed by a pause and revealing an intelligible purpose.

Alfred G. Gardiner

The structure of every sentence is a lesson in logic.   *John Stuart Mill*

A sentence should read as if its author, had he held a plough instead of a pen, could have drawn a furrow deep and straight to the end.

Henry David Thoreau

SEE ALSO STYLE, WRITING.

SENTIMENT

The jam on the bread, while sentimentality is jam without bread.   *Sydney J. Harris*

Sentiments are for the most part traditional; we feel them because they were felt by those who preceded us.   *William Hazlitt*

The poetry of the imagination.

Alphonse M. de Lamartine

Intellectualized emotion, emotion precipitated ...in pretty crystals by the fancy.

James Russell Lowell

The sediment of emotion.   *Anon.*

SENTIMENTALISTS

The barrenest of all mortals.   *Thomas Carlyle*

Talkers who mistake the description for the thing, saying for having.   *Ralph Waldo Emerson*

Persons who, seeing that the sentiments please, counterfeit the expression of them.

Ralph Waldo Emerson

They who seek to enjoy without incurring the Immense Debtorship for a thing done.

George Meredith

A cynic at heart. Indeed sentimentality is merely the bank-holiday of cynicism.   *Oscar Wilde*

Simply one who desires to have the luxury of an emotion without paying for it.   *Oscar Wilde*

SENTIMENTALITY

Ostentatious parading of excessive and spurious emotion...the mark of dishonesty, the inability to feel.   *James Baldwin*

Twin-sister to Cant.   *Thomas Carlyle*

That's what we call the sentiment we don't share.

Graham Greene

The name we give to any sentiment we are incapable of feeling intensely.   *Sydney J. Harris*

A superstructure covering brutality. *Carl G. Jung*

The emotional promiscuity of those who have no sentiment.   *Norman Mailer*

Only sentiment that rubs you up the wrong way.

William Somerset Maugham

The string of sensualism.   *George Meredith*

Feeling acquired below cost.   *Arthur Schnitzler*

Having a good cry for its own sake.

Myron Schueller

The error of supposing that quarter can be given or taken in mortal conflicts.

George Bernard Shaw

A failure of feeling.   *Wallace Stevens*

An emotion feigned or unearned. *John W. Sullivan*

The triumph of sugar over a mind that was diabetic to begin with.   *Anon.*

SERIOUSNESS

The very next step to being dull.

Joseph Addison

The devotion of all the faculties. *Christian N. Bovee*

The seasoning of eloquence.   *Victor Hugo*

Enthusiasm moulded by reason.   *Blaise Pascal*

The only refuge of the shallow.   *Oscar Wilde*

The world's original sin. If the cavemen had known how to laugh, history would have been different.   *Oscar Wilde*

SEE ALSO SOLEMNITY.

SERMON

SEE PREACHERS, PREACHING.

SERVANT

Hewers of wood and drawers of water.
                        Bible: Joshua, IX, 21.

He that is greatest among you shall be your servant.   *Bible: Matthew, 23, 11.*

The neutral utility of a home.
                        Eugene E. Brussell

A great man's overfed great man, what the Scotch call Flunkey.   *Thomas Carlyle*

(One who is) never in the way and never out of the way.   *Charles 2*

To pile the fire, to split the wood, to cut up the carcass, to roast the flesh, to pour out the wine—in these offices the humble serve the rich.
                        Homer

A tyrant without ears, eyes, organs, dimensions, passions.   *Elbert Hubbard*

The face of a pig, the ears of an ass, the feet of a stag, a padlock on his mouth.
                        Christopher Johnson

A real godsend, but... 'tis a rare bird in the land.
                        Martin Luther

Formerly one who performed menial tasks around the home for wages. At present, one who receives welfare from the government.
                        Hyman Opataschu

Nothing but eyes and feet.   *Johann C. Schiller*

A solemn processional of one.
                        Pelham G. Wodehouse

SERVICE

Pressed into service means pressed out of shape.
                        Robert Frost

The concept of doing something for nothing while doing someone for something.
                        Leonard L. Levinson

They serve God well, who serve his creatures.
                        Caroline Norton

Christianity.   *Theodore Parker*

The basis of all worthy enterprise.
                        Principles of Rotary, 1, 1905.

The vocation of every man and woman...to serve other people.   *Leon Tolstoy*

The object of love.   *Woodrow Wilson*

Doing good as a result of a positive decision.
                        Anon.

SEE ALSO ACTION, DEEDS, DUTY, PUBLIC OFFICE.

SERVILITY

To lick.   *English Proverb*

The instinct of superiority in its lowest form.
                        Elbert Hubbard

The politician's virtue.   *Elbert Hubbard*

A means of getting on.   *Elbert Hubbard*

Kissing the hand which oppresses you.
                        Adapted from Phaedrus

Wit that can creep, and pride that licks the dust.
                        Alexander Pope

SEVENTY

SEE OLD AGE.

SEX (LOVE)

(When) the loin lies down with the limb.
                        Conrad Aiken

In love-making, as in the other arts, those do it best who cannot tell how it is done.
                        James M. Barrie

An appetite placed in humans to insure breeding. It has in turn bred, as a sideproduct, interesting and often ludicrous customs. Its suppression has led to ugly perversions and cruelty.
                        Jonathan Benter

(When) not integrated and transfigured by spirit is always evidence of man's subjugation to the genus.   *Nicholas Berdyaev*

A great and mysterious motive force in human life.   *William Brennan 2*

The ability to make love frivolously is the chief characteristic which distinguishes human beings from the beasts.   *Heywood Broun*

(Something) popular because it's centrally located.   *Shannon Carse*

The pleasure is momentary, the position ridiculous, and the expense damnable.
                        Lord Chesterfield

A wholly satisfying link between two affectionate people from which they emerge unanxious, rewarded and ready for more.
                        Alexander Comfort

The great amateur art.   *David Cort*

The last refuge of the miserable.   *Quentin Crisp*

Physiological expenditure... a superficial way of self-expression.   *Salvador Dali*

A trick to perpetuate the species.
                        Jerry Dashkin

The central problem of life.   *Havelock Ellis*

To use the word "sex" intelligently, means to connote by it more than a specific sensory excitement. It involves the whole affectional life of man, and a major part of his motive power in every realm of creativity.   *Harry Emerson Fosdick*

A contact of epidermises.   *French Proverb*

The primal scene.   *Sigmund Freud*

Finding the cool satisfaction of heaven in the heated embers of the pit.   *Warren Goldberg*

Like wrestling—a contact of epidermises.
                        Warren Goldberg

Grandmother called it a "sin"; mother called it an "affair"; daughter calls it an "experience."
                        Sydney J. Harris

A perfectly normal, almost commonplace, activity—an activity...of the same nature as dancing or tennis.   *Aldous Huxley*

A sport, a recreation, a pastime.
                        Aldous Huxley

A two-way treat.   *Franklin P. Jones*

The sign that the lovers have nothing to refuse each other; that they belong wholly to each other.
                        Jacques Leclercq

The formula by which one and one makes three.
                        Leonard L. Levinson

The monstrosity of sexual intercourse outside marriage is...trying to isolate one kind of union (the sexual) from all other kinds of union which were intended to go along with it and make up the total union.   *Clive S. Lewis*

'Tis the Devil inspires this evanescent ardor, in order to divert the parties from prayer.
                        Martin Luther

A very holy subject.   *Geddes MacGregor*

Something that is often regulated by historical puritanism through law.   *Rollo May*

An expression of deep personal love and a means to the deepening, perfecting and sanctifying of that love.   *Thomas Merton*

The ersatz or substitute religion of the 20th century.   *Malcolm Muggeridge*

Sex touches the heavens only when it simultaneously touches the gutter and the mud.
                        George Jean Nathan

The poor man's polo.   *Clifford Odets*

The work of our...ability to imagine, which is no longer an instinct, but exactly the opposite: a creation.   *José Ortega y Gasset*

The rehearsal of a communion of a higher nature.
                        Coventry Patmore

Nothing but the motor memory of previously remembered pleasure.   *Wilhelm Reich*

Something that children never discuss in the presence of their elders.   *Arthur S. Roche*

A clever imitation of love. It has all the action but none of the plot.   *William Rotsler*

Consists essentially of respect for the other person, and unwillingness to use that person solely as a means of personal gratification.
                        Bertrand A. Russell

A lapse from one marriage into many.
                        Saint Clement

A noble and immense inspiration; to the naturalist it is a thin veil and prelude to the self-assertion of lust.   *George Santayana*

An irresistable attraction and an overwhelming repugnance and digust.   *George Bernard Shaw*

There is never any real sex in romance; what is more, there is very little, and that of a very crude kind, in ninety-nine hundredths of our married life.   *George Bernard Shaw*

The continuum of human behaviour.
John Updike

An emotion in motion.   *Mae West*

The tabasco sauce which an adolescent national palate sprinkles on every course in the menu.
Mary D. Winn

Sex merely expresses the totality of differences between male and female.   *Solly Zuckerman*

SEE ALSO BACHELOR, LOVE, LOVERS, LUST, MARRIAGE, PASSION, WOMEN.

SEXES (MEN AND WOMEN)

The vast mass of men have to depend on themselves alone; the vast mass of women hope or expect to get their life given to them.
William Bolitho

The whole world was made for man, but the twelfth part of man for woman; man is the whole world and the breath of God; woman the rib and crooked piece of man.   *Thomas Browne*

Man's fate and woman's are contending powers; each strives to dupe the other in the game—guilt to the victor—to the vanquished shame.
Adapted from Edward G. Bulwer-Lytton

The first...great experiments in the social subdivision of labor.   *Samuel Butler 2*

We should regard loveliness as the attribute of woman, and dignity as the attribute of man.
Cicero

Man's conclusions are reached by toil. Woman arrives at the same by sympathy.
Ralph Waldo Emerson

Most men and women are merely one couple more.   *Ralph Waldo Emerson*

Man is fire and woman tow; the devil comes and sets them in a blaze.   *Thomas Fuller*

Woman submits to her fate; man makes his.
Emile Gaboriau

Time and circumstance, which enlarge the views of most men, narrow the views of women almost invariably.   *Thomas Hardy*

Words are women, deeds are men.
George Herbert

A man is as good as he has to be, and a woman as bad as she dares.   *Elbert Hubbard*

The silliest woman can manage a clever man; but it needs a clever woman to manage a fool.
Rudyard Kipling

On one issue...men and women agree: they both distrust women.   *Henry Louis Mencken*

Woman wants monogamy;
Man delights in novelty.
Love is woman's moon and sun;
Man has other forms of fun.
Woman lives but in her lord;
Count to ten and man is bored.   *Dorothy Parker*

All the pursuits of men are the pursuits of women also, and in all of them a woman is only a lesser man.   *Plato*

Men are more eloquent than women made, but women are more difficult to persuade.
Adapted from Thomas Randolph

Men work and think, but women feel.
Christina Rossetti

A man says what he knows, a woman says what will please.   *Jean-Jacques Rousseau*

The only way for a woman to provide for herself decently is for her to be good to some man that can afford to be good to her.
George Bernard Shaw

Woman's dearest delight is to wound man's self-conceit, though man's dearest delight is to gratify hers.   *George Bernard Shaw*

There are three sexes,—men, women, and clergymen.   *Sydney Smith*

Of all the calamities that befall mortal man, nothing is worse, or ever will be worse, than woman.   *Sophocles*

Three sexes in America—men, women, and professors.   *Joel E. Spingarn*

When a man fronts catastrophe on the road, he looks in his purse—but a woman looks in her mirror.   *Margaret Turnbull*

All the reasoning of men is not worth one sentiment of women.   *Voltaire*

There is only one real tragedy in a woman's life. The fact that her past is always her lover, and her future invariably her husband.   *Oscar Wilde*

Women represent the triumph of matter over mind, just as men represent the triumph of mind over morals.   *Oscar Wilde*

There are three sexes—men, women, and tenors.

Anon.

SEE ALSO BACHELOR, HUSBAND, LOVE, LOVERS, MAN, MARRIAGE, WOMAN.

SHAKESPEARE, WILLIAM (1564-1616)

He walked in every path of human life, felt every passion, and to all mankind does now, will ever, that experience yield which only his own genius could acquire.   *Adapted from Mark Akenside*

Others abide our question. You are free. We ask and ask; you smile and are still, out-topping knowledge.   *Adapted from Matthew Arnold*

Shake was a dramatist of note;
He lived by writing things to quote.

Henry C. Bunner

The chief of all poets...the greatest intellect who, in our recorded world, has left record of himself in the way of literature.

Thomas Carlyle

The greatest genius that perhaps human nature has yet produced.   *Samuel Taylor Coleridge*

He is of no age—nor of any religion, or party, or profession. The body and substance of his works came out of the unfathomable depths of his own oceanic mind.   *Samuel Taylor Coleridge*

His want of erudition was a most happy and productive ignorance; it forced him back upon his own resources, which were exhaustless.

Charles Caleb Colton

His mind and hand went together, and what he thought he uttered with that easiness that we have scarce received from him a blot in his papers.

Condell and Heminge

He of all men best understands the English language, and can say what he will.

Ralph Waldo Emerson

A punning fool, bringing to the job far more enthusiasm than judgment.   *Clifton Fadiman*

An intellectual ocean, whose waves touched all the shores of thought.   *Robert G. Ingersoll*

He was not of an age, but for all time.

Ben Jonson

A life of Allegory: his works are the comments on it.   *John Keats*

He breathed upon dead bodies and brought them into life.   *Walter Savage Landor*

The great poet who foreruns the ages, anticipating all that shall be said!

Adapted from Henry Wadsworth Longfellow

The greatest poet that ever lived.

Thomas B. Macaulay

I know of no more heartrending reading than Shakespeare. How a man must have suffered to be so much in need of playing the clown.

Friedrich W. Nietzsche

He seems to have known the world by intuition, to have looked through nature at one glance.

Alexander Pope

The pride of nature and the shame of schools; born to create and not to learn from rules.

Adapted from Charles Sedley

A savage with sparks of genius which shone in a dreadful darkness of night.   *Voltaire*

A great playwright, a great humorist, the sweetest laughter in the world.   *Herbert G. Wells*

The greatest one-line writer of all times.   *Anon.*

SHAME

SEE DISGRACE.

SHAW, GEORGE BERNARD (1856-1950)

A man made after supper out of one of Ibsen's plays.   *Robert Blatchford*

The Irish smut-dealer.   *Anthony Comstock*

God created people of flesh and blood, but you, my friend, can only create elfin creatures of wit, humor and grace.   *Albert Einstein*

A playwright who knew all of the answers, but none of the questions.   *Harold Hobson*

A wingless angel with an old maid's temperament.   *James G. Huneker*

(A man who) discovered himself and gave ungrudgingly of his discovery to the world.

Hector H. Munro

He refused to give more than amusement...Shaw was...by preference a passionless man...The sight of a woman deeply in love with him annoyed him. *Bertha Newcombe*

Nobody can differ with me: you might as well differ from the Almighty about the orbit of the sun. *George Bernard Shaw*

The messenger boy of a new era.

Maurice Weinstein

An excellent man; he has not an enemy in the world, and none of his friends like him.

Oscar Wilde

I go out to amuse the dead, while you go out of your way to pain the living. *Oscar Wilde*

The way Shaw believes in himself is very refreshing in these atheistic days when so many believe in no God at all. *Israel Zangwill*

SHELLEY, PERCY BYSSHE (1792-1821)

A beautiful and ineffectual angel, beating in the void his luminous wings in vain.

Matthew Arnold

He would have died a Tory had he lived to be fifty—and president of the Bible Society.

Augustine Birrell

The least selfish and the mildest of men—a man who has made more sacrifices of his fortune and feelings for others than any I ever heard of.

Lord Byron

He had a fire in his eye, a fever in his blood, a maggot in his brain, a hectic flutter in his speech, which mark out the philosophic fanatic.

William Hazlitt

He was a liar and a cheat; he paid no regard to truth, nor to any kind of moral obligation.

Robert Southey

SHIP

A prison. *Robert Burton*

She walks the waters like a thing of life, and seems to dare the elements to strife.

Adapted from Lord Byron

(Something) worse than a gaol. There is, in a gaol, better air, better company, better conveniency of every kind. *Samuel Johnson*

Being in jail with the chance of being drowned.

Samuel Johnson

(A) packet of assorted miseries.

Rudyard Kipling

Ships are but boards. *William Shakespeare*

Your ships are wooden walls. *Themistocles*

SEE ALSO SAILOR, SEA.

SHREW

A woman who dries up her husband's glands.

Anon.

A woman who causes her husband not to care whether his glands are dried up. *Anon.*

A woman who dries up her husband's brain.

Anon.

A force which cannot be mastered by reason.

Anon.

That part of the wife which is not feminine.

Anon.

A woman who wears the pants, while her mate wears the hair shirt. *Anon.*

SEE ALSO WIFE, WOMAN.

SHYNESS

SEE BASHFULNESS.

SICKNESS

SEE ILLNESS, PAIN.

SIGHT

We see through a glass, darkly.

Bible: Corinthians, XIII, 12.

The keenest of all our senses. *Cicero*

The greatest thing a human soul ever does in this world...To see clearly is poetry, prophecy and religion all in one. *John Ruskin*

The highest bodily privilege...which man has derived from his Creator. *Sydney Smith*

We see things not as they are, but as we are.

Henry M. Tomlinson

SEE ALSO EYE, PROPHECY, VISION.

SILENCE

Silence is not golden, it's yellow.

Thomas Anderson

A still noise. *Josh Billings*

One of the hardest arguments to refute.

Josh Billings

The honor of wise men, who have not the infirmity, but the virtue of taciturnity.

Thomas Browne

The severest criticism. *Charles R. Buxton*

The element in which great things fashion themselves together. *Thomas Carlyle*

(Something) more eloquent than words.

Thomas Carlyle

Unbearable repartee. *Gilbert Keith Chesterton*

Often guilt instead of golden. *Harold Cochran*

A friend who never betrays. *Confucius*

A solvent that destroys personality, and gives us leave to be great and universal.

Ralph Waldo Emerson

Wisdom's best reply. *Euripides*

Knowledge on ice. *William Fairbanks*

The space surrounding every action and every communion of people. *Dag Hammarskjöld*

One great art of conversation. *William Hazlitt*

A healing for all ailments. *Hebrew Proverb*

The fence around wisdom. *Hebrew Proverb*

The essential condition of happiness.

Heinrich Heine

A conversation with an Englishman.

Heinrich Heine

A trick of the human gullet that conceals weakness or emptiness. *Elbert Hubbard*

The sharper sword. *Robert U. Johnson*

(Something which) propagates itself . . . the longer talk has been suspended the more difficult it is to find anything to say. *Samuel Johnson*

The best resolve for him who mistrusts himself.

La Rochefoucauld

Three silences there are: the first of speech, the second of desire, the third of thought.

Henry Wadsworth Longfellow

The best of all medicines. *Megilla, 18a.*

The *exodus* from slavery toward the possession of the Kingdom. *Peter Minard*

Not merely an absence of noise. Real Silence begins when a reasonable being withdraws from the noise in order to find peace and order in his inner sanctuary. *Peter Minard*

Strength. *Ovid*

Man's chief learning. *Palladas*

A figure of speech, unanswerable, short, cold, but terribly severe. *Theodore Parker*

The greatest persecution. *Blaise Pascal*

True silence is the rest of the mind; it is to the spirit what sleep is to the body, nourishment and refreshment. *William Penn*

An answer to a wise man. *Plutarch*

The highest wisdom of a fool. *Francis Quarles*

The only successful substitute for brain.

Maurice Samuel

The decoration of the illiterate.

Sanskrit Proverb

The most perfect expression of scorn.

George Bernard Shaw

Prayer begins by *talking* to God, but it ends by listening to Him. In the face of Absolute Truth, silence is the soul's language. *Fulton J. Sheen*

The gratitude of true affection.

Richard Brinsley Sheridan

Occasional flashes of silence make conversation delightful. *Adapted from Sydney Smith*

Admission. *Talmud: Yebamot, 87b.*

The universal refuge, the sequel to all dull discourses and all foolish acts, a balm to our very chagrin. *Henry David Thoreau*

Having nothing to say and saying it. *Anon.*

Mastery over the lips. *Anon.*

That inner room which is man's paradise. *Anon.*

Always a dangerous observer. *Anon.*

Conversation with a bore. *Anon.*

The fool's greatest defense. *Anon.*

SEE ALSO TACT, TALK, TONGUE, WORDS.

SIMPLICITY

The characteristic of all high bred deportment in every country. *James Fenimore Cooper*

To be simple is to be great.

Ralph Waldo Emerson

The really great of the earth. *Heinrich Heine*

Affected simplicity is a subtle form of imposture.

La Rochefoucauld

In all things the supreme excellency.

Henry Wadsworth Longfellow

An exact medium between too little and too much. *Joshua Reynolds*

The peak of civilization. *Jessie Sampter*

The art of art, the glory of expression and the sunshine of the light of letters. *Walt Whitman*

SIN

Three elements...first, that the deed was one that ought not to have been done...because it was opposed to what is intrinsically right...Secondly, the idea of sin implies that the sinner himself is the doer of the deed...Thirdly, it is the characteristic of sin that the fuller knowledge that the harmful deed is sinful comes after the act.

Felix Adler

Ignorance in motion. *Ian Aird*

Sin was not sent to earth. Man himself created it.

Apocrypha: Enoch, 98.4.

Sin lies in the scandal. *Aphra Behn*

The works of the flesh.

Bible: Galatians, V, 19.

The desire of one man to live on the fruits of another's labor. *James Bronterre*

A description of our entire situation, one of separation from God, alienation from him, arising out of our rebellion, our refusal to do his will, our insistence upon following our own wills.

Robert M. Brown

Man can emancipate himself from his Creator and make himself his own lord. That is what the Bible calls sin. *Emil Brunner*

Adultery, fornication, murder, theft, swearing, lying, covetousness, witchcraft, sedition, heresies. *John Bunyan*

That within us which deserves the hatred of God.

John Calvin

Hoping for another life and...eluding the implacable grandeur of this life. *Albert Camus*

The result of collaboration. *Stephen Crane*

A natural principle in man lowering him, deadening him, pulling him down by inches to the mere animal plane, blinding reason, searing conscience, paralyzing will. *Henry Drummond*

That which we call sin in others is experiment for us. *Ralph Waldo Emerson*

Guilt. *Sigmund Freud*

Insanity. *Hebrew Proverb*

Sin is not offense against God, but against our humanity. *Emil G. Hirsch*

Desires and other passions...are in themselves no sin. No more are the actions that proceed from those passions, till they know a law that forbids them. *Thomas Hobbes*

Not infrequently...an apprenticeship to sainthood. Many of the insights of the saint stem from his experience as a sinner. *Eric Hoffer*

Perverted power. The man without capacity for sin has no ability to do good. *Elbert Hubbard*

To believe things without evidence.

Thomas Henry Huxley

Naught that delights is sin. *Ben Jonson*

Converting tools into ideals.

Mordecai M. Kaplan

The breaking of one's own integrity.

D. H. Lawrence

The essence of Jewish-Christianity.

Busso Loewe

A departure from God. *Martin Luther*

The word sin in the Bible...means all the circumstances that act together and excite us to what is done; in particular, the impulses operating in the depths of our hearts. *Martin Luther*

The great staple of history, and the sole object of law.   *Frederick W. Maitland*

Ignorance.   *Christopher Marlowe*

The refusal of the creature to his God who invites him to union with Him.   *Columba Marmion*

To feel guilty about sex.   *Rollo May*

Pride, covetousness, lust, anger, gluttony, envy and sloth.   *John McAffrey*

People are no longer sinful, they are only immature or underprivileged or frightened or, more particularly, sick.   *Phyllis McGinley*

Rebellion against God.   *John Henry Newman*

It is a traitor's act who aims at the overthrow and death of His sovereign.   *John Henry Newman*

Man's self-desecration par excellence.
                                    Friedrich W. Nietzsche

(Something) indispensable to every society organized on an ecclesiastical basis; they are the only reliable weapons of power.
                                    Friedrich W. Nietzsche

The black spot which my bad act makes, seen against the disk of the Sun of Righteousness.
                                    Charles H. Parkhurst

Disease, deformity, weakness.   *Plato*

Conduct that tends to destroy more values than it creates, either for the actor or other sentient beings whom it affects.   *J. B. Pratt*

Anything that separates us from God.
                                    Alexander Purdy

Not in the act, but in the choice.   *John Ruskin*

A kind of lying.   *Saint Augustine*

Two causes: either from not seeing what we ought to do, or from not doing what we see ought to be done.   *Saint Augustine*

A state of mind, not an outward act.
                                    William Sewell

The seven deadly sins...food, clothing, fire, rent, taxes, respectability and children.
                                    George Bernard Shaw

The infidelity of man to the image of what he ought to be in his eternal vocation as an adopted son of God.   *Fulton J. Sheen*

An attempt to annihilate God.   *Bruno Webb*

The basic formula of all sin is: frustrated or neglected love.   *Franz Werfel*

An attempt to control the immutable and unalterable Laws of everlasting Righteousness, Goodness and Truth, upon which the Universe depends.   *Benjamin Whichcote*

Failure to make that adaptation to God which the growing life requires.   *Henry N. Wieman*

There is no sin except stupidity.   *Oscar Wilde*

Hatred of God, despair, unbelief, formal heresy, blasphemy.   *Christopher Wilmot*

Ugliness.   *Frank Lloyd Wright*

SEE ALSO ATHEISM, DEVIL, EVIL, GOOD AND BAD, HELL, JUDGMENT DAY, ORIGINAL, WICKEDNESS.

SINCERITY

To speak the words you mean.
                    Adapted from Thomas Bailey Aldrich

Not what you assume to be good or bad but what you are.   *Theodore Barbae*

Private sincerity is a public welfare.
                                    C. A. Bartol

Not the outward form but the foundation within.
                                    Samuel Taylor Coleridge

To speak nothing with God, but what is the sense of a single unfeigned heart.
                                    Samuel Taylor Coleridge

A proof of both a just frame of mind, and of a good tone of breeding. It is a quality that belongs equally to the honest man and to the gentleman.
                                    James Fenimore Cooper

Plain dealing.   *Ralph Waldo Emerson*

A mental attitude acquired after long practice by man, in order to conceal his ulterior motives.
                                    Elbert Hubbard

Bluffing only a part of the time.
                                    Elbert Hubbard

To lack invention, imagination or character.
                                    Elbert Hubbard

An openness of heart.   *La Rochefoucauld*

Just what I think, and nothing more nor less.
                                    Henry Wadsworth Longfellow

What our friends think about us when our backs are turned.   *Jimmy Lyons*

The quality that comes through on television.
                    Richard Milhous Nixon

As my mouth, so my heart.
                    Talmud: Megilla, 16a.

To practice more than your tongue says.
                    Adapted from Henry David Thoreau

To be the same person when one is with oneself; that is to say, alone.   *Paul Valéry*

To live a creed.   *Robert Zwickey*

Being yourself in any direction.   *Anon.*

A pose which puts you on guard.   *Anon.*

To be consistent with your conscience.   *Anon.*

To be nude.   *Anon.*

To shoot the way one shouts.   *Anon.*

To be perfect in your part.   *Anon.*

To give one's self for a principle.   *Anon.*

SEE ALSO HONESTY, TRUTH.

SINNER

One who...supposes that he is able to stand in God's presence because of his correctness and accomplishments, and does not understand that God demands the *entire* man.   *Rudolf Bultmann*

A man who makes no pretensions to being good on one day out of seven.   *Mary W. Little*

Man is a sinner not because he is finite but because he refuses to admit that he is.
                    Reinhold Niebuhr

Every one of us...We are men, not Gods.
                    Petronius

A person of violent practice, and one who doth unnatural acts.   *Benjamin Whichcote*

SEE ALSO DEVIL, HELL, SAINT, WICKED-NESS.

SIXTY

The age when one has spent twenty years in bed and over three years in eating.   *Anon.*

The time when one often finds new ways to use what he already knows.   *Anon.*

SEE ALSO OLD AGE.

SKEPTIC

A skeptic has no notion of conscience, no relish for virtue, nor is under any moral restraints from hope or fear. Such a one has nothing to do but to consult his ease, and gratify his vanity, and fill his pocket.   *Jeremy Collier*

A bad citizen...he seeks the selfishness of property and the drowsiness of institutions.
                    Ralph Waldo Emerson

One who laughs in order not to weep.
                    Adapted from Anatole France

I am ready to reject all belief and reasoning, and can look upon no opinion even as more probable or likely than another.   *David Hume*

Not one who doubts, but one who examines.
                    Charles A. Sainte-Beauve

One who won't take know for an answer.
                    Joan Tepperman

Skeptic always rhymes with septic; the spirit died of intellectual poisoning.   *Franz Werfel*

A dogmatist. He enjoys the delusion of complete futility.   *Alfred North Whitehead*

One who cannot quite believe nor dare disbelieve in central issues.   *Anon.*

SEE ALSO AGNOSTIC, DOUBT, PESSIMIST.

SKEPTICISM

A total disbeliever in human reason.
                    Henry B. Adams

Means not intellectual doubt alone, but moral doubt.   *Thomas Carlyle*

Whenever philosophy has taken into its plan religion it has ended in skepticism.
                    Samuel Taylor Coleridge

The mark and even the pose of the educated mind.
                    John Dewey

The first step on the road to philosophy.
                    Denis Diderot

Slow suicide.   *Ralph Waldo Emerson*

The spirit that always denies.

Johann W. Goethe

Through his skepticism the modern man is thrown back upon himself; his energies flow towards their source and wash to the surface those psychic contents which are at all times there, but lie hidden in the silt as long as the stream flows smoothly in its course.   *Carl G. Jung*

Believing nothing and being on your guard against everything.   *Latin Proverb*

The first attribute of a good critic.

James Russell Lowell

Skepticism, riddling the faith of yesterday, prepares the way for the faith of tomorrow.

Romain Rolland

The chastity of the intellect.   *George Santayana*

An exercise, not a life.   *George Santayana*

A discipline fit to purify the mind of prejudice and render it all the more apt, when the time comes, to believe and to act wisely.

George Santayana

The beginning of faith.   *Oscar Wilde*

SEE ALSO DOUBT, PESSIMISM.

SKILL

Skill to do comes of doing.

Ralph Waldo Emerson

A superb and necessary instrument but it functions at its highest level only when it is guided by a mature mind and an exalted spirit.

Richard H. Guggenheimer

An unconquered army.   *George Herbert*

The manipulative techniques of human goal attainment and control in relation to the physical world.   *Talcott Parsons*

Something that God gives for the hands of men to carry out.   *Anon.*

SEE ALSO ABILITY, TALENT.

SKY

The spacious firmament on high.

Joseph Addison

The glory of God.   *Bible: Psalms, XVIX, 1.*

The roof of the world.   *Willa Cather*

Of all the visual impressions, the nearest akin to feeling.   *Samuel Taylor Coleridge*

That inverted Bowl.   *Omar Khayyam*

That beautiful old parchment in which the sun and the moon keep their diary.   *Alfred Kreymborg*

That little tent of blue.
Which prisoners call the sky.   *Oscar Wilde*

SEE ALSO HEAVEN.

SLANDER

A most serious evil; it implies two who do wrong, and the one who is doubly wronged.   *Artabanus*

The most dangerous of wild beasts.

Henry G. Bohn

Horrible dispraise.   *Dante*

Shipwreck by a dry tempest.   *George Herbert*

The worst of poisons which find an entrance into ignoble minds.   *Adapted from John Hervey*

A necessity of life; insomuch that a dish of tea in the morning or evening cannot be digested without this stimulant.   *Thomas Jefferson*

A snake . . . a winged one—it flies as well as creeps.

Douglas Jerrold

The revenge of a coward, and dissimulation his defense.   *Samuel Johnson*

(To) cut men's throats with whisperings.

Ben Jonson

A verdict of "guilty" pronounced in the absence of the accused, with closed doors, without defense or appeal, by an interested and prejudiced judge.

Joseph Roux

A vice that strikes a double blow, wounding both him that commits, and him against whom it is committed.   *Saurin*

Witness, and judge, and executioner of the innocent.   *Jeremy Taylor*

That foul bird of rapine whose whole prey is a man's good name.

Adapted from Alfred Lord Tennyson

Silky moths that eat an honest name.

James Thomson

The immortal daughter of self-love and idleness.

Voltaire

SEE ALSO CALUMNY, GOSSIP, LIBEL, SCANDAL.

SLANG

A conventional tongue with many dialects, which are as a rule unintelligible to outsiders.

Albert Barrere

The voice of the god that dwells in the people.

Ralcy Bell

The speech of him who robs the literary garbage carts on their way to the dumps.

Ambrose Bierce

Language serving its apprenticeship.

Henry T. Buckle

(That which fixes) into portable shape the nebulous ideas of the vulgar.   *John Hay*

A poor-man's poetry.   *John Moore*

A token of man's lively spirit ever at work in unexpected places.   *John Moore*

A kind of metaphor and metaphor...is a kind of poetry.   *John Moore*

Language that takes off its coat, spits on its hands, and goes to work.   *Carl Sandburg*

The lawless germinal element, below all words and sentences, and behind all poetry.

Walt Whitman

Sport-model language stripped down to get more speed with less horse-power.   *Anon.*

The language of street humor, of fast, high and low life.   *Anon.*

SLAVE

If man remains a material and economic being and his spiritual nature is regarded as an illusion of consciousness, then man remains a slave.

Nicholas Berdyaev

(Those who) dare not speak...dare not be suspected to think differently from their masters.

William Cobbett

Corrupted freemen are the worst of slaves.

David Garrick

One who can be bought.   *Arthur Guiterman*

A class to do the mean duties.

James H. Hammond

The very mudsills of society.

James H. Hammond

A person who gratifies his wants...through cringing flattery...and who tyrannizes over others whenever he has a chance.   *Elbert Hubbard*

Man's mind and not his master makes him slave.

Robert U. Johnson

They are slaves who fear to speak
For the fallen and the weak.

James Russell Lowell

They are slaves who dare not be
In the right with two or three.

James Russell Lowell

All spirits are enslaved which serve things evil.

Adapted from Percy Bysshe Shelley

He is led away by his pleasures and can neither see what is good for him nor act accordingly.

Baruch Spinoza

SEE ALSO EMANCIPATION, NEGRO.

SLAVERY

Where the annual elections end, there slavery begins.   *John Adams*

The great and foul stain upon the North American Union.   *John Quincy Adams*

A vice instituted and fostered in the American colonies by aristocratic and monarchical England.

Charles Bradlaugh

That which exists when one must deny what one is in order to live with integrity, even to a single man.   *Eugene E. Brussell*

A weed that grows in every soil.

Edmund Burke

Yoked with the brutes, and fettered to the soil.

Thomas Campbell

The one intolerable sort...is the slavery of the strong to the weak; of the great and noble-minded to the small and mean.   *Thomas Carlyle*

Too much liberty.   *Cicero*

Freedom and slavery! The one is the name of virtue, and the other of vice, and both are acts of the will.   *Epictetus*

Not being able to speak your thoughts.

Euripides

(That which) includes all other crimes...the joint product of the kidnaper, the pirate, thief, murderer, and hypocrite.   *Robert G. Ingersoll*

Ignorance.   *Robert G. Ingersoll*

A prison for the soul, a public dungeon.

Longinus

A flagrant violation of the institutions of America—direct government—over all the people, by all the people, for all the people.

Theodore Parker

To have a price, and to be bought for it.

John Ruskin

A man's inability to moderate and control his passions.   *Baruch Spinoza*

Subordination to the superior race.

Alexander H. Stephens

By the Law of Slavery, man, created in the image of God, is divested of the human character, and declared to be a mere chattel.   *Charles Sumner*

Government without the consent of the governed.

Jonathan Swift

Taking the produce of another by force.

Leon Tolstoy

That execrable sum of all villainies.

John Wesley

SEE ALSO COMMUNISM, EMANCIPATION, EQUALITY, FREEDOM, NEGRO, SERVILITY.

SLEEP

To strain and purify the emotions, to deposit the mud of life, to calm the fever of the soul, to return into the bosom of material nature...a sort of innocence and purification.   *Henry F. Amiel*

Death's younger brother.   *Mary Anthers*

Death without dying—living, but not Life.

Edwin Arnold

Still the best eraser in the world.   *O. A. Battista*

Brother of death.   *Thomas Browne*

So like death. I dare not trust it without my prayers.   *Thomas Browne*

A boundary between the things misnamed death and existence.   *Adapted from Lord Byron*

The golden chain that ties health and our bodies together.   *Thomas Dekker*

Divine oblivion of my sufferings.   *Euripides*

A short death.   *Phineas Fletcher*

Often the only occasion in which we cannot silence...conscience.   *Erich Fromm*

The incomplete experience of death.

Hanina: Geneses, XVII, 5.

A skill in relaxation and self-control.

Edmund Jacobson

A dull, stupid state of existence.   *William Law*

Death without the responsibility.

Francis Lebowitz

A holiday from reality.   *Victor Ratner*

The interest we have to pay on the capital which is called in at death; and the higher the rate of interest the more regularly it is paid, the further the date of redemption is postponed.

Arthur Schopenhauer

The death of each day's life...balm of hurt minds...chief nourisher in life's feast.

William Shakespeare

The beginning of health.   *Anon.*

Sleep is a reconciling,
A rest that peace begets.   *Anon.*

A home to the homeless.   *Anon.*

A cloak to cover our hurts and weariness.

Anon.

SEE ALSO DREAM.

SLOGANS

Powerful opiates for the conscience.

James B. Conant

An art for getting the people to respond enthusiastically.   *Anon.*

A substitute for facts.   *Anon.*

Something necessary to start masses of people toward real or imagined projects.   *Anon.*

SEE ALSO CANT, PROPAGANDA.

SLUM

The feeding-grounds of crime.   *Anatole France*

The measure of civilization.   *Jacob Riis*

A place that creates a personality of poverty.
Anon.

The blight that failed.   *Anon.*

A fun place for the rich to visit, but a poor place to stay.   *Anon.*

The dwelling-place of the misbegotten.   *Anon.*

The breeding place of rebellion.   *Anon.*

SEE ALSO POOR, POVERTY.

SMELL

SEE NOSE, PERFUME.

SMILE

Smiles form the channel of a future tear.
Lord Byron

(When perpetual) a pathetic mask.
P. K. Thomajan

An inexpensive way to improve one's looks.
Anon.

The whisper of a laugh.   *Anon.*

The food of love.   *Anon.*

SEE ALSO LAUGHTER.

SNOB

A lady who walks like a peacock.
Patience Abbe

(Those who) talk as if they had begotten their own ancestors.   *Herbert Agar*

One who suffers from claustrophobia of the heart.
Cyril Connolly

A fellow as wants to be taken for better bred, or richer, or cleverer, or more influential than he really is.   *Charles Lever*

The ark that floats triumphant over the democratic wave; the faith of the old world reposes in his breast, and he shall proclaim it when the waters have subsided.   *George Moore*

The word Snob belongs to the sourgrape vocabulary.   *Logan P. Smith*

Perpetual nosing after snobbery at least suggests the snob.   *Robert Louis Stevenson*

That which we call a snob, by any other name would still be snobbish.
William Makepeace Thackeray

He who meanly admires mean things.
William Makepeace Thackeray

The man who allows the manhood within him to be awed by a coronet is a snob. The man who worships mere wealth is a snob.
Anthony Trollope

One who mistakes respectability for character.
Anon.

One who takes pride in his name being paged at an airport.   *Anon.*

SNOBBERY

The pride of those who are not sure of their position.   *Berton Braley*

In one form or another . . . eternal and omnipotent, and bigger than humanity itself.
Frank M. Colby

Snobbery is but a point in time. Let us have patience with our inferiors. They are ourselves of yesterday.   *Isaac Goldberg*

A characteristic of recent riches, high society, and the skunk.   *Austin O'Malley*

A quality rough to common men, but honeying at the whisper of a lord.
Adapted from Alfred Lord Tennyson

Pride in status without pride in function.
Lionel Trilling

The way of all status-seekers.   *Anon.*

The prerogative of the rich.   *Anon.*

SNORING

The tuneful serenade of that wakeful nightingale, the nose.   *George Farquhar*

To sleep loudly. *Anon.*

Sleeping out loud. *Anon.*

SOBRIETY

To be without money, to be destitute.
Elbert Hubbard

To be unhappy. *Elbert Hubbard*

Christian sobriety is all that duty that concerns ourselves in the matter of meat and drink, and pleasures and thoughts. *Jeremy Taylor*

A Boston aristocrat. *Anon.*

SEE ALSO ABSTINENCE; TEMPERANCE.

SOCIABILITY

The art of unlearning to be preoccupied with yourself. *Oscar Blumenthal*

That every man strive to accommodate himself to the rest. *Thomas Hobbes*

SOCIALISM

The legitimate heir of liberalism, not only chronologically, but spiritually. *Eduard Bernstein*

Economically, it means the socialization of the means of production. *Ber Borochov*

Politically, the establishment of the dictatorship of the toiling masses. *Ber Borochov*

Emotionally, the abolition of the reign of egotism and anarchy which characterizes the capitalistic system. *Ber Borochov*

Government of the deeds by the duds and for the deeds. *Winston S. Churchill*

The philosophy of failure, the creed of ignorance and the gospel of envy. *Winston S. Churchill*

Socialism is not merely the labor question, it is before all things the atheistic question, the question of the form taken by atheism today, the question of the tower of Babel built without God, not to mount to Heaven from earth but to set up Heaven on earth. *Fëdor M. Dostoievski*

The sophistry of the so-called intelligentsia, and it has no place in the hearts of those who would fight for freedom and preserve democracy.
Samuel Gompers

The combination of religious sentimentality, industrial insanity, and moral obliquity.
F. J. Hearnshaw

The most consistent scheme of militarism. It puts us all into battalions...We are all under discipline, and our individuality is chilled and killed.
Emil G. Hirsch

Resolutions passed by a committee as a substitute for work. *Elbert Hubbard*

A sincere, sentimental, beneficent theory, which has but one objection...it will not work.
Elbert Hubbard

A...scheme of government by which man shall loiter rather than labor. *Elbert Hubbard*

A plan by which the inefficient, irresponsible, ineffective, unemployable and unworthy will thrive without industry, persistence or economy.
Elbert Hubbard

An earnest effort to get Nature to change the rules for the benefit of those who are tired of the game.
Elbert Hubbard

The survival of the unfit. *Elbert Hubbard*

Participation in profits without responsibility as to deficits. *Elbert Hubbard*

(When) slavery comes to life again: the state an assemblage of slaves without personal liberty.
William von Ketteler

The logical sequence of economic and sociological development. *Daniel Leon*

To extend civilization to all humanity.
William Liebknecht

The standard bearer of the second rate.
Gilbert Longden

The practical application of Christianity to life, and has in it the secret of an orderly and benign reconstruction. *James Russell Lowell*

To raise suffering to a higher level.
Norman Mailer

Christian socialism is but the holy water with which the priest consecrates the heartburnings of the aristocrat. *Karl Marx*

Simply the degenerate capitalism of bankrupt capitalists. Its one genuine object is to get more money for its professors. *Henry Louis Mencken*

The joint ownership by all members of the community of the instruments and means of production.   *John Stuart Mill*

The consequence that the division of all the produce among the body of owners must be a public act performed according to the rules laid down by the community.   *John Stuart Mill*

For the street-corner and the club-room it wears the flaming scarlet of class-war; for the intellectual its red is shot with tawny; for the sentimentalists it becomes a delicate rose-pink; and in clerical circles it assumes a virgin-white, just touched with a faint flush of generous aspiration.

Ramsay Muir

A fake, a comedy, a phantom, and a blackmail.

Benito Mussolini

A system which is workable only in heaven, where it isn't needed, and in hell, where they've got it.   *Cecil Palmer*

These monstrous views...these venomous teachings.   *Pope Leo XIII*

Slavery.   *Herbert Spencer*

The capitalism of the lower classes.

Oswald Spengler

A stage in social development from a society guided by the dictatorship of the proletariat to a society wherein the state will have ceased to exist.

Joseph Stalin

An outlet of passionate expression for the inferiority complex of the disinherited.

Herbert G. Wells

SEE ALSO COMMUNISM.

SOCIALIST

A man who, so far as he himself is concerned, considers a thing done when he has suggested it.

Elbert Hubbard

A man suffering from an overwhelming compulsion to believe what is not true.

Henry Louis Mencken

Those who undermine the workingman's instincts, his pleasure, his contentment with his petty existence—those who make him envious and teach him revenge.

Adapted from Friedrich W. Nietzsche

A prim little man with a white-collar job, usually a secret teetotaller and often with vegetarian leanings.   *George Orwell*

SOCIETY

Something in nature that precedes the individual.

Aristotle

Comfort, use, and protection.   *Francis Bacon*

One vast conspiracy for carving one into the kind of statue it likes.   *Randolph Bourne*

A partnership not only between those ... living...but between...those who are dead, and those who are to be born.   *Edmund Burke*

A contract.   *Edmund Burke*

One polished horde formed of two mighty tribes, the bores and the bored.

Adapted from Lord Byron

The vital articulation of many individuals into a new collective individual.   *Thomas Carlyle*

Four classes: Noblemen, Gentlemen, Gigmen, and Men.   *Thomas Carlyle*

Two great classes: those who have more dinners than appetite, and those who have more appetite than dinners.   *Nicolas Chamfort*

To join in community with the human race.

Cicero

The glare, and the heat, and noise, this congeries of individuals without sympathy, and dishes without flavor; this is society.   *Benjamin Disraeli*

It is a community of purpose that constitutes society.   *Benjamin Disraeli*

Only a self-protection against the vulgarities of the street and the tavern... 'Tis an exclusion and a precinct.   *Ralph Waldo Emerson*

An unprincipled decorum; an affair of clean linen and coaches, of gloves, cards, and elegance in trifles.   *Ralph Waldo Emerson*

A joint-stock company, in which the members agree for better securing of his bread to each shareholder, to surrender the liberty and culture of the eater.   *Ralph Waldo Emerson*

A masked ball, where every one hides his real character, and reveals it by hiding.

Ralph Waldo Emerson

When a man meets his fitting mate society begins. *Ralph Waldo Emerson*

Someone to act with us, someone to confide our villainies to, someone to approve them.
William Hazlitt

Primarily a protective cocoon for the mechanisms of thought. *Donald O. Hebb*

These are the pillars of society—education, charity, and piety. *Hebrew Proverb*

Commerce...and...command.
Robert Herrick

A strong solution of books.
Oliver Wendell Holmes 1

The spirit of truth and the spirit of freedom—they are the pillars of society. *Henrik Ibsen*

Rendering mutual service to men of virtue and understanding to make them acquainted with one another. *Thomas Jefferson*

Not a safe harbor...The great society is a place where men are more concerned with the quality of their goals than the quality of their goods.
Lyndon Baines Johnson

A place where the meaning of man's life matches the marvels of man's labors.
Lyndon Baines Johnson

The group to which an individual belongs...the ground on which he stands, which gives or denies him security and help. *Kurt Z. Lewin*

The union of men but not men themselves; the citizen may perish but man remains.
Charles de Montesquieu

Always a dynamic unity of two component factors: minorities and masses.
José Ortega y Gasset

Society is always, whether it will or no, aristocratic by its very essence...it is a society in the measure that it is aristocratic, and ceases to be such when it ceases to be aristocratic.
José Ortega y Gasset

Above all a spiritual reality in which men communicate knowledge to each other in the light of truth, in which they can enjoy their rights and fulfill their duties, and are inspired to strive for moral good. *Pope John XXIII*

In the Creator's plan, society is a natural means which man can and must use to reach his destined end. Society exists for man and not man for society. *Pope Pius XI*

The painful ceremony of receiving and returning visits. *Tobias G. Smollett*

(That which) exists for the benefit of its members; not the members for the benefit of society.
Herbert Spencer

A new master, a new spook, a new supreme being, which takes us into its service and allegiance. *Max Stirner*

A madhouse whose wardens are the officials and police. *August Strindberg*

Two classes: the shearers and the shorn. We should always be with the former against the latter. *Charles de Talleyrand*

Commonly but the virtue of pigs in a litter, which lie close together to keep each other warm.
Henry David Thoreau

Society was invented for a remedy against injustice. *William Warburton*

A lot of nobodies talking about nothing.
Oscar Wilde

A bore. But to be out of it is simply a tragedy.
Oscar Wilde

Oneself. *Oscar Wilde*

High society is for those who have stopped working and no longer have anything important to do.
Woodrow Wilson

The dreary intercourse of daily life.
William Wordsworth

The noble living and the noble dead.
William Wordsworth

SEE ALSO COMPANY, FRIEND, SOLITUDE.

SOCRATES, (469-399 B.C.)

The first who brought down philosophy from Heaven, introducing it into the abodes of men, and compelling them to study the science of life, of human morals, and the effects of things good and bad. *Cicero*

The character of Socrates does not rise upon me. The more I read about him, the less I wonder that they poisoned him. *Thomas B. Macaulay*

Wisest of men. *John Milton*

The lowest of the low: he was the mob.

Friedrich W. Nietzsche

SOLDIER

He whose blood makes the glory of the general.

Adapted from Henry G. Bohn

For he was of that noble trade
That demi-gods and heroes made,
Slaughter, and knocking on the head.

Samuel Butler 1

Christ's warrior. As such he should regard himself, and so he should behave.

Mikhail I. Dragomiroff

Mouths without hands, maintained at vast expense; in peace a charge, in war a weak defense.

Adapted from John Dryden

A man who gets a piece of gold on his chest for a piece of lead in his pants.

Adapted from Jay C. Flippen

A man whose business it is to kill those who never offended him, and who are the innocent martyrs of other men's iniquities.   *William Godwin*

(Those who) fight and die to advance the wealth and luxury of the great.   *Tiberius Gracchus*

Learning to suspend your imagination and live completely in the very second of the present with no before and no after.   *Ernest Hemingway*

Every citizen...This was the case with the Greeks and the Romans, and must be that of every free state.   *Thomas Jefferson*

Men...most apt for all manner of services and best able to support and endure the infinite toils and continual hazards of war.   *Henry Knyvett*

One of the world's noblest figures.

Douglas MacArthur

The sinews of war.   *Niccolo Machiavelli*

Soldiers are made on purpose to be killed.

Napoleon 1

They know no country, own no lord, their home the camp, their law the sword.

Adapted from Silvio Pellico

The soldier's trade...is not slaying, but being slain.   *John Ruskin*

Citizens of death's gray land.

Siegfried Sassoon

Food for power.   *William Shakespeare*

A Yahoo hired to kill in cold blood as many of his own species, who have never offended him, as possibly he can.   *Jonathan Swift*

Theirs not to make reply,
Theirs not to reason why,
Theirs but to do and die.   *Alfred Lord Tennyson*

The only carnivorous animal that lives in a gregarious state.   *Johann G. Zimmerman*

A man hired to murder for his country's cause.

Anon.

That heady and adventurous crew that by death only seek to get a living. They make scars their beauty and count loss of limbs the commendation of a proper man.   *Anon.*

SEE ALSO ARMY, CANNON, GENERAL, MILITARISM, MILITIA, WAR.

SOLEMNITY

A condition precedent to believing anything without evidence.   *Robert G. Ingersoll*

A trick of the body to hide the faults of the mind.

La Rochefoucauld

The shield of idiots.   *Charles de Montesquieu*

A disease.   *Voltaire*

SEE ALSO SERIOUSNESS.

SOLITUDE

Often the best society.   *William G. Benham*

In bad company.   *Ambrose Bierce*

A good place to visit, but a bad place to stay.

Josh Billings

The most comprehensive of rights, and the right most valued by civilized men.

Louis D. Brandeis

There is no such thing...nor anything that can be said to be alone and by itself, but God.

Thomas Browne

To roam along, the world's tired denizen, with none who bless us, none we bless.

Adapted from Lord Byron

A luxury of the rich. *Albert Camus*

The sum-total of wretchedness to man.
Thomas Carlyle

The soul's best friend. *Charles Cotton*

The mightiest of agencies . . . essential to man. All men come into this world alone; all leave it alone.
Thomas De Quincey

The beginning of all freedom.
William O. Douglas

Inspiration makes solitude anywhere.
Ralph Waldo Emerson

To go to the window and look at the stars.
Ralph Waldo Emerson

The safeguard of mediocrity . . . to genius the stern friend. *Ralph Waldo Emerson*

(Something) not estimated by the number of people who live together, but by the retirement from bad passions . . . Where such solitude is present there is indeed the closest companionship.
Desiderius Erasmus

A discipline . . . essential for those who would acquaint themselves with God and be at peace.
E. Herman

The only thing that can hold the balance true.
Elbert Hubbard

A state dangerous to those who are too much accustomed to sink into themselves.
Samuel Johnson

The audience-chamber of God.
Walter Savage Landor

The nurse of full-grown souls.
James Russell Lowell

The playfield of Satan. *Vladimir Nabokov*

(That which) makes us tougher toward ourselves and tender toward others: in both ways it improves our character. *Friedrich W. Nietzsche*

A state that fertilizes the creative impulse.
Max Nordau

The companion . . . so companionable.
Henry David Thoreau

The happiest of all lives. *Voltaire*

Divine retreat. *Edward Young*

The triumph of mind over chatter. *Anon.*

When God talks to you. *Anon.*

SEE ALSO CROWD, HERMIT, LONELINESS, QUIET, SILENCE.

SON

The continuance of a parent's hope.
Eugene E. Brussell

Your son at five is your master, at ten your slave, at fifteen your double, and after that, your friend or foe, depending on his bringing up.
Abraham Hasdai

There are four types of sons: the wise, the simple, the wicked, and the one who does not know enough to ask. *Mekilta*

The anchors of a mother's life. *Sophocles*

SEE ALSO BOY, CHILD, PARENTS, YOUTH.

SONG

That which is not worth saying is sung.
Pierre A. Beaumarchais

Somehow the very central essence of us . . . as if all the rest were but wrappings and hulls.
Thomas Carlyle

The daughter of prayer, and prayer is the companion of religion. *Francois de Chateaubriand*

(Something) more lasting than the riches of the world. *Padraic Colum*

The licensed medium for bawling in public things too silly or sacred to be uttered in ordinary speech. *Oliver Herford*

(Man's) most orderly and magnanimous utterance. *Ned Rorem*

Soft words with nothing in them make a song.
Adapted from Edmund Waller

A form which lightens care and work no matter how nonsensical it may be. *Anon.*

SEE ALSO BALLAD, MUSIC.

SOPHISTICATION

A life style focused on appearances.
Eugene E. Brussell

Particularly aware of nuances...merest hints ... (being) moved by suasion and respond (ing) to subtle stimuli. *Bergen Evans*

The art of getting drunk with the right people.
Leonard L. Levinson

The trusted weapon of defense against ridicule.
L. Wardlaw Miles

A wide experience of the wrong and evil of the world, combined with a modish tolerance and an amused interest. *L. Wardlaw Miles*

The spirit's foe. *George Santayana*

In politics, a push-button opportunist who manipulates people's emotions, beliefs and hopes in his own interest. *George Santayana*

The ability to do almost anything without feeling guilty. *Earl Wilson*

A little bit of knowledge about everything, and appearing above the battle. *Anon.*

The corruption of idealism by worldly experience.
Anon.

A grace acquired with maturity. *Anon.*

SOPHISTRY

The lawyer's chief weapon. *Michael Axt*

Equivocation or ambiguity of words and phrase.
Francis Bacon

A maze of quibbles and a fog of words.
Ambrose Bierce

To reason correctly from a false principle is the perfection of sophistry. *Delos C. Emmons*

Mostly a strong concoction of lies, infected by a drop of truth. *Arthur Schnitzler*

To say one thing and think another.
Publilius Syrus

Talking only to conceal the mind. *Anon.*

SEE ALSO LAWYERS, WORDS.

SORROW

Sorrow is knowledge. *Lord Byron*

The one poor word which includes all our best insight and our best love. *George Eliot*

To love what is great, and try to reach it and yet to fail. *George Eliot*

For sorrow's a woman a man may take
And know, till his heart and body break.
Samuel Hoffenstein

A kind of rust of the soul, which every new idea contributes in its passage to scour away.
Samuel Johnson

Wisdom. *John Keats*

A form of self-pity. *John Fitzgerald Kennedy*

The future tense of love. *Leonard L. Levinson*

Uneasiness in the mind, upon the thought of a good lost, which might have been enjoyed longer; or the sense of a present evil. *John Locke*

The great idealizer. *James Russell Lowell*

A silence in the heart. *Robert Nathan*

A rainy corner in your life. *Jean Paul Richter*

An invitation to go to God.
Antonin Sertillanges

Visitors that come without invitation.
Charles H. Spurgeon

The Spartan sauce which gives gusto to the remainder—viands of life, the broken meats of love. *Francis Thompson*

When the heart weeps for what it has lost.
Anon.

SEE ALSO SUFFERING, TEARS.

SOUL

The first actualization of a natural body potentially having life. *Aristotle*

The soul is not where it lives, but where it loves.
Henry G. Bohn

A mere spectator of the movements of its body.
Charles Bonnet

Purely phenomenal existence, an appearance incomplete and inconsistent, and with no power to maintain itself as an independent "thing."
Francis H. Bradley

A finite centre of immediate experience.
Francis H. Bradley

Something in us that can be without us and will be after us.   *Thomas Browne*

Soul is the man.   *Thomas Campion*

The aspect of ourselves that is specific of our nature and distinguishes man from all other animals.   *Alexis Carrel*

An image of the infinity of God.
William Ellery Channing

A never ending sigh after God.
Theodore Christlieb

A spark of the never-dying flame that separates man from all the other beings of earth.
James Fenimore Cooper

The soul is created in a place between Time and Eternity: with its highest powers it touches Eternity, with its lower Time.   *Meister Eckhart*

The Supreme Critic on the errors of the past and present, and the only prophet of that which must be.   *Ralph Waldo Emerson*

The wise silence; the universal beauty, to which every part and particle is equally related.
Ralph Waldo Emerson

Something or other which generates dreams and ideals, and which sets up values.   *John Erskine*

That unified being which...is evident only to itself; luminous to itself, to every other eye obscure.   *Gustav T. Fechner*

Feeling depth, the ability to reach someone. It's being a part of what today is all about.
Aretha Franklin

My body's guest and comrade.   *Hadrian*

A guest in our body, deserving of our kind hospitality.   *Hillel*

That inner consciousness which aspires.
Richard Jefferies

A portion of the Deity housed in our bodies.
Josephus Flavius

The mirror of an indestructible universe.
Gottfried W. von Leibnitz

That mysterious instrument.
Henry Wadsworth Longfellow

Sunbeams lifted higher.
Henry Wadsworth Longfellow

The human soul is one, though it has many diverse activities.   *Moses Maimonides*

A troublesome possession, and when man developed it he lost the Garden of Eden.
William Somerset Maugham

Our souls are like those orphans whose unwedded mothers die in bearing them: the secret of our paternity lies in their grave, and we must there learn it.   *Herman Melville*

An immortal guest.   *Hannah More*

A soul? Give my watch to a savage, and he will think it has a soul.   *Napoleon 1*

The place where man's supreme and final battles are fought.   *Abraham Neuman*

A god within each human breast.   *Ovid*

Vital spark of heav'nly flame.   *Alexander Pope*

The soul is nothing apart from the senses.
Protagoras

The life whereby we are joined into the body.
Saint Augustine

The perfect body is itself the soul.
George Santayana

Where the Supreme Good dwells...And unless the soul be pure and holy, there is no room in it for God.   *Seneca*

Mine eternal jewel.   *William Shakespeare*

My soul is myself; the well-spring or point of consciousness, or center of activity.
Upton Sinclair

The start for all other knowing, the test by which I judge all other data.   *Upton Sinclair*

A silent harp in God's quire, whose strings need only to be swept by the divine breath to chime in with the harmonies of creation.
Henry David Thoreau

The wife of the body. They do not have the same kind of pleasure or, at least, they seldom enjoy it at the same time.   *Paul Valéry*

Four thousand volumes of metaphysics will not teach us what the soul is.   *Voltaire*

Nobody knows how the idea of a soul...started. It probably had its origin in the natural laziness of mankind.   *John B. Watson*

That measureless pride which revolts from every lesson but its own.   *Walt Whitman*

SEE ALSO CHRISTIANITY, DEATH, ETERNAL RECURRENCE, GOD, IMMORTALITY, SALVATION.

SOVEREIGN

SEE KING, MONARCHY, QUEEN.

SOVEREIGNTY

Some power or other from which there is no appeal.   *Samuel Johnson*

An original, supreme, absolute, and uncontrollable earthly power.   *James Otis*

SEE ALSO AUTHORITY, KING, STATE.

SPACE PROGRAM

A completely new step in the evolution of man. For the first time, life will leave its planetary cradle, and the ultimate destiny of man will no longer be confined to these familiar continents that we have known so long.

Wernher von Braun

A continuing process with countless goals, but no final end.   *Arthur C. Clarke*

A truly awesome mark on the total timeline of mankind.   *Jonathan Eberhart*

A moral and esthetic venture. These are our cathedrals.   *Paul Goodman*

A book with many chapters.

William Greenwood

This is a new ocean, and I believe the United States must sail upon it.

John Fitzgerald Kennedy

(Exploration) so that our supreme aim may become clearer: the intelligent organization of life on the planet.   *Salvador de Madariaga*

A part of man's world.   *Richard Milhous Nixon*

A race between great rival powers.

Bertrand A. Russell

Venturing into measureless space for the enrichment of all mankind.   *Anon.*

SEE ALSO APOLLO SPACE PROGRAM, ASTRONAUTS, MOON.

SPAIN

A whale stranded upon the coast of Europe.

Edmund Burke

Renown'd romantic land!   *Lord Byron*

A nation swollen with ignorance and pride, who lick yet loathe the hand that waves the sword.

Adapted from Lord Byron

The land of war and crimes.   *Lord Byron*

(Where they) import tourists and export chambermaids.   *Carlos Fuentes*

SPANKING

Punishment that takes less time than reasoning and penetrates sooner to the seat of memory.

Will Durant

Applause backwards.   *Anon.*

SPEAKER

SEE ORATOR, SPEECH.

SPECIALIST

Knowledge . . . best served by an exclusive (or at least paramount) dedication of one mind to one science.   *Thomas De Quincey*

One who limits himself to his chosen mode of ignorance.   *Elbert Hubbard*

A man who knows more and more about less and less.   *William J. Mayo*

No man can be a pure specialist without being in the strict sense an idiot.   *George Bernard Shaw*

A man of one particular interest who has come into his own in the twentieth century.   *Anon.*

SPECIALIZATION

A kind of hypnotic trance wherein a person by centering his gaze on a given object renders the object smaller in proportion to his growing illusions.   *Adapted from Elbert Hubbard*

The ability to focus all your energies on one thing.   *Elbert Hubbard*

SPECIES

No one definition has satisfied all naturalists; yet every naturalist knows vaguely what he means when he speaks of a species. *Charles Darwin*

SPECTATOR

People who are interested in something they are not interested in at all. *Peter Altenberg*

Two kinds: those who passively react to something, and those who create along with it.
Eugene E. Brussell

Not the arbiter of the work of art. He is the one who is admitted to contemplate the work of art... to forget in its contemplation all the egotism that mars him. *Oscar Wilde*

SPECULATION

SEE GAMBLING, REFLECTION, THINKING.

SPEECH

Out of the abundance of the heart the mouth speaketh. *Bible: Matthew, XII, 34.*

That art of... stifling and suspending thought.
Thomas Carlyle

The image of life. *Democritus*

The music that can deepest reach,
And cure all ill, is cordial speech.
Ralph Waldo Emerson

Speech is power: speech is to persuade, to convert, to compel. *Ralph Waldo Emerson*

The true use of speech is not so much to express our wants as to conceal them. *Oliver Goldsmith*

The only benefit man hath to express his excellency of mind above other creatures.
Ben Jonson

The Instrument of Society. In all speech, words and sense are as the body and the soul.
Ben Jonson

Like a love letter. Ideally, you should begin by not knowing what you are going to say, and end by not knowing what you've said. *William A. Jowitt*

Speech was made to open man to man, and not to hide him; to promote commerce, and not betray it. *David Lloyd*

Civilization itself. The word—even the most contradictory word—preserves contact. It is silence that isolates. *Thomas Mann*

Speech has been given to man to express his thought. *Moliere*

A constant stratagem to cover nakedness.
Harold Pinter

Man's speech is like his life. *Plato*

The index and mirror of the soul.
Thomas W. Robertson

Man's most confused and egocentric expression.
Ned Rorem

The index of the mind. *Seneca*

Speech was given to the ordinary sort of men to communicate their mind, but to wise men whereby to conceal it. *Robert South*

The first principle of a free society.
Adlai Ewing Stevenson

The first duty of man... that is his chief business in this world. *Robert Louis Stevenson*

All speech, written or spoken, is a dead language, until it finds a willing and prepared hearer.
Robert Louis Stevenson

The mirror of the soul; as a man speaks, so he is.
Publilius Syrus

A faculty given to man to conceal his thoughts.
Charles de Talleyrand

Embroidered tapestries, since, like them, it must be extended in order to display its patterns, but when it is rolled up it conceals and distorts them.
Themistocles

A hazard; oftener than not it is the most hazardous kind of deed. *Miguel de Unamuno*

Human nature itself, with none of the articificality of written language.
Alfred North Whitehead

The specific moving power to the working out of speech was... but the human tendency to sociability. *William D. Whitney*

Thought's canal... thought's criterion, too.
Adapted from Edward Young

Steer horns—a point here, a point there and a lot of bull in between.   *Anon.*

SEE ALSO CONVERSATION, ELOQUENCE, FREE SPEECH, ORATORY, TALK, VERBOSITY.

SPIES

Merely a form of international courtesy, like exchange professors...In fact, they give a rather nice cosmopolitan air to the streets.

Robert Benchley

Spies are of no use nowadays. Their profession is over. The newspapers do their work instead.

Oscar Wilde

SPIRIT

The seat of the knowledge of God.   *Al-ghazzali*

An inward flame; a lamp the world blows upon but never puts out.   *Margot Asquith*

One simple, undivided, active being—as it perceives ideas it is called the *understanding,* as it produces or otherwise operates about them it is called the will.   *George Berkeley*

Then shalt the dust return to the earth as it was: and the spirit shalt return unto God who gave it.

Bible: Ecclesiastes, XII, 7.

The lamp of the Lord, searching all the inward parts.   *Bible: Proverbs, XX, 27.*

Not a thing apart...it is in every thought and every word and every act.

Benjamin N. Cardozo

That which determines the material.

Thomas Carlyle

The supreme fact, supreme over all changes of process and lasting through them all.

Arthur Clutton-Brock

Spirit is the real and eternal; matter is the unreal and material.   *Mary Baker Eddy*

Matter has its essence out of itself; Spirit is *self-contained existence.*   *Georg W. Hegel*

The spiritual is automatic, that is, its functioning is its essence.   *Nahman Krochmal*

A bird: if you hold on to it tightly, it chokes, and if you hold it loosely, it escapes.   *Israel S. Lipkin*

A vital breath of more ethereal air.

Henry Wadsworth Longfellow

The light militia of the lower sky.

Alexander Pope

The life of God within us.   *Saint Teresa*

Awareness, intelligence, recollection. It requires no dogmas.   *George Santayana*

A glass through which we can peer more deeply into reality than by purely rational instruments alone.   *Edmund W. Sinnott*

SEE ALSO ANGEL, IMMORTALITY, SOUL.

SPORTS

One of the few honourable battlefields left.

Daniel Blanchflower

A conflict between good and bad, winning and losing, praise and criticism.

Daniel Blanchflower

Mechanization of the body conceived as a robot, ruled by the principle of productivity.

Jean-Marie Brohm

An armoured apparatus for coercion...dominated by a phallocratic and fascistoid idea of virility.   *Jean-Marie Brohm*

The toy department of human life.

Jimmy Cannon

Hard work.   *Irvin S. Cobb*

A pleasure of the flesh.   *Bruce Kidd*

An order of chivalry, a code of ethics and aesthetics, recruiting its members from all classes and all peoples.   *René Maheu*

Sport is education, the truest kind of education, that of character.   *René Maheu*

War minus the shooting.   *George Orwell*

When a man wants to murder a tiger, he calls it sport; when the tiger wants to murder him, he calls it ferocity.   *George Bernard Shaw*

Sport is imposing order on what was chaos.

Anthony Storr

The English Country gentleman galloping after a fox—the unspeakable in full pursuit of the uneatable.   *Oscar Wilde*

A duel with nature, with one's own fear...fatigue, a duel in which body and mind are strengthened.   *Yevgeny Yevtushenko*

SEE ALSO FISHING, HUNTING.

SPRING

The flowers appear on the earth; the time of the singing of birds is come, and the voice of the turtle is heard in our land.

Bible: Solomon's Song, II, 12.

One of love's April fools.   *William Congreve*

Spring is a call to action, hence the disillusion, therefore April is called the cruelest month.

Cyril Connolly

It is a trap to catch us two,
It is planned for me and you.   *Mary C. Davies*

The spring's behaviour here is spent to make the world magnificent.

Adapted from John Drinkwater

All the veneration of Spring connects itself with love...Even the frog and his mate have a newer and gayer coat for this benign occasion.

Ralph Waldo Emerson

(A season) full of sweet days and roses.

George Herbert

Nature taking up its option on the world.

Leonard L. Levinson

The pleasant year's king.

Adapted from Thomas Nashe

(Spring) makes everything young again except man.   *Jean Paul Richter*

When life's alive in every thing.

Christina Rossetti

When a young man's fancy lightly turns—and turns—and turns.   *Helen Rowland*

It is the season now to go
About the country high and low,
Among the lilacs hand in hand,
And two by two in fairy land.

Robert Louis Stevenson

A true reconstructionist.   *Henry Timrod*

This is the time when bit by bit
The days begin to lengthen sweet

And every minute gained is joy—
And love stirs in the heart of a boy.

Katherine Tynan

Now every field is clothed with grass, and every tree with leaves; now the woods put forth their blossoms, and the year assumes its gay attire.

Vergil

Spring has come when you can put your foot on three daisies at once.   *Anon.*

A season that says it with flowers.   *Anon.*

Winter defrosting.   *Anon.*

SEE ALSO APRIL.

STAGE

SEE ACTING, DRAMA, THEATER.

STALIN, JOSEPH (1879-1953)

The chief father-figure of the Russian empire for a time. A butcher by trade.   *Eugene E. Brussell*

A combination of fanatic and man of action, with the fanatical tinge predominating.   *Eric Hoffer*

His disastrous blunders—the senseless liquidation of the kulaks and their offspring, the terror of the purge, the pact with Hitler, the clumsy meddling with the creative work of writers, artists, scientists—are the blunders of a fanatic.   *Eric Hoffer*

The soul of an Oriental despot.   *Nikolai Lenin*

The Russian Father Divine.   *Sinclair Lewis*

The most outstanding mediocrity of the Soviet bureaucracy.   *Leon Trotsky*

The master of ignorance and disloyalty.

Leon Trotsky

STARLET

One who rises from nothing to become nothing.

Max Gralnick

A girl a studio pays to act while she's looking for a husband.   *Thomas Jenk*

(Girls) trying to bust their way into the limelight.

Wallace Reyburn

A young girl who goes to fabulous parties with movie executives and has a wonderful future—providing she is not put into a movie. *Anon.*

SEE ALSO ACTOR, HOLLYWOOD.

STARS

The beauty and glory of heaven...gleaming ornaments in the heights of God.
Apocrypha: Ben Sira, XLIII, 9f.

Let there be lights in the firmament of the heaven to divide the day from the night.
Bible: Genesis, I, 14.

The pale populace of Heaven. *Robert Browning*

Golden fruits upon a tree all out of reach.
George Eliot

A device to show man his insignificance.
Elbert Hubbard

The forget-me-nots of the angels.
Henry Wadsworth Longfellow

Light to the misled and lonely traveller.
Adapted from John Milton

These blessed candles of the night.
William Shakespeare

'Tis Nature's system of divinity. *Edward Young*

Elder scripture written by God's own hand, scripture authentic, uncorrupted by man.
Adapted from Edward Young

Someone's sun. *Anon.*

SEE ALSO ASTROLOGY.

STARVATION

SEE HUNGER, POVERTY, STOMACH.

STATE

Wherever men are who know how to defend themselves. *Alcaeus*

Great engines moving slowly. *Francis Bacon*

Slavery. Worse, it is the silly parading of force ...Its essence is command and compulsion.
Mikhail A. Bakunin

The legal maimer of our will, the constant negation of our liberty. *Mikhail A. Bakunin*

(Ideally) a sort of central bookkeeping department, devoted to the service of society.
Mikhail A. Bakunin

The State is not a product of sin but one of the constants of the divine Providence and government of the world in its action against sin. It is therefore an instrument of divine grace.
Karl Barth

Our own sin magnified a thousand times.
Emil Brunner

A legal relation by which a supreme authority exists in a certain territory. *Paul Eltzbacher*

A machine for the oppression of one class by another; this is true of a democracy as well as of a monarchy. *Friedrich Engels*

A perfect body of free men, united together to enjoy common rights and advantages.
Hugo Grotius

Embodied morality. *Georg W. Hegel*

Mind, *per se.* *Georg W. Hegel*

A secular deity...the march of God in the world.
Georg W. Hegel

Human sin on the large scale...the product of collective sin. *Max Huber*

Made up of a considerable number of the ignorant and foolish, a small proportion of genuine knaves, and a sprinkling of capable and honest men, by whose efforts the former are kept in a reasonable state of guidance and the latter of repression.
Thomas Henry Huxley

High-minded men, men who know their duties, but know their rights, and, knowing, dare maintain these rights—this constitutes the State.
Adapted from William James

A society of men, over whom the state alone has a right to command and dispose. It is a trunk which has its own roots. *Immanuel Kant*

States...are to be considered as moral persons having a public will, capable and free to do right and wrong. *James Kent*

Collections of individuals, each of whom carries with him into the service of the community the same binding law of morality and religion which ought to control his conduct in private life.
James Kent

The word state is identical with the word war.
Peter A. Kropotkin

I am the state!   *Louis XIV*

An unnatural infringement upon human liberty...a perversion of life's inherent simplifications.   *Judah Löw*

States are not made. They grow slowly through centuries of pain, and grow correctly in the main, but only by certain laws of certain bits in certain jaws.   *Adapted from John Masefield*

The association of men, and not men themselves; the citizen may perish, and the man remain.
Charles de Montesquieu

The conscience and will of the people.
Benito Mussolini

That cawing rookery of committees and subcommittees.   *V. S. Pritchett*

God's ministry for the common good.
Antonio de Salazar

States are as men are; they grow out of human character.   *Max Stirner*

Only a group of men with human interests, passions, and desires, or, worse yet...only an obscure clerk hidden in some corner of a government bureau.   *William G. Sumner*

The people, legally united as an independent entity...the objectively revealed will of God.
Heinrich von Treitschke

The system of cages in an impoverished provincial zoo.   *Leon Trotsky*

SEE ALSO ANARCHY, GOVERNMENT, NATION.

STATESMAN

A man of common opinions and uncommon abilities.   *Walter Bagehot*

Somebody old enough to know his own mind and keep quiet about it.   *Bernard Baruch*

A disposition to preserve, and an ability to improve.   *Edmund Burke*

Most statesmen have long noses, which is very lucky because most of them cannot see further than the length of them.   *Paul Claudel*

Security to possessors; Facility to acquirers; and, Hope to all.   *Samuel Taylor Coleridge*

(One) who cannot afford to be a moralist.
Will Durant

(One who will) stand like a wall of adamant between the people and the sovereign.
William E. Gladstone

A politician seeking re-election.   *Max Gralnick*

(One who) makes the occasion, but the occasion makes the politician.   *G. S. Hillard*

A politician who is held upright by equal pressure from all directions.   *Eric A. Johnston*

Metternich approaches close to being a great statesman. He lies very well.   *Napoleon I*

A politician who places himself at the service of the nation. A politician is a statesman who places the nation at his service.   *George Pompidou*

A successful politician who is dead.
Thomas Reed

(Those) suspected of plotting against mankind, rather than consulting their interests, and are esteemed more crafty than learned.
Baruch Spinoza

A lidless watch of the public weal.
Alfred Lord Tennyson

Any politician it is considered safe to name a school after.   *William Vaughan*

A politician away from home.   *Anon.*

Not the greatest doer, but he who sets others doing with the greatest success.   *Anon.*

A man whose kindnesses proceed from principles of his own need.   *Anon.*

The craft of getting along with politicians.
Anon.

One who has a reputation for doing what he believes should be done, and not necessarily what others want him to do.   *Anon.*

A dead politician.   *Anon.*

One who makes righteousness listenable.
Anon.

SEE ALSO POLITICIAN.

STATESMANSHIP

The act of changing a nation from what it is to what it ought to be.   *William R. Alger*

The art of sweeping ugly realities under the rug.

Jerry Dashkin

The art of understanding and leading the masses...Its glory is to lead them, not where they want to go, but where they ought to go.

Joseph Joubert

The wise employment of individual meannesses for the public good.   *Abraham Lincoln*

In statesmanship get the formalities right, never mind the moralities.   *Mark Twain*

STATISTICIAN

An average guy.   *Harold Coffin*

A man who draws a mathematically precise line from an unwarranted assumption to a foregone conclusion.   *Anon.*

Like alienists—they will testify for either side.

Anon.

One who collects data and draws confusions.

Anon.

SEE ALSO RESEARCH, SCIENTIST.

STATISTICS

The most exact of false sciences.   *Jean Cau*

The object...is to discover methods of condensing information concerning large groups of allied facts into brief and compendious expressions suitable for discussion.   *Francis Galton*

(Something used) for support rather than illumination.   *Andrew Long*

The art of lying by means of figures.

Wilhelm Stekel

Mendacious truths.   *Lionel Strachey*

The heart of democracy.   *Simeon Strunsky*

A group of numbers looking for an argument.

Anon.

SEE ALSO FACT, RESEARCH.

STOMACH

One's internal environment.   *Samuel Butler 2*

The greatest of deities.   *Euripides*

A great part of a man's liberty.

Michel de Montaigne

The reason man does not mistake himself for a god.   *Friedrich W. Nietzsche*

A slave that must accept everything that is given to it, but which avenges wrongs as slyly as does the slave.   *Emile Souvester*

A clock.   *Jonathan Swift*

SEE ALSO APPETITE, DIGESTION, EATING, FOOD, HUNGER.

STORY

SEE FABLE, FICTION, MYTHOLOGY, NOVEL.

STRENGTH

SEE CHARACTER, FORCE, POWER.

STRIKE

A labor pain.   *Leonard L. Levinson*

A phenomenon of war.   *Georges Sorel*

STUBBORN

SEE OBSTINACY.

STUDENT

A set o' dull, conceited hashes
Confuse their brains in college classes;
They gang in stirks, and come out asses.

Robert Burns

A person who is learning to fulfill his powers and to find ways of using them in the service of mankind.   *Harold Taylor*

SEE ALSO EDUCATION, SCHOOL.

STUDY

Crafty men contemn studies; simple men admire them; and wise men use them.   *Francis Bacon*

Serves for delight, for ornament, and for ability.

Francis Bacon

Much study is a weariness of the flesh.

Bible: Ecclesiastes, XII, 12.

A possession of the mind, that is to say, a vehement motion made by some one object in the organs of sense, which are stupid to all other motions as long as this lasteth.   *Thomas Hobbes*

Concentration of the mind on whatever will ultimately put something in the pocket.
Elbert Hubbard

Smelling of the lamp.   *Ben Jonson*

The stuff that memory is made of, and memory is accumulated genius.   *James Russell Lowell*

A great country which no war profanes, no conqueror menaces.   *Gaston Paris*

The noblest exercise of the mind within doors, and most befitting a person of quality.
William Ramsey

(To learn lessons) not for life, but for the lecturer-room.   *Seneca*

Authority from other's books.
William Shakespeare

Endless labor.   *Anon.*

SEE ALSO CONCENTRATION, EDUCATION, KNOWLEDGE, LEARNING.

STUPIDITY

Nature's favorite resource for preserving steadiness of conduct and consistency of opinion.
Walter Bagehot

Unconscious ignorance.   *Josh Billings*

A character defense of turned in hostility.
Paul Goodman

Not always a mere want of intelligence. It can be a sort of corruption. It is doubtful whether the good of heart can be really stupid.   *Eric Hoffer*

Mainly just a lack of capacity to take things in.
Clive James

(One who is) not only dull himself, but the cause of dullness in others.   *Samuel Johnson*

Obstinacy and heat of opinion are the surest proof of stupidity. Is there anything so assured, resolved, disdainful, contemplative, solemn and serious, as the ass.   *Michel de Montaigne*

Talent for misconception.   *Edgar Allan Poe*

Not so much brain as ear-wax.
William Shakespeare

There is no sin but stupidity.   *Oscar Wilde*

Believing much, understanding little.   *Anon.*

SEE ALSO IGNORAMUS, IGNORANCE, MORON.

STYLE

What gives value and currency to thought.
Henry F. Amiel

A good style must, first of all, be clear. It must not be mean nor above the dignity of the subject. It must be appropriate.   *Aristotle*

Acquiring a particular quality by acting in a particular way.   *Adapted from Aristotle*

Have something to say, and say it as clearly as you can.   *Matthew Arnold*

To speak as the common people do, to think as wise men do.   *Roger Ascham*

A chaste and lucid style is indicative of the same personal traits in the author.   *Hosea Ballou*

The style is the man himself.   *George de Buffon*

Nothing more than the order and movement in which thoughts are set.   *George de Buffon*

Doing things not in any way but in the best way.
Gelett Burgess

The dress of thoughts.   *Lord Chesterfield*

A bad one is when the author shifts his style much more often than his clothes.
Adapted from Charles Churchill

A simple way of saying complicated things.
Jean Cocteau

The interaction of . . . personality and period.
Aaron Copland

It is style alone by which posterity will judge of a great work, for an author can have nothing truly his own but his style.   *Isaac D'Israeli*

A man's style is his mind's voice.
Ralph Waldo Emerson

How you say a thing.   *Robert Frost*

That which indicates how the writer takes himself and what he is saying...It is the mind skating circles around itself as it moves forward.

Robert Frost

The style of an author should be the image of his mind, but the choice and command of language is the fruit of exercise. *Edward Gibbon*

The living, visible garment of writing.

Max Gralnick

To make the words absolutely disappear into thought. *Nathaniel Hawthorne*

No style is good that is not fit to be spoken or read aloud with effect. *William Hazlitt*

The creation of one's own language.

Roger Hemings

In stating as fully as I could how things really were, it was often very difficult and I wrote awkwardly and the awkwardness is what they called my style. All mistakes and awkwardness are easy to see, and they called it style.

Ernest Hemingway

The hallmark of a temperament stamped upon the material at hand. *Emile Herzog*

The outgrowth of a man's individuality.

Josiah G. Holland

Clear arrangement. *Horace*

(If overdone) a ceratin manner or deportment which emanates from those who have neither manner nor deportment. *Elbert Hubbard*

A peculiar and individual manner of doing the unnecessary. *Elbert Hubbard*

Style...is formed very early in life, while the imagination is warm and impressions are permanent. *Thomas Jefferson*

A strict and succinct style is that, where you can take away nothing without loss, and that loss to be manifest. *Ben Jonson*

The mind's translation. *Abraham I. Kook*

A noble manner in an easy manner.

George Meredith

The perfection of good sense. *John Stuart Mill*

Less often the man than the concept he wishes his public to have.

Adapted from George Jean Nathan

A wonderful pickle that is able to preserve mediocrity of thought under favorable conditions for many centuries. *F. S. Oliver*

The chief stimulus of good style is to possess a full, rich, complex matter to grapple with.

Walter Pater

The unique word, phrase, sentence, paragraph, essay or song, absolutely proper to the single mental presentation or vision within.

Walter Pater

Uncommon things...said in common words.

Coventry Patmore

A constant and continual phrase or tenor of speaking and writing, extending to the whole tale or process of the poem or history, and not properly to any piece or member of a tale; but is of words, speeches, and sentences together, a certain contrived form and quality. *George Puttenham*

The physiognomy of the mind, and a safer index to character than the face.

Arthur Schopenhauer

Style has no fixed laws; it is changed by the usage of the people, never the same for any length of time. *Seneca*

Effectiveness of assertion...He who has nothing to assert has no style and can have none.

George Bernard Shaw

The immortal thing in literature.

Alexander Smith

The vehicle of the spirit. *Sydney Smith*

Proper words in proper places. *Jonathan Swift*

As to the adjective: When in doubt, strike it out.

Mark Twain

Knowing who you are, what you want to say, and not giving a damn. *Gore Vidal*

The ultimate morality of the mind.

Alfred North Whitehead

The faintly contemptible vessel in which the bitter liquid is recommended to the world.

Thornton Wilder

That which reveals the form and likeness of our minds. *Robert Zwickey*

SEE ALSO ESSAY, FASHION, LANGUAGE, LITERATURE, METAPHOR, ORATORY, WRITING.

SUBSIDY

A formula for handing you back your own money
with a flourish that makes you think it's a gift.

Jo Bingham

SUBURBIA

Opportunity for companionship and friendship...easy access to local services...certain
forms of security.   *Charles Adrian*

(The) focal point not only of our material activites
but of much of our moral and intellectual life as
well.   *Charles Adrian*

A place peopled with home-owning Republicans
who were once city-dwelling renting Democrats.

Eugene E. Brussell

A body of middle class people who work, pay
taxes, provide a success-stimulus for their children via communal activities, and repair their
homes. They are a people of disengagement as far
as the problems of the inner city is concerned.

Eugene E. Brussell

The Split-Level Trap.   *Gordon and Gunther*

Disturbia.   *Gordon and Gunther*

The home of the middle class.   *Louis Harris*

A box of your own in one of the freshair slums
we're building around the edges of America's
cities.   *John Keats*

A parasitical growth, and the religion which
serves it tries artificially to recollect the vision of
a simple rural and village life which no longer
exists.   *Franklin H. Littell*

A sort of green ghetto dedicated to the elite.

Lewis Mumford

There's a green one and a pink one
And a blue one and a yellow one,
And they're all made out of ticky-tacky
And they all look just the same.

Malvina Reynolds

Homes beside a freeway, a forest of television
aerials, a church and synagogue, a shopping
center, people of the same white, middle class
standards, centered around their children's activities. This is suburbia.   *Joan Tepperman*

Where the developer bulldozes out the trees, then
names the streets after them.   *William Vaughan*

The thinnest sham of a community...where a
clerk or a working man will shift his sticks from
one borough to another without ever discovering
what he has done.   *Herbert G. Wells*

A mere roost where (the commuter) comes at
day's end to go to sleep.   *Edward B. White*

Places in the country immediately outside a city
(depending) upon the technological advances of
the age: the automobile and rapid transit line,
asphalt pavement, delivery trucks, septic tanks
...and motor-driven pumps.

Robert C. Wood

A looking glass in which the character, behavior,
and culture of middle class America is displayed.

Robert C. Wood

A melting pot of executives, managers, white-
collar workers, successful or unsuccessful, who
may be distinguished only by the subtle variations
of the cars they drive.   *Robert C. Wood*

A reasonable reconstruction of our heritage.

Robert C. Wood

A city in miniature.   *Anon.*

A place which has proper people in proper places.

Anon.

Developments, not communities.   *Anon.*

A complete interpenetration of city and country, a
complete fusion of their different modes of life
and a combination of the advantages of both.

Anon.

Sorority home communities with kids.   *Anon.*

A projection of dormitory life into adulthood.

Anon.

A place where large fields of country are converted into large tracts of crab-grass.   *Anon.*

A lay version of Army post life.   *Anon.*

A womb with a view.   *Anon.*

A Russia, only with money.   *Anon.*

Child-centered communities where everyone is an
amateur psychologist or sociologist.   *Anon.*

A development centered around the shopping
center; in short, a captive market community.

Anon.

A place where small town friendships grow near
the big city.   *Anon.*

A return to an earlier, better America. *Anon.*

A crazy-quilt of discontinuities. *Anon.*

A place where the crab-grass grows greenest.

Anon.

Snobdivisions. *Anon.*

SEE ALSO COMMUTER, MIDDLE CLASS.

SUCCESS

Success depends on faith and good deeds...not upon the knowledge of the proofs which lead to them. *Isaac Abravanel*

What an individual feels or thinks...each (person)...has a different meaning of, and attitude toward, what constitutes success. *Alfred Adler*

Not to get ahead of other people, but to get ahead of ourselves. *Maltbie D. Babcock*

Success is full of promise until men get it, and then it is a last-year's nest from which the birds have flown. *Henry Ward Beecher*

A form of amusement, mostly sacred to those who have not brains enough to attain it.

Thomas Beer

The one unpardonable sin against one's fellows.

Ambrose Bierce

Whenever we use our native capacities to their greatest extent. *Smiley Blanton*

The secret of success is sincerity. Once you can fake that you've got it made. *Arthur Bloch*

Each person working out for himself the compromises that will bring the self-fulfillment he seeks.

Eugene E. Brussell

The one who, early in life, clearly discerns his object, and towards that object habitually directs his powers. *Edward G. Bulwer-Lytton*

The only infallible criterion of wisdom to vulgar judgments. *Edmund Burke*

The true touchstone of desert. *Lord Byron*

Following the pattern of life one enjoys most.

Al Capp

The power with which to acquire whatever one demands of life without violating the rights of others. *Andrew Carnegie*

The true road to...success in any line is to make yourself master of that line. *Andrew Carnegie*

Putting all your eggs in one basket and then watching the basket.

Adapted from Andrew Carnegie

Success depends on previous preparation, and without such preparation there is sure to be failure. *Confucius*

Self-expression at a profit. *Marcelene Cox*

Willingness, readiness, alertness and courtesy.

Henry P. Davison

Women pushing their husbands along.

Thomas R. Dewar

Moving to become better. *John Dewey*

The child of audacity. *Benjamin Disraeli*

Constancy of purpose. *Benjamin Disraeli*

Never one thing and seldom one person can make for a success. It takes a number of them merging into one perfect whole. *Marie Dressler*

If A equals success, then the formula is A equals X plus Y plus Z. X is work. Y is play. Z is keep your mouth shut. *Albert Einstein*

A successful man is he who receives a great deal from his fellowmen, usually...more than corresponds to his service to them. *Albert Einstein*

Finding a better method.

Ralph Waldo Emerson

Never to fail to get what you desire; never to fall into what you would avoid. *Epictetus*

A result, not a goal. *Gustave Flaubert*

(To) have one's ideas exclusively focused on one central interest. *Sigmund Freud*

Consists of outgrowing your father's notions.

Adapted from Landon C. Garland

A chemical compound of man with moment.

Philip Guedalla

The test is simple and infallible. Are you able to save money? *James J. Hill*

The sole and earthly judge of right and wrong.

Adolf Hitler

Finding unobjectionable means for individual self-assertion. *Eric Hoffer*

Every man who can be a first-rate something—as every man can be who is a man at all.

Josiah G. Holland

To write your name high upon the outhouse of a country tavern. *Elbert Hubbard*

To rise from the illusion of pursuit to the disillusion of possession. *Elbert Hubbard*

The realization of the estimate which you place upon yourself. *Elbert Hubbard*

An illusion to all except its victims.

Elbert Hubbard

Keeping your mind awake and your desire asleep.

Adapted from Moses Ibn Ezra

The bitch-goddess. *William James*

What we back ourselves to be and do.

William James

What definition did Jesus give of "success"? He said that true success is to complete one's life. It is to attain to eternal life; all else is failure.

Toyohiko Kagawa

Stick to it long enough. *Helen A. Keller*

(Something that comes to those who) have always been cheerful and hopeful. *Charles Kingsley*

Consists in concentrating all efforts at all times upon one point. *Ferdinand Lassalle*

Not the result of spontaneous combustion. You must set yourself on fire. *Reginald Leach*

Merely luck and pluck... luck in finding someone to pluck. *Israel E. Leopold*

Nothing more than doing what you can do well; and doing well whatever you do, without a thought of fame. *Henry Wadsworth Longfellow*

In ourselves are triumph and defeat.

Henry Wadsworth Longfellow

That old ABC—ability, breaks and courage.

Charles Luckman

Failure kicked to pieces by hard work.

Jimmy Lyons

To know how to wait. *Joseph de Maistre*

The things you must scramble and elbow for ... They are the swill of life...leave them to swine.

Edward S. Martin

Seem a fool, but be wise.

Charles de Montesquieu

Life's greatest adventure. *Arthur Morgan*

To be able to spend your life in your own way.

Christopher Morley

Success depends on three things: who says it, what he says, how he says it; and of these three things, what he says is the least important.

John Morley

A great liar. *Friedrich W. Nietzsche*

A combination of hard work and breaks.

Richard Milhous Nixon

Fidelity is seven-tenths of business success.

James Parton

To burn always with this hard, gemlike flame, to maintain this ecstasy, is success in life.

Walter Pater

(To) be present always at the focus where the greatest number of vital forces unite in their purest energy. *Walter Pater*

Its formula is just about the same as that for a nervous breakdown. *Anthony Randall*

I can give you a six-word formula for success: "Think things through—then follow through."

Eddie V. Rickenbacker

Knowing how to get along with people.

Theodore Roosevelt

The people who get up and look for the circumstances they want and, if they can't find them, make them. *George Bernard Shaw*

(A state that) covers a multitude of blunders.

George Bernard Shaw

How can they say my life isn't a success? Have I not for more than sixty years got enough to eat and escaped being eaten? *Logan P. Smith*

The reward of toil. *Sophocles*

An earnest desire to succeed. *Stanislaus*

He...who has lived well, laughed often, and loved much. *A. J. Stanley*

Go with the crowd. *William W. Story*

Having ten honeydew melons and eating only the top half of each one. *Barbra Streisand*

(To) be able to foresee possibilities, to estimate with sagacity the outcome in the future.

Franklin W. Taussig

Only he . . . who makes that pursuit which affords him the highest pleasure sustain him.

Henry David Thoreau

The necessary misfortune of life, but it is only to the very unfortunate that it comes early.

Anthony Trollope

A poison that should only be taken late in life and then only in small doses. *Anthony Trollope*

Not so much by the position that one has reached in life as by the obstacles which you have overcome while trying.

Adapted from Booker T. Washington

Find out what you like doing best and get some one to pay you for doing it.

Katharine Whitehorn

The gallantry with which appalling experiences are survived with grace. *Tennessee Williams*

Success begins in a fellow's will;
It's all in the state of mind. *Walter D. Wintle*

Playing both ends against the middle. *Anon.*

Never committing yourself one way or the other on major issues. *Anon.*

Consists of getting others to do your work.

Anon.

The condition which grew out of the fear of being left behind. *Anon.*

Doing one task well. *Anon.*

The end of hope. *Anon.*

Getting what you want. Happiness is wanting what you get. *Anon.*

Making promises and keeping them. *Anon.*

The degree to which other people envy you.

Anon.

The real succeeders in life are the losers who keep trying. *Anon.*

SEE ALSO ECONOMICS, FAILURE, HAPPINESS, LUCK, PERSEVERANCE, WEALTH, WORK.

SUFFERING

A purification of the soul. *Henry F. Amiel*

A sacred trial sent by Eternal Love, a divine dispensation meant to sanctify and ennoble us, an acceptable aid to faith, a strange initiation into happiness. *Henry F. Amiel*

The main condition of the artistic experience.

Samuel Beckett

For I reckon that the sufferings of this present time are not worthy to be compared with the glory which shall be revealed in us.

Bible: Romans, VIII, 18.

Spiritual insight, a beauty of outlook, a philosophy of life, and understanding and forgiveness of humanity. *Louis E. Bisch*

A cleansing fire that clears away triviality and restlessness. *Louis E. Bisch*

The birth-throes of transition to better things.

John E. Boodin

The means of inspiration and survival.

Winston S. Churchill

The sole origin or consciousness.

Fëdor M. Dostoievski

A sure sign that you are alive. *Elbert Hubbard*

Nine-tenths . . . is caused by others not thinking so much of us as we think they ought. *Mary Lyon*

Craving for pleasures, craving for becoming, craving for not becoming.

Mahavagga of the Vinya Texts.

(A state which) makes men petty and vindictive.

William Somerset Maugham

A test of faith. *J. Messner*

One of the great structural lines of human life.

John W. Sullivan

The language of imperfection.

Rabindranath Tagore

The essence of life, because it is the inevitable product of an unresolvable tension between a living creature's essential impulse to try to make itself into the centre of the Universe and its essential dependence on the rest of Creation and on the Absolute Reality. *Arnold J. Toynbee*

The substance of life and the root of personality, for it is only suffering that makes us persons.

Miguel de Unamuno

One of the ways of knowing you're alive.

Jessamyn West

A revelation. One discovers things one never discovered before.   *Oscar Wilde*

Making more money to meet obligations you wouldn't have if you didn't make so much money.

    Anon.

SEE ALSO EXPERIENCE, ILLNESS, MISERY, PAIN, SORROW, TRAGEDY.

SUICIDE

Allowing yourself to be conquered by misfortune and seeking refuge in death.

    Adapted from Agathon

To die in order to avoid anything that is evil and disagreeable.   *Aristotle*

Cheating doctors out of a job.   *Josh Billings*

Man's attempt to give a final human meaning to a life which has become humanly meaningless.

    Dietrich Bonhoeffer

An act of justice normal men have no stomach for.

    John Ciardi

The worst form of murder, because it leaves no opportunity for repentance.   *Churton Collins*

The effect of cowardice in the highest extreme.

    Daniel Defoe

A sin. Life has a purpose.

    Mohandas K. Gandhi

The simplest of human rights.

    Charlotte P. Gilman

Striving to outdo one's companions on the golf course and tennis court or in the swimming pool constitutes several socially acceptable forms of suicide.   *George Griffith*

Felony upon himself.   *Legal Phrase*

The severset form of self-criticism.

    Leonard L. Levinson

A bastard valor.   *Philip Massinger*

Suicide is a belated acquiescence in the opinion of one's wife's relatives.   *Henry Louis Mencken*

The extraordinary propensity of the human being to join hands with external forces in an attack on his own existence.   *Karl Menninger*

To desert from the world's garrison without the express command of him who has placed us there.

    Michel de Montaigne

It is the role of cowardice...to crouch in a hole, under a massive tomb, to avoid the blows of fortune.   *Michel de Montaigne*

To abandon the world.   *William Mountford*

Cowardice.   *Napoleon I*

Amid the miseries of our life on earth, suicide is God's best gift to man.   *Pliny I*

Self-slaughter.   *William Shakespeare*

Those who commit suicide are powerless souls, and allow themselves to be conquered by external causes repugnant to their nature.

    Baruch Spinoza

When one has no more hope...a duty.   *Voltaire*

An accusation against those you leave behind.

    Eli Wallach

Confession.   *Daniel Webster*

What every gentleman promises to do if he breaks his vow to his beloved.   *Anon.*

The way out for the weak.   *Anon.*

The final act brought on by the fear of one's mode of life.   *Anon.*

Insanity.   *Anon.*

SUMMER

The season of inferior sledding.

    Eskimo Proverb

The time for exploring: for visiting our own country or one of its regions; for seeing a foreign land; for learning more of nature.

    Gilbert Highet

There is something of summer in the hum of insects.   *Walter Savage Landor*

To some the gravestone of a dead delight, to some the landmark of a new domain.

    Adapted from Henry Wadsworth Longfellow

(A season that) hath all too short a date.

    William Shakespeare

Days dripping away like honey off a spoon.

    Wallace Stegner

The time of year that children slam the door they left open all winter.   *Anon.*

The most beautiful word in the English language.

    Anon.

SUNDAY

(A day that) clears away the rust of the whole week.   *Joseph Addison*

The one great poem of New England.
                                 Henry Ward Beecher

The core of our civilization, dedicated to thought and reverence.   *Ralph Waldo Emerson*

The golden clasp that binds together the volume of the week.   *Henry Wadsworth Longfellow*

Day of all the week the best,
Emblem of eternal rest.   *John Newton*

The day on which we all hold our common assembly, because it is the first day on which God, when He changed the darkness and matter, made the world; and Jesus Christ our Saviour, on the same, rose from the dead.   *Saint Justin*

A continual proclamation of the message of Easter: Christ is risen.   *Gustave Wingren*

The one day of the week we act hypocrtically.
                                              Anon.

SEE ALSO PREACHING, SABBATH.

SUNDAY SCHOOL

A prison in which children do penance for the evil conscience of their parents.
                                 Henry Louis Mencken

SUPERIOR MAN

He who surpasses or subdues mankind.
                                        Lord Byron

He who chooses the right with invincible resolution.   *William Ellery Channing*

(He who is) ready not only to take opportunities, but to make them.   *Charles Caleb Colton*

The superior man is dignified, but not proud; the inferior man is proud but not dignified.
                                            Confucius

(One who) is slow in his words and earnest in his conduct.   *Confucius*

There are three marks of a superior man: being virtuous, he is free from anxiety; being wise, he is free from perplexity; being brave, he is free from fear.   *Confucius*

The personification and type of the epoch for which God destines him.   *Jean M. d'Aubigné*

He who would master no one, and who would be mastered by none.   *Kahlil Gibran*

The uneasy obligation.   *William Hazlitt*

The superior man...stands erect by bending above the fallen. He rises by lifting others.
                                    Robert G. Ingersoll

They...who have the best heart—the best brain.
                                    Robert G. Ingersoll

Signposts on the road to humanity.
                                    Guiseppe Mazzini

The man...who lives in essential servitude. Life has no savour for him unless he makes it consistent in service to something transcendental...he does not look upon the necessity of serving as an oppression.   *José Ortega y Gasset*

Life lived as a discipline—the noble life.
                                  José Ortega y Gasset

He who is urged, by interior necessity, to appeal from himself to some standard beyond himself, superior to himself, whose service he freely accepts.   *José Ortega y Gasset*

He who contemns what he finds in his mind without previous effort, and only accepts as worthy of him what is still far above him and what requires a further effort in order to be reached.
                                  José Ortega y Gasset

(He who) rises to greatness if greatness is expected of him.   *Adapted from John Steinbeck*

SEE ALSO ARISTOCRAT, GENIUS, GREATNESS, HERO, MINORITY, NOBILITY.

SUPERSTITION

The reproach of the Deity.   *Francis Bacon*

The religion of feeble minds.   *Edmund Burke*

A force which has taken advantage of human weakness to cast its spell over the mind of almost every man.   *Adapted from Cicero*

A senseless fear of God.   *Cicero*

The giant shadow which the solicitude of weak mortality casts on the thin mist of the uncertain future.   *Adapted from Samuel Taylor Coleridge*

The weakness of the human mind; it is inherent in that mind; it has always been, and always will be.
Frederick the Great

The poetry of life.   *Johann W. Goethe*

Godless religion, devout impiety.   *Joseph Hall*

Scrambled science flavored with fear.
Elbert Hubbard

A premature explanation that overstays its time.
George Iles

The only religion of which base souls are capable.
Joseph Joubert

The poison of the mind.   *Joseph Lewis*

Something that has been left to stand over, like unfinished business, from one session of the world's witenagemot to the next.
James Russell Lowell

False and fraudulent notions with which old idolaters...mislead the ignorant masses in order to exploit them.   *Moses Maimonides.*

The greatest burden in the world...not only of ceremonies in the Church, but of imaginary and scarecrow sins at home.   *John Milton*

The belief that all stage kisses give no satisfaction to the actor or actresses.   *George Jean Nathan*

This vague ague of the mind.   *Walter Scott*

Religion which has grown incongruous with intelligence.   *John Tyndall*

Any practice or form of religion to which we are not accustomed.   *Voltaire*

A serpent which chokes religion in its embrace.
Voltaire

Superstition is to religion what astrology is to astronomy—the mad daughter of a wise mother.
Voltaire

Conscience without judgment.
Benjamin Whichcote

Mysticism with paranoia.   *Anon.*

SUPREME COURT

Our business is not to write laws to fit the day. Our task is to interpret the Constitution.
Hugo Black

The highest court of appeal. It determines our country's laws, and is totally immune to public sentiment. From it there is no appeal. It can be both a blessing and a curse.   *Eugene E. Brussell*

Has been viewed by the people as the true expounder of their Constitution.
Andrew Johnson

(Those who) interpret the law and leave to Congress the writing of law.
Richard Milhous Nixon

A frequent tyranny which imposes its will on every citizen in the country.   *Anon.*

SURGEON

A good medical man who can cut.
Martin H. Fischer

An eagle's eye, a lion's heart, a lady's hand.
John Ray

SEE ALSO DOCTORS.

SURGERY

Surgery does the ideal thing—it separates the patient from his disease. It puts the patient back to bed and the disease in a bottle.
Logan Clendening

The practice of medicine is a thinker's art, the practice of surgery a plumber's.
Martin H. Fischer

Operating on someone who has no place else to go.   *John Kirklin*

All practice is theory; all surgery is practice; ergo, all surgery is theory.   *Lanfranc*

By far the worst snob among the handicrafts.
Austin O'Malley

SEE ALSO DOCTORS, MEDICINE.

SURVIVAL

The desire to effect a continuation of group life which is rooted in a conviction of the worthwhileness of living.   *Eugene E. Brussell*

The art of lying to yourself heroically, continuously, creatively.   *Benjamin de Casseres*

Victory at all costs.   *Winston S. Churchill*

Meeting what is demanded of us in order to push on.   *Jerry Dashkin*

Moral control and the return to spiritual order.
                              Christopher Dawson

An interest in life, good, bad or peculiar.
                                     Grace Paley

A condition that exists when death does not call.
                                           Anon.

The accolade we give ourselves for not dying.
                                           Anon.

SEE ALSO EVOLUTION, LIFE, LIVING, NATURAL SELECTION.

SUSPICION

Superabundance of suspicion is a kind of political madness.   *Francis Bacon*

Suspicions that the mind, of itself, gathers, are but buzzes; but suspicions that are artificially nourished and put into men's heads by the tales and whisperings of others, have strings.
                                   Francis Bacon

There is one safeguard known generally to the wise, which is an advantage and security to all, but especially to democracies as against despots—suspicion.   *Demosthenes*

The friendship that one actress has for another.
                                  Eleonora Duse

The badge of base-born minds.   *Virginia Moore*

The companion of mean souls.   *Thomas Paine*

What people think other people are thinking.
                                           Anon.

SEE ALSO DOUBT, SKEPTICISM.

SWEARING

SEE PROFANITY, VULGARITY.

SWITZERLAND

Beautiful but dumb.   *Edna Ferber*

What a pale historic coloring; what a penury of relics and monuments! I pined for a cathedral or a gallery.   *Henry James*

An inferior sort of Scotland.   *Sydney Smith*

A land of grave people.   *Anon.*

A country whose conservatism is a way of life.
                                           Anon.

The country of banks and cautious views.
                                           Anon.

A nation of bankers, merchants and cheese eaters.
                                           Anon.

SYCOPHANT

SEE FLATTERER.

SYMBOLS

Whoever has the symbol has thereby the beginning of the spiritual idea; symbol and reality together furnish the whole.   *Odo Casel*

A simplification and subordination of the concrete complexity in order to point a moral.
                              Ralph Barton Perry

The primary mode of our becoming aware of things. They are the way we register meanings in our depths.   *Gail C. Richardson*

Symbols are directed toward the infinite which they symbolize and toward the infinite through which they symbolize it. They force the infinite down to finitude and the finite up to infinity. They open the divine for the human and the human for the divine.   *Paul Tillich*

Man's ultimate concern must be expressed symbolically, because symbolic language alone is able to express the ultimate.   *Paul Tillich*

The symbol or significant image, is not...a substitute for spiritual truth. It is rather the point where the physical and metaphysical meet—a half-way house where the world of things and the world of spirit unite.   *Evelyn Underhill*

SYMPATHY

Rejoice with them that do rejoice, and weep with them that weep.   *Bible: Romans, XII, 15.*

Dissolved selfishness.   *Ludwig Boerne*

A fellow-feeling.   *Robert Burton*

A right attitude to the riddles of the universe. You must tune up your heart to catch the music of the spheres.   *Morris R. Cohen*

Chords in the human mind.   *Charles Dickens*

A virtue unknown in nature.   *Paul Eipper*

Harmony of aim, not identity of conclusion, is the secret of the sympathetic life.
Ralph Waldo Emerson

An impulse toward ourselves through the heart of another.   *Elbert Hubbard*

Whatever may be extended to another that does not take the shape of money.   *Elbert Hubbard*

Two hearts tugging at one load.
Charles H. Parkhurst

A heart that understands.   *Victor Robinson*

Subconscious self-pity.   *Harry Ruby*

What you feel for a man you wish were somewhere else.   *John Steinbeck*

What you give to someone when you don't want to loan him money.   *Anon.*

What one woman offers to another for all the details.   *Anon.*

Your pain in my heart.   *Anon.*

SEE ALSO FELLOWSHIP, KINDNESS, PITY, TOLERANCE.

SYNAGOGUE

Any ten men.   *Felix Adler*

The synagogue alone speaks of the common striving of a group of Jews to establish a conscious relationship between themselves and God.
Simon Greenberg

Congregational worship and edification, conducted by the congregation through their own members.   *Robert T. Herford*

Schools . . . we call our houses of worship, and that is what they should be, schools for the grown-up.
Samson R. Hirsch

The one unfailing wellspring of Jewish feeling. There we pray together with our brethren, and in the act become participators in the common sentiment, the collective conscience, of Israel.
Joseph Morris

The strength of Judaism.   *Ernest Renan*

A community of people whom the rabbi cares about and who care about each other.
Steven Riskin

SEE ALSO JEWS, JUDAISM, RABBI.

T

TACT

The rare ability to keep silent while two friends are arguing, and you know both of them are wrong. *Hugh Allen*

Knowing how far we may go too far.
Jean Cocteau

Granting graciously what you cannot refuse safely, and conciliating those you cannot conquer.
Adapted from Charles Caleb Colton

The poise that refreshes. *Raymond J. Cvikota*

Tongue in check. *Susan Dytri*

A subtle form of flattery. *Max Gralnick*

A halter in the house. *George Herbert*

A kind of mind reading. *Sarah Orne Jewett*

The ability to stay in the middle without getting caught there. *Franklin P. Jones*

The ability to describe others as they see themselves. *Abraham Lincoln*

The art of convincing people that they know more than you do. *Raymond Mortimer*

The knack of making a point without making an enemy. *Howard W. Newton*

One of the first mental virtues, the absence of which is often fatal to the best of talents; it supplies the place of many talents.
W. G. Simms

To keep silent and draw one's own confusions.
Cornelia Otis Skinner

The unsaid part of what you think.
Henry Van Dyke

That rare talent for not quite telling the truth.
Anon.

To leave unsaid the wrong thing at the tempting moment. *Anon.*

The art of saying whatever is required—including nothing. *Anon.*

Intelligence of the heart. *Anon.*

Closing your mouth before someone feels the urge to. *Anon.*

SEE ALSO DIPLOMACY, MANNERS, POLITENESS, SILENCE.

TALENT

To do easily what is difficult for others.
Henry F. Amiel

A faucet; while it is open, one must write.
Jean Anouilh

A valued tormentor. *Truman Capote*

Every man has his proper gift of God, one after this manner, and another after that.
Bible: Corinthians, V, 7.

Reason manifested gloriously.

Marie J. de Chénier

(Something) everyone has at twenty five. The difficulty is to have it at fifty.   *Edgar Degas*

Every natural power.   *Ralph Waldo Emerson*

Each man has his vocation. Talent is the call.

Ralph Waldo Emerson

Habitual facility of execution.

Ralph Waldo Emerson

Profound sincerity is the only basis of talent.

Ralph Waldo Emerson

(The) power and courage to make a new road to new and better goals.   *Ralph Waldo Emerson*

The tools to him who has the ability to handle them.   *French Proverb*

Talent differs from genius, as voluntary differs from involuntary power.   *William Hazlitt*

The confidence that by persistence and patience something worthwhile will be realized. Thus talent is a species of vigor.   *Eric Hoffer*

That which is in a man's power; genius is that in whose power a man is.   *James Russell Lowell*

A gift which God has given us secretly, and which we reveal without perceiving it.

Charles de Montesquieu

You cannot define talent. All you can do is build a greenhouse and see if it grows.

William P. Steven

To have talent, one must have character: abilities and natural disposition by themselves make no talent.   *Rahel L. Varnhagen*

An infinite capacity for imitating genius.

Anon.

SEE ALSO SUCCESS, WORK.

TALK

To give the occasion; and again to moderate and pass to someone else; for then a man leads the dance.   *Francis Bacon*

The talk of the lips tendeth only to penury.

Bible: Proverbs, XIV, 23.

A substitute for creative work, and its worst enemy.   *Eugene E. Brussell*

Liquidation of serious projects.

Eugene E. Brussell

The fun of talk is to find out what a man really thinks, and then contrast it with the enormous lies he has been telling all dinner, and perhaps all his life.   *Benjamin Disraeli*

You can talk when you cease to be at peace with your thoughts.   *Kahlil Gibran*

The greatest of all Jewish sports.   *Harry Golden*

The four-letter word for psychotherapy.

Eric Hodgins

Like playing on the harp; there is as much in laying the hands on the strings to stop their vibration as in twanging them to bring out their music.   *Oliver Wendell Holmes 1*

To open and close the mouth rapidly while the bellows in the throat pumps out the gas in the brain.   *Elbert Hubbard*

The disease of the age.   *Ben Jonson*

All natural talk is a festival of ostentation...each accepts and fans the vanity of the other.

Robert Lewis Stevenson

As the man is, so is his talk.   *Publilius Syrus*

The means by which we cure our sorrow.   *Anon.*

SEE ALSO CONVERSATION, SPEECH, TONGUE.

TALMUD

A literary monument of the national hegemony established and maintained by the autonomous communities of Roman Palestine and Persian Babylonia.   *Simon M. Dubnow*

A monument embodying the efforts of the leaders to build a strong shell of the Law around the shattered kernel of the nation.

Simon M. Dubnow

The Catholicism of the Jews.   *Heinrich Heine*

A hierarchy of religious laws, which often treat of the drollest, most ridiculous subtleties, yet are so intelligently arranged...and coincide with such...logical force, that they constitute a formidable and colossal whole.   *Henrich Heine*

The inner meaning of Talmudism is unshakable trust in God and unreserved obedience to His declared will.   *Robert T. Herford*

A fortress which had helped the Jews to maintain their distinctiveness amidst the peoples.

Vladimir Solovyov

An index of free thinking.   *Israel Zangwill*

SEE ALSO JUDAISM.

TASTE

A discerning sense of decent and sublime, with disgust for things deformed in species.

Adapted from Mark Akenside

Essentially a master of tradition.

William C. Brownell

Genius creates, and taste preserves. Taste is the good sense of genius; without taste, genius is only sublime folly.   *Francois de Chateaubriand*

Nothing else than reason delicately put in force.

Marie J. de Chenier

Love of beauty is taste.   *Ralph Waldo Emerson*

A fine judgment in discerning art.   *Horace*

The literary conscience of the soul.

Joseph Joubert

The only morality.   *John Ruskin*

The instinctive and instant preferring of one material object to another without any obvious reason, except that it is proper to human nature in its perfection so to do.   *John Ruskin*

Fine taste is an aspect of genius itself, and is the faculty of delicate appreciation, which makes the best effects of art our own.   *Nathaniel P. Willis*

Nothing but a propensity for something that pleases you.   *Anon.*

SEE ALSO CUSTOM, FASHION, HABIT.

TAXES

Joseph made it a law over the land of Egypt unto this day, that Pharaoh should have the fifth part.

Bible: Genesis, XLVII, 26.

Burdens unnecessarily laid upon...by...governments.   *William H. Borah*

Tribute to the common treasury.

Edmund Burke

A fund to be divided between different interests with political claims upon the state.

Neville Chamberlain

The sinews of the state.   *Cicero*

To create a class of persons who do not labor, to take from those who do labor the produce of that labor, and to give it to those who do not labor.

William Cobbett

Consists in so plucking the goose as to get the most feathers with the least hissing.

Jean B. Colbert

The simplest leverage known to society for directing social impulses.   *Morris Ernst*

Something that is heavy but immune to gravity.

Max Gralnick

Simple robbery.   *Hillel*

The price we pay for civilized society.

Oliver Wendell Holmes 2

A payment exacted by authority from part of the community for the benefit of the whole.

Samuel Johnson

Under every form...a choice of evils.

David Ricardo

A diminution of freedom.   *Herbert Spencer*

The fine we pay for thriving.   *Anon.*

The other certainty.   *Anon.*

The dues charged to belong to a certain geographical area.   *Anon.*

The process by which money is collected from the people to pay the salaries of the men who do the collecting.   *Anon.*

TAX INVESTIGATOR

A bracket buster.   *Anon.*

A man of few but well chosen words.   *Anon.*

A fiction reader.   *Anon.*

Someone more concerned with how you spend your money than how the government spends it.

Anon.

TAXPAYER

Someone who works for the federal government, but who doesn't have to take a civil service examination.   *Ronald Reagan*

One who has the government on his payroll.

Anon.

TEA

(Something so) proportioned to the human constitution as to warm without heating, to cheer but not to inebriate. *George Berkeley*

A glorious insipidity. *Colley Cibber*

Slopkettle. *William Cobbett*

The cups that cheer but not inebriate.
William Cowper

There is a great deal of poetry and fine sentiment in a chest of tea. *Ralph Waldo Emerson*

A stimulant, a thirst quencher, and a drug, the greatest English common denominator.
Anthony Mayer

Where small talk dies in agonies.
Percy Bysshe Shelley

An affront to luncheon and an insult to dinner.
Mark Twain

The favorite drink of the refined. *Anon.*

TEACHER

The true teacher defends his pupils against his own personal influence. *Amos Bronson Alcott*

(One who) should have an atmosphere of awe, and walk wonderingly, as if he was amazed at being himself. *Walter Bagehot*

The child's third parent.
Hyman Maxwell Berston

(A) sallow, virgin-minded, studious martyr to mild enthusiasm. *Robert Browning*

One who makes himself progressively unnecessary. *Thomas Carruthers*

(One who) should be sparing of his smile.
William Cowper

The man who can make hard things easy.
Ralph Waldo Emerson

(One) who kindly sets a wanderer on his way.
Quintus Ennius

Two kinds: the kind that fill you with so much quail shot that you can't move, and the kind that just give you a little prod behind and you jump to the skies. *Robert Frost*

A person who lessons your knowledge.
Warren Goldberg

The vanity of teaching often tempts a man to forget he is a blockhead. *Lord Halifax*

Like torches, a light to others, waste and destruction to themselves. *Richard Hooker*

A person...who instills into the head of another person...the sum and substance of his or her ignorance. *Elbert Hubbard*

One who makes two ideas grow where only one grew before. *Elbert Hubbard*

One who sweeps his living from the posteriors of little children. *Adapted from Ben Jonson*

He is awkward, and out of place, in the society of his equals. He comes like Gulliver from among his little people, and he cannot fit the stature of his understanding to yours. *Charles Lamb*

The average schoolmaster is and always must be an ass, for how can one imagine an intelligent man engaging in so puerile an avocation?
Henry Louis Mencken

One who in his youth, admired teachers.
Henry Louis Mencken

Not one who knows the most, but the one who is most capable of reducing knowledge to that simple compound of the obvious and the wonderful which slips into the infantile comprehension.
Henry Louis Mencken

The best teacher of children...is one who is essentially childlike. *Henry Louis Mencken*

It is the mission of the pedagogue, not to make his pupils think, but to make them think right.
Henry Louis Mencken

The candle which lights others in consuming itself. *Giovanni Ruffini*

He who can, does. He who cannot, teaches.
George Bernard Shaw

The Christian teacher's problem; to study and to teach science so as to include—or at least not to exclude—the Christian view of nature.
F. Sherwood Taylor

Everybody who is incapable of learning has taken to teaching. *Oscar Wilde*

(Those who) liberate American citizens to think apart and to act together. *Stephen S. Wise*

One who doesn't care anything about what you know, and knows all about things you don't care about.   *Anon.*

The best raise fundamental questions without answering them.   *Anon.*

One who frees his students from extreme modernity.   *Anon.*

God's mind at work to help grow the best possible plants in God's garden.   *Anon.*

SEE ALSO COLLEGE, EDUCATION, LEARNING, MOTHER, SCHOOL, TEACHING, UNIVERSITY.

TEACHING

To know how to suggest.   *Henry F. Amiel*

It is always safe to learn, even from our enemies—seldom safe to venture to instruct, even our friends.   *Charles Caleb Colton*

To awaken joy in creative expression and knowledge.   *Albert Einstein*

The same persons telling to the same people the same things about the same things.
                          Greek Proverb

To cultivate talent until it ripens for the public to reap its bounty.   *Jascha Heifetz*

The object of teaching a child is to enable him to get along without his teacher.   *Elbert Hubbard*

There is no other method of teaching that of which anyone is ignorant but by means of something already known.   *Samuel Johnson*

To learn twice.   *Joseph Joubert*

Guidance of our mind.   *Joseph Joubert*

The art of assisting discovery.   *Mark Van Doren*

The result of continued search for greater insight and constant effort to improve skills and procedures.   *Kimball Wiles*

It is achieved...by study, by evaluation, by experimentation, and by revision of goals, theory, and techniques in the light of new data.
                          Kimball Wiles

To appear to have known all your life what you learned this afternoon.   *Anon.*

The profession that has ruined more novelists than alcohol.   *Anon.*

The liquidation of illiteracy.   *Anon.*

SEE ALSO BOOK, EDUCATION, LEARNING, PROFESSOR, SCHOOL, TEACHER.

TEARS

The tribute of humanity to its destiny.
                          William R. Alger

Summer showers to the soul.   *Alfred Austin*

The telescope by which men see far into heaven.
                          Henry Ward Beecher

The ease of woe.   *Richard Crashaw*

Rain upon the blinding dust of earth, overlying our hard hearts.   *Charles Dickens*

    The aftermark
Of almost too much love,
The sweet of bitter bark
And burning clove.   *Robert Frost*

The noble language of the eye.   *Robert Herrick*

The mark...of power. They speak more eloquently than ten thousand tongues.
                          Washington Irving

The best gift of God to suffering man.
                          John Keble

Remorse code.   *I. Masai*

The most efficient water power in the world—woman's tears.   *Wilson Mizner*

There are tears of grief and tears of joy, but I've yet to see someone whose eyes have grown red from tears of joy.   *Moritz Saphir*

Woman's weapons.   *William Shakespeare*

Holy water.   *William Shakespeare*

The great interpreter.
                          Adapted from Frederic R. Torrence

The silent language of grief.   *Voltaire*

The refuge of plain women, but the ruin of pretty ones.   *Oscar Wilde*

An activity that makes you feel better.   *Anon.*

SEE ALSO GRIEF, SORROW, TRAGEDY, WOMEN.

TEDIOUS

SEE BOREDOM.

TELEPHONE

An invention of the devil which abrogates some of the advantages of making a disagreeable person keep his distance.   *Ambrose Bierce*

The greatest nuisance among the conveniences, the greatest convenience among nuisances.
Robert Lynd

Some one invented the telephone,
And interrupted a nation's slumbers,
Ringing wrong but similar numbers.
Ogden Nash

A device to connect you with strangers.   *Anon.*

An ingenious invention used by juveniles to call other juveniles for long periods of time.   *Anon.*

A device which does not ask questions but must be answered.   *Anon.*

TELEVISION

A device that permits people who haven't anything to do to watch people who can't do anything.   *Fred Allen*

A kind of radio which lets people at home see what the studio audience is not laughing at.
Fred Allen

Radio fluoroscoped.   *Fred Allen*

The triumph of machinery over people.
Fred Allen

Television is called a medium because anything good on it is rare.   *Fred Allen*

A built-in mediocrity...just an adjunct of the advertising business.   *Dana Andrews*

The first truly democratic culture—the first culture available to everybody and...governed by what people want.   *Clive Barnes*

(Television) has re-created for the great modern democracies one of the conditions of the Greek city-state: all citizens can see and hear their leaders.   *Lord Brain*

Chewing gum for the eyes.   *John Mason Brown*

The longest amateur night in history.
Robert Carson

(An)...amusement park...a circus...We're in the boredom-killing business.   *Paddy Chayefsky*

Democracy at its ugliest.   *Paddy Chayefsky*

A stench in the nostrils of the ionosphere.
Lee De Forest

The bright grey blackboard.   *Henry Dieuzeide*

A medium of entertainment which permits millions of people to listen to the same joke at the same time and yet remain lonesome.

Thomas Stearns Eliot

An invention that permits you to be entertained in your living room by people you wouldn't have in your home.   *David Frost*

The eternal rectangle.   *Shelby Friedman*

A medium. So called because it is neither rare nor well-done.   *Ernie Kovacs*

Simply automated day dreaming.   *Leon Lovinger*

Nothing but auditions.   *Joseph L. Mankiewicz*

Where all little movies go when they're bad.
Ronald Poulton

A nightly national seance.   *Daniel Schorr*

The best gauge of our decay.   *John Stevenson*

Vidiot's delight.   *Anon.*

A device that enables you to see static as well as hear it.   *Anon.*

A device that some people dislike so much that they spend all night glaring at it.   *Anon.*

Radio with eye-strain.   *Anon.*

The visual cliché.   *Anon.*

Summer stock in an iron lung.   *Anon.*

An invention which has proven that sight has a noticeable aroma.   *Anon.*

The bland leading the bland.   *Anon.*

A vast cultural wasteland.   *Anon.*

Boob-tube.   *Anon.*

TELEVISION COMMERCIAL

The last refuge of optimism in a world of gloom.
Cedric Hardwicke

Photoelectric sell.   *Lane Olinghouse*

The opening and closing quarter hours of a half-hour show.   *Anon.*

TEMPER

SEE ANGER.

TEMPERANCE

A kind of regimen. *Joseph Addison*

Health, longevity, beauty, are other names for personal purity; and temperance is the regimen for all. *Amos Bronson Alcott*

Abstaining from indulgence. *Aristotle*

The best physic. *Henry G. Bohn*

The moderating of one's desires in obedience to reason. *Cicero*

Consists in foregoing bodily pleasures. *Cicero*

The exercise of our faculties and organs in such a manner as to combine the maximum of pleasure with the minimum of pain. *Norman Douglas*

The golden mean. *Horace*

A disposition of the mind which sets bounds to the passions. *Saint Thomas Aquinas*

An angelic exercise...A greater good than marriage. *Saint Augustine*

(Not) giving more to the flesh than we ought.
Adapted from Saint Gregory

Temperance knows that the best measure of the appetite is not what you want to take, but what you ought to take. *Seneca*

Not the absence of passion, but...the transfiguring of passion into wholeness. *Gerald Vann*

Under some circumstances...a duty...never a virtue, it being without any moral quality whatever. *Richard G. White*

Moderation in the things that are good and total abstinence from the things that are bad.
Frances E. Willard

The nurse of chastity. *William Wycherley*

SEE ALSO MODERATION.

TEMPTATION

The strange god in man. *Abin*

A stumbling-block or an occasion to fall.
Bible: Romans, XIV, 13.

The voice of the suppressed evil. *J. A. Hadfield*

Honest bread is very well—it's the butter that makes the temptation. *Douglas Jerrold*

An irresistible force at work on a moveable body.
Henry Louis Mencken

The fiend at my elbow. *William Shakespeare*

The cunning livery of hell.
William Shakespeare

The whole effort—the object—of temptation is to induce us to substitute something else for God. To obscure God. *R. H. Stewart*

SEE ALSO DEVIL, EVIL, SIN.

TEN COMMANDMENTS

A series of commandments, ten in number,—just enough to permit an intelligent selection for observance, but not enough to embarrass the choice.
Ambrose Bierce

A series of commandments which form the keystone of two major religions, Christianity and Judaism. *Eugene E. Brussell*

SEE ALSO BIBLE, COMMANDMENT.

TENSION

A function of freedom. Only the fully domesticated animal...can or should expect a life devoid of continuous tension. From tension...all human progress springs. *Felix Morley*

TERROR

A sudden madness and paralysis of the soul.
Hilaire Belloc

The stampede of our self-possession.
Antoine Rivarol

Mass hysteria. *Phillip Wylie*

Rumor on fire. *Anon.*

SEE ALSO FEAR.

TEXAN

Those who insist on remaining ranch hands or drill riggers despite ample resources for bettering their estate and persons. Their gestures of philanthropy run to Methodist universities, football teams and drum majorettes.

Adapted from Lucius Beebe

TEXAS

One great, windy lunatic.   *Socrates Hyacinth*

A state of mind.   *John Steinbeck*

A place with more cows and less milk, more rivers and less water, and you can look farther to see less than anywhere else on earth.   *Anon.*

The state where you look the most to see the least.

Anon.

THAMES, THE

Liquid history.   *John Burns*

The thronged river toiling to the main.

Hartley Coleridge

The great street paved with water, filled with shipping, and all the world's flags flying and seagulls dipping.

Adapted from John Masefield

Serene yet strong, majestic yet sedate, swift without violence, without terror great.

Adapted from Matthew Prior

That mysterious forest below London Bridge.

John Ruskin

At once London's highroad and its sewer.

John H. Wilson

London's liquid artery.   *Anon.*

SEE ALSO RIVER.

THANKSGIVING DAY

A day celebrated not so much to thank the Lord for blessings as for the sake of getting more.

Adapted from William Carleton

Once every year we throng upon a day apart to praise the Lord with feast and song in thankfulness of heart.

Adapted from Arthur Guiterman

The only day that is purely American.   *O. Henry*

A national holiday on which all the people who during the past year have survived earthquake, fire, housemaid's knee and death, overeat and thus thank God for his favoritism.

Elbert Hubbard

Over three centuries ago, our forefathers in Virginia and in Massachusetts far from home in a lonely wilderness set aside a time for Thanksgiving.   *John Fitzgerald Kennedy*

THEATER

A crisis which is resolved either in death or in the return to complete health.   *Antonin Artaud*

The genesis of creation. It will be done.

Antonin Artaud

The first serum that man invented to protect himself from the sickness of despair.

Jean-Louis Barrault

(No more) than the conclusion to a dinner or the prelude to a supper.   *Max Beerbohm*

The challenge of the mighty line.

John Drinkwater

Keen satire is the business of the stage.

George Farquhar

Nothing but heathenism.   *Henry Fielding*

A window open on the life of our fellow creatures.

Mario Fratti

That smaller world which is the stage.

Isaac Goldberg

Life's moving pictures.   *Matthew Green*

Everybody has his own theatre, in which he is manager, actor, prompter, playwright, scene-shifter, boxkeeper, doorkeeper, and audience.

Julius and Augustus Hare

A world.   *Oliver Wendell Holmes 1*

Simply what cannot be expressed by any other means...A complexity of words, movements, gestures that convey a vision of the world unexpressible in any other way.   *Eugene Ionesco*

A spiritual compulsion. Once it celebrated the gods. Now it broods over the fate of man.

Ludwig Lewisohn

The last free institution in the amusement world.

Richard Maney

A place for diverting representation.

Henry Louis Mencken

A place where you can hear every variety of cough.   *Rose Mortinson*

An undying institution because it educates its audience's emotions.   *George Jean Nathan*

An escape from reality.   *George Jean Nathan*

The notorious badge of prostituted strumpets and the lewdest Harlots.   *William Prynne*

Sinful, heathenish, lewd, ungodly Spectacles ... condemned in all ages, as intolerable Mischiefs to Churches, to Republics, to the manners, minds and souls of men.   *William Prynne*

A wonderful holiday.   *Anthony Richardson*

A tradition of villains and heroes.

George Bernard Shaw

SEE ALSO ACTOR, DRAMA.

THEFT

SEE THIEF

THEISM

If theism is true there is only one world. "In Him we live and move and have our being." There is no outside to God. The universe is His mental creation, as truly as our dreams are the products of our thoughts.   *Charles E. Garman*

The only metaphysical position that has any consistent answer to the problem of life. It affirms that there is one law of being for the entire universe.   *Charles E. Garman*

The simple worship of God.   *Voltaire*

Good sense not yet instructed by revelation.

Voltaire

SEE ALSO GOD, RELIGION.

THEIST

He knows the divine presence to be mediated through his human experience. He ... finds himself interpreting his experience in this way.

John Hicks

A man firmly persuaded of the existence of a supreme being as good as he is powerful, who has formed all things ... who punishes, without cruelty, all crimes, and recompenses with goodness all virtuous actions.   *Voltaire*

THEOCRACY

The synonym for a bleak and narrow, if not a fierce and blood-stained tyranny.

William Archer

Government of God ... the thing to be struggled for.   *Thomas Carlyle*

The theory of "theocracy" suggests the absolute rule of God, or a polity of passive obedience.

Ralph Barton Perry

THEOLOGIAN

Means to take up the burden of rational analysis, exposition, and argument.   *Robert L. Calhoun*

The first of the professions, because it is necessary for all times.   *Samuel Taylor Coleridge*

(Those whose) opinion of themselves is so great that they behave as if they were already in heaven.

Desiderius Erasmus

Their aim is always to wield despotic authority over men's consciences.   *Frederick the Great*

Precisely what his name indicates—a man who thinks, and then gives us the fruit of this thought, about God.   *Aelred Graham*

The theologian seems to be less a philosopher and more a social engineer and ... a social psychoanalyst.   *Shailer Matthews*

Every religious man is to a certain extent a theologian.   *John Henry Newman*

Every creative philosopher is a hidden theologian.

Paul Tillich

THEOLOGY

The science of the divine lie.

Mikhail A. Bakunin

Science of mind applied to God.

Henry Ward Beecher

That madness gone systematic which tries to crowd God's fullness into a formula and a system.

Joel Blau

Those wingy mysteries in divinity, and airy subtleties in religion.   *Thomas Browne*

A philosophical formula for buttressing a religion.   *Eugene E. Brussell*

A rational superstructure erected on the foundations of the Christian theology of revelation.

Christopher Dawson

The rhetoric of morals.   *Ralph Waldo Emerson*

Nothing else than anthropology.

Ludwig A. Feuerbach

Pathology hidden from itself.

Ludwig A. Feuerbach

Not what we know about God, but what we do not know about nature.   *Elbert Hubbard*

An engine planned for the purpose of bewildering humanity.   *Elbert Hubbard*

Antique and obsolete philosophy.

Elbert Hubbard

Obsolete psychology.   *Elbert Hubbard*

An attempt to explain a subject by men who do not understand it. The intent is not to tell the truth but to satisfy the questioner.   *Elbert Hubbard*

The effort to explain the unknowable in terms of the not worth knowing.   *Henry Louis Mencken*

(That which) is not only opposed to the scientific spirit; it is opposed to every other form of rational thinking.   *Henry Louis Mencken*

To be still searching what we know not, by what we know, still closing up truth to truth as we find it.   *John Milton*

My theology ... Is that the Universe Was Dictated But not Signed.   *Christopher Morley*

The fundamental and regulating principle of the whole Church system.   *John Henry Newman*

Reflection upon the reality of worship and an explication of it. As such it is a rational affair ... faith seeking to understand.   *Albert C. Outler*

The study of nothing.   *Thomas Paine*

Most noble of studies.   *Pope Leo XIII*

The art of drawing religion out of a man, not pumping it into him.   *Karl Rahner*

The chief aim of this science is to impart a knowledge of God, not only as existing in Himself, but also as the origin and end of all things, and especially of rational creatures.

Saint Thomas Aquinas

The best theology is ... a divine life.

Jeremy Taylor

The term "theo-logy" implies...a mediation, namely, between the mystery, which is *theos*, and the understanding, which is *logos*.   *Paul Tillich*

A science profound, supernatural, and divine, which teaches us to reason on that which we don't understand and to get our ideas mixed up on that which we do.   *Voltaire*

All theology is to the religious life of prayer, of mystical experience and of good works, as the theory of harmony is to music.   *Franz Werfel*

A blind man in a dark room searching for a black cat which isn't there—and finding it.   *Anon.*

SEE ALSO BELIEF, GOD, RELIGION.

THEORY

A hunch with a college education.   *J. A. Carter*

Those fine flowers which relieve the drabness of our existence and help to make the human scene worth while.   *Morris R. Cohen*

An imperfect generalization caught up by a predisposition.   *James A. Froude*

A possession for life.   *William Hazlitt*

(Something) that holds together long enough to get you to a better theory.   *Donald O. Hebb*

A species of thinking, and its right to exist is coexistensive with its power of resisting extinction by its rivals.   *Thomas Henry Huxley*

Something usually murdered by facts.   *Anon.*

THIEF

Every rascal is not a thief, but every thief is a rascal.   *Aristotle*

Opportunity makes a thief.   *Francis Bacon*

Thieves respect property. They merely wish the property to become their property that they may more perfectly respect it.

Gilbert Keith Chesterton

One who considers he is honest if he has no chance to steal.   *Hebrew Proverb*

(One who) believes everybody steals.

Edgar W. Howe

One who just has a habit of finding things before people lose them.   *Joe E. Lewis*

Not caught, not a thief.   *Russian Proverb*

SEE ALSO CRIME, CRIMINAL.

THINKERS

The chief dynamic of history.   *Eric Bentley*

In every epoch of the world, the great event, parent of all others.   *Thomas Carlyle*

The critical minority.   *Sigmund Freud*

The thinker looks for a universal truth that will help explain unique events.   *Eric Hoffer*

Thinkers help other people to think, for they formulate what others are thinking. No person writes or thinks alone—thought is in the air, but its expression is necessary to create a tangible Spirit of the Times.   *Elbert Hubbard*

One who destroys philosophies.
          Elbert Hubbard

One who makes others think.   *Elbert Hubbard*

A soldier in the army of intellectual liberty.
          Robert G. Ingersoll

A person who aims where your head ought to be.
          Anon.

SEE ALSO HERO, INTELLIGENT PERSON.

THINKING

As he thinketh in his heart, so is he.
          Bible: Proverbs, XXIII, 7.

The greatest torture in the world for most people.
          Luther Burbank

The magic of the mind.   *Lord Byron*

To think is to live.   *Cicero*

To think is to differ.   *Clarence S. Darrow*

Another attribute of the soul...here I discover what properly belongs to myself. This alone is inseparable from me. I am—I exist: this is certain; but how often? As often as I think.
          René Descartes

Fiction that helps us to live.   *Havelock Ellis*

The hardest task in the world.
          Ralph Waldo Emerson

The hardest work there is, which is the probable reason why so few engage in it.   *Henry Ford*

Every act of thinking is identical with the molecular activity of the brain—cortex that coincides with it.   *Auguste Forel*

Thinking renders one unfit for every activity.
          Anatole France

The mind's muscles hanging onto a problem.
          Eric Hoffer

A moment's thinking is an hour in words.
          Thomas Hood

What a great many people think they are doing when they are merely rearranging their prejudices.   *William James*

Reading furnishes the mind only with the materials of knowledge; it is thinking makes what we read ours.   *John Locke*

Packing thought close, and rendering it portable.
          Thomas B. Macaulay

It has little to do with logic and is not much conditioned by overt facts.
          Henry Louis Mencken

No occupation is at once idler and more fruitful.
          Michel de Montaigne

To speak low. To speak is to think aloud.
          F. Max Muller

The talking of the soul with itself.   *Plato*

Only a flash between two long nights, but this flash is everything.   *Henry Poincare*

To converse with oneself.   *Miguel de Unamuno*

One must forget what he happens to wish before he can become susceptible to what the situation itself requires...This transition is one of the great moments in many genuine thought processes...Real thinkers forget themselves in thinking.   *Max Wertheimer*

SEE ALSO CLARITY, CONCENTRATION, IDEAS, LOGIC, REFLECTION.

THOREAU, HENRY DAVID
(1817-1862)

Thoreau's quality is very penetrating and contagious; reading him is like eating onions—one must look out or the flavor will reach his own page.   *John Burroughs*

Few lives contain so many renunciations. He was bred to no profession; he never married; he lived alone; he never went to church; he never voted; he refused to pay a tax to the State; he ate no flesh, he drank no wine, he never knew the use of tobacco; and, though a naturalist, he used neither trap nor gun. *Ralph Waldo Emerson*

The bachelor of thought and Nature.

Ralph Waldo Emerson

He thought everything a discovery of his own, from moonlight to the planting of acorns and nuts by squirrels. This is a defect in his character, but one of his chief charms as a writer.

James Russell Lowell

With his almost acid sharpness of insight, with his almost animal dexterity in act, there went none of that large, unconscious geniality of the world's heroes. He was not easy, not ample, not urbane, not even kind. *Robert Louis Stevenson*

For many, the American who spoiled success.

Anon.

The founder of the passive-resistance movement.

Anon.

THOUGHT

One of the manifestations of human energy.

Brooks Adams

A strenuous art—few practice it: and then only at rare times. *David Ben-Gurion*

A gift men and women make for themselves. It is earned...by effort. *Louis D. Brandeis*

The soul of act. *Robert Browning*

Feelings gone to seed. *John Burroughs*

The work of brain and nerve. *Richard Burton*

As near to God as we can get, it is through this that we are linked with God. *Samual Butler 2*

The blight of life. *Lord Byron*

It is the *Thought* of man...by which man works all things whatsoever. All that he does and brings to pass is the vesture of a Thought.

Thomas Carlyle

The universal consoler. *Nicolas Chamfort*

The key which unlocks the doors of the world.

Samuel M. Crothers

Man carries the world in his head, the whole astronomy and chemistry suspended in a thought.

Ralph Waldo Emerson

Thought makes everything fit for use.

Ralph Waldo Emerson

The senses collect the surface facts of matter...It was sensation; when memory came, it was experience; when mind acted, it was knowledge; when mind acted on it as knowledge, it was thought.

Ralph Waldo Emerson

The property of him who can entertain it and of him who can adequately place it.

Ralph Waldo Emerson

The seed of action. *Ralph Waldo Emerson*

The only conceivable prosperity that can come to us. *Ralph Waldo Emerson*

In all men, thought and action start from a single source, namely, feeling. *Epictetus*

The gaseous ashes of burned-out thinking, the excretion of mental respiration.

Oliver Wendell Holmes 1

Mental dynamite. *Elbert Hubbard*

A mirror: it shows man the ugliness and the beauty within him. *Moses Ibn Ezra*

An action of a particular organization of matter, formed for that purpose by its creator.

Thomas Jefferson

Every thought is something in itself—the false as well as the true. The false are simply weeds that we can't use in our housekeeping.

Georg C. Lichtenberg

My companions.

Henry Wadsworth Longfellow

Thought alone is eternal. *Owen Meredith*

It is thought, and thought alone, that divides right from wrong; it is thought, and thought only, that elevates or degrades human deeds and desires.

George Moore

Two distinct classes...those that we produce in ourselves by reflection...and those that bolt into the mind of their own accord. *Thomas Paine*

An idea in transit. *Pythagoras*

We are thought. Thought leads us. Therefore, the secret of our destiny lies here: in regulating our thoughts. *Antonin Sertillanges*

Dreams till their effects be tried.

William Shakespeare

The grand prerogative of mind. *Jane Taylor*

Thought breeds thought. It grows under your hands. *Henry David Thoreau*

Thought depends absolutely on the stomach, but in spite of that, those who have the best stomachs are not the best thinkers. *Voltaire*

The process by which human ends are ultimately answered. *Daniel Webster*

What you are today, what you will be tomorrow. *Anon.*

SEE ALSO CONCENTRATION, GENIUS, GREATNESS, IDEAS, REASON, REFLECTION, THINKERS, THINKING.

THOUGHT, FREE

SEE ALSO FREE THINKING.

THRIFT

SEE BUDGETING, MISERLINESS.

THRONE

SEE KING, MONARCHY.

TIME

An immense ocean, in which many noble authors are...swallowed up. *Joseph Addison*

One's best friend, teaching best of all the wisdom of silence. *Amos Bronson Alcott*

Something that we ain't got nothing but. *American Saying*

A very shadow that passeth away. *Apocrypha: Wisdom of Solomon, II, 5.*

The author of authors. *Francis Bacon*

The greatest innovator. *Francis Bacon*

A dressmaker specializing in alterations. *Faith Baldwin*

The stuff life's made of. *David Belasco*

Time exists because there is activity...Time is the product of *changing realities*, beings, existences. *Nicholas Berdyaev*

A file that wears and makes no noise. *Henry G. Bohn*

The only true purgatory. *Samuel Butler 2*

The avenger. *Lord Byron*

The beautifier of the dead,
Adorner of the ruin, comforter
And the only healer when the heart
hath bled. *Lord Byron*

The illimitable, silent, never-resting thing... rolling, rushing on, swift, silent, like an all-embracing oceantide, on which we and all the Universe swim. *Thomas Carlyle*

A ripener. No man is born wise. *Miguel de Cervantes*

A River without Banks. *Marc Chagall*

A system of folds which only death can unfold. *Jean Cocteau*

A great manager: it arranges things well. *Pierre Corneille*

(The) greatest and longest established spinner of all...His factory is a secret place, his work noiseless, and his hands are mutes. *Charles Dickens*

Time is money...And very good money too to those who reckon interest by it. *Charles Dickens*

The great physician. *Benjamin Disraeli*

Nothing absolute; its duration depends on the rate of thought and feeling. *John Draper*

The surest poison. *Ralph Waldo Emerson*

Time is an herb that cures all diseases. *Benjamin Franklin*

My estate: to Time I'm heir. *Johann W. Goethe*

A circus always packing up and moving away. *Ben Hecht*

The rider that breaks youth. *George Herbert*

A noiseless file. *George Herbert*

The press-agent of genius. *Elbert Hubbard*

An eternal guest that banquets on our ideals and bodies. *Elbert Hubbard*

An illusion—to orators. *Elbert Hubbard*

A tyranny to be abolished.   *Eugene Jolas*

Nothing else but something of eternal duration become finite, measurable and transitory.
                                    William Law

The shadow on the dial, the striking of the clock...these are but arbitrary and outward signs, the measure of Time, but not Time itself. Time is the Life of the Soul.
                        Henry Wadsworth Longfellow

An available instrument for reaching the Eternal.
                                    John W. Lynch

A great legalizer, even in the field of morals.
                                Henry Louis Mencken

A part of eternity, and of the same piece with it.
                                Moses Mendelssohn

Eternity begun.   *James Montgomery*

A flowing river.   *Christopher Morley*

The devourer of things.   *Ovid*

A stream which glides smoothly on and is past before we know.   *Ovid*

What we want most, but ... what we use worst.
                                    William Penn

Time is change, transformation, evolution.
                                    Isaac L. Peretz

The eternal tomorrow.   *Isaac L. Peretz*

The wisest counsellor of all.   *Pericles*

The moving image of eternity.   *Plato*

The soul of this world.   *Plutarch*

The Devil is the Prince of Time.
And God is the King of Eternity.
Time without end, that is Hell.
Perfect presence, that is Eternity.
                                Denis de Rougemont

Nothing else than protraction, but of what I know not; and I marvel, if it be not of the mind itself.
                                Saint Augustine

A sandpile we run our fingers in.
                                    Carl Sandburg

That which in all things passes away.
                                Arthur Schopenhauer

The form under which the will to live has revealed to it that its efforts are in vain.
                                Arthur Schopenhauer

The agent by which at every moment all things in our hands become as nothing, and lose all value.
                                Arthur Schopenhauer

Time is the school in which we learn,
Time is the fire in which we burn.
                                Delmore Schwartz

Nothing is ours except time.   *Seneca*

The king of men.   *William Shakespeare*

The sea in which men grow, are born, or die.
                                    Freya Stark

The only critic without ambition.
                                    John Steinbeck

The most valuable thing a man can spend.
                                    Theophrastus

A storm in which we are all lost.
                                William C. Williams

The tyrant of the body.   *Anon.*

The stuff between paydays.   *Anon.*

A great healer but a very poor beautician.
                                        Anon.

The arbitrary division of eternity.   *Anon.*

SEE ALSO CLOCK, DAY, ETERNITY, LIFE, PAST, PRESENT (THE), TODAY, YEAR, YESTERDAY.

TIPS

A sum of money that is more than you can afford and less than the waiter expected.
                                Cynic's Cyclopaedia

Wages paid to other people's hired help.   *Anon.*

TOASTMASTER

A man who eats a meal he doesn't want so he can get up and tell a lot of stories he doesn't remember to a lot of people who've already heard them.
                                    George Jessel

One who speaks a few appropriated words.
                                    Earl Wilson

One who goes around introducing people who need no introduction.   *Anon.*

TOBACCO

The softest consolation, next to that which comes from heaven. *Edward G. Bulwer-Lytton*

A good cigar is as great a comfort to a man as a good cry to a woman.
Edward G. Bulwer-Lytton

The ruin and overthrow of body and soul.
Robert Burton

Pernicious weed. *William Cowper*

The tomb of love. *Benjamin Disraeli*

Believing we do something when we do nothing is the first illusion of tobacco.
Ralph Waldo Emerson

Tobacco was surely designed.
To poison and destroy mankind. *Philip Freneau*

The only excuse for Columbus's misadventure in discovering America. *Sigmund Freud*

A damned dirty habit and a vice.
D. N. Goldstein

A branch of the sin of drunkenness.
James 1 of England

A custom loathsome to the eye, harmful to the brain, dangerous to the lungs.
James 1 of England

A shocking thing—blowing smoke out of your mouths into other people's mouths, eyes and noses, having the same thing done to us.
Samuel Johnson

Roguish tobacco . . . good for nothing but to choke a man, and fill him full of smoke and embers.
Ben Jonson

A conspiracy against womanhood. It owes its origin to that scoundrel, Sir Walter Raleigh, who was likewise the founder of American slavery.
John H. Kellogg

A lone man's companion, a bachelor's friend, a hungry man's food, a sad man's cordial, a wakeful man's sleep, and a chilly man's fire.
Charles Kingsley

A woman is only a woman, but a good cigar is a smoke. *Rudyard Kipling*

One of the leading causes of statistics.
Fletcher Knebel

My evening comfort and my morning curse.
Charles Lamb

Heaven's last, best gift, my ever new delight.
John Milton

That hell fume in God's clean air.
Carry Nation

An Indian weed. *Walter Scott*

An acknowledged poison. *Jesse Torrey*

A product you find only in Cuba. *Anon.*

A dangerous habit in search of contentment.
Anon.

SEE ALSO CIGARETTE.

TODAY

To those leaning on the sustaining infinite, to-day is big with blessings. *Mary Baker Eddy*

The here-and-now is no mere filling of time, but a filling of time with God. *John Foster*

Yesterday's pupil. *Benjamin Franklin*

Yesterday's effect and tomorrow's cause.
Phillip Gribble

The hearse that carries the dreams of yesterday to the cemetery. *Elbert Hubbard*

The blocks with which we build.
Henry Wadsworth Longfellow

Cash in hand—SPEND it! *John W. Newbern*

(A day which) is always different from yesterday.
Alexander Smith

The obscurest epoch. *Robert Louis Stevenson*

SEE ALSO DAY, PRESENT (THE), TIME, YESTERDAY.

TOLERANCE

Never mean enough to despise a man because he was ignorant, or because he was poor—or because he was black. *John A. Andrew*

Tolerance in the sense of moderation or superior knowledge or scepticism is actually the worst form of intolerance. *Karl Barth*

He maketh his sun to rise on the evil and on the good, and sendeth rain on the just and on the unjust. *Bible: Matthew, V, 45.*

To gently scan your brother man.   *Robert Burns*

The central figure in tolerance is the person, infinitely worthy of respect.   *John Cogley*

Implies a respect for another person, not because he is wrong or even because he is right, but because he is human.   *John Cogley*

Means that we shall give our enemies a chance.

Morris R. Cohen

The herb of spontaneous growth in the soil of indifference.   *Samuel Taylor Coleridge*

Live and let live.   *David Fergusson*

The lowest form of human cooperation...the drab, uncomfortable, halfway house between hate and charity.   *Robert I. Gannon*

To tolerate is to insult.   *Johann W. Goethe*

(Something that) ought in reality to be a transitory mood. It must lead to recognition. To tolerate is to affront.   *Johann W. Goethe*

The only real test of civilization.   *Arthur Helps*

An agreement to tolerate intolerance.

Elbert Hubbard

The best religion.   *Victor Hugo*

(Giving) to every other human being every right that you claim for yourself.   *Robert G. Ingersoll*

Another word for indifference.

William Somerset Maugham

A species of tyranny.   *Comte de Mirabeau*

Not the opposite of intoleration, but...the counterfeit of it. Both are despotisms. The one assumes to itself the right of withholding the liberty of conscience, and the other of granting it.

Thomas Paine

(Something) defined in the spirit of that great play of Sophocles, where Antigone says, "I was not born to share men's hatred, but their love."

Sarvepalli Radhakrishnan

The result of flattening high-mindedness out.

George Saintsbury

It implies a confession that there are insoluble problems upon which even revelation throws but little light.   *Frederic Temple*

The appurtenance of humanity. We are all full of weakness and errors, let us mutually pardon each other our follies—it is the first law of nature.

Voltaire

Toleration has been summed up in the words, "Let both grow together until the harvest."

Alfred North Whitehead

The ability to smile when someone else's child behaves as badly as your own.   *Eugene Yasenak*

SEE BROTHERHOOD, CHRISTIANITY, FELLOWSHIP, FOREBEARANCE, MERCY, RELIGION, SYMPATHY.

TOMB

SEE GRAVE, MONUMENT.

TOMORROW

One of the greatest labor-saving inventions of today.   *Vincent T. Foss*

An old deceiver, and his cheat never goes stale.

Samuel Johnson

The mysterious, unknown guest.

Henry Wadsworth Longfellow

The only day in the year that appeals to a lazy man.   *Jimmy Lyons*

The ambushed walk avoided by the circumspect...the fatal rock on which a million ships are wrecked.   *Walter Mason*

My country.   *Romain Rolland*

Always the busiest day of the week.

Richard Willis

The day when idlers work, and fools reform, and mortal men lay hold on heaven.   *Edward Young*

SEE ALSO FUTURE, TIME.

TONGUE

That which is good or bad among men.

Adapted from Anacharsis

The neck's enemy.   *Arabian Proverb*

That which should be trained to say, "I do not know," lest you be trapped into falsehood.

Babylonian Talmud

A fire, a world of iniquity.

Bible: James, III, 6.

A sharpened arrow.   *Bible: Jeremiah, IX, 7.*

The pen of a ready writer.

Bible: Psalms, XIV, 1

The magic of the tongue is the most dangerous of all spells.   *Edward G. Bulwer-Lytton*

When a man dies, the last thing that moves is his heart; in a woman her tongue.
George Chapman

(A thing) framed for articulation.
Ralph Waldo Emerson

A wild beast; once let loose it is difficult to chain.
Baltasar Gracian

The tongue is not steel, yet it cuts.
George Herbert

The greatest of man's treasures.   *Hesiod*

A windy satisfaction.   *Homer*

The only edged tool that grows keener with constant use.   *Washington Irving*

The inextinguishable passion of a woman, coeval with the act of breathing.   *Alain R. Le Sage*

A sharper weapon than the sword.   *Phocylides*

An unruly evil.   *Anon.*

SEE ALSO CONVERSATION, ELOQUENCE, GOSSIP, MOUTH, ORATORY, SPEECH, TALK, VERBOSITY, WORDS.

TORAH, THE

A mystic, almost cosmic, conception. The torah is the tool of the Creator; with it and for it He created the universe . . . It is the highest idea and the living soul of the world.   *Hayim N. Bialik*

An expression for the aggregate of Jewish teachings.   *Louis Ginzberg*

Divine teaching upon all and everything that concerns religion.   *Robert T. Herford*

The real Torah is not merely the written text of the Five Books of Moses; the real Torah is the meaning enshrined in that text, as expounded . . . and unfolded . . . by successive generations of sages and teachers in Israel.   *Joseph H. Hertz*

The whole of the sacred tradition, especially as expressed in all the writings of the faith, from the Bible to the present.   *Arthur Hertzberg*

The whole content of revelation.
George F. Moore

The distillation of the soul of Israel into the written words of its classic literature, in the institutions in which it has taken shelter . . . the

indwelling of the divine spirit in living souls as expressed in the genius of Israel.
Abraham A. Neuman

SEE ALSO JEWS, JUDAISM, SYNAGOGUE.

TOTALITARIANISM

The kingdom of Satan.   *Nicholas Berdyaev*

A violation of the personal rights which man's very nature gives him; and consequently it is an insult to God, the Creator of man's nature.
Francis J. Connell

The . . . Absolute State, which recognizes only individuals, which counts it citizens like heads of cattle, which tramples personality and makes zoos out of its universities . . . the end of everything worth living for.   *Robert I. Gannon*

A system in which no disagreement on ends is allowed . . . The end justifies the means, which therefore range from persuasion to coercion, from compromise to terror.   *Hans Simons*

A system of government with absolute control of the people's lives for real or imagined good.
Anon.

SEE ALSO DESPOTISM, DICTATORSHIP, TYRANNY.

TOWN

(A place where) people take what they can use without surrendering their way of life.
Granville Hicks

A place where even a haircut changes the whole appearance of the community.   *Kin Hubbard*

A hive of glass
Where nothing unobserved can pass.
Charles H. Spurgeon

A place where everybody knows whose check is good and whose wife isn't.   *Jack Sterling*

A place where there is nothing to buy with money.
Rebecca West

Grass roots life.   *Robert C. Wood*

The natural home of democracy.
Robert C. Wood

Where there is no place to go where you shouldn't be.   *Alexander Woollcott*

Where everybody knows what everybody else is doing—and all buy the weekly newspaper to see how much the editor dares to print.   *Anon.*

A place where nobody is too many.   *Anon.*

A place where everybody knows your credit rating.   *Anon.*

A community proud of its traffic congestion.
          Anon.

A republic in miniature.   *Anon.*

A place usually divided by a railroad, a main street, two churches, and a lot of opinions.
          Anon.

A place where you are known by your first name and last scandal.   *Anon.*

A place where the only things that goes out after 10 p.m. is the lights.   *Anon.*

TOYS

Life in miniature.   *Philip Kirkham*

Something a child uses to break all his other toys with.   *Anon.*

TRADE

SEE COMMERCE.

TRADITION

Means giving votes to...our ancestors. It is the democracy of the dead.   *Wystan H. Auden*

The continuity of nature and history.
          Leon Blum

Hearsays, mere words.   *Thomas Carlyle*

Tradition means giving votes to the most obscure of all classes, our ancestors. It is the democracy of the dead.   *Gilbert Keith Chesterton*

A great retarding force, the *vis inertiae* of history.
          Friedrich Engels

That body of revealed truths, received by the Apostles, from the lips of Christ Himself or told them by the Holy Ghost.   *Pietro Gasparri*

A form of salvation through ossification.
          Elbert Hubbard

A clock which tells what time it was.
          Elbert Hubbard

The fence of the law.   *Jewish Proverb*

The mother of religion.   *Jean B. Lacordaire*

Group efforts to keep the unexpected from happening.   *Mignon McLaughlin*

Lies...not in knowing too much, but rather in not knowing enough to think things through.
          Anne C. Moore

A living social process constantly changing, constantly in need of criticism, but constant also as the continuing memory, value system and habit structure of a society.   *Helmut R. Niebuhr*

Continuity.   *James A. Pike*

Inherited passions and loyalties.
          Richard Poirier

Anything handed down.   *Tertullian*

That part of history which has proven to be of value for the present age.   *Robert Zwickey*

SEE ALSO CIVILIZATION, CULTURE, CUSTOM, HERITAGE, HISTORY, RELIGION.

TRAGEDY

An imitation of an action that is serious, complete, and of a certain magnitude, effecting through pity and fear the proper catharsis, or purgation, of emotions.   *Aristotle*

Tragedy represents the life of princes; comedy serves to depict the actions of the people.
          Francois Aubignac

There can be no tragedy without a struggle; nor can there be genuine emotion for the spectator unless something other and greater than life is at stake.   *Ferdinand Brunetiere*

All tragedies are finished by a death.
          Lord Byron

The climax of every tragedy lies in the deafness of its heros.   *Albert Camus*

Not so much what men suffer, but rather what they miss.   *Thomas Carlyle*

That there should one man die ignorant who had the capacity for knowledge.   *Thomas Carlyle*

Tragedy must be something bigger than life, or it would not effect us. In nature the most violent passions are silent; in tragedy they must speak, and speak with dignity too.   *Lord Chesterfield*

The tragedy of life is not death but what dies inside a man while he lives—the death of genuine feeling, the death of inspired response...of the awareness that makes it possible to feel the pain or the glory of other men in oneself.

Norman Cousins

A very solemn lecture, inculcating a particular Providence and showing it plainly protecting the good, and chastising the bad.   *John Dennis*

That men know so little of men.

William Du Bois

To grow up.   *Helen Hayes*

A struggle between two rights.   *Georg W. Hegel*

One can play comedy; two are required for melodrama; but a tragedy demands three.

Elbert Hubbard

True tragedy may be defined as a dramatic work in which the outward failure of the principal personage is compensated for by the dignity and greatness of his character.   *Joseph Wood Krutch*

The difference between what is and what might have been.   *Alfred North Whitehead*

Not unhappiness. It resides in the solemnity of the remorseless working of things...in terms of human life by incidents which in fact involve unhappiness. For it is only by them that the futility of escape can be made evident.

Alfred North Whitehead

In this world there are only two tragedies. One is not getting what one wants, and the other is getting it.   *Oscar Wilde*

Retirement without a hobby.   *Anon.*

The utter impossibility of changing what you have done.   *Anon.*

SEE ALSO DEATH, LIFE, SORROW, SUFFERING.

TRAMP

SEE VAGABOND.

TRANSLATION

All translation is commentary.   *Leon Baeck*

At best an echo.   *George Borrow*

Like viewing a piece of tapestry on the wrong side where though the figures are distinguishable yet there are so many ends and threads that the beauty and exactness of the work is obscured.

Miguel de Cervantes

Trying to pour yourself into an invisible glass so that you take the shape of your vessel and transmit the author's light and flavor.   *Nevill Coghill*

Siphoning a bottle of wine into a pail of water.

Leonard L. Levinson

There is no translation except a word-for-word translation.   *George Moore*

Not versions but perversions.   *Saint Jerome*

The best translations...are those that depart most widely from the originals—that is, if the translator is himself a good poet.   *Edmund Wilson*

TRAVEL

Travel, in the younger sort, is a part of education; in the elder, a part of experience.

Francis Bacon

There are two classes of travel: first class, and with children.   *Robert Benchley*

From going to and fro in the earth, and from walking up and down in it.   *Bible: Job, I, 7.*

The ruin of all happiness. There's no looking at a building here after seeing Italy.

Frances Burney

The whole object...is not to set foot on foreign land; it is...to set foot on one's own country as a foreign land.   *Gilbert Keith Chesterton*

Too often...instead of broadening the mind, (it) merely lengthens the conversation.

Elizabeth Drew

A fool's paradise.   *Ralph Waldo Emerson*

One way of lengthening life, at least in appearance.   *Benjamin Franklin*

(A) childish delight in being somewhere else.

Sigmund Freud

An experience we shall always remember, or an experience which, alas, we shall never forget.

Julius Gordon

Liberty, perfect liberty, to think, feel, do just as one pleases.   *William Hazlitt*

An expensive trial of strength.   *Jonathan Miller*

TRAVELLER

A brutality. It forces you to trust strangers and to lose sight of all that familiar comfort of home and friends.   *Caesar Pavase*

Not to go anywhere, but to go...travel for travel's sake. The great affair is to move.

Robert Louis Stevenson

Something you enjoy three weeks after unpacking.   *Anon.*

SEE ALSO VACATION.

TRAVELLER

I have been a stranger in a strange land.

Bible: Exodus, II, 22.

If you will be a traveller, have always...two bags very full, that is one of patience and another of money.   *John Florio*

One who travels many miles to have his picture snapped in front of statues.   *Max Gralnick*

A traveller must have the back of an ass to bear all, a tongue like the tail of a dog to flatter all, the mouth of a hog to eat what is set before him, the ear of a merchant to hear all and say nothing.

Thomas Nashe

One who absorbs countries like vitamin pills— one a day.   *Anon.*

TREACHERY

SEE CALUMNY.

TREATY

The promise of a nation.   *Fisher Ames*

In international politics, the union of two thieves who have their hands so deeply inserted in each other's pocket that they cannot separately plunder a third.   *Ambrose Bierce*

An agreement which ceases to be when the parties come into conflict.

Adapted from Otto von Bismarck

A feeble candle...a flicker of light where there has been no light.   *Mike Mansfield*

A system under which the faithful are always bound and the faithless always free.

Robert G. Vansittart

An agreement between two nations to cross their fingers.   *Anon.*

An agreement which is binding on the weaker party only.   *Anon.*

SEE ALSO FOREIGN RELATIONS.

TREE

The ship that will cross the sea; the staff for our country's flag; shade from the hot sun.

Adapted from Henry Abbey

The tree is known by his fruit.

Bible: Matthew, XII, 33.

An object that moves some to tears, to others only a green thing that stands in the way.

Adapted from William Blake

Something that stands in one place for fifty years and then suddenly jumps out in front of your car.

Anon.

TRIAL

A formal inquiry designed to prove and put upon record the blameless characters of judges, advocates and jurors.   *Ambrose Bierce*

All trial is the investigation of something doubtful.   *Samuel Johnson*

Ordeal by battle. For the broadsword there is the weight of evidence; for the battleaxe the force of logic; for the sharp spear, the blazing gleam of truth; for the rapier, the quick and flashing knife of wit.   *Lloyd P. Stryker*

SEE ALSO JUDGE, LAW, LAWYERS.

TRINITY

There are three that bear record in Heaven, the Father, the Word, and the Holy Ghost, and these three are one.   *Bible: John, V, 7.*

The affirmation of a full rich life in God as distinct from all abstract and barren conceptions of his being.   *William A. Brown*

Practically, it is the affirmation that the true nature of God must be learned from his historic revelation in Christ, and from the experience which Christ creates.   *William A. Brown*

It affirms that the mystery of God is to be defined by means of the character of Jesus Christ.

Langdon Gilky

It asserts that the love which we see is Jesus Christ, and experience in the Holy Spirit, is one with the eternal power and being of Almighty God.   *Langdon Gilky*

God...recognized as Spirit only when known as the Triune.   *Georg W. Hegel*

"When the fullness of the time was come, God sent his Son," is the statement in the Bible. This means nothing else than that *self-consciousness* has reached the phase of development whose resultant constitutes the Idea of Spirit.

Georg W. Hegel

The mere Abracadabra of the mountebanks calling themselves the priests of Jesus.

Thomas Jefferson

Three are one, and one is three; and yet the one is not three, and the three are not one...This constitutes the craft.   *Thomas Jefferson*

The three persons in the Godhead are three in one sense and one in another. We cannot tell how— and that is the mystery.   *Samuel Johnson*

The three Persons of the Blessed Trinity are one and the same God, having one and the same divine nature, or substance.   *John McCaffrey*

To attribute to the Father those works of the divinity in which power excels, to the Son those in which wisdom excels, and those in which love excels to the Holy Ghost.   *Pope Leo XIII*

The Trinity is One God.   *Saint Augustine*

We recognize one God, but only in the attributes of Fatherhood, Sonship, and Procession, both in respect of cause and effect and perfection of substance.   *Saint John the Baptist*

Power, Love, Wisdom—there you have a real trinity which makes up the Jewish God.

Israel Zangwill

SEE ALSO CHRIST, CHRISTIANITY.

TRIUMPH

SEE VICTORY.

TROUBLE

The tools by which God fashions us for better things.   *Henry Ward Beecher*

(Mistaking) sex for love, money for brains, and transistor radios for civilization.

Daniel Bennett

What you make it.   *Edmund V. Cooke*

A hallucination that affords a sweet satisfaction to the possessor.   *Elbert Hubbard*

A plan of nature whereby a person is diverted from the humiliation of seeing himself as others see him.   *Elbert Hubbard*

Any interesting topic of conversation.

Elbert Hubbard

The next best thing to enjoyment; there is no fate in the world so horrible as to have no share in either its joys or sorrows.

Henry Wadsworth Longfellow

Fear of one's self.   *Wilhelm Stekel*

The one product in which the supply exceeds the demand.   *Anon.*

A baby that grows.   *Anon.*

Something partial to wetness—to tears and liquor.

Anon.

SEE ALSO MISFORTUNE, SUFFERING, WORRY.

TRUST

SEE CONFIDENCE, FAITH.

TRUMAN, HARRY S. (1884-1974)

He read tirelessly the material given to him; listened intently to the arguments; and then he decided, clearly and firmly. Once a matter was decided, he went on to new problems and had little time or inclination to rehash the old ones.

Dean Acheson

It is not unusual for a President to be rebuffed by Congress. What is a little unusual is for a Chief Executive, repeatedly rebuffed, to refuse to change his tactics.   *Felix Belair 2*

He is both the product and the embodiment of the American faith which is...a faith for the world. He speaks that faith in the language of his country-men. Moscow understands what he says, as well as Independence and Iowa.

Jonathan Daniels

Mr. Truman did everything except have himself shot from the mouth of a cannon.

Edward T. Folliard

Here is to be seen no flaming leadership, little of what could be called scholarship and no more that is profound. But it is very good and human and courageous. Common sense shines out of it, and political experience. *Arthur Krock*

A scrapper. *New York Sun*

A beaten man who refuses to stay licked. *New York Sun*

An ordinary man; not an average man . . . but an ordinary man who must make do without any special endowments of genius, intellect, or charm. His strength lay in his ability to do the best he could with what he had and not to despair over what he did not have. *Cabell Phillips*

Neither in manner, speech, nor appearance does he present any of the outward attributes of forcefulness or dignity or command out of which the popular image of leadership is compounded. *Cabell Phillips*

A tidy administrator without being a slave to routine or organization charts. *Cabell Phillips*

(Truman was) right on all the big things, wrong on most of the little ones. *Sam Rayburn*

Truman is accustomed to having political offices he didn't seek thrust upon him. *William M. Reddig*

At no time had I presumed to possess a special gift of omniscience in dealing with what we had to face. I never felt that I was in any sense the indispensable man. *Harry S. Truman*

I . . . never hesitated to do the things I thought necessary, regardless of whether they were popular or not. *Harry S. Truman*

I never take a problem to bed with me at night. *Harry S. Truman*

The Small Man who was in simple fact to become much bigger than the Large Man (Franklin D. Roosevelt) in big things. *William S. White*

The Missouri machine politician. *Anon.*

TRUTH

Truth and good are one. *Mark Akenside*

The secret of eloquence and of virtue, the basis of moral authority; it is the highest summit of art and life. *Henry F. Amiel*

Truth indeed is one name for Nature, the first cause of all things true. *Marcus Aurelius*

It is the characteristic of truth to need no proof but truth. *Jeremy Bentham*

An ingenious compound of desirability and appearance. *Ambrose Bierce*

Everything possible to believe is an image of truth. *William Blake*

Knowing when to lie and when not to. *Samuel Butler 2*

Truth is like the use of words, it depends greatly on custom. *Samuel Butler 2*

That which seems true to the best and most competent men of any given age and place where truth is sought. It is what these men can acquiesce in with the least discomfort. *Samuel Butler 2*

The foe of tyrants, and the friend of man. *Thomas Campbell*

The first casualty in time of war. *Boake Carter*

The highest thing that man may keep. *Geoffrey Chaucer*

A species of revelation. *Samuel Taylor Coleridge*

The object of philosophy, but not always of philosophers. *John C. Collins*

The aim of the superior man. *Confucius*

A river that is always splitting up into arms that reunite. Islanded between the arms, the inhabitants argue for a lifetime as to which is the main river. *Cyril Connolly*

What keeps honest men poor. *Jerry Dashkin*

Patient, cooperative inquiry operating by means of observation, experiment, record, and controlled reflection. *John Dewey*

When you have eliminated the impossible, whatever remains, however improbable, must be the truth. *Arthur Conan Doyle*

The highest compact we can make with our fellow. *Ralph Waldo Emerson*

The knowledge of what is just and lawful. *Epictetus*

A profound sea, and few there be who dare wade deep enough to find out the bottom on't. *George Farquhar*

Not having to guess what a candidate means. *Gerald Ford*

The unexpressed and the inexpressible.
Egon Friedell

Two elements are needed to form a truth—a fact and an abstraction.   *Remy de Gourmont*

(That which) is not for or against anything; truth simply is.   *Aelred Graham*

Truth is *many*. There are as many truths as there are things and causes of action and contradictory principles at work in society.   *William Hazlitt*

Whatever is reasonable is true, and whatever is true is reasonable.   *Georg W. Hegel*

The name of God is truth.   *Hindu Proverb*

The road I can't help traveling.
Oliver Wendell Holmes 2

If more men accept a doctrine than reject it, and those who accept it are more intelligent than its opponents, it is as near the truth as we can get at present.   *Edgar W. Howe*

Nothing is true except a few fundamentals every man has demonstrated for himself.
Edgar W. Howe

The opinion that still survives.   *Elbert Hubbard*

A prejudice raised to an axiom.
Elbert Hubbard

That which serves us best in expressing our lives.
Elbert Hubbard

The heart of morality.   *Thomas Henry Huxley*

The name of whatever proves itself to be good in the way of belief, and good, too, for definite, assignable reasons.   *William James*

Only the expedient in the way of our thinking, just as "the right" is only the expedient in the way of our behaving.   *William James*

A property of certain of our ideas. It means their "agreement," with "reality." ... True ideas are those that we can assimilate, validate, corroborate and verify.   *William James*

A relation between two things, an idea, on the one hand, and a reality outside of the idea, on the other.   *William James*

Since there is no complete truth, our movement toward it is itself the only form in which truth can achieve completion in existence, here and now.
Karl Jaspers

Man's proper good, and the only immortal thing ... given to our mortality to use.
Ben Jonson

Every truth is true only up to a point. Beyond that, by way of counter-point, it becomes untruth.
Sören Kierkegaard

Two kinds ... those of reasoning and those of fact. The truths of reasoning are necessary and their opposite is impossible; the truths of fact are contingent and their opposite is possible.
Gottfried W. von Leibnitz

The measure of knowledge, and the business of understanding.   *John Locke*

Where you find the general permanent voice of humanity agreeing with the voice of your conscience.   *Joseph Mazzini*

The smallest atom ... represents some man's bitter toil and agony; for every ponderable chunk of it there is a brave truthseeker's grave upon some lonely ash-dump and a soul roasting in hell.
Henry Louis Mencken

A word which each one understands in his own way, according to his own needs, as it suits him.
Mendele

A quality belonging primarily to judgments ... a judgment is true when and only when it states a fact.   *William P. Montague*

The strong compact in which beauty may sometimes germinate.   *Christopher Morley*

Truth means facts and their relations, which stand towards each other pretty much as subjects and predicates in logic.   *John Henry Newman*

The opinion which is fated to be ultimately agreed to by all who investigate it.
Charles S. Peirce

What men kill each other for.   *Herbert Read*

Truth is polygonal. I never feel sure that I have got it until I have contradicted myself five or six times.   *John Ruskin*

Rightness perceptible to the mind alone ... Rightness distinguishes it from every other thing which is called rightness ... Truth and rightness and justice define each other.   *Saint Anselm*

A jewel which should not be painted over; but it may be set to advantage and shown in a good light.   *George Santayana*

My way of joking...It's the funniest joke in the world.   *George Bernard Shaw*

The one thing that nobody will believe.
                                                   George Bernard Shaw

The strongest argument.   *Sophocles*

Not to state the true facts, but to convey a true impression; truth in spirit, not truth to the letter, is the true veracity.   *Robert Louis Stevenson*

Phrases, ways of speaking words.   *Max Stirner*

The system of propositions which have an unconditional claim to be recognized as valid.
                                                        Alfred E. Taylor

The rarest quality in an epitaph.
                                                   Henry David Thoreau

Man discovers truth by reason only, not by faith.
                                                           Leon Tolstoy

The matching of our human minds with something akin to them.   *David E. Trueblood*

A fruit which should not be plucked until it is quite ripe.   *Voltaire*

All truths are half-truths. It is trying to treat them as whole truths that plays the devil.
                                                Alfred North Whitehead

A generic quality with a variety of degrees and modes.   *Alfred North Whitehead*

A truth in art is that whose contradictory is also true.   *Oscar Wilde*

Something that is stranger than fiction, but not as popular.   *Anon.*

SEE ALSO ART, BEAUTY, BIBLE, CHRISTIANITY, FACT, GOD, HISTORY, HONESTY, JUSTICE, LITERATURE, MINORITY, PHILOSOPHY, POETRY, POWER, PROPHECY, PROVERBS, REALITY, SCIENCE, STYLE, WISDOM.

TWAIN, MARK (1835-1910)

The Lincoln of literature.   *William D. Howells*

He never wrote a line that a father could not read to a daughter.   *William Howard Taft*

I think he mainly misses fire: I think his life misses fire: he might have been something; he comes near to being something: but he never arrives.   *Walt Whitman*

A noteworthy male whose narratives sparkle like ale.   *Anon.*

This Prince of the Grin, who once fathered Huck Finn, and holds the world by the tale.   *Anon.*

TWENTIETH CENTURY

The first century since life began when a decisive part of the most articulate section of humanity has not merely ceased to believe in God, but has deliberately rejected God...the century in which this religious rejection has taken a specifically religious form.   *Whittaker Chambers*

Only the nineteenth speaking with a slightly American accent.   *Philip Guedalla*

The century of the common man.

                                                         Henry Wallace

A time of momentous revolution and incessant ferment along secular lines.   *Robert Zwickey*

TYRANNY

A surrender of those inestimable privileges to the arbitrary will of vindictive tyrants.

                                                         Samuel Adams

An exercise of irresponsible power.

                                                       Edward Bellamy

Every wanton and causeless restraint of the will of the subject, whether practiced by a monarch, a nobility, or a popular assembly.

                                                    Willaim Blackstone

The worst of treasons.   *Lord Byron*

To compel men not to think as they do, to compel men to express thoughts that are not their own.

                                                        Milovan Djilas

Tyranny is but the act of a mortal, here today and in the grave tomorrow.   *Issac Ibn Pulgar*

Oppression, and Sword-law.   *John Milton*

The wish to have in one way what can only be had in another.   *Blaise Pascal*

Irresponsible power.   *William Pinkney*

Where law ends, tyranny begins.   *William Pitt*

The rule of the many by the few...the rule of the few by the many is tyranny also, only of a less intense kind.   *Herbert Spencer*

Merely the most vigorous kind of rule, springing out of, and necessary to, a bad state of man.

Herbert Spencer

The normal pattern of government.

Adlai Ewing Stevenson

TYRANTS

Our own affections.   *William Alexander*

A cruel lord, who, by force or by craft...has obtained power over any realm or country...they love rather to work their own profit, though it be to the harm of the land, than the common profit of all.   *Alfonso the Wise*

The most dangerous preachers of liberty.

Ludwig Boerne

The worst...are those which establish themselves in our own breasts.   *William Ellery Channing*

All men...if they could.   *Daniel Defoe*

He who endeavors to control the mind by force.

Robert G. Ingersoll

A money-loving race.   *Sophocles*

Nothing but a slave turned inside out.

Herbert Spencer

The sovereign...who knows no laws but his caprice.   *Voltaire*

One who believes in freedom—for himself.

Anon.

A power-loving race.   *Anon.*

One raised in blood, in blood established, and ruling with blood.   *Anon.*

U

UMBRELLA

A portable roof. *Leonard L. Levinson*

Civilization defying the elements.
Leonard L. Levinson

The stamp of respectability...the acknowledged index of social position.
Robert Louis Stevenson

Something strangers take away. *Anon.*

UNBELIEF

SEE AGNOSTICISM, ATHEISM.

UNCONSCIOUSNESS

A realm of potential hell. *Sigmund Freud*

The deep well of...cerebration. *Henry James*

Hidden powers. *Fritz Kunkel*

The unconsciousness of man is the consciousness of God. *Henry David Thoreau*

SEE ALSO FREUD, FREUDIANISM, PSYCHO-ANALYSIS.

UNDERSTANDING

A man only understands what is akin to something already existing in himself.
Henry F. Amiel

The wealth of wealth. *William G. Benham*

Not the logical, argumentative, but the intuitive; for the end of understanding is not to prove and find reasons, but to know and believe.
Thomas Carlyle

To understand is to complicate.
Lucien Lefebvre

Learning the grounds of one's own opinions.
John Stuart Mill

Mutual praise and pity. *Dorothy Parker*

Hearing in retrospect. *Marcel Proust*

The soil in which grow all the fruits of friendship.
Woodrow Wilson

SEE ALSO INTUITION, MIND, REASON.

UNDERTAKER

One who is permitted to sign his correspondence "Eventually yours." *Anon.*

One who always lets you down. *Anon.*

One who always carries out what he undertakes.
Anon.

SEE ALSO FUNERAL, GRAVE.

UNHAPPINESS

SEE MISERY, SORROW, SUFFERING.

UNION

All for one; one for all.   *Alexander Dumas*

Strength.   *German Proverb*

We two.   *Ovid*

Three unions in this world: Christ and the Church, husband and wife, spirit and flesh.

Saint Augustine

UNION, LABOR

SEE LABOR UNIONS.

UNIVERSE

A crank machine.   *Alfonso the Wise*

Mutation.   *Marcus Aurelius*

A single life comprising one substance and one soul.   *Marcus Aurelius*

The universal order and the personal order are nothing but different expressions and manifestations of a common underlying principle.

Marcus Aurelius

One vast symbol of Good.   *Thomas Carlyle*

A collector and conservator, not of mechanical energy...but of persons.   *Pierre de Chardin*

A great smelting-pot.   *Chuang-tzu*

One commonwealth of which both gods and men are members.   *Cicero*

The footprint of the divine goodness.   *Dante*

System and gradation. Every god is there sitting in his sphere.   *Ralph Waldo Emerson*

The Incarnation of God, and the Personality of Man.   *Michael Fairless*

Not a machine, but an organism, with an indwelling principle of life. It was not made, but it has grown.   *John Fiske*

Nothing less than the progressive manifestation of God.   *John B. Haldane*

An immense and unbroken chain of cause and effect.   *Paul H. d'Holbach*

The universe is not hostile, nor yet is it friendly. It is simply indifferent.   *John Holmes*

(It) can best be pictured as consisting of pure thought...a mathematical thinker.   *James Jeans*

Matter and void alone.   *Thomas Jefferson*

An invisible piece of writing in which we can now and then decipher a letter or a word and then it's gone again.   *Arthur Koestler*

The sum total of all sums total.   *Lucretius*

Nothing but one individual being...there is no vacuum whatever therein.   *Moses Maimonides*

A handful of sand.   *David McCord*

The manifestation of eternal and indestructible matter, and nothing more.   *Benito Mussolini*

A handful of dust which God enchants.

Theodore Parker

An infinite sphere whose centre is everywhere, its circumference nowhere.   *Blaise Pascal*

The plots of God are perfect. The Universe is a plot of God.   *Edgar Allan Poe*

(Something that) is true for all of us and different for each of us.   *Marcel Proust*

The universe is anonymous.

W. Winwood Reade

Great is this organism of mud and fire, terrible this vast, painful, glorious experiment.

George Santayana

A wonderful and immense engine.

George Santayana

One of God's thoughts.   *Johann C. Schiller*

The progressive manifestation of Spirit.

Milton Steinberg

The outward manifestation of Mind, Energy, of spirit, or to use the older and better word, of God.

Milton Steinberg

A wheel. Upon it are all creatures...subject to birth, death, and rebirth. Round and round it turns, and never stops.

Svetasvatara Upanishad

An intelligent design.   *William F. Swann*

The diffused energy of the supreme Brahman.

Puranas Visnu

An intelligence test.   *Heathcote Williams*

SEE ALSO EARTH, STARS, WORLD.

UNIVERSITY

Home of lost causes, and forsaken beliefs, and unpopular names, and impossible loyalties!
Matthew Arnold

Sophistry and affectation.   *Francis Bacon*

(Where one learns) to believe; first, to believe that others know that which they know not; and after, that themselves know that which they know not.
Francis Bacon

(Where) individualism is dreaded as nothing else, wherein manufactories of patent drama, business schools and courses for the propagation of fine embroidery are established on the order of the monied.   *Thomas Beer*

A collection of books.   *Thomas Carlyle*

(A place that) brings out all abilities including incapacity.   *Anton Chekhov*

What a college becomes when the faculty loses interest in students.   *John Ciardi*

A place of light, of liberty, and of learning.
Benjamin Disraeli

The best university...is the gauntlet of the mob.
Ralph Waldo Emerson

A place hostile to geniuses.
Adapted from Ralph Waldo Emerson

Fit for nothing but to debauch the principles of young men, to poison their minds with romantic notions of knowledge and virtue.
Henry Fielding

An institution consciously devoted to the pursuit of knowledge, the solution of problems, the critical appreciation of achievement, and the training of men at a really high level.   *Abraham Flexner*

A tributary to a larger society, not a sanctuary from it.   *Bartlett Giametti*

A conversation about wisdom.
Alfred W. Griswold

A place where...men send their sons who have no aptitude for business.   *Elbert Hubbard*

A place wherein the youthful mind is taught the danger of thinking.   *Elbert Hubbard*

A plan for...the exaltation of athletics.
Elbert Hubbard

The medieval university looked backwards; it professed to be a storehouse of old knowledge...The modern university looks forward, and is a factory of new knowledge.
Thomas Henry Huxley

Not the transformation of undergraduates into fountains of information...Its business is the very different task of teaching the student how facts are converted into truth.   *Harold J. Laski*

A college with a stadium seating over 40,000.
Leonard L. Levinson

An institution of higher yawning.
Leonard L. Levinson

A place where those who hate ignorance may strive to know, where those who perceive truth may strive to make others see.   *John Masefield*

A stony-hearted step-mother.   *John Milton*

Not ivory towers; they are advanced guards exploring the path of life for the people.
Gamal Abdel Nasser

An Alma Mater, knowing her children one by one, not a foundry, or a mint, or a treadmill.
John Henry Newman

A place of instruction where universal knowledge is professed.   *John Henry Newman*

The canary in the coalmine...the most sensitive barometer of social change.   *James Perkins*

A fool's brain digests philosophy into folly, science into superstition, and art into pedantry. Hence University education.
George Bernard Shaw

A thought-control center.   *Joan Tepperman*

The use of a university is to make young gentlemen as unlike their fathers as possible.
Woodrow Wilson

SEE ALSO BOOK, COLLEGE, EDUCATION, KNOWLEDGE, LEARNING, PROFESSOR, SCHOOL.

UTOPIA

Imaginary commonwealths.   *Francis Bacon*

Straws to which those who cling have no real hope.   *Emil Brunner*

The future . . . lighted . . . with the radiant colors of hope.
John Fiske

The idea . . . will always be found as chimerical as that of a perfect and immortal man.
David Hume

The most magnificent promises of impossibilities.
Thomas B. Macaulay

SEE ALSO PROGRESS, REFORM.

V

VACATION

Recess between assignments.   *Warren Goldberg*

A period of increased and pleasurable activity when your wife is at the seashore.

Elbert Hubbard

What you take when you can no longer take what you've been taking.   *Earl Wilson*

Something which seems like fun—after you've rested at home for a month.   *Anon.*

A time enjoyed to the extent that there is no place like home.   *Anon.*

A system whereby the tired become exhausted.

Anon.

The time when you need half the clothes and twice the money you took.   *Anon.*

SEE ALSO TRAVEL.

VAGABOND

They were strangers and pilgrims on the earth.

Bible: Hebrews, XI, 13.

He who goes from country to country, guided by the blind impulse of curiosity.

Oliver Goldsmith

A man who builds palaces and lives in shacks. He rides the rods, reaps the harvest and stands in the bread line.   *Adapted from Godfrey Irwin*

Friends and lovers have we none, nor wealth, nor abode.   *Adapted from John Masefield*

One who straggles his way through the world without hope, without habitation, without sustenance, without faith.

Medieval Legal Definition

The vagabond, when rich, is called a tourist.

Paul Richard

An untough tramp.   *Joan Tepperman*

I seem to myself like water and sky,
A river and a rover and a passer-by.

Ridgely Torrence

Wanderers of the street.   *William Wordsworth*

VALUES

SEE BELIEF, CREED, CULTURE, GOD, RELIGION.

VANITY

The normal desire to win the approval of others.

Hamilton Basso

The pride of Nature.   *William G. Benham*

Every man at his best state.

Bible: Psalms, XXXIX, 5.

An itch for the praise of fools.

Robert Browning

That divine gift which makes woman charming.

Benjamin Disraeli

Vanity is the mother, and affectation is the ... daughter; vanity is the sin, and affectation is the punishment; the first may be called the root of self-love, the other the fruit.   *Lord Halifax*

A single quality that is shared by all great men...I mean by "vanity" only that they appreciate their own worth.   *Yussef Karsh*

The greatest of all flatterers.   *La Rochefoucauld*

The name of the machinery that makes swelled heads.   *Jimmy Lyons*

To go about by our proportions and conjectures to guess at God...And to govern Him, and the world according to our capacity and laws.

Michel de Montaigne

Cruelty was the vice of the ancient, vanity is that of the modern world. Vanity is the last disease.

George Moore

Vanity, vanity, all is vanity
That's any fun at all for humanity.   *Ogden Nash*

The polite mask of pride.

Friedrich W. Nietzsche

The desire to live an imaginary life in the minds of others.   *Adapted from Blaise Pascal*

Sickness... imagining yourself to be perfect.

Jallaludin Rumi

The quicksand of reason.   *George Sand*

The highest form... is the love of fame.

George Santayana

Keeps persons in favor with themselves who are out of favor with all others.

William Shakespeare

To say that a man is vain means merely that he is pleased with the effect he produces on other people.   *Anon.*

The self-love centered vulgarization of the heart.

Anon.

SEE ALSO BOASTER, CONCEIT, EGOISM, PRIDE, SELF-LOVE.

VATICAN

SEE CHURCH (ROMAN CATHOLIC), PAPACY.

VENGEANCE

SEE CAPITAL PUNISHMENT, REVENGE.

VERBOSITY

Uncurbed, unfettered, uncontrolled of speech.

Aristophanes

The habit of common and continuous speech...a system of mental deficiency.   *Walter Bagehot*

Shooting without aiming.   *William G. Benham*

Volleys of eternal babble.   *Samuel Butler 1*

Thinking too little, talking too much.

Adapted from John Dryden

The reinless lips that will own no master.

Euripides

The talk of empty-headed, vain and tiresome babblers...thought that comes from the lips and not from the heart.   *Aulus Gellius*

Parting aimlessly.   *Max Gralnick*

In that manner vulgarly, but significantly, called rigmarole.   *Samuel Johnson*

Saying something when there's nothing to be said.

Samuel Johnson

The disease of talking.   *Ben Jonson*

Superfluous breath.   *William Shakespeare*

SEE ALSO CONVERSATION, GOSSIP, TALK.

VERSE

SEE POETRY.

VICE

A miscalculation of chances, a mistake in estimating the value of pleasures and pains. It is false moral arithmetic.   *Jeremy Bentham*

A creature of such heinous mein, that the more you see of it the better you like it.

Adapted from Finley Peter Dunn

The senses gone astray.   *David Grayson*

Whatever was passion in the contemplation of man, being brought forth by his will into action.

James Harrington

The greatest part of human gratification.

Samuel Johnson

Servility. *Karl Marx*

The vice which offends no one is not really vice.

Michel de Montaigne

A monster. *Alexander Pope*

(Something) we first endure, then pity, then embrace. *Alexander Pope*

What were once vices are not the manners of the day. *Seneca*

Instruments to plague us. *William Shakespeare*

A waste of life. Poverty, obedience and celibacy are the canonical vices. *George Bernard Shaw*

Discord, war, and misery.

Percy Bysshe Shelley

SEE ALSO SIN, WICKEDNESS.

VICE-PRESIDENT

The most insignificant office that ever the invention of man contrived or his imagination conceived. *John Quincy Adams*

A mere Doge of Venice. *John Quincy Adams*

A vice-president is a person who finds a molehill on his desk in the morning and must make a mountain out of it by five p.m. *Fred Allen*

Echo men...who follow in the wake of the big executive and echo his sentiments as they are expressed. *Fred Allen*

A member of the team...able to step into the Presidency smoothly in case anything happens.

Dwight David Eisenhower

The role...is exactly what the President makes it.

Dwight David Eisenhower

A spare tire on the automobile of government.

John Nance Garner

The tranquil and unoffending role.

Thomas Jefferson

A man in a cataleptic state: he cannot speak; he cannot move; he suffers no pain; and yet he is perfectly conscious of everything that is going on about him. *Thomas R. Marshall*

I think the Vice-President should do anything the President wants him to do.

Richard Milhous Nixon

The man with the best job in the country...All he has to do is get up every morning and say, "How's the President?" *Will Rogers*

A man only a heartbeat away from the presidency.

Adlai Ewing Stevenson

A cow's fifth teat. *Harry S. Truman*

Like the last cookie on the plate. Everybody insists he won't take it, but somebody always does. *William Vaughan*

He sits around in the parks, and feeds the pigeons, and takes walks, and goes to the movies. *Anon.*

The forgotten fellow and amiable nonentity.

Anon.

An obscure personage who takes over if and when the President dies. *Anon.*

VICTORIAN AGE

An age wanting in moral grandeur and spiritual health. *Matthew Arnold*

A blessed period of peace and prosperity... Despite its limitations, it was a good, solid, happy time of English life at its best.

S. M. Ellis

VICTORY

Victory is of the Lord.

Bible: Proverbs, XXI, 31.

Not merely...the conquest of the battlefield, but...the destruction of physical and moral forces and this is usually attained only in the pursuit after the battle is won.

Karl von Clausewitz

A thing of the will. *Ferdinand Foch*

War engenders war, and victory defeat. Victory is a Spirit. *Anatole France*

A matter of staying power. *Elbert Hubbard*

The greatest victory is defeat. *Henrik Ibsen*

No longer a truth. It is only a word to describe who is left alive in the ruins.

Lyndon Baines Johnson

Vain noise and tumult.   *Moses Luzzatto*

That which must be bought with the lives of young men to retrieve the errors of the old.

Gordon R. Munnoch

Redemption purchased for men's hope at a cost so terrible that only defeat could be more bitter.

Gordon R. Munnoch

The most dangerous moment.   *Napoleon I*

A crown, or else a glorious tomb!

William Shakespeare

Victories do not make peace. Victories only stop wars...like the notice "to be continued" that comes after each chapter of a serialized novel.

Avraham Shlonsky

With the development of modern technology, "victory" in war has become a mockery.

Adlai Ewing Stevenson

Fighting the good fight and vanquishing the demon that tempts us within.

Adapted from William W. Story

Victory is always where there is unanimity.

Publilius Syrus

To gain land and lose lives.   *Anon.*

Defeat—in the atomic age.   *Anon.*

SEE ALSO BATTLEFIELD, CONQUER, WAR.

VILLAGE

SEE TOWN.

VIOLENCE

SEE FORCE, WAR.

VIRGIN BIRTH

Behold, a virgin shall conceive and bear a son and shall call his name Immanuel.

Bible: Isaiah, VII, 14.

Once the great glove of Nature was taken off His hand. His naked hand touched her...The whole soiled and weary universe quivered at this direct injection of essential life—direct, uncontaminated, not drained through all the crowded history of nature.   *Clive S. Lewis*

A Virgin conceived, a Virgin bore, and after birth was a Virgin still.   *Saint Augustine*

The first begotten of God, our master Jesus Christ, was born of a virgin, without any human mixture.   *Saint Justin Martyr*

SEE ALSO CHRIST.

VIRGINIAN

Patriotism with a Virginian is a noun personal. It is the Virginian himself and something over. He loves Virginia *per se*...he loves her for herself and for himself—because she is Virginia and—everything else beside.   *J. G. Baldwin*

The Virginians have little money and great pride, contempt of Northern men, and great fondness for a dissipated life.   *Noah Webster*

VIRGINITY

The state of virginity consecrated to God...is a marriage with Jesus Christ Himself.   *A. Carre*

Sweet self-love.   *John Davies*

A frozen asset.   *Clare Boothe Luce*

The virtue which opens up your heart to the truest, greatest, and most encompassing love on earth: the service of Christ and of souls.

Pope John XXIII

A very efficacious means for devoting oneself to the service of God.   *Pope Pius XII*

A fair-built steeple without bells.   *Henry Porter*

It is a free offering to the Lord.   *Saint Augustine*

Peevish, proud, idle, made of self-love, which is the most inhibited sin in the canon.

William Shakespeare

A woman's highest gift for the marriage bed.

Anon.

SEE ALSO CHASTITY, SELF-DENIAL.

VIRTUE

Reverence for superiors, respect for equals, regard for inferiors—these form the supreme trinity of the virtues.   *Felix Adler*

Self-control and understanding, righteousness and courage.

Apocrypha: Wisdom of Solomon, IV, 1.

A mean state between two vices, the one of excess and the other of deficiency. *Aristotle*

Virtue and sense are one. *John Armstrong*

A woman's lack of temptation and man's lack of opportunity. *Ambrose Bierce*

Certain abstentions. *Ambrose Bierce*

Virtue does not consist in the absence of the passions, but in the control of them.

Josh Billings

A man's virtue is in his behavior in the face of his destiny. *Lyman Bryson*

To be serviceable, must, like gold, be alloyed with some commoner but more durable metal.

Samuel Butler 1

Victorious resistance to one's vital desire.

James Branch Cabell

The first virtue is to restrain the tongue. *Cato*

Blood is an inheritance, virtue an acquisition.

Miguel de Cervantes

Reason in practice. *Marie J. de Chénier*

A habit of the mind, consistent with nature and moderation and reason. *Cicero*

Gravity, magnanimity, earnestness, sincerity, kindness. *Confucius*

Crimes by exaggeration. *Alexander Dumas*

Adherence in action to the nature of things.

Ralph Waldo Emerson

It consists in a perpetual substitution of being for seeming. *Ralph Waldo Emerson*

Forebearance. *F. Scott Fitzgerald*

Whatever behavior fits a given situation.

Johann W. Goethe

A mean between vices, remote from both extremes. *Horace*

Consists in fleeing vice. *Horace*

Every quality of the mind which is useful or agreeable to the person himself or to others.

David Hume

Wisdom is knowing what to do next; virtue is doing it. *David S. Jordan*

Most frequently vices disguised.

La Rochefoucauld

Feeling or habit. *Georg C. Lichtenberg*

That which is thought praiseworthy; and nothing else but that which has the allowance of public esteem. *John Locke*

To resist all temptation to evil.

Thomas R. Malthus

An angel, but she is a blind one, and must ask of Knowledge to show her the pathway that leads to her goal. *Horace Mann*

The fount whence honor springs.

Christopher Marlowe

Virtue's but a word. *Philip Massinger*

An intellectual force of the soul which so rules over animal suggestions or bodily passions that (it) easily attains that which is absolutely and simply the best. *Henry More*

Virtue is nothing if not difficult. *Ovid*

Doing good to mankind, in obedience to the will of God, and for the sake of everlasting happiness.

William Paley

Wisdom, courage, temperance, justice. *Philo*

A kind of health, beauty and good habit of the soul. *Plato*

Although virtue receives some of its excellencies from nature, yet it is perfected by education.

Quintilian

Objectivity, courage, and a sense of responsibility.

Arthur Schnitzler

Consists, not in abstaining from vice, but in not desiring it. *George Bernard Shaw*

Insufficient temptation. *George Bernard Shaw*

Peace, and happiness and harmony.

Percy Bysshe Shelley

Women's virtue is man's greatest invention.

Cornelia Otis Skinner

Action in accord with the laws of one's own nature. *Baruch Spinoza*

Life under the direction of reason.

Baruch Spinoza

The performance of pleasant actions.

James Stephens

Repose of mind. *James Thomson*

Eccentric.   *Mark Twain*

Only a plaster, the scar of a surgical operation.
Rahel L. Varnhagen

Justice for others, courage for ourselves.
Rahel L. Varnhagen

Compensation to the poor for the want of riches.
Horace Walpole

Glory's voice.   *Henry K. White*

A constant struggle against the laws of nature.
Anon.

SEE ALSO CHARITY, CHASTITY, DEEDS, GOOD, GOOD AND BAD, HONESTY, MORALITY, PHILANTHROPY, PIETY, SALVATION, WISDOM.

VISION

And it shall come to pass afterward, that I will pour out my Spirit upon all flesh; and your sons and your daughters shall prophesy, and your old men shall dream dreams.   *Bible: Joel, II, 28.*

A waking dream.

Henry Wadsworth Longfellow

The fool's paradise, the statesman's scheme; the air-built castle, and the golden dream; the maid's romantic wish, the chemist's flame.

Adapted from Alexander Pope

A bolt of nothing, shot at nothing.

William Shakespeare

The art of seeing things invisible.

Jonathan Swift

Vision looks inward and becomes a duty. Vision looks outward and becomes aspiration. Vision looks upward and becomes faith.

Stephen S. Wise

A strong perception beyond the reach of the senses.   *Robert Zwickey*

SEE ALSO DREAM, IMAGINATION, PROPHECY, REVELATION.

VOCATION

When you have learned to believe in God's purpose for you as an individual.

John S. Bonnell

Each individual has his own kind of living assigned to him by the Lord as a sort of sentry post so that he may not heedlessly wander throughout life.   *John Calvin*

Every vocation is ultimately founded on the salutary selfishness by which an individual, despite the whole world, seeks to save his own immortal soul.   *M. Raymonds*

A falling in love with God.   *Fulton J. Sheen*

The test... is the love of the drudgery it involves.
Logan P. Smith

Employment in honest trades and offices is a serving of God.   *Jeremy Taylor*

The vocation of every man and woman is to serve other people.   *Leon Tolstoy*

SEE ALSO HAPPINESS, LABOR, WORK.

VOICE

A second face.   *Gerard Bauer*

An arrow for the heart.   *Lord Byron*

A man's style is his mind's voice.

Ralph Waldo Emerson

(That which is) on the borderline between the physical and the spiritual.   *Isaac L. Peretz*

Nothing but flogged air.   *Seneca*

An index of character.   *Anon.*

VOLTAIRE (1694-1778)

Historian, bard, philosopher, combined.
Lord Byron

The flippant Frenchman.   *Matthias Claudius*

The Scripture was his jest-book.

William Cowper

An apostle of Christian ideas; only the names were hostile to him.   *Ralph Waldo Emerson*

I know this author cannot be depended on with regard to facts; but his general views are sometimes sound and always entertaining.

David Hume

(One who) did more for human liberty than any other man who ever lived or died.

Robert G. Ingersoll

The prince of buffoons. *Thomas B. Macaulay*

The child spoiled by the world which he spoiled.
Baronne de Montolieu

The godless arch-scoundrel.
Wolfgang Amadeus Mozart

His forte lay in exposing and ridiculing the superstitions which priestcraft, united with state-craft, had interwoven with governments...He merits the thanks rather than the esteem of mankind. *Thomas Paine*

One of those heroes who liked better to excite martyrs than be one. *Horace Walpole*

VOTING

Voices...numbered and not weighed.
Francis Bacon

The instrument and symbol of a freeman's power to make a fool of himself and a wreck of his country. *Ambrose Bierce*

The government of a house by its nursery.
Otto von Bismarck

The notion that a man's liberty consists in giving his vote at election...and saying, "Behold, now, I too have my twenty-thousandth part of a Talker in our National Palaver." *Thomas Carlyle*

The honest and independent and fearless exercise of your own franchise...a trust confided to you not for your private gain but for the public good.
Catholic Bishops of the U.S., 1840.

A public trust. *Grover Cleveland*

The freeman casting, with unpurchased hand.
Oliver Wendell Holmes 1

The first duty of democracy.
Lyndon Baines Johnson

The basic right without which all others are meaningless. It gives people—people as individuals—control over their own destinies.
Lyndon Baines Johnson

Simply a way of determining which side is the stronger without putting it to the test of fighting.
Henry Louis Mencken

A weapon that comes down as still
  As snowflakes fall upon the sod;

But executes a freeman's will,
  As lightning does the will of God.
John Pierpont

Something that shows which hot air blows the best. *Anon.*

Picking the lesser of evils. *Anon.*

SEE ALSO BALLOT, ELECTIONEERING, POLITICIAN, POLITICS.

VOYAGE

SEE TRAVEL.

VULGARITY

The garlic in the salad of taste. *Cyril Connolly*

An inadequate conception of the art of living.
Mandell Creighton

Words that make you squint in print.
D. H. Lawrence

The eighth sin...and worse than all the others put together, since it perils your salvation in this world. *James Russell Lowell*

Vulgarity is only in concealment of truth, or affectation. *John Ruskin*

Simple and innocent vulgarity is merely an untrained and undeveloped bluntness of body and mind; but in true, inbred vulgarity there is...callousness which in extremity becomes capable of every sort of bestial habit and crime, without fear, without pleasure, without horror, and without pity.
John Ruskin

That vice of civilization which makes man ashamed of himself and his next of kin.
Solomon Schechter

At bottom, the kind of consciousness in which the will completely predominates over the intellect, where the latter does nothing more than perform the service of its master, the will.
Arthur Schopenhauer

No crime is vulgar, but all vulgarity is crime.
Oscar Wilde

Simply the conduct of other people.
Oscar Wilde

SEE ALSO PROFANITY.

W

WAGNER, RICHARD (1813-1883)

One cannot do a greater disservice to Wagner than by bringing his music into a concert hall. It is created solely for the theatrical stage, and that is where it belongs. *Johannes Brahms*

No hypocrite. He says what he means, and he usually means something nasty.

James G. Huneker

He presented the mythology of music at the same time with that of the world; in that he bound the music to the things and made them express themselves in music. *Thomas Mann*

A melodramatic rhetorician of the senses.

Friedrich W. Nietzsche

The counterpoison against all that is German.

Friedrich W. Nietzsche

A disease. Everything he touches falls ill: he has made music sick. *Friedrich W. Nietzsche*

(A composer whose) music is better than it sounds. *Mark Twain*

My destiny is solitude, and my life is work.

Richard Wagner

By nature I am luxurious, prodigal, and extravagant, much more than . . . all the old emperors put together. *Richard Wagner*

I like Wagner's music better than any other music. It is so loud that one can talk the whole time without people hearing what one says.

Oscar Wilde

WAR

The science of destruction. *J. S. Abbott*

The most successful of our cultural traditions.

Robert Ardrey

A luxury which only the small nations can afford.

Hannah Arendt

A biological necessity of the first order.

Friedrich von Bernhardi

A temporary abdication of ethical and humane standards. *John Mason Brown*

A racket . . . The cost of operations is always transferred to the people who do not profit.

Smedley Butler

A brain-spattering, windpipe-slitting art—unless her cause by right be sanctified. *Lord Byron*

Men slaying each other like wild beasts.

Andrew Carnegie

(Something that begins) ten years before the first shot is fired. *K. K. Casey*

The concentration of all human crimes. It turns man into a beast of prey.

William Ellery Channing

A catalog of mistakes and misfortunes.

Winston S. Churchill

A time when the laws are silent. *Cicero*

An act of violence whose object is to constrain the enemy, to accomplish our will.
Karl von Clausewitz

Nothing but a duel on a large scale.
Karl von Clausewitz

The continuation of state policy with other means.
Karl von Clausewitz

The province of chance.   *Karl von Clausewitz*

An instrument of policy.   *Karl von Clausewitz*

Much too important a matter to be left to the generals.   *Georges Clemenceau*

The best amusement of our morning meal.
Samuel Taylor Coleridge

A passion play performed by idiots.
William Corum

A phase in the life-effort of the state towards completer self-realization.   *J. A. Cramb*

The highest perfection of human knowledge.
Daniel Defoe

The trade of kings.   *John Dryden*

The essence of war is fire, famine and pestilence. They contribute to its outbreak; they are among its weapons; they become its consequences.
Dwight David Eisenhower

War gratifies... the combative instinct of mankind, but it gratifies also the love of plunder, destruction, cruel discipline, and arbitrary power.
Charles W. Eliot

That condition which uses man's best to do man's worst.   *Adapted from Harry Emerson Fosdick*

The crassest opposition to the psychical attitude imposed on us by the cultural process.
Sigmund Freud

Instruments for dealing with international conflicts.   *Frans A. von Geusaw*

The chief pursuit of ambitious minds.
Edward Gibbon

A perpetual violation of every principle of religion and humanity.   *Edward Gibbon*

The most simple affirmation of life. Supress war, and it would be like trying to suppress the processes of nature.   *Joseph P. Goebbels*

A disaster to the soldier; to the general a spectacle.   *Isaac Goldberg*

A perpetual struggle with embarrassments.
Colmar von der Goltz

A shield for economic failures.   *Max Gralnick*

The perfect type of Hell.   *Fulke Greville*

An activity that makes rattling good history: but peace is poor reading.   *Thomas Hardy*

A crime. Ask the infantry and ask the dead.
Ernest Hemingway

Death's feast.   *George Herbert*

The only proper school of the surgeon.
Hippocrates

The acquiring of the right of sovereignty by victory.   *Thomas Hobbes*

Three principal causes ... competition ... diffidence ... glory.   *Thomas Hobbes*

Consists not in battle only, or the act of fighting; but in a tract of time, wherein the will to contend by battle is sufficiently known.
Thomas Hobbes

The great failure of man.   *Cordell Hull*

Nine times out of ten... murder in uniform.
Douglas W. Jerrold

It appears ingrafted on human nature; it passes even for an act of gentleness, to which the love of glory alone, without any other motive, impels.
Immanuel Kant

A war between the governments of two nations is a war between all the individuals of the one and all the individuals of... the other.   *James Kent*

An outrage... against simple men.
T. M. Kettle

(The) failure of human wisdom.
Andrew B. Law

A part of a whole, and that whole—politics.
Nikolai Lenin

That attractive rainbow that rises in showers of blood.   *Abraham Lincoln*

A blood-stained stagger to victory.
David Lloyd George

The greatest plague that can afflict humanity; it destroys religion...states...families. Any scourge is preferable to it.   *Martin Luther*

The application of the mechanics of force to human nature.   *Douglas MacArthur*

The essence of war is violence.

Thomas B. Macaulay

The only study of a prince. He should consider peace only as a breathing-time, which gives him leisure to contrive, and furnishes ability to execute, military plans.   *Niccolo Machiavelli*

The only sport that is genuinely amusing. And it is the only sport that has any intelligible use.

Henry Louis Mencken

The beginning of all war may be discerned not only by the first act of hostility, but by the counsels and preparations foregoing.

John Milton

Part of God's world order.   *Helmuth von Moltke*

A natural calamity whether victorious or not.

Helmuth von Moltke

The same reasons that make us quarrel with a neighbor cause war between two princes.

Michel de Montaigne

The business of barbarians.   *Napoleon 1*

Organized barbarism, an inheritance of the savage state, however disguised or ornamented.

Napoleon 3

The contention between two or more states through their armed forces for the purpose of overpowering each other and imposing such conditions of peace as the victor pleases.

Lassa F. Oppenheim

An evil and it is often the lesser evil. Those who take the sword, perish by the sword, and those who don't take the sword perish by smelly diseases.   *George Orwell*

(When) each government accuses the other of perfidy, intrigue and ambition, as a means of heating the imagination of their respective nations, and incensing them to hostilities.

Thomas Paine

It is not the object of war to annihilate those who have given provocation for it, but to cause them to mend their ways; not to ruin the innocent and guilty alike, but to save both.   *Polybius*

Warfare seems to signify blood and iron.

Quintilian

An ugly mob-madness, crucifying the truth-tellers, choking the artists, side-tracking reforms, revolutions, and the working of social forces.

John Reed

A contagion.   *Franklin Delano Roosevelt*

The needy bankrupt's last resort.

Nicholas Rowe

Like children's fights—all meaningless, pitiless and contemptible.   *Jallaludin Rumi*

A transfer of property from nation to nation.

Leon Samson

The much vaunted crime of slaughtering whole peoples.   *Seneca*

A most pestilential nuisance.

George Bernard Shaw

There is only one virtue, pugnacity; only one vice, pacifism. That is an essential condition of war.   *George Bernard Shaw*

A method of killing people.

George Bernard Shaw

The stateman's game, the priest's delight, the lawyer's jest, the hired assassin's trade.

Adapted from Percy Bysshe Shelley

War is hell.   *William T. Sherman*

War is cruelty, and you cannot refine it.

William T. Sherman

A state into which the mass of mankind rush with a greatest avidity, hailing official murderers...as the greatest and most glorious of human creatures.   *Sydney Smith*

The primeval policy of all living things...to the extent that...combat and life are identical, for when the will to fight is gone, so is life itself.

Oswald Spengler

All wars are civil wars. All killing is fratricidal.

Adlai E. Stevenson

The great force for forging a society into a solid mass.   *William G. Sumner*

That mad game the world so loves to play.

Jonathan Swift

An effort to make the laws of God and nature take sides with one party.   *Henry David Thoreau*

A drastic medicine for ailing humanity.
Henrich von Treitschke

The unfolding of miscalculations.
Barbara Tuchman

A game, but unfortunately the cards, counters, and fishes suffer by an ill run more than the gamesters.   *Horace Walpole*

The transformation of a man into a thing.
Simone Weil

Consists in getting at what is on the other side of the hill.   *Arthur W. Wellington*

Fear cloaked in courage.
William Westmoreland

A sort of dramatic representation, a...dramatic symbol of a thousand forms of duty.
Woodrow Wilson

A lucky turn-up of patronage for the minister, whose chief merit is the art of keeping himself in place.   *Mary Wollstonecraft*

Man—arranged for mutual slaughter.
William Wordsworth

The diplomat's vacation period.
Robert R. Young

A series of mathematical problems, to be solved through proper integration and coordination of men and weapons in time and space.
Georgi Zhukov

Pure hell—when you're getting licked.   *Anon.*

A business that ruins those who succeed in it.
Anon.

A period of intense boredom punctuated by moments of acute fear.   *Anon.*

Fertilization of the land on a vast scale.   *Anon.*

SEE ALSO ARMS, ARMY, BATTLE, BAT-TLEFIELD, CANNON, FIGHTING, GENERAL, MILITARISM, MILITIA, PEACE, SELF-DE-FENSE, SOLDIER, VICTORY.

WARRIOR

SEE SOLDIER.

WASHINGTON, D.C.

A city that goes around in circles.
John Mason Brown

A city of temporaries, a city of just-arriveds and only-visitings, built on the shifting sands of politics, filled with people passing through.
Allen Drury

Where an insignificant individual may trespass on a nation's time.   *Ralph Waldo Emerson*

Means Washington Demands Cash.
Jack Herbert

An endless series of mock palaces clearly built for clerks.   *Ada L. Huxtable*

A city of Southern efficiency and Northern charm.   *John Fitzgerald Kennedy*

City of magnificent vistas.   *Pierre C. L'Enfant*

A city where a political leader learns that the number of his friends goes up and down with his standing in the public-opinion polls.
Richard Milhous Nixon

It is us inescapably.   *Joel Sayre*

A city where one can relax—provided one is a congressman.   *Anon.*

The country's pressure point.   *Anon.*

First in war, first in peace, and last in the American League.   *Anon.*

A city of politicians and a lot of marble.   *Anon.*

SEE ALSO CONGRESS, PRESIDENCY, SEN-ATORS.

WASHINGTON, GEORGE (1732-1799)

A gentleman of one of the first fortunes upon the continent...sacrificing his ease, and hazarding all in the cause of his country.
John Quincy Adams

His talents...were adapted to lead without dazzling mankind, and to draw forth and employ the talents of others without being misled by them.
Fisher Ames

The father of his country.   *Francis Bailey*

A Virginia buckskin.   *Edward Braddock*

The greatest man that ever lived in this world uninspired by divine wisdom.

Henry Brougham

Here is a fine, fearless, placid man, perfectly well seated in the center of his soul, direct and pure.

Joseph Delteil

The Genius of these lands.   *Philip Freneau*

Washington is now only a steel engraving. About the real man who lived and loved and hated and schemed, we know but little.

Robert G. Ingersoll

He errs as other men do, but errs with integrity.

Thomas Jefferson

His mind was great and powerful, without being of the very first order; his penetration strong... and as far as he saw, no judgment was ever sounder.   *Thomas Jefferson*

A nobleness to try for,
A name to live and die for.   *George P. Lathrop*

A leader who could be induced by no earthly motive to tell a falsehood, or to break an engagement, or to commit any dishonorable act.

William E. Lecky

A citizen, first in war, first in peace, first in the hearts of his countrymen.   *Henry Lee*

The mightiest name on earth. On that name an eulogy is expected. Let none attempt it. In solemn awe pronounce the name and in its naked, deathless splendor leave it shining on.

Abraham Lincoln

Soldier and statesman.   *James Russell Lowell*

Friend of all climes, and pride of every age.

Thomas Paine

First Citizen of the Earth.   *James J. Roche*

The great ornament of human kind.   *Ezra Stiles*

The one man equal to his trust.   *Walt Whitman*

WATER

The first of things.   *John S. Blackie*

The natural, temperate and necessary beverage for the thirsty.   *Clement of Alexandria*

The greatest necessity of the soldier.

Napoleon 1

The noblest of the elements.   *Pindar*

The only drink for a wise man.

Henry David Thoreau

Liquid that freezes slippery side up.   *Anon.*

WEALTH

Not an end of life, but an instrument of life.

Henry Ward Beecher

Power.   *Edmund Burke*

A sacred trust which its possessor is bound to administer in his lifetime for the good of the community.   *Andrew Carnegie*

A good name.   *Miguel de Cervantes*

The savings of many in the hands of one.

Eugene V. Debs

Wisdom. He that's rich is wise.   *Daniel Defoe*

Consists not in having great possessions but in having few wants.   *Epicurus*

The thing most honored among men, and the source of the greatest power.   *Euripides*

Not his who has it, but his who enjoys it.

Benjamin Franklin

A...device of fate whereby men are made captive and burdened with responsibilities.

Elbert Hubbard

Owing nothing.   *Hungarian Proverb*

The general centre of inclination, the point to which all minds persevere an invariable tendency.

Samuel Johnson

What one is able to do without with dignity.

Immanuel Kant

Neither goodness, nor wit, nor talent, nor strength, nor delicacy. I don't know exactly what it is: I am waiting for someone to tell me.

Jean de La Bruyère

A thousand dollars a day—and expenses.

Pierre Lorillard

An excellent thing, for it means power, it means leisure, it means liberty.   *James Russell Lowell*

A great means of refinement; and it is a security for gentleness, since it removes disturbing anxieties.   *Ik Marvel*

Any income that is at least $100 more a year than the income of one's wife's sister's husband.

Henry Louis Mencken

A pretty promoter of intelligence, since it multiplies the avenues for its reception.

Donald G. Mitchell

A contented mind.   *Mohammed*

The product of man's capacity to think.

Ayn Rand

Evidence of greatness.   *Thomas B. Reed*

The possession of the valuable by the valiant.

John Ruskin

Life.   *John Ruskin*

A hostile comrade, a domestic enemy.

Saint John Chrysostom

Gilded torture.   *Saint Cyprian*

To have what is necessary; and, secondly, to have what is enough.   *Seneca*

A power usurped by the few, to compel the many to labor for their benefit.   *Percy Bysshe Shelley*

Good wife and health.   *Charles H. Spurgeon*

Only power, like steam, or electricity, or knowledge.   *William G. Sumner*

To be thought rich is as good as to be rich.

William Makepeace Thackeray

A matter of personal outlook.   *Anon.*

Like muck, which stinks in a heap, but spread around, makes the earth fruitful.   *Anon.*

The greatest force for good when spent wisely.

Anon.

SEE ALSO BANK, CAPITAL, DOLLAR, GOLD, LUXURY, MONEY, POSSESSIONS, PROPERTY, RICHES.

WEAPONS

SEE ARMS, CANNON.

WEATHER

The discourses of fools.   *Thomas Fuller*

A literary specialty, and no untrained hand can turn out a good article on it.   *Mark Twain*

Every man's chatter.   *Edward B. White*

WEDDING

A ceremony at which two persons undertake to become one, one undertakes to become nothing, and nothing undertakes to become supportable.

Ambrose Bierce

When the blind lead the blind.

George Farquhar

Same old slippers,
  Same old rice,
Same old glimpse of
  Paradise.   *William J. Lampton*

A hymeneal orgy.   *Henry Louis Mencken*

The point at which a man stops toasting a woman and begins roasting her.   *Helen Rowland*

A ceremony in which rings are put on the finger of the lady and through the nose of the gentleman.

Herbert Spencer

A funeral where you smell your own flowers.

Anon.

SEE ALSO BRIDE, HONEYMOON, MARRIAGE, NIAGARA FALLS, WIFE.

WEED

A plant whose virtues have not yet been discovered.   *Ralph Waldo Emerson*

A flower in disguise.   *James Russell Lowell*

An unloved flower.   *Ella W. Wilcox*

A plant with nine lives.   *Anon.*

A thriving garden plant.   *Anon.*

SEE ALSO GARDEN, GARDENING.

WEEKEND

To the husband, when repairs are done around the house. To the bachelor, a time for philandering.

Eugene E. Brussell

WELL-BRED

Differs, if at all, from high breeding only as it gracefully remembers the rights of others, rather than gracefully insists on its own rights.

Thomas Carlyle

The characteristic...is to converse with...inferiors without insolence, and with...superiors with respect and ease. *Lord Chesterfield*

Tenderness, compassion and good nature...that you show in any place. *William Law*

SEE ALSO BREEDING (MANNERS), GENTLEMAN, MANNERS.

WEST, THE OLD

A place where men were men and smelled like horses. *Judy Canova*

Out where the handclasp's a little stronger, out where the smile dwells a little longer—that's where the West begins.

Adapted from Arthur Chapman

Those who rested there made a fresh deal all around. *Brete Harte*

(A place) won by men on horseback—and is being lost to men on bulldozers. *Harry Karns*

The land of the heart. *George P. Morris*

This worthless area, this region of savages and wild beasts...of cactus and prairie dogs.

Daniel Webster

A corner of heaven itself. *D. Eardley Wilmot*

A place that lacked water and society. *Anon.*

A land unmortgaged. *Anon.*

A place that saw the greatest transmigration of greenhorns since the Children of Israel left Egypt.

Anon.

A place to get away from something, to get something. *Anon.*

A good land irrigated by a lot of sweat. *Anon.*

WHISKEY

The devil's right bower. *Elbert Hubbard*

I like it, I always did, and that is the reason I never use it. *Robert E. Lee*

A torchlight procession marching down your throat. *George W. Russell*

Trouble put up in liquid form. *Gideon Wurdz*

A popular cold remedy that won't cure a cold.

Anon.

The only enemy that man has succeeded in loving. *Anon.*

That which makes you see double and feel single.

Anon.

SEE ALSO DRINKING, DRUNKENNESS.

WHITE HOUSE

SEE PRESIDENCY, PRESIDENT.

WHITMAN, WALT (1819-1892)

We go to Whitman for his attitude toward life and the universe; we go to fortify our souls...for his cosmic philosophy incarnated in a man.

John Burroughs

The Christ of the modern world.

John Burroughs

A Balaam come to judgment. *Aleister Crowley*

He was harmonized, orchestrated, identified with the program of being. *Zona Gale*

Mr. Whitman's muse is at once indecent and ugly, lascivious and gawky, lubricious and coarse.

Lafcadio Hearn

He departed from all received forms, and indulged in barbarous eccentricities.

Henry Cabot Lodge

A large, shaggy dog, just unchained, scouring the beaches of the world and baying at the moon.

Robert Louis Stevenson

Democracy's divine protagonist.

Francis H. Williams

WHORE

SEE PROSTITUTE.

WICKEDNESS

Anything the old cannot enjoy. *Anton Chekhov*

Wholehearted sin. *Leonard L. Levinson*

Weakness. *John Milton*

To wish to appear wicked. *Quintilian*

A sickness. *Voltaire*

A myth invented by good people to account for the curious attraction of others. *Oscar Wilde*

SEE ALSO EVIL, IMMORALITY, SIN, VICE.

WIDOW

The most perverse creatures in the world.
Joseph Addison

A rudderless boat. *Chinese Proverb*

What's a widow but an axle broke, whose one part falling, neither part can move.
Adapted from John Davies

The financial remains of a love affair.
George Jean Nathan

Those . . . too wise for bachelors to wed.
Alexander Pope

Marilla W. Ricker has often told us that widows are divided into two classes—the bereaved and relieved. She forgot the deceived—the grass widows. *Victor Robinson*

A widow must be a mourner. *Jeremy Taylor*

One who is sadder but wiser. *Anon.*

SEE ALSO FUNERAL.

WIFE

A joy to her husband; she shall double the days of his life. *Apocrypha; Ben Sira, XXVI, 1.*

Double strife. *Francis Bacon*

Young men's mistresses; companions for middle age; and old men's nurses. *Francis Bacon*

A slave who demands to be set on a throne.
Honoré de Balzac

A sweetheart is a bottle of wine;
A wife is a wine bottle. *Charles Baudelaire*

And Adam said, This is now bone of my bones, and flesh of my flesh. *Bible: Genesis, II, 18.*

The weaker vessel. *Bible: Peter, III, 7.*

A crown to her husband.
Bible: Proverbs, XII, 1.

She looketh well to the ways of her household, and eateth not the bread of idleness.
Bible: Proverbs, XXXI, 27.

The first wife is matrimony, the second company, the third heresy. *Henry G. Bohn*

Man's best possession. *Robert Burton*

Poison to the dearest sweets of love.
John Dryden

The soul of a great household; she introduces order there for temporal welfare and future salvation. *Francois de Fenelon*

A man's mental mate, and his competitor in the race for power. *Elbert Hubbard*

He that outlives a wife whom he has loved, sees himself disjoined from the only mind that has the same hope, fears, and interest. *Samuel Johnson*

Your tillage. *Koran, 2.*

That sovereign bliss. *David Mallett*

The bourgeois sees in his wife a mere instrument of production. *Karl Marx*

A former sweetheart. *Henry Louis Mencken*

One who is sorry she did it, but would undoubtedly do it again. *Henry Louis Mencken*

Heaven's last best gift. *John Milton*

Home means wife. *Mishna: Yoma, I, 1.*

A person who reminds one that her allowance is not as big as her alimony would be.
Vaughn Monroe

A man's wife is his compromise with the illusion of his first sweetheart. *George Jean Nathan*

One who will do anything for her husband except stop criticizing and trying to improve him.
John B. Priestly

A man's best fortune or his worst. *John Ray*

The partner of my soul. *Nicholas Rowe*

My better half. *Philip Sidney*

A fellow-farer true through life.
Robert Louis Stevenson

An ideal wife is any woman who has an ideal husband. *Booth Tarkington*

No woman is a wife who is not a mother too.
Welsh Proverb

The clog of all pleasure, the luggage of life.
John Wilmot

A tourniquet—she stops your circulation.

Anon.

One who stands by a man in all the trouble he wouldn't have if he hadn't married.   *Anon.*

One who knows everything except why she married you.   *Anon.*

A companionable vessel.   *Anon.*

A housekeeper who gets bed and boredom.

Anon.

SEE ALSO BRIDE, MARRIAGE, MOTHER, WOMAN.

WILDE, OSCAR (1854-1900)

The most enchanting company in the universe.

Max Beerbohm

A delicate design that lay like lace
Upon the purple velvet of disgrace.   *John Macy*

If, with the literate, I am
Impelled to try an epigram,
I never seek to take the credit;
We all assume that Oscar said it.

Dorothy Parker

The one person I would like to meet in heaven.

George Bernard Shaw

What has Oscar in common with art? except that he dines at our tables and picks from our platters the plums for the puddings he peddles in the provinces. Oscar...has the courage of the opinions...of others.   *James McNeill Whistler*

WILL

The God of the universe.

Michael J. Berdichevsky

The master of the world. Those who want something, those who know what they want, even those who want nothing, but want it badly, govern the world.   *Ferdinand Brunetiere*

That by which the mind chooses anything.

Jonathan Edwards

The education of the will is the object of our existence.   *Ralph Waldo Emerson*

The slaves of the accumulated influence of our interior companionships.

Harry Emerson Fosdick

Faith and persistency.   *Aldous Huxley*

A faculty to chose *that only* which reason independent of inclination recognizes as practically necessary, i.e., as good.   *Immanuel Kant*

A faculty of determining oneself to action in accordance with the conception of certain laws.

Immanuel Kant

That which has all power; it makes heaven and it makes hell; for there is no hell but where the will of the creature is turned from God, nor any heaven but where the will of the creature works with God.

William Law

The will is taken for the deed.   *Legal Maxim*

Nothing but the power, or ability, to prefer or choose.   *John Locke*

A beast of burden. If God mounts it, it wishes and goes as God wills; if Satan mounts it, it wishes and goes as Satan wills. Nor can it choose its rider...The riders contend for its possession.

Martin Luther

Character in action   *William McDougall*

By *will*, or rational appetite in general, we mean the faculty of inclining towards or striving after some object defined simply as the *capacity of self-determination.*   *John A. O'Brien*

One of the principal organs of belief, not that it forms belief, but because things are true or false according to the side on which we look at them.

Blaise Pascal

Nothing more than a particular case of the general doctrine of assocation of ideas, and therefore a perfectly mechanical thing.   *Joseph Priestly*

The foundation of all being; it is part and parcel of every creature, and the permanent element in every thing.   *Arthur Schopenhauer*

The only permanent and unchangeable element in the mind...it...gives unity to consciousness and holds together all its ideas and thoughts, accompanying them like a continuous harmony.

Arthur Schopenhauer

A simple homogeneous mental state, forming the link between feeling and action, and not admitting of subdivisions.   *Herbert Spencer*

Will and understanding are one and the same.

Baruch Spinoza

The pump of appetite.   *Lope de Vega*

The Will is the Man.   *John Wilson*

SEE ALSO CHARACTER, CHOICE, DEEDS,
FREE WILL, SUCCESS, VICTORY.

WILL, FREE

SEE FREE WILL.

WILSON, WOODROW (1856-1924)

He is standing at the throne of a God whose
approval he won and has received.

Newton D. Baker

He was the sole out-post for that world-old hope
that humanity can never quite release; he gave his
heart, his life, his soul to hold our eyes upon the
gleam of lasting peace.

Adapted from S. Omar Barker

The man who imposed himself as the supreme
head of the continental empire of the United
States. Who, further, handled that colossal power
as if it were a sword in his hand . . . With this and
the power of his thought he ends the war. And then
in person he sets out to save humanity by ending
war for ever.   *William Bolitho*

It was harder to de-bamboozle this old Presbyterian than it had been to bamboozle him, for
the former involved his belief in and respect for
himself.   *John M. Keynes*

The university president who cashiered every
professor unwilling to support Woodrow Wilson
for the first vacancy in the Trinity.

Henry Louis Mencken

A very adroit . . . (but not forceful) hypocrite.

Theodore Roosevelt

He had made our statesmanship a thing of empty
elocution. He has covered his fear of standing for
the right behind a veil of rhetorical phrases. He
has wrapped the true heart of the nation in a
spangled shroud of rhetoric.

Theodore Roosevelt

The most perfect example we have produced of
the culture which has failed and is dying out.

Lincoln Steffens

No man ever more fully exemplified the adage
that the pen is mightier than the sword.

Mark Sullivan

WINE

An unreliable emissary: I sent it down to my
stomach, and it went up to my head!

Judah Al-Harizi

The blood of grapes.   *Bible: Genesis, XLIX, 2.*

A mocker.   *Bible: Proverbs, XX, 1.*

A turn-coat; first a friend, and then an enemy.

Thomas Fuller

Created only to comfort mourners and requite
sinners.   *Hanan, Sanhedrin, 70a.*

A food.   *Oliver Wendell Holmes 1*

(A drink) pernicious to mankind; it unnerves the
limbs, and dulls the noble mind.   *Homer*

An infallible antidote to commonsense and seriousness.   *Elbert Hubbard*

An excuse for deeds otherwise unforgivable.

Elbert Hubbard

A traitor not to trust.   *Robert U. Johnson*

Makes a man mistake words for thoughts.

Samuel Johnson

Old men's milk.   *Medieval Latin Phrase*

The beginning of all sin.   *Menahem Meiri*

The most healthful and most hygienic of bev-
erages.   *Louis Pasteur*

A remedy for the moroseness of old age.   *Plato*

It first seizes the feet; it is a crafty wrestler.

Plautus

It transformeth a man into a beast, decayeth
health, poisoneth the breath, destroyeth natural
heat, deformeth the fact, rotteneth the teeth, and
maketh a man contemptible.   *Walter Raleigh*

The first weapon that devils use in attacking the
young.   *Saint Jerome*

Bottled poetry.   *Robert Louis Stevenson*

The divine juice of September.   *Voltaire*

One of the noblest cordials in nature.

John Wesley

SEE ALSO CHAMPAGNE, DRINKING, DRUNK-
ENNESS.

WINTER

Clouds, and storms. *James Thomson*

When the electric-blanket lights come on to mark the progress of the cold front. *William Vaughan*

The season when we try to keep the house as warm as it was in the summer, when we complained about the heat. *Anon.*

The reason why California and Florida boast of high real estate value. *Anon.*

SEE ALSO CHRISTMAS, FEBRUARY.

WISDOM

Consists in the highest use of the intellect for the discernment of the largest moral interest of humanity. *Felix Adler*

Working for the better from the love of the best. *Felix Adler*

Wisdom comes by suffering. *Aeschylus*

In calamity not to cherish anger against the gods. *Aeschylus*

Consists in rising superior both to madness and to common sense, and in lending one's self to the universal delusion without becoming its dupe. *Henry F. Amiel*

The soul's natural food. *Jacob Anatoli*

The spirit of human love. *Apocrypha: Wisdom of Solomon, I, 6.*

The wisdom of this world is foolishness with God. *Bible: Corinthians, III, 19.*

Vexation. *Bible Ecclesiastes, I, 18.*

Days should speak, and multitude of years should teach wisdom. *Bible: Job, XXXII, 7.*

The beginning of wisdom is: Get wisdom. *Bible: Psalms, CXI, 10.*

A special knowledge in excess of all that is known. *Ambrose Bierce*

Pain is the father, and love the mother of wisdom. *Ludwig Boerne*

Keeping a sense of the fallibility of all our views and opinions. *Gerald Brenan*

The highest achievement of man. *Thomas Carlyle*

The sad smile with which we recognize our own motives in a fool. *John Ciardi*

The knowledge of things human and divine and of the cause by which those things are controlled. *Cicero*

Pretending to know and believe more than we really do. *William Congreve*

To stand prepared to meet the worst. *Adapted from Nathaniel Cotton*

Never to repent and never to reproach others, these are the first steps to wisdom. *Denis Diderot*

A collection of platitudes. *Norman Douglas*

Two words—wait and hope. *Alexander Dumas*

To finish the moment, to find the journey's end in every step of the road, to live the greatest number of good hours. *Ralph Waldo Emerson*

To see the miraculous in the common. *Ralph Waldo Emerson*

Knowing when you can't be wise. *Paul Engle*

The ability to do good and to abandon sin. *Jonah Gerondi*

To read aright the present, and to march with the occasion. *Homer*

Knowing what to do next. *Herbert C. Hoover*

Denotes the pursuing of the best ends by the best means. *Frances I. Hutcheson*

Knowing what to overlook. *William James*

(Consists of) knowing what to do next; virtue in doing it. *David Starr Jordan*

The science of happiness. *Gottfried W. von Leibnitz*

The means of attaining the lasting contentment which consists in the continual achievement of a greater perfection or at least in variations of the same degree of perfection. *Gottfried W. von Leibnitz*

Learning aged in wood. *Leonard L. Levinson*

To recognize that there is an original Being . . . and that all . . . exist only through the reality of His being. *Moses Maimonides*

To know that which before us lies in daily life.

Adapted from John Milton

The faculty of judging from the very viewpoint of . . . Creator and Father.   *Peter Minard*

To take things as they are . . . to endure what we cannot evade . . . to live and die well.

Michel de Montaigne

The truest wisdom . . . is a resolute determination.

Napoleon 1

The final wisdom of life requires not the annulment of incongruity but the achivement of serenity within and above it.   *Reinhold Neibuhr*

The chief aim . . . is to enable one to bear with the stupidity of the ignorant.   *Pope Sixtus I*

Being wise in time.   *Theodore Roosevelt*

All things that pass
Are wisdom's looking-glass.

Christina Rossetti

The greatest good.   *Saint Augustine*

Wise in words . . . wise in deeds.   *Saint Gregory*

To believe the heart.   *George Santayana*

Taking all things as much as possible seriously, but nothing too gravely.

Adapted from Arthur Schnitzler

Palpable falsehood till it come and utter itself by my side.   *Henry David Thoreau*

Inward silence.   *John Greenleaf Whittier*

Something divided into two parts:
(a) having a great deal to say;
(b) not saying it.   *Anon.*

Making the most of all that comes, the least of all that goes.   *Anon.*

SEE ALSO BOOK, EXPERIENCE, JUDGMENT.

WISE

This wisest man is he who does not believe that he is.   *Nicolas Boileau*

They only are wise who know that they know nothing.   *Thomas Carlyle*

They call him the wisest man to whose mind that which is required occurs.   *Cicero*

The wise man does nothing of which he can repent, nothing against his will, but does everything nobly, consistently, soberly, rightly.

Cicero

He . . . who does not grieve for the things which he has not, but rejoices for those which he has.

Epictetus

Man is wise only in search of wisdom; when he imagines he has attained it, he is a fool.

Solomon Ibn Gabirol

A reputation that is built by agreeing with everybody.   *Jewish Saying*

Anyone who follows a middle course.

Moses Maimonides

Who is wise? He who learns from everybody.

Mishna: Abot, IV, 1.

Those who drink old wine and see old plays.

Plautus

To know how little can be known.

Alexander Pope

To see all other's faults, and feel our own.

Alexander Pope

The wisest man preaches no doctrines; he has no scheme; he sees no rafter, not even a cobweb, against the heavens. It is clear sky.

Henry David Thoreau

A wise man will not communicate his thoughts to unprepared minds, or in a disorderly manner.

Benjamin Whichcote

Knowing yourself and not telling anyone.

Anon.

WISH

SEE HOPE.

WIT

Educated insolence.   *Artistotle*

A sharp and clever remark, usually quoted, and seldom noted.   *Ambrose Bierce*

A treacherous dart . . . the only weapon with which it is possible to stab oneself in one's own back.

Geoffrey Bocca

The best safety valve modern man has evolved; the more civilization, the more repression, the more need for wit.   *Abraham Brill*

Reason which is chastely expressed.
                                    Marie J. de Chénier

Wit is so shining a quality that everybody admires it; most people aim at it, and few love it except in themselves.   *Lord Chesterfield*

It pleases only the mind, and never distorts the countenance.   *Lord Chesterfield*

(Something which) makes its own welcome, and levels all distinctions.   *Ralph Waldo Emerson*

The thing that helps us play the fool with more confidence.   *Thomas Fuller*

A form of lightening calculation.   *Russell Green*

Humor is the electric atmosphere; wit is the flash.
                                    Hugh R. Haweis

The rarest quality to be met with among people of education, and the most common among the uneducated.   *William Hazlitt*

The salt of conversation, not the food.
                                    William Hazlitt

An unruly engine, widely striking sometimes a friend, sometimes the engineer.
                                    George Herbert

To be witty is not enough without sufficient wit to avoid having too much of it.
                                    Adapted from Emile Herzog

Two things: celerity of imagining (that is, swift succession of one thought to another), and steady direction to some approved end.
                                    Thomas Hobbes

The thing that fractures many a friendship.
                                    Elbert Hubbard

The clash and reconcilement of incongruities, the meeting of extremes round a corner.
                                    Leigh Hunt

The terse intrusion into an atmosphere of serene mental habit of some uncompromising truth.
                                    Philander Johnson

That which is at once natural and new; that which, though not obvious, is, upon its first production, acknowledged to be just.   *Samuel Johnson*

A combination of dissimilar images, or discovery of occult resemblances in things apparently unlike.   *Samuel Johnson*

The true touchstone of wit is the impromptu.
                                    Moliere

The most rascally, contemptible, beggarly thing on the face of the earth.   *Arthur Murphy*

The epitaph of an emotion.
                                    Friedrich W. Nietzsche

A justness of thought and a facility of expression, or (in the midwive's phrase) a perfect conception with an easy delivery.   *Alexander Pope*

Nature to advantage dressed, what often was thought but never so well expressed.
                                    Adapted from Alexander Pope

There's no possibility of being witty without a little ill-nature; the malice of a good thing is the barb that makes it stick.
                                    Richard Brinsley Sheridan

Consists in knowing the resemblance of things which differ, and the difference of things which are alike.   *Anne Louise de Staël*

The sudden marriage of ideas which before their marriage were not perceived to have any relation.
                                    Mark Twain

Wit is the only wall
Between us and the darkness.   *Mark Van Doren*

The unexpected explosion of thought.
                                    Edwin P. Whipple

WITCH

Atheists.   *Thomas Browne*

They are neither man nor woman—
They are neither brute nor human,
They are Ghouls!   *Edgar Allan Poe*

The weird sisters.   *William Shakespeare*

WITS

Those who jest with good taste.   *Aristotle*

Brutes.   *Caron de Beaumarchais*

The man who sees the consistency in things.
                                    Gilbert Keith Chesterton

Great wits are sure to madness near allied, and thin partitions do their bounds divide.

Adapted from John Dryden

Sayer of *bons mots* . . . bad character.

Blaise Pascal

(A wit) needs to be pitied, being the only person in an atmosphere of social relaxation who cannot relax. The man who is famous for witty flings is never off-duty. *Hesketh Pearson*

SEE ALSO COMEDIAN, HUMORIST.

WOMAN

Largely the product of the romantic imagination of men. *Charles Angoff*

An inferior man. *Aristotle*

A creature between man and the angels.

Honoré de Balzac

The man is not of the woman; but the woman of the man. Neither was the man created for the woman; but the woman for the man.

Bible: Corinthians, II, 8-9.

To men a man is but a mind . . . But woman's body is the woman. *Ambrose Bierce*

An animal usually living in the vicinity of man, and having a rudimentary susceptibility to domestication. *Ambrose Bierce*

Being a woman is a terribly difficult task, since it consists principally in dealing with men.

Joseph Conrad

One of nature's agreeable blunders.

Hannah Cowley

A species that cannot love an automobile.

Bernard De Voto

Every woman is a science. *John Donne*

(She) inspires us to great things—and prevents us accomplishing them. *Alexander Dumas*

Woman exists chiefly to demonstrate to man the Lord's sense of humor. *Ninon T. Fleckenstein*

A microcosm: and rightly to rule her requires as great talents as to govern a state. *Samuel Foote*

A creature that carries her weapons on her.

Warren Goldberg

A sometime thing. *Du Bose Heyward*

A woman is only a woman, but a good cigar is a smoke. *Rudyard Kipling*

A frail vessel. *Martin Luther*

One man's lady is another man's woman; sometimes, one man's lady is another man's wife. Definitions overlap but they almost never coincide. *Russell Lynes*

A person who would rather have a caress than a career. *Elizabeth Marbury*

Although the story goes that woman was contrived from Adam's rib, I have a different theory. In her public sense, she sprang full-panoplied out of his imagination. *Phyllis McGinley*

An evil, and he is a lucky man who catches her in the mildest form. *Menander*

The last thing man will civilize.

George Meredith

A tyrant until she's reduced to bondage, and a rebel until she's well beaten. *George Meredith*

The substance of our lives . . . All other things are irrelevancies. *George Moore*

The second mistake of God.

Friedrich W. Nietzsche

A desirable calamity. *Palladius*

A teabag—you can't tell how strong she is until you put her in hot water. *Nancy Reagan*

The peg on which the wit hangs his jest, the preacher his text, the cynic his grouch, and the sinner his justification. *Helen Rowland*

The Devil's agent. *Russian Proverb*

An evil no household should be without.

Russian Proverb

A sort of intermediate stage between a child and a man. *Arthur Schopenhauer*

That undersized, narrow-shouldered, broad-hipped, and short-legged race.

Arthur Schopenhauer

A ministering angel. *Walter Scott*

A female of the human species, and not a different kind of animal. *George Bernard Shaw*

The baggage of life. *John Suckling*

A distinct race. *Talmud: Sabbath, 62a.*

The confusion of man. *Vincent of Beauvais*

Picturesque protests against the mere existence of common sense. *Oscar Wilde*

The companions, not the satellites of men.
Emma Willard

A biped with two hands, two feet, two breasts, two eyes and two faces. *Anon.*

A multiplication table for the human species.
Anon.

A person who will look in a mirror any time—except when she is pulling out of a parking space.
Anon.

SEE ALSO COQUETTE, COSMETICS, COURTESAN, HAIR, HUSBAND, LADY, LOVE, LOVERS, MARRIAGE, MOTHER, MOTHERHOOD, SEX (LOVE), SEXES (MEN AND WOMEN), SHREW, VIRGINITY, WIDOW, WIFE, WOMEN.

WOMEN

The weaker sex, to piety more prone.
William Alexander

A device invented by Providence to keep the wit of man well sharpened by constant employment.
Arnold Bennett

Here's to woman! Would that we could fall into her arms without falling into her hands.
Ambrose Bierce

A sweetheart is milk, a bride is butter, And a wife—is cheese. *Ludwig Boerne*

An animal, and an animal not of the highest order. *Edmund Burke*

Only children of a larger growth.
Lord Chesterfield

(One) to be talked to as below men, and above children. *Gilbert Keith Chesterton*

Women will be as pleasing to men as whiskey when they learn to improve as much with age.
Franklin Dane

Women are door-mats. *Mary C. Davies*

Theirs is the only useless life.
Benjamin Disraeli

The latest thing in clothes is usually the woman you've been waiting for. *John Dobina*

Like pictures; of no value in the hands of a fool till he hears men of sense bid high for the purchase.
George Farquhar

A sweet poison. *French Proverb*

Like death: they pursue those who flee from them, and flee from those who pursue them.
German Proverb

(A creature) created for the comfort of men.
James Howell

A being to get rid of or to secure—to run away from, or with, as the case may be.
Elbert Hubbard

(One who) would rather marry a poor provider any time than a poor listener. *Kin Hubbard*

Those who look like angels until you see them crunching bread and herring. *Jewish Saying*

As the faculty of writing has been chiefly a masculine endowment, the reproach of making the world miserable has always been thrown upon the women. *Samuel Johnson*

The shadows of men. *Ben Jonson*

Children whom I would rather give a sugar plum than my time. *John Keats*

(A species) more deadly than the male.
Rudyard Kipling

Women have simple tastes. They can get pleasure out of the conversation of children in arms and men in love. *Henry Louis Mencken*

Saints in the church, angels in the street, devils in the kitchen, and apes in your bed.
Thomas Middleton

Women have two weapons—cosmetics and tears.
Napoleon 1

They are all saints abroad, but ask their maids what they are at home. *Charles H. Spurgeon*

(Creatures who) are wiser than men because they know less and understand more.
James Stephens

Two types of women: those who wear well and those who wear little. *Walter Streightiff*

(Those who) like not only to conquer, but to be conquered. *William Makepeace Thackeray*

Wicked women bother one. Good women bore one. That is the only difference between them.
Oscar Wilde

A decorative sex . . . They represent the triumph of matter over mind. *Oscar Wilde*

Sphinxes without secrets. *Oscar Wilde*

Looking glasses possessing the . . . power of reflecting the figure of man at twice its natural size. *Virginia Woolf*

Those who inspire us to do masterpieces, and then get in the way of our carrying them out. *Anon.*

The wild life of a country. Morality corresponds to game laws. *Anon.*

One who needs no eulogy—she speaks for herself. *Anon.*

The obstinate sex. *Anon.*

An infinity of cosmetics. *Anon.*

One who never opens her mouth unless she has nothing to say. *Anon.*

Demons that make us enter Hell through the door of Paradise. *Anon.*

SEE ALSO BACHELOR, BEAUTY, BRIDE, COSMETICS, COURTESAN, GIRLS, HUSBAND, LADY, LOVE, LOVERS, MARRIAGE, MISTRESS, MOTHER, PROSTITUTE, SEX (LOVE), SEXES (MEN AND WOMEN), SHREW, VIRGINITY, WIDOW, WIFE, WOMAN.

WONDER

Implies the desire to learn. *Aristotle*

The basis of worship. *Thomas Carlyle*

The seed of our science. *Ralph Waldo Emerson*

The attitude of reverence for the infinite values and meaning of life, and of marveling over God's purpose and patience in it all. *George W. Fiske*

The root of knowledge. *Abraham J. Heschel*

The effect of novelty upon ignorance. *Samuel Johnson*

The purpose of contemplative life. *Charles Morgan*

To begin to understand. *José Ortega y Gasset*

The feeling of a philosopher, and philosophy begins in wonder. *Plato*

WORDS

The tokens current and accepted for conceits, as moneys are for values. *Francis Bacon*

Words are but wind. *Richard Barnfield*

An unnecessary stain on silence and nothingness. *Samuel Beckett*

Pegs to hang ideas on. *Henry Ward Beecher*

And the word was made flesh and dwelt among us. *Bible: John, I, 14.*

The saddest words of tongue or pen are those you didn't think of then. *Betty Billipp*

An attempt to grip and dissect that which in ultimate essence is as ungrippable as a shadow. *Samuel Butler 2*

The clothes that thoughts wear—only the clothes. *Samuel Butler 2*

Words are things, and a small drop of ink, falling like dew upon a thought, produces that which makes thousands, perhaps millions think. *Lord Byron*

A word's enough to raise mankind to kill. *Lord Byron*

Words are what hold society together. *Stuart Chase*

The dress of thoughts; which should no more be presented in rags, tatters, and dirt, than your person should. *Lord Chesterfield*

Words are used to express meaning; when you understand the meaning, you can forget about the words. *Chuang-tse*

A weathercock for ev'ry wind. *John Dryden*

Living, protean things. They grow, take roots, adapt to environmental changes like any plant or animal. *Bergen Evans*

An arrow let fly. *Thomas Fuller*

Articulate words are a harsh clamor and dissonance. When man arrives at his highest perfection, he will again be dumb! *Nathaniel Hawthorne*

The only things that last forever. *William Hazlitt*

Words are women, deeds are men. *George Herbert*

The skin of a living thought and may vary greatly in color and content according to the circumstances and time in which it is used.
Oliver Wendell Holmes 2

The soul's ambassadors, who go abroad upon her errands to and fro.   *James Howell*

The humming-birds of the imagination.
Elbert Hubbard

Power to mould men's thinking, to canalize feeling, to direct willing and acting.
Adapted from Aldous Huxley

Tools which automatically carve concepts out of experience.   *Julian Huxley*

Words are like bodies, and meanings like souls.
Abraham Ibn Ezra

A man coins not a new word without some peril and less fruits; for if it happen to be received, the praise if but moderate; if refused, the scorn is assured.   *Ben Jonson*

Man's refusal to accept the world as it is.
Walter Kaufmann

The most powerful drug used by mankind.
Rudyard Kipling

The signs of our ideas only, and not...things themselves.   *John Locke*

Water—...it moves in any direction.
Bernard Malamud

Apt words have power to suage
The tumors of a troubl'd mind.   *John Milton*

Every word is a preconceived judgment.
Friedrich W. Nietzsche

Things to kill time until emotions make us inarticulate.   *Arthur S. Roche*

They sing. They hurt. They teach. They sanctify. They were man's first, immeasurable feat of magic. They liberated us from ignorance and our barbarous past.   *Leo C. Rosten*

The opiate of the intellectuals.   *Leo C. Rosten*

Words are loaded pistols.   *Jean-Paul Sartre*

Servants to shallow fools.   *William Shakespeare*

Weapons.   *Percy Bysshe Shelley*

A powerful agent.   *Mark Twain*

A symbol, and its meaning is constituted by the ideas, images, and emotions, which it raises in the mind of the hearer.   *Alfred North Whitehead*

The gate of scholarship.   *Woodrow Wilson*

Tools of force and persuasion.   *Anon.*

SEE ALSO ELOQUENCE, LANGUAGE, POETRY, PROSE, RHETORIC, SEMANTICS, SILENCE, SLANG, SOPHISTRY, SPEECH, STYLE, TONGUE, WRITING.

WORK

The real essence...is concentrated energy.
Walter Bagehot

A remedy against all ills.   *Charles Baudelaire*

A high human function...the most dignified thing in the life of man.   *David Ben-Gurion*

A dangerous disorder affecting high public functionaries who want to go fishing.
Ambrose Bierce

All work...is noble; work alone is noble...A life of ease is not for any man, nor for any god.
Thomas Carlyle

The grand cure for all the maladies and miseries that ever beset mankind.   *Thomas Carlyle*

A life purpose.   *Thomas Carlyle*

The prerogative of intelligence, the only means to manhood, and the measure of civilization. Savages do not work.   *Calvin Coolidge*

The finest expression of the human spirit.
Walter Courtenay

Work is work if you're paid to do it, and it's pleasure if you pay to be allowed to do it.
Finley Peter Dunne

The sire of fame.   *Euripides*

The salvation of the race.   *Henry Ford*

Love made visible.   *Kahlil Gibran*

Paid struggle.   *Max Gralnick*

A social duty.
Grand Council of Fascism, 1927.

The greatest thing in the world, so we should always save some of it for tomorrow.
Don Herold

A form of nervousness.   *Don Herold*

An easy solution of the problems which confront the autonomous individual. *Eric Hoffer*

The goose that lays the golden egg. Payrolls make consumers. *George Humphrey*

Useful work is worship...the highest form of prayer. *Robert G. Ingersoll*

The yeast that raises the dough. *Irish Digest*

Exercise continued to fatigue. *Samuel Johnson*

The safe and general antidote against sorrow.
Samuel Johnson

Work is half one's life—and the other half, too.
Erich Kastner

Something...which must be done, whether you like it or not. *James Russell Lowell*

An activity reserved for the dullard. It is the very opposite of creation, which is play, and which just because it has no *raison d'être* other than itself is the supreme motivating power in life.
Henry Miller

The law of life and its best friend. *Lewis Morris*

Work expands so as to fill the time available for its completion (and) the thing to be done swells in importance and complexity in a direct ratio with the time to be spent. *C. Northcote Parkinson*

A necessity for man. Man invented the alarm-clock. *Pablo Picasso*

What you do so that some time you won't have to do it any more. *Alfred Polgar*

A continuation of the labor of Jesus Christ Himself. *Pope John XXIII*

Two kinds: first, altering the position of matter at or near the earth's surface relatively to other such matter; second, telling other people to do so. The first kind is unpleasant and ill paid; the second is pleasant and highly paid. *Bertrand A. Russell*

To work is to pray. *Saint Augustine*

The significance of the individual.
Jean-Paul Sartre

To serve God in his calling. *Richard Steele*

The inevitable condition of human life, the true source of welfare. *Leon Tolstoy*

An incidental means of spiritual edification.
Arnold J. Toynbee

Consists of whatever a body is obliged to do, and play consists of whatever a body is not obliged to do. *Mark Twain*

Activity for wages that is detrimental to the health. *Benjamin Twore*

The sweetest of pleasures.
Luc de Vauvenargues

My life. *Richard Wagner*

The curse of the drinking classes. *Oscar Wilde*

Work is something you want to get done; play is something you just like to be doing.
Harry Wilson

Drudgery in disguise. *Anon.*

The easiest activity man has invented to escape boredom. *Anon.*

SEE ALSO DUTY, FARMING, LABOR, PU-RITANISM, VOCATION.

WORKERS

The sons of little men. *Robert Burns*

Soldiers with different weapons but the same courage. *Winston S. Churchill*

Those who rely for work upon the ventures of confident and contented capital.
Grover Cleveland

The saviors of society, the redeemers of the race.
Eugene V. Debs

The slave of the bourgeoisie. *Friedrich Engels*

The author of all greatness and wealth.
Ulysses S. Grant

The wealth of a country. *Theodor Herzl*

It is by working that we become workers.
Latin Proverb

Those who live exclusively...by their own labor and who do not grow rich through the labor of others. Besides wage-earners it includes the small farmers and small shopkeepers.
William Liebknecht

The basis of all government, for the plain reason that they are the most numerous.
Abraham Lincoln

Mechanic slaves. *William Shakespeare*

Living pulleys of a dead machine.
Percy Bysshe Shelley

Mere wheels of work and articles of trade.
Percy Bysshe Shelley

The American worker is merely a capitalist without money.
George Sokolsky

A man who goes to work before 9 a.m.
Anon.

Those who count the clock oftenest.
Anon.

WORLD

A corpse, and they who seek it are dogs.
Arabian Proverb

A great poem.
Philip J. Bailey

God's workshop for making men.
Henry Ward Beecher

A board with two kinds of holes in it, and the square men have got into the round holes and the round men into the square holes.
George Berkeley

To me the world is one gallows.
Hayyim N. Bialik

A spacious burial-field strewn with death's spoils.
Adapted from Robert Blair

A mirror: what looks in looks out. It returns only what you lend it.
Ludwig Boerne

(A place) inhabited by beasts, but studied and contemplated by man.
Thomas Browne

A small parenthesis in eternity.
Thomas Browne

I count it not an inn but a hospital, and a place not to live, but to die in.
Thomas Browne

Where all the heaviest wrongs get uppermost.
Elizabeth Barrett Browning

A gambling table so arranged that all who enter the casino must play, and all must lose more or less heavily in the long run, though they win occasionally by the way.
Samuel Butler 2

A republic of mediocrities.
Thomas Carlyle

A thoroughfare full of woe.
Geoffrey Chaucer

A country which nobody ever yet knew by description; one must travel through it one's self to be acquainted with it.
Lord Chesterfield

(A place which) does not end with the life of any man.
Winston S. Churchill

A scene of changes.
Abraham Cowley

A vast house of assignation to which the filing system has been lost.
Quentin Crisp

An inn, and death the journey's end.
John Dryden

A great factory or shop of power.
Ralph Waldo Emerson

A divine dream, from which we may presently awake to the glories and certainties of day.
Ralph Waldo Emerson

A proud place, peopled with men of positive quality, with heroes and demigods standing around us, who will not let us sleep.
Ralph Waldo Emerson

The world is all a carcass and vanity,
The shadow of a shadow, a play
And in one word, just nothing.
Owen Felltham

Nothing but craft and cozenage.
John Fletcher

A ladder for some to go up and some down.
Thomas Fuller

A singularly stupendous fool.
Johann W. Goethe

A beautiful book, but of little use to him who cannot read it.
Carlo Goldoni

It is merely zero; but with Heaven before it, it means much.
Baltasar Gracian

Nothing but vanity cut out into several shapes.
Lord Halifax

That cold accretion...so terrible in the mass ... so unformidable, even pitiable in its units.
Thomas Hardy

That great baby.
William Hazlitt

A volume larger than all the libraries in it.
William Hazlitt

If the world were good for nothing else, it is a fine subject for speculation.
William Hazlitt

The world stands on three pillars: law, worship, and charity.
Hebrew Proverb

The world is what I share with others.
Martin Heidegger

A fine place and worth fighting for.

Ernest Hemingway

A stage which God and nature do with actors fill.

Adapted from John Heywood

The truth of the existence of God.

William E. Hocking

A wilderness where tears are hung in every tree.

Thomas Hood

A great mob, and nothing will influence it so much as the lash.   *Edgar W. Howe*

Only the first rude essay of some infant deity, who afterwards abandoned it, ashamed of his lame performance.   *David Hume*

There are two worlds; the world that we can measure with line and rule, and the world that we feel with our hearts and imagination.

Leigh Hunt

A fair: people gather for a while, then part; some profit and rejoice, others lose and grieve.

Joseph Ibn Pakuda

An enemy cloaked as a friend. *Immanuel of Rome*

The sum total of all its beings and events now.

William James

Nothing more than a larger assembly of beings, combining to counterfeit happiness which they do not feel.   *Samuel Johnson*

(A place) where there is much to be done and little to be known.   *Samuel Johnson*

A practical joke of God, like a bad day.

Franz Kafka

A sum of appearance, and must have some transcendent ground.   *Immanuel Kant*

A league of rogues against the true people, of the vile against the generous.   *Giacomo Leopardi*

An expensive hotel: you pay dearly for each pleasure.   *Israel S. Lipkin*

The Ten Commandments backwards, a mask and picture of the Devil.   *Martin Luther*

An antechamber to the next. Prepare yourself here that you may be admitted to the banquet hall there.   *Mishna: Abot, IV, 16.*

A strange affair.   *Moliere*

An endless seesaw.   *Michel de Montaigne*

This world is all a fleeting show,
For man's illusion given.   *Thomas Moore*

The pictured scroll of worlds within the soul.

Adapted from Alfred Noyes

The sum total of our vital possibilities.

José Ortega y Gasset

That portion of destiny which goes to make up our life.   *José Ortega y Gasset*

My country.   *Thomas Paine*

An imperceptible point in the ample bosom of nature.   *Blaise Pascal*

A community we recognize but where our relationships are not felt.   *William Pfaff*

God's epistle to mankind—his thoughts are flashing upon us from every direction.   *Plato*

A place of exile, and not . . . our true country.

Pope Leo XIII

A kind of spiritual kindergarten, where millions of bewildered infants are trying to spell "God" with the wrong blocks.

Edwin Arlington Robinson

Always a caricature of itself, always pretending to be something quite other than what it actually is.

Adapted from George Santayana

Something that had better not have been.

Arthur Schopenhauer

A ghastly drama of will-to-live divided against itself.   *Albert Schweitzer*

This great stage of fools.   *William Shakespeare*

A stage where every man must play a part.

William Shakespeare

A looking-glass, and gives back to every man the reflection of his own face.

William Makepeace Thackeray

A comedy to those that think, a tragedy to those that feel.   *Horace Walpole*

A stage, but the play is badly cast.   *Oscar Wilde*

A funny paper read backwards. And that way it isn't so funny.   *Tennessee Williams*

The world is everything that is the case.

Ludwig Wittgenstein

A prophecy of worlds to come.   *Edward Young*

A place that grows smaller as postal rates grow larger. *Anon.*

A place where nothing is had for nothing. *Anon.*

A puzzle with a peace missing. *Anon.*

SEE ALSO EARTH, UNIVERSE.

WORMS

Your worm is your only emperor for diet; we fat all creatures else to fat us, and we fat ourselves for maggots. *William Shakespeare*

The end of our living. *Anon.*

The last experience. *Anon.*

SEE ALSO DEATH, GRAVE.

WORRY

The killer. *Jerry Dashkin*

A god, invisible but omnipotent. It steals the bloom from the cheek and lightness from the pulse; it takes away the appetite, and turns the hair gray. *Benjamin Disraeli*

The crosses which we make for ourselves by overanxiety. *François de Fénelon*

A morbid anticipation of events which never happens. *Russell Green*

Interest paid on trouble before it becomes due. *William R. Inge*

Interest paid by those who borrow trouble. *George W. Lyon*

A thin stream of fear trickling through the mind. If encouraged, it cuts a channel into which all other thoughts are drained. *Arthur Somers Roche*

The only insupportable misfortune of life. *Henry St. John*

A complete cycle of inefficient thought revolving about a pivot of fear. *Anon.*

SEE ALSO FEAR.

WORSHIP

The daily bread of patience. *Honoré de Balzac*

Where two or three are gathered together in my name, there am I in the midst of them. *Bible: Matthew, XVIII, 20.*

A man climbing the altar stairs to God. *Dwight Bradley*

Transcendent wonder. *Thomas Carlyle*

A way of living, a way of seeing the world in the light of God...to rise to a higher level of existence, to see the world from the point of view of God. *Abraham J. Heschel*

Not a petition to God; it is a sermon to ourselves. *Emil G. Hirsch*

The special sphere of the will in religion. *William E. Hocking*

Doing your duty and acting according to the rules of reason. *Georg C. Lichtenberg*

The free offering of ourselves to God. *James Martineau*

This solitary repsonse to reality. *Bernard E. Meland*

Turning from the periphery of life to the core of existence. In this solitary moment it is as if one entered into the scheme of things. *Bernard E. Meland*

Devotion to an ideal. *John Henry Newman*

The soul offering plain truth. *Philo*

The best of sacrifices, the full and truly perfect obligation of noble living. *Philo*

The first way to worship the gods is to believe in the gods. *Seneca*

The process by which we first define God. *Willard L. Sperry*

To quicken the conscience by the holiness of God...to open the heart to the love of God, to devote the will to the purpose of God. *William Temple*

An adventure of the spirit, a flight after the unattainable. *Alfred North Whitehead*

The practice of commitment by ritual, symbol, self-examination, and assembly. *Henry N. Wieman*

SEE ALSO CHURCHES, PIETY, PRAYER, RELIGION, REVERENCE, SYNAGOGUE.

WRITERS

A category of human being for whom his work ought to speak for itself.   *Isaac Asimov*

Writers, like teeth, are divided into incisors and grinders.   *Walter Bagehot*

The writer of art has in mind the psychology of his characters; the writer of trash, the psychology of his readers.   *Solomon Bickel*

If he is not truth's ordained priest, then he is fit only for the scrapheap.   *Georg M. Brandes*

A simple-minded person...He's not a great mind, he's not a great thinker, he's not a great philosopher, he's a story-teller.

Erskine Caldwell

The Hero as Man of Letters will be found discharging a function for us which is ever honourable, ever the highest; and was once well known to be the highest.   *Thomas Carlyle*

A perpetual priesthood.   *Thomas Carlyle*

(One who writes about himself) but has his eye always on that thread of the universe which runs through himself, and all things.

Ralph Waldo Emerson

Talent alone cannot make a writer. There must be a man behind the book.   *Ralph Waldo Emerson*

It is his privilege to help man endure by lifting his heart, by reminding him of the courage and honor and hope and pride and compassion and piety and sacrifice which have been the glory of his past.

William Faulkner

Valuable colleagues...their testimony is to be rated very highly, because they had a way of knowing many of the things between heaven and earth which are not dreamed of in our philosophy...they draw upon sources that we have not yet made accessible to science.   *Sigmund Freud*

The portrayal of the psychic life of human beings is...his most special domain; he has always been the forerunner of science.   *Sigmund Freud*

(Those who) salvage from the whirlpool of their emotions the deepest truths, to which we others have to force our way, ceaselessly groping amid torturing uncertainties.   *Sigmund Freud*

A two-way channel, who must humbly offer the use of his voice to the life ever-lasting.

William Gerhardie

Apprentices in a craft where no one ever becomes a master.   *Ernest Hemingway*

One who has had an unhappy childhood.

Joseph Hergesheimer

They...write the things they think other folks think they think.   *Elbert Hubbard*

Great writers leave us not just their works, but a way of looking at things.   *Elizabeth Janeway*

There are two literary maladies—writer's cramp and swelled head. The worst of writer's cramp is that it is never cured; the worst of swelled head is that it never kills.   *Coulson Kernahan*

(One who would) trade a hundred contemporary readers for ten readers in ten years and one reader in a hundred years.   *Arthur Koestler*

Someone who can make a riddle out of an answer.

Karl Kraus

Two kinds...those who are and those who aren't. With the first, content and form belong together like soul and body; with the second, they match each other like body and clothes.   *Karl Kraus*

The mark of a really great writer is that he gives expression to what the masses of mankind think or feel without knowing it. The mediocre writer simply writes what everyone would have said.

Georg C. Lichtenberg

A spectator, looking at everything with a highly critical eye.   *Bernard Malamud*

A dreamer and a conscious dreamer.

Carson McCullers

A prostitute. First I did it to please myself, then ... my friends, and finally I did it for money.

Ferenc Molnar

Good writers have two things in common: they prefer being understood to being admired, and they do not write for the overcritical and too shrewd reader.   *Friedrich W. Nietzsche*

The Faust of modern society, the only surviving individualist in a mass age. To his orthodox contemporaries he seems a semi-madman.

Boris Pasternak

To become immortal our great writers first have to die of hunger.   *Moritz Saphir*

A spiritual anarchist, as in the depth of his soul every man is.   *William Saroyan*

He neither walks with the multitude nor cheers with them. The writer who is a real writer is a rebel who never stops.   *William Saroyan*

A frustrated actor who recites his lines in the hidden auditorium of his skull.   *Rod Serling*

A purveyor of amusement for people who have not wit enough to entertain themselves.

George Bernard Shaw

Paper-blurrers.   *Philip Sidney*

The first writers are first and the rest, in the long run, nowhere but in anthologies.

Carl Van Doren

(One who) must be willing . . . to take chances, to risk making a fool of himself—or even to risk revealing the fact that he is a fool.

Jessamyn West

Writers write for themselves and not for their readers, and that art has nothing to do with communication between person and only with the communication between different parts of a person's mind.   *Rebecca West*

People who talk to themselves for a living.

Anon.

SEE ALSO ARTISTS, AUTHOR, BOOK, CREATIVITY, FICTION, LITERATURE, NOVELISTS, PEN, POETS, PROSE, STYLE, WORDS, WRITING.

WRITING

A dangerous and contagious disease.

Pierre Abélard

All writing is a process of elimination.

Martha Albrand

Learning to say nothing, more cleverly every day.

William Allingham

A way of life in itself.   *Sherwood Anderson*

An artificial activity . . . a lonely and private substitute for conversation.   *Brooks Atkinson*

To have conversations with oneself.

Alan Ayckbourn

Write to the mind and heart, and let the ear glean after what it can.   *Philip J. Bailey*

Simply talking on paper and in time learning what not to say.   *Beryl Bainbridge*

For me, writing was an act of love. It was an attempt not to get the world's attention, it was an attempt to be loved.   *James Baldwin*

Take a few sheets of paper and for three days in succession write down, without falsification or hypocrisy, everything that comes into your head. Write what you think . . . and when the three days are over you will be amazed at what novel and startling thoughts have welled up in you.

Ludwig Boerne

A kind of double living. The writer experiences everything twice. Once in reality and once in that mirror which waits always before or behind him.

Catherine D. Bowen

One writes best in a cellar on a rainy day.

Van Wyck Brooks

The talent of concealing technique.

Eugene E. Brussell

Selecting experience suited to your talent and a lot of backside power.   *Eugene E. Brussell*

A victory against death.   *Michel Butor*

The long journey to recover, through the detours of art, the two or three simple and great images which first gained access to his heart.

Albert Camus

The true reign of miracles.   *Thomas Carlyle*

An adventure. To begin with, it was a toy, and amusement; then it became a mistress, and then a master, and then a tyrant.   *Winston S. Churchill*

Giving the reader the most knowledge in the least time.   *Adapted from Charles Caleb Colton*

The true function . . . is to produce a masterpiece; no other task is of any consequence.

Cyril Connolly

By the power of the written word to make you hear, to make you feel . . . before all, to make you see. That, and no more, and it is everything.

Joseph Conrad

An excuse to live . . . in fantasy land, where you can create, direct and watch the products of your own head.   *Monica Dickens*

When I want to read a book I write one.

Benjamin Disraeli

(People) write for their country, their sect: to amuse their friends or annoy their enemies.

George Douglas

All writing comes by the grace of God.

Ralph Waldo Emerson

He that writes to himself writes to an eternal public. *Ralph Waldo Emerson*

A kind of skating which carries off the performer where he would not go. *Ralph Waldo Emerson*

To create out of the materials of the human spirit something which did not exist before.

William Faulkner

(The) need to create an alternative world.

John Fowles

The only respectable work a girl can do in bed.

Victor Fredericks

All there is to writing is having ideas. To learn to write is to learn to have ideas. *Robert Frost*

Writing is busy idleness. *Johann W. Goethe*

An activity in which the dreariness of labor and the loneliness of thought is substituted for conversation. *Warren Goldberg*

Writing is putting one's obsessions in order.

Jean Grenier

Whatever an author puts between the two covers of his book is public property; whatever of himself he does not put there is his private property, as much as if he had never written a word.

Gail Hamilton

At best...a lonely life. *Ernest Hemingway*

Springs from a maladjustment to life, or from an inner conflict which the adolescent (or grown man) cannot resolve in action...a method of resolving a conflict. *Emile Herzog*

No man but a blockhead ever wrote except for money. *Samuel Johnson*

The only end of writing is to enable the readers better to enjoy life or better to endure it.

Samuel Johnson

(That which) the mind conceives with pain, but brings forth with delight. *Joseph Joubert*

Merely the dregs of experience. *Franz Kafka*

The writer writes in order to teach himself, to understand himself, to satisfy himself; the publishing of his ideas, though it brings gratification, is a curious anticlimax. *Alfred Kazin*

A form of prayer. *John Keats*

I get up in the morning, torture a typewriter until it screams, then stop. *Clarence B. Kelland*

It is the glory and merit of some men to write well, and of others not to write at all.

Jean de La Bruyère

When the pen becomes a clarion.

Adapted from Henry Wadsworth Longfellow

A great evil. There is no measure or limit to this fever of writing; everyone must be an author; some out of vanity, others for the sake of money and gain. *Martin Luther*

To the man with an ear for verbal delicacies ... there is in writing the constant joy of sudden discovery, of happy accident.

Henry Louis Mencken

To rouse the inward vision. *George Meredith*

A voyage of discovery. *Henry Miller*

I speak to my paper as I speak to the first person I meet. *Michel de Montaigne*

The point of good writing is knowing when to stop. *Lucy M. Montgomery*

Not to say what we can all say, but what we are unable to say. *Anais Nin*

A craft. You have to take your apprenticeship in it like anything else. *Katherine Ann Porter*

Make 'em laugh; make 'em cry; make 'em wait.

Charles Reade

Having a sheet of paper, a pen and not...an idea of what you're going to say. *Francoise Sagan*

To be able to enter into the skin of people.

Georges Simenon

The clumsy attempt to find symbols for the wordlessness. *John Steinbeck*

A different name for conversation.

Laurence Sterne

The product of someone's neurosis.

William Styron

To scratch your head, and bite your nails.

Jonathan Swift

The art of applying the seat of the pants to the seat of the chair. *Mary Heaton Vorse*

An exercise in the use of language...It is drama, speech and events that interest me.

Evelyn Waugh

I write in order to discover on my shelf a new book which I would enjoy reading, or to see a new play that would engross me.   *Thorton Wilder*

Writing is a coy game you play with your unconscious.   *Thorton Wilder*

A disease. You can't stop it.
William C. Williams

I just sit at the typewriter and curse a bit.
Pelham G. Wodehouse

The art of putting black words on white paper in succession until the impression is created that something has been said.   *Alexander Woollcott*

Living alone in a room.   *Anon.*

SEE ALSO ART, AUTHOR, CREATIVITY, LANGUAGE, LITERATURE, PEN, POETS, PROSE, STYLE, WRITERS.

Y

YANKEE

In Europe an American. In the Northern States a New Englander. In the Southern States, a Damyank. *Anon.*

A tourist who visits the southern states and spends his money. *Anon.*

YAWN

A silent shout. *Gilbert Keith Chesterton*

Something that makes two yawners. *French Proverb*

The pains and penalties of idleness. *Alexander Pope*

Honesty undisguised. *Anon.*

A pertinent remark. *Anon.*

Nature's provision for letting married men open their mouths. *Anon.*

SEE ALSO BORE, BOREDOM.

YEAR

Drops of time. *Matthew Arnold*

Black oxen. *Gertrude Atherton*

A tale that is told. *Bible: Psalms, XC, 9.*

A period of three hundred and sixty-five disappointments. *Ambrose Bierce*

All sorts of things and weather
Must be taken in together,
To make up a year. *Ralph Waldo Emerson*

The specious panorama of a year
But multiplies the image of a day.
Ralph Waldo Emerson

The year doth nothing else but open and shut.
George Herbert

Dreams . . . death alone can tell their meaning.
Abraham Ibn Ezra

SEE ALSO DAY, LIFE, TIME.

YESTERDAY

A short-change artist from whom we can never recover. *Elbert Hubbard*

One evil less and one memory more.
Elbert Hubbard

The tomorrow that got away.
Leonard L. Levinson

And all our yesterdays have lighted fools the way to dusty death. *William Shakespeare*

SEE ALSO PAST.

YOUNG

SEE YOUTH.

YOUTH

(Those who) have exalted notions because they have not yet been humbled by life or learned its necessary limitations.   *Aristotle*

Quick to hope.   *Aristotle*

A fast gallop over a smooth track to the bright horizon.   *Harold Azine*

The time of great expectations for yourself and expectation of others for you—to be fulfilled at an unspecified time called "Someday."

Harold Azine

(They who) embrace more than they can hold, stir more than they can quiet, fly to the end without consideration of the means.   *Francis Bacon*

One of the worst things that can happen to an American child nowadays.   *Russell Baker*

Someone who is young enough to know every-thing.   *James M. Barrie*

The age of striving and selfishness.

Arthur Brisbane

Youth means love.   *Robert Browning*

Life's morning march.   *Thomas Campbell*

To all the glad season of life; but often only by what it hopes, not by what it attains, or what it escapes.   *Thomas Carlyle*

The joy of the young is to disobey—but the trouble is, there are no longer any orders.

Jean Cocteau

The feeling that will never come back any more—the feeling that I could last forever, outlast the sea, the earth, and all men.   *Joseph Conrad*

Young heads are giddy, and young hearts are warm, and make mistakes for manhood to re-form.   *Adapted from William Cowper*

A blunder.   *Benjamin Disraeli*

When we...are confident in our opinions, sure that we possess the whole truth.

Thomas Stearns Eliot

A person who has a wolf in his stomach.

English Proverb

The best time to be rich, and the best time to be poor.   *Euripides*

A disease from which we all recover.

Dorothy Fuldheim

A feeling of eternity...To be young is to be as one of the Immortal Gods.   *William Hazlitt*

The young are prodigal of life from a super-abundance of it.   *William Hazlitt*

The time of life when one believes he will never die.   *William Hazlitt*

A lunatic.   *Hindu Proverb*

(One) quick in temper but weak in judgment.

Homer

The ability to see beauty. Anyone who keeps the ability to see beauty never grows old.

Franz Kafka

A habit with some so long they cannot part with it.

Rudyard Kipling

A continual intoxication.   *La Rochefoucauld*

A fever of reason.   *La Rochefoucauld*

The age of disinterestedness, enthusiasm, and ready sacrifice.   *Ferdinand Lassalle*

Elbowing self-conceit.   *James Russell Lowell*

A defect...that we outgrow only too soon.

James Russell Lowell

Beautiful is youth because it never comes again.

George Jean Nathan

To be young is to hope...to love simply and naturally...to rejoice in one's own health and strength, and in that of all human beings, and of the birds of the air and the beetles in the grass.

Max Nordau

The season of credulity.   *William Pitt*

Youth sees too far to see how near it is to seeing farther.   *Edwin Arlington Robinson*

A time of disillusionment, anger, rebellion and loneliness...when we discover who we are, what the world is, and the elusive nature of our rela-tionship to it.   *L. M. Schulman*

A wonderful thing; what a crime to waste it on children.   *George Bernard Shaw*

Youth is wholly experimental.

Robert Louis Stevenson

The time to go flashing from one end of the world to the other both in mind and body; to try the manners of different nations; to hear the chimes at midnight. *Robert Louis Stevenson*

Not a time of life—it is a state of mind.
Samuel Ullman

A temper of the will, a quality of the imagination, a vigor of the emotions. It is a freshness of the deep spring of life. *Samuel Ullman*

(One who) must be strong, unafraid, and a better taxpayer than its father. *Harry V. Wade*

A man or woman before it is ready or fit to be seen. *Evelyn Waugh*

A silly, vapid state. *Carolyn Wells*

Life as yet untouched by tragedy.
Alfred North Whitehead

Those who are always ready to give to those older than themselves the full benefit of their inexperience. *Adapted from Oscar Wilde*

The most conservative people I have ever dealt with. *Woodrow Wilson*

A time stranger than fiction. *Anon.*

Means a predominance of courage over timidity, of the appetite of adventure over the love of ease.
Anon.

A fire, and the years are a pack of wolves who grow bolder as the fire dies down. *Anon.*

SEE ALSO ADOLESCENCE, BOY, BOYHOOD, CHILDREN, GIRLS.

Z

ZEAL

Like fire, it wants both feeding and watching.
William G. Benham

A certain nervous disorder afflicting the young and inexperienced. *Ambrose Bierce*

A dreadful termagant. *Samuel Butler 1*

Zeal without knowledge is the sister of folly.
John Davies

A strong, steady, uniform, benevolent affection; but false zeal is a strong, desultory, boisterous, selfish passion. *Nathaniel Emmons*

Fire without light. *English Proverb*

Violent zeal for truth hath an hundred to one odds to be either petulancy, ambition, or pride.
Jonathan Swift

Persecuting zeal... Hell's fiercest fiend!
James Thomson

What we do which in a calmer condition we would not do. *Robert Zwickey*

SEE ALSO FANATICISM.

ZIONISM

The Jewish people's unending attempt to build homelessness into a home. *Meir Ben-Horin*

The Holy Land, where land is made holy and holiness made land. *Meir Ben-Horin*

The creation of a new type of Jew. In place of the Jew who is a victim of the... material and who worships lifeless things a Jew is to appear whose life is rooted in the spirit, who is animated by love and sacrifice. *Hugo Bergmann*

To create for our people a national center, the influence of which on the diaspora will be spiritual only. *Ahad HaAm*

The return of the Jews to Judaism, before their return to the Jewish land. *Theodor Herzl*

To create for the Jewish people a publicly recognized and legally secured home in Palestine.
Theodor Herzl

A nationalist movement and a social revolution. To the orthodox Jew it is also a religious movement. *Eric Hoffer*

One man persuading another man to give money to a third man to go to Palestine.
Arthur Koestler

The affirmation of our personality... in ourselves, our spirit, our destiny to be worthy of our past. *Bernard Lazare*

To be a Zionist is to be a Jew... Jews who are not Zionists at heart, are not Jews.
Benjamin Mandelstamm

It belongs completely to the series of messianic movements which have continuously existed within Judaism. *Franz Rosenzweig*

Not a mere national or chauvinistic caprice, but the last desperate stand of the Jews against annihilation. *Arthur Ruppin*

The half-conscious instinct of a people integrating past and future together into the totality of the will to live and to be itself and only itself.

Stephen S. Wise

SEE ALSO ISRAEL.

ZOO

A place devised for animals to study the habits of human beings. *Oliver Herford*

A garden scented by wild animals.

Jimmy Lyons

A form of idle and witless amusement, compared to which a visit to a penitentiary, or even to a State Legislature in session, is informing, stimulating and ennobling. *Henry Louis Mencken*

A place which prevents people from getting at the animals. *Anon.*

Index

C

H

K